British Master Tax Guide 2010–

CCH
a Wolters Kluwer business

Wolters Kluwer
145 London Road
Kingston upon Thames
KT2 6SR
Telephone: (0) 844 561 8166
Facsimile: +44 (0) 208 547 2638
Email: cch@wolterskluwer.co.uk
Website: www.cch.co.uk

This publication is sold with the understanding that neither the publisher nor the authors, with regard to this publication, are engaged in rendering legal or professional services. The material contained in this publication neither purports, nor is intended to be, advice on any particular matter.

Although this publication incorporates a considerable degree of standardisation, subjective judgment by the user, based on individual circumstances, is indispensable. This publication is an aid and cannot be expected to replace such judgment.

Neither the publisher nor the authors can accept any responsibility or liability to any person, whether a purchaser of this publication or not, in respect of anything done or omitted to be done by any such person in reliance, whether sole or partial, upon the whole or any part of the contents of this publication.

Legislative and other material

While copyright in all statutory and other materials resides in the Crown or other relevant body, copyright in the remaining material in this publication is vested in the publisher.

The publisher advises that any statutory or other materials issued by the Crown or other relevant bodies and reproduced and quoted in this publication are not the authorised official versions of those statutory or other materials. In the preparation, however, the greatest care has been taken to ensure exact conformity with the law as enacted or other material as issued.

Crown copyright legislation is reproduced under the terms of Crown Copyright Policy Guidance issued by HMSO. Other Crown copyright material is reproduced with the permission of the controller of HMSO. European Communities Copyright material is reproduced with permission.

Telephone Helpline Disclaimer Notice

Where purchasers of this publication also have access to any Telephone Helpline Service operated by Wolters Kluwer (UK), then Wolters Kluwer's total liability to contract, tort (including negligence, or breach of statutory duty) misrepresentation, restitution or otherwise with respect to any claim arising out of its acts or alleged omissions in the provision of the Helpline Service shall be limited to the yearly subscription fee paid by the Claimant.

© 2010 Wolters Kluwer (UK) Limited

ISBN 978-1-84798-314-5

British Library Cataloguing-in-Publication Data

A catalogue record for this book is available from the British Library.

Typeset in-house at Wolters Kluwer (UK) Ltd
Printed and bound in Italy by Legoprint-Lavis (TN)

British Master Tax Guide
2010–11

British Master Tax Guide
2010-11

About the authors

Julie Clift BA (Hons.) CTA worked at Arthur Andersen and then at Ernst & Young, mainly specialising in personal tax issues. She then joined *The Tax Journal* as Deputy Editor before returning to practice as a Tax Editor in Deloitte & Touche's Tax Policy Group. She joined CCH as a Senior Technical Editor in 2003 and has worked on some of their leading tax products, including the *British Tax Reporter* and the *Inheritance Tax Reporter*. Julie is a Chartered Tax Adviser and a member of the Chartered Institute of Taxation.

Jon Fursdon BSc(Hons) FCA CTA is a specialist in corporate tax and the wider tax aspects of owner managed business. He was a tax partner with Deloitte & Touche until 2002 and then with Grant Thornton UK LLP until June 2008. Jon now runs his own tax consultancy business advising clients and other firms of accountants on business related tax matters. He is a member of the Chartered Institute of Tax Corporation Tax Technical Committee.

Sarah Laing is a Chartered Tax Adviser. She has been writing professionally since joining CCH Editions in 1998 as a Senior Technical Editor, contributing to a range of highly regarded publications including the *British Tax Reporter*, *Taxes – The Weekly Tax News*, the Red & Green legislation volumes, *Hardman's*, *International Tax Agreements* and many others. She became Publishing Manager for the tax and accounting portfolio in 2001 and later went on to help run CCH Seminars (including ABG Courses and Conferences).

Sarah originally worked for the Inland Revenue in Newbury and Swindon Tax Offices, before moving out into practice in 1991. She has worked for both small and Big 4 firms. She now works as a freelance author providing technical writing services for the tax and accountancy profession.

Sarah is a director and news editor of TaxationWeb Limited (www.taxationweb.co.uk), which provides free information and resources on UK taxes to taxpayers and professionals.

Michael Steed trained with Coopers & Lybrand (now PWC), passing his ATT exams in 1992 and ATII (now CTA) VAT specialist route in 1994. He gained FTII status in 1995 with his thesis on VAT groups. He gained practical experience of both indirect and direct taxes while working for Coopers. Michael is Kaplan's leading authority on indirect taxes and works closely with both practice and industry clients providing highly bespoke products to meet their exact training needs.

Preface

The *British Master Tax Guide 2010–11* is designed primarily to assist practitioners in understanding tax liabilities and entitlements for the tax year 2010–11. It is designed not only to answer those questions which arise in the preparation of tax returns for the year, but also to provide information on the tax consequences flowing from decisions and transactions faced by taxpayers. The Guide also provides a concise but clear guide to tax for students and others who come to the subject for the first time.

The Guide has ten major chapters. The first chapter provides key dates, rates and other checklists collated in a user-friendly section. The second chapter provides a brief overview of the tax system. The third details the charge to income tax and includes full details of all the reliefs and deductions available. Similar treatments of corporation tax, capital gains tax, inheritance tax, value added tax, National Insurance contributions and other indirect taxes follow. The final chapter deals with overseas aspects of taxation.

At the beginning of each of the main chapters, there is a 'What's New' and a 'Key Points' section. 'What's New' gives a concise listing of new developments in that particular area since last year whilst 'Key Points' is a concise listing of the major issues in that area.

The Guide explains the rules affecting everyday business and personal tax questions in the simplest possible way. Examples are included throughout which illustrate the text and show how these rules apply. There are also extensive links to the in-depth commentary which can be found in CCH's *British Tax Reporter* and *British Value Added Tax Reporter*. The Guide rests on the firm foundation of legislation, statements of practice, extra-statutory concessions and other non-statutory sources, and decisions of the courts; references to which are included on separate law and source lines at the end of each paragraph for easy reference. All relevant provisions of the *Finance Act* 2010 and *Finance (No. 2) Act* 2010 have been reflected.

An exhaustive case table, legislation finding list and topical index facilitate access to the Guide.

I am grateful to Michael Steed (Value Added Tax and Indirect Taxes chapters), Julie Clift (Inheritance Tax chapter) and Jon Fursdon (Corporation Tax chapter) for their contributions.

September 2010

What's new?

INCOME TAX

- For 2010–11, the starting rate of income tax for savings is 10 per cent, the basic rate is 20 per cent, the higher rate is 40 per cent and the additional rate is 50 per cent (see 50).
- For 2010–11, the basic rate limit is £37,400 (see 50).
- The additional rate of 50 per cent is payable on taxable income exceeding £150,000 (see 50).
- For 2010–11, the 10 per cent savings rate applies to savings income only, with a limit of £2,440. If an individual's taxable non-savings income is above this limit then the 10 per cent savings rate will not be applicable (see 50).
- For 2010–11, the basic personal allowance is £6,475 (2009–10: £6,475) (see 1851), the age-related personal allowance is £9,490 (2009–10: £9,490) for those aged 65 to 74, and £9,640 (2009–10: £9,640) for those aged 75 or over (see 1874), and the married couple's allowance is £6,965 (2009–10: £6,965) for those aged 75 or over (see 1874).
- For 2011–12 the basic personal allowance will rise to £7,475. However, the basic rate limit for 2011–12 will be reduced, so that higher rate taxpayers will not benefit from the increase in the personal allowance (see 1851).
- The rate applicable to discretionary and accumulation trusts rises to 50 per cent for 2010–11. Such trusts have a basic rate band of £1,000 from 6 April 2007 (see 989).
- From 2010–11, the basic personal allowance will be subject to a single income limit of £100,000. Where an individual's adjusted net income is below or equal to the £100,000 limit, they will continue to be entitled to the full amount of the basic personal allowance. If adjusted net income exceeds the £100,000 limit, the personal allowance will be reduced by 1 for every 2 above the income limit. The personal allowance may be reduced to nil from this income limit (see 1850).
- From 2010–11 there are three rates of tax for dividends. Dividends otherwise taxable at the 20 per cent basic rate will continue to be taxable at the 10 per cent dividend ordinary rate and dividends otherwise taxable at the 40 per cent higher rate will continue to be taxable at the 32.5 per cent dividend upper rate. Dividends otherwise taxable at the new 50 per cent additional rate will be taxable at a new 42.5 per cent dividend additional rate.
- For 2010–11 the figure for calculating car fuel benefit rises to £18,000 (£16,900 for 2009–10) (see 403).
- From 2010–11, the lower threshold for company car emissions is reduced to 130g/km. It will be reduced further to 125g/km from 2011–12.
- The £80,000 cap is to be withdrawn from the calculation of company car benefit from 6 April 2011 (see 402).
- For 2010–11 the annual Individual Savings Account (ISA) savings limit is £10,200 (£5,100 in cash). From April 2011 the savings limit will be increased annually in line with inflation (see 1921).

- The child element of child tax credit is £2,300 for 2010–11. The threshold for working tax credit remains unchanged at £6,420 and the withdrawal rate is 39 per cent for 2010–11 (see 1847).
- The annual investment allowance (AIA), available to businesses of all sizes for investment in most plant and machinery, is doubled from £50,000 to £100,000 from April 2010 (see 2366).
- A new anti-avoidance measure is introduced for certain arrangements entered into on or after 24 March 2010. The new measure disallows property loss relief against general income to the extent that the loss is attributable to AIA, but only where tax avoidance was a main purpose of the arrangements (see 2366).
- The categories of expenditure qualifying for accelerated allowances for energy-saving or environmentally beneficial (water-efficient) technologies are to be revised. The general category of compact heat exchangers will be removed, as will the sub-technology of liquid pressure amplification. In the water-efficiency category, the criteria for tax and showers will be tightened. The date of the changes is not yet known but they will be made by Treasury Order prior to the summer 2010 parliamentary recess (see 2376).
- The special allowance for certain buildings in enterprise zones (EZAs) will be withdrawn from April 2011 (see 2380).
- From 1 April 2010 individuals may only deduct foreign income tax from any foreign income where they have included the foreign tax in their taxable income calculation. Legislation is also introduced to reaffirm the scope of the targeted DTR anti-avoidance rule (see 1550).
- In relation to payments received on or after 6 April 2010, a new measure, similar to the current tax exemption for payments to adopters, will mean that certain payments to special guardians, and to certain carers looking after children under a residence order, will be exempt from income tax.
- The *Pensions Act* 2008 received Royal Assent on 26 November 2008. The government plans to introduce certain reforms contained in the Act from 2012 (see 429).
- Income tax relief on pension contributions will be restricted to basic rate for individuals with earnings of £150,000 or more from 6 April 2011. *Finance Act* 2009 contains anti-forestalling provisions preventing those potentially affected from seeking to forestall this change by increasing pension savings in excess of their normal regular pattern on or after 22 April 2009 (see 429).

CORPORATION TAX

- For the financial year 2010 the main rate of corporation tax is 28 per cent (see 3092); the full or main rate applies if profits exceed the upper profits limit (namely £1,500,000). The main rate of corporation tax will reduce to 27 per cent for the financial year 2011. For North Sea Oil and Gas ring fence companies the 2010 main rate of corporation tax is 30 per cent.
- For the financial year 2010, the small profits rate (formerly, the small companies' rate) is unchanged at 21 per cent (see 3092). For North Sea Oil and Gas ring fence companies the 2010 small companies rate is 19 per cent.

- The new *Corporation Tax Act* 2010 which is the second of two corporation tax acts rewriting the corporation tax code became effective for accounting periods ending on or after 1 April 2010 (see 3001).
- The *Taxation (International and Other Provisions) Act* 2010 has been introduced with effect for accounting periods ending on or after 1 April 2010. This act rewrites the legislation, in particular, on transfer pricing, double tax relief and the 2009 worldwide debt cap provisions.
- The *Corporation Tax Act* 2010 has renamed 'small companies' rate' the 'small profits rate' (see 3092) and has rewritten the provisions on charges on income and renamed them 'charitable donations relief' (which, since 2005, was the last remaining category of expenditure that fell within the definition of charge on income) (see 3059).
- New provisions have been introduced to restrict the availability of capital allowances following, broadly, a change in ownership of a company (see 3034).
- New provisions have been introduced to prevent corporation tax relief where a loan made by a close company to a participator is written off (see 3036).
- Changes have been made to the conditions applying to the exemption from the loan relationship charge when an impaired debt becomes held by a connected company (see 3036).
- An extended definition of charity has been introduced (see 3059).
- A new anti-avoidance provision restricting the relief available on gifts of shares to charities has been introduced (see 3059).
- The amount of the annual investment allowance has been increased from £50,000 to £100,000 with effect from 1 April 2010 (see 3034).
- A new penalty regime for failure to notify chargeability to corporation tax has been introduced (see 4952).
- HMRC have published their views on the inheritance tax consequences of company contributions to employee benefit trusts (see 4278).
- Various extra-statutory concessions have been enacted, including those allowing a negligible value claim where an asset is transferred between group companies on a no gain/no loss basis (see 3684), preventing a reduction in the base cost of a shares for CGT purposes where a transfer of an asset at an undervalue by a close company is taxable on the recipient as employment income or as a distribution (see 4278) and allowing the value of shares disposed of by a transferee company (who acquired them from another group company under a no gain/no loss transfer) to a third party to be the appropriate proportion of the value of any larger holding held by the transferor company at 31 March 1982 (see 3684).
- HMRC have published their views on the meaning of 'ordinary share capital' in the context of overseas companies following the decision in *Swift v HMRC* (see 3653).
- The dividend exemption for demergers has been extended to companies resident in EU member states (see 3200).
- HMRC have announced a delay in the introduction of managed payment plans (see 4966).
- The government has confirmed that distributions of a capital nature will be exempt from corporation on income under the new distribution exemption that applies for distributions made on or after 1 July 2009 (see 3085).

- HMRC have published guidance on the form of accounts that need to be included with a corporation tax return (see 4952).
- An additional test for the extent that losses of a company owned by a consortium can be surrendered as group relief is to be introduced (see 3812).
- Electronic filing of corporation tax returns using XBRL will be compulsory where an accounting period ends after 31 March 2010 (see 4952).
- HMRC have published the most commonly asked questions and answers in relation to the Role of Senior Accounting Officer introduced for large companies and groups (see 4959).
- The following Court decisions have been reported:
- The Upper Tribunal decision in *Dawsongroup Limited v R & C Commrs* on the meaning of investment business and expenses of management (see 4553).
- The decision in *Laerstate BV v R & C Commrs* on the meaning of central management and control for the purposes of determining whether a company is resident in the UK for UK tax purposes (see 3014).
- The decision in *Research & Development Partnership Ltd v R & C Commrs* that under the pre-2009 penalty regime, reliance on another can in some situations be a reasonable excuse (see 4980).
- The decision in *FCE Bank plc* that the non-discrimination clause of the UK-US double tax treaty enables group relief to be claimed under the pre-2000 group relief rules (see 3809).
- The decision in *Philips Electronics UK Ltd v R & C Commrs* that the requirement for the consortium relief link company to be UK resident is contrary to EU law and the subsequent announcement of correcting legislation (see 3809).
- Two further decisions in the ongoing *Marks and Spencer plc v R & C Commrs* case concerning the availability of group relief on the overseas losses of foreign companies, this time in relation to the quantification of the amount of the losses and the time on which group relief claims are taken to be made when made in a series (see 3809).
- The decision in *First Nationwide v R & C Commrs* concerning the criteria for determining whether a distribution received from a foreign company is of an income nature or capital nature (see 3085).

CAPITAL GAINS TAX

- For 2008–09 onwards the standard rate of capital gains tax is 18 per cent for individuals (see 5410).
- A higher rate of capital gains tax of 28 per cent is introduced in respect of disposals on or after 23 June 2010. The new rate replaces the 18 per cent rate in respect of trustees and personal representatives. For individuals, however, it applies in addition to the 18 per cent rate; the actual rate applicable will be determined by the aggregate of the individual's taxable income and chargeable gains (see 5410).
- The annual exemption is equal to £10,100 for 2009–10 and 2010–11 (see 6150).
- The annual exemption for most trusts is £5,050 for 2009–10 and 2010–11.
- For disposals occurring in the period 6 April 2010 to 22 June 2010, the limit for entrepreneurs' relief is £2m (£1m prior to 6 April 2010). For disposals occurring on or after 23 June 2010, the limit is £5m (see 5293).
- FA 2010 contained legislation relating to foreign currency bank accounts.

- The provisions of ESC D50, relating to compensation receipts, have been enacted from 6 April 2010 (see 5080).

INHERITANCE TAX

- The inheritance tax threshold has been frozen at £325,000 for 2010–11 to 2014–15.
- New inheritance tax penalty regime for documents filed on or after 1 April 2010.

VAT

- The standard rate of VAT is due to rise from 17.5% to 20% on 4 January 2011.
- VAT registration limits increased from 1 April 2010 (see 8256).
- The new VAT and services rules came into effect on 1 January 2010 (aka the new VAT package); this extends the scope of the reverse charge (see 7820).
- Revised car fuel scale charges for VAT come into force with effect from 1 May 2010 (see 7762).
- The concession that allows employment businesses supplying temporary staff to choose whether to charge VAT on the staff costs charged to their clients was withdrawn from 1 April 2009.
- From 1 August 2009, it is possible to revoke options to tax made on the introduction of the legislation. Revised legislation sets out procedures to be followed if an election is revoked (see 8230).
- A new regime for charging penalties for errors came into effect on 1 April 2009 (see 8520).
- From 1 April 2010, VAT returns that are paper filed must be accompanied by cleared funds by the due date and not just an uncleared cheque.
- From April 2010 all businesses with taxable turnover above £100,000 and all newly registered businesses must file their VAT returns online. Online filers must also pay online.

NATIONAL INSURANCE CONTRIBUTIONS

- The lower earnings limit for Class 1 NIC is increased to £97 a week for 2010–11 (see 110 for tables).
- The upper earnings limit for Class 1 NIC is £844 a week for 2010–11.
- The primary threshold for Class 1 NICs for 2010–11 is £110 per week.
- Class 2 NICs for 2010–11 are £2.40 per week (£3.05 for share fishermen).
- The Class 2 NIC small earnings exemption limit is £5,075 for 2010–11.
- The Class 3 NIC rate is £12.05 per week for 2010–11.
- The Class 4 NIC lower and upper earnings limits for 2010–11 are £5,715 and £43,875 respectively.
- From 6 April 2010 expenses payments to ministers of religion in respect of heating, lighting, cleaning and gardening in connection with living accommodation provided with the employment will not attract NICs (see 8780 for tables).
- HMRC are consolidating their PAYE databases into one, which will mean that an individual's total employment position can be accessed by staff on one screen.

INDIRECT TAXES

- A new electronic customs project aims to replace existing hybrid paper/electronic format transactions with EC-wide electronic ones. A modernised Customs Code has been adopted by the EC Commission (see 9510).
- The rate of Bingo duty was reduced from 22% to 20% on 29 March 2010 (see 9680).
- Cider duty rates which were increased in the March 2010 Budget were reduced in the emergency Budget in June 2010 (see 9710).
- The tobacco duty regime has been slightly amended for long cigarettes. From 1 January 2011, cigarettes longer than 8cm will be treated as two cigarettes for duty purposes (see 9720).
- In excise duties, the old paper-based system of controlling goods moving duty-free between EC Member States has gone from 1 April 2010. It has been replaced with an electronic system – the EMCS (see 9740).
- In excise duties, the REDS has gone from April 2010. The regime has been replaced with a new person, the Registered Consignee (see 9750).
- The standard rate of IPT is due to rise to 6% and the selected higher rate is due to rise to 20% on 4 January 2011 (see 9800).
- Stamp duty land tax relief was extended to cover new zero carbon flats from 1 October 2007. The relief is time-limited and will expire on 30 September 2012 (see 10216).
- The Government is developing a new duty on aviation which is plane-based rather than passenger-based (see 9760).
- The standard rate of landfill tax for active waste has been increased to £48 per tonne from 1 April 2010. It is expected to rise to £56 per tonne in April 2011. The lower rate for inactive waste remains at £2.50 per tonne (see 9950).
- Rates of climate change levy are increasing from 1 April 2011 (see 10025).
- The standard rate for aggregates levy is £2.20 per tonne from 1 April 2011 (see 10040).

OVERSEAS ASPECTS

- Finance Act 2010 contains legislation to clarify that the definition of a relevant person for remittance basis purposes includes subsidiaries of non-resident companies which would be close companies if they were resident in the UK. The change took effect from 6 April 2010.
- To ensure compliance with certain aspects of the Human Rights Act 1998, legislation was introduced by Finance Act 2009, which took effect from 6 April 2010, to withdraw the entitlement for non-resident individuals who previously qualified for UK personal tax allowances and reliefs solely by virtue of being a Commonwealth citizen (see 11700).

Contents

Key Data

GENERAL

5   Finance Acts

Year	Budget		Royal Assent	
1982	9 March	1982	30 July	1982
1983	15 March	1983	13 May	1983
1983 (No. 2)	15 March	1983	26 July	1983
1984	13 March	1984	26 July	1984
1985	19 March	1985	25 July	1985
1986	18 March	1986	25 July	1986
1987	17 March	1987	15 May	1987
1987 (No. 2)	17 March	1987	23 July	1987
1988	15 March	1988	29 July	1988
1989	14 March	1989	27 July	1989
1990	20 March	1990	26 July	1990
1991	19 March	1991	26 July	1991
1992	10 March	1992	16 March	1992
1992 (No. 2)	10 March	1992	16 July	1992
1993	16 March	1993	27 July	1993
1994	30 November	1993	3 May	1994
1995	29 November	1994	1 May	1995
1996	28 November	1995	29 April	1996
1997	26 November	1996	19 March	1997
1997 (No. 2)	2 July	1997	31 July	1997
1998	17 March	1998	31 July	1998
1999	9 March	1999	27 July	1999
2000	21 March	2000	28 July	2000
2001	7 March	2001	11 May	2001
2002	17 April	2002	24 July	2002
2003	9 April	2003	10 July	2003
2004	17 March	2004	22 July	2004
2005	16 March	2005	7 April	2005
2005 (No. 2)	16 March	2005	20 July	2005
2006	22 March	2006	19 July	2006
2006	22 March	2006	19 July	2006
2007	21 March	2007	19 July	2007
2008	12 March	2008	21 July	2008
2009	22 April	2009	21 July	2009
2010	24 March	2010	8 April	2010
2010 (No. 2)	22 June	2010	27 July	2010

7   Retail Prices Index

The Retail Prices Index (RPI), issued by the Department of Employment, is used to calculate the indexation allowance for capital gains tax purposes. Certain personal and other reliefs are also linked to the RPI, subject to Parliament determining otherwise.

With effect from February 1987 the reference date to which the price level in each subsequent month is related was changed from 'January 1974 = 100' to 'January 1987 = 100'.

Movements in the RPI in the months after January 1987 are calculated with reference to January 1987 = 100. (With a base of January 1974 = 100, January 1987's RPI was 394.5). A new formula has been provided by the Department of Employment for calculating movements in the index over periods which span January 1987:

'The index for the later month (January 1987 = 100) is multiplied by the index for January 1987 (January 1974 = 100) and divided by the index for the earlier month (January 1974 = 100). 100 is subtracted to give the percentage change between the two months.'

CCH has prepared the following table in accordance with this formula:

	1982	1983	1984	1985	1986	1987	1988	1989	1990	1991
Jan.		82.61	86.84	91.20	96.25	100.0	103.3	111.0	119.5	130.2
Feb.		82.97	87.20	91.94	96.60	100.4	103.7	111.8	120.2	130.9
March	79.44	83.12	87.48	92.80	96.73	100.6	104.1	112.3	121.4	131.4
April	81.04	84.28	88.64	94.78	97.67	101.8	105.8	114.3	125.1	133.1
May	81.62	84.64	88.97	95.21	97.85	101.9	106.2	115.0	126.2	133.5
June	81.85	84.84	89.20	95.41	97.79	101.9	106.6	115.4	126.7	134.1
July	81.88	85.30	89.10	95.23	97.52	101.8	106.7	115.5	126.8	133.8
Aug.	81.90	85.68	89.94	95.49	97.82	102.1	107.9	115.8	128.1	134.1
Sept.	81.85	86.06	90.11	95.44	98.30	102.4	108.4	116.6	129.3	134.6
Oct.	82.26	86.36	90.67	95.59	98.45	102.9	109.5	117.5	130.3	135.1
Nov.	82.66	86.67	90.95	95.92	99.29	103.4	110.0	118.5	130.0	135.6
Dec.	82.51	86.89	90.87	96.05	99.62	103.3	110.3	118.8	129.9	135.7

	1992	1993	1994	1995	1996	1997	1998	1999	2000	2001
Jan.	135.6	137.9	141.3	146.0	150.2	154.4	159.5	163.4	166.6	171.1
Feb.	136.3	138.8	142.1	146.9	150.9	155.0	160.3	163.7	167.5	172.0
March	136.7	139.3	142.5	147.5	151.5	155.4	160.8	164.1	168.4	172.2
April	138.8	140.6	144.2	149.0	152.6	156.3	162.6	165.2	170.1	173.1
May	139.3	141.1	144.7	149.6	152.9	156.9	163.5	165.6	170.7	174.2
June	139.3	141.0	144.7	149.8	153.0	157.5	163.4	165.6	171.1	174.4
July	138.8	140.7	144.0	149.1	152.4	157.5	163.0	165.1	170.5	173.3
Aug.	138.9	141.3	144.7	149.9	153.1	158.5	163.7	165.5	170.5	174.0
Sept.	139.4	141.9	145.0	150.6	153.8	159.3	164.4	166.2	171.7	174.6
Oct.	139.9	141.8	145.2	149.8	153.8	159.5	164.5	166.5	171.6	174.3
Nov.	139.7	141.6	145.3	149.8	153.9	159.6	164.4	166.7	172.1	173.6
Dec.	139.2	141.9	146.0	150.7	154.4	160.0	164.4	167.3	172.2	173.4

	2002	2003	2004	2005	2006	2007	2008	2009	2010	2011
Jan.	173.3	178.4	183.1	188.9	193.4	201.6	209.8	210.1	217.9	
Feb.	173.8	179.3	183.8	189.6	194.2	203.1	211.4	211.4	219.2	
March	174.5	179.9	184.6	190.5	195.0	204.4	212.1	211.3	220.7	
April	175.7	181.2	185.7	191.6	196.5	205.4	214.0	211.5	222.8	
May	176.2	181.5	186.5	192.0	197.7	206.2	215.1	212.8	223.6	
June	176.2	181.3	186.8	192.2	198.5	207.3	216.8	213.4		
July	175.9	181.3	186.8	192.2	198.5	206.1	216.5	213.4		
Aug.	176.4	181.6	187.4	192.6	199.2	207.3	217.2	214.4		
Sept.	177.6	182.5	188.1	193.1	200.1	208.0	218.4	215.3		
Oct.	177.9	182.6	188.6	193.3	200.4	208.9	217.7	216.0		
Nov.	178.2	182.7	189.0	193.6	201.1	209.7	216.0	216.6		
Dec.	178.5	183.5	189.9	194.1	202.7	210.9	212.9	218.0		

Key Data

12 PAYE thresholds

Tax year	Amount	
	Weekly **£**	**Monthly** **£**
2010–11	125.00	540.00
2009–10	125.00	540.00
2008–09	116.00	503.00
2007–08	100.00	435.00
2006–07	97.00	420.00
2005–06	94.00	408.00
2004–05	91.00	395.00
2003–04	89.00	385.00

Note

The figures for 2008–09 were increased from £105 (weekly) and £453 (monthly) from 7 September 2008 (as a result of the changes made during the year to the personal allowance). As a result, employers were required to add 60 to the previous tax code number for all L codes in time for the first payday on or after 7 September 2008 (e.g. 543L became 603L). The emergency tax code was 543L for paydays before 7 September 2008 but rose to 603L for paydays on or after that date.

Under normal circumstances, employers need not deduct tax for employees who earn less than the above amounts.

The PAYE monthly and weekly thresholds are calculated arithmetically from the personal allowance (SI 2003/2682, reg. 9(8)).

13 PAYE returns

PAYE returns: deadlines

Forms	Date	Provision	Penalty provisions
P14, P35, P38 and P38A	19 May following tax year	*Income Tax (Pay As You Earn) Regulations* 2003 (SI 2003/2682), reg. 73 and 74	TMA 1970, s. 98A
P60 (to employee)	31 May following tax year	*Income Tax (Pay As You Earn) Regulations* 2003 (SI 2003/2682), reg. 67	TMA 1970, s. 98A
P9D and P11D	6 July following tax year	*Income Tax (Pay As You Earn) Regulations* 2003 (SI 2003/2682), reg. 85–87	TMA 1970, s. 98
P46 (Car)	3 May, 2 August, 2 November, 2 February	*Income Tax (Pay As You Earn) Regulations* 2003 (SI 2003/2682), reg. 90	TMA 1970, s. 98

PAYE returns: penalties

Changes from April 2009

A new penalty regime has been introduced for returns for periods commencing on or after 1 April 2008 and where the return is due on or after 1 April 2009. Penalties are determined as a percentage of potential lost revenue. The percentage to be applied is determined according to whether the inaccuracy giving rise to the penalty was 'careless' (up to 30 per cent) 'deliberate but not concealed' (up to 70 per cent) or 'deliberate and concealed' (up to 100 per cent).

Earlier periods

Penalties (fixed, but see ESC B46) imposed for delays (TMA 1970, s. 98A)

Forms	First 12 months	Thereafter
P14, P35, P38 and P38A	£100 per 50 employees per month	Additional penalty not exceeding 100% of the tax and NIC payable for the year but remaining unpaid by 19 April following end of tax year

Penalties (mitigable) that may be imposed for delays (TMA 1970, s. 98)

Forms	Initial	Continuing
P9D and P11D	£300 per return	£60 per day

Penalties that may be imposed for incorrect returns

Forms	Provision TMA 1970	Penalty
P14, P35, P38 and P38A	s. 98A	Maximum of 100% of tax underpaid (s. 98A(4))
P9 and P11D	s. 98	Maximum penalty £3,000 (s. 98(2))

Interest on certain PAYE paid late

Where an employer has not paid the net tax deductible by him under PAYE to the collector within 14 days of the end of the tax year, the unpaid tax carries interest at the prescribed rate from the reckonable date until the date of payment. Certain repayments of tax also attract interest.

Interest on Class 1, 1A and 4 National Insurance contributions

From 19 April 1993 interest is charged on Class 1 contributions unpaid after the fourteenth day after the end of the tax year in which they were due. Interest is due on Class 1A contributions unpaid 14 days after the end of the tax year in which they were due to be paid.

For assessments issued after 18 April 1993 interest can be charged on overdue Class 4 contributions at the prescribed rate.

Law: SSCBA 1992, Sch. 1, para. 6(2), (3)

PAYE electronic communications: penalties (reg. 205 failures)

Penalties for tax year 2010–11 and later years
(SI 2003/2682, reg. 210AA)

Table 9ZA

Number of employees (note 1)	Penalty
1–5	£100
6–49	£300
50–249	£600
250–399	£900
400–499	£1,200
500–599	£1,500
600–699	£1,800
700–799	£2,100
800–899	£2,400

Number of employees (note 1)	Penalty
900–999	£2,700
1,000 or more	£3,000

Note

(1) Number of employees for whom particulars should have been included with the relevant annual return.

Penalties for tax year 2009–10
(SI 2003/2682, reg. 210A)

Table 9

Number of employees (note 1)	Penalty
1–5	£0
6–49	£100
50–249	£600
250–399	£900
400–499	£1,200
500–599	£1,500
600–699	£1,800
700–799	£2,100
800–899	£2,400
900–999	£2,700
1,000 or more	£3,000

Note

(1) Number of employees for whom particulars should have been included with the relevant annual return.

Penalties for tax year 2004–05 to 2008–09
(SI 2003/2682, reg. 210A)

Former table 9

Number of employees (note 1)	Penalty
1–49	£0
50–249	£600 (but see note 2)
250–399	£900

Number of employees (note 1)	Penalty
400–499	£1,200
500–599	£1,500
600–699	£1,800
700–799	£2,100
800–899	£2,400
900–999	£2,700
1,000 or more	£3,000

Note

(1) Number of employees for whom particulars should have been included with the specified information.

(2) But nil for tax year 2004–05 only (50–249 employees).

PAYE electronic communications: penalties (reg. 205A failures)

Penalties for tax quarter ending 5 April 2010 and for tax year 2010–11

(SI 2003/2682, reg. 210B)

Table 9A

Number of items (note 1)	Penalty
1–5	£0
6–49	£100
50–149	£300
150–299	£600
300–399	£900
400–499	£1,200
500–599	£1,500
600–699	£1,800
700–799	£2,100
800–899	£2,400
900–999	£2,700
1,000 or more	£3,000

Key Data

Note

[1] Number of items of specified information the employer has failed to deliver in the tax quarter. (Each item mentioned in reg. 207(1) paras. (a) to (d) counts as a separate item of specified information.)

PAYE surcharges

(SI 2003/2682, reg. 203)

Specified percentage for each default in a surcharge period	
Default number (within the surcharge period)	Specified percentage %
1	0.00
2	0.00
3	0.17
4	0.17
5	0.17
6	0.33
7	0.33
8	0.33
9	0.58
10	0.58
11	0.58
12 and more defaults	0.83

14 PAYE codes

The PAYE code enables an employer or payer of pension to make any changes announced in the Budget. The codes are as follows:

L   tax code with basic personal allowance;
P   tax code with full personal allowance for those aged 65–74;
Y   tax code with full personal allowance for those aged 75 or over;
T   tax code used where HM Revenue & Customs reviewing other items in tax code. Also used where HM Revenue & Customs asked not to use other codes;
K   total allowances are less than total deductions.

Note

Codes A and H are no longer applicable for 2003–04 onwards. Code V is obsolete from April 2009 (as all individuals born before 6 April 1935 and qualifying for Married Couple's allowance (MCA) will be aged 75 and over during the tax year ended 5 April 2010. MCA is therefore due at the higher rate).

Other codes

The codes BR, DO, OT and NT are generally used where there is a second source of income and all allowances have been included in tax code which is applied to first or main source of income.

15 Rates of interest on overdue tax

The following tables give the rates of interest applicable under FA 1989, s. 178 and prescribed rates of interest (VATA 1994, s. 74 and former TMA 1970, s. 89). The rates apply to interest charged on overdue tax, with the exception of inheritance tax. From 6 February 1997 the rate for corporation tax diverges, see below.

Period of application		Rate %
From 29 September	2009	3
From 24 March	2009 to 28 September 2009	2.5
From 6 January	2009 to 26 January 2009	4.5
From 6 December	2008 to 5 January 2009	5.5
From 6 November	2008 to 5 December 2008	6.5
From 6 January	2008 to 5 November 2008	7.5
From 6 August	2007 to 5 January 2008	8.5
From 6 September	2006 to 5 August 2007	7.5
From 6 September	2005 to 5 September 2006	6.5
From 6 September	2004 to 5 September 2005	7.5
From 6 December	2003 to 5 September 2004	6.5
From 6 August	2003 to 5 December 2003	5.5
From 6 November	2001 to 5 August 2003	6.5
From 6 May	2001 to 5 November 2001	7.5
From 6 February	2000 to 5 May 2001	8.5
From 6 March	1999 to 5 February 2000	7.5
From 6 January	1999 to 5 March 1999	8.5
From 6 August	1997 to 5 January 1999	9.5
From 6 February	1997 to 5 August 1997	8.5
From 6 February	1996 to 5 February 1997	6.25
From 6 March	1995 to 5 February 1996	7
From 6 October	1994 to 5 March 1995	6.25
From 6 January	1994 to 5 October 1994	5.5
From 6 March	1993 to 5 January 1994	6.25
From 6 December	1992 to 5 March 1993	7
From 6 November	1992 to 5 December 1992	7.75
From 6 October	1991 to 5 November 1992	9.25
From 6 July	1991 to 5 October 1991	10
From 6 May	1991 to 5 July 1991	10.75
From 6 March	1991 to 5 May 1991	11.5

Notes

Fixed by Treasury order under SI 1989/1297.

Rates of interest on overdue corporation tax

With effect for **interest** periods commencing on 6 February 1997, the rates of interest for the purposes of late paid or unpaid corporation tax are different from those for other taxes. From that date, the rate of interest on late paid or unpaid corporation tax will depend on the accounting period for which the tax is due and, under self-assessment, the nature of the tax due.

Self assessment

For accounting periods within the self assessment regime (or CTSA – APs ending on or after 1 July 1999), these rates are distinct from those for periods before the start of self assessment because the interest is an allowable deduction for tax purposes (see below).

In addition, there are separate provisions for:

- overpaid instalments of corporation tax (which benefit from a more favourable rate – for details of payment by instalments, see below); and
- other liabilities such as the final liability due on the date specified in accordance with the table below.

Pre-self assessment

For accounting periods before the start of self assessment, there are two rates of interest applicable to all unpaid/late paid tax depending on whether the accounting period is within the Pay and File regime (APs ending after 30 September 1993) or note (i.e. periods ending before 1 October 1993).

CTSA (APs ending on or after 1.7.99)

1. Unpaid CT (other than underpaid instalments)

Period of application	Rate %
From 29 September 2009	3
24 March 2009 to 28 September 2009	2.5
27 January 2009 to 23 March 2009	3.5
6 January 2009 to 26 January 2009	4.5
6 December 2008 to 5 January 2009	5.5
6 November 2008 to 5 December 2008	6.5
6 January 2008 to 5 November 2008	7.5
6 August 2007 to 5 January 2008	8.5
6 September 2006 to 5 August 2007	7.5
6 September 2005 to 5 September 2006	6.5
6 September 2004 to 5 September 2005	7.5
6 December 2003 to 5 September 2004	6.5
6 August 2003 to 5 December 2003	5.5
6 November 2001 to 5 August 2003	6.5
6 May 2001 to 5 November 2001	7.5

Period of application	Rate %
6 February 2000 to 5 May 2001	8.5
6 March 1999 to 5 February 2000	7.5

2. Underpaid instalments

Period of application	Rate %
From 16 March 2009	1.50
16 February 2009 to 15 March 2009	2.00
19 January 2009 to 15 February 2009	2.50
15 December 2008 to 18 January 2009	3.00
17 November 2008 to 14 December 2008	4.00
20 October 2008 to 16 November 2008	5.50
21 April 2008 to 19 October 2008	6.00
18 February 2008 to 20 April 2008	6.25
17 December 2007 to 17 February 2008	6.50
16 July 2007 to 16 December 2007	6.75
21 May 2007 to 15 July 2007	6.50
22 January 2007 to 20 May 2007	6.25
20 November 2006 to 21 January 2007	6.00
14 August 2006 to 19 November 2006	5.75
15 August 2005 to 13 August 2006	5.50
16 August 2004 to 14 August 2005	5.75
21 June 2004 to 15 August 2004	5.50
17 May 2004 to 20 June 2004	5.25
16 February 2004 to 16 May 2004	5
17 November 2003 to 15 February 2004	4.75
21 July 2003 to 16 November 2003	4.5
17 February 2003 to 20 July 2003	4.75
19 November 2001 to 16 February 2003	5
15 October 2001 to 18 November 2001	5.5
1 October 2001 to 14 October 2001	5.75
13 August 2001 to 30 September 2001	6
21 May 2001 to 12 August 2001	6.25
16 April 2001 to 20 May 2001	6.5
19 February 2001 to 15 April 2001	6.75

Period of application	Rate %
20 April 2000 to 18 February 2001	7
21 February 2000 to 19 April 2000	8

Pre-CTSA

Period of application	Rate % pre-Pay and File	Rate % post-Pay and File
From 29 September 2009	3	3
24 March 2009 to 28 September 2009	2	1.75
27 January 2009 to 23 March 2009	2.75	2.75
6 January 2009 to 26 January 2009	3.5	3.5
6 December 2008 to 5 January 2009	4.25	4.25
6 November 2008 to 5 December 2008	5	5
6 January 2008 to 5 November 2008	5.75	6
6 August 2007 to 5 January 2008	6.5	6.75
6 September 2006 to 5 August 2007	5.75	6
6 September 2005 to 5 September 2006	5	5.25
6 September 2004 to 5 September 2005	5.75	6
6 December 2003 to 5 September 2004	5.25	5
6 August 2003 to 5 December 2003	4.25	4.25
6 November 2001 to 5 August 2003	5	5
6 May 2001 to 5 November 2001	5.75	6
6 February 2000 to 5 May 2001	6.5	6.75
6 March 1999 to 5 February 2000	5.75	5.75
6 January 1999 to 5 March 1999	6.5	6.5
6 August 1997 to 5 January 1999	7.25	7.5
6 February 1997 to 5 August 1997	6.25	6.25

Rates of interest on overpaid corporation tax

With effect for **interest** periods commencing on 6 February 1997, the rates of interest for the purposes of overpaid corporation tax are different from those for other taxes. The rate of interest on overpaid corporation tax will depend on the accounting period for which the tax is due and, under self assessment, the nature of the tax repayable.

Self assessment

For accounting periods within the self assessment regime (CTSA), i.e. APs on or after 1 July 1999, the rates of interest on repayments of overpaid corporation tax are distinct from those for pre-CTSA periods, because the interest is taxable (see below).

In addition, there are separate provisions for:

- overpaid instalments of corporation tax; and
- payments of corporation tax made after the normal due date.

Pay and File and earlier periods

For accounting periods within Pay and File (APs ending after 30 September 1993) and accounting periods before Pay and File, interest on overpaid corporation tax, repayments of income tax and payments of tax credits in respect of franked investment income received is given at the appropriate rate shown in the relevant table below.

CTSA (APs ending on or after 1 July 1999)

1. Overpaid CT (other than overpaid instalments and early payments of CT not due by instalments)

Period of application	Rate %
From 29 September 2009	0.5
27 January 2009 to 28 September 2009	0
6 December 2009 to 26 January 2009	1
6 December 2008 to 5 January 2009	2
6 November 2008 to 5 December 2008	3
6 January 2008 to 5 November 2008	4
6 August 2007 to 5 January 2008	5
6 September 2006 to 5 August 2007	4
6 September 2005 to 5 September 2006	3
6 September 2004 to 5 September 2005	4
6 December 2003 to 5 September 2004	3
6 August 2003 to 5 December 2003	2
6 November 2001 to 5 August 2003	3
6 May 2001 to 5 November 2001	4
6 February 2000 to 5 May 2001	5
6 March 1999 to 5 February 2000	4
6 January 1999 to 5 March 1999	5

Key Data

2. Overpaid instalments and early payments of CT not due by instalments

Period of application	Rate %
From 21 September 2009	0.5
16 March 2009 to 20 September 2009	0.25
16 February 2009 to 15 March 2009	0.75
19 January 2009 to 15 February 2009	1.25
15 December 2008 to 18 January 2009	1.75
17 November 2008 to 14 December 2008	2.75
20 October 2008 to 16 November 2008	4.25
21 April 2008 to 19 October 2008	4.75
18 February 2008 to 20 April 2008	5.00
17 December 2007 to 17 February 2008	5.25
16 July 2007 to 16 December 2007	5.50
21 May 2007 to 15 July 2007	5.25
22 January 2007 to 20 May 2007	5.00
20 November 2006 to 21 January 2007	4.75
14 August 2006 to 19 November 2006	4.50
15 August 2005 to 13 August 2006	4.25
16 August 2004 to 14 August 2005	4.50
21 June 2004 to 15 August 2004	4.25
17 May 2004 to 20 June 2004	4.00
16 February 2004 to 16 May 2004	3.75
17 November 2003 to 15 February 2004	3.5
21 July 2003 to 16 November 2003	3.25
17 February 2003 to 20 July 2003	3.50
19 November 2001 to 16 February 2003	3.75
15 October 2001 to 18 November 2001	4.25
1 October 2001 to 14 October 2001	4.50
13 August 2001 to 30 September 2001	4.75
21 May 2001 to 12 August 2001	5.00
16 April 2001 to 20 May 2001	5.25
19 February 2001 to 15 April 2001	5.5

Period of application	Rate %
21 February 2000 to 18 February 2001	5.75
24 January 2000 to 20 February 2000	5.5
15 November 1999 to 23 January 2000	5.25
20 September 1999 to 14 November 1999	5.00
21 June 1999 to 19 September 1999	4.75
19 April 1999 to 20 June 1999	5.00
15 February 1999 to 18 April 1999	5.25
18 January 1999 to 14 February 1999	5.75
Before 18 January 1999	6.00

Pay and File

Period of application	Rate %
From 29 September 2009	0.5
27 January 2009 to 28 September 2009	0.00
6 January 2009 to 26 January 2009	0.5
6 December 2008 to 5 January 2009	1.25
From 6 November 2008 to 5 December 2008	2
From 6 January 2008 to 5 November 2008	2.75
6 August 2007 to 5 January 2008	3.50
6 September 2006 to 5 August 2007	2.75
6 September 2005 to 5 September 2006	2
6 September 2004 to 5 September 2005	2.75
6 December 2003 to 5 September 2004	2
6 August 2003 to 5 December 2003	1.25
6 November 2001 to 5 August 2003	2
6 May 2001 to 5 November 2001	2.75
6 February 2000 to 5 May 2001	3.5
6 March 1999 to 5 February 2000	2.75
6 January 1999 to 5 March 1999	3.25
6 August 1997 to 5 January 1999	4
6 February 1996 to 5 August 1997	3.25
6 March 1995 to 5 February 1996	4

Key Data

Period of application	Rate %
6 October 1994 to 5 March 1995	3.25
6 January 1994 to 5 October 1994	2.5
1 October 1993 to 5 January 1994	3.25

Pre-Pay and File

Period of application	Rate %
From 29 September 2009	0.5
24 March 2009 to 28 September 2009	2.00
27 January 2009 to 23 March 2009	2.75
6 January 2009 to 26 January 2009	3.5
6 December 2008 to 5 January 2009	4.25
From 6 November 2008 to 5 December 2008	5
From 6 January 2008 to 5 November 2008	5.75
6 August 2007 to 5 January 2008	6.5
6 September 2006 to 5 August 2007	5.75
6 September 2005 to 5 September 2006	5
6 September 2004 to 5 September 2005	5.75
6 December 2003 to 5 September 2004	5
6 August 2003 to 5 December 2003	4.25
6 November 2001 to 5 August 2003	5
6 May 2001 to 5 November 2001	5.75
6 February 2000 to 5 May 2001	6.5
6 March 1999 to 5 February 2000	5.75
6 January 1999 to 5 March 1999	6.5
6 August 1997 to 5 January 1999	7.25
6 February 1996 to 5 August 1997	6.25
6 March 1995 to 5 February 1996	7
6 October 1994 to 5 March 1995	6.25
6 January 1994 to 5 October 1994	5.5
6 March 1993 to 5 January 1994	6.25
6 December 1992 to 5 March 1993	7
6 November 1992 to 5 December 1992	7.75

Period of application	Rate %
6 October 1991 to 5 November 1992	9.25
6 July 1991 to 5 October 1991	10
6 May 1991 to 5 July 1991	10.75
6 March 1991 to 5 May 1991	11.5

Inheritance tax

Dates at which rates applicable	Chargeable transfers made on death %	Chargeable transfers not made on death %
From 29 September 2009	3	3
From 24 March 2009 to 28 September 2009	0	0
From 27 January 2009 to 23 March 2009	1	1
From 6 January 2009 to 26 January 2009	2	2
From 6 November 2008 to 5 January 2009	3	3
From 6 January 2008 to 5 November 2008	4	4
From 6 August 2007 to 5 January 2008	5	5
From 6 September 2006 to 5 August 2007	4	4
From 6 September 2005 to 5 September 2006	3	3
From 6 September 2004 to 5 September 2005	4	4
From 6 December 2003 to 5 September 2004	3	3
From 6 August 2003 to 5 December 2003	2	2
From 6 November 2001 to 5 August 2003	3	3
From 6 May 2001 to 5 November 2001	4	4
From 6 February 2000 to 5 May 2001	5	5
From 6 March 1999 to 5 February 2000	4	4
From 6 October 1994 to 5 March 1999	5	5
From 6 January 1994 to 5 October 1994	4	4
From 6 December 1992 to 5 January 1994	5	5

Key Data

Dates at which rates applicable	Chargeable transfers made on death %	Chargeable transfers not made on death %
From 6 November 1992 to 5 December 1992	6	6
From 6 July 1991 to 5 November 1992	8	8
From 6 May 1991 to 5 July 1991	9	9

Note

Rate change by order under the *Taxes (Interest Rate) Regulations* 1989 (SI 1989/1297).

From 16 December 1986 a single rate of interest has been prescribed in relation to all chargeable transfers, whether or not made on death.

Value added tax

Default interest on certain VAT recoverable by assessment is calculated at the following rates:

Date	Rate %
From 29 September 2009	3
From 24 March 2009 to 28 September 2009	2.5
From 27 January 2009 to 23 March 2009	3.5
From 6 January 2009 to 26 January 2009	4.5
From 6 December 2008 to 5 January 2009	5.5
From 6 November 2008 to 5 December 2008	6.5
From 6 September 2006 to 5 November 2008	7.5
From 6 September 2005 to 5 September 2006	6.5
From 6 September 2004 to 5 September 2005	7.5
From 6 December 2003 to 5 September 2004	6.5
From 6 September 2003 to 5 December 2003	5.5
From 6 November 2001 to 5 September 2003	6.5
From 6 May 2001 to 5 November 2001	7.5
From 6 February 2000 to 5 May 2001	8.5
From 6 March 1999 to 5 February 2000	7.5
From 6 January 1999 to 5 March 1999	8.5
From 6 July 1998 to 5 January 1999	9.5
From 6 February 1996 to 5 July 1998	6.25
From 6 March 1995 to 5 February 1996	7
From 6 October 1994 to 5 March 1995	6.25
From 6 January 1994 to 5 October 1994	5.5
From 6 March 1993 to 5 January 1994	6.25
From 6 December 1992 to 5 March 1993	7
From 6 November 1992 to 5 December 1992	7.75
From 6 October 1991 to 5 November 1992	9.25
From 6 July 1991 to 5 October 1991	10
From 6 May 1991 to 5 July 1991	10.75
From 6 March 1991 to 5 May 1991	11.5
From 6 November 1990 to 5 March 1991	12.25
From 1 April 1990 to 5 November 1990	13

Key Data

For the default surcharge payable in respect of many non-payments or underpayments of VAT and for the serious misdeclaration penalty, see 8516 and 8528.

Interest on overpaid VAT arises under VATA 1994, s. 78 in certain cases of official error:

Period of application		Rate %
From 29 September 2009		0.5
From 27 January 2009 to	28 September 2009	0
From 6 January 2009 to	26 January 2009	1
From 6 December 2008 to	5 January 2009	2
From 6 November 2008 to	5 December 2008	3
From 6 September 2006 to	5 November 2008	4
From 6 September 2005 to	5 September 2006	3
From 6 September 2004 to	5 September 2005	4
From 6 December 2003 to	5 September 2004	3
From 6 September 2003 to	5 December 2003	2
From 6 November 2001 to	5 September 2003	3
From 6 May 2001 to	5 November 2001	4
From 6 February 2000 to	5 May 2001	5
From 6 March 1999 to	5 February 2000	4
From 6 January 1999 to	5 March 1999	5
From 1 April 1997 to	5 January 1999	6
From 6 February 1993 to	31 March 1997	8
From 16 October 1991 to	5 February 1993	10.25

Note

Generally, a repayment under VATA 1994, s. 78 in relation to any claim made after 18 July 1996 is not made for more than three years after the end of the applicable period to which it relates.

20 Plant and machinery – overview of allowances from April 2008

The following is a summary of the main plant and machinery allowances available from 6 April 2008. The cross references to commentary relate to *CCH British Tax Reporter*.

Description	Detail	Notes	Commentary
Annual investment allowance	Full relief for first £50,000 (adjusted pro rata for shorter or longer periods).	1. Restricted relief for periods spanning 1 or 6 April 2008. 2. AIA can cover long-life asset and integral features, as well as standard P&M. 3. Groups and certain other related parties share a single amount.	¶236-400ff.

Description	Detail	Notes	Commentary
First-year allowances (100%) for cars	Cars with CO_2 emissions not exceeding 110g/km.	Threshold reduced from 120g/km from 1 April 2008.	¶237-450ff.
Other first-year allowances (100%)	Still available for certain energy-saving assets; environmentally beneficial assets; refuelling stations; plant used in ring-fence trades.	Payable tax credits available for company losses created by allowances re energy-saving or environmentally beneficial expenditure.	Energy-saving plant: ¶237-400. Environmentally beneficial assets: ¶237-600. Refuelling stations: ¶237-500. Ring-fence trades: ¶237-550.
Writing-down allowances (20%)	Standard rate of WDA for assets, including cars but excluding those assets attracting relief at just 10% as below.	1. Reduced from 25% for P&M only for expenditure incurred from 1 April or 6 April (CT or income tax). 2. £3,000 restriction for cars remains in place, but new system to apply from April 2009.	¶238-050ff.
Writing-down allowances (10%)	Reduced rate of WDA applies to certain 'special rate' expenditure, covering long-life assets, integral features, thermal insulation.	1. Transitional provisions apply for periods spanning 1 or 6 April 2008. 2. AIAs (see above) are available for this expenditure. 3. Higher emission cars will have 10% WDAs from April 2009.	Long-life assets: ¶239-500ff. Integral features: ¶243-400ff. Thermal insulation: ¶246-030. Cars: ¶237-450ff.
Balancing allowances		No change from April 2008.	¶238-100ff.
Balancing charges		No change from April 2008.	¶238-125ff.

Plant and machinery: first-year allowances – from April 2008 (CAA 2001, s. 52)

Changes were made to first-year allowances from April 2008. Subject to the general exclusions listed below, full 100 per cent allowances are still available for the following types of expenditure incurred by a business of any size. If full FYAs are not claimed, WDA is normally available at 20 per cent on a reducing balance basis.

Nature of expenditure	Authority (CAA 2001)	Notes
Energy-saving plant or machinery	s. 45A–45C	Loss-making companies may claim tax rebate
Cars with very low CO_2 emissions	s. 45D	Threshold tightened from April 2008
Plant or machinery for certain refuelling stations	s. 45E	
Plant or machinery (other than a long life asset) for use by a company wholly in a ring fence trade	s. 45F	
Environmentally beneficial plant or machinery	s. 45H–45J	Loss-making companies may claim tax rebate

Plant and machinery: first-year allowances – general

No first-year allowances are available, for a business of any size, for:

- expenditure incurred in the final chargeable period;
- cars (other than those with very low CO_2 emissions);
- certain ships and railway assets;
- long-life assets (other than plant or machinery for use by a company wholly in a ring fence trade, in which case a 24 per cent FYA is available if such expenditure is a LLA);
- plant or machinery for leasing;
- in certain anti-avoidance cases where the obtaining of a FYA is linked to a change in the nature or conduct of a trade;
- where an asset was initially acquired for purposes other than those of the qualifying activity;
- where an asset was acquired by way of a gift;
- where plant or machinery that was provided for long funding leasing starts to be used for other purposes.

Plant and machinery: first-year allowances – medium-sized enterprises (CAA 2001, s. 52)

Medium-sized enterprises are entitled to all the allowances listed in the table above. Until April 2008, they were also entitled to a 40 per cent FYA on any other plant and machinery. The removal of these other allowances means that the size distinction ceases to be relevant for capital allowance purposes.

All FYAs are subject to the general exclusions listed above.

Plant and machinery: first-year allowances – small enterprises (CAA 2001, s. 52)

Small enterprises are entitled to all the allowances listed in the table above. Until April 2008, they were also entitled to the additional allowances referred to at ¶2-020. The first-year allowance rate of 40 per cent was, however, increased to 50 per cent for the years 2004–05, 2006–07 (but not 2005–06) and 2007–08 (and for financial years 2004, 2006 and 2008 (but not 2005)).

The removal of these other allowances from 2008 means that the size distinction ceases to be relevant for capital allowance purposes.

All FYAs are subject to the general exclusions listed above.

Plant and machinery: writing-down allowances (CAA 2001, s. 56)

	From April 2008	Before April 2008
Standard WDAs	20%	25%
Long-life assets	10%	6%
Overseas leasing	10%	10%
Integral features	10%	25% (i.e. treated as other P&M)
Cars over £12,000	Lower of £3,000 or 20%	Lower of £3,000 or 25%
Thermal insulation	10%	25% (but restricted to industrial buildings)

Integral features (CAA 2001, s. 33A)

The following assets are designated as integral features:

- electrical systems (including lighting systems);
- cold water systems;
- space or water heating systems, powered systems of ventilation, air cooling or air purification, and any floor or ceiling comprised in such systems;
- lifts, escalators and moving walkways; and
- external solar shading.

The draft legislation had proposed an additional category (active facades) but these were not in the event added to the list.

Expenditure on thermal insulation and long-life assets is also allocated to the 'special rate' pool.

Definition of small and medium-sized enterprises

This concept was relevant for capital allowances purposes up to 31 March or 5 April 2008 (respectively for corporation tax and income tax purposes).

A company or business is a *small enterprise* if:

- it qualifies (or is treated as qualifying) as small under the *Companies Act* 2006, s. 382, for the financial year of the company in which the expenditure is incurred; and
- it is not a member of a medium or large group (*Companies Act* 2006, s. 466) at the time the expenditure is incurred.

A company or business is a *small or medium-sized enterprise* if:

- it qualifies (or is treated as qualifying) as small or medium-sized under the *Companies Act* 2006, s. 382, for the financial year of the company in which the expenditure is incurred; and
- it is not a member of a large group (*Companies Act* 2006, s. 466) at the time the expenditure is incurred.

Under the *Companies Act* 2006, s.382, a company qualifies as small or medium-sized for a financial year if two or more of the requirements shown below are met in that and the preceding financial year. A group is small or medium-sized under the *Companies Act* 2006, s.466 in a year in which it satisfies two or more of the requirements per relevant category, as shown in the tables below.

There are two tables set out below. The first table is in respect of years ending on or after 30 January 2004 (but see exception below) and takes into account the changes made by the *Companies Act 1985 (Accounts of Small and Medium-Sized Enterprises and Audit Exemption) (Amendment) Regulations* 2004 (SI 2004/16). The second table is in respect of years ending before 30 January 2004. However, as an exception, the second table applies also to a financial year that only ends on or after 30 January 2004 by reason of an exercise of the power (conferred by the *Companies Act* 2006, s. 392) to alter the accounting reference date, by the giving of a notice (namely, Form 225, *Change of accounting reference date*) to the Registrar of Companies on or after 9 January 2004.

The first table is as follows:

Type of company	Requirements	
Small company	Turnover	Not more than £5.6m
	Balance sheet total	Not more than £2.8m
	Number of employees	Not more than 50
Medium-sized company	Turnover	Not more than £22.8m
	Balance sheet total	Not more than £11.4m
	Number of employees	Not more than 250

25

Key Data

Type of company	Requirements	
Small group	Aggregate turnover	Not more than £5.6m net (or £6.72m gross)
	Aggregate balance sheet total	Not more than £2.8m net (or £3.36m gross)
	Aggregate number of employees	Not more than 50
Medium-sized group	Aggregate turnover	Not more than £22.8m net (or £27.36m gross)
	Aggregate balance sheet total	Not more than £11.4m net (or £13.68m gross)
	Aggregate number of employees	Not more than 250

The second table is as follows:

Type of company	Requirements	
Small company	Turnover	Not more than £2.8m
	Balance sheet total	Not more than £1.4m
	Number of employees	Not more than 50
Medium-sized company	Turnover	Not more than £11.2m
	Balance sheet total	Not more than £5.6m
	Number of employees	Not more than 250
Small group	Aggregate turnover	Not more than £2.8m net (or £3.6m gross)
	Aggregate balance sheet total	Not more than £1.4m net (or £1.68m gross)
	Aggregate number of employees	Not more than 50
Medium-sized group	Aggregate turnover	Not more than £11.2m net (or £13.44m gross)
	Aggregate balance sheet total	Not more than £5.6m net (or £6.72m gross)
	Aggregate number of employees	Not more than 250

Expenditure unaffected by statutory restrictions re buildings

The restrictions in CAA 2001, s. 21 and 22(buildings, structures and other assets) do not apply to expenditure in List C at CAA 2001, s. 23. List C, as amended at items 2, 3 and 6 by *Finance Act* 2008 with effect for expenditure incurred from 1 or 6 April 2008, is as follows:

(1)   Machinery (including devices for providing motive power) not within any other item in this list.

(2)   Gas and sewerage systems provided mainly

    (a)   to meet the particular requirements of the qualifying activity;

    (b)   to serve particular plant or machinery used for the purposes of the qualifying activity.

(3)   [omitted by *Finance Act* 2008].

(4)   Manufacturing or processing equipment; storage equipment (including cold rooms); display equipment; and counters, checkouts and similar equipment.

(5)   Cookers, washing machines, dishwashers, refrigerators and similar equipment; washbasins, sinks, baths, showers, sanitary ware and similar equipment; and furniture and furnishings.

(6)   Hoists.

(7)   Sound insulation provided mainly to meet the particular requirements of the qualifying activity.

(8)   Computer, telecommunication and surveillance systems (including their wiring or other links).

(9)   Refrigeration or cooling equipment.

(10) Fire alarm systems; sprinkler and other equipment for extinguishing or containing fires.

(11) Burglar alarm systems.

(12) Strong rooms in bank or building society premises; safes.

(13) Partition walls, where moveable and intended to be moved in the course of the qualifying activity.

(14) Decorative assets provided for the enjoyment of the public in hotel, restaurant or similar trades.

(15) Advertising hoardings; signs, displays and similar assets.

(16) Swimming-pools (including diving boards, slides and structures on which such boards or slides are mounted).

(17) Any glasshouse constructed so that the required environment (namely, air, heat, light, irrigation and temperature) for the growing of plants is provided automatically by means of devices forming an integral part of its structure.

Key Data

(18)   Cold stores.

(19)   Caravans provided mainly for holiday lettings.

(20)   Buildings provided for testing aircraft engines run within the buildings.

(21)   Moveable buildings intended to be moved in the course of the qualifying activity.

(22)   The alteration of land for the purpose only of installing plant or machinery.

(23)   The provision of dry docks.

(24)   The provision of any jetty or similar structure provided mainly to carry plant or machinery.

(25)   The provision of pipelines or underground ducts or tunnels with a primary purpose of carrying utility conduits.

(26)   The provision of towers to support floodlights.

(27)   The provision of

    (a)   any reservoir incorporated into a water treatment works; or
    (b)   any service reservoir of treated water for supply within any housing estate or other particular locality.

(28)   The provision of

    (a)   silos provided for temporary storage; or
    (b)   storage tanks.

(29)   The provision of slurry pits or silage clamps.

(30)   The provision of fish tanks or fish ponds.

(31)   The provision of rails, sleepers and ballast for a railway or tramway.

(32)   The provision of structures and other assets for providing the setting for any ride at an amusement park or exhibition.

(33)   The provision of fixed zoo cages.

Items 1–16 of the above list do not, however, include any asset with the principal purpose of insulating or enclosing the interior of a building or of providing an interior wall, floor or ceiling that is intended to remain permanently in place.

Industrial buildings, hotels and sports pavilions; agricultural buildings and structures

These allowances are being phased out. To achieve this, the following percentages are applied to the writing-down allowances that would otherwise be available for industrial buildings, hotels and sports pavilions and agricultural buildings and structures.

Financial year beginning	Tax year	Percentage
1 April 2007 and earlier	2007–08 and earlier	100 per cent

Financial year beginning	Tax year	Percentage
1 April 2008	2008–09	75 per cent
1 April 2009	2009–10	50 per cent
1 April 2010	2010–11	25 per cent
1 April 2011 and later	2011–12 and later	0 per cent (ie no further allowances given)

Where a chargeable period straddles the financial or tax year, the WDA is to be apportioned on a strict time basis.

The restriction applies both to the standard four per cent WDA and to the higher WDA available for some used buildings.

No initial allowances are available.

Enterprise zones: industrial buildings, hotels, commercial buildings or structures

The following allowances are available for certain buildings in enterprise zones [1](industrial buildings; hotels and commercial buildings or structures[2]):

Date expenditure incurred	Initial allowance	Writing down allowance
Contract to be made within 10 years of site being included within the enterprise zone (but not expenditure incurred over 20 years after the date of the site being included)	100%	25%

Notes

[1] Areas designated by Orders made under the *Local Government, Planning and Land Act* 1980 or equivalent Northern Ireland legislation (CAA 2001, s. 298(3)).

[2] Buildings or structures used for the purposes of a trade, profession or vocation (but not an industrial building or qualifying hotel) or used as offices; but not a dwelling-house (CAA 2001, s. 281).

Business premises renovation allowances (CAA 2001, s. 360Aff.)

Date expenditure incurred	Initial allowance	Writing down allowance
On or after 11 April 2007	100%	25%

Flat conversion allowances (CAA 2001, s. 393Aff.)

Date expenditure incurred	Initial allowance	Writing down allowance
On or after 11 May 2001	100%	25%

Dredging allowances (CAA 2001, s. 484ff.)

Date expenditure incurred	Initial allowance	Writing down allowance
On or after 1 April 1986	Nil	4%

Mineral extraction allowances (CAA 2001, s. 394ff.)

Date expenditure incurred	Initial allowance	Writing down allowance
On or after 1 April 1986	Nil	25%

Research and development allowances (CAA 2001, s. 437ff.)

Date expenditure incurred	Initial allowance	Writing down allowance
On or after 5 November 1962	100%	No provision for WDAs

Patent allowances (CAA 2001, s. 464ff.)

Date expenditure incurred	Initial allowance	Writing down allowance
On or after 1 April 1986	Nil	25%

Know-how allowances (CAA 2001, s. 452ff.)

Date expenditure incurred	Initial allowance	Writing down allowance
On or after 1 April 1986	Nil	25%

Assured tenancy allowances (CAA 2001, s. 490ff.)

Date expenditure incurred	Initial allowance	Writing down allowance
1 April 1986 to 31 March 1992	Nil	4%

Enterprise zones

Enterprise zones can be valid for up to 20 years in total. Those that still fall within that 20-year period are as follows:

Statutory instrument	Area	Start date
1989/145	Inverclyde	3 March 1989
1989/794	Sunderland (Castletown and Doxford Park)	27 April 1990
1989/795	Sunderland (Hylton Riverside and Southwick)	27 April 1990
1993/23	Lanarkshire (Hamilton)	1 February 1993
1993/24	Lanarkshire (Motherwell)	1 February 1993
1993/25	Lanarkshire (Monklands)	1 February 1993
1995/2624	Dearne Valley (Barnsley, Doncaster, Rotherham)	3 November 1995
1995/2625	Holmewood (North East Derbyshire)	3 November 1995
1995/2738	Bassetlaw	16 November 1995
1995/2758	Ashfield	21 November 1995
1995/2812	East Durham (No. 1 to No. 6)	29 November 1995
1996/106	Tyne Riverside (North Tyneside)	19 February 1996
1996/1981	Tyne Riverside (Silverlink North Scheme)	26 August 1996
1996/1981	Tyne Riverside (Silverlink Business Park Scheme)	26 August 1996
1996/1981	Tyne Riverside (Middle Engine Lane Scheme)	26 August 1996
1996/1981	Tyne Riverside (New York Industrial Park Scheme)	26 August 1996
1996/1981	Tyne Riverside (Balliol Business Park West Scheme)	26 August 1996
1996/2435	Tyne Riverside (Baltic Enterprise Park Scheme)	21 October 1996
1996/2435	Tyne Riverside (Viking Industrial Park – Wagonway West Scheme)	21 October 1996
1996/2435	Tyne Riverside (Viking Industrial Park – Blackett Street Scheme)	21 October 1996
1996/2435	Tyne Riverside (Viking Industrial Park – Western Road Scheme)	21 October 1996

30   Interest factor tables

Inland Revenue Press Release 72/99, issued 11 March 1999, states that 'legislative changes to the basis on which interest is calculated, and increased use of computers, have lead to disuse of the tables'. New interest factor tables are, therefore, no longer produced.

Repayment supplement

Repayment supplement was introduced in 1975. Until 5 February 1997, the relevant interest factors were identical to those applying in the case of investigation settlements (below). However, in the case of repayment supplement the tax month to which the interest factor applies ends on the fifth of that month and not on the first, as with investigation settlement interest. The table, which applies in relation to repayments made other than under Pay and File, incorporates the interest change to four per cent p.a. which came into operation on 6 January 1999.

Table of interest factors as at fifth of month

	5 Jan	5 Feb	5 Mar	5 Apr	5 May	5 Jun	5 Jul	5 Aug	5 Sept	5 Oct	5 Nov	5 Dec
1975	1.242	1.2495	1.257	1.2645	1.272	1.2795	1.287	1.2945	1.302	1.3095	1.317	1.3245
1976	1.332	1.3395	1.347	1.3545	1.362	1.3695	1.377	1.3845	1.392	1.3995	1.407	1.4145
1977	1.422	1.4295	1.437	1.4445	1.452	1.4595	1.467	1.4745	1.482	1.4895	1.497	1.5045
1978	1.512	1.5195	1.527	1.5345	1.542	1.5495	1.557	1.5645	1.572	1.5795	1.587	1.5945
1979	1.602	1.6095	1.617	1.6245	1.632	1.6395	1.647	1.6545	1.662	1.6695	1.677	1.6845
1980	1.692	1.702	1.712	1.722	1.732	1.742	1.752	1.762	1.772	1.782	1.792	1.802
1981	1.812	1.822	1.832	1.842	1.852	1.862	1.872	1.882	1.892	1.902	1.912	1.922
1982	1.932	1.942	1.952	1.962	1.972	1.982	1.992	2.002	2.012	2.022	2.032	2.042
1983	2.0487	2.0554	2.062	2.0687	2.0754	2.082	2.0887	2.0954	2.102	2.1087	2.1154	2.122
1984	2.1287	2.1354	2.142	2.1487	2.1554	2.162	2.1687	2.1754	2.182	2.1887	2.1954	2.202
1985	2.2087	2.2154	2.222	2.2287	2.2354	2.2445	2.2537	2.2628	2.2720	2.2812	2.2903	2.2995

	5 Jan	5 Feb	5 Mar	5 Apr	5 May	5 Jun	5 Jul	5 Aug	5 Sept	5 Oct	5 Nov	5 Dec
1986	2.3087	2.3178	2.3270	2.3362	2.3453	2.3545	2.3637	2.3728	2.3799	2.3870	2.3940	2.4019
1987	2.4098	2.4178	2.4257	2.4336	2.4411	2.4468	2.4555	2.4624	2.4693	2.4768	2.4843	2.4918
1988	2.4987	2.5056	2.5125	2.5193	2.5262	2.5327	2.5391	2.5456	2.5537	2.5618	2.5708	2.5797
1989	2.5887	2.5983	2.6079	2.6175	2.6271	2.6367	2.6462	2.6564	2.6666	2.6768	2.6871	2.6979
1990	2.7088	2.7196	2.7304	2.7413	2.7521	2.7629	2.7738	2.7846	2.7954	2.8063	2.8171	2.8273
1991	2.8375	2.8477	2.8579	2.8675	2.8771	2.8861	2.8950	2.9033	2.9116	2.9200	2.9277	2.9354
1992	2.9431	2.9508	2.9585	2.9663	2.9740	2.9817	2.9894	2.9971	3.0048	3.0125	3.0202	3.0267
1993	3.0326	3.0384	3.0442	3.0494	3.0546	3.0598	3.0650	3.0702	3.0755	3.0807	3.0859	3.0911
1994	3.0963	3.1009	3.1055	3.1101	3.1147	3.1193	3.1238	3.1284	3.1330	3.1376	3.1428	3.1480
1995	3.1532	3.1584	3.1636	3.1694	3.1753	3.1811	3.1869	3.1928	3.1986	3.2044	3.2103	3.2161
1996	3.2219	3.2278	3.2330	3.2382	3.2434	3.2486	3.2538	3.2591	3.2643	3.2695	3.2747	3.2799
1997	3.2851	3.2903	3.2937	3.2970	3.3003	3.3037	3.3070	3.3103	3.3143	3.3182	3.3222	3.3261
1998	3.3301	3.3340	3.3380	3.3419	3.3459	3.3498	3.3538	3.3578	3.3618	3.3657	3.3697	3.3736
1999	3.3776	3.3809	3.3842	3.3876	3.3909	3.3942	3.3976	3.4009	3.4042	3.4076	3.4109	3.4142
2000	3.4176	3.4209	3.4242	3.4276	3.4309	3.4342	3.4376	3.4409	3.4442	3.4476	3.4509	3.4542
2001	3.4576											

35 Foreign exchange rates

2009–10 Foreign exchange rates

Average rates for the year to 31 December 2009 and the year to 31 March 2010

Country	Unit of currency	Average for the year to 31 December 2009		Average for the year to 31 March 2010	
		Currency units per £1	Sterling value of currency unit £	Currency units per £1	Sterling value of currency unit £
Algeria	Algerian Dinar	113.373	0.0088204	115.670	0.0086453
Argentina	Peso	5.8426	0.17116	6.0580	0.16507
Australia	Australian Dollar	1.9923	0.50193	1.8829	0.5311
Bahrain	Dinar	0.5896	1.69607	0.6005	1.66528
Bangladesh	Taka	108.191	0.0092429	110.103	0.0090824
Barbados	Barbados Dollar	3.1280	0.31969	3.1853	0.31394
Bolivia	Boliviano	10.9794	0.09108	11.1804	0.089442
Botswana	Pula	11.0911	0.090163	10.8900	0.091827
Brazil	Real	3.1109	0.32145	2.9799	0.33558
Brunei	Brunei Dollar	2.2743	0.4397	2.2677	0.44098
Bulgaria	Lev	2.1974	0.45508	2.2063	0.45325
Burma	Kyat	10.0277	0.099724	10.2089	0.097954
Burundi	Burundi Franc	1929.10	0.00051838	1959.83	0.00051025
Canada	Canadian Dollar	1.7801	0.56177	1.7398	0.57478
Cayman Islands	C.I. Dollar	1.2851	0.77815	1.3067	0.76529
Chile	Chilean Peso	870.827	0.0011483	854.751	0.0011699
China	Yuan	10.7044	0.09342	10.8798	0.091913
Colombia	Colombia Peso	3358.97	0.00029771	3183.33	0.00031414
Congo (Dem Rep)	Congolese Franc	1263.11	0.0007917	1354.89	0.00073807
Costa Rica	Colon	898.802	0.0011126	906.539	0.0011031
Cuba	Cuban Peso	1.5673	0.63804	1.5935	0.62755
Czech Republic	Koruna	29.8025	0.033554	29.3613	0.034058
Denmark	Danish Krone	8.3581	0.11964	8.4083	0.11893

2009–10 Average foreign exchange rates (cont'd)

Average rates for the year to 31 December 2009 and the year to 31 March 2010

Country	Unit of currency	Average for the year to 31 December 2009		Average for the year to 31 March 2010	
		Currency units per £1	Sterling value of currency unit £	Currency units per £1	Sterling value of currency unit £
Egypt	Egyptian £	8.6820	0.11518	8.8012	0.11362
El Salvador	Colon	13.7107	0.072936	13.9391	0.071741
Ethiopia	Ethiopian Birr	18.7056	0.05346	19.7973	0.050512
European Union	Euro	1.1235	0.89008	1.1298	0.88511
Fiji Islands	Fiji Dollar	3.0833	0.32433	3.1723	0.31523
French Cty/Africa	CFA Franc	736.978	0.0013569	739.927	0.0013515
French Pacific Islands	CFP Franc	133.979	0.0074639	134.515	0.0074341
Gambia	Dalasi	41.6103	0.024033	42.4940	0.023533
Ghana	Cedi	2.2426	0.44591	2.3068	0.4335
Grenada/Wind. Isles	East Carib Dollar	4.2229	0.2368	4.3023	0.23243
Guyana	Guyana Dollar	316.241	0.0031621	322.95	0.0030965
Honduras	Lempira	29.6097	0.033773	30.1084	0.033213
Hong Kong	HK Dollar	12.1317	0.082429	12.3810	0.080769
Hungary	Forint	316.187	0.0031627	308.141	0.0032453
Iceland	Icelandic Krona	193.524	0.0051673	200.920	0.0049771
India	Indian Rupee	75.6294	0.013222	75.5588	0.013235
Indonesia	Rupiah	16175.8	0.000061821	15601.1	0.000064098
Iran	Rial	15443.8	0.000064751	15770.0	0.000063412
Iraq	New Iraqi Dinar	1802.03	0.00055493	1838.48	0.00054393
Israel	Shekel	6.1341	0.16302	6.1280	0.16319
Jamaica	Jamaican Dollar	137.646	0.007265	141.387	0.0070728
Japan	Yen	146.366	0.0068322	148.193	0.006748
Jordan	Jordanian Dinar	1.1077	0.90277	1.1278	0.88668
Kenya	Kenyan Shilling	120.848	0.0082749	121.942	0.0082006
Korea (South)	Won	1993.87	0.00050154	1924.48	0.00051962
Kuwait	Kuwaiti Dinar	0.4508	2.21828	0.4582	2.18245
Laos	New Kip	13295.8	0.000075212	13502.7	0.000074059
Latvia	Lats	0.7936	1.26008	0.7975	1.25392
Lebanon	Lebanese Pound	2348.60	0.00042579	2391.71	0.00041811
Libya	Libyan Dinar	1.9538	0.51182	1.9751	0.5063
Lithuania	Litas	3.8793	0.25778	3.8949	0.25675
Malawi	Kwacha	221.896	0.0045066	229.365	0.0043599
Malaysia	Ringgit	5.5051	0.18165	5.5113	0.18145
Mauritius	Mauritius Rupee	49.8915	0.020043	49.6959	0.020122
Mexico	Mexican Peso	21.0920	0.047411	20.8849	0.047881
Morocco	Dirham	12.6491	0.079057	12.7327	0.078538
Nepal	Nepalese Rupee	121.294	0.0082444	120.696	0.0082853
N'nd Antilles	Antilles Guilder	2.8053	0.35647	2.8523	0.35059
New Zealand	NZ Dollar	2.4870	0.40209	2.3637	0.42307
Nicaragua	Gold Cordoba	31.9532	0.031296	32.8596	0.030433
Nigeria	Naira	234.162	0.0042706	239.591	0.0041738
Norway	Nor Krone	9.8078	0.10196	9.6327	0.10381
Oman	Rial Omani	0.6022	1.66058	0.6132	1.63079
Pakistan	Pakistan Rupee	127.926	0.007817	132.082	0.0075711

Key Data

33

2009–10 Average foreign exchange rates (cont'd)

Average rates for the year to 31 December 2009 and the year to 31 March 2010

Country	Unit of currency	Average for the year to 31 December 2009		Average for the year to 31 March 2010	
		Currency units per £1	Sterling value of currency unit £	Currency units per £1	Sterling value of currency unit £
Papua New Guinea	Kina	4.2283	0.2365	4.2584	0.23483
Paraguay	Guarani	7783.09	0.00012848	7779.04	0.00012855
Peru	New Sol	4.6983	0.21284	4.6586	0.21466
Philippines	Peso	74.5322	0.013417	75.1918	0.013299
Poland	Zloty	4.8775	0.20502	4.7177	0.21197
Qatar	Riyal	5.6946	0.1756	5.7982	0.17247
Romania	New Leu	4.7645	0.20989	4.7312	0.21136
Russia	Rouble	49.7386	0.020105	48.6544	0.020553
Rwanda	Franc	891.257	0.001122	908.223	0.0011011
Saudi Arabia	Riyal	5.8657	0.17048	5.9728	0.16743
Seychelles	Rupee	21.1657	0.047246	19.6567	0.050873
Sierra Leone	Leone	5314.64	0.00018816	5723.55	0.00017472
Singapore	Singapore Dollar	2.2711	0.44032	2.2719	0.44016
Solomon Islands	SI Dollar	12.4682	0.080204	12.7244	0.078589
Somali Republic	Shilling	2161.21	0.0004627	2236.85	0.00044706
South Africa	Rand	13.0021	0.076911	12.4676	0.080208
Sri Lanka	Rupee	180.184	0.0055499	183.205	0.0054584
Sudan	Sudanese Pound	3.6544	0.27364	3.7308	0.26804
Surinam	Dollar	4.3020	0.23245	4.3741	0.22862
Swaziland	Lilangeni	12.9656	0.077127	12.3156	0.081198
Sweden	Krona	11.9491	0.083688	11.7215	0.085313
Switzerland	Franc	1.6968	0.58935	1.6961	0.58959
Syria	Pound	72.0249	0.013884	73.1795	0.013665
Taiwan	Dollar	51.6003	0.01938	51.7867	0.01931
Tanzania	Shilling	2071.20	0.00048281	2118.02	0.00047214
Thailand	Baht	53.6478	0.01864	53.7107	0.018618
Tonga Islands	Pa'anga	3.1526	0.3172	3.1071	0.32184
Trinidad & Tobago	Dollar	9.8537	0.10148	10.0652	0.099352
Tunisia	Dinar	2.1093	0.47409	2.1345	0.46849
Turkey	New Lira	2.4264	0.41213	2.4160	0.41391
Uganda	New Shilling	3177.46	0.00031472	3237.06	0.00030892
United Arab Emirates	Dirham	5.7445	0.17408	5.8497	0.17095
Uruguay	Peso Uruguay	35.2328	0.028383	34.3153	0.029142
USA	US Dollar	1.5633	0.63967	1.5962	0.62649
Venezuela	Bolivar Fuerte	3.3620	0.29744	1/4/09 to 10/1/10: 0.28987 11/1/10 to 31/3/10: 0.14969*	1/4/09 to 10/1/10: 3.4498 11/1/10 to 31/3/10: 6.6804*
Vietnam	Dong	28019.6	0.000035689	28974.5	0.000034513
Yemen	Rial	318.436	0.0031403	329.603	0.0030340
Zambia	Kwacha	7870.74	0.00012705	7741.14	0.00012918

* Rate shown for Venezuela from 11/1/10 is 'petro-dollar' rate, preferential rate is fixed at 2.6 to the US dollar

Table of spot rates on 31 December 2009 and 31 March 2010

		Table of Spot rates on 31 December 2009 and 31 March 2010			
		31 December 2009		**31 March 2010**	
Country	Unit of Currency	Currency units per £1	Sterling value of currency unit £	Currency units per £1	Sterling value of currency unit £
Australia	Australian Dollar	1.7956	0.55692	1.6527	0.60507
Canada	Canadian Dollar	1.6930	0.59067	1.5390	0.64977
Denmark	Danish Krone	8.3750	0.1194	8.3459	0.11982
European Union	Euro	1.1255	0.88849	1.1211	0.89198
Hong Kong	HK Dollar	12.5217	0.079861	11.7783	0.084902
Japan	Yen	150.335	0.0066518	141.739	0.0070552
Norway	Nor Krone	9.3287	0.1072	9.0038	0.11106
South Africa	Rand	11.8914	0.084094	11.1401	0.089766
Sweden	Krona	11.5302	0.086729	10.9171	0.091599
Switzerland	Franc	1.6693	0.59905	1.5967	0.62629
USA	US Dollar	1.6149	0.61923	1.5169	0.65924

2008–09 Foreign exchange rates

		Average rates for the year to 31 December 2008 and the year to 31 March 2009			
		Average for the year to 31 December 2008		**Average for the year to 31 March 2009**	
Country	Unit of currency	Currency units per £1	Sterling value of currency unit £	Currency units per £1	Sterling value of currency unit £
Algeria	Dinar	119.634	0.0083588	112.768	0.0088678
Argentina	Peso	5.8413	0.17119	5.559	0.17989
Australia	Australian Dollar	2.1869	0.45727	2.1814	0.45842
Bahrain	Dinar	0.6979	1.43287	0.6472	1.54512
Bangladesh	Taka	126.837	0.0078841	117.481	0.008512
Barbados	Barbados Dollar	3.7036	0.27001	3.4337	0.29123
Bolivia	Boliviano	13.4418	0.074395	12.2272	0.081785
Botswana	Pula	12.5687	0.079563	12.2141	0.081873
Brazil	Real	3.3579	0.29781	3.3307	0.30024
Brunei	Brunei Dollar	2.6016	0.38438	2.4531	0.40765
Bulgaria	Lev	2.4496	0.40823	2.3525	0.42508
Burma	Kyat	11.9263	0.083848	11.0485	0.09051
Burundi	Burundi Franc	2196.36	0.0004553	2060.04	0.00048542
Canada	Canadian Dollar	1.9615	0.50981	1.9112	0.52323
Cayman Islands	C.I Dollar	1.5166	0.65937	1.4031	0.71271
Chile	Chilean Peso	956.952	0.001045	946.012	0.0010571
China	Yuan	12.8301	0.077942	11.7475	0.085124
Colombia	Colombia Peso	3608.31	0.00027714	3535.02	0.00028288
Congo (Dem Rep)	Congolese Franc	1032.28	0.00096873	1023.63	0.00097692
Costa Rica	Colon	973.351	0.0010274	928.677	0.0010768
Cuba	Cuban Peso	1.826	0.54765	1.7008	0.58796
Czech Republic	Koruna	31.2163	0.032035	30.6209	0.032657
Denmark	Danish Krone	9.3823	0.10658	8.971	0.11147

2008–09 Average foreign exchange rates (cont'd)

Average rates for the year to 31 December 2008 and the year to 31 March 2009

Country	Unit of currency	Average for the year to 31 December 2008		Average for the year to 31 March 2009	
		Currency units per £1	Sterling value of currency unit £	Currency units per £1	Sterling value of currency unit £
Egypt	Egyptian £	10.0716	0.099289	9.3599	0.10684
El Salvador	Colon	16.1864	0.06178	14.9744	0.066781
Ethiopia	Ethiopian Birr	17.8542	0.056009	17.1711	0.058237
European Union	Euro	1.2586	0.79453	1.2042	0.83043
Fiji Islands	Fiji Dollar	2.9203	0.34243	2.8305	0.35329
French Cty/Africa	CFA Franc	821.42	0.0012174	788.89	0.0012676
French Pacific Islands	CFP Franc	149.33	0.0066966	143.417	0.0069727
Gambia	Dalasi	40.9522	0.024419	39.7935	0.025130
Ghana	Cedi	1.9891	0.50274	1.9975	0.50063
Grenada/Wind. Isles	E Carib Dollar	4.9999	0.200004	4.6356	0.21572
Guyana	Guyana Dollar	377.743	0.0026473	349.056	0.0028649
Honduras	Lempira	34.9474	0.028614	32.3282	0.030933
Hong Kong	HK Dollar	14.4291	0.069304	13.354	0.074884
Hungary	Forint	312.999	0.0031949	311.844	0.0032067
Iceland	Icelandic Krona	159.163	0.0062829	167.632	0.0059654
India	Indian Rupee	79.9647	0.012506	78.1871	0.01279
Indonesia	Rupiah	17758.16	0.000056312	17352.65	0.000057628
Iran	Rial	17472.49	0.000057233	16415.66	0.000060917
Iraq	New Iraq Dinar	2209.16	0.00045266	2024.15	0.00049403
Israel	Shekel	6.6178	0.15111	6.2823	0.15918
Jamaica	Jamaican Dollar	134.301	0.007446	130.009	0.0076918
Japan	Yen	192.26	0.0052013	173.793	0.005754
Jordan	Jordanian Dinar	1.3114	0.76254	1.2159	0.82244
Kenya	Kenyan Shilling	126.93	0.0078784	122.243	0.0081804
Korea (South)	Won	2016.25	0.00049597	2052.65	0.00048718
Kuwait	Kuwaiti Dinar	0.4978	2.00884	0.468	2.13675
Laos	New Kip	16140.15	0.000061957	14709.12	0.000067985
Latvia	Lats	0.8802	1.13611	0.848	1.17925
Lebanon	Lebanese Pound	2792.83	0.00035806	2584.94	0.00038686
Libya	Libyan Dinar	2.2503	0.44439	2.1135	0.47315
Lithuania	Litas	4.3238	0.23128	4.1526	0.24081
Malawi	Kwacha	260.21	0.003843	241.322	0.0041438
Malaysia	Ringgit	6.1456	0.16272	5.858	0.17071
Mauritius	Mauritius Rupee	52.2565	0.019136	50.51	0.019798
Mexico	Mexican Peso	20.4908	0.048802	20.3173	0.049219
Morocco	Dirham	14.2196	0.070325	13.5629	0.073731
Nepal	Nepalese Rupee	128.535	0.00778	125.743	0.0079527
N'nd Antilles	Antilles Guilder	3.3106	0.30206	3.0628	0.3265
New Zealand	NZ Dollar	2.6107	0.38304	2.657	0.37636
Nicaragua	Gold Cordoba	35.8091	0.027926	33.5155	0.029837
Nigeria	Naira	219.909	0.0045473	214.921	0.0046529
Norway	Nor Krone	10.3359	0.09675	10.1688	0.09834
Oman	Rial Omani	0.7129	1.40272	0.661	1.51286
Pakistan	Pakistan Rupee	129.686	0.0077109	127.419	0.0078481

2008–09 Average foreign exchange rates (cont'd)

Average rates for the year to 31 December 2008 and the year to
31 March 2009

Country	Unit of currency	Average for the year to 31 December 2008		Average for the year to 31 March 2009	
		Currency units per £1	Sterling value of currency unit £	Currency units per £1	Sterling value of currency unit £
Papua New Guinea	Kina	4.8787	0.20497	4.5214	0.22117
Paraguay	Guarani	8020.51	0.00012468	7557.59	0.00013232
Peru	New Sol	5.3906	0.18551	5.1117	0.19563
Phillipines	Peso	81.9749	0.012199	78.9259	0.01267
Poland	Zloty	4.3869	0.22795	4.5008	0.22218
Qatar	Riyal	6.7405	0.14836	6.2508	0.15998
Romania	New Leu	4.6269	0.21613	4.5851	0.2181
Russia	Rouble	45.8837	0.021794	46.5529	0.021481
Rwanda	Franc	1011.52	0.00098861	944.62	0.0010586
Saudi Arabia	Riyal	6.9462	0.14396	6.4408	0.15526
Seychelles	Rupee	17.1243	0.058397	19.1079	0.052334
Sierra Leone	Leone	5518.12	0.00018122	5152.67	0.00019407
Singapore	Singapore Dollar	2.613	0.3827	2.4609	0.40636
Slovakia	Koruna (to 31.12.08) (Euro from 1.1.09)	39.0363	0.025617	1.4.08 to 31.12.08: 37.7155 (Euro from 1.1.09)	1.4.08 to 31.12.08: 0.026514 (Euro from 1.1.09)
Solomon Islands	SI Dollar	14.1409	0.070717	13.2045	0.075732
Somali Republic	Shilling	2594.15	0.00038548	2388.10	0.00041874
South Africa	Rand	15.1357	0.066069	14.8671	0.067263
Sri Lanka	Rupee	200.476	0.0049881	188.497	0.0053051
Sudan	Sudanese Pound	3.8614	0.25897	3.6671	0.2727
Surinam	Dollar	5.0768	0.19697	4.6968	0.21291
Swaziland	Lilangeni	15.1142	0.066163	14.863	0.067281
Sweden	Krona	12.0887	0.082722	12.0213	0.083186
Switzerland	Franc	1.9979	0.50053	1.8833	0.53098
Syria	Pound	92.5003	0.010811	83.5987	0.011962
Taiwan	Dollar	58.2406	0.01717	54.854	0.01823
Tanzania	Shilling	2213.92	0.00045169	2111.78	0.00047353
Thailand	Baht	61.599	0.016234	58.3223	0.017146
Tonga Islands	Pa'anga	3.521	0.28401	3.3988	0.29422
Trinidad & Tobago	Dollar	11.5893	0.086286	10.7217	0.093269
Tunisia	Dinar	2.2674	0.44103	2.1824	0.45821
Turkey	New Lira	2.3965	0.41728	2.3961	0.41734
Uganda	New Shilling	3164.28	0.00031603	3045.77	0.00032832
United Arab Emirates	Dirham	6.8011	0.14704	6.3059	0.15858
Uruguay	Peso Uruguay	38.4107	0.026034	36.5457	0.027363
U S A	US Dollar	1.8511	0.54022	1.7138	0.5835
Venezuela	Bolivar Fuerte	3.9764	0.25148	3.6867	0.27125
Vietnam	Dong	30510.83	0.000032775	28859.78	0.00003465
Yemen	Rial	368.639	0.0027127	341.543	0.0029279
Zambia	Kwacha	6878.11	0.00014539	6952.69	0.00014383

Key Data

Table of spot rates on 31 December 2008 and 31 March 2009

| | | Table of Spot rates on 31 December 2008 and 31 March 2009 | | | |
| | | 31 December 2008 | | 31 March 2009 | |
Country	Unit of Currency	Currency units per £1	Sterling value of currency unit £	Currency units per £1	Sterling value of currency unit £
Australia	Australian Dollar	2.0622	0.48492	2.0630	0.48473
Canada	Canadian Dollar	1.7749	0.56341	1.8034	0.55451
Denmark	Danish Krone	7.6987	0.12989	8.0409	0.12436
European Union	Euro	1.0344	0.96674	1.0796	0.92627
Hong Kong	HK Dollar	11.1429	0.089743	11.1085	0.090021
Japan	Yen	130.332	0.0076727	141.572	0.0070635
Norway	Nor Krone	10.0673	0.099331	9.6781	0.10333
South Africa	Rand	13.2920	0.075233	13.6312	0.073361
Sweden	Krona	11.3697	0.087953	11.8499	0.084389
Switzerland	Franc	1.5303	0.65347	1.6298	0.61357
U S A	US Dollar	1.4378	0.69551	1.4334	0.69764

2007–08 Foreign exchange rates

| | | Average rates for the year to 31 December 2007 and the year to 31 March 2008 | | | |
| | | Average for the year to 31 December 2007 | | Average for the year to 31 March 2008 | |
Country	Unit of currency	Currency units per £1	Sterling value of currency unit £	Currency units per £1	Sterling value of currency unit £
Algeria	Algerian Dinar	139.34	0.007177	137.08	0.007295
Argentina	Peso	6.2363	0.160351	6.283	0.15916
Australia	Australian Dollar	2.3907	0.418286	2.3153	0.431916
Bahrain	Bahrain Dinar	0.754	1.32626	0.7562	1.322401
Bangladesh	Taka	138.02	0.007245	138.23	0.007234
Barbados	Barbados Dollar	4.0023	0.249856	4.0151	0.24906
Bolivia	Boliviano	15.7073	0.063665	15.5431	0.064337
Botswana	Pula	12.2795	0.081437	12.4328	0.080432
Brazil	Real	3.8951	0.256733	3.7214	0.268716
Brunei	Brunei Dollar	3.0127	0.331928	2.9581	0.338055
Bulgaria	Lev	2.8506	0.350798	2.7593	0.362411
Burma	Kyat	12.8474	0.077837	12.8986	0.077528
Burundi	Burundi Franc	2180.06	0.0004587	2246.85	0.0004451
Canada	Canadian Dollar	2.1484	0.465473	2.0725	0.482501
Cayman Islands	C.I. Dollar	1.7029	0.587234	1.6912	0.591296
Chile	Chilean Peso	1043.21	0.0009586	1007.89	0.0009922
China	Yuan Renminbi	15.2109	0.065742	14.944	0.066916
Colombia	Colombia Peso	4150.21	0.00024095	4009.40	0.00024941
Congo (Dem Rep)	Congolese Franc	1111.48	0.0008997	1116.84	0.0008954

2007–08 Average foreign exchange rates (cont'd)

Average rates for the year to 31 December 2007 and the year to 31 March 2008

Country	Unit of currency	Average for the year to 31 December 2007		Average for the year to 31 March 2008	
		Currency units per £1	Sterling value of currency unit £	Currency units per £1	Sterling value of currency unit £
Costa Rica	Colon	1033.37	0.0009677	1025.41	0.0009752
Cuba	Cuban Peso	1.9787	0.505382	1.9719	0.507125
Cyprus	Cyprus Pound (up to 31/12/07) (Euro from 1/1/08)	0.8494	1.177302	1/4/07 to 31/12/07: 0.84398 (Euro from 1/1/08)	1/4/07 to 31/12/07: 1.184865 (Euro from 1/1/08)
Czech Republic	Koruna	40.4435	0.024726	38.2403	0.02615
Denmark	Danish Krone	10.8900	0.091828	10.5702	0.094606
Egypt	Egyptian £	11.2921	0.0885575	11.226	0.089079
El Salvador	Colon	17.5503	0.056979	17.6071	0.056795
Ethiopia	Ethiopian Birr	18.0963	0.055260	18.4057	0.054331
European Union	Euro	1.4604	0.684755	1.4178	0.70532
Fiji Islands	Fiji Dollar	3.2178	0.310771	3.1500	0.31746
French Cty/Africa	C.F.A. Franc	956.12	0.0010459	925.47	0.0010805
French Pacific Islands	C.F.P. Franc	173.82	0.005753	168.25	0.005944
Gambia	Dalasi	49.573	0.020172	46.5553	0.02148
Ghana	Ghanaian Cedi	1/1/07 to 30/6/07: 18264.02 1/7/07 to 31/12/07: 1.927	1/1/07 to 30/6/07: 0.00005475 1/7/07 to 31/12/07: 0.518950	1/4/07 to 30/6/07: 18434.15 1/7/07 to 31/3/08: 1.9257	1/4/07 to 30/6/07: 0.00005425 1/7/07 to 31/3/08: 0.519286
Grenada/Wind. Isles	East Caribbean Dollar	5.4032	0.185076	5.4204	0.184488
Guyana	Guyanese Dollar	406.10	0.0024624	409.02	0.002445
Honduras	Lempira	37.8929	0.02639	38.016	0.026305
Hong Kong	H.K. Dollar	15.6114	0.064056	15.659	0.063861
Hungary	Forint	366.12	0.002731	356.86	0.002802
Iceland	Icelandic Krona	127.99	0.007813	128.36	0.00779
India	Indian Rupee	82.6063	0.012106	80.7528	0.012383
Indonesia	I.Rupiah	18294.55	0.00005466	18425.14	0.00005427
Iran	Iranian Rial	18566.81	0.00005386	18630.05	0.00005368
Iraq	Iraq Dinar	2510.79	0.0003983	2479.81	0.00040325
Israel	Shekel	8.2105	0.121795	7.9471	0.125832
Jamaica	Jamaican Dollar	138.11	0.007241	140.35	0.007125
Japan	Japanese Yen	235.6273	0.004244	229.3116	0.0043609
Jordan	Jordanian Dinar	1.4178	0.705318	1.4222	0.703136
Kenya	Kenya Shilling	134.68	0.007425	134.00	0.007463
Korea (South)	Won	1861.77	0.0005371	1877.73	0.0005326
Kuwait	Kuwaiti Dinar	0.5687	1.758396	0.5618	1.779993
Laos	New Kip	19225.02	0.00005202	18955.83	0.00005275
Latvia	Lats	1.0206	0.979832	0.9855	1.014713
Lebanon	Lebanese Pound	3026.21	0.00033045	3035.80	0.0003294
Libya	Libyan Dinar	2.519	0.396983	2.4937	0.401011
Lithuania	Litas	5.0329	0.198694	4.8715	0.205275

Key Data

2007–08 Average foreign exchange rates (cont'd)

Average rates for the year to 31 December 2007 and the year to 31 March 2008

Country	Unit of currency	Average for the year to 31 December 2007		Average for the year to 31 March 2008	
		Currency units per £1	Sterling value of currency unit £	Currency units per £1	Sterling value of currency unit £
Malawi	Malawi Kwacha	280.16	0.0035693	281.54	0.003552
Malaysia	Ringgit	6.8706	0.145548	6.7553	0.148032
Malta	Maltese Lira (up to 31/12/07) (Euro from 1/1/08)	0.6271	1.594642	1/4/07 to 31/12/07: 0.62236 (Euro from 1/1/08)	1/4/07 to 31/12/07: 1.606799 (Euro from 1/1/08)
Mauritius	Mauritius Rupee	62.0963	0.016104	59.8987	0.016695
Mexico	Mexican Peso	21.8598	0.045746	21.8287	0.045811
Morocco	Dirham	16.3605	0.061123	15.9354	0.062753
Nepal	Nepalese Rupee	132.02	0.007575	129.13	0.007744
N'nd Antilles	Antilles Guilder	3.5895	0.27859	3.6011	0.277693
New Zealand	N.Z. Dollar	2.7195	0.367715	2.6436	0.378272
Nicaragua	Gold Cordoba	37.0597	0.026983	37.6291	0.026575
Nigeria	Nigerian Naira	251.46	0.003977	246.92	0.00405
Norway	N. Krone	11.7296	0.085254	11.3122	0.0884
Oman, Sultanate of	Rial Omani	0.7702	1.298364	0.7726	1.294331
Pakistan	Pakistan Rupee	121.51	0.00823	122.81	0.008143
Papua New Guinea	Kina	5.8123	0.172049	5.7172	0.174911
Paraguay	Guarani	10055.95	0.00009944	9823.32	0.0001018
Peru	New Sol	6.2554	0.159862	6.1231	0.163316
Phillipines	Phillipine Peso	92.1586	0.010851	88.695	0.011275
Poland	Zloty	5.4989	0.181855	5.2082	0.192005
Qatar	Qatar Riyal	7.2833	0.1373	7.3053	0.136887
Romania	Leu	4.8646	0.205567	4.8313	0.206984
Russia	Rouble	51.1028	0.019568	50.1627	0.019935
Rwanda	Rwanda Franc	1096.84	0.0009117	1098.52	0.0009103
Saudi Arabia	Saudi Riyal	7.4983	0.133364	7.5217	0.132949
Seychelles	Rupee	13.6354	0.073339	14.6353	0.068328
Sierra Leone	Leone	5972.91	0.0001674	5987.38	0.000167
Singapore	Singapore Dollar	3.0131	0.331884	2.9616	0.337655
Slovakia	Koruna	49.234	0.020311	47.1771	0.021197
Solomon Islands	S.I. Dollar	14.509	0.068923	14.6865	0.06809
Somali Republic	Shilling	2745.39	0.0003642	2770.69	0.0003609
South Africa	Rand	14.1085	0.070879	14.3067	0.069897
Sri Lanka	Rupee	221.39	0.004517	221.61	0.004512
Sudan	Sudanese Dinar (up to 30 June 2007) Sudanese Pound (from 1 July 2007)	1/1/07 to 30/6/07: 397.24 1/7/07 to 31/12/07: 4.1168	1/1/07 to 30/6/07: 0.0025174 1/7/07 to 31/12/07: 0.242907	1/4/07 to 30/6/07: 400.6417 1/7/07 to 31/3/08: 4.0913	1/4/07 to 30/6/07: 0.002496 1/7/07 to 31/3/08: 0.244418
Surinam	Surinam Guilder	5.5045	0.18167	5.5224	0.181081
Swaziland	Lilangeni	14.0461	0.071194	14.3204	0.069830
Sweden	Swedish Krona	13.5236	0.073945	13.1967	0.075776

2007–08 Average foreign exchange rates (cont'd)

Average rates for the year to 31 December 2007 and the year to
31 March 2008

Country	Unit of currency	Average for the year to 31 December 2007		Average for the year to 31 March 2008	
		Currency units per £1	Sterling value of currency unit £	Currency units per £1	Sterling value of currency unit £
Switzerland	Swiss Franc	2.4010	0.416498	2.3261	0.429896
Syria	Syrian Pound	103.71	0.009642	103.50	0.009662
Taiwan	T. Dollar	65.7326	0.015213	65.258	0.015324
Tanzania	Shilling	2481.21	0.000403	2437.04	0.0004103
Thailand	Thai Baht	68.5207	0.014594	67.7565	0.014759
Tonga Islands	Pa'Anga	3.908	0.255885	3.8389	0.260491
Trinidad & Tobago	Trinidad & Tobago Dollar	12.6152	0.079269	12.6561	0.079013
Tunisia	Dinar	2.5590	0.390778	2.5108	0.398279
Turkey	Turkish Lira	2.6067	0.383627	2.5166	0.397362
Uganda	New Shilling	3451.92	0.0002897	3429.98	0.00029155
United Arab Emirates	U.A.E Dirham	7.3481	0.13609	7.3712	0.135663
Uruguay	Uruguayan Peso	46.9076	0.021319	45.3662	0.022043
U.S.A	U.S. Dollar	2.0020	0.499493	2.0080	0.497998
Venezuela	V. Bolivar (2007) Bolivar Fuerte (2008)	5357.25	0.00018666	1/4/07 to 31/12/07: 4665.73 1/1/08 to 31/3/08: 4.2501	1/4/07 to 31/12/07: 0.00021433 1/1/08 to 31/3/08: 0.235287
Vietnam	Dong	32241.04	0.000031016	32340.43	0.00003092
Yemen	Rial	398.84	0.0025073	400.27	0.0024983
Zambia	Zambian Kwacha	7984.03	0.00012525	7769.02	0.00012872
Zimbabwe	Z. Dollar	01/01/07 to 5/9/07: 496.04 6/9/07 to 31/12/07: 61053.83	01/01/07 to 5/9/07: 0.00201596 6/9/07 to 31/12/07: 0.000016379	1/4/07 to 5/9/07: 500.60 6/9/07 to 31/3/08: 60335.72	1/4/07 to 5/9/07: 0.0019976 6/9/07 to 31/3/08: 0.000016574

Table of spot rates on 31 December 2007 and 31 March 2008

Country	Unit of Currency	31 December 2007		31 March 2008	
		Currency units per £1	Sterling value of currency unit £	Currency units per £1	Sterling value of currency unit £
Australia	Australian Dollar	2.2671	0.441092	2.1773	0.459284
Canada	Canadian Dollar	1.9646	0.509009	2.0393	0.490364
Denmark	Danish Krone	10.1522	0.098501	9.3536	0.106911
European Union	Euro	1.3615	0.734484	1.2543	0.797257
Hong Kong	H. K. Dollar	15.5215	0.064427	15.4685	0.064648
Japan	Japanese Yen	222.380	0.0044968	197.826	0.0050549
Norway	N. Krone	10.8087	0.092518	10.1000	0.099010
South Africa	Rand	13.6045	0.073505	16.1515	0.061914
Sweden	S.Krone	12.8656	0.077727	11.7858	0.084848
Switzerland	Swiss Franc	2.2536	0.443734	1.9658	0.508699
U.S.A	U.S. Dollar	1.9906	0.502361	1.9875	0.503145

Key Data

41

2006–07 Foreign exchange rates

		Average rates for the year to 31 December 2006 and the year to 31 March 2007			
		Average for the year to 31 December 2006		Average for the year to 31 March 2007	
Country	Unit of currency	Currency units per £1	Sterling value of currency unit £	Currency units per £1	Sterling value of currency unit £
Algeria	Algerian Dinar	134.0142	0.0074619	136.9221	0.00730342
Argentina	Peso	5.652	0.17692852	5.8223	0.17175343
Australia	Australian Dollar	2.4448	0.409031	2.4739	0.40422006
Bahrain	Bahrain Dinar	0.6952	1.43843498	0.7141	1.40036409
Bangladesh	Taka	127.3866	0.007850119	131.2303	0.007620191
Barbados	Barbados Dollar	3.6879	0.27115703	3.7884	0.26396368
Bolivia	Boliviano	14.7464	0.06781316	15.1462	0.06602316
Botswana	Pula	10.8192	0.092428276	11.4887	0.08704205
Brazil	Real	4.0028	0.24982512	4.0789	0.24516414
Brunei	Brunei Dollar	2.9251	0.341868654	2.9649	0.337279504
Burma	Kyat	11.8406	0.08445518	12.1615	0.08222670
Burundi	Burundi Franc	1846.6517	0.000541521	1932.3958	0.000517492
Canada	Canadian Dollar	2.0901	0.47844601	2.1567	0.4636713
Cayman Islands	C.I Dollar	1.5712	0.636456212	1.6242	0.615687723
Chile	Chilean Peso	977.173	0.00102336	1010.6452	0.00098947
China	Renminbi	14.7126	0.067968952	14.9935	0.066695568
Colombia	Colombia Peso	4348.138	0.00022998	4441.0926	0.00022517
Congo Dem (Rep) Zaire	Congolese Franc	859.2795	0.00116377	935.6975	0.00106872
Costa Rica	Colon	946.8613	0.001056121	981.3863	0.001018967
Cuba	Cuban Peso	1.8483	0.54103771	1.901	0.526038927
Cyprus	Cyprus Pound	0.8434	1.185677022	0.8508	1.175364363
Czech Republic	Koruna	41.4016	0.024153656	41.5989	0.024039097
Denmark	Danish Krone	10.9397	0.09141018	11.0014	0.0908975
Egypt	Egyptian £	10.5864	0.09446082	10.8563	0.09211241
El Salvador	Colon	16.1758	0.061820745	16.6369	0.060107352
Ethiopia	Ethiopian Birr	16.1638	0.06186664	16.7003	0.059879164
European Union	Euro	1.4666	0.68184917	1.475	0.6779661
Fiji Islands	Fiji Dollar	3.2042	0.312090381	3.2532	0.307389647
French Cty/Africa	C.F.A. Franc	960.8382	0.001040758	967.3428	0.00103376
French Pacific Islands	C.F.P. Franc	174.6763	0.005724875	175.8587	0.005686383
Gambia	Dalasi	51.8573	0.019283688	53.0478	0.018850923
Ghana	Ghanaian Cedi	16916.4967	0.0000591139	17447.0667	0.0000573162
Grenada/Wind. Isles	East Caribbean Dollar	4.9787	0.20085565	5.1144	0.19552636
Guyana	Guyanese Dollar	350.4058	0.00285383	365.1609	0.00273852
Honduras	Lempira	34.9226	0.028634752	35.9179	0.027841271
Hong Kong	H.K. Dollar	14.3132	0.06986558	14.724	0.0679163
Hungary	Forint	386.9914	0.002584037	388.1129	0.00257657
Iceland	Icelandic Krona	128.9847	0.00775286	133.7177	0.00747844
India	Indian Rupee	83.4523	0.01198289	85.6028	0.01168186

2006–07 Average foreign exchange rates (cont'd)

Average rates for the year to 31 December 2006 and the year to 31 March 2007

Country	Unit of currency	Average for the year to 31 December 2006		Average for the year to 31 March 2007	
		Currency units per £1	Sterling value of currency unit £	Currency units per £1	Sterling value of currency unit £
Indonesia	I.Rupiah	16875.1042	0.0000592589	17253.2658	0.00005796
Iran	Iranian Rial	16908.4704	0.000059142	17424.415	0.0000573907
Iraq	Iraq Dinar	2699.6693	0.00037042	2685.7928	0.00037233
Israel	Shekel	8.2066	0.12185314	8.2179	0.12168559
Jamaica	Jamaican Dollar	121.3518	0.00824050	125.8431	0.00794640
Japan	Japanese Yen	214.3005	0.0046663447	221.4527	0.004515637
Jordan	Jordanian Dinar	1.3066	0.76534517	1.3422	0.74504545
Kenya	Kenya Shilling	132.9039	0.0075423	135.298	0.00739109
Korea(South)	Won	1757.86	0.000568874	1794.2808	0.000557326
Kuwait	Kuwaiti Dinar	0.535	1.869158879	0.5483	1.82381908
Laos	New Kip	18530.2392	0.0000539658	18804.8133	0.0000531779
Lebanon	Lebanese Pound	2780.1683	0.00035969	2859.8993	0.00034966
Libya	Libyan Dinar	2.4064	0.41555851	2.4467	0.40871378
Malawi	Malawi Kwacha	251.0676	0.003983	262.3102	0.00381228
Malaysia	Ringgit	6.7564	0.148007815	6.832	0.14637002
Malta	Maltese Lira	0.63	1.58730159	0.6338	1.57778479
Mauritius	Rupee	57.9506	0.017256077	60.4041	0.01655517
Mexico	Mexican Peso	20.0984	0.0497552	20.8418	0.04798050
Morocco	Dirham	16.186	0.061781787	16.3655	0.061104152
Nepal	Nepalese Rupee	133.8618	0.007470391	137.3187	0.007282329
N'nd Antilles	Antilles Guilder	3.3084	0.302260912	3.4027	0.293884268
New Zealand	N.Z. Dollar	2.8425	0.35180299	2.8853	0.34658441
Nicaragua	Gold Cordoba	32.1564	0.031098008	33.5507	0.029805637
Nigeria	Nigerian Naira	236.971	0.00421993	242.9804	0.00411556
Norway	N. Krone	11.8095	0.08467759	11.9303	0.0838202
Oman, Sultanate of	Rial Omani	0.7099	1.408649	0.7293	1.371178
Pakistan	Pakistan Rupee	111.1701	0.00899522	114.5979	0.00872616
Papua New Guinea	Kina	5.5053	0.181643144	5.6454	0.177135367
Paraguay	Guarani	10373.1821	0.0000964024	10251.0069	0.0000975514
Peru	New Sol	6.0317	0.165791	6.1252	0.163260
Phillipines	Phillipine Peso	94.5009	0.01058191	95.5121	0.01046988
Poland	Zloty	5.7126	0.17505164	5.7668	0.173406395
Qatar	Qatar Riyal	6.7125	0.148976	6.8958	0.145016
Romania	Leu	5.1527	0.19407301	5.1239	0.19516384
Russia	Rouble (market)	50.0151	0.019993962	50.6508	0.019743025
Rwanda	Rwanda Franc	1010.6548	0.000989458	1042.4532	0.000959276
Saudi Arabia	Saudi Riyal	6.9151	0.144611	7.1037	0.140772
Seychelles	Rupee	10.2716	0.097355816	10.8403	0.09224837
Sierra Leone	Leone	5461.5218	0.0001830992	5631.4166	0.0001775752
Singapore	Singapore Dollar	2.9308	0.341204	2.966	0.337154
Solomon Islands	S.I. Dollar	13.597	0.073545635	13.9149	0.07186541
Somali Republic	Shilling	2615.015	0.000382407	2599.6275	0.00038467
South Africa	Rand	12.4976	0.08001536	13.341	0.0749569
Sri Lanka	Rupee	191.8051	0.00521363	200.1501	0.00499625

43

2006–07 Average foreign exchange rates (cont'd)

Average rates for the year to 31 December 2006 and the year to 31 March 2007

Country	Unit of currency	Average for the year to 31 December 2006		Average for the year to 31 March 2007	
		Currency units per £1	Sterling value of currency unit £	Currency units per £1	Sterling value of currency unit £
Sudan	Sudanese Dinar	399.0983	0.002505648	397.5664	0.002515303
Surinam	Surinam Guilder	5.0713	0.197188098	5.218	0.191644308
Swaziland	Lilangeni	12.6018	0.079353743	13.4435	0.074385391
Sweden	Swedish Krona	13.5672	0.07370718	13.593	0.0735673
Switzerland	Swiss Franc	2.3074	0.43338823	2.3425	0.42689434
Syria	Syrian Pound	96.5596	0.010356298	99.2471	0.010075861
Taiwan	New T. Dollar	59.9643	0.01667659	61.8966	0.01615598
Tanzania	Shilling	2311.7583	0.00043257	2411.6028	0.00041466
Thailand	Thai Baht	69.7902	0.014328659	69.3549	0.01441859
Tonga Islands	Pa'Anga	3.7453	0.267001308	3.8224	0.261615739
Trinidad & Tobago	Trinidad & Tobago Dollar	11.58	0.08635579	11.9098	0.083964
Tunisia	Dinar	2.4507	0.40804668	2.4998	0.400032
Turkey	Turkish Lira	2.6492	0.3774724	2.7546	0.363029
Uganda	New Shilling	3375.2477	0.000296275	3440.7299	0.00029064
United Arab Emirates	U.A.E Dirham	6.7727	0.147652	6.9571	0.143738
Uruguay	Uruguayan Peso	44.2834	0.022581825	45.5669	0.02194575
U.S.A	U.S. Dollar	1.8424	0.54277030	1.8932	0.5282062
Venezuela	V.Bolivar	5044.842	0.00019822	5747.9573	0.00017397
Vietnam	Dong	29567.2417	0.00003382	30455.15	0.00003284
Yemen	Rial	364.4703	0.002743708	376.1672	0.002658392
Zambia	Zambian Kwacha	6622.279	0.00015101	7244.9871	0.00013803
Zimbabwe	Z. Dollar	01/01/06–3/8/06 = 178951.06 04/08/06–31/12/06 = 476.63	01/01/06–03/08/06 = 0.00000558812 04/08/06–31/12/06 = 0.00209806	01/04/06–03/08/06 = 185137.83 04/08/06–31/03/07 = 481.06	01/04/06–03/08/06 = 0.00000540138 04/08/06–31/03/07 = 0.00207874

Table of spot rates on 31 December 2006 and 31 March 2007

Country	Unit of Currency	31 December 2006		31 March 2007	
		Currency units per £1	Sterling value of currency unit £	Currency units per £1	Sterling value of currency unit £
Australia	Australian Dollar	2.4779	0.40356754	2.4279	0.41187858
Canada	Canadian Dollar	2.2776	0.43905866	2.2627	0.44194988
Denmark	Danish Krone	11.0641	0.09038241	10.9789	0.09108381
European Union	Euro	1.4842	0.67376364	1.4735	0.67865626
Hong Kong	H K Dollar	15.2213	0.06569741	15.3265	0.06524647
Japan	Japanese Yen	233.204	0.00428809	231.586	0.00431805
Norway	N.Krone	12.1859	0.08206206	11.9723	0.08352614
South Africa	Rand	13.7994	0.07246692	14.2247	0.07030025
Sweden	S.Krone	13.3928	0.07466699	13.7611	0.07266861
Switzerland	Swiss Franc	2.3891	0.41856766	2.3945	0.41762372
U.S.A	U.S. Dollar	1.9572	0.51093399	1.9614	0.50983991

2005–06 Foreign exchange rates

Country	Unit of currency	Average rates for the year to 31 December 2005 and the year to 31 March 2006			
		Average for the year to 31 December 2005		Average for the year to 31 March 2006	
		Currency units per £1	Sterling value of currency unit £	Currency units per £1	Sterling value of currency unit £
Algeria	Algerian Dinar	132.3118	0.0075579	130.3635	0.007671
Argentina	Peso	5.3182	0.188033545	5.2768	0.189508793
Australia	Australian Dollar	2.3862	0.419076356	2.37825	0.420477
Bahrain	Bahrain Dinar	0.6859	1.457938	0.6729	1.486105
Bangladesh	Taka	116.7483	0.00856544	117.237	0.00853
Barbados	Barbados Dollar	3.639	0.274800769	3.57	0.28011204
Bolivia	Boliviano	14.666	0.068185	14.36	0.069638
Botswana	Pula	9.2512	0.10809409	9.51	0.10515
Brazil	Real	4.4133	0.226588	4.1126	0.24316
Brunei	Brunei Dollar	3.0182	0.33132331	2.9546	0.33846
Burma	Kyat	11.6811	0.085608	11.4616	0.08725
Burundi	Burundi Franc	1920.5317	0.0005207	1839.63	0.00054
Canada	Canadian Dollar	2.2063	0.45324752	2.1598	0.46300941
Cayman Islands	C.I Dollar	1.501	0.66622252	1.4774	0.67686
Chile	Chilean Peso	1018.873	0.000981	975.9229	0.001025
China	Renminbi	14.8666	0.0672488	14.4759	0.06908
Colombia	Colombia Peso	4227.3334	0.000236556	4107.4241	0.00024346
Congo Dem (Rep) Zaire	Congolese Franc	886.8474	0.00112759	864.3402	0.00115695
Costa Rica	Colon	869.6228	0.00114992	869.708	0.00115
Cuba	Cuban Peso	1.8162	0.55060015	1.7815	0.56132
Cyprus	Cyprus Pound	0.8438	1.18511496	0.8417	1.18807
Czech Republic	Koruna	43.66	0.02290426	43.1314	0.02318
Denmark	Danish Krone	10.8991	0.0917507	10.93255	0.09146997
Egypt	Egyptian £	10.538	0.094895	10.2955	0.09713
El Salvador	Colon	15.8952	0.06291207	15.5912	0.06414
Ethiopia	Ethiopian Birr	15.7915	0.06332521	15.5295	0.06439
European Union	Euro	1.4626	0.68371393	1.4664	0.681956
Fiji Islands	Fiji Dollar	3.0678	0.32596649	3.0556	0.32727
French Cty/Africa	C.F.A. Franc	959.9	0.00104178	961.102	0.00104
French Pacific Islands	C.F.P. Franc	174.5057	0.00573047	174.724	0.00572
Gambia	Dalasi	51.7924	0.01930785	50.3634	0.01986
Ghana	Ghanaian Cedi	16513.74	0.00006	16225.61	0.00006
Grenada/Wind. Isles	East Caribbean Dollar	4.9126	0.203558197	4.8195	0.2074904
Guyana	Guyanese Dollar	335.8187	0.0029778	334.5235	0.002989
Honduras	Lempira	34.1971	0.02924225	33.6188	0.02975
Hong Kong	H.K. Dollar	14.1526	0.07065839	13.9682	0.0715911
Hungary	Forint	363.5366	0.00275075	367.705	0.00272
Iceland	Icelandic Krona	114.2941	0.008749	113.7708	0.00879
India	Indian Rupee	80.099	0.012485	78.8637	0.01268

2005–2006 Foreign exchange rates (cont'd)

		Average for the year to 31 December 2005		Average for the year to 31 March 2006	
Country	Unit of currency	Currency units per £1	Sterling value of currency unit £	Currency units per £1	Sterling value of currency unit £
Indonesia	I.Rupiah	17636.33	0.0000567	17323.1629	0.0000577
Iran	Iranian Rial	16299.03	0.0000614	16111.9	0.000062
Iraq	Iraq Dinar	2667.384	0.000375	2620.743	0.000382
Israel	Shekel	8.1539	0.122641	8.1412	0.12283
Jamaica	Jamaican Dollar	112.8199	0.008864	112.3691	0.00889924
Japan	Japanese Yen	200.1041	0.0049974	201.2374	0.0049693
Jordan	Jordanian Dinar	1.2893	0.7756147	1.2648	0.79064
Kenya	Kenya Shilling	137.2843	0.007284	132.8881	0.007525
Korea (South)	Won	1852.275	0.00053988	1797.1	0.00056
Kuwait	Kuwaiti Dinar	0.5313	1.882176	0.5213	1.91828
Laos	New Kip	17674.3833	0.0000566	18440.6	0.0000542
Lebanon	Lebanese Pound	2744.3486	0.0003644	2687.5416	0.00037209
Libya	Libyan Dinar	2.3765	0.420787	2.3642	0.422976
Malawi	Malawi Kwacha	214.9901	0.004651	220.5461	0.004534
Malaysia	Ringgit	6.8872	0.145196887	6.7233	0.14873648
Malta	Maltese Lira	0.6285	1.59109	0.6293	1.58907
Mauritius	Rupee	53.4296	0.01602025	53.3423	0.01874685
Mexico	Mexican Peso	19.8317	0.050424	19.1852	0.05212
Morocco	Dirham	16.1185	0.06204051	16.0777	0.0622
Nepal	Nepalese Rupee	127.9483	0.00781566	125.954	0.00794
N'nd Antilles	Antilles Guilder	3.251	0.30759766	3.1888	0.3136
New Zealand	N.Z. Dollar	2.5815	0.387372	2.5841	0.38698193
Nicaragua	Gold Cordoba	29.7796	0.03358003	29.6126	0.03377
Nigeria	Nigerian Naira	241.7492	0.004137	235.493	0.00425
Norway	N. Krone	11.7178	0.08641325	11.6878	0.85559301
Oman, Sultanate of	Rial Omani	0.7006	1.427348	0.6873	1.4549687
Pakistan	Pakistan Rupee	108.417	0.009224	106.6047	0.0093804
Papua New Guinea	Kina	5.5303	0.18082202	5.4038	0.18505
Paraguay	Guarani	11239.12	0.0000889	10913.66	0.0000916
Peru	New Sol	5.9931	0.166859	5.9161	0.16903
Phillipines	Phillipine Peso	100.0778	0.009992226	96.8521	0.010325021
Poland	Zloty	5.5982	0.17862884	5.8289	0.17156
Qatar	Qatar Riyal	6.622	0.151012	6.4968	0.15392193
Romania	Leu	1/1/05-30/6/05 = 53404.4 1/7/05-31/12/05 = 5.2643	1/1/05-30/6/05 = 0.000018725 1/7/05-31/12/05 = 0.189959	1/1/05-30/6/05 = 53483.7 1/7/05-31/12/05 = 5.2306	1/1/05-30/6/05 = 0.000018697 1/7/05-31/12/05 = 0.191183
Russia	Rouble (market)	51.3674	0.0194676	50.4621	0.01982
Rwanda	Rwanda Franc	991.2927	0.00100878	967.81	0.00103
Saudi Arabia	Saudi Riyal	6.8237	0.146548	6.6944	0.14937859
Seychelles	Rupee	10.0265	0.0997357	9.8347	0.10168
Sierra Leone	Leone	5017.596	0.000199	5130.52	0.000195
Singapore	Singapore Dollar	3.0264	0.330425588	2.9663	0.337120318

2005–2006 Foreign exchange rates (cont'd)

Average rates for the year to 31 December 2005 and the year to
31 March 2006

Country	Unit of currency	Average for the year to 31 December 2005		Average for the year to 31 March 2006	
		Currency units per £1	Sterling value of currency unit £	Currency units per £1	Sterling value of currency unit £
Solomon Islands	S.I. Dollar	13.3353	0.07498894	13.1391	0.07611
Somali Republic	Shilling	4614.7308	0.0002167	3841.33	0.00026
South Africa	Rand	11.5723	0.08641325	11.4532	0.0873119
Sri Lanka	Rupee	182.1193	0.005491	180.6241	0.0053644
Sudan	Sudanese Dinar	442.4396	0.0022602	424.337	0.00236
Surinam	Surinam Guilder	4.9568	0.20174306	4.8734	0.2052
Swaziland	Lilangeni	11.5501	0.08657934	11.4034	0.08769
Sweden	Swedish Krona	13.5776	0.07365072	13.67855	0.073107
Switzerland	Swiss Franc	2.2681	0.440898	2.2756	0.43944
Syria	Syrian Pound	94.8321	0.01054495	93.0719	0.01074
Taiwan	New T. Dollar	58.4213	0.017117045	57.7011	0.01733
Tanzania	Shilling	2051.1569	0.00048753	2052.1933	0.0004873
Thailand	Thai Baht	73.1459	0.013671306	72.1171	0.0138663
Tonga Islands	Pa'Anga	3.253	0.30740855	3.2585	0.30689
Trinidad & Tobago	Trinidad & Tobago Dollar	11.3985	0.087730842	11.1882	0.08937988
Tunisia	Dinar	2.3573	0.424214	2.3656	0.422726
Turkey	Turkish Lira	2.4483	0.408447	2.4068	0.415489
Uganda	New Shilling	3234.669	0.000309	3221.231	0.00031
United Arab Emirates	U.A.E Dirham	6.6827	0.14964012	6.5562	0.152527379
Uruguay	Uruguayan Peso	44.461	0.0224916	43.1552	0.0231722
U.S.A	U.S. Dollar	1.8195	0.54960154	1.79738	0.556365
Venezuela	V.Bolivar	4916.2392	0.000203408	4751.6019	0.00021046
Vietnam	Dong	28797.3333	0.000035	28298.4	0.000035
Yemen	Rial	348.0178	0.00287342	345.207	0.0029
Zambia	Zambian Kwacha	8104.899	0.000123	7310.1153	0.0001368
Zimbabwe	Z. Dollar	1/1/05-21/10/05 = 22764.44 22/10/05-31/12/05 = 118470.7	1/1/05-21/10/05 = 0.0000439 22/10/05-31/12/05 = 0.00000844	1/1/05-21/10/05 = 27676.3 22/10/05-31/12/05 = 144586.5	1/1/05-21/10/05 = 0.000036 22/10/05-31/12/05 = 0.0000069

Table of spot rates on 31 December 2005 and 31 March 2006

Country	Unit of currency	30 December 2005 (31 December is a Saturday)		31 March 2006	
		Currency units per £1	Sterling value of currency unit (£)	Currency units per £1	Sterling value of currency unit (£)
Australia	Australian Dollar	2.3403	0.427296	2.4326	0.411083
Canada	Canadian Dollar	2.0054	0.498654	2.0235	0.494193
Denmark	Danish Krone	10.8558	0.092117	10.6962	0.093491
European Union	Euro	1.4554	0.687096	1.4333	0.697691
Hong Kong	H K Dollar	13.3109	0.075126	13.4598	0.074295
Japan	Japanese Yen	202.268	0.004944	204.660	0.004886
Norway	N.Krone	11.6245	0.086025	11.3835	0.087846

| Country | Unit of currency | 30 December 2005 (31 December is a Saturday) | | 31 March 2006 | |
		Currency units per £1	Sterling value of currency unit (£)	Currency units per £1	Sterling value of currency unit (£)
South Africa	Rand	10.8885	0.09184	10.6926	0.935226
Sweden	S.Krone	13.6629	0.073191	13.5185	0.073973
Switzerland	Swiss Franc	2.2681	0.440898	2.2668	0.44115
U.S.A	U.S. Dollar	1.7168	0.582479	1.7346	0.576502

2004–05 Foreign exchange rates

| Country | Unit of currency | Average rates for the year to 31 December 2004 and the year to 31 March 2005 | | | |
| | | Average for the year to 31 December 2004 | | Average for the year to 31 March 2005 | |
		Currency units per £1	Sterling value of currency unit £	Currency units per £1	Sterling value of currency unit £
Algeria	Algerian Dinar	131.4975	0.007605	132.9205	0.007523
Argentina	Peso	5.402	0.18512	5.4508	0.18346
Australia	Australian Dollar	2.4912	0.401412974	2.4986	0.400224126
Bahrain	Bahrain Dinar	0.6917	1.445713	0.6968	1.435132
Bangladesh	Taka	108.9708	0.00917677	11.5317	0.008966
Barbados	Barbados Dollar	3.6574	0.273418	3.6848	0.271385
Bolivia	Boliviano	14.5681	0.068643	14.7661	0.067723
Botswana	Pula	8.5620	0.11679514	8.5027	0.117610
Brazil	Real	5.3511	0.18688	5.2779	0.18947
Brunei	Brunei Dollar	3.0908	0.32354083	3.0890	0.323729
Burma	Kyat	11.7790	0.08496850	11.8660	0.08427
Burundi	Burundi Franc	1941.2442	0.00051513	1963.573	0.000509
Canada	Canadian Dollar	2.3840	0.4194631	2.3573	0.4242141
Cayman Islands	C.I Dollar	1.5106	0.66198861	1.523	0.656599
Chile	Chilean Peso	1116.725	0.000895	1118.999	0.000894
China	Renminbi	15.1577	0.06597307	15.2827	0.065433
Colombia	Colombia Peso	4803.50	0.000208	4674.58	0.0002139
Congo Dem (Rep) Zaire	Congolese Franc	753.258	0.00132757	797.5428	0.00125385
Costa Rica	Colon	805.2731	0.00124181	830.7517	0.001204
Cuba	Cuban Peso	1.8314	0.54603036	1.8465	0.541565
Cyprus	Cyprus Pound	0.8572	1.16658889	0.8509	1.175226
Czech Republic	Koruna	47.0014	0.02127596	45.652	0.021905
Denmark	Danish Krone	10.9655	0.0911868	10.9121	0.0916414
Egypt	Egyptian £	11.3764	0.08791269	11.2929	0.08855
El Salvador	Colon	16.028	0.06239082	16.1604	0.06188
Ethiopia	Ethiopian Birr	15.7273	0.0635837	15.8847	0.062954
European Union	Euro	1.474	0.67842605	1.467	0.68166326
Fiji Islands	Fiji Dollar	3.1709	0.31536788	3.1678	0.315676
French Cty/Africa	C.F.A. Franc	966.9058	0.00103423	960.6808	0.001041
French Pacific Islands	C.F.P. Franc	175.0749	0.00571184	174.5547	0.005729
Gambia	Dalasi	53.9398	0.01853919	54.2474	0.018434

2004–2005 Foreign exchange rates (cont'd)

Average rates for the year to 31 December 2004 and the year to 31 March 2005

Country	Unit of currency	Average for the year to 31 December 2004		Average for the year to 31 March 2005	
		Currency units per £1	Sterling value of currency unit £	Currency units per £1	Sterling value of currency unit £
Ghana	Ghanaian Cedi	16488.517	0.00006064	16679.57	0.000059953
Grenada/Wind. Isles	East Caribbean Dollar	4.9525	0.2019182	4.99	0.2004008
Guyana	Guyanese Dollar	328.4189	0.0030449	330.8431	0.0030226
Honduras	Lempira	33.3949	0.02994469	34.0669	0.029354
Hong Kong	H.K. Dollar	14.268	0.70087	14.3762	0.069559
Hungary	Forint	369.4715	0.00270657	362.5755	0.002758
Iceland	Icelandic Krona	128.2386	0.007798	125.1205	0.0079923
India	Indian Rupee	82.9188	0.01206	82.8631	0.0120681
Indonesia	I.Rupiah	16422.433	0.0000608	16916.541	0.0000591
Iran	Iranian Rial	15816.065	0.0000632	16145.573	0.0000619
Iraq	Iraq Dinar	1/1/04-20/2/04 = 0.5734 21/2/04-31/12/04 = 2368.6802	1/1/04-20/2/04 = 1.74398325 21/2/04-31/12/04 = 0.00042217	2697.8116	0.0003707
Israel	Shekel	8.2138	0.1217463	8.2195	0.1216619
Jamaica	Jamaican Dollar	111.4187	0.0089752	112.6457	0.0088772
Japan	Japanese Yen	198.065	0.00505	198.171	0.00505
Jordan	Jordanian Dinar	1.3007	0.7688168	1.3102	0.7632423
Kenya	Kenya Shilling	145.2923	0.0068827	145.9332	0.0068525
Korea(South)	Won	2084.2033	0.0004798	2029.15	0.000493
Kuwait	Kuwaiti Dinar	0.5408	1.8491124	0.5435	1.8399264
Laos	New Kip	14397.408	0.000069456	14498.05	0.000068974
Lebanon	Lebanese Pound	2778.0553	0.00036	2798.3398	0.0003574
Libya	Libyan Dinar	2.3891	0.4185677	2.3908	0.41827
Malawi	Malawi Kwacha	198.5154	0.0050374	200.7741	0.0049807
Malaysia	Ringgit	6.9715	0.1434412	7.023	0.1423893
Malta	Maltese Lira	0.6306	1.5857913	0.6286	1.5908368
Mauritius	Rupee	50.5845	0.0197689	52.2987	0.0191209
Mexico	Mexican Peso	20.6952	0.0483204	20.9278	0.0477833
Morocco	Dirham	16.256	0.06151575	16.1825	0.061795
Nepal	Nepalese Rupee	132.5356	0.00754514	132.6487	0.007539
N'nd Antilles	Antilles Guilder	3.2781	0.30505476	3.3052	0.302554
New Zealand	N.Z. Dollar	2.7591	0.362437	2.7339	0.3657778
Nicaragua	Gold Cordoba	29.0374	0.03443835	29.5863	0.033799
Nigeria	Nigerian Naira	246.3451	0.0040593	246.7575	0.0040526
Norway	N. Krone	12.347	0.080991	12.1438	0.082347
Oman, Sultanate of	Rial Omani	0.7064	1.4156285	0.7117	1.4050864
Pakistan	Pakistan Rupee	107.2052	0.009327	108.9175	0.0091813
Papua New Guinea	Kina	5.7518	0.17385862	5.7245	0.174688
Paraguay	Guarani	10949.034	0.000953257	11145.829	0.0000897
Peru	New Sol	6.2532	0.1599181	6.2005	0.1612773
Phillipines	Phillipine Peso	102.9065	0.0097176	103.0777	0.0097014
Poland	Zloty	6.6646	0.15004651	6.0596	0.165027

2004–2005 Foreign exchange rates (cont'd)

		Average rates for the year to 31 December 2004 and the year to 31 March 2005			
		Average for the year to 31 December 2004		Average for the year to 31 March 2005	
Country	Unit of currency	Currency units per £1	Sterling value of currency unit £	Currency units per £1	Sterling value of currency unit £
Qatar	Qatar Riyal	6.6804	0.1496916	6.7288	0.1486149
Romania	Leu	59678.391	0.00001675	58049.01	0.000017226
Russia	Rouble (market)	52.6246	0.01900252	52.7342	0.018963
Rwanda	Rwanda Franc	1026.683	0.00097401	1031.425	0.00097
Saudi Arabia	Saudi Riyal	6.8814	0.1453193	6.9322	0.1442543
Seychelles	Rupee	10.1103	0.09890903	10.1938	0.098098
Sierra Leone	Leone	4501.4316	0.0002222	4552.6395	0.0002197
Singapore	Singapore Dollar	3.0974	0.3228514	3.0937	0.3232375
Solomon Islands	S.I. Dollar	13.6055	0.07349969	13.6218	0.073412
Somali Republic	Shilling	5035.7142	0.00019858	5293.099	0.000189
South Africa	Rand	11.81	0.084674	11.5364	0.086682
Sri Lanka	Rupee	185.8561	0.0053805	187.8602	0.0053231
Sudan	Sudanese Dinar	472.2258	0.00211763	471.232	0.002122
Surinam	Surinam Guilder	5.0088	0.19964862	5.0407	0.198385
Swaziland	Lilangeni	11.7582	0.08504703	11.5018	0.086943
Sweden	Swedish Krona	13.4526	0.07433507	13.3494	0.07491
Switzerland	Swiss Franc	2.2757	0.4394252	2.2596	0.4425562
Syria	Syrian Pound	92.1296	0.01085427	94.1199	0.010625
Taiwan	New T. Dollar	61.0875	0.01637	60.6512	0.0164877
Tanzania	Shilling	1995.077	0.0005012	2008.9023	0.0004978
Thailand	Thai Baht	73.7457	0.0135601	73.9875	0.0135158
Tonga Islands	Pa'Anga	3.6061	0.27730789	3.6002	0.277762
Trinidad & Tobago	Trinidad & Tobago Dollar	11.3504	0.0881026	11.488	0.0870474
Tunisia	Dinar	2.2834	0.4379434	2.3029	0.4342351
Turkey	Turkish Lira	2614460.3	0.00000038248	1/4/04-31/12/04 = 2672509.6 1/1/05-31/3/05 = 2.4998	1/4/04-31/12/04 = 0.00000037418 1/1/05-31/3/05 = 0.4000320
Uganda	New Shilling	3314.5158	0.0003017	3248.728	0.0003078
United Arab Emirates	U.A.E Dirham	6.7388	0.1483944	6.7884	0.1473101
Uruguay	Uruguayan Peso	52.5696	0.0190224	50.9267	0.0196361
U.S.A	U.S. Dollar	1.8318	0.5459111	1.8445	0.5421523
Venezuela	V.Bolivar	5128.1466	0.000195	4997.8741	0.0002001
Vietnam	Dong	28839.666	0.000035	29110.77	0.000034
Yemen	Rial	338.4705	0.00295447	342.6463	0.002918
Zambia	Zambian Kwacha	8742.492	0.0001144	8790.4958	0.0001138
Zimbabwe	Z. Dollar	1/1/04-23/1/04 = 1505.5 24/1/04-31/12/04 = 9319.984	1/1/04-23/1/04 = 0.00947867 24/1/04-31/12/04 = 0.00010729	10335.445	0.00009675

Table of spot rates on 31 December 2004 and 31 March 2005

Country	Unit of currency	31 December 2004		31 March 2005	
		Currency units per £1	Sterling value of currency unit (£)	Currency units per £1	Sterling value of currency unit (£)
Australia	Australian Dollar	2.4491	0.4001441	2.4428	0.409366
Canada	Canadian Dollar	2.3003	0.4347259	2.2861	0.437426
Denmark	Danish Krone	10.5068	0.0951764	10.8316	0.092322
European Union	Euro	1.4125	0.7079646	1.454	0.687757
Hong Kong	H K Dollar	14.9229	0.0670111	14.7377	0.067853
Japan	Japanese Yen	196.732	0.0050831	202.112	0.004947
Norway	N.Krone	11.6281	0.0859986	11.9316	0.083811
South Africa	Rand	10.8163	0.0924531	11.7604	0.085031
Sweden	S.Krone	12.7584	0.0783797	13.3089	0.075137
Switzerland	Swiss Franc	2.1832	0.4580432	2.2523	0.443990
U.S.A	U.S. Dollar	1.9199	0.5208605	1.8896	0.529212

Key Data

INCOME TAX

50 Income tax rates

2010–11

	Taxable income band £	Tax rate %	Tax on band £
Basic rate	1–37,400	20	7,480.00
Higher rate	37,400–150,000	40	45,040
Additional rate	Over 150,000	50	

Rate on non-dividend savings income	10% up to £2,440 20% up to basic rate limit 40% up to higher rate limit 50% thereafter
Dividend ordinary rate	10% up to basic rate limit
Dividend higher rate	32.5% up to higher rate limit
Dividend additional rate	42.5% above higher rate limit
Trust rate	50%
Dividend trust rate	42.5%

2009–10

	Taxable income band £	Tax rate %	Tax on band £
Basic rate	0–37,400	20	7,480.00
Higher rate	Over 37,400	40	

Rate on non-dividend savings income	10% up to £2,440 20% up to basic rate limit 40% thereafter
Rate on dividend income	10% up to basic rate limit 32.5% thereafter
Trust rate	40%
Dividend trust rate	32.5%

2008–09

	Taxable income band £	Tax rate %	Tax on band £
Basic rate	0–34,800	20	6,960.00
Higher rate	Over 34,800	40	

Rate on non-dividend savings income	10% up to £2,320 20% up to basic rate limit 40% thereafter
Rate on dividend income	10% up to basic rate limit 32.5% thereafter
Trust rate	40%
Dividend trust rate	32.5%

2007–08

Taxable income band £	Tax rate[1] %	Tax on band £
0– 2,230	10	223
2,231–34,600	22	7,121.40
Over 34,600	40	

Note

[1] Savings income, other than dividends, is taxed at 10% up to the starting rate limit, at 20% above the starting rate limit and up to the basic rate limit, and at 40% above that. UK Dividend income is taxed at 10% up to the basic rate limit and at 32.5% thereafter.

2006–07

Taxable income band £	Tax rate[1] %	Tax on band £
0– 2,150	10	215
2,151–33,300	22	6,853
Over 33,300	40	

Note

[1] Savings income, other than dividends, is taxed at 10% up to the starting rate limit, at 20% above the starting rate limit and up to the basic rate limit, and at 40% above that. UK Dividend income is taxed at 10% up to the basic rate limit and at 32.5% thereafter.

2005–06

Taxable income band £	Tax rate[1] %	Tax on band £
0– 2,090	10	209
2,091–32,400	22	6,668
Over 32,400	40	

Note

[1] Savings income, other than dividends, is taxed at 10% up to the starting rate limit, at 20% above the starting rate limit and up to the basic rate limit, and at 40% above that. UK Dividend income is taxed at 10% up to the basic rate limit and at 32.5% thereafter.

2004–05

Taxable income band £	Tax rate[1] %	Tax on band £
0– 2,020	10	202
2,021–31,400	22	6,463
Over 31,400	40	

Note

[1] Savings income, other than dividends, is taxed at 10% up to the starting rate limit, at 20% above the starting rate limit and up to the basic rate limit, and at 40% above that. UK Dividend income is taxed at 10% up to the basic rate limit and at 32.5% thereafter.

2003–04

Taxable income band £	Tax rate[1] %	Tax on band £
0– 1,960	10	196
1,961–30,500	22	6,278
Over 30,500	40	

Note

[1] Savings income, other than dividends, is taxed at 10% up to the starting rate limit, at 20% above the starting rate limit and up to the basic rate limit, and at 40% above that. UK Dividend income is taxed at 10% up to the basic rate limit and at 32.5% thereafter.

56 Personal reliefs

Note: Individuals earning in excess of £100,000 have a reduced personal allowance from 2010–11 (FA 2009, s. 4)

Type of relief	2010–11 £	2009–10 £	2008–09 £	2007–08 £	2006–07 £	2005–06 £	2004–05 £
Personal allowance							
Age under 65	6,475	6,475	6,035	5,225	5,035	4,895	4,745
Age 65–74	9,490	9,490	9,030	7,550	7,280	7,090	6,830
Age 75 & over	9,640	9,640	9,180	7,690	7,420	7,220	6,950
Married couple's allowance[1]							
Born after 6 April 1935	–	–	–	–	–	–	–
Born before 6 April 1935; Age up to 74	–	6,865	6,535	6,285	6,065	5,905	5,725
Born before 6 April 1935; Age 75 & over	6,965	6,965	6,625	6,365	6,135	5,975	5,795
Minimum amount of allowance	2,670	2,670	2,540	2,440	2,350	2,280	2,210
Maximum income before abatement of reliefs for older taxpayers:	22,900	22,900	21,800	20,900	20,100	19,500	18,900
Abatement income ceiling Personal allowance:							
Age 65–74	28,930	28,930	27,790	25,550	24,590	23,890	23,070
Age 75 & over	29,230	29,230	28,090	25,830	24,870	24,150	23,220
Married couples allowance							
Born before 6 April 1935; Age up to 74	–	37,320	35,780	33,240	32,020	31,140	30,100
Born before 6 April 1935; Age 75 & over	37,820	37,820	36,260	33,680	32,440	31,540	30,390
Blind person's allowance	1,890	1,890	1,800	1,730	1,660	1,610	1,560
Life assurance relief (policies issued before 14 March 1984)	12.5% of premiums	12.5% of premiums	12.5% of premiums	12.5% of premiums	12.5% of premiums	12.5% of premiums	12.5% of premiums
'Rent-a-room' limit	4,250	4,250	4,250	4,250	4,250	4,250	4,250

Notes

[1] Relief is given at a rate of 10%.

Working tax credit – maximum rates 2005–06 to 2010–11

Element	2010–2011 £	2009–10 £	2008–09 £	2007–08 £	2006–07 £	2005–06 £
Basic element	1,920	1,890	1,800	1,730	1,665	1,620
Disability element (see note below)	2,570	2,530	2,405	2,310	2,225	2,165
30-hour element	790	775	735	705	680	660
Second adult element	1,890	1,860	1,770	1,700	1,640	1,595
Lone parent element	1,890	1,860	1,770	1,700	1,640	1,595
50-plus element;						

Key Data

Element	2010–2011 £	2009–10 £	2008–09 £	2007–08 £	2006–07 £	2005–06 £
(a) working over 16 but less than 30 hours per week	1,320	1,300	1,235	1,185	1,140	1,110
(b) working over 30 hours per week (see note below)	1,965	1,935	1,840	1,770	1,705	1,660
Childcare element: percentage of eligible costs up to weekly maximum of:	80%				70%	70%
• for one child	£175				£175	£135
• for two or more	£300				£300	£200

Child tax credit – maximum rates 2005–06 to 2010–11

Element	Circumstance	2010–11 £	2009–10 £	2008–09 £	2007–08 £	2006–07 £	2005–06 £
Family	Normal case	545	545	545	545	545	545
	Where there is a child under the age of one	1,090	1,090	1,090	1,090	1,090	1,090
Individual	Each child or young person	2,300	2,235	2,085	1,845	1,765	1,690
	Each disabled child or young person	5,015	4,905	4,625	4,285	4,115	3,975
	Each severely disabled child or young person	6,110	5,980	5,645	5,265	5,060	4,895

Income thresholds and withdrawal rates 2005–06 to 2010–11

	2010–11	2009–10	2008–09	2007–08	2006–07	2005–06
First income threshold	£6,420	£6,420	£6,420	£5,220	£5,220	£5,220
First withdrawal rate	39%	39%	39%	37%	37%	37%
Second income threshold	£50,000	£50,000	£50,000	£50,000	£50,000	£50,000
Second withdrawal rate	6.67%	6.67%	6.67%	6.67%	6.67%	6.67%
First threshold for those entitled to Child Tax Credit only	£16,190	£16,040	£15,575	£14,495	£14,155	£13,910
Income disregard	£25,000	£25,000	£25,000	£25,000	£25,000	£2,500

Working Tax Credits – Daily rates 2005–06 to 2010–11

Credit element	2005–06 Daily rate £	2006–07 Daily rate £	2007–08 Daily rate £	2008–09 Daily rate £	2009–10 Daily rate £	2010–11 Daily rate £
Basic element of WTC	4.44	4.57	4.73	4.94	5.18	5.27
30-hour element of WTC	1.81	1.87	1.93	2.02	2.13	2.17
Second adult or lone parent element of WTC	4.37	4.50	4.65	4.85	5.10	5.18

Credit element	2005–06 Daily rate £	2006–07 Daily rate £	2007–08 Daily rate £	2008–09 Daily rate £	2009–10 Daily rate £	2010–11 Daily rate £
Disability element of WTC	5.93	6.10	6.32	6.59	6.94	7.05
Severe disability element of WTC	2.52	2.59	2.68	2.80	2.95	3.00
50-plus element of WTC, (16 hours +)	3.04	3.13	3.24	3.39	3.57	3.62
50-plus element of WTC, (30 hours +)	4.55	4.67	4.84	5.05	5.31	5.39

Working Tax Credits – Maximum daily rates for childcare 2005–06 to 2010–11

	2005–06 Daily rate £	2006–07 Daily rate £	2007–08 Daily rate £	2008–09 Daily rate £	2009–10 Daily rate £	2010–11 Daily rate £
One child	25.00	25.00	25.00	25.00	25.00	25.00
Two or more children	42.86	42.86	42.86	42.86	42.86	42.86

Child Tax Credits – Maximum daily rates 2005–06 to 2010–11

	2005–06 Daily rate £	2006–07 Daily rate £	2007–08 Daily rate £	2008–09 Daily rate £	2009–10 Daily rate £	2010–11 Daily rate £
Credit element						
Family element	1.50	1.50	1.49	1.50	1.50	1.50
– child under one year old (baby rate)	2.99	2.99	2.98	2.99	1.50	1.50
Child element	4.31	4.84	5.05	5.72	6.13	6.31
Disability element	6.27	6.44	6.67	6.96	7.32	7.44
Severe disability element	2.53	2.59	2.68	2.80	2.95	3.00

58 Payment dates 2009–10

(TMA 1970, s. 59A, 59B)

Tax is paid on 31 January next following the year of assessment as a single sum covering capital gains tax and income tax on all sources. Interim payments on account may be required. No interim payments are required for a year of assessment if the tax paid by assessment for the preceding year was less than £500 or 20% of the total tax liability for that year. This threshold will rise to £1,000 for payments on account due in January and July 2010. These will normally be half the amount of the net tax payable for the preceding year, but may be reduced to half the current year's liability if less. Net tax is previous year's tax after taking off tax deducted at source and tax on dividends. For 2009–10 the following due dates apply:

First interim payment	31 January 2010
Second interim payment	31 July 2010
Final balancing payment	31 January 2011

Note

If a return is not issued until after 31 October 2009 and the taxpayer has notified chargeability by 5 October 2009, the due date for the final payment becomes three months from the issue of the return (TMA 1970, s. 57B).

59 Time-limits for elections and claims

In the absence of any provision to the contrary, under self-assessment for the purposes of income tax, the normal rule is that claims are to be made within five years from 31 January next following the tax year to which they relate, previously six years from the end of the relevant chargeable period.

In certain cases the Board *may* permit an extension of the strict time-limit in relation to certain elections and claims.

Provision	Time-limit	Statutory reference
Averaging of profits of farmers or creative artists	12 months from 31 January next following end of the second tax year concerned	ITTOIA 2005, s. 222
Stock transferred to a connected party on cessation of trade to be valued at higher cost or sale price	2 years from end of accounting period in which trade ceased	ICTA 1988, s. 100(1C), ITTOIA 2005, s. 175
Post-cessation expenses relieved against income and chargeable gains	12 months from 31 January next following the tax year	ITA 2007, s. 96, ITTOIA 2005, s. 257(4)
Current and preceding year set-off of trading losses	12 months from 31 January next following the tax year loss arose	ITA 2007, s. 64, 71
Three-year carry-back of trading losses in opening years of trade	12 months from 31 January next following the tax year loss arose	ITA 2007, s. 72
Carry-forward of trading losses	5 years from 31 January next following tax year in which loss arose	ITA 2007, s. 83
Carry-back of terminal losses	5 years from 31 January next following tax year	ITA 2007, s. 89
Certain plant and machinery treated as 'short life' assets (income tax elections)	12 months from 31 January next following the tax year in which ends the chargeable period in which the qualifying expenditure was incurred	CAA 2001, s. 85
Transfer between connected parties of certain assets, eligible for capital allowances, at tax-written down value	2 years from date of sale	CAA 2001, s. 570(5)

60 Car, fuel and van benefits

Car benefit charges: normal rules

The benefit is calculated on a percentage of the list price of the car appropriate to the level of the car's CO_2 emissions, as follows:

- 15 per cent of the list price of cars emitting up to the lower threshold of emissions of carbon dioxide in grams per kilometre;
- increased by one per cent per 5g/km over the lower threshold, but

- capped at 35 per cent of the list price.

The lower threshold for each year from 2002–03 is as follows (ITEPA 2003, s. 139):

Tax year	Lower threshold (in g/km)
2010–11	130
2009–10	135
2008–09	135
2007–08	140
2006–07	140
2005–06	140
2004–05	145
2003–04	155
2002–03	165

If the exact CO_2 emissions figure does not end in 0 or 5, it should be rounded *down* to the nearest 5g/km before applying the above figures.

From 6 April 2008, lower rates apply to qualifying low emissions cars.

Discounts are given for cars using alternative fuels and technologies.

Diesel supplement

There is usually a three per cent penalty loading on diesel cars (subject to 35 per cent cap).

For years to 5 April 2006, no loading was applied to diesel cars that met the Euro IV emissions standard.

From 6 April 2006, the diesel loading applies to *all* diesel cars first registered from 1 January 2006 (as well as to older cars not meeting the standard).

Car benefit charges: table of taxable percentages

This table provides the 'appropriate percentage' figures for calculating the taxable benefit of a company car, based on CO_2 emissions figures for petrol cars (based on ITEPA 2003, s. 139, as amended).

CO_2 emissions (See note 1)	2010–11 %	2008–09 to 2009–10 %	2005–06 to 2007–08 %	2004–05 %	2003–04 %	2002–03 %
120	See note 2	See note 2				
130	15	15	15	15	15	15
135	16	15	15	15	15	15
140	17	16	15	15	15	15
145	18	17	16	15	15	15
150	19	18	17	16	15	15

CO_2 emissions (See note 1)	2010–11 %	2008–09 to 2009–10 %	2005–06 to 2007–08 %	2004–05 %	2003–04 %	2002–03 %
155	20	19	18	17	15	15
160	21	20	19	18	16	15
165	22	21	20	19	17	15
170	23	22	21	20	18	16
175	24	23	22	21	19	17
180	25	24	23	22	20	18
185	26	25	24	23	21	19
190	27	26	25	24	22	20
195	28	27	26	25	23	21
200	29	28	27	26	24	22
205	30	29	28	27	25	23
210	31	30	29	28	26	24
215	32	31	30	29	27	25
220	33	32	31	30	28	26
225	34	33	32	31	29	27
230	35	34	33	32	30	28
235	35	35	34	33	31	29
240	35	35	35	34	32	30
245	35	35	35	35	33	31
250	35	35	35	35	34	32
255	35	35	35	35	35	33
260	35	35	35	35	35	34
265	35	35	35	35	35	35

Notes

(1) The actual CO_2 emissions figure, if it is not a multiple of five, should be rounded down to the nearest multiple of five before applying this table.

(2) Since 6 April 2008, a new 10 per cent appropriate percentage has applied to company cars with CO_2 emissions of 120g/km or less (a 'qualifying low emissions car' or 'QUALEC').

Qualifying low emissions cars

From 6 April 2008, a lower tax charge is made if the vehicle is a 'qualifying low emissions car' ('QUALEC') for the tax year in which it is provided as a company car. In such a case, the appropriate percentage will be 10 per cent for petrol cars (but with a three per cent penalty loading, so a figure of 13 per cent, for most diesel cars).

A car is a QUALEC if its CO_2 emissions figure does not exceed the limit for the year, as specified at ITEPA 2003, s. 139(3A). For 2008–09, that limit is 120g/km.

Alternative fuel cars: current rules

Type of car	*Discounted charge*
Battery electric cars	15% of list price, less 6% discount – ie 9% of list price
Bi-fuel gas and petrol cars manufactured or converted before type approval	Appropriate percentage of list price, less 2% discount
Hybrid electric and petrol cars	Appropriate percentage of list price, less 3% discount
Cars capable of running on E85 fuel	Appropriate percentage of list price, less two per cent discount. (But NB discount applies only from 6 April 2008)
Note: the cost of conversion is ignored for bi-fuel gas and petrol cars converted after type approval, but no additional percentage discount is given.	

Alternative fuel cars: periods to 5 April 2006

Type of car	*Discounted charge*
Battery electric cars	15% of list price, less 6% discount – ie 9% of list price.
Hybrid electric cars	Appropriate percentage of list price, less 2% discount and a further 1% discount for each full 20 g/km that the CO_2 emissions figure is below the lower threshold.
Cars using liquid petroleum gas (LPG) or compressed natural gas (CNG) Cars running on road fuel gas alone	Appropriate percentage of list price, less 1% discount and a further 1% discount for each full 20 g/km that the CO_2 emissions figure is below the lower threshold.
Bi-fuel cars (both gas and petrol) *Cars first registered on or after 1 January 2000, and approved for running on both petrol and gas*	Appropriate percentage of list price applying to gas CO_2 emissions, less 1% discount and a further 1% discount for each full 20 g/km that the CO_2 emissions figure is below the lower threshold.

Type of car	Discounted charge
Cars first registered before 1 January 2000, and petrol cars that are retro-fitted	Appropriate percentage of list price applying to petrol CO_2 emissions, less 1% discount.

Fuel benefit charges: current rules

Since 6 April 2003, the additional taxable benefit of free fuel provided for a company car has been calculated using the same CO_2 figures as are used for calculating the company car charge.

The CO_2 percentage figure is applied to a fixed amount in accordance with the following table:

	£
2008–09	16,900
2007–08	14,400
2006–07	14,400
2005–06	14,400
2004–05	14,400
2003–04	14,400

The fuel benefit is reduced to nil if the employee is required to make good the full cost of all fuel provided for private use, and does so.

A proportionate reduction is made where the company car is only available for part of the year, where car fuel ceases to be provided part-way through the year, or where the benefit of the company car is shared.

The annual figure is expected to increase in line with RPI each year from April 2009.

Fuel types

Where there is a fuel benefit, employers must notify the Revenue of the type of fuel (or other power) by entering the appropriate 'key letter' on the form P11D. The key letters are as follows:

Key letter	Fuel or power type description
P	Petrol
D	Diesel not meeting Euro IV standard
L	Diesel meeting Euro IV standard
E	Electric only
H	Hybrid electric
B	Gas only, or bi-fuel with approved CO_2 emissions figure for gas when first registered (which must be from 1 January 2000)
G	Car manufactured to be capable of running on E85 fuel
C	Conversion, and all other bi-fuel cars with an approved CO_2 emissions figure for petrol only when first registered

In *Employer's Bulletin* 17, the Revenue wrote that:

'we have been asked to make it clear that the key letter shown in the P11D (Guide) refers to the car, not to the fuel in isolation.'

61 HMRC authorised mileage rates

Advisory fuel rates for company cars

HMRC have published rates that can be used for reimbursement of private mileage by company car drivers to their employers.

Rates applying from 1 June 2010

Engine size	Petrol	Diesel	LPG
1400cc or less	12p	11p	8p
1401cc to 2000cc	15p	11p	10p
Over 2000cc	21p	16p	14p

Rates applying from 1 December 2009*

Engine size	Petrol	Diesel	LPG
1400cc or less	11p	11p	7p
1401cc to 2000cc	14p	11p	8p
Over 2000cc	20p	14p	12p

Petrol hybrid cars are treated as petrol cars for this purpose.

* The rates have effect for all journeys made from 1 December 2009.

Rates applying from 1 July (or 1 June) 2009

Engine size	Petrol	Diesel	LPG
1400cc or less	10p	10p	7p
1401cc to 2000cc	12p	10p	8p
Over 2000cc	18p	13p	12p

Petrol hybrid cars are treated as petrol cars for this purpose.

Rates applying from 1 January 2009 (or 2 December 2008*)

Engine size	Petrol	Diesel	LPG
1400cc or less	10p	11p	7p
1401cc to 2000cc	12p	11p	9p
Over 2000cc	17p	14p	12p

Petrol hybrid cars are treated as petrol cars for this purpose.

* The rates were announced on 2 December 2008, to have effect from 1 January 2009. However, HMRC then added the following comment:

'HMRC is content for the new rates to be implemented immediately where employers are able and wish to do so.'

Rates applying from 1 July 2008

Engine size	Petrol	Diesel	LPG
1400cc or less	12p	13p	7p
1401cc to 2000cc	15p	13p	9p
Over 2000cc	21p	17p	13p

Rates applying from 1 January 2008

Engine size	Petrol	Diesel	LPG
1400cc or less	11p	11p	7p
1401cc to 2000cc	13p	11p	8p
Over 2000cc	19p	14p	11p

Rates applying from 1 August 2007

Engine size	Petrol	Diesel	LPG
1400cc or less	10p	10p	6p
1401cc to 2000cc	13p	10p	8p
Over 2000cc	18p	13p	10p

Rates applying from 1 February 2007

Engine size	Petrol	Diesel	LPG
1400cc or less	9p	9p	6p
1401cc to 2000cc	11p	9p	7p
Over 2000cc	16p	12p	10p

Rates applying from 1 July 2006 to 31 January 2007

Engine size	Petrol	Diesel	LPG
1400cc or less	11p	10p	7p
1401cc to 2000cc	13p	10p	8p
Over 2000cc	18p	14p	11p

Rates applying from 1 July 2005 to 30 June 2006

Engine size	Petrol	Diesel	LPG
1400cc or less	10p	9p	7p
1401cc to 2000cc	12p	9p	8p
Over 2000cc	16p	13p	10p

Rates applying from 6 April 2004 to 30 June 2005

Engine size	Petrol	Diesel	LPG
1400cc or less	10p	9p	7p
1401cc to 2000cc	12p	9p	8p
Over 2000cc	14p	12p	10p

Rates applying to 5 April 2004

Engine size	Petrol	Diesel	LPG
1400cc or less	10p	9p	6p
1401cc to 2000cc	12p	9p	7p
Over 2000cc	14p	12p	9p

Mileage allowance payments

Statutory mileage rates 2002–03 onwards

From April 2002, statutory rates are set for mileage allowance payments (ITEPA 2003, s. 230). An employer may reimburse business mileage at more or less than the statutory rates; any excess is taxable and any shortfall is tax deductible.

Kind of vehicle	Rate per mile
Car or van	40p for the first 10,000 miles 25p after that
Motorcycle	24p
Cycle	20p

62 Taxable state benefits

The following benefits are liable to income tax (ITEPA 2003, s. 577, 580, 660).

Rates were most recently updated by the *Social Security Benefits Up-rating Regulations* 2008 (SI 2008/667).

Benefit	Weekly rate from						
	April 2010 £	April 2009 £	April 2008 £	April 2007 £	April 2006 £	April 2005 £	April 2004 £
Bereavement allowance	97.65	95.25	90.70	87.30	84.25	82.05	79.60
Carer's allowance	53.90	53.10	50.55	48.65	46.95	45.70	44.35
Dependent adults with retirement pension[1] with carer's allowance[1] with severe disablement allowance	57.05 31.70 31.90	57.05 31.70 31.90	54.35 30.20 30.40	52.30 29.05 29.25	50.50 28.05 28.05	49.15 27.30 27.50	47.65 26.50 26.65

Industrial death benefit:
Widow's pension
Permanent rate –
    higher
    lower
	
	97.65
	29.30
		
		95.25
		28.58
			
			90.70
			27.21
				
				87.30
				26.19
					
					84.25
					25.28
						
						82.05
						24.62
							
							79.60
							23.88

Benefit	Weekly rate from						
	April 2010 £	April 2009 £	April 2008 £	April 2007 £	April 2006 £	April 2005 £	April 2004 £
Incapacity benefit (long term)							
Rate	91.40	89.80	84.50	81.35	78.50	76.45	74.15
Increase for age:							
higher rate	15.00	15.65	17.75	17.10	16.50	16.05	15.55
lower rate	5.80	6.55	8.90	8.55	8.25	8.05	7.80
Incapacity benefit (short term)							
Higher rate:							
under pensionable age[2]	81.60	80.15	75.40	72.55	70.05	68.20	66.15
over pensionable age[2]	91.40	89.80	84.50	81.35	78.50	76.45	74.15
Non-contributory retirement pension							
Standard rate	58.50	57.05	54.35	52.30	50.50	49.15	47.65
Age addition (at age 80)	0.25	0.25	0.25	0.25	0.25	0.25	0.25
Retirement pension							
Standard rate	97.65	95.25	90.70	87.30	84.25	82.05	79.60
Age addition (at age 80)	0.25	0.25	0.25	0.25	0.25	0.25	0.25
Widow's pension[3]							
Pension (standard rate)	97.65	95.25	90.70	87.30	84.25	82.05	79.60
Widowed parent's allowance	97.65	95.25	90.70	87.30	84.25	82.05	79.60

Notes

[1] No new claims for adult dependency increases payable with the state retirement pension or the carer's allowance may be made on or after 6 April 2010. Adult dependency increases already in payment immediately before 6 April 2010 are being phased out between 2010 and 2020.

[2] Pensionable age is 60 for women, 65 for men. From 6 April 2020, the state pension age for women will be 65, the same as for men. From 2010, women's state pension age is being gradually increased to bring it up to age 65 by 2020.

[3] Bereavement allowance replaced widow's pension from 9 April 2001 for all new claims by widows and widowers.

Website: www.dsdni.gov.uk/benefit_rates
www.rightsnet.org.uk/pdfs/Ben_Rates_2007_2008.pdf

63 Non-taxable state benefits

The following UK social security benefits are wholly exempt from tax (ITEPA 2003, s. 677(1), except where indicated otherwise. See also EIM 76100):

Benefit rates

Key Data

Benefit	Weekly rate from						
	April 2010 £	April 2009 £	April 2008 £	April 2007 £	April 2006 £	April 2005 £	April 2004 £
Attendance allowance							
Higher rate (day and night)	71.40	70.35	67.00	64.50	62.25	60.60	58.80
Lower rate (day or night)	47.80	47.10	44.85	43.15	41.65	40.55	39.35
Child benefit[2]							
For the eldest qualifying child	20.30	20.00	18.80	18.10	17.45	17.00	16.55
For each other child	13.40	13.20	12.55	12.10	11.70	11.40	11.05
Constant attendance allowance							
Exceptional rate	116.80	115.00	109.60	105.40	101.80	99.20	96.20
Intermediate rate	87.60	86.25	82.20	79.05	76.35	74.40	72.15
Normal maximum rate	58.40	57.50	54.80	52.70	50.90	49.60	48.10
Part-time rate	29.20	28.75	27.40	26.35	25.45	24.80	24.05
Exceptionally severe disablement allowance	58.40	57.50	54.80	52.70	50.90	49.60	48.10
Disability living allowance (care component)							
Higher rate	71.40	70.35	67.00	64.50	62.25	60.60	58.80
Middle rate	47.80	47.10	44.85	43.15	41.65	40.55	39.35
Lower rate	18.95	18.65	17.75	17.10	16.50	16.05	15.55
Disability living allowance (mobility component)							
Higher rate	49.85	49.10	46.75	45.00	43.45	42.30	41.05
Lower rate	18.95	18.65	17.75	17.10	16.50	16.05	15.55
Incapacity benefit (short term)[3]							
Lower rate:							
under pensionable age[4]	68.95	67.75	63.75	61.35	59.20	57.65	55.90
over pensionable age[4]	87.75	86.20	81.10	78.05	75.35	73.35	71.15

Notes

[1] Child special allowance and child dependency increases with retirement pension, widow's benefit, short-term incapacity benefit at the higher rate and long-term incapacity benefit, invalid care allowance, severe disablement allowance, higher rate individual death benefit, unemployability supplement and short-term incapacity benefit if beneficiary over pension age.

[2] Child benefit increases for 2009 were paid from January rather than April 2009.

[3] Incapacity benefit (and contributory employment & support allowance) are taxable, under the *Income Tax (Earnings and Pensions) Act* 2003, except for short-term benefit payable at the lower rate. There is no tax charge, however, if the recipient started receiving invalidity benefit or sickness benefit before 6 April 1995 and has continued receiving incapacity benefit since then.

[4] Pensionable age is 60 for women, 65 for men. From 6 April 2020, the state pension age for women will be 65, the same as for men. From 2010, women's state pension age is gradually being increased to bring it up to age 65 by 2020.

64   Official rate of interest

(ITEPA 2003, s. 181)

The official rate of interest is used to calculate the cash equivalent of the benefit of an employment-related loan which is a taxable cheap loan. HMRC normally set a single rate in advance for the whole tax year and gave a commitment in January 2000, that (following announcement of the rate for any given tax year) the official rate may be reduced but will not be increased in the light of interest rate changes generally.

The official rate of interest was reduced with effect from 6 April 2010 and figures for recent periods have been as follows:

Date	Rate %	SI No.
From 6 April 2010	4.00	SI 2010/415
From 1 March 2009 to 5 April 2010	4.75	SI 2009/199
From 6 April 2007 to 28 February 2009	6.25	SI 2007/684
From 6 January 2002 to 5 April 2007	5.00	SI 2001/3860

The *average* official rates of interest are given below. These should be used if the loan was outstanding throughout the tax year and the normal averaging method of calculation is being used.

Year	Average official rate %
2009–10	4.75
2008–09	6.10
2007–08	6.25
2006–07	5.00
2005–06	5.00
2004–05	5.00
2003–04	5.00

65 Official rate of interest – foreign currency loans

The official rate of interest for certain employer-provided loans in Japanese yen or Swiss francs has been set as follows:

Loans in Swiss francs	
Date	**Rate %**
From 6 July 1994	5.5
From 6 June 1994 to 5 July 1994	5.7
Loans in Japanese yen	
Date	**Rate %**
From 6 June 1994	3.9

Note

There is no tax charge if all the employee's cheap or interest-free loans total no more than £5,000. Alternatively, where the employee's cheap or interest-free loans total more than £5,000, there is no tax charge in respect of 'non-qualifying' loans totalling no more than £5,000. A 'non-qualifying' loan is one in respect of which interest paid does not qualify for relief under ITA 2007, s. 24(1) (ignoring the exclusion of MIRAS loans) and is disallowed in computing the charge on trading profits.

The lower 'official rate' of interest for taxing loans in a foreign currency where interest rates in that country are significantly lower than interest rates in the UK only applies to a loan in another country's currency, to a person who normally lives in that country and has actually lived there in the year or previous five years.

Law: ITA 2007, s. 24(1)

67 Relocation allowance

Statutory relief

Tax relief for relocation expenses in relation to payments made or expenses provided in connection with an employee's change of residence where the employee's job or place of work is changed is generally subject to a statutory maximum from 6 April 1993. The maximum allowance is:

From	Maximum allowance £
6 April 1993	8,000

Law: ITEPA 2003, s. 288

68 Incidental overnight expenses

Benefits, reimbursements and expenses provided by an employer for employees' minor, personal expenditure whilst on business-related activities requiring overnight accommodation away from home are not taxable provided that the total amount reimbursed, etc. does not exceed the relevant maximum amount(s) per night, multiplied by the number of nights' absence. If the limit is exceeded the whole amount provided remains taxable.

	Authorised maximum per night	
From	**In UK** **£**	**Outside the UK** **£**
6 April 1995	5	10

Law: ITEPA 2003, s. 241

CORPORATION TAX

70 Corporation tax rates

Financial year	Full rate %	Small companies' rate %	Profit limit for small companies' rate (lower limit)	Profit limit for small companies' marginal relief (upper limit)	Marginal relief fraction for small companies	Starting rate %	Profit limit for starting rate (lower limit)	Profit limit for starting rate marginal relief (upper limit)	Marginal relief fraction for starting rate
2010	28	21	300,000	1,500,000	7/400	(5)	(5)	(5)	(5)
2009	28	21	300,000	1,500,000	7/400	(5)	(5)	(5)	(5)
2008	28	21	300,000	1,500,000	7/400	(5)	(5)	(5)	(5)
2007	30	20	300,000	1,500,000	1/40	(5)	(5)	(5)	(5)
2006	30	19	300,000	1,500,000	11/400	(5)	(5)	(5)	(5)
2005	30	19	300,000	1,500,000	11/400	0	10,000	50,000	19/400
2004	30	19	300,000	1,500,000	11/400	0	10,000	50,000	19/400

Notes

(1) The lower and upper limits for the small companies' rate and the small companies' marginal relief, as well as the similar lower and upper limits for the starting rate, are reduced proportionally:
- for accounting periods of less than 12 months, and
- in the case of associated companies, by dividing the limits by the total number of non-dormant associated companies.

(2) For companies with ring fence profits, the rates are as above except that:
- for financial years 2007, 2008, and 2009, the small companies' rate of tax is 19 per cent and the marginal relief fraction for small companies is 11/400; and
- for financial years 2008, 2009 and 2010, the main rate is 30 per cent.

For authorised unit trusts and open ended investment companies, the rate of corporation tax for a financial year is the rate at which income tax at the basic rate is charged for the year of assessment which begins on 6 April in that financial year (20 per cent for the financial year 2009). It was announced in the 2009 Pre-Budget Report that the Government is considering applying a reduced rate of corporation tax to income from patents from 2013.

(3) 'Close investment holding companies' do not receive the benefit of the small companies' rate or the starting rate and so are taxable entirely at the full rate regardless of the level of their profits.

(4) From 1 April 2006, the starting and non-corporate distribution rates are replaced with a new single banding for small companies set at the existing small companies' rate. The small companies' rate therefore applies to companies with taxable profits between £0 and £300,000.

(5) From 1 April 2004 to 31 March 2006, the benefit of the start5ng rate and marginal starting rate relief applied only to undistributed profits and profits distributed to other companies. Profits chargeable to corporation tax below the threshold for the small companies' rate that had been distributed to non-company shareholders were subject to a minimum rate (the 'non-corporate distribution rate': NCD rate which, for the financial years

2004 and 2005, was the equivalent to the small companies' rate). Profits distributed to other bodies subject to corporation tax were disregarded for the purpose of establishing whether the NCD rate applied.

Effective marginal rates

For marginal small companies' relief and marginal starting rate relief, there is an effective rate of tax in the margin, i.e. between the lower and upper limits given for each in the preceding table, which exceeds the full rate. These marginal rates are not prescribed by statute, but are derived from theappropriatee corporation tax rates and fractions. The applicable rates are as follows:

Financial year	Marginal small companies' rate %	Marginal starting rate %
2010	29.75	(1)
2009	29.75	(1)
2008	29.75	(1)
2007	32.5	(1)
2006	32.75	(1)
2005	32.75	23.75
2004	32.75	23.75

(1) From 1 April 2006, the starting rate is replaced with a new single banding for small companies set at the existing small companies' rate. The small companies' rate therefore applies to small companies with taxable profits between £0 and £300,000.

Marginal relief

$$\text{Deduction} = (\text{Upper Limit} - \text{Profits}) \times \frac{\text{Basic profits}}{\text{Profits}} \times \text{Marginal Relief Fraction}$$

'**Profits**' means profits as finally computed for corporation tax purposes *plus* franked investment income *excluding* franked investment income from companies in the same group. Distributions are treated as coming from within the group if they are received from a company which is a 51 per cent subsidiary or a consortium company, the recipient being a member of the consortium. For distributions received on or after 1 July 2009, the reference to franked investment income (and the exclusion for franked investment income received from group companies) includes distributions that are exempt from tax under the new broad exemption for distributions.

'**Basic profits**' means profits as finally computed for corporation tax purposes (also known as 'profits chargeable to corporation tax').

Similar provisions apply for calculating marginal relief for the starting rate effective from 1 April 2000.

74 Due dates

Liability	Due date
Mainstream tax (TMA 1970, s. 59D)	Nine months and one day after end of an accounting period[1]
Mainstream tax in instalments[2]:	The 14th day of the seventh, tenth, 13th and 16th months after start of a 12 month accounting period.
Income tax on interest, annual payments etc.	14 days after end of return period.[3]
Charge on loans to participators (CTA 2010, s. 455)	Nine months and one day after the end of the accounting period in which the loan was advanced.

Notes

[1] FA 2009, s. 111 provides for companies to enter into voluntary payment plans with HMRC under which corporation tax liabilities can be paid in instalments spread equally before and after the due date. It should be noted that only corporation tax payable in accordance with TMA 1970, s. 59D (i.e. tax payable nine months and one day after the end of the accounting period) can be the subject of a managed payment plan. This excludes corporation tax payable by large companies in accordance with the quarterly instalment payment scheme. In addition, companies which have entered into a group payment arrangement can not enter into a managed payment plan. The payment plans will be launched in April 2011.

[2] TMA 1970, s. 59E and SI 1998/3175 provide for the payment of corporation tax by 'large' companies (defined in accordance with the small profits marginal relief upper limit) in instalments.

Companies which are 'large' because of the number of associated companies or because of substantial dividend income will not have to pay by instalments if their corporation tax liabilities are less than £10,000. Companies which become 'large' in an accounting period, having previously had profits below the upper limit, may be exempt from instalment arrangements in certain circumstances. Groups containing 'large' companies are able to pay corporation tax on a group-wide basis.

For accounting periods ending after 30 June 2005, corporation tax and the supplementary charge payable by oil companies on ring fence profits are payable in three equal instalments. Corporation tax due on other profits (i.e. non-ring fence) continues to be payable in quarterly instalments as above.

The payment dates for the three instalments once the transitional period (see below) has passed are as follows:

(1) one-third payable six months and 13 days from the start of the accounting period (unless the date for instalment (3) is earlier);

(2) one-third payable three months from the first instalment due date (unless (3) is earlier); and

(3) the balance payable 14 days from the end of the accounting period (regardless of the length of the period).

Transitional arrangements apply for the first accounting period affected. These arrangements leave the first two quarterly instalments unchanged (at one-quarter each of the estimated liability for the period) but then require payment of the remainder of the estimated liability on ring fence profits for that accounting period to be paid on the new third instalment date.

(3) Return periods end on 31 March, 30 June, 30 September, 31 December and at the end of an accounting period.

The requirement for companies to deduct and account for income tax on certain payments is removed with effect for payments after 31 March 2001 of:

- interest, royalties, annuities and other annual payments made to companies within the charge to UK corporation tax on that income; and
- interest on quoted Eurobonds paid to non-residents.

78 Time-limits for elections and claims

In the absence of any provision to the contrary, the normal rule is that claims are to be made within six years from the end of the relevant chargeable period (FA 1998, Sch. 18, para 46(1)) for accounting periods within self-assessment.

In certain cases the Board *may* permit an extension of the strict time-limit in relation to certain elections and claims.

Provision	Time limit	References
Stock transferred to a connected party on cessation of trade to be valued at higher cost or sale price	2 years from end of accounting period in which trade ceased	CTA 2009, s. 167(1)–(4)
Carry-forward of trading losses	Relief is given automatically	CTA 2010, s. 45
Set-off of trading losses against profits of the same, or an earlier, accounting period(1)	2 years from end of accounting period in which loss incurred	CTA 2010, s. 37(7)
Group relief	Claims to group relief must be made (or withdrawn) by the later of: (1) 12 months after the claimant company's filing date for the return for the accounting period covered by the claim; (2) 30 days after a closure notice is issued on the completion of an enquiry(2); (3) 30 days after HMRC issue a notice of amendment to a return following the completion of an enquiry (issued where the company fails to amend the return itself); or (4) 30 days after the determination of any appeal against an HMRC amendment (as in (3) above).	FA 1998, Sch. 18, para. 74
Set-off of loss on disposal of shares in unquoted trading company against income of investment company	2 years from end of accounting period	CTA 2010, s. 70(4)
Surrender of company tax refund within group	Before refund made to surrendering company	CTA 2010, s. 963(3)

Provision	Time limit	References
Election to reallocate a chargeable gain or an allowable loss within a group [3]	2 years from end of accounting period during which the gain or loss accrues	TCGA 1992, s. 171A
Relief for a non-trading deficit on loan relationships (including any non-trading exchange losses)	2 years from end of period in which deficit arises, or, in the case of a claim to carry forward the deficit, 2 years from end of the accounting period following the deficit period, or within such further period as the Board may allow	CTA 2009, s. 460(1)

[1] The carry-back period is extended to three years for accounting periods ending in the period 23/11/08 to 24/11/2010 (FA 2009, s. 23, Sch. 6).

[2] 'Enquiry' in the above does not include a restricted enquiry into an amendment to a return (restricted because the time limit for making an enquiry into the return itself has expired), where the amendment consists of a group relief claim or withdrawal of claim. These time limits have priority over any other general time limits for amending returns and are subject to HMRC permitting an extension to the time limits.

[3] Following the enactment of the *Finance Act* 2009, it is now possible for chargeable gains and allowable losses to be transferred within a group. For gains and losses made before 21 July 2009, this result could only be achieved by electing for the notional transfer of an asset before its disposal to a third party (TCGA 1992, s. 171A prior to the changes made by FA 2009, s. 31, Sch. 12). The election had to be made jointly on or before the second anniversary of the end of the actual vendor group company's accounting period in which it made the disposal.

CAPITAL GAINS TAX

80 Rates, annual exemption, retirement relief, chattel exemption

Tax year	Annual exempt amount		Chattel exemption (max sale proceeds)[1]	Rate	
	Individuals, PRs[2], trusts for mentally disabled[3] £	Other trusts[3] £	£	Individuals %	Trustees and PRs %
2010–11	10,100	5,050	6,000	18[4]	18
2009–10	10,100	5,050	6,000	18[4]	18
2008–09	9,600	4,800	6,000	18[4]	18
2007–08	9,200	4,600	6,000	10/20/40[4]	40
2006–07	8,800	4,400	6,000	10/20/40[4]	40
2005–06	8,500	4,250	6,000	10/20/40[4]	40
2004–05	8,200	4,100	6,000	10/20/40[4]	40
2003–04	7,900	3,950	6,000	10/20/40[4]	34
2002–03	7,700	3,850	6,000	10/20/40[4]	34
2001–02	7,500	3,750	6,000	10/20/40[4]	34
2000–01	7,200	3,600	6,000	10/20/40[4]	34

Notes

[1] Where disposal proceeds exceed the exemption limit, marginal relief restricts any chargeable gain to $^5/_3$ of the excess. Where there is a loss and the proceeds are less than £6,000 the proceeds are deemed to be £6,000.

[2] For year of death and next two years in the case of personal representatives (PRs) of deceased persons.

[3] Multiple trusts created by the same settlor; each attracts relief equal to the annual amount divided by the number of such trusts (subject to a minimum of 10% of the full amount).

[4] For 2000–01 to 2007–08, capital gains are taxed as top slice of income at:

- starting rate to the extent to the starting rate limit;
- lower rate to the extent above the starting rate limit but to the basic rate limit; and
- higher rate to the extent above the basic rate limit.

81 Due dates

1996–97 and subsequent years

(1) Where a tax return for the tax year was issued to the taxpayer before 1 November of the following tax year, the due date of payment of capital gains tax for the tax year is 31 January following the end of the tax year in which the gain arises; and

(2) where a tax return for the tax year was issued to the taxpayer after 31 October of the following tax year, the due date of payment of capital gains tax for the tax year is three months after the date that the tax return was issued to the taxpayer.

82 Time-limits for elections and claims

In the absence of any provision to the contrary, under self-assessment the normal rule is that claims are to be made within five years from 31 January next following the tax year to which they relate, otherwise the limit is six years from the end of the relevant chargeable period (TMA 1970, s. 43(1)).

For details of time-limits relating to payment of tax, see 74.

In certain cases the Board *may* permit an extension of the strict time-limit in relation to certain elections and claims.

Provision	Time-limit	References
Post-cessation expenses relieved against gains	12 months from 31 January next following the tax year in which expenses paid	ITA 2007, s. 96
Trading losses relieved against gains	12 months from 31 January next following the tax year loss arose	ITA 2007, s. 64 and 71
Value of asset negligible	2 years from end of tax year (or accounting period if a company) in which deemed disposal/reacquisition takes place	TCGA 1992, s. 24(2)
Re-basing of all assets to 31 March 1982 values	Within 12 months from 31 January next following the tax year of disposal (or 2 years from end of accounting period of disposal if a company)	TCGA 1992, s. 35(6)
50% relief if deferred charge on gains before 31 March 1982	Within 12 months from 31 January next following the tax year of disposal (or 2 years from end of accounting period of disposal if a company)	TCGA 1992, s. 36 and Sch. 4, para. 9(1)
Variation within 2 years of death not to have CGT effect	6 months from date of variation (election not necessary for variations on or after 1 August 2002)	TCGA 1992, s. 62(7)
Specifying which "same day" share acquisitions (through employee share schemes) should be treated as disposed of first	Date of earliest disposal	TCGA 1992, s. 105A
Replacement of business assets (roll-over relief)	5 years from 31 January next following the tax year (or 6 years from the end of the accounting period if a company) Replacement asset to be purchased between 12 months before and 3 years after disposal of old asset	TCGA 1992, s. 152(1)
Disapplication of incorporation relief under TCGA 1992, s. 162	2 years from 31 January following the end of the year of assessment in which the business is transferred	TCGA 1992, s. 162A

Provision	Time-limit	References
Disposal of asset and re-investment in qualifying company (prior to 30 November 1993, applied only to disposal of qualifying shares or securities) (re-investment relief) (repealed for 1998–99 onwards)	5 years from 31 January next following the tax year	Former TCGA 1992, s. 164A(2)
Hold-over of gain on gift of business asset	5 years from 31 January next following the tax year	TCGA 1992, s. 165(1)
Determination of main residence	2 years from acquisition of second property (see ESC D21)	TCGA 1992, s. 222(5)
Irrecoverable loan to a trader	2 years from end of tax year (or accounting period if a company) otherwise effective from date claimed (see SP 8/90)	TCGA 1992, s. 253(3)
Retirement relief: ill-health grounds (pre 2003–04)	12 months from 31 January next following the year of assessment in which the disposal occurred	Former TCGA 1992, Sch. 6, para. 5(2)

83 Entrepreneurs' relief (from 6 April 2008 onwards)

Chargeable gains arising on disposals of qualifying business assets on or after 6 April 2008 are to be reduced by $^4/_9$ths before being charged to tax at the flat rate of 18%.

The qualifying gains eligible for this reduction are limited to a cap of £1m during the lifetime of the individual, or, in the case of a trustees' disposal, the lifetime of the qualifying beneficiary. That limit is increased to £2m in respect of disposals on or after 6 April 2010.

Transitional provisions allow relief to be claimed in certain circumstances where gains deferred from disposals made on or before 5 April 2008 subsequently become chargeable.

84 Exemptions and reliefs

Taper relief

(applies to individuals, trustees and personal representatives, NOT companies)

Introduced for gains realised on or after 6 April 1998 and before 6 April 2008. Indexation allowance to 5 April 1998 (see below) may also be available.

The chargeable gain is reduced according to how long the asset has been held or treated as held after 5 April 1998. Non-business assets acquired prior to 17 March 1998 qualify for an addition of one year to the period for which they are treated as held after 5 April 1998.

The taper is generally applied to the net chargeable gain for the year after deduction of any losses of the same tax year and of any losses carried forward from earlier years.

The amount of taper relief depends on:

(a)   the number of whole years in the qualifying holding period; and

(b) the amounts of the chargeable gain treated as:

(i) a gain on the disposal of a business asset; and

(ii) a gain on the disposal of a non-business asset.

The rules for determining the amounts of the chargeable gain that are treated as (i) a gain on the disposal of a business asset and (ii) a gain on the disposal of a non-business asset are set out in former TCGA 1992, Sch. A1, para. 3.

With respect to defining a business asset, the conditions for shares to qualify as business assets are set out in former TCGA 1992, Sch. A1, para. 4 and the conditions for other assets to qualify as business assets are set out in former para. 5.

The tables below show the percentage of chargeable gain that is subject to capital gains tax; i.e., after taper relief. Hence, if the percentage of gain chargeable is 100 per cent, then taper relief is 0 per cent; if the percentage of gain chargeable is 95 per cent, then taper relief is 5 per cent, and so on.

Business assets

Number of complete years after 5.4.98 for which asset held	Percentage of gains chargeable	
	All years from 2002–03 to 2007–08	2001–02
0	100	100
1	50	87.5
2	25	75
3	25	50
4 or more	25	25

Non-business assets

Number of complete years after 5.4.98 for which asset held	Percentage of gains chargeable (all years from 2001–02 to 2007–08)
0	100
1	100
2	100
3	95
4	90
5	85
6	80
7	75
8	70
9	65
10 or more	60

Key Data

85 Treatment of shares and other securities (after 5 April 1998)

Pooling for capital gains tax (but not corporation tax) ceased for acquisitions on or after 6 April 1998.

Disposals after 5 April 1998 are identified with acquisitions in the following order:

(1)   same day acquisitions (under existing rule);

(2)   acquisitions within the following 30 days;

(3)   previous acquisitions after 5 April 1998 on last-in first out (LIFO) basis;

(4)   any shares in 'pool' as at 5 April 1998;

(5)   any shares held at 5 April 1982; and

(6)   any shares aquired before 6 April 1965.

If the above identification rules fail to exhaust the shares disposed of, they are identified with subsequent acquisitions.

Law: TCGA 1992, s. 106A

86 Enterprise Investment Scheme

(TCGA 1992, s. 150A and Sch. 5B)

Under the Enterprise Investment Scheme (EIS), income tax relief, CGT deferral relief and CGT disposal relief may be available and claimed. The income tax relief is based on the amount subscribed by a qualifying individual for eligible shares in a qualifying company. Income tax relief may be withdrawn under certain circumstances. With regards to the CGT reliefs:

(1)   CGT Deferral Relief – Gains arising on the disposal of any asset can be deferred against subscriptions made by a qualifying individual for eligible shares in a qualifying company. For shares issued on or after 6 April 1998, shares no longer have to have EIS Income Tax Relief attributable to them in order to qualify for CGT Deferral Relief. The defered gains may crystallise on the disposal of the shares.

(2)   CGT Disposal Relief – Gains arising on the disposal by a qualifying individual of eligible shares in a qualifying company are exempt from CGT provided the shares have been held for a minimum period or the EIS Income Tax Relief has not been withdrawn.

'Qualifying individual' is basically someone who is not connected with the qualifying company.

'Eligible shares' are basically ordinary unquoted shares in a company.

'Qualifying company' is basically an unquoted company existing wholly for the purposes of carrying on a 'qualifying trade', or whose business consists entirely in the holding of shares in, or the making of loans to, one or more 'qualifying subsidiaries'.

'Qualifying trade' is basically one that is conducted on a commercial basis with a view to realising profits other than specifically excluded activities.

'Qualifying subsidiary' is basically one carrying on a qualifying trade.

87 Roll-over relief

To qualify for roll-over or hold-over relief on the replacement of business assets, the items must be appropriate business assets and the reinvestment must take place within 12 months before, or three years after, the disposal of the old asset. For hold-over relief, the replacement asset is a depreciating asset (an asset with a predictable useful life of no more than 60 years).

Classes of assets qualifying for relief:

* land and buildings occupied and used exclusively for the purposes of a trade;
* fixed plant or machinery;
* ships, aircraft, hovercraft;
* satellites, space stations and spacecraft (including launch vehicles);
* goodwill;
* milk quotas, potato quotas and (from 29 March 1999) fish quotas;
* ewe and suckler cow premium quotas; and
* payment entitlements under the single payment scheme.

Law: TCGA 1992, s. 155

STAMP DUTIES

89 Rates, penalties and interest

Conveyance or transfer on sale of shares and securities (FA 1999, Sch. 13, para. 3)

Instrument	Rate of tax after 26 October 1986 %
Stock transfer	$1/_2$[(1)(2)]
Conversion of shares into depositary receipts	$1 1/_2$[(3)]
Take overs and mergers	$1/_2$[(1)(2)]
Purchase by company of own shares	[(1)(2)]
Letters of allotment	$1/_2$

Notes

(1) Because duty at $^{1}/_{2}\%$ is equivalent to £5 per £1,000 of consideration and duty is rounded up to the next multiple of £5 (FA 1999, s. 112(1)(b)), duty is effectively £5 per £1,000 (or part of £1,000) of consideration.

(2) Loan capital is generally exempt from transfer on sale duty subject to specific exclusions (designed to prevent exemption applying to quasi-equity securities) (FA 1986, s. 79).

(3) FA 1986, s. 67(3).

Transfers of property (consideration paid)

Rates from 23 March 2006

Rate (%)	All land in the UK	
	Residential	**Non-residential**
Zero	£125,000	£150,000
1	Over £125,000–£250,000	Over £150,000–£250,000
3	Over £250,000–£500,000	Over £250,000–£500,000
4	Over £500,000	Over £500,000

Rates from 17 March 2005

Rate (%)	All land in the UK	
	Residential	**Non-residential**
Zero	£120,000	£150,000
1	Over £120,000–£250,000	Over £150,000–£250,000
3	Over £250,000–£500,000	Over £250,000–£500,000
4	Over £500,000	Over £500,000

Rate (%)	Land in disadvantaged areas	
	Residential	**Non-residential**
Zero	£150,000	All
1	Over £150,000–£250,000	
3	Over £250,000–£500,000	
4	Over £500,000	

Note:

Disadvantaged area relief for non-residential land transactions is not available for non-residential land transactions with an effective date on or after 17 March 2005.

However, the relief is preserved for:

- the completion of contracts entered into and substantially performed on or before 16 March 2005;
- the completion or substantial performance of other contracts entered into on or before 16 March 2005, provided that there is no variation or assignment of the contract or sub-sale of the property after 16 March 2005 and that the transaction is not in consequence of the exercise after 16 March 2005 of an option or right of pre-emption.

New leases (lease duty)

Duty on rent

Rate (%)	Net present value of rent	
	Residential	Non-residential
Zero	£0–£125,000	£0–£150,000
1	Over £125,000	Over £150,000

Note:

When calculating duty payable on the 'NPV' (net present value) of leases, reduce the 'NPV' calculation by the following before applying the 1% rate:

- Residential – £125,000 (£120,000 prior to 23 March 2006);
- Non-residential – £150,000.

Duty on premium is the same as for transfers of land (except special rules apply for premium where rent exceeds £600 annually).

The rate of stamp duty/stamp duty reserve tax on the transfer of shares and the securities is unchanged at 0.5% for 2006–07.

Rates from 1 December 2003 (implementation of stamp duty land tax)

Transfers of property (consideration paid)

Rate (%)	All land in the UK	
	Residential	Non-residential
Zero	£60,000	£150,000
1	Over £60,000–£250,000	Over £150,000–£250,000
3	Over £250,000–£500,000	Over £250,000–£500,000
4	Over £500,000	Over £500,000

Rate (%)	Land in disadvantaged areas	
	Residential	Non-residential
Zero	£150,000	All
1	Over £150,000–£250,000	
3	Over £250,000–£500,000	
4	Over £500,000	

Note

FA 2003, s. 125 confirms that property that is not land, shares or interests in partnerships is no longer subject to stamp duty from 1 December 2003.

Conveyance or transfer on sale of other property (e.g. freehold property)

Rates from 9 April 2003 to 30 November 2003

Rate (%)	All property	Disadvantaged areas	
		Residential	Non-residential
Zero	£0–£60,000	£0–£150,000	All
1	Over £60,000–£250,000	Over £150,000–£250,000	
3	Over £250,000–£500,000	Over £250,000–£500,000	
4	Over £500,000	Over £500,000	

Rates prior to 9 April 2003 (FA 1999, Sch. 13, para. 4)

Instruments executed	Thresholds			
	Up to £60,000	Over £60,000 up to £250,000	Over £250,000 up to £500,000	Over £500,000
On or after 28 March 2000[1]	Nil	1%	3%	4%
On or after 16 March 1999[2]	Nil	1%	2.5%	3.5%

Notes

[1] Transfers executed on or after 28 March 2000 unless in pursuance of a contract made on or before 21 March 2000.

[2] Transfers executed on or after 16 March 1999 unless in pursuance of a contract made on or before 9 March 1999.

Stamp duty at the appropriate rate is charged on the *full* amount of the certified value, not just on any excess over a threshold.

Fixed duties (FA 1999, s. 112(2))

In relation to instruments executed on or after 1 October 1999, the amount of fixed stamp duty is £5.

Duty (pre-1/10/99)	Amount
Conveyance or transfer – miscellaneous	50p
Declaration of trust	50p
Duplicate or counterpart	50p
Exchange or partition	50p
Leases – small furnished letting	£1
miscellaneous	£2
Release or renunciation	50p
Surrender	50p

Note

FA 2003, s. 125 confirmed that property that is not land, shares or interests in partnerships is no longer subject to stamp duty from 1 December 2003.

Leases (and agreements for leases) (FA 1999, Sch. 13, para. 11–13)

Rates for instruments executed after 27 March 2000

Term (FA 1999, Sch. 13, para. 12(3))	Rate %
Under 7 years or indefinite:	
• rent £5,000 or less	Nil
• over £5,000	1
Over 7 but not over 35 years	2
Over 35 but not over 100 years	12
Over 100 years	24

Notes

Leases for a definite term of less than one year: fixed duty of £5 (FA 1999, Sch. 13, para. 11 with effect from 1 October 1999).

Where a furnished property lease is granted for a premium, this will be subject to stamp duty with the nil rate only applying if the annual rent does not exceed £600 per annum.

An agreement for lease is liable to stamp duty as if it were an actual lease, but if a lease is subsequently granted which is in conformity with the agreement, or which relates to substantially the same property and term of years as the agreement, the duty on the lease is reduced by the duty already paid on the agreement.

Duty on new leases from 1 December 2003

Duty on rent

| Rate (%) | Net present value of rent | |
	Residential	Non-residential
Zero	£0–£60,000	£0–£150,000
1	Over £60,000	Over £150,000

Notes

These rates were introduced by FA 2003, s. 56 and Sch. 5.

Duty on *premium* is the same as for transfers of land (except special rules apply for premium where rent exceeds £600 annually).

Penalty for late presentation of documents for stamping

Documents executed after 30 September 1999 (SA 1891, s. 15B)

Type of document	Penalties applicable if document presented for stamping more than
Document executed in UK	30 days after execution
Document executed abroad relating to UK land and buildings	30 days after execution (wef Royal assent to FA 2002)
Other document executed abroad	30 days after document first received in UK[1]

Note

[1] Free standing penalty (see table further below) may apply if written information confirming date of receipt in UK is incorrect.

The maximum penalties are:

- £300 or the amount of duty, whichever is less; on documents submitted up to one year late; and
- £300 or the amount of duty, whichever is greater; on documents submitted more than one year late.

Mitigated penalties due on late stamping

The Stamp Office publishes tables (booklet SO10) of mitigated penalty levels that will be applied in straightforward cases.

Cases involving ad valorem duties

Months late	Up to £300	£300–£700	£705–£1,350	£1,355–£2,500	£2,505–£5,000	Over £5,000
Under 3	Nil	£20	£40	£60	£80	£100
Under 6	£20*	£40	£60	£80	£100	£150
Under 9	£40*	£60	£80	£100	£150	£200
Under 12	£60*	£80	£100	£150	£200	£300
Under 15	15% of the duty or £100 if greater					
Under 18	25% of the duty or £150 if greater				See	
Under 21	35% of the duty or £200 if greater				below	
Under 24	45% of the duty or £250 if greater					

Note

* Or the amount of the duty if that is less.

Cases over one year late involving duty over £5,000 and any case over two years late are considered individually.

Cases involving fixed duties

	Maximum penalty per document	Penalty after mitigation
Up to 12 months late	£5	Nil (100% mitigation)
Over 12 months late	£300	According to circumstances

In all cases above the penalties will not apply if the person responsible for stamping can show a 'reasonable excuse' for the failure to submit the document(s) within the time-limit. Interest is due on any unpaid penalty.

Free standing penalties (maximum amount)

- fraud in relation to stamp duty; (£3,000)
- failure to set out true facts, relating to stamp duty liability, in a document; (£3,000)
- failure to stamp document within 30 days of issue of a Notice of Decision on Adjudication; (£300)
- failure to allow inspection of documents; (£300)
- registering or enrolling a chargeable document that is not duly stamped; (£300)
- circulating a blank transfer; (£300)
- issuing an unstamped foreign security. (£300)

Duties abolished since March 1985

Duty	Effective date of abolition
Ad valorem	
• Capital duty	Transactions after 15 March 1988 – documents stamped after 21 March 1988
• Gifts inter vivos	Instruments executed after 18 March 1985, stamped after 25 March 1985

Key Data

Duty	Effective date of abolition
• Life assurance policy duty	Instruments executed after 31 December 1989
• Transfers on divorce etc.	Instruments executed after 25 March 1985
• Unit trust instrument duty	Instruments executed after 15 March 1988, stamped after 21 March 1988
• Variations and appropriations on death	Instruments executed after 25 March 1985
• Transfers of loan capital (subject to specific exclusions) generally (replaced previous provisions excepting certain categories of loan capital)	Instruments executed after 31 July 1986
• Duty on Northern Ireland bank notes etc.	1 January 1992
• Transfers of intellectual property	Instruments executed after 27 March 2000
• Transfers to Registered Social Landlords	Instruments executed after 28 July 2000
• Stamp duty reserve tax on transfers of units or shares in collective investment schemes held in individual pension accounts (IPAs)	Transactions from 1 April 2001
• Transfers of land and leases in designated disadvantaged areas (for consideration/ premium up to £150,000)	Instruments executed after 29 November 2001
• Transfers of goodwill	Instruments executed after 22 April 2002
• Transfers of debts	tba (late 2003)
Fixed duties	
• Agreement or contract made or entered into pursuant to the Highways Act. Appointment of a new trustee, and appointment in execution of a power of any property. Covenant. Deed of any kind whatsoever, not liable to other duties. Letter of power of attorney. Procuration. Revocation of any use or trust of any property by any writing, not being a will. Warrant of attorney. Letter of allotment and letter of renunciation. Scrip certificate, scrip.	Instruments executed after 25 March 1985
• Categories within the *Stamp Duty (Exempt Instruments) Regulations* 1987 (SI 1987/516):	Instruments executed after 30 April 1987
A. Trust vesting instrument	
B. Transfer of bequeathed property to legatee	
C. Transfer of intestate property to person entitled	
D. Certain appropriations on death	
E. Transfer to beneficiary of entitlement to residue	
F. Certain transfers to beneficiaries entitled under settlements	
G. Certain transfers in consideration of marriage	
H. Transfers in connection with divorce	

Duty	Effective date of abolition
I. Transfers by liquidator to shareholder J. Grant of easement for no consideration K. Grant of servitude for no consideration L. Conveyance as voluntary disposition for no consideration M. Variations on death N. Declaration of trust of life policy	Instruments executed after 30 September 1999

Note

FA 2003, s. 125 confirmed that property that is not land, shares or interests in partnerships is not subject to stamp duty from 1 December 2003.

Stamp duty reserve tax

Principal charge (FA 1986, s. 87)

Subject matter of charge	Rate of tax %
Agreements to transfer chargeable securities[1] for money or money's worth	0.5
Renounceable letters of allotment	0.5
Shares converted into depositary receipts	1.5
but transfer of shares or securities on which stamp duty payable	1
Shares put into clearance system	1.5
but transfer of shares or securities on which stamp duty payable	1

Note

[1] Chargeable securities = stocks, shares, loan capital, units under unit trust scheme (FA 1986, s. 99(3)).

Interest on stamp duty and stamp duty reserve tax (SDRT)

In respect of instruments executed on or after 1 October 1999, interest is chargeable on stamp duty that is not paid within 30 days of execution of a stampable document, wherever execution takes place (*Stamp Act* 1891, s. 15A). Interest is payable on repayments of overpaid duty, calculated from the later of 30 days from the date of execution of the instrument, or lodgement with the Stamp Office of the duty repayable (FA 1999, s. 110). Interest is rounded down (if necessary) to the nearest multiple of £5. No interest is payable if that amount is under £25. The applicable interest rate is as prescribed under FA 1989, s. 178.

SDRT carries interest as follows:

- interest is charged on SDRT paid late (TMA 1970, s. 86 via SI 1986/1711, reg. 13);
- repayments of SDRT carry interest from the date that SDRT was paid (FA 1989, s. 178 via SI 1986/1711, reg. 11); and
- similarly, SDRT is repaid with interest if an instrument is duly stamped within six years of the date of the agreement (FA 1986, s. 92).

For interest periods from 1 October 1999 onwards, the rate of interest charged on underpaid or late paid stamp duty and SDRT exceeds that on repayments:

Period of application	Rate %	
	Underpayments	Repayments
From 6 September 2006	7.50	3.00
6 September 2005 to 5 September 2006	6.50	2.25
6 September 2004 to 5 September 2005	7.50	3.00
6 December 2003 to 5 September 2004	6.50	2.25
6 August 2003 to 5 December 2003	5.50	1.50
6 November 2001 to 5 August 2003	6.50	2.25
6 May 2001 to 5 November 2001	7.50	3.50
5 February 2000 to 5 May 2001	8.50	4.00
1 October 1999 to 5 February 2000	7.50	3.00

INHERITANCE TAX

90 Inheritance tax rates: general

There is a tapered reduction in the tax payable on transfers between seven and three years before death where the death occurs on or after 18 March 1986 (see below).

The following tables may be used for the purposes of 'grossing up' calculations (see 6620). The lower and upper limit of each rate-band may be ascertained by reference to the first column in each table and the rate of tax by reference to the second column.

94 Lifetime transfers: 2002 onwards

Lifetime transfers on or after 6 April 2010

Portion of value		Rate of tax %
Lower limit £	Upper limit £	
0 325,000	325,000 –	Nil 20

Grossing up table

Gross cumulative total £	Gross rate of tax %	Inheritance tax on band £	Cumulative inheritance tax payable £	Net cumulative total £	Tax on each £ over net cumulative total for grossing up
325,000 Over 325,000	Nil 20	Nil –	Nil –	325,000 –	$1/4$ –

Lifetime transfers on or after 6 April 2009

Portion of value		Rate of tax %
Lower limit £	Upper limit £	
0 325,000	325,000 –	Nil 20

Grossing up table

Gross cumulative total £	Gross rate of tax %	Inheritance tax on band £	Cumulative inheritance tax payable £	Net cumulative total £	Tax on each £ over net cumulative total for grossing up
325,000	Nil	Nil	Nil	325,000	$^1/_4$
Over 325,000	20	–	–	–	–

Lifetime transfers on or after 6 April 2008

Portion of value		Rate of tax %
Lower limit £	Upper limit £	
0	312,000	Nil
312,000	–	20

Grossing up table

Gross cumulative total £	Gross rate of tax %	Inheritance tax on band £	Cumulative inheritance tax payable £	Net cumulative total £	Tax on each £ over net cumulative total for grossing up
312,000	Nil	Nil	Nil	312,000	$^1/_4$
Over 312,000	20	–	–	–	–

Lifetime transfers on or after 6 April 2007

Portion of value		Rate of tax %
Lower limit £	Upper limit £	
0	300,000	Nil
300,000	–	20

Grossing up table

Gross cumulative total £	Gross rate of tax %	Inheritance tax on band £	Cumulative inheritance tax payable £	Net cumulative total £	Tax on each £ over net cumulative total for grossing up
300,000	Nil	Nil	Nil	300,000	$^1/_4$
Over 300,000	20	–	–	–	–

Lifetime transfers on or after 6 April 2006

Portion of value		Rate of tax
Lower limit £	Upper limit £	%
0	285,000	Nil
285,000	–	20

Grossing up table

Gross cumulative total £	Gross rate of tax %	Inheritance tax on band £	Cumulative inheritance tax payable £	Net cumulative total £	Tax on each £ over net cumulative total for grossing up
285,000	Nil	Nil	Nil	285,000	$^1/_4$
Over 285,000	20	–	–	–	–

Lifetime transfers on or after 6 April 2005

Portion of value		Rate of tax
Lower limit £	Upper limit £	%
0	275,000	Nil
275,000	–	20

Grossing up table

Gross cumulative total £	Gross rate of tax %	Inheritance tax on band £	Cumulative inheritance tax payable £	Net cumulative total £	Tax on each £ over net cumulative total for grossing up
275,000	Nil	Nil	Nil	275,000	$^1/_4$
Over 275,000	20	–	–	–	–

Lifetime transfers on or after 6 April 2004

Portion of value		Rate of tax
Lower limit £	Upper limit £	%
0	263,000	Nil
263,000	–	20

Grossing up table

Gross cumulative total £	Gross rate of tax %	Inheritance tax on band £	Cumulative inheritance tax payable £	Net cumulative total £	Tax on each £ over net cumulative total for grossing up
263,000	Nil	Nil	Nil	263,000	$^1/_4$
Over 263,000	20	–	–	–	–

Lifetime transfers on or after 6 April 2003

Portion of value		Rate of tax %
Lower limit £	Upper limit £	
0	255,000	Nil
255,000	–	20

Grossing up table

Gross cumulative total £	Gross rate of tax %	Inheritance tax on band £	Cumulative inheritance tax payable £	Net cumulative total £	Tax on each £ over net cumulative total for grossing up
255,000	Nil	Nil	Nil	255,000	$^1/_4$
Over 255,000	20	–	–	–	–

Lifetime transfers on or after 6 April 2002

Portion of value		Rate of tax %
Lower limit £	Upper limit £	
0	250,000	Nil
250,000	–	20

Grossing up table

Gross cumulative total £	Gross rate of tax %	Inheritance tax on band £	Cumulative inheritance tax payable £	Net cumulative total £	Tax on each £ over net cumulative total for grossing up
250,000	Nil	Nil	Nil	250,000	$^1/_4$
Over 250,000	20	–	–	–	–

97 Reliefs

	Rate of relief for disposals			
Type of relief	**before 10/3/92** %	**10/3/92– 31/8/95** %	**1/9/95– 5/4/96** %	**on or after 6/4/96** %
Agricultural property (IHTA 1984, s. 115ff.)[1]				
Vacant possession or right to obtain it within 12 months	50	100	100	100
Tenanted land with a vacant posession value	50	100	100	100
Entitled to 50% relief at 9 March 1981 and not since able to obtain vacant possession	50	100	100	100
Agricultural land let on or after 1 September 1995	N/A	N/A	100	100
Other circumstances	30	50	50	50
Business property (IHTA 1984, s. 103ff.) *Nature of property*				
Business or interest in business	50	100	100	100
Controlling shareholding in quoted company	50	50	50	50
Controlling shareholding in unquoted[2] company	50	100	100	100
Settled property used in life tenant's business	50/30[3]	100/50[3]	100/50[3]	100/50[3]
Shareholding in unquoted[2] company: more than 25% interest	50[4]	100	100	100
Minority shareholding in unquoted[2] company: 25% or less	30[5]	50	50	100
Land, buildings, machinery or plant used by transferor's company or partnership	30	50	50	50

Notes

[1] From 6 April 1995, short rotation coppice is regarded as agricultural property.

[2] With effect from 10 March 1992 'unquoted' means shares not quoted on a recognised stock exchange and therefore includes shares dealt in on the Unlisted Securities Market (USM) or Alternative Investment Market (AIM).

[3] The higher rate applies if the settled property is transferred along with business itself (*Fetherstonhaugh & Ors v IR Commrs* [1984] BTC 8,046).

[4] 30% if a minority interest transferred before 17 March 1987, or if transferor had not held at least 25% interest throughout preceding two years.

[5] The relief was 20% for transfers after 26 October 1977 but before 15 March 1983.

Taper relief

Years between gift and death		Percentage of full tax charge at death – rates actually due
More than	**Not more than**	%
3	4	80
4	5	60
5	6	40
6	7	20

Law: IHTA 1984, s. 7(4)

Quick succession relief

| Years between transfers | | Percentage applied to |
More than	Not more than	formula below
0	1	100
1	2	80
2	3	60
3	4	40
4	5	20

Formula

Tax charge on earlier transfer $\times \dfrac{\text{Increase in transferee's estate}}{\text{Diminution in transferor's estate}}$

Law: IHTA 1984, s. 141

Exemptions

Annual and small gift exemption

	On or after 6 April 1981 £	6 April 1980 to 5 April 1981 £	6 April 1976 to 5 April 1980 £
Annual	3,000	2,000	2,000
Small gift	250	250	100

Law: IHTA 1984, s. 19, 20

Gifts in consideration of marriage
(IHTA 1984, s. 22)

Donor	Exemption limit £
Parent of party to the marriage or civil partnership	5,000
Remote ancestor of party to the marriage or civil partnership	2,500
Party to the marriage or civil partnership	2,500
Any other person	1,000

Gift by UK-domiciled spouse or civil partner to non-UK domiciled spouse or civil partner
(IHTA 1984, s. 18)

Transfer on or after	Exemption limit £
9 March 1982	55,000

98   Due dates for delivery of accounts

Nature of transfer	Due Date
Chargeable lifetime transfer	Later of: – 12 months after end of month in which transfer occurred – 3 months after person became liable
Potentially exempt transfers which have become chargeable	12 months after end of month in which death of transferor occurred
Transfers on death	Later of: – 12 months after end of month in which death occurred – 3 months after personal representativers first act or have reason to believe an account is required
Gifts subject to reservation included in donor's estate at death	12 months after end of month in which death occurred
National heritage property	6 months after end of month in which chargeable event occurred

Values below which no account required

Excepted lifetime chargeable transfers on and after 6 April 2007	£
Where the property given away, or in which the interest subsists, is wholly attributable to cash or quoted stocks and securities, the cumulative total of all chargeable transfers made by the transfer in the seven years before the transfer must not exceed the nil rate band.	
Where the property given away, or in which the interest subsists, is wholly or partly attributable to property other than cash or quoted stocks and securities: (1) the value transferred by the chargeable transfer together with the cumulative total of all chargeable transfers made by the transferor in the seven years before the transfer must not exceed 80 per cent of the relevant IHT nil rate band; (2) the value transferred must not exceed the nil rate band that is available to the transferor at the time the disposal takes place.	
Excepted lifetime chargeable transfers on and after 1 April 1981 to 5 April 2007	
Transfer in question, together with all other chargeable transfers in same 12-month period ending on 5 April	10,000
Transfer in question, together with all previous chargeable transfers during preceding ten years	40,000

Excepted estates

Domiciled in the United Kingdom

Deaths on and after	But before	Total gross value[(1)] £	Total gross value of property outside UK £	Total value of settled property £	Aggregate value of 'specified transfers' £
6 April 2009	5 April 2010	325,000[(1), (2)]	100,000	150,000	150,000
6 April 2008	5 April 2009	312,000[(1), (2)]	100,000	150,000	150,000
6 April 2007	5 April 2008	300,000[(1), (2)]	100,000	150,000	150,000
6 April 2006	5 April 2007	285,000[(1), (2)]	100,000	150,000	150,000
6 April 2005	5 April 2006	275,000[(1), (2)]	100,000	150,000	150,000
6 April 2004	5 April 2005	263,000[(1), (2)]	100,000	150,000	150,000
6 April 2003	5 April 2004	240,000	75,000	100,000	100,000
6 April 2002	6 April 2003	220,000	75,000	100,000	100,000
6 April 2000	6 April 2002	210,000	50,000	–	75,000
6 April 1998	5 April 2000	180,000	30,000	–	50,000
6 April 1996	5 April 1998	180,000	30,000	–	50,000
6 April 1995	5 April 1996	145,000	15,000	–	–
1 April 1991	6 April 1995	125,000	15,000	–	–
1 April 1990	1 April 1991	115,000	15,000	–	–
1 April 1989	1 April 1990	100,000	15,000	–	–
1 April 1987	1 April 1989	70,000	10,000	–	–

Notes

[(1)] The aggregate of the gross value of that person's estate, the value transferred by any specified transfers made by that person, and the value transferred by any specified exempt transfers made by that person, must not exceed the IHT threshold. (Where the deceased dies after 5 April and before 6 August and application for probate or confirmation is made before 6 August in the same year as death, the inheritance tax threshold used is that for the preceding tax year.)

[(2)] An estate will qualify as an excepted estate where the gross value of the estate, plus the chargeable value of any transfers in the seven years to death, does not exceed £1,000,000 and the net chargeable estate after deduction of spouse or civil partner and/ or charity exemption **only** is less than the IHT threshold.

[(3)] For deaths on or after 6 April 2002, the limit applies to the aggregate of the gross value of the estate *plus* the value of 'specified transfers' which is extended and includes chargeable transfers, within seven years prior to death, of cash, quoted shares or securities, **or an interest in land and furnishings and chattels disposed of at the same time to the same person** (excluding property transferred subject to a reservation or property which becomes settled property).

For deaths on or after 6 April 1996 but before 6 April 2002, this limit applies to the total gross value of the estate *plus* the value of any transfers of cash or of quoted shares or securities made within seven years before death.

(4) If any of the sections IHTA 1984, s. 151A–151C dealing with alternatively secured pension funds apply by reason of an individual's death, that individual's estate does not qualify as an excepted estate (SI 2006/2141).

99 Due dates for payment of inheritance tax

Transfer	Due Date
Chargeable lifetime transfers between 6 April and 30 September	30 April in following year
Chargeable lifetime transfers between 1 October and 5 April	6 months after end of month in which transfer made
Potentially exempt transfers which become chargeable	6 months after end of month in which death occurred
Transfers on death; extra tax payable on chargeable lifetime transfers within seven years before death	6 months after end of month in which death occurred

Law: IHTA 1984, s. 226

VALUE ADDED TAX

100 VAT rates

Period of application	Standard rate %	Higher rate %
From 1/1/10	17.5	N/A
1/12/08–31/12/09	15	N/A
1/4/91–30/11/08	17.5	N/A
18/6/79–31/3/91	15	N/A
12/4/76–17/6/79	8	12.5
1/5/75–11/4/76	8	25*
18/11/74–30/4/75	8	25†
29/7/74–17/11/74	8	N/A
1/4/73–28/7/74	10	N/A

Notes

The increase from 1 January 2010 in the standard rate to 17.5 per cent from 15 per cent is as planned by the Chancellor of the Exchequer in his Pre-Budget Report of November 2008, but that plan may change.

* Re petrol, electrical appliances and luxury goods.

† Re petrol.

(1) Supplies of fuel and power for domestic, residential and charity non-business use and certain other supplies are charged at five per cent (VATA 1994, Sch. 7A).

(2) Imports of certain works of art, antiques and collectors' items are charged at an effective rate of five per cent from 27 July 1999 (VATA 1994, s. 21(4)–(6) as inserted by FA 1995, s. 22(1) and as amended by FA 1999, s. 12(1)(b)).

(3) The zero rate has applied from 1 April 1973 to date.

102 Registration limits

Taxable supplies

Period of application	Past turnover (£)[1]		Future turnover (£)[1]
	1 year	Unless turnover for next year will not exceed	30 days[2]
From 1/4/10	70,000	68,000	70,000
1/5/09–31/3/10	68,000	66,000	68,000
1/4/08–30/4/09	67,000	65,000	67,000
1/4/07–31/3/08	64,000	62,000	64,000
1/4/06–31/3/07	61,000	59,000	61,000
1/4/05–31/3/06	60,000	58,000	60,000
1/4/04–31/3/05	58,000	56,000	58,000
10/4/03–31/3/04	56,000	54,000	56,000
25/4/02–9/4/03	55,000	53,000	55,000
1/4/01–24/4/02	54,000	52,000	54,000
1/4/2000–31/3/01	52,000	50,000	52,000
1/4/99–31/3/2000	51,000	49,000	51,000
1/4/98–31/3/99	50,000	48,000	50,000
1/12/97–31/3/98	49,000	47,000	49,000
27/11/96–30/11/97	48,000	46,000	48,000

Notes

[1] Value of taxable supplies at the zero rate and all positive rates are included.

[2] A person is liable to register if there are reasonable grounds for believing that the value of his taxable supplies in the period of 30 days then beginning will exceed this limit.

Supplies from other member states – distance selling

Period of application	Cumulative relevant supplies from 1 January in year to any day in same year £
From 1/1/93	exceed 70,000

Notes

(VATA 1994, Sch. 2; Leaflet 700/1A).
If certain goods subject to excise duty are removed to the UK the person who removes the goods is liable to register in the UK because all such goods must be taxed in the country of destination. There is no de minimis limit.

Acquisitions from other member states

Period of application	Cumulative relevant acquisitions from 1 January in year to end of any month in same year £
From 1/4/10	70,000
1/5/09–31/3/10	68,000
1/4/08–30/4/09	67,000
1/4/07–31/3/08	64,000
1/4/06–31/3/07	61,000
1/4/05–31/3/06	60,000
1/4/04–31/3/05	58,000
10/4/03–31/3/04	56,000
25/4/02–9/4/03	55,000
1/4/01–24/4/02	54,000
1/4/2000–31/3/01	52,000
1/4/99–31/3/2000	51,000
1/4/98–31/3/99	50,000
1/1/98–31/3/98	49,000

Assets supplied in the UK by overseas persons

From 21 March 2000, any person without an establishment in the UK making or intending to make 'relevant' supplies must VAT register, regardless of the value of those supplies (VATA 1994, Sch. 3A). 'Relevant' supplies are taxable supplies of goods, including capital assets, in the UK where the supplier has recovered UK VAT under the eighth or thirteenth VAT directive. This applies where:

(1) the supplier (or his predecessor in business) was charged VAT on the purchase of the goods, or on anything incorporated in them, and has either claimed it back or intends to do so; or

(2) the VAT being claimed back was VAT paid on the import of goods into the UK.

104 De-registration limits

Taxable supplies

Period of application	Future turnover £
From 1/4/10	68,000
1/5/09–31/3/10	66,000
1/4/08–30/4/09	65,000
1/4/07–31/3/08	62,000
1/4/06–31/3/07	59,000
1/4/05–31/3/06	58,000
1/4/04–31/3/05	56,000
10/4/03–31/3/04	54,000
25/4/02–9/4/03	53,000
1/4/01–24/4/02	52,000
1/4/00–31/3/01	50,000
1/4/99–31/3/2000	49,000
1/4/98–31/3/99	48,000

Supplies from other member states

Period of application	Past relevant supplies in last year to 31 December £	Future relevant supplies in immediately following year £
From 1/1/93	70,000	70,000

Acquisitions from other member states

Period of application	Past relevant acquisitions in last year to 31 December £	Future relevant acquisitions in immediately following year £
From 1/4/10	70,000	70,000
1/5/09–31/3/10	68,000	68,000

Period of application	Past relevant acquisitions in last year to 31 December £	Future relevant acquisitions in immediately following year £
1/4/08–30/04/09	67,000	67,000
1/4/07–31/3/08	64,000	64,000
1/4/06–31/3/07	61,000	61,000
1/4/05–31/3/06	60,000	60,000
1/4/04–31/3/05	58,000	58,000
10/4/02–31/3/04	56,000	56,000
25/4/02–9/4/03	55,000	55,000
1/4/01–24/4/02	54,000	54,000
1/4/2000–31/3/01	52,000	52,000
1/4/99–31/3/2000	51,000	51,000
1/4/98–31/3/99	50,000	50,000
1/1/98–31/3/98	49,000	49,000

Special Accounting Limits

Cash accounting: admission to the scheme

Period of application	Annual turnover limit £
From 1/4/07	1,350,000
1/4/04–31/3/07	660,000
1/4/01–31/3/04	600,000
1/4/93–31/3/01	350,000
1/10/90–31/3/93	300,000
1/10/87–30/9/90	250,000

Notes

Annual turnover limit includes zero-rated supplies, but excludes any capital assets previously used in the business. Exempt supplies are also excluded.

A person must withdraw from the cash accounting scheme at the end of a prescribed accounting period if the value of his taxable supplies in the one year ending at the end of the prescribed accounting period has exceeded £1,600,000 (from 1 April 2007) (*Value Added Tax (Amendment) (No. 2) Regulations* 2007 (SI 2007/768)).

Outstanding VAT on supplies made and received while using the cash accounting scheme may be brought to account on a cash basis for a further six months after withdrawal from the scheme, but only where withdrawal was voluntary or because the turnover threshold was exceeded.

Annual accounting: admission to the scheme

Period of application	Annual turnover limit £
From 1/4/06	1,350,000
1/4/04–31/3/06	660,000
1/4/01–31/3/04	600,000
9/4/91–31/3/01	300,000

Notes

Annual turnover limit includes positive and zero-rated supplies but excludes any supplies of capital assets and any exempt supplies.

A person must withdraw from the annual accounting scheme at the end of a prescribed accounting period if the value of his taxable supplies in the one year ending at the end of the prescribed accounting period has exceeded £1,600,000 (£825,000 between April 2004 and 31 March 2006) (*Value Added Tax Regulations* 1995 (SI 1995/2518), Pt. VII).

Flat-rate scheme: admission to the scheme

Period of application	Annual taxable turnover limit[1] £	Annual total turnover limit [2] £
Returns ending after 10 April 2003	150,000	187,500
Returns ending after 25 April 2002	100,000	125,000

Notes

[1] Zero-rated and positive rated supplies excluding VAT. Exempt supplies are excluded.

[2] Total of VAT-exclusive taxable turnover and exempt and/or other non-taxable income.

[3] Net VAT liability is calculated by applying a flat-rate percentage to the VAT-inclusive turnover. The flat-rate percentage depends upon the trader sector (Notice 733).

106 VAT on private fuel

From 1 May 2010

For prescribed accounting periods beginning after 30 April 2010, the following table applies to assess output tax due on fuel used by cars for private journeys if it was provided at below cost from business resources (VATA 1994, s. 57(3)).

Fuel scale charges for 12-month period

CO$_2$ band, g/km	VAT fuel scale charge, 12 month period, £
120 or less	570.00
125	850.00
130	850.00
135	910.00
140	965.00
145	1,020.00
150	1,080.00
155	1,135.00
160	1,190.00
165	1,250.00
170	1,305.00
175	1,360.00
180	1,420.00
185	1,475.00
190	1,530.00
195	1,590.00
200	1,645.00
205	1,705.00
210	1,760.00
215	1,815.00
220	1,875.00
225	1,930.00
230 or more	1,985.00

Fuel scale charges for 3-month period

CO$_2$ band, g/km	VAT fuel scale charge, 3 month period, £
120 or less	141.00
125	212.00
130	212.00
135	227.00
140	241.00
145	255.00
150	269.00

CO₂ band, g/km	VAT fuel scale charge, 3 month period, £
155	283.00
160	297.00
165	312.00
170	326.00
175	340.00
180	354.00
185	368.00
190	383.00
195	397.00
200	411.00
205	425.00
210	439.00
215	454.00
220	468.00
225	482.00
230 or more	496.00

Fuel scale charges for 1-month period

CO₂ band, g/km	VAT fuel scale charge, 1 month period, £
120 or less	47.00
125	70.00
130	70.00
135	75.00
140	80.00
145	85.00
150	89.00
155	94.00
160	99.00
165	104.00
170	108.00
175	113.00
180	118.00
185	122.00
190	127.00
195	132.00
200	137.00
205	141.00
210	146.00

CO$_2$ band, g/km	VAT fuel scale charge, 1 month period, £
215	151.00
220	156.00
225	160.00
230 or more	165.00

1 January 2010 to 30 April 2010 (17.5 per cent rate)

The standard rate of VAT rose to 17.5 per cent from 15 per cent with effect from 1 January 2010, but there was no change to the amount of the fuel scale in VATA 1994, s. 57(3) which applies from 1 May 2009. However, the VAT on such charges must take account of the change in the standard rate.

Where the standard rate of 17.5 per cent applies, the following table applies to assess output tax due on fuel used by cars for private journeys if it was provided at below cost from business resources (VATA 199, s. 57(3)).

Fuel scale charges for 12-month period

CO$_2$ band, g/km	VAT fuel scale charge, 12 month period, £	VAT on 12 month charge, £	VAT exclusive 12 month charge, £
120 or less	505.00	75.21	429.79
125	755.00	112.45	642.55
130	755.00	112.45	642.55
135	755.00	112.45	642.55
140	805.00	119.89	685.11
145	855.00	127.34	727.66
150	905.00	134.79	770.21
155	960.00	142.98	817.02
160	1,010.00	150.43	859.57
165	1,060.00	157.87	902.13
170	1,110.00	165.32	944.68
175	1,160.00	172.77	987.23
180	1,210.00	180.21	1,029.79
185	1,260.00	187.66	1,072.34
190	1,310.00	195.11	1,114.89
195	1,360.00	202.55	1,157.45
200	1,410.00	210.00	1,200.00
205	1,465.00	218.19	1,246.81
210	1,515.00	225.64	1,289.36
215	1,565.00	233.09	1,331.91
220	1,615.00	240.53	1,347.47
225	1,665.00	247.98	1,417.02

CO₂ band, g/km	VAT fuel scale charge, 12 month period, £	VAT on 12 month charge, £	VAT exclusive 12 month charge, £
230	1,715.00	255.43	1,459.57
235 or more	1,765.00	262.87	1,502.13

Fuel scale charges for 3-month period

CO₂ band, g/km	VAT fuel scale charge, 3 month period, £	VAT on 3 month charge, £	VAT exclusive 3 month charge, £
120 or less	126.00	18.77	107.23
125	189.00	28.15	160.85
130	189.00	28.15	160.85
135	189.00	28.15	160.85
140	201.00	29.24	171.76
145	214.00	31.87	182.13
150	226.00	33.66	192.34
155	239.00	35.60	203.40
160	251.00	37.38	213.62
165	264.00	39.32	224.68
170	276.00	41.11	234.89
175	289.00	43.04	245.96
180	302.00	44.98	257.02
185	314.00	46.77	267.23
190	327.00	48.70	278.30
195	339.00	50.49	288.51
200	352.00	52.43	299.57
205	365.00	54.36	310.64
210	378.00	56.30	321.70
215	390.00	58.09	331.91
220	403.00	60.02	342.98
225	416.00	61.96	354.04
230	428.00	63.74	364.26
235 or more	441.00	65.68	357.32

Fuel scale charges for 1-month period

CO₂ band, g/km	VAT fuel scale charge, 1 month period, £	VAT on 1 month charge, £	VAT exclusive 1 month charge, £
120 or less	42.00	6.26	35.74
125	63.00	9.38	53.62
130	63.00	9.38	53.62

Key Data

CO_2 band, g/km	VAT fuel scale charge, 1 month period, £	VAT on 1 month charge, £	VAT exclusive 1 month charge, £
135	63.00	9.38	53.62
140	67.00	9.98	57.02
145	71.00	10.57	60.43
150	75.00	11.17	63.83
155	79.00	11.77	67.23
160	83.00	12.36	70.64
165	88.00	13.11	74.89
170	92.00	13.70	78.30
175	96.00	14.30	81.70
180	100.00	14.89	85.11
185	104.00	15.49	88.51
190	109.00	16.23	92.77
195	113.00	16.83	96.17
200	117.00	17.43	99.57
205	121.00	18.02	102.98
210	126.00	18.77	107.23
215	130.00	19.36	110.64
220	134.00	19.96	114.04
225	138.00	20.55	117.45
230	142.00	21.15	120.85
235 or more	147.00	21.89	125.11

From 1 May 2008, VAT fuel scale charges have changed. The former VAT fuel scale charges (see below), which were based on the engine size and fuel type of a car, have been replaced by a fuel scale charge based solely on the CO_2 rating of a car. Businesses must use the new scales from the start of their first accounting period beginning on or after 1 May 2008.

From 1 May 2009 to 31 December 2009 (15 per cent VAT rate)

For prescribed accounting periods *beginning* after 30 April 2009, where the standard rate of 15 per cent applies, the following table applies to assess output tax due on fuel used by cars for private journeys if it was provided at below cost from business resources (VATA 1994, s. 57(3)).

The standard rate of VAT is due to rise to 17.5 per cent from 15 per cent with effect from 1 January 2010, but there will probably be no change to the amount of the fuel scale charge in VATA 1994, s. 57(3) which applied from 1 May 2009. However, the VAT on such charges must take account of the change in the standard rate.

Fuel scale charges for 12-month period

CO₂ band, g/km	VAT fuel scale charge, 12 month period, £	VAT on 12 month charge, £	VAT exclusive 12 month charge, £
120 or less	505.00	65.87	439.13
125	755.00	98.48	656.52
130	755.00	98.48	656.52
135	755.00	98.48	656.52
140	805.00	105.00	700.00
145	855.00	111.52	743.48
150	905.00	118.04	786.96
155	960.00	125.22	834.78
160	1,010.00	131.74	878.26
165	1,060.00	138.26	921.74
170	1,110.00	144.78	965.22
175	1,160.00	151.30	1,008.70
180	1,210.00	157.83	1,052.17
185	1,260.00	164.35	1.095.65
190	1,310.00	170.87	1,139.13
195	1,360.00	177.39	1,182.61
200	1,410.00	183.91	1,226.09
205	1,465.00	194.09	1,270.91
210	1,515.00	197.61	1,317.39
215	1,565.00	204.13	1,360.87
220	1,615.00	210.65	1,404.35
225	1,665.00	217.17	1,447.83
230	1,715.00	223.70	1,491.30
235 or more	1,765.00	230.22	1,534.78

Fuel scale charges for 3-month period

CO₂ band, g/km	VAT fuel scale charge, 3 month period, £	VAT on 3 month charge, £	VAT exclusive 3 month charge, £
120 or less	126.00	16.43	109.57
125	189.00	24.65	164.35
130	189.00	24.65	164.35
135	189.00	24.65	164.35
140	201.00	26.22	174.78
145	214.00	27.91	186.09
150	226.00	29.48	196.52

CO$_2$ band, g/km	VAT fuel scale charge, 3 month period, £	VAT on 3 month charge, £	VAT exclusive 3 month charge, £
155	239.00	31.17	207.83
160	251.00	32.74	218.26
165	264.00	34.43	229.57
170	276.00	36.00	240.00
175	289.00	37.70	251.30
180	302.00	39.39	262.61
185	314.00	40.96	273.04
190	327.00	42.65	284.35
195	339.00	44.22	294.78
200	352.00	45.91	306.09
205	365.00	47.61	317.39
210	378.00	49.30	328.70
215	390.00	50.87	339.13
220	403.00	52.57	350.43
225	416.00	54.26	361.74
230	428.00	55.83	372.17
235 or more	441.00	57.52	383.48

Fuel scale charges for 1-month period

CO$_2$ band, g/km	VAT fuel scale charge, 1 month period, £	VAT on 1 month charge, £	VAT exclusive 1 month charge, £
120 or less	42.00	5.48	36.52
125	63.00	8.22	54.78
130	63.00	8.22	54.78
135	63.00	8.22	54.78
140	67.00	8.74	58.26
145	71.00	9.26	61.74
150	75.00	9.78	65.22
155	79.00	10.30	68.70
160	83.00	10.83	72.17
165	88.00	11.48	76.52
170	92.00	12.00	80.00
175	96.00	12.52	83.48
180	100.00	13.04	86.96
185	104.00	13.57	90.43
190	109.00	14.22	94.78

Key Data

CO₂ band, g/km	VAT fuel scale charge, 1 month period, £	VAT on 1 month charge, £	VAT exclusive 1 month charge, £
195	113.00	14.74	98.26
200	117.00	15.26	101.74
205	121.00	15.78	105.22
210	126.00	16.43	109.57
215	130.00	16.96	113.04
220	134.00	17.48	116.52
225	138.00	18.00	120.00
230	142.00	18.52	123.48
235 or more	147.00	19.17	127.83

From 1 December 2008–30 April 2009 (15 per cent VAT rate)

When the standard rate of VAT fell to 15 per cent from 17.5 per cent with effect from 1 December 2008, there was no change to the amount of the fuel scale charge in VATA 1994, s. 57(3) which applied from 1 May 2008. However, the VAT on such charges must take account of the change in the standard rate. The revised amounts are shown in the tables in Annex D to the HMRC guide *VAT – Change in the standard rate: a detailed guide for VAT-registered businesses* and are reproduced below.

Fuel scale charges for 12-month period

CO₂ band,	VAT fuel scale charge, 12 month period, £	VAT on 12 month charge, £	VAT exclusive 12 month charge, £
120 or less	555.00	72.39	482.61
125	830.00	108.26	721.74
130	830.00	108.26	721.74
135	830.00	108.26	721.74
140	885.00	115.43	769.57
145	940.00	122.61	817.39
150	995.00	129.78	865.22
155	1,050.00	136.96	913.04
160	1,105.00	144.13	960.87
165	1,160.00	151.30	1,008.70
170	1,215.00	158.48	1,056.52
175	1,270.00	165.65	1,104.35
180	1,325.00	172.83	1,152.17
185	1,380.00	180.00	1,200.00
190	1,435.00	187.17	1,247.83

CO$_2$ band,	VAT fuel scale charge, 12 month period, £	VAT on 12 month charge, £	VAT exclusive 12 month charge, £
195	1,490.00	194.35	1,295.65
200	1,545.00	201.52	1,343.48
205	1,605.00	209.35	1,395.65
210	1,660.00	216.52	1,443.48
215	1,715.00	223.70	1,491.30
220	1,770.00	230.87	1,539.13
225	1,825.00	238.04	1,586.96
230	1,880.00	245.22	1,634.78
235 or more	1,935.00	252.39	1,682.61

Fuel scale charges for 3-month period

CO$_2$ band,	VAT fuel scale charge, 3 month period, £	VAT on 3 month charge, £	VAT exclusive 3 month charge, £
120 or less	138.00	18.00	120.00
125	207.00	27.00	180.00
130	207.00	27.00	180.00
135	207.00	27.00	180.00
140	221.00	28.83	192.17
145	234.00	30.52	203.48
150	248.00	32.35	215.65
155	262.00	34.17	227.83
160	276.00	36.00	240.00
165	290.00	37.83	252.17
170	303.00	39.52	263.48
175	317.00	41.35	275.65
180	331.00	43.17	287.83
185	345.00	45.00	300.00
190	359.00	46.83	312.17
195	373.00	48.65	324.35
200	386.00	50.35	335.65
205	400.00	52.17	347.83
210	414.00	54.00	360.00
215	428.00	55.83	372.17
220	442.00	57.65	384.35
225	455.00	59.35	395.65
230	469.00	61.17	407.83
235 or more	483.00	63.00	420.00

Key Data

Fuel scale charges for 1-month period

CO₂ band,	VAT fuel scale charge, 1 month period, £	VAT on 1 month charge, £	VAT exclusive 1 month charge, £
120 or less	46.00	6.00	40.00
125	69.00	9.00	60.00
130	69.00	9.00	60.00
135	69.00	9.00	60.00
140	73.00	9.52	63.48
145	78.00	10.17	67.83
150	82.00	10.70	71.30
155	87.00	11.35	75.65
160	92.00	12.00	80.00
165	96.00	12.52	83.48
170	101.00	13.17	87.83
175	105.00	13.70	91.30
180	110.00	14.35	95.65
185	115.00	15.00	100.00
190	119.00	15.52	103.48
195	124.00	16.17	107.83
200	128.00	16.70	111.30
205	133.00	17.35	115.65
210	138.00	18.00	120.00
215	142.00	18.52	123.48
220	147.00	19.17	127.83
225	151.00	19.70	131.30
230	156.00	20.35	135.65
235 or more	161.00	21.00	140.00

From 1 May 2008 – 30 November 2008 (17.5 per cent VAT rate)

For prescribed accounting periods *beginning* after 30 April 2008, where the standard rate of 17.5 per cent applied, the following table applies to assess output tax due on fuel used by cars for private journeys if it was provided at below cost from business resources (VATA 1994, s. 57(3)).

Fuel scale charges for 12-month period

CO₂ band, g/km	VAT fuel scale charge, 12 month period, £	VAT on 12 month charge, £	VAT exclusive 12 month charge, £
120 or less	555.00	82.66	472.34
125	830.00	123.62	706.38
130	830.00	123.62	706.38

CO₂ band, g/km	VAT fuel scale charge, 12 month period, £	VAT on 12 month charge, £	VAT exclusive 12 month charge, £
135	830.00	123.62	706.38
140	885.00	131.81	753.19
145	940.00	140.00	800.00
150	995.00	148.19	846.81
155	1,050.00	156.38	893.62
160	1,105.00	164.57	940.43
165	1,160.00	172.77	987.23
170	1,215.00	180.96	1,034.04
175	1,270.00	189.15	1,080.85
180	1,325.00	197.34	1,127.66
185	1,380.00	205.53	1,174.47
190	1,435.00	213.72	1,221.28
195	1,490.00	221.91	1,268.09
200	1,545.00	230.11	1,314.89
205	1,605.00	239.04	1,365.96
210	1,660.00	247.23	1,412.77
215	1,715.00	255.43	1,459.57
220	1,770.00	263.62	1,506.38
225	1,825.00	271.81	1,553.19
230	1,880.00	280.00	1,600.00
235 or more	1,935.00	288.19	1,646.81

Fuel scale charges for 3-month period

CO₂ band, g/km	VAT fuel scale charge, 3 month period, £	VAT on 3 month charge, £	VAT exclusive 3 month charge, £
120 or less	138.00	20.55	117.45
125	207.00	30.83	176.17
130	207.00	30.83	176.17
135	207.00	30.83	176.17
140	221.00	32.91	188.09
145	234.00	34.85	199.15
150	248.00	36.94	211.06
155	262.00	39.02	222.98
160	276.00	41.11	234.89
165	290.00	43.19	246.81
170	303.00	45.13	257.87

CO$_2$ band, g/km	VAT fuel scale charge, 3 month period, £	VAT on 3 month charge, £	VAT exclusive 3 month charge, £
175	317.00	47.21	269.79
180	331.00	49.30	281.70
185	345.00	51.38	293.62
190	359.00	53.47	305.53
195	373.00	55.55	317.45
200	386.00	57.49	328.51
205	400.00	59.57	340.43
210	414.00	61.66	352.34
215	428.00	63.74	364.26
220	442.00	65.83	376.17
225	455.00	67.77	387.23
230	469.00	69.85	399.15
235 or more	483.00	71.94	411.06

Fuel scale charges for 1-month period

CO$_2$ band, g/km	VAT fuel scale charge, 1 month period, £	VAT on 1 month charge, £	VAT exclusive 1 month charge, £
120 or less	46.00	6.85	39.15
125	69.00	10.28	58.72
130	69.00	10.28	58.72
135	69.00	10.28	58.72
140	73.00	10.87	62.13
145	78.00	11.62	66.38
150	82.00	12.21	69.79
155	87.00	12.96	74.04
160	92.00	13.70	78.30
165	96.00	14.30	81.70
170	101.00	15.04	85.96
175	105.00	15.64	89.36
180	110.00	16.38	93.62
185	115.00	17.13	97.87
190	119.00	17.72	101.28
195	124.00	18.47	105.53
200	128.00	19.06	108.94
205	133.00	19.81	113.19
210	138.00	20.55	117.45

CO$_2$ band, g/km	VAT fuel scale charge, 1 month period, £	VAT on 1 month charge, £	VAT exclusive 1 month charge, £
215	142.00	21.15	120.85
220	147.00	21.89	125.11
225	151.00	22.49	128.51
230	156.00	23.23	132.77
235 or more	161.00	23.98	137.02

Key Data

108   Value added tax – 'blocked' input tax

Any input tax charged on the following items is 'blocked', i.e. non-recoverable (see 8058):

- Motor cars, other than certain motor cars acquired by certain persons but after 31 July 1995 (1) any person can recover input tax on motor cars used exclusively for business and (2) only 50 per cent of VAT on car leasing charges is recoverable if lessee makes any private use of the car and if the lessor recovered the VAT on buying the car.
- Entertainment, except of employees.
- In the case of claims by builders, articles of a kind not ordinarily installed by builders as fixtures in new houses.
- Goods supplied under a second-hand scheme.
- Goods imported for private purposes.
- Non-business element of supplies to be used only partly for business purposes. This may contravene European law where the supplies are of goods: strictly the input tax is deductible, but output tax is due on non-business use. VAT on supplies not intended for business use does not rank as input tax, so cannot be recovered.
- Goods and services acquired by a tour operator for resupply as a designated travel service.
- Domestic accommodation for directors and their families to the extent of domestic purpose use.

In addition, 'exempt input tax' is not recoverable (see 8060). From 10 March 1999 the partial exemption simplification rule that allowed some businesses to claim back all their input tax, providing that their exempt input tax is only incurred in relation to certain exempt supplies, has been abolished.

NATIONAL INSURANCE CONTRIBUTIONS

110   NIC rates

Class 1 contributions

Class 1 primary (employee) contributions 2010–11	
Lower earnings limit (LEL)[1]	£97 weekly £421 monthly £5,044 yearly
Primary threshold	£110 weekly £476 monthly £5,715 yearly
Upper earnings limit (UEL)	£844 weekly £3,656 monthly £43,875 yearly
Upper accrual point (UAP)	£770 weekly £3,337 monthly £40,040 yearly
Rate on earnings up to primary threshold[1]	0%
Not contracted-out rate	11% on £110.01 to £844 weekly 1% on excess over £844
Contracted-out rate	9.4% on £110.01 to £770 weekly 11% on £770.01 to £844 weekly 1% on excess over £844
Reduced rate[2]	4.85% on £110.01 to £844 weekly 1% excess over £844 (no rebate even if contracted-out)

Notes

[1] Earnings from the LEL, up to and including the primary threshold (PT), count towards the employee's basic state pension, even though no contributions are paid on those earnings. Similarly, earnings between the LEL and the primary threshold count towards the employee's entitlement to certain benefits including the second state pension (S2P). Employees in contracted-out employment earn no S2P rights and receive a rebate of contributions of 1.6 per cent. This applies from the LEL to the UAP, so earnings from LEL to PT attract a 'negative' contribution of 1.6 per cent and the rate for earnings from PT to UAP becomes 9.4 per cent.

Monthly and annual LEL, UEL and UAP figures are calculated per SI 2001/1004, reg. 11.

[2] The reduced rate applies to married women or widows with a valid certificate of election.

Class 1 contributions

Class 1 primary (employee) contributions 2009–10	
Lower earnings limit (LEL)[1]	£95 weekly £412 monthly £4,940 yearly
Primary threshold	£110 weekly £476 monthly £5,715 yearly
Upper earnings limit (UEL)	£844 weekly £3,656 monthly £43,875 yearly
Upper accrual point (UAP)	£770 weekly £3,337 monthly £40,040 yearly
Rate on earnings up to primary threshold[1]	0%
Not contracted-out rate	11% on £110.01 to £844 weekly 1% on excess over £844
Contracted-out rate	9.4% on £110.01 to £770 weekly 11% on £770.01 to £844 weekly 1% on excess over £844
Reduced rate[2]	4.85% on £110.01 to £844 weekly 1% excess over £844 (no rebate even if contracted-out)

Notes

[1] Earnings from the LEL, up to and including the primary threshold (PT), count towards the employee's basic state pension, even though no contributions are paid on those earnings. Similarly, earnings between the LEL and the primary threshold count towards the employee's entitlement to certain benefits including the second state pension (S2P). Employees in contracted-out employment earn no S2P rights and receive a rebate of contributions of 1.6 per cent. This applies from the LEL to the UAP, so earnings from LEL to PT attract a 'negative' contribution of 1.6 per cent and the rate for earnings from PT to UAP becomes 9.4 per cent.

Monthly and annual LEL, UEL and UAP figures are calculated per SI 2001/1004, reg. 11.

[2] The reduced rate applies to married women or widows with a valid certificate of election.

Class 1 contributions

Class 1 primary (employee) contributions 2008–09	
Lower earnings limit (LEL)[1]	£90 weekly £390 monthly £4,680 yearly
Primary threshold	£105 weekly £453 monthly £5,435 yearly
Upper earnings limit (UEL)	£770 weekly £3,337 monthly £40,040 yearly
Rate on earnings up to primary threshold	0%
Not contracted-out rate	11% on £105.01 to £770 weekly 1% on excess over £770
Contracted-out rate	9.4% on £105.01 to £770 weekly 1% on excess over £770
Reduced rate[2]	4.85% on £105.01 to £770 weekly 1% excess over £770

Notes

[1] Earnings from the lower earnings limit (LEL), up to and including the primary threshold will count towards the employee's basic 'flat rate' state pension, even though no contributions will have been paid on those earnings. Similarly, earnings between the LEL and the primary threshold count towards the employee's entitlement to certain benefits, including the second state pension. Monthly LEL and upper earnings limit (UEL) figures are calculated as per SI 2001/1004, reg. 1 (as amended by SI 2008/133). The equivalent annual figures are calculated as 52 × the weekly figure (NIM 12021).

[2] The reduced rate applies to married women or widows with a valid certificate of election. Men over 65 and women over 60 pay no primary contributions, though employers still pay the secondary contribution at the usual rate. People under 16 and their employers pay no contributions.

Key Data

Class 1 contributions

Class 1 primary (employee) contributions 2007–08[1]	
Lower earnings limit (LEL)[2]	£87 weekly £377 monthly £4,524 yearly
Primary threshold	£100 weekly £435 monthly £5,225 yearly
Rate up to primary threshold	0%
Rate between primary threshold and UEL (not contracted-out)	11%
Rate between primary threshold and UEL (contracted-out)	9.4%
Rate on earnings above UEL	1%
Reduced rate on earnings between primary threshold and UEL[3]	4.85%
Upper earnings limit (UEL)	£670 weekly £2,905 monthly £34,840 yearly

Notes

[1]   Class 1 contributions are earnings related. Employees must pay primary Class 1 contributions on that part of their earnings which exceeds the primary threshold at the main rate of 11 per cent and on one per cent on earnings above the UEL.

[2]   Earnings from the LEL, up to and including the primary threshold will count towards the employee's basic 'flat rate' state pension, even though no contributions will have been paid on those earnings. Similarly, earnings between the lower earnings limit (LEL) and the primary threshold will count towards the employee's entitlement to certain benefits including the additional pension (SERPS), or, from April 2002, the second state pension.

[3]   The reduced rate applies to married women or widows with a valid certificate of election. Men over 65 and women over 60 pay no primary contributions, though employers still pay the secondary contribution at the usual rate. People under 16 and their employers pay no contributions.

Class 1 contributions

Class 1 primary (employee) contributions 2006–07[1]	
Lower earnings limit (LEL)[2]	£84 weekly £364 monthly £4,368 yearly
Primary threshold	£97 weekly £420 monthly £5,035 yearly
Rate up to primary threshold	0%
Rate between primary threshold and UEL (not contracted-out)	11%
Rate between primary threshold and UEL (contracted-out)	9.4%
Rate on earnings above UEL	1%
Reduced rate on earnings between primary threshold and UEL[3]	4.85%
Upper earnings limit (UEL)	£645 weekly £2,795 monthly £33,540 yearly

Notes

[1]   Class 1 contributions are earnings related. Employees must pay primary Class 1 contributions on that part of their earnings which exceeds the primary threshold at the main rate of 11 per cent and on one per cent on earnings above the UEL.

[2]   Earnings from the LEL, up to and including the primary threshold will count towards the employee's basic 'flat rate' state pension, even though no contributions will have been paid on those earnings. Similarly, earnings between the lower earnings limit (LEL) and the primary threshold will count towards the employee's entitlement to certain benefits including the additional pension (SERPS), or, from April 2002, the second state pension.

[3]   The reduced rate applies to married women or widows with a valid certificate of election. Men over 65 and women over 60 pay no primary contributions, though employers still pay the secondary contribution at the usual rate. People under 16 and their employers pay no contributions.

Class 1 contributions

Class 1 primary (employee) contributions 2005–06[1]	
Lower earnings limit (LEL)[2]	£82 weekly £355 monthly £4,264 yearly
Primary threshold	£94 weekly £407 monthly £4,888 yearly
Rate up to primary threshold	0%
Rate between primary threshold and UEL (not contracted-out)	11%
Rate between primary threshold and UEL (contracted-out)	9.4%
Rate on earnings above UEL	1%
Reduced rate on earnings between primary threshold and UEL[3]	4.85%
Upper earnings limit (UEL)	£630 weekly £2,730 monthly £32,760 yearly

Notes

[1] Class 1 contributions are earnings related. Employees must pay primary Class 1 contributions on that part of their earnings which exceeds the primary threshold at the main rate of 11 per cent and on one per cent on earnings above the UEL.

[2] Earnings from the LEL, up to and including the primary threshold will count towards the employee's basic 'flat rate' state pension, even though no contributions will have been paid on those earnings. Similarly, earnings between the lower earnings limit (LEL) and the primary threshold will count towards the employee's entitlement to certain benefits including the additional pension (SERPS), or, from April 2002, the second state pension.

[3] The reduced rate applies to married women or widows with a valid certificate of election. Men over 65 and women over 60 pay no primary contributions, though employers still pay the secondary contribution at the usual rate. People under 16 and their employers pay no contributions.

Class 1 contributions

Class 1 primary (employee) contributions 2004–05[1]	
Lower earnings limit (LEL)[2]	£79 weekly £343 monthly £4,108 yearly
Primary threshold	£91 weekly £395 monthly £4,732 yearly
Rate up to primary threshold	0%
Rate between primary threshold and UEL (not contracted-out)	11%
Rate between primary threshold and UEL (contracted-out)	9.4%
Rate on earnings above UEL	1%
Reduced rate on earnings between primary threshold and UEL[3]	4.85%
Upper earnings limit (UEL)	£610 weekly £2,643 monthly £31,720 yearly

Notes

[1] Class 1 contributions are earnings related. Employees must pay primary Class 1 contributions on that part of their earnings which exceeds the primary threshold at the main rate of 11 per cent and on one per cent on earnings above the UEL.

[2] Earnings from the LEL, up to and including the primary threshold will count towards the employee's basic 'flat rate' state pension, even though no contributions will have been paid on those earnings. Similarly, earnings between the lower earnings limit (LEL) and the primary threshold will count towards the employee's entitlement to certain benefits including the additional pension (SERPS), or, from April 2002, the second state pension.

[3] The reduced rate applies to married women or widows with a valid certificate of election. Men over 65 and women over 60 pay no primary contributions, though employers still pay the secondary contribution at the usual rate. People under 16 and their employers pay no contributions.

Class 1 contributions

Class 1 primary (employee) contributions 2003–04[1]	
Lower earnings limit (LEL)[2]	£77 weekly £334 monthly £4,004 yearly
Primary threshold	£89 weekly £385 monthly 4,628 yearly
Rate up to primary threshold	0%
Rate between primary threshold and UEL (not contracted-out)	11%
Rate between primary threshold and UEL (contracted-out)	9.4%
Rate on earnings above UEL	1%
Reduced rate on earnings between primary threshold and UEL[3]	4.85%
Upper earnings limit (UEL)	£595 weekly £2,579 monthly £30,940 yearly

Key Data

Notes

[1] Class 1 contributions are earnings related. Employees must pay primary Class 1 contributions on that part of their earnings which exceeds the primary threshold at the main rate of 11 per cent and on one per cent on earnings above the UEL.

[2] Earnings from the LEL, up to and including the primary threshold will count towards the employee's basic 'flat rate' state pension, even though no contributions will have been paid on those earnings. Similarly, earnings between the lower earnings limit (LEL) and the primary threshold will count towards the employee's entitlement to certain benefits including the additional pension (SERPS), or, from April 2002, the second state pension.

[3] The reduced rate applies to married women or widows with a valid certificate of election. Men over 65 and women over 60 pay no primary contributions, though employers still pay the secondary contribution at the usual rate. People under 16 and their employers pay no contributions.

Class 1 secondary (employer) contributions 2010–11	
Secondary earnings threshold	£110 weekly £476 monthly £5,715 yearly
Not contracted-out rate	12.8% on earnings above threshold

Class 1 secondary (employer) contributions 2010–11	
Contracted-out rate[1]	9.1% for salary-related (COSR) and 11.4% for money-purchase (COMP) schemes on earnings from secondary threshold to UAP (plus 3.7% and 1.4% rebates for earnings from LEL to secondary threshold), then 12.8% above UAP

Notes

[1] As for employees, earnings between the LEL and the ST will count towards the employee's entitlement to S2P. Employers with contracted-out occupational pension schemes receive a rebate of contributions for scheme members of 3.7 per cent (COSR) or 1.4 per cent (COMP). This applies from the LEL to the UAP, so earnings from LEL to ST attract a 'negative' contribution and the rate for earnings from ST to UAP is reduced as shown

Class 1 secondary (employer) contributions 2009–10	
Secondary earnings threshold	£110 weekly £476 monthly £5,715 yearly
Not contracted-out rate	12.8% on earnings above threshold
Contracted-out rate[1]	9.1% for salary-related (COSR) and 11.4% for money-purchase (COMP) schemes on earnings from secondary threshold to UAP (plus 3.7% and 1.4% rebates for earnings from LEL to secondary threshold), then 12.8% above UAP

Notes

[1] As for employees, earnings between the LEL and the ST will count towards the employee's entitlement to S2P. Employers with contracted-out occupational pension schemes receive a rebate of contributions for scheme members of 3.7 per cent (COSR) or 1.4 per cent (COMP). This applies from the LEL to the UAP, so earnings from LEL to ST attract a 'negative' contribution and the rate for earnings from ST to UAP is reduced as shown

Class 1 secondary (employer) contributions 2008–09	
Secondary earnings threshold	£105 weekly £453 monthly £5,435 yearly
Not contracted-out rate	12.8% on earnings above threshold

Key Data

Class 1 secondary (employer) contributions 2008–09	
Contracted-out rate	9.1% for salary-related (COSR) and 11.4% for money-purchase (COMP) schemes on earnings from secondary threshold to the UEL, then 12.8% on earnings above the UEL

Class 1 secondary (employer) contributions 2007–08[4]	
Earnings/secondary threshold	£100 weekly £435 monthly £5,225 yearly
Rates (not contracted-out)	12.8% above earnings threshold
Rates (contracted-out)[5]	9.1% for salary-related (COSR) and 11.4% for money-purchase (COMP) schemes (including 3.7% and 1.4% rebates for earnings from LEL to earnings threshold), then 12.8% above UEL.

Notes

[4] Class 1 contributions are earnings related. Employers must pay secondary Class 1 contributions on that part of an employee's earnings which exceeds the earnings threshold, without limit (i.e. without capping).

[5] With contracted-out salary related (COSR) schemes there is an employer's NIC rebate of 3.7% of earnings above the employer's earnings threshold, up to and including the upper earnings limit. With contracted-out money purchase (COMP) schemes there is an employer's NIC rebate of 1.4% of earnings above the employer's earnings threshold, up to and including the upper earnings limit, and a further age-related rebate is paid by the Inland Revenue National Insurance Contributions Office directly to the scheme (see table).

Class 1 secondary (employer) contributions 2006–07[4]	
Earnings/secondary threshold	£97 weekly £420 monthly £5,035 yearly
Rates (not contracted-out)	12.8% above earnings threshold
Rates (contracted-out)[5]	9.3% for salary-related (COSR) and 11.8% for money-purchase (COMP) schemes (including 3.5% and 1% rebates for earnings from LEL to earnings threshold), then 12.8% above UEL.

Notes

(4)   Class 1 contributions are earnings related. Employers must pay secondary Class 1 contributions on that part of an employee's earnings which exceeds the earnings threshold, without limit (i.e. without capping).

(5)   With contracted-out salary related (COSR) schemes there is an employer's NIC rebate of 3.5% of earnings above the employer's earnings threshold, up to and including the upper earnings limit. With contracted-out money purchase (COMP) schemes there is an employer's NIC rebate of 1.0% of earnings above the employer's earnings threshold, up to and including the upper earnings limit, and a further age-related rebate is paid by the Inland Revenue National Insurance Contributions Office directly to the scheme (see table).

Class 1 secondary (employer) contributions 2005–06(4)	
Earnings/secondary threshold	£94 weekly £407 monthly £4,888 yearly
Rates (not contracted-out)	12.8% above earnings threshold
Rates (contracted-out)(5)	9.3% for salary-related (COSR) and 11.8% for money-purchase (COMP) schemes (including 3.5% and 1% rebates for earnings from LEL to earnings threshold), then 12.8% above UEL.

Notes

(4)   Class 1 contributions are earnings related. Employers must pay secondary Class 1 contributions on that part of an employee's earnings which exceeds the earnings threshold, without limit (i.e. without capping).

(5)   With contracted-out salary related (COSR) schemes there is an employer's NIC rebate of 3.5% of earnings above the employer's earnings threshold, up to and including the upper earnings limit. With contracted-out money purchase (COMP) schemes there is an employer's NIC rebate of 1.0% of earnings above the employer's earnings threshold, up to and including the upper earnings limit, and a further age-related rebate is paid by the Inland Revenue National Insurance Contributions Office directly to the scheme (see table).

Class 1 secondary (employer) contributions 2004–05(4)	
Earnings/secondary threshold	£91 weekly £395 monthly £4,732 yearly
Rates (not contracted-out)	12.8% above earnings threshold

Rates (contracted-out)[5]	9.3% for salary-related (COSR) and 11.8% for money-purchase (COMP) schemes (including 3.5% and 1% rebates for earnings from LEL to earnings threshold), then 12.8% above UEL.

Notes

[4] Class 1 contributions are earnings related. Employers must pay secondary Class 1 contributions on that part of an employee's earnings which exceeds the earnings threshold, without limit (i.e. without capping).

[5] With contracted-out salary related (COSR) schemes there is an employer's NIC rebate of 3.5% of earnings above the employer's earnings threshold, up to and including the upper earnings limit. With contracted-out money purchase (COMP) schemes there is an employer's NIC rebate of 1.0% of earnings above the employer's earnings threshold, up to and including the upper earnings limit, and a further age-related rebate is paid by the Inland Revenue National Insurance Contributions Office directly to the scheme (see table).

Class 1 secondary (employer) contributions 2003–04[4]	
Earnings/secondary threshold	£89 weekly £385 monthly £4,615 yearly
Rates (not contracted-out)	12.8% above earnings threshold
Rates (contracted-out)[5]	9.3% for salary-related (COSR) and 11.8% for money-purchase (COMP) schemes (including 3.5% and 1% rebates for earnings from LEL to earnings threshold), then 12.8% above UEL.

Notes

[4] Class 1 contributions are earnings related. Employers must pay secondary Class 1 contributions on that part of an employee's earnings which exceeds the earnings threshold, without limit (i.e. without capping).

[5] With contracted-out salary related (COSR) schemes there is an employer's NIC rebate of 3.5% of earnings above the employer's earnings threshold, up to and including the upper earnings limit. With contracted-out money purchase (COMP) schemes there is an employer's NIC rebate of 1.0% of earnings above the employer's earnings threshold, up to and including the upper earnings limit, and a further age-related rebate is paid by the Inland Revenue National Insurance Contributions Office directly to the scheme (see table).

Flat-rate rebate Class 1 contracted-out rebates 2002–03 to 2009–10

	COSR (salary related) %	COMP (money purchase) %
Employees	1.6	1.6
Employers	3.7	1.4 + age-related percentage

Class 1A contributions

From 6 April 2000, employers (but not employees) pay NICs on an annual basis on benefits in kind provided to employees earning at the rate of £8,500 p.a. or more or to directors. The Class 1A rate for 2009–10 is 12.8 per cent. Contributions for the year 2008–09 are due on 19 July 2009.

From 5 April 1991 to 5 April 2000, employers (but not employees) paid NICs on an annual basis on cars or fuel provided for the private use of employees earning at the rate of £8,500 p.a. or more or for directors. The liability is calculated on the income tax car and fuel scale rates.

Rate of Class 1B contributions

From 6 April 1999 Class 1B contributions are payable by employers on the amount of emoluments in a PAYE settlement agreement (PSA) which are chargeable to Class 1 or Class 1A NICs, together with the total amount of income tax payable under the agreement. Class 1B contributions are charged at a rate equal to the secondary rate of NICs (12.8 per cent in 2009–10), with power for the Secretary of State to alter the rate by statutory instrument; but not so as to increase it to more than two per cent above the rate applicable at the end of the preceding year.

Class 2 contributions

Rates and SEE limit

Tax year	Weekly contribution rate			Small earnings exceptional limit £
	Rate £	Share fishermen £	Volunteer development workers £	
2010–11	2.40	3.05	4.75	5,075
2009–10	2.40	3.05	4.75	5,075
2008–09	2.30	2.95	4.50	4,825
2007–08	2.20	2.85	4.35	4,635
2006–07	2.10	2.75	4.20	4,465
2005–06	2.10	2.75	4.10	4,345
2004–05	2.05	2.70	3.95	4,215

Class 3 contributions

Class 3 contributions are paid voluntarily by persons not liable for contributions, or who have been excepted from Class 2 contributions, or whose contribution record is insufficient to qualify for benefits. They are paid at a flat rate.

Rate and earnings factor

Tax year	Weekly contribution rate £
2010–11	12.05
2009–10	12.05
2008–09	8.10
2007–08	7.80
2006–07	7.55
2005–06	7.35
2004–05	7.15
2003–04	6.95
2002–03	6.85
2001–02	6.75

Class 4 contributions

Self-employed people whose profits or gains are over a certain amount have to pay Class 4 contributions as well as Class 2 contributions.

Percentage rate and earnings limits

Tax year	Percentage rate %	Annual lower earnings limit £	Annual upper earnings limit £	Maximum contribution £
2010–11	8	5,715	43,875	(1)
2009–10	8	5,715	43,875	(1)
2008–09	8	5,435	40,040	(1)
2007–08	8	5,225	34,840	(1)
2006–07	8	5,035	33,540	(1)
2005–06	8	4,895	32,760	(1)
2004–05	8	4,745	31,720	(1)
2003–04	8	4,615	30,940	(1)

(1) Contributions are payable at the rate of one per cent on profits above the upper earnings level.

Law: SSCBA 1992, Sch. 1, para. 6(2) and (3)

INDIRECT TAXES

114 Insurance Premium Tax

Rate

Imposed on certain insurance premiums where the risk is located in the UK (FA 1994, Pt. III).

Period of application	Standard rate %	Higher rate %
From 1 July 1999	5	17.5
1 April 1997 to 30 June 1999	4	17.5
1 October 1994 to 31 March 1997	2.5	n/a

Note

[1] From 1 August 1998, the higher rate applies to all travel insurance.

Interest payable on certain assessments

Since 6 Februaury 1996, interest on insurance premium tax is charged at the same rate as under VATA 1994, s. 74.

116 Landfill Tax

Landfill tax was introduced on 1 October 1996 and is collected from landfill site operators (FA 1996, Pt. III).

Exemption applies to mining and quarrying waste, dredging waste, pet cemeteries and waste from the reclamation of contaminated land.

From 1 October 1999, exemption applies to inert waste used in restoring licensed landfill sites, including the progressive backfilling of active mineral workings.

Type of waste	Rate (per tonne) £
Inactive waste	
From 1 April 2008	2.50
To 31 March 2008	2.00
Active waste:	
From 1 April 2010	48
From 1 April 2009	40
From 1 April 2008	32
1 April 2007 to March 2008	24
1 April 2006 to 31 March 2007	21
1 April 2005 to 31 March 2006	18
1 April 2004 to 31 March 2005	15

Type of waste	Rate (per tonne) £
1 April 2003 to 31 March 2004	14
1 April 2002 to 31 March 2003	13
1 April 2001 to 31 March 2002	12
1 April 2000 to 31 March 2001	11
1 April 1999 to 31 March 2000	10
1 October 1996 to 31 March 1999	7

The lower rate of tax, which applies to land filled with inactive or inert wastes listed in the *Landfill Tax (Qualifying Material) Order* 1996 (SI 1996/1528), is £2.00 per tonne.

Interest payable on underdeclared landfill tax (FA 1996, Sch. 5, para. 26)

Since 1 April 1997, interest on landfill tax is charged at the same rate as under VATA 1994, s. 74.

Environmental trusts

Site operators making payments to environmental trusts set up for approved environmental purposes can claim a tax credit up to 90 per cent of their contribution – subject to a maximum of 20 per cent of their landfill tax bill in a 12-month period. From 1 August 1999, operators using the scheme have up to an additional month every quarter to claim tax credits. On 15 October 1996, Customs approved an independent body, ENTRUST, as the regulator of environmental trusts. It is responsible for enrolling environmental bodies, maintaining their operation and ensuring that all expenditure complies with the landfill tax requirements.

118   Aggregates Levy

Rate

Period of application	Rate (per tonne) £
From 1 April 2008	1.95
1/4/02–31/3/08	1.60

There is no registration threshold for aggregates levy. Any person who commercially exploits aggregate in the UK after 31 March 2002 may be liable to register with Customs and account for aggregates levy (FA 2001, Sch. 4 and the *Aggregates Levy (Registration and Miscellaneous Provisions) Regulations* 2001 (SI 2001/4027), reg. 2).

Generally, 'aggregate' means any rock, gravel or sand together with any other substances which are for the time being incorporated in or naturally occurring with it.

Key Data

'Commercially exploited' generally means in the course or furtherance of a business the earliest of (FA 2001, s. 16):

- removal from:
  - the originating site;
  - a connected site that is registered under the same name as the originating site; or
  - a site where it had been intended to apply an exempt process to it, but this process was not applied;
- agreement to supply to another person;
- use for construction purchases; and
- mixing with any material or substance other than water, except in permitted circumstances.

Interest payable on underdeclared aggregates levy (FA 2001, Sch. 5, para. 5ff.)

Since 1 April 2002, interest on aggregates levy is charged at the same rate as under VATA 1994, s. 74.

Overview

Overview

- Taxes may be direct or indirect.
- Direct taxes include income tax (see 240ff.), corporation tax (see 3000ff.), capital gains tax (see 5000ff.) and inheritance tax (see 6505ff.).
- Indirect taxes include VAT (see 7700ff.), stamp duty (see 10100ff.), stamp duty reserve tax (see 10150ff.), customs duties (see 9500ff.), excise duties (see 9650ff.), air passenger duty (see 9760ff.), insurance premium tax (see 9800ff.), landfill tax (see 9950) and council tax (see 10050ff.).
- Tax law is derived from various sources – Acts of Parliament (primary legislation) (see 168); orders and regulations, usually made by statutory instrument (secondary legislation) (see 174); European legislation (see 175) and case law (see 177).
- Interpretation of tax law is aided by various non-statutory sources, including statements of practice, extra-statutory concessions (although HMRC are currently undergoing a process of giving concessions statutory effect), departmental leaflets and pamphlets, Revenue interpretations and decision and internal guidance manuals (see 176).
- Tax law distinguishes between items of an income nature and of a capital nature (see 186).
- Income and capital gains tax are charged by reference to a year of assessment (or tax year) which runs from 6 April to the following 5 April (see 183).
- Corporation tax is charged by reference to financial years. A financial year runs from 1 April to the following 31 March (see 183).
- Income tax is a tax on profits or gains of an income nature (see 195).
- Capital gains tax is a tax on chargeable gains resulting from chargeable disposals by chargeable companies (see 195 and 5000ff.).
- Corporation tax is a tax on profits, including income and capital gains, of a company (see 195 and 3000ff.).
- Inheritance tax is a tax on transfers of value made by individuals, executors and trustees (see 195 and 6505ff.).

Overview

A BRIEF HISTORY OF TAXATION

150   The introduction of income tax

In order to help finance the Napoleonic wars, the then prime minister, William Pitt, introduced income tax as a temporary measure. Income taxation, however, brought with it the necessity that the taxpayer must reveal his income. This was most unpopular and when the then prime minister, Henry Addington, re-introduced income tax in 1803 he chose a method of classifying income by its source and charged each source of income separately under a Schedule. Using this method, a taxpayer's total income could not be ascertained without assessing and computing his income under each source or Schedule.

Income tax was last introduced by Sir Robert Peel in 1842 as a three-year temporary measure, but it has been with us ever since. There have been four consolidations since 1842, in the *Income Tax Acts* 1918 and 1952 and in the *Income and Corporation Taxes Acts* 1970 and 1988.

The Tax Law Rewrite Project was commissioned with the task of rewriting tax legislation into a more logical and 'user-friendly' format. The publication of the *Income Tax (Earnings and Pensions) Act* 2003 (ITEPA 2003) covers income from employments, pensions and social security benefits and replaces the former Schedule E. The *Income Tax (Trading and Other Income) Act* 2005 (ITTOIA 2005) covers income from trades, professions and vocations, income from property, savings income and investments. It replaced the six cases of former Schedule D, Schedule A and Schedule F. The *Income Tax Act* 2007 covers basic provisions about the charge to income tax, income tax rates, calculations and personal reliefs. It also deals with specific reliefs, such as EIS, VCT, etc. and trusts.

See *British Tax Reporter* ¶102-000.

151   The National Insurance Scheme

The National Insurance Scheme first came into effect in 1948. It was based on proposals made in a government report on Social Insurances and Allied Services – the so-called 'Beveridge Report'. The original plan was for flat rate contributions to be paid into the scheme so that flat rate benefits could be paid out. Graduated pension arrangements were grafted onto the scheme in 1959, so that employees were required to contribute an amount based on a percentage of their earnings in return for enhanced pensions. In 1975 the rules were consolidated into a single scheme, which forms the crux of the National Insurance regime as it is today.

As indicated above, the original principle was that all benefits were contributory. Since the introduction of the scheme, there has been increasing divergence of the contributions side from the benefits side, so that in recent times, benefits far outpace contributions. Indeed, there have been an increasing number of non-contributory benefits for which entitlement does not depend upon an individual having contributed to the fund.

152 The addition of taxation on capital gains

Any system of taxation that failed to tax capital profits or gains would effectively be providing an open invitation to avoid tax. A taxpayer would simply devote more time to the making of capital profits to avoid liability to tax. It is, therefore, not surprising that capital gains are now taxed. It was not, however, until 1962 that a tax on short-term capital gains was introduced. This taxed gains on land made within three years of acquisition and all other gains made within six months of acquisition. The gain was treated as unearned income and taxed under former Sch. D, Case VII.

In 1965 capital gains tax (CGT) was introduced which taxed capital gains not already covered by the short-term capital gains legislation. In 1971 the government abolished income tax on short-term capital gains, and CGT became the only tax on capital gains.

The statutory provisions relating to CGT are now to be found in the *Taxation of Chargeable Gains Act* 1992, subject to amendment or supplementation by subsequent Finance Acts. This 1992 Act includes provisions relating to the taxation of chargeable gains by way of corporation tax as well as CGT. It should be noted that there are still some capital receipts that fall to be taxed as income, e.g. lease premiums and reverse premiums (see 1260, 1290) (see also 1448).

Until 1985, gains from development land were taxed separately from capital gains. The last of this series of taxes, development land tax, was imposed from 1976 until its abolition in the Budget of 19 March 1985. Its rationale was to tax any gain over and above the current use value of the land at an appreciably higher rate than the CGT rate (then 30 per cent). At the time of its abolition in 1985, development land tax was charged at 60 per cent.

For the early part of its history, CGT was charged at a significantly lower rate than the higher rates of income tax. This encouraged the proliferation of sophisticated devices whereby an income profit could be 'turned into' a capital gain (e.g. 'bond washing'). The scope for this kind of fiscal alchemy was reduced, but not eliminated, by anti-avoidance legislation such as the accrued income scheme (1985: see 1378). Only when in 1988 CGT rates were aligned with the basic and higher rates of income tax, and capital gains became taxed as the highest part of a taxpayer's income, did this kind of anti-avoidance lose much of its purpose. From 1999–2000 CGT rates were aligned with those for savings income so that gains in excess of the annual exempt amount were charged at 20 per cent where the gains when added to total income were below the basic rate limit and 40 per cent where they exceeded that limit. From 6 April 2008, CGT is payable at a flat rate of 18 per cent (see 5410).

See *British Tax Reporter* ¶102-450.

154 History of taxation on death

The notion of taxing a deceased person's estate is a long-standing one in the UK tax system. As a deceased's personal representatives are obliged to gather in all the property formerly belonging to him, the administration of an estate represents an ideal tax point.

The value attributable to the personal property comprised in an estate has been taxable since 1694, and from 1894, with the introduction of estate duty, broadly speaking the entire estate of a deceased person has been subject to tax. Further, from 1965 to 1971, death was also the occasion of a charge to capital gains tax (CGT).

Estate duty was abolished upon the introduction of capital transfer tax (CTT) in 1975. Whilst CTT preserved the notion of taxing the estate of the deceased, it additionally introduced the novel concept of charging lifetime transfers of wealth cumulatively to tax. However, since the *Finance Act* 1986, CTT has itself been replaced by inheritance tax, which retains the principal features of CTT but is confined in its operation to the taxation of deceased persons' estates, transfers of capital made within seven years of death, and lifetime transfers into certain settlements. The inheritance tax represents in many ways a return to the estate duty system. The statutory provisions relating to inheritance tax are to be found in the *Inheritance Tax Act* 1984 (previously known as the *Capital Transfer Tax Act* 1984) as amended and supplemented by subsequent Finance Acts.

See *British Tax Reporter* ¶600-000.

156 Development of the taxation of companies

The *Joint Stock Companies Act* 1844 heralded the first of the statutory registered companies. This was superseded by the former *Companies Act* 1985 and now the *Companies Act* 2006. Notwithstanding this, no separate code of taxation for companies appeared until 1965 when corporation tax was introduced (although companies were previously subject to income tax and profits tax). The *Income and Corporation Taxes Act* 1988, as amended and supplemented, principally by parts of the Finance Acts receiving Royal Assent between 1988 and 1996, embodied the main corporation tax provisions.

Most of the provisions applying for corporation tax purposes have now been rewritten by the *Corporation Tax Act* 2009 and the *Corporation Tax Act* 2010. Many provisions dealing with international matters have been rewritten by the *Taxation (International and Other Provisions) Act* 2010. The enactment of the *Corporation Tax Act* 2010 and the *Taxation (International and Other Provisions) Act* 2010 effectively brought the Tax Law Rewrite Project to an end (see 150).

See *British Tax Reporter* ¶102-400.

159 The introduction of VAT

The UK joined what was then the European Economic Community in 1973. The treaty establishing the Community stated that one of its aims was the harmonisation of turnover taxes of member states. As a result, member states were encouraged to adopt a broadly common tax on value added. The UK's obligations in this respect were met with the introduction of VAT in 1973.

There have been a number of attempts to further harmonise the taxes that were introduced in each of the member states, but there remain considerable divergences, both in rates and in those items that are subject to charge.

See *British VAT Reporter* ¶1-100.

THE SOURCES OF TAX LAW

165 The legality of taxation

For the levying of taxes to be legal they must have the authority of Parliament. The Bill of Rights of 1688 states (in olde English!) that: 'levying moneys for or to the use of the Crowne by preference of prerogative without grant of parliament ... is illegale'. Similar provision is made in Scotland by the Claim of Right 1689. It follows then that there is no such thing as a common law tax (though 'cheating the Revenue' is a common law crime: see 2659).

See *British Tax Reporter* ¶103-000.

168 Acts of Parliament

The various taxation provisions are made known to us primarily through statutes. The more important ones are the *Corporation Tax Act* 2009; the *Corporation Tax Act* 2010; the *Taxation (International and Other Provisions) Act* 2010; the *Taxation of Chargeable Gains Act* 1992, the *Inheritance Tax Act* 1984; the *Value Added Tax Act* 1994, the *Social Security Contributions and Benefits Act* 1992, the *Income Tax (Earnings and Pensions) Act* 2003, the *Income Tax (Trading and Other Income) Act* 2005 and the *Income Tax Act* 2007. The *Taxes Management Act* 1970, the *Customs and Excise Management Act* 1979 and the *Social Security Administration Act* 1992 regulate the institutions involved in the imposing and collecting of the main taxes, and the *Capital Allowances Act* 2001 the granting of capital allowances. In some parts, Customs and Excise leaflets go further than providing a useful explanation of the views of Customs and actually have the effect of law: particular examples of this are the parts of Notice 700 (*The VAT guide*) which relate to the records to be retained by traders, and the booklets concerning retail schemes and second-hand goods schemes. Other legislative sources include statutory instruments, made by government departments under the authority of 'enabling' Acts of Parliament, and European Community legislation.

Overview

The *Commissioners for Revenue and Customs Act* 2005 received Royal Assent on 7 April 2005. The Act provides the legal basis for the new integrated department, Her Majesty's Revenue and Customs (HMRC), and the new independent prosecutions office, Revenue and Customs Prosecutions Office. These departments were launched on 18 April 2005.

Income tax is perhaps unusual in that it has to be imposed year-by-year by way of a Finance Act (though the legislation authorises the continuity of operation of the administrative machinery). Such Finance Acts also make amendment to the other main statutes and provide additional rules to implement government policy changes or to target avoidance. Social Security changes are also made by statutes other than the annual Finance Act.

Statute entrusts HMRC with the 'care and management' of income tax, corporation tax and CGT.

Law: TMA 1970, s. 1(1); ICTA 1988, s. 820

See *British Tax Reporter* ¶103-050.

171 Provisional collection of taxes

Parliament imposes income tax separately for each year of assessment (tax year) by passing the yearly Finance Act. The legislation provides that the Income Tax Acts' provisions continue to apply in a new tax year despite the fact that the Finance Act may not have, as yet, been given Royal Assent. Section 820 does not impose the tax or allow deductions without the Finance Act being in force but allows the continuity of the administration connected with the Acts to continue.

The Finance Bill does not normally receive the Royal Assent until the end of July or start of August after the beginning of the tax year on 6 April, which means that a vacuum is created when there is no provision authorising payment or deductions of tax. Therefore, at the conclusion of the Budget debate, the House of Commons passes resolutions declaring that they are to have statutory effect under the *Provisional Collection of Taxes Act* 1968. This states that income tax which was in force in the previous financial year is to be renewed, reimposed or any income tax in force at present is to be varied, abolished or repealed. The resolutions may make changes to the previous year's income tax before being reimposed. The 1968 Act also applies to corporation tax, petroleum revenue tax, stamp duty reserve tax, certain VAT provisions, and duties of customs and excise (there is no similar requirement in relation to NIC).

The resolutions then have the same effect as would an Act of Parliament. This statutory effect is for a limited period only however. The House of Commons must give a Bill, which includes provisions that will achieve what the resolutions provide, a second reading within 30 sitting days or the resolutions lose their effect. If the provisions in the Bill that support the resolutions are rejected during the passage of the Bill, or an Act is passed giving effect to the provisions, or Parliament is dissolved or prorogued, the statutory effect of the resolutions is lost.

To allow employers time to update their payroll systems following a March Budget, no change as a result of the statutory indexation of income tax rates and allowances needs to be made for PAYE purposes until after 17 May in the relevant tax year.

Law: ICTA 1988, s. 820

See *British Tax Reporter* ¶103-150.

174   Regulations, orders, statutory instruments

Finance legislation in recent times increasingly contains provisions which empower administrative bodies to make 'secondary' legislation, and prescribes the purpose and extent of their powers to do so. The Treasury and HMRC are empowered to make orders or regulations, usually by means of statutory instrument or – in the case of double taxation treaties – the sovereign is empowered to make an Order in Council. The legislation provides for control of statutory instruments by Parliament by either requiring approval of the draft by the House of Commons before they are made or by making them subject to annulment by resolution of the House of Commons (or either House).

Law: ICTA 1988, s. 788

See *British Tax Reporter* ¶103-500.

175   European Community legislation

The UK became a member of what is now the European Union by virtue of the Treaty of Accession of 1972, and the *European Communities Act* 1972, which incorporates the treaties establishing the Communities into UK law. There are three types of European Community legislation.

- *Regulations* of the Council of Ministers and the Commission are directly applicable in member states and do not depend for their enforcement on the passing of national legislation. In the UK they have direct effect.
- *Directives* are generally binding but require to be separately enacted within member states. In the UK, this is done either by Act of Parliament or by subordinate legislation.
- *Decisions* are addressed to individual member states and are binding on them alone (e.g. those authorising derogations in the UK from the sixth VAT directive).

Most EC taxation law is concerned with VAT and duties of customs and excise: the UK law on VAT derives from EC law, notably the sixth directive on VAT. Note, however:

- Directive 77/799 of 19 December 1977 which provides for mutual assistance between the Revenue authorities of member states with a view to preventing international tax evasion and avoidance;
- Directive 90/434 and Directive 90/435 of 23 July 1990, on the tax treatment of cross-

border mergers and payment of dividends by subsidiaries to parent companies in different member states.

In addition, the convention on the elimination of double taxation in connection with the adjustment of profits of associated enterprises (Convention 90/436 of 23 July 1990), which seeks to address transfer pricing issues, has been ratified, and entered into force on 1 January 1995.

Law: ECA 1972, s. 2; Directive 77/388 of 17 May 1977 (OJ 1977 L145/1)

See *British Tax Reporter* ¶103-800.

176 Non-legislative sources

HMRC often issue statements in which they make known their views on the correct interpretation of statute, or the way in which they propose to apply certain rules. In addition, they may announce a relaxation in their approach to a particular statutory provision, where to adhere strictly to it would cause undue administrative difficulties, or hardship to the taxpayer. Such statements of practice and extra-statutory concessions (ESCs) lack the force of law and do not affect a taxpayer's rights on appeal. However, a taxpayer may rely on those concessions except where an attempt is made to use them for the purpose of tax avoidance; Customs concessions are generally limited in number and scope and do not carry the same weight.

From 6 April 2009, HMRC have powers to give statutory effect to concessions (FA 2008, s. 160). The *Enactment of Extra-Statutory Concessions Order* 2009 (SI 2009/730) enacted 16 existing HMRC ESCs and is the first in a series of Orders which are planned to be made using this power.

Departmental press releases are also a useful source of information on topical issues: the intention to legislate is often announced in a press release, and it is established practice to bring a law into force retrospectively from the date on which the intention to legislate is so announced. Press releases are also the medium for announcing new extra-statutory concessions or statements of practice.

Interpretations of various points of tax law are often published in the *HMRC Brief*. Such interpretations are qualified by an important caveat that particular cases may turn on their own facts or context, and that there may be circumstances where the interpretation would not apply. In addition, there may be circumstances in which the Board would find it necessary to argue for a different interpretation in appeal proceedings. *HMRC Brief* also contains articles which give an insight into the thinking of HMRC head office specialists.

In a further step towards greater openness, the HMRC internal guidance manuals are now freely available.

Proposals for future tax legislation on difficult or controversial matters are increasingly set out in consultative documents.

See *British Tax Reporter* ¶103-520.

177   The function of the courts

In order to understand the function of the courts, a distinction must first be made between what is fact and what is law, for it is only upon the second of these two issues that the court will adjudicate.

The former general and special commissioners, VAT and Duties and Section 706 Tribunals (the latter dealing with appeals in respect of the income tax anti-avoidance rules governing transactions in securities) have been replaced from April 2009 with a new tribunals system. This means that the role of the general commissioners (and clerks) no longer exists. Existing judges, special commissioners and members of the VAT and Duties and Section 706 Tribunals have been transferred into the new system. The tax tribunals now hear appeals in respect of both direct and indirect taxes in the UK.

A taxpayer in dispute with HMRC may normally take the matter to the First-tier Tribunal (Tax Chamber) or the Upper Tribunal. The Upper Tribunal hear appeals on points of law from the First-tier Tribunal, although a small number of tax appeals are transferred from the First-tier Tribunal to the Upper Tribunal. Appeal hearings of the First-tier Tribunal are available locally, via a network of 130 hearing centres across the country.

The courts today are finding that they are called upon to interpret statutes containing provisions which are far more complex than was necessary in the days when the various taxes were first introduced. One reason for this is that with the increasing burden of taxation, taxpayers and their professional advisers have spent ever increasing funds and time in trying to arrange their affairs so that they minimise their liability under the legislation. Parliament has therefore responded by drafting more complex provisions.

Avoidance schemes have now reached such a state of complexity that the courts have on occasion seen fit to depart from the strict wording approach of Lord Donovan (see 180) and look at the purpose behind transactions.

See *British Tax Reporter* ¶102-850.

180   Interpretation or construction

The fact that tax is a statutory creature (see 165) and the ability of the courts only to hear appeals based upon an error of law (see 177) means that they will, in most cases, find it necessary to construe the words of the statute to ascertain their applicability to the facts in question. All statutes are subject to certain rules of interpretation, but whereas with non-fiscal legislation the courts may resolve any absurdity by looking at the spirit and intendment of the Act, they are more reluctant to do so with fiscal legislation. In 1970 Lord Donovan outlined the rules governing the interpretation of tax legislation:

'First, the words are to be given their ordinary meaning. They are not to be given some other meaning simply because their object is to frustrate legitimate tax avoidance devices. As Turner J. said in his (albeit dissenting) judgment in *Marx* v. *Inland Revenue Commissioners* ... moral precepts are not applicable to the interpretation of revenue statutes.

Secondly, " ... one has to look merely at what is clearly said. There is no room for any intendment. There is no equity about a tax. There is no presumption as to a tax. Nothing is to be read in, nothing is to be implied. One can only look fairly at the language used": *per* Rowlatt J. in *Cape Brandy Syndicate* v. *Inland Revenue Commissioners* ... (approved by Viscount Simons L.C. in *Canadian Eagle Oil Co. Ltd.* v. *The King* ...)

Thirdly, the object of the construction of a statute being to ascertain the will of the legislature, it may be presumed that neither injustice nor absurdity was intended. If therefore a literal interpretation would produce such a result, and the language admits of an interpretation which would avoid it, then such an interpretation may be adopted ...

Fourthly, the history of an enactment and the reasons which led to its being passed may be used as an aid to its construction.'

Therefore if the words are ambiguous the taxpayer is entitled to the benefit of the doubt but if there is no ambiguity the words must take their natural meaning however great the hardship to the taxpayer.

In a later House of Lords case some attention was focused on the general principles of construing fiscal legislation in the light of tax avoidance schemes. Lord Steyn indicated that an approach that followed a narrow, literalistic interpretation of such statute was outmoded when he said:

'During the last 30 years there has been a shift away from literalist to purposive methods of construction. Where there is no obvious meaning of a statutory provision the modern emphasis is on a contextual approach designed to identify the purpose of a statute and to give effect to it. But under the influence of the narrow *Duke of Westminster* doctrine tax law remained remarkably resistant to the new non formalist methods of interpretation ... Tax law was by and large left behind as some island of literal interpretation ... the intellectual breakthrough came in 1981 in *Ramsay*, and notably in Lord Wilberforce's seminal speech ... It marked the rejection by the House [of Lords] of pure literalism in the interpretation of tax statutes'

The House of Lords has decided that Parliamentary material (in that case, *Hansard*) may, in limited circumstances, be used to ascertain the *intention* of Parliament when enacting legislation. A majority of the House held that, subject to the question of Parliamentary privilege, the rule excluding reference to *Hansard* should be relaxed where:

- legislation was ambiguous or obscure, or led to absurdity;
- the material relied on consisted of statements by a minister or other promoter of a Bill, together with any other Parliamentary material necessary to understand such statements and their effect;
- the statements relied on were clear.

The UK law on VAT derives from EC law, notably the sixth directive on VAT. Under the Treaty of Rome, the government is obliged to enact the UK law in such a way as to implement the provisions contained in the European directives and regulations. Consequently, it is sometimes possible to refer to the EC legislation for guidance on the interpretation of the UK law. Furthermore, if the UK law fails to implement the EC law, the citizen is entitled to rely on the EC law where it has direct effect in the UK.

Law: Directive 77/388 of 17 May 1977 (OJ 1977 L145/1); *IR Commrs v Hinchy* [1960] AC 748; *Mangin v IR Commrs* [1971] AC 739; *Pepper (HMIT) v Hart* [1992] BTC 591; *IR Commrs v McGuckian* [1997] BTC 346

See *British Tax Reporter* ¶104-000.

183   Tax periods

Liability to both CGT and income tax is in respect of a 'year of assessment' (or 'tax year'), beginning on 6 April and ending on 5 April in the following year. Liability to corporation tax, however, is in respect of a 'financial year' (see 3027), which begins on 1 April and ends on 31 March in the following year. While liability arises by reference to a 'year of assessment' or a 'financial year', it does not necessarily follow that it is the income or gain made during those periods that is taxed. Where income or gain is taxed in the year of assessment or financial year in which it arises, tax is said to be calculated on a 'current year' basis. Where it is charged in the year of assessment or financial year following that in which it arises, tax is said to be charged on a 'preceding year' basis. However, all sources of income were moved to a current year basis to coincide with the introduction of self-assessment in 1996–97.

For VAT, a trader is normally required to make VAT returns and provisional attributions of input tax for each prescribed accounting period (VAT return period: see 8166), and then review this for his VAT tax year, i.e. a period of 12 months ending on 31 March, 30 April or 31 May, depending upon the business' VAT accounting period.

Class 1, Class 2 and Class 3 NIC are recorded for the purposes of computing benefit entitlement on the basis of years ending on 5 April, although (unlike income tax) National Insurance contributions of those classes do not arise on an annual or annualised basis and liability within each tax year is calculated by reference to earnings paid in an earnings period, for Class 1, and by reference to contribution weeks for Class 2 and Class 3; contributions of Class 1A arise on an annual basis while Class 4 contribution liability is linked to tax liability on income arising from a trade, profession or vocation.

Law: ITA 2007, s. 4(3), (5); CTA 2010, s. 1119 and Sch. 1, paras. 248, 689(3); *Value Added Tax Regulations* 1995 (SI 1995/2518), reg. 99(3)

See *British Tax Reporter* ¶102-000.

186   Income or capital

Tax law generally makes a distinction between capital and income items when analysing receipts and expenditure. This distinction was more important in the days when income tax was calculated at progressive rates while capital gains were taxed at a flat rate of 30 per cent. In general a sum which is derived from the sale of a capital item will not give rise to an income receipt but it does not follow that what is a capital expense to one party is necessarily a capital receipt to the other party.

Example

X owns a factory, manufacturing toys. He sells his factory to Y who deals in buying and selling commercial properties. In X's hands the receipt is capital; in Y's hands the expense is an income (or revenue) expense. Capital items include any profit-making apparatus of the business. For further details of the distinction, see 630.

The Tax Acts give no general definition of income, but a receipt, to be taxable, must fall within one of the heads of charge listed in the Acts if it is to be charged to income tax or corporation tax as income. Income is taxed according to the source from which it arises: e.g. the profits of a trade are taxed under the special rules of CTA 2010, Part 2 in the case of corporation tax and ITTOIA 2005, Pt. 2 in the case of income tax. The source of income must, as a general rule, exist in the year in which the income arose.

Example

A taxpayer (an individual) who is not domiciled in the UK and who receives bank interest in Jersey could close the account and remit the interest to the UK in the financial year after the one in which the interest arose and that interest would not be taxable. The reason is that, for non-domiciliaries, liability arises on a remittance basis and in the tax year in which the liability arose the source, i.e. the bank account, had ceased to exist.

See *British Tax Reporter* ¶106-100.

GENERAL PRINCIPLES OF DIRECT TAXATION

195   Liability to tax

Income tax is a tax on profits or gains of an income nature. It is therefore necessary to distinguish them from gains of a capital nature (see 630). The Taxes Acts do not define either income or capital.

Capital gains tax is a tax on certain gains of a capital nature. Broadly, it seeks to tax chargeable gains resulting from chargeable disposals of chargeable assets by chargeable persons.

Corporation tax is a tax on profits, including income and chargeable gains.

Inheritance tax is altogether different and applies to transfers of value.

In general a sum received from the sale of a capital item will be a capital sum and will not attract income taxation. Capital items are defined widely and include such things as contracts under which the business operates to make profits, know-how and any other profit-making apparatus of the business.

In general, the basic liability to tax is in each case given without reference to the circumstances of the person concerned. The scope of charge is then limited in certain cases. However, there is also a generally accepted principle that the extent of a territory's taxation should not exceed its national boundaries – this is generally determined by 'residence' (see 213, 214), 'ordinary residence' (see 216) and 'domicile' (see 219) or the location of the 'source' of income or gains (see 201). Where the rules of other territories also impose tax in accordance with this principle relief may be provided to limit any double taxation.

See *British Tax Reporter* ¶148-050.

201 The source doctrine

Income profits are charged by reference to their source. For a receipt to be taxable it must have a source under the provisions of one of the Taxes Acts. If it has not it will not be taxable. Moreover, the source must normally be in existence at the time when liability arises. Sources outside the UK may be subject to separate rules of calculation.

Capital taxation is also determined in part by the location of assets or property.

See *British Tax Reporter* ¶102-150.

204 Form and substance

The words of a taxing statute must clearly lay the burden of tax upon the taxpayer. If they do not the taxpayer will not be taxed purely because it was the intention of the legislature that the taxpayer be taxed. It is, however, up to the court to decide upon the legal rights of the parties and in doing so they will not be influenced by nomenclature. Where the transactions are a sham or constitute a blatant scheme for tax avoidance, the court may decide to look at their substance or end result to determine how they should be taxed.

Cases starting with *WT Ramsay Ltd v IR Commrs* [1982] AC 300 and *Furniss (HMIT) v Dawson* [1984] BTC 71 have established that where there:

- is a *pre-ordained series* of transactions or *single composite* transaction,
- are steps inserted with no commercial purpose other than the avoidance of tax,

149

the court may ignore the inserted steps and tax the transaction, or series of transactions, accordingly.

Transactions regarded as a sham

Only bona fide transactions are to be taken into account for tax purposes, 'shams' being ignored. An avoidance scheme in pursuance of which a chain of companies was set up and the declaration of a dividend out of capital reserve which was created by the passing of a sum of money along the chain and the creation of an alleged dealing loss of £3m (approximately) was held not to be trading. These cases set the scene for the later development of the *Furniss v Dawson* doctrine.

Law: *Johnson v Jewitt (HMIT)* (1961) 40 TC 231; *WT Ramsay Ltd v IR Commrs* [1982] AC 300 and *Furniss (HMIT) v Dawson* [1984] BTC 71

See *British Tax Reporter* ¶103-050.

207 Methods of collecting tax

There are two methods of collecting tax. The first is by direct assessment. This is done by HMRC assessing the amount that the taxpayer is liable to pay, or, from 1996–97, by the taxpayer producing a self-assessment.

The second method is by deduction of tax at source by the person who makes the payment to the taxpayer. In principle, the payer then sends that deducted tax to HMRC.

See *British Tax Reporter* ¶116-000.

210 Grossing up

Income may be received which has already had tax deducted from it at source, i.e. before it is received. Where this is done a calculation must be made to ascertain the gross figure which forms part of the taxpayer's total income. The process of calculating this gross figure is called 'grossing up'. The calculation is as follows:

Multiply the net amount received by the grossing-up fraction.
The grossing-up fraction is 100 divided by (100 less the basic rate of tax).

Example

If £160 is received after the basic rate income tax of 20% has been deducted, the grossed-up figure is as follows:

$$£160 \times \frac{100}{100 - 20}$$

$$£160 \times \frac{100}{80} = £200$$

Therefore £200 is the grossed-up figure.

Example

If £160 is received after the basic rate income tax of 40% has been deducted, the grossed-up figure is as follows:

$$£160 \times \frac{100}{100 - 40}$$

$$£160 \times \frac{100}{60} = £266.67$$

Therefore £266.67 is the grossed-up figure.

A special grossing up process is required for inheritance tax. Tax in respect of a disposition made by a transferor which is chargeable is calculated by reference to the reduction in value of his estate. If he also agrees to pay any tax due the reduction in his estate is that much greater. A complex grossing up of the value of the disposition is required (see 6620).

See *British Tax Reporter* ¶110-700.

213 Residence of individuals

The meaning of 'residence' for tax purposes is the same as its everyday English meaning. In *The Oxford English Dictionary*, the word 'reside' is defined as:

> 'To dwell permanently or for a considerable time, to have one's settled or usual abode, to live in or at a particular place.'

It is for the tribunal to decide whether a taxpayer is resident or not in any tax year and because this is a question of fact it is one with which the courts will not interfere unless no tribunal acting reasonably could have come to that decision on the evidence available (see 177). In practice, the matter will often be decided on the basis of a residence ruling by HMRC.

To be resident, an individual must, generally, be physically present in the UK during some part of the year of assessment. Where a person is present for any period whereby he is regarded as resident for that time, he is strictly also regarded as resident for the whole of the tax year. There is no statutory provision for splitting a tax year in relation to residence (but there are concessions in this area).

A Commonwealth citizen (or citizen of the Republic of Ireland) who is ordinarily resident in the UK is regarded as resident in the UK where he has left the country for only occasional residence abroad. 'Occasional residence' is not defined, but a person who for a number of years spent the major part of each year living abroad in hotels was held to have left the UK for only occasional residence abroad.

In deciding if one is resident or not in the UK, the following factors should be considered. Where there is no standard pattern of working hours (35–40 being considered as a typical UK working week), HMRC will look to determine *full-time* employment in the cases below on the basis of the nature of the job and local conditions or practices; it might include several concurrent part-time jobs.

See *British Tax Reporter* ¶111-200.

(1) Physical presence in UK – the six-month rule

Any person who spends six months or longer in the UK in the tax year in question will be regarded as resident in the UK for that year. In calculating the six-month period, days and hours are taken into consideration. Any day in which an individual is present in the UK at midnight will count as a day's presence. Days spent in transit, even involving changes between methods of transport, will not count as a day's residence, unless the individual carries out activities that are substantially unrelated to the transit process (e.g. a business meeting).

One is still resident in the UK if one's residence abroad is temporary. It is possible to be resident in more than one country at any one time.

Once there has been a finding that a taxpayer is resident in the UK then he is treated as resident for the whole of that tax year. HMRC, however, will allow a tax year to be split so that a taxpayer will be treated as resident in the UK for only part of that tax year in four situations:

(1) where an individual comes to the UK to take up permanent residence or to stay for at least three years; or

(2) where an individual comes to the UK to take up employment which is expected to last for a period of at least two years; or

(3) where an individual ceases to reside in the UK if he has left for permanent residence abroad; or

(4) where an individual leaves the UK to take up full-time employment abroad, and:

   (a) he is absent from the UK for a complete tax year;
   (b) his visits to the UK do not exceed six months in the tax year in question and do not average three months per year.

See *British Tax Reporter* ¶111-450.

(2) Established ordinary residence

Where a person has been ordinarily resident (see 216) in the previous tax year but goes abroad for an occasional residence, he will be treated as remaining resident in the UK.

Occasional residence must mean a period in excess of six months abroad each year otherwise his presence in the UK for more than six months in a particular tax year would mean a finding of residence under the six-month rule.

When applying the above concession, the day of arrival in or the days of departure from the UK are included in the period of residence in the UK.

The period of six months after which an individual is treated as resident in the UK is taken to be 182 days. The 182 days must fall within a tax year. It is possible therefore to spend a continuous period in excess of 182 days in the UK and still not be resident there. The last 181 days before 6 April and the first 181 days after 5 April could be spent in the UK without there being an automatic finding of residency. It does not follow, however, that because one spends less than six months in the UK in a particular tax year that one will not be resident in that year.

See *British Tax Reporter* ¶112-200.

(3) *UK visits and temporary residence*

It has already been made clear that if an individual spends six months or more of any tax year in the UK he will be resident there for tax purposes. If he spends less than six months in the UK he may or may not be resident depending upon whether the visits are frequent and substantial: HMRC consider the regularity of the visits and the reason for them. It is more likely that a taxpayer will be resident in the UK if his visits are regular and form part of his way of life. If the nights spent in the UK on average amount to more than three months per tax year for four years, then the taxpayer will be resident from the first year. HMRC regard visits as sufficiently regular if they are on average for periods of three months or more per tax year. In applying the three-month rule any day in which an individual is present in the UK at midnight will count as a day's presence.

> ### Example
>
> Bruce, who was previously resident in Australia, takes up a post as manager of a group's European operations, a post involving work in several countries and expected to last for five years. He moves his wife and family to the UK. His intention from the outset is to spend two months of each year in the UK and the rest of his time elsewhere in Europe, either working or on holiday. In these circumstances and in the absence of special facts, the visits in each year are for a temporary purpose only and Bruce would be treated as a short-term visitor, and not resident in the UK for each year where the limits set out below were not exceeded.

HMRC treat a short-term visitor (i.e. a person who visits the UK for only limited periods in one or more tax years) as resident for a tax year if he is in the UK for 183 days or more in the tax year.

Alternatively, a person who visits the UK regularly and after four tax years his visits during those years average 91 days or more per tax year, is treated as resident from the fifth tax year. (Any days spent in the UK for exceptional reasons beyond the visitor's control, for example the illness of the visitor or of a member of his immediate family, are not counted for this purpose.) However, HMRC will treat the visitor as resident from 6 April of the first year if it is clear when he first comes to the UK that he intends making such visits; and he is treated as resident from 6 April of the tax year in which he decides to make such visits where he makes his decision before the start of the fifth tax year.

Example

Erik comes to the UK with no definite residence intentions but his visits during the tax years xxx1–2 to xxx4–5 average 93 days a tax year. HMRC will treat Erik as resident from 6 April xxx5.

Example

Francoise comes to the UK during the tax years xxx1–2, intending that between then and 5 April xxx5, her visits will average at least 91 days a tax year. HMRC treat Francoise as resident from 6 April xxx1.

Example

Gregor first comes to the UK during the tax years xxx1–2 with no definite residence intention and spends 60 days there. He returns to the UK during xxx2–3 and decides that he will come regularly in future years and that his visits will average at least four months a tax year. HMRC will treat Gregor as resident from 6 April xxx2.

CGT charge on temporary non-residents

For the CGT charge on temporary non-residents, see 5702.

Law: FA 2008, s. 24; ITA 2007, s. 829, 831; TCGA 1992, s. 9(3); *R & C Commrs v Grace*[2009] EWCA Civ 1082; *Levene v IR Commrs* [1928] AC 217; *Wilkie v IR Commrs* [1952] Ch 153

Source: ESC A11, *Residence in the United Kingdom: year of commencement or cessation of residence*; ESC A78, *Residence in the United Kingdom: accompanying spouse*; SP 2/91, *Residence in the UK: visits extended because of exceptional circumstances*; HMRC6: *Residence, domicile and the remittance basis*

See *British Tax Reporter* ¶111-650.

214   Residence of companies

Company residence is important because a UK-resident company is taxed on its worldwide profits, whereas a non-resident company is taxed generally only on profits arising from its operations in the UK (see 3014).

Three rules apply in determining if a company is resident in the UK for corporation tax purposes:

- the incorporation rule whereby a company which is incorporated in the UK is UK resident;
- the case law rule whereby a company which has its central management and control in the UK is UK resident; and
- the tie-breaker rule whereby a company which is treated as non-UK resident by any double taxation arrangements is non-UK resident for corporation tax purposes despite the application of the incorporation or case law rules.

European Companies (or Societas Europaea, SEs) and European Co-operative Societies (or Societas Co-operative Europaea, SCEs) will be regarded as UK resident for tax purposes if they transfer their registered office from another EU member state to the UK. Any other place given by rule of law is to be disregarded in determining their residence status. In addition, they will not cease to be regarded as UK resident merely because of a subsequent transfer of their registered office out of the UK.

Any liabilities or obligations which arise under self-assessment will continue to apply where a UK-resident company ceases to be resident as a direct consequence of the formation of an SE by a merger of companies, whether or not the UK company ceases to exist; where it does cease to exist, those liabilities and responsibilities will fall on the SE. Similar provisions apply if an SE transfers its registered office outside the UK (and ceases to be UK resident) in respect of liabilities before then.

A company which is resident in the UK is liable to corporation tax on its worldwide profits. A company which is not resident in the UK is liable to corporation tax only if it trades in the UK through a permanent establishment. A non-resident company not trading in the UK through a PE/branch or agency is not liable to corporation tax but, generally, such a company is assessed to income tax on income arising from sources within the UK.

Where a non-resident company receives any payment from which income tax has been deducted, it may set the amount of income tax deducted against any assessment for corporation tax on that income. The company is not entitled to a repayment of income tax until the assessment for the accounting period is finally determined and a repayment appears due. Where the non-resident company is an overseas life insurance company, only a limited amount of the income tax is available for set-off.

Special provisions apply to certain foreign subsidiaries of UK-resident companies, such subsidiaries being referred to in the legislation as 'controlled foreign companies' (see 4713). It was announced as part of the 2009 Pre-Budget Report that, following the introduction of a broad exemption for distributions, discussions would take place regarding the possibility of a move to exemption for the profits of foreign branches of UK-resident companies.

There are also special provisions which apply to the foreign element of certain companies and their funds. In general, such companies are subject to corporation tax rather than income tax and the special provisions relate to the corporation tax charge rather than the rare circumstances in which a company is subject to income tax, although in some cases the provisions apply in respect of all revenue taxes.

Law: CTA 2009, s. 14–18; F(No. 2)A 2005, s. 61; *De Beers Consolidated Mines Ltd v Howe* [1906] AC 455; *Unit Construction Co Ltd v Bullock* [1960] AC 351

Source: SP 1/90, *Company residence*

See *British Tax Reporter* ¶764-000.

216 Ordinary residence

It is possible to be resident but not ordinarily resident and vice versa. Capital gains tax is payable by those who are resident *or* ordinarily resident. It is therefore envisaged that one can be ordinarily resident without being resident. If, for example, an individual was abroad for a full tax year, he may well be ordinarily resident without being resident.

Ordinary residence connotes continuity or habitual residence. Unlike domicile, intention to remain in the UK has no bearing on whether one is ordinarily resident in the UK. In one case, a woman of Australian domicile was placed in a sanatorium in the UK shortly after her arrival there in 1885. She remained there until her death 54 years later. The High Court held that she was ordinarily resident in the UK despite the fact that she was there against her will.

The House of Lords has reconsidered the meaning of the words 'ordinarily resident' in the UK in a case which involved overseas students and their entitlement to local education authority grants. Lord Scarman said that ordinarily resident referred to a man's abode in a particular place or country which he had adopted voluntarily and, for settled purposes, as part of the regular order of his life for the time being (whether of a short or long duration). The settled purpose might be one or several, and it might be specific or general, and it might be for a limited period. Education, business or profession, employment, health, family and a love of a particular place were all common reasons for a choice of regular abode. The test is not a *real home* test.

Except in certain cases where an individual has accommodation available to him in the UK, HMRC are prepared to allow a grace period of three years for an individual coming to the UK to establish whether he is to be ordinarily resident.

A statement of practice explains how the ordinary residence of an individual who comes to the UK not intending to stay for three years or more is determined. The statement indicates that ordinary residence will, in these circumstances, normally apply from the beginning of the tax year after the third anniversary of the person's arrival in this country; if the individual buys accommodation or acquires it on a lease for three years or more or if he/she decides to stay beyond that time, ordinary residence will commence from the beginning of the tax year in which the event occurs or the decision is made (or the day of arrival if this is later). This has been the practice for some time for those taking up employment here. The treatment of others is now being brought into line with that of employees.

Law: *Levene v IR Commrs* [1928] AC 217; *IR Commrs v Lysaght* [1928] AC 234; *Re Mackenzie* [1941] Ch 69; *R v Barnet London Borough Council, ex parte Shah* [1983] 2 AC 309

Source: SP 3/81, *Individuals coming to the UK: ordinary residence*; SP 17/91, *Residence in the UK: when ordinary residence is regarded as commencing where the period to be sent here is less than three years*; HMRC6: *Residence, domicile and the remittance basis*

See *British Tax Reporter* ¶112-200.

219 Domicile

Domicile is important largely for inheritance tax purposes whereas CGT and income tax are founded mainly on residence. Domicile is where the individual has a settled intention permanently to reside. Everybody must have a domicile, one cannot be without one and a person can only be domiciled in one place at any one time.

Under English law, a person has either a domicile of origin, a domicile of dependency, or a domicile of choice. Until 1 January 1974, the domicile of a married woman was dependent on her husband; thereafter, a married woman is capable of having a separate domicile.

See *British Tax Reporter* ¶113-550.

(1) Domicile of origin

Domicile of origin follows that of the father or, if illegitimate, that of the mother and will, in the case of adults, apply in the absence of a domicile of choice. The domicile of a minor is dependent on that of the father if legitimate, and on the mother if illegitimate, and will change according to whether the parent acquires a new domicile of choice.

(2) Domicile of choice

At the age of 16 an individual acquires the right to a domicile of choice. To establish a domicile of choice there must be evidence of fact and intention. The required fact would be habitual residence in the country where it is alleged that the domicile is established, and the required intention would be the intention to abandon the domicile of origin and establish a permanent home in the country of choice. In one case, the taxpayer, with a domicile of origin in the UK, failed to establish a domicile of choice in Guernsey when she remained in the UK during school and university terms to complete her education. Until a domicile of

Overview

choice is established, the domicile of origin continues. Once a domicile of choice is abandoned, the domicile of origin is revived and continues until another domicile of choice is established.

See *British Tax Reporter* ¶113-600.

(3) Domicile by operation of law

For any given purpose a person may be considered to be domiciled in the UK irrespective of domicile under general law. There is a deemed domicile provision in relation to inheritance tax (see 6540).

Domicile for tax purposes of overseas electors

In order to determine a person's domicile for inheritance tax, income tax or CGT purposes on or after 6 April 1996 (or for the purposes of the deemed domicile rule, considered at 6540, on or after 6 April 1993), any action taken by a person in becoming an overseas elector or voting in an overseas election is disregarded. This rule applies unless the taxpayer in question wishes such an action to be taken into account.

Companies' domicile

A company's domicile is its country of registration.

Law: FA 1996, s. 200; *Gasque v IR Commrs* [1940] 2 KB 80; *Re Clore (dec'd)* [1984] BTC 8,101; *Plummer v IR Commrs* [1987] BTC 543

Source: HMRC6: *Residence, domicile and the remittance basis*

See *British Tax Reporter* ¶764-450.

223   Taxation of spouses

A husband and wife are treated as independent taxpayers. This applies for income tax and CGT; it has always been the case for inheritance tax. This independent treatment affects a number of reliefs but principally 'personal allowances' (see 1850ff.) and the 'annual exemption' applying to CGT (see 6150). Transfers between spouses are generally on a no gain/no loss basis for CGT purposes and are exempt from inheritance tax (see 5500, 7192). There are a number of other CGT provisions relating to spouses (see 5460ff.).

Jointly held property

If, after 1989–90, a husband and his wife who is 'living with' him (see 1862) are beneficially entitled to income from property held in their names, they will be treated as entitled to it in equal shares unless they make a joint declaration (on form 17) to the contrary. The declaration has effect in relation to income arising on or after its date;

however, a declaration made before 6 June 1990 also had retrospective effect. The declaration is ineffective if:

- notice of it is not given to the officer (on form 17) within 60 days of its making; or
- the spouses' interests in the property do not correspond to their interests in the income.

Once validly made, the declaration continues in effect unless and until the spouses' interests in either the income or capital cease to accord with the declaration.

From 6 April 2004, distributions (usually dividends) from jointly-owned shares in close companies are no longer automatically split 50/50 between husband and wife but are taxed according to the actual proportions of ownership and entitlement to the income.

Gains are apportioned according to the beneficial interests of the spouses at the date of disposal; if the split is unclear, HMRC will usually accept that it is in equal shares. However, where a declaration is made for income tax HMRC will presume that the same split applies for CGT (see 5502).

In one case, the taxpayer had instructed the Department of Social Security to pay his retirement pension into his wife's bank account and claimed that, since he had not received the income, he was not liable to pay tax on it. A special commissioner held that the taxpayer had not disclaimed his pension into his wife's bank account; he had assigned it to his wife, and in so doing he exercised dominion over it by directing to whom it should be paid.

Law: ITA 2007, s. 836, 837; *Meredith-Hardy v McLellan (HMIT)* (1995) Sp C 42

See *British Tax Reporter* ¶504-100.

224 Taxation of infants

There is a statutory duty on 'every person . . . who is chargeable' to income tax or CGT for a particular tax year and who has not received a notice to make a return of his total income and gains (see 2550) to give notice of his chargeability to HMRC not later than six months after the end of that year. 'Every person . . . chargeable' includes a child under the age of 18: in effect the obligation to make a return in respect of non-settled property will fall upon the child's parent or guardian (see 987). Such a parent, etc. may also be held responsible for any tax chargeable on the child.

Law: TMA 1970, s. 73; *R v Newmarket Income Tax Commrs, ex parte Huxley* (1916) 7 TC 49.

See *British Tax Reporter* ¶154-000.

225 Same-sex couples

The *Civil Partnership Act* 2004 (CPA 2004), which gives legal recognition to same-sex couples, became law in November 2004 and came into effect on 5 December 2005. Broadly, the Act allows same-sex couples to make a formal legal commitment to each other by entering into a civil partnership through a registration process. A range of important rights and responsibilities flows from this, including legal rights and protections. One of the key taxation areas that is affected by this legislation is inheritance tax where transfers between partners are now exempt.

In addition, only one property owned by a couple who are civil partners, whether that property is owned solely or jointly, may be treated as the principal private residence of either of them at any time for the purposes of capital gains tax private residence relief (see 6220). Transfers of assets between civil partners living together will be on a no-gain no-loss basis for CGT purposes.

Legislation relating to all areas of taxation, social security benefits and NICs has been amended to reflect the introduction of CPA 2004. Broadly, references to husband, wife, ex-husband, ex-wife, spouse, ex-spouse, surviving spouse, widow and widower include civil partner, former civil partner and surviving civil partner under the terms of CPA 2004. References to 'step' relations and 'in-laws' are also to be interpreted to include relationships arising from a civil partnership.

Source: *Tax Bulletin*, Issue 80, December 2005

DEALING WITH HMRC

226 HMRC powers and taxpayer rights

Taxpayer Charter

HMRC are statutorily required to maintain a Charter. The current Charter, entitled *Your Charter*, sets out standards of behaviours and values for HMRC to aim at when dealing with taxpayers and others. Legislation also requires the Commissioners for HMRC to report annually on how well HMRC is doing in meeting Charter standards.

HMRC are entitled to:

(1) enquire into any tax return, or any claim or election included in the return (or made outside it) – provided they follow the proper procedure within the appropriate time-limit;

(2) by written notice, require a taxpayer to:

   (a) produce such documents as are in his possession or power and as may reasonably require for the purpose of determining whether (and to what extent) his tax return (or any amendment made to it) is incomplete or incorrect; and

(b) provide such accounts and particulars as they may reasonably require for that purpose.

They can do so only after issuing an enquiry notice to the taxpayer and only if they want the information for the purpose of enquiring into the return (or claim) or an amendment to it. The taxpayer does not have to provide original documents. He can provide photocopies but must make the original available for inspection if required and must allow copies to be taken.

(3) by written notice, require a taxpayer to produce such documents (and accounts, etc.) as HMRC reasonably require for the purpose of making a determination of the amount of tax payable where they determine that income should be calculated in a specific manner.

(4) subject to safeguards, require a taxpayer to:

(a) deliver such documents as are in his possession or power and may contain information relevant to any tax liability to which the taxpayer may be subject or to the amount of any such liability; or

(b) provide such information as may reasonably be required as being relevant to (or to the amount of) a tax liability of the taxpayer.

A TMA 1970, s. 20 notice ('a s. 20 notice') cannot be served unless:

(a) the officer has given the taxpayer a reasonable opportunity to deliver the documents in question (he cannot apply to the tribunal under (c) before he has done this);

(b) the officer is authorised by the Board for the purpose of TMA 1970, s. 20 (most senior officers will be so authorised);

(c) the officer has obtained the consent of the tribunal – who are satisfied that HMRC are justified in issuing a s. 20 notice.

A s. 20 notice:

(i) cannot extend to 'personal records' or journalistic material;

(ii) cannot require the taxpayer to provide original documents, a photocopy will suffice – although, if so required, the original must be made available (e.g. at your office) for inspection;

(iii) cannot require the taxpayer to deliver documents or furnish particulars relating to the conduct of any pending appeal by him; and

(iv) cannot be served by an officer on a barrister, advocate or solicitor – only the Board of HMRC itself can serve such a notice;

(5) subject to safeguards, require any person to deliver to HMRC such documents as are in that person's possession or power which, in the officer's reasonable opinion, may contain information relevant to the tax liability of any other person.

The safeguards in (4)(a)–(c) again apply (with the person on whom the notice is served, rather than the taxpayer, having been given the opportunity to volunteer the information). In addition:

(d)   except where the notice is served by the Board, rather than an officer, the information must relate to a named taxpayer – unless the application was authorised by order of the Board of HMRC and made to the tribunal and the tribunal has consented to the name not being given, because the identity of the taxpayer is not known to HMRC;

(e)   where a notice is given under (a), the person on whom it is served can give a counternotice to the officer that it would be onerous to comply with it, and unless the two agree what information should be disclosed, the objection then needs to be considered by the tribunal and the notice does not need to be complied with unless and until they confirm it;

(f)   the notice cannot require documents the whole of which originate more than six years before the date of the notice – but the tribunal can specifically exclude this restriction if they believe that tax may have been lost owing to the fraud of the taxpayer; and

(g)   a notice cannot be given in relation to a deceased taxpayer more than six years after the death.

The safeguards under (4)(i)–(iv) again apply. In addition:

(v)   the person on whom the notice is served can elect to make the documents available for inspection by HMRC, instead of sending them copies – but he is required to allow them to take copies of (or extracts from) such documents;

(vi)   a copy of the notice must be given to the taxpayer concerned, unless the tribunal decides otherwise, on the basis that to do so could prejudice the assessment or collection of tax, or HMRC has reasonable grounds for suspecting the taxpayer of fraud; and

(vii)   the notice cannot require an auditor to make available his working papers, or a tax adviser to make available 'relevant communications';

(6)   call for the papers of a 'tax accountant' who has been convicted of a tax offence, or has had a penalty imposed on him under TMA 1970, s. 99;

(7)   enter premises with a search warrant and search there. This must be issued by a circuit judge (or a sheriff in Scotland, or a county court judge in Northern Ireland) and various formalities have to be complied with;

(8)   remove anything found on premises which they have entered with a search warrant and to search anyone found on those premises (subject to safeguards); or

(9)   require returns to be made by specified categories of people.

HMRC have no power:

(1)   to interview the taxpayer;

(2)   to interview any other person;

(3)   to enter any premises without a search warrant;

(4) to require a third party to furnish particulars, i.e. information, as opposed to documents;

(5) to require a taxpayer to produce information in any particular, format, e.g. by completing a non-statutory form; or

(6) to require or remove original documents – except where they have a search warrant.

However, the tribunal:

(1) has the power to issue a witness summons to require any person to attend an appeal hearing to give evidence – they almost certainly cannot require the taxpayer to give evidence against himself; nor can they require an auditor or tax adviser to produce documents that are protected from a s. 20 notice;

(2) still have the power to serve notice on any party to an appeal (other than HMRC) directing him:

   (a) to deliver such particulars as they may require for the purpose of determining any of the issues in the proceedings; and

   (b) to make available for inspection by the tribunal or by HMRC all such books, accounts or other documents in his possession or power as may be specified or described in the notice, being books, accounts or other documents which, in the opinion of the tribunal, consist of or may contain information relevant to the subject matter of the proceedings.

In practice, the HMRC officer's ability under TMA 1970, s. 19A (see above) to obtain documents, accounts and particulars, e.g. to require the creation of documents that do not exist, and the completion of non-statutory forms, etc. means that the tribunal's use of these powers is a rare event.

The taxpayer has the right:

(1) to complain to the officer in charge, or the Regional Director if an HMRC officer is not complying with the Taxpayer's Charter, or one of HMRC's codes of practice;

(2) to complain to the Adjudicator if a complaint has been made to the Regional Director and the taxpayer is not satisfied with the response;

(3) to ask his MP to raise a complaint with the Parliamentary Ombudsman (as an alternative to the Adjudicator) or to ask his MP to raise his complaint with ministers;

(4) to ask the tribunal to require HMRC to close an enquiry opened under the self-assessment rules; and

(5) to appeal to the tribunal against most decisions by HMRC.

Law: FA 2009, s. 92; TMA 1970, s. 9A, 12AC, 13–19, 19A(1), 19A(2), 19A(2A), 20(1), 20C, 20CC, 21–28; FA 1998, Sch. 18; *Transfer of Tribunal Functions and Revenue and Customs Appeals Order* 2009 (SI 2009/56); *Orders for the Delivery of Documents (Procedure) Regulations* 2000 (SI 2000/2875)

Source: *Your Charter* is available online at www.hmrc.gov.uk/charter; *Prosecution policy of the Board of Inland Revenue* is available online at www.hmrc.gov.uk/prosecutions/prosecution-policy.htm

See *British Tax Reporter* ¶180-000.

227   Disclosure

Clients have an obligation under self-assessment to submit tax returns which, to the best of their knowledge and belief, are correct and complete. The HMRC officer has the power to enquire into returns to check that taxpayers have fulfilled that obligation.

Under self-assessment, disclosure is important for the following reasons.

- A major benefit to taxpayers is the concept of finality. If a return has not been selected for enquiry within (normally) 12 months of filing, HMRC cannot subsequently open that year unless they can make a 'discovery'. Disclosure limits the circumstances in which HMRC can displace the finality of a self assessment and make a discovery assessment. HMRC cannot base a discovery on information that had previously been made available to them before the enquiry window closed if the HMRC officer could have been reasonably expected, on the basis of that information, to be aware of the under-assessment. From 1 April 2010, if HMRC discover that tax has been lost they can make an assessment to recover the tax lost at any time up to four years from the end of the year of assessment.
- In the vast majority of cases where a return is selected for enquiry, it will be for an 'aspect' enquiry. In these aspect cases the HMRC officer will be doubtful about one or two entries on the return, and will just be checking these and will not be enquiring into the whole return. An aspect enquiry can be prevented by identifying areas where something looks odd and volunteering information to explain the oddity. HMRC can turn aspect enquiries into full enquiries, so volunteering information could forestall a full enquiry too.
- If fraud or negligence can be shown there is no protection from discovery. HMRC might try to categorise mistakes by the taxpayer or his agent as negligence. Their chances of establishing this are lessened by disclosure. With fraud or negligence the time-limit for making discovery assessments is currently extended for up to 20 years after 31 January following the self-assessment year. However, FA 2008 amended TMA 1970, s. 36(1), from 1 April 2010, so that an assessment on a person in a case involving a loss of income tax or capital gains tax brought about carelessly by the person may be made at any time not more than six years after the end of the year of assessment to which it relates.

The disclosure of information that might debar discovery is only regarded as made available to HMRC if it is:

(1)   information that is contained in the taxpayer's self-assessment tax return (or in a claim outside the return) for that year (or either of the two previous years) or in any accounts, statements or documents accompanying the return (or claim);

(2)   information contained in any document, accounts or particulars produced to HMRC for the purpose of its enquiries into the return (or into the claim);

(3)   other information, the existence and relevance of which could reasonably be expected to be inferred by HMRC from information within (1) or (2); and

(4)   other information, the existence and relevance of which is notified in writing by the taxpayer to HMRC.

Where the taxpayer is a partner, information contained in the partnership return and accompanying statements is similarly protected.

In relation to (2), it is worth noting that when HMRC close an enquiry, the taxpayer has finality for that year. HMRC have only one bite at the cherry and not only cannot reopen an enquiry for that year on information provided during the course of the enquiry, but also on other information provided on or with the return. However, if new information indicating an under-assessment comes into HMRC's possession the discovery provisions can be used to reopen that year.

It should particularly be noted that information within (1), i.e. that accompanying a return or claim, is automatically protected if its relevance to the return should be obvious to the HMRC officer. Information supplied separately (i.e. within (4)) is protected only if the taxpayer makes it clear to which return it applies and the relevance of the information to that return.

Of course, there is a question mark over what an HMRC officer could have been reasonably expected to be aware of. HMRC's view is that the taxpayer should point out to the HMRC officer the relevance to the taxpayer's affairs of the information that is sent, as that would prevent such an argument being raised. That is undoubtedly correct. But it is also undoubtedly correct that there are many categories of information where it is obvious that it is relevant to the taxpayer's tax position.

Indeed, HMRC do not seriously question that an officer ought to know that accounts and computations, CGT computations and many other documents accompanying a return will contain information that is likely to be relevant to the taxpayer's self-assessment. Accordingly, such information is automatically protected. What HMRC had in mind was that if, for instance, a 96-page sale agreement is sent with the return, an officer could not reasonably be expected to be aware of something tucked away on p. 85 that cast doubts on the tax treatment adopted.

However, most tribunals are likely to decide that the officer could reasonably be expected to realise that the sale agreement was sent with the return because it had a relevance to the taxpayer's liability. A reasonable officer, confronted with the 96 pages, could be expected at least to realise that the identity of the vendor, the amount of the consideration, and possibly the identity of the purchaser was relevant information, even though he could not be expected to study the agreement fully just in case there was something else important to the tax position, and thus be aware of the few lines on p. 85 that the taxpayer thought made the agreement conditional, or whatever.

It is only where the relevance of a document is not apparent that consideration needs to be given to drawing the officer's attention to why it is being disclosed.

There have been differences of opinion over whether accounts, CGT computations, dividend schedules and similar documents should automatically be sent with the return. One school of thought says that since computations have been prepared, they may as well be submitted to HMRC, but the opinion that seems to be prevailing is: why bother, unless you believe that they add something to the return? It is this opinion that is in accord with HMRC's wishes.

What is indisputable is that when a return is sent to HMRC, consideration needs to be given as to whether it may be sensible to volunteer additional information and, if so, how much information. Disclosure may mean attaching a document to the return. It may mean attaching a statement explaining an entry. It may mean putting a note in the white space on the return. Indeed, if anything is attached to a return, a note detailing the attachments should be entered in the white space. The enclosures are likely to be separated from the return when it is processed, so the officer reviewing the return should be alerted to the fact that additional information has been submitted.

Consideration should be given as to whether to disclose appropriate information without reference to the client, or whether this should be agreed with the client first. Most clients will leave this decision to their tax adviser, and in this situation, the position should be made clear in the initial engagement letter.

Ethical issues and responsibilities exist in relation to disclosure and it is important that these factors are also given careful consideration.

The rules for corporation tax self-assessment are broadly the same as for income tax. A major difference is that accounts must be sent with a corporation tax self-assessment (CTSA) return. Unlike with Pay and File, details of loans to participators must also be sent with the corporation tax return. Where a company controls an overseas company which is a controlled foreign company (CFC), information in relation to the CFC is also required as part of the return. The corporation tax return also contains an optional page for directors' remuneration. If the information to complete this is readily available it is sensible to complete it. HMRC like to try to tie in remuneration shown in a company's accounts with the returns of the individual directors. Accordingly if this page is not completed they may consider opening an enquiry in order to obtain the requisite information.

Law: FA 2008, Sch. 39, para. 7; *Finance Act 2008, Schedule 39 (Appointed Day, Transitional Provision and Savings) Order* 2009 (SI 2009/403); ; TMA 1970, s. 29(6), (7); *Sokoya v R & C Commrs* [2009] TC 00125

228 Returns, records and assessments

Tax returns

Taxpayers retain ultimate responsibility for their tax returns. They cannot avoid penalties for omissions by blaming their accountant. It is important to ensure that the client appreciates that even though his agent has completed the return, it remains his or her responsibility. When sending a tax return to a client for signature, it is sensible:

- to make clear which year it relates to;
- to ask clients to review it;
- to ask clients to check in particular that all sources of income have been included for that year and that all allowances to which they are entitled have been claimed – they ought to know what income they have even though in many cases you cannot expect them to know if the amount is correct (e.g. it is probably unrealistic to expect them to check the dividend list against the dividend vouchers even if they are sent back with the return); and
- to point out any 'grey' areas and any assumptions that have been made in arriving at the figures.

It is also sensible to attach copies of any additional information to the return when sending for signature. This ensures that the client is aware of all proposed disclosures.

Client records

The self-assessment legislation imposes record-keeping requirements. These can be found in TMA 1970, s. 12B for income tax. For the self employed, it requires records to be kept and preserved for:

- all amounts received and expended in the course of the trade, profession or business and the matters for which the receipts and expenditure take place and,
- where a trade involves dealing in goods, all the sales and purchases of goods made during the course of the trade.

The records have to be kept for the five years from 31 January following the self-assessment year. The maximum penalty for not keeping and retaining records is £3,000, but HMRC have given assurances that this penalty legislation will only be used in the most serious cases, and it needs authorisation by their Compliance Division. Instead, their officers are advised to make an appropriate loading of the penalty under TMA 1970, s. 95, if they can (see HMRC *Enquiry Manual* EM4500ff.).

The self-assessment legislation imposes similar obligations on companies. The records have to be kept until the sixth anniversary of the end of the accounting period. HMRC have stated that the records that a company is required to keep for Companies Act purposes will satisfy the corporation tax record-keeping requirement (*Tax Bulletin*, Issue 37, October 1998). However, there is one exception which relates to transfer pricing (see 10860). Where a company enters into transactions with an associated person who is resident outside the UK, it must use arm's length prices to calculate its tax liability if the prices actually used are different and result in lower taxable profits. HMRC consider that all companies, however small, must establish whether or not its transfer prices are arm's length prices and must record the result of its pricing review. The work needed to do this will depend on the company. HMRC do not expect a small company to carry out the sort of economic analysis that they expect large companies to have done. At a minimum a small company should have a written statement setting out why it believes its transfer prices to be arm's length prices. It needs to be realised that the transfer pricing does not apply only to sales and purchases of goods. It applies to all transactions with overseas associates including loan interest, management charges, royalties, etc. (Further guidance on transfer pricing record keeping can be found in *Tax Bulletin*, Issue 37.)

Estimates, valuations and provisional figures

There is nothing to stop a taxpayer using estimates in his self-assessment calculations, and there is no statutory requirement to disclose where estimates have been used. However, if a figure on the face of the return is estimated, it is common sense to indicate this fact on the return. If figures in the client's business accounts are estimated, consideration should be given as to whether either an individual item, or the aggregate of estimated items, is a material figure in the context of the accounts. If it is not, there is probably no point in disclosing it if it is a genuine estimate, i.e. a considered opinion as to the amount wholly and exclusively incurred for the purpose of the business. Common sense suggests that any material figure ought to be disclosed. If it is not and the return is selected for enquiry, the client runs the risk of HMRC questioning whether the return can be said to be correct. Also HMRC could use the non-disclosure to make a discovery at a later date.

The same applies to valuations. There is no duty to disclose the use of a valuation (except where this is specifically required by the tax return form itself; e.g. in relation to CGT) but consideration needs to be given as to whether or not the existence of a valuation ought, as a matter of prudence, to be disclosed.

HMRC interpret case law as requiring provisional figures to be disclosed and they include a box on the self-assessment return to be ticked if provisional figures are included. If this is not done, HMRC might view it as an attempt to mislead and look at the possibility of imposing a penalty. It is also common sense to indicate in the 'Additional Information' box (white space) which figures are provisional. HMRC accept that they cannot send back a return as incomplete where provisional figures are included and the additional information box has not been completed. However, returns with provisional figures are routinely selected for aspect enquiries by officers from HMRC's mandatory review list. They might also seek to impose a penalty where they felt the use of a provisional figure was unjustified. This is a sensitive area for HMRC. They do not wish to see any further erosion of the finality of the 31 January filing date through the use of estimated or provisional figures.

Joint filing

HMRC have issued a statement (1 September 2009) which confirms the introduction of a new joint filing facility. This follows a recommendation from Lord Carter's 2006 review. This is optional and will allow companies to reduce administrative burdens by allowing for one account to be filed online which will satisfy the requirements for both HMRC and Companies House.

Law: *Finance Act 2008, Schedule 37 (Appointed Day) Order* 2009 (SI 2009/402); FA 2008, s. 115; TMA 1970, s. 12B

229 Enquiries

Serious Organised Crime Agency

The *Serious Organised Crime and Police Act* 2005 received Royal Assent on 7 April 2005. The Act established a single powerful agency to lead the fight against organised crime – the Serious Organised Crime Agency (SOCA). The Act includes a power for designated members of SOCA staff, police constables and officers of HMRC, acting under the supervision of the Director of Public Prosecutions, the Director of Revenue & Customs Prosecutions or the Lord Advocate, to compel people to co-operate with an investigation by answering questions and producing relevant documents. This power is applicable in connection with various offences. However, those of particular interest from a tax point of view are offences under s. 72 of the *Value Added Tax* 1994 (fraudulent evasion of VAT, etc.) and the common law offence of cheating the public revenue – in each case where the alleged loss, or potential loss, to the public revenue from the offence is £5,000 or more.

The *Serious Crime Act* 2007 received Royal Assent on 30 October 2007. Among the many measures that it introduces, the Act extends HMRC's existing surveillance powers to a wider range of criminal activity to combat organised tax crime.

Specialist enquiry sections

There are a number of specialist enquiry offices that are outside the district network. The main one is Special Civil Investigations (SCI) Office. If a letter is received from the SCI, the tax practitioner needs to work on the basis that either:

- HMRC suspect serious fraud;
- they suspect that there is a significant amount of undeclared income – not necessarily fraudulently; they may simply disagree with a view taken by the taxpayer that an item is not taxable; or
- if the client has entered into a tax avoidance scheme, HMRC want to investigate whether it has been carried out properly, or they can find a flaw in its implementation.

The SCI Office works collaboratively with colleagues in other parts of HMRC, most notably the Anti-Avoidance Group (AAG), the Large Business Service (LBS) and Corporation Tax & Value Added Tax (CT & VAT) to increase efficiency and to meet the requirements of HMRC.

The other main unit is Special Trades Investigation Unit (STIU). This is similar to SCI but is almost exclusively concerned with suspected fraud.

The STIU has offices in London and Leicester. It deals almost exclusively with the CMT ('cut, make and trim') sector of the clothing industry in Leicester, Birmingham and the east end of London. Whilst this is a small section it is very active in its particular sphere and has had a significant impact in raising PAYE/National Insurance contributions compliance levels in this sector. A significant proportion of businesses in the CMT sector of the clothing industry are run by Asian immigrants or second generation UK domiciles of Asian origin. STIU receives a great deal of information (often anonymous in origin) concerning the use of illegal immigrants as direct labour or out-workers by bona fide UK businesses. The employment of illegal immigrants significantly increases the risk that PAYE will not be operated on wages paid to the worker. Whilst there appears to be no provision for information to be swapped between the Home Office and HMRC concerning the use of illegal immigrants by employers, nevertheless STIU is likely to be in the forefront of government agencies with an interest in the provisions of the *Asylum and Immigration Act* 1996.

The Agricultural Compliance Unit is also a subsidiary unit of SCI based in Leeds and deals with self-employed gang masters in order to ensure that they operate the PAYE rules on gangs of casual workers utilised by farmers at peak times during harvesting. There has been an increased tendency in recent years for casual workers in the agricultural sector to be recruited from unemployed peasant workers from Eastern Europe. There is a significant risk that these workers may contravene immigration control regulations and that wages will be paid in cash without deduction of tax under the PAYE regulations.

Criminal Taxes Unit

Alongside HMRC's Spring Departmental Report 2006, an announcement was made that a new Criminal Taxes Unit (CTU) would be set up. The unit works with the police, SOCA and the Assets Recovery Agency to identify those who have amassed wealth from crime but have paid little or no tax. The CTU will use taxation as a way of disrupting crime.

Self-assessment district enquiries

Enquiries under self-assessment are aimed at:

- encouraging voluntary compliance; and
- detecting and correcting non-compliance.

There are two types of enquiry:

(1) full enquiries into all the constituent parts of the accounts and the underlying records; and

(2) aspect enquiries – where HMRC want to raise questions on only one or two specific aspects of the return.

Some full enquiries will be randomly selected (roughly, one in every 1,000 returns). These are selected centrally at the beginning of the tax year. The intention is to test the self-assessment system.

Other enquiry cases are selected by the area risk, intelligence and analysis team, based on risk management. HMRC have limited resources and need to target them. They have a reason for starting an enquiry – although they are not allowed to tell the taxpayer what it is. They will, however, say whether the enquiry is to be a full or aspect enquiry.

A case that starts an aspect enquiry could, of course, develop into a full enquiry. The HMRC *Enquiry Manual* states:

'The working of cases under SA, using records examination, correspondence, interviews, negotiations and so on, will inevitably be similar to the way cases were worked previously. The opening of enquiries should be less contentious because they won't be presented as "investigations" resulting from dissatisfaction with the return.

We will aim to develop a more neutral and less confrontational approach to the opening of enquiries. This, with new information powers and the development of teamworking, should enable enquiries to be completed more quickly.

There should be greater emphasis on improving taxpayer's record keeping standards so that errors do not recur in future . . .

Best practice should include

- the preparation of a plan for each enquiry case to
- assess the risks present at the start of the enquiry
- identify the actions and information needed to address these risks
- provide for the risks and actions to be updated as the enquiry progresses
- increased consideration of underlying records in both full and aspect enquiries
- greater concentration on field visits, to gather information, to conduct interviews and to examine records on site (the new SA powers do not, however, give us an automatic right of access to business premises)
- greater emphasis on coordination of enquiries into returns with other compliance activities.'

Compliance checks

A revised framework for compliance checks was introduced from 1 April 2009 which changed the way that HMRC conduct enquiries, visits and inspections. The reformed provisions introduced significant changes to the HMRC management of compliance checks across most taxes including income tax, capital gains tax, VAT, PAYE, the construction industry scheme and corporation tax.

Finance Act 2008, Sch. 36, 37 and 39 contain the legislation for the new regime. In summary, Sch. 36 gave HMRC one set of new powers covering all the taxes concerned. This includes powers to visit businesses (without the right of appeal) and inspect the premises, assets and records, and to ask taxpayers and third parties for more information and documents. FA 2008, s. 114 provides the powers to access premises and inspect any computer used by the business.

The *Police and Criminal Evidence Act 1984 (Application to Revenue and Customs) Order 2007 (Amendment) Order* 2010 (SI 2010/360) came into force on 19 March 2010, which extended the application of the Act to national minimum wage investigations. It also applies provisions of the Act not previously applied to criminal investigations conducted by HMRC.

Further rules, contained in Sch. 37 and 39 are designed to provide greater flexibility in setting record-keeping requirements after 1 April 2009, along with new time-limits for assessment and claims which came into force fully from April 2010 (some transitional arrangements came into force from 1 April 2009). HMRC also have a new power enabling them to correct obvious errors in a tax return based on information held.

There is now a four-year time-limit for assessments and claims, a reduction from six years for income tax, capital gains tax and corporation tax and an increase from three years for VAT; reductions in extended assessment time-limits; a streamlined process for closing corporation tax assessments; a new statutory ban on inspecting purely private dwellings without consent; a statutory requirement for HMRC to give at least seven days' prior notice of a visit, unless either an unannounced visit is necessary, or a shorter period is agreed; a new requirement that unannounced visits must be approved beforehand by a specially trained HMRC officer; and a statutory requirement on HMRC to act reasonably.

The legislation, Codes of Practice and guidance governing the revised regime contain certain safeguards for businesses and taxpayers. Broadly, in carrying out compliance checks:

- HMRC's powers must be used reasonably and proportionately;
- taxpayers should be clear about when a compliance check begins and ends;
- HMRC officers do not have the right to enter any parts of premises that are used solely as a dwelling, whether to carry out an inspection or to examine documents produced under an information notice. They can, however, enter if invited;
- unannounced visits will be made where agreement has been given by an authorised HMRC officer.

In addition to examining statutory records (such as PAYE deduction working sheets and expenses payments records), HMRC often ask for supplementary information to enable them to ascertain and quantify a tax position. Examples of supplementary information may include appointment diaries, notes of board meetings, correspondence, commercial employment contracts, explanations and schedules. Under the new framework, an information notice for supplementary information must be reasonable, proportionate, and reasonably required to check the tax position. There is a right of appeal against an information notice unless the First-tier Tribunal has approved the issue of the notice. Agreement is required from an authorised HMRC officer before asking for tribunal approval.

There may be occasions where HMRC cannot get information and documents from the taxpayer or wish to check the accuracy of information and documents provided. Where HMRC think it is necessary to gather information by using a third party notice, they must have the approval of the person whose tax position is being checked and the independent First-tier Tribunal before the notice can be issued. Agreement of an authorised officer within HMRC is required before the request is referred to the First-tier Tribunal. Officers cannot inspect or require auditors or tax advisers to produce documents which ask for or give advice to a client about their tax affairs.

By way of a taxpayer safeguard, there are certain things that HMRC are not allowed to request. Such items include information relating to the conduct of appeals against HMRC decisions, legally privileged information, information about a person's medical or spiritual welfare, and journalistic material.

There are also some time constraints relating to information that may be requested. This includes information over six years old, which can only be included in a notice issued by or with the approval of an authorised HMRC officer. In addition HMRC cannot give a notice in respect of the tax position of a dead person more than four years after the person's death.

Powers can be exercised before a return is received in certain circumstances. This could include a situation where there is a reason to believe that a taxpayer did not notify chargeability to tax, did not register for VAT if required, or is operating in the informal economy.

Penalties

HMRC may seek to impose a penalty where a taxpayer:

- fails to comply with an information notice;
- conceals, destroys or otherwise disposes of documents required by an information notice;
- conceals, destroys or otherwise disposes of documents that they have been notified are, or likely to be, required by an information notice; or
- deliberately obstructs an inspection that has been approved by the First-tier Tribunal.

There are three types and amounts of penalty:

- a standard penalty of £300;
- a daily penalty of up to £60 for every day that the failure or obstruction continues after the date the standard penalty is assessed;
- a tax-related penalty.

Daily or tax-related penalties cannot be considered unless a standard penalty, in respect of the failure or obstruction, has been assessed. Moreover, they can only be assessed by, or applied with, the agreement of an authorised HMRC officer.

A tax-related penalty is in addition to the standard penalty and any daily penalties. The amount of the penalty is decided by the Upper Tribunal based on the amount of tax at risk.

A person is not liable to a penalty if they have a reasonable excuse for:

- failing to comply with an information notice;
- obstructing an inspection;

and they remedy that as soon as the excuse ends. The excuse will then be treated as continuing until the correction is made. Normally, daily penalties will not be assessed after the failure has been remedied.

See *British Tax Reporter* ¶184-000.

Avoiding enquiries

Tax practitioners should be conscious of how enquiries start and try to avoid letting a client exhibit one of the signs that prompts an enquiry.

If there is something in the accounts that is likely to prompt an enquiry by HMRC, provide an explanation to HMRC when the return is submitted – this can influence the decision whether or not to investigate a case flagged as suspicious by the computer.

Try to persuade clients to keep good records, particularly of cash transactions, and to write them up promptly and regularly. If the agent can show that the records are very good, this can sometimes speed up a full enquiry.

If a client's affairs are complex, try to keep them up to date – and hopefully ward off the risks of a SCO scrutiny.

Do not be obstructive to reasonable HMRC enquiries – but at the same time, do not be afraid to ask why they need the information, if a request is considered to be unreasonable. If information is not provided, HMRC may try to obtain it from another source. This has three disadvantages:

- it will not be known what information they have been able to obtain;
- if an officer has to go to an effort to obtain information from third parties, it becomes very difficult to persuade him that his enquiries are unjustified; and
- valuable 'brownie points' that are to be gained for co-operation may be lost.

If HMRC have issued a business economic note in respect of a client's trade, get hold of it and read it before the accounts are prepared – and if the client's business departs radically from the norm, tell the officer why when the return is submitted.

What prompts an investigation?

The sort of things in accounts that influence the local tax office to select a return for a full enquiry are:

- low gross profit margin compared to similar business;
- low profit figures, or a low turnover compared to similar businesses;
- the relationship of certain expenses to income, as compared with similar businesses (e.g. a taxi driver's earnings depend on his mileage, which reflects in the cost of fuel);
- if employees earn more than the proprietor;
- if turnover is low in relation to the number of employees;
- the business is of the type where cash is involved and other traders tend to understate income or overstate expenses;
- low drawings;
- if the business was acquired as a going concern and the turnover is significantly less than that of the previous owner;
- if the accountant or other person preparing the accounts has historically submitted a number of unsatisfactory accounts for other clients; or

- where entries on the proprietor's tax returns suggest a large unexplained source of wealth (e.g. purchase of investments, premature redemption of a mortgage).

HMRC can accumulate a lot of information to suggest that a taxpayer derives income from a particular source. Some areas they would cover are:

- advertisements in newspapers (particularly local newspapers);
- returns of bank and building society interest;
- press reports of burglaries;
- investigative journalism; and
- information deriving from investigation of other people.

If that source is not shown in the accounts, they become suspicious. Observations of HMRC employees:

- 'I wonder who drives that white Rolls Royce with the personalised number plate?'
- 'That house looks well furnished; how does he do it on an income of £12,000 a year?'
- 'The chap who moved into that big house that I pass on my way to work each morning doesn't seem to be on our books; I wonder why not?'

Informers' letters – bear in mind:

- the 'X factor' (ex-spouse; ex-partner; ex-employee) – they all tend to know a lot about a client's affairs;
- jealous neighbours; and
- the fact that HMRC do not ignore anonymous letters.

Civil fraud procedures

Current procedures for civil investigation in cases of suspected serious tax fraud were introduced from 1 September 2005. The procedures are set out in *Code of Practice* 9 (2005) and apply to investigations commenced after 1 September 2005. Existing cases at that date were worked to a conclusion under the old Inland Revenue *Hansard* procedures.

Broadly, the new procedure is wholly civil, removing the threat of prosecution for the original tax offence. HMRC retain the option to consider prosecution for a materially false disclosure or materially false statement with intent to deceive. Interviews are no longer conducted under caution and tape-recorded. Investigations under the Civil Investigation of Fraud procedure cover both direct and indirect taxes where appropriate.

The civil investigation of fraud (CIF) procedures that HMRC introduced in September 2005 to deal with serious indirect and direct tax fraud in a consistent manner were extended from 1 July 2006. Up until then, the Special Civil Investigations (SCI) Unit was solely responsible for applying the new procedures. From 1 July 2006, the SCI Unit shares this responsibility with new specialist teams that have been set up within the National and Local Compliance divisions of HMRC to operate the new procedures. HMRC intend to take on a greater number of cases under the CIF procedures as a result of this move.

175

Law: *Finance Act 2009, Schedule 47 (Consequential Amendments) Order* 2009 (SI 2009/2035); *Finance Act 2008*, Sch. 36, 37, 39; *Serious Organised Crime and Police Act* 2005; *Commissioners for Revenue and Customs Act* 2005, s. 5; FA 1998, Sch. 18; TMA 1970, s. 19A, 20; *Finance Act 2008, Schedule 35 (Appointed Day and Savings) Order* 2009 (SI 2009/404); *Finance Act 2008, Schedule 37 (Appointed Day) Order* 2009 (SI 2009/402); *Finance Act 2008, Schedule 39 (Appointed Day, Transitional Provision and Savings) Order* 2009 (SI 2009/403); *Serious Organised Crime and Police Act 2005 (Commencement No. 5 and Transitional and Transitory Provisions and Savings Order* 2006 (SI 2006/378); *Serious Organised Crime and Police Act 2005 (Commencement No. 1, Transitional and Transitory Provisions) Order* 2005 (SI 2005/1521); *Afsar v R & C Commrs* (2007) Sp C 645; *Floyd v R & C Commrs* (2007) Sp C 646

Source: HMRC *Compliance Handbook*; IR *Enquiry Manual*; HMRC Brief 16/10: *Changes to time limits for assessments and claims*

Website: www.opsi.gov.uk/act/acts2005/20050015.htm
www.hmrc.gov.uk/leaflets/cop9-2005.htm

See *British Tax Reporter* ¶180-000; ¶183-100; ¶183-400; ¶185-500; ¶195-450.

230 Disclosure of tax avoidance schemes

New rules came into force from 1 August 2004, which require promoters and, in some cases, users, to provide HMRC with information ('disclosure') about certain direct tax schemes under which obtaining a tax advantage might be one of the main benefits. The rules were further extended from 1 August 2006. The three key changes effective from that date are:

● for income tax, corporation tax and capital gains tax purposes, the range of disclosable tax arrangements is no longer limited to employment or financial products. Under the revised rules, they potentially include any tax arrangement relating to any aspect of those taxes;

● for income tax, corporation tax and capital gains tax purposes, the range of disclosable tax arrangements is no longer limited by a series of filters. Instead a tax arrangement becomes disclosable if any one of a series of 'hallmarks' applies;

● disclosure of newly implemented 'in-house' tax arrangements relating to income tax, corporation tax and capital gains is now due within 30 days of implementation, rather than by the filing date for the return period in which the first transaction of the tax arrangement was implemented.

The regulations governing disclosure of avoidance schemes were amended from 1 September 2009 to include references to pension schemes.

Promoters of schemes, or the taxpayers themselves, are now obliged to make disclosure of specific information within five days of the scheme being made available by the promoter, or implemented by the taxpayer. This means that HMRC will be aware of the scheme before it has been put to any widespread use.

Disclosures may be made online via the HMRC website (www.hmrc.gov.uk/aiu/index.htm).

Promoters

Responsibility for making a disclosure to HMRC lies initially with a 'promoter'. There are four categories of persons who are to be regarded as promoters (but subject to exclusions):

(1) designers of the proposal;

(2) marketers of the proposal;

(3) designers of the arrangements as implemented; and

(4) organisers/managers implementing the arrangement.

Prescribed information

The prescribed information to be notified by a promoter has been specified as sufficient information as might reasonably be expected to enable an officer of the Board to comprehend the manner in which the proposal, or arrangements, as the case may be, is, or are, intended to operate. In particular, the following information is required:

- the promoter's name and address;
- the provision(s) by virtue of which the proposal, or arrangements (as the case may be) is, or are, notifiable;
- a summary of the proposal or arrangements and any name by which it, or they, are known;
- an explanation of each element of the arrangement or proposed arrangements and the way in which they are structured, from which the tax advantage is expected to arise; and
- the statutory provisions on which the expected tax advantage is based.

The prescribed information to be notified by a scheme user is the same as for a promoter above, except that the scheme user must also supply their name and address and that of the promoter (if any).

Hallmark schemes

From 1 August 2006, the schemes required to be disclosed are those that fall within certain hallmarks as prescribed by the *Tax Avoidance Schemes (Prescribed Descriptions of Arrangements) Regulations 2006* (SI 2006/1543). The regulations contain hallmarks (descriptions of arrangements in line with the system used for VAT). If a scheme falls within any one hallmark then it will be notifiable. The hallmarks fall into the following three categories:

(1) three generic hallmarks that target new and innovative schemes;

(2) a hallmark that targets mass marketed tax products; and

(3) hallmarks that target areas of particular risk.

The three generic hallmarks are derived from the existing 'filters' of confidentiality, premium fee and off-market terms.

Two specific hallmarks concern:

(1) schemes intended to create tax losses to offset income or capital gains tax; and

(2) certain leasing schemes.

Penalties

Failure by promoters or scheme users to comply with their obligations to notify prescribed information in respect of notifiable proposals and arrangements or failure by promoters to inform clients of the scheme reference number, renders them liable to the following penalties:

- an initial penalty of up to £5,000; and
- a further penalty of up to £5,000 for each day the failure continues after the imposition of the initial penalty.

Scheme users who fail to supply the prescribed information required in their returns are liable to a penalty of:

- £100 for the first failure;
- £500 for a second failure; and
- £1,000 for every failure thereafter.

Law: FA 2004, Part 7; TMA 1970, s. 98C; *Tax Avoidance Schemes (Prescribed Descriptions of Arrangements) (Amendment) Regulations* 2009 (SI 2009/2033); *Tax Avoidance Schemes (Information) (Amendment) Regulations* 2007 (SI 2007/2153); *Tax Avoidance Schemes (Prescribed Descriptions of Arrangements) Regulations* 2006 (SI 2006/1543); *Tax Avoidance Schemes (Information) (Amendment) Regulations* 2006 (SI 2006/1544)

Source: AAG6: *Disclosure of Avoidance Scheme – Notification of scheme reference number*

Website: www.hmrc.gov.uk/ria/disclosure-guidance.pdf

THE APPEALS SYSTEM

235 Introduction

The tax appeals system has been completely reformed from 1 April 2009.

The way in which appeals against HMRC decisions were handled up to 1 April 2009 was inherited from the two predecessor departments (namely HM Inland Revenue and HM Customs & Excise). The system reflected both developments over a period of time and the different approaches of those two former departments. Appeals were made to different tribunals, and different appeal and review processes operated in different areas depending on the particular tax or scheme involved. Since the merger of the two departments, HMRC had been considering the alignment and modernisation of the administration of appeals, particularly in the context of the Review of Powers that was looking at taxpayer safeguards and the reform of the tribunal system being developed by the Ministry of Justice. A consultation document entitled *HM Revenue and Customs and the Taxpayer: Tax Appeals against decisions by HMRC* was published in October 2007 and a *Summary of Responses and Future Direction* was published in March 2008.

The *Tribunals Courts and Enforcement Act* 2007 (TCEA 2007), sponsored by the Ministry of Justice (MoJ), is the first relevant piece of legislation governing the new regime. The Act received Royal Assent on 19 July 2007 and provides for a new two-tier tribunal structure subdivided into chambers (see below).

TCEA was followed by legislation in *Finance Act* 2008, s. 124, which gave the Treasury power, by secondary legislation, to make provisions for:

- reviews of HMRC decisions; and
- changes to appeals administration procedures,

and details the matters that such an Order might cover.

The subsequent *Transfer of Tribunal Functions and Revenue and Customs Appeal Order* 2009 (SI 2009/56) provides for the actual transfer of the functions of former tax tribunals to the new tribunals established under TCEA 2007 (broadly effective from 1 April 2009). The Order also makes consequential amendments to legislation relating to tax tribunals and the appeals they consider. In addition the Order makes changes to HMRC appeals and review processes and related administrative changes.

Law: *Tribunals Courts and Enforcement Act* 2007; *Transfer of Tribunal Functions and Revenue and Customs Appeal Order* 2009 (SI 2009/56); *Finance Act* 2008, s. 124

Source: HMRC Brief 10/09; HMRC guidance: COP 9

See *British Tax Reporter* ¶190-000.

236 Overview of the Tribunal system

Range of work

The new tribunal does not affect just tax cases. It incorporates a wide range of previously independent tribunals from the Meat Hygiene Appeals Tribunal and the Antarctic Act Tribunal to the Information Tribunal and the Special Educational Needs and Disability Tribunal through to the Social Security Tribunal, the Social Security Commissioner and the Lands Tribunal.

The two tribunals

One of the most important changes introduced by the new system is the fact that the new system introduces two different tribunals into the tax litigation process. These two new tribunals are known as:

- the First-tier Tribunal (TCEA 2007, s. 3(1)); and
- the Upper Tribunal (TCEA 2007, s. 3(2)).

The persons hearing cases in the tribunals are referred to as judges or other members (collectively, referred to as 'members'), depending on their qualifications.

The vast majority of cases will be first heard by the First-tier Tribunal which should therefore be considered as the successor to the general and special commissioners.

Under the old system, appeals from the commissioners or the VAT and Duties Tribunal would (in England and Wales) almost invariably be heard by the Chancery Division of the High Court – some cases occasionally being able to 'leapfrog' this stage to be heard by the Court of Appeal.

Under the new system, appeals from the First-tier Tribunal will invariably be heard by the Upper Tribunal. The Upper Tribunal is a superior court of record and will therefore have the same status as the High Court itself. Indeed, it is expected that the Upper Tribunal will often be presided over by High Court judges or (in Scotland) judges of the Court of Session.

Furthermore, the Upper Tribunal may exercise the same authority, powers and privileges and rights as those Higher Courts in relation to:

- the attendance and examination of witnesses;
- the production and inspection of documents; and
- all other matters incidental to the Upper Tribunal's functions.

Appeals from the Upper Tribunal will be heard by the Court of Appeal (in England and Wales and in Northern Ireland) or the Court of Session (in Scotland).

Law: TCEA 2007, s. 3, 11 and 25; *First-tier Tribunal and Upper Tribunal (Chambers) Order* 2008 (SI 2008/2684); *First-tier Tribunal and Upper Tribunal (Chambers) (Amendment No. 3) Order* 2009 (SI 2009/1590); *Qualifications for Appointment of Members to the First-tier Tribunal and Upper Tribunal (Amendment) Order* 2009 (SI 2009/1592).

Judicial review

Another major change is that judicial review powers (previously the preserve of the High Court and the Court of Session) can now be exercised by the Upper Tribunal.

Law: TCEA 2007, s. 15

See *British Tax Reporter* ¶190-350.

Chambers in the First-tier Tribunal

Tax matters are handled by a specialist tax chamber of the First-tier Tribunal (the 'Tax Chamber'). However, it should be noted that tax credit appeals are dealt with in the Social Entitlement Chamber.

Chambers in the Upper Tribunal

In the Upper Tribunal, there will be fewer chambers. Appeals from the Social Entitlement Chamber of the First-tier Tribunal will all be dealt with by the Administrative Appeals Chamber of the Upper Tribunal.

Again, tax matters are heard by a specialist finance and tax chamber of the Upper Tribunal.

Law: *Tribunal Procedures (Amendment No. 2) Rules* 2009 (SI 2009/1975); *R (on the application of Hankinson) v R & C Commrs* [2009] EWHC 1774 (Admin)

237 Bringing cases to the tribunal

One of the changes that is introduced under the new system is the giving to taxpayers a greater control over the listing of a hearing before a tribunal, particularly in direct tax cases. Historically, the request for a hearing was generally made by the tax office when negotiations reached an impasse. Whilst this definitely simplified matters for taxpayers (as it removed one level of bureaucracy from them), there was often a perceived 'closeness' between the tax authorities and the independent appeal commissioners.

Once a taxpayer appeals against a decision by HMRC (in writing to HMRC), there are now three possible courses of action. Either:

(1)   the taxpayer can make a formal request that HMRC review the matter in question;

(2)   HMRC may offer a review of the matter to the taxpayer; or

(3)   the taxpayer may notify the appeal directly to the First-tier Tribunal.

Whichever approach is taken, it does not prevent the parties from settling the dispute by mutual agreement.

If a taxpayer requires HMRC to review the matter, HMRC must set out their initial view of the matter within:

- 30 days of their receipt of the request for the review; or
- such longer period as is reasonable.

A request may not be made (and HMRC may not be required to conduct a review) if either:

- the taxpayer has already requested a review in relation to the matter;
- HMRC have already offered a review in relation to the matter; or
- the taxpayer has already notified the First-tier Tribunal of the appeal.

When HMRC offer a review to the taxpayer, the offer must include HMRC's view of the matter in question. The taxpayer then has 30 days (starting with the date stated on HMRC's offer of a review) to request that HMRC conduct a review. It is imperative that taxpayers note this time-limit carefully, because failure to accept the offer of a review will mean that the dispute will be treated as settled (in accordance with HMRC's views of the matter). Furthermore, the taxpayer may not withdraw from any agreement under s. 54(2) (requests to repudiate or resile from agreement). However, the matter may still be taken to the First-tier Tribunal (see below).

HMRC may not offer a review (and HMRC may not be required to conduct a review) if either:

- the taxpayer has already requested a review in relation to the matter;
- HMRC have already offered a review in relation to the matter; or
- the taxpayer has already notified the First-tier Tribunal of the appeal.

Nature of review

There are three outcomes of a review: the original HMRC view will be either upheld, varied or cancelled.

The nature and extent of the review will depend on what appears to be appropriate to HMRC in the particular circumstances. However, HMRC must bear in mind the steps taken by HMRC in first deciding the matter and any steps taken by any person seeking to resolve the disagreement.

The review must also take into account any representations made by the taxpayer, provided that they are made sufficiently early to give HMRC a reasonable opportunity to consider them. To avoid difficulties with this hurdle, it is therefore suggested that the representations be included in the request for a review (or the acceptance of the offer of the review).

Law: TMA 1970, s. 49E

Timescale for a review

HMRC must notify the taxpayer of their conclusions of the review and their reasoning within a 45-day period (unless the parties agree a different timescale). That 45-day period runs:

- in a case where the taxpayer requested the review, from the day on which HMRC notified the taxpayer of their initial view of the matter; and
- in a case where the taxpayer accepted HMRC's offer of a review, from the day on which HMRC received the acceptance of the offer.

The conclusions reached by the review are then deemed to stand (as a TMA 1970, s. 54(1) agreement) and the taxpayer is unable to withdraw from this deemed agreement under s. 54(2) (requests to repudiate or resile from agreement).

If HMRC fail to give their conclusions within the 45-day period (or such other period as agreed), then the initial HMRC view is deemed to stand (as a s. 54(1) agreement) and the taxpayer is unable to withdraw from this deemed agreement under s. 54(2) (requests to repudiate or resile from agreement). HMRC are required to notify the taxpayer of the conclusion that is deemed to have been reached.

This provision begs the question: what is the point of asking HMRC for a review? Not only are there concerns about the effectiveness of a review, especially if HMRC reviewers will not be able to diverge from HMRC policy; however, if HMRC fail to meet their own 45-day time-limit, then the parties are deemed to have agreed to the original HMRC position that was subject to the review in the first place. If taxpayers wish to avoid this 'Catch 22' situation, then they should try to agree with HMRC for an extension of the 45-day period so that HMRC cannot argue that they have run out of time.

In either case, however, the matter may still be taken on appeal to the First-tier Tribunal.

For appeals made to HMRC before 1 April 2009, where no appeal had been lodged with the general or special commissioners, any review that is offered or requested before 1 April 2010 will be subject to a 90-day review period rather than the 45-day period. This is subject to any agreement between the parties to vary the review period.

Law: TMA 1970, s. 49E and 49F; *Transfer of Tribunal Functions and Revenue and Customs Appeal Order* 2009 (SI 2009/56), Sch. 3, para. 5

Notification of appeal to the tribunal

Once HMRC have been notified that their decision is to be appealed against, the taxpayer may notify the First-tier Tribunal of the appeal. Once this is done, it will be for the tribunal to decide the matter.

However, different procedures apply if either:

* HMRC have given their view of the matter following a review under s. 49B; or
* HMRC have given their view of the matter when offering a review under s. 49C.

Notification of appeal to the tribunal (after review)

Once a review has been concluded (or once the period for the review expires without HMRC notifying the taxpayer of their conclusion), the taxpayer may notify the First-tier Tribunal of the appeal. This should generally be done within a 30-day period.

If the taxpayer is late in notifying the First-tier Tribunal of the appeal then the appeal may not proceed unless the tribunal gives permission.

Once the tribunal has been notified of the appeal, the tribunal will decide the matter in question.

The operation of the period for notifying the tribunal depends on the circumstances of the case:

- If HMRC have notified the taxpayer of their conclusions following the review, the period to appeal runs for 30 days starting with the date on the notice on which HMRC state their conclusions of the review.
- If HMRC have failed to conclude the review in time (usually within 45 days), the taxpayer may notify the tribunal of the appeal at any time between:
  - the conclusion of the review period (usually 45 days); and
  - the 30th day following HMRC giving the document under s. 45E(9) – the deemed conclusion of the review (being in accordance with the original decision).

Notification of appeal to the tribunal (after review offered but not accepted)

Although the review procedures are likely to catch out many taxpayers, the option of not accepting an offer of a review could be even more troublesome for taxpayers.

As previously noted, an offer of a review must be accompanied by a statement of HMRC's position (TMA 1970, s. 49C(2)). Furthermore, a taxpayer's failure to accept the offer of the review within 30 days will mean that the HMRC view will be deemed to have been accepted by both parties as their settled position from which the taxpayer cannot withdraw.

The taxpayer will, however, have the opportunity to notify the First-tier Tribunal of the appeal in such circumstances and the tribunal will decide the matter. Nevertheless, the timing will be critical.

If the notification to the tribunal is within the 30-day period (i.e. within the 30 days after the date of the document by which HMRC sends the offer of a review), then the matter can be heard by the tribunal without any additional hurdle.

However, if the tribunal is notified later (for example, because the taxpayer is unaware of the consequences of not accepting the offer of a review), then the appeal may not proceed to the tribunal unless the tribunal gives permission.

Law: TMA 1970, s. 49H(1), (4)

Procedure if no review offered or requested

In direct tax cases, the taxpayer will usually have the opportunity to request a review at the same time as notifying HMRC of the appeal against the decision. However, the taxpayer may not necessarily do this and there is no obligation on HMRC to offer one. In such circumstances, the parties will be able to continue to discuss matters until such time as the taxpayer either requests a review or applies directly to the tribunal or HMRC formally offers a review. Then, the procedures discussed above will be triggered.

See *British Tax Reporter* ¶190-380.

Income Tax

Income Tax

Income Tax

WHAT'S NEW

- For 2010–11, the starting rate of income tax for savings is 10 per cent, the basic rate is 20 per cent, the higher rate is 40 per cent and the additional rate is 50 per cent (see 50).
- For 2010–11, the basic rate limit is £37,400 (see 50).
- The additional rate of 50 per cent is payable on taxable income exceeding £150,000 (see 50).
- For 2010–11, the 10 per cent savings rate applies to savings income only, with a limit of £2,440. If an individual's taxable non-savings income is above this limit then the 10 per cent savings rate will not be applicable (see 50).
- For 2010–11, the basic personal allowance is £6,475 (2009–10: £6,475) (see 1851), the age-related personal allowance is £9,490 (2009–10: £9,490) for those aged 65 to 74, and £9,640 (2009–10: £9,640) for those aged 75 or over (see 1874), and the married couple's allowance is £6,965 (2009–10: £6,965) for those aged 75 or over (see 1874).
- For 2011–12 the basic personal allowance will rise to £7,475. However, the basic rate limit for 2011–12 will be reduced, so that higher rate taxpayers will not benefit from the increase in the personal allowance (see 1851).
- The rate applicable to discretionary and accumulation trusts rises to 50 per cent for 2010–11. Such trusts have a basic rate band of £1,000 from 6 April 2007 (see 989).
- From 2010–11, the basic personal allowance will be subject to a single income limit of £100,000. Where an individual's 'adjusted net income' is below or equal to the £100,000 limit, they will continue to be entitled to the full amount of the basic personal allowance. If 'adjusted net income' exceeds the £100,000 limit, the personal allowance will be reduced by £1 for every £2 above the income limit. The personal allowance may be reduced to nil from this income limit (see 1850).
- From 2010–11 there are three rates of tax for dividends. Dividends otherwise taxable at the 20 per cent basic rate will continue to be taxable at the 10 per cent dividend ordinary rate and dividends otherwise taxable at the 40 per cent higher rate will continue to be taxable at the 32.5 per cent dividend upper rate. Dividends otherwise taxable at the new 50 per cent additional rate will be taxable at a new 42.5 per cent dividend additional rate.
- For 2010–11 the figure for calculating car fuel benefit rises to £18,000 (£16,900 for 2009–10) (see 403).
- From 2010–11, the lower threshold for company car emissions is reduced to 130g/km. It will be reduced further to 125g/km from 2011–12.
- The £80,000 cap is to be withdrawn from the calculation of company car benefit from 6 April 2011 (see 402).
- For 2010–11 the annual Individual Savings Account (ISA) savings limit is £10,200 (£5,100 in cash). From April 2011 the savings limit will be increased annually in line with inflation (see 1921).
- The child element of child tax credit is £2,300 for 2010–11. The threshold for working tax credit remains unchanged at £6,420 and the withdrawal rate is 39 per cent for 2010–11 (see 1847).
- The annual investment allowance (AIA), available to businesses of all sizes for investment in most plant and machinery, is doubled from £50,000 to £100,000 from April 2010 (see 2366).
- A new anti-avoidance measure is introduced for certain arrangements entered into on or after 24 March 2010. The new measure disallows property loss relief against general income to the extent that the loss is attributable to AIA, but only where tax avoidance was a main purpose of the arrangements (see 2366).
- The categories of expenditure qualifying for accelerated allowances for 'energy-saving' or 'environmentally beneficial' (water-efficient) technologies are to be revised. The general category of compact heat exchangers will be removed, as will

the sub-technology of liquid pressure amplification. In the water-efficiency category, the criteria for tax and showers will be tightened. The date of the changes is not yet known but they will be made by Treasury Order prior to the summer 2010 parliamentary recess (see 2376).

- The special allowance for certain buildings in enterprise zones (EZAs) will be withdrawn from April 2011 (see 2380).
- From 1 April 2010 individuals may only deduct foreign income tax from any foreign income where they have included the foreign tax in their taxable income calculation. Legislation is also introduced to reaffirm the scope of the targeted DTR anti-avoidance rule (see 1550).
- In relation to payments received on or after 6 April 2010, a new measure, similar to the current tax exemption for payments to adopters, will mean that certain payments to special guardians, and to certain carers looking after children under a residence order, will be exempt from income tax.
- The *Pensions Act* 2008 received Royal Assent on 26 November 2008. The government plans to introduce certain reforms contained in the Act from 2012 (see 429).
- Income tax relief on pension contributions will be restricted to basic rate for individuals with earnings of £150,000 or more from 6 April 2011. *Finance Act* 2009 contains anti-forestalling provisions preventing those potentially affected from seeking to forestall this change by increasing pension savings in excess of their normal regular pattern on or after 22 April 2009 (see 429).

KEY POINTS

- Income tax is a charge on receipts, profits or gains (see 240).
- There are three main rates of income tax – the starting rate (which applies to savings income only from 2008–09), the basic rate and the higher rate – special rates apply to dividends (see 50).
- Tax is collected either by direct assessment or by deduction at source (see 2775ff.).
- HMRC have various enforcement powers at their disposal to ensure collection and recovery of tax (see 2801ff.).
- Income from employment, pensions and social security is dealt with under the provisions of ITEPA 2003 (see 250ff.).
- Certain benefits in kind are taxable on all employees irrespective of their level of earnings (see 312ff.), whereas other benefits are taxable only on P11D employees and directors (see 382ff.).
- Profits from trades, professions and vocations are taxed under ITTOIA 2005 (see 555ff.).
- Under self-assessment, income tax is charged directly on the partners in a partnership (see 750ff.).
- Special rules apply to certain categories of taxpayers, including charities (see 900ff.), farmers and market gardeners (see 940ff.); mining concerns (see 960ff.) and Lloyd's underwriters (see 970ff.).
- Special rules apply to tax the income of trusts and deceased person's estates (see 985ff.).
- Income from property is taxed under the tax on property income rules of ITTOIA 2005 (see 1200ff.).
- Foreign income may be taxable in the UK, depending on the recipient's residence and domicile status. Relief is available to prevent double taxation (see 1550ff.).
- There are various deductions and reliefs to which an individual may be entitled in computing his or her income tax liability (see 1840ff.).

- Allowable business expenses are taken into account in computing taxable business income (see 2150ff.).
- Depreciation is not an allowable expense in computing tax profits, instead capital allowances (effectively depreciation for tax purposes) may be available (see 2324ff.).
- Under the self-assessment regime, taxpayers can work out their own tax and pay the tax due by the payment date. HMRC will work out the tax for those taxpayers not wishing to perform their own calculation provided the return is submitted by 31 October.

GENERAL FRAMEWORK OF INCOME TAX

240 Introduction to income tax

Income tax is a tax on income, but also on some capital receipts (see 1448).

The taxation of employment income is generally charged under the provisions of ITEPA 2003 from 6 April 2003.

The *Income Tax Act* 2007 received Royal Assent on 20 March 2007 and came into force on 6 April 2007. The Act covers basic provisions about the charge to income tax, income tax rates, the calculation of income tax liability, and personal reliefs; various specific reliefs (including relief for losses, the enterprise investment scheme, venture capital trusts, community investment tax relief, interest paid, gift aid and gifts of assets to charities); specific rules about trusts, deduction of tax at source, manufactured payments and repos, the accrued income scheme and tax avoidance; and general income tax definitions.

The *Income Tax (Trading and Other Income) Act* 2005 (ITTOIA 2005) received Royal Assent on 24 March 2005 and took effect from 6 April 2005. The Act covers the taxation of trading, property, savings and investment and miscellaneous income.

Certain persons are exempt from all taxes on income and gains, while some are specifically exempt from income tax. Certain income is also exempt from income tax.

Law: ITA 2007; ITTOIA 2005; ITEPA 2003; *Salisbury House Estate Ltd v Fry* [1930] AC 432; *Mitchell and Edon v Ross* [1962] AC 813

See *British Tax Reporter* ¶110-000.

244 Proforma income tax computation

The amount of a person's income to which the income tax rates are to be applied is generally known as 'taxable income'.

Income Tax

Taxable income is statutory 'total income' less amounts *deductible from* total income, as opposed to amounts *deductible in computing* total income.

To find a person's ('the taxpayer') liability to income tax for a tax year, the following steps are applied:

Step 1 – Identify the amounts of income on which the taxpayer is charged to income tax for the tax year. The sum of those amounts is 'total income'. Each of those amounts is a 'component' of total income.

Step 2 – Deduct from the components the amount of any relief (under a provision listed below) to which the taxpayer is entitled for the tax year. The sum of the amounts of the components left after this step is 'net income'.

Step 3 – Deduct from the amounts of the components left after Step 2 any allowances to which the taxpayer is entitled for the tax year (under ITA 2007, Pt. 3 Ch. 2 or ICTA 1988, s. 257 or 265 (individuals: personal allowance and blind person's allowance)).

At Steps 2 and 3, the reliefs and allowances are deducted in the way which will result in the greatest reduction in the taxpayer's liability to income tax (ITA 2007, s. 25(2)).

Step 4 – Calculate tax at each applicable rate on the amounts of the components left after Step 3 (see 50 for rates).

Step 5 – Add together the amounts of tax calculated at Step 4.

Step 6 – Deduct from the amount of tax calculated at Step 5 any tax reductions to which the taxpayer is entitled for the tax year (under a provision listed below).

Step 7 – Add to the amount of tax left after Step 6 any amounts of tax for which the taxpayer is liable for the tax year under any provision listed below.

The result is the taxpayer's liability to income tax for the tax year.

Reliefs

If the taxpayer is an individual, the provisions referred to at Step 2 above are broadly as follows:

(a)   early trade losses relief;
(b)   share loss relief;
(c)   gifts of shares, securities and real property to charities, etc.;
(d)   payments to trade unions or police organisations;
(e)   pension schemes: relief under net pay arrangement: excess relief;
(f)   pension schemes: relief on making of claim;
(g)   trade loss reliefs: against general income; carry-forward loss relief; terminal loss relief; and post-cessation relief;

(h)   property reliefs: carry-forward; against general income; and post-cessation;

(i)   employment loss relief against general income;

(j)   loss relief against miscellaneous income;

(k)   interest payments; annual payments and patent royalties;

(l)   manufactured dividends on UK shares: payments by non-companies; manufactured interest on UK securities: payments not otherwise deductible;

(m)   plant and machinery allowances in a case where the allowance is to be given effect under CAA 2001, s. 258 (special leasing of plant and machinery);

(n)   industrial buildings allowances, in a case where the allowance is to be given effect under CAA 2001, s. 355 (buildings for miners, etc.: carry-back of balancing allowances);

(o)   patent allowances in a case where the allowance is to be given effect under CAA 2001, s. 479 (persons having qualifying non-trade expenditure);

(p)   deduction for liabilities related to former employment;

(q)   strips of government securities: relief for losses;

(r)   listed securities held since 26 March 2003: relief for losses: persons other than trustees); and

(s)   relief for patent expenses.

Tax reductions

If the taxpayer is an individual, the provisions referred to at Step 6 above are broadly as follows:

(a)   tax reductions for married couples and civil partners;

(b)   EIS relief;

(c)   VCT relief;

(d)   Community investment tax relief;

(e)   qualifying maintenance payments;

(f)   payments for benefit of family members;

(g)   spreading of patent royalty receipts;

(h)   relief for interest on loan to buy life annuity;

(i)   top slicing relief;

(j)   relief for deficiencies;

(k)   double taxation relief;

(l)   relief for foreign tax where no double taxation arrangements;

(m)   relief for qualifying distribution after linked non-qualifying distribution; and

(n)   relief where foreign estates have borne UK income tax.

Tax reductions are deducted in the order which will result in the greatest reduction in the taxpayer's liability to income tax for the tax year

If the taxpayer is an individual, the provisions referred to at Step 7 above are broadly as follows:

(a)   gift aid: charge to tax;

(b)   pension schemes: the short service refund lump sum charge;

(c)   pension schemes: the special lump sum death benefits charge;

Income Tax

193

(d) pension schemes: the unauthorised payments charge;

(e) pension schemes: the unauthorised payments surcharge;

(f) pension schemes: the lifetime allowance charge;

(g) pension schemes: the annual allowance charge; and

(h) social security pension lump sum.

Law: ITA 2007, s. 23, 24, 25, 26–30

See *British Tax Reporter* ¶148-400.

EMPLOYEES AND THE CHARGE ON EMPLOYMENT INCOME

INTRODUCTION: SCOPE OF THE CHARGE ON EMPLOYMENT INCOME

250 The charge on employment income

Income tax was formerly charged under Sch. E. The *Income Tax (Earnings and Pensions) Act* 2003 (ITEPA 2003), which received Royal Assent on 6 March 2003, replaced the Sch. E legislation with a charge on employment income. The charge applies in respect of:

- emoluments from any office or employment (see 252ff.);
- pensions (see 420ff.);
- other income directed to be charged under the charge on employment income, e.g. certain social security benefits (see 365ff.), certain contributions by employers to retirement benefit schemes (see 430ff.) and certain termination payments (see 438ff.).

Income tax is generally charged on a receipts basis rather than on earnings.

It is generally accepted that liability falls on the holder of the office or employment and that it is not possible to assign the right to income to avoid that liability. Although distinction perhaps needs to be drawn between the income and any underlying right, a taxpayer's instructions, say, for payment of his state retirement pension into his wife's bank account does not amount to a disclaimer of the pension, which remains taxable on him.

Law: ITEPA 2003, s. 6(1), 7(2), (3), 10(2); *Meredith-Hardy v McLellan* (1995) Sp C 42; *Dewar v IR Commrs* [1935] 2 KB 351

See *British Tax Reporter* ¶405-000.

252 The meaning of 'office'

An 'office' (see 250) has been judicially described as:

> 'a subsisting, permanent, substantive position, which had an existence independent of the person who filled it, which went on and was filled in succession by successive holders ... '

Company directors are the most numerous examples of office holders.

However, a rigid requirement that the office be permanent is no longer appropriate, nor is it vouched by any decided case, and continuity need not be regarded as an absolute qualification. Although an office is often associated with some constituent instrument (creating and defining it but more than a job description), or some degree of public relevance and formality of appointment, none of these is essential.

The question whether a person is the holder of an office is a mixed question of fact and law, involving the application of the facts as found to the proper legal meaning of the word 'office' in the charge on employment income (see 250).

Law: *McMenamin (HMIT) v Diggles* [1991] BTC 218; *Edwards (HMIT) v Clinch* [1982] BTC 109; *Great Western Railway Co v Bater* [1922] 2 AC 1

See *British Tax Reporter* ¶400-010.

253 Employed or self-employed?

Employees are taxed under entirely different provisions from those which tax the self-employed. It is therefore necessary to distinguish an employment from a trade, profession or vocation.

In deciding whether a contract of service exists, all the relevant facts are looked at and weighed in the balance. Some of the more obvious facts are as follows.

Income Tax

For employment	*Against employment*
Control by another over the manner in which the work is performed.	No control by another over the manner in which the work is done.
The person performing the work is restricted from delegating his work to another.	The person performing the work is free to delegate his duties to another.
The person performing the work does not bear the losses nor keep the profits.	The person performing the work bears the losses and keeps the profits.
Tax and National Insurance contributions are withheld by the person for whom the work is done.	No tax or National Insurance contributions are withheld from payments.
The parties agree employment.	The parties agree self-employment.
The person for whom the work is done provides the tools and equipment.	The person performing the work provides his own tools.
The person for whom the work is done lays down regular and defined hours of work.	The person performing the work is free to decide when he wishes to work.
The person for whom the work is done cannot withhold payment.	The person for whom the work is done is free to withhold payment until the work is performed as agreed.
The person for whom the work is done can dismiss.	The person for whom the work is done cannot dismiss the worker or cancel the work once the work is agreed, without compensation.
The person for whom the work is done has an obligation to provide work and to pay the 'employee' when no work is available.	There is no obligation to provide the 'employee' with work, or to pay him when no work is available.

Individually, the above points do not prove the existence or otherwise of a contract of employment. A HMRC leaflet (IR 56, *Employed or self-employed?*) gives useful guidance on what HMRC regard as important criteria. However, they are points which influence the decision whether such a contract exists. The list is not exhaustive, and any fact which appears relevant in a particular case is taken into account and considered. The important factor is the actual performance of the contract.

Law: ITEPA 2003, s. 4; *Athenaeum Club v R & C Commrs* [2010] TC00325; *Sherburn Aero Club Limited v R & C Commrs* TC00006; *Hall (HMIT) v Lorimer* [1993] BTC 473; *Andrews v King (HMIT)* [1991] BTC 338; *Sidey v Phillips (HMIT)* [1987] BTC 121; *Walls v Sinnett (HMIT)* [1987] BTC 206; *Warner Holidays v Secretary of State for Social Services* [1983] ICR 440; *Fall (HMIT) v Hitchen* [1973] 1 WLR 286; *Market Investigations Ltd v Minister of Social Security* [1969] 2 QB 173; *Ready Mixed Concrete (South East) Ltd v Minister of Pensions and National Insurance* [1968] 2 QB 497; *Davies (HMIT) v Braithwaite* [1931] 2 KB 628

Website: www.hmrc.gov.uk/leaflets/c1.htm

See *British Tax Reporter* ¶400-050.

260   Agency workers

Certain agency workers are charged to tax under the provisions of ITEPA 2003 as employees rather than under ITTOIA 2005 as self-employed persons. The agency for which they work applies the PAYE scheme to them and deducts tax and NICs accordingly.

The workers affected are those who:

● are under an obligation to render personal services to a client; and
● are subject to the right of supervision, direction or control as to the manner in which they render those services; and
● are supplied to the client by an agency; and
● are under an obligation to render those services under the terms of a contract between the worker and the agency.

Only expenses permitted for employees (see 1990) can be deducted from earnings as an agency worker.

Law: ITEPA 2003, s. 44; *Bhadra v Ellam (HMIT)* [1988] BTC 25; *Brady (HMIT) v Hart (trading as Jaclyn Model Agency)* [1985] BTC 373

See *British Tax Reporter* ¶407-500.

265   Personal service companies

From 6 April 2000, anti-avoidance provisions apply to prevent workers avoiding tax and National Insurance contributions (NICs) (see 8732) by offering their services through an intermediary, such as a personal service company. The legislation is widely referred to as the IR 35 rules after the number of the 1999 Budget press release in which they were first announced. To assist workers in determining whether they are within the scope of the rules, HMRC will provide an opinion on a contract if submitted together with any relevant details of recent engagements. Details of this service are given on the HMRC website.

With effect from 9 April 2003, income received by domestic workers, including nannies and butlers, in respect of services provided after this date via an intermediary, are caught by the intermediaries legislation. This anti-avoidance measure means that workers who would otherwise be treated as employees, if they were engaged directly, can no longer avoid paying tax and NICs on any payments of salary by using a service company. Additional tax and NICs may have to be paid on the 'deemed payment' (see below).

Broadly, the 'IR 35' rules provide that:

Income Tax

(1) where an individual ('the worker') personally performs, or has an obligation personally to perform, services for the purposes of a business carried on by another person ('the client');

(2) the performance of those services by the worker is referable to arrangements involving a third party, rather than referable to a contract between the client and the worker; and

(3) the circumstances are such that, were the services to be performed by the worker under a contract between him and the client, he would be regarded as employed in the employed earner's employment by the client,

then the relevant payments and benefits are treated as emoluments paid to the worker in respect of his or her employment. These rules apply irrespective of whether the client is a person with whom the worker holds any office or employment. Under the rules, a deemed salary payment, subject to tax under PAYE, may fall to be made to the worker on 5 April at the end of the tax year. The tax and NICs due on this deemed payment must be accounted for by 19 April.

To ascertain whether a deemed salary payment falls to be made, and the extent of any such payment, the following procedure should be followed.

Step 1

Find the total amount of all payments and other benefits received by the intermediary in the year in respect of the relevant engagements and reduce that figure by five per cent.

Step 2

Add to the result of Step 1 the amount of any 'payments and benefits' received by the worker (or the worker's family: ITEPA 2003 s. 61(3)(b)) in respect of 'relevant engagements' during the tax year, from any person other than the intermediary, where such amounts are not chargeable to income tax as employment income and would be so chargeable if the worker were employed by the client.

This rule ensures that any amounts paid directly to the worker as part of an arrangement to avoid the application of these provisions is caught.

Step 3

Deduct the amount of any expenses met in the year by the intermediary, or (from 6 April 2002) met by the worker and reimbursed by the intermediary, that would have been deductible from the emoluments of the employment if the client had employed the worker and the expenses had been met by the worker out of those emoluments. For 2002–03 onwards, where the intermediary provides a vehicle for the worker, deduct any mileage allowance that would have been available had the worker been directly employed and provided their own vehicle.

If the result of applying Step 3, or at any later point, is nil or a negative amount, there is no deemed employment payment. Neither, by implication, is there a deductible deemed amount.

Step 4

Deduct the amount of any capital allowances in respect of expenditure incurred by the intermediary that could have been claimed by the worker had he been employed by the client and had incurred the expenditure.

Step 5

Deduct any contributions made in that year for the benefit of the worker by the intermediary to an approved retirement benefit scheme or personal pension plan that if made by an employer for the benefit of an employee would not be chargeable to income tax as income of the employee.

Step 6

Deduct the amount of any employer's NIC paid by the intermediary for the year in respect of the worker.

Step 7

Deduct the amount of any payments or other benefits received in the year by the worker from the intermediary that are chargeable to income tax under Sch. E and do not represent items in respect of which a deduction was made at step 3 above. From 6 April 2002, mileage allowance payments and passenger payments are deemed to be chargeable under the charge on employment income provisions (formerly Sch. E) and therefore included in the amount to be deducted.

If the result at this point is nil or a negative amount, there is no deemed charge on employment income.

Step 8

Assume that the result of Step 7 represents an amount together with employer's National Insurance contributions on it, and deduct what (on that assumption) would be the amount of those contributions. The result of this 'netting down' is the deemed employment payment.

Example

Peter and Monica offer their services through a service company. The shares in the service company are owned equally by Peter and Monica. During the tax year 2007–08, they each undertake some engagements that fall to be classified as relevant engagements under the new rules. They also undertake some other engagements that are not relevant engagements.

During the year, the service company received income of £50,000 in respect of relevant engagements undertaken by Peter and a further £30,000 in respect of relevant engagements undertaken by Monica. The company also has further income of £40,000, which is not derived from relevant engagements.

The company pays a salary of £30,000 to both Peter and Monica. Employer's NIC of £3,171 is paid in respect of each salary payment ((£30,000 − £5,225) × 12.8%). The company also makes a contribution of £5,000 each to a registered employer's pension scheme.

Peter incurs travelling expenses of £2,500 in relation to the relevant engagements undertaken by him, and Monica incurs travelling expenses of £1,000 in relation to the relevant engagements undertaken by her.

At the end of the tax year, the company must calculate whether a deemed payment falls to be made. This is calculated as follows:

	Peter £	Monica £
Income from relevant engagements	50,000	30,000
Less: travelling expenses	(2,500)	(1,000)
pension contributions	(5,000)	(5,000)
employer's NICs paid in year	(3,067)	(3,067)
5% deduction for expenses	(2,500)	(1,500)
(£50,000/£30,000 × 5%)	36,933	19,433
Less: salary paid in year	(30,000)	(30,000)
		(10,567)
Deemed payment and employer's NIC	6,933	
Less: employer's NIC		
$\dfrac{12.8}{112.8} \times £6,933$	(786)	
Deemed salary payment	6,147	

No deemed salary payment falls to be made to Monica as the salary paid to her during the year exceeds the intermediary's income from relevant engagements that she undertook during the year after taking account of relevant expenses.

However, a deemed salary payment of £6,054 falls to be made to Peter on 5 April 2008.

Interaction with construction industry deduction scheme

It may be that the company income on which the deemed salary payment is based has already suffered a tax deduction under the construction industry scheme. These deductions may be repaid once the company submits its accounts, but in the meantime there may be an unfortunate cash-flow effect.

In order to avoid this, HMRC have issued ESC C32, which provides relief from interest on late payment of tax and NIC under the personal service company rules to the extent that the liability is offset by repayments due under the construction industry scheme. It is a condition that CIS repayments are claimed before 31 January following the tax year to which the deemed salary payment relates.

Law: ITEPA 2003, Pt. 2, Ch. 8; FA 2000, s. 60 and Sch. 12; *Autoclenz Ltd v Belcher* [2009] EWCA Civ 1046; *Dragonfly Consulting Ltd v R & C Commrs* (2008) EWHC 2113 (Ch); *Jones v Garnett (HMIT)* [2007] UKHL 35; *Island Consultants Ltd v R & C Commrs* (2007) Sp C 618

Source: Inland Revenue *Tax Bulletin* (issue 45, February 2000); Inland Revenue *Tax Bulletin* (issue 47, June 2000)

Website: www.hmrc.gov.uk/ir35/index.htm

See *British Tax Reporter* ¶407-600.

267   Managed service companies

Finance Act 2007 contained provisions that deem dividend (and indeed any other non-employment) income to be employment income where individuals provide their services through managed service companies (MSCs) and their income is not already treated as employment income. This means MSCs have to operate and account for PAYE tax and NICs on all payments that individuals receive for services provided through the MSC. If the MSC does not pay the tax and NICs, HMRC will be able to recover them from others, principally the MSC's director and the person who provided the company and management services for the company to the individual.

Broadly, MSCs are personal service companies, often referred to as 'managed personal service companies' or 'composites'.

In a composite company scheme before the FA 2007 changes led to their virtual disappearance, several (typically 10 to 20) otherwise unrelated workers were made worker-shareholders of the company. The size of the company was restricted to ensure that profits did not exceed the threshold for the small companies' rate of corporation tax. Each worker usually held a different class of share in the company. This enabled the company to pay different rates of dividend to each worker, and in practice the dividend received would be directly related to the company's income from the end client for work undertaken by that worker.

In a managed personal service company (MPSC) scheme, in contrast to a composite company, there was only one worker per company structure. The MSC scheme provider performed similar functions for MPSCs as for composite companies – it usually provided a director and exercised financial and management control of the company (e.g. operating the bank account, invoicing, preparing accounts and tax returns, etc. leaving the worker simply to provide the service to the end user), typically performing this function for many MPSCs.

Income Tax

The MSC was used to save both tax and NICs. Many contractors working through MSCs had a company paying them a salary of around £5,000, to use up their personal allowance and earn them a deemed contribution record. Because the company typically took on numerous short-term contracts in different places, the worker was also able to claim tax- and NIC-free home-to-work travel expenses, as each location was a temporary workplace for that employment. The company paid corporation tax at 19 per cent on the profit (after deducting the scheme provider's charges), and paid out the net by way of dividend. To the extent that the worker was a basic rate taxpayer, there was no further tax to pay, and for higher rate earners the effective tax rate was only 25 per cent on the dividend received. Crucially, dividends are classed as investment income, not earnings, so NIC liability did not arise.

HMRC believed that most of these MSC schemes involved working arrangements that fell foul of the IR35 rules (see 265), but when faced with nearly a quarter of a million such companies HMRC's compliance teams could not cope with challenging them. Some of the workers were from overseas and had left the UK by the time questions could be asked of their companies, and others simply put their companies into liquidation in order to avoid being challenged.

The anti-avoidance provisions introduced by FA 2007 do not try to change the status of the workers, who are always employees and/or directors and therefore 'employed earners'. Instead, they deem any non-employment payments (in effect, dividends) made by a MSC to be earnings for NIC and PAYE purposes. Unlike IR35, the rules create the liability at the time of payment, not at the end of the tax year. Note that the PAYE liability was backdated to 6 April 2007, but the NIC regulations could not be laid before Royal Assent to the Act, so they applied only from 6 August 2007.

They also solve the problem of runaway workers and liquidated employers by creating transfer of debt rules that enable HMRC to pursue the scheme providers for any unpaid liabilities. It is hardly surprising that MSC schemes closed down quickly when their liabilities were no longer avoidable (or indeed easy to evade for the unscrupulous).

Law: FA 2007, Sch. 3; ITEPA 2003, s. 61A–61J, 688A; *Income Tax (Pay as You Earn) (Amendment No. 3) Regulations* 2007 (SI 2007/2296); *Income Tax (Pay as You Earn) (Amendment No. 2) Regulations* 2007 (SI 2007/2069); *Social Security (Contributions) (Amendment No. 5) Regulations* 2007 (SI 2007/2068); *Social Security Contributions (Managed Service Companies) Regulations* 2007 (SI 2007/2070); *Social Security Contributions and Benefits Act 1992 (Modification of Section 4A) Order* 2007 (SI 2007/2071)

Source: HMRC: *MSC Guidance: Chapter 9 and Section 688A ITEPA and Transfer of Debt: MSCs*

See *British Tax Reporter* ¶400-010.

TAXABLE EARNINGS

273 Taxable earnings

Under the provisons of ITEPA 2003 the charge to tax on employment income is a charge to tax on general earnings and specific employment income. 'Taxable earnings' and 'taxable specific income' are two new labels used to identify income at various stages from which it arises to when it becomes chargeable to tax in a particular tax year.

Law: ITEPA 2003, s. 10(2); *Wilcock (HMIT) v Eve* [1994] BTC 490; *Mairs (HMIT) v Haughey* [1993] BTC 339; *Shilton v Wilmshurst (HMIT)* [1991] BTC 66; *Hamblett v Godfrey (HMIT)* [1987] BTC 83; *Pritchard (HMIT) v Arundale* [1972] Ch 229; *Hochstrasser (HMIT) v Mayes* [1960] AC 376

See *British Tax Reporter* ¶412-000.

274 Earnings

'Earnings' means:

- any salary, wages or fee;
- any gratuity or other profit or incidental benefit of any kind obtained by the employee if it is money or money's worth; or
- anything else that constitutes an emolument of the employment.

'Money's worth' means something that is of direct monetary value to the employee, or capable of being converted into money or something of direct monetary value to the employee.

The most obvious forms of earnings arising from an office or employment are the salary, wages, fees or commissions payable, in cash or by cheque. Other receipts or non-cash benefits in kind may be directly regarded as emoluments and therefore taxable; particular regard should be given to:

- gifts, awards and prizes (see 285);
- rewards for future services (see 275);
- restrictive covenants (see 283);
- contractual entitlement (see 277);
- receipts from third parties (see 284; 285);
- tips (see 285);
- non-cash benefits of lower-paid employees (see 288);
- reductions in wages in return for benefits (see 279); and
- discharging an obligation of the employee (see 292).

As far as non-cash benefits in kind are concerned, some benefits are taxable irrespective of the level of an individual's earnings (see 312ff.); certain other benefits are treated as

Income Tax

203

emoluments for employees earning at a rate of £8,500 a year or more (including benefits in kind and expenses not covered by a dispensation) and for directors (see 382ff.).

For the treatment of reimbursed expenses and round-sum allowances, see 322.

Law: ITEPA 2003, s. 62; *O'Leary v McKinlay (HMIT)* [1991] BTC 37

See *British Tax Reporter* ¶412-000.

275 Reward for future services

A receipt that is remuneration for future services may be taxable despite the element of non-recurrence or the fact that the employee did not expect it (see 285).

Payments made to induce a person to enter into employment are taxable if they represent an advance of salary.

Law: *Glantre Engineering Ltd v Goodhand (HMIT)* [1982] BTC 396; *Pritchard (HMIT) v Arundale* [1972] Ch 229; *Riley (HMIT) v Coglan* [1967] 1 WLR 1300; *Jarrold (HMIT) v Boustead* [1964] 1 WLR 1357

See *British Tax Reporter* ¶412-450.

277 Contractual entitlement

The fact that an employee is contractually entitled to a payment is not conclusive in establishing that the payment was either taxable or non-taxable.

See further 284 and 285.

Law: *Jarrold (HMIT) v Boustead* [1964] 1 WLR 1357; *Denny v Reed (HMIT)* (1933) 18 TC 254

See *British Tax Reporter* ¶412-400.

279 Reductions in wages in return for benefits

If a benefit is directly received in exchange for a reduction in wages or salary, the benefit could be regarded as money's worth chargeable as emoluments (without reference to specific benefits legislation): the 'salary sacrifice' may represent the amount into which the benefit could be converted.

It may be much more tax-efficient from the point of view of an employee earning less than £8,500 a year to receive a wage plus a non-convertible benefit, such as a car or private medical insurance, than to receive a higher wage with a requirement that the wage be expended in a particular way. This is known as the *Heaton v Bell* trap after the case in which the principle was established. However, it should be noted that subsequent to this case legislation was introduced to make it clear that where an employee is offered the choice of a car or cash he is taxed on whichever he chooses.

Although a farm worker is by statute entitled to opt for higher wages in lieu of free board and lodging, he is not taxed on the latter's value if, when his wages are added to it (see 386), he remains lower-paid.

Law: ITEPA 2003, s. 119; *Heaton (HMIT) v Bell* [1970] AC 728

283 Restrictive covenants

The provisions relating to the taxation of payments for entering into restrictive covenants currently apply where an individual holds, has held or is about to hold an office or employment, and he gives in connection with his holding of the employment an undertaking the tenor or effect of which is to restrict him in the conduct of his activities. It is immaterial that the undertaking may be qualified, or even unenforceable.

In the situations above, any payment made in respect of the undertaking, or its total or partial fulfilment, either to the individual or to any other person, which would not otherwise be treated as an emolument of the office or employment (see 273), is so treated, and tax under the charge on employment income is chargeable for the tax year in which it is paid.

The circumstances in which HMRC do not charge tax under the above provisions in respect of certain undertakings made by individuals under a financial settlement when their employment is terminated are set out in a statement of practice. The statement makes it clear that where sums are paid in settlement of financial claims relating to the employment which the employee could have pursued in law, and the employee accepts that the sums payable satisfy claims and legal rights to which he may be entitled under the terms of his employment or statutory provisions, then a charge does not arise. However, a charge under that provision may arise where an agreement contains specific provisions as to the employee's conduct or activities which involve an undertaking going beyond the settlement of existing claims and rights which he may have against the employer.

Payments caught by the charge are deductible by the employer (see 2240).

Law: ITEPA 2003, s. 225, 226; *Vaughan-Neil v IR Commrs* [1979] 1 WLR 1283

Source: SP 3/96, *Section 313 ICTA: Termination payments made in settlement of employment claims*

See *British Tax Reporter* ¶423-500.

Income Tax

284 Receipts from third parties

The fact that a payment is received from someone other than the employer is not a bar to its assessment as an emolument. The test for liability to tax is whether the payment is received as a reward for services. The fact that the payment is unlikely to be repeated further assists in a finding that the payment is non-taxable. However, where there is an element of expectation on the part of the employee to receive the payment, or it can be said to be reasonable to expect that the payment will be made, then it may well be held to be taxable.

Entertainment provided by a third party to employees is not taxable on the employees (see 383).

For the tax treatment of gifts and tips, etc., see 285.

Law: *Wright v Boyce (HMIT)* [1958] 1 WLR 832; *Moorhouse (HMIT) v Dooland* [1955] Ch 284; *Blakiston v Cooper* [1909] AC 104

See *British Tax Reporter* ¶437-850.

285 Gifts, awards, prizes and tips

A gift received from an employer or third party by an employee is not automatically tax-free. It is taxable if it is received as a reward for services past, present or future (or simply, if it is provided by reason of the individual's employment by way of voucher or, in the case of an employee earning at a rate of £8,500 a year or more or a director, otherwise: see 318, 382). Some factors of relevance in deciding whether a voluntary payment, benefit or perquisite may escape tax are as follows.

- Whether, from the recipient's standpoint, it accrues to him as a reward for services.
- If his contract of employment entitles him to receive the payment there is a strong ground for holding that it accrues by virtue of the employment and is therefore remuneration.
- The fact that a voluntary payment is of a periodic or recurrent character affords a further, though less cogent, ground for the same conclusion.
- If it is made in circumstances which show it is given by way of a present or testimonial on grounds personal to the recipient (e.g. a collection made for a vicar of a given parish because he is so poor, or a benefit for a professional cricketer in recognition of his long and successful career), then the proper conclusion is likely to be that it is not a reward for services and is therefore not taxable.

Awards made under most staff suggestion schemes are tax-free (ITEPA 2003, s. 321 and 322, formerly ESC A57).

Long service awards

Tax is not charged in respect of certain awards made to directors and employees as testimonials to mark long service. Such awards must take the form of tangible articles or shares in an employing company (or another group company), costing the company up to £50 per year of service; the recipient must have completed at least 20 years' service and have had no similar award within the previous ten years.

For gifts received on retirement or dismissal, see 438ff.

Taxed award schemes

Employers who provide non-cash incentive awards and prizes (e.g. cameras or holidays), and most of those who provide such prizes for employees of third parties, can operate HMRC's 'taxed award scheme'. Such schemes:

- allow the provider of the incentive to pay the tax due on the award, so that the incentive for the recipient is not blunted by having to pay tax on it; and
- provide an economical means of collecting the tax due (in bulk, instead of from individual recipients).

Before an incentive campaign begins, the provider enters into a contract with HMRC's Incentive Award Unit (for the address and contact details, see 1) to pay the tax on the total value of the awards to be made. The provider can pay tax at different rates: there are separate contracts for different rate schemes.

The amount of the tax payable is worked out on the grossed-up value (see 210) of the award to the recipient. Providers must give recipients details of the tax paid so that they can complete their tax returns, or claim repayment if appropriate. Providers give HMRC details of recipients so that any higher-rate tax can be collected.

Most awards under taxed award schemes are suitable for inclusion in a PAYE settlement agreement (see 2750) instead of a taxed award scheme. However, a third party who provides awards to the employees of another and who wishes to pay the employees' tax bill must use a taxed award scheme.

An information pack on the scheme can be obtained from the Incentive Award Unit.

Christmas parties and gifts provided by third parties

Gifts made by a third party to any employee are not taxable provided the cost does not exceed £250 in any tax year: if the cost is, say, £251, all of the £251 is assessable. The same concession allows employers to provide one or more annual events at a cost of up to £150 per head without the employees incurring tax liability in respect of the benefit. The limit of £150 applies from 2003–04 onwards.

Tips and service charges

Tips are generally part of an employee's taxable income in the same way as his other earnings (see 284). However, not all employees return full details of the tips they receive. Therefore, HMRC may estimate the tips earned on the basis of the facts available to ensure that the correct amount of tax is paid. Before doing this, HMRC establish first who is in a

Income Tax

position to receive them. Wherever possible they negotiate agreed figures with the employees concerned or with their representative where large numbers are employed at any one establishment.

For the PAYE position in relation to tips, see 2784.

Law: ITEPA 2003, s. 323 (Long service awards), s. 264 (Annual parties and functions), s. 270 and 324 (Small gifts from third parties), s. 703 (PAYE settlement agreements); *Wicks v Firth (HMIT)* [1982] BTC 402; *Moore v Griffiths (HMIT)* [1972] 1 WLR 1024; *Ball (HMIT) v Johnson* (1971) 47 TC 155; *Moorhouse (HMIT) v Dooland* [1955] Ch 284; *Calvert (HMIT) v Wainwright* [1947] KB 526; *Reed (HMIT) v Seymour* [1927] AC 554

See *British Tax Reporter* ¶412-450.

288 Non-cash benefits of lower-paid employees

It is not only cash payments given to an employee that are taxable under the general charge on employment income provisions (see 250). The charge applies to money or money's worth.

'Money's worth' means those things that can be converted into money by the employee. The taxable amount for an employee earning less than £8,500 a year is the amount of money into which he can lawfully convert the benefit, whether or not he does so. It follows that if a restriction is placed upon the use of the benefit by the employer so that the employee cannot convert it into money without being in breach of the condition, he is not taxed on it, provided the restriction is not a sham, e.g. the gift to the employee could only be sold to a scrap merchant. Speaking of the position of employees earning at a rate of less than £8,500 per annum, Lord Reid declared in a House of Lords case:

'In my judgment the recipient of a perquisite other than a sum of money can be assessed and can only be assessed, on the amount of money which he could have obtained by some lawful means by the use or in place of the perquisite.

I say by lawful means because I see no ground for HMRC being entitled to disregard a genuine condition restricting the recipient's right to use or dispose of the perquisite. But of course if any restrictive condition is a sham or inserted simply to defeat the claims of HMRC it can be disregarded.'

Payment in the form of a tradable asset is a payment by the employer for the purposes of PAYE (see 2784).

For the tax charge on benefits provided for employees earning at a rate of £8,500 p.a. or more and for directors, see 382ff.

Law: *Heaton (HMIT) v Bell* [1970] AC 728; *Laidler v Perry (HMIT)* [1966] AC 16

See *British Tax Reporter* ¶412-850.

292 Discharging an employee's obligation

The amount upon which an employee earning less than £8,500 a year is taxable in respect of a benefit in kind is the second-hand value or the amount he would receive for it if he sold it (see 288). However, this rule does not apply if the employer gives cash to the employee to buy goods or discharges a debt that the employee has incurred. If either is the case, the employee is taxed at the full cost to the employer of providing the benefit. Hence, if an employer pays his employee's council tax, the cost is to be part of the employee's emoluments (though the employer may obtain a business deduction for it: see 2240).

The same principle applies where the employer releases the employee from an obligation owed to the employer. If the employer discharges a debt of the employee in respect of something from which the employee is entitled to an exemption, such as living accommodation (see exceptions to charge in 314), those exceptions still apply and the employee is only charged, at the cost to the employer, on payments to which the exemption does not apply.

Example 1

In order to induce the employee to stay in the house in which he was living the company paid his various outgoings. It was held that he was correctly assessed on an amount equal to the cost to the employer of discharging the employee's debts.

Example 2

An employee agreed with her employer that, while she was away from work on a nine-month course of study, her employer would advance to her, on loan, the pay that she would have earned had she been working. The arrangement was that the loan need not be repaid if she remained with her employer for a further 18 months upon her return. She did so. The loan was cancelled and it was held that she had been correctly assessed on the amount of the loan.

Law: *Richardson (HMIT) v Worrall* [1985] BTC 508; *Clayton (HMIT) v Gothorp* (1971) 47 TC 168; *Nicoll (HMIT) v Austin* (1935) 19 TC 531

See *British Tax Reporter* 412-850.

293 Medical treatment and insurance

If an employee or director undergoes medical treatment or diagnosis and the employer reimburses the employee, or settles his personal medical bill, the amount reimbursed, etc. is taxable (see 292).

However, if the employer contracts direct with the provider of the medical services, no taxable benefit arises for non-P11D employees (see 382ff.), as conversion into cash is not possible (see 288). For directors and P11D employees, the cash equivalent of the benefit is the cost incurred by the employer in providing the treatment, less any amount which the employee or director makes good (see 388). However, there is no such benefit where:

- the director or P11D employee is provided with medical treatment outside the UK (including in-patient treatment); and
- the need for the treatment arises while the employee is outside the UK for the purpose of performing the duties of his employment.

'Medical treatment' includes all forms of treatment for, and all procedures for diagnosing, any physical or mental ailment, infirmity or defect.

One health screening and one medical check-up per employee per year may be treated as exempt from the charge to income tax and NICs.

Medical insurance

Employers commonly contribute to medical insurance schemes for their employees. Members of the employee's family or household are sometimes covered. Any premium paid by the employer in respect of a policy under which the *employer* is the insured person is not a benefit chargeable on the employee.

However, a premium paid by the employer in respect of a policy under which the *employee* (or a member of his family or household) is the insured person, less any part of the premium which the employee makes good (see 388), constitutes a chargeable benefit in the case of directors and P11D employees. (The benefit is not taxable for a non-P11D employee, as conversion into cash is not possible: see 288.) However, there is no such taxable benefit where the employee, etc. is provided with medical treatment outside the UK and the need for it arises while the employee is outside the UK for the purpose of performing the duties of his employment.

Law: ITEPA 2003, s. 325; *Income Tax (Exemption of Minor Benefits) (Revocation) Regulations* 2009 (SI 2009/695)

Source: Revenue Interpretation, Inland Revenue *Tax Bulletin*, May 1993, p. 74

Website: www.hmrc.gov.uk/bulletins/index.htm

See *British Tax Reporter* ¶437-900.

294   Sickness, maternity, paternity, adoption and disability payments

Employees are taxed under the charge on employment income provisions of ITEPA 2003 on sick pay or disability pay (paid to them or to members of their family or household) where such payments have been arranged with the employer. Statutory maternity pay (SMP), statutory paternity pay (SPP), statutory adoption pay (SAP) and statutory sick pay (SSP) paid by the employer are also taxable under these charging provisions.

A lump sum received under a life, accident or sickness insurance policy is not normally regarded as income for tax purposes. From 6 April 1996, continuing benefits from certain policies are also exempt (see 1366); otherwise, there is a standard 12-month period for exemption of benefits received in respect of a fall in earnings caused by ill-health or disability.

For the tax treatment of social security benefits received in respect of disability, etc. see 365ff.

Law: ITEPA 2003, s. 221, 660

Website: www.hmrc.gov.uk/calcs/ssp.htm

See *British Tax Reporter* ¶420-050.

295   New Deal 50plus payments

Employment credits or training grants paid under the New Deal 50plus scheme are exempt from income tax. The exemption applies in respect of payments from the start date of the scheme (25 October 1999).

Law: FA 2000, s. 84

See *British Tax Reporter* ¶490-550.

298   Relocation expenses and benefits

Certain relocation expenses and benefits paid on behalf of, reimbursed to, or provided for employees who are obliged to move with their job or in order to start a new job are exempt from tax.

Specified costs incurred in the tax year of the move or the following tax year are exempt up to a limit of £8,000. Eligible benefits include those in respect of disposal, acquisition and the new residence itself (or abortive acquisition), transport of belongings, travelling and subsistence. PAYE need not be applied to relocation packages, even if the £8,000 limit is exceeded – the benefits will instead be reported in the P11D or P9D. If the inspector is satisfied that flat rate allowances do no more than reimburse employees' eligible expenses, they may be paid gross in similar fashion. Strictly, an interest-free bridging loan is not an eligible expense but, if the rest of the employee's relocation package does not use up the £8,000 exemption the balance can be converted into a number of days' relief by which the income tax charge on the beneficial loan (see 406) is reduced. Relief for international travel continues to be available under other provisions (see 1574).

For guaranteed selling price schemes operated by employers in respect of employees' homes, see 388.

Law: ITEPA 2003, Pt. 4, Ch. 7

Website: www.hmrc.gov.uk/guidance/relocation.htm

See *British Tax Reporter* ¶433-850.

302   Incidental overnight expenses

To reduce the burden on employers of identifying and reporting to HMRC what would otherwise be taxable expenses, certain minor personal expenditure are exempt from tax. The exemption applies to amounts of personal expenditure up to £5 per night in the UK and £10 for each night overseas. If this limit is exceeded, the whole amount is taxable. Thus, in most cases, it is still necessary to analyse the receipts submitted with employees' expenses claims.

Law: ITEPA 2003, s. 240

Source: *Personal Incidental Expenses – Guidance Notes for Employers*

See *British Tax Reporter* ¶432-900.

304   Work-related training

Certain work-related training may be provided free of tax. The exemption applies both to that funded by an employer and that funded by a third party.

To qualify for the exemption, the training must be 'work-related'. This covers any training course or other activity designed to impart, instil, improve or reinforce any knowledge or skills or personal qualities which are, or are likely to be useful to the employee in performing the duties of any 'relevant employments' or which will qualify or better qualify the employee to undertake any relevant employment or such charitable or voluntary activities which could be undertaken in connection with the relevant employment. An employment is a 'relevant employment' if it is the employee's current job or a job which he is to hold with his employer or a person 'connected' with his employer (see 3826).

The expenditure covered by the exemption is limited to the cost of providing the training plus any 'related costs', such as the cost associated with an assessment or obtaining a qualification.

A number of specific exclusions from the exemption ensure that it is restricted to genuine work-related training. For example, the exemption is unavailable to the extent that the 'training' is actually for recreation, entertainment, reward or offered as an inducement. Activity which is partly work-related training and partly recreation is apportioned.

The transfer of assets under the guise of work-related training is also excluded from the exemption, except where, for example, an employee is provided with stationery, books or other written material, audio or video tapes and compact or floppy disks as part of the work-related training.

Incidental overnight expenses in connection with the training are tax-free to the same degree as those paid to an employee away on a business trip (see 302).

Law: ITEPA 2003, s. 240, 250

See *British Tax Reporter* ¶432-500.

308   Miscellaneous exemptions and concessions

The following do not constitute taxable earnings for employees or directors:

- employers' contributions to approved retirement benefit schemes, etc. or personal pension schemes;
- priority share allocations (see 340);
- cash in lieu of miners' free coal, or the free coal itself;
- awards in respect of long-service or staff suggestions (see 285);
- financial assistance, etc. for travel either: from home to work for the severely disabled; or when public transport is disrupted; or when employees are occasionally required to work until at least 9 p.m.; or for offshore oil and gas, etc. workers travelling to and from the mainland (see 1580, 1994); or for members of the armed forces (see 318); or for additional travelling and subsistence costs for 'away' jobs, etc. (see 2000);
- clergymen's reimbursed/settled council tax (or other statutory amounts) if the premises belong to the charity or organisation, etc. and lower-paid clergymen's reimbursed/settled heating, cleaning or similar expenses;
- costs either reimbursed, etc. in respect of work-related training (see 304) or incurred by an employer with a view to retraining present or past employees (see 2241);
- scholarship income, including certain payments of up to £7,000 (£5,500 before 6 April 1992) for attending sandwich courses and certain education allowances under the Overseas Service Aid Scheme (see 408); sponsorship by the Home Office for training as a trainee probation officer on a two-year postgraduate course was, in one case, held to be within this exemption;
- a pension, lump sum, etc. to be given on an employee's death or retirement to a member of his family or household and pensions in respect of awards of the Victoria Cross or various other medals, etc.;
- grants or resettlement payments, etc. made to individuals ceasing to be MPs or MEPs;
- free or subsidised canteen meals (see 412) or meal vouchers of up to 15p a day (see 2000);
- employer-provided workplace nurseries (see 409);
- vouchers exchangeable for the use of sports or recreational facilities (see 318);
- small gifts by third parties (see 285);
- employers' expenditure on certain social events (see 285);

Income Tax

- incidental overnight expenses of up to £5 per night in the UK, or £10 per night outside the UK paid by the employer (see 302);
- mobile telephones (see 415);
- the provision of routine health checks (see 293);
- uniforms provided as a necessary part of employment duties;
- payments under the New Deal 50plus scheme (see 295);
- works bus services (see 417);
- the provision of certain computer equipment for use by the employee (see 416);
- provision of cycles and cyclists' safety equipment (see 418);
- small amounts of private use of items provided by the employer for use in the employee's work (see 396); and
- contributions by employers towards additional household costs incurred by employees who work some or all of the time at home. For payments of up to £3.00 per week (£2.00 per week prior to 2008–09), no supporting evidence is required to obtain the income tax exemption. For payments of more than £3.00 per week, supporting evidence is required (see 383).

See also 383.

Law: ITEPA 2003, s. 242, 243, 244, 290, 291, 306, 307, 320, 638

See *British Tax Reporter* ¶437-450.

BENEFITS COVERED BY ALL-EMPLOYEE LEGISLATION

312 All-employee charge on benefits

Certain benefits are dealt with by specific legislation and are taxable (or exempt), irrespective of the level of earnings of the employee or office holder (see 314–322). This does not affect the charge under general provisions where benefits can be directly regarded as earnings (see 273ff.).

Specific provisions also apply to charge other benefits received by employees earning £8,500 p.a. or more (P11D employees) and directors (see 382ff.).

314 Living accommodation

A director or employee, or a member of his family or household (see 386) who is provided with accommodation, such as a company house or flat, rent-free or at a nominal rent, is generally liable to tax on it under the provisions of ITEPA 2003, Pt. 3, Ch. 5 (irrespective of his rate of pay). The main charge is based on the greater of the 'annual value' and rent paid by the 'person providing the accommodation' less, in either case, any sums made good by the employee. The 'annual value' is usually the gross rateable value of the property, adjusted for Scottish property, but is the open market rental for property outside the UK or property rented from a connected person.

Note that the charge is avoided if the employee pays rent of an amount at least equal to the benefit otherwise computed under these provisions.

Where a property is provided as living accommodation to more than one employee or director in the same period, the amounts chargeable on each is reduced so that the total does not exceed the amount which would have been chargeable had the property been provided as living accommodation to a single employee.

Exceptions

There is no charge to tax in the following circumstances.

- It is necessary for the proper performance of the employee's duties that he resides in the accommodation. It must be the nature of the duties of his employment that make it necessary for him to reside there (e.g. a lighthouse keeper) and not just a condition imposed by his employer. This exception, sometimes called 'representative occupation', does not apply to directors.
- The accommodation is provided for the better performance of the duties of his employment, and his is one of the kinds of employment in the case of which it is customary for employers to provide living accommodation for employees: e.g. hostel wardens. In deciding whether the practice is customary, statistical evidence, the time for which the practice has continued and whether it is generally accepted are factors to be considered. This exception does not apply to directors.
- There being a special threat to his security, special security arrangements are in force and he resides in the accommodation as part of those arrangements, e.g. the prime minister's occupation of 10 Downing Street.
- The employer is an individual and the accommodation is provided in the normal course of his domestic, family or personal relationships, e.g. to a domestic servant.
- The accommodation is provided by a local authority (see 5800) on terms no more favourable than those on other accommodation it provides, e.g. a council house for a council employee.
- The accommodation is provided temporarily by way of subsistence for an MP, member of the Scottish Parliament or the devolved assemblies for Wales and Northern Ireland, or other person holding an office or position within the *Ministerial and other Salaries Act 1975*, or to a member of that person's family or household.

Expensive accommodation

In addition to the standard charge above, there is a further charge where the cost to the employer exceeds £75,000. Here, the charge is the excess multiplied by the 'official rate of interest' (at the beginning of the tax year: see 406) less any excess rent. HMRC do not seek an additional charge under these provisions where the main charge is calculated on the basis of the market rental.

Income Tax

The cost is the actual cost to the employer, not the value of the property when it is occupied by the employee except, broadly, where the employer owned the property throughout the six years ending with the employee's first occupation. Each property can be considered separately for the purposes of the £75,000 test.

In ascertaining the cost of providing the accommodation, any improvement expenditure must be added to the acquisition cost. From this may be deducted any sums reimbursed by the tenant. The figure in respect of excess rent is the amount by which the rent paid by the employee is greater than the value to him of the accommodation as determined under the general charge (i.e. 'annual value').

Example

Sam, on 6 April 1997, took up residence in a house provided by his employer. His employer bought the property in July 1991 for £300,000 and installed a sauna at a further cost of £10,000. Sam pays rent that is £5,000 in excess of the annual value.

Thus the cost of provision is £300,000 + £10,000 = £310,000.

As the official rate of interest on 6 January 2008 was 6.25% the additional charge for 2007–08 is £9,687 ((£310,000 −75,000) × 6.25%) − £5,000).

If the taxpayer earns at a rate of £8,500 a year or more or is a director, a charge may also arise in respect of other expenses connected with the accommodation, e.g. rates, heating, provision of furniture, etc. (see 398).

Law: ITEPA 2003, Pt. 3, Ch. 5, s. 108; *Vertigan v Brady (HMIT)* [1988] BTC 99; *Stones v Hall (HMIT)* [1988] BTC 323; *Tennant v Smith* [1892] AC 150

Source: ESC A56, *Benefits in kind; the tax treatment of accommodation in Scotland provided for employees*

318 Vouchers and credit cards

Where a voucher other than a 'cash voucher' (see 320) is provided for an employee (whatever his rate of pay) by reason of his employment, there is generally a charge on the employee (although some exemptions apply – for example where the voucher is for the provision of a benefit that would, if provided directly, be tax-free). It may arise in the tax year in which the expense is incurred or the voucher is received or used but it is reduced by amounts the employee reimburses or amounts deductible if the employee had incurred the expense himself.

A benefit received by an employee (whatever his annual pay) through the use of a credit card or credit-token is also taxed as an emolument. It arises in the tax year in which the card or token is used but it is reduced by amounts deductible if the employee had incurred the expense himself or amounts he reimburses. The definition of 'credit-token' refers to a card, token, document or other thing given to a person by another person who undertakes:

- that on the production of it (whether or not some other action is also required) he will supply money, goods and services (or any of them) on credit; or
- that where, on the production of it to a third party (whether or not some other action is also required), the third party supplies money, goods and services (or any of them), he will pay the third party for them (whether or not taking any discount or commission).

In either case, the liability of the employee will be the cost to the employer (or other person bearing the cost) of providing the voucher, token and goods/services obtained. If, as a result of its use, the user obtains money or goods which are tradable (or the voucher itself is tradable), the appropriate amounts are also brought within the PAYE scheme (see 2784); if the employee does not reimburse the tax to the employer within 30 days of the deemed payment in point, that tax is treated as an additional PAYE income of the employee.

Use of a credit token or voucher by a relation of the employee is treated as if it were use by the employee.

Exclusions

The rules do not apply where a voucher or credit-token is exchangeable for the right to make use of most types of in-house (or shared-employer) sporting or recreational facilities or is provided by a person other than the employer to obtain alternative entertainment for the employee. Nor are they applicable where a voucher or token is used to provide parking (including, since 1999–2000, parking for cycles and motor cycles) at or near the workplace. There are also exemptions for certain travel vouchers, warrants for particular journeys and allowances and payments for travel or leave by members of the armed forces. There is no charge on certain meal vouchers (see 412, 2000). See also 302 regarding incidental overnight expenses.

HMRC have the power to make regulations to remove from a tax charge a voucher or credit token used to provide an otherwise tax-exempt employee benefit.

Law: *Finance Act* 2006, s. 63; ITEPA 2003, Pt. 3, Ch. 4

Source: SP 6/85, *Incentive awards*

320   Cash vouchers

A 'cash voucher' is a document or stamp exchangeable for a sum of money not substantially less than its cost of provision where the sum for which it is exchangeable would have been chargeable to tax if received directly, i.e. where it is not a gift or otherwise exempt.

Cash obtained by virtue of cash vouchers given by employers to their employees would generally be chargeable to tax as emoluments under the charge on employment income provisions (ITEPA 2003) (see 274). However, this rule is overridden by a provision treating

Income Tax

as emoluments the amounts for which they are capable of being exchanged, unless they are paid under approved schemes. Such vouchers are also generally within the PAYE system (see 2784); if the employee does not reimburse the tax to the employer within 30 days of the deemed payment in point, that tax is treated as an additionalemolumentsof the employment.

Law: ITEPA 2003, Pt. 3, Ch. 4

321 Employee liability and indemnity insurance

In certain circumstances employees are entitled to a deduction for the costs of meeting or defending claims to do with liabilities arising out of their work, or insuring against those costs; equally, no tax liability arises on the employee when such costs are met by the employer. The deduction is available provided expenditure relates to a 'qualifying liability' (broadly an act or omission of a person in the capacity of office holder or employee, or a claim in respect of such an act or omission, but not including any deduction where it would be illegal for the employer to insure against them), or where a premium relates to a 'qualifying contract of insurance' (which is widely defined). A similar relief is available in respect of expenditure defrayed by former employees which occurred in the year in which the employment ceased, or in the following six years, and where the payment would have been allowable as above but for the fact that the employment ceased.

Normal rules apply to the timing of relief. Generally, relief is available in the year in which the payment is made against the emoluments of that year for the employment in respect of which the payment arises. In relation to ex-employees, relief reduces the employee's total income of the year (and, if that income is insufficient, his excess chargeable gains over allowable losses for that year).

Law: ITEPA 2003, s. 346; FA 1995, s. 92

Website: www.hmrc.gov.uk/bulletins/index.htm

322 Reimbursed expenses and round-sum allowances

The reimbursement of an expense incurred in the performance of an employee's duties is not generally regarded as a perquisite or other amount which would fall within the meaning of the term 'emoluments' (see 274).

If, however, the amount reimbursed to the employee is excessive, the excess could be regarded as emoluments and taxable as such. Further, any round-sum allowance made 'by reason of employment' (see 273) to cover expenses incurred, or to be incurred, is generally regarded as an emolument rather than a reimbursement of actual expenses on the facts of each case. There will be exceptions to this rule on specific facts (see 302 regarding incidental overnight expenditure). Further, where an individual receives an allowance in respect of duties performed outside his controlled duties as an employee, it may not be 'for acting as an employee'.

HMRC have introduced a set of benchmark scale rates that employers can use to make certain day subsistence payments free of tax and National Insurance contributions to employees who incur allowable business travel expenses.

Contributions by an employer of up to £3.00 per week (£2.00 per week prior to 2008–09) towards additional household costs incurred by employees working at home may be paid tax free (see 383).

If the employee earns at a rate of £8,500 or more a year, expenses payments made by the employer which would not otherwise be chargeable to tax are treated as emoluments and are assessable (see 382). The level of reimbursed expenses may take the employee into this category (see 386, but see 302 regarding incidental overnight expenditure).

There are special exemptions for payments in respect of travel assistance during strikes or for the disabled (see 308), of pure training (see 304) or retraining (of the sort set out at 2241), of subsistence (see 2000), of rates but probably not council tax for certain employer-provided accommodation and of special allowances or expenses for civil servants abroad, armed forces, reserve or auxiliary forces and clergymen.

Where any amount is treated as taxable emoluments, an employee may claim a deduction to the extent that his expenses have been incurred wholly, exclusively and necessarily in the performance of his duties. A dispensation may be granted for regular payments which would be taxable but for which the employee could later claim relief (see 1991).

Law: *Donnelly (HMIT) v Williamson* [1982] BTC 11; *Owen v Pook (HMIT)* [1970] AC 244

Website: www.hmrc.gov.uk/manuals/eimanual/EIM05230.htm

EMPLOYEE SHARE SCHEMES

323 Share incentives generally

All shares and securities acquired in connection with an employment come within the scope of the employment-related securities regime, including shares acquired by directors or employees on the formation of a company. The rules also extend to rights or opportunities to acquire securities, and to benefits in connection with shares and securities that are not otherwise chargeable to tax. They cover cases where the securities, or opportunities or rights to acquire the securities, are provided by a person other than the employer, and where the securities are not directly received by the employee.

In general the treatment of remuneration received through shares and other forms of security follows the main principle that applies to other forms of remuneration such as cash and benefits. That principle is to charge to income tax and National Insurance contributions (NICs) the value that the employee receives as reward for his services at the time he has access to that value.

Income Tax

In deciding whether the employee has received reward for services in connection with securities, it is necessary to look at the extent to which, if at all, the employee has given consideration other than services. If, for example, the employee has paid the full market value for a simple share received from his or her employer, then there will be no employment reward and no charge to income tax and NICs on acquisition of the share. Any future normal commercial growth in the value of the share is within the capital gains tax regime.

Similarly, if an employee is given a free share as a reward for services, and pays income tax and NICs on the full value of that share, then the employee is exposed to exactly the same potential financial loss if the venture fails as he or she would have been having risked his or her own funds from the outset. Future normal commercial growth in value of such a security is also within the capital gains regime.

In more complex situations, the employee may receive a share as a reward for services, with the acquisition structured so that the value is acquired at some future point, contingent on some future event or condition being fulfilled and as a reward for future services. This right or opportunity is not dissimilar to a share option. When that opportunity crystallises and the employee receives the benefit of that value, then the rules also tax that benefit.

An employee earning at a rate of £8,500 or more a year (or a director) who acquires shares at less than market value under an opportunity available by reason of his employment may be treated as if his employer has lent him that amount interest-free (see 410).

Relief for National Insurance contributions on share option gains is dealt with at 8784.

Relief is given in respect of CGT for amounts charged to income under these provisions (see 5925).

Law: FA 2003, s. 140, Sch. 22; ITEPA 2003, s. 471–487; *Hunt (HMIT) v Murphy* [1992] BTC 28; *Ball (HMIT) v Phillips* [1990] BTC 470; *Abbott v Philbin (HMIT)* [1961] AC 352

Source: HMRC *Employee Share Schemes Manual*; *Tax Bulletin*, Special Edition (May 2005)

Website: www.hmrc.gov.uk/shareschemes/index.htm

See *British Tax Reporter* ¶464-000.

324 Unapproved schemes

Unapproved share schemes may take various forms, including unapproved share option schemes and share incentives. Employees and officers may be offered the opportunity to acquire shares in their capacity as employees and officers, such incentives including:

- formal incentive schemes, such as employee benefit trusts;

- individual service agreements;
- pre-emption rights, especially in the case of directors;
- flotations or public offers;
- management buy-outs; or
- one-off offers to individuals or groups of individuals.

Also falling under the heading of unapproved schemes are (for example) the following:

- share acquisitions at an undervalue;
- participation in public offers;
- share sales at an overvalue;
- conditional acquisition of shares;
- acquisition of convertible shares; and
- lifting of restrictions on shares, growth in value of shares in dependent subsidiaries and shares providing special benefits.

Although unapproved schemes do not have the tax advantages associated with the approved schemes, they are useful in some circumstances. Because they do not need to meet the stringent conditions for HMRC approval, they are more flexible in their application and can be better tailored to the needs of the organisation. They are often used where the company wishes to reward selected employees only and where this is not possible within the confines of an approved scheme. Unapproved schemes are often cheaper and quicker to set up and there is no approval process that has to be undertaken.

Law: ITEPA 2003, Pt. 7, Ch. 1–5

326   Key tax charges in employee shares

Where a participating employee exercises an option under an approved scheme, there will always be a charge to income tax on exercise. There is no exception to this rule. The income tax charge is calculated as follows:

Value of shares at date of exercise	x
Less: Cost of shares	(x)
Charge at date of grant (if any)	(x)
Taxable income	x

The grant of an option by an employer to an employee is a disposal of an asset by the employer (the option itself) and an acquisition of that asset by the employee at that time. Where the grant of the option is in recognition of past, present or future office or employment services, which would be the case where the obtaining of the option was by reason of holding the office or employment as a director or an employee, the market value rule that would apply is disapplied in determining the employer's disposal proceeds of the option (and the employee's cost of acquiring the option) for capital gains tax purposes. Therefore, the gain realised by the employer on the grant of the option is computed as follows:

(1) actual consideration received for granting the option; *less*

(2)   the cost of providing the option (if any).

When the option is exercised by the employee, the grant and exercise of the option become a single transaction. Thus, at the time of exercising the option, the grant of the option ceases to be a disposal by the employer, or an acquisition by the employee, of an asset. Any capital gains tax paid in respect of the grant of the option is set off or refunded. It should be noted that the cessation of the option on its exercise does not amount to a disposal of the option by the holder (i.e. employee).

Where an employee is granted an option to acquire shares in his employer or some related company, there are potential income tax charges:

- on the grant of an option under an approved company share option plan where any amount paid for the grant plus the amounts payable to acquire the shares is less than the market value of the shares at the date of the grant. The granting of any other employment-related options does not give rise to an income tax charge;
- on the exercise of the option, where the market value of the shares acquired exceeds the amount paid for them. The employee must be UK resident at the time the option was granted.

An income tax charge may also arise where an option is assigned or surrendered without being exercised.

The market value rule

Where the option is granted over shares which are already in existence (i.e. they are currently held by another shareholder or some form of trust), the disposal of the shares on the exercise of the option and the corresponding acquisition by the employee would normally fall within TCGA 1992, s. 17 because the option would have been granted in recognition of the employee's services and as a result the consideration for both the disposal and acquisition would be the market value of the shares at that time. However, following the decision in *Mansworth v Jelley*[2003] BTC 3, the market value rule does not apply. Instead, the consideration for the disposal and acquisition will be the actual exercise price.

The *Mansworth v Jelley* case concerned the amount which should be taken as the 'cost' of the shares acquired under an option granted to an employee. Mr Jelley was non-resident when the options were granted although resident when they were exercised. Therefore there was no income tax charge, which would otherwise have been treated as part of his cost for CGT purposes. That being the case his cost would have been merely the amount paid to acquire the shares on the exercise of the option, so that the whole of his profit would have been liable to CGT. However, a vital point (and one overlooked by many, including HMRC) was that the shares he received were already in existence (probably held by some form of trust) and so he could argue successfully that the market value rule in TCGA 1992, s. 17 applied because his acquisition was a transaction not at arm's length and/or was in recognition of his services as an employee. So his base cost was the market value of the shares when he acquired them, which being the same as the sale proceeds, meant that there was no capital gain and the whole of his profit escaped tax. TCGA 1992, s. 144A was introduced with effect from 10 April 2003 to deny the use of the market value rule in circumstances where assets are acquired as a result of the exercise of an option.

(If the shares acquired by Mr Jelley had been issued to him by the company, the market value rule could not have applied as this requires the transaction to be both an acquisition and a disposal and the company does not make a disposal when it issues shares.)

Computation of gains or losses

The current position is therefore that, if the employee subsequently disposes of shares which were acquired on the exercise of the option, then, regardless of whether those shares were in existence prior to his acquisition, the gain or loss on that disposal is computed as follows:

(1)   disposal proceeds; *less*

(2)   the actual consideration paid for the shares on exercise of the option; *less*

(3)   any amount(s) charged to income tax as a result of being granted the option or the acquisition of the shares.

Shares acquired by the exercise of options prior to 10 April 2003

It is theoretically possible (but highly improbable) that taxpayers still hold shares which were acquired before 10 April 2003 by the exercise of employment-related options. Following the decision not to appeal against the Court of Appeal's ruling in *Mansworth v Jelley*, HMRC issued a technical note which advised that in all cases where shares were acquired on the exercise of an option prior to 10 April 2003, the gain or loss on the subsequent disposal of the shares was to be computed by deducting from the sale proceeds:

● the market value of the shares at the time the option was exercised; *plus*
● any amount chargeable to income tax on the exercise of that option.

This advice was heavily criticised at the time. In particular Counsel for Mr Jelley described the guidance as 'incomplete and seriously muddled'. HMRC had overlooked two key aspects of the case:

(1)   the market value rule cannot apply where the shares were issued by the company to the employee. That rule does not apply unless there is both an acquisition and a disposal and the company does not make a disposal when it issues shares;

(2)   the income tax charge is treated as a element of the acquisition cost under TCGA 1992, s. 38, but, if the market value rule applies, s. 38 is displaced. The two are thus incompatible.

It took six years before HMRC admitted that the guidance they had issued in 2003 was incorrect (*Revenue & Customs Brief* 30/09, issued on 12 May 2009). It accepted that, where the market value rule applied, that was the full measure of the acquisition cost; it was not to be augmented by the amount of any income tax charge.

This 'new understanding' was to be applied to cases where there was an open enquiry.

The *Mansworth* case only affects unapproved share option schemes and EMIs. It does not affect the treatment of gains arising under SAYE option schemes or CSOPs.

Law: FA 2006, s. 92; TMA 1970, s. 33 and 43; *Mansworth v Jelley*[2002] BTC 270

See *British Tax Reporter* ¶465-000.

327 Restricted securities

Where employees acquire securities (or an interest in securities) by reason of their employment, their value (less anything paid for them) will generally be taxable as employment income. If the securities have restrictions or conditions attached to them, including risk of forfeiture, then those restrictions will affect the value and, generally, the securities will be worth less than they would be without those restrictions (this depression in value is often referred to as a 'discount').

The legislation provides that the employee is charged to income tax and NICs when additional value in a security is accessed as a result of lifting a restriction. Each restriction placed on securities will have a proportionate effect on its market value. Each time a restriction is lifted or varied there will be a charge based on the market value of the discount relating to that restriction which represents the proportion of the securities' value that was not taxed on acquisition.

The charge is calculated using a formula. In the simplest case (where there is only one restriction) the charge is equal to the restriction's effect on the market value of the securities at the time it is lifted. The result is that the employee is taxed on the whole share in two stages – an amount at acquisition relating to the unrestricted proportion of the securities and the balance when the restriction is lifted. By focusing on proportions of the securities' market value at each event, the legislation ensures that capital growth on previously taxed proportions is not included in the computation of the income gain.

Exceptions

There are three situations where securities would be 'restricted securities' but for this specific provision excepting them. If the only restrictions on the securities are covered by this section then the securities are outside the scope of ITEPA 2003, Pt. 7, Ch. 2 and are not therefore taxed under the provisions of these rules. These situations are as follows:

- the securities are unpaid (or partly paid) and will be forfeited if the balance is not paid up when required – provided there is nothing that might specifically prevent the payment being made;
- a requirement to dispose of the securities on cessation of employment for misconduct (commonly known as a 'bad leaver' provision); and
- the securities are redeemable for payment.

The legislation provides that no charge to tax arises on the receipt of the securities where the securities are restricted under restrictions covered by ITEPA 2003, s. 423(2) (forfeitable securities), and that restriction will cease within five years from acquisition. In other words, there must be a risk that the securities will be forfeited within five years of receipt, and if that were to happen the person holding them would not receive their full market value. Where this situation arises there is no income tax charge on the receipt of the securities, unless they are 'partly paid' securities within Pt. 7, Ch. 3C, or are acquired under conversion rights within Pt. 7, Ch. 3, or securities option rights within Pt. 7, Ch. 5.

Law: ITEPA 2003, s. 435–446

See *British Tax Reporter* ¶465-125.

328 Approved share option schemes

To encourage share ownership, the government have introduced various tax-advantaged share option schemes (known as 'approved' schemes). Provided that certain conditions are met, normally there is no charge to income tax under general principles on the grant or exercise, etc. of an option (see 324) where shares are acquired under an approved share option scheme.

For details of the various tax-approved schemes, see 329ff.

Website: www.hmrc.gov.uk/manuals/ersmmanual/index.htm

See *British Tax Reporter* ¶469-650.

329 Company share option schemes

Company share option plans (CSOPs) are HMRC-approved, tax advantageous share option plans. The schemes are discretionary, allowing the company to select the directors and employees it wishes to reward. Options are granted to the employee/director. No income tax is payable on grant. Normally there is no income tax payable on the increase in value of the shares between grant and exercise provided that certain conditions have been met. For capital gains tax purposes, the cost of the shares is normally the price paid for them.

The value of shares for which a person may hold options under any approved scheme established by his employer or any associated company is limited to £30,000.

The share price must be specified at the time the option is granted and must not be manifestly less than their market value at that time.

The employee must not exercise his option less than three years or more than ten years after the date on which it was granted. Previously, approved options could only be exercised once every three years. However, FA 2003, s. 139, Sch. 21, removes the charge to income tax on a second option exercise within three years of a previous exercise. This is designed to make schemes easier for companies to administer and to give employees in such schemes more flexibility. There are special provisions on exercise in relation to individuals who die (see eligible participants, below).

The procedure for obtaining approval is substantially the same as that for approved savings-related share option schemes (see 330).

The rules do not affect share options which were granted before 6 April 1984.

It is possible within limits to subject shares within an approved scheme to restrictions where the restriction is either attached to all shares of the same class or requires that the directors and employees sell all the shares upon cessation of employment and that shares be sold when acquired, if the acquisition of the shares occurs after cessation of employment. Restrictions which are not permissible include those attaching to shares which limit the holder's freedom to dispose of the shares, or their proceeds of sale, or to exercise any right conferred by the shares; they do not include restrictions imposed by the Stock Exchange Model Rules for Securities Transactions by Directors, nor to any terms of a loan relating to repayment or security.

Eligible participants

Only full-time directors and employees may participate in a scheme approved before 1 May 1995. The 'full-time' requirement is removed in respect of schemes approved on or after that date.

However, a company may include provisions in a scheme which permit options to be exercised by participators who, by the time of the exercise, may no longer be full-time employees. A provision may also be included allowing options to be exercised by the personal representatives of a deceased participator; in such cases, the exercise must take place within one year of the employee's death but subject to the ten-year limit.

Any person having 'a material interest' in a close company is ineligible to participate in an approved share scheme involving that company. Broadly, a person has a 'material interest' for this purpose if he, alone or with any 'associate(s)' (see 4268) beneficially owns or is able to control more than ten per cent of the ordinary share capital of the company or on the company's liquidation would be entitled to more than ten per cent of its assets. Excluded from consideration are the personal shareholdings of fellow beneficiaries, though trust shares remain to be aggregated. A 'close company' for present purposes is, in brief, one which is controlled by five or fewer 'participators' (see 4256) or over half the assets of which could be distributed on its liquidation between five or fewer participators or director participators.

Companies of which a jointly-owned company (JOC) has control can join in approved share schemes run by either of the JOC's parent companies. Consent will only be given where an undertaking has been given by the grantor of the relevant share scheme to notify HMRC of changes in the ownership or control of any of the appropriate parties. For rights granted before 21 December 1992 the concession applied only to the JOC, and it is unlikely that the rights could be altered without jeopardising the scheme.

Law: ITEPA 2003, Pt. 7, Ch. 7, Sch. 3, para. 46, Sch. 4, para. 34; FA 1996, s. 114, 115, Sch. 16; *IR Commrs v Reed International plc* [1995] BTC 373; *IR Commrs v Eurocopy plc* [1991] BTC 459

Website: www.hmrc.gov.uk/shareschemes/csop_general.htm
www.hmrc.gov.uk/shareschemes/csop_general_ees.htm
www.hmrc.gov.uk/shareschemes/index.htm
www.hmrc.gov.uk/bulletins/index.htm

See *British Tax Reporter* ¶477-250.

330   Approved savings-related share options

As regards savings-related share option schemes, providing certain rules imposed by HMRC are complied with, no charge is made on the grant or exercise of the option or on the increased value of the shares (for such charges, see 324). There are a number of conditions to be fulfilled to obtain approval, including the following:

- the shares must be bought through a certified contractual savings scheme and any loans must not be payable before a date approved by HMRC except where the employee dies or leaves his job before that date;
- the price paid for the shares must not be less than 80 per cent of their market value when purchased;
- all employees or directors must be able to participate in the scheme, except individuals who have held five per cent of the share capital of a close company (see 4250) in the last 12 months;
- all those who have worked for a qualifying period must be permitted to participate in the scheme (the qualifying period must not exceed five years);
- the shares must be fully paid ordinary shares which are non-redeemable and they must be either quoted on a stock exchange or be shares in a subsidiary company.

An approved scheme must not permit a person's total contributions under certified contractual savings schemes linked to approved schemes to exceed £250 a month or impose a minimum contribution on the amount of a person's contributions which exceeds £10 a month.

Provisions on jointly-owned companies apply in the same way as for share option schemes (see 328).

As with approved share option schemes it is possible to subject shares within savings-related share option schemes to restrictions connected with the termination of employment (see 328).

On a takeover of a company, scheme participants may exchange their rights of option in shares of the company taken over for equivalent rights in the acquiring company or another company. Scheme rules may be changed so that an exchange of rights is permissible and such a transaction will not give rise to a CGT charge.

Law: FA 2003, s. 139, Sch. 21; ITEPA 2003, Sch. 3, 4

Website: www.hmrc.gov.uk/shareschemes/index.htm

See *British Tax Reporter* ¶475-800.

335   Enterprise management incentives

In nine cases out of ten, if a company qualifies for the selective Enterprise Management Incentives (EMIs) scheme, and takes the project to fruition, it will end up implementing that scheme. This is due to a combination of great flexibility and particularly attractive tax breaks for employees. For disposals up to 5 April 2008, they were able to obtain full business asset taper relief two years from the day on which options were granted, in the right circumstances. This meant a maximum 10 per cent tax rate for a higher-rate taxpayer with no risk to the individual at all.

They still benefit from the relatively low rates of capital gains tax, compared with 41 per cent combined for income tax and NIC. Further, with effect from 6 April 2008, those employees holding sufficient shares to qualify for entrepreneurs' relief (at least 5 per cent of the ordinary shares and voting rights), enjoy an effective rate of 10 per cent on the first £5m of lifetime gains.

The major factors that might prevent qualification for EMIs are

- the working hours requirement;
- the gross assets limit for the company or group of £30m;
- the restrictive qualification with regard to trading which eliminates, among others, property developers and accountants, and
- the individual limit on shares under option at any time, which currently stands at £120,000, having increased from £100,000 from 6 April 2008.

With effect from 21 July 2008, an additional limit on the number of employees was imposed. This prevented companies or groups with 250 or more employees from participating.

There is also an overall limit of £3m on the total value of shares that can be held under option at any time for each company (or group), although it is highly unlikely in practice that this will stop any but a handful of companies that might be interested in implementing an EMI scheme.

These are simple, flexible option arrangements that almost allow the company to draw up its own arrangements in an atmosphere of complete freedom. Options can be offered at any price and with an exercise date that could be as soon as the next week, should that prove attractive. Further, the arrangements are administratively simple as there is no need to obtain HMRC approval in advance of commencing an agreement.

This means that, at least in theory, a company could draw up an agreement and put an EMI scheme into place on the day that they first thought of it. In practice, it is at least advisable to obtain both an agreed share valuation and clearance that the company is a qualifying company with HMRC before embarking.

Obviously it is important to remember that formal agreement documentation is required.

Law: ITEPA 2003, s. 527–541; FA 2000, s. 62 and Sch. 14; *Income Tax (Limits for Enterprise Management Incentives) Order* 2008 (SI 2008/706)

Source: HMRC leaflet: *Enterprise Management Incentives – A guide for employees, employers and advisers*

Website: www.hmrc.gov.uk/shareschemes/index.htm
www.proshare.org.uk

See *British Tax Reporter* ¶480-700.

340   Priority share allocations for employees

Where a company makes a public offer of shares, employees are often given priority rights so that if the offer is over-subscribed, the employees will receive either their full allocation, or, where there is a scaling-down, more shares than a member of the public who subscribed for the same number; without special provision a tax charge could arise (see 323). There are two possible charges: the benefit of priority and the discount.

No taxable benefit accrues from such a share allocation where the offer is at a fixed price or by tender, the employees or directors are entitled to a priority allocation at the fixed price or at the lowest price successfully tendered, and not more than ten per cent of the shares on offer are subject to employee/director priority. Further, all the persons entitled to the priority allocation must be so entitled 'on similar terms', though discrimination according to pay level, length of service, etc. is allowed. In relation to offers made after 25 July 1990, the 'similar terms' test is not failed where persons who are not directors or employees of the company have a smaller entitlement to shares in the company than those who are, if:

- those who are not employees, etc. are nonetheless entitled, by reason of their employment and in priority to the public, to share allocations in another company which are offered to the public at the same time; and
- the total entitlement of each of those persons is on a par with the entitlement of comparable employees, etc. of the first-mentioned company.

From 16 January 1991, the discount is not covered by the above exemption to the extent that it exceeds a 'registrant discount', i.e. one which is available to directors/employees but which is also available (or for which a suitable alternative is offered) to those individual members of the public who are allocated at least 40 per cent of the rest of the shares.

Income Tax

229

The condition that a maximum of ten per cent of the shares offered can be subject to employee/director priority is also modified where the offer to the public is part of an arrangement which includes other offers of shares of the same class in the same company or is made after 15 January 1991 and is part of an offer to the public consisting of a package of shares in two or more companies where employees/directors are entitled to shares in just one (or some) of them. Where there is such an arrangement and employee/director priority applies only to one of those offers, the percentage limit above is both ten per cent of all the shares and 40 per cent of the shares subject to that offer; in the case of the packaged, multi-company offer the limit is ten per cent of each share on offer.

Law: ITEPA 2003, Pt. 7, Ch. 10

Website: www.hmrc.gov.uk/shareschemes/index.htm

See *British Tax Reporter* ¶482-650.

354 Share incentive plans

Share incentive plans (formerly known as the all-employee share scheme) were introduced from 28 July 2000. From that date employees can be awarded shares in a tax and NIC-efficient fashion through the means of a share incentive plan. The plan, which is an all-employee scheme and which replaced approved profit-sharing schemes has the following key features:

- employers can give employees up to £3,000 of shares each year, free of tax and National Insurance;
- some or all of the shares can be awarded to employees for reaching performance targets;
- employees will be able to buy partnership shares out of their pre-tax salary, to a maximum of £1,500, free of tax and National Insurance; and
- employees can match partnership shares by giving employees up to two free shares for each partnership share that they buy.

An approvals process applies. HMRC operate a helpline (0207) 438 6718/7231/6756 proving guidance on all aspects of the plans. In addition, detailed guidance, including model rules and trust deeds are available on the HMRC website.

Law: FA 2003, s. 139, Sch. 21; FA 2000, s. 47 and Sch. 8

Source: *Share Incentive Plans – A Guide for employees*

Website: www.hmrc.gov.uk/shareschemes/index.htm
www.proshare.org.uk

See *British Tax Reporter* ¶469-650.

355 Research institution spinout companies

Where the method by which employees share in the rewards of the exploitation of their own intellectual property is via shares in a so-called 'spinout' company, from 2 December 2004, the tax charge on the employee will no longer depend on the value of that property at the time of transfer. The purpose of this rule is intended to encourage the formation of such companies by institutions such as universities, health trusts and the like. Where a company has been established and shares passed to employees before then, an election may be made (to be submitted by 15 October 2005) that tax and NIC on the employee be payable at a later date when the company is commercially successful.

Law: FA 2005, s. 20

P11D EMPLOYEES AND DIRECTORS

382 Selective charge on expenses and cash equivalent of benefits

Special rules (see 384–415) apply to payments in respect of expenses and to benefits of any kind given to 'employees earning at the rate of £8,500 p.a. or more' known as 'P11D employees' (from the end-of-year return form which employers must send to HMRC: see 2576) and 'directors'.

Expenses and benefits given to a P11D employee are deemed to be provided by reason of his or her employment. The measure of the taxable benefit is its cash equivalent value. Unless the value is determined by a specific statutory provision (see 383) for those benefits where specific charging provisions exist, the cash equivalent value is determined in accordance with the general charging provisions; the cash equivalent value being the cost to the employer of providing the benefit, less any amount made good by the employee (see further 388).

Law: ITEPA 2003, s. 70–72

Source: Booklet 480, *Expenses and benefits: a tax guide*

Website: www.hmrc.gov.uk/biks/index.htm

See *British Tax Reporter* ¶412-850.

Income Tax

383 Exceptions from the general charge

Specific charging provisions

Certain benefits are specifically charged under provisions separate from the general benefits charge on a director or P11D employee (see 382). The provisions prescribe the calculation to be applied in determining the cash equivalent value of the benefit. For example, special rules apply to:

- employer-provided vans (see 400), cars and petrol (see 402, 403);
- mileage allowances (see 405);
- beneficial loans (see 406);
- directors' tax paid by employers (see 407);
- scholarships (see 408); and
- shares acquired at an undervalue (see 410).

Exemptions

Certain benefits are exempt from the general benefits charge altogether. For example:

- mobile telephones, subject to certain conditions (from 1999–2000: see 415);
- prior to 6 April 2006, the first £500 of annual benefit to an employee, where computer equipment is lent free or at low-cost by the employer (see 416);
- employer-provided and supported bus services (see 417);
- most in-house sporting or recreational facilities (including shared-employer facilities). From 2005–06, the exemption for the tax charge on subsidised meals (see 412) and recreational benefits is extended to persons other than employees who work on the premises of an employer who provides such benefits for their employees;
- accommodation provided on the employer's premises for the employee to enable him to carry out his duties;
- the giving of a lump sum pension or gratuity on the death or retirement of the employee;
- the provision of canteen meals to all staff (see 412);
- medical treatment or insurance provided in respect of an overseas business trip (see 293);
- entertainment and hospitality provided by third parties otherwise than in consideration of specific services;
- workplace nurseries (see 409);
- car (and, since 1999–2000, motor cycle and cycle) parking facilities at or near the workplace;
- bicycles and cycling safety equipment provided for employees' commuting journeys (see 418);
- certain incidental overnight expenses (see 302);
- security assets and services (see 2020);
- contributions by employers towards additional household costs incurred by employees who work some or all of the time at home. For payments of up to £3.00 per week, no supporting evidence is required to obtain the income tax exemption. For payments of more than £3.00 per week, supporting evidence is required. *Tax Bulletin*, Issue 68,

December 2003 includes an interpretation entitled 'Teleworkers: reimbursed expenses and benefits for employees working at home'; and
- from 2005–06, pensions advice and information provided, on behalf of employers, to employees of up to £150 per employee per year.

Law: ITEPA 2003, s. 237, 240, 241, 265, 307, 313, 317(1), 325, 718

Source: Booklet 480, *Expenses and benefits: a tax guide*

Website: www.hmrc.gov.uk/biks/index.htm

See *British Tax Reporter* ¶432-000.

384   Meaning of 'director'

A 'director' is a member of the board of directors or similar body, or if the company's affairs are managed by one person, that person. If the company's affairs are managed by the members themselves, a member is a director for tax purposes. In addition, any person upon whose instructions the directors of the company are accustomed to act is also a director, but there is an exception made for solicitors and other professional advisers who advise the company in their professional capacity. They are not treated as directors by doing so.

A person is not treated as a director if:

(1)   his total emoluments from the company are at the rate of £8,500 or more (see 386);

(2)   he has no 'material interest' in the company, and either:

    (a)   he is a 'full-time working director'; or

    (b)   the company is non-profit making (i.e. it is not a trading company and does not hold investments) or is established for purely charitable purposes.

Broadly, a person has a material interest for present purposes if he, alone or with any associate(s) (see 4268), beneficially owns or is able to control more than five per cent of the ordinary share capital of the company or on the company's liquidation would be entitled to more than five per cent of its assets.

Law: ITEPA 2003, s. 67, 216(3), 223(8)

See *British Tax Reporter* ¶413-000.

Income Tax

386 Whether employee earns at the rate of £8,500 p.a. or more

In determining whether the £8,500 threshold (see 382) is reached (and thus whether an employee is within the benefit regime applying to P11D employees and directors), the following items are included in the calculation unless they are covered by a dispensation:

- emoluments chargeable under the charge on employment income provisions;
- payments by way of expenses;
- benefits chargeable on P11D employees and directors;
- living accommodation provided by the employer;
- amounts chargeable in respect of cash and credit tokens; and
- tax accounted for by the employer (because PAYE could not be applied) and not reimbursed by the employee.

However, the calculation is performed *before* the deduction of expenses other than:

- contributions to a superannuation scheme in respect of which the individual is entitled to tax relief as an expense;
- contributions to an approved payroll giving scheme.

Example

Ruby is paid £5,000 a year. She is also provided with a company car, the cash equivalent value of which is £3,500. Her employer also provides private medical insurance, the cost of which is £300 a year. Ruby meets expenses of £225 from her emoluments that are deductible for tax purposes and contributes £100 to an approved payroll giving scheme.

For the purposes of determining whether Ruby is a P11D employee, she has emoluments of:

	£
Salary	5,000
Add: car	3,500
private medical insurance	300
	8,800
Less: contribution to approved payroll giving scheme	(100)
	8,700

Ruby's emoluments exceed the £8,500. For the purposes of this calculation her deductible expenses of £225 are not taken into account.

Double counting of costs relating to car and car fuel benefits in calculating total earnings for the £8,500 benefits threshold is removed by concession (ESC A104). The strict letter of tax law means the value of these benefits should be added to the value of the benefits received under separate rules governing car and car fuel benefit charges. In practice this could result in an employee going over the £8,500 limit as a result of having the same benefit added in twice.

Law: ITEPA 2003, s. 66(4), 216(1)–(4), 217(1), 218(1), (3), (4), 219(5), (6)

Source: ESC A104

See *British Tax Reporter* ¶419-600.

388 General charge on benefits

Unless a benefit is covered by a specific provision that dictates how the cash equivalent of the benefit is to be calculated, for tax purposes, the measure of a benefit provided to a P11D employee or a director is its cash equivalent value as calculated in accordance with the general charging provision as follows:

	£
Cost to employer	x
Less: amount made good by employee	(x)
Cash equivalent value	x

> ### Example
>
> As a reward for meeting her sales targets, Polly's employer gives her a luxury hamper. The hamper cost £300. Polly makes no contribution towards the cost. The cash equivalent value of the benefit is thus the cost to Polly's employer of providing the hamper, i.e. £300.

Where the benefit comprises facilities shared between the person to whom the benefit is provided and others (e.g. cheap school fees for a child of a teacher at an independent school) only the additional direct costs (or 'marginal costs') are taken into account in calculating the cash equivalent and not the total cost of providing the facilities which might include a rateable proportion of overheads and other expenses.

VAT

Where the cost to the employer includes VAT, the cash equivalent of the benefit is computed using the VAT-inclusive cost, even if the VAT element is subsequently recovered by the employer.

Law: ITEPA 2003, s. 201–203; *Mairs (HMIT) v Haughey* [1992] BTC 373; *Pepper (HMIT) v Hart* [1992] BTC 591

Source: Booklet 480; *Expenses and benefits: a tax guide*; Revenue Interpretation, Inland Revenue *Tax Bulletin*, Issue 16, April 1995; SP A7, *Benefits in kind: VAT*

Website: www.hmrc.gov.uk/biks/index.htm
www.hmrc.gov.uk/employers/index.htm

Income Tax

www.hmrc.gov.uk/bulletins/index.htm

See *British Tax Reporter* ¶412-850.

390   Minor benefits

The Treasury has a general power to make regulations to exempt minor benefits from the general charge on benefits in kind. Benefits exempted under this head include welfare counselling (from August 2001), cyclists' breakfasts and lunchtime use of works buses (from April 2002), and, from 9 July 2002, hearing aids and other equipment, services or facilities made available to disabled employees, to enable them to fulfil the duties of their employment..

The exemption was extended from 6 April 2002 so as to remove from the charge to tax any non-cash voucher evidencing entitlement to a minor benefit, if the minor benefit itself would be exempt.

Law: ITEPA 2003, s. 210(1), (2), 266(4), (5)

See *British Tax Reporter* ¶432-050.

394   Assets transferred

Where an asset is transferred to an employee or director, several factors need to be taken into account in determining the cash equivalent value of the resultant benefit.

P9D employees

If the asset is transferred to a P9D employee, or a member of his or her family or household, the basic rule is that the employee is taxed on the second-hand value of the asset, less any amount made good by the employee.

Asset transferred to P11D employee/director before it has depreciated

However, where the asset is transferred to a P11D employee or a director, the cash equivalent will depend on whether the asset has been used or depreciated at the time of transfer and whether it has previously been placed at the employee or director's disposal.

In the situation that an asset is transferred before it has been used or has depreciated, the cash equivalent value is the greater of the:

- cost of providing the asset; or
- its second-hand value,

less any amount made good by the employee.

Asset transferred to a P11D employee or director after it has depreciated or has been used

Where an asset is transferred to a P11D employee or director after it has been used or has depreciated, the cash equivalent value of the resultant benefit is the market value of the asset at the date of transfer less any amount made good by the employee.

Asset transferred after being made previously available to the P11D employee/director

It may be the case that the asset is lent to the employee/director before being transferred to him or her. In this situation, the cash equivalent value of the resultant benefit is the higher of:

- the market value at the date of transfer, and
- the market value when the asset was first made available for use by the employee/director, less any amounts charged in respect of that benefit,

less any amounts made good by the employee/director.

From 6 April 2005, no tax charge arises where employees/directors buy computers or bicycles from their employer, provided that the bicycle or computer has previously been loaned to them or to another employee, and that they pay market value (see 394).

Law: FA 2005, s. 16 and 17; ITEPA 2003, s. 203(2), (3), 206, 208

Source: Booklet 480, *Expenses and Benefits, a tax guide*

Website: www.hmrc.gov.uk/biks/index.htm
www.hmrc.gov.uk/employers/index.htm

See *British Tax Reporter* ¶437-950.

396 Assets placed at employee's disposal

Where an asset is placed at the disposal of a P11D employee or a director for his or her private use, the cash equivalent value of the resultant benefit is the higher of:

- 20 per cent of the market value of the asset when it was first made available for use by an employee; and
- the annual rent or hire charge of the asset,

plus any costs incurred in the tax year less in association with the provision of the asset, less any amount made good by the employee.

Example

David's employer lent him a fridge and a freezer for his personal use. The assets were first made available in 2001 when they had market values of £400 and £600 respectively. In 2010–11, David's employer pays for an annual service contract covering both appliances. The contract costs £100. David makes no contribution towards the costs.

The taxable benefit charged on David, a P11D employee, in 2010–11 is £300, calculated as follows:

	£	£
Fridge – higher of		
• 20% market value when first made available (20% × £400)	80	
• annual hire/rent	Nil	
		80
Freezer – higher of		
• 20% market value when first made available (20% × £600)	120	
• annual hire/rent	Nil	
		120
		200
Add: associated costs		100
		300
Less: amount made good by employee		(Nil)
Cash equivalent value		300

It should be noted that the charge arises where the asset is *available* for private use, even if no actual private use takes place.

If the asset is land, the annual value is the amount that the land would reasonably be expected to produce on a yearly letting.

For the position where ownership of the asset is transferred to an employee having been previously placed at his disposal, see 394.

Incidental private use

No charge arises in respect of incidental private use of assets which are used by the employee in performing the duties of his or her employment. For the exemption to be in point, the private use must not be 'significant'.

However, the exemption will not extend to small amounts of private use of certain high value assets (the assets in question to be specified by a Treasury Order).

Law: ITEPA 2003, s. 203(2), (3), 205, 206, 207(1), 316; FA 2000, s. 57 and Sch. 10

Source: Booklet 480, *Expenses and Benefits, a tax guide*

Website: www.hmrc.gov.uk/employers.index.htm

See *British Tax Reporter* ¶413-500.

398 Living accommodation and related expenses

The provision of living accommodation is a taxable benefit whatever the recipient's rate of pay; however, there are exceptions to the charge (see 314).

Where an employee earning at a rate of £8,500 p.a. or more, or a director, has the running expenses of his accommodation paid by his employer, that will constitute a benefit chargeable to tax in accordance with the general charging provisions (see 388). However, the amount of the charge is partially exempt from tax where the employee qualifies for a job-related exemption (see 314). The partial exemption reduces what would otherwise be a charge on the full cost of the provision of such expenses as lighting, heating, repairs, cleaning, maintenance, and decoration to an amount not exceeding ten per cent of the emoluments of the employee, less any amount paid by the employee for them; 'emoluments' for these purposes means the employee's total emoluments, including any emoluments of any employment with an associated company, but after making certain deductions.

Law: ITEPA 2003, s. 99(1), (2), 100, 314, 315

Source: Booklet 480, *Expenses and benefits: a tax guide*

See *British Tax Reporter* ¶414-500.

400 Vans used by employees

Where a company van is available for the private use of a P11D employee or a director, a taxable benefit arises. The tax treatment of vans provided by the employer currently works on the basis of a fixed charge per van, irrespective of the cost of the van. As such, the legislation concerning vans is simpler than that governing the taxation of company cars.

There is no tax charge if the van is not in fact used for private purposes.

For those who are liable to tax on the provision of a company van, the taxable benefit is a fixed amount of £3,000, but a reduction may be made if there is shared use of the van, there is a period in the year during which the van is not available for private use, or the employee makes contributions for private use of the van.

There is no fuel benefit where the benefit of the van itself is exempt. In other cases, the taxable cash equivalent of free fuel is £550 per year from 6 April 2010 (£500 per year between 6 April 2007 and 5 April 2010).

Income Tax

239

Shared vans

Changed rules for shared vans were introduced from 6 April 2005, representing a considerable simplification of the previous position.

The current rules apply where a van is made available by the same employer to more than one employee, and where both employees may use the van for private purposes.

The taxable benefit is first calculated in accordance with normal principles. A reduction is then given for any periods during which the van is unavailable. To recognise that the benefit of the van is shared between more than one employee, a further reduction is then made 'on a just and reasonable basis'. Discretion as to what is just and reasonable will presumably be left to employers unless HMRC suspect deliberate manipulation of the rules. Subject to the following paragraph, use by all employees is included in the calculation, even if an individual is not in fact chargeable to tax on the van benefit because he earns less than £8,500 – still possible, in theory at least, for a part-time worker.

There is a complication where two employees who share a van are members of the same family or household. Suppose, for example, that they have equal use of a van, with unrestricted private use. The overall taxable benefit would be £3,000 and in the ordinary way this might therefore be split £1,500 to each. However, if one of the two is in lower-paid employment (broadly, earning less than £8,500 per year) then he or she might escape any tax liability on the van. In this case, the other member of the same family or household would still pay tax on the full value of £3,000.

Example

John is sole shareholder of his own building company. He drives a van and uses it for both private and business purposes. John employs his 17-year-old son, Steve, in the business, paying him £5,000 per year for ten hours per week. Steve is also allowed to drive the vehicle and father and son make roughly equal use of the van overall, in each case with unrestricted private use.

The overall taxable benefit is £3,000. In the ordinary way, this might therefore be split £1,500 to each. However, as Steve is in lower-paid employment, he would escape any tax liability on the van. In this case, his private use is ignored and John will pay tax on the full value of £3,000.

This anti-avoidance rule does not apply where the two employees are unconnected.

Law: ITEPA 2003, s. 114, 115, 155, 157, 161, 169A; *Car and Van Fuel Benefits Order 2010* (SI 2010/406)

Source: Booklet 480, *Expenses and benefits: a tax guide*

Website: www.hmrc.gov.uk/guidance/it-vans.htm

See *British Tax Reporter* ¶416-000.

402 Company cars

A car that is placed at an employee's disposal is generally termed a 'company car'. Where such a car is available for the private use of a P11D employee or a director, the car is taxed as a benefit in kind.

System from April 2002

From April 2002, the system for taxing the private use of company cars was replaced with a new regime. From that date, the charge is based on a percentage of the car's price, graduated according to carbon dioxide emission levels. The charge started at 15 per cent of the list price for cars emitting 165 grams per kilometre (g/km) or less of carbon dioxde (CO_2) in 2002–03, increasing in increments of one per cent for each additional 5g/km of CO_2 emitted, to a maximum of 35 per cent of the list price. Diesel cars attract a supplement of three per cent, but the supplement is capped so that the maximum charge of 35 per cent of the list price is not exceeded. (Note that although the three per cent supplement waiver for Euro IV diesel cars was withdrawn from 6 April 2006 for all diesel cars registered on or after 1 January 2006, it will apply to all diesel cars, including those approved to the Euro IV standard and first registered before 1 January 2006 from 2011–12.)

See the table at 60 for full details of rates.

The old business mileage discounts have been abolished from the start of the new regime. Also abolished is the age discount for cars over four years old at the end of the tax year. The list price remains as determined under the old system (see below). The rules in relation to classic cars, and the treatment of contributions by employees, either to the cost of the car, or for its private use, also remain unchanged (see below). A minor change is made the formula used to determine the reduced cash-equivalent value of the benefit when the car is unavailable for private use for part of the tax year. The time apportionment calculation is now based on the actual number of days in the year, rather than a blanket 365; the cash-equivalent value of the benefit being multiplied by A/B, where A is the number of days in the year when the car was available and B is the number of days in the year. In practical terms, this means that in a leap year, the calculation will be based on 366 days, rather than 365, as was the case prior to 2002–03.

> ### Example
>
> Frank drives a petrol car with a list price of £20,000. The car was first registered in March 2005 and has CO_2 emissions of 198g/km. The car is a company car and is available for Frank's private use throughout the tax year. To find the appropriate percentage, the emissions figure of 198g/km is rounded down to the nearest 5g/km, i.e. 195g/km. From the table at 60, the appropriate percentage for 2009–10 is 27 per cent.

> Applying this to the list price of £20,000 gives a cash equivalent value of the benefit derived from Frank's private use of £5,400 (£20,000 × 27 per cent). In 2010–11, the appropriate percentage is 28 per cent and the cash equivalent value of the benefit is £5,600 (£20,000 × 27 per cent).

To provide a continuing incentive for employees and employers to choose environmentally-friendly vehicles, a new 10 per cent band commenced from 2008–09 onwards for cars that emit 120g/km or less of CO_2. Electric cars are specifically excluded from these measures as they continue to qualify for a nine per cent rate. Alternatively fuelled cars may be eligible for the 10 per cent rate but the existing discounts for LPG, bi-fuel or hybrid cars only apply if the car is taxed at a rate above 10 per cent. With the three per cent supplement the lowest charge for a diesel car will be 13 per cent unless it is approved for Euro IV standards and was first registered before 1 January 2006, when the rate will be 10 per cent. Note that the three per cent supplement waiver applies to all diesel cars, including those approved to the Euro IV standard and first registered before 1 January 2006 from 2011–12.

From 6 April 2008, the appropriate percentage for calculating car benefits can be reduced by 2 per cent for cars capable of running on bioethanol or on a mixture of 85 per cent bioethanol and unleaded petrol (commonly known as E85).

Automatic cars for disabled drivers

Where the holder of a disabled person's badge has to use an automatic car, the benefit is calculated on the basis of the emissions figure for an equivalent manual car.

Cars with no omissions figures

The basic car benefit charge is the car's price multiplied by the percentage charge appropriate to the car's age and engine size (including any diesel supplement).

Cars first registered before 1 January 1998

Since 1 January 1998, car manufacturers have been required to report CO_2 emissions for all new cars on sale in the EC. However, there are no reliable sources of CO_2 emissions data for cars first registered before this date. Consequently, cars registered prior to 1 January 1998, which have an internal combustion engine within one or more reciprocating pistons, will be taxed in accordance with the following table.

Cylinder capacity in cubic centimetres	Appropriate percentage %
1,400 or less	15
1,401–2,000	22
2,001 or more	32

Miscellaneous points

HMRC have published guidance on the application of the company car rules in three specific situations where problems can arise in applying the law strictly:

- test and experimental cars;
- demonstrator and courtesy cars; and
- employees with frequent changes of car ('averaging').

The guidance applies for 2009–10 and later years and can be found on the HMRC website at www.hmrc.gov.uk/cars/averaging.pdf.

Income Tax

Flowchart: determining the cash equivalent value of the benefit

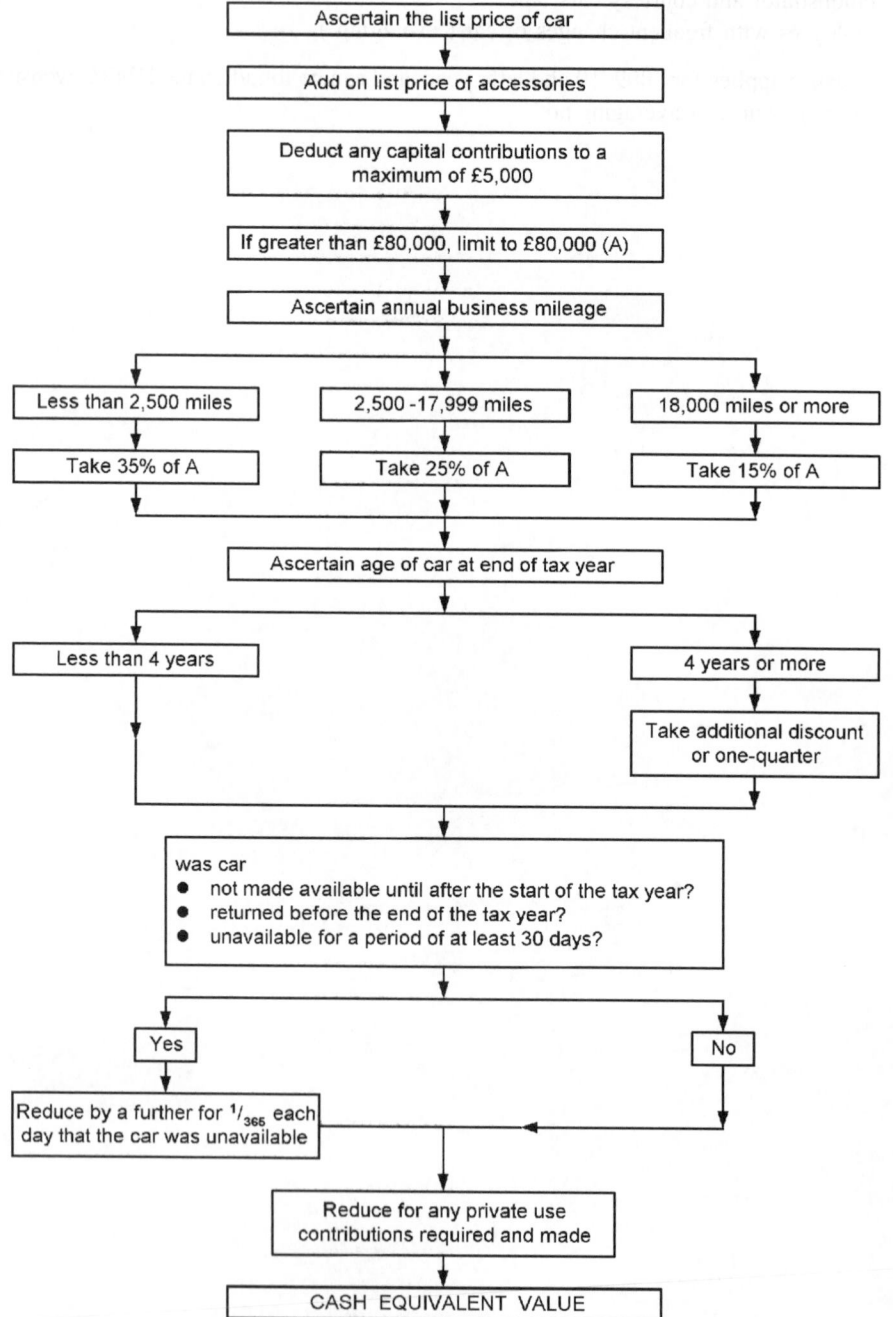

Classic cars

Special rules apply to 'classic cars'. These are cars that are more than 15 years old at the end of the tax year and in respect of which the market value is greater than the list price and the market value is at least £15,000. In the calculation of the cash equivalent of the benefit, the list price is replaced by the market value.

Emergency vehicles

From 2004–05 no liability arises where an emergency vehicle is made available to an employee for private use, but where the terms on which it is made available prohibit its use otherwise than when the employee is on call or engaged in on-call commuting.

Law: FA 2008, s. 47; FA 2006, s. 59; FA 2004, s. 81; ITEPA 2003, s. 114–148, 167, 169; FA 1999, s. 47, 52; *Income Tax (Car Benefits) (Replacement Accessories) Regulations* 1994 (SI 1994/777); *IR Commrs v Quigley* [1995] BTC 356; *Brown v Ware (HMIT)* (1995) Sp C 29; *Gurney (HMIT) v Richards* [1989] BTC 326

Source: Booklet 480, *Expenses and benefits: a tax guide*

Website: www.hmrc.gov.uk/guidance/it-vans.htm
www.hmrc.gov.uk/biks/index.htm
www.roads.detr.gov.uk/vehicle/fuelcon/index.htm

See *British Tax Reporter* ¶415-050.

403 Fuel benefits

The taxable benefit arising where an employer provides an employee with free fuel for private motoring in a company car is linked to the level of the car's carbon dioxide emissions, providing symmetry with the regime that has applied since 6 April 2002 to tax the benefit derived from the private use of a company car. For 2003–04 and subsequent tax years, the cash equivalent of the benefit of free fuel will be found by applying the percentage figure used in the car benefit calculation to an amount set by the Treasury. This amount is £18,000 from 2010–11 onwards (£16,900 for 2008–09 and 2009–10).

The annual charge may be apportioned where free fuel is withdrawn part way through the tax year, provided that it is not reintroduced before the end of the tax year.

Law: ITEPA 2003, s. 149–153; *Car and Van Fuel Benefits Order* 2010 (SI 2010/406); *Income Tax (Cash Equivalents of Car Fuel Benefits) Order* 1999 (SI 1999/684)

Source: Booklet 480, *Expenses and benefits: a tax guide*; 490, *Employee travel, a tax and NICs guide*

Website: www.hmrc.gov.uk/biks/index.htm

www.hmrc.gov.uk/employers/index.htm

See *British Tax Reporter* ¶416-000.

405 Mileage allowances

Employers are required to use the HMRC system for working out and reporting any taxable part of payments made to employees for the expenses of business travel in privately owned cars, vans, motorcycles and cycles. There is a tax-free approved amount that employers can pay to employees using their own vehicles for business travel. If an employer pays more than the approved amount, the excess will be charged to tax. Employers will need to include the excess when completing forms P9D or P11D. The tax-free approved amount is expressed in terms of pence per mile. For current rates, see 61.

Passenger payments

Passenger payments up to the approved rate for business travel (see 61) may be made to an employee for carrying passengers in his/her own car or van or in the company's car or van.

Source: Booklet 480 *Employer's Further Guide to PAYE and NICs*

See *British Tax Reporter* ¶416-650.

406 Beneficial loans

Where a low-interest or interest-free loan is made to a P11D employee or to a director, a tax charge arises on the cash equivalent of the benefit of the loan, with allowance for any potential relief in respect of interest paid on certain loans. Similarly, where a loan to such an individual is written off (whether or not a 'soft loan' and whether or not a 'qualifying loan'), the amount written off is treated as a taxable emolument unless the write-off occurs on death.

Loans by a close company to one of its directors may in some cases be aggregated for the purposes of determining the interest paid and the benefit so arising; before 1996–97, this applied to many more cases of loans between the same borrower and lender.

Before 1995–96, any loan which replaced a beneficial loan was treated as the original loan. From 6 April 1995, the replacement loan is not automatically a beneficial loan, but the same tests apply to determine whether the replacement is a beneficial loan. The effect of this is to remove an obstacle to the provision of replacement loans to employees. An employer who wishes to stop providing cheap or interest-free loans to employees can now transfer the loans to a subsidiary of a commercial lender set up for the purpose without the loans automatically becoming taxable. Under the old rules the loans would have been treated as beneficial loans even if the subsidiary made commercial loans to the general public, but this is not now the case.

The exemption from the charge to tax on beneficial loans applying to loans made to employees on the same terms as to members of the public ('ordinary commercial loans' is widened from 6 April 2000 to include loans to employees that are varied to bring them onto ordinary commercial terms. Also from 6 April 2000, the exemption is extended to cover lending by an employer who supplies goods or services on credit. For years prior to 2000–01, the exemption applied only to loans made by the employer in the ordinary course of his business, which includes lending money. This extension ensures that employees receiving the same credit arrangements as other customers, for example payment in arrears for gas and electricity, are not inadvertently caught by the beneficial loan provisions.

In relation to arrangements entered into on or after 22 March 2006, cheap loans provided by employers to their employees which do not involve the payment of interest are taxed in the same way as conventional employee loans, i.e. on the difference between the interest (or its equivalent) payable by the employee and the amount of interest that would be payable at the official rate.

A loan made to an employee's spouse, his spouse's parents, grandparents, children, grandchildren, brothers, sisters, or their spouses, is treated as if it were made to the employee unless he can show that he received no benefit from it.

Loans made in the normal course of domestic, family or personal relationships are exempt from the soft loan provisions including, from 6 April 1994, personal loans within families where the employer is a close company. Similarly exempt from 6 April 1994 are loans which employers provide to employees on the same terms as loans they make to the public.

Small loans

An exemption applies to remove certain small loans from the beneficial loans provisions. From 1994–95, all soft loans may be omitted if they total £5,000 or less; failing this, all non-qualifying loans (such as season ticket loans) may be disregarded if they total £5,000 or less.

With effect from 1995–96, if the original loan is replaced by another loan from the same employment (an 'employment-related loan'), or replaced by a non-employment-related loan, which in turn is replaced by an employment-related loan, then the loans are all treated, for the purposes of averaging, as the same loan. This seeks to prevent exploitation of the part months which may occur at the beginning or end of each of the various loans.

Taxable amount in respect of beneficial loans

There are alternative methods for determining the cash equivalent of beneficial loans. The standard method is that the average amount of the loan which is outstanding at either end of the tax year is multiplied by the average official rate of interest for the year in question (see 64) and there is then subtracted the interest actually paid (the cash equivalent of any loan which is not outstanding for the whole of the tax year is reduced by a proportionate amount and there are special rules for multiple loans). The alternative method may be employed if the inspector requires or if the taxpayer elects for it: this uses a daily basis of calculation.

247

The Treasury is able to set a lower official rate (see 65) for loans in a foreign currency where interest rates are significantly lower than in the UK.

Example 1

George's employer makes him a loan interest-free. The balance outstanding at 5 April 2009 is £10,000. He repays £6,000 on 15 January 2010 so that the balance on 5 April 2010 is £4,000.

Standard method

$$\frac{(£10,000 + £4,000)}{2} \times 6.10\% = \qquad \underline{\underline{£427}}$$

Alternative method	£
£10,000 × $^{284}/_{365}$ × 6.10%	475
£4,000 × $^{81}/_{365}$ × 6.10%	54
	$\underline{\underline{529}}$

Beneficial loans where all the interest qualifies for tax relief are exempted from charge.

Law: *Finance Act* 2006, s. 97; ITEPA 2003, s. 173–191; *West (HMIT) v O'Neill; West (HMIT) v Crossland* [1999] BTC 32; *Grant v Watton (HMIT)* [1999] BTC 85; *Harvey v Williams (HMIT) (No. 2)* (1998) Sp C 168; *Euro Fire Ltd v Davison (HMIT); Hill v Davison (HMIT)* [1997] BTC 191

Source: SP 7/79, *Benefits in kind – cheap loans – advances for expenses*; Booklet 480, *Expenses and benefits: a tax guide*

Website: www.hmrc.gov.uk/employers/ebik/ebik2/loans.htm
www.hmrc.gov.uk/employers/index.htm

See *British Tax Reporter* ¶417-000.

407 Director's tax paid by employer

Where a person is employed as a 'director' (see 384) of a company and the company fails to deduct tax under PAYE from his emoluments but accounts to HMRC for the tax, any tax for which the director does not reimburse the company is treated as a benefit received by the director and is chargeable as an emolument of his employment.

Law: ITEPA 2003, s. 223

See *British Tax Reporter* ¶420-100.

408   Scholarships

It is not unusual for employers to offer, as incentives to attract employees, scholarships for the education of employees' children. Except as noted below, any scholarship payments made to a child of a 'director' (see 384) or to the child of an 'employee earning at a rate of £8,500 p.a. or more' (see 386) are taxed as benefits in kind where they are made as a result of 'arrangements entered into by an employer, or a connected person'.

The charge arises in accordance with the general charging provisions (see 382).

Scholarships not affected

For the general exemption from tax for scholarship income, see 308.

The charging provisions do not apply to scholarships awarded out of a fund or under a scheme where 75 per cent or more of the scholarships (by value) go to scholars otherwise than by reason of their parents' employment, i.e. not more than 25 per cent of payments are made for children of directors or higher-paid employees by reason of their employment. The 25 per cent test excludes from the charge to tax only those awards where the connection between the award and the parent's employment is purely fortuitous.

Special provisions apply to scholarships taken up before 6 April 1984.

Law: ITEPA 2003, s. 211–215

Source: SP 4/86, *Scholarship and apprenticeship schemes at universities and technical colleges*; Booklet 480, *Expenses and benefits: a tax guide*

See *British Tax Reporter* ¶419-150.

409   Employer-provided childcare

A statutory exemption applies to remove from the charge to tax employer-provided childcare in a workplace nursery or similar facility. The exemption to tax applies if the following conditions are satisfied:

- the employee has 'parental responsibility' for the child or resides with it or, being the employee's child or stepchild, he maintains it at his expense;
- the care is provided on premises that are not wholly or mainly used as a private dwelling;
- *either* the care is provided on premises which are made available by the employer alone *or* the care is provided under arrangements made by persons who include the employer and which make him at least partly responsible for financing and managing the care provision; *and*
- in a case where 'the registration requirement applies, it is met'.

The registration requirement applies where either the premises or the carer must be registered under various care statutes and the requirement is met if the premises or person are so registered.

According to HMRC, to satisfy the condition that the care must be provided under arrangements which make the employer at least partly responsible for financing and managing the care provision (see above), the employer's role must be a real one which renders him accountable for his actions if things go wrong.

'Parental responsibility' means all the rights, duties, powers, responsibilities and authority which by law a child's parent has in relation to the child and his property.

'Care' means any form of care or supervised activity, provided on a regular or an irregular basis, but does not extend to supervised activity primarily provided for educational purposes.

For the purposes of the exemption, a 'child' is someone under the age of 18.

For 2005–06 , employees could receive up to £50 per week for childcare free of tax and NICs where the employer contracts with an approved childcarer, or provides childcare vouchers for the purpose of paying an approved childcarer. This limit was increased to £55 per week for 2006–07 onwards.

Law: FA 2005, s. 15; FA 2004, s. 78; ITEPA 2003, s. 318; *Income Tax (Qualifying Child Care) Regulations* 2008 (SI 2008/2170)

Source: HMRC Technical Note (www.hmrc.gov.uk/employers/ employersupportedchildcare.pdf); HMRC information (www.hmrc.gov.uk/childcare): *Employer supported childcare short guide for small and medium businesses*; *Childcare tax and National Insurance contributions – employers' factsheet*; *Employer supported childcare short guide for childcarers*; Inland Revenue *Tax Bulletin*, Issue 34, April 1998; Booklet 480, *Expenses and benefits: a tax guide*

Website: www.hmrc.gov.uk/biks/index.htm
www.hmrc.gov.uk/employers/index.htm
www.hmrc.gov.uk/bulletins/index.htm
www.hmrc.gov.uk/childcare/index.htm

See *British Tax Reporter* ¶437-650.

410   Shares acquired at undervalue

Acquisition of the shares

Where, under an opportunity 'available by reason of his employment', an employee or director acquires shares at less than their market value when fully paid, or without payment at all, the difference between market value and the amount paid by the employee is treated as a notional loan to him, unless the benefit is otherwise charged to tax (as it often is: see 324). Any payment subsequently made by the employee will reduce the notional outstanding loan. The loan will cease to exist when the shares are fully paid or when the employee dies. In the meantime, the loan is taxed year by year or on other termination (see 406).

Disposal of the shares

Where the employee or director disposes of the beneficial interest in the shares or he is released from his obligation to pay for them or the debt is written off, etc. the amount so written off (the corresponding amount of the loan) is treated as an emolument of the employee's employment and is taxable (see 406).

A disposal by the director or employee of the shares, at more than their market value, results in the excess over market value being treated as an emolument of the employee's employment. A disposal on death is excluded but a disposal after leaving the job still attracts the charge to tax.

Application of provisions

The above provisions apply to shares acquired by persons who are (or are about to be) employed as employees earning at a rate of £8,500 p.a. or more (see 386), or directors (see 384), and those 'connected with' them (see 1260). The provisions do not apply to 'approved profit-sharing schemes', while there are interaction rules with charges for 'approved share option schemes' (see 328).

Law: ITEPA 2003, s. 192–197; *IR Commrs v Herd* [1993] BTC 245

412 Provision of subsidised meals

The provision by employers of meals in a canteen in which meals are provided for staff generally is exempted from the charge on directors and P11D employees (see 384, 386). By concession, tax is not charged on such meals, or on the use of any ticket or token to obtain such meals, if the meals are provided on a reasonable scale and either:

- all employees may obtain free or subsidised meals on a reasonable scale, whether on the employer's premises or elsewhere; or
- the employer provides free or subsidised meal vouchers for staff for whom meals are not provided.

The concession does not apply, in the case of a hotel, catering or similar business, to free or subsidised meals provided for its employees in a restaurant or dining room at a time when meals are being served to the public, unless part of it is designated as being for the use of staff only.

From 6 April 2002, cyclists' breakfasts were exempted under the minor benefits provisions (see 390). No tax charge arose in repsect of the first six such breakfasts provided to cyclists' in the tax year. If a cyclist was provided with more than six breakfasts, the excess over six was taxed. Further regulations came into force with effect from 25 June 2003, which completely remove this limit and consequently completely remove the charge on cyclists' breakfasts with effect from that date.

From 2005–06, the exemption for the tax charge on subsidised meals and recreational benefits is extended to persons other than employees who work on the premises of an employer who provides such benefits for their employees.

Law: ITEPA 2003, s. 266, 317; *Income Tax (Exemption of Minor Benefits) Regulations 2002 (SI 2002/205)*

Source: Booklet 480, *Expenses and benefits: a tax guide*

Website: www.hmrc.gov.uk/biks/index.htm
www.hmrc.gov.uk/employers/index.htm

415 Mobile telephones

For 1999–2000 and subsequent tax years, an employer-provided mobile telephone (including one mounted in a car, van or heavier commercial vehicle) which is used for private calls is exempted from any income tax charge in accordance with the general charging provision (see 382).

A 'mobile telephone' is one not physically connected to a land line (including a car telephone), but not telepoint telephones or cordless extensions to domestic telephones.

From 6 April 2006, this exemption applies where only one mobile phone or similar device is lent to an employee but it must not be lent to his or her family or household. If the phone was first made available to the employee or member of his or her household before 6 April 2006 no charge arises. No charge will be due where provision of the phone is facilitated by the use of a voucher or credit token.

For years prior to 1999–2000, a standard charge of £200 per phone applied.

Law: *Finance Act* 2006, s. 60; ITEPA 2003, s. 319

Source: Booklet 480, *Expenses and benefits: a tax guide*

416 Computer equipment

Prior to 6 April 2006, the first £500 of the annual benefit in kind of a computer borrowed from an employer was exempted. From 2006–07 onwards this exemption has been removed. Equipment first made available to the employee, or his or her family, before 6 April 2006 is unaffected by the change.

Law: *Finance Act* 2006, s. 61; FA 2005, s. 17; FA 2004, s. 79; FA 1999, s. 45

Source: Booklet 480, *Expenses and benefits: a tax guide*

Website: www.hmrc.gov.uk/employers/index.htm

417   Works bus services

With effect from 6 April 1999, any benefits attributable to an employee as a result of an employer either directly providing a works bus service or subsidising, in any way, a public transport bus service, areexempt from the general benefit-in-kind charge (see 382). Where such a benefit is made available through a ticket or voucher, any charge under the non-cash voucher rules is also exempted.

To qualify for this exemption for a works bus service, the buses used must have a seating capacity of 12 or more (a 'large' bus) and the facility must be available to employees generally. However, to make it easier for smaller employers to offer such a service, from 6 April 2002, the exemption is extended to allow the service to be provided by means of a minibus, which has a seating capacity of at least nine but not more than 12 seats. To ensure that safety is not compromised by unscrupulous employers squeezing additional seats into vehicles such as people carriers to bring them within the definition of 'minibus', the exemption will only apply to vehicles originally constructed to carry nine or more seats.

Where a subsidy is provided to a bus service operator, the fares paid by employees must not be lower than non-employee passengers' fares. The exemption only extends to bus services that convey employees on 'qualifying journeys'; these are trips between:

- an employee's home and workplace; or
- one workplace and another.

However, from 6 April 2002 employees may benefit from lower fares without a benefit arising, so long as the service is a local stopping service. From the same date, the definition of a qualifying journey is amended to accommodate the situation where the bus is used for only part of the journey to work.

Law: ITEPA 2003, s. 242; FA 1999, s. 45

Source: Booklet 480, *Expenses and benefits: a tax guide*

Website: www.hmrc.gov.uk/employers/index.htm

418   Bicycles and cycling safety equipment

The benefit of bicycles and cycling safety equipment provided by employers to employees for their commuting journey is exempt from the general benefit-in-kind charge (see 382).

From 6 April 2005, no tax charge arises where employees buy bicycles from their employer, provided that the bicycle has previously been loaned to them or to another employee, and that they pay market value.

Law: FA 2005, s. 16 and 17; ITEPA 2003, s. 244; FA 1999, s. 50

Source: Booklet 480, *Expenses and benefits: a tax guide*

Website: www.hmrc.gov.uk/employers/index.htm

419   Eye tests and spectacles

The provision by an employer of eyecare tests and/or corrective spectacles for VDU users is exempt from 2006–07 onwards. The exemption applies irrespective of whether the costs are paid directly, reimbursed or provided by means of a voucher.

There are two conditions that must be met. Condition A is that the provision of the test or appliances is required by the *Health and Safety at Work etc Act* 1974. Condition B is that tests and glasses are made available generally to employees working with VDUs.

Law: ITEPA 2003, s. 320A

PENSIONS INCOME

420   Charge to tax on pensions

ITEPA 2003, as well as charging emoluments from employment (see 250), charges:
- every annuity, pension or stipend payable by the Crown or out of the public revenue of the UK or of Northern Ireland;
- any pension that is paid otherwise than by or on behalf of a person outside the UK;
- any pension or annuity payable in the UK to a UK resident (or widow, child or dependant thereof) by certain foreign governments in respect of foreign service.

For the scope of the pensions charge generally and other amounts treated in a like manner, see 422.

Law: ITEPA 2003, s. 1

See *British Tax Reporter* ¶313-000.

422   Scope of pensions charge

The basic charge to tax in respect of pensions, etc. (see 420) covers pension benefits received from either of the following principal types of arrangement:

- retirement benefit schemes (sometimes referred to as 'occupational pension schemes'), for which there are certain reliefs in respect of contributions and lump sum commutations but in respect of which employers' contributions may be taxable on the employee (see 429ff.);
- state retirement pensions.

There is no statutory definition of a 'pension', though the term specifically includes a voluntary pension. The *Shorter Oxford English Dictionary* defines the word as:

> 'an annuity or other periodical payment made, especially by a government, a company or an employer of labour, in consideration of past services or of the relinquishments of rights, claims or emoluments.'

Thus the word seems to connote an element of recurrence and to exclude a lump sum payment.

Concessions

By concession, a special or additional pension paid to a person who has retired because he is disabled following an injury at work, or because of a work related illness, is not taxed.

Also by concession, full or partial exemption from income tax is given, depending upon the exact level of foreign service, where the employment giving rise to the benefits was largely carried on abroad. The foreign service requirements are the same as for the similar exemption in respect of golden handshakes (see 1583).

Registered schemes

Payments made by a registered pension scheme are either authorised payments or unauthorised payments. There are two types of authorised payment:

- authorised member payments; and
- authorised employer payments.

Likewise, unauthorised payments are either unauthorised member payments or unauthorised employer payments. For these purposes, the term 'payment' includes a transfer of assets and any other transfer of money's worth.

The taxable pension income for a tax year is the full amount of the pension under the registered pension scheme that accrues in that year, irrespective of what is actually paid. The person who is liable for the charge to tax on the pension accrued in the tax year is the person receiving or entitled to the pension under the registered pension scheme.

Income Tax

Lump sums under registered pension schemes

Certain lump sums may be paid by a registered pension scheme without giving rise to a liability to income tax. The exemption from income tax applies to:

- a pension commencement lump sum;
- a serious ill-health lump sum;
- a refund of excess contribution lump sum;
- a defined benefits lump sum death benefit;
- an uncrystallised funds lump sum death benefit; or
- a transfer lump sum death benefit.

However, the existence of this exemption does not limit the operation of the lifetime allowance charge (see 432).

A short service refund lump sum under a registered pension scheme is subject to income tax in accordance with FA 2004, s. 205, but not otherwise.

A lump sum under a registered pension scheme that is:

- a pension protection lump sum death benefit;
- an annuity protection lump sum death benefit; or
- an unsecured pension fund lump sum death benefit,

is subject to tax under FA 2004, s. 206 but not otherwise.

Where a trivial commutation lump sum or a winding-up lump sum is paid to a member of a registered pension scheme, the member is treated as having taxable pension income for the year in which the payment is made equal to the amount of the lump sum. However, if immediately before the lump sum is paid, the member has not become entitled to any of the benefits under the pension scheme, the amount of the taxable pension income is 75 per cent of the lump sum. This means that in these circumstances, 25 per cent of the lump sum is tax-free.

Authorised surplus payments charge

A charge to tax, known as the authorised surplus payment charge arises where an authorised surplus payment is made to a sponsoring employer by an occupational pension scheme that is a registered pension scheme. The person who is liable to the authorised surplus payments charge is the scheme administrator, irrespective of whether the scheme administrator and the sponsoring employer are resident, ordinarily resident or domiciled in the UK.

The charge does not apply to any authorised surplus payment to the extent that, in the absence of this charge, the sponsoring employer would have been exempt, or entitled to claim exemption from income tax or corporation tax in respect of it, or if the sponsoring employer is a charity.

The rate of tax that is charged in respect of the authorised surplus payment is 35 per cent.

An authorised surplus payment in respect of which income is charged under the surplus authorised payments charge is not treated as income for any purposes of the Tax Acts.

The scheme administrator has a liability to account and pay the tax due using the Accounting for Tax Return.

Recycling of lump sums

Following the introduction of the new pensions regime, the Government became concerned that the increased contributions limits combined with the tax-free lump sum could result in individuals over the age of 50 making contributions to pension schemes, taking out the lump sum free from tax and reinvesting the funds, thus receiving further tax relief. Legislation was subsequently introduced in the *Finance Act* 2006, taking effect from 6 April 2006, to counter this perceived abuse.

Where the anti-recycling rules apply, the pension scheme is treated as having made an unauthorised payment, giving rise to a 40 per cent charge on the member. The amount of the unauthorised payment is the amount of the lump sum which can be offset against the lifetime allowances. This does, however, mean that no charge will arise if the individual concerned has already fully utilised the lifetime allowance. The rules apply if:

- the amount of the contributions paid by or on behalf of, or in respect of, the member to the pension scheme, or to any other registered pension scheme, is significantly greater than it would otherwise be;
- the member envisaged that that would be so (when the lump sum was paid or, if earlier, when the increased contributions were made to the scheme); and
- the increased contributions were made as a result of the lump sum.

The rules are very widely drawn and are designed to catch any deliberate decision to reinvest some of the lump sum received. However, there are two exemptions to the rules. No unauthorised payment will arise if:

- the lump sum received (when aggregated with any other lump sum received in the previous year) is less than or equal to one per cent of the standard lifetime allowance on that day; or
- the amount by which the pension contribution is increased is 30 per cent or less than the amount of the lump sum.

Income Tax

Example

Fred took a lump sum from his pension scheme of £40,000. He usually invested £10,000 per annum in the scheme but since he had received the lump sum, he decided to invest £30,000. The additional contributions represent more than 30% of the lump sum and the lump sum represents more than 1% of the lifetime allowance. Therefore the recycling provisions are likely to bite.

Tax charges on unauthorised payments

Payments made by a registered pension scheme are either authorised payments or unauthorised payments. Unauthorised payments may be either unauthorised member payments or unauthorised employer payments.

An unauthorised member payment is a payment by a registered pension scheme to or in respect of a member of the pension scheme that is not an authorised member payment or a payment that is specifically treated as an unauthorised member payment by virtue of the legislation.

An unauthorised employer payment is a payment by a registered pension scheme that is an occupational pension scheme to or in respect of a sponsoring employer that is not an authorised employer payment or a payment that is specifically treated as an unauthorised member payment by virtue of the legislation.

The FA 2006 extended the definition of 'member' and 'sponsoring employer' to include ex-members and former sponsoring employers for the purposes of the unauthorised payments charge.

The payment of an unauthorised payment can generate up to three tax charges:

- the unauthorised payments charge;
- the unauthorised payments surcharge; and
- the scheme sanction charge.

Unauthorised payments charge

Where a registered pension scheme makes an unauthorised payment, a tax charge arises. That charge is known as an unauthorised payments charge.

The nature of the unauthorised payment determines who is liable for the unauthorised payments charge. If the payment is an unauthorised member payment that is made before the member's death, the tax liability falls on the member to or in respect of whom the payment is made. If the payment is an unauthorised member payment that is made after the member's death, the tax liability falls on the recipient of that payment. If the payment is an unauthorised employer payment, the tax liability rests with the sponsoring employer to or in respect of whom the payment is made. In the event that the liability falls on more than one person, those persons are jointly and severally liable to the charge in respect of the payment. A person is liable for the unauthorised payments charge irrespective of whether or not that person, any other person with liability for the charge, and the scheme administrators are resident, ordinarily resident or domiciled in the UK.

The rate of tax charged in respect of the unauthorised payments charge is 40 per cent.

An unauthorised payment may also be subject to the unauthorised payments surcharge and the scheme sanction charge, as well as the unauthorised payments charge. However, an unauthorised payment is not treated as income for any purposes of the Tax Acts.

The scheme administrator should report details of any payment of an unauthorised payment in the Event Report.

Unauthorised payments surcharge

A charge to income tax is where a surchargeable unauthorised member payment is made by a registered pension scheme. The charge is known as the unauthorised payments surcharge.

Surchargeable unauthorised payments are surchargeable unauthorised member payments and surchargeable unauthorised employer payments.

A payment is a surchargeable unauthorised member payment if it is an unauthorised payment that together with any other unauthorised member payments made in a surcharge period equals or exceeds the surcharge threshold. The surcharge threshold is reached if the unauthorised payments percentage reached 25 per cent.

The surcharge period is the period that starts with the reference date and ends on the earlier of 12 months following the reference date and the day on which the surcharge threshold is reached. This means that if in any 12-month period, unauthorised member payments made by the registered pension scheme are less than the surcharge threshold, the unauthorised payments surcharge will not apply.

The rate of charge in respect of the surchargeable unauthorised payment is 15 per cent.

The person liable for the charge depends on the circumstances. If the surchargeable unauthorised member payment was made before the member's death, the liability for the charge falls on the member in respect of whose arrangement the payment was made. If the surchargeable member payment is made after the member's death, the recipient is liable for the charge. In the case of a surchargeable employer payment, it is the sponsoring employer to or in respect of whom the payment is made who is liable for the charge. If more than one person is liable to the surcharge, those persons are jointly and severally liable. A person remains liable to the surcharge irrespective of whether that person, any other person who is liable and the scheme administrator are resident, ordinarily resident or domiciled in the UK.

Scheme sanction charge

The scheme administrator is liable to a charge to income tax, known as the scheme sanction charge, where in any one tax year, one or more scheme chargeable payments are made by a registered pension scheme. If the scheme is treated as having been wound up, the liability falls on the person who was the scheme administrator immediately before the winding-up. A person liable to the scheme sanction charge is liable irrespective of whether that person or any other person who is liable to the scheme sanction charge are resident, ordinarily resident or domiciled in the UK.

The scheme sanction charge for any tax year is a charge at the rate of 40 per cent in respect of the scheme chargeable payment, or the aggregate of the scheme chargeable payments, made by the pension scheme in the tax year. However, if the scheme chargeable payment is an unauthorised payment, or any of the scheme chargeable payments are unauthorised payments and tax charged in relation to that payment, or any of those payments under the unauthorised payments charge has been paid, a deduction is made from the amount of tax that would otherwise be chargeable as the scheme sanction charge. The deduction is the lesser of:

- 25 per cent of the scheme chargeable payment, or the aggregate amount of such of the scheme chargeable payments as are tax-paid; and
- the amount of tax which has been paid in respect of the unauthorised payments charge in relation to the scheme chargeable payments, or in relation to such of the scheme chargeable payments as are tax-paid.

A scheme chargeable payment is tax-paid if the whole or part of the tax chargeable in relation to it in respect of the unauthorised payments charge has been paid.

Foreign and other special pensions

Foreign pensions (i.e. pensions payable by or on behalf of a person outside the UK), including voluntary pensions, are chargeable under former Sch. D, Case V if they do not fall within the ITEPA 2003 provisions.

There are certain exemptions and reliefs for parliamentary pension funds and foreign and overseas pension funds.

Any pension or allowance which relates to death due to service in the armed forces of the Crown or wartime service in the merchant navy or war injuries or to peacetime service in the armed service of the Crown before 3 September 1939, or any pension or allowance payable by a country other than the UK which is of a character substantially similar to those mentioned above, is not treated as income and is not therefore subject to income tax.

Law: FA 2006, s. 161 and Sch. 23; FA 2004, s. 160, 161, 207; ITEPA 2003, s. 579B, C, Pt. 9: Pension income; ESC A62; *Rockliffe v R & C Commrs* [2009] TC 00124

Source: HMRC *Registered Pension Schemes Manual* RPSM04100040; ICAEW Technical Release TR 851; Law Society's *Gazette* 7 October 1992

See *British Tax Reporter* ¶313-000.

PENSION TAX REGIME FROM 6 APRIL 2006

429 Introduction

Pensions taxation reform applies from 6 April 2006. From that date, known as A-Day, a single unified tax regime applies in place of the eight previous regimes. The post A-Day rules apply to all types of schemes and to all members of those schemes, regardless of when they joined. Under the unified regime, there are no limits on the amount that an individual can save in a pension scheme. However, there are limits on the amount of pension savings that qualify for tax relief.

The tax advantages are only available to registered pension schemes.

An individual who is a UK taxpayer is entitled to tax relief on contributions of up to 100 per cent of UK earnings. Non-taxpayers receive £25 from HMRC for each £100 that they contribute, up to a maximum of £3,600 a year. Employers are entitled to tax relief on any contributions that they make to a pension scheme. The relief for pension contributions is given on the same basis as relief for other forms of business expenditure.

Under the unified regime, there are two controls on an individual's tax-relieved pension savings. The first is the annual allowance (see 431). This is set at £255,000 for 2010–11. If in the tax year the increase in the value of an individual's pension savings or their contributions (including any employer contributions) exceeds the annual allowance, the excess is charged to tax at 40 per cent. The second control is the lifetime allowance (see 432). This is set at £1.8m for 2010–11. If when an individual takes his or her benefits from the pension scheme, total pension savings exceed the lifetime allowance, the excess is subject to a tax charge of 40 per cent.

Rules apply to determine when a person can take pension benefits. From 6 April 2010, every pension scheme must have an age limit of 55. Formerly there was an upper limit of 75, by which an individual must start taking pension benefits. However, this restriction has been removed in relation to persons who reach 75 on or after 22 June 2010. The rules allow scheme members to take a proportion of overall benefits in the form of a tax-free lump sum. Subject to the scheme rules, this can be up to 25 per cent of the pension fund subject to the amount of the lifetime allowance at the time.

Law: F(No. 2)A 2010, s. 6 and Sch. 3; FA 2007, s. 68–70 and Sch. 8–20 and 27 (Pt. 3); FA 2006, Pt 7; FA 2005, Pt. 5; *Registered Pension Schemes (Standard Lifetime and Annual Allowances) Order* 2010 (SI 2010/922); *Registered Pension Schemes (Modification of the Rules of Existing Schemes) Regulations* 2009 (SI 2009/3055); FA 2004, Pt. 4; *Taxation of Pension Schemes (Transitional Provisions) (Amendment No. 2) Order* 2009 (SI 2009/1989); *Special Annual Allowance Charge (Application to Members of Currently-Relieved Non-UK Pension Schemes) Order* 2009 (SI 2009/2031); *Pension Schemes (Application of UK Provisions to Relevant Non-UK Schemes) (Amendment) Regulations* 2009 (SI 2009/2047)

Website: www.hmrc.gov.uk/pensionschemes/pts.htm

See *British Tax Reporter* ¶306-000.

430 Registered pension schemes

A registered pension scheme is one that is registered with HMRC. A registered pension scheme qualifies for special tax privileges that are not available to pension schemes that are not registered.

A pension scheme must be a registered pension scheme in order to benefit from the tax reliefs available. An application for registration must be made to HMRC. The application must contain such information as is reasonably required by HMRC and must be in the specified form. The application must be accompanied by a declaration that the application is made by the scheme administrator and by such other declarations by the scheme administrator that are reasonably required. Such declaration may include a declaration that the instrument or agreement by which the pension scheme is constituted do not entitle any person to unauthorised payments. An application for registration must be made by the scheme administrator.

Once an application for registration has been made, the decision as to whether to register the scheme or not rests with HMRC. However, HMRC must register a scheme unless it appears that the information contained in the application is incorrect or any declaration accompanying it is false. HMRC must notify the scheme administrator of the decision made in regard to the application for registration. Unless the decision is not to register the scheme, the notification must state the date from which the registration is effective.

Those promoting (and in some cases those using) schemes and arrangements designed to produce a tax advantage relating to registered pension schemes are obliged to report these to HMRC. Entering into a registered pension scheme based on standardised documentation is not, however, a reportable event.

A pension scheme can only be registered if certain conditions are met.

From 6 April 2007 an application to register a pension scheme, that is not an occupational pension scheme, can be made only if the pension scheme has been established by a person who has (or persons who have) permission from the Financial Services Authority (FSA) to establish in the UK a personal pension scheme or a stakeholder pension scheme.

In the event that HMRC decide not to register a pension scheme, the scheme administrator can appeal against that decision. The time-limit for making an appeal is 30 days from the date on which the scheme administrator was notified of the decision not to register the pension scheme. The tribunal must decide whether the scheme should be registered. If they decide it should not be registered, they must dismiss the appeal. However, if they decide the scheme should be registered, the pension scheme is treated as being a registered pension scheme from the date of the commissioners' determination.

De-registration

HMRC may withdraw the registration of a pension scheme. The notification must state the date on and after which the pension scheme will not be a registered pension scheme.

The registration of a pension scheme can only be withdrawn if it appears to HMRC that:

- the amount of the scheme chargeable payments made by the pension scheme during any 12-month period exceeds the de-registration threshold;

- the scheme administrator fails to pay a substantial amount of tax, or interest on tax, due from the scheme administrator in accordance with the pension tax rules;
- the scheme administrator fails to provide information required to be provided to HMRC and that failure is significant;
- any information contained in the application for registration of the pension scheme is incorrect in a material particular;
- any declaration accompanying that application or the provision of other information to HMRC is false in a material particular; or
- there is no scheme administrator.

Law: FA 2004, s. 153, 154, 156, 157; TMA 1970, s. 46(1)

Source: HMRC *Registered Pension Schemes Manual*, RPSM02300030

See *British Tax Reporter* ¶306-525.

431 Annual allowance

The annual allowance for 2010–11 is £255,000.

The annual allowance charge is at the rate of 40 per cent in respect of the amount by which the total pension input amount exceeds the amount of the annual allowance. This excess is not treated as income for any purposes of the Tax Acts.

Liability for the annual allowance charge falls on the individual who is the member of the registered pension schemes. The individual is liable to the annual allowance charge irrespective of whether the individual and the scheme administrator of the pension scheme or schemes concerned is resident, ordinarily resident or domiciled in the UK.

The total pension input amount is arrived at by aggregating the pension input amounts in respect of each arrangement relating to the individual under a registered pension scheme of which the individual is a member. The pension input amount depends on the nature of the arrangements. However, if before the end of the tax year, the individual has become entitled to all the benefits that may be provided to the individual under the arrangement or has died, there is no pension input amount.

Law: *Registered Pension Schemes (Standard Lifetime and Annual Allowances) Order* 2010 (SI 2010/922)

432 Lifetime allowance

The lifetime allowance is one of the controls on the amount of tax-free pension savings to which an individual is entitled. Each individual has a set level of benefits that can be drawn from the registered pension scheme without triggering a tax charge. This limit is known as the lifetime allowance.

Income Tax

The lifetime allowance is expressed as a capital value, which is set at a particular level for each tax year. The amount set is known as the standard lifetime allowance. For 2010–11 the standard lifetime allowance is £1,800,000.

In certain circumstances the individual may be entitled to an enhanced lifetime allowance. The enhanced allowance is available where one or more lifetime allowance enhancement factors operate in relation to a benefit crystallisation event in relation to an individual at the time of the benefit crystallisation event (benefit crystallisation events are set out in FA 2004, s. 216). The enhanced allowance is found in accordance with the formula:

$$SLA = (SLA \times LAEF)$$

SLA   is the standard lifetime allowance at the time of the benefit crystallisation event; and

LAEF   is the lifetime enhancement factor that operates with respect to the benefit crystallisation event, the individual (or individuals if more than one of them) or the aggregate of them.

The standard lifetime allowance may also be reduced in certain circumstances where the individual is permitted to draw the pension before normal retirement age.

Lifetime allowance charge

A charge to income tax, known as the lifetime allowance charge, arises where a benefit crystallisation event occurs in relation to an individual who is a member of one or more registered pension schemes and either the first lifetime allowance charge condition or the second lifetime allowance charge condition is met.

First lifetime allowance charge condition

The first lifetime allowance charge condition is that the whole or any part of the individual's lifetime allowance is available on the benefit crystallisation event, but the amount crystallised by the benefit crystallisation event exceeds the amount of the individual lifetime allowance that is available on the benefit crystallisation event (as set out in FA 2004, s. 216).

Second lifetime allowance charge condition

The second lifetime allowance charge condition is that none of the individual's lifetime allowance is available on the benefit crystallisation event (as set out in FA 2004, s. 216).

Amount of the charge

The lifetime allowance charge is charged on the chargeable amount. The charge is at the rate of 55 per cent on so much of the chargeable amount, if any, as constitutes a lump-sum amount and at the rate of 25 per cent in respect of so much, if any, of the chargeable amount as constitutes the retained amount

The chargeable amount comprises the aggregate of the basic amount and any amount that is treated as forming part of the lump sum amount or the retained amount. For these purposes, the basic amount depends on whether the first lifetime allowance charge condition or the second lifetime allowance charge condition is met. If the first lifetime allowance charge condition is met, the basic amount is the amount by which the amount crystallised by the benefit crystallisation event exceeds the amount of the individual's lifetime allowance available on it and if the second lifetime allowance charge condition is met, the basic amount is the amount that is crystallised by the benefit crystallisation event.

The lump sum amount is the aggregate of so much of the basic amount as is paid as a lump sum to the individual or a lump sum death benefit in respect of the individual amount that is treated as forming part of the lump sum amount. Where any tax that is payable as a result of the lifetime allowance charge on the lump sum amount is covered by a scheme-funded payment, it is itself treated as forming part of the lump sum amount.

The retained amount is the aggregate of so much of the basic amount as is not paid as a lump sum to the individual or a lump sum death benefits in respect of the individual and any amount that is treated as forming part of the retained amount. Where any of the tax that is payable as a result of the lifetime allowance charge on the retained amount is covered by a scheme-funded payment, it is itself treated as forming part of the retained amount.

An amount of tax is treated as covered by a scheme-funded tax payment if the tax is paid by the scheme administrator. The chargeable amount is not treated as income for any purpose of the Tax Acts.

Liability for the lifetime allowance charge falls on the individual and the scheme administrator, and their liability is joint and several. Where the liability arises by the payment of a relevant lump sum death benefit, the liability for the lifetime allowance charge falls on the person to whom it is paid.

If more than one relevant lump sum death benefit is paid in respect of an individual and tax is not chargeable on the whole amount of all of them, the total amount of tax payable is apportioned on a just and reasonable basis between the recipients of the lump sum death benefits.

Liability to the lifetime allowance charge arises irrespective of when the person, any other person who is liable and the scheme administrator (if so liable) are resident, ordinarily resident or domiciled in the UK .

Law: FA 2004, s. 215–217; *Special Annual Allowance Charge (Protected Pension Input Amounts) Order 2010 (SI 2010/429); Registered Pension Schemes (Standard Lifetime and Annual Allowances) Order 2010 (SI 2010/922)*

See *British Tax Reporter* ¶306-000.

433 Unregistered pension schemes

Registered pension schemes enjoy opportunities for tax privileged pension saving not available to schemes that are not registered.

Schemes that were approved pension schemes immediately prior to 6 April 2006 are automatically registered pension schemes after that date, unless the scheme administrator opts out of automatic registration. Schemes that were not approved prior to 6 April 2006 will not be registered pension schemes after that date unless the schemes are registered as such. Similarly, schemes set up after 6 April 2006 that are not registered will not be registered pension schemes and will not attract the associated tax benefits.

TERMINATION PAYMENTS

438   Nature and treatment of termination payments

Whether a payment made to a director or employee on the termination of his office or employment is taxable depends on whether the payment was made by way of reward for services (see 273), or whether it is made to compensate the employee, etc. for the loss of his rights in respect of his employment, etc. It is only the former which is taxable on general principles (though those payments which escape tax on general principles are usually now caught in part by specific provisions: see 440). It is now accepted that genuine non-statutory redundancy payments are not within the former, even if they form part of an employee's terms of employment.

Similar arguments apply to partial termination payments by way of a reduction in duties or the emoluments therefrom. Payments made for such a reduction are generally taxable. However, payments have escaped the general principle where they related to compensation for giving up certain financial advantages which would have accrued and commutation of pension rights. Payment under a termination clause agreed following a move between subsidiaries, resented by the director but enforced by the parent company, has been held to be an emolument rather than damages.

Payments in lieu of notice

The term 'payment in lieu of notice' (PILON) is not a tax term and may be used to describe a number of differing payments made on termination of employment. The exact nature of the payment, rather than the label ascribed to it, will determine the tax consequences. The following table summaries the tax position for various payments commonly described as PILONs.

Nature of payment	*Tax implications*
Notice is given but not worked commonly referred to as 'gardening leave'), salary for the notice period being paid as a lump sum	There is no payment in lieu. The salary payment is taxed as normal under ITEPA 2003, s. 6(1)
Contractual arrangements provide for PILON to be paid as an alternative to notice	The PILON replaces the salary that would have been payable had proper notice been given. It is a chargeable emolument under ITEPA 2003, s. 6(1)
Employer and employee agree at the time of termination that the employment is to be terminated without proper notice, but on making of a PILON	No contractual PILON. Payment is a termination payment chargeable under ITEPA 2003, s. 401
Contractual arrangements do not provide for a PILON. The employer terminates the contract and tenders a PILON	No contractual PILON. Payment represents liquidated damages and is taxed under ITEPA 2003, s. 401

Where a professional person also holds an office and is paid compensation in respect of its termination, that payment is assessable under the charge on employment income provisions and not under the charge on business profits provisions (former Sch. D).

Statutory redundancy payments and similar 'employer's payments' are exempt from tax under the charge on employment income provisions.

'Outplacement counselling' and related fees or travelling expenses are also, for most employees and office holders, exempt from tax to the extent that they are provided in the UK.

For more details of the rules concerning ex gratia payments, see 422.

Law: ITEPA 2003, s. 309, 310; *Clinton v R & C Commrs* (2009) TC 00278; *Cornell v R & C Commrs* [2009] TC 00108; *SCA Packaging Ltd v R & C Commrs* [2007] EWHC 270 (Ch); *Brander & Ors v R & C Commrs* (2007) Sp C 610; *EMI Group Electronics Ltd v Coldicott (HMIT)* [1999] BTC 294; *Antelope v Ellis (HMIT)* (1995) Sp C 41; *Mairs (HMIT) v Haughey* [1993] BTC 339; *IR Commrs v Brander & Cruickshank* [1971] 1 WLR 212; *Dale (HMIT) v de Soissons* (1950) 32 TC 126; *Wales (HMIT) v Tilley* [1942] 2 KB 169; *Cameron v Prendergast (HMIT)* [1940] AC 549; *Hunter (HMIT) v Dewhurst* (1932) 16 TC 605

Income Tax

Source: SP 1/94, Non-statutory lump sum redundancy payments

See *British Tax Reporter* ¶437-000.

440 Tax treatment of termination payments

The rules applying to tax termination payments were revised from April 1998. From that date, to the extent that their amount exceeds £30,000, payments and other 'benefits' which are not otherwise chargeable to tax (see 438) are specifically charged under the charge on employment income provisions if they are received in connection with:

- the termination of a person's office or employment, or
- any change in its duties or emoluments.

This had the effect that, technically, some benefits that would have been exempt if provided in connection with continuing employment, could be taxed in connection with a termination or change of duties.

See *British Tax Reporter* ¶437-000.

442 Termination settlement agreements

Payments and benefits received after 5 April 1998 under a termination settlement agreement are taxable for the year in which they are received, rather than (as previously) being treated as income of the year of termination or change.

For these purposes, 'benefit' includes anything which, if received for performing the duties of the employment, would be (apart from any exemption):

- an emolument of the employment (see 273ff.), or
- taxable as an emolument of the employment (see 312, 382ff.).

A cash benefit is treated as received:

- when payment is made of or on account of the benefit, or
- the recipient becomes entitled to require payment of or on account of the benefit.

A non-cash benefit is treated as received when it is used or enjoyed.

The rules apply to all payments and other benefits received directly or indirectly in consideration or in consequence of, or otherwise in connection with, the termination or change:

(1) by the employee or former employee;

(2) by the spouse or civil partner, or any relative or dependant of the employee or former employee; or

(3) by the personal representatives of the former employee.

A payment or other benefit which is provided on behalf, or to the order, of the employee or former employee is treated as received by the employee or former employee.

The following are excluded from charge.

(1) Payments, etc. made on account of injury to or 'disability' of the employee, or where termination of employment is as a consequence of the employee's death. A 'disability' can be caused by a slow deterioration in mental or physical health, as well as a sudden affliction.

(2) Terminal grants, gratuities or other lump sums paid to members of the armed forces.

(3) Benefits under pension schemes run by the government of an overseas Commonwealth territory, or compensation for career loss, interruption of service or disturbance made in connection with any constitutional change in such a territory to a person who, before the change, was employed in the territory's public service (this effectively re-enacts previous provisions).

Application of £30,000 threshold

The application of the £30,000 threshold is as follows:

(1) payments and benefits in respect of different employments with the same or an 'associated' employer are aggregated;

(2) if the payments, etc. are received in different tax years, the £30,000 is set against payments, etc. received in earlier years before those of earlier later years (thus reflecting that payments, etc. are now chargeable as they are received); and

(3) within any particular tax year, any outstanding exemption is allocated first to cash benefits as they are received, any balance at the end of the year being set against the aggregate value of non-cash benefits received in the year.

Exclusion or reduction of charge in case of foreign service

Relief is available in respect of payments in relation to 'foreign service'. Full exemption continues to be given from the charge where the period of foreign service meets one of three tests.

Where there has been foreign service but on a scale insufficient to qualify for exemption as above, the charge is proportionately reduced (as previously). However, a taxpayer is not entitled to this relief in so far as the relief, together with any personal relief allowed to him, would reduce the income on which he is chargeable below the amount of income tax which he is entitled:

(1) to charge against any other person; or

(2) to deduct from any payment he is liable to make.

Income Tax

269

Valuation of benefits

The amount of a payment or other benefit is:

(1)   in the case of a cash benefit, the amount received; and

(2)   in the case of a non-cash benefit, the 'cash equivalent' of the benefit.

The 'cash equivalent' of a non-cash benefit is whichever is the greater of:

(1)   the amount which would be chargeable to tax if the benefit were an emolument of the employment chargeable to tax under ITEPA 2003 (former Sch. E, Case I) (see 250) (which would catch a benefit which has risen in value since acquisition); or

(2)   the cash equivalent of benefits under non-approved pension schemes (see 422), which largely follows the counterpart rules for employee benefits (see 382).

Notional interest treated as paid if amount charged in respect of beneficial loan

Where a person is taxable under the present provisions on the cash equivalent of a beneficial loan, relief is given which mirrors that available to employees for 'notional interest' payable on a beneficial loan that attracts interest relief (see 406).

Giving effect to the charge to tax

Tax under the present provisions is charged on the employee or former employee, whether or not he or she is the recipient of the payment or other benefit. After the death of the employee or former employee, any outstanding charge is attached to his or her estate (as previously).

Reporting requirements

Employers must provide a report by the 6 July after the tax year in which any termination award is made. (This relaxes the previous requirement of a report within 30 days of the tax year end.)

For more details of the rules concerning ex gratia payments, see 422.

Law: ITEPA 2003, s. 401–404; *Income Tax (Pay As You Earn) Regulations* 2003 (SI 2003/2682); *The Tax and Civil Partnership Regulations* 2005 (SI 2005/3229); *Colquhoun* [2010] TC 00348

See *British Tax Reporter* ¶437-000.

444   The treatment of damages

An employee may commence or threaten legal proceedings for wrongful dismissal or breach of contract. Any payment made in settlement of such a claim is treated as a payment in

University of Chester, Seaborne Library

Title: British master tax guide : 2010-11/
Julie Clift... [et al.]
ID: 36132628
Due: 18-02-14

Total items: 1
28/01/2014 21:12

Thank you for using Self Check

4

compensation for loss of office and is chargeable as a specific termination payment, and the usual exemptions apply to it where appropriate (see 440).

Damages for wrongful dismissal or for breach of contract are to put the innocent party in the same position that he would have been in had the contract been carried out. In most instances the employee would have been liable to tax on the payment. A deduction can accordingly be made to allow for tax from such payments so that the employee is in no better position than he would have been in had there been no breach of contract. This is known as the rule in *Gourley's* case.

Limitations to the Gourley rule

The following limitations to the *Gourley* rule should be noted:

- income tax is only deducted if such tax would have been deducted had there not been a breach of contract; and
- the damages, etc. themselves must not be the subject of a charge to tax.

In the case of damages for wrongful dismissal and breach of contract, the taxpayer would have paid tax on the payments as wages or salary if there had been no breach of contract, but such damages are charged to tax allowing the first £30,000 to be tax-free (see 440). The excess over £30,000, therefore, does not fall within the *Gourley* rule, whereas the first £30,000 does.

Law: *British Transport Commission v Gourley* [1956] AC 185

See *British Tax Reporter* ¶437-000.

BUSINESS INCOME

550 Profits from trades, professions and vocations – liability

From 6 April 2005, profits arising from a trade, profession or vocation are taxed under the provisions of the *Income Tax (Trading and Other Income) Act* 2005 (ITTOIA 2005).

If a proprietor of a business wishes to show that he is not the person who carries on the trade and is not entitled to the profits, he has to prove that they accrue to someone else.

Law: ITTOIA 2005, s. 5; *Alongi v IR Commrs* [1991] BTC 353

See *British Tax Reporter* ¶200-000.

Income Tax

TRADES

555 Introduction to meaning of 'trade'

The word 'trade' is incompletely defined in the legislation. 'Trade', it is stated, includes 'every trade, manufacture, adventure or concern in the nature of a trade': without a definition of 'trade', this is of limited assistance. The only thing to do, as Lord Denning MR once declared, is to look at the usual characteristics of a trade and see how the transaction under consideration measures up to them. While some activities are deemed to be trades by statute (see 556) for the most part, decided cases must be studied, to distinguish the borderline between trading and other activities: most of such cases fit easily within one or more of the 'badges of trade' (see 560).

Entertainers

Notwithstanding the fact that they treat most entertainers as employees, HMRC by concession continue to treat those with 'reserved Sch. D status' as self-employed (see 253).

Law: *JP Harrison (Watford) Ltd v Griffiths (HMIT)* (1962) 40 TC 281

See *British Tax Reporter* ¶201-000.

556 Statutory trades

(1) Farming and market gardening (except woodlands)

All 'farming' and 'market gardening' in the UK, and the occupation of other UK land (except woodlands) managed on a commercial basis with a view to profits, are treated as a trade, the profits from which are taxed under ITTOIA 2005 (see further 940ff.).

(2) Woodlands

Profits from occupying land which comprises 'woodlands or is being prepared for use for forestry purposes' are not taxable under ITTOIA 2005 as being profits from the 'commercial occupation of land' (see above).

Timber merchants are taxed on their profits under ITTOIA 2005 on general principles.

Law: ITTOIA 2005, s. 9–16; *Jaggers (t/a Shide Trees) v Ellis (HMIT)* [1997] BTC 571

See *British Tax Reporter* ¶201-000.

558 Trade v investment

The holding of an asset would seem to require that it be either an investment (whether as a capital asset of a business or otherwise) or an item of trading stock; the term investment in this sense does not imply any overwhelming desire to make a profit (see also 571). Lord Wilberforce said in a House of Lords case:

'What I think is not possible is for an asset to be both trading stock and permanent investment at the same time, nor to possess an indeterminate status – neither trading stock nor permanent asset. It must be one or the other, even though, and this seems to be legitimate and intelligible, the [taxpayer] in whatever character it acquires the asset, may reserve an intention to change its character.'

In the case, properties acquired by a group for retention were sold on the liquidation of the group and the decision to liquidate did not turn capital profits into trading profits (see also 3689).

Where a person buys an article or item for investment rather than trade, the following factors are usually present.

- A feeling on his part that he will enjoy the possession or use of the item purchased, apart from the pleasure he will feel at its increase in value.
- An intention to keep the article or item for a reasonable time. What is considered to be a reasonable time? The buyer must keep the item for long enough to make it clear that he did have the feeling mentioned above. However, a resale by the buyer almost immediately will not necessarily mean that he is trading if he has a good reason to sell (see 570).

A gain made from the sale of assets held for investment may give rise to a charge under the CGT provisions (see 5000ff.) but is not subject to income tax (see further the 'badges of trade' at 560).

Law: *Simmons (as liquidator of Lionel Simmons Properties) v IR Commrs* [1980] 1 WLR 1196; *Kirkby v Hughes (HMIT)* [1993] BTC 52; *Koenigsberger v Mellor (HMIT)* [1995] BTC 292

Source: SP 14/91, *Tax treatment of transactions in financial futures and options*; SP 15/91, *The treatment of transactions in financial futures and options*

See *British Tax Reporter* ¶200-275.

560 The 'badges of trade'

To find the characteristics of a trade it is helpful to look at the case law in some detail. In order to make the matter a little easier, the principles were categorised within six badges or identifying features of trading by the (Radcliffe) Royal Commission on the Taxation of Profits and Income in 1954 (Cmd. 9474). The categories are subject-matter (see 562), period of ownership (see 564), frequency of the transactions (see 566), supplementary work (see

568), circumstances responsible for sale (see 570) and motive (see 571). In 1986, Browne-Wilkinson V-C has enumerated slightly different badges, though he has subsequently redefined his entire approach to the consideration of trading (see 555).

Source: *Marson (HMIT) v Morton* [1986] BTC 377

See *British Tax Reporter* ¶200-600.

562   Badge of trade: subject-matter

'*While almost any form of property can be acquired to be dealt in, those forms of property, such as commodities or manufactured articles, which are normally the subject of trading, are only very exceptionally the subject of investment. Again property which does not yield to its owner an income or personal enjoyment merely by virtue of its ownership is more likely to have been acquired with the object of a deal than property that does*' (Radcliffe Report: see 560).

In one case, a merchant in agricultural machinery was offered 44 million yards of aircraft linen which he bought and sold at a considerable profit. To do so he found it necessary to set up a business to handle sales of it to the public. Because of the nature of the subject-matter involved (and admittedly because he had set up a business to sell it) the court held that the resale of the aircraft linen was a trading transaction.

In another case, a money-lender on business abroad bought one million rolls of toilet paper. He sold the toilet paper to a single purchaser on his return to the UK and made a profit of £10,000. The Court of Session, in holding that the taxpayer was engaged in an adventure in the nature of a trade, said that he:

> 'made himself liable for the purchase of this vast quantity of toilet paper obviously for no other conceivable purpose than that of reselling it at a profit.'

In another Court of Session case, a woodcutter who had never previously traded in whisky bought three lots of it and sold them two years later at a profit. The court said the nature of the transaction is important. Some things are bought for pleasure, but not vats of whisky. The size of the transaction also is important. A very large transaction can be evidence that the taxpayer never intended to keep the asset.

Law: *Martin v Lowry (HMIT)* [1927] AC 312; *Rutledge v IR Commrs* (1929) 14 TC 490; *IR Commrs v Fraser* (1942) 24 TC 498

See *British Tax Reporter* ¶200-600.

564 Badge of trade: period of ownership

'*Generally speaking, property meant to be dealt in is realised within a short time after acquisition. But there may be exceptions to this as a universal rule*' (Radcliffe Report: see 560).

A case which demonstrates this concerned a taxpayer who was in a position to purchase land at a favourable price. However, he could not raise a loan. To get over this problem he contracted to sell the land to a purchaser, at a profit, before he had contracted to buy it. It was this fact that persuaded the High Court to hold the transaction to be an adventure in the nature of trade.

The knowledge alone that a purchase will increase in value is insufficient evidence upon which to find that a transaction is in the nature of trade. Many people buy things to keep and enjoy but at the same time they know that they will increase in value and may be sold at a profit. Where, however, the resale at a profit appears to be the only reason for the purchase, the inference drawn will be that the taxpayer is trading.

In another case, a farmer bought two fields and sold one with planning permission nine months later. He repeated this a few months later with the second field. In holding that he was liable to tax under former Sch. D, Case I, the High Court said the motive for resale was important. A taxpayer may unexpectedly be offered money but a quick resale always invites close scrutiny of the transaction.

Law: *Turner v Last (HMIT)* (1965) 42 TC 517; *Johnston (HMIT) v Heath* [1970] 1 WLR 1567

See *British Tax Reporter* ¶200-600.

566 Badge of trade: the frequency of the transactions

'*If realisations of the same sort of property occur in succession over a period of years or there are several such realisations at about the same date a presumption arises that there has been dealing in respect of each*' (Radcliffe Report: see 560).

This statement is well illustrated by a case where a taxpayer started a driving school and later sold it at a profit. He then set up and sold some 30 driving schools. The High Court held that the sales which followed the first had tainted the first, so that it too was a trading transaction. This does not mean that a single transaction cannot be a trading transaction (see 562). It would appear that there may not have been, initially, any intention to sell the first driving school from the outset but the subsequent sales led the court to believe that there must have been.

In another case, a taxpayer bought and resold a spinning mill. Then, in partnership with friends, he repeated the transaction four times. The High Court said that one transaction does

Income Tax

not usually give rise to a finding of trading but systematic repetition raises an inference of trading.

Another case concerned a mathematician with £100,000, who wanted to produce £7,000 per year. He went to auctions and bought up endowment policies on other people's lives to produce the income. The Court of Appeal said that it was not necessary to buy and sell to be trading. Because of the huge number of policies or the frequency of the transactions, the court held him to be trading.

An isolated transaction involving the purchase, development, and resale of land may not be regarded as trading where the development is a subsidiary purpose of the acquisition and sale.

Law: *Pickford v Quirke (HMIT)* (1927) 13 TC 251; *Barry v Cordy (HMIT)* (1946) 28 TC 250; *Leach v Pogson (HMIT)* (1962) 40 TC 585; *Kirkham v Williams (HMIT)* [1991] BTC 196

See *British Tax Reporter* ¶200-600.

568   Badge of trade: supplementary work

'*If the property is worked up in any way during the ownership so as to bring it into a more marketable condition, or if any special exertions are made to find or attract purchasers, such as the opening of an office or large-scale advertising, there is some evidence of dealing. For when there is an organised effort to obtain profits there is a source of taxable income. But if nothing at all is done, the suggestion tends the other way*' (Radcliffe Report: see 560).

A number of cases illustrate this point. In one such case, a ship repairer, a blacksmith and an employee of a fish salesman bought a cargo ship and converted it into a steam drifter which was then sold at a profit. They had never done this sort of work before nor were they connected persons. Lord President Clyde said that this was more than just a purchase and resale. They had actually spent money on making the asset something else. The court held the venture to be a trading transaction.

In another case, the taxpayers were members of different firms. They bought three lots of brandy, shipped it to London where it was blended, mixed and packaged before being sold by the taxpayers. This required expertise. The Court of Appeal held this to be trading.

The supplementary work must change the asset

To polish, clean or otherwise prepare an asset for sale so that it will attract the best price will not be considered to be trading. In one case, a taxpayer bought two metal stills. Having carried out considerable work on the stills consisting mainly of removing a sticky glue from them, he then sold them individually to each of two companies which he controlled. The Court of Appeal declined to disturb the general commissioners' finding of fact that he was not trading. The courts will not disturb a finding of fact by the commissioners if it was one which there was evidence to support, notwithstanding that a different body of commissioners might have reached a different finding on the same evidence (see 177).

In another case, a grocer and newsagent who lived over his shop noticed a house for sale. He went to the auction, bought it on impulse, and then decided that he did not want to live in the house. He then obtained planning permission for the land and sold it at a vast profit. The Crown conceded that the original purchase of the house as a residence was not in the course of trade. Taking steps to enhance its value did not make him a trader. However, it should be noted that the Court of Appeal also said that improving land often indicates trading, particularly where the taxpayer's business is connected with land.

Law: *Cape Brandy Syndicate v IR Commrs* [1921] 2 KB 403; *IR Commrs v Livingstone* (1926) 11 TC 538; *Jenkinson (HMIT) v Freedland* (1961) 39 TC 636; *Taylor v Good (HMIT)* [1974] 1 WLR 556

See *British Tax Reporter* ¶200-600.

570 Badge of trade: circumstances responsible for sale

A quick resale leads to an inference of trading, but if the asset is sold in response to 'a sudden emergency or opportunity calling for ready money, that negatives the idea that any plan of dealing prompted the original purchase' (Radcliffe Report: see 560).

In one case, the taxpayer built 2,500 houses. Some were for letting and some for resale. The letting business started losing money and the taxpayer decided to sell the letting houses. The High Court said this was a forced sale and was not trading.

Law: *West v Phillips (HMIT)* (1958) 38 TC 203

See *British Tax Reporter* ¶200-600.

571 Badge of trade: motive

The taxpayer's motive was considered to be a significant factor by the Radcliffe Report (see 560).

Where there is clear evidence upon which it can be decided whether a taxpayer is trading, the taxpayer's motive is irrelevant. However, where the evidence is ambiguous, the taxpayer's motive can be considered. A clear intention to buy and resell quickly at a profit will be taken to be trading if in fact the taxpayer does resell quickly. A desire to make a profit is not, per se, sufficient evidence to support a finding of trading. It is clear that a desire to make a profit is uppermost in the minds of all who buy for investment. But where that desire is not coupled with an intention to hold the item as one would hold an investment, it will assist in a finding of trading.

Income Tax

277

The question of motive becomes more important where the taxpayer buys for investment and quickly thereafter changes his mind and decides to sell, or where he buys with the sole intention of reselling the asset at a profit but then realises that he likes the asset and decides to keep it for the enjoyment he derives from it. Providing that there is clear evidence that the asset was bought for investment, a quick resale will not make the transaction an adventure in the nature of trade (see 570). The reason for sale will rather be looked upon as an unforeseen contingency. To be unexpectedly offered a good price for the asset could be an unforeseen contingency, but enjoyment derived from an expectation of price rise will not assist in a finding that the asset is held for investment.

If a decision is made by the taxpayer shortly after the purchase to retain an asset (which was bought with the intention of reselling it at a profit) because he enjoys using or having it (apart from the enjoyment derived from a knowledge that the asset is increasing in value), then clearly when he later comes to sell it he will not be held to be trading. If, on the other hand, the taxpayer intends to sell as soon as possible, but cannot find a buyer for a considerable time, he is much more likely to be considered to be trading. In one case, the Court of Session, in deciding that very question, decided that the taxpayer was not trading. The taxpayer had bought four houses with a view to resale and had instructed his agents to sell whenever a suitable opportunity arose. He sold them three years later. Lord Keith said that the intention to resell some day at a profit is not in itself sufficient to attract tax.

In another case, the Court of Appeal said that in addition to bearing badges of trade, a trading transaction must have a commercial purpose: if the sole purpose of the transaction was to obtain a fiscal advantage, it was impossible to postulate the existence of any commercial purpose. However, the House of Lords has effectively refuted this view, implying that the decision pertained to the fact that a transaction whose effect was fiscal alchemy was not trading (see 555). In the Court of Appeal case, the issue was whether the company was trading when it assumed liability for the risk of foreign exchange losses from another company in the same group. The object was to convert capital losses to revenue losses which could then be set-off against trading profits. The court held that the company was not trading in respect of these transactions. They had no commercial justification in the group context.

Law: *IR Commrs v Reinhold* (1953) 34 TC 389; *Overseas Containers (Finance) Ltd v Stoker (HMIT)* [1989] BTC 153; *Ensign Tankers (Leasing) Ltd v Stokes (HMIT)* [1992] BTC 110

See *British Tax Reporter* ¶200-600.

572 Mutual trading

It is a basic rule that,

'No man ... can trade with himself [or] make ... taxable profit by dealing with himself.'

In other words, a person's taxable profits must derive from sources outside himself.

The 'mutuality' principle has been ascribed to this rule and is a principle which has been developed by the courts over a long period. For mutuality to apply there must be a class of contributors to a common fund, all of who are entitled to participate in the surplus. Where all the participators in the surplus are contributors to the common fund, then the participators are trading mutually and any surplus made from the venture is not assessable. A distribution of fund assets on its dissolution may give rise to a taxable receipt on the contributor.

Outsiders

Where the mutual trade has dealings with outsiders and those dealings produce profits, then those profits are assessable under ITTOIA 2005. This point is demonstrated by a case where the members of a golf club paid an annual subscription and were allowed to use the facilities of the club. Non-members were allowed to use the facilities upon the payment of green fees. The High Court held that profits made from the green fees were assessable under former Sch. D, Case I. A Revenue 'interpretation' (see 176) reiterates this view and adds that even where visitors become 'temporary members' of a golf club, the income received from their use of the club's facilities is taken into account for tax purposes unless their rights are the same as those of full members (e.g. including a right to vote at meetings and generally to exercise control over the running of the club).

Liabilities and rights

There must be a balance between the amount which the member contributes to the fund and that which he draws from it.

In one case, hotel owners paid more in membership fees to a club so that their guests could use club facilities. The Privy Council held that the hotel owners were trading with the club because they contributed a great deal more than other members but received the same benefits in return.

However, a special commissioner has held that equality of rights was not an essential requirement. A club had two classes of membership: 'ordinary' and 'associate'. Associate members were non-voting, were not involved in the management of the club's affairs and were not entitled to a share in the club's assets on dissolution. The mutual trading exemption applied to surpluses in respect of business with both classes.

HMRC have published an 'interpretation' (see 176) on the taxation of members' sports clubs.

Law: ITTOIA 2005, s. 104; *Dublin Corporation v M'Adam*(1887) 2 TC 387; *Carlisle and Silloth Golf Club v Smith (HMIT)* [1913] 3 KB 75; *Fletcher v Jamaica Income Tax Commissioner* [1972] AC 414; *Westbourne Supporters of Glentoran Football Club v Brennan (HMIT)* (1995) Sp C 22

Website: www.hmrc.gov.uk/bulletins/index.htm

See *British Tax Reporter* ¶203-000.

573 Illegal trading

Whilst there are conflicting dicta on the matter, it now seems clear that the profits of an illegal trade are taxable. Profits obtained from shipping whisky to the US during prohibition have been held taxable, as have profits from illegal wagering contracts. The profits of prostitution have also been held to be trading income assessable under former Sch. D, Case I.

Law: *Partridge v Mallandaine* (1886) 18 QBD 276; *Lindsay v IR Commrs* (1932) 18 TC 43; *IR Commrs v Aken* [1990] BTC 352

See *British Tax Reporter* ¶200-925.

574 The realisation of trade assets

Where a trade goes into liquidation, the mere realisation of assets after discontinuance of the trade will not constitute trading if it is incidental to the liquidation. A whisky broker who was compelled to discontinue trading due to ill health and sold his business and whisky to another person has been held not to be trading.

However, it is possible for the realisation of assets to be trading. In one case, two wine and spirit merchants sent a letter to customers explaining that they were about to retire and asking if they wished to buy stock. The process of discontinuance took about one year during which time stock was still being bought in to fulfil contracts of sale agreed previously. The House of Lords said that they were trading.

The executors of a sole trader are normally not regarded as trading. However, if they go beyond what is necessary for prudent winding up of the estate they can be found to be trading. The executor of a deceased partner does not become a partner. However, should the executor associate himself with the surviving partners in trading activities, he may be treated as trading in partnership with them.

Law: *J & R O'Kane & Co v IR Commrs* (1922) 22 TC 303; *Marshall's Exors v Joly (HMIT)* (1936) 20 TC 256; *Newbarns Syndicate v Hay (HMIT)* (1939) 22 TC 461; *IR Commrs v Nelson* (1939) 12 TC 716; *Pattullo's Trustees v IR Commrs* (1955) 36 TC 87

See *British Tax Reporter* ¶202-500.

PROFESSIONS AND VOCATIONS

584 Introduction to the meaning of profession or vocation

The same problem presents itself in defining 'profession or vocation' with respect to the charge of business income (see 550) as is found with 'trade' (see 560). There is no definition in statute. In practice, there is no need to distinguish between professions (see 586) and vocations (see 587).

See *British Tax Reporter* ¶202-000.

586 'Profession'

A 'profession' involves work requiring purely intellectual skill or manual labour dependent upon purely intellectual skill. However, while the activities of a person may on the above tests amount to a profession, he may still be employed. If so, his emoluments are taxed under ITEPA 2003 and not under ITTOIA 2005 (see 253). An example of this would be a barrister employed by a company.

Law: *IR Commrs v Maxse* [1919] 1 KB 647

See *British Tax Reporter* ¶202-000.

587 'Vocation'

In a case concerning partners who went to the races as bookmakers and punters, it was said that the term 'vocation' is analogous to calling: the way in which a man passes his life.

In another case, the taxpayer's sole means of livelihood was betting on horses which he did from a private residence with bookmakers at starting prices. The High Court held that the profits were not assessable. This was not a vocation: the taxpayer was simply addicted to betting.

Law: *Partridge v Mallandaine* (1886) 18 QBD 276; *Graham v Green (HMIT)* [1925] 2 KB 37

See *British Tax Reporter* ¶202-050.

ANNUAL PROFITS FROM BUSINESS

588 Calculation of taxable business profits

Once it is established that a person is engaged in a trade, profession or vocation (see 555, 584ff.), his 'annual profits' must be ascertained because it is only these which are liable to income tax (see 550).

Unless there is an explicit provision otherwise:

- statutory references to 'receipts' and 'expenses' are to be taken as items brought into account as credits and debits in computing profits, there being no implication thereby that any amount is actually received or paid; and

- the rules used to compute profits for trades, professions and vocations must be used to compute losses.

Law: ITTOIA 2005, s. 26(1)–(2), 27(1)–(3)

See *British Tax Reporter* ¶210-000.

590 True and fair view

Taxable business profits are usually computed on an earnings basis: i.e. on sums earned in the period of account as opposed to sums received (the cash basis). Professions and vocations may only use the cash basis after their first three years, where appropriate and provided the taxpayer gives certain undertakings (for barristers, see below). However, with respect to periods of account beginning after 6 April 1999, profits for present purposes must be computed on a basis which gives a 'true and fair view', subject to any adaptations necessary to comply with specific tax law. Thus the use of non-standard accounting bases (such as the cash basis) in calculating such profits will not be possible (but see below).

Barristers and advocates in early years of practice

HMRC have generally always allowed barristers to compute their profits on a cash basis. Despite the above change, barristers (and advocates in Scotland) may use either a cash or other non-earnings basis acceptable to HMRC to calculate their profits for periods of account ending during their first seven years of practice. The chosen basis must be used consistently and must be changed to the statutory 'true and fair view' basis (see above) after seven years (earlier changeover is permitted but once made is irrevocable).

A charge to tax may arise on this change of basis (see 591). The charge is spread over ten tax years.

There is, however, an option to increase an instalment payment. Notice must be given in writing on or before 31 January following the tax year in question, and must state the amount that is to be paid. The amount can be any figure up to the balance of the total adjustment charge owing. Future instalments are then re-calculated.

Law: ITTOIA 2005, s. 25, 160, 227–240

Source: SP A3, *Barristers – the cash basis*; SP A27, *Accounts on a cash basis*

See *British Tax Reporter* ¶205-620.

591   Change of accounting basis

Finance Act 2002 altered the treatment of changes in accounting basis, where the first period of account affected by the change ends on or after 1 August 2001. For changes in earlier periods, see below.

Where a business moves from one valid basis for computing its profits for tax to another valid basis, an adjustment must be made to ensure that there is no double-counting or omission of receipts or expenses because of the change. This works by comparing the amount by which profits have been understated (or losses overstated) on the old basis, with the amount by which profits have been overstated (or losses understated) on the old basis. This results in either a positive adjustment, which is then charged to tax, or a negative adjustment, which is treated as an allowable deduction.

The rules do not apply where the change is occasioned by an amendment to statute, because there will be specific transitional provisions governing the change.

Calculation of the adjustment

The calculation of the adjustment is divided into two steps.

Step one

Work out by how much profits were understated (or losses overstated) on the old basis. This is done by aggregating the following four amounts.

(1)   Receipts which the new basis would place in a period of account before the change, but which have not been recognised under the old basis. That is to say, receipts which would otherwise fall out of account.

(2)   Expenses which have already been recognised under the old basis, but under the new basis are brought into account in a period of account after the change. That is to say, expenses which would otherwise be double-counted.

(3)   Deductions for opening stock or work in progress on the new basis to the extent that they are not matched by credits for closing stock or work in progress on the old basis, or to the extent that the deduction is greater than the closing credits because of the difference in basis.

(4)   Amounts in respect of depreciation that were not the subject of a tax adjustment in the last period of account before the change, but for which a tax adjustment is required on the new basis. This refers specifically to the inclusion of depreciation in figures for stock, a practice which HMRC consider to have been ended by recent case law. Any amount which would otherwise fall out of account on the resulting enforced change of practice is swept up in this item.

Step two

From the figure arrived at in step one, the amount by which profits were overstated (or losses understated) on the old basis is deducted. This comprises the following amounts.

Income Tax

(1)   Receipts which have already been recognised under the old basis, but which would not have been so recognised had the new basis applied. That is to say, receipts which would otherwise be double counted.

(2)   Expenses that would otherwise drop out of account because the old basis would place them in a period of account after the change, whereas the new basis would place them before the change.

(3)   Credits for closing stock or work in progress on the old basis that are not matched by deductions for opening stock or work in progress on the new basis, or to the extent that the closing credits are higher than the opening deduction because of the difference in basis.

Any amount that is included in this calculation cannot also be deducted in computing profits for a period of account.

Note that there is no equivalent of item 4 in step one, because this particular adjustment can only work in one direction – i.e. to correct an understatement of profit (or overstatement of loss).

Giving effect to the adjustment

If the result of the two steps described above is a positive figure, then that amount is chargeable to tax.

For income tax purposes, the charge is under ITTOIA 2005, Pt 2, Ch. 17, and is deemed to arise on the last day of the first period of account under the new basis. For corporation tax purposes, the amount chargeable is treated as a receipt arising on the last day of the first period of account under the new basis.

If the result of the two steps described above is a negative figure, it is treated as an expense of the trade, profession or vocation arising on the last day of the first period of account under the new basis.

Deferred revenue expenditure

There used to be a divergence of accounting and tax treatment in the case of certain revenue expenditure that, for accounting purposes, was taken to the balance sheet and then amortised over several periods of account. The tax treatment was often to allow the expenditure when incurred.

Accounting and tax treatment have since converged, so that the expenditure is allowed as it is taken to the profit and loss account. However, where the expenditure had been allowed in full under the old basis, the effect of applying the change in basis rules (see step one, item two above) would be to bring in as a positive adjustment all amounts still to be taken to the profit and loss account.

Therefore, in order to leave the tax treatment on the 'incurred' basis undisturbed, the rules are overridden, so that no adjustment is necessary on a change of accounting basis to the new understanding. As a corollary, any amount previously allowed before the change is disallowed for periods after the change.

Deferral of charge

There is a deferral of the tax charge arising from a positive adjustment in two circumstances:

- Where there is a change in tax treatment affecting amounts included in the calculation of stock or work in progress; or
- Where the positive adjustment arises in respect of a change in tax treatment of depreciation (see specifically step one, item four above).

In these circumstances, the tax charge is deferred until the asset in question is realised (by sale, exchange, appropriation or otherwise) or written off.

Application to partnerships

Where a business is carried on in partnership, the amount of any adjustment is computed, for income tax purposes, as if the partnership were an individual resident in the UK.

The general rule is that each partner's share of the adjustment charge is calculated according to the profit-sharing arrangements in force for the twelve months prior to the date of the change of basis.

Any election concerning the adjustment charge must be made jointly by all those who were partners in the twelve months preceding the change of basis.

Law: ITTOIA 2005, s. 227–240

See *British Tax Reporter* ¶206-300.

592 Spreading of bunched income of authors and other artists

Creative artists can make an average claim if profits from a qualifying trade fluctuate from one tax year to the next. Qualifying creative works means literary, dramatic, musical or artistic works, or designs created by the taxpayer personally, or if in partnership, by one or more of his partners.

An averaging claim may be made if the taxpayer has been carrying on the qualifying trade for at least two consecutive tax years and either:

- relevant profits for one of the tax years are less than 75 per cent of the profits for the other; or
- relevant profits for one (but not both) years are nil.

An averaging claim must be made not later than 12 months after 31 January next following the end of the later tax year to which it relates.

Law: ITTOIA 2005, s. 221–224

See *British Tax Reporter* ¶268-300.

596 Sale of income derived from personal activities

Where arrangements are made for the exploitation of income derived from professional activities by placing some other person in a position to enjoy all or any part of their income and, as part of those arrangements or in connection with or in consequence of them, the individual or any other person receives a capital sum and the main object or one of the objects was the avoidance or reduction of income tax, then the capital sum received is chargeable under ITTOIA 2005 (formerly Sch. D, Case VI) as income and not capital.

> ### Example
>
> A high income earner could in the absence of this provision form a company, and sell to the company in consideration for shares issued by the company, his rights in future income. The individual would then simply sell the shares (which apart from this provision are a capital item) and be liable only for capital gains tax on them instead of income tax.

Law: ITA 2007, s. 776

See *British Tax Reporter* ¶269-000.

602 Timing and nature of business results

A person's annual profits from business (see 588ff.) are computed in accordance with generally accepted accounting practice ('GAAP'). His gross profit is the difference between sales made (whether or not he has received cash) and the cost of purchases (purchases adjusted for opening and closing stock, etc.: see 652). To obtain net taxable profits, add to gross profit other 'chargeable trading receipts' (see 626ff.) and deduct 'allowable revenue expenses' (see 2150ff.) incurred (whether or not paid). Where a customer does not pay this will give rise to a bad debt in due course (see 2174).

Trading income is taxable when the trader has fulfilled all conditions necessary to earn it.

Law: *Eckel v Board of Inland Revenue (Trinidad and Tobago)* [1989] BTC 94

See *British Tax Reporter* ¶210-700.

CHARGEABLE BUSINESS RECEIPTS

626   Extent to which business receipts are chargeable

All trading-related receipts count in the computation of 'chargeable business income' (see 602) unless they fall into one of the following categories:

- income arising from outside the scope of the taxpayer's trade, profession or vocation (see 628);
- capital receipts (see 630);
- receipts already taxable by deduction at source (see 635).

There are also various types of receipt for which specific rules have developed either through the courts or by way of statute. In particular, adjustments may be made for undervalue sales, etc. (see 636), certain windfall gains (see 640, 642) and the eventual recovery of bad debts (see 648). There are also rules affecting foreign exchange gains (see 650).

See *British Tax Reporter* ¶220-000.

628   Income outside the scope of the taxpayer's business

Profits from activities outside the taxpayer's trade, profession or vocation do not give rise to a charge to tax as a profit of the trade, etc.

Income from investments held by a trader is prima facie investment income, but may in certain circumstances be brought into account as a trading receipt. Whether it may or may not be so treated depends on the nature of the trade. Decided cases show that the nature of the trade must be such that it can fairly be said that the making and holding of investments at interest is an integral part of the trade.

A person's exploitation of anything produced in the course of his profession cannot be regarded as outside its scope.

Receipts arising outside the scope of the taxpayer's existing trade, whilst not being receipts from that trade, may nevertheless be regarded as the receipts of another (i.e. different) trade or may simply constitute capital receipts (see 5000ff.). Motor mileage allowances for volunteer services are, in the case of taxi drivers and the like, trading receipts as they are received in connection with the taxpayer's trade.

Law: *Scott (HMIT) v Ricketts* [1967] 1 WLR 828; *Simpson (HMIT) v John Reynolds & Co (Insurances) Ltd* [1975] 1 WLR 617; *Wain v Cameron (HMIT)* [1995] BTC 299; *Nuclear-Electric plc v Bradley (HMIT)* [1996] BTC 165

See *British Tax Reporter* ¶220-000.

Income Tax

630 Distinguishing capital and revenue receipts

Revenue receipts must be distinguished from capital receipts, because it is normally only revenue receipts which are chargeable to income tax. Gains from capital receipts normally attract capital gains tax (CGT). However, the equalisation of income tax and CGT rates (see 5000) greatly reduces the importance of the distinction.

What is income and what is capital is a question of law, rather than a question of fact. However, the question has to be answered in the light of all the circumstances, and the weight to be given to a particular circumstance depends on common sense, rather than any single legal principle.

There are two well-known tests for distinguishing a revenue receipt from a capital one, though both of them are of limited value, as will be shown further in this paragraph. The first test is to distinguish receipts which relate to assets which form part of the permanent structure of the business. An example of this would be machinery the sale of which would give rise to a capital receipt.

The second test is to distinguish between circulating and fixed capital. A fixed capital asset is retained in the business with the object of making profits. An example of this would again be machinery. Circulating capital, on the other hand, is acquired to be used or sold. An example would be the raw materials used in the business.

While the above two tests are of some help, they do not resolve all the problems. What is established is that certain types of receipts will be treated in a particular way. The position is summarised in the table below.

Capital	Revenue
Receipts from sale of business assets Sale of fixed assets is a capital receipt, although a profit on the sale of trading stock constitutes an income receipt *Receipts for the sale or destruction of the taxpayer's profit-making apparatus* *Receipts in return for restrictive convenants* Payments received in return for the sterilisation of assets are capital receipts, although treatment of lump sums for 'exclusivity agreements' depends on purpose of payment *One-off receipts* A one-off receipt strongly, but not conclusively suggests a capital receipt	*Payments in lieu of trading receipts* Including: • agreed damages for loss of profits arising from delay in repairs • damages in excess of repair costs to cover lost profits • compensation for increased revenue expenditure • damages for negligence of agents resulting in a trading loss • rebates against price due for goods supplied *Recurring receipts* Recurring receipts are more likely to be revenue receipts

Law: ITTOIA 2005, s. 105, 207; *Glenboig Union Fireclay Co Ltd v IR Commrs* (1921) 12 TC 427; *Burmah Steam Ship Co Ltd v IR Commrs* (1930) 16 TC 67; *Van den Berghs Ltd v Clark (HMIT)* [1935] AC 431; *Kelsall Parsons & Co v IR Commrs* (1938) 21 TC 608; *Thompson (HMIT) v Magnesium Elektron Ltd* (1943) 26 TC 1; *Barr, Crombie & Co Ltd v IR Commrs* (1945) 26 TC 406; *Davies (HMIT) v Shell Company of China Ltd* (1951) 32 TC 133; *Orchard Wine and Spirit Co v Loynes (HMIT)* (1952) 33 TC 97; *Higgs (HMIT) v Olivier* [1952] Ch 311; *Evans Medical Supplies Ltd v Moriarty (HMIT)* [1957] 1 WLR 288; *Jeffrey (HMIT) v Rolls-Royce Ltd* [1962] 1 WLR 425; *London and Thames Haven Oil Wharves Ltd v Attwooll (HMIT)* [1967] Ch 772; *Murray (HMIT) v Imperial Chemical Industries Ltd* [1967] Ch 1038; *Ryan (HMIT) v Crabtree Denims Ltd* [1987] BTC 289; *Donald Fisher (Ealing) Ltd v Spencer (HMIT)* [1989] BTC 112; *Deeny v Gooda Walker Ltd (in vol liq)* [1996] BTC 144; *Tanfield Ltd v Carr (HMIT)* (1999) Sp C 200

Website: www.hmrc.gov.uk/bulletins/index.htm

See *British Tax Reporter* ¶220-000.

633   Taxation of 'know-how' sales

A trader's receipts from the sale of know-how are nowadays only treated as capital receipts if the sale accompanied the sale of part or all of his business and if he and the buyer do not elect otherwise. Non-traders' receipts from know-how sales may attract income tax under ITTOIA 2005. 'Know-how' is orthodoxly defined (see 2398).

Law: ITTOIA 2005, s. 192–195

See *British Tax Reporter* ¶220-850.

635   Business receipts already taxable by deduction at source

Since the provisons under which earnings from employment, etc. and trading income is charged to tax are mutually exclusive (see 240), it is clear that the same income must not be taxed twice. Any sum received under deduction of tax is therefore not included in a trading computation.

See *British Tax Reporter* ¶220-000.

636   Dispositions at an undervalue and stock taken for own use

A trader could reduce his profits and as a consequence his liability to tax by selling his stock at less than it is worth or by giving it away. This would benefit somebody else at his expense. However, if he does so, for tax purposes he must bring into his accounts a figure representing the market value of the goods sold. The authority for this is the case of *Sharkey v Wernher*. Lady Wernher owned a stud farm, the profits of which were assessed under former Sch. D, Case I. She also owned racing stables. At the racing stables she trained horses which she had bred at the stud farm. The racing stables were a hobby; thus any profit was not assessable and any loss not allowable. She transferred five horses from the stud farm to the racing stables. It was admitted that some figure had to be entered in the accounts of the farm to represent the disposition of trading stock but it was contended that the appropriate figure was the cost of breeding the horses rather than their market value. The House of Lords decided that the correct figure was the market value of the horses transferred.

The effect of Sharkey v Wernher

The rule in *Sharkey v Wernher* not only means that it is possible for a trader to trade with himself (e.g. a grocer who supplied his family with goods off the shelf of his shop would be required to enter market value in his books as if he had made the same profit on their sale as he would have done had he sold them to the public), but that he must enter the market value in his books if he throws the stock away.

Further, the rule affects both the accounts of the disponor and the accounts of the recipient of those goods. The recipient of goods given gratuitously to him must enter the market value of those goods in his books and cannot value his stock at nil.

The *Sharkey v Wernher* rule applies to most non-commercial disposals of trading stock. It follows from the necessity that there be a disposal of trading stock that the rule is confined to taxpayers who are assessed on an earnings basis. For the distinction between earnings and cash basis, see 590.

It also follows that the rule does not apply to services given without payment (e.g. by a professional person). The reason is that there is no disposal of trading stock. In one case, an author assigned the copyright in a book to his father. HMRC sought to assess the author on the market value of the book. The Court of Appeal held that the rule in *Sharkey v Wernher* did not apply, even though the expenses of writing the book had been allowed in his accounts.

There are also special statutory rules in relation to bodies of persons, e.g. partnerships (see 759) or companies (see 3042).

Gifts of equipment made to schools and other institutions

The rule in *Sharkey v Wernher* does not apply to gifts, made after 18 March 1991 to educational institutions designated in regulations made by the various Secretaries of State for Education and Science, etc. of equipment manufactured, sold or used in the course of the taxpayer's trade. The long list of qualifying establishments includes local education authority-maintained schools in England, Wales and Northern Ireland, grant-maintained schools, independent schools administered by educational charities, public and self-governing schools (in Scotland), universities, and most other higher education establishments.

The above relief has effectively been extended to all charitable causes on or after 27 July 1999.

Gifts in kind for relief in poor countries

The rule in *Sharkey v Wernher* does not apply to gifts of trading stock for educational or medical projects in designated countries or territories made before the end of December 2000, under a scheme launched in 1998.

Law: ITTOIA 2005, s. 107–110; *Taxes (Relief for Gifts) (Designated Educational Establishments) Regulations (Northern Ireland)* 1992 (SI 1992/109); *Sharkey (HMIT) v Wernher* [1956] AC 58; *Petrotim Securities Ltd v Ayres (HMIT)* [1964] 1 WLR 190; *Ridge Securities Ltd v IR Commrs* [1964] 1 WLR 479; *Mason (HMIT) v Innes* [1967] Ch 1079

See *British Tax Reporter* ¶216-350.

640   Ex gratia business receipts

Sometimes receipts take on the appearance of gifts. That is, they are made without legal obligation. Such receipts may escape income tax (see 628) if the following conditions are met:

- the payment must be unsolicited and unexpected;
- if a business connection existed between the donor and recipient then this must have ended before the voluntary payment is made;
- the payment must not be for past services;
- the payment must not be a retainer or an advance payment for further services;
- the payment must not be compensation for loss of business.

If the payment is merely to supplement the trader's income, then it will not escape income tax.

Law: *Simpson (HMIT) v John Reynolds & Co (Insurances) Ltd* [1975] 1 WLR 617; *IR Commrs v Falkirk Ice Rink Ltd* (1975) 51 TC 42

See *British Tax Reporter* ¶220-000.

642   Deposits and unclaimed money

Where a trader receives money from or on behalf of a customer which the trader is supposed to repay and the customer neglects to claim it, the unclaimed money is not a trading receipt. The money never belonged to the trader, was never part of his income and cannot subsequently become so.

However, sometimes the money becomes the trader's by operation of law (as in relation to unclaimed surpluses on a pawnbroker's sale of unredeemed pledges) and in such cases it may be held to be a trading receipt. If the payment was strictly a deposit (i.e. it goes towards the cost of whatever is ordered), then this is a trading receipt even though whatever was ordered was not collected.

Law: *Morley (HMIT) v Tattersall* (1938) 22 TC 51; *Jay's the Jewellers Ltd v IR Commrs* (1947) 29 TC 274; *Elson (HMIT) v Prices Tailors Ltd* [1963] 1 WLR 287

See *British Tax Reporter* ¶220-050.

646   Stock lending

Stock lending is a long established practice that enables securities dealers, in return for a fee, to 'borrow' securities (including shares) from institutions such as insurance companies or pension funds when they need them in order to deliver on sales. The dealer undertakes to replace them at a later date with securities of the same kind and amount.

From 1 July 1997, the previous income tax and CGT restrictions were removed from the borrowing and lending of UK equities. However, anti-avoidance legislation prevents stock lending being used to switch dividend income from one person to another for tax reasons. If a stock lending arrangement does not provide for manufactured payments (see 1375) to be made, then such payments will be deemed to have been made.

Law: ITA 2007, s. 596; TCGA 1992, s. 271(9); FA 1997, Sch. 10;

See *British Tax Reporter* ¶221-000.

648   Debts: release or receipt after write off

If a trade debt is incurred and the creditor later releases the debt (otherwise than under a 'voluntary arrangement' under the *Insolvency Act* 1986 after 29 November 1993), then the debtor has in fact made a profit which is taxable on release (for releases post-cessation, see 662).

Note that without a formal release from the debt, the amount is not taxable under the statute. However, it is HMRC view that, with effect for accounting periods that start from 1 January 2002 onwards, normal accounting practice should determine the tax treatment of debts that are written off, but not formally released. Accordingly, if the debtor writes the amount back to the profit and loss account, there is no need for a tax adjustment, and it will therefore be taxed.

> ### Example
>
> John owes Thomas £100. Thomas later releases John from the debt. John has therefore made a profit of £100 which is taxable in the period of release.

If a trader eventually receives more than he *originally* estimated he would, then the excess must be related back and the accounts of that period should be reopened. This rule only applies to receipts which are analogous to trade debts.

Example

Peter agrees to supply Ian with goods at a price to be agreed under a certain formula. The agreement is made in 2008. Peter enters a notional price into his books for 2009–10. He is assessed to tax on this notional figure in 2009–10. Subsequently under the formula for ascertaining the price he receives more than the notional amount that he entered in his books and on which he was taxed. The difference between the notional price and the actual price has to be entered into his books for 2008–09 as a trading receipt on which he will be taxed. This will obviously involve reopening his accounts for that year.

If, however, after a debt is written off for tax purposes (or a specific provision is made against it), a trader recovers the amount, it will be treated as a receipt of the trade on receipt.

Law: ITTOIA 2005, s. 97; *Bristow (HMIT) v William Dickinson & Co Ltd* (1946) 27 TC 157

See *British Tax Reporter* ¶223-100.

650   Gains from foreign currency transactions

A profit or loss may arise to a trader when the foreign exchange rates alter.

Statutory rules were introduced in 1993 dealing with the taxation of companies' foreign exchange differences in 1993 (see 3035).

For the relationship with tax on chargeable gains, see 5221.

Law: *Landes Bros v Simpson (HMIT)* (1934) 19 TC 62; *Imperial Tobacco Co Ltd v Kelly (HMIT)* (1943) 25 TC 292; *Davies (HMIT) v Shell Company of China Ltd* (1951) 32 TC 133; *Pattison (HMIT) v Marine Midland Ltd* [1983] BTC 448

Source: SP 1/87, *Exchange rate fluctuations*

TRADING STOCK AND WORK IN PROGRESS

652   Valuation of stock in trade in continuing business

Stock in trade is that portion of the goods purchased for resale by a trader but which is not yet sold and can include such things as contracts and land. At any given time, a trader may have goods which are ready for sale and he may have some which are in the process of

Income Tax

being made ready; these items are known as work in progress – both are also generally classed as stock.

From 12 March 2008 a long established rule, which has effect where goods are appropriated into or from trading stock other than by way of trade, has been put on a statutory footing. In such circumstances, the profits of the trade for tax purposes should be adjusted to replace the cost of the stock or the actual proceeds with their market value.

Since taxable profits from business are computed in accordance with generally accepted accounting principles, the cost of sales (deducted from turnover to produce gross profit) is calculated by reference to movements in stock, i.e. in very broad terms:

gross profit = turnover − (purchases + opening stock − closing stock)

so that stock directly affects taxable profit. Where a property development company carries forward interest as part of work in progress in the balance sheet, no trading deduction can be claimed until it is effectively charged as part of the cost of sales; conversely, no adjustment need be made to reflect any disallowance until that time (allowance as a charge on income is unaffected, relief being given when the interest is paid).

Stock is valued at the end of each period of account for tax purposes at the lower of cost or market value. The trader may value each item of stock individually at the lower of cost or market value. As stock normally increases in value it is usual to value it at cost price, thus reducing the trader's profit. However, if items of stock decrease in value, then obviously market value will be used. If someone donates stock to a trader to start him in business then the trader may bring in that stock at market value.

Example

Roger, a grocer, is set up in his business by Jack who provides all of Roger's stock. If Roger put down in his accounts no value for his opening stock, then his profits would be extremely high when he came to enter the sale price in his books. HMRC allow the trader in these circumstances to value his opening stock at open market value. This will naturally mean lower profits and a lower liability to tax than if he had brought in the opening stock at cost, which was free.

An element of prudence has to be balanced with a degree of expectation. Lord Pearson has said:

'that the correct principle is that goods should not be written down price unless there really is a loss actual or prospective. So long as the fall in prevailing prices is only such as to reduce prospective profit, the initial valuation at cost should be retained.'

Example of trading accounts

Trading account for the year ended 30 June 2009

	£	£
Sales		105,000
Less: cost of goods sold–		
stock on hand 1 July 2008	20,000	
purchases	80,000	
	100,000	
Less: stock on hand at 30 June 2009	(30,000)	
		(70,000)
Gross profit for the year ended 30 June 2009		35,000

Trading account for the year ended 30 June 2010

	£	£
Sales		170,000
Less: cost of goods sold–		
stock on hand 1 July 2009	30,000	
purchases	120,000	
	150,000	
Less: stock on hand at 30 June 2010	(20,000)	
		(130,000)
Gross profit for the year ended 30 June 2010		40,000

No general rule can be laid down for valuing work in progress for tax purposes. The method used will depend on which is best fitted to the trade in question.

There are particular problems in relation to farmers (see 940ff.).

Long-term contracts

HMRC now accept that there is no longer a tax rule which denies provisions for anticipated losses or expenses. This means in particular that accurate provisions for foreseen losses on long-term contracts (e.g. in the construction industry) made in accordance with correct accounting practice will be tax deductible. A statement of practice on the subject has accordingly been withdrawn.

Market value of stock

Market value is taken to be that market in which the trader would normally sell his stock, be it wholesale or retail.

Cost price of stock

Identification of stock
Quite often stock is mixed and stored together so that it is impossible to tell the cost price of each particular item.

> **Example**
>
> A coal merchant buys five tons of coal at £30 per ton in August 2010 and ten tons of coal at £35 per ton in September 2010. All the coal is stored together so there is no indication what part of the stock cost £30 per ton and what cost £35 per ton.

In practice HMRC accept all those methods recognised by the accountancy profession so long as they do not violate the taxing statutes.

The answer usually adopted and generally accepted by the courts to this problem is known as first-in, first-out (FIFO). This means that the first to be sold will be considered to be the first acquired. Thus in the above example the first five tons of coal sold by the trader will be brought into his trading accounts at £30 per ton.

The opposite method known as last-in, first-out (LIFO) has been rejected by the courts as unsuitable for tax purposes.

Another method commonly used for valuing stock at cost is the 'average cost' method. The average cost of the stock is arrived at by adding together all the stock and dividing this into the total price paid for all that stock.

> **Example**
>
> A coal merchant buys four tons of coal at £25 per ton and four tons of coal at £15 per ton and ten tons of coal at £20 per ton. He has bought 18 tons at a total cost of £360. If the cost of £360 is divided by the amount 18 tons, the average cost of £20 per ton is arrived at.

Other methods which are used and accepted by HMRC are the 'adjusted selling price' method and the 'standard cost' method. The 'adjusted selling price' is used when it is impractical to value such items at cost individually. In this case the cost price is taken to be the selling price less the normal mark up. This applies only where the selling prices are full selling prices. This is not normally the position, so HMRC accept value as marked prices less the normal mark up. This 'adjusted selling price' method is quite often used by the department stores.

The 'standard cost' method is a method whereby a standard price is chosen by the trader to be the cost price of his stock. However, this will not be accepted by HMRC unless the standard chosen closely reflects the current market value.

There is also the base stock method of valuation which assumes the necessity for a minimum or basic amount of stock which is necessary for the operation of the business. The base stock is valued at cost as at the date of the manufacturing process to which it relates and quantities in excess of the base stock are valued by some other method. This method is not accepted by HMRC for tax purposes.

Attribution of overheads

There are two accepted methods in arriving at cost.

- The 'direct cost' method which only takes account of the actual cost of the labour and materials used.
- The 'on cost' method or 'indirect cost' method which also takes account of the general overheads, e.g. heating, lighting, etc.

Law: FA 2008, s. 37; *Kelsall Parsons & Co v IR Commrs* (1938) 21 TC 608; *IR Commrs v Cock Russell & Co Ltd* (1949) 29 TC 387; *Rellim Ltd v Vise (HMIT)* (1951) 32 TC 254; *Minister of National Revenue v Anaconda American Brass Ltd* [1956] AC 85; *Duple Motor Bodies Ltd v Ostime (HMIT)* [1961] 1 WLR 739; *BSC Footwear Ltd v Ridgway (HMIT)* [1972] AC 544; *Symons (HMIT) v Weeks* [1983] BTC 18

Website: www.hmrc.gov.uk/bulletins/index.htm

See *British Tax Reporter* ¶224-650.

654 Change from one valid method to another

According to a statement of practice (which was withdrawn on 20 July 1999), when a change is made from one valid method of stock valuation to another (see 652), the opening stocks figure in the year of change must remain the same as the closing figure for the preceding year. Thus a tax-free uplift cannot be obtained where the opening stocks of one year exceed those of the previous year. See also 636, 660.

Law: *Pearce (HMIT) v Woodall-Duckham Ltd* (1978) 51 TC 271; *R v IR Commrs, ex parte SG Warburg & Co Ltd* [1994] BTC 201

See *British Tax Reporter* ¶224-900.

660 Stock valuation on discontinuance of trade

When a trade is discontinued or, except as noted below, is deemed discontinued (see 675ff.) any trading stock belonging to the trade at the time of discontinuance must be valued at market value at discontinuance.

However, if:

- the stock is sold to a UK trader; *and*
- the cost of it is deductible in computing the new trader's profits,

then the value of the stock will be taken to be the price the trader paid for it. For sales taking place after 24 July 2002, it is possible to make a just and reasonable apportionment of the consideration received where stock is transferred along with other assets.

Income Tax

Example of rule

Ten years ago Rupert, an art dealer, bought a painting for £2,000. He does not keep it on open display (or if he does he prices it much too highly). He now ceases to trade, with the painting unsold and worth an estimated £22,000. He cannot avoid income tax by bringing the painting into his final accounts at cost and later selling it privately for £25,000. £22,000 is the figure which he will bring into his final accounts.

Example of exception

Sebastian discontinues in trade. He sells his stock to an unconnected UK trader, Max, who enters the cost of this stock in his books as a deduction. Sebastian can enter into his accounts the price Max paid for his stock. Usually this exception will make very little difference to the basic rule of valuing at market value on discontinuance, since most traders will want to sell their goods at market value.

Where the transferor and transferee are 'connected', the arm's length price rather than the actual transfer price (subject to the possibility of a joint election made by the parties in certain circumstances) is to be used for the valuation of the stock transferred.

If a sole trader dies and, as a result, the trade is discontinued, stock will be valued in the normal way, at the lower of cost price or market value.

The above provisions (with the exception of the 'new rules' relating to transfer of stock on a discontinuance) apply to work in progress of professions and vocations with the proviso that the excess of the market value or sale price of the work in progress over cost can be taxed as a post-cessation receipt (see 662). However, an election to do this must be made within 12 months of discontinuance.

Example

Robert, an architect, discontinues his profession. The value of his work in progress at discontinuance is taken to be the amount it would have realised if sold on the open market at the discontinuance.

Any dispute concerning such transfer between trades, professions or vocations is dealt with in the same way as an appeal.

Law: ITTOIA 2005, s. 173–186

See *British Tax Reporter* ¶225-600.

662 Post-cessation receipts

This paragraph deals with all sums received after the trade, profession or vocation has been discontinued, including debts released after discontinuance (see 675ff.). These sums must be in respect of work carried out before the discontinuance. The legislation has made a distinction between the case where profits are calculated on an 'earnings basis' and the case where profits are calculated on a conventional basis. It is still net sums which are ultimately chargeable and amounts charged do not cease to be earned income. It is implicit that the charge arises on receipt except that the taxpayer may elect for a relating-back to the discontinuance.

Under self-assessment, where a claim is made to treat the receipt as received on the date of discontinuance (or date of the change of basis, where relevant), the claim is to be related to the year in which the sum is received (the 'later year'), with effect being given to it by an increase in the amount of tax payable for that later year (see 2684).

(1) Earnings basis

The earnings basis accounts for all income earned, e.g. bills delivered for work done by the firm even though cash has not yet been received, and all debits, e.g. expenses incurred but not yet paid for.

Where the earnings basis is used to determine profits, then all sums not brought into account before discontinuance, or debts released (other than after 29 November 1993 under a 'voluntary arrangement' under the *Insolvency Act* 1986), are chargeable to tax under ITTOIA 2005 (former Sch. D, Case VI).

(2) Cash basis or conventional basis

Whereas the 'earnings basis' takes account of all income earned and expenses incurred, the 'cash basis' may leave out of account such things as work in progress. The conventional basis is used to describe any method of calculating profits other than the earnings basis and would include the cash basis. Accounts must be prepared on an earnings basis, except for barristers in the early years of their practice (see 590).

Where the cash basis is used to determine profits, then tax is charged on those sums which are not brought into account on that basis and not otherwise chargeable or which would not have been brought into account before discontinuance if the 'earnings basis' had been used, in the latter instance, because:

- the date on which the sums became due fell after the discontinuance; or
- the date on which the amount due was ascertained fell after the discontinuance.

There is a specific relief for certain individuals born before 6 April 1917.

(3) Exceptions

The following post-cessation receipts are, in most cases, excluded from the above provisions:

- sums representing income arising outside the UK received by or on behalf of a person not resident in the UK;
- a lump sum paid to the personal representatives of an author or designer as consideration for the assignment of the copyright or design right;
- sums paid in consideration of the transfer of trading stock or work in progress at discontinuance.

(4) Particular receipts

Sums received in payment of a debt are treated as not brought into account if a deduction has already been allowed.

Special rules apply to transfers of the right to receive debts, etc.

Law: ITTOIA 2005, s. 241–257

See *British Tax Reporter* ¶223-000.

WHETHER CONTINUANCE OF TRADE

675   Assessing beginning and cessation of trade

It is important for tax purposes to know when a trade has commenced and when it has ceased. On a discontinuance, trading stock may have to be uplifted to market value (see 660). Relief for trading losses depends upon a continuing trade (see 2290ff.).

It is usually quite clear when a trade commences though care must be taken to distinguish between trading and investment or other activities (see 555ff.) and between trading activity and preparation for trading activity. This is of less importance since 1980, when pre-trading expenditure became allowable as a trading loss on the day when the trade actually starts (see 2260).

In one case, the directors of a company between June and October arranged for premises and plant and for the supply of trading stock. They engaged a works manager in August and work commenced in October. It was held that the trade commenced in October and that the activity before October was preparation for trading activity.

However, it is not always clear when a trade has ceased. In particular, an existing trade may have continued as the same trade notwithstanding that it has:

- expanded or contracted (see 677);

- ceased temporarily (see 678);
- changed ownership by way of succession (see 752).

The Court of Session has indicated that, in respect of the transfer of a business to a company, a farming business is capable of being moved from one piece of land to another without being brought to an end. All farming businesses carried on by one person are treated as one trade (see 940).

Law: *Birmingham & District Cattle By-Products Co Ltd v IR Commrs* (1919) 12 TC 92; *Gordon v IR Commrs; IR Commrs v Gordon* [1991] BTC 130

677 Expansion or contraction of trade and continuing trade

Where a trader expands or reduces the scope of his trade this will not necessarily be regarded as either, in the former case, the commencement of a new trade or, in the latter case, as a discontinuance of the trade (but see 752 on successions).

> ### *Example 1*
>
> A trader who has two shops selling sports goods decides to open a third shop also selling sports goods. This will not generally be regarded as the commencement of a new business.

> ### *Example 2*
>
> A trader has five shops all selling wine. He decides to close one of them. This will not generally be regarded as the cessation of a business.

It should be noted that any expansion of trade should be of the same nature as the previous trade.

It is a question of fact in each case whether a trade has been expanded or a new trade commenced (or a succession has taken place). An illustrative case, showing current thinking, involved taxpayers who had carried on the business of a fish and chip shop for a number of years. They bought an existing fish and chip shop business five miles away. Immediately on acquiring the new shop the taxpayers changed its name and ran the business in their own style with their daughter in charge. The High Court upheld the general commissioners' right to reject HMRC's analysis of the facts that the second business was the same as before: they found that the taxpayers had not succeeded to that business but expanded their own trade into new premises.

Generally, losses of an existing business can be brought forward from previous years and set off against the profits of the acquired business by virtue of the nature of relief for losses in respect of any trade (see 2290ff.).

Law: *Maidment (HMIT) v Kibby* [1993] BTC 291

678 Trade ceased temporarily

A business may have a slack period in which little or no work can be done. This may involve closing the business down. If the same business is reactivated at a later date then it will not usually be regarded as permanently discontinued and/or as the commencement of a new business (see 675), but it is all a question of degree. The reactivated business must be substantially the same as before.

PARTNERSHIPS

750 Partnerships: general

The existence of a partnership is a question of fact. What is agreed between the parties is not conclusive of its existence; neither is the existence of a partnership agreement. For taxation purposes, a partnership is a trade or profession carried on by two or more persons jointly and a limited partnership is a partnership for tax purposes.

There are some differences in law between English and Scottish partnerships. For example, although a partnership is a legal person in Scotland, in England and Wales it is the individual members of a partnership who are trading and not the partnership itself.

However, for taxation purposes provisions generally apply to partnerships in the UK irrespective of their form. Income tax in respect of partners chargeable thereto has historically been assessed jointly in the name of the partnership. Under self-assessment income tax is assessed directly on the partners. Partners chargeable to corporation tax have always been assessed directly (see 762).

Law: *Partnership Act* 1890, s. 4(2); ITTOIA 2005, s. 848; *Morden Rigg & Co and R B Eskrigge & Co v Monks* (1923) 8 TC 450; *Dickenson v Gross (HMIT)* (1927) 11 TC 614

See *British Tax Reporter* ¶286-000.

Source: *Business Brief* 30/04, 19 November 2004, 'VAT and partnership "shares"'

751 Limited liability partnerships

Where a limited liability partnership (LLP) carries on a trade, profession or other business with a view to profit, from 6 April 2001:

- all the activities of the partnership are treated as carried on in partnership by its members (rather than by the partnership as such);
- anything done by, or in relation to the partnership for the purposes of, or in connection

with, any of its activities is treated as done by, to or in relation to the members as partners; and

- the property of the partnership is treated as held by the members as partnership property.

This treatment applies where the LLP is no longer trading with a view to profit and the cessation is temporarary. Where there is a permanent cessation, the above treatment applies in the period of winding up provided that the winding up is not for reasons connected with the avoidance of tax, nor is it unreasonably prolonged. However, this treatment ceases on the appointment of a liquidator or, if earlier, the making of a winding up order by the court.

Law: ITTOIA 2005. s. 863

See *British Tax Reporter* ¶289-750.

752 Membership changes

Under the self-assessment regime as it applies to partnerships (see 750), a change in the personnel carrying on a partnership business triggers provisions treating the business as permanently discontinued at the date of the change and a new business as having commenced if none of the original partners continues to carry on the business thereafter.

Where a partner joins or leaves a partnership, the commencement and cessation rules apply to him individually. A sole trader who takes on a partner is treated as continuing to trade, and the partner is treated as commencing to trade. Conversely, when a business goes from a partnership to a sole trader, the latter is treated as continuing and the other partner(s) as ceasing. If partners dissolve the partnership but each continues with part of the business, the partnership business ceases and the commencement provisions apply to the businesses run by the ex-partners.

A change in the personal representatives or trustees who carry on a trade is not treated as a discontinuance.

Law: ITTOIA 2005, s. 246

Source: SP 9/86, *Partnership mergers and demergers*

See *British Tax Reporter* ¶287-650.

754 Partners' salaries and interest on capital

In England and Wales (unlike Scotland) a partnership is not a legal entity. Thus, a partnership cannot enter into a contract of employment with an equity partner and such a partner cannot be the employee of the remaining partners – the same person cannot be both master and servant.

Income Tax

If, therefore, an equity partner is, by virtue of the terms of the agreement of partnership, entitled to salary or wages, he is merely entitled to an allocation of profits before the general division among the partners. This compares with some salaried partners who, by the nature of the particular arrangement in point, are more akin to employees.

The tax consequences of the legal position that equity partners' salaries are not deductible in arriving at the net partnership income (or net partnership loss) poses no problem where the adding back of salaries results in the individual interests of both partners in the net income or net loss showing either a surplus or a deficiency.

Example 1

Alex and Ben are in partnership. Alex is the only active partner and receives a salary of £20,000 p.a. as manager. The profits and losses (calculated after deducting Alex's salary) are to be shared equally. Profits of £15,000 are made in the basis year after deducting Alex's salary.

		£
Partnership profit (after Alex's salary deducted)		15,000
Add: Alex's salary		20,000
Assessable income		35,000
Allocation of assessment:	£	
Alex: salary	20,000	
plus 50% of balance (£15,000)	7,500	
		27,500
Ben: 50% of balance (£15,000)		7,500
Total		35,000

Example 2

Charlie and David are partners in a firm. The partnership agreement provides for salaries to be paid as follows:

Charlie = £10,000

David = £5,000

Profits or losses remaining after an allowance for the salaries has been made are shared equally between Charlie and David. The firm makes a loss in a tax year of £20,000 after the salaries have been deducted. The tax-allowable loss is restricted to:

	£	£
Partnership loss		(20,000)
Less: Charlie's salary	10,000	
David's salary	5,000	
		15,000
Tax loss		(5,000)
Allocation of loss:	£	£
Charlie: salary	10,000	
Less: 50% of loss of 20,000	(10,000)	
		—
David: salary	5,000	
Less: 50% of loss of 20,000	(10,000)	
		(5,000)
Total		(5,000)

However, it is in cases where the distribution between the partners in accordance with the partnership agreement results in a surplus for one partner and a deficiency for the other that problems arise.

The basic position can be summarised as follows:

- Where, before taking partners' salaries into account, there is a *net partnership income* for tax purposes, the partner whose entitlement (including salary) shows a surplus is taxed on the whole of the net partnership income; no loss for tax purposes is allowable to the other partner.
- Where, before taking partners' salaries into account, there is a *net partnership loss*, the partner whose entitlement (including salary) shows a deficiency is entitled to the whole of the net partnership loss; no amount is assessable to the other partner.

Interest on capital

Interest paid to a partner on capital which he contributes to the partnership is likewise not an allowable expense but rather an allocation of profit. However, a partner who makes, for the purpose of the partnership, any actual payment or advance beyond the amount of capital which he has agreed to contribute is entitled (in the absence of a contrary agreement) to simple interest at five per cent per annum. Such interest constitutes an allowable expense of the partnership and attracts an income tax charge (see 1366ff.).

Law: *Partnership Act* 1890, s. 24(3); *Heastie (HMIT) v Veitch & Co* (1933) 18 TC 305

See *British Tax Reporter* ¶287-200.

756   Partnership income

Partnership income is apportioned according to the shares current in the tax year even though, before self-assessment, the assessment may be based on profits of an earlier period. Salaries paid to partners and interest on capital contributed by partners are deducted from the partnership profits before the shares of each partner are ascertained (see 754). Where a partnership involves a company slightly different rules apply (see 762).

Other income of a trading partnership is computed as if the partnership were a UK-resident individual (with the residence condition only applying from 1995–96 onwards), and allocated according to sharing ratios in the period covered by the computation. This is achieved by treating such income as if it were profits, gains or losses of a trade or profession. If the other income is untaxed, then, for basis periods purposes, all sources of untaxed income are pooled and treated as arising from a separate deemed trade.

Although property income is generally taxed on a tax year basis from 1995–96 (see 1200ff.), under self-assessment the members of a partnership are still taxed on the accounts basis.

HMRC have clarified the treatment of partnership income from jointly owned property. Consider two individuals carrying on business in partnership with land-owning and trading activities arranged such that:

- the partnership business comprises both a business trading income source and a property income source: the income from the property income source will be assessable using the basis periods that apply for the business trading income source;
- there are two separate businesses and two separate partnerships, albeit partnerships between the same two individuals: the income from the property source will be assessable on a tax year basis;
- the letting income is not ancillary to the trading (former Sch. D, Case I/II) partnership source, and the letting activity cannot be described as the carrying on of a business: the income arising is not assessable as partnership income and each share will be assessable as the personal income of the individuals.

A partner cannot assign his income to another person for tax purposes.

For the application of the loan relationships, foreign exchange and financial instruments legislation to partnerships that include companies, see SP 4/98.

Law: ITTOIA 2005, s. 851(1)–(2), 854–855; *Hadlee v Commr of Inland Revenue (New Zealand)* [1993] BTC 133

Source: SP 4/98

Website: www.hmrc.gov.uk/bulletins/index.htm

See *British Tax Reporter* ¶287-000.

759 Transactions between the partnership and individual partners

Transactions between the partnership and an individual partner are subject to transfer pricing rules. The actual sale proceeds or actual purchase price as appropriate may be adjusted so as to prevent the avoidance of UK tax; thus sales at an overvalue or undervalue may be prevented. The provisions may apply where the buyer or seller is a body of persons, including a partnership, and there is common control with the other party – in the case of a partnership control is determined by reference to a right to more than 50 per cent of the assets or income (for details of the anti-avoidance provision.

Transfers of trading stock may fall within the above provisions or may alternatively be subject to further provisions (see 636).

Assets owned by an individual partner but used in the partnership trade may attract capital allowances on general principles or, in the case of machinery or plant, by statute.

Law: ITA 2007, s. 995; CAA 2001, s. 264

See *British Tax Reporter* ¶287-000.

760 Post-cessation receipts

The provisions relating to sums received after permanent discontinuance (see 662) also apply to any deemed discontinuance on changes of partners (see 752). However, if the right to receive the sums has been transferred to the partnership, as constituted after the change, the sums are treated as receipts of the trade, etc. in the period in which they are received.

Law: ITTOIA 2005, s. 98(1)–(3), 251(4), 310(1)–(3), 355(4)

See *British Tax Reporter* ¶287-000.

762 Partnerships with company members

A company may be a member of a partnership, with other companies and/or with one or more individuals. Where a partnership involves a company the general rules for computing income profits and losses are modified, as set out below.

In the case of partnership trading income, profits ('profits' does not here include chargeable gains) and losses are computed as if the partnership were a UK-resident company (except in the case of a corporate partner which is a company resident outside the UK). This is in order to ascertain the corporation tax liability of the company partner. However, although tax is computed applying corporation tax principles (with reference to accounting periods), initially distributions are ignored and no adjustment is made for charges on income or capital allowances and charges; also, no deduction is made in any accounting period for losses incurred in an earlier accounting period.

A change in the persons carrying on a trade is treated as a transfer of the trade to a different company if a company continues to be a member of the partnership but is not also a company which was a partner before the change. Thus, a transfer of the trade might give rise to balancing charges in relation to capital allowances. A company's share in the profits and losses of any accounting period is calculated according to its entitlement during that period. Corporation tax is charged as if that share was derived from a trade carried on by the company alone in its corresponding accounting period or periods.

If one or more individuals are partners, income tax is charged as if all the partners had been individuals except that, before self-assessment – generally from 1997–98 and immediately in relation to partnerships whose trades, professions or vocations are set up and commenced after 6 April 1994 – their shares of profits are computed by reference to both the computations made for corporation tax and their shares of profits in respect of the conventional basis periods.

Law: CTA 2009, s. 77(5), 1262; *Ensign Tankers (Leasing) Ltd v Stokes (HMIT)* [1992] BTC 110

See *British Tax Reporter* ¶289-300.

764 Partnership retirement annuities

In some cases agreements to pay partnership annuities to retired partners might constitute 'settlements' and thus be caught by the anti-avoidance provisions discussed at 1070ff. Normally, however, they will not be settlements, having been made for full consideration.

See *British Tax Reporter* ¶287-000.

766 General partnership losses

As with profits, partnership losses are divided among partners according to their respective shares. For losses generally, see 2290ff.

Briefly, a partner is entitled to loss relief, for his share of the partnership loss, against other income of the same tax year and against any income of the following year (in so far as relief has not already been given) if he is still a partner in the firm.

However, *Finance Act* 2004 introduced a measure, subject to certain transitionary provisions, to restrict loss relief available to non-active general partners and non-active members of limited liability partnerships. Broadly, the amount which may be given otherwise than against income consisting of profits arising from the trade only to the extent that:

- the amount given; or
- the aggregate amount,

does not exceed the amount of the individual's contribution to the trade at the end of the tax year in question.

A loss (in so far as relief has not already been given) may be carried forward by the partner and set against his share of the profits of the trade, etc. for subsequent years (see 2292).

Each partner may choose whether he prefers the former ('carry-across') relief or 'carry-forward' relief. The calculation of the two reliefs may vary where partnership profit-sharing ratios are changed because for carry-across relief (where the loss is generally treated as arising in the tax year in which the accounting period ends), the relevant profit-sharing ratio is that existing during *the tax year* in which the accounting period ends. For carry-forward relief the relevant profit-sharing ratio is that existing during *the accounting period* in which the loss arose.

Upon the death or retirement of a partner, losses which have not been relieved cannot be carried forward. However, the relief described in 2304 (carry-back of terminal losses) may apply in such cases.

Terminal loss relief applies on a permanent discontinuance of a trade, etc. which includes a deemed discontinuance on a change in partners (see 752). A person who continues to be a partner after the deemed discontinuance is not entitled to terminal loss relief (though he continues to be entitled to carry forward his losses).

Relief for losses in the early years of a trade may be available (see 2302).

From 2 December 2004, limited recourse or non-repayable loans, or other reimbursable amounts are excluded from being treated for tax purposes as part of the partner's contribution to a trade, thereby preventing that partner from benefiting from loss relief in excess of the actual amounts lost or at risk. The rules apply to individual partners in limited partnerships, limited liability partnerships, partners who spend less than ten hours per week actively carrying on a partnership trade, and any partners who have claimed film-related losses.

Law: ITA 2007, s. 110; *The Partnerships (Restrictions on Contributions to a Trade) Regulations* 2005 (SI 2005/2017)

See *British Tax Reporter* ¶287-600.

767 Limited partnership losses

A limited partnership is one in which one or more members have limited liability provided that at least one member has unlimited liability.

When a limited partnership makes a trading loss the partners are entitled to make a claim for relief from income tax in the same way as a partner in an ordinary partnership (see 766). The limited partner's share of the loss is restricted to the amount of his capital contribution. Only that amount can be set off against his other income. The restriction applies to both individual and company partners. It applies not only to limited partners in partnerships restricted under the *Limited Partnership Act* 1907 but also to persons participating in other joint venture arrangements where the liability is limited in a similar way by contract, agreement or guarantee or by the laws of other countries. Any balance of a limited partner's share of the partnership loss which cannot be relieved against other income because of this restriction may be carried forward and set against the limited partner's share of any future profits from the partnership. This restriction did not apply to periods beginning before 20 March 1985.

See 766 regarding a restriction for loss relief available to non-active members of partnerships.

Law: ITA 2007, ss. 56, 104, 110; *Reed (HMIT) v Young* [1986] BTC 242

See *British Tax Reporter* ¶289-500.

768 Personal reliefs: partnerships

Partners may claim 'personal reliefs' (see 1850) according to their respective shares and interests. Any partner's personal reliefs may be set off against the share of tax attributed to him. Any excess of allowances over tax due on his partnership share can be set off against any other income that he might have.

Law: ITA 2007, Part 3

See *British Tax Reporter* ¶286-350.

800 European Economic Interest Groupings (EEIGs)

The tax regime for European Economic Interest Groupings (EEIGs) broadly provides that:

- any trade or profession carried on by an EEIG is treated as carried on in partnership by the members of the grouping (any member's share of UK trading operations of a group managed and controlled abroad being chargeable in the same way as a non-resident trading in the UK); and
- disposals of assets by an EEIG are treated for tax purposes as disposals by members of the grouping of their shares of the assets concerned;

and income tax or corporation tax, as the case may be, is then charged if appropriate on the profits and gains attributed to the separate members of the grouping.

For returns by EEIGs, see 2589.

Law: ITA 2007, s. 842 and Sch. 1

See *British Tax Reporter* ¶765-450.

SPECIAL TAXPAYERS

CHARITIES

900   Special treatment for charities

Charities are favourably treated for tax purposes. A 'charity' is defined as 'any body of persons or trust established for charitable purposes only'. Whether a purpose is charitable is a question largely answered by case law and reference should be made to one of the standard textbooks. A training and enterprise council (or TEC, donations to which may be deductible: see 2154) has been held not to be a charity.

A new definition for tax purposes of charities and other organisations entitled to UK charity tax reliefs applies from 1 April 2010. One condition that must be satisfied to fall within the new definition is that the managers of the body are 'fit and proper persons' to be its managers.

The British Museum, the Natural History Museum, the Historic Buildings and Monument Commission and the National Heritage Memorial Fund enjoy the same exemptions available to charities generally.

A gain is not a chargeable gain (and, therefore, not liable to CGT) if it accrues to a charity and is applicable and applied for charitable purposes (see 6189). For the inheritance tax exemption for gifts to charities, see 7195. For covenanted payments to charity, see 1073.

Law: FA 2010, Sch. 6; ITTOIA 2005, s. 108(4), 878(1); *IR Commrs v Oldham Training and Enterprise Council* [1996] BTC 539

Source: HMRC press release 8 July 2010: *Detailed guidance on the fit and proper persons test*

See *British Tax Reporter* ¶138-050.

901   Exemptions for charities' trading or investment income

Charities benefit from a number of exemptions in relation to their trading and investment income. These are summarised below.

311

Rents

Exemption is given, upon a claim being made, from income tax in respect of the rents or other receipts from land vested in trustees for charitable purposes, so far as the rents are applied to charitable purposes only.

Interest, annuities, dividends

Charities are exempt from tax in respect of:

- yearly interest or other annual payments or equivalent foreign income (see 1366ff.); or
- any distribution charged under former Sch. F or equivalent foreign income.

Tax credits from 6 April 1999

The treatment of tax credits was changed radically with effect from 6 April 1999 (i.e. for the tax year 1999–2000 and later tax years). The amount of tax credit attaching to distributions by UK companies was been reduced from 20 per cent to ten per cent. At the same time, substantially all entitlement to payment of tax credits has been removed, other than tax credits payable under double taxation agreements.

Charities (and also heritage bodies and scientific research organisations) were compensated for the loss of the payment of tax credits after 5 April 1999. The compensation, which was funded by central government funds, was phased out over a five-year period. The compensation had to be claimed within two years from the tax year in which the distribution was made.

Income from trade

Prior to 22 March 2006, charities were exempt from income tax under ITTOIA 2005 in respect of trading income if the profits were applied solely for the purposes of the charity and either:

- the trade was exercised in the course of the actual carrying out of a primary purpose of the charity (e.g. school education); or
- the work in connection with the trade was mainly carried out by beneficiaries of the charity. The Court of Session has held that an association, whose object was to promote and conduct concerts, etc. was exempt from tax on its income from admission charges to its musical festival: the competitors were the beneficiaries of the charity and they did the most essential part of the work in conducting the festival.

For chargeable periods commencing on or after 22 March 2006 (FA 2006, s. 56), this relief is extended to charities where the trade is undertaken only partly for the primary (charitable) purposes, or is only carried out by the beneficiaries of the charity. From that date, relief will be given on the profits that can be reasonably attributed to the part of the trade carried on for the primary purpose or to the part carried out by the beneficiaries.

From 6 April 2000, for charitable trusts, and for accounting periods beginning on or after 1 April 2000 in relation to charities that are companies, the exemption for a charities trading income is widened to encompass small trades, provided that the following conditions are met:

- the income must be applied solely for the purposes of the charity; and
- the gross income (before expenses) must be within the limits of the greater of £5,000 and whichever is the lesser of £50,000 and 25 per cent of the charity's income.

The condition is met if at the beginning of the period the charity had a reasonable expectation that its gross income would be within the limit. Where the period in question is less than 12 months, the £5,000 and £50,000 limits are reduced proportionately.

The extension of the relief introduced by FA 2006 (see above) will particularly help charities where more than ten per cent of their trading activity is not attributable to their primary charitable purpose. Where charities operate a small trade not for the primary purpose of the charity, they may continue to obtain relief under the exemption for small trades.

Universities

The Financial Secretary to the Treasury has commented on Revenue discussions with university representatives on the tax treatment of consultancy earnings, holiday lettings and conference facilities:

> 'The Inland Revenue has explained that universities are entitled to the same tax exemptions as other charities. Trading profits are exempt only where the trade is exercised in the course of the actual carrying out of a primary purpose of the charity, or where the work in connection with the trade is mainly carried out by beneficiaries of the charity. Profits from other trading activities are likely to be taxable, in the same way as for other traders. The outcome in each case depends on its particular facts.'

Trading activities for charitable purposes

Profits of bazaars, jumble sales and similar activities arranged by voluntary organisations to raise funds for charity are usually exempt from tax provided a range of conditions are met.

Covenanted payments from associated trading companies

Where the trade is carried on by a company whose shares are held by the charity, any profits from the trade are exempt from tax if the company covenants to make payments to the charity equal to its profits. HMRC have confirmed that this arrangement will not constitute a tax ineffective 'scheme' within *Furniss v Dawson*.

Lottery income

Profits accruing to a charity from a lottery are exempt from tax, provided that they are applied solely to the charity's purposes and the lottery is promoted in accordance with the *Lotteries and Amusements Act* 1976, s. 3 or 5, or the corresponding Northern Ireland legislation. This exemption applies to chargeable periods beginning after 31 March 1995 in the case of a company, and after 5 April 1995 in any other case.

Income Tax

Law: FA 2006, s. 56; ITTOIA 2005, s. 385(1), 397(1), (6); FA 2000, s. 46; F(No. 2)A 1997, s. 28, 35; FA 1993, s. 80; F(No. 2)A 1992, s. 28; FA 1989, s. 59; *IR Commrs v Glasgow Musical Festival Association* (1926) 11 TC 154; *IR Commrs v National Book League* [1957] Ch 488; *Furniss (HMIT) v Dawson* [1984] BTC 71; *Guild & Ors (as trustees of the William Muir (Bond 9) Ltd Employees' Share Scheme) v IR Commrs* [1993] BTC 267

Source: ESC C4, *Trading activities for charitable purposes*; former ESC B9; IR 75 *Tax relief for charities*; Technical Release 588

Website: www.hmrc.gov.uk/leaflets/c10.htm

See *British Tax Reporter* ¶140-000.

902 Charitable donations by individuals: gift aid

A specific relief, 'gift aid', is available to individuals in respect of certain single gifts in money to charities (relief for covenanted payments is available under other provisions: see 1073, 1840). Gifts are made net of basic rate tax, which charities reclaim from HMRC; higher-rate relief is also available to donors. Charities will be given a 2 per cent transitional relief for gift aid donations to compensate for the reduction in the basic rate of tax from 22 per cent to 20 per cent in 2008–09.

From 6 April 2000, the scheme was extended to include donations by Crown servants, members of the UK armed forces serving overseas and foreign donors. Prior to that date, the scheme was limited to UK residents. Also from 6 April 2000, the scheme is extended to donors who pay capital gains tax and who pay tax at below the basic rate.

For the gift to 'charity' (see 900), to be a 'qualifying donation', it must constitute a sum of money; and:

- be subject to no repayment condition;
- prior to 6 April 2000, not be a 'covenanted payment to charity' (see 1073);
- not fall within the payroll deduction scheme (see 904);
- not be conditional on or associated with, or part of an arrangement involving, the acquisition of property by the charity, otherwise than by way of gift, from the donor or a person 'connected with' him (see 1260).

From 6 April 2000, payments made under deeds of covenants are brought within the gift aid scheme.

Qualifying donations are treated as 'covenanted payments to charities' (see 1073) of an amount equal to their grossed-up value (see 210). Thus, where basic rate income tax is 20 per cent, a gift of £800 is treated as one of £1,000, and the donor may deduct £1,000 in computing his total income, including for higher rate and starting rate purposes. To the extent that the gross donation is matched by the donor's taxable income, the donor is charged to tax at the basic rate for the tax year of the donation, without distinguishing the payment. To the extent that the gross donation is not matched by the donor's taxable income, the donor is assessable and chargeable with basic rate tax. However, if HMRC find that a non-taxpayer's donation has been included in a gift aid claim from a charity, they pursue the charity for the shortfall rather than the donor.

For gifts made on or after 6 April 2003, relief for gift aid payments may be set against the previous year's liability. An election for this must be made on or before the date the tax return for the previous year is delivered, but in any case no later than the 31 January filing date. There must be enough income and gains in the previous year to cover the donation. The election does not affect the position of the recipient.

From 1 November 2005, charities are no longer required to send donors a written record of an oral declaration providing certain conditions are met.

Certain heritage and conservation charities may offer free admission in return for a donation without the admission counting as a benefit for gift aid purposes. This exemption was extended from 6 April 2006 to any type of charity that grants the right to pay to view its property. However, if a donation is made instead of paying an admission charge, gift aid will only apply to the whole of the gift if:

- the right of admission is for an unrestricted number of visits over a period of at least one year; or
- the right of admission is for less than one year but the gift is at least 10 per cent more than the amount any member of the public would have to pay for the same right of admission. If there is not a comparable admission ticket, the value of the right of admission will count towards the benefit limit for gift aid purposes (25 per cent of the donation, up to a maximum of £250 in any year).

The effect is that, for admissions after 5 April 2006, charities can no longer simply reclassify admission fees as donations subject to gift aid.

Where an individual makes a donation to a charity and receives the right of admission in consequence, the right of admission is, in restricted circumstances, disregarded as a benefit to the donor in determining whether the donation is eligible for gift aid relief.

It is possible for an individual to authorise for a repayment of tax due to be given to charity via the gift aid scheme. Such an election is made on the individual's self-assessment return form.

In the charity's hands, a qualifying donation is treated as an annual payment from which basic rate tax has been deducted, thus entitling the charity to reclaim that tax from HMRC provided certain procedures have been followed (see 901).

For charitable donations by companies, see 3059.

Law: FA 2008, s. 53; ITA 2007, Pt. 8, Ch. 2; *LCC v Attorney-General* (1900) 4 TC 265

Website: www.hmrc.gov.uk/leaflets/c10.htm

Income Tax

www.hmrc.gov.uk/charities/chapter3-insert.htm

See *British Tax Reporter* ¶116-000.

903 Gifts of shares and securities, etc. to charities

From 6 April 2000, as regards gifts by individuals, and from 1 April 2000, as regards gifts by companies (see 3059) tax relief is available for gifts of qualifying investments to a charity.

Where the donor is an individual, he or she will benefit from an income tax deduction for the full market value of the qualifying investment at the date of the gift, plus incidental expenses of transfer, less any consideration or benefit received. This relief is in addition to capital gains tax relief available for gifts of shares, securities and other assets to a charity.

Qualifying investments

The following constitute qualifying investments:

- shares or securities that are listed or dealt in on a recognised stock exchange;
- units in an authorised unit trust;
- shares in an open-ended investment company;
- an interest in an offshore fund; and
- from April 2002, a freehold interest or leashold interest in land and buildings in the UK.

The relief

The amount of relief (known as the 'relevant amount') is, in the case of a gift, the market value at the time of the disposal. Where the disposal is at an undervalue, the relevant amount is the difference between the market value at the date of the disposal and the amount of value of any consideration received. In the hands of the charity, the base cost of the investment for capital gains tax purposes is reduced by the relevant amount, or to nil if the relevant amount exceeds the base cost. Incidental costs of disposal are taken into account in computing the relevant amount where the disposal is at an undervalue, although the base cost is not reduced for such incidental expenses.

Law: ITA 2007, Pt. 8, Ch. 3

See *British Tax Reporter* ¶116-000.

904 Payroll deduction scheme donations

Under the payroll deduction scheme an employee's donation to 'charity' (900) from his pay-packet, subject to an annual limit, attracts tax relief. Relief is available where:

- an employee suffers deduction of tax under PAYE;
- the employer operates an approved scheme for the deduction of charitable donations;

- the employee authorises the employer to make the deductions;
- the employer pays the deducted sums to an approved agent;
- the approved agent pays the deducted sums to a charity or charities; and
- the sums deducted constitute gifts from the employee to the charity and are not paid under a covenant.

The deduction of a donation to charity under the scheme occurs before PAYE is applied, thus giving relief by means of a 'net pay' arrangement.

There are regulations under which payroll deduction schemes are approved.

For relief for expenses incurred by the employer, see 2240.

Law: FA 2003, s. 146; FA 2000, s. 38; ITEPA 2003, s. 713; *Charitable Deductions (Approved Schemes) Regulations* 1986 (SI 1986/2211)

See *British Tax Reporter* ¶458-000.

905 Community amateur sports clubs

From April 2002, amateur sports clubs that register as community amateur sports clubs (CASCs) are given various tax reliefs and exemptions similar to those given to a charity. Broadly, prior to 2003–04, the club will not be taxed if its trading income does not exceed £15,000 per year, and its rental income does not exceed £10,000 per year, as long as all that income is applied in providing facilities for and promoting participation in one or more eligible sports (to be defined in regulations).

The corporation tax threshold for CASCs was doubled with effect from 1 April 2004. CASCs are exempt from corporation tax if their trading income is less than £30,000 or where their gross property income is less than £20,000. CASCs which do not exceed these thresholds do not have to complete an annual tax return.

A CASC is treated as a charity for the purpose of Gift Aid donations by individuals (see 902), although membership fees may not be treated as gifts. The CASC will be able to reclaim basic rate tax on donations. The treatment of a CASC as a charity also means that gifts and bequests to it are free of IHT (see 7195) and exempt from CGT (see 6189). Relief is also available on gifts from businesses (see 636) and for gifts of plant and machinery.

CASCs wishing to claim a repayment from HMRC should use Revenue form R68 (CASC).

Law: FA 2004, s. 56

Source: Revenue guidance on multi-sports clubs: www.hmrc.gov.uk/casc/casc_guidance.htm

See *British Tax Reporter* ¶144-175.

907 Large charities with non-qualifying expenditure: restricted exemptions

For chargeable periods commencing before 22 March 2006, the tax exemptions available to a charity (see 901) were restricted if, in its chargeable period:

- its 'relevant income and gains' were not less than £10,000; and
- its 'relevant income and gains' exceeded its 'qualifying expenditure'; and
- it incurred non-qualifying expenditure.

'Relevant income and gains' means income otherwise so exempted from tax and income taxable notwithstanding those provisions, taken together with capital gains exempted from CGT (see 5800) and gains which are chargeable notwithstanding that exemption.

'Qualifying expenditure' means any expenditure made for charitable purposes only and includes qualifying investments and qualifying loans. Payment made to overseas bodies is not qualifying expenditure unless the charity concerned has taken such steps as may be reasonable to ensure that the payment is applied for charitable purposes.

Where the three conditions above were met exemption from tax was not available in respect of so much of the excess of relevant income and gains over qualifying expenditure as did not exceed the non-qualifying expenditure.

This restriction on exemption from tax had no application to small charities, that is those the sum of whose taxable income and gains in a chargeable period did not exceed £10,000. The limit did not operate to protect two or more charities who acted in concert to engage in transactions to avoid tax.

Where in a chargeable period the sum of qualifying and non-qualifying expenditure exceeds the relevant income and gains of that period, some or all of the excess may be carried back and treated as the non-qualifying expenditure of an earlier period.

In respect of non-charitable expenditure incurred in a chargeable period commencing on or after 22 March 2006, the *de minimis* income limit of £10,000 is removed and there is a technical change to the way in which the restriction of income attracting relief is calculated. Where there is an excess of non-charitable expenditure over total income in the current year, the excess can still be carried back to an earlier period.

Where a charity's own exemption from tax is limited by these rules, higher rate tax relief for covenantors will be similarly restricted (see 1073, 1840).

Law: ITA 2007, Part 10; ITTOIA 2005, s. 878(1)

See *British Tax Reporter* ¶142-000.

909   Grants paid by one charity to another

A sum received by a charity by way of a grant from another charity is chargeable to income tax as income of the payee charity, but is treated as if it were an annual payment thereby eligible for exemption from tax if applied for charitable purposes (see 901).

Law: ITA 2007, s. 523

See *British Tax Reporter* ¶138-050.

911   Covenanted payments by subsidiary to parent

Where a subsidiary company pays a covenanted sum to its parent charity, such a sum must be paid under deduction of income tax if the payer company is to treat the sum so paid as a charge on income (see 3055ff.). The parent charity may reclaim the tax so paid provided it satisfies the conditions for exemption from income tax. A statement of practice sets out a HMRC procedure for provisional repayment of tax deducted at source to minimise cashflow disadvantages for charities.

Source: SP 3/87, *Repayment of tax to charities on covenanted and other income*; IR 75, *Tax reliefs for charities*

Website: www.hmrc.gov.uk/leaflets/c10.htm

See *British Tax Reporter* ¶138-050.

913   Substantial donors

Additional restrictions have been placed on transactions that can take place on or after 22 March 2006 (unless a contract was entered into earlier), between a charity and its substantial donors without the charity's tax relief being restricted.

Broadly, an individual or a company will be treated as a 'substantial donor' if they give the charity £25,000 or more in any 12-month period, or £100,000 over a six-month period, both for the chargeable period in which they exceed these limits and the following five chargeable periods. The limits apply only to amounts on which tax relief has been claimed.

The 'substantial donor' rules apply to various specified transactions unless the transaction is otherwise exempt, or where HMRC is satisfied that a charity has engaged in it for genuine commercial reasons, or on terms that are no less beneficial to the charity than those that might be expected of an identical arm's length transaction, so long as the transaction is not part of an arrangement for the avoidance of tax.

Income Tax

The rules do not apply to a disposal at less than market value by a substantial donor to a charity to which the 'gifts of shares, securities and real property to charity' rules (see 903), or the capital gains 'gifts to charities' (see 6189) rules apply.

Where a charity takes part in any one of the specified transactions that are not otherwise exempt, any payments made by the charity in connection with the transaction will be treated as non-charitable expenditure. Where the transaction is not on arm's length terms, any difference between the actual terms and arm's length terms, so far as it favours the substantial donor, will be treated as non-charitable expenditure and the charity will have its tax relief restricted.

Law: FA 2006, s. 54

923 Scientific research associations

The exemptions applying to charities, the procedures for reclaiming tax deducted at source, the treatment of tax credits associated with dividends from UK companies and HMRC's information powers (see 901) also apply to certain scientific research associations. The exemptions are available where:

- the object of an association is 'scientific research' which may lead to or facilitate an extension of any class or classes of trade approved by the Department of Trade and Industry; and
- the memorandum of association or other similar instrument regulating the functions of the association precludes the direct or indirect payment, or transfer, to any of its members of any of its income or property by way of dividend, gift, bonus, etc. (except for reasonable payment for goods, labour, services, or reasonable interest or rent).

Law: CTA 2010, s. 469

Source: ESC C31, *Scientific research associations*

See *British Tax Reporter* ¶144-165.

FARMING CONCERNS AND MARKET GARDENERS

940 Farming concerns and market gardeners: introduction

All farming and market gardening in the UK is treated as the carrying on of a trade (or part of a trade) chargeable under ITTOIA 2005, s. 9.

'Farming' consists of occupying land for the purposes of husbandry but excluding market gardening. 'Market gardening' consists of occupying land (other than for the growth of hops) as a nursery or garden for the sale of produce.

Share farming

'Share farming' is a method of farming where the owner or tenant of farm land (the landowner) enters into a contract with a working farmer (the share farmer). Typically:

- the landowner provides the farm land and buildings, fixed equipment and machinery, major maintenance of the buildings and his expertise;
- the share farmer provides labour, field and mobile machinery and his expertise;
- other costs such as seed, fertilisers and feed are shared. If there is a livestock enterprise then ownership of the animals is shared on the basis that each party owns a share in each animal;
- each party is rewarded by a share in the produce of the farm which he is free to sell as he likes; and
- each party produces his own accounts and is responsible for his own tax and VAT returns.

HMRC consider that both parties to a genuine share farming agreement are carrying on a 'farming' business for tax purposes.

Grants to farmers

Payments to taxpayers by way of grants cause difficulty and general rules are problematic since it is the precise purpose of the grant in each case which is critical – however, some guidance is available as set out below.

- Amounts received by farmers to make good a possible loss or temporary loss of income are generally taxable as income. Hence, the first premium under the EC Dairy Herd Conversion Scheme has been treated as taxable under former Sch. D, Case I, where it was held that under the scheme taxpayers gave up the right to continue producing milk for supply and sale but neither lost nor surrendered any capital assets (the conversion premium was for expected loss during the exchange from dairy cows to beef cattle which would be taxable if received). HMRC have confirmed that a payment of superlevy made after a farmer has exceeded his milk quota is an allowable trading deduction.
- Aid under the Oilseeds Support Scheme 1992 is generally to be treated as a subsidy towards the selling price; hence, accounts should recognise the payments as income for tax purposes at the time the crop is sold and, if best estimates are used until final figures are available, the inspector may decide to agree the computation and adjust the amount in the following period.

All farming by same person to be treated as one trade

All farming (but not market gardening) carried on by one person (or partnership or body of persons) is treated as one trade. Thus, a farming company which bought one farm in Scotland and soon after sold a farm in England was (being engaged in a continuous trade) entitled to carry forward losses and unused capital allowances from the English farming business to the Scottish one.

Income Tax

321

Law: ITTOIA 2005, s. 9–11; *Bispham (HMIT) v Eardiston Farming Co (1919) Ltd* [1962] 1 WLR 616; *IR Commrs v Biggar* [1982] BTC 332

Website: www.hmrc.gov.uk/bulletins/index.htm

See *British Tax Reporter* ¶270-500.

942 Relief for fluctuating profits from farming

Because personal reliefs which are unused in one tax year cannot be carried forward or backward to another tax year (see 1850), and because of the progressive nature of income tax liability, a person who earns, say, £40,000 in one tax year and £10,000 in the next pays more income tax than a similarly placed person who earns £25,000 in each of two succeeding tax years. Special relief is accordingly available to individuals and partnerships engaged in a 'farming or market gardening business' (see 940) to take account of fluctuating profits.

Farming, for these purposes, includes the intensive rearing of livestock or fish on a commercial basis for the production of food for human consumption.

The relief

If in two consecutive tax years, the profits assessable in one are 70 per cent or less of those in the other, the profits of both years can be averaged. A year in which a loss is incurred is, for the purposes of the relief, deemed to be a year of nil profit. Loss relief is, nevertheless, still available.

The introduction of self-assessment changed the method of dealing with capital allowances in the computation of profits, and consequently it also changes the measure of profits to be used in an averaging claim. For trades which commenced on or after 6 April 1994 regardless of the years covered by the claim, and for other trades where the claim is for 1996–97 and 1997–98 or a later pair of years, 'profits' for the purpose of averaging are the net trading profits *after* the deduction or addition of capital allowances and balancing charges.

In either case, the profits to be taken are the profits before any deduction for losses.

A claim for the relief must be made in writing within two years of the end of the second tax year to which the claim relates. Under self-assessment, the claim is to be related to the later year, with any necessary adjustments in respect of the earlier year being given in the later year (see 2684).

The average profits for the second year can provide the basis for averaging the profits for years two and three.

> **Example**
>
> Andrew, a farmer, has profits as follows:
>
> Year 1 £30,000
>
> Year 2 £10,000
>
> Year 2 profits are less than 70 per cent of Year 1 profits. Andrew claims the relief.
>
> His profits for each of Year 1 and Year 2 will be deemed to be:
>
> $$\frac{£30,000 + £10,000}{2} = £20,000$$
>
> The profits in Year 3 are £10,000. Andrew again claims relief. His profits for Years 2 and 3 will each be adjusted to:
>
> $$\frac{£20,000 + £10,000}{2} = £15,000$$

There is a marginal relief where profits for one year are more than 70 per cent but less than 75 per cent of the profits of the other year.

A claim for relief cannot be made for a year of commencement or discontinuance.

Law: ITTOIA 2005, s. 221–225

See *British Tax Reporter* ¶272-300.

944 Restriction of loss relief for farming

In general, any loss incurred in 'farming or market gardening' (see 940) is unavailable for loss relief by offset against general income (see 2296ff.) if in each of the prior five years a loss was incurred (disregarding capital allowances) in carrying on that trade, i.e. losses can only be relieved against general income for five years. The restriction also applies to capital allowances related to the loss.

Law: ITA 2007, s. 67

See *British Tax Reporter* ¶272-850.

946 Treatment of livestock, tillages and harvested crops

The treatment and valuation of stock-in-trade is a particular problem for farmers. This applies to livestock, tillages, harvested crops, etc. As a general rule, animals kept for farming are treated as trading stock; however, animals are not so treated where the farmer makes an election for 'the herd basis' (see below). A number of long-standing practices

Income Tax

were called into question by HMRC, their views being set out in a business economic note (BEN 19) issued in April 1993. HMRC later commented on their revised practice in ascertaining the cost of harvested crops (from 85 per cent of market value to 75 per cent thereof) and clarified further the areas in which they expected changes to valuation methods: full waygoing valuations, dilapidations reserves, certificates under the 1942 NFU arrangement and production animals taken at cull value.

The herd basis

Where animals are treated as part of the trading stock, payments and receipts for animals bought and sold are dealt with in the accounts in the usual way. Trading stock will have to be revalued at the end of the period of account. However, where an election for the herd basis is made, the initial cost of the herd, and of any animal added to the herd which is not a replacement animal, is not deducted in the accounts as an expense and the value of the herd is not brought into account.

Generally, where an animal is sold, or dies, and is replaced, the proceeds of sale are included as a trading receipt and the cost of the replacement animal is deductible as an expense. It is not always clear whether the acquisition of one animal is necessarily a 'replacement' for another. HMRC have confirmed that inspectors will accept that replacement treatment is applied where an animal is brought into the herd within 12 months of the corresponding disposal. If the interval is longer than 12 months, replacement treatment may be accepted if the facts of the case support it.

Where at least 20 per cent of the herd is sold within a 12-month period, and is not replaced within five years, any profit or loss is treated as a capital profit or loss. However, no chargeable gain will accrue on disposal as animals are wasting assets which are tangible moveable property (see 5330).

An election for the herd basis can only be made in relation to 'production herds': i.e. herds of animals of the same species kept wholly or mainly for the sake of the products which they produce for the farmer to sell, e.g. dairy herds. An election must be made in writing and must specify the class of herds to which it relates. An election is irrevocable and normally must be made within two years of the end of the first chargeable period for which the farmer is chargeable under ITTOIA 2005, or is given relief for trading losses against general income. In commencement cases, the time-limit is extended to two years after the end of the first period of account if that is later.

The herd basis extends to cases where several farmers hold shares in one animal for the purposes of a herd, or in animals forming part of a herd.

Where there is a change in any of the persons carrying on the farming trade, HMRC view is that the herd basis election made by the old 'farmer' ceases and the new 'farmer' can decide whether to make a fresh election.

Capital allowances cannot be claimed in respect of animals in respect of whom the herd basis is used to compute profits.

Law: ITTOIA 2005, Pt. 2, Ch. 8

See *British Tax Reporter* ¶271-000.

MINING CONCERNS

960 Mining concerns identified for tax purposes

Profits of mines, quarries (including gravel pits, sand pits and brickfields) and alum mines and works are chargeable under ITTOIA 2005, s. 12 as if from a trade.

Mines, oil wells and other sources of mineral deposits, being of a wasting nature, require special treatment as regards capital allowances (see 2386ff.).

Law: ITTOIA 2005, s. 12

See *British Tax Reporter* ¶265-500.

962 Mining royalties

Rent paid in respect of any land or easement used, occupied or enjoyed in connection with any mining concern (and also certain other concerns: see 556) is generally charged to tax under ITTOIA 2005 (see 960). The rent was, before 1 May 1995, subject to deduction of income tax at source (see 1368, 1370) as if it were a patent royalty, unless it was rendered in the produce of the concern, in which case it is charged under former Sch. D, Case III (see 1366).

Mineral royalties subject to deduction of tax at source were not allowable as deductions in computing trading profits (see 2174).

Half of the royalties are treated as chargeable gains.

Law: ITTOIA 2005, s. 319, 340

See *British Tax Reporter* ¶265-050.

LLOYD'S UNDERWRITERS

970 Lloyd's underwriters: introduction

An applicant may be elected as an underwriting member of Lloyd's from 1 January in a calendar year. Groups of members get together to form syndicates to provide insurance.

Each member is known as a Name and each syndicate is run by a managing agent. It became possible to admit corporate members from 1 January 1994 (see 4580).

Each Name underwrites a risk with unlimited liability but is not held responsible for the whole of the syndicate's debts.

A Name may be a working Name, i.e. one who works full-time in the ambit of Lloyd's, or may be purely an investor who delegates responsibility for investment, etc. to an underwriting agent. A Name will often be a member of several syndicates and will have a members' agent to look after his various interests. The Corporation of Lloyd's or the syndicate managers hold the Name's investments as bare trustees.

A Name does not receive any distribution profits from the syndicate during the first three calendar years – each trading account remains open for at least three years. The syndicate draws up accounts to 31 December each year and the accounts are not finalised (remain open) for a further two years, when any outstanding claims are valued and reinsured.

The taxation of Lloyd's underwriters was reformed retrospectively for most purposes (for years after 1991–92) but not for profits or losses in respect of ancillary trust funds arising before 6 April 1993, nor in relation to the deemed disposal and reacquisition of assets in the premiums trust fund for the underwriting year (calendar year) 1993.

Under self-assessment, for 1994 and subsequent accounts, profits are assessed in the tax year corresponding to that in which the results are declared and distributed. For example, the 2006 account closed on 31 December 2006 and the results are declared in 2009. As the underwriting year 2009, the year in which the results are declared, corresponds to the tax year 2009–10, the profits of the 2006 account are assessed in 2009–10. This basis of assessment is known as the 'distribution year basis'.

Profits from underwriting business are chargeable as trading profits and are earned income. Underwriting losses can be set off in the same way as trading losses.

Assets in premiums trust funds are treated as acquired and disposed of each underwriting year, with the exception of certain UK securities where an exemption applies for particular non-resident holders.

Gains or losses on the disposal of assets in funds other than a premiums trust fund or the new special reserve fund continue to be subject to CGT and are not brought within the computation of trading profits.

Distributions relating to assets held in a corporate member's ancillary trust fund, or employed by it in its underwriting business are to be included in its trading profits, without taking into account the associated tax credit.

Relief for payments ('reinsurance to close' premiums) which one syndicate makes to its successor to take over its outstanding liabilities is available to the extent that the payments are fair and reasonable having regard to the liabilities transferred.

Rules give relief for payments and charge receipts in respect of loss insurance and of the new Lloyd's High Level Stop Loss Fund; relief is also provided for payments made to transfer to someone else a member's rights and liabilities in respect of business he has underwritten – a 'quota share contract'.

The final tax year of a member's underwriting business is generally that in which his deposit at Lloyd's is repaid, subject, in cases of death, to the final year not being later than the year in which the underwriter dies.

Amendments have been made , from 1 January 2006 for corporation tax and 6 April 2006 for income tax, to the powers for making regulations relating to Lloyd's underwriters. Broadly, FA 1993, Sch. 19 has been repealed and future legislation will be made by Statutory Instrument. This allows for greater flexibility when amending and modernising the current procedures by, for example, allowing for electronic filing of syndicate returns and by applying self-assessment principles to the determination of syndicate profits. (Lloyd's managing agents are required to make returns to HMRC of syndicate profits and losses, computed for tax purposes.)

Law: FA 1993, s. 176

See *British Tax Reporter* ¶639-350.

972 Requirements as to special reserve funds

A special reserve fund is made up of funds set aside each year by a Lloyd's Name out of his profits to meet potential future liabilities (see 970).

Tax deductibility is available for up to 50 per cent of a member's profits transferred to an approved reserve each year subject to an overall fund value limit of 50 per cent of the member's overall premium limit. Income and gains on assets within the fund will be free of tax. Withdrawals from the fund will be required, notably, to meet losses and where the member ceases underwriting, and will be treated as trading income.

Where the funds are released after trading has ceased, from 31 December 1999, all sums released from the special reserve fund, including accumulated profits to the date of disposal, are brought into charge.

Law: FA 1993, s. 175, Sch. 20; *Lloyd's Underwriters (Equalisation Reserves) (Tax) Regulations* 2009 (SI 2009/2039); *Lloyd's Underwriters (Special Reserve Fund) Regulations*

1999 (SI 1999/3308); *Lloyd's Underwriters (Special Reserve Fund) Regulations* 1995 (SI 1995/353)

See *British Tax Reporter* ¶639-350.

974 Payment of tax by Lloyd's underwriters' agents

Since, from underwriting year 1994, syndicate profits are assessed for the tax year corresponding to the underwriting year in which the profits are declared, modifications of the self-assessment rules are not required. For example, profits for the 2004 underwriting account are declared in 2007, corresponding to the tax year 2007–08. Under self-assessment, tax is payable on the same dates as are for other trades generally, i.e. for 2007–08 (2004 underwriting account) tax on syndicate income falls due on 31 January 2008, 31 July 2008 and 31 January 2009.

Law: FA 1993, s. 173, 182, Sch. 19; *Lloyd's Underwriters (Tax) Regulations* 1995 (SI 1995/351); *Blackburn (HMIT) v Keeling*

See *British Tax Reporter* ¶639-350.

INCOME OF TRUSTS AND DECEASED PERSONS' ESTATES

985 Operation of trusts

The question 'what is a trust?' is a matter of general trust law. Briefly, a 'trust' is an obligation imposed on trustees (who may be individuals or corporate bodies) to hold and deal with trust property in particular ways (which may be specified in the trust deed) for the benefit of specified persons, or a class of beneficiaries or, if charitable, for particular purposes. The person providing the trust property (the settlor) may be among the beneficiaries.

A 'settlement' is, basically, a trust which creates successive interests in trust property. Such interests may be in income or capital, as between those with a life interest or remaindermen. They may have no life interest or other interest in possession, e.g. a discretionary trust.

From 6 April 2006, 'settled property' is redefined as any property held in trust other than property held as nominee, bare trustee for a person absolutely entitled, an infant or disabled person. References in the legislation to a settlement are construed as references to settled property and the meaning of settlement is determined by case law. This measure effectively aligns what is treated as a settlement for the general purposes of income tax and tax on chargeable gains (see also 1071 for further commentary on the new definitions of settor and settlement contained in *Finance Act* 2006).

For the purpose of determining liability for income tax, the liability of trustees to tax on income of a trust fund must not be confused with the liability of a beneficiary to tax on distributions from a trust fund.

The rate of tax borne by trustees depends largely on whether the trust is a discretionary trust or whether a beneficiary is absolutely entitled to the trust income.

For the incidence of CGT on trusts and settlements, see 5550ff. For the incidence of inheritance tax on trusts and settlements, see 6880ff.

Reasons for creating a trust

Since time immemorial trusts have been formed to avoid some unpleasant consequence, and the non-tax reason must not be forgotten. However, trusts and tax planning have a long history. In medieval times they were used to avoid feudal dues.

These days, there are many reasons for establishing a trust over property, including mitigation of tax. For example, a trust may be set up to save income tax. A settlor, whose income is taxed at the higher rate, could transfer the income-producing capital to trustees. They would hold it for beneficiaries taxed at much lower rates or who could offset their personal allowances or other reliefs against their income from the trust.

However, the main tax reason for creating many trusts is to pass property during the lifetime of the settlor to trustees for beneficiaries to reduce the burden of inheritance tax on death. A person may wish to make a gift but a settlor may also want to prevent a beneficiary from taking control of the gifted property too soon. Alternatively, the settlor might want to retain the maximum flexibility over the ultimate destination of the property for as long as possible. By making a gift into trust (whether in lifetime or by will) the settlor can achieve these objectives as well as securing the inheritance tax advantages that would apply to an outright gift.

Trusts are frequently set up for purposes other than tax mitigation and may be used:

- to hold property for those who cannot manage their affairs, such as minors or mentally incapacitated persons;
- to hold property for persons in succession as when property is left to A for life thereafter to B;
- to protect spendthrifts from themselves;
- to preserve maximum flexibility in the event of unforeseeable circumstances. The discretionary trust is the ideal vehicle to achieve this objective;
- to benefit charity.

In some cases, trusts represent an ideal or convenient legal regime for certain activities (e.g. pension funds and unit trusts). In other cases trusts may be imposed by law. This happens when, for example, a person dies intestate and property passes to minors under the intestacy law.

Income Tax

How to create a trust

A trust may be established by a settlor during lifetime ('inter vivos') or by will, or it may arise automatically if someone dies intestate (i.e. without making a will). An inter vivos trust may be oral but it is eminently desirable to set out all the necessary provisions in a formal deed. Indeed, if the trust property comprises land it is generally the case that the trust must be evidenced in writing. A will must be in writing and satisfy certain other formalities as to execution unless it is made by a person on active service in the armed forces, or a mariner or seaman at sea.

The creation of trusts by deed or will is very much the province of lawyers and advice must be taken.

In particular it is essential that the trust document should set out in full everything that is required. Once it is executed a trust may not be altered unless the trustees have been given powers of variation. This is unlike a contract where the parties are free to agree to subsequent changes. A will can always be changed at any time before death provided the necessary formalities as to execution are observed. Even after death, a deed of variation, formerly called a deed of family arrangement, may be effective for capital gains tax and inheritance tax but not income tax.

The *Trustee Act* 1925 and *Trusts of Land and Appointment of Trustees Act* 1996 apply, unless and except to the extent that the trust instrument provides to the contrary. These Acts contain a number of useful automatic provisions. The trust document does not need to set out these provisions specifically unless variations are to be made. Other Acts and case law provide a general framework but considerable thought must be given to the contents of the document. For example, it is usual to provide very wide powers of investment. Unless this is done, trustees must invest only in investments authorised by the *Trustee Investments Act* 1961. These investment powers have recently been extended so that, for example, trustees may proceed with an investment without taking advice where they judge this a reasonable course of action.

In setting up a trust, there must be what are commonly called three certainties:

(1)   the certainty of words;

(2)   the certainty of subject matter; and

(3)   the certainty of objects of the trust.

If the trust fails in these certainties it will not be effective under trust law and, as a result, may not achieve the desired tax savings.

Trust documentation

Since 6 April 1991 tax offices have in general ceased to ask for a copy of every new family trust document. Instead they rely on information shown by trustees, settlors and beneficiaries in their annual tax returns or repayment claims. When a new trust is created, trustees are sent a form which asks them to give some basic factual information about the identities of the trustees and settlor and whether the trustees can accumulate income or distribute it at their discretion. This does not alter the examination of deeds for inheritance tax purposes by the Capital Taxes Offices.

HMRC will seek further information only where necessary, and only exceptionally will they ask to see trust deeds, wills or other documents. That may happen if, for example, an inspector is not satisfied with a tax return or repayment claim, or if the taxpayer is unsure of the effect of the document and the issue cannot be resolved in some other way.

Trust provisions

Beneficial interests

Analysis and classification of the particular type of beneficial interest is essential for tax purposes. This is discussed in more detail in the sections dealing with each tax.

When a trust is set up, the tax consequences of the precise beneficial interests created must be borne in mind.

(1) Income or capital: a beneficiary may have an interest in income only. A life interest is a right to receive income for life or for a set period. An annuity might be given. This is a right to receive specified periodical payments for a specified period that could be for life. A beneficiary may have only an interest in capital. This would be where, for example, property is left to A for life and thereafter to B. B has an interest only in capital and will take that capital when A dies.

(2) In possession or in remainder or reversion: this is where property is held on trust for A for life and then for B. A has an 'interest in possession' which has been described as a present right of enjoyment. B has an 'interest in remainder' which is deferred until after A's death. This is sometimes called a 'reversionary interest'. B would be known as a 'remainderman' or 'reversioner'.

(3) Vested or contingent: where property is held on trust for A for life, the remainder to such of the children of A as attain the age of 21, A has a vested interest. A does not need to satisfy any conditions to be entitled to it. A's children have contingent interests. Each child's interest will become vested if and when he or she reaches 21 years of age.

(4) Determinable and defeasible: if property is held on trust for A (a widow) until she remarries, A's interest is determinable because she is only entitled to enjoy it until she remarries. An interest is defeasible if, though vested, it can be subsequently lost. This would be the case if, for example, property is held for the children of A if they attain 18. If no one reaches 18 the trust would fail because there would be no certainty of objects. This is why trust deeds leave the funds to a charity. The charity has a vested interest but one which will be defeated if a child of A attains 18. Its interest will be in possession if in the meanwhile it is entitled to the income ('the intermediate income') but in remainder if the income goes to A's children. Often the vested interest of a beneficiary is defeasible because the trustees have a power of appointment enabling them to pay income or capital to another beneficiary.

Income Tax

(5)   Mere *spes*: a beneficiary under a discretionary trust has a mere *spes* (a Latin word meaning hope). Unless and until the trustees decide to pay something, income or capital, the beneficiary is entitled to nothing. Trustees of such a trust therefore enjoy enormous flexibility. They can usually accumulate income for the period permitted by law and are not bound to know who has a vested interest in capital until the end of the maximum period permitted by law. They are also usually given wide powers to change the nature of the trust, particularly the beneficial interests, and an absolute discretion over who amongst the class of beneficiaries may receive income and capital and in what shares.

Trusts and powers

A *trust* is mandatory. If the trustees fail in their duty the court will enforce it at the suit of any beneficiary. A *power* is discretionary. Trustees may choose whether or not to exercise a power and if they decide not to, the court will not compel them to do so.

It is often important to determine whether a provision is a *trust* or a *power*. A trust to distribute income with a power to accumulate means that income must be paid out unless all trustees agree to accumulate it. A trust to accumulate income with power to distribute it means that one trustee can insist income be accumulated. The distinction between a trust to sell with a power to retain, and a power of sale in relation to trust property, is similar, but the importance of a trust for sale has declined following the *Trusts of Land and Appointment of Trustees Act* 1996.

Trustees, particularly of discretionary trusts, are often given powers of appointment. These are powers to alter the beneficial interests in income and capital by taking these away from one beneficiary, or class, and giving them to another. Such powers may permit the creation of new trusts, sub-trusts, alterations in the size of shares, and distributions to other trusts, even foreign trusts.

Accumulations and perpetuity

The law does not permit trust income to be accumulated indefinitely (whether under a trust or power). It lays down six maximum periods, the most common of which is the period of 21 years from the date of the deed for a lifetime settlement or from the date of death for a will trust.

In addition, income may be accumulated during the minority of any minor beneficiary.

Once the permitted accumulation period has expired, the income must be distributed.

The property comprised in the trust fund must become vested in a beneficiary or beneficiaries within the 'perpetuity period', i.e. the maximum period permitted by law. The name reflects the law's intention to prevent a settlor from tying up property in trust for generations without any limit. Property must vest within the lifetime of a living person plus 21 years, or, if specifically chosen, within a period of up to 80 years, from the date when the settlement commenced. The settlor must choose the period required. Some trusts, such as charitable trusts and pension funds, are exempt from the perpetuity rule.

If, at the outset, it seems possible that some interests may not vest within the perpetuity period, it is permitted to wait and see for a period which is broadly similar to the perpetuity period. If an interest vests within the wait and see period the trusts are valid.

Power of maintenance

Under the *Trustee Act* 1925 trustees have a power to pay or apply income to or for the maintenance, education or benefit of a beneficiary who is an unmarried minor (under the age of 18) but must otherwise accumulate it. It is essential that the gift should 'carry the intermediate income' and that the settlor should not exclude this section of the Act unless similar trusts are set out in the settlement document. Most trusts allow this part of the *Trustee Act* 1925 to be implied, though many vary its terms slightly. They may, for example, enable the trustees to exercise their discretion subjectively, as they may think fit, rather than objectively. Provided the trustees do not act unreasonably, a subjective discretion is less open to challenge than an objective requirement.

This section of the *Trustee Act* 1925 (s. 31) should be expressed to apply whether the minor's beneficial interest is vested or contingent. It has two main effects:

(1)   During minority, the trustees have a discretion to pay the income out for the maintenance, education or benefit of a beneficiary, but otherwise they must accumulate it.

(2)   When the minor attains 18, or marries earlier, they must pay income from then on until the beneficiary's interest vests, is defeated or the beneficiary dies. Accumulations of income not paid out during minority will go to the beneficiary if the interest vests on attaining 18 but, if not, they are added to capital. As a result, the accumulations would only pass to the beneficiary if the beneficiary attains a vested interest in capital. Such a vesting of capital would arise, for example, where the beneficiary attains 25 in a trust contingent on attaining 25.

A minor who marries under 18 is treated as ceasing to be a minor but pre-1970 trusts have 21 as the relevant age.

Power of advancement

Section 32 of the *Trustee Act* 1925 allows trustees to advance 50 per cent of the prospective share of capital to any beneficiary. Most trust documents vary this to 100 per cent. It is a type of special power that is exercisable by a trustee resolution and is read into every trust unless excluded. If a beneficiary's interest is defeated, the advance does not have to be repaid but it is taken into account on final distribution.

Law: *Finance Act* 2006, s. 88, 89 and Sch. 12 and 13; *Trustee Act* 1925, s. 31, 32; *Sinclair v Lee* [1993] Ch 497

See *British Tax Reporter* ¶350-000; ¶354-300.

Income Tax

TRUSTEES' INCOME TAX POSITION

987 Trustees generally

The provisions of tax legislation frequently refer to 'the person' or 'any person'. 'Person' is defined in the *Interpretation Act* 1978 as including a body of persons. It follows that such provisions are apt to cover trustees of a settlement, as well as individuals.

Where a valid trust has been created and trustees receive income from the settled property which is held on trusts, other than bare trusts, the trustees are chargeable to income tax in respect of that income in accordance with the rules applicable to the income. The basis of this is that the trustees either receive or are entitled to this income (and in most cases both receive and are entitled to the income) and hence are, for example, within the charging provisions in respect of:

- trading profits;
- property business profits;
- interest;
- dividend and dividend related income; and
- miscellaneous income.

Trustees are treated as a deemed single person, distinct from the actual persons who are (from time to time) the trustees of the settlement, who are jointly (but not jointly and severally), entitled to the settled property. They are liable to income tax on income arising from the settled property independently of the settlor and the beneficiaries. Where different trust assets are held by different persons, then (unless a sub-funding election is in place) all such persons are treated as one.

Changes of the individual trustees are ignored. Thus, if a sole trustee carries on a trade, then his resignation as trustee and the substitution of another individual in his stead does not give rise to a cessation and recommencement of that trade.

Tax may be assessed and charged on and in the name of any one or more of 'the relevant trustees': i.e. the trustees to whom the income arises and any subsequent trustees of the settlement.

Trustees are not 'individuals' and are accordingly not entitled to personal allowances or other reliefs which are only available to individuals; nor are they subject to progressive rates of tax (see, however, 989 in respect of the 'trust' rates of tax on income which is accumulated or paid at the trustees' discretion).

Double taxation agreements

Trustees are regarded as a deemed 'person' and not as individuals. Any provision in a double tax agreement which is applicable to a 'body of persons' is potentially applicable to trustees. It is necessary, therefore, to look at any relevant double taxation agreement to see whether this overrides the domestic law in relation to their tax residence. Where, by application of their domestic laws, the two parties to the agreement would regard the settlement as being resident in both countries for the same year, the agreement will specify which of the two shall be treated as the residence of the trust and relief within the agreement will be available to the trustees against liabilities arising in the other country.

Trustees' management expenses

Because the charge to income tax is on income received by the trustees, the expenses of the trustees in administering the trust are not deductible. The measure of the income is in accordance with the normal rules. However, the trust rates charged on discretionary and accumulation trusts are not charged on that part of the income of such a trust which is used to defray appropriate trust management expenses (see 991). The trust income that is used to pay the expenses is only liable at the usual rates of income tax (see 989).

Income charged on settlor

Income of a settlement is treated as income of the settlor if he or his spouse retains any interest in the trust property or if the income is paid to, or applied for the benefit of, his minor unmarried child. In addition, capital sums paid to the settlor may be treated as his income to the extent that it falls within the amount of income available up to the end of the year of payment.

Where a settlement is within one or more of these provisions, the trustees are not liable at the special trust rates on the income, but continue to be liable at basic rate, or dividend ordinary rate on savings and dividend income. The income arising in the settlement is then treated as part of the settlor's total income, higher rates of tax being levied accordingly. In these circumstances, the settlor has a right to recover from the trustees the higher rate tax he pays on that income. Conversely, where a repayment is available to the settlor because his lower rate band and personal allowances are not absorbed by other income, that repayment must be paid to the trustees or the person entitled to the income under the terms of the settlement.

Further, the income treated as belonging to the settlor is income before deduction of any trust expenses. Therefore, the R185 issued by the trustees to the settlor should show the income assessable at the rate at which tax was deducted at source, not the reduced income that would have been assessable at the special trust rates.

Where income arising in a settlement is treated as the settlor's income, he should complete the Trusts page T1, boxes 7–14 after reviewing the guidance in Helpsheet HS 270.

Trustees acting for incapacitated persons

The trustee, guardian, tutor, etc. of any incapacitated person is in a special position. He is assessable and chargeable to income tax to the extent that the incapacitated person would be charged and assessed. This is so where the trustee, etc. has the direction, control or management of the property of the incapacitated person, whether or not that person resides in the UK.

Income Tax

A new tax regime applies from 6 April 2004 for certain trusts with vulnerable beneficiaries. Certain trusts and beneficiaries can elect into the regime and, where a claim for special tax treatment is made for a tax year, no more tax will be payable in respect of the relevant income and gains of the trust for that year than would be paid had the income and gains accrued directly to the beneficiary.

Income and gains arising from the property held on qualifying trusts for the benefit of a vulnerable person is eligible for the alternative tax treatment. The special treatment does not apply in cases where the settlor is regarded as having an interest in the property from which the qualifying trusts income arose.

Broadly, the amount of income tax relief under the new regime is the difference between two amounts. The first of those amounts is what (were it not for the new rules) the income tax liability of the trustees would be in respect of the qualifying trusts income for the tax year. The second amount is the amount of extra tax to which the vulnerable person would be liable if the qualifying trusts income were that person's own income.

For details on the special CGT treatment available, see 5595.

Law: ITA 2007, s. 474; FA 1989, s. 151(4); *Reid's v IR Commrs* 14 TC 512; *Dawson v IR Commrs* [1989] BTC 200; *Williams v Singer* [1921] 1 AC 65; *Aikin v Macdonald's Trustees* (1894) 3 TC 306

See *British Tax Reporter* ¶350-100.

989   Rate of tax for discretionary trusts

Special rates of tax (termed the 'trust rate' and the 'dividend trust rate') are levied on settlement income which is either accumulated or is payable at the discretion of the trustees or of some other person and is not within one of a narrow group of exclusions.

The trust rate for 2009–10 was 40 per cent and the dividend trust rate was 32.5 per cent. From April 2010, the trust rate increased to 50 per cent and the dividend trust rate increased to 42.5 per cent.

Income which is excluded from the charge comprises:

● income which, before it is distributed, is the income of someone other than the trustees (e.g. the settlor);
● income from property that is held for a superannuation fund relating to an undertaking carried on outside the UK and not held as a member of a property investment LLP; and
● income from a 'relevant housing body', e.g. a local authority, social landlord, charitable housing trust, etc. From that date, the exclusion was extended to cover private landlords as well.

However, there are 11 categories of receipt which are charged at the special trust rates, that within category 1 (see below) is charged at the dividend trust rate whilst the remainder are charged at the trust rate. The specified categories are:

(1)   an amount received or receivable on a company's purchase of own shares (including a redemption or repayment of shares) or on the purchase of rights to acquire such shares;

(2)   amounts chargeable under the accrued income scheme;

(3)   offshore income gains;

(4)   deemed income arising to an employee share ownership trust;

(5)   amounts treated as receipts of a property business (lease premiums, etc.);

(6)   profits from deeply discounted securities;

(7)   chargeable event gains on life assurance policies, other than policies held on charitable trusts;

(8)   profits arising from transactions in deposits;

(9)   profits on disposals of futures and options involving guaranteed returns, except where the profits are chargeable on the settlor, or where the profits arise to charitable trustees or those of a superannuation fund;

(10)   amounts received in respect of sales of foreign dividend coupons; and

(11)   deemed income arising under the anti-avoidance provisions for transactions in land.

For the purposes of the special trust rates, personal representatives are not 'trustees'. However, where personal representatives pay (on or before the completion of the administration of the estate) a sum which represents income that has arisen during the period of administration to trustees of a will trust (who are commonly the same individuals as the personal representatives), this sum is treated as income of the trustees; and if this income is to be accumulated or payable at their discretion, it attracts a charge to income tax at the special rate. Where this happens, the sum is treated as having borne tax at the applicable rate for grossing up basic amounts of estate income.

Relief for the first slice of trust rate income

With effect from 2005–06 onwards, the special trust rates do not apply to the first slice of the 'trust rate income', i.e. the income which would have otherwise attracted tax at the special trust rates (it is therefore the income remaining after any allowable trustees' expenses have been deducted). Instead, the normal income tax rates (currently the basic rate and dividend ordinary rate) apply as appropriate.

For 2005–06, this relief applied to the first £500, but for 2006–07 onwards, it was increased to the first £1,000.

This relief is applied to the first or lowest slice of the 'trust rate income', where dividend income is taken as the higher slice of that income followed by income chargeable at the

337

basic rate. For years 2005–06 to 2007–08 inclusive, there were also the lower rate and the savings rate to contend with and the order was that a source of income suffering a lower rate of tax than another was a higher slice. The relief is thus set against income bearing a higher rate of tax in priority to that bearing a lower rate.

For 2006–07 onwards, where the same person is the settlor in respect of more than one current settlement, the band is divided equally between those settlements. However, the minimum band to be available to any settlement is £200. Where there is more than one settlor in respect of a settlement, the available band is found by calculating it for each person separately and then taking the lowest figure, but again this is subject to a £200 de minimis.

Where trustees make discretionary distributions to beneficiaries which are their income for tax purposes, the income is treated as an amount from which tax payable at the trust rate has been deducted. Trustees have to have paid sufficient income tax to cover the amount of that deemed deduction, which is available as a tax credit to the beneficiary, and is disclosed as such on the form R185 (Trust Income), otherwise additional tax becomes payable.

Income tax paid by the trustees at the trust rate or dividend trust rate (less the 10 per cent non-payable tax credit) goes into the 'tax pool'. This pool can be used to cover the amount of the deemed deduction, with the trustees paying any additional tax to cover a shortfall. Any tax charged at the basic rate (but not at the dividend ordinary rate) as a result of the relief for the first slice of trust rate income can be added to the tax pool and can be used to cover the amount of the deemed deduction. However, it will be seen that effectively the relief restricts the amount of tax going into the tax pool and, where all discretionary income is in fact distributed, there will be an additional amount of tax levied on the trustees.

Law: FA 2009, s. 6(4); ITA 2007, s. 479–487; FA 2005, s. 14; FA 2004, s. 29; F(No. 2)A 1997, s. 31–33, Sch. 4, para. 16, Sch. 6, para. 11; *Carver v Duncan (HMIT); Bosanquet v Allen (HMIT)* [1985] BTC 248

Website: www.hmrc.gov.uk/bulletins/index.htm

See *British Tax Reporter* ¶351-100.

991 Payments under discretionary trusts

Income received by a discretionary trust is liable to tax at the rate applicable to trusts and, for 2007–08 onwards, is subject to a basic rate band of £1,000 (see 989). This income is assessed for the year in which it arises. If the income is not distributed until a later year, when the rate of tax has increased, then the trustees are liable to make an additional payment of tax, effectively representing the difference in rates, i.e. they deduct an amount of tax at source.

Discretionary payments by trustees are treated as income of the payee, received net after the rate applicable to trusts. The tax treated as deducted is assessable on the trustees.

Law: ITA 2007, s. 499–503; FA 2006, Sch. 12 and 13; FA 2004, s. 29; F(No. 2)A 1997, s. 20, Sch. 4, para. 15; *Stevenson (HMIT) v Wishart* [1987] BTC 283

See *British Tax Reporter* ¶354-800.

993 Trustees' remuneration

Some trust instruments specify a fixed remuneration to which trustees are entitled. This remuneration is regarded as an annual payment under ITTOIA 2005 (see 1366ff.).

Source: *Jones v Wright* (1927) 13 TC 221; *Baxendale (HMIT) v Murphy* [1924] 2 KB 494

See *British Tax Reporter* ¶351-950.

TAX POSITION OF THE BENEFICIARY

1001 General

The gross equivalent of the income received from a settlement is treated as part of the total income of the recipient for the tax year in which it is actually received, if paid at the discretion of the trustees, or if the beneficiary has an interest in possession in the year in which it arises. Credit for tax deducted by the trustees is given to the beneficiary, who may use the tax credit on the certificate R185 supplied to him to satisfy his own liability to income tax. The beneficiary is responsible for any tax liability in excess of that shown on the certificate and can claim repayment where his own tax liability on the income from the trust is less than that on the certificate.

Under English law a beneficiary with an interest in possession in a trust is treated as entitled to the income of the trust as it arises, but this is not the position under Scots law. In order that beneficiaries under Scottish trusts should not be put at a disadvantage compared with their English counterparts, and that they should be able to enjoy the benefit of the lower rates on interest and dividends where appropriate, the rights of a beneficiary under a UK-resident trust subject to Scots law are, from 1993–94, deemed to include the same right to income as under English law.

Bare trustees for minor or incapacitated person

A trustee having the direction, control or management of property held on bare trusts for a minor is assessable and chargeable to income tax in respect of income arising from that property. The quantum of the liability is calculated as if the income arose directly to the minor himself and no regard is taken of the personal circumstances of the individual trustee. It is thus possible for the trustee to claim repayment of income tax by reference to the personal allowance available to the minor.

The trustee of a minor is also subject to any liability to higher rates of tax, calculated with respect to the total income of that minor. Furthermore, in relation to such a charge, a trustee is answerable for all matters required to be done by the Income Tax Acts for assessment and payment of income tax on behalf of the minor. However, the trustee in this situation may retain out of money coming into his hands sufficient to reimburse him for tax charged and he is entitled to an indemnity in respect of payments made in pursuance of the Income Tax Acts. The above provisions also apply to incapacitated persons.

Further, where the beneficial owner is a minor, his parent, guardian (or, in Scotland before 25 September 1991, his tutor) is liable, not only for tax levied in respect of the minor's income but also in respect of any payment arising from neglect or refusal to pay that tax. He is therefore liable to pay any appropriate interest or penalties. A parent, etc. is similarly indemnified as against the minor in respect of all sums so paid. These provisions only apply if the income arises from property which is held on bare trusts.

Nominees or bare trustees for a person *sui juris*

Where the beneficial owner of the property that gives rise to the income is *sui juris* (i.e. of full age and legal capacity), the provisions of TMA 1970, s. 72 (see above) have no application. The general rule is that the bare trustee or nominee is ignored and the income taxed on the beneficial owner.

Law: TMA 1970, s. 72, 73; *Hamilton-Russell's Executors v IR Commrs* (1943) 25 TC 200; *Corbett v IR Commrs* [1938] 1 KB 567

See *British Tax Reporter* ¶350-250 and ¶350-300.

1003   Income applied for trust beneficiary's benefit

Income applied at the discretion of trustees for the maintenance, education or benefit of a beneficiary is treated as the beneficiary's income in the year of receipt. The beneficiary is treated as having received the grossed up amount (see 991). However, it should be remembered that in some cases the income is treated as that of the settlor and not of the beneficiary (e.g. where the beneficiary is an infant child of the settlor – see 1075) in which case the larger rate does not apply (though if the settlor is liable to higher rate tax, so will the trust income be chargeable).

The following payments by trustees have been held to be income of the beneficiary:

- the payment of rates in respect of a house which a beneficiary was entitled to occupy under the terms of a settlement; and
- the payment of outgoings in respect of a mansion (which the beneficiary was entitled 'to occupy, use and enjoy'), the expenses of keeping up the mansion as a residence, and the expenses of maintaining game for sport.

Law: *IR Commrs v Miller* [1930] AC 222; *Sutton v IR Commrs* (1929) 14 TC 662; *Drummond v Collins* [1915] AC 1011

See *British Tax Reporter* ¶353-200.

1005 Payments to trust beneficiaries out of capital

Whether or not a payment is treated as having been made out of trust income or capital is usually of significance only if the beneficiary is entitled absolutely to both income and capital of the trust fund. In such a case payments to the beneficiary out of income retain their income character whilst payments to the beneficiary out of capital retain their character as capital. In other cases, it is the character of the payments in the hands of the beneficiary which is important.

> ### Example
>
> Terry, the testator, directs trustees to pay his widow £4,000 out of income of the trust fund and, where the income is not sufficient to meet this obligation, the trustees are to raise and pay the balance out of capital. The payments out of capital are annual payments charged under ITTOIA 2005 (see 1366) and are part of the widow's total income.

Law: *Stevenson (HMIT) v Wishart* [1987] BTC 283; *Brodie's Will Trustees v IR Commrs* (1933) 17 TC 432

See *British Tax Reporter* ¶353-150.

1006 Non-discretionary trusts

Non-discretionary trusts

Tax law regards the beneficiary of a trust with an interest in possession, as owning the income from the trust as it arises. This is typically the position of a life tenant who is a beneficiary entitled to income for life.

From 6 April 1993, UK and overseas dividend income was chargeable at the lower rate of 20 per cent and from 6 April 1996 savings income is also chargeable at that rate. From 6 April 1999, dividends are chargeable at the rate of ten per cent. The trustees will account for tax at basic rate on all other non-dividend investment income. The lower rate of 20 per cent only applies for savings income. The question then arises whether the beneficiary is liable to higher rates or has available reliefs that give a repayment of tax.

Effectively the beneficiary of a fixed interest trust can, unlike the trustees, obtain relief for administration expenses, but only at the higher rate. Trust expenses are set first against dividend income, then savings income and then other income when calculating the income available for distribution to the beneficiary.

To the extent that the beneficiary's income is liable to tax at the higher rate, there will be a further income tax liability on the beneficiary of 20 per cent (40 − 20) on non-dividend savings income. In effect, the beneficiary is treated as if receiving the savings income direct.

Example

Trustees receive income in 2007–08 of £1,000 rent (net of expenses), dividends of £900 and interest of £400 from which tax has been deducted at source. They pay expenses relating to income of £200. The beneficiary (B) has a life interest. If the beneficiary's top slice of income is within the basic rate tax band, no relief is given for expenses but there will be no further income tax on the income:

	Income received £	Tax credit/ tax deducted £	Gross income £
Property income	780	220	1,000
Interest	400	100	500
Dividends	900	100	1,000
	2,080	420	2,500

If B is liable to tax at the higher rate of 40 per cent there will be a further liability to income tax over and above that paid by the trustees. Also, relief will be given to expenses but only for the excess liability and first against dividend income.

	Income received £	Tax credit/ tax deducted £	Gross income £
Dividends	900	100	1,000
Expenses	(200)	(22)	(222)
	700	78	778
Property income	780	220	1,000
Interest	400	100	500
	1,880	398	2,278

For calculating the additional liability, £1,500 will be taxed at 40 per cent with a tax credit of £330. £778 will be taxed at 32.5 per cent with a tax credit of £78.

Discretionary and accumulation trusts

Sums paid to beneficiaries under discretionary and accumulation trusts are paid at the exercise of the trustees' discretion and are taxable on the beneficiary on the basis of receipt of the income, albeit that there is no entitlement.

A beneficiary who receives income is treated as receiving an amount from which tax has been deducted (currently at 40 per cent) and is taxable on the gross (with a credit for the tax withheld).

Where the income is paid by a UK-resident trustee, tax at the rate applicable to trusts, will have been deducted from the income and accounted for on payments from trusts where there is discretion as to payment or a power to accumulate. In either case, trust income received by a beneficiary and which has borne tax is the income of the beneficiary, grossed up to take account of the tax.

Example

David, a beneficiary of the Ward Discretionary Trust, receives trust income of £1,276 in 2007–08. The income has borne tax at 40 per cent (the rate applicable to trusts). David is treated as having received £2,126 (£1,276 grossed up at 40 per cent). In making his tax return David will be entitled to a tax credit of £850 (£2,126 − £1,276). Where the beneficiary's total income brings him into higher rates, then further tax will be due on trust income received or to which he is entitled.

Trust income received by children

Almost the only way to move substantial amounts of taxable income from parent to child is a discretionary trust. Most settlements on children either contain a power for the trustees to accumulate income, discretion over its distribution or both. A discretionary trust, especially an accumulation and maintenance trust, can have considerable inheritance tax advantages. The income tax position, however, is less satisfactory. Parents who settle assets on trust for their children are not assessed on the *undistributed* income of the trust. This is advantageous for parents who expect to finance the children's higher education through an accumulation and maintenance trust. If, however, the income is used for secondary education, when the children are still minors, there are substantial tax charges. The tax credit on dividends is effectively lost. Most significantly, the trustees will not be able to distribute the entire amount of a dividend to a beneficiary since they will need to retain part of it to pay the tax liability. Trustees should consider accumulating income or investing in assets other than shares, where income is paid gross.

It should also be noted that for 2006–07 a basic rate band of £1,000 applies to all trusts paying tax at the 'rate applicable to trusts', so that trusts with small amounts of taxed income will have no further liability and no obligation to submit a self-assessment return if the amount of income received annually by the trust does not exceed this threshold.

Example 1

Andrew settles shares on discretionary trusts for his children, giving the trustees power to accumulate the income for 21 years. The trustees receive £9,000 of dividends from UK companies in 2007–08. The tax position of the trustees is as follows:

Income Tax

	£
Dividends received	9,000
Tax credit	1,000
Income of trustees	10,000
Less: s. 568 tax (32.5%)	(3,250)
Available for distribution to beneficiaries	6,750
Tax due from trustees	3,250
Less: tax credit	(1,000)
Additional tax due	2,250

The trustees decide to distribute £6,750 to Andrew's ten-year old daughter Martha, who has no other income. This is treated as a payment net of tax at the trust rate of 40 per cent.

	£
Paid to Martha	6,750
Gross up ($\times \,{}^{100}/_{60}$)	11,250
Tax due from trustees	
£11,250 @ 40%	4,500
Less: tax paid	(2,250)
Tax payable on distribution	2,250

Unless the trustees have an additional £2,250 which they can apply to meet the tax liabilities, they will only be able to pay out 60 per cent of the net dividends, that is £5,400. This figure will represent £9,000 of gross income in Martha's hands. The trustees' liability on the distribution becomes £1,350, which is the difference between the £3,600 due on the distribution and the £2,250 additional tax due on the receipt of the dividend.

Example 2

Martha will be entitled to a repayable tax credit. If she has no other income for 2007–08, her tax position will be as follows. The first column assumes that the trustees are able to meet the tax liabilities out of other funds while the second column assumes that they cannot do so.

	£	£
Martha's tax:		
Gross income	11,250	9,000
Less: personal allowance	(4,895)	(4,895)
Taxable income	6,355	4,105
Income tax		
£2,090/£2,090 @ 10%	209	209
£4,265/£2,015 @ 20%	853	403
	1,062	612
Less: tax paid by trustees	(2,250)	(1,350)
Repayment due to Martha	1,188	738

If Martha had owned the shares outright, she would have received £9,000 without any further tax liabilities. She will actually receive either £7,938 (£6,750 distribution plus £1,188 tax repayment), if the trustees have other assets out of which they can pay the tax, or £6,138 (£5,400 plus £738) if the dividend has to cover the trustees' tax liabilities. (This example ignores any effect of the £1,000 basic rate band applying to trusts.)

Benefits in kind

Beneficiaries of UK trusts are not taxed on benefits in kind (e.g. the notional value of the right to occupy rent-free accommodation owned by the trustees). There is no charge comparable to that which applies to benefits from an employment. Payment of rates and other outgoings would be taxable in the same way as a cash payment. Such a payment merely represents an indirect payment of income to a beneficiary.

Capital payments taxed as income

In principle, payments of capital to beneficiaries are not taxable as income in the recipient's hands though they may give rise to a liability to CGT or inheritance tax. Where a capital payment is made to the settlor it may be taxed as income.

Where a beneficiary is entitled only to capital it is unlikely that HMRC will seek to tax capital distributions as income but problems arise where the beneficiary is or may also be entitled to income. Examples include the situation where:

(1) a life tenant is entitled to the income of the trust for life but the trustees may have power to appoint capital to him or her. This is now very common;

(2) a beneficiary under a discretionary trust may be eligible to receive either income or capital, subject to the trustees exercising their discretion in the beneficiary's favour;

(3) a minor beneficiary is usually in the position that the trustees have discretion to pay sums for maintenance during minority but must accumulate the balance.

If capital payments are made to a life tenant under a power to augment income or defray living expenses, they will be liable to income tax.

Income Tax

345

In other cases this is less likely if the payments are not regular or if the purpose is to meet a 'capital' commitment such as the purchase of a house or car or to set up in business.

Payments to minors from accumulated income in a trust by their parents will be taxed as the income of their parents (see above) but otherwise payments out of accumulated income are capital, unless made for an income purpose. Often accumulated income will specifically be added to capital but this does not alter the tax treatment in the hands of the recipient.

Payment of school fees causes particular difficulty. HMRC adopt a fluid policy, treating each case on its special facts. The most that can be said is that payment of a composition fee may well be treated as capital but payments of fees on a term-by-term basis could well be taxed as income.

Loans by trustees are not generally liable to income tax. Trustees must be careful if they make a loan to the settlor or his or her spouse or repay a loan made by either of them. Such a transaction could cause the settlor to be liable to income tax on the amount lent or repaid up to the amount of accumulated trust income or, as to any excess, future trust income of the next ten years.

A payment by way of a loan or repayment of a loan by a company in which the trustees own shares is also caught under these rules if within five years before or after it there is an associated payment by the trustees to the company (e.g. a loan or subscription for shares).

Liability to income tax is not affected by the fact that the trustees charge the payment to capital rather than income. The important point is the nature of the receipt in the recipient's hands.

It should not be automatically assumed that income tax treatment is unfavourable. If beneficiaries are liable to rates of tax lower than those borne by the trustees, trustees will be able to make distributions without further income tax liability and the beneficiary may even be eligible to make repayment claims. This may be preferable to making distributions of capital involving possible CGT or inheritance tax liabilities.

See *British Tax Reporter* ¶351-100.

1007 Treatment of trust beneficiary's income

A beneficiary's share (as grossed up: see 210) of the income of a trust fund forms part of his total income (see 244) in the tax year in which it arises. The income is from the trust and not from the underlying property; hence, except in relation to discretionary trusts (see below), the grossing up process is at the *basic rate* by virtue of the deduction at source being under the normal rules for payments out of profits chargeable to income tax, etc. in the hands of the trustees (see 1368, 1370).

> **Example**
>
> In 2008–09 Dwight is entitled to a personal relief of £6,035 (see 1851). His only income is trading income (adjusted for tax) of £4,000 and trust income of £2,310 (received under deduction of basic rate income tax). His total income is thus £6,887 (i.e. £4,000 + (£2,310 × $^{100}/_{80}$)) and his tax liability should be £85.20 (i.e. 10% × (£6,887 − £6,035)). As Dwight has already suffered £577 by deduction he can reclaim the balance of £491.80 from HMRC.

Although trustees are not entitled to deduct management expenses in calculating the trust's tax liability (see 987), such expenses are deductible in ascertaining the beneficiary's income.

A discretionary beneficiary who receives, as income, payments from a trust is treated as receiving an amount net of a rate equivalent to the rate applicable to trusts for the year of payment (see 991).

Where payments are made to a beneficiary under the *Trustee Act* 1925, s. 31 (see 1001) from an accumulation and maintenance trust, tax is likewise deducted at the rate applicable to trusts and is in this instance treated as income of the settlor.

Source: *Macfarlane v IR Commrs* (1929) 14 TC 532

See *British Tax Reporter* ¶353-200.

1009   Claims in respect of trust beneficiaries' income

Claims on behalf of incapacitated persons are made by the trustees. In other cases, claims must be made by the beneficiary in receipt of income. Claims for repayment relating to trust income which forms part of the beneficiary's total income as it arises must be made within six years of the end of the tax year in which the income arises.

See *British Tax Reporter* ¶353-200.

1010   Trusts with vulnerable beneficiary

New rules took effect from 6 April 2004 which created a new tax regime for certain trusts with vulnerable beneficiaries. Under the provisions, certain trusts and beneficiaries are able to elect into the regime and, where a claim for special tax treatment is made for a tax year, no more tax will be payable in respect of the relevant income and gains of the trust for that year than would be paid had the income and gains accrued directly to the beneficiary.

Income and gains arising from the property held on qualifying trusts for the benefit of a vulnerable person are eligible for the new tax treatment. The special treatment does not apply in cases where the settlor is regarded as having an interest in the property from which the qualifying trusts income arose.

Income Tax

Broadly, the amount of income tax relief under the new regime is the difference between two amounts. The first of those amounts is what (were it not for the new rules) the income tax liability of the trustees would be in respect of the qualifying trusts income for the tax year. The second amount is the amount of extra tax to which the vulnerable person would be liable if the qualifying trusts income were that person's own income.

With regards to CGT, the special capital gains tax treatment applies in relation to chargeable gains arising to the trustees of a settlement if the following conditions are met in relation to the tax year in question:

- chargeable gains ('qualifying trusts gains') arise in the tax year to the trustees on the disposal of settled property held on qualifying trusts for the benefit of a vulnerable person;
- the trustees would be chargeable to CGT in respect of those gains were it not for the application of the new rules in FA 2005, Ch. 4;
- the trustees are resident or ordinarily resident in the UK during any part of the tax year; and
- the trustees make a claim for special tax treatment for the tax year.

Under the new rules, the trustees' liability to CGT for the tax year will be reduced by an amount determined by using a formula set out in the legislation. Broadly, the amount is equal to the difference between two quantities. The first quantity is the CGT liability that the trustees would have in respect of the qualifying trusts gains were it not for the new regime contained in FA 2005. The second quantity is the amount of extra tax to which the vulnerable person would be liable to under the new rules, subject to making certain assumptions, in relation to the qualifying trusts gains.

Law: FA 2005, s. 23–45 and Sch. 1

Source: *Tax Bulletin*, Issue 78, August 2005 (Changes to the taxation of trusts introduced by the Finance Act 2005)

ESTATES OF DECEASED PERSONS

1030 Death, personal representatives and administration period

When a person dies his property passes to his personal representatives, i.e. either executors appointed by his will or administrators of his estate appointed by the court. Personal representatives are liable for any tax liability of the deceased to the extent that there are sufficient assets of the deceased coming into their hands to meet the debt. Any one or more of several personal representatives is assessable and chargeable in respect of estate income. A personal representative who neglects or refuses to pay may be proceeded against as any other defaulter; but the personal representative may deduct any payments of tax made out of the assets of the deceased.

A personal representative may also be assessed to tax in respect of income (and chargeable gains) accruing to the deceased but not assessed on him. Such an assessment cannot be made later than three years after the tax year in which the deceased died.

A specific legatee is generally entitled to income from the property in point from the date of the testator's death, while a general legatee may only be entitled to interest in respect of the value of the property and then only from a given date (see 1038). A residuary legatee has no interest in any particular asset of the estate until the residue has been ascertained. So far as not covered by specific legacies therefore, the income of the estate is the income of the personal representatives (though by special provision payments to residuary legatees are to be treated as their income: see 1032, 1034). Of course, if the personal representatives appropriate specific assets to a residuary beneficiary, the income of the appropriated assets is the income of the beneficiary.

Any charge on the personal representatives is at the basic rate. The income is computed in the usual way appropriate to the source of income and the appropriate reliefs and deductions are taken into account. When certain payments and deemed payments are added to the aggregate income of estates, they are treated, for 1995–96 and successive tax years, as made after deduction of tax at the appropriate rate. The payments affected include certain chargeable event gains which arise to personal representatives in connection with certain life annuities and policies.

Payments to beneficiaries of estates in administration which are funded out of

- *non*-qualifying distributions (see 3076 for definition) and are received after 1 July 1997; or
- distributions received after 1998–99;

are treated as made under deduction of non-repayable lower rate, etc. tax. Without this change, such payments would be treated as paid under deduction of repayable tax. The change ensures that beneficiaries are taxed in the same way as if they had received the distribution direct.

Personal representatives cannot utilise personal reliefs against estate income nor are administration expenses deductible in computing tax payable. However, personal reliefs to which the deceased was entitled can be used by his personal representatives against income of the deceased.

Example

Trevor, the testator, dies unmarried on 10 July 2010. Trevor's executors are entitled to set off his full personal allowance of £6,475 for 2010–11 (see 1851) against his income tax liability for that year.

Income Tax

When the administration of the estate is complete, the personal representatives hold the property as trustees until such time as the property vests in the beneficiaries or in other trustees, and 987ff. will apply to the income arising from the estate.

All personal representatives are treated as UK resident where any personal representative is so resident provided that the deceased was resident, ordinarily resident or domiciled in the UK (see 213ff.) at his death.

UK and foreign estates

A foreign estate is one which is not a UK estate. A 'UK estate' is defined as an estate, the income of which comprises only income which either:

- has borne UK income tax by deduction; or
- is directly assessable to UK income tax on the personal representatives.

To be a UK estate the personal representatives must not be entitled to claim exemption from UK income tax (in respect of any part of the income of the estate) by reason of their residence or ordinary residence outside the UK.

Law: ITTOIA 2005, s. 651, 680; TMA 1970, s. 40, 74; *R v Income Tax Acts Special Purposes Commrs, ex parte Dr Barnardo's Homes* (1921) 7 TC 646

See *British Tax Reporter* ¶362-000.

1031 The administration period

This is the period between the date of death of a deceased and the completion of the administration of his estate, which takes place when all the debts and legacies have been paid or provided for and the residue of the estate is ascertained and can be distributed either outright to beneficiaries or to the trustees of any continuing trust.

Excepted estates

To simplify the administration of smaller estates, executors do not need to file accounts where the estate does not exceed a prescribed limit. See 98 regarding present and past prescribed limits.

Executors or administrators of straightforward smaller estates ('excepted estates') do not have to deliver an account to HMRC. For valid excepted estates personal representatives obtain a grant of representation simply by swearing a revised form of oath for the Probate Registry that the various criteria have been satisfied. However, HMRC have 35 days from the making of the first full grant to the deceased to call for an account and does so in about two per cent of cases.

An estate qualifies as excepted only where:

- the deceased died domiciled in the UK;

- the total gross value of the estate before deduction of any debts, together with the value of any gifts as mentioned below, does not exceed the prescribed annual limit;
- the estate consists only of property which has passed under the deceased's will or intestacy, or by nomination, or beneficially by survivorship. Where any of the value of an estate relates to joint property passing by survivorship, it is the value of the deceased's beneficial interest in that property which counts for the purposes of the prescribed limit (£325,000 from 6 April 2009);
- any estate assets situated outside the UK have a total value of not more than £100,000; and
- any taxable lifetime transfers made within seven years of the deceased's death consisted only of cash, quoted shares or quoted securities with a total gross value not exceeding the prescribed limit. Previously such transfers would have ruled out the excepted estates procedure.

The excepted estates procedure does not apply where the deceased had:

- within seven years of the death made a chargeable or potentially exempt transfer other than transfers of cash, etc.;
- made a gift with reservation of benefit which either continued until death or ceased within seven years before the death;
- enjoyed an interest in possession in settled property at, or within seven years before, the death.

Personal representatives are required to include details of the transfers made by the deceased within seven years preceding death. This is, of course, unless the estate is an excepted estate.

Income tax and capital gains tax

Personal representatives are either executors or administrators. They administer the estate. They collect income in and are liable to pay the tax on it. This income is then attributed to the beneficiaries.

From 6 April 1999, payments to beneficiaries out of estates funded by dividend income will be treated as made after deduction of a non-refundable tax credit of ten per cent and then taxed on the recipient as if he or she had received the dividend.

A beneficiary entitled to a specific legacy under the will is taxable on the income arising from it from the date of death unless the executors have to use the income to pay debts. Residuary beneficiaries are taxed on estate income initially on the basis of what they receive. There is a subsequent adjustment to the actual income of each tax year of the administration period. Beneficiaries are only liable to higher rates as the executors will have borne tax at basic rate or the ten per cent rate for dividends. They may be entitled to a repayment of tax treated as borne by the executors.

In the early stages of an administration it may be difficult for the executors to know the level of future costs such as tax on gross income like rents, and therefore how much of the income they can distribute to beneficiaries. Reserves prudently retained by the trustees for tax and other costs may mean that further distributions are made in a later tax year. This may also happen if fresh income sources come to light after initial distributions.

Where a beneficiary has a right to income only, any distributions are taxed in the tax year they are received, but if any 'excess' is due at the end of the administration this is income for tax in the year the administration is completed. It is not now necessary to re-open the beneficiary's tax affairs for previous years in these circumstances.

Where a beneficiary is absolutely entitled to part or the whole of the residuary estate, the due share of income is calculated and matched against payments received. Any excess of entitlement after the first year of the administration is brought forward and added to the entitlement for the succeeding year, so that it is available for matching against payments in that year. Only payments that exceed the total income entitlement, up to and including the year in which the payment is made, escape income tax at this stage. This procedure applies for all years, and any final balance paid at the end of the administration period is taxed as the beneficiary's income at that stage.

Where a deed of variation is put into effect, and provided the original beneficiary had an absolute interest and had received no payment from the estate, any income tax liability arises on the new beneficiary who actually receives the income.

For gains arising on disposals occurring on or before 22 June 2010, personal representatives are liable to CGT at the rate of 18 per cent. Where disposals occur on or after 23 June 2010, the rate is 28 per cent. Personal representatives can claim the same annual exemption for the year of death and the next two. On death a deceased's assets are deemed to be disposed of and re-acquired at market value but without chargeable gain or allowable loss. In effect, the base cost for the personal representatives is the market value at death. If these assets are distributed in kind a beneficiary inherits the assets at market value at death. This is then the beneficiary's base cost. This differs from the position of interest in possession trusts where there is a capital gain on a beneficiary obtaining the asset.

1032 Income of person with limited interest in residue

Special provisions apply to persons with limited interests in the residue of the whole or part of an estate during the administration period (or part of it) (see 1030).

A person is deemed to have a limited interest if he does not have an absolute interest and the income of the residue (or part of it) would be properly payable to him, or directly or indirectly paid for his benefit, if the residue had been ascertained at the commencement of the administration period. A life interest is a limited interest.

Any sum paid during the administration period in respect of a limited interest is, subject to adjustment on the completion of administration (or its Scottish equivalent), deemed to have been paid as income in the tax year in which the sum was paid. Where the sum is paid in respect of a limited interest which has ceased during the administration, the sum paid after the interest has ceased is deemed to have been paid in the last tax year in which the interest subsisted. Personal representatives may be treated as residuary beneficiaries in such a way that the deemed income forms part of the estate of a second deceased person. The legislation also caters for discretionary payments.

In the case of a 'UK estate' (see 1030) the personal representatives will have paid tax at the former Sch. F ordinary rate and any sum paid to a beneficiary is treated as a net amount after the application of that rate. Payments are made first out of payments bearing tax at that rate and there are provisions for effecting a reasonable apportionment of amounts between persons with different interests. Since 6 April 1999, similar treatment has applied to income deemed to have borne (non-repayable) tax at the 'Schedule F ordinary rate' (see 1030): such income is treated as if it were chargeable to income tax, and while the beneficiary cannot reclaim the tax credit, his basic rate liability is treated as satisfied.

In the case of a 'foreign estate' (see 1030), the sum paid is treated as gross income chargeable under ITTOIA 2005, Pt 5, Ch. 6 with a possible proportionate reduction on proof of tax deduction in respect of the aggregate income of the estate.

In respect of discretionary payments out of income, beneficiaries are treated as receiving income on which tax has been paid at the basic rate or, in the case of payments routed through trustees, at the rate applicable to trusts.

A residuary beneficiary who is neither resident nor ordinarily resident in the UK may claim to have his income from an estate in the course of administration treated as if it had arisen directly to him, so that he will not be liable to tax on, for example, foreign source income of the estate.

On the completion of the administration of an estate, where an amount remains payable in respect of a limited interest, the amount is deemed to have been paid as income of the tax year in which the administration period ends; if the sum is deemed to be paid in respect of an interest which ceased before the end of the administration period, then it is deemed to have been paid in respect of the last tax year in which that interest subsisted.

In many cases, therefore, adjustments will have to be made to assessments already made on the beneficiary during the administration period. The adjustments may be made within three years of 31 January following the end of the tax year in which administration of that estate was completed.

Law: ITTOIA 2005, Pt 5, Ch. 6

Source: ESC A14, *Deceased person's estate: residuary income received during the administration period*

See *British Tax Reporter* ¶364-600.

1034 Income of person with absolute interest in residue

Special provisions apply to persons who, during the administration period (or part of it), have an absolute interest in the whole or part of the residue of the estate of the deceased (see 1030). A person is deemed to have an absolute interest if and so long as the capital of the residue (or of the relevant part) would, if the residue had been ascertained, be properly payable to him or, directly or indirectly, payable for his benefit.

A person entitled to an absolute interest may receive payments during the administration period made out of either income or capital and these have to be distinguished. This is done by first calculating the residuary income during such part of the administration period in which the beneficiary had an absolute interest.

The 'residuary income' is ascertained by deducting from the income of the estate for that year:

- annual interest, annuities or other annual payments for that year which are a charge on residue (see below), except for any interest, etc. which is allowable in computing the income of the estate;
- management expenses (unless allowable in computing the aggregate income of the estate) which, in the absence of any express provision in a will, are properly chargeable to income;
- the income of the estate to which any person is specifically entitled as a devisee or legatee.

There is also a reduction in residuary income by way of relief for higher rate tax purposes where accrued income has also been included in the value of the estate for inheritance tax purposes; the reduction is the grossed-up value (see 210) of inheritance tax attributable to the accrued income net of accrued liabilities.

The importance of calculating the residuary income lies in the fact that any sum paid during the administration period in respect of the absolute interest is deemed to have been paid as income to the extent that it does not exceed the residuary income for that year (less basic rate tax for that year in the case of a UK estate). Personal representatives may be treated as residuary beneficiaries in such a way that the deemed income forms part of the estate of a second deceased person. The legislation caters for successive absolute interests and discretionary payments.

Where any deductions exceed the amount of residuary income, the excess may be carried forward and treated as an amount to be deducted from the aggregate income of the estate for the following year.

In the case of a 'UK estate' (see 1030), the sum deemed to have been paid as income includes the amount by which the aggregated income entitlement of the person for the tax year exceeds the aggregate of all the sums which have been paid (as income) to that person in respect of that absolute interest. It is, therefore, grossed up (see 210) at the basic, lower or Sch. F ordinary rate (see 1030) in force for the year of payment; payments are made first out of payments bearing tax at basic rate and there are provisions for effecting a reasonable apportioning of amounts between persons with different interests. Where the lower or Sch. F ordinary rate applies, the income is then taxable in the hands of the beneficiary (or intermediate trustees) at that rate as the top slice of income. In the case of a 'foreign estate' (see 1030), the amount paid is treated as gross income with a possible proportionate reduction on proof of tax deduction in respect of the aggregate income of the estate.

A residuary beneficiary who is neither resident nor ordinarily resident in the UK may claim to have his income from an estate in the course of administration treated as if it had arisen directly to him, so that he will not be liable to tax on, for example, foreign source income of the estate.

On the completion of administration certain adjustments may be necessary, giving rise to additional assessments or a claim for relief. Any further or adjusted assessment or claim for relief may be made within three years beginning with 31 January following the tax year in which the administration of the estate is completed.

Charges on residue

'Charges' on residue means the following liabilities (to the extent that the liabilities fall ultimately on residue) properly payable out of the estate and interest payable in respect of those liabilities:

- funeral, testamentary and administration expenses and debts;
- general legacies, demonstrative legacies, annuities and any sum payable out of residue under an intestacy;
- any other liabilities of the personal representatives;
- (relating to Scotland only) any sums required to meet claims in respect of legal rights by the surviving spouse or children.

Thus, for example, interest payable in respect of a general legacy is a charge on residue and is not taken into account in calculating residuary income. In Scotland, sums required to meet certain claims by a surviving spouse or child are also charges on residue.

Law: ITTOIA 2005, Pt 5, Ch 6

Source: ESC A14, *Deceased person's estate: residuary income received during the administration period*; former ESC A13, *Adminstration of estates: beneficences of income received during the administration period*

See *British Tax Reporter* ¶364-800.

1038 Income of legatees and annuitants

In the case of a specific legacy, the legatee is entitled to the income (subject to a contrary provision in the will) from the relevant property from the date of the testator's death. The income from the property, therefore, forms part of the legatee's total income as it arises, notwithstanding the general charge on the personal representatives (see 1030).

In the case of a general legacy, the legatee is entitled to interest at five per cent. If the legacy is an immediate one, the interest is generally payable (subject to a contrary provision in the will) only after the end of the executor's year. Such interest is charged to tax under ITTOIA 2005 (former Sch. D, Case III) (see 1366) as part of the legatee's total income. However, a legatee may refuse to accept payment of the interest and in such instances the interest is only treated as his income if there is identifiable income which he can claim, e.g. from a fund set aside to meet the legacy.

In general an annuitant is not entitled to the capital value of his annuity though he is entitled to have a fund set aside to secure the annuity. The first instalment of the annuity is payable only at the end of the executor's year but (subject to a contrary intention) the annuity runs from the testator's death and forms part of the annuitant's total income from that date.

In some cases, and in particular where the estate is insufficient to provide an annuity fund and also to pay the pecuniary legacies in full, the annuitant is entitled to the actuarial value of his annuity (duly abated, if necessary). This is regarded as a capital payment and is not included in the annuitant's total income. Thus, payments made in respect of an annuity are regarded as capital payments where the payments are made before it is discovered that the income of the estate is insufficient to pay the annuity in full.

References in a will or codicil to payments by reference to the former 'surtax' and 'standard rate' are treated as if they were to higher rate(s) and basic rate.

Law: *IR Commrs v Hawley* [1928] 1 KB 578; *Dewar v IR Commrs* [1935] 2 KB 351; *IR Commrs v Lady Castlemaine* (1943) 25 TC 408; *Spens v IR Commrs* [1970] 1 WLR 1173

See *British Tax Reporter* ¶365-250.

SETTLEMENTS: ANTI-AVOIDANCE

SETTLEMENTS AND THE TRANSFER OF INCOME

1070   Avoidance of tax on income using settlements

There are specific anti-avoidance provisions designed to prevent higher-rate taxpayers reducing their liability to tax by giving away the right to receive income. 'Settlements' (see 1071) have often been used by taxpayers to alienate, or transfer to another, a portion of their income. Basically, the theoretical possibilities have been as set out below.

- S transfers to B a portion of his income each year (an 'income settlement'). If the obligation to B is a legally binding one, then, ignoring the special provisions relating to such 'settlements', the payments to B would be a 'charge' on the income of S. He would retain basic rate tax and would escape liability to tax at the higher rate. B may be entitled to reclaim the whole or part of the basic rate tax deducted depending on his personal tax liability.

- S transfers capital to trustees to hold for the benefit of B (a 'capital settlement'). Ignoring the special provisions, this would effectively divest S of any tax liability on the income derived from that capital.

The provisions prevent certain 'settlements' being effective at all for the purpose of taxes on income whilst other provisions only prevent certain settlements being effective for the purpose of the 'settlor' avoiding higher rate tax. In the latter case the beneficiary retains the right to make a claim for repayment of basic rate tax in appropriate circumstances. These provisions affect only the tax treatment of the settlement income and not any rights or obligations under the general law.

The legislation relating to settlements has been substantially amended with effect for 1995–96 and later years.

Law: *Bird & Anor v R & C Commrs*(2008) Sp C 720

See *British Tax Reporter* ¶355-450.

1071   Meaning of 'settlement' and 'settlor' for income tax

In general terms, a 'settlement' is the creation of a trust with successive interests; but, for the purposes of the income tax anti-avoidance provisions (see 1070), 'settlement' is much more widely defined to include any disposition, trust, covenant, agreement or arrangement.

From 6 April 2006, 'settled property' is redefined as any property held in trust other than property held as nominee, bare trustee for a person absolutely entitled, an infant or disabled person. References in the legislation to a settlement are construed as references to settled property and the meaning of settlement is determined by case law. This measure effectively aligns what is treated as a settlement for the general purposes of income tax and tax on chargeable gains. The effect is that income tax will be charged on income arising to the trustees of a 'settlement' with the definition of settlement being derived from existing trust law and case law, and 'settled property' being defined in the tax legislation. The existing definition of settlement in ITTOIA 2005, s. 620 still applies for the purposes of the settlements anti-avoidance legislation.

'Settlor'

A 'settlor' is any person who makes a settlement. He is deemed to have made a settlement if he makes or enters into the settlement directly or indirectly and, in particular, if:

- he has directly or indirectly provided or undertaken to provide funds for the purpose of the settlement; or

Income Tax

357

- he has made a reciprocal arrangement with any other person for that other person to make or enter into the settlement.

Finance Act 2006 inserted new ICTA 1988, s. 685B for income tax purposes to define a settlor. This is based on the wider definition in the settlements anti-avoidance legislation. The measure is effective from 6 April 2006 and affects settlements whenever created. A person is a settlor in relation to a settlement if it was made (or treated as made) by that person directly or indirectly or if it arose on his or her death. A settlor of property means that which is settled or derived from settled property and a person is treated as having made a settlement if he or she has provided (or undertaken to do so) property directly or indirectly for the settlement. If A enters into a settlement where there are reciprocal arrangements with B, B is treated as the settlor for these purposes.

Finance Act 2006 also inserts new ICTA 1988, s. 685C which takes effect from 6 April 2006 in relation to settlements whenever created. The new section identifies the settlor where there is a transfer of property between settlements made for no consideration or less than full consideration. Where property is disposed of from settlement 1 and acquired by settlement 2 (even if in a different form), the settlor(s) of settlement 1 will be treated as the settlor(s) of settlement 2 unless the transfer occurs because of a will variation.

Finance Act 2006 also contains a measure to identify the settlor in relation to will and intestacy variations occurring on or after 6 April 2006 regardless of the deceased's date of death. The measure applies where there is a variation in accordance with TCGA 1992, s. 62(6) and property which was not settled property under the will becomes settled. In this case a person mentioned in the group below is treated as having made the settlement and providing the property for it:

- a person who immediately before the variation was entitled to the property, or to property from which it derives, absolutely as legatee (as defined);
- a person who would have become entitled to the property, or to property from which it derives, absolutely as legatee but for the variation;
- a person who immediately before the variation would have been entitled to the property, or to property from which it derives, absolutely as legatee but for being an infant or other person under a disability; and
- a person who would, but for the variation, have become entitled to the property, or to property from which it derives, absolutely as legatee if he had not been an infant or other person under a disability.

If property would have been comprised in a settlement as a result of the deceased's will but the effect of the variation is that it becomes comprised in another settlement, the deceased will be treated as the settlor. He or she will also be the settlor if an existing settlement of which the deceased was settlor becomes comprised in another settlement. In both cases the deceased is treated as having made the settlement immediately before his or her death unless the settlement arose on the person's death.

Law: *Finance Act* 2006, s. 88, 89 and Sch. 12 and 13; ITTOIA 2005, s. 620(1)–(3); *Yates (HMIT) v Starkey* [1951] Ch 465; *Crossland (HMIT) v Hawkins* [1961] Ch 537; *IR Commrs v Mills* [1975] AC 38; *IR Commrs v Plummer* [1980] AC 896; *IR Commrs v Levy* [1982]

BTC 235; *Harvey (HMIT) v Sivyer* [1985] BTC 410; *Butler (HMIT) v Wildin* [1988] BTC 475

Source: HMRC leaflet: *A Guide to the Settlements Legislation for Small Business Advisers* (www.hmrc.gov.uk/practitioners/guide_sba.pdf)

See *British Tax Reporter* ¶355-750.

1073   Covenanted payments to charity

Charitable covenants are exempt from the provisions treating income of settlements in which the settlor retains an interest as the settlor's income.

Covenanted payments to charity remain a relatively efficient form of giving since the payer is often eligible for higher rate relief (see 1840).

A 'covenanted payment to charity' is defined as a payment made under a covenant which:

- is not made in consideration of money or money's worth (but rights of admission to view wildlife or property held by a charity do not count as consideration: see 901);
- is in favour of a body of persons or a trust established for charitable purposes;
- requires the annual payments to be made for a period which may exceed three years; and
- is not capable of earlier termination without the consent of the persons for the time being entitled to the payments.

Companies, as well as individuals, can take advantage of these provisions (covenanted donations to charity being charges on income: see 3061).

Charities receiving covenanted payments may generally reclaim the tax deducted from HMRC (see 901).

For one-off charitable payments under the gift aid scheme, see 902.

Law: ITTOIA 2005, s. 627(2), 727(1), Sch. 2, para. 132(1)–(2); *Racal Group Services Ltd v Ashmore* [1995] BTC 406

See *British Tax Reporter* 355-450.

SETTLEMENTS ON CHILDREN

1075   Payments to minor unmarried children of settlor

If a settlement is not caught by the provisions outlined at 1078, but income from it is paid during the settlor's lifetime to or for the benefit of a minor unmarried child of the settlor, that income is treated for all tax purposes as the settlor's income for the tax year in which it is so paid. A 'minor' is defined as a person under 18 years of age, and a 'child' as including a stepchild and an illegitimate child, while references in this provision to payments include payments in money or money's worth.

Where there is accumulated income in the settlement, any kind of payment to a minor unmarried child of the settlor is treated as a payment of income to the extent that it matches available retained or accumulated income. 'Available retained or accumulated income' is the total income that has arisen under the settlement since it began, excluding:

- income treated as income of the settlor or a beneficiary;
- income paid to or for the benefit of a beneficiary other than a minor unmarried child of the settlor, whether as income or as capital; and
- income applied in defraying expenses of the trustees which were properly chargeable to income, notwithstanding any express provision of the trust.

Where an offshore income gain accrues to a bare trustee or nominee for a minor beneficiary, the gain is treated, for the purposes of the charge on offshore income gains, as income paid to the beneficiary. Accordingly, if the beneficiary is a minor unmarried child of the settlor, the gain is converted into income chargeable on the settlor.

Income of no more than £100 paid to a minor unmarried child of the settlor in any tax year is not treated as that of the settlor.

1999 changes

Where a trust is set up after 8 March 1999 by parents on behalf of minor unmarried children which, for tax purposes, is treated as a bare trust because the children are entitled to the income and capital of the trust, any income arising from the trust, whether paid for the child's benefit or accumulated, is taxed as the parents' income; likewise, the income from new funds added to existing trusts after that date. However, the charge does not apply where the total income from all settlements by the same parent for the same child does not exceed £100 in any tax year.

Law: ITTOIA 2005, s. 629–632

See *British Tax Reporter* ¶355-600.

1077 Maintenance payments to children

An arrangement whereby a divorced or separated parent undertakes to maintain his minor child is still treated as a 'settlement' and no tax relief is available.

Law: ITTOIA 2005, s. 727–730, Sch. 2, para. 146; *Sherdley v Sherdley* [1987] BTC 273; *Harvey (HMIT) v Sivyer* [1985] BTC 410; *Morley-Clarke v Jones (HMIT)* [1985] BTC 460

Source: *Practice Direction* [1983] 1 WLR 800

See *British Tax Reporter* ¶355-650.

BENEFIT RETAINED BY SETTLOR

1078 Settlor retaining an interest

The rules on revocable settlements and settlements where the settlor retains an interest were recast for years after 1994–95. The rules are not restricted to undistributed income and they apply to all settlements whenever made.

The basic rule is that during the settlor's lifetime, settlement income is to be treated as income of the settlor for all tax purposes unless it arises from property in which the settlor has no interest. The question whether the settlor has an interest in any property is addressed by the provisions which follow.

A settlor has an interest in settled property if there is any possibility of the property or any 'derived property' being paid to the settlor, or the settlor's spouse, or applied for their benefit in any circumstances whatever. The term 'derived property', in relation to the settled property, is given a specific, if wide, definition. It can mean any of the following:

- income from the settled property;
- other property 'directly or indirectly representing the proceeds of' the settled property;
- other property 'directly or indirectly representing the proceeds of' the income of the settled property;
- income from such proceeds.

Where the settled property or derived property cannot be paid to the settlor or his spouse while someone else is alive unless that person becomes bankrupt or assigns or charges his interest, the settlor will not be regarded as having an interest while that person is under the age of 25. Furthermore, there are four circumstances in which property may become payable to the settlor or his spouse without triggering a charge on the settlor:

- the bankruptcy of a possible beneficiary;
- a possible beneficiary assigning or charging his beneficial interest;
- in the case of a marriage settlement, the death of both parties to the marriage and all or any of the children of the marriage;
- the death of a child of the settlor who had become beneficially entitled to the property or any derived property on or before the age of 25.

If property is payable to a possible future spouse, a separated spouse or a widow or widower of the settlor, the settlement income is not caught by these provisions. This is a relaxation of the former rule that income from settlements which can benefit a future spouse of the settlor is deemed to be income of the settlor for tax purposes. A separation must be by court order or by separation agreement, or take place in such circumstances that the separation is likely to be permanent.

The following do not constitute a settlement for the purposes of these provisions:

- an outright gift between spouses (but see below);
- an irrevocable allocation of pension rights between spouses under a relevant statutory scheme;
- income from settlements made by one party to a marriage to provide for the other party following a divorce or annulment, or a separation pursuant to a court order, a separation agreement or in such circumstances that the separation is likely to be permanent;
- annual payments made by an individual for bona fide commercial reasons in connection with his trade, profession or vocation; and
- covenanted payments to charity.

The outright gift exclusion does not apply to the following:

- a gift which does not carry a right to the whole of the income from the gifted property;
- a gift which consists wholly or substantially of a right to income;
- a gift which is subject to conditions; and
- a gift the subject-matter of which, or any derived property from which, will or may become payable to or applicable for the benefit of the donor in any circumstances whatever.

Law: ITTOIA 2005, s. 622–627

Source: former SP A30, *Settlements: benefit to settlor's future spouse*; HMRC guidance – Businesses, Individuals and the Settlements Legislation – Part II, 4 December 2003; Tax Bulletin, Issue 64 (April 2003); Revenue response to CIOT, ICAEW Tax Faculty, ICAS, ACCA, ATT, AAT, FSB and Working Together Representatives paper on Tax Bulletin 64 Article on the Settlements Legislation (November 2003)

See *British Tax Reporter* ¶355-500.

1081 Nature of charge and other provisions

Tax chargeable on the settlor is treated as the highest part of the settlor's income barring termination payments and gains on chargeable events associated with certain policies. The same deductions and reliefs are available to the settlor as if the income treated as his had actually been received by him.

Adjustments between settlor and trustees

A settlor who pays tax is entitled to recover the tax paid from the trustees or from any person to whom the income is payable under the settlement, and as conclusive evidence of payment of tax he may require HMRC to certify the amount of income charged to tax, and the amount of tax paid. Conversely, a person who receives a repayment of tax in excess of his entitlement must repay the excess to the trustee or the appropriate beneficiary. Any question as to the amount of such a payment, or as to any apportionment where more than one beneficiary is entitled, is to be decided by the tribunal, whose decision is final.

Settlements by two or more settlors

Where there is more than one settlor, the code applies separately to each settlor as if he were the only settlor in relation to the property or income originating from him. Payments of income to a minor unmarried child of the settlor are only taken into account, in relation to each settlor, to the extent that they emanate from income originating from that settlor, and other such payments to the extent that they represent retained or accumulated income which has originated from that settlor.

'Property originating from a settlor' is property which that settlor has provided for the settlement, and property representing it or accumulated income from it, including an apportioned part of any property which represents both it and other property. 'Income originating from a settlor' includes both income from property which originates from the settlor, and income which the settlor has provided. A settlor is treated as providing property or income which has been provided by another person under reciprocal arrangements with the settlor, but not property which the settlor has provided under reciprocal arrangements with another person.

Power to obtain information

HMRC have wide powers to obtain information from any party to a settlement. Any notice requiring such information must give the recipient at least 28 days in which to respond.

Law: ITTOIA 2005, s. 619–648

See *British Tax Reporter* ¶356-000.

CAPITAL SUMS PAID TO SETTLOR

1097   Capital sums paid by trustee to settlor as income

'Capital sums' (see below) paid directly or indirectly by the trustees of a 'settlement' (see 1071) to the settlor are treated as the income of the settlor (for all income tax purposes), except to the extent that the payment exceeds the amount of 'income available' up to the end of that tax year. Where the capital sum does exceed the income available, the excess is treated as the income of the settlor for following years to the extent that the payment does not fall within the amount of income available up to the end of the year of payment, but does fall within the amount of income available up to the end of the following ten years.

'Income available' is, basically, the aggregate of undistributed income arising in the year in question and in any previous year, less:

- capital payments already treated as the settlor's income;
- settlement income which is treated as the settlor's income under the provisions outlined at 1075, 1078; and
- basic rate tax on undistributed income not otherwise treated as the settlor's income.

Example

Stuart, the settlor, receives in May 2005 a capital payment of £100,000. The undistributed income of the settlement is as follows:

	£
2006–07	20,000
2007–08	30,000
2008–09	40,000
2009–10	50,000

There is no undistributed income for 2005–06 or earlier years.

The sum of £100,000 is treated as Stuart's income in the following amounts and tax years:

	£
2006–07	20,000
2007–08	30,000
2008–09	40,000
2009–10	10,000
	100,000

Capital sums

A 'capital sum' is:

- any loan (see below) or repayment of a loan; and
- any other sum not paid as income and which is not paid for full consideration in money or money's worth.

Certain sums (which would not otherwise be so treated) are treated as capital sums paid to the settlor by the trustees of a settlement. These are sums which:

- are paid by the trustees to a third party at the settlor's direction or because of the assignment by him of his right to receive it; or
- are otherwise paid or applied by them for the benefit of the settlor.

A capital sum is paid to the settlor if it is paid directly or indirectly to the settlor, the settlor's spouse, or jointly to the settlor (or his or her spouse) and another person.

Loans

If the capital sum paid to the settlor (or spouse, etc.) is a loan only, then no part of the loan is treated by these provisions as the settlor's income for any tax year after that in which the loan is wholly repaid.

Deemed tax deduction

Any sum treated by these provisions as the income of the settlor is treated as income grossed up at the basic rate of tax applicable to the year of payment.

Income tax is chargeable under ITTOIA 2005 and the settlor is entitled to set off against that tax the lesser of:

- basic rate tax for that year on the amount treated as his income; or
- the tax charged.

Law: ITTOIA 2005, s. 622, 633(1)–(5)

See *British Tax Reporter* ¶357-600.

1098   Capital sums paid by company connected with settlement as income

Capital sums (see 1097) paid to a settlor by a company connected with a settlement which also receives an associated payment from the trustees of the settlement are treated in the same way as amounts paid direct by the trustees (see 1097); the onus is on the settlor receiving such a sum and on the trustees to show that there was no associated payment. An 'associated payment' is, broadly, any payment or transfer at an undervalue within five years either side or any capital sum; a company is 'connected with a settlement' if it is a close company (or would be if UK-resident) and the trustees are participators or is controlled by such a company. There are certain exemptions for short-term (less than 12-month) loans.

A capital sum to which this provision applies is treated as having been paid to the settlor in the year of payment to the extent that the sum falls within the total of associated payments made up to the end of the year in which they are made. To the extent that the capital sum is not treated as paid to the settlor in the year of payment, it is treated as having been paid to the settlor in the following year (so long as it falls within the total of associated payments to the end of that year) and so on for each subsequent year.

Law: ITTOIA 2005, s. 641

See *British Tax Reporter* ¶357-850.

MAINTENANCE FUNDS FOR HISTORIC BUILDINGS

1103   Election for maintenance fund for historic buildings to avoid income charges on settlor

The trustees of a maintenance fund for historic buildings (see 7040ff.) may elect for the exclusion of certain settlement provisions in relation to any tax year, or part. If they do so:

- income arising in that year from property comprised in the settlement which would otherwise be treated as the income of the settlor (see 1070ff.) is not so treated; and
- sums applied in that year out of the property in the settlement for the maintenance, repair or preservation of, or making provisions for public access to, qualifying property (see

Income Tax

7349) are not treated as the income of the settlor if they otherwise would have been so treated by the provisions outlined at 1097, or because the settlor has an interest in the property (see 1078ff.).

Also, where gains arising under the settlement would otherwise have been deemed to be the settlor's gains for the purpose of applying the settlor's rates to non-discretionary trusts (see 5420), that rule will not apply where an election is in force.

If a settlement relates partly to historic buildings, etc. and partly to other property, it is treated as two separate settlements.

The election must be made within one year of 31 January following the end of the tax year to which it relates; before self-assessment, two years from the end of the tax year).

Income of the settled property which is treated as the income of the settlor (see 1070ff.) and is applied in reimbursing the settlor for expenditure incurred in the maintenance, repair, etc. of qualifying property is not to be treated as reducing deductible expenditure, in computing the profits of the trade, where the settlor is carrying on the trade of showing his property.

Law: ITA 2007, s. 507–510

See *British Tax Reporter* ¶354-500.

1104 Exit charge where property leaves maintenance fund for historic buildings

Where property (whether capital or income) comprised in a maintenance fund is applied for any purpose other than the maintenance, repair or preservation of the heritage property, or for the benefit of a heritage body or charity (see 7198), an exit charge arises on the whole of the income which has not been so applied, and which has arisen either since the last such exit charge, or since the settlement began. The rate of charge is equivalent to the higher rate of tax for the tax year during which the charge arises, reduced by the rate applicable to trusts (see 989) for the year. The charge is in addition to any tax otherwise chargeable but does not apply to income deemed to be that of the settlor (see 1070ff.).

The exit charge also bites where any property leaves the settlement and devolves otherwise than on a heritage body or charity, or where the Treasury direction confirming the maintenance fund's privileged status (see 7371) ceases to have effect. However, it does not apply if property is simply transferred from one maintenance fund to another.

Law: ITA 2007, s. 512

See *British Tax Reporter* ¶354-500.

INCOME FROM PROPERTY

INCOME FROM LAND AND BUILDINGS

1200   Changes to the taxation of income from land

The taxation of income from land and buildings changed radically, for income tax purposes from 1995–96 onwards, and for corporation tax purposes from 1 April 1998.

With effect from 6 April 2005, income from property is taxed under the provisions of the *Income Tax (Trading and Other Income) Act* 2005 (ITTOIA 2005).

Income tax and corporation tax under ITTOIA 2005 are charged on any business which exploits rights over land in the UK to produce rents or other receipts. Moreover, to the extent that any transaction is entered into for exploiting, as a source of rents or other receipts, any such estate, etc. the transaction is deemed to have been entered into in the course of such a business. Thus a 'receipt' (see below) from a one-off or casual letting which may lack the degree of organisation usually associated with a business may be chargeable.

Receipts, in relation to any land, include:

- any payment for a licence to occupy or otherwise to use any land or in respect of exercising any other right over the land; and
- rental charges, ground annuals and (in Scotland) feu duties, and any other annual payments reserved in respect of, or charged on or issuing out of, the land.

Excluded from the charge are profits:

- charged to tax by virtue of the provisions outlined at 940, 962, 2174, respectively relating to farming and market gardening, mines, quarries and similar concerns, rents from mines, etc. or rent from electric line wayleaves;
- from letting tied premises, the rent from which is deemed to be a trading receipt (see 556).

Rents for 'caravans' confined to use at a single UK location and for permanently moored houseboats come within the property business income tax charge. 'Caravan', for this purpose, broadly means any structure designed or adapted for human habitation which is capable of being moved. Sums payable, or valuable consideration provided, by a tenant or licensee for the use of furniture also come within the rules, unless they constitute receipts of a trade which consists in, or involves, the making available of furniture for use in premises (including caravans and houseboats).

'Land' includes buildings and other structures, land covered with water, and any estate, interest, easement, servitude or right in or over land.

Income Tax

367

For rent a room relief, see 1254.

Law: ITTOIA 2005, s. 264; FA 1998, s. 38, Sch. 5; *Interpretation Act* 1978, Sch. 1; *Caravan Sites and Control of Development Act* 1960, s. 29(1)

Source: HMRC *Property Income Manual*

Website: www.hmrc.gov.uk/manuals/pimmanual/index.htm

See *British Tax Reporter* ¶300-000.

1205 Chargeable persons

Under ITTOIA 2005, it is the person who is receiving or entitled to the income from the property who is charged to tax. It is important to note that beneficial entitlement may be unnecessary as far as, for example, an estate agent or other agent in receipt of such property is concerned.

Law: ITTOIA 2005, s. 271

Source: HMRC *Property Income Manual*

Website: www.hmrc.gov.uk/manuals/pimmanual/index.htm

See *British Tax Reporter* ¶304-160.

1210 Computational rules

Income tax under ITTOIA 2005 is computed on the full amount of the profits arising in the tax year.

Subject to any express contrary rules, such profits are computed as if the trading income deductions rules were, in general, applicable (see 2040). All businesses and transactions carried on or entered into by a person or partnership are treated as a single business for the purposes of ITTOIA 2005.

HMRC may consider landlords who let multiple properties to be running a rental business and, therefore, recommend them to check online at www.hmrc.gov.uk/findout (click on 'landlord') to find out whether they are liable for tax.

The charge and mutual business

Property business activities conducted on a mutual basis (see 572) are treated (from 1998–99 or 1 April 1998 for companies) as if there was no mutual relationship. Any surplus from such activities is treated as a profit (and any deficit as a loss) if it would be so treated were the business not mutual. The person who receives or is entitled to the profit (see above), or to whom the profit arises for corporation tax purposes, is the person who would satisfy that description were the business not mutual.

Apportionment of rents on sale of land

Where, on disposal, a rental payment is apportioned between the vendor and purchaser, the income is split between the parties, and the party with no interest in the land at the time the amount was due is deemed to have received his share at the date by reference to which the apportionment is made.

Law: ITTOIA 2005, s. 264, 270(1), 272(2), 275(2)–(3), 320–321

Source: HMRC *Property Income Manual*

Website: www.hmrc.gov.uk/manuals/pimmanual/index.htm
www.hmrc.gov.uk/bulletins/index.htm

See *British Tax Reporter* ¶300-000.

1254   Rent a room scheme

In relation to people who let furnished rooms in their homes, there is a 'rent a room' relief. The relief applies to owner occupiers and tenants. Gross annual rents which do not exceed £4,250 are exempt from income tax; those who receive gross annual rents in excess of £4,250 can choose between paying tax on the excess (but forgoing relief for allowable expenses) or on the actual profit in the usual way. If someone else receives income in such circumstances when the property is the individual's only or main residence, the individual's rent a room limit is reduced by half to £2,125.

Example 1

Lenny lets furnished accommodation in his house for £115 a week (£5,980 a year). As he incurs expenses of £2,000, his profit is £3,980. The amount of gross rent he receives (£5,980) exceeds the basic limit (£4,250) by £1,730. Lenny will be taxed on the profits derived from the let in the normal way (i.e. on £3,980). But if he makes the alternative basis election, he will only be taxed on £1,730.

Example 2

Lara lets furnished accommodation in her house, and provides meals, cleaning and a laundry service, for £115 a week (£5,980 a year). As she incurs expenses of £4,600, her profit is £1,380. The amount of gross rent she receives (£5,980) exceeds the basic limit (£4,250) by £1,730. Lara will be taxed on the profits derived from the let in the normal

---

Income Tax

way (i.e. on £1,380). Were she to make the alternative basis election, she would be taxed on £1,730.

Law: ITTOIA 2005, Pt 7, Ch. 1

Website: www.hmrc.gov.uk/individuals/tmaletting-my-home.shtml

See *British Tax Reporter* ¶303-000.

1255   Furnished holiday letting income

The letting of furnished holiday accommodation constitutes a property income business and the basis period rules, as well as most of the business income rules for calculating profits (see 2150ff.), accordingly apply. However, the letting of furnished holiday accommodation in the UK is currently treated in an especially beneficial way, i.e. as a trade.

All the commercial lettings of furnished holiday accommodation made by a particular person or partnership are treated as one trade. The profit or loss has to be calculated, in practice, separately from other property income business profits and losses in order to see whether advantage can be taken of the above benefits. However, any overall profit is included in the general property income business result, as is any loss unless used separately against other income.

Benefits of furnished holiday lettings

The main benefits for the taxpayer of treatment as a trader are as follows:

- losses are not restricted to property business income but can be set against general income (see below) or capital gains (see 2299);
- capital allowances are available for expenditure on plant and machinery acquired for purposes of the letting (see 2364);
- CGT roll-over reliefs are available, where applicable and subject to the usual rules; likewise, relief for gifts of business assets and in respect of loans to traders (see 6305);
- the income attracts retirement annuity or personal pension relief.

It should nevertheless be noted that the 'rent-a room' exemption (see 1254) may prove more advantageous to the taxpayer.

Conditions to be satisfied

The above treatment applies only where there is a 'commercial letting' of 'furnished holiday accommodation' which is situated in the UK.

'Commercial letting'
'Commercial letting' requires that the property be let:

(1)   on a commercial basis, and

(2)   with a view to the realisation of 'profits'.

'Profits' here means the 'commercial', not the 'tax adjusted', profit.

It should be noted that HMRC take the view that the required income profit motive may be displaced where the taxpayer's motive is the acquisition of a second, or retirement, home, or securing a long-term capital profit on disposing of the property. Claimants may also fail the above requirements where the size of the mortgage used to purchase the property is so large that the projected profitability is jeopardised or the commercial credibility of the scheme as a whole is, consequently, questionable even though individual lettings are on a commercial basis. In such cases, HMRC expect a written business plan to be prepared, with credible figures.

Where the taxpayer seeks relief for losses in the early years of a trade (see 2302), there is an additional, *objective*, condition that profits could reasonably be expected to be realised in the year of the loss or within a reasonable time thereafter. HMRC's view is that this test must be considered for each year for which relief is claimed and that it is necessary to look at the year of the loss and whatever, on the facts, is a reasonable time thereafter. And they dissent from a special commissioner's view that this relief is available so long as profits may be expected not later than a reasonable time after the end of the statutory four-year period:

> 'We consider that "reasonable time" depends on the facts and, particularly, the nature of the loss making activity. In general, our view is that this should be a fairly short period. But, in the context of capital intensive activities, such as furnished holiday lettings, we would normally expect there to be a reasonable and realistic expectation of profits emerging within five years from the date of the commencement of the activities.'

'Furnished holiday accommodation'

For accommodation to qualify as 'furnished holiday accommodation', the tenants or licensees must be entitled to use of some furniture and it must comply with certain requirements in relation to the appropriate 12-month period, below. They are:

(1)   that it is *available* for commercial letting to the public generally as holiday accommodation for periods which total not less than 140 days; and

(2)   it is actually let for at least 70 days; and

(3)   for a period of at least seven months it is not normally in the same occupation for a continuous period exceeding 31 days (this means that calendar month bookings do not break the conditions).

The seven-month period can be broken up during the year and need not be continuous. However, it does include the period of 70 days when the accommodation is actually let, as above.

The appropriate 12-month period for which the conditions must be satisfied is in general the tax year or accounting period in question except:

- where the accommodation in question was not let as furnished accommodation in the tax year or accounting period preceding the year in which it is so let, then, for the purposes of compliance with the tests for the current year, the 12 months beginning with the date on which the accommodation was so let in the current tax year or accounting period is relevant; and

- where the accommodation was let as furnished accommodation in the preceding tax year or accounting period, but is not so let in the following tax year or accounting period, then for the purposes of compliance with the test for the current year reference is made to the 12 months ending on the date on which he ceased to let it in the current year.

Where the taxpayer has let out other furnished properties which satisfy all three of these conditions, except that the 70-day letting test is not met, then he may make a claim to 'average' the properties for this purpose. However, qualifying accommodation may not be specified in more than one claim for any one year or period.

Furnished holiday letting losses

A person who makes a loss on all properties let as furnished holiday accommodation, taken together, can elect whether to set the loss against his general income for either the tax year in which the loss was made or the previous year in the same way as trading losses (see 2296ff.). Any loss not claimed against general income must be set first against any other property business profits of the same year, any balance remaining being carried forward and set against the first available profits (see 2292).

If the loss to any extent consists of capital allowances for plant and machinery (see 2364), the whole loss can be set against any other property business losses of the same year or, where appropriate, carried forward against profits of the same business in later years.

Where a property business is made up *solely* of furnished holiday lettings, any losses can either be set against general income or carried forward.

However, a person whose property income business is made up partly of furnished holiday lettings and partly of other land and property can choose whether to set any loss from furnished holiday lettings against his general income. Any losses not claimed against general income must be set first against any other property income business profits in the same tax year, any balance being set against the first available profits of the same business in later tax years.

Carry-back of losses in early years

For carry-back of a loss in the early years of a furnished holiday letting, see 'Commercial letting' above.

Law: ITTOIA 2005, s. 323–326; *Walls v Livesey (HMIT)* (1995) Sp C 4; *Brown v Richardson (HMIT)* (1997) Sp C 129

Source: *HMRC Property Income Manual*

Website: www.hmrc.gov.uk/manuals/pimmanual/index.htm

www.hmrc.gov.uk/bulletins/index.htm

See *British Tax Reporter* ¶303-100.

1260 Treatment of lease premiums as rent

The legislation relating to lease premiums, etc. is largely unchanged by the introduction of the rules relating to property income businesses (see 1200ff.), with amendments being made to include references to the new system.

Premiums in respect of leases of more than 50 years' duration are charged to CGT. Grants, variations, surrenders and other lump sum payments in respect of leases which do not exceed 50 years are charged partly to CGT and partly to income tax under the property income provisions (see 1264, 1268, 1270); such 'short leases' are also potentially subject to charges under ITTOIA 2005 (former Sch. D, Case VI) in the case of a sale with a right to reconveyance or leaseback (see 1274, 1276) or of a profit on sale (see 1278). The duration of a lease is determined by reference to certain specific principles (see 1262).

A 'lease' includes an agreement for a lease as well as any tenancy, but does not include a mortgage. A 'premium' includes:

'any like sum, whether payable to the immediate or a superior landlord or to a person connected [see below] with the immediate or a superior landlord.'

'Connected persons' in relation to an individual are his spouse or relative (i.e. brother, sister, ancestor or lineal descendant), or his relatives' spouses, or trustees of a settlement of which he (or an individual connected with him) is the settlor, or a partner or a partner's spouse or relative, or a company of which he, or he and persons connected with him, have control (see 3826).

Law: ITTOIA 2005, s. 306–307, 364, 878–879

See *British Tax Reporter* ¶300-115.

1262 The duration of a lease

There are rules for determining the duration of a 'lease' (see 1260), as follows.

- Where the terms of the lease or any other circumstances render it unlikely that the lease will continue beyond a date falling before the expiry of the term of the lease and the premium was not substantially greater than it would have been (on certain specified assumptions) had the term been one expiring on that date, the duration of the lease is calculated to that earlier date.
- Where there is provision for the extension of the lease beyond a given date by notice given by the tenant, account may be taken of any circumstances making it likely that the lease will be so extended.
- Where the tenant, or a person connected with him (see 3826), is, or may become,

373

entitled to a further lease or the grant of a further lease (whenever commencing) on the same premises, or on premises including the whole or part of the same premises, the term of the lease may be treated as not expiring before the term of the further lease.

In applying the above it is assumed that all parties concerned act as they would act if they were at arm's length and that, where an unusual benefit is conferred by the lease, the benefit would not have been conferred had the lease been for a period ending on the likely date of determination, rather than on the actual date. The likely date of determination is in most cases the end of the period of the lease. An unusual benefit would be any benefit other than the right to enjoy the beneficial occupation of the premises or the right to receive a reasonable commercial rent in respect of them.

Law: ITTOIA 2005, s. 303–305

See *British Tax Reporter* ¶300-115.

1264 Short leases: portion of premium treated as rent

Premiums arising on the grant of 'leases' (see 1260) which do not exceed 50 years are taxed as part income (i.e. deemed rentals) and part capital gain (for the meaning of 'premium', see 1260; for the duration of a lease, see 1262). To ascertain what part of the premium falls to be taxed as income and what part is the capital element, a formula exists by which the appropriate part of the premium to be charged to income tax can be ascertained, i.e. the amount of the premium minus one-fiftieth of that amount for each complete period of 12 months (other than the first) in the duration of the lease.

Example

Anna grants Emma a lease for $21\frac{1}{2}$ years for a premium of £10,000.

	£
Premium	10,000
Less: $(21 - 1) \times 2\% \times £10,000$	(4,000)
Amount assessable under ITTOIA 2005	6,000

The part of the premium chargeable is taxable in full in the chargeable period in which the lease is granted.

Where provision is made in the lease for the tenant to carry out work instead of paying a premium, the amount by which the landlord's estate has been increased in value by the provision requiring the work to be done is treated as a premium. However, if the work is of a type which, if the landlord and not the tenant were obliged to carry it out, would be deductible from the rent under general rules or as an expense of a property income business, the rule does not apply.

A complex form of relief may also be available (and continues to be available in the case of a property income business), if the premium arises on the grant of a sub-lease out of a head lease in respect of which a charge under these provisions has previously been made; also if a charge would have been made except for any exemption from tax); similarly, relief may be available if the previous charge arose as a result of the grant of a lease at undervalue (see 1278).

Where it appears to an inspector that the amount chargeable affects the tax liability of any other person, he may notify those other persons of the amount he proposes to charge. All parties may then object if they so wish and the amount will be determined by the tribunal as if it were an appeal.

The various payments under the present provisions are taxable in full in the chargeable period in which payment is received.

In general, the whole of a discounted premium is taxable in the relevant chargeable period. However, there is a relief where a premium is payable by instalments: originally, a taxpayer who satisfied HMRC that he would otherwise suffer undue hardship could elect to pay the tax chargeable by such instalments as HMRC might allow over a period not exceeding eight years. As this did not fit with self-assessment, the income or corporation tax payer now has the option to pay tax by instalments over the eight-year period.

Law: ITTOIA 2005, s. 277–279

See *British Tax Reporter* ¶300-120.

1268 Short leases: lump-sum rents and surrender payments

Where, under the terms subject to which a 'lease' (see 1260) is granted, a sum becomes payable by the tenant in lieu of the whole or part of the rent for any period, that sum is deemed to be a premium and a notional rent arises when it becomes payable by the tenant. The lump sum or premium is treated as relating only to the period of the lease for which the payment was made in lieu of rent. The sum may thus be taxable to the extent which applies in relation to premiums generally under short leases (see 1264).

> ### Example
>
> A landlord grants a lease of 31 years. The lease provides that the landlord can demand a lump sum after ten years of £40,000 in lieu of rent for the remainder of the lease. The £40,000 is deemed to be a premium payable for a lease of 21 years (31 − 10).

Where, under the terms subject to which a lease is granted, a sum becomes payable by the tenant as consideration for the surrender of the lease (brought to an end by an agreement between landlord and tenant), that sum is deemed to be a premium and a notional rent arises when it becomes payable by the tenant. The premium is taken to be paid in consideration of the lease from the date of commencement to the date of surrender. The sum may thus be taxable to the extent which applies in relation to premiums generally under short leases (see 1264). If, however, surrender is agreed between landlord and tenant after the lease has commenced, the above provision will not apply and CGT only will be chargeable on the surrender payment.

Example

The landlord grants a lease for 31 years with a surrender clause and the tenant surrenders in accordance with the clause after ten years for the stipulated figure of £20,000. The £20,000 is treated as a premium applicable to the duration of the lease from commencement to surrender (i.e. ten years).

Law: ITTOIA 2005, 279–280

See *British Tax Reporter* ¶300-130.

1270 Short leases: payments to waive or vary the terms of the lease as income

Where a sum becomes payable by the tenant, otherwise than by way of rent, in consideration for a variation of any term of the 'lease' (see 1260), that sum is deemed to be a premium in the year when the contract providing for the variation or waiver was entered into. The sum may thus be taxable to the extent which applies in relation to premiums generally under short leases (see 1264). The premium is treated as attributable to the period during which the waiver or variation is to have effect, i.e. the duration of the lease to which the variation or waiver applied. (Payments in point paid to a person other than the landlord are assessable only if paid to a person who in relation to the landlord is a 'connected person' (see 3826).

Example

The landlord grants a lease of 31 years. Under the provisions in the lease the tenant has an option to take a further term provided he observes all the conditions of the lease. If the tenant fails to do so after ten years have elapsed but then pays the landlord £10,000 to waive his (the landlord's) right to object to a further term being taken, that £10,000 would be treated as a premium attributable to that period of the lease over which the variation or waiver occurred, i.e. 21 years.

Law: ITTOIA 2005, s. 313(5); *Banning v Wright (HMIT)*[1972] 1 WLR 972

See *British Tax Reporter* ¶300-140.

1274 Short leases: sale proceeds as income where right of reconveyance

In addition to the anti-avoidance provisions relating to the duration of the lease (the lease term for tax purposes being determined in a specific way: 1262), there are also provisions designed to prevent specific avoidance schemes in connection with leasebacks (see 1276) or reconveyances (see below).

Where the terms subject to which an estate or interest in land is sold provide that it shall be, or may be required to be, reconveyed at a future date to the vendor or a person 'connected' (see 3826) with him, the vendor may be chargeable to tax under ITTOIA 2005 (former Sch. D, Case VI) (or the sum may be treated as received as income of a property income business). The charge is on any amount by which the price at which the estate or interest is sold exceeds the price at which it is to be reconveyed, or, if the earliest date at which in accordance with those terms it would fall to be reconveyed is a date two years or more after the sale it is discounted in accordance with the provisions taking only a portion of premiums as income (see 1264).

Where the terms of the sale do not stipulate a date for reconveyance and the price varies with the date of reconveyance, the price of the reconveyance is taken to be the lowest possible under the terms of the sale. The vendor may reclaim (up to six years after the reconveyance) that amount of the tax assessed on him which exceeds the amount which would have been assessed had the date been treated as the date fixed by the terms of sale.

Where it appears to an inspector that the amount chargeable affects the tax liability of any other person, he may notify those other persons of the amount he proposes to charge; all parties may then object if they so wish and the amount will be determined by the tribunal as if it were an appeal.

Law: ITTOIA 2005, s. 284, 286

See *British Tax Reporter* ¶300-160.

1276 Short leases: sale and leaseback income charges

In addition to the anti-avoidance provisions which deal with the duration of the lease (the lease term for tax purposes being determined in a specific way: see 1262) and those which deal with the sale of land with the right to reconveyance (see 1274), the legislation deals with ascertaining the charge to tax where land is sold and the agreement contains a provision for its lease back to the vendor or a person connected with him (rather than a reconveyance as such).

The amount of the premium payable on the grant of the lease plus the value at the date of sale of the right to purchase the reversion when the lease is granted is taken to be the

Income Tax

reconveyance price for the purposes of the rules set out in 1274. The date of reconveyance is deemed to be the date of the grant of the lease.

> ### Example
>
> A landlord sells the property to the tenant for £30,000 but the agreement gives the landlord the right to take a 999-year lease for £15,000 after ten years.
>
> If the value of the reversion was £500, the landlord would be charged as follows:
>
> £30,000 − (£15,000 + £500) = £14,500 over ten years, discounted in accordance with the provisions treating only a portion of any premium as income (see 1264).

This type of transaction is frequently used, not as a means of avoidance, but as a bona fide commercial method to finance the development of land; therefore, an express proviso excludes situations where the lease is granted and begins to run within one month after the sale.

The amount deemed to have been received is taken into account in computing Sch. A profits in the period in which the estate or interest is 'sold'. The estate or interest is treated as 'sold' when any of the following occurs:

(1) an unconditional contract for its sale is entered into;

(2) a conditional contract for its sale becomes unconditional; or

(3) an option or right of pre-emption is exercised requiring the vendor to enter into an unconditional contract for its sale.

Where it appears to an inspector that the amount chargeable affects the tax liability of any other person, he may notify those other persons of the amount he proposes to charge; all parties may then object if they so wish and the amount will be determined by the tribunal as if it were an appeal.

Law: ITTOIA 2005, s. 285–286, 301–302

See *British Tax Reporter* ¶304-600.

1278 Short leases: premium foregone treated as income

Where a lease of not more than 50 years (see 1262) is granted at less than its market value, the difference between the amount for which it was granted and the market value of the lease is called 'the amount foregone'.

On a subsequent first assignment of the lease by the tenant, any consideration over and above the premium on the grant of the undervalued lease, is chargeable to income tax under ITTOIA 2005 in the assignor's hands. The amount so chargeable is limited by the 'amount foregone' and is discounted in accordance with the provisions treating only a portion of any premium as income (see 1264) as if it had arisen on the original grant of the lease. The balance of the 'amount foregone' is carried forward to subsequent assignments until used up: at each stage the relevant excess is the excess of consideration for the assignment in question over the consideration previously given.

The amount of any 'excess' is taken into account in computing property income profits in the period in which the payment is due.

Because future assignees of the lease may not know if the lease has been previously granted at an undervalue, the grantor or any assignor or assignee of the lease may submit a statement to HMRC showing whether or not a charge to tax arises and the inspector must, if he is satisfied with the accuracy of the statement, certify its accuracy.

Where it appears to an inspector that the amount chargeable affects the tax liability of any other person, he may notify those other persons of the amount he proposes to charge; all parties may then object if they so wish and the amount will be determined by the tribunal as if it were an appeal.

Law: ITTOIA 2005, s. 282–283, 300

See *British Tax Reporter* ¶300-110.

1290   Reverse premiums

Reverse premiums are the sums landlords pay to induce potential tenants to take a lease.

Reverse premiums received on or after 9 March 1998 are taxable as revenue receipts. However, the charge to tax does not apply to a premium to which the recipient was entitled immediately before that date, arrangements made on or after that date being ignored for this purpose.

Inducements

The legislation taxes 'a payment or other benefit by way of inducement'. Such an inducement may take the form of a cash payment by the landlords, a period of rent-free occupation, a contribution to the tenant's costs or the assumption by landlord of the tenant's liabilities. However, not all such inducements are caught by the rules. The following table summarises those inducements that are taxable under the reverse premium provision and those that are not.

Income Tax

Taxable	Non-taxable
• Cash payments • Contributions towards specified tenant's costs, e.g. relocation costs, start-up costs or fitting-out costs • Sums paid to third parties to meet obligations of the tenant, e.g. rent to a landlord due under an old lease or a capital sum to terminate such a lease • An effective payment of cash by other means, e.g. the landlord writing off a sum owed by the tenant	• The grant of a rent-free period of occupation • The replacement by agreement of an existing rent with a lower rent because market conditions have made the original rent onerous • A new lease by agreement without an onerous condition present in former lease

Broadly, inducements are caught if they involve the laying out of money. Benefits representing amounts foregone or deferred are not generally caught as they do not involve an outlay.

Tax treatment of receipts by way of reverse premiums

For tax purposes, a reverse premium is treated as a revenue receipt taxable under ITTOIA 2005.

The timing of the charge generally follows accepted principles of commercial accounting, the broad effect of which is to spread the reverse premium over the period of the lease, or to the first rent review, whichever is the shorter. See, however, the anti-avoidance provision below.

Arrangements not at arm's length

An anti-avoidance provision aims at preventing the exploitation of timing differences by the grant of a lease to a connected person on clearly uncommercial terms (e.g. a 25-year lease with no rent review clause).

Exclusions

The above provisions do not apply to a payment or benefit:

- if or to the extent that it is taken into account under the capital allowances provision relating to subsidies, contributions, etc. to reduce the recipient's expenditure qualifying for allowances (see 2336);
- received in connection with a relevant transaction where the person entering into the transaction is an individual and the transaction relates to premises occupied or to be occupied as his only or main residence; or
- to the extent that it is consideration for the transfer of an estate or interest in land which

constitutes the sale in a 'sale and leaseback transaction' as described in ICTA 1988, s. 779(1), (2).

Law: ITTOIA 2005, s. 311, Sch. 2 , para 28, 72, 99, 101–103; *Commr of Inland Revenue (New Zealand) v McKenzies (NZ) Ltd* [1988] 2 NZLR 736; *Commr of Inland Revenue (New Zealand) v Wattie*[1998] BTC 438

Website: www.hmrc.gov.uk/bulletins/index.htm

See *British Tax Reporter* ¶300-190.

1300   Transactions in land: anti-avoidance

Transactions designed to avoid tax on the sale of land by direct or indirect means are taxed as income under ITTOIA 2005 (former Sch. D, Case VI) (see 1430). Some of the transactions caught are normal developments of land. To the extent that capital gains are now taxed at income tax rates in the case of individuals and the full corporation tax rate in the case of companies, the importance of the provisions is diminished.

The provisions are nevertheless very wide in scope, applying to all persons (which include companies and unincorporated bodies), whether or not resident in the UK. However, the land in question (or part of it) must be situated in the UK for the provisions to apply.

These provisions apply wherever:

- land, or any property deriving its value from land (including shares in a land-owning company), is acquired with the sole or main object of realising a gain from disposing of the land; or
- land is held as trading stock; or
- land is developed with the sole or main object of realising a gain from disposing of the land when developed;

and any gain of a capital nature is obtained from the disposal of the land, by the person acquiring, holding or developing the land, or by any 'connected person' (see 3826) or, where any arrangement or scheme is effected in respect of the land which enables a gain to be realised by any indirect method, or by any series of transactions, by any person who is a party to, or concerned in, the arrangement or scheme, and whether any such person obtains the gain for himself or for any other person.

Supplementary provisions ensure that the rules apply to many transactions whereby a person indirectly benefits, though where one person is assessed to tax in respect of consideration receivable by another person there is a right of recovery. However, the operation of the provisions is restricted where a company holds land as trading stock, or where a company owns 90 per cent or more of the ordinary share capital (directly or indirectly) of another company which holds land as trading stock, and there is a disposal of shares in either the land trading company or the holding company, and all the land so held is disposed of in the normal course of trade by the company which held it, and all the opportunity of profit or gain in respect of the land arises to that company.

Adjustments have been upheld in respect of:

- the grant by trustees of a lease of land to a developer, with a clause ensuring that the premium payable should be linked with the prices obtained from the sale of the underleases following the redevelopment of the land;
- the sale of properties through the medium of Bahamian companies.

HMRC are given powers to obtain such information as they think necessary for these purposes. Conversely, the taxpayer can apply for advance clearance or can request confirmation after the fact that HMRC will not challenge any transaction.

Law: ITA 2007, Pt. 13, Ch. 3; *Page (HMIT) v Lowther*[1983] BTC 394; *Sugarwhite v Budd (HMIT)*[1988] BTC 189

See *British Tax Reporter* ¶304-600.

1305   Rent factoring

Rent factoring is the sale of the right to receive rents. The right to receive rents over a period of time is valuable, but a business may prefer to realise that value upfront, rather than over the period of the lease. The right to receive the rents is therefore sold for a lump sum that realises most of the value but which also allows the purchaser, usually a bank or other finance house, to make a commercial profit from the receipt of the rents over time.

In some circumstances the lump sum may be taxable as income but the transactions could be structured so that the lump sum would not be brought into charge as income of the seller (i.e. a capital sum). Where the lump sum is capital it could effectively escape taxation, either because of costs that could reduce the gain to nil (or nearly so) or because of the availability of capital losses.

This type of tax avoidance was addressed by *Finance Act* 2004 by ensuring that, where the right to receive all or part of the rental stream arising from a lease of plant and machinery is sold or otherwise transferred to another person, the proceeds are brought into charge as income if they would not otherwise be brought into account as income.

See *British Tax Reporter* ¶300-042.

1320   Real estate investment trusts

The regime for Real Estate Investment Trusts ('UK-REITs' and 'Group REITs') took effect from 1 January 2007. It is part of a trend in various countries, including the USA, Germany, Japan and Australia, to encourage property investment by offering a fund in which investors can buy shares or units, and which is 'look-through' for taxation purposes – the liability falling not on the fund but on the investor.

UK-REITs must be publicly listed on a stock exchange, so that the method of investment is to purchase shares in the open market.

The legislation provides an alternative taxation treatment for listed companies that invest substantially in real property held as part of a property rental business. To comply with the conditions laid down, such a company must distribute at least 90 per cent of its profits from its property rental business each year.

The alternative taxation treatment on offer consists of exemption from corporation tax for the investing company, in so far as it carries on a property rental business that meets the conditions; instead, liability to income tax or corporation tax falls on the shareholder in respect of the distributions from the UK-REIT that they receive. This replaces the normal UK taxation regime whereby the company to which the profits accrue is charged to corporation tax on them, and the shareholder then receives a dividend which may or may not in practice give rise to a further liability to tax.

A company that meets the conditions may give notice to enter the UK-REIT regime for any accounting period commencing on or after 1 January 2007. A new accounting period starts on entry into the regime. Tax penalties may arise if the company leaves the regime before ten years have expired.

There are conditions that the company's property rental business, the income arising from that business, and the company itself must meet if the notice given is to be valid. Failure to meet these and other conditions or requirements of the regime once the UK-REIT is in existence can lead to a tax charge or cessation of UK-REIT status. The Group REIT regime, and the regime for joint ventures, also contain special rules. Directors and advisers should in particular be aware of the increased accounting requirements for Group REITs, and for single company UK-REITs that have a 40 per cent interest in a joint venture company.

A number of compliance rules are framed so as to ensure that a 'minor or inadvertent' breach of the rules will not result in UK-REIT status being invalid. Some rules are of an 'x strikes and you're out' nature, intended to enable a company or group that takes its responsibilities seriously to survive without harm in spite of the occasional breach. Major breaches, on the other hand, can result in UK-REIT status being denied from the start, or from the beginning of an accounting period that ended some time ago. The risks arising from this need no emphasis.

With the introduction of the UK-REIT regime, the legislation relating to housing investment trusts was repealed.

Law: FA 2006, Part 4

See *British Tax Reporter* ¶788-000.

Income Tax

INVESTMENT INCOME

DIVIDENDS AND UNIT TRUST INCOME RECEIVABLE

1350   Dividends receivable

Where a company makes a 'qualifying distribution' (see 3076) to an individual shareholder who is resident in the UK, he generally receives a tax credit. He is treated as if he received an amount of income equal to the cash amount (or value) plus the tax credit; such credit then reduces his income tax liability for the financial year in which the distribution is made and any excess remaining over his tax liability is paid back to him. By this method, the tax paid by the company on its income is partially imputed to the shareholder (see further 3004).

Special rates of income tax apply to dividend income. These rates are known as the dividend ordinary, the dividend upper rate and (since 6 April 2010) the dividend additional rate . The charge to tax at the dividend rates is subject to any other provisions of the Income Tax Acts that provide for income to be charged at different rates of income tax in some circumstances.

Dividend ordinary rate

As far as individuals are concerned, income tax is charged at the dividend ordinary rate on an individual's dividend income which would otherwise be charged to income tax at the basic rate (or, previously, the starting rate) and which is not relevant foreign income charged on the remittance basis.

Income tax is also charged at the dividend ordinary rate on the dividend income of persons other than individuals which would otherwise be charged at the basic rate and which is not relevant foreign income, unless the income in question is charged at another rate by other provisions of the Income Tax Acts, e.g. the certain trustees and unauthorised unit trusts.

The dividend ordinary rate is set at 10 per cent and, as dividends and distributions from UK companies carry a tax credit equal to 10 per cent of the aggregate value of the dividend and the tax credit itself, no additional tax is due on this category of income which falls within the basic rate limit.

Dividend upper rate

Individuals are charged to income tax at the dividend upper rate on dividend income which would otherwise be chargeable at the higher rate of tax. The dividend upper rate is set at 32.5 per cent. The tax credit attaching to dividends and distributions from UK companies is set against the tax charged at the dividend upper rate. The dividend upper rate does not apply to relevant foreign income charged in accordance with ITTOIA 2005, s. 832.

Dividend additional rate

Individuals are charged to income tax at the dividend additional rate on dividend income which would otherwise be chargeable at the additional rate of tax. The dividend additional rate is set at 42.5 per cent. The tax credit attaching to dividends and distributions from UK companies is set against the tax charged at the dividend additional rate.

The dividend additional rate does not apply to relevant foreign income charged in accordance with ITTOIA 2005, s. 832.

Dividend income

The dividend rates apply to dividend income. Dividend income comprises:

- dividends and distributions from UK companies;
- dividends and 'relevant foreign distributions' from non-UK resident companies. A relevant foreign distribution is a distribution, other than a dividend, corresponding to taxable distributions from UK companies;
- stock dividends from UK-resident companies; or
- the release of a loan to a participator in a close company.

Example 1

Martha is a non-taxpayer. She receives a dividend of £1,000 in 2008–09. The dividend has an associated tax credit of £111.11 ($^1/_9$). The tax credit is not repayable, thus Martha effectively suffers tax of £111.11 on her dividend.

Example 2

Ellie receives a dividend of £1,000 in 2008–09. She has other income of £5,700. She has taxable income of £776 (£5,700 + gross dividend £1,111 (£1,000 × $^{100}/_{90}$) − personal allowance of £6,035). The dividend, forming the top slice of Ellie's income is taxable at 10 per cent. The tax on the dividend is £111 (£1,111 × 10%), exactly matched by the associated tax credit.

Example 3

George receives a dividend of £1,000 in 2008–09. He has other income of £20,000. His taxable income is £15,076 (£20,000 + gross dividend of £1,111 (£1,000 × $^{100}/_{90}$) − personal allowance of £6,035). The dividend falls in the basic rate band and as such is taxed at the dividend rate of 10 per cent. The tax due in respect of the dividend (£111, i.e. £1,111 × 10%) is exactly matched by the associated tax credit.

Income Tax

Example 4

Hannah earns £300,000 in 2008–09. She also receives a dividend of £1,000. The dividend is treated as the top slice of her income, being taxed at the rate of 32.5 per cent. Additional tax payable in respect of the dividend is as follows:

	£
Gross dividend – £1,000 × $^{100}/_{90}$	1,111
Tax thereon at 32.5%	361
Less: tax credit (£1,111 × 10%)	(111)
Additional tax payable	250

Arrangements to pass on value of tax credit

Since 2 July 1997, pension funds have not been entitled to payment of tax credits attaching to qualifying distributions that they receive. The use of such tax credits is limited to set-off against any tax due on qualifying distributions received.

There is a consequential restriction, operative from 2 July 1997, on the set-off or payment of a tax credit attaching to a UK distribution where there are arrangements to pass on the benefit to a person (e.g. a pension fund) who would not have been able to make such use of the tax credit had that person received the distribution direct. This is designed to prevent the circumvention of the inability to obtain payment of tax credits by making arrangements, directly or indirectly, with a third party which can utilise the tax credit and then pass back the resulting benefit.

Law: ITA 2007, s. 13; ITTOIA 2005, Pt. 4, Ch. 3

Source: IR press release, 30 March 1988

See *British Tax Reporter* ¶321-000.

1358   Unit trust income receivable

The tax treatment of income arising in respect of investment through a unit trust depends upon whether the trust is authorised. Authorised unit trusts are generally treated as companies subject to corporation tax while unauthorised unit trusts are treated as trusts subject to income tax.

Income from underlying investments made through authorised unit trusts are effectively treated as those of the trustees rather than of the ultimate investors (the precise way in which effect is given to this differs depending upon the circumstances, as noted below). There is a deemed 'full-payout' of scheme income. For distribution periods of such a scheme beginning after 31 March 1994, the scheme may distinguish in its accounts whether amounts are to be paid out wholly as dividends (and in part as FIDs if desired) or wholly as yearly interest; non-resident investors can register to receive such interest without deduction of tax where it derives from eligible assets (for special provisions for corporate recipients, see 3027). Previously, the amount available for pay-out was treated as dividends but with certain exceptions for fixed interest trusts (or 'gilt unit trusts').

For unauthorised unit trusts, unit holders are liable to tax on amounts which are paid out or reinvested in the fund for their benefit, those amounts being treated as reaching unit holders with basic rate tax having been deducted by the trustees.

(Investment trusts are companies whose distributions are taxable in the usual manner: see 1350.)

Law: ITTOIA 2005, s. 372–381; *Authorised Investment Funds (Tax) (Amendment) Regulations* 2009 (SI 2009/2036); *Authorised Investment Funds (Tax) Regulations* 2006 (SI 2006/964)

See *British Tax Reporter* ¶321-000.

INTEREST, ANNUITIES AND OTHER ANNUAL PAYMENTS

1366 The income charge on annual payments, including interest

The following items are charged to tax under ITTOIA 2005.

- Any interest of money, whether yearly or otherwise, or any 'annuity' (see 1396) or other 'annual payment' (see below and 1398), whether such payment is payable within or out of the UK, either as a charge on any property of the person paying the same by virtue of any deed or will or otherwise, or as a reservation out of it, or as a personal debt or obligation by virtue of any contract. This applies whether it is received and payable half-yearly or at any shorter or more distant periods, but excludes any payment chargeable under the tax on property income rules (former Sch. A). The Court of Appeal has held that interest credited to the taxpayer's account but retained by the bank as security for a debt was taxable as interest to which the taxpayer was entitled: although he never received the interest, he received the benefit of it since his liability for the debt was reduced. Investors in certain unit trusts are deemed to receive interest (see 1358).
- All discounts (see 1400).
- Income, formerly with the exception of income charged under Sch. C (see 1402), from securities bearing interest payable out of the public revenue (including those which the Treasury has directed are gross payment securities).

There are certain exempt forms of interest, such as that on certain National Savings, TESSAs and ISAs (see 1372, 1921). Interest on compensation paid in respect of certain mis-sold personal pensions, buy-out contracts and retirement annuity contracts is also exempt.

Generally, certain annual payments made by an individual, that individual's personal representative or a Scottish partnership involving an individual are not taxable if they fall due after 14 March 1988. Specifically excluded from this exemption (and therefore still within the charge to tax) are the following:

- payments of interest;
- payments made for bona fide commercial reasons in connection with the individual's trade, profession or vocation;
- certain payments for non-taxable consideration; and
- certain maintenance payments (see 1404).

Other exempt annual payments include benefits paid under certain 'self-contained' insurance policies to those who make arrangements to protect themselves from financial losses caused by accident, sickness, disability, infirmity or unemployment, or from the cost of long-term care. Benefits received under employers' group policies and passed on to an employee are also exempt if and to the extent that the employee has contributed to the premiums. Benefits are not exempt where they fall to be taken into account in computing the insured's trading or similar profits, or where the insured person was entitled to deduct the premiums in the computation of his income tax liability. (From 1 October 1996, HMRC treat benefits paid under insurance policies taken out by medical practitioners in respect of locum and fixed practice expenses in the event of the policyholder's incapacity or illness as taxable professional receipts, and the premiums as deductible.) In general, the above provisions take effect after 5 April 1996, but if the insurance policy provided benefits that are linked to mortgage repayments or other specified commitments the exemption has retrospective effect.

Certain other income is specifically directed to be charged under ITTOIA 2005: e.g. certain rents (see 962), interest paid by registered industrial and provident societies (see 4670), loans against life assurance policies (see 1465), and under-deductions from payments made before passing of the annual Finance Act.

HMRC take no action to pursue liability where a non-resident receives untaxed interest which cannot be assessed in the name of a UK trustee or of a UK agent or branch which manages or controls the interest (see 1672). This also applies to discount, to profits on disposal of certificates of deposit (see 1448), to dividends paid gross by building societies (see 1372) and gains from 'deep gain securities' (see 1401) or payments representing interest in respect of a general client account, paid gross by a bank, etc. or building society by virtue of being exempt from the basic rate deduction requirements (see 1372).

Law: ITA 2007, s. 7, 12, 16, 18; *Peracha v Miley (HMIT)*[1990] BTC 406

See *British Tax Reporter* ¶330-000.

1368   Gross or net: payments out of profits or gains brought into the charge to income tax

Subject to the important exceptions noted below, where an 'annuity' (see 1396) is paid, or an 'annual payment' (see 1398) is made, in a tax year when the payer has sufficient income chargeable to income tax to match the gross payment, the payer has a right to deduct a sum equal to basic rate income tax thereon, i.e. 20 per cent for 2008–09. That deducted sum is treated as income tax paid by the payee. The payment, less tax, fully discharges the payer's obligation to the payee. The computation of the payee's total income must include the gross amount of the payment, i.e. the amount actually received plus the amount of the tax deducted by the payer. The payee usually receives a certificate showing the relevant amounts and may otherwise demand one.

The payer's taxable income includes the amount which he is liable to pay to the payee. The payer therefore compensates himself by keeping the tax he has deducted from the payment made to the payee. Personal allowances are available to the payer as though his income excluded the gross amount of the payment made to the payee (see 1850).

Although the payer's taxable income includes an amount equivalent to the payments, such profits are generally taxable only at the lower or basic rate, i.e. the payments attract higher rate relief.

A tenant who fails to deduct tax from rent paid to a non-resident landlord may not be able to set off the amount which should have been deducted against subsequent payments. This contrasts with views expressed in relation to the requirement that tax must be deducted when amounts are paid out of funds not chargeable to income tax (see 1370).

Similar provisions apply to:

- sums paid in respect of the user of a patent (see 1406); and
- before 1 May 1995 mining, etc. rents and royalties (see 962).

Exceptions

Irrespective of the above, the following annual payments may not be made under deduction of income tax:

- payments (other than interest) falling due after 14 March 1988 and made otherwise than under covenant to charity, or made otherwise than for bona fide commercial reasons in connection with the individual's trade, profession or vocation;
- payments (other than interest) made for non-taxable consideration – the statutory provisions nullify the 'reverse annuity' decisions that regular payments to a charity in return for a capital sum were annuities or annual payments within these provisions.

These payments do not attract tax in the payee's hands and are not deductible by the payer for income tax purposes.

Income Tax

Repayment or direct assessment

A payee who is not required to pay tax at a rate below the higher rate may reclaim from HMRC the tax which the payer has deducted (see 2687 for time-limits).

A payee who is liable to tax at higher than the deducted rate (and in calculating the tax rate applicable to him, the gross amount of the payment he received must be included in his total income), is directly assessed or makes a self-assessment on the tax owing.

HMRC will not make repayment of sums of £50 or less during the tax year, but only after the end of the appropriate tax year.

Law: ITTOIA 2005, s. 727–729, Sch. 2, para. 147; *Tenbry Investments Ltd v Peugeot Talbot Motor Co Ltd*[1992] BTC 547; *IR Commrs v Crawley*[1987] BTC 112

1370   Gross or net: payments made out of profits or gains which are not brought into the charge to income tax

Subject to the important exceptions noted in 1368, where an 'annuity' (see 1396) or 'annual payment' (see 1398) (other than interest) is paid in a tax year when the payer lacks sufficient taxable income fully to match the gross payment, the payer must deduct income tax from the payment and to account to HMRC for it. The deduction is made at the basic rate, i.e. 20 per cent for 2008–09. The payment, less basic rate tax, made to the payee discharges the payer's obligation to the payee. The payee usually receives a certificate showing the relevant amounts and may otherwise demand one.

Where a payment is made in a later tax year than that in which it fell due, an allowance is made where the payment, if made on the due date, could have been paid wholly or partly out of taxed income.

All chargeable profits must be exhausted before it can be said that the payment is made other than out of profits or gains brought into the charge to tax.

Similar provisions apply to:

● sums paid in respect of the user of a patent (see 1406);
● before 1 May 1995, mining, etc. rents and royalties (see 962).

A temporary failure to deduct tax may, in some cases, be corrected by deducting amounts from subsequent payments. The Court of Appeal held that, although the right to deduct was lost when a payment was completely made, weekly payments of maintenance were instalments of a yearly amount which was completely made at the end of the year. A tax year approach may be appropriate, though there is some doubt that in relation to leases, the payment of four quarterly instalments is more relevant. Where the payer ultimately fails to deduct the required tax, HMRC either assesses the payer despite the fact that he has not deducted tax from the payment or assesses the payee directly under former Sch. D, Case III.

The requirements are apparently unaffected by an EC Council directive dealing with the abolition, in certain cases, of withholding taxes on interest and royalty payments made between parent companies and subsidiaries in different member states.

Law: ITA 2007, Pt. 15; FA 2004, Pt. 3, Ch. 6; EC Directive 90/435; *Tenbry Investments Ltd v Peugeot Talbot Motor Co Ltd*[1992] BTC 547; *Johnson v Johnson*[1946] P 205; *Taylor v Taylor*[1938] 1 KB 320

Source: ESC A16, *Annual payments (other than interest) paid out of income not brought into charge to income tax*

1372   Gross or net: interest

Investments with banks and building societies

In respect of interest on most deposits made by individuals with savings institutions, the bank, building society, etc. must deduct and account for basic rate tax, i.e. 20 per cent for 2008–09; the tax deducted is repayable where appropriate, though non-taxpayers can complete a certificate permitting gross payment. The payee usually receives a certificate showing the relevant amounts and may otherwise demand one.

The scheme applies in principle to any building society or any person who receives deposits in the course of business as a prescribed deposit-taker.

Interest is effectively excluded from the scheme if it is paid to, or to a trust (including a discretionary or accumulation trust after 5 April 1996) for, or for the estate of, an individual who is not ordinarily resident in the UK. Interest on certain other special deposits is also excluded. In particular, interest can be paid gross to investors in the following circumstances:

- on payments to tax-exempt charities (see 900, 901);
- on payments to companies (including unincorporated associations such as clubs or societies), local authorities and health service bodies;
- on payments to the trustees of unit trust schemes; and
- on certificates of deposit (including paperless ('dematerialised') certificates) and sterling or foreign currency time deposits providing that the loan is not less than £50,000 and is repayable within five years;
- on general client deposit accounts;
- on accounts held at overseas branches of UK and foreign banks and building societies;
- under 'repos' (see 1378).

Persons not ordinarily resident may also be excluded from certain HMRC audit powers (see 4650, 4700) and having made a declaration of status can request that they be excluded from the payer's general statutory interest return (see 2594). Separate provisions ensure that interest payable to such persons is not caught by other deduction at source rules.

Distributions and interest in respect of quoted securities issued by building societies are subject to a direct tax deduction requirement equivalent to that for non-bank interest (see below) rather than this scheme (interest payable by a deposit-taker on any security may fall directly within such non-bank regime on definitional grounds, although generally covered by the exclusions); this does not apply to certain certificates of deposit issued in paperless ('dematerialised') form, which are 'gross payments' under the scheme.

Non-taxpayers

Non-taxpayers can complete a certificate claiming gross payment. If a building society incorporates, the registration is carried forward (see 4652). Gross interest registration forms can be signed by a parent, spouse, son or daughter of a mentally incapacitated person; a receiver or other person appointed by the court to manage the affairs of such a person can also register on their behalf. The TaxBack pages of the HMRC website (www.hmrc.gov.uk/taxback/index.htm), also explain some important points and contain a copy of the relevant form (R85):

- a parent or guardian can register a child's account if the child's total income is expected to be below the tax threshold, although registration is not possible if interest of £100 or more arises on money provided by either parent;
- a separate form needs to be completed for each account;
- completed forms should be taken to the bank, building society, etc. which will make the necessary arrangements;
- each joint holder who does not expect to be taxable should complete a form and where, say, two individuals have a joint account and only one of them expects to be a non-taxpayer, the institution may offer to pay gross interest on the non-taxpayer's share of the interest (where tax is deducted it will be reclaimable).

There is a maximum penalty of £3,000 for a person making a false declaration in order to receive gross interest or failing to notify the institution of becoming liable to tax. HMRC have indicated that the penalty will not be applied where taxpayers have acted in good faith; in these cases, an assessment, or coding adjustment, would be made to collect any tax which was due.

People claiming a repayment of the tax deducted from bank and building society interest do not need to wait until the end of the tax year, so long as the amount at stake is £50 or more. Those who are entitled to self-certify may be able to obtain repayment of tax previously deducted in the same year by completing R85 and submitting it to the bank, building society, etc. (not all payers will agree to this). Others who believe that they may be entitled to a repayment will need to complete R95 (incorporated in the above leaflet, or via contact with their tax office).

Client moneys

Tax on dividends paid gross by building societies and payments representing interest in respect of a general client account, paid gross by a bank, etc. or building society by virtue of being exempt from the basic rate deduction requirements, is not generally pursued from non-residents (see 1366). The following HMRC-approved aide-memoire deals with the tax treatment of interest received on clients' money in most normal situations.

Aide-memoire of normal situations

Type of account	*Payment of interest by bank or building society*	*Consequences*
A Designated – where subject to tax deduction.	Net	Pay net to client, who gets basic rate tax credit. No further tax deductions for non-residents (unless the solicitor is assessable as an agent).
B Designated – where paid gross (client money generally).	Gross	Pay gross to client who is assessable on payment as gross income. No deduction of tax for non-residents (unless the solicitor is assessable as agent).
C Bank and building society general client account deposit – always paid gross (client money generally and stake money).	Gross	Pay gross to client who in turn is assessable on payment as gross income; in practice solicitor assessed on net interest after setting-off this payment. No deduction of tax for non-residents.

Interest paid by and to companies

Where annual interest chargeable to tax under former Sch. D, Case III is paid by a company, a partnership of which a company is a member, or any person to another person whose usual place of abode is outside the UK, the payer must deduct income tax. However, there is no such obligation in the case of certain specified payments, including payments to a person within the charge to corporation tax in respect of interest on an advance from a bank. Where interest is paid to a company within the charge to corporation tax, the receipt is taxed under the loan relationships provisions (see 3037ff.). If the loan relationship is for trade purposes, yearly interest received will be a credit which falls to be taxed as part of the company's profit. However, the obligation to deduct income tax remains.

Gilt interest

Interest received on gilt-edged securities, where taxable, is charged under ITTOIA 2005 (formerly Sch. D, Case III). Before 6 April 1998 most gilt interest received by individuals was normally paid after the deduction of tax. There were some exceptions to this basic rule, relating to:

- interest on gilts purchased via the National Savings Stock Register; and
- interest on certain gilts, issued on special terms, held by persons who are not resident in the UK (so-called FOTRA securities: see 1650).

For companies from 23 November 1995, interest on certain gilt-edged securities may be paid without deduction of tax.

From 6 April 1998 existing recipients of gilt interest which is subject to the deduction of income tax at source can apply to receive interest gross if they wish to.

Income Tax

Law: ITA 2007, s. 892, 893; FA 1998, s. 37; F(No. 2)A 1997, s. 37; TMA 1970, s. 99A; *Income Tax (Gilt-Edged Securities) (Gross Payments of Interest) Regulations* 1995 (SI 1995/2934); *Income Tax (Deposit-Takers) (Interest Payments) Regulations* 1990 (SI 1990/2232), reg. 1–9

Website: www.hmrc.gov.uk/bulletins/index.htm

1374 Non-bank interest

Where 'yearly interest' (see 2249) is chargeable to tax and is paid:

- otherwise than in a fiduciary or representative capacity, by a company or local authority; or
- by or on behalf of a partnership of which a company is a member; or
- by a person to another person whose usual place of abode is outside the UK (other than to a UK branch outside the scope of any treaty exemption),

then the person by or through whom the payment is made must, on making the payment, deduct out of it a sum representing the amount of basic rate income tax thereon in force for that year. This does not apply to certain interest including the following:

- interest payable in the UK on an advance from a bank carrying on a genuine banking business in the UK (this can include UK branches of overseas banks); or
- interest paid by such a bank in the ordinary course of that business (see 4700).

Accordingly, in the above two cases the payment is made without deduction of income tax. Where tax is deducted, the payee usually receives a certificate showing the relevant amounts and may otherwise demand one.

Annual interest paid after 8 October 1991 is eligible for gross payment if the terms and conditions of the borrowing (whether for capital or revenue purposes) are broadly the same as those offered by the other UK banks on comparable borrowings; however, interest on certain loans, relating to the capital structure of a bank is to be treated as subject to withholding.

Where tax is deducted on making the payment, the payer must deliver up that tax to HMRC. Until the rate has been fixed for any tax year, tax is accounted for at the rate applicable in the previous year (though Budget resolutions are usually made in sufficient time for them to be applied); where the rate falls, any over-deduction must be made good either by payment or by adjustment of the following interest payment. Where agreements refer to amounts less tax or of fixed net amount, they are taken to refer to the gross amount if no deduction is required.

Subject to special provisions for interest on quoted Eurobonds, MIRAS interest, public revenue dividends (see 1402) and foreign dividends (see 1654), other types of interest, whether yearly or 'short', are paid gross without any deduction being made by the payer.

Except in relation to certain of the special provisions, above, the requirements are apparently unaffected by an EC Council directive dealing with abolition of withholding taxes on interest and royalty payments made between parent companies and subsidiaries in different member states.

Law: ITA 2007, s. 874–879; *Provisional Collection of Taxes Act* 1968, s. 2; EC Directive 90/435

Source: SP 4/96, *Income tax: interest paid in the ordinary course of business*

Website: www.hmrc.gov.uk/bulletins/index.htm

See *British Tax Reporter* ¶331-300.

1375   Gross or net: manufactured dividends or interest

Manufactured payments are made by one party to a transaction in securities to a second party. They take the place of 'real' payments of interest or dividends that the second party would have received but for the transaction. They arise in a variety of situations, but in particular when stock is lent or sold under a repurchase agreement. From 1 July 1997, the previous complex legislation concerning manufactured dividends was replaced by simplified provisions. Regulations about manufactured interest and dividends provide detailed rules about how the tax due each quarter from those involved is to be accounted for (see below).

Manufactured interest on UK securities

Manufactured interest is any payment by one of the parties to a contract (or other arrangement) for the transfer of UK securities to the other party, which represents a periodical payment of interest on those securities. In relation to the manufacturer, the interest is treated for tax purposes as if it were an annual payment to the recipient, but is neither annual interest nor an amount payable wholly out of profits or gains brought into charge for income tax purposes. The manufacturer is liable to make an annual return of such payments.

A payer who is resident and trading in the UK should deduct tax from the payment at the lower rate, unless the payment relates to either manufactured gilt interest or other interest which is normally paid gross. The gross amount of the payment is deductible in computing the amount of his profits for tax purposes and in the recipient's hands the manufactured interest is treated as if it were real taxed interest. However, if the payer is not resident and trading in the UK, the recipient must account for income tax of an amount equal to that which the payer would have had to deduct had he been resident and trading in the UK.

The interest manufacturer must provide a tax voucher to the recipient showing the gross and net amounts of the manufactured interest, the tax deducted and the date of payment.

Accounting for tax

The machinery for collecting income tax on company payments applies, with modifications, to payments of manufactured interest on UK securities received by UK-resident companies (or non-resident companies which receive such payments for the purposes of a trade carried on by them in the UK through a branch or agency) from non-resident interest manufacturers. The recipient companies (or any person claiming title through them) are treated as if the payment received had borne income tax by deduction. Provision is made for liability for tax in circumstances where the interest manufacturer in question is in receipt of the real interest of which the manufactured interest is representative.

Manufactured interest on gilts

Tax does not have to be deducted from manufactured interest on gilt and certain other securities, either by the manufacturer or the recipient.

Manufactured dividends on UK equities

A manufactured dividend paid by a UK-resident company is treated in the same way as its real counterpart, subject to treatment as a dividend (with a responsibility to account for ACT until its abolition from 6 April 1999: see 3000). In all other cases, an amount equivalent to the ACT which would have been due had the payer been a UK-resident company must be paid over to HMRC. This should be paid by the manufacturer, if he has a presence in the UK, or the recipient.

In either case the payer must provide a voucher to the recipient in the same way as if the manufactured payment were a real dividend. The voucher should show the amount of the manufactured dividend, the date of payment and the amount of tax credit to which the recipient is entitled.

Provided that the dividend manufacturer is UK-resident and is not a company, the amount of the manufactured dividend actually paid, together with an amount equal to the notional ACT, is allowed as a deduction in computing profits for income tax. However, where the payer is a non-resident company, no deduction is allowed.

Accounting for tax

Provision is made for accounting for tax in relation to manufactured dividends on UK equities other than manufactured dividends paid by UK-resident companies. The tax accounted for on manufactured dividends on UK equities by UK branches of non-resident companies can be set off against corporation tax on their profits.

Manufactured dividends representative of foreign income dividends

A manufactured overseas dividend is a payment, representative of an overseas dividend, made by one party to a transfer of overseas securities to the other. The payment was treated as a foreign income dividend (see 1350) made by the manufacturer until 5 April 1999 (when the foreign income dividend scheme was abolished). The manufacturer was not liable to account for ACT on it.

The recipient of a manufactured overseas dividend was treated for tax purposes as having received a foreign income dividend. He too was not liable to account for ACT on the amount received.

Where the dividend manufacturer was UK-resident and not a company, he was entitled to deduct, in computing his profits for tax purposes, an amount equivalent to the net manufactured payment made. He could not deduct an amount equal to the notional ACT on the payment.

The payer had to provide a tax voucher to the recipient in the same way as if the payment had been a real foreign income dividend. The voucher showed the amount of the manufactured dividend, the date of payment and the fact that the dividend carried no entitlement to a tax credit, etc.

Stock lending and deemed manufactured payments

From 1 July 1997, the legislation relating to transfers of equities under approved stock lending arrangements (see 646) was repealed, as was legislation relating to the tax treatment of interest earned on cash collateral provided in connection with certain stock lending arrangements, and stock lending does not give rise to an income tax charge. (Similar changes have been made to the CGT rules.) As there are now no restrictions on terms under which stock lending is carried out, anti-avoidance legislation prevents stock lending being used to switch dividend income from one person to another for tax reasons. If a stock lending arrangement does not provide for manufactured payments to be made, then such payments are deemed to have been made stock lending arrangements.

Sale and repurchase of securities: deemed manufactured payments

Price adjustments made in lieu of 'manufactured payments' under agreements for the sale and repurchase of securities are treated in the same way as actual manufactured payments.

Manufactured dividends after 6 April 1999

As a consequence of the abolition of the requirement to account for advance corporation tax (ACT) on actual distributions with effect from 6 April 1999 (see 1350), it is confirmed that ACT will not have to be provided for on manufactured dividends either.

Unallowable purpose provision

Finance Act 2004 introduced an 'unallowable purpose' rule for manufactured payments. It applies only where the manufactured payment is made by a company. Broadly, 'relevant tax relief' is restricted where that relief is attributable to manufactured payments made by a company in pursuance of arrangements having an unallowable purpose. The restriction applies only to the extent that, on a just and reasonable basis, the relief is attributable to the unallowable purpose. However, before the new rule can apply the following conditions must be met:

- a company must make, or be deemed to make, a manufactured payment in pursuance of arrangements to which it is party; and
- the arrangements, or any transaction entered into in pursuance of them, must have an unallowable purpose.

Arrangements have an unallowable purpose at any time where the purposes for which the company is party to the arrangements or to any transaction in pursuance of them or to any related transaction include a purpose which is not amongst the business or other commercial purposes of the company. The business or commercial purposes of a company are defined to exclude the purpose of any part of its activities which is outside the scope of corporation tax. Tax avoidance is an unallowable purpose if it is the main or one of the main purposes for which the company is party to the arrangements. Tax avoidance means a purpose that consists in securing a tax advantage for the manufacturer or any other person. Where the relevant conditions are met, then relevant tax relief attributable to the manufactured payment is disallowed on a just and reasonable basis. The restriction can apply only to the company that makes the payment. It follows that where that person would not otherwise receive relief for the payment, for instance because it is representative of a dividend on UK equities and the manufacturer is not within the scope of ITTOIA 2005, s. 366(1) then the rule can have no effect.

The rule will not operate where any relief for the manufactured payment could be restricted under the existing unallowable purpose rule in the loan relationships legislation. For accounting periods starting on or after 1 April 2004, the new management expense rules contain an unallowable purpose rule. Again, the new manufactured payments rule will not apply where relief is restricted under this provision.

Relevant tax relief is any of the following:

- any deduction in computing profits or gains for the purposes of corporation tax;
- any deduction against total profits;
- any debit brought into account under the loan relationship provisions; and
- the surrender of any amount by way of group relief.

The basic rule is that the new rules apply to all manufactured payments made on or after 2 July 2004, subject to certain transitional provisions.

Law: FA 2004, s. 136, 137; FA 1997, Sch. 10; *Manufactured Interest (Tax) Regulations 1997* (SI 1997/992); *Manufactured Dividends (Tax) Regulations 1997* (SI 1997/993)

See *British Tax Reporter* ¶331-350.

1376   Interest on damages

Where the courts award interest on damages or debts, the position appears to be that, except as noted below, if the interest is paid for more than one year it is yearly interest upon which tax must be paid (see 1366). The fact that the payee's tax rate may be affected because the interest is paid to him all in one year is irrelevant. If the person paying the interest is an individual he must pay the interest as a gross sum and the payee will be responsible for the tax. But if the payer is a company or a local authority, tax must be deducted from the payment before it is made (see 1372).

Interest on damages for personal injuries are excluded from the above and are exempt if awarded by a UK court. (This extends to foreign court awards if the interest is exempt from tax in the appropriate territory.) Where such damages are paid by way of an annuity, the sum paid is, after 1 May 1995, to be paid without deduction of tax. This also applies to criminal injuries compensation paid after 8 November 1995 by way of an annuity.

Law: ITTOIA 2005, s. 731–734

1377   Interest on overpaid student loan repayments

Borrowers will start making loan repayments under the income-contingent student loans scheme from April 2000. For borrowers paying tax under PAYE, HMRC will collect the repayments, based on income, from their employers. A borrower who, at the end of the loan, turns out to have paid too much will get a refund with interest which will be tax-free.

Law: ITTOIA 2005, s. 753

1378   'Bondwashing': accrued income scheme on purchase/ sale of interest on securities

Interest or dividends on stocks and shares do not become 'income' until they become due and payable. No apportionment of interest which actually becomes due and payable is made over the period in respect of which it is paid. Certain anti-avoidance provisions have been introduced to prevent the avoidance of tax by broadly purchasing shares or securities just after a dividend or interest has been paid and selling them just before a dividend or interest becoming due, or by sale and repurchase around a dividend or interest payment.

Sale and repurchase of securities

Sale and repurchase transactions (REPOs) involve the sale for cash and repurchase of the same or similar securities by the 'original holder' at a repurchase price fixed at the time of the original transfer to the 'interim holder'. Any fluctuations in market value are therefore borne by the original holder, who must repurchase the securities at a fixed price. The difference between the sale and repurchase price of securities (the price differential) is treated as interest assessable under former Sch. D, Case III (see 1366) on the recipient for the purposes of the Taxes Acts. (Correspondingly, the payer can treat the difference between purchase and repurchase prices as an interest expense for tax purposes.)

Where, before 6 November 1996, the original owner of securities agreed to sell or transfer those securities and in the same or a collateral agreement:

- agreed to buy back or reacquire the securities (or similar securities); or
- acquired an option, which he subsequently exercised, to buy back or reacquire the securities (or similar securities),

then, if the interest on the securities was receivable by someone other than the owner, the interest was deemed to be the original owner's interest and if the interest was paid without deduction of tax, that owner was chargeable to tax under former Sch. D, Case VI (see 1430ff.) in respect of the interest as his income, but was entitled to a tax credit for any tax which the income was shown to have borne.

Securities covered by the accrued income scheme (below) are excluded from these provisions (by order effective from 9 June 1988) but may, instead, be subject to similar rules within the manufactured payment regime (see 1375).

Transfer of interest

Where the owner of a security transfers only the right to receive the interest from it, the interest is deemed to be that of the owner of the security for tax purposes.

Accrued income scheme

If the owner of securities sells them just before a certain date (fixed by the stock exchange), he will not be entitled to that year's interest on them. The new owner will receive it. This is called selling 'cum dividend' or 'cum interest'. If the securities are sold after that date, the original owner will remain entitled to that year's interest despite the fact that the securities have been transferred to a new owner. This is called selling 'ex dividend' or 'ex interest'.

Under the 'accrued income scheme', where securities are transferred, accrued interest reflected in the value of the securities is taxed separately as income at the lower rate (ten per cent for 2005–06), instead of the basic rate, of tax from 1998–99 though not for trustees or taxpayers liable at the higher rate. The seller is treated as entitled to the proportion of interest which has accrued since the last interest payment. The purchaser is entitled to relief of the same amount. Where securities are sold ex dividend the tax charge falls on the transferee, in respect of interest attributable to the remainder of the interest period.

If the amounts to which a person is treated as entitled in a particular period exceed the amounts of relief, he is charged to income tax under former Sch. D, Case VI (see 1430ff.) on the difference. If the relief exceeds the amount of deemed interest, the taxpayer is entitled to an allowance. The sale and repurchase of securities can, in certain REPO arrangements, be excluded from the application of the accrued income scheme.

The scheme does not apply where the seller:

- carries on a trade and the sale is taken into account in computing his trading profits;
- did not hold securities with a nominal value exceeding £5,000 during the tax year in which the interest period ends (this limit applies to husband and wife jointly);
- was neither resident nor ordinarily resident in the UK during any part of the period in question; or
- is taxed on the interest under manufactured payment rules (see 1375).

Special provisions may apply in relation to securities held by a company associated with the issuer, so as to establish both a time and a method for determining the quantum of chargeable income deemed to arise in relation to such debts (see 3027).

Purchase and sale of securities

Special provisions apply where there is a purchase of securities by a person (called the first buyer) and then a subsequent sale by him, the result of which being that the interest becoming payable in respect of those securities is received by the first buyer.

These provisions vary according to whether the first buyer is a dealer in securities and whether he is entitled to exemptions. Dealers are discouraged from buying and selling securities in this way by reducing the amount which they can deduct for tax purposes in respect of the accrued dividend and, from 2 July 1997, requiring them to include all distributions from such securities in the calculation of trading profit. Market makers are exempt from these anti-bondwashing provisions, and they do not apply in the case of certain REPO agreements. Relief extends to all principal traders on LIFFE, in relation to hedging transactions and transactions entered into as a result of the exercise of options.

The charge will not generally arise if the period between the purchase and sale is more than six months or, in the case of most options, one month.

Interest payable under REPOs after 30 July 1997 does not trigger the above provisions.

The accrued income scheme (above) generally takes precedence over the above provisions, so that securities acquired by the first buyer after 27 February 1986 are covered by that scheme.

Law: ITTOIA 2005, s. 151–154; *Income Tax (Dealers in Securities) Regulations* 1992 (SI 1992/568)

See *British Tax Reporter* ¶341-550.

1395 Securities issued in tranches: additional returns

Where securities of a given class are not all issued at the same time, but in stages ('tranches') any additional return paid to the second or subsequent issue to compensate for the fact that interest is accruing on the earlier issue(s) is treated as interest.

Income Tax

The deemed interest in point will then be chargeable to tax in the same way as actual interest (see 1366).

Law: ITA 2007, s. 845

See *British Tax Reporter* ¶337-300.

1396 Annuities

An annuity is *always* an annual payment, but *not all* annual payments are annuities. Annuities usually comprise income bought from insurance companies.

Annuities are specifically included within the charge to tax in respect of annual payments (see 1366).

An annuity has been described as income purchased with a sum of money when the capital has gone and has ceased to exist, the principal having been converted into an annuity.

Debts paid by instalments are not annuities because liability for the capital sum remains.

A purchased life annuity (see 1898) is actuarially dissected into non-taxable capital and taxable income elements, the income element being received net of basic rate income tax; the mortality tables have been revised with effect where the first payment begins to accrue on or after 1 March 1992.

Annuities from FSAVC schemes

A flaw in the original legislation has meant that pensions paid as a result of free-standing additional voluntary contribution (FSAVC) retirement schemes could be taxable in the same manner as purchased annuities above: i.e. with a non-taxable capital element. However, the intention was that annuities from FSAVC schemes should be taxed in full in the same way as other pensions for which tax relief has been given for the contributions, and the legislation has accordingly been amended to achieve this. The amendment is deemed to have always applied.

Law: ITTOIA 2005, s. 717–724; *Lady Foley v Fletcher*(1858) 28 LJ Exch 100

See *British Tax Reporter* ¶342-150.

1398 Annual payments

The charge to tax as income on annual payments refers to any interest, annuity or other annual payment (see 1366). In general, those annual payments other than interest or annuities in point are those which are construed along the same lines as interest and annuities. However, decided cases indicate that annual payments must be:

- capable of continuing for more than one year;
- payable under a binding legal obligation;
- of an income nature; and
- subject to the provision of permitted benefits by charities (see 901), pure income profit in the hands of the recipient.

See *British Tax Reporter* ¶330-000.

1400 Discounts generally

Where a bill or promissory note is bought by someone before it matures, the price the buyer will pay for it will be less than the value of it on maturity. The profit the buyer will make on maturity is called a discount (see 1366) unless it is a trading profit.

In one case, the Court of Appeal said that trustees had acquired a promissory note before maturity at less than its face value. On maturity they had made a profit which was a plain case of a discount received on a discounting transaction. Whether a receipt was of an income or capital nature was dependent on the facts. In the present case, the only proper conclusion was that the excess received was of an income nature, and so it was chargeable under former Sch. D, Case III as a discount.

There are special rules for certain securities issued at a large discount (see 1401).

Law: *Ditchfield (HMIT) v Sharp* [1983] BTC 360

1401 Securities with significant discounts

Background

As part of the reform of provisions dealing with corporate debt or 'loan relationships' (see 3036), the income tax treatment of securities issued at a significant discount became divorced from that applicable for corporation tax. From 1996–97 a charge to income tax is made in respect of relevant discounted securities (RDSs) with the abolition altogether of provisions relating to deep discount securities and deep gain securities (including qualifying convertible securities and qualifying indexed securities).

Relevant discounted securities

An income tax charge arises on sale, exchange, gift, redemption, conversion or death by reference to the proceeds (or deemed proceeds) less acquisition cost and incidental costs. A RDS is, subject to specific exclusions, any security issued at a deep gain, i.e. more than one-half of one per cent of the redemption price for each year of the security's life (or 15 per cent for a security with a life of more than 30 years).

Income Tax

> ### Example
>
> Dickens plc issues a security on 1 January 2000 at 80 for redemption on 31 December 2004 at 100.
>
> Discount is $((100 - 80)/100) \times 100 = 20$.
>
> This is more than 0.5×5, so the security is an RDS.

Each of the following is expressly not an RDS:

- shares;
- unstripped gilts;
- life assurance policies;
- capital redemption policies;
- securities issued under the same prospectus where the preponderance of the securities so issued are not RDSs;
- 'excluded indexed securities', i.e. chargeable assets for which the redemption value is found by increasing its issue price in the same proportion as the change in value of specified assets or an index over them (excluding the RPI).

A loss may be set against other income for the tax year on the making of a claim within one year of 31 January next following the year of loss, i.e. some 22 months. Allowable incidental costs can increase a loss but cannot turn a profit into a loss. There are special rules for losses of trusts, pension funds and charities.

Market value is substituted on a transfer between connected persons, for a consideration not in money or money's worth or not at arm's length.

There are special rules for securities issued in separate tranches and for gilt strips.

The definition of a 'relevant discounted security' has been amended to block an avoidance device that relied on a weakness in the previous definition. The defining test now applies to the discount at maturity, and at any occasion on which the security may be redeemed (except for redemptions triggered by a default, which is unlikely to happen).

This applies to:

- any transfer of a security on or after 15 February 1999; or
- any occasion on or after 15 February 1999 on which the holder of a security becomes entitled to any payment on its redemption.

Deep discount securities

In relation to securities issued after 13 March 1984 and until 1996–97, where a company issued securities at a 'deep discount', an income tax charge arose when an investor disposed of or redeemed his securities.

Securities are issued at a 'deep' discount where the difference between the issue price and the redemption price exceeds $^1/_2$ per cent per year over the life of the security, or 15 per cent overall. For example, securities issued at 75 for redemption in ten years at 100 are deep discount securities. The issue price does not include any 'additional return' representing accrued interest in relation to securities issued in tranches (see also 1395). Zero coupon bonds issued as part of a bond-stripping exercise, usually at varying discounts and redeemable so as to effect the true interest and redemption payments, are generally deep discount securities.

The discount is treated as income accruing over the life of the security, so that an investor will be charged on the income deemed to accrue during his period of ownership. When a company issues deep discount securities, it must show on the certificate the income element deemed to accrue during each income period (i.e. each period for which interest is paid) from issue to redemption.

Where an investor acquires or disposes of securities midway through an income period, a straight-line apportionment is made to determine the accrued income at the date of acquisition or disposal.

Example 1

On 1 March 1996, Alicia acquires a holding of 1,000 deep discount securities issued by X Ltd at 45 for redemption at 100. She resells the holding on 1 November 2000. Interest is paid on the securities on 1 January and 1 July each year. According to the information supplied by X Ltd, the 'adjusted issue price' of the securities on various dates is as follows:

1 January 1996	58.25
1 July 1996	62.62
1 July 1999	90.18
1 January 2000	96.33

Accrued income price at acquisition = $58.25 + {}^1/_3 (62.62 - 58.25)$
  = 58.25 + 1.46
  = 59.71

Accrued income price at disposal = $90.18 + {}^2/_3 (96.33 - 90.18)$
  = 90.18 + 4.10
  = 94.28

Income element = 94.28 − 59.72
  = 34.56

Alicia will be charged to tax on the income element of 34.56, i.e. on £345.60 in respect of her 1,000 units.

It will be seen from the above example that the purchaser's acquisition and disposal prices are irrelevant with regard to the income tax charge. In addition to the calculation of the

Income Tax

income element, as above, a separate calculation must be made to determine whether a CGT liability also arises.

Example 2

The facts are as in example 1. Alicia acquired her holding in 1996 for £605 and sold it in 1999 for £925.

	£	£
Selling price		925
Less: acquisition cost	605	
income element	345	
		(950)
Capital loss		(25)

Any difference between the acquisition cost and the disposal or redemption proceeds which is greater or less than the accrued income is normally taxed as a capital gain or loss.

A company issuing deep discount securities may treat the accrued income as a charge on income incurred at the end of each income period (see 3147). Special provisions may apply in relation to securities held by a company associated with the issuer, so as to establish both a time and a method for determining the quantum of chargeable income deemed to arise in relation to such debts (see 3027).

Deep gain securities

Before 1996–97, a deep gain security was a security issued at a discount of more than $\frac{1}{2}$ per cent per year or more than 15 per cent overall but which incorporated at least one variable feature (e.g. variable coupon or uncertain redemption proceeds). Without special provision, many ordinary bonds carrying a full coupon and issued at a small discount may be capable of delivering an uplift of more than the specified percentage if they carry terms permitting bondholders to be repaid on the occurrence of events prejudicial to their interests (either by default or at their option: so-called 'events of default' or 'event risk' clauses); the discount was therefore, in many of these cases, calculated as if such a redemption were ignored. Where such securities were disposed of after 14 March 1989 the entire difference between acquisition cost and disposal or redemption proceeds was taxed as income.

Example

On 23 August 1991 a company issued a security at a price of £67. The security is redeemable on two different dates, 31 August 1997 or 30 May 2002. The redemption price on the first date is £69 and on the second date £78.

Applying the two alternative tests:

(1)   the amount payable on redemption on the 1997 date less 15% is £58.65;

the amount payable on redemption on the 2002 date less 15% is £66.30;

---

the issue price is not below these figures and so is not more than 15% below the redemption price;

(2) the issue price plus $\frac{1}{2}$% for each complete year to the 1997 date is:

£67 + (3% × 67) = £69.01

the issue price plus $\frac{1}{2}$% for each complete year to the 2002 date is:

£67 + (5% × 67) = £70.35

the redemption price exceeds the above figure for the 2002 date so that there is a deep gain.

Note: the discount in this example would not result in the security being a deep discount security.

Special provisions may apply in relation to securities held by a company associated with the issuer, so as to establish both a time and a method for determining the quantum of chargeable income deemed to arise in relation to such debts (see 3027).

Excluded from the rules for deep gain securities are the following.

(1) *Qualifying convertible securities* (former FA 1990, Sch. 10). These are securities issued after 9 June 1989 which:

    (a)   are convertible into the ordinary share capital of the issuing company;

    (b)   provide the investor with the option of 'putting' the bond back to the issuer; and

    (c)   meet certain other qualifying conditions.

The 'put' premium is separated into annual income components taxable on the investor.

(2) *Qualifying indexed securities*. These are indexed securities meeting detailed qualifying conditions. Such securities may be linked to a published general index (e.g. the RPI) or, for quoted securities, an index of shares quoted on a recognised stock exchange (e.g. FT-SE 100). They may incorporate nominal floors to their redemption value but HMRC object to a formula being used to restrict the impact of the index on the interest paid; it is also HMRC's view that the recognised stock exchange whose published index is used in determining the amount payable on redemption should also be the stock exchange on which the security is quoted.

Law: FA 1999, s. 65; former ICTA 1988, Sch. 4; former FA 1989, Sch. 11

Website: www.hmrc.gov.uk/bulletins/index.htm

See *British Tax Reporter* ¶337-000.

1402   Investment in public funds

From 1996–97 to 2004–05, all investments in public funds and profits from securities bearing interest payable out of the public revenue of the UK or Northern Ireland were charged under Sch. D, Case III. The rules relating to the deduction of tax in respect of public revenue dividends (i.e. any income paid in respect of securities which is paid out of the UK public revenue except interest on local authority stock) are in ITA 2007, Pt. 15, Ch. 5: in particular, s. 892, which provides that:

> 'The person by or through whom the payment is made must, on making the payment, deduct from it a sum representing income tax on it at the savings rate in force for the tax year in which it is made.'

Law: ITA 2007, Pt. 15, Ch. 5

See *British Tax Reporter* ¶344-450.

1404   Maintenance receivable on separation and divorce

Following separation or divorce, maintenance payment arrangements are often made between the spouses. Most maintenance payments are periodical payments which would fall to be taxed in the same way as other annual payments (see 1398). However, there are special rules for certain types of payment.

Voluntary payments have never been taxable for the recipient.

Legally binding payments, whether under a court order or an agreement, are not taxable if they fall due after 14 March 1988 unless they are made in pursuance of 'existing obligations' at that date. From 6 April 2000, this is also the case in relation to arrangements made prior to 15 March 1988.

Law: ITTOIA 2005, s. 727(1); *Morley-Clarke v Jones (HMIT)*[1985] BTC 460

See *British Tax Reporter* ¶355-650.

1406   Patent royalties

Patent royalties may be annual payments (see 1398) as well as trade or professional receipts. UK patents only last 20 years and are, therefore, wasting assets (see 6158).

A UK resident who sells patent rights for a capital sum is charged to income tax on the receipt on the net proceeds. An election may be made either for such a sum to be chargeable only in the period of receipt (e.g. where the sale is at a loss) or for spreading of the sum over six years. Under self-assessment, such an election must be made to HMRC in writing before the first anniversary of 31 January following the tax year of receipt or payment. Previously, it had to be made within two years of the chargeable period in which the amount was received or paid, as the case might be.

A non-UK resident who sells UK rights for a capital sum is charged to income tax, but the purchaser will deduct tax from the payment and account for it to HMRC (see 1683); this is subject to relief under any double taxation agreement (see 1780).

Law: ITTOIA 2005, s. 587–590; *Patents Act* 1977, s. 25

See *British Tax Reporter* ¶343-300.

1408 'Tax-free' arrangements for making annual payments

Where an 'annual payment' (see 1398) is expressed to be made free of tax it is in fact made after tax where a deduction should have been made (see 1368).

The usual way of clarifying the situation is to use the formula 'the payment of such an amount as shall, after the deduction of basic rate income tax for the time being in force, bear the sum of £x p.a. in the payee's hands'. Such a formula is typical, for example, in deeds of covenant.

If the payee is liable to the higher rate of tax he will bear this without recourse to the payer, and if the payee is not liable to income tax he can claim repayment without having to account to the payer for the tax reclaimed. The gross amount of the payment will vary only with a variation in the rate of basic rate tax (see 50).

Annuities under wills

An arrangement to pay an 'annuity' (see 1396) free of tax constitutes an arrangement to pay an amount which, after basic rate tax has been deducted from it, leaves the desired amount in the hands of the payee. The payee is then liable for any higher rate tax which may be due on the payment. Where a payment under a will is directed to be paid free of tax, the direction is treated as one to pay an amount which leaves the amount directed to be paid to the payee, in the payee's hands, after basic rate tax has been deducted from it. In addition, for the payment to be tax-free, the payee will have to be indemnified for any excess tax that he may have to bear because he is a higher rate taxpayer.

Thus, an arrangement to pay an annuity free of tax is void, but this does not apply to a direction under a will though the effect is essentially the same for a basic rate taxpayer.

Law: TMA 1970, s. 106(2); *Re Pettit* [1922] 2 Ch 765

1410 Child Trust Fund

All children born since September 2002 have received an initial voucher worth at least £250, with those from low-income families receiving an additional £250 paid directly into their accounts, making £500 in total. However, as announced on 24 May 2010, government contributions to CTFs will be reduced to a basic £50 from August 2010. Contributions will cease completely from 1 January 2011.

Since April 2010, the government have been contributing £100 every year to the CTF accounts of all disabled children, with severely disabled children receiving £200 per year. The payments started in April 2010 for children in receipt of Disability Living Allowance at any point during the 2009–10 tax year. As noted above, all government contributions to CTFs will cease from 1 January 2011.

A further universal payment of £250 has formerly been made to the child at age seven, with children from low-income families receiving £500. However, as announced on 24 May 2010, such contributions ceased with effect from August 2010.

With regards to tax, there will be no tax to pay on the income or gains arising on the monies in the account, provided the person entitled to the fund is UK resident at the time the fund is paid out. This makes CTFs a particularly attractive and tax-efficient way of saving for parents and carers wondering how they will ever be able to afford seemingly ever-increasing educational fees.

There are three types of CTF account to choose from. Before deciding on the type of account to open, parents will need to consider their attitude towards risk and return, for example, whether they want to put their child's money in a very safe account, where there will not be a risk but the return on the money might not be so high, or whether they might take a small risk to try and get a higher return. The three main types of CTF account are as follows:

(1) savings accounts;

(2) accounts that invest in shares; and

(3) stakeholder CTF accounts.

Stakeholder accounts are the government's preferred way of saving. The following table shows the key differences between the two:

Stakeholder	Non-stakeholder
Must have exposure to shares	Need not be exposed to shares
Some investments are prohibited (see below)	Almost unrestricted investment choice
Maximum provider charge is 1.5% of the account's value per year	No maximum provider charge
Minimum contribution not exceeding £10	Minimum contribution may be more or less than £10
The account must provide a 'lifestyling' facility (see below)	'Lifestyling' is not compulsory

Both types of account have the following features in common:

- only children born on or after 1 September 2002 are eligible;
- all payments are a gift to the child and cannot be reclaimed;
- the money can only be paid out to the child and is locked in until they are 18;
- tax-efficient growth; and
- up to £1,200 per year may be paid into each account.

A stakeholder account must meet certain requirements, in particular:

- the account must include at least some exposure to equities;
- the underlying investments must represent a mixture of assets which is both appropriate and suitable for long-term savings for a child;
- any underlying investments held directly (rather than indirectly – for example through a collective investment scheme) for the CTF account must not be, or include:

  - investment trust shares or securities;
  - collective investment scheme shares, if these are dual priced;
  - with-profits endowment policies or rights in contracts of insurance whose value is linked to shares in a dual-priced fund;
  - company shares;
  - company securities whose value could fall below 80 per cent of their purchase price;
  - cash in bank or building society deposit or share accounts whose interest rate is more than one per cent below the Bank of England base rate; and
  - depositary interests in any of the above.

- it must be possible, starting no later than the child's 13th birthday, to gradually move the underlying investments into lower risk assets (such as cash and government bonds) to reduce the chance of losses. This is commonly referred to as 'lifestyling';
- the minimum payment amount which the CTF account manager will accept must not be more than £10; and
- the total regular charges which can be made by the CTF account manager must not be more than 1.5 per cent a year.

Assuming investment growth of seven per cent per annum (and annual charges of 1.5 per cent) a monthly investment of £25 would produce a payout at age 18 of £9,761. A £100 per month investment on similar terms would yield £37,078. Although stakeholder CTF accounts must meet certain government requirements, this does not of course mean that they will be suitable for everyone, nor that they are guaranteed to perform well.

The registered contact, i.e. the person who opens a CTF account for a child, will be responsible for managing the account for the child. This includes keeping account statements safe, letting the relevant people know if there is a change of address, and changing the account or provider, depending on the child's best interests. The registered contact, and the child, when he or she has turned 16, can change account or CTF provider at any time. The account stops being a CTF account on the child's 18th birthday. The young adult, then has full access to the money in the account and can use it how he or she thinks best. It's important to consider the best ways to use the money and even to seek advice on the best ways to invest, if this is what the child chooses to do.

Law: *Child Trust Funds (Amendment No. 2) Regulations* 2010 (SI 2010/836); *Child Trust Funds (Amendment) Regulations* 2010 (SI 2010/582); *Child Trust Funds (Amendment) Regulations* 2009 (SI 2009/475); *Child Trust Funds (Amendment No. 2) Regulations* 2009 (SI 2009/694); *Child Trust Funds (Amendment No. 3) Regulations* 2006 (SI 2006/3195)

Source: www.childtrustfund.gov.uk

Website: www.hmrc.gov.uk/ria/annex-b-impact-assessment.pdf

TRANSACTIONS IN SECURITIES: ANTI-AVOIDANCE

1416   Introduction

ITA 2007, Pt. 13, Ch. 1 contains anti-avoidance rules that apply to certain transactions in securities. Before they were rewritten for income tax purposes in ITA 2007, the rules for both income tax and corporation tax were in ICTA 1988, s. 703–709.

These provisions on transactions in securities are a very wide-ranging set of anti-avoidance rules. They originated, in 1960, as a response to a fairly closely defined group of tax avoidance devices which went under the name of 'dividend-stripping'.

Because of other changes in tax law, primarily the introduction of corporation tax in 1965, the dividend-stripping schemes of the 1950s would not now work in any event. In its basic form, as exemplified by the case of *Griffiths v JP Harrison (Watford) Ltd* [1963] AC 1, the scheme consisted of purchasing a company which was pregnant with undistributed profit, and then declaring a large dividend, the net amount of which was roughly equal to the total profit available for distribution. The company – minus its profits – was then sold at a loss. The dealer set this loss against the dividend income, and was therefore entitled to a repayment of the tax notionally deducted when the dividend was paid, so effectively making a profit on the transactions equal to the amount of that tax.

A series of statutory measures designed to prevent tax being avoided in this way were countered by more sophisticated schemes. Finally, what is now ITA 2007, Pt. 13, Ch. 1 was enacted, originally as FA 1960, s. 28, 29 and 43(4).

Where the legislation does apply, the income tax advantage is cancelled. This may be by assessment, by denying the right to a repayment, by requiring the return of a repayment already made, or by a recalculation of profits, gains, or a liability to tax.

Law: ITA 2007, Pt. 13, Ch. 1; *Griffiths v JP Harrison (Watford) Ltd*[1963] AC 1

See *British Tax Reporter* ¶339-300.

1420   The 'prescribed circumstances'

If ITA 2007, Pt. 13, Ch. 1 is to apply to cancel an income tax advantage, three conditions must be met:

(1)   There must be a transaction in securities or more than one such transaction.

(2)   A person must have obtained, or must be in a position to obtain, an income tax advantage in consequence of the transaction or transactions.

(3)   One or more of the following circumstances must be present.

   (a)   Circumstance A: the person receives an abnormal amount by way of dividend and the amount received is used for exemptions or reliefs;
   (b)   Circumstance B (repealed for transactions taking place after 5 April 2008): the person becomes entitled to a deduction in computing profits or gains because of a fall in value of the securities;
   (c)   Circumstance C: a person who is the other party to certain similar transactions receives in a tax-free form a sum representing company assets, future receipts or trading stock;
   (d)   Circumstance D: in connection with a distribution made by certain companies, the person receives in a tax-free form a sum representing company assets, future receipts or trading stock;
   (e)   Circumstance E: in connection with certain transactions, the person receives share capital in a tax-free way, and that capital is redeemed.

Even if the above three conditions are met, the legislation will not apply to cancel the income tax advantage if the person can show:

● that the transaction or transactions were carried out for genuine commercial reasons or in the ordinary course of making investments; and
● that the obtaining of an income tax advantage was not the main object of the transaction (or, where there is more than one transaction, of any of them).

Law: ITA 2007, s. 684

See *British Tax Reporter* ¶339-360.

1422   Meaning of 'tax advantage'

The legislation does not apply unless the taxpayer is in a position to obtain, or has obtained, an 'income tax advantage' in consequence of the transaction in securities. Even if such an advantage has been obtained, there will be no cancellation of it if the taxpayer can show that the transaction or transactions were effected for genuine commercial reasons or in the ordinary course of making investments, and that the income tax advantage was not a main object of the transaction or transactions.

In relation to the potential income charge to cancel a tax advantage from a transaction in securities (see 1416), a tax advantage means:

- a 'relief' (including a tax credit), or increased relief, from tax;
- a repayment or increased repayment, of income tax; or
- the avoidance or reduction of a charge to income tax or an assessment to income tax or the avoidance of a possible assessment thereto.

HMRC have to show that a tax advantage has been obtained. It is then for the taxpayer to show that obtaining a tax advantage was not a main object of the transaction.

The charge does not apply to any transaction in securities where the taxpayer shows first that it was carried out for bona fide commercial reasons and that obtaining a tax advantage was not the main object of the transaction or one of them. An advance clearance procedure exists (see 1426).

Law: ITA 2007, s. 683; *Grogan v R & C Commrs* [2009] TC 00187; *Marwood Homes Ltd v IR Commrs* (1996) Sp C 106; *IR Commrs v Universities Superannuation Scheme Ltd* [1997] BTC 3

Website: www.hmrc.gov.uk/bulletins/index.htm

See *British Tax Reporter* ¶339-570.

1424   Cancellation of tax advantage

Once it is shown that a transaction in securities resulted in an unacceptable tax advantage (see 1416), HMRC may counteract the advantage by:

- raising a tax assessment;
- nullifying a right to repayment of tax;
- requiring the return of a repayment already made;
- computing or recomputing profits or gains or a liability to tax,

on such basis as HMRC may specify by notice.

Law: ITA 2007, s. 698

See *British Tax Reporter* ¶340-350.

1425   Appeals

A person on whom a counteraction notice has been served may appeal on the grounds that:

(a)   s. 684 (person liable to counteraction of income tax advantage) does not apply to the person in respect of the transaction or transactions in question; or

(b)   the adjustments directed to be made are inappropriate.

An appeal may be made only by giving notice to the Commissioners for Her Majesty's Revenue and Customs within 30 days of the service of the counteraction notice. On an appeal, the tribunal may affirm, vary or cancel the counteraction notice, or affirm, vary or quash an assessment made in accordance with the notice.

Law: ITA 2007, s. 705

See *British Tax Reporter* ¶340-290.

1426   Clearance procedure: tax advantage from transactions in securities

A procedure exists for advance clearance of transactions in which there is a potential tax advantage which may be challenged by HMRC (see 1416). Where the taxpayer provides HMRC with details of the transactions concerned, HMRC must either give or refuse clearance, or request further details, within 30 days.

HMRC will only refuse clearance where they would actually take action to cancel the tax advantage.

Law: ITA 2007, s. 701

See *British Tax Reporter* ¶340-350.

Income Tax

PROFITS OF AN INCOME NATURE NOT CHARGED ELSEWHERE

1430   Charge on miscellaneous income

When the *Income Tax (Trading and Other Income) Act* 2005 came into force on 6 April 2005 it swept away, at least for income tax purposes, the schedular system which had applied with modifications since 1803. As a consequence, many of the categories of 'annual profits or gains' which were specifically to be charged under Sch. D Case VI, are now to be charged under a particular Part of ITTOIA 2005.

For example, trading receipts received after the permanent cessation of the trade were formerly charged to income tax under Case VI by virtue of ICTA 1988, s. 103(1). They are now charged under ITTOIA 2005, Pt. 2, Ch. 18 by virtue of s. 242.

Similarly, income from furnished lettings came within Case VI but is now chargeable as property income under ITTOIA 2005, Pt. 3, along with income which was previously assessed under Sch. A.

The modern equivalent of Case VI is ITTOIA 2005, Pt. 5. This contains a number of chapters which bring into charge specific sources of income which are not otherwise chargeable under Pt. 2 as trading income, Pt. 3 as property income, Pt. 4 as savings income or ITEPA 2003 as employment income.

Law: ITTOIA 2005, Pt. 5; *Trustees of Earl Haig v IR Commrs* (1939) 22 TC 725; *Attorney-General v Black* (1871) LR 6 Exch 308

See *British Tax Reporter* ¶129-000.

LIFE POLICIES, LIFE ANNUITIES AND CAPITAL REDEMPTION POLICIES

1460   Gains on life assurance policies, investment bonds, etc.

Gains on certain life assurance policies, life annuity contracts and capital redemption policies are subject to higher rate tax as income of an individual investor. These include 'securitised' or 'second-hand' life policies or contracts (in relation to most assignments after 25 June 1982) and 'investment bonds'.

See further 1465ff.

See *British Tax Reporter* ¶310-100.

1465   Chargeable events

Subject to the matters below, the charge (see 1460) generally arises on:

- the death of the person whose life is insured;
- the maturity of the policy;
- the surrender of rights;
- the assignment of rights for money or money's worth; or
- the annual excess of withdrawals over a permitted five per cent annual level,

as far as is relevant to the type of investment in point.

Policies taken out before 20 March 1968 are exempt, as are 'qualifying' policies (see 1880) once the premiums have been paid for ten years or, if less, three-quarters of the term for which the policy is to run (in the case of an endowment policy). Where changes are made to a qualifying policy, the exemption may be lost. However, by concession, there will be no tax charge on benefits arising on subsequent maturity or surrender, provided a number of specific circumstances apply. It is uneconomical for insurers to collect premiums on policies made at least 20 years ago because of the small sums involved, and they can now stop collecting these amounts without loss of tax exemption to policy holders.

'Free gifts' provided to investors after 6 December 1993 are ignored if they cost no more than £30. In certain circumstances, a notional tax credit is given when an insurance company has suffered tax, as a proxy for the policy holder, on the underlying gains and income accruing during the term of a policy.

The gain so charged is treated as part of the individual's total income for the purposes of higher rate tax. Top-slicing relief is available (see 1883). If the rights are held by personal representatives the amount of the gain so charged is part of the aggregate income of the deceased.

Law: ITTOIA 2005, s. 473–526

Source: ESC A96, *Old life insurance policies: insurer stopping collection of premiums*; ESC B42, *'Free gifts' and insurance contracts*

See *British Tax Reporter* ¶311-350.

1470   Guaranteed income bonds

The tax treatment of payments to policy holders under certain life insurance policies, including guaranteed income bonds providing a series of regular payments, was clarified in 1997: the payments are dealt with under the special rules for life assurance policies (see 1465), rather than as interest or annual payments. The clarification is fully retrospective and reflects the insurance industry's previous practice.

Law: ITTOIA 2005, s. 504(1)–(4), (7)

See *British Tax Reporter* ¶702-850.

1475   Deceased or non-resident settlors

With effect generally from 6 April 1998, provisions have been introduced to close a perceived loophole when a life assurance policy is held in a UK or foreign trust and the settlor is either dead or non-resident. A gain on a life assurance, etc. policy chargeable as

Income Tax

outlined at 1465 can be taxed as income of UK trustees. The new provisions ensure that, if the policy is held in a foreign trust or similar vehicle, the gain may be taxed as income of a UK resident, to the extent that he receives a benefit. If the gain is taxable on the settlor, no further charge arises on the trustees or beneficiaries.

Law: ITTOIA 2005, s. 461–533

See *British Tax Reporter* ¶355-800.

1480   Overseas life assurance business

A gain on a capital redemption or life assurance policy which forms part of the overseas life assurance business (OLAB) of a UK insurer will be taxed at an individual's marginal rate, rather than at the difference between the basic rate and the marginal rate. Such policies can only be acquired by non-residents, and the insurer is not taxable on income and gains in the OLAB fund. Accordingly, where the policy holder becomes resident in the UK and a 'chargeable event' (see 1465) has happened after he becomes resident and after 16 March 1988, no credit for basic rate tax will be available. This provision primarily targets the sale of such policies to UK expatriates prior to their return to the UK.

Law: ITTOIA 2005, s. 474–476, Sch. 2, para. 113; FA 1998, s. 88

See *British Tax Reporter* ¶310-750.

1482   Non-resident life assurance policyholders

To bring the treatment of non-residents with life assurance policies more into line with the treatment of non-residents with other forms of income, by concession:

- the provisions of former statement of practice 11/80 (withdrawn from 5 April 1999) are extended so that tax is not due on gains where an individual or a company is not UK-resident in the relevant period;
- in certain circumstances, UK insurers do not have to send HMRC information about gains made by non-resident policyholders; and
- an individual who comes to the UK to take up permanent residence or to stay for at least two years who needs to change the terms of a personal portfolio bond to take advantage of transitional relief will have two years in which to do so.

The concessionary treatment applies from 6 April 1999.

Source: ESC B53; former SP 11/80, *Liability under Chapter II of Part XIII ICTA 1988, on gains arising on life and capital redemption policies and life annuities*

See *British Tax Reporter* ¶310-750.

1485   Personal portfolio bonds

Following a 1997 decision, a charge to tax has been imposed on 'personal portfolio bonds'. Such a bond is a policy of life assurance where the assets backing the policy and giving rise to the benefits under the policy are personal to the individual policy holder, who may have significant control over those assets. Such policies retain many of the benefits of direct investment, while the policy holder is able to defer taxation of investment income and gains by choosing the date of surrender, or to escape taxation altogether by becoming non-resident before the policy is surrendered.

Law: ITTOIA 2005, 526(1)–(2); FA 1998, s. 89; *Personal Portfolio Bonds (Tax) Regulations* 1999 (SI 1999/1029); *IR Commrs v Willoughby* [1997] BTC 393

See *British Tax Reporter* ¶311-900.

1490   Information

Insurance companies have three months within which to supply details of chargeable events (see 1465) to HMRC. Non-UK life insurers selling into the UK are now required to have a UK tax representative to provide such information.

Law: ITTOIA 2005; FA 1998, s. 87; ICTA 1988, s. 552–552B (repealed in part); *Life Assurance and Other Policies (Keeping of Information and Duties of Insurers) Regulations* 1997 (SI 1997/265); *Overseas Insurers (Tax Representatives) Regulations* 1999 (SI 1999/881)

1495   Accident insurance policies

HMRC do not regard accident insurance policies as giving rise to 'taxable gains' (see 1465) if they:

- afford protection against the risk of dying only if death is as a result of an accident; and
- have no investment content; and
- do not acquire a surrender value (other than one equal to a proportion of the premium paid which is refundable if the policy is terminated early or in other circumstances).

An accident insurance policy which provides cover against disablement only (not death) as a result of an accident is not a policy of life insurance and so is unaffected. Policy benefits may otherwise be chargeable to tax, for example as receipts of a trade or profession; any such charge is unaffected.

Source: SP 6/92, *Accident insurance policies: chargeable events and gains on policies of life insurance*

See *British Tax Reporter* ¶514-750.

FOREIGN INCOME AND DOUBLE TAXATION

1550   Introduction to foreign income

The tax treatment of income derived from overseas sources, or of income arising in the UK to someone from abroad, often depends on whether the person liable to tax is resident, ordinarily resident or domiciled in the UK. These terms are explained in more detail in 213, 216, 219ff. Double tax relief (see 1780ff.) might apply in cases of income having a foreign source and in cases of dual residence, where the UK and another jurisdiction both claim taxing rights under their domestic fiscal regimes.

Non-resident partners

In the case of a partnership, under self-assessment (i.e. from 1994–95 for trades, etc. set up and commenced after 5 April 1994, and from 1997–98 for other trades, etc.), a non-resident's share of partnership profits is treated as arising from a trade carried on in the UK by the non-resident partner alone. Equivalent provisions for non-resident companies which are members of partnerships ensure that corporate partners only pay UK tax on their share of partnership profits arising in the UK. The non-resident company's share is treated as arising from a trade carried on by it through a UK branch or agency.

Law: ITTOIA 2005, s. 857–858

Source: HMRC6: *Residence, domicile and the remittance basis*

Website: www.hmrc.gov.uk/leaflets/c9.htm

See *British Tax Reporter* ¶288-500.

EMPLOYEES' FOREIGN INCOME

1560   The charge to tax on foreign income

In general, whether income arising from an employment is subject to tax depends upon the 'residence' (see 213) and 'ordinary residence' of the taxpayer (see 1572). 'Domicile' is important in so far as emoluments may then become foreign emoluments eligible for relief (see 1570).

The place of performance of duties is also critical. For a discussion of incidental duties, see 1572. Where duties are ordinarily performed in the UK, emoluments during any absence from employment are related to UK duties unless, but for that absence, they would have been emoluments for duties performed outside the UK; an airline pilot's rest days were not attributable to duties performed outside the UK – in order to bring himself within the exception, the taxpayer would have to show that had he worked on those days his actual duties would have been performed outside the UK and it did not matter that most of his time was spent on duties abroad.

Resident and ordinarily resident

Except in relation to such foreign emoluments as are mentioned above, any person who is resident and ordinarily resident in the UK is liable to income tax on the whole of his earnings wherever earned and irrespective of whether they are remitted to the UK. The taxpayer may be entitled to a special deduction where his duties are carried out wholly or partly outside the UK (see below) and in many cases double taxation relief will apply (see 1780ff.).

Resident but not ordinarily resident

An employee resident but not ordinarily resident in the UK is liable to tax on earnings from duties performed in the UK, under ITEPA 2003, s. 25 and 26. There was formerly a deduction for foreign emoluments (see below).

The relative levels of the emoluments received here and abroad may not reflect the relative duties performed here and abroad. The split may be made simply to suit the employee's convenience and there may be scope for tax planning in this area. He may, therefore, be remitting to the UK emoluments received abroad but attributable to the UK duties. Each case must be studied on its facts.

HMRC will accept that the total emoluments may be apportioned between UK and overseas duties on the basis of working days, unless there are special circumstances.

Not resident

An employee who is not resident in the UK is only liable to tax on earnings from duties performed in the UK, under ITEPA 2003, s. 27.

Basis of charge

Emoluments are taxed in the year in which they are received, rather than earned. However, liability to the charge depends on residence and/or ordinary residence in the tax year in which the emoluments are earned.

Example 1

A bonus of £5,000 earned in 2008–09 when the employee was resident and ordinarily resident in the UK is chargeable to UK income tax and will be assessed for 2009–10 when it is received even if, following a move abroad, the employee is not resident in 2009–10.

Income Tax

Example 2

In the converse situation, an overseas resident who comes to work in the UK and is resident here in 2009–10 is not chargeable on a bonus received in 2009–10 but earned in 2008–09 when he was not resident here.

The charge to income tax remains fundamentally the same, with the same available deductions (see below).

Available deductions

There is a 100 per cent deduction for seafarers' earnings derived from duties performed abroad where there is a 'qualifying period' consisting of at least 365 days (see 1567).

Other deductions, in respect of expenses, etc. are generally available in the same way irrespective of residence, ordinary residence or domicile (see 1990).

Law: ITEPA 2003, s. 38; *Langley v R & C Commrs* (2007) Sp C 642; *Leonard v Blanchard (HMIT)* [1993] BTC 138

Source: SP 1/09, *Employees resident but not ordinarily resident in the UK: general earnings chargeable under sections 15 and 26 Income Tax (Earnings and Pensions) Act 2003 (ITEPA) and application of the mixed fund rule under sections 809Q onwards of the Income Tax Act 2007 (ITA)*; HMRC6: *Residence, domicile and the remittance basis*

Website: www.hmrc.gov.uk/leaflets/c9.htm

See *British Tax Reporter* ¶111-150.

1567 Foreign earnings deduction for seafarers

The 100 per cent deduction in determining the foreign earnings which are brought into charge to income tax (see 1560) was withdrawn for all office holders, and for all employees except seafarers, with effect from 17 March 1998. The definition of seafarers has also been clarified to exclude explicitly those employed on offshore installations for oil or gas exploration or extraction. *Finance Act* 2004 includes a measure to redefine 'offshore installation' to ensure that from 6 April 2004, FED remains available only to the parts of the shipping sector for whom it was intended.

The foreign earnings deduction is thus unavailable to non-seafarers for emoluments attributable to 'qualifying periods' (see below) beginning on or after 17 March 1998, or to emoluments attributable to qualifying periods beginning before that date but received thereafter. The deduction remains available for emoluments attributable to qualifying periods beginning before 17 March 1998 and received before that date. For such relief, there must still be a full qualifying period, but part of it can fall after that date.

The deduction is calculated by reference to emoluments for the qualifying period *after* allowing such deductions as pension contributions, expenses and capital allowances.

To qualify for the 100 per cent deduction, the duties of the employment must be:

- performed wholly or partly outside the UK; and
- performed in the course of a qualifying period consisting of at least 365 days, falling wholly or partly in any tax year.

For this purpose, seamen (and, before the deduction's withdrawal, aircrew) are generally treated as performing their duties abroad where the voyage (or journey) or any part of it begins or ends outside the UK; this applies notwithstanding the provision which treats such duties as performed in the UK for most purposes (see 1572). The days which a seafarer can spend in the UK as part of a qualifying period of absence are 183 days or one-half of the total days.

From 6 April 2011, the seafarers' earnings deduction is extended so that seafarers resident in the EU or EEA can also claim the deduction on their earnings as a seafarer where those earnings are liable to UK income tax.

Where duties of the employment are performed partly outside the UK, the earnings subject to the deduction are determined on a reasonable basis (see also 1578).

The European Commission has requested the UK to change its income tax provisions that allow a tax deduction for the earnings of seafarers who are resident in the UK but do not allow the same deduction for seafarers who are not resident in the UK.

Where a period of leave immediately follows a qualifying period, the earnings attributable to that leave generally qualify for the 100 per cent deduction (such period not being part of a qualifying period: see below).

A 'qualifying period'

A 'qualifying period' is a period of consecutive days which consists of days of absence from the UK. The qualifying period need not coincide with a complete tax year in order to take advantage of the deduction.

The date of departure from the UK counts as a day of absence (the test being whether an individual is present in the UK at midnight on a particular day); the date of arrival does not. Days spent abroad on holiday can be included towards the 365-day period.

For seafarers who have previously been resident in the UK and who return to the UK following a period of absence abroad during which they have not been resident or ordinarily resident in the UK, such absences are not taken into account when calculating the qualifying period.

Income Tax

Law: FA 2004, s. 136; ITEPA 2003, s. 378; FA 1998, s. 63; *Spowage v R & C Commrs* [2009] TC 00110; *Torr v R & C Commrs and related appeals*(2008) Sp C 679; *Robins (HMIT) v Durkin* [1988] BTC 195

Source: SP 18/91

Website: www.hmrc.gov.uk/bulletins/index.htm

See *British Tax Reporter* ¶459-000.

1570   Foreign emoluments

A person may be entitled to a deduction from his earnings where the earnings from his employment are 'foreign emoluments'. Foreign emoluments are the earnings of a person who is:

- not 'domiciled' (see 219) in the UK, and
- the earnings are derived from an office or employment which is with an employer who is not 'resident' (see 213, 214) in the UK or the Republic of Ireland.

The position of non-UK domiciles who are not in receipt of foreign emoluments is the same as that for UK domiciles, i.e. the employee may be entitled to the 100 per cent deduction.

Foreign emoluments of an employee resident and ordinarily resident in the UK are charged to tax only on the value of the earnings remitted to the UK if the duties are performed wholly outside the UK. An employee in receipt of foreign emoluments who is resident but not ordinarily resident in the UK and whose duties are performed wholly or partly abroad is liable to tax on the overseas earnings only to the extent remitted to the UK (see 1560). A person in receipt of foreign emoluments who is not resident in the UK is not liable to tax on his earnings except upon the earnings of duties performed in the UK (see 1560).

For provisions preventing the loading of earnings where an individual has more than one job, see 1578.

Law: ITEPA 2003, s. 378

Source: HMRC6: *Residence, domicile and the remittance basis*

Website: www.hmrc.gov.uk/leaflets/c9.htm

See *British Tax Reporter* ¶406-550.

1572   Incidental duties: employments partly overseas

Duties performed in the UK which are merely incidental to duties performed abroad are treated as if they were performed abroad.

For the purpose of the 100 per cent deduction for seafarers (see 1567), incidental duties performed abroad are treated as performed in the UK where the duties of the employment are in substance performed in the UK.

Whether duties performed in the UK are 'incidental duties' is a question of fact. It is the nature of the duties which is the most significant factor, but the time spent on such duties is also a factor to be taken into account.

The following duties appear to be regarded as incidental or not incidental to duties performed abroad (see booklet HMRC6).

Not incidental	Incidental
(1) *Directors' meetings* A company director, usually working abroad, attends directors' meetings in the UK. (2) *Three months or more* Duties performed for an aggregate period of three months or more.	(1) *Overseas representative* An overseas representative of a UK employer comes to the UK to report to the employer or receive fresh instructions. (2) *Training* An overseas employee visiting the UK for a training period not exceeding three months in a year and where no productive work is done by him in that time.

Law: ITEPA 2003, s. 39(1), (2), 341(6), (7), 376(4), (5); *Robson v Dixon (HMIT)* [1972] 1 WLR 1493

Source: HMRC6: *Residence, domicile and the remittance basis*

Website: www.hmrc.gov.uk/leaflets/c9.htm

See *British Tax Reporter* ¶406-600.

1574   Travel expenses: employees' overseas duties

Travelling expenses incurred by an employee necessarily in the performance of his duties may be deducted in computing his assessable income (see 1990ff.). It is sometimes difficult to establish that the expenses have been necessarily incurred (see 1992).

Income Tax

425

Expenses incurred in connection with certain overseas duties – either travel to take up a foreign employment with duties wholly overseas (and returning to the UK at the end of that employment), board and lodging while there or in travelling between an employment whose duties are at least partly overseas and any other employment – are eligible for relief if the employee is:

- resident and ordinarily resident in the UK (see 213, 216); and
- the earnings are not foreign emoluments (see 1570).

Expenses are apportioned where travel is partly for another purpose.

Where an employer provides travel facilities for an employee or reimburses an employee the cost of travel, the employee is entitled to a deduction of so much of the cost of the travel facilities or sum reimbursed as falls to be treated as his emoluments.

This rule applies to:

- travel between any place in the UK and the place of performance of any of those duties outside the UK (and any return journey) by the spouse or any child of the employee;
- travel from any place in the UK to the place of performance of any of those duties (and any return journey) by an employee whose duties are performed partly outside the UK and can only be performed outside the UK; and
- travel from the place of performance of any duties of an office or employment outside the UK to any place in the UK (and any return journey) by an employee absent from the UK performing the duties of an office or employment which can only be performed outside the UK.

Similar provisions apply with regard to the travel expenses of non-UK domiciled employees.

Before the travel expenses of the spouse or any child of the employee can attract the beneficial treatment, further conditions need to be met.

Travel expenses of spouse and children

The travelling expenses of the spouse or any child of a resident and ordinarily resident employee from and to the UK are allowable as a deduction, in certain cases, from the emoluments of the employee where the employee is absent from the UK for a continuous period of at least 60 days for the purpose of performing the duties of one or more employments and:

- the spouse or any child of the employee accompanies him at the beginning of the period of absence; or
- visits him during that period.

The child must be aged under 18 at the beginning of the outward journey. Similar deductions are allowed where the employee visits his spouse or any child of his in the UK.

These provisions apply for a maximum of two outward and two return journeys by the same person in any tax year.

Similar provisions apply to the travel expenses of the spouse and any child of an employee not domiciled in the UK.

Law: ITEPA 2003, s. 341, 342, 373, 374

Source: HMRC6: *Residence, domicile and the remittance basis*; IR 490, *Employee travel. A tax and NICs guide for employers*

Website: www.hmrc.gov.uk/leaflets/c9.htm

See *British Tax Reporter* ¶455-580.

1578 More than one job: tax avoidance through overseas earnings

Special provisions apply where the employee has two or more employments. These provisions are largely designed to prevent the 'loading' of earnings onto the overseas employment in order to avoid tax.

Where the duties of an employment and any associated employment (see below) are wholly performed abroad, the deductions referred to above will apply to all the earnings of the employment.

The 100 per cent deduction for seafarers and the deduction relating to 'foreign emoluments' (see 1567, 1570) apply to only a proportion of the earnings from the employment abroad where the duties of the employment or any associated employment are *not* performed wholly outside the UK. That proportion is one which is shown by the employee to be reasonable having regard to the nature of the duties and the time devoted to them within the UK and abroad and other relevant circumstances.

An employment is an 'associated employment' of another employment for these purposes if they are with the same person or with persons associated with each other. A company is associated with another if one of them has control of the other or both are under the control of the same person or persons. An individual or partnership is associated with another person (whether or not a company) if one of them has control of the other or both are under the control of the same person or persons.

Law: ITEPA 2003, s. 23(3), 24, 329(1), 331(2)

Source: HMRC6: *Residence, domicile and the remittance basis*

Website: www.hmrc.gov.uk/leaflets/c9.htm

See *British Tax Reporter* ¶406-550.

Income Tax

1580   Special employees with foreign income

Diplomats

Diplomats and diplomatic staff are entitled to a number of exemptions from tax.

Visiting forces

Emoluments paid by the government of any designated country (basically, countries which are members of NATO are exempt from income tax where they are paid to a member of a visiting force of the designated country and that person is not a British citizen, a British Dependent Territories citizen or a British Overseas citizen.

Crown servants

The duties of Crown servants are, in general, treated as being performed in the UK. This is so where the duties are of a public nature and the emoluments are paid out of the public revenue of the UK or of Northern Ireland. The nature of the Civil Service and its duties are prima facie public. By concession, tax is not charged in the case of unestablished staff engaged locally if they are non-UK resident and are paid less than London staff.

Allowances given to any Crown servant representing compensation for the extra cost of having to live abroad in order to perform their duties are not regarded as income. Such allowances are not, therefore, liable to tax. To qualify for the exemption, the allowances must be certified by the Minister for the Civil Service as representing such compensation.

Oil rig workers

UK territorial waters are generally considered to be 12 nautical miles. The territorial sea is deemed to be part of the UK for the purposes of income, capital gains and corporation taxes.

The UK is also extended to certain parts of the continental shelf for tax purposes. Any earnings from an employment in connection with exploration or exploitation activities are treated as earnings for duties performed in the UK. This is so where the earnings are in respect of duties performed in an area of the continental shelf designated by Order in Council under the *Continental Shelf Act* 1964, s. 1(7). A non-UK resident company operating in such an area must make tax deductions under the PAYE system from employees' emoluments if the company has a 'tax presence' in the UK.

The benefit of free transportation of offshore oil and gas rig workers to and from the mainland, and of necessary overnight accommodation near the mainland departure point, are not charged to income tax.

Law: ITEPA 2003, s. 28, 299, 305; *Territorial Sea Act* 1987, s. 1; *Diplomatic Privileges Act 1964; Visiting Forces (Income Tax and Death Duties) (Designation) Order* 1964 (SI 1964/924); *Visiting Forces and Allied Headquarters (Income Tax and Death Duties)*

(Designation) Order 1961 (SI 1961/580); *Clark (HMIT) v Oceanic Contractors Inc* [1982] BTC 417; *Graham v White (HMIT)* [1972] 1 WLR 874

See *British Tax Reporter* ¶435-000.

1583 'Golden handshakes' where foreign service

Compensation payments made to employees for loss of office, etc. are wholly exempt from tax where the duties of the employment included 'foreign service'. Foreign service is such service during which the employee was not both resident and ordinarily resident in the UK or else the emoluments of the service qualify for the 100 per cent deduction (see 440; 1567).

If the employee has been in foreign service, but this is insufficient to give full exemption from tax (see 440), part of the golden handshake may still be non-taxable. The amount which is not taxable will depend on the length of the foreign service in relation to the total length of service.

The foreign service, in general, must comprise one of the following:

- three-quarters of the whole period of service; or
- the last ten years where the period of service exceeded ten years; or
- where the period of service exceeded 20 years, one-half of that period, including any ten of the last 20 years.

Law: FA 1998, Sch. 9

1585 Personal reliefs for non-residents

Non-UK residents are not entitled to 'personal reliefs' (see 1850ff.) except where the individual is:

- a Commonwealth (including a British) citizen or citizen of the Republic of Ireland (or, from 1996–97, otherwise a European Economic Area (EEA) national);
- a person who is or has been a Crown servant;
- a widow (or from 1990–91, a widower) of a Crown servant;
- a missionary;
- a person in the service of a British protectorate;
- a resident of the Isle of Man or Channel Islands;
- a person who has been resident in the UK but is now resident abroad for the sake of his health or the health of a member of his family who resides with him.

In these cases, the non-resident is entitled to the personal reliefs to which residents are entitled.

Most Hong Kong residents who were British Dependent Territories citizens were expected to have registered as British Nationals (Overseas) by 1 July 1997, when the Hong Kong

Income Tax

429

Special Administrative Region came into existence, and therefore continue to be entitled to UK personal reliefs from that date. Of those not registering, only those who are citizens of other Commonwealth countries and/or the EEA will continue to benefit from the reliefs.

To ensure compliance with certain aspects of the *Human Rights Act* 1998, from 6 April 2010, entitlement for non-resident individuals who previously qualified for UK personal tax allowances and reliefs *solely* by virtue of being a Commonwealth citizen will be withdrawn. Whilst the vast majority of individuals affected will still benefit through other means such as Double Taxation Treaties, citizens of Bahamas, Cameroon, Cook Islands, Dominica, Maldives, Mozambique, Nauru, Niue, St Lucia, St Vincent & the Grenadines, Samoa, Tanzania, Tonga, and Vanuatu may be affected.

Law: FA 2009, s. 5; ITA 2007, s. 35

Source: HMRC6: *Residence, domicile and the remittance basis*

Website: www.hmrc.gov.uk/bulletins/index.htm
www.hmrc.gov.uk/leaflets/c9.htm

See *British Tax Reporter* ¶158-000.

REMITTANCE OF INCOME

1600   Importance of remittances

In most cases it is unimportant whether income of a person subject to UK tax arising abroad is remitted or sent back to the UK. In the majority of cases income is taxed on an 'arising basis'. However, in some situations, income is only charged to UK tax if received in the UK.

Income falling within ITTOIA 2005 is usually charged on an arising basis; but the remittance basis applies where the resident taxpayer is not domiciled in the UK or is a Commonwealth (including a British) citizen (or citizen of the Republic of Ireland) and is not ordinarily resident (see 216) in the UK. In the case of any income liable to tax on a remittance basis, tax is charged on the amount received in the UK on a current year basis.

Income falling within ITEPA 2003 is charged to tax on a remittance basis. Such income comprises emoluments of a person resident in the UK (see 213) whether or not ordinarily resident there (see 216) and derived from duties performed abroad.

It is not always easy to ascertain if amounts have been remitted to the UK (see 1603). Emoluments are treated as received in the UK if they are paid, used or enjoyed in the UK, or transmitted or brought to the UK; amounts treated as remitted which are not directly received are sometimes known as 'constructive remittances'. In the case of a person ordinarily resident in the UK, income applied outside the UK in satisfaction of any debt incurred in the UK (or overseas, if the money lent is brought into or received in the UK) is treated as received in the UK.

Income received in a tax year after the source of the income has ceased to exist is not taxable on the remittance basis so long as the remittance is not in the same tax year.

No loss can ever arise on income taxed on the remittance basis.

Law: ITEPA 2003, s. 33; *Joffe v Thain (HMIT)* (1956) 36 TC 199

Source: HMRC6: *Residence, domicile and the remittance basis*

Website: www.hmrc.gov.uk/leaflets/c9.htm

See *British Tax Reporter* ¶370-000.

1603   Whether income remitted to UK

Income considered as remitted to the UK need not necessarily be paid to the taxpayer (for the definition of remittance in relation to emoluments, see 1600); but income which is properly alienated abroad to another person is not regarded as remitted to the UK by the original owner if the new owner sends that money to the UK.

It is sometimes difficult to distinguish between income and capital, but, in general, the proceeds of investments purchased abroad with income that would be taxable if remitted are liable to tax as income if those proceeds are themselves remitted.

The fact that sums remitted are derived from a bank overdraft is not in itself sufficient to establish that the remittance is out of capital.

However, investments purchased out of income before taking up residence in the UK may be realised and the money remitted without liability.

Law: *Walsh v Randall (HMIT)* (1940) 23 TC 55; *Carter (HMIT) v Sharon* (1936) 20 TC 229; *Timpson's Exors v Yerbury (HMIT)* [1936] 1 KB 645; *Fellowes-Gordon v IR Commrs* (1935) 19 TC 683; *Kneen (HMIT) v Martin* [1935] 1 KB 499

Source: HMRC6: *Residence, domicile and the remittance basis*

Website: www.hmrc.gov.uk/leaflets/c9.htm

See *British Tax Reporter* ¶370-250.

Income Tax

1605 Delayed remittances

Difficulties may arise where income is liable to tax only when remitted to the UK (see 1600) if the taxpayer is prevented from remitting the income until some later stage when rates of tax may be higher. Relief can be obtained on making a claim. For the relief to apply the taxpayer must:

- have been prevented from transferring the income to the UK, either by the laws of that territory or any executive action of its government or by the impossibility of obtaining foreign currency in that territory; and
- have used reasonable endeavour to transfer the income.

Law: ITEPA 2003, s. 35–37

Source: HMRC6: *Residence, domicile and the remittance basis*

Website: www.hmrc.gov.uk/leaflets/c9.htm

See *British Tax Reporter* ¶370-900.

1607 Unremittable overseas income

Persons (including companies) who are liable to tax on their overseas income wherever it arises are (for example, because of foreign exchange controls) sometimes unable to remit the income to the UK. This can cause hardship in some cases. In certain circumstances, therefore, the overseas income will not be taken into account in assessing that person to tax.

Unremittable overseas income is the income arising abroad which:

- a person is prevented from transferring to the UK, either by the laws of that territory or any executive action of its government or by the impossibility of obtaining foreign currency in that territory;
- the person has used reasonable endeavour to transfer; and
- that person has not realised in some other currency which he is not prevented from transferring to the UK.

To take advantage of this relief, a claim must be made not later than the first anniversary of the 31 January from the end of the tax year (or, in the case of companies, two years from the end of the accounting period) in which the income arises. The relief will be given only as long as the three conditions above continue to be satisfied, i.e. the tax liability is only postponed, not removed.

Any appeal against an assessment where these provisions apply is to be made to the tribunal.

Law: ITTOIA 2005, s. 841–845

Source: HMRC6: *Residence, domicile and the remittance basis*

Website: www.hmrc.gov.uk/leaflets/c9.htm

See *British Tax Reporter* ¶371-000.

TRADES, PROFESSIONS AND VOCATIONS: FOREIGN INCOME

1620   Charge on foreign income from trade, profession or vocation

Income of a UK resident derived from a trade, profession or vocation (see 550ff.) which is carried on wholly abroad is liable to tax only if it was remitted to the UK where he is:

- not domiciled in the UK (see 219); or
- a Commonwealth (including a British) citizen or a citizen of the Republic of Ireland and is not 'ordinarily resident' (see 216) in the UK.

For whether income is remitted, see 1603.

In all other cases the income of a resident is liable to tax whether or not the income is remitted. Income arising in the Republic of Ireland is treated as if it arose in the UK but is nevertheless entitled to the same deductions (and subject to the same limitation of reliefs) as apply to trades, etc. carried on abroad.

The income of a non-resident derived from a trade carried on wholly abroad is not liable to tax. However, a non-resident trading in the UK through a branch or agency is liable to tax on consequent profits (see 1622).

For double tax relief, see 1780ff.

Law: ITTOIA 2005, s. 7(4)

See *British Tax Reporter* ¶293-000.

1622   Trading in the UK

A 'non-UK resident' (see 213) trading in the UK is only liable to UK tax where he is trading through a branch or agency.

What constitutes a trade is dealt with at 555ff. Whether a person is trading in the UK through a branch or agency is a question of fact, but the distinction has to be made between trading with the UK and trading in the UK: soliciting orders in the UK will not by itself constitute trading in the UK. An important factor is whether the contract for sale or supply of services was made abroad, but the contract may not be conclusive.

Law: *Firestone Tyre and Rubber Co Ltd v Lewellin (HMIT)* [1957] 1 WLR 464; *FL Smidth & Co v Greenwood* (1922) 8 TC 193; *Grainger & Son v Gough* [1896] AC 325

See *British Tax Reporter* ¶293-350.

1624 UK resident trading wholly abroad

An individual who is resident in the UK and carries on a trade, profession or vocation wholly abroad, either alone or in partnership, is liable to tax on all his income from such a trade. The income is assessed on a current year basis. Losses, etc. can only be set off against the income of that or another overseas source, foreign emoluments (see 1570), other overseas income (see 1654ff.) and certain pensions (see 1640, 1642).

However, a person who is not domiciled in the UK or else is a Commonwealth (including a British) citizen (or a citizen of the Republic of Ireland) who is not ordinarily resident in the UK is liable only on a remittance basis (see 1600).

Law: ITTOIA 2005, s. 7, 19, 227

See *British Tax Reporter* ¶293-150.

1625 Expenses connected with foreign trades

Special rules apply to travel expenses and board and lodging expenses incurred by an individual taxpayer whose trade, profession or vocation is carried on wholly outside the UK, and who has failed to satisfy HMRC that he is not domiciled here or else, being a Commonwealth (including a British) citizen (or a citizen of the Republic of Ireland), is not ordinarily resident here.

Where the rules apply the travel and board and lodging expenses are to be treated as deductible provided that the taxpayer's absence from the UK is wholly and exclusively for the purpose of performing the function of the foreign trade.

In certain conditions travel expenses of the taxpayer's spouse and any child of his are deductible.

Travel between foreign trades is also deductible, subject to conditions.

Law: ITTOIA 2005, s. 92–94

See *British Tax Reporter* ¶293-400.

1630   Non-resident entertainers and sportsmen

There is a system of withholding basic rate income tax from payments made to visiting, non-resident entertainers and sports personalities (see 1673). Except where the activity in point is performed in the course of an office or employment, it is treated as if it were a trade, profession or vocation exercised in the UK and the income from it plus payments connected with it are chargeable on a current year basis; it is stated that regulations dealing with the system generally can provide specifically for losses and reliefs.

Law: ITTOIA 2005, s. 13–14

See *British Tax Reporter* ¶293-550.

FOREIGN PENSIONS

1640   Foreign pensions

Generally, pensions of UK residents are assessed to tax under the charge on employment income provisions (see 420), but in the case of foreign pensions the assessment is under the income from foreign possessions rules. These are pensions which:

- are paid by or on behalf of a person outside the UK; *and*
- are not pensions charged to income tax in respect of overseas public service (see 1642).

If a foreign pension or increase is granted retrospectively and the pension is chargeable to tax on an arising basis, the full amount of the award, including arrears, is assessable in one sum. However, where it is to the taxpayer's advantage, the tax is calculated as if the arrears (after making the deduction mentioned below) arose in the years to which they relate.

A pension or annual payment paid by or on behalf of an employer outside the UK to an ex-employee (or his widow, child, relative or dependant) is assessed under the income on foreign possessions rules even if paid voluntarily.

Foreign pensions paid to a UK resident are only liable to tax if remitted to the UK where the person entitled to the pension is:

- not 'domiciled' in the UK (see 219); or
- a Commonwealth (including a British) citizen or a citizen of the Republic of Ireland and is not 'ordinarily resident' (see 216) in the UK.

In most other cases, the pension is liable to tax whether or not it is remitted. Pensions which have their source abroad and are not taxed on a remittance basis are eligible for a ten per cent deduction. Pensions arising in the Republic of Ireland are treated as if they arose in the UK, but nevertheless attract the ten per cent deduction unless the pensioner is either not domiciled in the UK or, being a Commonwealth (including a British) or Irish citizen, is not ordinarily resident in the UK. Pensions payable under German or Austrian law in compensation to victims of Nazi persecution are exempt from income tax altogether.

Law: ITTOIA 2005; *Albon v IR Commrs* [1999] BTC 138; *Aspin v Estill (HMIT)* [1987] BTC 553

See *British Tax Reporter* ¶320-050.

1642 Pensions from overseas public service

Certain overseas public service pensions and annuities paid to UK residents are assessed on a current year basis, but nevertheless attract a ten per cent deduction. These are pensions which are:

(1)   payable in the UK;

(2)   so payable through any public department, officer or agent of the government of any country forming part of the British dominions or any country mentioned in the *British Nationality Act* 1981, Sch. 3 or any British protectorate;

(3)   paid to a person (or his widow, child, relative or dependant) who has been employed in the service of the Crown or in the service of such a territory as in (2) above; and

(4)   paid in respect of that service.

This provision does not apply where the payment is out of the public revenue of the UK or of Northern Ireland.

Law: ITEPA 2003, s. 615

See *British Tax Reporter* ¶320-250.

FOREIGN INVESTMENT INCOME

1650 UK government securities: foreign income

An exemption from tax applies to UK government securities issued by the Treasury with a condition that the interest is not liable to tax where evidence is provided that the beneficial ownership of the securities is in a person not ordinarily resident in the UK though other conditions may be imposed – often termed FOTRA securities since they are free of tax to residents abroad.

The number of securities which are exempt varies with the redemption of old securities and the issue of new securities (the list current at any time may be obtained from FICO (International)). The income will not be exempt where, by any provision of the Tax Acts, it is deemed to be the income of any other person who is ordinarily resident in the UK. Special regard must be had to the anti-avoidance provisions concerning the transfer of assets by virtue of which income becomes payable to persons abroad (see 1700).

Banks and approved stockbroking firms can obtain block exemption from income tax on behalf of various overseas customers, irrespective of whether the relevant securities have been held for at least two dividend dates.

A non-resident who is trading in the UK would ordinarily be exempt where the interest forms part of the trading receipts; but in all cases to date, except with regard to the 3¹/₂ per cent War Loan, the Treasury has modified the exemption so as not to apply to trades or businesses carried on in the UK.

Special rules apply to non-resident banks, insurance companies and dealers in securities carrying on business in the UK.

Law: ITTOIA 2005, s. 73, 714, 716; FA 1996, Sch. 28

See *British Tax Reporter* ¶371-100.

1652   Foreign government securities: foreign income

From 1996–97, overseas public revenue dividends fall within the ambit of provisions relating to 'foreign dividends' (see 1654).

Previously, although deduction of tax under Sch. C was broadly cast so as to apply to almost anyone in the UK handling such dividends, exemptions were provided in relation to securities held in a recognised clearing system or on proof that the person owning the securities, and entitled to the proceeds, was not resident in the UK.

See *British Tax Reporter* ¶371-200.

1654   Foreign dividends

Whether a dividend emanates from a foreign possession depends upon the residence of the company.

From 1993–94, the foreign dividends above are generally charged at the same rate of income tax as UK dividends (see 1350).

Paying and collecting agents

Foreign dividends can be subject to a form of tax deduction or payment on account of the person entitled to them. The rules for UK paying agents and collecting agents were replaced in 1996. Foreign dividends now encompass overseas public revenue dividends (see formerly 1652). The replacement of the old rules involves little substantive change, but rather a reorganisation of the rules together with the codification (in some instances through regulations) of existing administrative practice.

Income Tax

Three requirements have to be met before a receipt becomes subject to the collecting agent rules:

(1)   a person of a specified type (bank, coupon dealer or person acting in the course of a trade or profession – including acting as a custodian of holdings – but not someone merely clearing a cheque);

(2)   performs a relevant function;

(3)   as a result of which he receives or otherwise realises the value of foreign dividends or quoted Eurobond interest (a 'relevant receipt').

Income tax deducted or to be accounted for is due and payable to HMRC 14 days after the end of the month in which the 'chargeable date' falls, i.e. the date on which the foreign dividends or quoted Eurobond interest obtained by a collecting agent are paid or the date on which the collecting agent sells or otherwise realises coupons for them.

For 2000–01 and with deemed effect for 1999–2000, the rate of income tax deducted by paying and collecting agents in relation to foreign income dividends is ten per cent.

Abolition of paying and collection agents regime

The paying and collecting agents regime was abolished from April 2001. Since that date, agents do not have to deduct income tax when paying or collecting interest on quoted UK Eurobonds or foreign income dividends and interest. Additionally, from that date, a new definition of 'quoted Eurobond' applies, meaning that bonds will not have to be issued in bearer form to be free of withholding tax.

Law: FA 2000, s. 111; FA 1996, Sch. 7; *Income Tax (Paying and Collecting Agents) Regulations* 1996 (SI 1996/1780); *Income Tax (Interest on Quoted Eurobonds) Regulations* 1996 (SI 1996/1779); EC Directive 90/435; *Bradbury v English Sewing Cotton Co Ltd* [1923] AC 744

See *British Tax Reporter* ¶371-350.

1656   Local authority securities in foreign currency

Interest on certain securities quoted in foreign currencies is paid without deduction of income tax and, so long as the beneficial owner is not resident in the UK, is exempt from income tax (but not corporation tax). Such securities are those issued by local authorities and statutory corporations which are the subject of a Treasury direction.

Law: ITTOIA 2005, s. 755–756;

See *British Tax Reporter* ¶132-900.

1658   Annual interest as foreign income

Income from foreign 'securities' is charged under ITTOIA 2005 (former Sch. D, Case IV). Deep discounts on certain securities are specifically charged under this head (see 1401).

The person by or through whom a payment is made of annual interest of money chargeable to tax must deduct lower rate income tax (basic rate tax before 1996–97) before making the payment if the payment is to a person whose usual place of abode is outside the UK (see 1372). The tax deducted must be accounted for to HMRC. An exemption is provided for interest paid to non-resident holders of quoted Eurobonds held in a recognised clearing system (Euroclear, CEDEL, First Chicago Clearing Centre).

For provisions requiring paying or collecting agents for foreign interest to deduct tax, see 1654.

Where interest is paid gross to a non-resident (notably in the case of certain bank and building society interest: see 1372), HMRC will not pursue the income tax liability unless the person is chargeable in the name of a trustee, agent or branch in the UK (see 1672).

See *British Tax Reporter* ¶371-100.

1660   Rent from properties outside the UK

Rent and other receipts from properties outside the UK are charged to tax under ITTOIA 2005. The profits or losses are normally calculated in the same way as those of a property income business (see 1200ff.). However, the property income business approach does not apply where the taxpayer is entitled to the benefit of the remittance basis (see below).

All businesses and transactions carried on or entered into by a person or partnership are treated as a single business (an 'overseas property business'). However, separate computations may be necessary for tax credit relief purposes where there are properties in different countries (see 1780ff.).

Where a person carries on a business of letting property situated in the UK and an overseas property business, the two businesses are treated separately. The special provisions relating to relief in respect of certain travel connected with foreign trades (see 1625), and furnished holiday lettings (see 1255) are disregarded in computing the profit or loss of an overseas property business. (For corporation tax, see 3133.)

Example
Example
David travels to Tuscany and spends two weeks redecorating the villa which he lets to holidaymakers. The following week he goes on a walking holiday in the area. None of his travel costs are tax deductible (see 2040, 2154).

Income Tax

Losses from overseas property business

Except for losses of a trade, etc. carried on wholly abroad, before 1998–99 there was no provision for relief for foreign income losses. However, deficiencies from overseas lettings could be carried forward and set off against future income from the same property. Currently, as all overseas lettings are treated as a single business (see above), excess expenditure on one such letting is automatically set against surplus receipts from other such lettings. Any overall loss can only be carried forward and set against future foreign rental business profits. See further 2062.

Remittance basis

The remittance basis (see 1600) applies to rental income from overseas lettings where the taxpayer:

- is not 'domiciled in the UK' (see 219); or
- is a Commonwealth (including a British) citizen, or a citizen of the Republic of Ireland, and is not 'ordinarily resident in the UK' (see 216).

Law: ITTOIA 2005, s. 261, 265–365

Source: ESC B25, *Capital allowances: asssets leased outside the United Kingdom – transitional provisions: syndicated leases*

Website: www.hmrc.gov.uk/leaflets/c13.htm

See *British Tax Reporter* ¶370-100.

1663   Annual payments as foreign income

The remittance basis (see 1600) applies to annual payments and similar income from foreign possessions where the taxpayer is not 'domiciled in the UK' (see 219) or in certain cases, is not 'ordinarily resident in the UK' (see 216). In other cases such income is charged on an arising basis (i.e. on the full amount of the income arising).

Exempt annual payments include benefits paid under certain 'self-contained' insurance policies to those who make arrangements to protect themselves from financial losses caused by accident, sickness, disability, infirmity or unemployment, or from the cost of long-term care.

Law: ITTOIA 2005, s. 227, 229, 269, 610–617, Sch. 1, para. 606–607, 609

See *British Tax Reporter* ¶371-100.

1664   EU Savings Directive

Directive 2003/48/EC on the 'taxation of savings income in the form of interest payments' was adopted by the Council on 3 June 2003 and entered into force on 1 July 2005. It directs each member state to introduce legislation requiring businesses and public bodies established in that state (referred to as 'paying agents') who pay interest to, or collect interest on behalf of, EU-resident individuals, to report details of the payments and the payees to the tax authorities (art. 8). The Directive also requires that information relating to residents of another member state be passed on to the authorities in that state (art. 9). A paying agent will be obliged to establish the identity and state of residence of the beneficial owner of the interest and in particular where there is evidence to suggest that the recipient is not the beneficial owner. Rules are provided setting out the minimum steps the agent must take to establish the identity and residence position of the beneficial owner (art. 2 and 3). Where the contractual relationship between the paying agent and the beneficial owner was established before 1 January 2004, the agent is to establish the owner's identity and residence position by reference to information at its disposal and with regard to the existing anti-money laundering legislation in force in its state of establishment implementing Directive 91/308/EEC (art. 2(a), 3(a)). Where the contractual relationship was established on or after 1 January 2004, or, where no contractual relationship exists, transactions take place after that date, the agent will have to establish identity and state of residence by reference to the owner's name, address and 'tax identification number' (if one exists) obtained from a passport, official identity card or 'any other documentary proof of identity presented by the beneficial owner' (art. 2(b), 3(b)). Member states were required to adopt the legislation necessary to implement the terms of the Directive by 1 January 2004 with a view to bringing it into force from 1 January 2005 (art. 17). However, the Council, using its powers under art. 17(3), decided to defer the start date to 1 July 2005, as it did not consider that the conditions set out in art. 17 for the Directive to come into force would be satisified by the original date.

Law: FA 2003, s. 199; *Reporting of Savings Income Information (Amendment) Regulations* 2005 (SI 2005/1539); *Reporting of Savings Income Information Regulations* 2003 (SI 2003/3297)

Website: www.hmrc.gov.uk/esd-guidance/newguidance-v4.rtf

See *British Tax Reporter* ¶103-835.

ASSESSMENT AND COLLECTION OF TAX ON FOREIGN INCOME

1670   PAYE and payment of tax on employees' foreign income

Tax will often be deducted by the employer under the PAYE system in respect of employees' earnings (see 2784). Entitlement to deductions will be taken account of as far as possible in the PAYE codings. However, this is not always possible: an employee working and paid abroad by a foreign employer may be directly assessed. HMRC will generally make an estimated assessment and tax will be collected in four equal instalments.

A non-UK resident company operating in a designated area of the continental shelf must operate the PAYE system if it has a 'taxable presence' in the UK.

Law: *Income Tax (Pay As You Earn) Regulations* 2003 (SI 2003/2682); *Clark (HMIT) v Oceanic Contractors Inc* [1982] BTC 417

See *British Tax Reporter* ¶496-350.

1671   Income from property assessments on non-residents

Income tax of persons normally living abroad arising from property in the UK has been charged, from 6 April 1996, by way of deduction at source by the agent for the property or, where there is no agent, from the tenant, with a final settling-up with the non-resident under self-assessment. These arrangements replace earlier ones. Tenants who pay rent of £100 or less per week do not have to operate the scheme unless asked to do so by HMRC. Non-residents may apply to HMRC for approval to receive their UK property income with no tax deducted provided:

- their UK tax affairs are up to date;
- they have never had any obligations in relation to UK tax; or
- they do not expect to be liable to UK income tax;

and they undertake to comply with all their UK tax obligations in the future. The regulations also set out details of annual information returns to be made by letting agents and tenants who have to operate the scheme, as well as other information to be supplied to HMRC on request. Landlords are non-residents for the purposes of the scheme if they have a usual place of abode outside the UK.

Law: ITA 2007, s. 971; *Taxation of Income from Land (Non-residents) Regulations* 1995 (SI 1995/2902)

Website: www.hmrc.gov.uk/leaflets/c9.htm

See *British Tax Reporter* ¶293-400.

1672   Non-residents trading through a branch or agency

Where non-residents carry on a trade in the UK through a permanent establishment (see 4500), for the purposes of self-assessment, HMRC will, broadly, treat that permanent establishment as the non-resident's 'UK representative', and look to it for the performance of various tax obligations. Certain persons are excluded from being a UK representative.

The amount of income tax chargeable for any tax year on the total income of any person who is not resident in the UK is limited to the sum of:

(1) tax deducted, or treated as deducted, at source (including tax credits) from income received under deduction of tax; and

(2) tax on the non-resident's total income computed without regard to:

   (a) income taxable under Sch. C (before 1996–97), former Sch. D, Case III and former Sch. F;
   (b) gains from disposals of certificates of deposit;
   (c) various social security benefits;
   (d) income arising from transactions carried out on the non-resident's behalf by brokers and investment managers who are not treated as the non-resident's UK representative;
   (e) income designated for this purpose by the Treasury in regulations;
   (f) personal allowances;
   (g) relief under any double tax treaty.

The limitation on charge does not apply to the income of non-resident trustees if any of the trust's beneficiaries is an individual ordinarily resident in the UK or a company resident in the UK. 'Beneficiaries' are broadly defined to include both actual and potential beneficiaries who:

- are or ever might become entitled to receive income from the trust; or
- have income from the trust paid to them or applied for their benefit by legitimate exercise of the trustees' discretion;

and 'trust' income includes capital derived from accumulated income.

The above provisions replace a concession under which, where interest or certain other payments were paid gross to a non-resident (notably in the case of certain bank and building society interest: see 1372), HMRC did not pursue the income tax liability unless the person was chargeable in the name of a trustee, agent or branch in the UK.

Source: SP 15/91, *The treatment of investment managers and their overseas clients*

See *British Tax Reporter* ¶293-450.

1673   Payment of tax by foreign entertainers and sportsmen

Where a payment is made in respect of an appearance by a non-resident entertainer or sportsman in the UK the payer must deduct tax at the basic rate. This rule does not apply if:

- the payment is below £1,000;
- the recipient has agreed a lower or nil rate of withholding tax with HMRC.

Regulations give definitions of 'entertainers' and 'sportsmen', and detail the activities covered by the rules, the types of income subject to withholding, the deduction of expenses and the administration arrangements in connection with the procedure. The rules apply to fees and prize money, and also to associated income from advertising, sponsorship and endorsements. The deduction at source cannot be avoided by directing payment to a third party.

Tax is assessed on a current-year basis (see 1630).

Law: ITTOIA 2005, s. 13–14; *Income Tax (Entertainers and Sportsmen) Regulations* 1987 (SI 1987/530)

See *British Tax Reporter* ¶293-550.

1674   Returns for foreign secondees

An employer must, if required so to do, prepare and deliver to HMRC a return relating to persons who are or have been employed by him (see 2573). Where a person performs the duties of an office or employment in the UK for a continuous period of at least 30 days and the employment is with a non-UK resident but the duties are performed for the benefit of a UK resident (or person carrying on a trade, profession or vocation in the UK), then the person benefiting from those services may be required to make a return of the name and address of the 'employee'.

Law: FA 1974, s. 24

See *British Tax Reporter* ¶170-100.

INTELLECTUAL PROPERTY ROYALTIES AS FOREIGN INCOME

1680   Copyright royalties as foreign income

Certain copyright or design royalties paid to an owner of the copyright, etc. who does not usually live in the UK are to be paid after deducting income tax at the basic rate. The tax retained must be accounted for to HMRC.

The amount of the payment of royalties can be reduced by any agent's commission before deducting income tax if the royalties are paid through an agent resident in the UK and he is entitled, as against the owner of the copyright, etc. to deduct commission. Copyright royalties include authors' public lending rights and the rules relating to returns and penalties for failure to deliver a return in respect of fees, commissions, etc. (see 2597) also apply accordingly.

Law: ITA 2007, s. 906, 907(1)

1683   Patent right disposals: foreign income

Basic rate income tax is deducted in accordance with the usual mechanism for deducting basic rate tax at source (see 1370) from the proceeds of sale of any UK patent by a non-resident and the proceeds (consisting wholly or partly of a capital sum but net of any capital cost attributable) are taxed on a current year basis. The seller can elect to have the proceeds of sale (net of any acquisition cost) treated as the income of the year of receipt and of the five succeeding years as if one-sixth was received in each tax year.

Law: ITTOIA 2005, s. 587–599

TRANSFER OF INCOME/ASSETS ABROAD

1700   Deemed income where transferor receives benefit of transfer abroad

Overseas income of a person who is 'resident' (see 213) and 'domiciled' (see 219) abroad is not liable to tax in the UK. Special anti-avoidance provisions prevent an individual (or his spouse) who is ordinarily resident in the UK from obtaining a tax advantage by transferring his assets abroad in such a way that the income is paid to persons who are resident or domiciled abroad but is in some manner still enjoyed by the resident himself.

An attempt has been made to tighten these rules. For income arising on or after 26 November 1996, the rules apply:

- whatever the ordinary residence of the individual when the transfer is made;
- where a purpose of the transfer is to avoid any form of direct taxation (e.g. capital taxation).

For the purposes of the provisions, 'assets' include property or rights of any kind (e.g. 'assets' were held to include rights under a contract of employment. As an important safeguard, the rules do not apply where the transfer of assets is not made to avoid tax or where the transfer is a genuine commercial transaction not designed to avoid tax. Irrespective of residence otherwise, companies incorporated outside the UK are always treated as non-resident for present purposes, bringing transfers of assets to them potentially within the anti-avoidance provisions.

The income of any such transfer is regarded as that of the individual making the transfer where he has power to enjoy the income and, in particular, where:

- the income is used for his benefit; or
- the income increases the value of any assets held by or for him; or
- he receives or is entitled to receive any benefit out of that income or money which represents that income; or
- he may become entitled to enjoy the income through the exercise of any power

Income Tax

445

(e.g. where he is a member of a class of beneficiaries who may be entitled to income if a power within the trust is exercised); or

- he is able directly or indirectly to control the way the income is applied (a right to direct investments is not included, nor a power of appointment in connection with capital payments.

A transferor is also liable to tax on the income of the assets transferred if he is entitled to receive any capital sum the payment of which is in any way connected with the transfer. 'Capital sum' means:

- any sum paid or payable as a loan or repayment of a loan; and
- any other sum which is not income and which is not paid for full consideration in money or money's worth.

Any sum which a third person becomes entitled to receive is treated as a capital sum to which an individual becomes entitled if the third person's entitlement is at the individual's direction or is because of an assignment by the individual of his right to receive it.

Income is not treated as an individual's for any tax year merely because he has received a loan if the loan is wholly repaid before the beginning of that year.

These provisions apply only to the person (or that person's spouse) who made the original transfer of assets). However, further provisions concerning the transfer of assets abroad were enacted in 1981 to extend the charge to benefits received by others (see 1701).

An individual who is domiciled abroad is not liable to tax on income deemed to be his if it in fact had been his income and he would not have been liable to tax on it by reason of his domicile (this prevents these anti-avoidance provisions disrupting the normal operation of the remittance basis applying to non-domiciliaries; see 1600ff.).

Law: ITA 2007, Part 13, Ch. 2; *IR Commrs v Botnar* [1999] BTC 267; *IR Commrs v Willoughby* [1997] BTC 393; *IR Commrs v Brackett* [1986] BTC 415; *Vestey v IR Commrs* [1980] AC 1148; *Lord Vestey's Exors v IR Commrs* (1949) 31 TC 1

See *British Tax Reporter* ¶129-700.

1701 Deemed income where non-transferor receives benefit from transfer abroad

Anti-avoidance provisions dealing with the transfer of income-producing assets abroad generally charge only the transferor (see 1700). Additional provisions attack non-transferors who receive a similar benefit.

They apply where assets are transferred abroad (where the purpose or one of the purposes is to avoid tax) and:

- income becomes payable to a person 'resident' (see 213) or 'domiciled' (see 219) outside the UK; *and*
- an individual 'ordinarily resident' (see 216) in the UK (and who is not the original transferor) receives a benefit out of the assets transferred.

The amount of the benefit is treated as the income of the recipient and charged to UK tax accordingly, and he is liable to income tax upon it in the year of receipt. This is so long as the amount received is not more than the relevant amount of income from the transferred assets which can be used for his benefit.

The relevant amount of income is the income up to and including the tax year in which the benefit is received. Any part of the benefit received which exceeds this relevant amount of income is taxed as the income of the next or subsequent years when it is covered by income which can be used for his benefit.

Example

A Bahamian settlement is established in 1999–2000 to avoid tax. The beneficiaries do not include the settlor or his wife. The income of the settlement is as follows:

	£
1999–2000	30,000
2000–01	50,000
2001–02	2,700
2002–03	50,000
2003–04	100,000

In 2002–03 beneficiary A (ordinarily resident in the UK) receives £140,000.

The settlement income to 5 April 2002 totals £132,700; only £132,700 will be taxed in 2002–03. The rest may be taxed as A's income in 2003–04 and subsequent years.

No income is to be taken into account more than once in charging tax under these provisions. HMRC have a discretion to apportion the income as it considers just and reasonable where there is more than one person liable under these provisions, including those charging the transferor (see 1700). The tribunal has jurisdiction to review such a decision.

An individual who is domiciled abroad is not liable to tax on income deemed to be his if in fact it had been his income and he would not have been liable to tax on it by reason of his domicile (this prevents these anti-avoidance provisions disrupting the normal operation of the remittance basis applying to non-domiciliaries; see 1600ff.).

Law: ITA 2007, Part 13, Ch. 2; *A beneficiary v IR Commrs* (1999) Sp C 190

See *British Tax Reporter* ¶129-700.

DOUBLE TAX RELIEF

1780   Tax treaties

The UK has concluded a large number of tax treaties with other countries to avoid international double taxation and to prevent fiscal evasion. Tax treaties covering all usual areas of possible double taxation (comprehensive agreements) have been made. A list of all current and pending Tax Treaties can be found on the HMRC website at www.hmrc.gov.uk/international/in_force.htm.

Law: TIOPA 2010, Pt. 2; Convention 90/436

Website: www.hmrc.gov.uk/cnr/dtdigest.pdf
www.hmrc.gov.uk/international/dtr-guidance.htm

See *British Tax Reporter* ¶170-050.

1783   Types of double tax relief

There are different kinds of relief from double taxation.

- *Relief by treaty exemption* – certain categories of income are exempted from tax in whole or in part in one or other of the countries which are parties to the 'double taxation agreement' or 'double tax treaty' (see 1780).
- *Relief by treaty credit* – tax charged in one country may be available as a credit in the other.
- *Unilateral relief* – where there is no provision for double taxation relief, any foreign tax paid may nevertheless be available as a credit in calculating UK tax.
- *Relief by deduction* – the taxpayer can treat the foreign tax paid as a deduction from his taxable income (for example, the foreign tax suffered may be 'inadmissible' for credit relief: see 1789).

The provision made for double tax relief also apply to capital gains and chargeable gains of companies.

Whether HMRC will admit a foreign tax for unilateral double taxation relief in relation to business profits is determined by examining the tax within its legislative context in the foreign territory and deciding whether it serves the same function as income tax and corporation tax serve in the UK in relation to such profits (see 1789).

For the calculation and effect of the available relief, see 1789, 1792.

Effect must be given to agreements, decisions or opinions in connection with transfer pricing made in accordance with the arbitration convention (see 1780) whether by assessment or discharge or repayment of tax.

Law: TCGA 1992, s. 277(1); TIOPA 2010, Pt. 2

See *British Tax Reporter* ¶170-150.

1786 Model treaty provisions as typically used in the UK

Two chief methods of relieving double taxation are adopted in 'tax treaties' (see 1780). First, taxing rights over certain classes of income are reserved entirely to the country of residence of the person deriving the income. Secondly, all other income may be taxed (in some cases, only to a limited extent) by the country of origin of that income; if the country of residence of the recipient also taxes that income, it must grant a credit against its tax for the tax levied by the country of origin (see 1783).

Many tax treaties are based on the 1977 or 1992 Model Convention published by the Organisation for Economic Co-operation and Development. They usually provide that a national from one territory should not be treated more harshly than a national from the other territory (a 'non-discrimination clause'; though the EC Treaty (formerly known as the Treaty of Rome) requires similar treatment within the EC, as noted at 1780): the matter in point must fall within the provision for the reliefs effected by arrangements agreed with foreign governments.

Some of the usual exemption provisions of treaties are noted below, but it is emphasised that each treaty must be looked at individually for its specific provisions.

Business profits

The profits of any business carried on by a resident of country A is taxable only in country A unless the business is carried on in country B through a permanent establishment (a fixed place of business, e.g. a branch, office, factory or mine) in country B. Where this is the case, the profits of the business are taxable in country B, but only to the extent that those profits are attributable to the permanent establishment.

Shipping, inland waterways and air transport

Profits from the operation of ships, aircraft or inland waterways transport are taxable only in the country in which the place of effective management of the relevant enterprise is situated.

Interest, dividends, royalties, non-government pensions

Interest, dividends, patent and copyright royalties, and non-government pensions are often taxable only in the country of residence or are taxed at a reduced rate in the other country. Recipients of dividends are often entitled to a proportion of the tax credit to which a UK-resident would have been entitled (see 1350). Where a tax credit on a dividend is to be determined subject to a deduction based on the aggregate of the dividend plus the tax credit, the deduction is calculated on the gross amount of the dividend and the tax credit, without any allowance for the deduction itself.

Professional services

The income of a person in respect of professional services is generally only taxable in the country in which he is resident, unless he has a fixed base regularly available to him in the other country for the purpose of providing his services. However, actors, musicians and athletes are generally liable to tax in both countries.

Salaries and wages

Most salaries and wages are generally taxable only in the country of residence unless the employment is exercised in the other country, in which case income derived from such employment is also taxable in the other country. However, usually the treaty will contain a provision that the salary, etc. is only taxable in the country of residence if:

- the taxpayer is present in the other country for an aggregate period not exceeding 183 days in the relevant tax year;
- the salary, etc. is paid by, or on behalf of, an employer who is not resident in the other country; and
- the payments are not borne by a permanent establishment which the employer has in the other country.

However, actors, musicians and athletes are generally liable to tax in the country in which they perform.

Government salaries and pensions

Government pensions, salaries, etc. are generally taxable only in the country responsible for paying the pensions, salaries, etc. However, the income is only taxable in the other country if the services are rendered in that country and the taxpayer is resident in, or is a citizen of, that country.

Students

Students temporarily abroad for the purposes of education are generally not taxable on their grants and other income reasonably necessary for maintenance and education.

Teachers

A resident of country A who visits country B for the purpose of teaching is usually exempt from tax in country B on the income derived from his teaching. The normal proviso is that the period of temporary residence in country B does not exceed two years.

Personal allowances and reliefs

Many double tax agreements provide that individuals who are resident in country A are entitled to the same personal allowances, reliefs, and deductions for the purposes of tax in country B as subjects of country B who are not resident in that country.

Often the double taxation agreement will exclude entitlement to the personal allowances, etc. where the income consists solely of dividends, interest or royalties.

Law: TIOPA 2010, Pt. 2

See *British Tax Reporter* ¶170-300.

1789 Effect of exemptions under double tax treaties

If a double tax treaty provides an exemption from tax or a partial exemption from tax in a particular territory (see 1783), the amount in respect of which tax is exempt may nonetheless be brought fully into account in the UK – there is very little relief for 'tax spared' in the other territory, except in the case of transfers of foreign branches of UK-resident companies between EC member states (see below) and in the case of certain interest.

There is an element of tax sparing provided by virtue of EC provisions. A UK-resident company transferring a foreign branch activity between EC member states may be exempt from tax in the territory in which the branch subsisted (in accordance with the mergers directive); chargeable gains in respect of the transfer may be netted with allowable losses (see 4088) and the resultant taxable amount may be subject to double tax relief on the basis of the tax which would have been payable but for the exemption.

Non-resident companies carrying on business in the UK are unable to claim relief for losses incurred as a result of the exemption of dividends, interest or royalty income under a double taxation convention. For accounting periods beginning before 30 November 1993, the restriction applied only to dividends and interest received by non-residents carrying on business as a bank, insurance company or dealer in securities.

Law: TIOPA 2010, Pt. 2; EC Directive 90/434

See *British Tax Reporter* ¶170-750.

1792 Calculation of double tax credit relief available

In many cases, double tax agreements provide that where there is no deduction or exemption from UK tax, credit is to be given for any foreign tax which is paid and which corresponds to income tax whilst similar credit is given by 'unilateral relief' (see 1783); this reduces the amount of UK tax chargeable except in certain cases where a non-resident company is connected with a state or province of a foreign territory which operates a 'unitary tax' regime. In general, a claim for relief by way of credit for foreign tax must be made within the period ending five years from 31 January following the end of the tax year within which the income falls to be charged to tax (before self-assessment, a period of six full years). For tax spared when a UK-resident company transfers a foreign branch activity between EC member states, see 1789.

Income Tax

From 17 March 1998, taxpayers who have claimed relief for foreign tax must notify HMRC if there is an adjustment to the amount of foreign tax and the relief claimed has become excessive as a consequence. This requirement clarifies taxpayers' obligations under self-assessment.

For trades, professions and vocations, there are special rules relating to the years of commencement and cessation.

An overseas dividend manufacturer may have his right to double tax relief restricted, in particular, in respect of tax credits on overseas dividends received when the tax credits have been offset against tax due on manufactured overseas dividends paid or when the overseas dividends have been effectively paid on to a non-resident (see 1375).

Where no credit is allowable the foreign tax may be deducted (see 1794). A person may elect that any treaty provision giving credit is ignored.

Where transitional rules apply to average (or scale down) profits or income under self-assessment, double tax relief may be treated similarly.

Thin capitalisation

Some treaties contain thin capitalisation provisions, restricting relief or exemption where the size of loans is greater than would be expected between unrelated parties (or their terms are more beneficial to the lender). In this regard, it is specifically provided that, for interest paid after 14 May 1992, account should be taken in the UK of whether the loan would have been made at all, whether it would have been of such size and whether the rate and other terms would have been of that order. HMRC have confirmed that the absence of cross-default and cross-guarantee provisions, etc. in an intra-group loan will not be taken into account as regards the terms on which a loan is made.

Finance Act 2004 introduces measures to merge the current thin capitalisation requirements and subsume them within the general transfer pricing rules. The new rules will end transfer pricing and thin capitalisation requirements for small and medium-sized enterprises in most circumstances from 1 April 2004.

Law: FA 2004, s. 30–37 and Sch. 5; TIOPA 2010, Pt. 2; *Yates (HMIT) v GCA International Ltd (formerly Gaffney Cline and Associates Ltd)* [1991] BTC 107

Source: SP 7/91, *Double taxation relief: business profits: unilateral relief*; TAX 5/93

Website: www.hmrc.gov.uk/leaflets/c13.htm

See *British Tax Reporter* ¶171-350.

1794 Foreign tax as an expense

If no credit is allowable (or taken: see 1792) the foreign tax may be deducted so that only the net income is charged to UK tax.

Law: TIOPA 2010, s. 112

See *British Tax Reporter* ¶171-350.

RELIEFS AND DEDUCTIONS FOR INCOME TAX

NATURE OF INCOME TAX RELIEFS AND DEDUCTIONS

1840 Types of income tax relief or deduction

There are various tax reductions and reliefs to which an individual is entitled or which are available for the purposes of income tax generally. These can be categorised as items which:

- produce income which is exempt from tax, such as investments in personal equity plans and personal pension schemes;
- are deductible in computing income from a particular source or offset against income from a particular source, such as employment expenses (see 1990), business expenses (see 2150) and personal pension scheme contributions;
- are deductible in computing total income (known as 'charges on income': see below);
- can be offset against total income, such as with certain losses, and the personal allowance; and
- give rise to credits against tax (known as 'income tax reductions': see below).

Charges on income

Charges on income include, or have at some time included, certain 'annual payments' (see 1398), qualifying interest (see 1884), medical insurance premiums (see 1925) and maintenance payments (see 1882).

Some payments give rise to income tax reductions (see below).

Further, except in relation to certain existing obligations at 15 March 1988, any payment which is made by an individual and which would ordinarily be chargeable to income tax under ITTOIA 2005 (see 1366) in the hands of the payee cannot be a charge on the payer's income (though the payment becomes exempt for the payee) unless it is:

- a payment of interest;
- a covenanted payment to charity (see 1073);
- a payment made for bona fide commercial reasons in connection with the payer's trade, profession or vocation; and

- an annual payment made for non-taxable consideration.

There are special rules for maintenance payments which are discussed at 1882.

If relief as a charge is permitted, there are certain payments which are not deductible, or not wholly deductible, for higher rate tax purposes, e.g. covenanted payments to charity are restricted if the charity is not wholly exempt (see 907). Most covenants provide for a 'net' payment and the change in the basic rate of income tax may result in the charity receiving a lesser sum; that amount is not matched by an equivalent higher rate saving for the payer.

Offsets against total income

There are a number of personal reliefs from income tax available to individuals, depending on their circumstances; there are also a number of loss reliefs which are given in respect of an amount of income equal to any loss. In general, deductions may be set off against total income in the way which is most favourable to the taxpayer. However, personal reliefs are deducted after other deductions: thus to the extent that other deductions claimed reduce taxable income, personal reliefs may be lost (see example at 2297).

The amount of each personal relief is determined for each tax year. From 1994–95, the personal allowance, the blind person's allowance and life assurance premium relief are obtained by deducting set amounts from or offsetting them against an individual's total income, depending on his circumstances; other allowances are given by income tax reduction, as set out below (for eligibility, see 1850; for amounts see 56).

For reliefs for business losses against general income, see 2296ff., 2302. For the income tax relief for losses on shares in unquoted trading companies, see 5940.

Income tax reductions

Double tax relief has always been available in suitable circumstances by way of credit against tax otherwise payable (see 1792).

From 1994–95, basic rate tax on the following amounts has also been relieved in this manner:

- enterprise investment scheme (see 1930ff.);
- medical insurance premiums relief (see 1925);
- qualifying maintenance payments (see 1882);
- married couple's allowance, additional personal allowance and widow's bereavement allowance (see 1851ff.).

An effective order of offset is given by the amounts respectively taken into account before any particular reduction is determined (see 244).

From 2000–01, the married couple's allowance is withdrawn for most couples (see 1853ff.), the additional personal allowance is totally withdrawn and the widow's bereavement allowance is withdrawn for new claimants.

Law: ITA 2007, s. 23, 900; ITTOIA 2005, s. 727(1); FA 1996, s. 147

See *British Tax Reporter* ¶154-000.

1843 Claims for income tax reliefs and deductions

Deductions are usually given automatically. Reliefs and allowances generally have to be claimed by the taxpayer (see 2684).

If no specific time-limit is provided, a claim for relief must generally be made within four years from the end of the tax year to which it relates (see 2687).

See *British Tax Reporter* ¶184-200.

PAYABLE TAX CREDITS

1845 Introduction to tax credits

Tax credits come in a variety of forms. Some are true tax credits – that is to say they may only be used to reduce an amount of tax that is due. If no tax is due they are lost. The relief under the Enterprise Investment Scheme falls into this category (subject to a limited carry-back facility – see 1934). The tax credits brought in to replace social security benefit payments (working tax credit and child tax credit are different in character. They are 'payable' tax credits, and do not have to be covered by a comparable tax liability. Indeed, they are not actually set against an income tax liability, but are paid out directly by HMRC.

From 5 December 2005, the *Civil Partnerships Act* 2004 came into effect and ensures that same-sex couples are now treated in the same way as husband and wife couples.

Overview of tax credits

Very broadly, the WTC is payable to people in low-paid work, and the CTC to people with children, whether in work or not.

Tax credits are payable in full to people on income support or income-based jobseeker's allowance, or those whose income is very low. The maximum amount is then tapered away at 39 per cent as income rises. While the WTC minus the childcare element disappears fairly low down the income distribution, the childcare element and the CTC is retained as the claimants' income rises – and when the level of benefit finally dwindles away, there is still universal, tax-free, child benefit.

Income Tax

The WTC is available to couples with children, lone parents and people with a disability who are over 16 years of age and who work for at least 16 hours a week, and to others aged 25 or over who work at least 30 hours a week. From 31 March 2006, the whole of the WTC is payable directly to the claimant.

Tax credits have to be claimed. Any claim can be backdated by up to three months provided the conditions for entitlement are satisfied during the intervening period. Credits are awarded for a tax year, from 6 April to the following 5 April. If however a claim is made part-way through the year, the award period starts with the date of claim, subject to backdating. Certain changes in claimants' personal circumstances will also entitle HMRC to bring the award to an immediate end.

The claimants' entitlement is assessed, initially, on the basis of the previous tax year's income, and current circumstances. At the end of the award period the claimant's entitlement is adjusted to reflect the actual income of that period. If the claimant's income has fallen, more credit will be due. If it has risen by more than £2,500 above the level at which it was originally assessed, an overpayment may have arisen, which is recoverable at the discretion of HMRC.

The system can also recognise changes in a claimant's personal or financial circumstances during the year. Certain changes in circumstances have to be notified to the Revenue within three months, but many do not. Changes in income do not have to be notified as they are reflected in the year-end 'reconciliation'. Any change that increases a claimant's award, if notified, can be backdated by three months, but no more.

The calculation of a tax credit award is a complicated process. First, a claimant's circumstances are reviewed to find out which of several elements of the WTC and CTC they are entitled to. Then those elements are added together to reach the 'maximum' credit. The result is then tapered away as the claimant's income rises above a fixed threshold. Even when the tax credit award has dwindled away to nothing, at an income usually of about £58,000 a year, the claimant is still left with child benefit.

Neither tax credit, nor child benefit, is counted as taxable income.

A claim to tax credits may be made by an individual, a couple, or a polygamous unit. A claim is a 'joint claim' if made by a couple, or the members of a polygamous unit, and a 'single claim' if made by a single person. If a member of a couple or a polygamous unit wishes to make a claim, it must be a joint claim. In any case, every claimant, whether claiming singly or jointly, must be over 16 years of age, and be 'in the UK'.

Residence for tax credits purposes is different from the income tax concept. The statutory requirement for claimants to be 'in the United Kingdom' is expanded in the *Tax Credits (Residence) Regulations* 2003 (SI 2003/654) on which the Tax Credits Technical Manual (TCTM) is regarded by HMRC as an authoritative commentary. Broadly, a person who is not 'ordinarily resident' in the UK is regarded as not in the UK for this purpose; but HMRC take the view that 'ordinary residence' here has a different meaning from 'ordinary residence' for income tax. However, as will be seen, some anomalous situations arise as a result of the peculiar set of rules. Practitioners will need to be wary of potential clashes between the two systems, and should be particularly alert to HMRC's declared readiness to change its mind on a person's residence status.

Law: *Tax Credits Act* 2002; *Tax Credits Up-rating Regulations* 2009 (SI 2009/800); *Tax Credits (Miscellaneous Amendment) (No. 2) Regulations* 2009 (SI 2009/2887)

See *British Tax Reporter* ¶160-000.

1846   Working Tax Credit

The basic element of WTC

Claimants with children or a disability are eligible for WTC provided they work at least 16 hours a week and are aged 16 or over, or qualify for the 50 plus element (see below). Workers with neither children nor a disability are eligible provided they work at least 30 hours a week and are aged 25 or over. Gaps between jobs of up to seven days are ignored.

Other elements of WTC

Provided they are eligible for the basic element of WTC, claimants to WTC may be entitled to various other elements, based on their circumstances (for a table of the amounts of these elements, see 56):

- A second adult element. This is automatic where a joint claim to WTC is made, unless one of the claimants is over 50 and the 50 plus element is payable (see below).
- A lone parent element, where a single claim is made and the claimant is responsible for a child or children.
- A 30 hour element. This is designed to encourage those with a disability, or families with children, to move to full-time work. Couples with children will be entitled to it if one of the couple works at least 30 hours a week, or if they jointly work 30 hours a week, provided that one of them works at least 16 hours. Note that, for the purposes of claiming the child care element of WTC (see below) both partners in a couple must work for at least 16 hours a week.
- A disability element. Joint claimants may each claim this if they both qualify.
- A severe disability element. Joint claimants may each claim this if they both qualify.
- A 50 plus element. This is available to those aged 50 or over who are returning to work following a period of at least six months out of the labour market. It is divided into two rates – one for those working at least 16 hours, and one for those working at least 30 hours. Joint claimants may each claim the 50 plus element if they both qualify for it. Note that from 2012, the 50 plus element will be removed from the working tax credit.

The child care element

Families are eligible for the child care element where a lone parent or both partners in a couple work at least 16 hours a week. It is paid directly to the main carer by HMRC, either weekly or four-weekly at the claimant's choice. It is worth up to 70 per cent of qualifying

457

childcare costs, although a maximum limit to those costs is set (see 56 for a table showing the maximum costs). Child care costs are calculated on the basis of the average weekly cost, either using the four weeks immediately prior to the claim, or, in the case of monthly payments, multiplying by 12 and dividing by 52.

From 18 July 2009 changes have been made to the childcare registration arrangements governing tax credits. This is due to new childcare laws in England. The changes affect childcare providers who have been approved under the Childcare Approval Scheme, for example a nanny, and foster carers who work as childminders From 18 July 2009 the Childcare Approval Scheme no longer exists and the provider must be registered with Ofsted to allow the claimant to get tax credits help for childcare costs. Foster carers who work as childminders will have to officially register with Ofsted.

Any 'relevant' change in child care costs must be reported to HMRC. A relevant change occurs where:

- there is any change in the child care provided; or
- there is an increase or decrease in child care costs of £10 a week or more for a four week period.

The four week rule is designed to prevent the need to notify one-off variations. Where the changed sum is paid in each of the four weeks the need to notify is triggered.

When a relevant change occurs, the child care element of WTC must be recalculated. It is important to note that where child care costs decrease, and therefore less WTC is due, the recalculation will be made from the week following the four week period of the change. Where costs increase, so that more WTC is due, the recalculation is made from the later of:

- the first day of the week in which the change occurred; and
- the first day of the week in which falls the date three months prior to the change being notified to HMRC.

Hence, there is the possibility of obtaining the increase from the first day of the four week period (any decrease begins from the end of the four week period) – but any delay in notification of more than three months will mean a loss of credit.

Law: *Tax Credits Up-rating Regulations* 2010 (SI 2010/981)

Source: Leaflet WTC2: *A Guide to child tax credit and working tax credits*; Leaflet WTC6: *Child Tax Credit and Working Tax Credit – Other types of help you may be able to get*

See *British Tax Reporter* ¶164-000.

Website: www.hmrc.gov.uk/leaflets

1847 Child tax credit

The CTC brings together support for children from the diverse provisions of WFTC, DPTC, the children's tax credit, income support and income-based jobseeker's allowance. Claimants do not have to be in work. Child tax credit is expected to benefit 5.75 million families and can affect those on incomes well above £60,000 p.a. It is paid by HMRC directly to the main carer.

Children are eligible up to 1 September following their 16th birthday. The credit remains payable after that date for those in full-time, non-advanced, education up to the age of 19. From 6 April 2006, child tax credit may be paid to families of 16–19 year olds on unwaged work-based training programmes. The credit may also be payable beyond a young person's 19th birthday, either until they finish their course of education or training or they reach the age of 20.

The usual test to be applied is that the child is 'normally living with' the claimant(s). Where there are competing claims, the test is who has the 'main responsibility' for the child. This is subject to a joint election as to who has the main responsibility, but in the absence of such an election HMRC will decide on the information available.

Child tax credit remains payable for up to eight weeks following the death of a child.

Elements of CTC

The following elements make up CTC entitlement (see 56 for amounts):

- A family element. This is the basic element, paid to all families eligible for CTC and taking the place of the children's tax credit. A higher family element is available for the year following the birth of a child.
- A child element for each child in the family. Note that the baby element of CTC will be scrapped from April 2011.
- A disabled child element, where disability living allowance is payable or the child is registered blind.
- An enhanced disabled child element for families caring for a child with severe disability, where the highest rate of the care component of disability living allowance is payable.

Law: *Tax Credits (Miscellaneous Amendments) (No. 2) Regulations* 2008 (SI 2008/2169); *Child Tax Credit Regulations* 2002 (SI 2002/2007)

Source: Leaflet WTC2: *A Guide to child tax credit and working tax credits*; Leaflet WTC6: *Child Tax Credit and Working Tax Credit – Other types of help you may be able to get*

See *British Tax Reporter* ¶165-000.

Income Tax

1848 Calculating the tax credit

An award of tax credit lasts for a tax year, and this may have to be divided into 'relevant periods'. A relevant period is a part of the period of award (i.e. the tax year) where there is no change to the elements of WTC which the claimant is entitled to, and no relevant change in child care costs or arrangements (see 1849). Thus, a fluctuation in income does not trigger a new relevant period, but changes in circumstances (such as a material change in working hours) do. It follows that if there is no change in circumstances during the tax year, then the relevant period is the whole tax year.

Note that there is an extended definition of 'relevant period' where both WTC and CTC are claimed (see below).

The general method of calculation is to compute the maximum that can be claimed, and then to reduce this figure if income exceeds the threshold (see 56).

Income for tax credit purposes

'Income' is the gross income (i.e. before tax and NIC) of the claimant or, in the case of a joint claim, of the couple for a tax year. This is deemed to include 'notional' income – items which would otherwise be capital, like stock dividends, and items which are treated for tax purposes as the individual's income, like trust income where the settlor retains an interest, or payments to unmarried minor children. There are anti-avoidance provisions to ensure that income is not artificially reduced so as to increase credit entitlement.

Income for tax credit purposes is arrived at in a series of steps, as follows.

Step one
Add together:

- pension income;
- investment income;
- property income;
- foreign income; and
- notional income.

Each of these items is subject to complex definition in regulations. HMRC have given detailed guidance in the notes accompanying claim forms.

If the sum of these items is £300 or less, it is treated as nil. If it is more than £300, only the excess is carried forward to the next stages in the computation.

Step two
Add together:

- employment income;
- social security income;

- student income (grants); and
- miscellaneous income – i.e. income taxed under Schedule D Case VI.

Once again, these items are subject to detailed regulations, but there is extensive guidance available in the notes accompanying claim forms.

Step three
Add together the results of steps one and two.

Step four
Calculate trading income/loss. Add the income or deduct the loss from the result of step three.

Deductions
In calculating income for tax credit purposes the following may be deducted.

- any banking charge or commission for conversion of income into sterling;
- charitable donations under the gift aid scheme; and
- contributions to an approved retirement benefits scheme, an approved retirement annuity contract, or an approved personal pension scheme.

Calculating WTC

The first step is to calculate the maximum daily rate for each of the elements of WTC to which the claimant is entitled, other than the child care element (see below). This is done by dividing the annual maximum figures (see 56) by the number of days in the tax year, and rounding up to the nearest penny.

Having calculated the daily entitlement, the maximum rate for the relevant period is obtained by multiplying the daily rate by the number of days in the relevant period.

Income Tax

Example

Roger is registered blind and works full-time. From 1 September 2009 he chooses to work part-time, working 20 hours. His maximum rate of WTC is found as follows:

Relevant period 6.4.2009–31.8.2009 (148 days)	£
Basic element: $\dfrac{\pounds1,890}{365} = \pounds5.17 \times 148 =$	765.16
30 hour element: $\dfrac{\pounds775}{365} = \pounds2.12 \times 148 =$	313.76
Disability element: $\dfrac{\pounds2,530}{365} = \pounds6.93 \times 148 =$	1,025.64
Maximum rate for relevant period	2,104.56
Relevant period 1.9.2009–5.4.2010 (217 days)	
Basic element: $\pounds5.17 \times 217 =$	1,121.89

Disability element: £6.93 × 217 =	1,503.81
Maximum rate for relevant period	2,625.70

The maximum rate for the relevant period is then reduced by 39 per cent (rounding down to the nearest penny) of any income falling above a designated threshold (see 56). The annual threshold and income figures are apportioned between relevant periods (rounding income down to the nearest penny and the threshold up to the nearest penny).

The child care element

The calculation for the child care element for the relevant period is slightly different, since child care costs are reckoned on a weekly basis. The costs for the relevant period are found by obtaining an annual figure (multiply weekly cost by 52) and apportioning this using the number of days in the tax year and the number of days in the relevant period.

This must then be compared with the maximum that may be paid. Once again, the figure for the relevant period must be computed. The relevant maximum figure is divided by seven, rounded up to the nearest penny, and multiplied by the number of days in the relevant period.

The lower of the two figures (the actual child care costs of the relevant period and the maximum allowable for the relevant period) is then multiplied by 80 per cent (rounding up to the nearest penny). The result is the maximum rate of child care element for the relevant period.

Example

Tom and Barbara start the tax year 2007–08 paying £350 per week in child care costs. On 1 September, one of their two children starts school, but they still pay for out of school hours child care. Nonetheless, the overall cost reduces to £290 per week. The maximum rate for the child care element of WTC is as follows:

Maximum rate for relevant period 6.4.2007–31.8.2007 (148 days)

	£
Actual cost:	
$£350 \times \dfrac{52}{365} \times 148 =$	7,379.72
Maximum:	
$\dfrac{£300}{7} = £42.85 \times 148 =$	6,341.80
Maximum rate is therefore: £6,341.80 × 80%	5,073.44

Maximum rate for relevant period 1.9.2007–5.4.2008 (217 days)	
Actual cost:	
$£290 \times \dfrac{52}{365} \times 217 =$	8,965.37
Maximum:	
$£42.85 \times 217$	9,298.45
Maximum rate is therefore: $£8,965.37 \times 80\%$	7,172.30

If income is high enough to result in a reduction of credit greater than the other elements of WTC, the excess is set against the child care element.

Calculating CTC

An award of CTC is also for a tax year, and may have to be divided into relevant periods. A relevant period for CTC purposes is any part of the period of award where the maximum rate of CTC to which the claimant is entitled stays the same. Since the maximum rate is calculated before any reduction on account of income, changes in income will not trigger the end of a relevant period. However, changes in circumstances which affect the gross amount of CTC due (such as the birth of another child) will.

If WTC is being claimed at the same time as CTC, the definition of a relevant period is different. In addition to the requirement that the maximum rate of CTC stay the same, the two requirements for WTC relevant periods must also be met (i.e. no change in the elements of WTC the claimant is entitled to, and no relevant change in child care costs or arrangements).

The first step in calculating the rate of CTC for a relevant period is to compute the maximum daily rate. Divide the annual maximum amounts (see 56) by the number of days in the tax year, rounding up to the nearest penny. This figure is then multiplied by the number of days in the relevant period.

Where only CTC is being claimed, the threshold figure is straightforward (see 56). However, where both WTC and CTC are claimed the threshold figure is the greater of:

- the annual figure; or
- the amount of income needed to absorb all entitlement to WTC.

This produces some very fiddly computations, but fortunately the practical effect is simply to carry forward to CTC any amount of reduction left over from the WTC calculation. This carried forward figure of reduction may be set against all elements of CTC apart from the family element, which is subject to a different rate of reduction (see below).

The annual threshold and income figures are apportioned between relevant periods (rounding income down to the nearest penny and the threshold up to the nearest penny) where necessary.

Income Tax

Reducing the family element of CTC

A separate rate of reduction of 6.67 per cent applies to the family element of CTC (see 56). It is applied to income above the greater of:

- £50,000; and
- the income needed to absorb all other elements of WTC and CTC.

Once again, this gives rise to fiddly computations, but a simpler method is to adjust the carried forward figure of reduction for the new rate.

Note that from April 2011, the income threshold for the withdrawal of the family element of child tax credit (CTC) will be reduced from £50,000 to £40,000 and the withdrawal rate will be increased from 6.67 per cent to 41 per cent.

Law: *Tax Credits (Definition and Calculation of Income) Regulations* 2002 (SI 2002/2006); *Tax Credits (Income Thresholds and Determination of Rates) Regulations* 2002 (SI 2002/2008)

See *British Tax Reporter* ¶165-500.

1849   Making and adjusting claims

Initial claims to WTC and CTC are based on current circumstances and the previous tax year's income. On the basis of this information HMRC will make an initial decision as to the award of tax credit. HMRC are empowered to require what further information or evidence they need for this decision from the claimant(s) or from an employer.

It is possible for intermediaries such as the citizens advice bureau to act on behalf of an individual in cases concerning both tax credits and child benefits. In order for the intermediary to be recognised by HMRC a form TC689 must be completed by both the individual concerned and the target intermediary.

Claims may be backdated for up to three months.

An appeal may be brought against HMRC's initial decision on the award of tax credit.

Adjustments to claims during the period of award

Claims to WTC and CTC will run for 12 months unless there is a change in circumstances or income. The system provides for adjustments to be made during the year. Tax credit awards can be affected by:

- changes in the adults heading a household;
- changes in the circumstances giving entitlement to tax credits or the various elements of those tax credits; or
- changes in income.

Changes in circumstances

There are two changes of circumstance where it is compulsory to inform HMRC:

- Changes in the adults heading a household. This is because an award of tax credit is made to a household based on the income of those adults. Any change signifies the end of that particular claim.
- Use of qualifying child care changes or the weekly cost varies by £10 or more (see 1846).

Changes should be notified to HMRC within one month.

Apart from these mandatory notifications, it is up to the claimant whether to tell HMRC about changes in their circumstances during the year that increase or reduce entitlement to tax credit. Provided notification is within one month of the change, increased entitlement will run from the date of that change – otherwise the increased entitlement will run from the date of notification (thus, missing this deadline will result in a loss of some of the tax credit that would have been due for the year). It should be noted that changes reducing entitlement always run from the date of that change, so significant overpayments may be run up if HMRC are not informed.

Changes in income

HMRC will respond to all notifications of a decrease in income (and thus an increase in tax credit due) during the year. However, if the claimant does not inform HMRC during the year, no credit is lost – the change will form part of the end-of-year adjustment.

Increases in income are subject to a £2,500 disregard. That is to say, the first £2,500 of any increase in income is ignored. The disregard only operates in the year of the increase.

Example

Stephen is a lone parent who works full-time and has one child. In 2008–09 he earned £8,000. At the start of 2009–10 he gets a better job and expects to earn £11,500.

Stephen's rise in income of £3,500 is above the £2,500 disregard, and will thus reduce his entitlement to tax credit. He does not have to inform HMRC, but if he does not he will be faced with the recovery of any overpayment for 2009–10 during 2010–11. His entitlement to tax credit for 2009–10 will be calculated as if his income were £9,000 (£11,500 − £2,500). However, for 2010–11, entitlement will be based on the actual income of 2009–10, i.e. £11,500.

An appeal may be brought against HMRC's decision to adjust an award of tax credit.

Finalising claims

At the end of the year a renewal form will be issued by HMRC. The renewal form asks for confirmation of circumstances and income (or an estimate of income) for the year just finished so that HMRC may finalise the claim for that year. It also provides the basis for the

Income Tax

next year's claim. Whilst HMRC are awaiting the return of the renewal form the existing level of credit will continue.

Claimants must normally respond to the renewal notice by 6 July following the year end.

Thus, the year end sees HMRC having to make adjustments to the amount of credit paid out during the year. If credit has been underpaid, HMRC will make a single payment of the amount they owe. If credit has been overpaid, HMRC will recover the excess by adjusting the credit due in the following year, or through the PAYE code, or, as a last resort, through a one-off demand. Recovery of over-payments will be subject to a code of practice.

HMRC's 'finalising' decision on a claim may be appealed.

Investigations

HMRC may enquire into the entitlement of the claimant(s) to tax credit and to the amount of tax credit. In order to pursue their enquiries they may require information from the claimant(s) or an employer. As for income tax, HMRC must give notice that they are opening an enquiry, and also give notice when their enquiry is finished. Also like income tax, the claimant may ask the tribunal to direct HMRC to close their enquiry.

HMRC may adjust tax credit claims after an income tax enquiry, although their decision may be appealed.

Penalties

There is a penalty of up to £3,000 for fraudulently or negligently making an incorrect statement or declaration in connection with a claim for tax credit, or for supplying incorrect information or evidence in response to a notice requiring information. This applies also to any person acting for another in connection with the claim or notice. The penalty is imposed by a HMRC determination. An appeal may be lodged with the tribunal.

Failure to comply with a request for information or evidence, or with the requirements of a renewal notice, may result in an initial penalty of up to £300, after proceedings in front of the tribunal. Their decision may be appealed to the High Court. Continued failure results in a penalty of up to £60 per day, to be imposed by HMRC (an appeal against the determination may be lodged with the tribunal).

Where notification of a change in circumstances is mandatory (see above), failure to do so results in a fine of up to £300. This is imposed by HMRC determination, and appeal is to the tribunal.

Fraud

There is an offence of being 'knowingly concerned' in any fraudulent activity undertaken with a view to obtaining payments of a tax credit. This carries a maximum penalty of seven years' imprisonment, or a fine, or both.

HMRC powers, in cases where serious fraud is suspected, to seek judicial authority to order the production of documents or to enter premises with a warrant to obtain documents apply equally to tax credits. Once documents have been requested under these powers it is an offence to tamper with them, or destroy them.

Interest

Where an overpayment occurs because of fraud or neglect, HMRC may decide that all, or any part of, the overpayment is to carry interest. Interest runs from 30 days following the 'appropriate date', which is:

- in a case where the overpayment arises because the claimant was never entitled to the credit, the date of HMRC's decision to terminate the award; and
- in any other case, the date given in the end-of-year renewal notice – normally 6 July following the year to which it relates.

HMRC must issue a notice stating their decision regarding interest, and the notice must refer to the right of appeal against the decision.

Penalties carry interest from the date on which they become due and payable. However, HMRC may reduce the amount of interest due, including down to nil, if they think it appropriate.

Law: *Tax Credits Act* 2002; *Working Tax Credit (Entitlement and Maximum Rate) (Amendment) Regulations* 2010 (SI 2010/918); *Tax Credits Up-rating Regulations* 2010 (SI 2010/981); *Tax Credits (Provision of Information) (Functions Relating to Health) Regulations* 2003 (SI 2003/731); *Tax Credits (Polygamous Marriages) Regulations* 2003 (SI 2003/742); *Tax Credits (Claims and Notifications) Regulations* 2002 (SI 2002/2014); *Tax Credits (Appeals) (No. 2) Regulations* 2002 (SI 2002/3196); *The Social Security Commissioners (Procedure) (Tax Credits Appeals) Regulations* 2002 (SI 2002/3237)

Website: www.hmrc.gov.uk/forms/tc689.pdf

See *British Tax Reporter* ¶162-000.

PERSONAL RELIEFS

1850 Nature of personal reliefs

The various personal reliefs are available to UK residents and, in certain cases, non-residents (see 1585). Personal reliefs cannot be carried forward or backwards to other tax years. For interaction with other reliefs and deductions, see 1840.

The personal allowance, the blind person's allowance and life assurance premium relief are obtained by deducting set amounts from or offsetting them against an individual's total income (see 1851, 1878, 1880, respectively).

Income Tax

From 2000–01, the married couple's allowance is withdrawn for most couples (see 1853ff.).

The necessary claims are normally made in the tax return in respect of the previous year's income. For the time-limit for claims, see 1843.

Law: ITA 2007, Pt 3

See *British Tax Reporter* ¶154-000.

1851   Personal allowance

Every individual, irrespective of sex and marital status, who is liable to income tax is entitled to a personal allowance of £6,475 for 2010–11 (remaining unchanged from 2009–10). For a table of recent allowances, see 56. The individual may deduct this amount from his total income, along with any other deductions to which he may be entitled, and will then be taxed on the remainder. If the individual earns less than the personal allowance to which he is entitled for that year, he will not be liable to income tax.

Example 1

In 2010–11 Amanda's only taxable income comprises business profits of £10,220. She is a single woman aged 35.

	£
Earnings	10,220
Less: personal allowance	(6,475)
Taxable income	3,745

	£
Tax on £3,745 @ 20%	749

Example 2

In 2010–11 Bella's only income comprises earnings of £5,500. Since this figure is less than the personal allowance of £6,475 she will not have to pay any income tax.

The necessary claim is normally made in the tax return in respect of the previous year's income (see 1850).

For taxpayers aged over 65, see 1874.

Law: ITA 2007, s. 23, 35; *Income Tax (Indexation) (No. 3) Order* 2008 (SI 2008/3023); *Income Tax (Indexation) (No. 4) Order* 2008 (SI 2008/3024)

See *British Tax Reporter* ¶155-000.

1853 Married couple's allowance

The married couple's allowance was withdrawn for most couples from 6 April 2000. It is only available after that date where at least one party to the marriage was born before 6 April 1935.

Entitlement to the allowance

In addition to the 'personal allowance' (see 1851), a 'married couple's allowance' was available to a claimant who proves that at some time in the tax year he is a married man whose wife is 'living with' him (this term means more than living under the same roof: see 1862).

A marriage is generally accepted as valid if it is made in accordance with the law of the country in which it was performed and of the country of domicile of the parties though the allowance is unavailable in respect of 'common law' relationships. However, no more than one married couple's allowance is available in any tax year.

For the tax treatment applicable in the year of marriage, see 1856.

Transfer of married couple's allowance to wife

A wife may as a result of an election be entitled to the basic allowance (or a one-half share of it) irrespective of the level of her husband's income (see below); any allowance unused by an individual may be transferred to the other spouse.

For married couple's allowance to be so transferable, the husband (or from 1993–94, the wife) has to give to the inspector written notice, within six years after 31 January following the end of the tax year to which the notice relates (before self-assessment, six years from the end of the tax year); such notice is irrevocable.

A wife can opt to receive a one-half share of the basic allowance (even if the greater allowance for the elderly is in point) or the couple can agree to allocate the basic allowance wholly to the wife; the husband can elect to revert to the half-share basis. Any of these elections will normally take effect from the beginning of the tax year *following* that in which it is made (except in the year of marriage or within a 30-day grace period if prior notification has been given); an election continues in force until the year after it is withdrawn or replaced by a new election.

The amount of married couple's allowance that can be transferred to a wife during a tax year is limited to the minimum level of allowance due that year. The level is set to increase each year in line with the retail prices index (RPI) unless an alternative amount is announced in the annual Budget.

Income Tax

Restriction of allowance to those reaching 65 before 2000–01

The married couple's allowance was abolished from April 2000 for couples under 65, nor will people be able to make new claims for the allowance when they or their spouse reach 65 after 5 April 2000. However, where persons born before 5 April 1935 newly get married, they or their spouse will still be eligible to claim the allowance (see 1874).

Law: ITA 2007, Pt 3, Ch 3; *Rignell (HMIT) v Andrews* [1990] BTC 306; *Nabi v Heaton (HMIT)* [1983] BTC 359

Source: IR 80, *Income tax and married couples*

See *British Tax Reporter* ¶156-000.

1856 Married couple's allowance in the year of marriage

The married couple's allowance remains available after 5 April 2000 to newly married couples after that date where at least one party to the marriage was born before 5 April 1935.

The married couple's allowance (see 1853) has effect in relation to any claim by a man who 'becomes married' in the tax year for which the claim is made, and who has not previously, in that year, been entitled to the allowance (by reason of a previous marriage), as if the allowance were reduced, for each month of that year ending before the date of marriage, by one-twelfth. A 'month' means a month beginning with the sixth day of a month of the calendar year, i.e. it is a tax month. The reduced allowance can be wholly transferred to the wife or shared equally with the wife in the usual way, though an election to transfer can be made in the year of marriage with effect for that year (see 1853).

For the monthly reduction for recent tax years, see 56.

> ### Example
>
> Hubert, born in July 1929, marries Winifred on 24 December 2009. Hubert's reduced married couple's allowance for 2009–10 is £6,965 − ($^{8}/_{12}$ × 6,965) = £2,322.

Law: ITA 2007, s. 54, 55

Source: IR 80, *Income tax and married couples*

See *British Tax Reporter* ¶155-500.

1862   Husband and wife: year of separation, divorce

There may be a number of consequences for personal reliefs in the year in which a couple separate or divorce, as set out below. For the tax treatment of maintenance payments, see 1882.

Separation

A married woman is treated as living with her husband unless:

- they have been separated by a court order or by deed of separation; or
- they are in fact separated in such circumstances that the separation is likely to be permanent.

When a married couple first so separate, they should advise their tax office. They may claim personal allowances for the tax year of separation. In that year if the husband is entitled to the married couple's allowance, he remains entitled to the full allowance for that year. The allowance may be transferred to the wife or shared equally with her in the usual way; both parties remain entitled to their individual personal allowances, of course (see 1851).

See also transitional provisions for separated couples at 1853.

Divorce

On a divorce, 'married couple's allowance' (see 1853), to the extent that it was previously available, ceases to be available in the tax year in no part of which the couple were both:

- married; and
- 'living together' (see above).

Both parties remain entitled to their individual personal allowances, of course (see 1851).

Law: ITA 2007, s. 1011

See *British Tax Reporter* ¶155-550.

1864   Husband and wife: year of annulment or death

Annulment

Where a marriage is annulled (treated as having never taken place) the married couple's allowance (see 1853) granted for previous years will not be affected.

Wife's death

A wife's death does not reduce her widower's married couple's allowance (if still available to him) (see 1853) for the tax year of death.

Income Tax

Husband's death

A deceased husband's personal representatives may request that any of the married couple's allowance (see 1853) for the year of his death which could not be used against his income be transferred to his widow.

See *British Tax Reporter* ¶156-300.

1874   Allowances for the elderly

Increased personal allowance

An elderly individual, irrespective of marital status, is entitled to a 'personal allowance' (see 1851) at an increased level. Deduct contributions to personal pension schemes in arriving at income for these purposes (see ESC A102). There is a table of allowances for recent years at 56.

Married couple's allowance

Although the married couple's allowance was withdrawn from 6 April 2000, it remains available where at least one party to the marriage was born before 6 April 1935, even if the marriage did not take place until after 5 April 2000.

For 1999–2000 and earlier years, the married couple's allowance (see 1853) was available at an increased level where either the man or his wife is elderly.

Where the age-related married couple's allowance is available after 6 April 2000, it is relieved only at the rate of ten per cent; this is effected by a reduction in the income tax otherwise payable (see 1850). The relief was also at ten per cent for 1999–2000.

It is only the basic married couple's allowance which can be freely transferred between spouses from 1993–94 (see 1853).

These increased levels of the personal allowance and married couple's allowance are initially given for the tax year in which the sixty-fifth or seventy-fifth birthday falls, or would have fallen but for earlier death within that year.

The age-related allowances are tapered away from people with income above a specified limit (see below), down to a new minimum level. For 2010–11, the minimum amount of married couple's allowance is £2,670.

Income limit

Married couples each have their own 'income limit' – £22,900 for 2010–11, above which the age-related personal allowances are reduced, the income of a wife not being aggregated with that of her husband. However, neither may transfer any unused part of that limit to the other. To the extent that a husband's total income exceeds the income limit, the maximum age-related married couple's allowance is reduced by one-half of the excess, less any reduction already made to his personal allowance, until it reaches the minimum amount of married couple's allowance (see 1853).

Example

Hugo and Wendy are a cohabiting married couple, both aged 69, with respective total incomes in 2007–08 of £25,900 and £11,000.

Hugo's personal allowance

	£
Hugo's total income	25,900
Less: income limit	(20,900)
Excess	5,000

Hugo's age-related personal allowance (£7,550) is reduced by one-half of the excess (i.e. by £2,500) to £5,050; however, no taxpayer gets less than the basic personal allowance, and this is accordingly Hugo's personal allowance for 2007–08.

Married couple's allowance

The age-related married couple's allowance (£6,285 in 2007–08) is reduced by one-half of Hugo's income over the income limit (i.e. by £2,500) *less* the actual reduction (of £2,325 (£7,550 − £5,225)) already made to his personal allowance: i.e. the £6,285 allowance is reduced to £6,110 (£6,285 − (£2,500 − £2,325)).

Wendy's personal allowance

As Wendy's income does not exceed the £20,900 limit, she is entitled to the full (increased) personal allowance of £7,550.

The increased personal and married couple's allowances are also available to or in respect of a person who would have attained 65 (or 75) in the tax year but for dying in that year. Thus if a taxpayer would have become 65 (or 75) on 1 April 2008 but died on 30 June 2007, he would still be entitled to all of his increased personal allowance for 2007–08 for offset against his income for the period from 6 April 2007 to 30 June 2007.

For the tax treatment applicable to the year of marriage, see 1856.

Law: ITA 2007, Pt 3, Ch 3

Source: IR 80, *Income tax and married couples*

See *British Tax Reporter* ¶156-000.

Income Tax

1878   Blind person's allowance

An allowance of £1,890 for 2010–11 (remaining unchanged from 2009–10) is available to a person who proves that he is a registered blind person for all or part of a tax year. For the amount of the allowance for recent years, see 56.

A person who becomes entitled to the blind person's allowance by being registered blind will also be granted the allowance for the previous tax year, if, at the end of that year, he had obtained proof of blindness subsequently used to qualify for registration. This concession is intended to prevent people losing the allowance because of delays in the registration process.

A blind married man whose wife is 'living with' him (see 1862) can transfer the allowance to her if and to the extent that he lacks sufficient income against which to use the allowance after making all other available deductions except those listed at 1853. Where it is the wife who is entitled to blind person's allowance, she may likewise transfer any unusable part of it to her husband. Before these transfer provisions can apply, the person entitled to the allowance must have given to the inspector an irrevocable written notice, not later than the fifth anniversary of the 31 January (or, before self-assessment, not later than six years) from the end of the tax year to which the notice relates, that the provisions should apply. Such a notice also operates as a notice to transfer married couple's allowance (see 1853).

A registered blind person means a person registered as blind under the *National Assistance Act* 1948 or Northern Ireland counterpart.

Law: ITA 2007, s. 38–40

Source: ESC A86, *Blind person's tax allowance*

See *British Tax Reporter* ¶157-000.

1879   Foster carers relief

Foster carers relief was introduced with effect from 6 April 2003. The relief applies to individuals who provide foster care services to local authorities, either directly or indirectly. The relief replaced the former treatment of income from fostering and consists of two elements:

(1)   foster carers whose gross receipts from foster care do not exceed an individual limit (see below) in a year are exempt from tax on their income from foster care; and

(2)   foster carers whose gross receipts from foster care exceed the individual limit. Individuals who fall into this category will be able to choose between:

- computing their business profits using the normal rules; or
- treating as their profit the amount by which their gross receipts from foster care exceed their individual limit.

The individual limit is made up of two elements:

(1)   a fixed amount per residence of £10,000 for a full year; and

(2)   an additional amount per child for each week, or part week, that the individual provides foster care. The amounts are £200 a week for a child aged under 11 and £250 a week for a child aged 11 or older.

Law: ITTOIA 2005, Pt 7, Ch. 2; FA 2003, s. 176, Sch. 36

Website: www.hmrc.gov.uk/individuals/foster-carers.htm
www.hmrc.gov.uk/individuals/adult-placement-carers.htm

See *British Tax Reporter* ¶164-050.

1880   Life assurance premium relief

Life assurance premium relief ('LAPR') has been abolished for policies issued after 13 March 1984. For insurances made before that date, taxpayers are entitled to relief on $12^1/_2$ per cent of the premiums paid on qualifying policies. The insurance must be on the taxpayer's life, or that of his/her spouse and relief will be available regardless of which spouse pays the premium. Relief continues after divorce in respect of premiums paid by one party on the other's life if they were married when the policy was taken out but were divorced after 5 April 1979. This treatment extends to premiums paid by a divorced person on a policy taken out before the marriage. The person paying the premium must be 'resident in the UK' (see 213) when the payment is made and the payment must be made to a UK company or a UK branch of an overseas company.

Relief is also available for certain payments made to secure a deferred annuity for any widow, widower or child of the claimant after death.

Law: ITA 2007, Pt 8, Ch 6

Source: ESC A31, *Life assurance premium relief by deduction: pre-marriage policies*

See *British Tax Reporter* ¶310-900.

1882   Relief for maintenance payments

Tax relief for maintenance payments is withdrawn with effect from 5 April 2000, except where one or both parties to the marriage are aged 65 or over on that date.

For those who remain eligible for relief, the rules previously applying to arrangements made after 15 March 1988 apply to all maintenance payments, irrespective of whether the arrangement were set up before that date (previously known as 'Existing obligations'. These rules are summarised below.

Income Tax

The rules set out below apply for 2000–01 and later tax years in respect of those maintenance payments which continue to attract relief (see above), irrespective of the date on which the arrangement was made and for 1999–2000 and earlier years, to all arrangements made after 15 March 1988.

Where relief is not otherwise available, payments under a court order or agreement within the EU to a divorced or separated wife or husband (who has not remarried) for:

- their own maintenance; or
- the maintenance of a child of the marriage,

will be eligible for relief – a 'qualifying maintenance payment'. The extension to other EU member states has effect for payments due from 6 April 1992.

Maintenance assessed by the Child Support Agency qualifies for relief from 6 April 1993 in the same way as maintenance paid under a court order; maintenance collected by the Agency on behalf of a divorced or separated spouse will qualify for tax relief in the same way as if payment were made to the spouse.

The maximum amount eligible for relief for any year is equal to:

- the payments due in that year; and
- the minimum married couple's allowance for that year (£2,670 for 2010–11).

Relief is given by reducing the tax liability by 10 per cent of the amount eligible for relief, or by reducing the tax liability to nil, whichever is the lower. In reducing the tax liability to nil, reductions for married couple's allowance, children's tax credit, additional personal allowance and widow's bereavement allowance are ignored.

From 2000–01, those receiving maintenance payments under pre-15 March 1988 arrangements are not taxed on the payments they receive.

Law: ITA 2007, Pt 8, Ch 5

Website: www.hmrc.gov.uk/bulletins/index.htm

See *British Tax Reporter* ¶115-650.

1883 Relief for gains on life policies and investment bonds

Gains on certain life assurance policies, life annuity contracts and capital redemption policies (including 'investment bonds') are subject to higher rate tax as income of an individual (see 1460ff.).

Relief is afforded to such gains by way of top-slicing relief. The gain which is charged is averaged over the years the investment has been held and it is only then added to the individual's other income for the tax year in point to determine whether higher rate tax is payable. Any higher rate tax so calculated is then multiplied by the number of years the investment has been held.

See *British Tax Reporter* ¶310-900.

RELIEF FOR INTEREST PAYMENTS

1884 Nature of relief against income tax for interest payments

Income tax relief (at various effective rates) is available for an interest payment if it relates to one of the specified categories of loan, below.

Relief is not granted in the following circumstances:

- where interest is paid on an overdraft or under credit card arrangements;
- where interest is paid at a rate greater than a reasonable commercial rate (in which case the excess is ineligible for relief);
- where the main benefit of the arrangement is the reduction of tax;
- where relief is sought by a company within the charge to corporation tax (see 3061).

Interest paid as a revenue rather than capital item on money borrowed wholly and exclusively for the purposes of a trade, profession or vocation is not subject to the foregoing restrictions (see 2150ff.). There are provisions intended to prevent any double deductions for interest.

Categories of qualifying loan

Interest relief is available on loans applied for the following purposes:

- to purchase machinery and plant (see 1886);
- in acquiring an interest in a close company (see 1888);
- in acquiring an interest in a co-operative (see 1890);
- in acquiring shares in an employee-controlled company (see 1892);
- in acquiring an interest in a partnership (see 1894);
- to pay inheritance tax (see 1896);
- to purchase a life annuity where the borrower is 65 years old or more (see 1898).

The giving of credit to a purchaser under any sale is treated as the making of a loan to defray money applied by him in making the purchase.

Where only part of a loan satisfies the conditions for interest relief, only a proportion of the interest will be eligible for relief. That proportion is one which is equal to the proportion of the loan fulfilling those conditions at the time the money is applied.

Full interest relief is generally available on a joint loan to a husband and wife where only one of them satisfies the qualifying conditions as respects investment in a close company or partnership and that spouse makes the payments or they are made out of a joint account.

Income Tax

Form of relief

Relief generally takes the form of a deduction from or offset against total income in respect of the interest paid. However, as with mortgage interest, from 1994–95, if relief is not available at source, relief for interest on a loan to purchase a life annuity is given by way of a reduction in the income tax otherwise payable, though the rate of relief in this case remains the basic rate; an effective order of offset of reliefs (see 244) is provided (for relief at source, see 1898). Any necessary apportionment of the interest where a loan is used the purpose of purchasing such annuity and for other qualifying purposes is made on a specified basis.

Where an individual would obtain relief in respect of interest on a loan but the loan is on preferential terms and is obtained by reason of his employment, no taxable benefit ultimately arises (the benefit is effectively offset by relief for the deemed interest) (see 406).

Indirect recoveries of capital

If at any time after the application of the proceeds of the loan, the borrower has recovered capital from the close company, employee-controlled company, co-operative or partnership (but does not use it in repayment of the loan) he is treated as repaying the loan (in whole or in part) so that the interest eligible for relief, and payable for any period after capital is recovered, is reduced by an amount equal to the interest on the capital recovered.

The borrower is treated as having recovered capital if he receives consideration for the sale, exchange or assignment of his ordinary shares in the close company or of his shares in the co-operative or of his interest in the partnership. Capital is deemed to have been recovered if the company, etc. repays the loan or the partnership returns capital to the borrower. HMRC view is that the conversion of loan stock into ordinary shares is an assignment of the loan stock to the company (in exchange for shares), so that relief ceases.

Claim for relief

As a general rule, a claim (see 1843) must be made for interest relief. The person making the claim must supply the inspector with a written statement from the lender which contains the following information:

- the date when the debt was incurred;
- the amount of the debt when incurred;
- the interest paid in the tax year for which the claim is made; and
- the name and address of the debtor.

Local authorities and building societies (or companies carrying out similar business) are excluded from this requirement. HMRC forms can be used but are not required.

Law: ITA 2007, s. 383

Website: www.hmrc.gov.uk/bulletins/index.htm

1886 Interest on loan to buy machinery or plant

Interest attracts income tax relief (see 1884) where it is paid by an individual member of a partnership to buy machinery or plant if the partnership is entitled to capital allowances in respect of that machinery, etc.

An employee or director is entitled to such interest relief if he is entitled to a capital allowance (or would be so entitled but for some contribution made by his employer) for machinery or plant belonging to him and used for the purposes of his office or employment (e.g. a car: see 1997).

In cases both of partnerships and employments, the relief is available for interest payable up to three years from the end of the tax year in which the debt was incurred.

Where the plant or machinery is used only partly for the purposes of the trade, etc. or the employment, then a just and reasonable apportionment is made of the interest eligible for relief.

Law: ITA 2007, s. 388–391

See *British Tax Reporter* ¶115-200.

1888 Interest on loan to invest in a close company

Interest paid on a loan made to an individual may be eligible for income tax relief (see 1884) if the money is borrowed:

(1) to acquire ordinary shares of a qualifying 'close company' (see 4253);

(2) in making a loan to a qualifying close company where the loan is used wholly and exclusively for the business of the company or of any associated qualifying close company; or

(3) in satisfying an earlier loan which would have qualified for interest relief.

A close company is a qualifying close company if it falls within one of the types of company excluded from being a close investment-holding company (see 4283).

Relief will generally be denied unless either of the conditions set out below is satisfied. However, the following points should be noted:

- HMRC are willing to allow relief for interest, following a reorganisation involving an exchange of shares after the loan proceeds are applied, provided the conditions for relief would have been met had the loan been a new loan taken out to invest in the new business entity; and
- relief has been allowed where taxpayers borrowed money to buy shares in a close company formed to put into effect a management buy-out, even though the company had not started trading when the loans were taken out: the High Court said that if a loan was

made and shares subscribed to enable a company to acquire a business, it could be said that the company existed for the purpose of carrying on that business and that the acquisition of the business was the means by which that purpose was to be achieved and not an end in itself (*Lord (HMIT) v Tustain* [1993] BTC 447).

(1) Investors with a 'material interest'

The company must be a qualifying close company at the time the interest is paid and the borrower must have a material interest in the company. Basically, an individual has a material interest if he, alone or with any associate(s) (see 4268), owns beneficially or is able to control more than five per cent of the ordinary share capital of the company or would be entitled to more than five per cent of the assets on a winding up, etc. (for accounting periods beginning before 1 April 1989: five per cent of the apportionable income). As well as holding a material interest, the claimant must also show that he has not recovered any capital from the company apart from any amount taken into account in reducing the interest eligible for relief (see 1884). If the company exists wholly or mainly to hold investments or other property, the borrower must not use property held by the company as a residence unless he has spent the majority of his time in the management or conduct of the company's business or that of an associated company (see 4271).

Note that the definition of 'associate' for the purpose of establishing a material interest prevents the personal shares of other trust beneficiaries being aggregated with those of the participator. The effect is that close company interest relief is not available where a material interest has been artificially created by a token trust holding.

(2) Investors managing the company

At the time the interest is paid the company must be a qualifying close company and the borrower must hold shares of the company. Up to the date of the interest payment, the borrower must have worked for the majority of his time in the management or conduct of the company or of an associated company. He must also show that he has not recovered any capital up to the time interest is paid apart from any amount taken into account in reducing the interest eligible for relief (see 1884).

Relief in respect of shares acquired is denied if the acquirer or his spouse claims EIS relief in respect of them. Relief continues to be denied whatever relief is claimed under the *new* EIS (which combines the old EIS relief with reinvestment relief for CGT: see 1930).

Law: ITA 2007, s. 392–395

Source: ESC A43, *Interest relief: investments in partnerships, co-operatives, close companies, and employee-controlled companies*; SP 3/78, *Close companies: income tax relief for interest on loans applied in acquiring an interest in a close company*

See *British Tax Reporter* ¶115-200.

1890   Interest on loan to invest in a co-operative

A co-operative is a common ownership enterprise or a co-operative enterprise as defined in the *Industrial Common Ownership Act* 1976, s. 2.

Interest paid by an individual (the borrower) on a loan to buy shares in a co-operative or its subsidiary may be eligible for income tax relief (see 1884) if the loan is made after 10 March 1981 and at the time the interest is paid, the co-operative continues to be a co-operative; the borrower must for the greater part of his time have been an employee of the co-operative or its subsidiary from the time the loan is applied to the time of the interest payments. He must also show that he has not recovered any capital from the co-operative before the interest payment except for any amount taken into account in reducing the interest eligible for relief (see 1884).

Law: ITA 2007, s. 401

See *British Tax Reporter* ¶115-350.

1892   Interest on loan to invest in an employee-controlled company

Interest may be eligible for income tax relief (see 1884) if it is paid on a loan made to an individual to acquire ordinary shares in an employee-controlled company or to pay off another loan which would have qualified for interest relief.

Conditions for relief

Relief will only be given if the following conditions are satisfied:

(1)   the company must be (from the date on which the shares are acquired to the date on which interest is paid):

   (a)   an unquoted company resident only in the UK, and
   (b)   a trading company or the holding company of a trading company,

(2)   the shares must be acquired before, or not later than 12 months after, the date on which the company first becomes an employee-controlled company;

(3)   during the tax year in which the interest is paid, the company must either:

   (a)   first become an employee-controlled company, or
   (b)   be employee-controlled throughout a period of at least nine months;

(4)   the individual must be a full-time employee of the company from the date of buying the shares to the date on which the interest is paid. Relief will continue to be given for interest paid up to 12 months after the taxpayer has ceased to be a full-time employee;

(5)   the taxpayer must not have recovered any capital from the company unless that amount is treated as a repayment of the loan in whole or in part (see 1884).

What is an employee-controlled company?

A company is an employee-controlled company at any time when at least 50 per cent:

- of the issued ordinary share capital of the company; and
- of the voting power in the company,

is beneficially owned by persons who are full-time employees of the company.

Where an individual owns beneficially more than ten per cent of the issued ordinary share capital or controls more than ten per cent of the voting power in the company, the excess over ten per cent is not regarded as being owned by a full-time employee.

Law: ITA 2007, s. 396

See *British Tax Reporter* ¶115-400.

1894   Interest on loan to invest in partnership

Interest on a loan to an individual attracts income tax relief (see 1884) if the loan is used to defray money applied in the following ways:

- to purchase a share in a partnership;
- to contribute capital to a partnership, or advance money to it, where it is used wholly for the purposes of the business carried on by the partnership; or
- to pay off another loan interest on which would have been eligible for relief.

The individual must be a member of the partnership but not a limited partner throughout the period from the application of the loan until the interest is paid. He must also show that, up to the date interest is paid, he has not recovered any capital from the partnership apart from any amount taken into account in reducing the interest eligible for relief (see 1884).

Interest may also be eligible for relief if a loan is used by a partner to buy land occupied by the partnership.

Law: ITA 2007, s. 398–400

See *British Tax Reporter* ¶115-450.

1896   Interest on loan to pay inheritance tax

Interest on a loan made to personal representatives of a deceased person attracts income tax relief (see 1884) if the loan is applied either:

- to pay, before the grant of representation, inheritance tax on the deceased's personal estate; or
- to pay off another loan, interest on which would be eligible for relief as above.

Only interest paid in the first year of the making of the original loan is eligible for relief.

Where, in the year interest is paid, income is insufficient for full relief to be given, relief may be given against income of preceding tax years (taking the earliest year first) and, if still unrelieved, relief may be given against income of succeeding tax years.

Law: ITA 2007, s. 403–405

See *British Tax Reporter* ¶115-550.

1898   Interest on loan to purchase life annuity

Life annuities are sold by specialist plan providers and normally form part of a home income plan. Interest paid on a loan to purchase a life annuity attracts income tax relief (see 1884) if the following conditions are satisfied:

(1)   the loan must have been made before 9 March 1999;

(2)   the loan must be made as part of a scheme under which at least 90 per cent of the loan is applied in purchasing a life annuity ending with the death of the borrower or the survivor of the borrower and two or more annuitants;

(3)   at the time the loan is made the borrower and any other annuitant must be at least 65 years old;

(4)   the loan must be secured on land in the UK or Republic of Ireland and the borrower, or one of the annuitants, must own an estate or interest in that land;

(5)   for any loan made after 26 March 1974, the annuitant must use the land on which the loan is secured as his only or main residence at the time the interest is paid, or within 12 months of leaving the property, must intend to dispose of it, and take steps actually to do so; and

(6)   the interest must be payable by the borrower or by one of the annuitants.

In respect of payments of interest made after 6 April 2000, relief is fixed at 23 per cent (the basic rate of tax in 1999–2000), rather than being linked to the prevailing basic rate of tax. Similarly the ceiling for loans is fixed at £30,000 and is not re-set annually.

As regards (1) above, a loan made on or after 9 March 1999 may be treated as made before that date if it is made in pursuance of an offer in writing made by the lender before that date. This ensures that anyone who was in the process of taking out a loan on that date and whose application was well advanced will still be entitled to relief.

As regards (5) above, with effect from 27 July 1999, these conditions are relaxed and the borrower will no longer lose relief simply because he stops using, as his only or main residence, the property on which the loan is secured. This change ensures that a borrower can move, say, into a nursing home, without losing relief.

Also borrowers are able to move house or re-mortgage without moving (for example, to obtain a lower interest rate, or to increase the size of the loan) without losing their existing relief. A new loan made after 26 July 1999 qualifies for relief if either:

- it is applied wholly in paying off the old (qualifying) loan; or
- if only partially applied in paying off the old loan, not less than nine-tenths of the new part is applied to the purchase of a qualifying annuity.

Interest on a loan made after 26 March 1974 only attracts relief on an amount up to the 'qualifying maximum' – for recent years the figure has been £30,000; if interest is payable by two or more persons, interest payable by each is eligible for relief on a proportion of the total eligible interest.

Tax relief for interest payments on loans within these provisions is given in most cases through MIRAS, i.e. *basic* rate tax is to be deducted and retained by the borrower from the interest payments before the payments are made. The deduction continues to be at basic rate, even though MIRAS is applied to home loans, etc. at ten per cent after 5 April 1998.

Law: ITA 2007, s. 385

See *British Tax Reporter* ¶115-600.

1921   Individual savings accounts

Individual savings accounts (ISAs) are stand-alone savings products which started on 6 April 1999. Interest, dividends and capital gains held within ISAs are not liable to income tax or CGT.

An ISA can be made up of an investment in cash, or investments like stocks and shares or insurance. Individual savers are able to invest in two separate ISAs in any one tax year: one cash ISA and one stocks and shares ISA.

All individuals who are both resident and ordinarily resident in the UK for tax purposes and are aged 18 or over have the same opportunity to subscribe to the new account, and husbands and wives each have their own annual limit.

The limit for annual investment into ISAs has been increased from £7,200 to £10,200, up to £5,100 of which can be saved in cash. The new limits apply from 6 October 2009 to people aged 50 and over in 2009–10, and for all investors from 2010–11 onwards.

Law: ITTOIA 2005, s. 697; *Individual Savings Account (Amendment No. 2) Regulations 2009* (SI 2009/1994); *Individual Savings Account (Amendment) Regulations 2010* (SI 2010/835); *Individual Savings Account (Amendment) Regulations 2009* (SI 2009/1550); *Individual Savings Account (Amendment No. 3) Regulations 2008* (SI 2008/3025);

Individual Savings Account (Amendment) Regulations 2007 (SI 2007/2119); *Individual Savings Account Regulations* 1998 (SI 1998/1870)

See *British Tax Reporter* ¶321-500.

1925 Medical insurance premiums relief

Policies taken out or renewed after 1 July 1997

Relief on premiums paid on annual contracts for private medical insurance (PMI) for the over 60s is withdrawn for policies taken out, or renewed, on or after 2 July 1997. There is an exception for the situation where a contract is finalised before 1 August 1997, but where arrangements were made before 2 July 1997 (even though the contract was not final by that date).

Premiums under annual contracts already in existence on 2 July 1997, and contracts falling within the exception (see above), qualify for relief until the end of the contract, provided that premiums were received by the insurer before 6 April 1999.

Law: F(No. 2)A 1997, s. 17; FA 1996, Sch. 18, para. 12; former FA 1989, s. 54–56; *Private Medical Insurance (Tax Relief) Regulations* 1989 (SI 1989/2387); *Private Medical Insurance (Disentitlement to Tax Relief and Approved Benefits) Regulations* 1994 (SI 1994/1518); *Sturgeon v Matthews (HMIT)* (1995) Sp C 45

See *British Tax Reporter* ¶103-820.

ENTERPRISE INVESTMENT SCHEME

1930 Introduction

The enterprise investment scheme (EIS) was introduced to encourage new equity investment in trading companies by providing tax incentives to investors. These incentives take the form of an income tax reduction, a capital gains tax exemption and a capital gains tax deferral (see 5923).

Any company which carries on a qualifying activity wholly or mainly in the UK can issue shares under the EIS. A qualifying activity comprises the carrying on of a qualifying trade, the preparation for carrying on such a trade or the research and development for use in such a trade. There is no requirement for the company to be incorporated here. Additionally, any investor with a UK tax liability qualifies for EIS relief regardless of whether he is UK-resident. Both of these measures were designed to help to attract foreign investors into the UK.

Income Tax

The range of qualifying trades in which a company wishing to issue EIS shares may engage is strictly prescribed. Prohibited activities include those such as dealing in goods (other than wholesale and retail distribution), leasing, receipt of royalties and licence fees, property development, shipbuilding, production of coal and steel, the operation of hotels, nursing homes and residential care homes and the provision of legal and accounting services.

Various anti-avoidance measures exist to counter attempts to protect the investor from risk and to prevent him from realising value from the company as a result of his investment. These measures will result in the withdrawal or reduction of relief.

The prescribed periods

The legislation lays down a number of conditions relating to the investor, the issuing company and the 'relevant shares' which must be satisfied for certain periods. In addition, relief, once given, may be withdrawn or reduced on the occurrence of certain events with those periods.

There are three periods prescribed, all of which terminate immediately before the 'termination date' relating to the share issue, which is the third anniversary of the issue (ITA 2007, s. 256). The periods differ only in their start dates, which are:

- Period A: either the incorporation of the company or a date two years before the share issue;
- Period B: the share issue;
- Period C: 12 months before the share issue.

Income tax relief

An investor obtains income tax relief for EIS investments at the 'EIS Rate' of 20 per cent on the amount of his investment in eligible shares in the tax year, subject to an overall limit of £500,000. He may make a claim for relief in respect of some or all of the shares included in the issue.

The relief is given by means of a reduction in his income tax liability at Stage 6 of the prescribed method of calculation. That reduction cannot reduce the liability to less than nil. In other words, it cannot create a repayment. For years prior to 2008–09 the rate was equal to the lower rate of tax applicable in the year, which was also 20 per cent.

Where there is more than one tax reduction to be made at Step 6 for a tax year, a prescribed order of priority is set out.

Carry-back relief

Subject to the overall maximum relief allowable for any year (i.e. £500,000 for 2008–09 onwards), an individual may claim relief in one tax year for amounts invested in qualifying shares in the immediately following year.

For 2009–10 onwards the whole of the following year's qualifying investment can be carried back to the extent that the total relief claimed in the earlier year does not exceed £500,000. Thus an investment in 2009–10 can be carried back to 2008–09.

For investments in years to 2008–09, carry-back was restricted to one-half of the investment made in the period 6 April to 6 October in that year. For those years there was also a monetary limit; the maximum that could be carried back was £50,000. Thus, for example if EIS shares were subscribed for on 30 September 2008, up to half of the amount subscribed for could be carried back and treated as if it were a subscription in 2007–08, provided that the maximum subscription limit (£400,000 for 2007–08) had not already been reached.

Eligibility for income tax relief

Relief is available in respect of an amount subscribed for shares in the issuing company where:

- 'relevant shares' are issued to the individual;
- he is a 'qualifying investor' in relation to those shares;
- the issuing company is a 'qualifying company';
- the shares are issued in order to raise money for a qualifying business activity and the funds raised are so employed; and
- the amounts subscribed in the tax year at least total £500 (unless the subscription is made via an approved investment fund).

Pre-arranged exits

In relation to shares issued after 1 July 1997, relief cannot be given where, at the time of an investment, certain exit arrangements are in place which guarantee the investor a way of disposing of the shares at the end of the qualifying period, effectively turning the whole investment into a low-risk venture. Broadly, relief is denied where the terms of the issue include, or there already exist at the time of issue, arrangements for repurchasing or exchanging the shares, ceasing the trade, disposing of assets of the company or otherwise providing some form of protection or guarantee for the investor.

Law: ITA 2007, Pt 5; *Finance Act 2008, Section 31 (Specified Tax Year) Order* 2008 (SI 2008/3165); *Taylor & Anor v R & C Commrs* (2009) TC 00277

Source: SP 6/98, *Enterprise investment scheme, venture capital trusts, capital gains tax reinvestment relief and business expansion scheme: loans to investors*

Website: www.hmrc.gov.uk/eis/eis-index.htm

See *British Tax Reporter* ¶323-000.

Income Tax

1932 Individuals, companies and activities qualifying for EIS relief

Qualifying investors

There is no requirement for an investor to be resident or ordinarily resident in the UK. However there is little point in investing under the EIS unless the individual has a UK income tax liability against which relief can be set.

There are three requirements that an investor must satisfy:

- he must not be 'connected with the issuing company';
- no 'linked loan' must be made to the investor or his associates by any person at any time in Period A (see 1930);
- he must subscribe for the shares for genuine commercial reasons and not as part of some scheme or arrangement which has a main purpose of avoiding tax.

The investor and directors may not be connected with the company during the relevant period. The relevant period begins two years before the EIS shares are issued and ends immediately before the termination date. The termination period is the third anniversary of the later of the share issue date and the trade commencement date (i.e., where the trade for which the shares were issued had begun after the share issue date).

A person is 'connected with' the company if he is (or an associate of his is) in relation to that company or any 51 per cent subsidiary of it:

- a partner;
- an employee;
- a director who receives or becomes entitled to a payment which does not fall within a given list of bona fide commercial payments unless he was unconnected with the company before his investment and he receives remuneration commensurate with his duties as director;
- a person who controls it (see 4265) or who is entitled to over 30 per cent of the company's assets available for distribution to its equity holders on a winding-up or any person with, or entitled to acquire, over 30 per cent of the issued share capital, loan capital or voting power in the company.

An individual will not fail to qualify for relief solely because he or she (or any associate) held any subscriber shares at a time when the company in question had not yet begun to carry on any trade or business, and had not yet begun to make any preparations for doing so.

Qualifying company

To obtain EIS relief, the individual must invest wholly in cash in a qualifying company. A 'qualifying company' is one which is, throughout the period beginning on the share issue date and ending on the third anniversary of the later of the share issue date and the trade commencement date (i.e. where the trade for which the shares were issued had commenced after the share issue date):

- an unquoted company which is not controlled by another company or persons connected with such other company, so that companies dealt in on the Unlisted Securities Market are excluded from the scheme;
- in existence largely to carry on one or more qualifying trades or to be the holding company (and/or funding company) of one or more qualifying subsidiaries;
- from 19 July 2007 there is a requirement that qualifying companies must have fewer than 50 employees at the date on which the relevant shares or securities are issued.

A company can be a qualifying subsidiary of an EIS company if it is a 51 per cent subsidiary (except a property management subsidiary or a subsidiary which carries on the trade, or research and development, in question – these have to be 90 per cent subsidiaries).

From 19 July 2007, a new investment limit applies to a company raising money under the EIS. For an 'investment' to qualify for relief, the company (or group of companies) must have raised no more than £2m under any or all of the venture capital schemes (EIS, CVS, VCT) in the 12 months ending on the date of the relevant investment. If the limit is exceeded, none of the shares or securities within the issue that causes the condition to be breached will qualify for relief under the EIS or CVS, or rank as a qualifying holding for a VCT.

A company ceases to satisfy the conditions for being a qualifying company when it ceases to trade or is wound-up or dissolved unless for bona fide commercial reasons resulting in the distribution of its assets to members within a specified time. If such a bona fide winding-up is initiated as promptly as circumstances permit, HMRC will ignore any short gap between the cessation of trading and the passing of the winding-up resolution. The appointment of an administrative receiver has no effect on the company's status.

Proposed changes to legislation with effect from 6 April 2010

In order to comply with EC rules on State Aid to industry, certain changes in the EIS legislation are required. These are:

- a new requirement is to be introduced that the issuing company is not 'in difficulty'. The European Commission regards a firm as being in difficulty where it is unable, whether through its own resources or with the funds it is able to obtain from its owner/shareholders or creditors, to stem losses which, without outside intervention by the public authorities, will almost certainly condemn it to going out of business in the short or medium term (*Community Guidelines for Rescuing Restructuring Firms in Difficulty*, (2004/C244/02)) and;
- the requirement that the qualifying business activity is to be carried on wholly or mainly within the UK is to be replaced with a requirement that the issuing company must have a permanent establishment in the UK. The definition of 'permanent establishment' will be based upon Art. 5 of the OECD Model Tax Convention.

Unquoted status

A fundamental condition of EIS was that the EIS company must be unquoted when it issues the shares and remain unquoted for three full years after the issue. For shares issued on or

Income Tax

after 7 March 2001 (2001 Budget day), this requirement is replaced with conditions that only apply when the EIS shares are issued. These conditions are:

(1)   the EIS company is unquoted; and

(2)   no arrangements exist for either:

    (a)   the company to become unquoted; or
    (b)   it to become a subsidiary of a company which has plans to become unquoted.

The company will not lose its unquoted status if its shares are listed on an unrecognised exchange (such as the AIM – alternative investment market) which then becomes recognised after the EIS shares are issued.

Gross assets test

A gross assets test applies in order to confine EIS relief to investment in smaller companies. The issuing company's assets (together with the assets of all other companies, if any, in the company's group) must not exceed £7m (£15m prior to 2006–07) immediately before the issue of shares, and must not exceed £8m (£16m prior to 2006–07) immediately afterwards. A statement of practice sets out HMRC's general approach in applying this gross assets test.

Use for a qualifying business activity

The investment period in which a manager has to invest 90 per cent of the funds raised by an approved EIS fund was extended from 6 October 2006 from six months to 12 months. A qualifying business activity can encompass a qualifying trade, research and development intended to lead to such a trade or oil exploration, provided in each case that for the first five years in which the trade is carried on it is carried on wholly or mainly in the UK.

Where an investment is made in a parent company which would otherwise qualify for EIS relief, it is not disqualified merely because one or more of its subsidiaries carries on non-qualifying activities, provided that the group as a whole qualifies. Certain activities by either the parent or any of its subsidiaries (e.g. intra-group loans and the holding and managing of property used for the group's activities) are disregarded or ignored when applying the rules concerning qualifying activities.

Whether a qualifying trade is or will be carried on wholly or mainly in the UK will turn on its precise facts and circumstances. HMRC have said that, in general, in looking to see whether this test is satisfied, the total activities of the trade will be taken into account and that no single factor is in itself likely to be decisive in any particular case; a company may carry on some of these activities outside the UK and yet satisfy the requirement, provided that the major part, i.e. over one-half, of the aggregate of these activities takes place inside the UK.

Qualifying trade

A 'qualifying trade' is one which is not excluded by statute. The trade must be carried on a commercial basis with an intention to realise profits. With the exception of certain research and development activities and short-term ship chartering, it excludes banking, insurance, money lending, debt factoring, hire-purchase financing or other financial services, leasing or receiving royalties or licence fees, providing legal or accounting services, dealing in shares, commodities, securities, financial instruments, futures, land or goods (except in the course of an ordinary trade of wholesale and retail distribution) providing facilities for a trade (other than carried on by its parent) controlled by the same person and consisting of excluded trades and (after 16 March 1998) property development, farming and market gardening, forestry activities and timber production, operating and managing hotels and comparable establishments, or property used as such, and operating or managing nursing or residential care homes, or property used as such. From 2008–09 excluded activities also include shipbuilding and coal and steel production. The Treasury can amend the list of disqualified activities by order.

In relation to those companies carrying out research and development within the scope of the relief, 'research and development' is limited to any activity which is intended to result in a patentable invention (within the meaning of the *Patents Act* 1977) or in a computer program. The fact that the company's income is substantially from royalties or licence fees will not exclude it from qualification, provided that those royalties or fees are attributable to research and development activities and provided that such activities are continued during the period in question.

Using the money raised: time-limit

Prior to 22 April 2009, the legislation specified that 80 per cent of the monies raised from an EIS share issue must be used within 12 months of the share issue (or within 12 months of the commencement of trading if later). The remaining 20 per cent of the monies raised had to be used within the later of 24 months of the share issue or the commencement of trading. However, FA 2009 relaxed this time-limit, so that all money raised by the issue of shares must be wholly employed in a qualifying activity within two years of the EIS share issue, or (if later) within two years of the qualifying activity commencing. The use to which the monies raised must be put, within the specified time-limit, is a 'qualifying business activity'.

These conditions are not treated as failed if some of the funds are applied for a non-qualifying purpose provided the amount so used is 'not significant'. No guidance is given regarding the meaning of 'not significant', but in other contexts a proportion may be regarded as 'significant' once it exceeds five per cent. In the absence of detailed guidance, this level could probably be argued as being the measure of a significant amount.

In *Forthright (Wales) Ltd v HMIT*, the company was formed to take over an existing business (FMS) which provided management services to an accountancy firm. The monies obtained on the issue of shares (nearly £300,000) were used to settle liabilities taken over from FMS and to pay dividends to its shareholders, some of whom were employees of the company who had agreed to be remunerated by way of dividend. It was held that the payments of FMS's liabilities and dividends to investors (as opposed to employees) using money raised by the share issue did not employ the money wholly for the purposes of the (otherwise) qualifying trade. The dividends paid to employees who had agreed to be paid through dividends rather than wages were found to be made for the purposes of the trade. The payments of the former trader's liabilities and significant dividends (30 per cent of the

491

total) to non-employee investors were not made for the purposes of the company's trade and so the claim for EIS relief failed (at the commissioners and High Court).

Law: FA 2009, Sch. 55; FA 2008, s. 31, 32 and Sch. 11; FA 2007, s. 51 and Sch. 16; ITA 2007, Pt 5

Source: *Brief* 77/09

See *British Tax Reporter* ¶323-000.

1934 Scope of EIS relief available

Relief under the EIS is available where an individual who qualifies for the relief subscribes for eligible shares in a suitable company, provided the money raised is employed by the company within a specified time. For discussion of whether an individual qualifies for relief, the suitability of a company and the time period involved, see 1932. For claims, see 1936.

Eligible shares are new ordinary shares which, throughout the period beginning with the date on which they are issued and ending immediately before the termination date for those shares, carry no present or future preferential right to be redeemed. The termination date is the third anniversary of the later of the share issue date and the trade commencement date (i.e. where the trade for which the shares were issued had begun after the share issue date).

Prior to 2009–10 and subject to the overall annual limit of £500,000 (from 6 April 2008; £400,000 prior to then), an individual could claim relief in one tax year (say, 2008–09) for one-half of any amount invested in qualifying shares before 6 October in the following year (i.e. before 6 October 2009). The maximum amount that an investor could request to carry back in this way was £50,000. FA 2009 extended the carry-back period so that for 2009–10 onwards, investors may carry back the full amount subscribed for shares (subject to the EIS qualifying limit). The amount of the subscription carried back is treated as though it related to a share issue made in the previous tax year.

The minimum investment required to attract EIS relief is £500, except in the case of purchases by 'approved investment funds' (see 1946).

Relief for any tax year is attributed pro rata to shares subscribed for (or treated as subscribed for) in that year, treating any bonus issue as if it were in the same year as the original investment; a withdrawal of relief is treated in a similar way.

Any gain on disposal of EIS shares is generally exempt but, where a loss arises, that loss is effectively reduced by the amount of income tax relief given (see 5925). An individual may claim income tax relief for any loss if he would have satisfied the necessary conditions (see 5940) had the investee company been a qualifying trading company.

Law: FA 2009, Sch. 55; ITA 2007, Pt 5

See *British Tax Reporter* ¶323-000.

1936   Claiming EIS income tax relief

To obtain EIS relief, an investor must submit a claim:

- not before the qualifying activity has been carried on for four months, and
- no later than the fifth anniversary of the 31 January following the tax year in which the shares were issued.

However, a claim can be made if the company concerned commences the qualifying business activities but is wound up, or dissolved without winding up, before the end of the four-month period, provided the winding up/dissolution is for bona fide commercial reasons and not as part of a scheme or arrangement in which one of the main purposes is to avoid tax. Similarly if, having commenced the activities, the issuing or any other company goes into administration or receivership within four months, a claim may still be made.

Law: ITA 2007, s. 158(1), 176, 202

See *British Tax Reporter* ¶323-100.

1938   Withdrawal of EIS relief: general

'EIS relief' (see 1930) will generally be withdrawn by assessment for the tax year for which the relief was given if it is subsequently found that it was not due. Except in the case of fraudulent or negligent conduct, no such withdrawal will be made:

- by reason of any event occurring after the taxpayer has disposed of all the shares (unless he remains connected) or after his death;
- because the company is not a qualifying company, unless the company has notified the inspector that this is the case and he has informed the company that, as a result, relief obtained by any individual was not due; or
- more than six years after the tax year in which the event occurs or, if later, in which the funds must be employed.

Withdrawals may be made by reference to a number of events, including sale (see 1939), receipt of value from the company (1940) and replacement capital (see 1942). There are provisions requiring the investor, the company and, in some cases, other persons to notify HMRC within 60 days if the conditions for relief cease to be satisfied; HMRC also have other information gathering powers in this respect.

There are rules determining the date from which interest on overdue tax will run in respect of additional tax resulting from a withdrawal.

Income Tax

Law: ITA 2007, s. 234, 235

See *British Tax Reporter* ¶323-650.

1939 Withdrawal of EIS relief: disposal of shares

Where, following receipt of 'EIS relief' (see 1930), a shareholder sells the shares at an arm's length price (or the shares become subject to a call or put option) within the relevant period, relief will be withdrawn on a first-in/first-out (FIFO) basis by reference to the amount which he receives for their sale; if such a sale is not at arm's length, his whole relief for those shares will be withdrawn. This does not apply to a disposal to one's spouse if they are living together at that time; the transferee spouse then steps into the shoes of the transferor.

The relevant period begins on the share issue date and ends immediately before the termination date. The termination date is the third anniversary of the later of the share issue date and the trade commencement trade (i.e. the trade for which the shares were issued began after the share issue date).

For the nature of any withdrawal, see 1938.

Law: ITA 2007, s. 209–212

See *British Tax Reporter* ¶323-650.

1940 Withdrawal of EIS relief: members receiving value from the company

Where, for the purposes of 'EIS relief' (see 1930), an individual subscribes for eligible shares in a company and receives any value from the company (or a 51 per cent subsidiary of it) at any time in the 'period of restriction', the amount of the relief to which he is entitled in respect of those shares will be reduced by reference to the value received; reasonable directors' remuneration is excluded.

The period of restriction begins 12 months before the issue of the shares and ends immediately before the termination date. The termination date is the third anniversary of the later of the share issue date and the trade commencement date (i.e. where the trade for which the shares were issued had begun after the date the shares were issued).

For this purpose, an individual also receives value if any person connected with the company (see 1932) either purchases any of its share capital or securities which belong to the individual or pays him for giving up any right in relation to any of the company's share capital or securities.

Equally, where a shareholder other than a claimant receives value from the company, by way of a repayment, redemption or repurchase of capital, every individual who qualified for relief is subject to a proportionate clawback.

For the nature of any withdrawal, see 1938.

Law: ITA 2007, s. 213–223

See *British Tax Reporter* ¶323-850.

1942   Withdrawal of EIS relief: replacement capital

A taxpayer will not be granted 'EIS relief' (see 1930) where he has an opportunity to receive back from someone other than the company the 'additional' capital he has subscribed, as set out below (as regards value received from the company, see 1940). The company itself is not disqualified and so new investors can obtain relief for additional capital subscribed for shares in that company.

As a general rule, an individual is not entitled to relief where at any time in the 'relevant period' (i.e. the period beginning on the share issue date and ending on the termination date, which is the third anniversary of the later of the date of the share issue and the date of the commencement of the trade for which the shares were issued) – or, in the case of certain directors, at any time before the termination date – the company or its subsidiary takes over a trade or trade assets and either:

● the individual had more than a 50 per cent interest in the previous trade and has a similar interest in the new trade; or
● the individual 'controlling' (see 4265) the company also controlled another company which previously carried on the trade.

There are various definitions which apply for this purpose and the concept is extended to situations in which the company takes over another company. For the nature of any withdrawal, see 1938.

Law: ITA 2007, s.224–234

See *British Tax Reporter* ¶324-050.

1946   Approved EIS investment funds

An individual investor may obtain 'EIS relief' (see 1930) where an approved investment fund invests on his behalf in a number of qualifying companies (see 1932). HMRC have full power to approve the investment and must be satisfied that the managers of the fund are reputable and capable of handling the necessary administration. Since 15 March 1988, relief has been granted when the fund closes rather than the date the share issue is made, provided

Income Tax

90 per cent of the individual's subscription has been invested within six months of the fund closure.

Law: ITA 2007, s. 250(3), 251(1), (2)

See *British Tax Reporter* ¶325-350.

VENTURE CAPITAL TRUSTS

1950 Overview of VCTs

A 'venture capital trust' (VCT) is essentially a specific type of investment trust which invests in unquoted trading companies. Individual investors in VCTs receive various tax incentives:

- for shares issued on or after 6 April 2004 (but before 6 April 2006), the rate of income tax relief available was 40 per cent. For 2006–07 onwards the rate of income tax relief is 30 per cent;
- for 2004–05 onwards the maximum amount invested for which tax reliefs can be obtained was increased from £100,000 to £200,000 per tax year;
- exemption from income tax on distributions paid by VCTs (see 1956);
- prior to 2004–05, deferral of CGT on a chargeable gain from the disposal of an asset where the gain is invested in new VCT shares. From 6 April 2004, it is no longer possible to defer CGT by reinvesting gains in VCT shares (see 5925); and
- exemption from CGT on the disposal of ordinary shares in VCTs, whether or not they were new shares when acquired (see 5925).

VCTs are exempt from corporation tax on any capital gain arising on disposal of their investments.

A VCT is defined as a company which is not close and which has obtained HMRC's approval, satisfying the conditions below; the grant of approval can be made retrospective to the date of the application.

Proposed changes to legislation with effect from 6 April 2010

In order to comply with EC rules on State Aid to industry, certain changes in the VCT legislation are required. These are:

- a new requirement is to be introduced that the issuing company is not 'in difficulty'. The European Commission regards a firm as being in difficulty where it is unable, whether through its own resources or with the funds it is able to obtain from its owner/ shareholders or creditors, to stem losses which, without outside intervention by the public authorities, will almost certainly condemn it to going out of business in the short or medium term (*Community Guidelines for Rescuing Restructuring Firms in Difficulty,* (2004/C244/02));
- the requirement that the relevant company's qualifying trade is to be carried on wholly

or mainly within the UK is to be replaced with a requirement that the issuing company must have a permanent establishment in the UK. The definition of 'permanent establishment' will be based upon Art. 5 of the OECD Model Tax Convention;

- the requirement that a VCT's shares must be included in the Official UK List is replaced with one requiring that the shares must be traded on an EU regulated market; and
- changes in the rules on the amount of a VCT's investment which must be held as equity. Currently VCTs are required to have 70 per cent of their investments in shares or securities as qualifying holdings and 30 per cent of the qualifying holdings held as equities. The changes will increase that 30 per cent requirement to 70 per cent.

Conditions to be satisfied

The conditions which a company must satisfy (in its most recent complete accounting period and in the accounting period during which the application for approval as a VCT is made) are as follows:

(1)   the company's income has been wholly or mainly derived from shares or securities;

(2)   from 19 July 2007 there is a requirement that qualifying companies must have fewer than 50 employees at the date on which the relevant shares or securities are issued;

(3)   generally, at least 70 per cent (by value) of its investments has been in shares or securities in 'qualifying holdings' (but see 1952);

(4)   at least 30 per cent of the qualifying holdings has been in holdings of eligible shares (defined, broadly, as ordinary shares carrying no preferential rights and no rights to be redeemed);

(5)   no holding in any company, other than another VCT (or a company which would qualify as a VCT if its ordinary shares were quoted on the Stock Exchange) amounts to more than 15 per cent of the company's investments;

(6)   the company's ordinary share capital has been quoted on the Stock Exchange;

(7)   the company has not retained more than 15 per cent of the income it derived from shares or securities;

(8)   from 6 April 2007 the conditions for approval and withdrawal of approval for VCTs have been amended so that all money held by or on a VCT's behalf is regarded as an investment when considering whether the conditions are met;

(9)   from 19 July 2007, a new investment limit applies to a company raising money under the venture capital schemes (VCT, EIS, CVS). For an 'investment' to qualify for relief under the EIS or CVS, or be treated as a qualifying holding of a VCT, the company (or group of companies) must have raised no more than £2m under any or all of the venture capital schemes in the 12 months ending on the date of the relevant investment. If the limit is exceeded, none of the shares or securities within the issue that causes the condition to be breached will qualify for relief under the EIS or CVS, or rank as a qualifying holding for a VCT.

Income Tax

Provisional approval

If all the conditions outlined above are not satisfied as regards the company's most recent complete accounting period, HMRC may nevertheless grant approval to a company in certain circumstances, if they are satisfied that:

- if any condition other than (1) or (2) above is not met, it will be met in the accounting period in which the application is made, or in the following accounting period;
- if condition (1) and/or (2) is not met, it will be met in an accounting period of the company beginning within three years of the date on which approval is given, or, if approval is given retrospectively, within three years of the time at which approval takes effect; and
- that any condition which will be met within the timescales outlined above will then continue to be met throughout subsequent accounting periods.

Withdrawal of approval

HMRC may, at any time, withdraw approval of a company as a VCT if they believe that the necessary conditions were not fulfilled at the time of granting of approval. Equally, approval may be withdrawn if:

- HMRC had given approval on the basis that a condition would be met in an accounting period, but the condition was not then met; or
- the company failed to meet any necessary conditions or regulations within the three-year period referred to above; or
- the company failed to meet the appropriate conditions in its most recent complete accounting period, or in the current one, but approval will not be withdrawn for this reason if the failure was anticipated at the time of the granting of provisional approval.

Withdrawal of approval will normally take effect at the time when the notice of withdrawal is given to the company. However, the withdrawal of provisional approval may, if the conditions were never completely satisfied, take effect as if the provisional approval had never been given.

Any assessment consequential on withdrawn approval may be made within three years of the date on which the notice of withdrawal is given, regardless of the normal rules on time-limits.

Merger and winding up

The *Finance Act* 2002 gives authority to the Treasury to make regulations to ensure that approval continues when a VCT is being wound up or when it merges with another VCT. Thus tax reliefs for investors will be preserved. Furthermore, some of the capital raised as part of a merger from a new issue of shares, which would normally be used to acquire more shares in unquoted trading companies, can be used to repay investors who wish to realise their investment. This applies to a winding up or merger after 16 April 2002.

Law: FA 2008, s. 32 and Sch. 11; ITA 2007, Pt 6

Website: www.hmrc.gov.uk/guidance/vct.htm

See *British Tax Reporter* ¶326-400.

1952 'Qualifying holding'

For the holding to be a 'qualifying holding', various requirements must be satisfied. In brief, these are:

- the relevant company must be unquoted;
- the relevant company must exist wholly for the purpose of carrying on one or more qualifying trades or be the parent company of a trading group;
- the money raised by the investment must be used wholly for the purposes of carrying of a qualifying trade or for preparing to carry on such a trade;
- *Finance Act* 2009 replaced the time-limits for the employment of money by companies receiving VCT investments with a single requirement that all money raised must be wholly employed within two years, or (if later), within two years of the qualifying activity commencing. This relaxation applies in respect of funds raised by VCTs from 22 April 2009;
- the maximum qualifying investment that a VCT can make in a single relevant company is £1m;
- before and after the issue of the holding; the relevant company's assets must not exceed, respectively, £7m and £8m (£15m and £16m prior to 2006–07);
- after 1 July 1997, the securities should not relate to a guaranteed loan; and
- after 1 July 1997, at least ten per cent of the trust company's investment must be in the form of ordinary non-preference shares and non-redeemable shares.

In addition, the shares or securities held by the VCT must satisfy various requirements, and must have been first issued by the relevant company to the trust company, and must have been held by the trust company ever since that time, if they are to be regarded as forming part of the trust company's qualifying holdings.

There is a requirement that a VCT must at all times have at least 70 per cent by value of its investments in qualifying holdings to retain approval. In some cases a VCT may be unable to dispose of a holding without breaching this condition. From 6 April 2007, when a VCT makes a cash realisation on the disposal of an investment that has been part of its qualifying holdings for at least six months, the disposal will be ignored for the next six months for the purpose of the 70 per cent test. This will give the VCT up to six months to reinvest or distribute the disposal proceeds.

Acquisitions for restructuring purposes

Where a VCT has invested in a company which, as part of its preparations for seeking a market flotation, becomes a wholly-owned subsidiary of a new holding company, the shares, etc. which the VCT holds in the latter company are generally treated as meeting the relevant VCT tax rules to the same extent as the shares, etc. in the original company.

Conversion of convertible shares and securities

Where a VCT exercises its conversion rights in respect of certain convertible shares or securities, the resulting shares are treated as qualifying to the same extent as the convertibles from which they were derived.

Law: FA 2009, Sch. 55; FA 2007, s. 51 and Sch. 16; ITA 2007, Pt 6, Ch 4

See *British Tax Reporter* ¶326-500.

1954 Relief from income tax on investment

Entitlement to claim relief

Individuals will have relief from income tax on dividends from VCTs in respect of investments of up to £200,000 per year for 2004–05 onwards (prior to this the limit was £100,000). In relation to shares issued after 6 April 2000 but prior to 6 April 2006, the minimum period is three years. From 6 April 2006 investors must hold their shares for a minimum of five years to qualify for income tax relief.

Relief will be given to an individual on an amount equal to his subscription, on his own behalf, for shares in a VCT, but no relief will be available for any amount so subscribed, which is in excess of £200,000. The individual must be aged 18 or over at the time of issue of the shares.

The maximum relief which can be given will be an amount which reduces the individual's liability to nil, and in determining an individual's liability this relief will be given before any reliefs given by way of an income tax reduction.

No relief will be given if the circumstances are such that any relief, which might previously have been given, would have had cause to be withdrawn and relief will not be available unless the shares were both issued and subscribed for, for bona fide commercial purposes, and not as part of any tax avoidance scheme. Tax relief is also denied in certain circumstances in which the issue of shares is related to the making of loans, or any equivalent act such as the giving of credit or the assignment of a debt. A statement of practice sets out the application of these rules.

Loss of investment relief

If investment relief has been given to an individual, it will be lost in whole or in part if the individual disposes of the shares in the VCT within the period of five years (i.e. for shares issued after 5 April 2006, otherwise the period is three years) beginning with the issue of those shares to that individual. If the original subscriber makes a disposal to his or her spouse, then the spouse is treated as if he or she was the original subscriber for the shares.

If the disposal within the five-year time-limit (three-year time-limit for shares issued before 6 April 2006) is by way of a bargain not at arm's length, then the relief is withdrawn in full, but if the disposal is at arm's length, then the amount of relief withdrawn is based on the consideration for the disposal.

Specific rules apply where it is necessary to identify which shares have been disposed of. If a VCT loses its approved status, then any person holding shares in that VCT is deemed to have disposed of them immediately before that time, and not at arm's length, with the result that all the relief previously granted will be withdrawn.

Assessment on withdrawal or reduction of relief

If relief, once given, needs to be withdrawn, it will be withdrawn by way of an assessment for the tax year in respect of which the relief to be withdrawn was originally given. No assessment will be made to withdraw or reduce relief as a result of an event occurring after the subscriber's death.

Provision of information

An individual investor should inform the inspector within 60 days, if he becomes aware of an event which would cause his relief to be reduced or withdrawn. Equally, an inspector may require an individual to supply any information (within a period of not less than 60 days) which the officer believes may be reasonably required regarding an event which may cause relief to be reduced or withdrawn. An officer may, without breaching confidentiality, inform a VCT that relief given by reference to a number or proportion of its shares has been given or claimed under these provisions.

Law: ITA 2007, Pt 6, Ch 2

See *British Tax Reporter* ¶326-700.

1956   Exemption from income tax on distributions

'Qualifying investor' and 'relevant distribution'

If a qualifying investor (see below) becomes beneficially entitled to a relevant distribution (see below) of a VCT, then the distribution is not regarded as income for any income tax purposes.

A qualifying investor is an individual aged 18 or over who is beneficially entitled to the distribution, either because he holds the shares in respect of which the distribution is made, or because the shares are held by a nominee of his (including the trustees of a bare trust of which the individual is the only beneficiary).

A relevant distribution, as regards a company which is a VCT, is one consisting of a dividend paid in respect of ordinary shares (i.e. shares forming part of the company's ordinary share capital) where the shares:

- were acquired by the person to whom the distribution is made at a time when the company was a VCT; and
- are not shares in excess of the permitted maximum (see below) for any year of investment.

A dividend is excluded from being a relevant distribution if it is paid in respect of profits or gains arising in an accounting period at the end of which the company was not a VCT. In addition, in relation to shares acquired on or after 9 March 1999, the shares must have been acquired for bona fide commercial purposes, and not part of a tax avoidance scheme.

Meaning of 'permitted maximum'

If an individual acquires, directly or via a nominee (see above), ordinary shares in a VCT, for bona fide commercial purposes (i.e. not as part of a tax avoidance scheme), he may so acquire shares to the value of £200,000 without exceeding the permitted maximum. The 'value' of shares acquired is taken to be market value as at the time of acquisition.

If the investor acquires new shares in a VCT in exchange for shares in another VCT (which were originally acquired in whole or in part within the permitted maximum for the year), then the value of the new shares is ignored in calculating the permitted maximum for the year in which the new shares were acquired. However, the new shares still qualify for distribution relief, with the proviso that if only part of the original shares qualified for such relief, then a similar part of the new shares continue so to qualify.

Where shares are acquired in excess of the permitted maximum, specific rules apply, broadly, to give relief on the first £200,000 worth acquired in any year. This would appear to mean that the shares on which tax relief on distributions is given may not be the same shares on which tax relief on investment (see 1954) is given. If an investor acquires *existing* shares for £30,000 and, later in the same year, subscribes for £200,000 worth of *new* shares, then tax relief on distributions will be given on the £30,000 existing shares and the first £170,000 new shares. However, tax relief on investment will be given on the £200,000 new shares subscribed for.

Law: FA 2007, s. 51 and Sch. 16; ITA 2007, Pt 6

See *British Tax Reporter* ¶326-750.

Community Investment Tax Relief

1960   Introduction

Community Investment tax relief was introduced by FA 2002, but much of the detail is dealt with in regulations. The legislation applies to investments made on or after 17 January 2002. Claims to relief may be made from 23 January 2003 onwards.

The scheme borrows much from the Enterprise Investment Scheme (EIS) with the position of the SME company in that scheme being taken by an accredited Community Development Finance Institution (CDFI). The investment in the CDFI may be in the form of a loan, shares or securities held for a five year period.

The investor, which may be a company, bank or an individual, can claim tax relief of up to 25% of the amount invested once a tax relief certificate has been issued by the CDFI, but the tax relief must be spread over the five year term of the investment giving only 5% tax relief per year. The tax relief reduces the investor's tax liability, and is limited by the amount of that liability. If the investor receives any significant value from the CDFI within a six year period starting one year before the date of the investment, the tax relief is withdrawn.

Law: ITA 2007, Pt 7

See *British Tax Reporter* ¶325-000.

1962 Conditions of investment

A number of conditions surround the CDFI, the investor and the type of investment.

Conditions for the CDFI

The objective of a CDFI must be to provide finance and financial advice to enterprises for disadvantaged communities, which include enterprises in disadvantaged areas and enterprises for disadvantaged groups.

The enterprises in which the CDFI may invest must be SMEs but they do not need to be incorporated. The finance provided by the CDFI to the SME must be in the form of a loan or equity investment, or a combination of the two. There are restrictions on property investment by the CDFI.

There will be two types of CDFI: those which invest only directly in enterprises for disadvantaged communities, known as 'retail' CDFIs, and those 'wholesale' CDFI bodies which invest in other CDFIs as well as directly in the community enterprises.

Conditions for the investor

An investor in the CDFI may be an individual, a partner, a company or a bank, but in each case the investor or any person connected with him, must not control the CDFI at any time during the five years immediately following the investment date.

Conditions for the investment

The investment in the CDFI can be in the form of a loan, shares or securities, all of which have particular conditions attached. However any investment in a CDFI can only qualify for tax relief under this scheme if there are no arrangements made to reduce the risk of that investment, such as a guarantee or insurance. Such prohibited arrangements do not include

Income Tax

not normal commercial arrangements which may be undertaken by a bank when lending as part of its business, such as a charge on property taken as security for a loan, or foreign currency hedging contracts.

Loans

The investment in the CDFI may be in the form of a loan that is either drawn down by the CDFI in full on the investment date, or is drawn down in stages over a period of up to 18 months after the investment date. Tax relief will only be given on the capital balance of the loan that has been drawn-down, (see tax relief below).

The loan must not be convertible into shares or securities that have rights to allow redemption within five years of the investment date, but the loan may be repayable in stages as follows:

- Nothing repayable in the first two years after investment;
- In the third year, up to 25% of the capital outstanding after two years;
- In the fourth year, up to 50% of the outstanding loan;
- In the fifth year, up to 75% of the outstanding loan.

These percentages may be altered by regulation.

Shares or securities

Any shares or securities received as part of an investment in a CDFI under this scheme must be subscribed for in cash and fully paid up on the date of the investment. They must also not have any rights to allow redemption within five years, or conversion into a loan or other shares or securities which could be redeemed within five years of the investment date. The shares or securities must not be jointly subscribed for, as the investor must be the sole beneficial owner of the shares at the date of the investment.

No tax avoidance motive

The standard anti-avoidance clause applies such that any investment will not receive tax relief if the main purpose of any scheme or arrangement under which the investment is made is the avoidance of tax.

Law: FA 2008, s. 54; ITA 2007, Pt 7

See *British Tax Reporter* ¶325-000.

1964   The tax relief

Tax relief under this scheme must be claimed on an annual basis at the rate of five per cent of the 'invested amount' (see below) for the tax year (or accounting period for a corporate investor) in which the investment date falls and the four subsequent tax years (or accounting periods). If the investment was by way of a loan the 'invested amount' will not necessarily be the amount of the loan made available at the beginning of the five-year investment period, (see below). The tax relief due under this scheme is a tax reducer rather than an allowance, so it cannot reduce the taxpayer's tax liability below zero.

The investor must receive a tax relief certificate from the CDFI before claiming any tax relief in respect of the investment.

Tax relief for shares and securities

For shares and securities the invested amount will normally be the amount subscribed for in cash. However where the investor has received a significant receipt of value (see below) which does not exceed the permitted levels the invested amount is treated as being reduced by the amount of value received.

Tax relief for loans

As an investment made as a loan may be drawn-down over an 18 month period and repaid in stages, (see conditions for the investment above) the 'invested amount' for the tax years or accounting periods corresponding to the five-year investment period is determined according to the average balance of the loan in the relevant 12-month investment period as follows:

Tax Year or accounting period:	Relevant investment period:	Invested amount calculated as:
1. In which the investment was made.	12 months from the date of investment.	The average capital balance, calculated on a daily basis in the relevant period of investment.
2. In which the first anniversary of the investment date falls.	12 months from 1st anniversary of date of investment.	The average capital balance, calculated on a daily basis in the relevant period of investment.
3, 4 or 5: In which the 2nd, 3rd or 4th anniversary of the investment date falls.	12 months from the anniversary of the investment date falling in the tax year or accounting period.	The average capital balance, calculated on a daily basis in the relevant period of investment, but subject to restriction.

If the amount of the loan is increased during the third, fourth or fifth years of the investment period the 'invested amount' is restricted to the average capital balance of the last six months of the second year of the five-year investment period. This ensures that tax relief is only given for loan capital which was made available from the start of the investment period, and drawn-down within 18 months of the investment date.

> ### Example
>
> S Ltd that makes up accounts for a calendar year, made a loan of £100,000 on 30 June 2002 to an accredited CDFI which is repayable at the rate of £10,000 per year from 1 July 2004. The relevant investment period for each accounting period runs from 30 June to 29 June. The tax relief due is calculated as follows:

Year	Average capital balance of loan in the relevant investment period	Tax relief due at 5% of capital balance in the relevant investment period
2002	£100,000	£5,000
2003	£100,000	£5,000
2004	£90,000	£4,500
2005	£80,000	£4,000
2006	£70,000	£3,500

If S Ltd advanced a further £50,000 on 1 July 2005, the capital balance for the year to 30 June 2006 would be £130,000 but the tax relief due for 2006 would be:

5% × £100,000 = £5,000

The 'invested amount' is restricted to the amount of the average capital balance between 1 January 2004 and 30 June 2004.

Order of set-off

The tax relief given under this scheme is only available after any relief due under the EIS, VCT scheme and corporate venturing relief has been taken, and before any double taxation relief due. Individuals must also retain sufficient income tax to cover any gift aid donations made.

Law: ITA 2007, Pt 7, Ch 5

See *British Tax Reporter* ¶325-000.

1966   Withdrawal or reduction of tax relief

When tax relief under this scheme must be reduced due say to a sale of the investment (see below), or it is found not to be due, the tax relief will be clawed back by way of an assessment under Sch. D, Case VI. However no tax relief will be clawed back if the event trigging the tax relief reduction occurs after the investor's death.

Example

P Ltd has a calendar accounting period and subscribed for £80,000 worth of shares in an accredited CDFI on 1 March 2003. It sold shares for £20,000 on the open market on 1 September 2007. The qualifying date for 2007 is 1 March 2008. The tax relief due is calculated as follows:

Year	Tax relief first claimed	Claw-back of tax relief
2003	5% × £80,000 = £4,000	5% × 20,000 = 1,000
2004	5% × £80,000 = £4,000	5% × 20,000 = 1,000
2005	5% × £80,000 = £4,000	5% × 20,000 = 1,000
2006	5% × £80,000 = £4,000	5% × 20,000 = 1,000
2007	Nil	No tax relief due as shares have been sold by the qualifying date.

Receipt of value

The receipt of value rules try to ensure that the funds invested in the CDFI cannot be returned to the investor in another guise either shortly before the investment date, or during the five-year investment period.

The investor will suffer a reduction or complete withdrawal of the tax relief given under this scheme if he (or a person connected with him) receives an amount that is not of 'insignificant value' (broadly less than £1,000 or insignificant compared with the investment) from the CDFI (or a person connected with it) during the restricted period. The restricted period is the period of six years beginning exactly one year before the investment date. Certain payments are excluded from this including the payment of dividends or other distributions (provided they do not exceed a normal return), and the discharge of an ordinary trade debt, where the credit given is not more than six months.

If the investment in the CDFI was as shares or securities, the investor is permitted to receive some value (ignoring insignificant amounts) from the CDFI before his tax relief is reduced. The permitted levels of receipts are as follows:

● Before the 3rd anniversary of the investment date: up to 25% of the invested capital;
● Before the 4th anniversary of the investment date: up to 50% of the invested capital;
● Before the 5th anniversary of the investment date: up to 75% of the invested capital.

If the value received exceeds these permitted levels all the tax relief in respect of the investment must be withdrawn.

If the value received is significant but does not exceed these permitted levels the 'invested amount' is treated as reduced by the value received, in respect of the tax year or accounting period in which the value was received and any later periods.

If the investment in the CDFI was a loan the receipt of value is treated as being a repayment of the loan made at the beginning of the year in which the value was received. However, if the value was received in the first 24 months of the period of restriction the deemed loan repayment is treated as being made on the investment date.

Multiple investments
If the investor has made more than one investment in the CDFI and receives a receipt of value within the period of restriction, the receipt of value is allocated against those

investments in proportion to the relative value of each investment in the year the receipt of value is received.

Loss of accreditation

If the CDFI losses its accreditation during the five-year investment period the investor will also lose its tax relief.

Investor becomes accredited

If the investor body becomes an accredited CDFI it will lose any further tax relief due on investments it has made under this scheme.

Early loan repayment

An investment in a CDFI made in the form of a loan may be partially repaid within the five-year investment period within prescribed limits. If the loan repayments exceed those limits by more than £1,000, or by an amount that is significant compared to the average capital balance of the relevant year of the investment period, all of the tax relief must be withdrawn.

Disposal of investment

Generally if an investor disposes of all or part of his investment in a CDFI within the five-year investment period he will lose all the tax relief due on that investment unless the disposal falls within one of the following circumstances:

- as part of the winding up or dissolving of the CDFI;
- as a deemed disposal the investment becomes of negligible value or is lost completely;
- the disposal is made after the CDFI has lost its accreditation; or
- sale of shares or securities as part of an arms-length bargain.

Where the shares or securities are sold the tax relief due is reduced by five per cent of the sale proceeds. If the shares are sold at book profit, five per cent of the proceeds will be more than the tax relief due so all the tax relief must be withdrawn. If the tax relief attributed to the shares is less than five per cent of the invested amount, say because the tax relief has been limited by the total tax liability of the investor, the reduction in the tax relief due to a sale is also proportionately reduced.

Example

P Ltd has a calendar accounting period and subscribed for £80,000 worth of shares in an accredited CDFI on 1 March 2003. It sold those shares for £20,000 on the open market on 1 September 2007. The qualifying date for 2007 is 1 March 2008. the tax relief due is calculated as follows:

Year	Tax relief first claimed	Claw-back of tax relief
2003	5% × £80,000 = £4,000	5% × 20,000 = 1,000
2004	5% × £80,000 = £4,000	5% × 20,000 = 1,000
2005	5% × £80,000 = £4,000	5% × 20,000 = 1,000
2006	5% × £80,000 = £4,000	5% × 20,000 = 1,000
2007	Nil	No tax relief due as shares have been sold by the qualifying date.

When an investor disposes of his shares or securities in a CDFI the normal pool rules do not apply. The shares or securities are treated as being disposed of on a first in first out basis.

Law: ITA 2007, Pt 7, Ch 6; FA 2002, Sch. 26, Pt. 6

See *British Tax Reporter* ¶325-000.

1968 Information requirements

If an investor disposes of his investment in the CDFI within the five-year investment period or receives a loan repayment or receipt of value that would create a claw-back or restriction of his tax relief under this scheme, he must inform HMRC of the circumstances within the following deadlines:

- *For individuals*: by 31 January following the end of the tax year in which the event occurred;
- *For companies*: within 12 months of the end of the accounting period in which the event occurred.

If a person connected to the investor receives value from the CDFI, the investor must inform HMRC within 60 days of becoming aware of the event.

Law: ITA 2007, Pt 7, Ch 7

See *British Tax Reporter* ¶325-000.

EMPLOYEES' AND DIRECTORS' EXPENSES

1990 Extent of employees' deductions

Employees and directors are charged to tax on all their 'emoluments' (see 250ff.). The legislation allows a few special deductions but, apart from these, relief for necessary expenses is only given where the money is expended wholly, exclusively and necessarily in the performance of the employee's duties.

See further 1992, 1994.

Income Tax

Law: ITEPA 2003, s. 327

See *British Tax Reporter* ¶454-000.

1991 Dispensations

In cases where the employer satisfies the inspector that his arrangements for paying expenses to employees are adequately controlled and the amounts would be fully covered by an expenses deduction, the inspector may give a dispensation. The effect of this is that the PAYE procedure will not apply to the expenses for which the dispensation has been given.

Dispensations are not given for 'round-sum' expense allowances nor where such action would allow an employee to escape the implications of various chargeable benefit-in-kind provisions (see 382).

An application for a dispensation should be made on form P11DX.

Dispensations given by HMRC also count for National Insurance contributions (NICs).

Law: ITEPA 2003, s. 65, Sch. 7, para. 15

Website: www.hmrc.gov.uk/bulletins/index.htm

1992 Deductibility of employees' general expenses

For an employee or director to be allowed a particular deduction, the following conditions must be satisfied:

- the employee, etc. must be obliged to incur and pay the expense as holder of the employment; and
- the expense must be wholly, exclusively and necessarily incurred in the performance of those duties (see 1990).

'Wholly and exclusively'

Wholly and exclusively means that there cannot be any dual purpose in incurring the expenditure. Thus expenditure which is partly incurred for personal purposes (e.g. on food or clothing), will be disallowed. However, HMRC may sometimes allow a proportionate part of the expenditure. See further 2028 and 2154.

Necessarily

The test for deduction of expenses under ITEPA 2003 is stricter than that applying for Sch. D purposes in that the expense must be necessarily incurred, as well as wholly and exclusively so. Thus the fact that an expense was wholly and exclusively incurred in the performance of the duties will not be sufficient to support a claim for relief if it were not also necessary that the employee incurred the expense.

The courts have interpreted this very narrowly. For instance, it has been held that an expense must be one that each and every holder of the office would incur, not peculiar to the circumstances of any particular incumbent.

In the performance of the duties of the employment

In the performance of the duties means that any expenses incurred before the employee's duties commence or after they terminate will not be allowed as a deduction. Thus, the expense of obtaining a job or a job qualification is not usually deductible.

Expenditure incurred by an employee to qualify himself, or to keep himself qualified, to perform the duties of the employment – such as expenditure by a professional person in keeping himself informed of developments in his professional field – would not be incurred in the performance of his duties in the statutory sense. It appears that it is irrelevant whether the actions might be regarded as necessary.

For travelling, etc. expenses, see 1994.

Law: ITEPA 2003, s. 336; *R & C Commrs v Decadt*; *Baird v Williams (HMIT)* [1999] BTC 228; *Fitzpatrick v IR Commrs (No. 2)* [1994] BTC 66; *Smith (HMIT) v Abbott* [1994] BTC 66; *Brown v Bullock (HMIT)* (1961) 40 TC 1

See *British Tax Reporter* ¶453-200.

1994　Employees' deductible travelling expenses

The tax treatment of employees' and directors' travelling and subsistence expenses was modernised and simplified from 6 April 1998.

Benchmark rates

HMRC introduced a new benchmark rate system from 6 April 2009. Employers can use the rates to make certain day subsistence payments free of tax and NICs to employees who incur allowable business travel expenses. Employers do not have to use the rates. They can reimburse their employees' actual expenditure or apply to HMRC to agree a scale rate appropriate for their business needs in a dispensation.

Qualifying travelling expenses

'Qualifying travelling expenses' are now deductible from emoluments (see 1990). These are:

(1)　amounts necessarily expended on travelling in the performance of the duties of the employment, etc.; or

(2) other expenses of travelling which:

(a) are attributable to the employee's, etc. necessary attendance at any place in performing the duties of the employment, etc., and

(b) are not expenses of 'ordinary commuting' or 'private travel' (see below).

HMRC regard 'travelling expenses' as including subsistence costs attributable to the journey in question.

Travel between group companies

Expenses of travel between places where duties are carried out for different offices or employments under or with companies in the same group are treated as necessarily expended in performing the duties to be performed at the destination.

Ordinary commuting and private travel

'Ordinary commuting' means travel between:

(1) the employee's home, or

(2) a place that is not a 'workplace' in relation to the employment,

(3) and a place which is a 'permanent workplace' in relation to the employment.

'Private travel' means travel between:

(1) the employee's home and a place that is not a workplace in relation to the employment, or

(2) between two places neither of which is a workplace in relation to the employment.

'Workplace' means a place at which the employee's attendance is necessary in performing the duties of the employment.

Travel between any two places which is for practical purposes substantially ordinary commuting or private travel is treated as ordinary commuting or private travel.

Permanent and temporary workplaces

For the purposes of (3) above, and subject to what follows below, 'permanent workplace' means a place which the employee regularly attends in performing the duties of the employment, and which is not a 'temporary workplace'. A 'temporary workplace' means a place which the employee attends in performing the duties of the employment for the purpose of performing a task of limited duration or for some other temporary purpose (see further below).

The 24-month rule and fixed term appointments

A place is not regarded as a temporary workplace if the employee's attendance is in the course of a 'period of continuous work' at that place:

(1) lasting more than 24 months, or

(2)   comprising all or almost all of the period for which the employee is likely to hold the employment,

or if the employee's attendance is at a time when it is reasonable to assume that it will be in the course of such a period.

A 'period of continuous work' at a place is a period over which, looking at the whole period and considering all the employment duties, the employment duties fall to be performed to a significant extent at that place.

Where there is a change, or a contemplated change, in the place at which the employment duties are to be carried out, the change is ignored if it does not have any substantial effect on the employee's journey or on the expenses of travelling.

Depots and bases

A place which the employee regularly attends in performing employment duties is treated as a *permanent* workplace if it is either:

(1)   the base from which the employment duties are performed, or

(2)   the place at which the tasks to be carried out in performing the employment duties.

Area-based employees

An employee is treated as having a permanent workplace consisting of an area if all the following conditions are met:

(1)   the employment duties are defined by reference to an area (whether or not they also require attendance at places outside the area);

(2)   in performing the employment duties the employee attends different places within the area;

(3)   none of the places which he or she attends in performing the employment duties is a permanent workplace; and

(4)   applying para. 4 and 5 above to the area as if it were a place, the area meets the conditions for being a permanent workplace.

Example

An employee's return journey from home to his permanent workplace costs him £7. No relief has ever been available for this expenditure.

The employee makes an occasional journey from home to a temporary workplace which costs £15 return. Relief is available for the full cost of the journey: £15.

Concessions in relation to the following should also be noted.

- Financial assistance (including subsistence), etc. when public transport is disrupted.
- Financial assistance, etc. for home-to-work travel for the severely disabled.

Income Tax

- Offshore oil and gas, etc. workers' travel to and from the mainland (see 1580).
- Payments for employees' late-night journeys home. An employee's late-night taxi fares home which are reimbursed by the employer may be income tax-free where the employee is occasionally required to work late, but those occasions are neither regular nor frequent. 'Late' means after 9 p.m. The term 'regular' means following a predictable pattern in the normal course of employment. The exemption will therefore not apply to, for example, bar staff who regularly work until after 11 p.m., or a cashier who must work late every Friday night to deal with the week's takings.
- Employers may pay tax-free (from 9 March 1999) for alternative transport to get car sharers home when exceptional circumstances, such as a domestic emergency, mean that the normal car sharing arrangements unavoidably break down. The concession aims to help employers promote car-sharing arrangements by their employees.

The last two concessions apply to a maximum of 60 journeys in a tax year.

See also 302 (incidental overnight expenses); 318 (members of the armed forces); 405 (mileage allowances); 2000 (subsistence costs).

Law: ITEPA 2003, s. 245–248, 337–342

Source: HMRC *Brief* 24/09

Website: www.hmrc.gov.uk/leaflets/c6.htm

See *British Tax Reporter* ¶454-000.

1997 Machinery and plant allowances

Employees and directors may be entitled to capital allowances in respect of machinery or plant (see 2360ff.) which is 'necessarily' provided for use in the performance of their duties.

However, in relation to an employee, etc. who uses his own 'mechanically propelled road vehicle' (or cycle, from 1999–2000) for work, only part of the capital expenditure on which was incurred for work purposes, the vehicle need *not* have been necessarily provided for use in the performance of his duties.

An employee's entitlement to balancing allowances (e.g. on leaving employment) is limited to a fraction (A/B) of the excess of 'qualifying expenditure' over 'disposal value' (see 2364), 'A' being the number of tax years for which he has claimed allowances, and 'B' being the number of tax years for which allowances fall to be made to him. Thus, if an employee chooses not to claim allowances in a period in which he is entitled to them, for instance because his income is insufficient to absorb them, his entitlement to balancing allowances is proportionately reduced, so that he cannot recoup the lost writing-down allowances at the end of his employment, or when the car ceases to belong to him.

See also 1886 (interest on loans to buy machinery).

Law: CAA 2001, s. 15(1), 36 and 262; FA 1999, s. 50; *White v Higginbottom* [1983] BTC 46

See *British Tax Reporter* ¶237-000.

1998 Allowable accommodation and residence expenses of employees

Like most expenses other than qualifying travelling expenses (see 1992, 1994), accommodation expenses, to be deductible, must be incurred wholly, exclusively and necessarily in the performance of an employee's or director's duties. Everyone has to live somewhere, so if an individual chooses to live a great distance from his place of work and stays at a hotel during the working week he will be unable to deduct the hotel expenses.

Example 1

Sue has jobs with two completely separate companies, one in London, and the other in Birmingham. She lives in London, but on those days when she works in Birmingham she stays in a hotel. The expenses of living in the hotel would not be deductible.

Example 2

Teresa has a job in London and is occasionally required to go to Liverpool on business. She stays in a hotel when in Liverpool. The hotel expenses in this case are deductible.

The cost of providing personal accommodation for employees by employers will form part of that employee's taxable emoluments whether or not it is deducted from that employee's wages or salary (see 314).

Employees required to work from home are permitted to deduct a proportion of many costs attributable to the property, including council tax.

Source: *Tax Bulletin*, Issue 69, October 2005 (homeworking expenses)

See *British Tax Reporter* ¶454-000.

2000 Employees' subsistence costs

The expense of meals is rarely necessarily incurred in the performance of one's duties, as required for it to be allowable (see 1990). Even if the expense is necessarily incurred, it would be unusual to find that the expense was incurred wholly and exclusively in the performance of an employee's duties. However, HMRC allow the tax-free issue of certain non-transferable meal vouchers to employees up to 15p for each working day.

Deduction is currently allowed of obligatory travelling expenses attributable to an employee's necessary attendance at any place in performing his employment duties (and which are not expenses of ordinary commuting or private travel); such expenses include subsistence costs attributable to the journey in question (see 1994). See also 302 as regards incidental overnight expenses.

Working rule agreements

Working rule agreements drawn up between employers' federations and trade unions set out the terms and conditions of a large number of employees in the construction and allied industries. HMRC have agreed that some of the modest travel and subsistence allowances which employees receive under these agreements will not be taxed. However, the employees covered can still choose relief under the ordinary rules. If so, they are entitled to relief for the full cost of business journeys *less* the amount of tax-free allowance received.

Lorry drivers' meals

Where travelling itself is an essential feature of an employee's duties ('travelling appointments'), with the result that he has to spend money on meals in restaurants or cafés above what he would spend if he had a fixed place or area of work or were able to get home for meals, a deduction may be allowed for the extra expenses necessarily incurred in the performance of the duties.

Drivers who qualify for consideration under this heading are those who are engaged full-time in travelling in the performance of their duties. By this is meant employment as a driver throughout the full normal working hours of each day, except those days when the employee cannot work by reason of sickness or other reasonable cause, or which are holidays or rest days. Jobs which entail only incidental travelling are not regarded as 'travelling appointments'.

Even full-time drivers are excluded from consideration if they travel only in a limited area. This is because they incur no additional expenses when at work from one day to the next, as they have an established pattern of expenditure on meals in the same way as any other employee who has to work at a distance from home and who cannot return home for lunch.

HMRC require claimants to give full details of the nature of their duties in addition to providing evidence of the expenditure actually incurred. In practice, relief is not restricted by reference to amounts of expenditure saved by not having meals at home or a fixed place of work.

In addition, HMRC have agreed with the Road Haulage Association an overnight allowance tax-free without need for detailed bills and vouchers, but subject to production of documentary evidence that the taxpayer was absent from home overnight and based at a particular depot.

Law: ITEPA 2003, s. 89

Website: www.hmrc.gov.uk/leaflets/c6.htm

See *British Tax Reporter* ¶455-000.

2002   Employees' business entertaining

Usually, there are no allowable deductions for business entertainment expenses. However, if the expenses are met out of a sum provided by the employer for business entertainment and:

- that sum is included in the employee's emoluments; and
- that sum was disallowed in computing the profits or losses of the trade,

that sum may be deductible if it satisfies the 'wholly, exclusively and necessarily' test (see 1990).

Law: ITEPA 2003, s. 356, 357

See *British Tax Reporter* ¶455-200.

2004   Fees and subscriptions to professional bodies

An employee or director may deduct an annual subscription paid to certain professional bodies and learned societies, etc. approved by HMRC. A lengthy list of approved bodies is published periodically by HMRC. It is available on the HMRC website at www.hmrc.gov.uk/list3/list3.htm.

Fees and contributions are also deductible:

- in respect of the retention of a name in the Register of Architects;
- in respect of the retention of a name in the dentists' register or on a roll or record kept for a class of ancillary dental workers;
- in respect of the retention of a name in either of the registers of ophthalmic opticians or in the register of dispensing opticians;
- by a registered patent agent;
- in respect of the retention of a name in the register of pharmaceutical chemists;
- to the Compensation Fund or Guarantee Fund payable on the issue of a solicitor's practising certificate;
- by a registered veterinary surgeon or by a person registered in the Supplementary Veterinary Register.

The above fees will be deductible if the fee is payable in respect of a registration (or retention of a name on a roll or record) or certificate which is a condition, or one of alternative conditions, of the performance of the duties of the office or employment.

Income Tax

HMRC generally permit relief for members of the ICAEW in respect of subscriptions to *Accountancy* on the basis that it is the official journal of the Institute and effectively part of the subscription to the Institute.

Entertainers' agency fees

In 1990 HMRC announced that actors and other performers engaged on standard Equity contracts would be moved from former Sch. D to Sch. E from 6 April 1990, unless their first appearance pre-dated 6 April 1987 (see 253). To secure engagements, most of such entertainers rely on theatrical agents, whose fees would be non-deductible under the strict rules of Sch. E (see 1990). However, from the same date actors, singers, musicians, dancers and theatrical artists may deduct from their chargeable emoluments fees, inclusive of VAT, paid to agents (including co-operative society arrangements), not exceeding $17^1/_2$ per cent of their emoluments in any tax year.

Law: ITEPA 2003, s. 343–345

See *British Tax Reporter* ¶455-000.

2006 Civil servants' expenses

Where persons such as civil servants are paid out of public funds, the Treasury will fix an amount representing the average amount spent wholly, exclusively and necessarily in the performance of their duties. The amount so fixed by the Treasury will then be deducted from salary when charging it to income tax. If a person actually has greater expenses than the amount fixed he will be able to deduct the actual expenses incurred wholly, exclusively and necessarily in the performance of his duties.

Law: ITEPA 2003, s. 328–330, 368

See *British Tax Reporter* ¶406-500.

2020 Security assets and services

A deduction is allowed in respect of expenditure incurred or reimbursed by an employer on the provision of security assets and security services which improve personal security. The security asset or service must be provided for the employee to meet a special threat to his personal physical security which arises wholly or mainly by virtue of the particular employment concerned. HMRC have given such examples of qualifying security assets and services as alarm systems, bullet-resistant windows in houses, floodlighting and security guards.

Law: FA 1989, s. 50–52

See *British Tax Reporter* ¶456-000.

2028 Tools and special clothing allowance

In some cases individuals will incur expenditure on the cost or upkeep of tools or special clothing necessary for work. By concession HMRC give flat-rate allowances for most classes of trade, which have been agreed with the trade unions concerned, without enquiring what any individual employee has actually spent. A £60 allowance for fire fighters was agreed with fire service unions in 1994.

Further categories of allowance have been introduced for healthcare workers for 1998–99 onwards. Tax relief on between £45 and £110 per year will be available to certain employees who have to wear a uniform and are not provided with laundry services by their employers.

Law: ITEPA 2003, s. 367

See *British Tax Reporter* ¶456-000.

PROPERTY INCOME DEDUCTIONS AND LOSSES

2040 Property business deductions

The profits of a property business are calculated in the same way as the profits of a trade, but are subject to certain limits (as set out in the table in ITTOIA 2005, s. 272). The following business deduction rules apply:

- business entertainment expenses;
- expenditure involving crime;
- redundancy payments;
- training courses for employees;
- counselling services for employees;
- consideration for restrictive undertakings;
- deductions on respect of certain emoluments;
- expenses connected with non-approved retirement benefit schemes;
- expenditure connected with providing security assets or services; and
- rules for computing profits and losses.

Law: ITTOIA 2005, s. 272, 274–275

See *British Tax Reporter* ¶300-000.

2041 Energy-saving items

From 6 April 2004, a landlord may claim up to £1,500 per property (per building prior to 2007–08) per tax year for expenditure incurred in respect of energy-saving items (such as

Income Tax

loft and cavity wall insulation, hot water system insulation, draught proofing and installation of floor insulation), where the expenditure is incurred in the course of a property income business. Where more than one person has an interest in the building concerned, the allowance may be apportioned accordingly.

From April 2007, the allowance is also available to corporate landlords who let residential properties.

Law: ITTOIA 2005, s. 312; FA 2004, s. 133; *Energy-Saving Items (Income Tax) Regulations* 2007 (SI 2007/3278)

2042 Deductions relating to land managed as one estate

Where land is managed as one estate, the owner can elect that deductions attributable to any of the land which is not let should be relieved against income from other parts of the estate, as if each had been let out on full-rent leases. These provisions have been extended to provide for loss relief to be available for set-off outside the estate where expenditure on land within the estate leased at a rent greater than its annual value exceeds the estate income. This is achieved by providing that the estate be divided into two parts when dealing with income and expenditure, with the parts relating respectively to land leased at a rent higher than its annual value, and land either not leased or leased at a rent equal to or lower than the annual value.

Expenditure on the first part can form a property business loss (see 2062), and thus be set against profits outside the estate, where it exceeds the income arising from both parts of the estate, to the extent that the second part is reduced by expenditure in the tax year and that brought forward from an earlier year. Expenditure on the second part can only be set against income from the estate and cannot form a property business loss (see 2062, 3133).

The above provisions are to be repealed for income tax purposes from 6 April 2001 and for corporation tax purposes from 1 April 2001.

Law: FA 1998, s. 39, Sch. 5, para. 7; ICTA 1988, s. 26

See *British Tax Reporter* ¶300-000.

2044 Maintenance funds for historic buildings

Adjustments are made where part of an estate is, or becomes, comprised in a maintenance fund for historic buildings, etc. This treatment has been modified for years after 1994–95, and from April 1998 for corporation tax purposes, to operate in the context of a property income business (see 1200ff.). Any excess expenditure remaining after relief is given under the provisions outlined at 2042 can be relieved as a property income business loss (see 2062, 3133).

The above provisions are to be repealed for income tax purposes from 6 April 2001 and for corporation tax purposes from 1 April 2001.

Law: FA 1998, s. 39; ICTA 1988, s. 27

See *British Tax Reporter* ¶300-000.

2046 Expenditure on making sea walls

Property income businesses may also attract an annual deduction for a twenty-first proportion of any expenditure on a wall or embankment erected to protect premises from the sea or a tidal river.

Law: ITTOIA 2005, s. 315–318

See *British Tax Reporter* ¶300-000.

2062 Property income business losses

Relief is provided for income tax losses arising in a property income business (see 1200) or an 'overseas property business' (see 1660).

Carry-forward relief

A loss sustained in a property income business is computed in the way in which property income profits are computed. Such a loss, sustained by an individual or partner in a tax year, is automatically carried forward to be set against the first available profits of that business. If those profits suffice to cover the loss, the taxpayer cannot opt to set off only part of the loss. If the business ceases with unrelieved losses, these cannot be carried forward to any new property income business subsequently set up.

Excess expenditure and interest

Unrelieved property income business excess expenditure and unrelieved furnished letting losses arising in years before 1995–96 are converted into losses to be set against the first available property income business profits after 1994–95. Similarly, where, on the change to the property income business rules, there is an excess of interest to be set against income from property which, but for the change, would have been carried forward against property income of a year or years after 1994–95, the unrelieved excess is converted into a loss to be set against the first available property income business profits after 1994–95.

Excess capital allowances

Where a taxpayer incurs a property income business loss, and:

Income Tax

- the capital allowances treated as expenses in computing the loss exceed the amount of any balancing charges treated as receipts in computing the loss; and/or
- the property income business has been carried on in relation to land which consists of or includes an agricultural estate to which allowable agricultural expenses, deducted in computing the loss, are attributable;

then the taxpayer may claim, in relation to the tax year of the loss or the following year, to have some or all of the capital allowances, or agricultural part of the loss, set against his *general* income. Before 1997–98, property income business losses attributable to excess capital allowances could not be set against other income of the same year.

Time-limit for claims

The above claim must be accompanied by all such amendments as may be needed of any self-assessment previously made by the claimant (see 2564). The claim cannot be made after the end of 12 months from 31 January following the end of the year to which it relates, though claims relating to 1995–96 could be made at any time before 6 April 1998.

For property income business losses for companies, see 3133.

Law: ITA 2007, s. 118–124; FA 1997, Sch. 15

See *British Tax Reporter* ¶300-000.

BUSINESS EXPENSES AND LOSSES

2150   Extent of relief for business expenses and losses

Taxable business income is calculated by deducting *all allowable* expenses incurred in the income year from the total assessable income earned during that year (see 1850). Note that it is the gross receipts from a business activity that are brought in as assessable income, not the net profits or gains according to commercial principles.

Losses or outgoings of a capital nature, even though incurred in the course of producing assessable income, are not generally deductible. Expenses or losses of a private or domestic nature are not deductible at all.

As to the treatment of trading stock for tax accounting purposes, see 652ff.

The Taxes Acts seldom *expressly* allow deductible expenses, though it is provided that only deductions which are expressly enumerated in the Acts are allowable. The usual form is that the Acts set out what is disallowed, and by implication what is not disallowed is allowed (see 2174); however, certain transactions are effectively ignored, e.g. certain stock lending arrangements are ignored on both the expenditure and income sides (see 646).

In order to be allowable, an expense must normally be of a revenue nature (see 2152) and incurred wholly and exclusively for the purposes of the trade (see 2154).

Timing

A long-established principle requires that, for tax purposes, expenditure should be taken into account when it is incurred (unless there is some overriding statutory provision or principle developed in the cases to the contrary).

There are special rules for spreading certain pension contributions (see 2240) and there is some uncertainty regarding lease rentals (see 2245).

Purely contingent liabilities cannot be recognised but statistical estimation of facts which had happened but were unknown does seem to be permissible. Hence, for example, the Privy Council has held that a figure for anticipated liability under warranties given with vehicles sold to remedy defects manifesting themselves within 12 months was deductible in computing profits.

Provisions for anticipated losses or expenses

A business makes a 'provision' where it expects to pay out money in the future and takes that probable expense into account when working out its current profits. The legislation requires a business to pay tax 'on the full amount of the profits or gains of the year of assessment' (no more and no less), and the courts until recently (see 2245) took the firm view that, for tax purposes, neither profit nor loss could be anticipated.

The Accounting Standards Board have now published Financial Reporting Standard 12 (FRS 12) (provisions, contingent liabilities and contingent assets), which considerably increases the requirements for making a provision. Compliance with FRS 12 is mandatory for all non-Small Entities companies for accounting periods ending after 22 March 1999, though a date has yet to be set for compliance by users of the FRS for Small Entities.

HMRC have announced that they are not pursuing appeals in a case concerning provisions for future rents and in another case concerning repairs provisions. They now accept that there is no longer a tax rule which denies provisions for anticipated losses or expenses. This means that the tax treatment of provisions has moved (in HMRC's words) 'substantially closer to UK generally accepted accounting practice'.

Law: ITTOIA 2005, s. 7(1), 200(4); *Herbert Smith v Honour (HMIT)* [1999] BTC 44; *Jenners, Princes Street Edinburgh Ltd v IR Commrs* (1998) Sp C 166; *Commr of Inland Revenue (New Zealand) v Mitsubishi Motors Ltd* [1996] BTC 398; *Gallagher v Jones (HMIT); Threlfall v Jones (HMIT)* [1993] BTC 310; *BSC Footwear Ltd v Ridgway (HMIT)* [1972] AC 544; *Duple Motor Bodies Ltd v Ostime (HMIT)* [1961] 1 WLR 739

Income Tax

2152   Capital or revenue expenditure

Revenue expenditure is allowable as a business expense provided it is incurred 'wholly and exclusively for the purposes of the trade, etc.' (see 2154) and is not specifically disallowed in the Taxes Acts (see 2174). Usually there is no problem in distinguishing between expenditure on revenue account and expenditure on capital account. Thus the cost of purchasing (whether by a single payment or by way of instalments of the lump sum cost) business premises is capital expenditure, while rent paid for business premises is revenue expenditure, and the cost of alterations, additions, improvements or renovations is capital, while the cost of repairs is revenue.

There is clearly some overlap between the various 'tests' below which have been suggested by the courts.

Fixed and circulating capital

Fixed capital and circulating capital should be distinguished. Fixed capital represents those assets which are retained and used in order to make profits, e.g. machinery used to make cars in a car factory is part of the fixed capital. Circulating capital on the other hand represents those assets which are bought and sold in the ordinary course of trade, e.g. machinery bought and sold by a trader in machinery is part of the circulating capital and the cost of it is deductible. In one case £733,649 claimed as the cost of winding up a North Sea Oil operation was held to be a non-deductible capital expense as the cost related to the profit-making structure of the business, i.e. fixed capital.

The cost of 'creating, acquiring or enlarging the permanent ... structure of which the income is to be the produce or fruit' is of a capital nature, while 'the cost of earning that income itself or performing the income-earning operations' is a revenue expense. Applying these dicta, the Privy Council has held that interest paid by a Hong Kong development company on a loan obtained for a capital project was a payment on capital account, which was therefore not deductible from its taxable profits: the fact that interest is income in the recipient's hands and a recurring and periodic payment does not necessarily mean that it is a revenue expense.

With respect to operations after 6 April 1989 expenditure on making good landfill sites for waste disposal qualifies as a revenue deduction for persons holding disposal or waste management licences (unless capital allowances are available): expenditure on preparing a site is written off according to the proportion of site capacity filled with waste in the appropriate period, and expenditure on making good a site is allowed as a trading expense in the period in which it is paid. Site preparation expenditure includes costs incurred before the disposal licence is granted or in obtaining such licence. Authorisations for the disposal of radioactive waste are added to the lists of relevant licences for trades begun after 31 March 1993; relief for site preparation is also extended for such companies to any expenditure which is incurred before trading starts.

Enduring benefit

In difficult cases the courts have held that, in the absence of special circumstances, expenditure is of a capital nature where it is made with a view to bringing into existence an asset or an advantage (tangible or intangible) for the enduring benefit of the trade or business.

One should perhaps look and see whether a capital asset is identifiable from the sum expended. The payment (to be of a capital nature) must be made for an enduring capital asset even if one of the advantages secured by the payment for the capital asset is an increased share in profits. The initial payment by a franchisee depends upon what it is for but, in HMRC's view, it is generally for substantial rights of an enduring nature to initiate or substantially extend a business and is together with any related professional fees; however, HMRC will accept that an appropriate part of the initial fee is for revenue items, such as stock or training of staff (not the franchisee), and hence allowable, where:

- the sum claimed in respect of revenue items fairly reflects the actual goods and services provided, and
- it is clear that those services are not separately charged for in the continuing fees.

Once-and-for-all expenditure on a capital asset

There has been distinguished as capital expenditure, 'once and for all expenditure on a capital asset to make it more advantageous'.

Preservation of trade

A payment to get rid of an obstacle to successful trading is a revenue and not a capital payment. However, the purpose of the taxpayer to preserve the trade is not determinative of the capital/income issue.

Software development costs

HMRC's view is that an in-house or contracted-out software project to ensure that existing computer systems could be adapted for the millennium would always be a revenue matter unless it was part of a major new project instituting other changes and the project was of a capital nature. Similarly, conversion-driven costs required in adapting computer systems for the euro are unlikely to be capital.

Law: ITTOIA 2005, s. 165–168; *Southern Counties Agricultural Trading Society v Blackler (HMIT)* (1999) Sp C 198; *Wharf Properties Ltd v Commr of Inland Revenue (Hong Kong)* [1997] BTC 173; *Croydon Hotel & Leisure Co v Bowen (HMIT)* (1996) Sp C 101; *Lawson (HMIT) v Johnson Matthey plc* [1992] BTC 324; *Rolfe (HMIT) v Wimpey Waste Management Ltd* [1989] BTC 191; *RTZ Oil & Gas Ltd v Elliss (HMIT)* [1987] BTC 359; *E Bott Ltd v Price (HMIT)* [1987] BTC 49; *Jeffs (HMIT) v Ringtons Ltd* [1985] BTC 585; *Whitehead (HMIT) v Tubbs (Elastics) Ltd* [1983] BTC 28; *Watney Combe Reid & Co Ltd v Pike (HMIT)* [1982] BTC 288; *Tucker (HMIT) v Granada Motorway Services Ltd* [1979] 1 WLR 683; *IR Commrs v Carron Co* (1968) 45 TC 18; *Commr of Taxes v Nchanga*

Consolidated Copper Mines Ltd [1964] AC 948; Anglo-Persian Oil Co Ltd v Dale (HMIT)
[1932] 1 KB 124; Mallett (HMIT) v Staveley Coal and Iron Co Ltd [1928] 2 KB 405; British
Insulated and Helsby Cables Ltd v Atherton (HMIT) [1926] AC 205

Website: www.hmrc.gov.uk/bulletins/index.htm

See *British Tax Reporter* ¶213-000.

2154 Expenditure not wholly and exclusively for business

To be deductible as a business expense (see 2150) the expenditure must be wholly and
exclusively laid out or expended for the purposes of the business. The word 'wholly' refers
to the quantum, i.e. how much is referable to business purposes. Thus if expenditure is not
wholly referable to a business purpose the excess will be disallowed as a deduction. The
word 'exclusively' means that if the expenditure was partly laid out for business purposes
and partly for personal purposes then the expenditure will be disallowed as a deduction.

However, even if there is such a duality of purpose HMRC will often allow apportionment if
accurate apportionment can be made. It should be noted that if the payment is solely for
business purposes then it will be deductible even if some private benefit is obtained by the
taxpayer. Where a taxpayer runs his business from home, a proportionate part of his costs
relating to the property will usually be allowed, including presumably council tax in the
same way as for employees required to work from home; HMRC have ceased to apply the
one-third rule of thumb for business use of a farmhouse (also reflected in a change to the
CGT rules at 6244).

Travelling expenses

Travelling expenses are not deductible unless they are wholly and exclusively for business
purposes. HMRC by concession usually allow a proportionate part of the travelling expenses
if there is duality of purpose (see above). Travelling expenses are allowed as a deduction
where the taxpayer is travelling from one place of work to another in the course of his
duties.

Where the cost of overnight accommodation is allowable as a business expense, HMRC
accept reasonable claims for the cost of evening meals and breakfast (as substantiated by
receipts or other records); in the case of long-distance self-employed lorry drivers a
deduction will be allowed whether such meals are taken as an adjunct to overnight
accommodation or where they spend the night in their cabs.

Law: ITTOIA 2005, s. 34; *McLaren v Mumford (HMIT)* [1996] BTC 490; *Redkite Ltd v
Inspector of Taxes* (1996) Sp C 93; *MacKinlay (HMIT) v Arthur Young McClelland Moores
& Co* [1989] BTC 587; *Mallalieu v Drummond (HMIT)* [1983] BTC 380

Website: www.hmrc.gov.uk/bulletins/index.htm

See *British Tax Reporter* ¶708-170.

2174   Statutory disallowances for business expenses

Expenditure not wholly and exclusively for trading purposes

See 2154.

Expenditure involving a criminal offence

Payments made as a result of blackmail or extortion, whether by terrorist groups or other criminals, or constituting the commission of a criminal offence (e.g. bribes), are disallowed.

Expenditure to maintain taxpayer or his family

No sum can be deducted in computing taxable business profits, in respect of any disbursements or expenses of maintenance of the taxpayer, his family or establishment, or any sums expended for any other domestic or private purposes distinct from business purposes.

Example

Alfie draws £150 a week from his business for personal expenditure. This will be disallowed as a deduction.

Rent for dwelling-house

The rent of a dwelling-house or domestic offices, or any part thereof, is not allowed as a deduction. However, if part of the premises is used for business purposes then up to a maximum of two-thirds of the rent paid is allowed as a deduction unless, having regard to all the circumstances, a greater sum should be allowed.

Example

Alison rents premises for £120 per week. One-third of the premises is used as her office in the course of her business. One-third of the rent, i.e. £40, will be allowed as a deduction.

Repairs and alterations

While sums expended for repairing premises occupied, or for supplying, repairing or altering any implements, utensils or articles employed for business purposes are deductible, capital expenditure (e.g. on improving business premises) is disallowed.

Income Tax

> ### Example 1
>
> Brandon replaces the single glazing in his factory with double glazing. This will not be an allowable deduction since it is capital employed in improving the premises.

Deductions for expenditure on disrepair existing at the time of purchase may well be disallowed, though deduction for expenditure on deferred repairs (i.e. disrepair existing at the time of purchase but not dealt with for good reason) may be allowed if there is a good reason for deferral.

> ### Example 2
>
> Archie purchases a ship for his business. It is unseaworthy, which is reflected in the purchase price of £500,000. Archie spends £150,000 on making it seaworthy and uses it for two years when further repairs costing £200,000 are required due to deterioration over that period. The £150,000 spent making the ship into a profit-making asset will not be allowed as a deduction since it is regarded as capital expenditure as the asset was incapable of being used when acquired and the purchase price reflected this. However, the further repairs costing £200,000 will be allowed as a deduction since it is revenue expenditure.

Non-trading losses

Any losses not connected with or arising out of the business is not allowed as a deduction.

Capital withdrawn from, or employed in, the business

Any capital withdrawn from, or any sum employed or intended to be employed as capital in the business, is not allowed as a deduction. This, however, does not include interest.

Notional interest

Any interest which might have been made if any such sums withdrawn as capital (above) or expended on improvements to business premises (above) had been laid out at interest is not allowed as a deduction.

> ### Example
>
> Amelia decides to replace the single glazing in her factory with double glazing. This will not be an allowable deduction since it is capital employed in improving the premises. Amelia cannot claim that she could have invested the money used for double glazing and earned interest on it and therefore the interest forgone should be allowed as a deduction.

Debts

Any debts, except bad debts proved to be such, trade debts given up by a creditor as part of a formal voluntary arrangement under the *Insolvency Act* 1986 or a compromise with creditors under the *Companies Act* 2006, s. 895(1) and 896, and doubtful debts to the extent that they are respectively estimated to be bad, will be disallowed as a deduction in arriving at the profits of the year in which the debts become bad or doubtful; in the case of the bankruptcy or insolvency of a debtor, the amount which may reasonably be expected to be received on any such debt will be deemed to be the value thereof. If the debt is later paid then it must be brought in as a trading receipt in the year in which it is paid (see 648).

Example

Annie, a trader, is owed money by Brenda for goods supplied in Year 1 and Annie decides to write the debt off as a bad debt. She is able to prove to HMRC that it is a bad debt and it is allowed as a deduction. However, in Year 5 Brenda pays the debt and Annie has to enter it into her books for that year as a receipt of her trade.

Relief is available for certain overseas trade debts. The legislation generally gives relief by deducting the appropriate amount from the trading profits of the 'accounting period' in which it is regarded as unremittable if it is outstanding for at least a year after the end of that period and meets certain general conditions. There are special provisions relating to companies holding debts with overseas governments.

A deduction may be permitted for a debt incurred in a prior trade proving to be irrecoverable after the deemed commencement of a new trade following a change in persons carrying it on, etc.

Average loss after adjustment

Any average loss beyond the actual amount of loss after adjustment will not be allowed as a deduction. This relates to marine, etc. insurance.

Insurance or indemnity

Any sum recoverable under an insurance or contract of indemnity will not be allowable as a deduction. HMRC treat benefits paid under insurance policies taken out by medical practitioners in respect of locum and fixed practice expenses in the event of the policyholder's incapacity or illness as taxable professional receipts, and the premiums as deductible.

Annuity or other annual payment

Any annuity or other annual payment (other than interest) payable out of profits will not be allowed as a deduction. This does not apply to payments made in earning profits but only to payments which are a charge on the profits and therefore paid under deduction of income tax.

Income Tax

Interest paid to non-residents

Any interest paid to a person not resident in the UK if and so far as it is interest at more than a reasonable commercial rate is not deductible (see further 2249).

Relevant loan interest

Relevant loan interest within MIRAS (other than interest deemed to be relevant loan interest pending notification of a change by the borrower to lender) is not allowed as a deduction.

Patent royalties

A royalty or other sum paid (under deduction of basic rate income tax: see 1368–1370) in respect of the user of a patent is disallowed as a deduction.

On the other hand, fees and expenses incurred in obtaining (or attempting to obtain) the grant of a patent, trade mark, etc. are allowable.

Mining rents and royalties

Any rent, royalty or other payment which, by ITTOIA 2005, s. 340 (in relation to payments made before 1 May 1995: see 962) or by ITTOIA 2005, s. 344, was subject to deduction of tax as if it were a royalty or other sum paid for the use of a patent, was disallowed as a deduction.

VAT penalties

The following are disallowed for all tax purposes:

(1) penalties under:

   (a) VATA 1994, s. 60–70 (see 8480ff.), FA 1994, s. 8–11 (excise); and
   (b) FA 1994, Sch. 7, para. 12–19 (insurance premium tax);

(2) interest under:

   (a) VATA 1994, s. 74 (see 8544), and
   (b) FA 1994, Sch. 7, para. 21 (insurance premium tax);

(3) surcharges under VATA 1994, s. 59 (see 8516).

As a corollary, any repayment supplement paid under VATA 1994, s. 79 (see 8522) is disregarded for all tax purposes.

Entertainment

Expenditure on business entertainment, including hospitality and most gifts, is disallowable unless provided in the ordinary course of the trade, profession or vocation (which is a trade, etc. relating to such activity) or for general advertising (though staff entertaining and certain promotional gifts are allowable: see 2246).

Law: ITTOIA 2005, s. 34, 35(1), 45–47, 55, 107–109; *Taylor v Clatworthy (HMIT)* (1996) Sp C 103; *Odeon Associated Theatres Ltd v Jones (HMIT)* [1973] Ch 288; *Law Shipping Co Ltd v IR Commrs* (1923) 12 TC 621

Website: www.hmrc.gov.uk/bulletins/index.htm

See *British Tax Reporter* ¶213-150.

2240   Payments for employees' benefit

The wages and salaries of employees are generally 'allowable business deductions' (see 2150) in the same way as other common payments made wholly and exclusively for the purposes of the business (see 2252). However, in the rare circumstances in which such amounts are not paid within the period of nine months from the end of the period of account, a deduction is denied until such emoluments are paid; special modifications apply to Lloyd's underwriters. Other payments made in connection with employees are set out below. See also 2241 (training costs).

Pension scheme contributions

Except as noted below, pension scheme contributions in respect of employees are generally allowable in the same way as pure wages.

Special contributions (as opposed to ordinary contributions) may have to be spread over a period depending upon the circumstances. The manner in which the Pension Schemes Office spreads such contributions was changed in August 1991, but later relaxed so as to allow the old rules to be used for accounting periods beginning before 1 September 1991 – the change involved spreading the whole contribution in accordance with the following table rather than spreading the excess over the normal level of contributions:

£0.5m–£1m	2 years
£1m–£2m	3 years
over £2m	4 years

The PSO's decision is not reviewable by the appeal tribunal.

An employer is only entitled to deduct payments to a non-approved retirement benefits scheme where, broadly, the employees who benefit are chargeable to income tax on the payments, though deductibility is to be determined on the general principles of business expenses (wholly and exclusively, etc.) or of investment companies' management expenses where payments or provisions are made in respect of the following (before 1996–97 relief was by concession):

(1)   a superannuation fund accepted as a wholly overseas fund; or

(2)   a retirement benefits scheme established outside the UK which is accepted as corresponding to an approved scheme, if the payments or provisions are made for the benefit of:

Income Tax

(a) employees who are in receipt of 'foreign emoluments' (see 1570); or

(b) employees who are not resident in the UK whose duties are performed wholly outside the UK.

With effect from periods of account ending after 5 April 1993 tax relief is only due for sums actually paid by employers into occupational pension schemes and not for provisions or accruals in respect of such payments; payments which are spread forward are unaffected. No deduction can, in any event, be allowed for sums paid into schemes after 5 April 1993 to the extent that provisions in excess of contributions actually paid have already been allowed for tax purposes.

Compensation

A compensation payment to get rid of an unsuitable employee is allowable if it was necessary for the business and was made for that purpose. The payment would not be deductible if the trade were discontinued or if it were made to compensate for loss of office when the company was taken over. However, compensation payments on cessation of trading (or partial discontinuance) are allowable up to three times the statutory redundancy payment.

Payroll giving: administrative costs

The expenses which an employer incurs in operating a 'payroll giving scheme' (see 904) are normally deductible on general principles. Relief specifically extends to payments made to an agent approved by HMRC for the purposes of directing payments to appropriate beneficiaries.

Employee trusts and share schemes

The deductibility of sums paid into employee trust funds is ordinarily determined according to general principles; however, there are exceptions for pension schemes (see above), share option scheme costs and costs/contributions relating to profit-sharing schemes or employee share ownership trusts (see 4850ff.).

Restrictive covenants

Restrictive covenant payments caught by the provisions outlined at 283 are deductible as expenses of a trade, profession or vocation, and from the expenses of management of an investment company.

Redundancy

Redundancy payments are generally an allowable deduction either under general principles or specifically. If the right to a tax deduction depends on statute, relief is due for the period of account in which the payment is made, and where the payment is made after the discontinuance it is regarded for this purpose as made on the last day on which the business is carried on.

Outplacement counselling

The costs of 'outplacement counselling', and related fees or travelling expenses, for redundant or potentially redundant employees are deductible, even if the redundancy arises out of the closing down of the business.

Benefits-in-kind

Benefit payments are usually deductible: i.e. expenditure which usually merely benefits the employee, e.g. for Christmas parties, is usually deductible since it fosters good industrial relations. This generally includes the situation in which an employer pays an employee's council tax.

National Insurance

Employers may deduct secondary Class 1, Class 1A and Class 1B National Insurance contributions when computing their taxable profits.

Law: ITTOIA 2005, s. 31, 35–36, 53, 69, 72–80, 865, 868, Sch. 1, para 594(2)–(3); FA 1999, s. 61; FA 1997, s. 65; *Kelsall (HMIT) v Investment Chartwork Ltd* [1994] BTC 16; *B W Noble Ltd v Mitchell (HMIT)* (1927) 11 TC 372; *IR Commrs v Anglo Brewing Co Ltd* (1925) 12 TC 803

Source: SP 11/81, *Additional redundancy payments*;

Website: www.hmrc.gov.uk/bulletins/index.htm

See *British Tax Reporter* ¶707-880.

2241   Staff training and development

The cost of general training and education in respect of the tasks and skills required of an employee to perform his duties are typically allowable as business expenses. Education of a special kind may be required in a particular trade and before 19 March 1991, employers could deduct payments made to provide special technical education necessary in a particular trade.

Where a business proprietor incurs costs in attending a training course, whether a deduction is available is largely a question of fact depending upon the course's purpose. If it is to extend or improve his or her professional knowledge or skills, it may well be capital expenditure and not deductible (see 2152); if it is to update his or her professional skills or knowledge it would generally be of a revenue nature and therefore allowable if it met the 'wholly and exclusively test' (see 2154).

Where an employer incurs relevant expenditure in connection with a qualifying course of training for an employee or ex-employee, and it is undertaken with a view to retraining the employee for work of a nature not within the employer's requirements, the expenditure is

Income Tax

nonetheless deductible as a 'business expense' (see 2150) by the employer, and the employee, etc. is not taxed on the expenditure. A training course qualifies if:

● it is designed to impart or improve skills or knowledge relevant to gainful employment or self-employment;
● it is entirely devoted to the teaching or practical application of the skills or knowledge;
● the duration does not exceed one year;
● all teaching takes place within the UK;
● the employee attends full-time;
● the employee has two years' service;
● it is available generally to employees (or a particular class of them) of that employer, and

a course is undertaken with a view to retraining if the employee commences the course whilst still employed or within one year of ceasing to be employed by the employer *and* he ceases to be employed within two years of the end of the course. Relevant expenses are:

● course fees;
● examination fees;
● cost of essential books;
● travelling expenses.

HMRC have outlined the circumstances in which expenditure by an employer on the training and development of employees may be disallowed either under the 'wholly and exclusively' rule (see 2154) or because for tax purposes it counts as capital (see 2152).

Law: ITTOIA 2005, s. 73–75, 107–108

Source: Inland Revenue *Tax Bulletin*, November 1991, p. 4, Issue 27, February 1997; Inland Revenue *Tax Bulletin*, Issue 64, April 2003

Website: www.hmrc.gov.uk/bulletins/index.htm

See *British Tax Reporter* ¶707-930.

2242 Legal and accountancy costs

Legal expenses are allowable as a 'business expense' (see 2150) where they relate to a revenue matter connected with the trade: e.g. allow legal expenses for recovering trade debts but not for recovering a loan to an employee. However, the legal cost of ascertaining or disputing profit is not strictly deductible, though in practice HMRC usually allow some deduction. If the legal expenses are incurred in relation to a capital asset then they are not deductible. Expenses on the redemption, repayment or purchase by a company of its own shares will generally be challenged by HMRC as capital rather than revenue under general principles (see 2152), as capital withdrawn (see 2174) or as failing the wholly and exclusively test (see 2154).

Accountancy expenses incurred in preparing accounts and agreeing tax liabilities are in practice normally deductible unless they relate to a tax investigation settlement (other than HMRC's in-depth examination of a particular year's accounts not resulting in penalties or interest nor in the adjustment of any other year's profits).

Accountancy expenses arising out of self-assessment enquiries

It is apparent that the above practice is incompatible with self-assessment procedures. HMRC have provided an interpretation of the current position which is as follows:

'Until such time as SP 16/91 is superseded the text below should be regarded as a statement of our practice, as it applies to self assessment enquiries.

Accountancy expenses arising out of self assessment enquiries

It is the practice to allow, in computing profits assessable under Case I and II of Schedule D, the normal accountancy expenses incurred in preparing accounts or accounts information and in assisting with the self assessment of tax liabilities.

Additional accountancy expenses arising out of an enquiry into the accounts information in a particular year's return will not be allowed where the enquiry reveals discrepancies and additional liabilities for the year of enquiry, or any earlier year, which arise as a result of negligent or fraudulent conduct.

Where, however, the enquiry results in no addition to profits, or an adjustment to the profits for the year of enquiry only and that adjustment does not arise as a result of negligent or fraudulent conduct, the additional accountancy expenses *will* be allowable.'

Law: *McKnight (HMIT) v Sheppard* [1999] BTC 236

Source: SP 16/91, *Accountancy expenses arising out of accounts investigation*; Revenue Interpretations, Inland Revenue *Tax Bulletin*, November 1991, p. 4, Issue 37, October 1998

Website: www.hmrc.gov.uk/bulletins/index.htm

See *British Tax Reporter* ¶708-470.

2243 Security assets or services for protecting proprietor

Revenue expenditure incurred in providing an individual with any security asset or service which meets a special threat to his personal physical security arising wholly or mainly by virtue of the particular business carried on by the taxpayer is deductible as a business expense (see 2150). HMRC have given such examples of security assets and services as alarm systems, bullet-resistant windows in houses and floodlighting. Expressly excluded as security assets are a car, ship, aircraft, dwelling or its appurtenant grounds. However, it does not prevent deductibility if the security asset becomes affixed to land or a dwelling.

If the security asset or service is not intended *solely* to improve personal physical security, a proportion of the expenditure is deductible.

If relief cannot be given against profits or gains the expenditure can be treated as capital expenditure for the purposes of capital allowances (see 2360).

Law: ITTOIA 2005, s. 81

See *British Tax Reporter* ¶707-530.

2244 Payments to protect or obtain level of profits

Licences or rates have to be paid for whether or not a profit is made and are therefore deductible as a 'business expense' (see 2150), whereas the payment of income tax is not deductible since it is merely an application of the profits.

Payments made to safeguard future profits are deductible, such as payments to care for crops which will only yield a harvest several years in the future. A payment for a restrictive covenant not to compete with the company has been held to be capital. However, the deduction of payments to present or former employees for restrictive covenants entered into by them after 8 June 1988 is now permitted.

The costs of a campaign to safeguard against nationalisation of the taxpayer's industry have also been held to be deductible.

Indemnity insurance premiums can be relieved against a professional person's tax liability; after retirement, relief is limited to offset against post-cessation receipts (for the taxation of post-cessation receipts, see 662). From 1 October 1996, HMRC treat premiums paid under insurance policies taken out by medical practitioners in respect of locum and fixed practice expenses in the event of the policyholder's incapacity or illness as deductible (and the benefits as taxable professional receipts).

Preservation of the level of profits should be contrasted with preservation of the trade itself. A payment to get rid of an obstacle to successful trading is a revenue and not a capital payment; however, the purpose of the taxpayer to preserve the trade may indicate that the payment is capital in nature (see 2152).

Law: ITTOIA 2005, s. 31, 69; *IR Commrs v Carron Co* (1968) 45 TC 18; *Morgan (HMIT) v Tate & Lyle Ltd* (1954) 35 TC 367; *Associated Portland Cement Manufacturers Ltd v Kerr (HMIT)* (1945) 27 TC 103; *Anglo-Persian Oil Co Ltd v Dale (HMIT)* [1932] 1 KB 124; *Vallambrosa Rubber Co v Farmer* (1910) 5 TC 529

Website: www.hmrc.gov.uk/bulletins/index.htm

See *British Tax Reporter* ¶708-500.

2245   Lease rentals

Rental payments are generally allowable as a business expense if they satisfy the usual 'wholly and exclusively' test (see 2154). However, if there is any question that the payments do not in any period reflect the use of that item for that period relief may be restricted. A portion of any lease premium may be deductible as a deemed rental, the amount taxed as income of the recipient being spread over the term of the lease (see 1260).

Finance leases

HMRC have set out the way they treat rentals payable under finance leases entered into after 11 April 1991. (A 'finance lease' is different from an operating lease under which the lessee rents an asset for a fixed period which is generally well short of its full life. Under an ordinary finance lease, the lessor, commonly part of a banking group, buys a physical asset and leases it to someone who will use it. The rental payments from the lessee are generally such that the full cost of the asset, plus an amount equivalent to interest, are returned to the lessor. The terms of the lease are such that the lessee has all, or substantially all, of the benefits of outright ownership. A finance leasing arrangement thus resembles an ordinary loan with interest, which is how it is treated in companies' commercial accounts.)

SSAP 21 essentially requires a finance lease to be capitalised in the lessee's balance sheet as an asset with a corresponding creditor. Rentals payable are apportioned between the finance element, charged to the profit and loss account, and the capital repayment which reduces the outstanding liability. The asset is depreciated over the shorter of the lease term and its useful life.

Law: ITTOIA 2005, s. 60–64, 74–75; *Gallagher v Jones (HMIT); Threlfall v Jones (HMIT)* [1993] BTC 310; *Duple Motor Bodies Ltd v Ostime (HMIT)* [1961] 1 WLR 739

Source: SP 3/91, *Finance Lease rental payments*

Website: www.hmrc.gov.uk/bulletins/index.htm

See *British Tax Reporter* ¶230-400.

2246   Payments to provide entertainment and promotional gifts

Expenditure on entertainment for trade purposes is disallowed (see 2174). However, provision for staff entertainment is allowed as a 'business expense' (see 2150). Reasonable entertainment expenses for overseas customers were allowed if provided by a UK trader but the relief has been withdrawn since 15 March 1988. Entertainment contracts already in existence on that date still qualify for relief.

Gifts which do not cost more than £10 per recipient per year (£50 for 2001–02), which conspicuously advertise the taxpayer's business and which are not food, drink, tobacco or gift tokens are allowed as a deduction. A deduction is also allowed if the gifts are products of the taxpayer's trade: e.g. a manufacturer of plastic footballs who gives some away to promote his product will be allowed a deduction in respect of them.

Other expenditure on gifts is not regarded as within the statutory disallowance provided that:

(1)   it satisfies the 'wholly and exclusively' test (see 2154);

(2)   the gift is made for the benefit of a body or association of persons established for educational, cultural, religious, recreational or benevolent purposes, and the body or association is:

    (a)   local in relation to the donor's business activities; and
    (b)   not restricted to persons connected with the donor;

(3)   the expenditure is reasonably small in relation to the scale of the donor's business.

The payment of an ordinary annual subscription to a local trade association by a non-member is similarly not regarded as a gift provided condition (1) is met.

For charitable donations, see also 902.

Law: ITTOIA 2005, s. 45(1) and 867(3); FA 1988, s. 72

Source: ESC B7, *Benevolent gifts for traders*

See *British Tax Reporter* ¶707-770.

2247   Remuneration of employees seconded to charities

If an employer temporarily makes available to a charity or educational body the services of one of his employees, any expenditure incurred by the employer which is attributable to the employment of that person is deductible as a 'business expense' (see 2150) as if his services continue to be available to the employer whilst he is working for the charity. As a general guideline, the expenditure includes the employee's salary which the employer continues to pay.

Law: ITTOIA 2005, s. 31(1)–(3)

See *British Tax Reporter* ¶708-000.

2248   Contributions to local enterprise agencies

Contributions to 'local enterprise agencies', 'training and enterprise councils' and 'local enterprise companies' (from 1 April 1990) and 'business link organisations' (from 30 November 1993) are deductible so long as the person making them does not receive any specific benefit by doing so.

Law: ITTOIA 2005, s. 82–85; FA 2000, s. 88

See *British Tax Reporter* ¶230-650.

2249   Interest and other costs of borrowing

Interest paid on loans to, or overdrafts of, a business is generally deductible as a 'business expense' (see 2150), under general principles, provided the interest is paid wholly and exclusively for the purposes of the business and at a reasonable rate of interest (see 2154, 2174); in the case of companies, the interest must be 'short' rather than 'annual' (see below) or, broadly, be payable on an advance from a bank. There are certain additional requirements for income tax purposes in relation to payments to non-residents (see also 1884, 2174). No deduction is allowed if the sole or main benefit to the payer from the transaction is a tax advantage.

It is not necessary for the loan to fall within one of the categories in respect of which an individual is permitted to deduct interest from total income, but interest which receives relief under those provisions may not also be deducted against business profits so as to give double relief.

No deduction is due if the loan effectively funds a proprietor's overdrawn current/capital account. In considering whether this is the case, accumulated realised profits must be distinguished from anticipated profits. A revaluation of business assets is therefore disregarded and the disallowance of the interest in point cannot be avoided by crediting the revaluation surplus to an overdrawn account.

Where a property development company charges disallowable interest to work in progress in accordance with 'correct' accounting practice, the interest need not be disallowed in the tax computation until it is effectively charged in the profits and loss account; conversely interest so charged is not allowable until it is similarly charged (see 652).

Incidental costs of business borrowings

Incidental costs of obtaining loan finance, such as fees, commissions, advertising and printing, are also specifically deductible in most cases. Such costs of taking out a life assurance policy as a pre-condition of receiving a loan would be included but the cost of the policy itself, i.e. the premiums, would, in HMRC's view be excluded. The deduction for incidental costs is given at the same time as any other deduction in computing profits for income tax purposes.

Yearly (annual) interest

The interest on loans capable of lasting longer than one year (whether or not they do in fact do so) is yearly interest and deciding whether interest is in fact 'yearly interest', regard is had to the loan agreement and the intention of the parties. A loan repayable on demand has been held to be an investment on which yearly interest was paid. Interest on an informal loan

Income Tax

replacing an overdraft by a parent company to its subsidiary has also been held to be yearly interest.

Law: ITTOIA 2005, s. 52, 58, 362(1)–(2); CTA 2009, s. 131; *Minsham Properties Ltd v Price (HMIT)* [1990] BTC 528; *Cairns v MacDiarmid (HMIT)* [1983] BTC 188; *Corinthian Securities Ltd v Cato* (1969) 46 TC 93

Website: www.hmrc.gov.uk/bulletins/index.htm

See *British Tax Reporter* ¶226-600.

2250   Theft: business deductions

A deduction as a 'business expense' (see 2150) is allowed if an irrecoverable loss by theft occurs in the course of the trader's business. Petty theft by an assistant from a shop till would be in the course of the business, but large scale misappropriation by a director would not.

Law: *Bamford (HMIT) v ATA Advertising Ltd* (1972) 48 TC 359

See *British Tax Reporter* ¶707-530.

2251   Expenditure on research and development

Revenue expenditure on research and development is specifically allowed as a deduction from profits. For the extended relief available for companies, see 4915.

The expenditure must be related to the trade carried on. Broadly, this means it must benefit the trade, of those employed in it. It must be undertaken by the trader or carried out on his behalf. Specifically excluded is expenditure on obtaining rights connected with research and development.

Subject to broadly the same conditions, especially as to the relevance of the research to the trade carried on, payments to scientific research associations and universities, colleges or similar institutions is also deductible.

Law: ITTOIA 2005, s. 87–88

See *British Tax Reporter* ¶230-500.

2252 Miscellaneous business expenses: deductibility

A number of common items, such as stationery, utilities, postage, etc. are allowable deductions if used wholly and exclusively for business purposes (where used partly for business, a fraction of the expenses may be allowed).

2260 Pre-trading expenditure

Expenditure incurred by a person for business purposes before the business commences is treated for income tax purposes as a trading loss incurred on the day trading starts (for relief, see 2290); the expenditure must not be incurred more than seven years before trading commences and must be such that it would have been allowable had trading commenced (see 2150). The time period in point was five years for those who started to trade before 1 April 1993.

HMRC's view is that pre-trading expenditure does not include costs incurred by persons other than the eventual trader.

Law: ITTOIA 2005, s. 57

Website: www.hmrc.gov.uk/bulletins/index.htm

See *British Tax Reporter* ¶203-150.

2290 Business losses: meaning for income tax

Business losses occur where allowable expenses exceed taxable receipts, and they may be relieved for income tax purposes in a variety of ways.

Under self-assessment, capital allowances are generally deducted as if they were a trade expense in arriving at the trading result (see 2324).

Relief applies to the commercial letting of furnished holiday properties as it applies to trading losses (see 1255). Note that the government intends to repeal the furnished holiday letting rules from 2010–11.

Where a person has made annual payments out of profits which have not been charged to income tax (see 1368) and those payments are wholly and exclusively for the purposes of a trade, profession or vocation, then the amount on which tax has been accounted for (see 1370) is treated as a loss sustained in the trade, etc. for 'carry-forward relief' (see 2292).

Allowable interest (see 1884) which exceeds available income, if laid out or expended 'wholly and exclusively' (see 2154) for the business purposes, is treated as a loss for the purposes of 'carry-forward relief' (see 2292) or 'terminal loss relief' (see 2304).

Income Tax

541

There is an extended right of offset against general income for opening years' losses (see 2302).

Law: ITA 2007, s. 88, 94

See *British Tax Reporter* ¶260-000.

2292 Business losses: income tax carry forward

Where a business 'loss' (see 2290) arises, relief may be obtained in some circumstances by carry forward against future income relating to the trade.

Where a person carrying on a business has suffered a loss therein which has not been wholly relieved under other provisions, he may make a claim (see 1843) that any of the unrelieved loss should be carried forward and set off against income from the same business in subsequent years: relief is given against the first subsequent tax year as far as possible and then against the next year, etc. indefinitely.

Under self-assessment the relief is computed by reference to the same periods of account as profits from that source. The claims procedure is simple – there is only one claim, effective as regards the year of loss and this must be made within five years of 31 January following the tax year to which it relates (see 2687), i.e. the year of loss.

Relief claimed under this route cannot also be claimed under any other provision.

Business transferred to a company

Where an individual transfers his business to a company for shares in that company and the shares are held by that individual throughout the tax year then he may claim (see 1843) that any unrelieved losses of his trade be carried forward and set against *any* income derived from the company (applicable equally to partnerships). Set-off must be primarily against earned income from the company, i.e. remuneration.

As with carry forward generally a deemed cessation on change in partners, etc. is effectively ignored.

Law: ITA 2007, s 83, 86

See *British Tax Reporter* ¶260-650.

2296 Business losses: income tax offset against general income

Where any person sustains a 'loss' (see 2290) in any trade, profession, employment or vocation carried on by him either solely or in partnership, he may make a claim (see 1843) for relief from income tax against income for certain periods. This 'sideways relief' is an offset against his total income (see 244). Relief for limited partners is restricted (see 767). If the income is insufficient to set off the loss then the outstanding loss may be carried forward (see 2292).

Any claim must be made by notice in writing given not later than 31 January which is 22 months after the end of the tax year in which the loss arose.

For late claims, see 2302.

A loss is not generally available for relief unless it is shown that, for the tax year in which the loss is claimed to have been sustained (i.e. at the end of that year or part), the trade was being carried on:

- on a commercial basis; and
- with a view to the realisation of profits in the trade (including a reasonable expectation thereof),

and, for this purpose, any cessation/recommencement deemed to have occurred before self-assessment on a change of partners is ignored.

Relief is also denied for a loss attributable to excess capital allowances on machinery, etc. let in the course of a part-time trade. This restriction does not apply where the trade consists of furnished holiday letting.

Farming and market gardening losses are often excluded if a loss was incurred in each of the prior five years (see 944).

Law: ITA 2007, 64–66; *Delian Enterprises (a partnership) v Ellis (HMIT)* (1999) Sp C 186; *Wannell v Rothwell (HMIT)* [1996] BTC 214; *Butt (HMIT) v Haxby* [1983] BTC 32

See *British Tax Reporter* ¶260-200.

2297 Offset against general income under self-assessment

Under self-assessment, relief may be given in respect of a person's business loss sustained for a tax year against income for the same year or income for the preceding year (apparently whether or not he carried on the business in that period); claims for current year losses take precedence over claims for losses carried back. A claim for carry-back is taken to relate to the later year (see 2684). See 2305 regarding a temporary extension to the carry back rules for 2008–09 and 2009–10.

The amount of any loss for a tax year is calculated on the same basis as is income (i.e. subject to opening and closing year rules, in respect of a period of account ending in that year), but a loss which would fall into two periods is not included in the second of those periods.

Income Tax

Example

Steve, a single man, makes up his accounts to 31 December each year. He has the following results:

			£
Accounts for year ending	31/12/06	Profit	500
	31/12/07	Loss	5,000
	31/12/08	Profit	5,000

His other income consists of dividends as follows:

2006–07	Dividends	4,995 (net of 10% tax)
2007–08	Dividends	3,600 (net of 10% tax)
2008–09	Dividends	1,800 (net of 10% tax)

Loss for year	£
2005–06	3,750

Loss for year 2007–08 can be relieved under:

either ITA 2007, s. 64(2)(a) against net statutory income of the same year;

or ITA 2007, s. 64(2)(b) against net statutory income of the preceding year, to the extent that he does not relieve the income by a claim for current year offset in 2007–08;

or ITA 2007, s. 83 carried forward against trading profits of *same* trade:

Assuming he makes no other claims, the alternative ways of relieving the 2007–08 loss are:

	ITA 2007		
	s. 64(2)(b)	s. 64(2)(a)	s. 83
	2006–07	2007–08	2008–09
	£	£	£
Trading profit	500	–	5,000
Less: ITA 2007, s. 83	–	–	(3,750)
Net trading income	–	–	1,250
Dividends	5,550	4,000	2,000
Net statutory income	6,050	4,000	3,250
Less: ITA 2007, s. 64(2)(b)	(3,750)	–	–
ITA 2007, s. 64(2)(a)	–	(3,750)	–
	2,300	250	3,250
Personal allowance restricted to	(2,300)	(250)	(3,250)
Taxable income	Nil	Nil	Nil
Wasted personal reliefs	2,735	4,975	2,785

In each case, part of the personal reliefs is lost. Here relief by way of carry forward seems best, in that the least amount of allowance is wasted.

Law: ITA 2007, s. 64

See *British Tax Reporter* ¶260-200.

2299 Business losses: income tax offset against chargeable gains

A 'business loss' (see 2290) may be offset against chargeable gains, whether arising on business or private assets, if the loss arises in a year after 1990–91.

The taxpayer may claim for the loss which exceeds general income in the same year against which a claim for offset could be made (see 2296ff.) to be offset against chargeable gains of the same year; if there is also insufficient general income in the following year to absorb the loss, the taxpayer may claim to set the excess loss against chargeable gains of that year. Once a claim for offset has been 'finally determined', the amount claimed is treated as an allowable loss and cannot be increased to take into account subsequent changes in circumstance: HMRC have indicated that the appropriate loss relief claim becomes final:

- 30 days after the inspector gives his decision on it; or
- when, after an appeal, agreement is reached between the taxpayer and HMRC; or
- when the tribunal determines an appeal; or
- when the courts decide an appeal,

and the point at which the inspector gives his decision would depend on the particular circumstances – for example, he could write agreeing the claim, or decide constructively by repaying tax, but any clear, unambiguous response of a positive nature would be regarded as constituting a determination. Claims are generally accepted even if not made (as strictly required) at the same time as claims for offset of trading losses against income.

The relief claimed may not exceed the amount on which the claimant would be chargeable to CGT, ignoring the annual exemption. Relief for capital losses in the same year is given in priority but relief for capital losses brought forward is not since the trading loss is treated as an allowable loss accruing in the year.

Example

Roger who has traded for many years as a builder, incurs a loss in the year ended 5 April 2009 of £16,200 (as adjusted). In the previous year, ended 5 April 2008, he has a trading profit of £10,000. In the year ended 5 April 2009 he has other income of £2,500 and net chargeable gains (on share disposals) of £8,600.

Roger is able to make a claim to set off £12,500 of the loss of the period ended 5 April 2009 against his general income. He can also claim to set off the remainder of the loss (£3,700) against the chargeable gains on the share disposal, though this may result in part of the benefit of the annual exemption being lost.

HMRC have provided some rules of thumb in determining the steps to go through in applying the relief:

(1) determine the 'relevant amount'. This is essentially the amount of unutilised trading loss available for relief under the present provision;

Income Tax

(2) then determine the 'maximum amount'. This is the amount on which the claimant would otherwise be chargeable to CGT for the year, ignoring the annual exempt amount;

(3) the 'maximum amount' is unaffected by a later reduction in the amount chargeable to CGT: for example, resulting from a roll-over relief claim.

Law: ITA 2007, s. 71

Website: www.hmrc.gov.uk/bulletins/index.htm

See *British Tax Reporter* ¶260-300.

2302 Business losses: income tax carry-back of losses in opening years

Where an individual carrying on a business sustains a 'loss' (see 2290) in:

- the tax year in which it is first carried on by him; or
- any of the next three tax years,

he may, by notice in writing given within one year of 31 January following the year of loss, make a claim for relief. A Revenue Interpretation sets out the circumstances in which late claims for the present relief (and for offset against general income, see 2296ff.) may be accepted. These are where the taxpayer or agent:

- had been misled by some relevant and uncorrected error on HMRC's part;
- had made an informal claim within the time-limit which fell short of a clear and unambiguous statement of what was being claimed but which he or she reasonably believed was an acceptable claim, and the need to formalise the claim was not, within the time-limit, pointed out by HMRC; or
- had effectively been prevented from making an in-date claim for reasons beyond his or her control.

Relief is given by carrying back that loss and setting it off against total income, being income for the three tax years last preceding that in which the loss is sustained, taking income for an earlier year before income for a later year. Under self-assessment a claim for carry-back is treated as if it related to the later year (see 2684).

If relief has already been given for the loss it cannot be claimed again.

Restrictions on relief are twofold:

- the trade must have been carried on throughout the period on a commercial basis and in such a way that profits in the trade could reasonably be expected to be realised in that period or within a reasonable time thereafter;
- relief is not given if at the time when the trade is first carried on by the trader he or she is married to and living with another individual who has previously carried on the trade

and the loss is sustained in a tax year later than the third tax year after that in which the trade was first carried on by the other individual.

Example

Elaine was employed for many years; her last three years' taxable earnings were:

- 2003–04: £25,000
- 2004–05: £28,000
- 2005–06: £29,000

She left employment on 31 March 2006 and commenced as a sole trader on 1 July 2006, making up her first accounts to 30 June 2007 (and to 30 June thereafter). Her tax adjusted, trading loss for the 12 months to 30 June 2007 (including capital allowances) was £36,000. She has no other income sources apart from those indicated. Her trading activities are unlikely to show significant profits for several years. The claims available to her under s. 72 are as shown below.

(1) Determine the losses available

		£
2006–07	(1 July 2006 – 5 April 2007) $^9/_{12}$ × £36,000 =	(27,000)
2007–08	(1 July 2006 – 30 June 2007) £36,000 – £27,000 =	(9,000)

(2) The earliest year for carry-back is:
(a) 2006–07 carry-back to 2003–04
(b) 2007–08 carry-back to 2004–05

(3) *2003–04*

	£
Income (Employment)	25,000
less	
Loss of 2006–07	(25,000)
	NIL

2004–05

	£	
Income (Employment)	28,020	
less		
Loss of 2006–07	(2,000)	(27,000 – 25,000)
	26,000	
Loss of 2007–08	9,000	
	17,000	

(4) *Loss of memorandum*

(a) loss of 2006–07	£27,000
used 2003–04	(25,000)
used 2004–05	(2,000)
(b) loss of 2007–08	£9,000
used 2007–08	(9,000)

Note

Once a loss has been carried back three years under a s. 72 claim any unused portion must be carried forward and set against income of the next year (as in the example, where

£2,000 of loss unused in 2003–04 is carried forward to 2004–05) even if it results in other allowances (e.g. personal allowance) being wasted.

Alternative claims are available to Elaine should she wish to make them. For example, she could set the loss of 2006–07 (£27,000) against the income of 2005–06 (final year of employment; £29,000) using s. 64. Such a claim would have been advantageous if she had sufficient income in 2005–06 to make her liable at the higher rate. A claim under s. 72, to carry back the loss of 2007–08 (the second year of trade) would still have been possible if such a s. 64 claim had been made.

The relief is also available to partnerships. Any deemed cessation/recommencement on a change in partners which is not a total change is ignored; under self-assessment this becomes irrelevant since the deeming rule is repealed in such cases.

Law: ITA 2007, s. 72

Website: www.hmrc.gov.uk/bulletins/index.htm

See *British Tax Reporter* ¶261-000.

2304 Business losses: income tax carry-back of terminal losses

Where a loss is made in the final year of trading, i.e. the 12 months before the date of discontinuance, unless relief has already been given for that loss it may be carried back and set against the profits of the same trade. Relief covers the year of cessation and the three previous years. Capital allowances are generally treated as trading deductions (see 2324) and are therefore automatically taken into account; before that, unrelieved capital allowances of the final 12 months may also be included in the claim. Relief is given as far as possible from the assessment for a later rather than an earlier year.

If the profits are insufficient for setting off the loss then any interest or dividends arising in that year which would be trading receipts but for the fact that they have already been taxed will be treated as profits and relief will be given accordingly by repayment or otherwise.

Example

Gordon has traded for many years, normally preparing accounts to 30 September each year; he ceases trade on 30 April 2008 producing seven-month accounts to that date. Tax adjusted results (including capital allowance claims) for his final periods of trading are a profit of £12,000 for the 12 months ending 30 September 2007 and a loss of £3,500 for the seven months to cessation on 30 April 2008. He has transitional overlap profit relief of £1,000 available. His terminal loss is for the year 2008–09 and will be:

(1) *Loss arising in final year* (2008–09)   £
    $1/_7 \times$ (£3,500)   (500)
    Overlap relief available   (1,000)
                                                                                               (1,500)

(2) *Loss of preceding year* (beginning 12 months prior to cessation.)
    Period 1/5/2007–5/4/2008   £
    (a) 1/5/2007–30/9/2007 $5/_{12} \times$ £12,000 =   5,000
    (b) 1/10/2007–5/4/2008 $6/_7 \times$ (£3,500) =   (3,000)

                                  Profit   2,000

    An overall profit is treated as a 'nil' loss   0
                                                                                               (£1,500)

The terminal loss of 2008–09 is £1,500. It can be used against trading profits of 2008–09 (in this case there are none); then carried back to 2007–08 where the profit of £12,000 can be relieved. If the loss were greater than the 2007–08 profit further carry backs to 2006–07 and 2005–06 would be possible.

The loss of £3,000 which was aggregated computationally with profits for the period 1 May 2007 to 30 September 2007 is still available for relief against other income under ITA 2007, s. 64, since it has not been utilised in the terminal loss claim.

Law: ITA 2007, s. 89

See *British Tax Reporter* ¶261-100.

2305 Temporary extension of trading loss carry-back

During 2008–09 and 2009–10 the period for which companies and unincorporated businesses making trading losses (including losses from professions or vocations) could be carried back against earlier profits was temporarily extended from one year to three years, with losses being carried back against later years first. The extended loss carry back period applied from 22 April 2009, to company trading losses in accounting periods ending between 24 November 2008 and 23 November 2010, and to trading losses incurred by unincorporated businesses in the tax years 2008–09 and 2009–10.

After losses have been carried back to the previous year, a maximum of £50,000 will be available for carry back to the earlier two years. A separate £50,000 limit applies to each 12 month period or tax year within the duration of the extension. For companies, this means a cap of £50,000 on the extended carry back of losses in accounting periods ending in the 12 months to 23 November 2009, and a separate £50,000 cap on the extended carry back of losses in accounting periods ending in the 12 months to 23 November 2010. For unincorporated businesses, a separate £50,000 cap applies to the extended carry back of losses incurred in each of the tax years 2008–09 and 2009–10.

Law: FA 2009, s. 23 and Sch. 6

Income Tax

2310 Relief for post-cessation expenditure

A specific relief is available to individuals for certain types of post-cessation expenditure. These include expenses connected with remedying or paying compensation for defective work or supplies, collecting debts, and debts which go bad. Relief is given by way of a reduction of income (and, where appropriate, chargeable gains) for the tax year in which the expense is paid. Such expenditure must be incurred within seven years of the cessation of trade, and a claim for the relief must be made within 12 months from 31 January following the end of the tax year in which the payment is made (in line with other claims under self-assessment). If a claim is made, certain connected receipts (mainly to do with insurance receipts) are specified as being taxable under the existing post-cessation receipts legislation (see 662).

HMRC have stated their views of a number of issues in their *Tax Bulletin*. In particular, professional indemnity insurance premiums for work undertaken in the course of the business are now almost always allowable (this supersedes HMRC's earlier view). The new relief exists alongside the rules already on the statute book for post-cessation receipts and expenses. Those rules provide that any loss or expense which would have qualified as a trading deduction had the business not ceased is relieved against post-cessation receipts; however, where the deductions exceed the post-cessation receipts for a tax year, the excess can only be carried forward and relieved against any post-cessation receipts arising in later years (see 662). Where an expense qualifies for sideways relief under the new rules as well as for carry-forward under the provision described above, the new rules thus take priority.

Law: ITTOIA 2005, s. 250, 349–352

Website: www.hmrc.gov.uk/bulletins/index.htm

See *British Tax Reporter* ¶260-650.

CAPITAL ALLOWANCES

2324 Nature of capital allowances

The cost and depreciation of a capital asset purchased by a trader are not allowed as deductions in computing his profits. However, capital allowances, which are a form of standardised depreciation, may be available.

The law relating to capital allowances is now largely found in the *Capital Allowances Act* 2001 which basically is the tax law rewrite version of *Capital Allowances Act* 1990.

The general rule is that capital allowances are included in the calculation of income for income tax purposes, or the calculation of profits for corporation tax purposes.

Major changes to capital allowance regime

Important changes to capital allowances were introduced in 2007, 2008 and 2009. The following notes provide an overview of the changes.

First-year allowances (plant and machinery)

The temporary 50 per cent rate of first-year allowances for small enterprises was extended for a further but final period of 12 months, to 31 March 2008 (corporation tax) or 5 April 2008 (income tax).

Abolition of most first-year allowances

The first-year allowances that were for many years given at 40 per cent (medium-sized enterprises) or 50 per cent (for some periods, for small enterprises, as above) were abolished for expenditure incurred after 31 March 2008 (corporation tax) or 5 April 2008 (income tax).

First-year allowances for all sizes of business were re-introduced on a temporary basis for expenditure incurred in the year 31 March 2010 (corporation tax) or 5 April 2010 (income tax). The allowances are given at 40 per cent. Such allowances are subject to the usual general exclusions and do not apply to 'special rate expenditure'.

Low emission cars

Under legislation already in place before FA 2008, the system of first-year allowances for certain low emission cars was due to come to an end for expenditure incurred after 31 March 2008 (corporation tax) or 5 April 2008 (income tax). The rules relating to expenditure on gas refuelling stations have likewise been extended, but again subject to change.

Green technology

First-year allowances for expenditure on other 'green' technology continue at 100 per cent but with the new option for companies to surrender losses arising from such expenditure in return for a cash payment.

Annual investment allowance (plant and machinery)

The concept of the 'annual investment allowance' (AIA) (see 2366) applies to expenditure incurred from 1 April 2008 (corporation tax) or 6 April 2008 (income tax). The AIA gives full tax relief for the first £100,000 of annual expenditure incurred by a business on plant and machinery in its chargeable period (increased from £50,000 for expenditure incurred from April 2010).

The introduction of the AIA coincides with the withdrawal of most first-year allowances and also with the increase in corporation tax rates for the smallest businesses.

The AIA offers full and immediate tax relief, for all sizes of business, for the first £100,000 of expenditure on plant and machinery in the year. The maximum annual allowance is proportionately increased or reduced if the chargeable period is greater or shorter than one year. In calculating the length of the chargeable period for these purposes, any time before 1 or 6 April 2008 is ignored. Thus a company with accounts drawn up for the year to 31 December 2008 is entitled to an AIA of just £37,500.

When the limit was increased from £50,000 to £100,000 from April 2010, the actual chargeable period is split into two notional periods, the second notional period beginning on 1 or 6 April 2010 (for corporation tax or income tax respectively).

Cars and expenditure on 'green' technology continue to be treated separately, but the AIA is available from April 2008 for expenditure on all other plant and machinery, including long-life assets and the new category of 'integral features'. Expenditure in excess of the annual £50,000 allowance may attract writing-down allowances in the same accounting period.

Reduction in rate of writing-down allowances for plant and machinery

The rate of writing-down allowances (WDAs) for plant and machinery in the general pool is reduced from 25 to 20 per cent for chargeable periods beginning from 1 or 6 April 2008 (for corporation tax and income tax respectively). A hybrid rate applies for chargeable periods straddling the date of change. Thus, for example, a company with a 31 December year end will have a hybrid rate of 21.25 per cent for the year to 31 December 2008, calculated as three months at 25 per cent and nine months at 20 per cent. Periods that are not of exactly 12 months will apply the same principle, based on the length of the period before and after the April 2008 change.

The same rates, and transitional arrangements, will apply to single asset pools, such as those for short-life assets. The company with the 31 December year end will therefore apply the same hybrid rate of 21.25 per cent to its short-life asset pool.

The reduction in the rate of WDAs is for plant and machinery allowances only. Many of the more minor allowances (e.g. flat conversion allowances (see 2394) and mineral extraction allowances (see 2396)) continue to have a 25 per cent WDA (though FCAs, for example, are normally given by way of a full initial allowance). See below for changes to industrial and agricultural buildings allowances.

Long-life assets

The rate of WDAs on long-life asset (LLA) expenditure increases from 6 to 10 per cent for chargeable periods beginning from 1 or 6 April 2008 (for corporation tax and income tax respectively). The effect is that LLA expenditure attracts relief at half the rate of most other assets, subject to the question of the annual investment allowance.

Integral features (plant and machinery)

With effect from April 2008, expenditure on 'integral features' has been treated separately from other capital expenditure for the purposes of claiming plant and machinery allowances. Expenditure on these integral features is excluded from the main capital allowances pool and writing-down allowances are given at a rate of 10 per cent (rather than the standard 20 per cent rate) on the reducing balance of the pool.

Payable tax credits (plant and machinery)

Loss-making companies that incur expenditure on certain 'green' technology from 1 April 2008 are able to claim a cash payment if they are otherwise unable to use their losses against their own profits or those of a group member (CAA 2001, s. 262A). The rules are directly linked to the first-year allowances that are given for expenditure on 'energy-saving' plant and machinery or 'environmentally beneficial' plant and machinery. In this way, companies can gain an immediate cash repayment rather than carrying losses forward indefinitely in the hope of obtaining relief when profits start to be realised in the future. See 2372 for commentary on this.

Cars

Capital allowances for cars were reformed for expenditure incurred from 1 or 6 April 2009 (for corporation tax and income tax respectively). The £3,000 annual cap on allowances for cars costing more than £12,000 was removed and a new system was introduced whereby allowances are linked to the CO_2 emissions of the vehicle.

Industrial and agricultural buildings allowances

From April 2008, WDAs on industrial (2386) and agricultural buildings (2392) are gradually being phased out, with final withdrawal of both regimes by April 2011. To prepare the way for final abolition, most balancing adjustments, and the recalculation of WDAs on sale, were effectively withdrawn from 21 March 2007.

Law: FA 2008, Part 3; FA 2007, s. 36 and 37; CAA 2001, s. 2; FA 1994, Sch. 20, para. 9

Source: HMRC Brief 66/08

See *British Tax Reporter* ¶235-000.

2330 Categories of expenditure/asset

The legislation dealing with capital allowances is a core part of the UK's tax system, with substantial amounts of money at stake. Capital allowances are of relevance to the great majority of businesses operating in the UK, from the largest conglomerate to the smallest business consisting of an individual with a van, a computer or even just a table.

The most familiar allowances are those available for capital expenditure on plant and machinery. For many businesses, however, expenditure on plant and machinery will determine only part of their overall capital allowance claims. Depending on the nature of the business, claims may be made under different rules in respect of any of the following:

- plant and machinery;
- industrial buildings or structure;
- renovation of business premises;
- agricultural buildings;
- flat conversions;
- mineral extraction;

- research and development;
- know-how;
- patents;
- dredging; and
- assured tenancies.

The distinction between assets qualifying for these various different types of allowance is not always clear-cut. There may, for example, be an overlap between plant and machinery and industrial buildings. Occasionally it is up to the taxpayer to decide whether to make a claim as plant and machinery on the one hand or as an industrial building or structure on the other.

For businesses carried on in a factory or similar premises, the key distinction between the effect of a claim for industrial buildings allowances (IBAs) and one for plant and machinery is likely to be the timing of the tax relief available. The timing difference can be significant and the cash flow implications crucial.

However, for businesses carried on in offices, for example, the distinction may be even more critical. If an asset can be shown to constitute plant or machinery then a reasonably generous rate of tax allowances may be due. If, on the other hand, the asset is deemed to be part of the building then no tax relief is due at all (though some relief may be available for fixtures in a building). There is no doubt that this can lead to borderline cases where the result is not a just one-off. However, the principles that govern the making of this distinction have been established over decades of legislation and case law. Therefore, the best that somebody carrying on a trade can do is to claim the maximum possible allowances that are due under the system.

Law: CAA 2001

See *British Tax Reporter* ¶235-000.

2332 Tax years and basis periods for income tax

Capital allowances are related to expenditure in the 'period of account', which is generally synonymous with its meaning in general accounting parlance (i.e. usually the period for which accounts are made up), though there are complications in the opening and closing years or where there is a change in accounting date. Where two basis periods overlap, the period common to both is deemed to fall in the first period only; where there is a 'gap period', the interval is treated as part of the first period of account. Where the accounts are made up to a date more than 12 months after the previous accounts date, the first 12 months is taken as one period with the remainder (up to a further 12 months) forming another period and so on.

Law: CAA 2001, s. 6

See *British Tax Reporter* ¶235-050.

2334 Timing and extent of expenditure included

Capital allowances are generally available by reference to certain expenditure incurred. Capital expenditure is normally treated as incurred for capital allowance purposes on the date when the obligation to pay it becomes unconditional, whether or not a later date for payment is specified. Where, however, any payment is due more than four months after the date when the obligation becomes unconditional, such payment is not taken to be incurred until it has to be paid. An anti-avoidance measure provides that where a date is inserted solely or mainly to accelerate entitlement to a capital allowance, the date is to be disregarded and the allowance will be given instead when payment is due.

Whether VAT is included in the extent of capital expenditure depends on the status of the taxpayer: a person who is not a taxable person for VAT will include all his VAT; a taxable person who makes only taxable supplies will include no VAT and a partly exempt person will be able to allocate VAT as appropriate. The capital allowances system also takes account of retrospective adjustments made under the VAT Capital Goods Scheme, to the amount of VAT payable on certain assets.

Law: ITTOIA 2005, s. 142; CAA 2001, s. 234–246

Source: SP B1, *Machinery or plant: changes from the 'renewals' to the capital allowances basis*

See *British Tax Reporter* ¶235-050.

2336 Subsidies and grants

Capital allowances are generally available by reference to certain expenditure incurred. Expenditure is not generally regarded as having been incurred by any person in so far as it has been or is to be met directly or indirectly by the Crown or by any government or public or local authority, whether in the UK or elsewhere, or by any person other than the first-mentioned person. This means that capital allowances may be claimed only on the cost of the asset less any grants or subsidies.

Where the expenditure met out of a grant, which is later repaid, and the grant would otherwise fall to be disregarded in giving allowances on the asset (see above), HMRC will treat the repayment as expenditure on which capital allowances may be given, provided the repayment falls to be taxed on the recipient through a balancing adjustment or as a trading receipt.

Law: CAA 2001, s. 532–536

Source: ESC B49, *Section 153 Capital Allowances Act 1990: grants repaid*

See *British Tax Reporter* ¶235-300.

2338 Contributions to expenditure

A person contributing to expenditure incurred by another person may be entitled to allowances if he does so for the purposes of a trade carried on or to be carried on by him. Each item of plant or machinery on which expenditure is incurred is treated separately, i.e. is not pooled (see 2384) with other assets.

Law: CAA 2001, s. 537–543

See *British Tax Reporter* ¶235-350.

2340 Capital allowances on a succession or sale to an affiliate

Where a person ceases to carry on activities relating to a trade, another person may begin to carry on those activities (typically transferring all the assets on which he has claimed capital allowances: see 2324). Alternatively, a person may dispose of all or any of these assets to an affiliate to enable that person to undertake or further his business activities.

If partners elect that, on an admission or retirement, the trade should be considered to continue, the successor partnership generally steps into the shoes of the predecessor as regards capital allowances. Otherwise, if there is a sale of assets on a succession or to an affiliate, the normal balancing adjustments will apply subject to the amendments set out below.

- For plant and machinery, if the parties are connected, there are provisions to ensure that the buyer obtains writing-down allowances only on the amount the seller brings into account, though they may elect for the transfer to be at tax written-down value − the normal rules (see 2364) would not disturb an agreed allocation of proceeds, unless there is some suggestion of avoidance; the required affiliation provides an extended definition of connected persons.
- For most other assets, if the parties are connected (or under common control) or the transaction is tax-structured, there will be taken to be a market value sale subject, in most cases, to an election to avoid any balancing charge by treating the sale as being at tax written-down value (WDV) if that is less than market value. From 16 March 1993, this was specifically extended to hotels and enterprise zone buildings, etc. and this has been further extended to include transfers before that date; the nil WDV applicable to capital expenditure on scientific research has also been brought into the rules. Special rules apply to patents and know-how (see 2402).

Law: CAA 2001, s. 265–268 and 537–560

See *British Tax Reporter* ¶235-450.

2360 Meaning of 'plant and machinery'

There is no statutory definition of 'plant and machinery' but it 'includes whatever apparatus is used by a businessman for carrying on his business – not his stock-in-trade ... but all goods and chattels, fixed or moveable ... which he keeps for permanent employment in his business'. The courts have held all of the following assets to be plant or machinery:

* books purchased by a practising barrister;
* a dry dock;
* a swimming pool at a caravan park;
* knives and lasts used by a shoe manufacturer together with machinery;
* moveable office partitioning;
* central heating plant, elevators, ventilation and air conditioning;
* alarms and sprinkler systems;
* concrete grain silos;
* apparatus providing hot water and electric lights;
* warehouse storage platforms;
* decorative window screens.

Notwithstanding the case law, HMRC have sought to prevent certain buildings and structures qualifying as plant, though buildings and structures which were already taken to have qualified on 30 November 1993 generally continue to do so. There are two statutory Tables of items regarded as 'buildings' and as 'structures and assets', which differentiate between those allowable and those disallowable (typically, the Tables seek to reflect decided cases on the subject). For example, the tables confirm that caravans provided mainly for holiday lettings may qualify as plant. By concession, the meaning of the word 'caravan' in this context was widened from its everyday meaning to that set out at 1200.

Boilers and water-filled radiators installed in a building as part of a space or water heating system are, by statute, fixtures.

The courts have held the following assets *not* to be machinery or plant:

* a canopy in a self-service petrol station;
* an inflatable cover for a tennis court;
* a prefabricated gymnasium and laboratory in a school;
* ordinary lighting in a department store;
* a vessel used as a floating restaurant;
* permanent quarantine kennels.

To determine whether a particular article is 'plant' of a trade, the nature of the trade being carried on must be considered. For example, murals in the office of the managing director of a trading company would not be 'plant' of the trading company, but murals on hotel walls have been held to be 'plant' of the hotel owners. It is a question of fact in each case. One test frequently used is whether the item in question performs some function in carrying on the trade or whether it merely forms part of the setting in which the trade is carried on.

Income Tax

An example of the degree of refinement required concerns glasshouses. HMRC stress the dependence on the facts in determining whether machinery, etc. allowances are available, their view being that the majority (which do not include sophisticated, computer-controlled equipment) will only qualify for agricultural buildings allowances (see 2392) though they concede that some may constitute plant.

The 'premises test' (above) and the entirety of other kinds of specialist construction have also been the subject of judicial consideration. In one case sophisticated car washing apparatus was held not to constitute plant. In another case a company was not entitled to machinery, etc. allowances for all of the capital expenditure it incurred on the provision of a large underground electrical sub-station. Only part of the expenditure related to plant, the remainder to premises.

Law: CAA 2001, s. 21–23, 71–73; *Family Golf Centres Ltd v Thorne (HMIT)* (1998) Sp C 150; *Bradley (HMIT) v London Electricity plc (No. 2)* [1996] BTC 451; *Attwood (HMIT) v Anduff Car Wash Ltd* [1996] BTC 44; *Gray (HMIT) v Seymours Garden Centre (Horticulture)* [1995] BTC 320; *Wimpy International Ltd v Warland (HMIT)* [1989] BTC 58; *IR Commrs v Scottish and Newcastle Breweries Ltd* [1982] BTC 187; *Yarmouth v France* (1887) 19 QBD 647

Source: ESC B16, *Fire safety: capital expenditure incurred on certain trade premises (A) in Northern Ireland, and (B) by lessons*; ESC B50

Website: www.hmrc.gov.uk/bulletins/index.htm

See *British Tax Reporter* ¶236-000.

2362 Fixtures not acquired by the taxpayer

To be eligible for plant and machinery allowances (see 2364) an asset must, prima facie, belong to the taxpayer in consequence of his incurring the expenditure in question. Expenditure by tenants on items which become fixtures would not, without further provision, qualify for allowances since fixtures belong by law to the owner of the freehold. There are also special provisions for contributions towards the cost of items belonging to other people.

To claim allowances, plant and machinery need generally to have belonged to a taxpayer (see 2364), but capital allowances are available to tenants who incur expenditure on machinery, etc. which becomes a landlord's fixture after installation: e.g. central heating or ventilating equipment forming part of the fabric of the building.

Taxpayers normally claim capital allowances in their tax returns. The claimant may now subsequently amend an incorrect claim to allowances on fixtures. (This would apply, for instance, where a claim by the purchaser of a building was reduced by an election to determine the apportionment of the cost of the building, or by a decision by the previous owner to claim allowances.) He must amend the return within three months of becoming aware that the claim was incorrect. Failure to do this attracts a penalty (see 2658).

A balancing charge or allowance will arise when the tenant leaves the premises (or similar) or ceases to trade.

An equipment lessor can obtain allowances by virtue of a joint election with a lessee if the equipment would have belonged to the latter had he incurred the expenditure.

For chargeable periods ending after 23 July 1996 in respect of expenditure incurred after that date:

- allowances cannot be given to equipment lessors on fixtures in dwelling-houses, and
- the lessee must be within the charge to tax on the profits of the trade or leasing activity for which the fixture is provided (and not, e.g. a local authority or charity), and must be entitled to allowances on the fixture. This rule was relaxed, subject to certain conditions, in the case of certain leases entered into after 18 March 1997, where the fact that the item is fixed is incidental to its being used as a chattel.

It was originally thought that where the equipment was leased before the lessee started to trade, allowances would be given from the start of that trade. However, in HMRC's view, an election could not be made before the lessee's trade had started. With effect for chargeable periods ending on or after 19 March 1997, the position was restored to what it was thought to have been before 1994.

Any assignment of the lessor's rights or the discharge of the obligations under the lease is treated as a sale by the lessor.

Where a trader acquires a lease by assignment and part of the price is referable to a fixture, he may become entitled to allowances in respect of it; however, two persons cannot become entitled to allowances in respect of the same fixture.

A trader who is granted a sublease may be entitled to allowances in respect of the price relating to a fixture if:

- neither the grantor nor any other person was entitled to allowances in respect of the fixture; or
- he jointly elects with the grantor to transfer the right to the allowances.

Other changes effective from 24 July 1996 include:

- the restriction of allowances in total to the original cost of the fixture (or where allowances were claimed on the fixture for periods before 24 July 1996, the cost price to the most recent claimant);
- the making of a joint election by the vendor and purchaser to determine how much of the sale price of a building is apportioned to fixtures; and
- the treatment of a fixture sold for less than its tax written-down value in order to accelerate allowances as sold at the tax written-down value.

Law: CAA 2001, s. 172–204; FA 2000, s. 79

Website: www.hmrc.gov.uk/bulletins/index.htm

See *British Tax Reporter* ¶236-400.

2364 Allowances for plant and machinery generally

Allowances are available in respect of expenditure on plant and machinery (see 2360) if a person who is carrying on a qualifying activity incurs qualifying expenditure. If a person carries on more than one qualifying activity then allowances must be calculated separately for each.

Plant and machinery allowances are given through a system of pooling, whereby most expenditure is merged within a single, ongoing calculation, the value of the pool increasing as new expenditure is incurred but reducing as allowances are given or sale proceeds are received.

Certain types of asset are not pooled as such (though the legislation uses the illogical term 'single asset pool'. A third category of assets can be pooled with one another but have to be kept separate from the main pool of expenditure.

For most businesses, capital allowances are from April 2008 given mainly by way of an annual investment allowance, giving full relief for expenditure in the year of up to £100,000 from April 2010 (£50,000 prior to April 2010).

First-year allowances are given in some cases, depending on the nature of the expenditure. Where available, such allowances are now always given at 100 per cent (i.e. full tax relief in the year in which the expenditure is incurred), though there is generally an option to accept a lower rate of allowance. Before April 2008, first-year allowances were also given for a much wider range of expenditure, but at a lower figure (typically 40 per cent) and only for small or medium-sized businesses. Where first-year allowances are available, no writing-down allowances are given for the same period. By contrast, the same expenditure may attract both an annual investment allowance and a writing-down allowance in the same period.

Balancing allowances or balancing charges may arise where an asset is sold or otherwise disposed of. Balancing charges can never exceed the total allowances that have been given for the asset in question.

See *British Tax Reporter* ¶236-000.

2366   Annual Investment Allowances

The concept of the 'annual investment allowance' (AIA) was announced in the Budget of March 2007 but first applies to expenditure incurred from 'the relevant date', defined as 1 April 2008 for corporation tax, and 6 April 2008 for income tax purposes.

In essence, the AIA gives full tax relief (similar in effect to a 100 per cent first-year allowance) for the first £100,000 (£50,000 prior to April 2010) of annual expenditure incurred by a business on plant and machinery. Expenditure must be incurred by a 'qualifying person', defined to mean an individual, a partnership consisting only of individuals, or a company. Expenditure is said to be 'AIA qualifying expenditure' if it is incurred by such a person and is not subject to any of the general exclusions (CAA 2001, s. 38B). The person claiming the allowance must own the plant or machinery at some time during the chargeable period for which the claim is made.

The declared purpose of the AIA is to 'target investment support on all businesses that are investing for growth and help alleviate the cash flow constraints which confront small and growing businesses'. The introduction of the AIA coincides with the withdrawal of most first-year allowances and also with changes in corporation tax rates.

The AIA offers full and immediate tax relief, for all sizes of business, for (broadly) the first £100,000 of expenditure on plant and machinery in the year. The AIA is made for the chargeable period in which the expenditure is incurred (but without the benefit of the pre-trading expenditure rules of CAA 2001, s. 12).

> ### Example
>
> A business spends £140,000 on general plant and machinery and £25,000 on integral features. It will wish to treat the whole of the latter as AIA qualifying expenditure so that the excess £115,000 (£140,000 plus £25,000, less £50,000) can attract allowances at the main WDA rate of 20 per cent rather than at the lower rate of 10 per cent.

Cars and expenditure on 'green' technology continue to be treated separately, but the AIA is available from April 2008 for expenditure on all other plant and machinery, including long-life assets and the new category of 'integral features'. Expenditure in excess of the annual £50,000 allowance may attract writing-down allowances in the same accounting period.

Where an asset is provided partly for purposes other than those of the qualifying activity carried on by the person, AIAs may be given to the extent that is just and reasonable in relation to the proportion in which the expenditure was incurred for the purposes of the qualifying activity. So if an asset costs £20,000, and is used one-quarter for private purposes, AIAs can be claimed on £15,000. It would seem to follow, from the way that the legislation is worded, that AIAs can be claimed on other expenditure of up to £35,000 (rather than £30,000).

Income Tax

The legislation specifies that a person may not claim an AIA and a first-year allowance in respect of the same expenditure. Now that all remaining first-year allowances are given at 100 per cent, the provision appears to be simply to remove any possibility of claiming double relief for the same expenditure.

Law: FA 2008, s. 74 and Sch. 24; CAA 2001, s. 38A, 51A, 52

See *British Tax Reporter* ¶236-400.

2368 First-year allowances

Important changes to the system of capital allowances were introduced from April 2008. These apply to expenditure incurred from 1 April (companies) or 6 April (those paying income tax). The introduction of the new annual investment allowance is discussed in detail at 2366.

Capital allowances were for many years typically given (by way of writing-down allowances (WDAs)) at the rate of one-quarter of the reducing value of an item of plant or machinery. The standard rate of WDA reduced from 25 to 20 per cent from April 2008, with a 10 per cent rate applying to certain expenditure.

For various reasons, Parliament has decided that it is appropriate in particular circumstances to allow tax relief at a faster rate. From April 2008, this is normally by way of the annual investment allowance discussed at 2366. Prior to that date, accelerated relief was available only by way of first-year allowances (FYAs). FYAs are not abolished completely from April 2008 but the most common FYAs, giving relief at 40 or 50 per cent for medium or small businesses, are withdrawn from that date. In reality, FYAs have been subject to frequent change in recent years.

For FYAs to be available, a person must incur 'first-year qualifying expenditure' and must own the asset in question at some time during the chargeable period in which the expenditure is incurred. Any first-year allowance is then made for that chargeable period.

Where an asset is provided partly for purposes other than those of the qualifying activity carried on by the person, FYAs may be given to the extent that is just and reasonable in relation to the proportion in which the expenditure was incurred for the purposes of the qualifying activity.

The legislation identifies several types of first-year qualifying expenditure. The following list takes account of the effect of *Finance Act* 2008, which formally removed from the legislation certain categories of expenditure:

Expenditure	Qualifying period	Rate	Authority (CAA 2001)	Comment
Incurred on energy-saving plant or machinery	From 1 April 2001	100%	s. 45A	Still available from April 2008. Payable tax credits available for companies (only) from that date.
Cars with low CO_2 emissions	From 17 April 2002	100%	s. 45D	Extended (with changes) from April 2008.
Incurred on P&M for gas refuelling station	From 17 April 2002	100%	s. 45E	Extended (and expanded) from April 2008.
Incurred on P&M for use in a ring fence trade	From 17 April 2002	24% or 100%	s. 45F	Special rules apply to this type of expenditure.
Incurred on environmentally beneficial P&M	From 1 April 2003	100%	s. 45H	Still available from April 2008. Payable tax credits available for companies (only) from that date.

Categories of expenditure removed by FA 2008

The most important categories of expenditure that ceased to apply from April 2008 were the standard 50 and 40 per cent FYAs given to small and medium-sized businesses.

Expenditure incurred for Northern Ireland purposes has not attracted special allowances since 12 May 2002 but was only formally removed from the capital allowances legislation by *Finance Act* 2008

Certain ICT expenditure incurred by 31 March 2004 attracted 100 per cent allowances. Again, these rules were only formally removed from the capital allowances legislation by *Finance Act* 2008.

Law: FA 2008, s. 75–79; CAA 2001, s. 52

See *British Tax Reporter* ¶237-000.

2370 Enhanced capital allowances

The term 'enhanced capital allowances' (ECAs) is often applied to expenditure under the following headings:

- energy-saving plant or machinery;
- low emission cars; and
- environmentally beneficial plant and machinery.

Income Tax

Although the capital allowances legislation does not use the term, there is some logic in it: all three categories relate to environmentally conscious expenditure and all offer businesses of whatever size the chance to gain full tax relief in the year in which the expenditure is incurred. Nevertheless, different rules apply and the best approach is to recognise the overlapping concepts but to apply the legislation on a case-by-case basis.

The mechanics of claiming ECAs are still fairly new and may represent unfamiliar territory for accountants and tax advisers. Under the energy-saving rules, for example, manufacturers need to register their products for inclusion on the Energy Technology List. The government website, www.eca.gov.uk, contains details of how to go about this. To be included, products must normally meet the scheme's published energy-efficiency criteria, though separate conditions are imposed for certain product types (including lighting).

Care is needed since, as the website states, 'it is the purchaser's responsibility to check with the manufacturer which of their products meet the criteria'. The end-user or his adviser therefore needs to go to the same website and, under 'product search', can choose (for example) to search for lamps. The site lists many thousands of items (and their manufacturers) that qualify under the energy-saving scheme. If the business wants to buy from a particular manufacturer, it can select that name, but often that will not be necessary.

Hiring and leasing of assets qualifying for enhanced allowances

The question of whether enhanced allowances are available for 'energy-saving' or 'environmentally beneficial' plant and machinery can be complex. As far as these two categories of asset are concerned, the position may be summarised as follows:

- generally speaking, expenditure on plant and machinery for leasing or letting on hire, does not qualify for FYAs;
- an amendment was made in 2003 so that the exclusion did not apply to the schemes for FYAs for environmentally beneficial technologies;
- energy-saving or environmentally beneficial technologies for leasing (but this amendment did not affect low emission cars qualifying under CAA 2001, s. 45D);
- but the denial of FYAs does not apply to 'background' plant and machinery, within the meaning of CAA 2001, s. 70R.

2372 Payable enhanced capital allowances

Loss-making companies that incur expenditure on certain 'green' technology from 1 April 2008 are able to claim a cash payment if they are otherwise unable to use their losses against their own profits or those of a group member (CAA 2001, s. 262A). The rules are directly linked to the FYAs that are given for expenditure on 'energy-saving' plant and machinery (see 2376) or 'environmentally beneficial' plant and machinery (see 2378). In this way, companies will gain an immediate cash repayment rather than carrying losses forward indefinitely in the hope of obtaining relief when profits start to be realised in the future.

The main features of the relief are as follows:

- relief will be given for expenditure incurred on technology currently qualifying for 100 per cent FYAs under either CAA 2001, s. 45A or s. 45H (respectively covering 'energy-saving' plant and 'environmentally beneficial' plant);
- the scheme will be available to companies (small, medium or large) but not to excluded companies, or to any sole traders, partnerships or other entities;
- companies will be able to surrender losses, to the extent that they are attributable to qualifying expenditure, so as to receive a percentage of the surrendered loss as a tax-free cash payment from HMRC.

A payment in respect of a first-year tax credit is not treated as income of the company for any tax purpose.

The draft legislation uses the term 'first-year tax credits' to describe the new form of tax relief. The guidance issued by HMRC in December 2007, on the other hand, opts for 'payable enhanced capital allowances'.

Excluded companies

A company is excluded from these rules if, at any time during the chargeable period in question, it is able to make a claim under any of the following provisions of ICTA 1988:

- rent, etc. of co-operative housing associations disregarded for tax purposes (s. 488);
- rent, etc. of self-build societies disregarded for tax purposes (s. 489);
- exemption from tax for charitable companies (s. 505); or
- exemption from tax for scientific research organisations (s. 508).

Anti-avoidance

A restriction is applied to the extent that a transaction is 'attributable to arrangements entered into wholly or mainly for a disqualifying purpose'. Arrangements are said to be entered into for a disqualifying purpose if their main object, or one of their main objects, is to enable a person to obtain a first-year tax credit to which the person would not otherwise be entitled, or a tax credit that is greater than would otherwise be the case.

The term 'arrangements' is defined to include 'any scheme, agreement or understanding, whether or not legally enforceable'.

Relevant first-year expenditure

A company's 'relevant first-year expenditure' means expenditure incurred from 1 April 2008 that is first-year qualifying expenditure under CAA 2001, s. 45A or s. 45H. In determining the date on which the expenditure was incurred for these purposes, the special rules relating to pre-trading expenditure are ignored. Expenditure treated as first-year qualifying expenditure by virtue of CAA 2001, s. 236 (additional VAT liability) is not 'relevant first-year expenditure'

The concept of 'relevant first-year expenditure' does not include expenditure incurred after 31 March 2013, but the Treasury may by order substitute a later date.

Income Tax

565

Surrenderable loss

A company is said to have a 'surrenderable loss' in a given chargeable period if, in that period:

- the company is entitled to a FYA under CA 2001, s. 45A or s. 45H;
- the expenditure is incurred on or after 1 April 2008;
- it is incurred for the purposes of a qualifying activity of which the profits are chargeable to corporation tax; and
- the company incurs a loss in that qualifying activity.

The amount of the surrenderable loss is the lower of the following figures:

- so much of the loss incurred in carrying on the qualifying activity as is unrelieved; or
- the amount of the FYA claimed in respect of the relevant first-year expenditure in the chargeable period in question.

Calculating the credit

Companies will be able to receive a percentage of the surrenderable loss as a cash repayment. That percentage figure is set at 19 per cent (whatever the size and corporation tax rate of the company), though the Treasury has the power to substitute a higher or lower figure. According to HMRC, 'the rate at which ECA tax credits are paid is linked to the small companies rate of corporation tax, which will be 21% from April 2008'. The guidance goes on to say that 'the Government considers that the proposed payment rate will be attractive to companies that are loss making, particularly in start-up situations where the losses may not be utilised for two or more years'.

That percentage figure will be applied to the amount of the 'surrenderable loss'.

Example 1

A company makes a profit of £50,000, before deduction of £90,000 of qualifying FYAs. The company thus has a loss of £40,000 which can be surrendered. The company will then receive a cash payment of £7,600 (£40,000 at 19 per cent).

Example 2

A second company makes a loss of £50,000, before deduction of £90,000 of qualifying FYAs. The company thus has an overall loss of £140,000 and its surrenderable loss is £90,000. The company can therefore surrender that £90,000 in return for a cash payment of £17,100 (£90,000 at 19 per cent).

A company may claim either the whole or part of the tax credit.

Upper limit on the tax credit

A cap is set on the amount of tax that can be reclaimed under these rules (CAA 2001, Sch. A1, para 2(2)). This cap is set, for each chargeable period, at the higher of:

- the level of the company's PAYE and NIC liabilities for payment periods ending in the chargeable period for which the claim has been made (see below); and
- £250,000.

The link to PAYE liabilities is on the grounds that the relief should in principle be restricted to those companies that have 'an active commercial presence in the UK'. Nevertheless, the alternative cap of £250,000 reflects the intention that the potential repayments should still be attractive for companies that have relatively low payroll costs but that still wish to invest in the new technologies. With a 19 per cent tax repayment rate, the £250,000 figure means that each company will be able to surrender losses of at least £1,315,789, regardless of the level of its PAYE and NICs liabilities.

The total amount of PAYE and NIC liabilities includes the following for any given payment period:

(1) the amount of income tax for which the company is required to account to HMRC for that period under the PAYE regulations, disregarding any deduction the company is authorised to make in respect of child tax credit or working tax credit; and

(2) the Class 1 NICs for which the company is required to account to HMRC for that period, disregarding any deduction the company is authorised to make in respect of payments of statutory sick pay, statutory maternity pay, child tax credit or working tax credit.

For these purposes, a payment period is defined to mean a period ending on the fifth day of a month, for which the company is liable to account to HMRC for income tax and NIC.

HMRC must pay to the company the amount specified in a claim. However, such an amount (and any interest thereon) may be applied first in discharging any corporation tax liability of the company.

If the company has any outstanding PAYE or Class 1 NIC liabilities for the chargeable period to which the claim relates then HMRC may withhold payment of the credit until those liabilities have been met.

If an enquiry is under way, HMRC have the discretion to make provisional payments while the return is still under enquiry, as they deem appropriate. Subject to that discretion, no payment of the credit needs to be made until the enquiries are completed.

Law: FA 2008. s. 79 and Sch. 25; CAA 2001, Sch. A1

See *British Tax Reporter* ¶242-000.

Income Tax

2374 Meaning of small or medium-sized enterprise (SME)

Several of the categories of first-year allowance have historically been available only to small or medium-sized enterprises, or just to small enterprises, though this distinction ceased from April 2008. As such, the commentary that follows is only relevant in relation to expenditure incurred before 1 or 6 April 2008 (for businesses paying corporation tax or income tax respectively).

CAA 2001 contained definitions under three categories, as follows, though all of these provisions were omitted by *Finance Act* 2008:

(1)   expenditure of small or medium-sized enterprises: companies;

(2)   expenditure of small or medium-sized enterprises: businesses; and

(3)   where the company is a member of a large or medium-sized group.

The company must satisfy two or more of the following requirements:

Small company	
Turnover	Not more than £5.6m
Balance sheet total	Not more than £2.8m
Number of employees	Not more than 50

Medium-sized company	
Turnover	Not more than £22.8m
Balance sheet total	Not more than £11.4m
Number of employees	Not more than 250

In addition, a small company must not be part of a large or medium-sized group, and a medium-sized company must not be part of a large group at the time the expenditure was incurred.

Expenditure incurred by a small or medium-sized enterprise could previously count as first-year qualifying expenditure as long as it was not within the general exclusions in CAA 2001, s. 44. In other words, this was a general type of FYA available for all but the largest businesses. First-year allowances given under this heading were generally at 40 per cent. However, this increased to 50 per cent, for small enterprises only, for expenditure incurred in various periods. As noted above, this type of FYA is withdrawn completely from April 2008.

2376 Energy-saving plant and machinery

First-year allowances (FYAs) are available at a rate of 100 per cent on expenditure on plant and machinery which falls into the category of 'energy-saving'. An equivalent relief is given for 'environmentally beneficial plant and machinery' which covers various types of water-related technology. Both of these types of allowance continue to be available after April 2008 (i.e. despite the withdrawal of most other FYAs from that date). Indeed, the value of these allowances is in some cases increased from 1 April 2008 as loss-making companies may from that date claim repayable tax credits based on this type of allowance. These credits are discussed at 2372.

Enhanced FYAs were extended from 17 April 2002 to lessors. The intention was that the availability of 100 per cent FYAs should enable lease rental payments to be reduced. This would in turn encourage lessees to use energy-efficient plant and machinery.

Expenditure on energy-saving plant and machinery qualifies for FYAs as long as it is not within the general exclusions identified at CAA 2001, s. 45A. Allowances under this heading are not restricted to small or medium-sized enterprises, and are given at 100 per cent. (The general exclusion with regard to leasing does not apply if the asset is provided for leasing under an excluded lease of background plant or machinery for a building.)

To qualify, the plant or machinery in question must meet certain energy-saving criteria specified by the Treasury. These criteria need to be met either when the expenditure is incurred or on the date the contract is entered into for the provision of the plant. This means that expenditure, not treated as qualifying when the contract is entered into, may nevertheless qualify if the list is suitably amended by the time the expenditure is incurred. This latter date is determined by CAA 2001, s. 5 (generally, as soon as there is an unconditional obligation to incur it). The Product List contains those products in the technology classes that have been accepted as meeting the published water-saving standards. Neither the product nor the installation normally needs to be separately certified, though each installation does need to be certified in certain cases, e.g. for efficient membrane filtration systems, which (according to HMRC guidance) are usually tailor-made for a particular application.

If only certain components of an item of plant meet the energy-saving criteria then the normal apportionment rules do not apply. Instead, the Treasury will specify the amount that will qualify under this heading for FYAs.

Products on the published Product List may be incorporated into other items of plant or machinery. In this case, it is necessary to identify the proportion of the expenditure incurred that qualifies for 100 per cent FYA, using tables included as part of the Product List. These specify the deemed expenditure qualifying for FYAs to be attributed to a particular product when incorporated into other equipment. The balance can still qualify for ordinary capital allowances.

What qualifies as 'energy-saving plant or machinery'?

The technologies that can qualify under the scheme are listed in the Energy Technology Criteria List which was issued on 1 April 2001. This list also contains the energy-saving standards that must be met for each of the different technologies. The Energy Technology Product List contains lists of the products that have been accepted as meeting those criteria.

The energy-saving criteria have been developed by the Department for Environment, Food and Rural Affairs (formerly the Department of the Environment, Transport and the Regions) and HMRC, in consultation with business and industry bodies.

The Treasury order, entitled the *Capital Allowances (Energy-saving Plant and Machinery) Order* 2001 (SI 2001/2541), as amended, gives statutory force to the lists, and also specifies the particular technologies to which subordinate rules apply.

The following are included in the criteria list of acceptable technologies:

- combined heat and power (CHP) capacity installed to provide heat and power to clearly identified end users, and certified as good quality by the CHPQA programme (known as the Qualifying Power Capacity: see www.chpqa.com);
- refrigeration equipment; boilers and add-ons; thermal screens; motors; variable speed drives (VSD); if the particular equipment is included in the list of approved products in the Energy Technology List; and
- lighting; pipe insulation; they meet the relevant energy-saving criteria in the Energy Technology List.

The FYAs are only available if the plant or machinery falls within the specified categories either:

- when the expenditure is incurred; or
- when the contract is entered into.

This means that expenditure, not treated as qualifying when the contract is entered into, may nevertheless qualify if the list is suitably amended by the time the expenditure is incurred. As a general rule, expenditure is incurred as soon as there is an unconditional obligation to incur it.

Additional certification

In some cases, plant or machinery must also be certified if it is to qualify for first-year allowances.

Such certificates will generally be issued by the Secretary of State for the DETR. However, for plant or machinery used or for use in Scotland, Wales or Northern Ireland, the certificate will be issued by the relevant devolved power.

A certificate may be revoked, in which case the certificate is treated as if it had never been issued. Any tax computations made on the understanding that a valid certificate had been issued will have to be amended accordingly.

If:

- a person has submitted a tax return on the basis of a valid certificate in respect of certain plant or machinery; or
- that person then discovers that the tax return is incorrect because the certificate has been revoked,

then that person must notify HMRC of the required amendment to the tax return within three months of the day on which the error came to light.

Example

Suppose U's tax return for the year ending 5 April 2007 is prepared on the basis of an entitlement to a 100 per cent FYA in respect of plant or machinery subject to a certificate.

The tax return is submitted on 7 October 2007. On 29 November 2007, the certificate is revoked. U learns of this on 24 March 2008 and realises immediately that the tax return is therefore incorrect.

U must therefore notify HMRC of any required adjustment by 23 June 2008.

Any taxpayer who does not notify HMRC in time may be subject to a penalty of £300 with additional daily penalties of £60.

Apportionments

Normally, if expenditure on plant or machinery needs to be apportioned because two or more items are bought in a single purchase, it is necessary to do a just and reasonable apportionment for both the seller and buyer.

However, a special apportionment rule applies to determine how much expenditure on an item of plant or machinery qualifies for the 100 per cent FYA if some components, but not all, qualify as energy-saving.

Amounts, which are the maximum expenditure on the component that can qualify for 100 per cent FYAs under the energy-saving rules, are set out in the product list.

So, if only one component is on the product list, then the amount qualifying for 100 per cent FYAs under the energy-saving rules will be the lower of:

- the amount actually incurred for the whole item of plant or machinery; and
- the amount specified on the Treasury Order.

Any actual expenditure in excess of the specified amount will qualify for plant or machinery allowances in the usual way, but not for 100 per cent FYAs by reason of the energy-saving rules.

Similarly, if two or more components are on the Product List, then the maximum amount qualifying for 100 per cent FYAs under the energy-saving rules is the sum of the relevant amounts specified on the list.

When must the expenditure be incurred?

The expenditure must be incurred after 31 March 2001. For income tax purposes, the new rules only apply for chargeable periods ending after 5 April 2001. Thus, any taxpayer who

Income Tax

has a chargeable period ending between 1 April and 5 April 2001 (inclusive) should take care that they do not incur the expenditure in that same short period.

Expenditure actually incurred before a qualifying activity commences is deemed to be incurred on the date that the trade commences. However, for businesses commencing after 31 March 2001, expenditure actually incurred before that date still does not qualify for the 100 per cent FYAs.

Law: *Capital Allowances (Energy-saving Plant and Machinery (Amendment) Order* 2008 (SI 2008/1916); *Capital Allowances (Energy-Saving Plant and Machinery) (Amendment) Order* 2009 (SI 2009/1863)

2378 Environmentally beneficial plant or machinery

First-year allowances are available at a rate of 100 per cent on expenditure on new plant and machinery that falls into the category of 'environmentally beneficial'. The relief mirrors that for 'energy-saving plant or machinery' (see 2376). Both of these types of allowance continue to be available after April 2008 (i.e. despite the withdrawal of most other FYAs from that date). Indeed, the value of these allowances is in some cases increased from 1 April 2008 as loss-making companies may from that date claim repayable tax credits based on this type of allowance. These credits are discussed at 2372.

The term 'environmentally beneficial plant and machinery' is used for certain water technology products. The idea is that the cash flow advantage of accelerated allowances should encourage businesses to invest in technology that either saves water or improves water quality. No allowances are due for used or second-hand plant or machinery or for long-life assets. According to HMRC, however, equipment will not cease to qualify due to the 'unused and not second-hand' rule solely because it is held as trading stock, is in the course of construction, or is in operation only for commissioning, testing or training (see www.hmrc.gov.uk/capital_allowances/eca-water-pt2.htm).

First-year allowances for environmentally beneficial plant or machinery are available to all businesses of whatever size or location, in contrast to some of the other types of FYAs, which are restricted to small or medium-sized enterprises. The expenditure must have been incurred on or after 1 April 2003.

Expenditure must be on plant or machinery that is 'unused and not second hand'. It must not be long-life expenditure and must not be ruled out by any of the 'general exclusions'.

The statute authorises the Treasury to make such orders as appear appropriate 'to promote the use of technologies, or products, designed to remedy or prevent damage to the physical environment or natural resources'. The Treasury is also permitted to require allowances to be given, in certain cases, only where a 'certificate of environmental benefit' is in force. Rules specify by whom such a certificate may be issued and the consequences if it is ever revoked. Revocation of the certificate imposes an obligation on a taxpayer who has claimed allowances to make an amended return within three months of becoming aware that the certificate was incorrect.

Law: FA 2003, s. 167, Sch. 30; CAA 2001, s. 45H–J

Source: *Capital Allowances (Environmentally Beneficial Plant and Machinery) Order* 2003 (SI 2003/2076)

See *British Tax Reporter* ¶237-600.

2380 Cars

The tax rules granting relief for business expenditure on cars were changed quite radically from April 2009.

The underlying principle has always been that a business should gain tax relief – at some stage – on the amount by which the value of a car has fallen over the period of ownership. If, for example, a business buys a car for £20,000 and sells it three years later for £7,500 then it will be able to reduce its taxable profits by £12,500 (albeit subject to a likely private use adjustment if the car is not owned by a company). What the tax system does not do, though, is to give tax relief on a timescale that mirrors commercial depreciation; rather, it contains its own fairly complex rules to determine the timing of the tax deductions.

The changes applying from April 2009 relate almost entirely to the timing of that tax relief. In the past, the main factor that determined the speed at which relief could be gained was the cost of the car: more expensive cars were discouraged by slowing down the percentage of relief that could be given in the early years. Now, the rate of relief is determined primarily by the level of engine emissions, the idea being to encourage businesses to buy cars that are more fuel efficient and that therefore have a less damaging environmental impact.

Definition of 'car'

The capital allowance definition of 'car' is now given at CAA 2001, s. 268A. The term covers any 'mechanically propelled road vehicle' except:

- a motor cycle;
- a vehicle of a construction primarily suited for the conveyance of goods or burden of any description (e.g. a van); or
- a vehicle of a type not commonly used as a private vehicle and unsuitable for such use (e.g. a police car).

The definition is similar (but not identical) to that used for the purposes of determining benefits in kind on company cars. As a result, some of the case law that has helped to hone the definition in that area of the legislation may be applied equally to the capital allowance definition.

Income Tax

Motor cycles

The exclusion of motor cycles was a change introduced from April 2009. This means that motor cycles are now treated for capital allowance purposes like any other asset, rather than being subject to the special rules applying for cars. One effect of this is that annual investment allowances are now available for motor cycles, whereas this was not previously the case.

Overview of new rules

Key features of the rules introduced from April 2009 are as follows:

- The former concept of 'expensive' cars is abolished and the rate of tax relief instead depends on the level of the vehicle's CO_2 emissions.
- Qualifying expenditure incurred from (broadly) 1 or 6 April 2009 (for corporation tax and income tax respectively) is normally allocated to one of the two main pools for plant and machinery. Expenditure on 'main rate cars' (broadly, those with emissions of up to 160g/km) goes into the main plant and machinery pool, attracting allowances at 20 per cent. Cars with higher emissions attract allowances at just 10 per cent in the 'special rate' pool.
- Cars with private use are kept in a single asset pool but the rate at which allowances are given is still determined by reference to the same emission principles.
- For cars bought before April 2009, allowances are normally calculated according to principles applying up to that date, though the transitional provisions are quite complex
- Car leases that began before 1 or 6 April 2009 broadly continue to be subject to the former rules. For new leases of vehicles above the 160g/km threshold, a flat rate disallowance is made, calculated as 15 per cent of 'relevant payments'. New cars with lower emissions will suffer no disallowance.
- Certain hire cars (e.g. taxis) that were formerly exempt from the restrictions for expensive cars are from April 2009 subject to the new rules. Conversely, motor cycles were previously classified as cars for capital allowance purposes but are excluded from the definition from April 2009.
- The 100 per cent first-year allowance for cars with very low emissions continues unchanged.

As noted above, the normal rule is that expenditure incurred from April 2009 is allocated either to the main plant and machinery pool or to the special rate pool, and attracts allowances at either 20 or 10 per cent accordingly.

Compared with the system applying before April 2009, the pooling of cars in this way may have a short-term advantage (as annual writing-down allowances are no longer capped at £3,000). However, the amended rules represent a significant cash-flow cost in the longer term as there will be no balancing allowance on sale of the vehicle. This will be disadvantageous for most cars but the change is especially severe for cars with higher emissions.

> ## Example
>
> A company director drives a company car with emissions of 170g/km. The vehicle is bought in year one for £40,000 and sold in year four for £18,000. Under the old rules, the company would obtain tax relief on £3,000 in each of years one to three, and £13,000 (by way of balancing allowance) in year four.
>
> Under the rules now applying, the company will initially be slightly better off, but will lose out badly when the car comes to be sold. Allowances will not be calculated separately for the car but will effectively be £4,000, £3,600, £3,240 and (adjusting for the sale proceeds) £1,116. The loss on the car is £22,000 but only just over half of that loss has attracted tax relief by the time the car comes to be sold. The rest of the relief will be obtained over an indefinite future period.

Meaning of 'main rate car'

The rate at which writing-down allowances are given depends on whether or not the car is a 'main rate car'. In simple terms, a main rate car will be added to the main plant and machinery pool (and will therefore attract allowances at 20 per cent) but any other car will go into the special rate pool, where allowances are given at just 10 per cent.

A 'main rate car' is defined as including three categories of vehicle:

- any car first registered before 1 March 2001;
- a car with low CO_2 emissions (as defined for these purposes: see below); or
- a car that is electrically propelled.

Low CO_2 emissions

For the purposes of this definition, a car has low CO_2 emissions if it meets both of the following conditions:

- when the car is first registered, it is so registered on the basis of a qualifying emissions certificate; and
- the applicable CO_2 emissions figure in relation to the car does not exceed 160g/km.

The Treasury may ('from time to time') alter the figure of 160g/km, and any order to this effect 'may contain transitional provision and savings'.

In the great majority of cases, it will be easy to determine whether or not the car has emissions of more than 160g/km. Nevertheless, the legislation does contain numerous technical definitions.

Writing-down allowances

Before April 2009, most business cars (specifically, those costing more than £12,000) were allocated to a single asset pool and allowances were therefore computed on a car-by-car basis. This principle no longer applies and the general rule is now that cars are pooled with other expenditure for the purposes of calculating writing-down allowances.

Income Tax

If a car is a 'main rate car' (see above), and if there is no private use of the vehicle (i.e. by a sole trader or member of a partnership) then the cost of the car is added to the main plant and machinery pool and allowances are given accordingly. There are no special rules to determine the treatment of such cars as they are not needed: in simple terms, the legislation has removed the requirement (formerly the first item at CAA 2001, s. 54(3)) to allocate these cars to a single asset pool.

Where there is private use of the main rate car, the car must be allocated to a single asset pool. The rate of allowance will still be the same (20 per cent) but this will then be subject to an adjustment to reflect private use.

Example

John is a sole trader. He buys a car for £20,000 in May 2009. The car has emissions of 135g/km.

John estimates that one-half of his use of the vehicle is for business purposes.

He initially calculates allowances for the year of £4,000 (£20,000 at 20%), but he then reduces this figure by half to reflect his private use. The allowances available are £2,000 and the value carried down to the next period of accounts is £16,000 (as he still deducts the whole of the £4,000).

Other cars

If the car is not a main rate car and if there is no private use, the cost of the vehicle will be added to the special rate pool, together with expenditure on long-life assets, integral features, etc. Allowances will be given accordingly, i.e. normally at 10 per cent of the reducing balance of the pool.

Law: CAA 2001, s. 104AA, 206

See *British Tax Reporter* ¶238-500.

2382   Other allowances and charges

CAA 2001 uses two key concepts to determine the amount of any entitlement to capital allowances or liability to balancing charges.

The two key terms are 'available qualifying expenditure' (AQE) and 'the total of any disposal receipts to be brought into account' (TDR).

The legislation then says, simply enough, that if AQE exceeds TDR then a writing-down allowance or balancing allowance will be due for the period in question. If the reverse is true then there will be a balancing charge for the period.

The principles apply equally to any single asset pools, any class pools and the main pool; see 2384 for details on how pooling operates. The only exception to the above is in respect of overseas leasing allowances where restrictions are applied in certain cases.

The allowance given where AQE exceeds TDR will always be a writing-down allowance except in the final chargeable period, when it will be a balancing allowance.

Law: CAA 2001, s. 55

2384 Pooling

Most businesses spend substantial amounts of money on plant and machinery, ranging from computer equipment to cars and other vehicles or to sophisticated electrical systems and many items which are specific to the trade in question. Clearly, it would be impractical to produce separate tax computations to claim relief on every individual item. For this reason the legislation provides for a 'pooling' system which enables most expenditure to be dealt with in a single computation.

The broad principle is therefore that expenditure has to be pooled for the purpose of calculating a person's entitlement to writing-down allowances and balancing allowances and any liability to balancing charges. If the same person carries on more than one qualifying activity, a separate pool (or set of pools) is required for each activity.

The legislation provides for a main pool but also for 'single-asset pools' and 'class pools'. Certain assets are stated to belong to the single-asset or class pools and all other expenditure is allocated to the main pool.

Single-asset pools

As the name suggests, such pools may contain expenditure relating to only one asset. Items in the following categories must go into a single asset pool (and no other items may do so):

- expensive cars bought (broadly) before April 2009;
- short-life assets;
- ships;
- items used partly for non-trade purposes;
- assets where a partial depreciation subsidy has been received; and
- plant and machinery contribution allowance payments.

Class pools

These are required for special rate expenditure within CAA 2001, s. 104C (previously for long-life assets: CAA 2001, s. 101), and for assets used for overseas leasing (CAA 2001, s. 107). From April 2008 expenditure on thermal insulation, on integral features and on long-life assets is allocated to a 'special rate pool', normally with the effect that allowances are given at 10 per cent rather than at any higher rate.

Income Tax

Law: FA 2008, s. 81 and 82 and Sch. 26; CAA 2001, s. 53–66

See *British Tax Reporter* ¶238-025.

2386 Industrial building allowances

Industrial Buildings Allowances (IBAs) were introduced in 1945, replacing an earlier regime of allowances for mills and factories. The aim of the new rules was to encourage post-war reconstruction for productive industry. As such, allowances were available for the construction costs of buildings used for manufacturing or processing.

The IBA regime applying up to 20 March 2007 was fundamentally the same as in 1945, though the original scope of the rules had been broadened to include, for example, certain hotels and commercial buildings. Rates of allowances have fluctuated, with initial allowances coming and going and with a doubling (from 1962) of the rate of the annual writing-down allowance from 2 to 4 per cent. The concept of the 'relevant interest' in a building has survived from the outset.

The IBA rules give tax relief for the depreciation suffered on factories or other industrial buildings, providing relief for the costs of construction over a 25-year period.

Normally, the giving of IBAs does not have any bearing on any capital gains tax (CGT) computations, except that a CGT loss may be restricted where IBAs have been given.

In a wholly unexpected announcement in the March 2007 Budget, the Chancellor announced that IBAs (and ABAs – see 2392) were to be phased out over a four-year period. According to the Explanatory Notes accompanying the subsequent 2007 Finance Bill, the allowances 'are to be withdrawn because they are anachronistic and poorly targeted'. Thus a form of tax relief that dates back, effectively, at least as far as the *Finance Act* 1919 is now perceived to have served its purpose. Section 84 of the *Finance Act* 2008 confirms that the IBA legislation ceases to apply in relation to expenditure incurred from 1 April 2011 (for corporation tax purposes) or 6 April 2011 (for income tax).

The *Finance Act* 2007 contained provisions that applied for most disposals made from 21 March 2007 and that prevented from that date the making of any balancing adjustments on disposals of industrial buildings (with the exception of disposals of buildings in enterprise zones).

The Explanatory Notes went further than this, however, and explained that 'the effective rate of WDAs for both regimes is reduced to 3 per cent from April 2008, to 2 per cent from April 2009 and to 1 per cent from April 2010. Finally, the allowances will be withdrawn altogether from 1 April 2011'. Legislation is contained in *Finance Act* 2008 to implement this phased withdrawal of the relief (FA 2008, s. 85).

Subject to the above comments, allowances are given at 4 per cent on a straight line basis, but at a different rate for a subsequent owner.

Before the change referred to above, the law was very much more complex when a building was sold within 25 years of first use:

- if it was sold at a profit, the owner would typically suffer a balancing charge at the point of sale to claw back any tax relief that had been given in earlier years;
- no such balancing adjustment was normally made, however, more than 25 years after the date on which the building was first used;
- this provided some important tax planning considerations. The grant of a long lease, for example, was not treated as a sale and so did not produce a balancing adjustment, though the parties were able to elect for alternative treatment;
- a person selling the factory, etc. at a loss within that 25-year period would normally have obtained tax relief for that loss, but adjusted for periods during which the building did not qualify;
- a subsequent buyer, if he continued to use the building for qualifying purposes, could obtain relief for the balance of the original expenditure; and
- the rules had some odd results in practice, not least in the way that the purchaser of a used building was treated. A person buying a building that was nearly 25 years old, for example, would often enjoy a very rapid rate of tax relief.

The three main conditions that need to be met if IBAs are to be obtained are as follows, and are all considered in more detail below:

- expenditure must be incurred on the construction of a building or structure;
- the building must be in use for a qualifying trade or other qualifying purpose; and
- the expenditure must be 'qualifying expenditure'.

An 'industrial building' is a building or structure which is in use as follows:

(1) for the purposes of a trade which consists in the manufacture of goods or materials or the subjection of goods or materials to any process, including their maintenance or repair; or

(2) for the purposes of a trade which consists in the storage of goods or materials:

    (a) to be used in the manufacture of other goods or materials; or

    (b) to be subjected, in the course of a trade, to any process; or

    (c) which, having been manufactured or produced or subjected in the course of a trade to any process, have not yet been delivered to any purchaser; or

    (d) on their arrival in any part of the UK from a place outside; or

(3) for certain other special trades or activities (broadly, these relate to mining, contract work for farmers, transport, sewerage and power generation),

and includes any building or structure (including sports pavilions) provided by the person carrying on such a trade or undertaking for the welfare of its workers involved therein. Toll roads are included from 6 April 1991 with the definition extended to highways from 6 April 1995 to encompass design, build, finance and operate (DBFO) schemes.

Income Tax

An 'industrial building' does not include a building in use as, or as part of, a dwelling-house, retail shop, showroom or office or for a 'purpose ancillary to the purposes of' a dwelling-house, shop, etc.

Wholesale supermarkets do not attract IBAs: buildings are only used for 'storage' within head (3) above if storage is an end in itself; and the checking, sorting, repackaging and labelling, etc. of the merchandise does not amount to a 'process' within head (2) above.

A part of an industrial building may be used for non-qualifying purposes without any restriction in the allowance for the building as a whole, so long as the expenditure on that part does not exceed 25 per cent of the expenditure on the whole building. Where the expenditure on the non-qualifying part is greater than 25 per cent only the expenditure on the industrial part qualifies for the allowance.

Where a building, etc. is outside the UK, the activity must be within the rules charging amounts to tax as a trade.

Law: FA 2008, s. 84–87; FA 2007, s. 36; CAA 2001, Pt. 3; *Girobank plc v Clarke (HMIT)* [1998] BTC 24; *(Holdings) Ltd v Luff (HMIT)* [1998] BTC 69; *Sarsfield (HMIT) v Dixons Group plc* [1998] BTC 288; *Walker v Smith (HMIT)* [1999] BTC 209

Source: Former ESC D20

Website: www.hmrc.gov.uk/bulletins/index.htm

See *British Tax Reporter* ¶246-750-.

2388   Enterprise zone buildings

The enterprise zone rules form part of the overall IBA legislation (see 2386). Unless otherwise specified, therefore, qualifying expenditure on an enterprise zone building will be treated for IBA purposes in the same way as any other qualifying expenditure.

Nevertheless, there are some key differences, including in particular the following:

- the abolition of most balancing adjustments for events occurring from 21 March 2007 does not apply for enterprise zone expenditure, but IBAs will be withdrawn even for enterprise zone expenditure from April 2011;
- at the time of abolition of IBAs, there will be a seven-year run-off period during which taxpayers may still face balancing charges;
- a wider range of buildings, specifically to include commercial buildings, can qualify under the enterprise zone rules than under the general IBA rules;
- an initial allowance is available for enterprise zone expenditure;
- if a full (100 per cent) initial allowance has not been taken, expenditure qualifies for writing-down allowances at a much faster rate;

- the tax treatment differs from the main IBA rules where buildings are bought that have already been used; and
- in view of the attractive tax benefits, the enterprise zone rules are subject to their own anti-avoidance legislation.

As indicated above, commercial buildings may be included in the list of buildings qualifying under the enterprise zone rules. For the avoidance of doubt, however, the other tax benefits just listed are not restricted to commercial buildings. All the tax advantages can apply equally to industrial buildings and qualifying hotels, as long as they fall within a designated enterprise zone and the expenditure is incurred within the specified time-limits.

As mentioned above, IBAs have been phased out since April 2007 and will be completely abolished from April 2011. As a general principle, this will apply for qualifying enterprise zone expenditure as it does for all other allowances under the IBA code.

For enterprise zone expenditure only, balancing adjustments can still be made. Furthermore, it will still be possible for a person to incur a balancing charge up to 5 April 2018 in relation to such expenditure (*Finance Act* 2008, Sch. 27, para. 31). More specifically, the balancing charge will (from April 2011) arise if:

- an initial allowance or writing-down allowance has been made under the IBA rules;
- an event occurs which would have given rise to a balancing charge under those rules; and
- a balancing event occurs within seven years of the date on which the building was first used.

Similarly, an initial allowance for qualifying enterprise zone expenditure will be withdrawn if:

- an event occurs which would have caused the allowance to be withdrawn if (from April 2011), CAA 2001, s. 307 had not been withdrawn; and
- a balancing event occurs within seven years of the end of the chargeable period for which the allowance was made.

For chargeable periods that start before 1 or 6 April 2011 (the 'relevant date' for corporation tax and income tax respectively), but end after that date, any writing-down allowances will only be given for the part of the period falling before that date. This is achieved (per *Finance Act* 2008, s. 86) by calculating the allowance for that period according to the following formula:

$$(DCPB/DCP) \times WDA$$

where:

DCPB   is the number of days in the chargeable period which fall before the relevant date;
DCP   is the number of days in the chargeable period; and
WDA   is the writing-down allowance to which the person would otherwise be entitled for the chargeable period.

Enterprise zones last for ten years from designation. For a list of such zones, see 20.

Law: FA 2008, s. 86; CAA 2001, s. 271(1)(b)(iv), 281, 298, 305, 310(1)(a); *Income Tax (Definition of Unit Trust Scheme) Regulations* 1988 (SI 1988/267)

See *British Tax Reporter* ¶246-000.

2390 Business Premises Renovation Allowance

Business Premises Renovation Allowances (BPRAs) apply to expenditure incurred in a period of at least five years from the start date. The original intention was that the relief would start to be available in 2005 but, in the event, the five-year period runs from 11 April 2007. The allowances offer 100 per cent upfront tax relief for the costs of renovating or converting certain unused business property in any of the 2,000 or so areas of the UK that are designated as disadvantaged. Allowances can be claimed by an individual or company incurring capital expenditure on bringing qualifying business premises back into business use. The allowances are available both to landlords and to businesses occupying their own properties.

The scheme of allowances offers full tax relief where, without the special rules, allowances might have been available at:

- 40, 25, 20 or 10 per cent (plant and machinery, taking account of changes applying from April 2008);
- 4 per cent, reducing eventually to zero (industrial buildings); or
- zero per cent – i.e. no allowances due for the bulk of the expenditure on certain offices and other commercial premises.

The allowances constitute 'state aid' and the timing of when the relief could start was therefore subject to EU approval.

Allowances are due only to the person incurring the expenditure. They can be clawed back if there is a sale or other 'balancing event' within seven years from the date on which the premises are first brought back into use (or on which they are first made suitable and available for letting). A subsequent purchaser of the property has no entitlement to allowances.

Entitlement to BPRAs depends on three conditions:

- a person must incur qualifying expenditure;
- that expenditure must be on a qualifying building; and
- the person must have the relevant interest in that building.

Law: CAA 2001, s. 360A; FA 2005, s. 92; *Finance Act 2005, Section 92 and Schedule 6 (Appointed Day) Order* 2007 (SI 2007/949); *Business Premises Renovation Allowances Regulations* 2007 (SI 2007/945)

See *British Tax Reporter* ¶246-750.

2392   Agricultural land and buildings

In a wholly unexpected announcement in the March 2007 Budget, the Chancellor announced that ABAs (and IBAs – see 2386) were to be phased out over a four-year period. According to the Explanatory Notes accompanying the subsequent 2007 Finance Bill, the allowances 'are to be withdrawn because they are anachronistic and poorly targeted'. Thus a form of tax relief that dates back for many decades is now perceived to have served its purpose.

The *Finance Act* 2007 contained provisions that applied immediately (i.e. for most disposals made from 21 March 2007) and that prevented any further balancing adjustments on disposals of agricultural buildings.

In addition, 'the effective rate of WDAs for both regimes was reduced to 3 per cent from April 2008, and will be reduced to 2 per cent from April 2009 and to 1 per cent from April 2010. Finally, the allowances will be withdrawn altogether from 1 April 2011'. *Finance Act* 2008 provides for the full withdrawal of the relief from 2011.

Subject to the above comments, allowances are normally given at 4 per cent on a straight line basis.

Expenditure must be 'qualifying expenditure' incurred by a person who has an interest in land in the UK. That land must be occupied wholly or mainly for the purposes of husbandry, and the expenditure must be incurred for the purposes of husbandry on that land (CAA 2001, s. 361(2)). A building overseas cannot be an agricultural building for ABA purposes.

Many features of the ABA system are similar to the IBA rules, including the following:

- allowances are made to the person with the relevant interest in the qualifying expenditure;
- no allowances are given on the cost of the land on which a building stands; and
- relief is normally given on a straight line basis at an annual rate of 4 per cent.

But other features of ABA are different from the IBA system, including (but not restricted to) the following:

- ABAs are given according to the time at which the expenditure is incurred, whether or not the building has been brought into use at that time;
- as long as the first use of the building is for the purposes of husbandry, allowances will continue to be given even if the use of the building changes;
- where there is a transfer of the relevant interest, the normal treatment has been that allowances simply continue for the new owner, without any balancing adjustment (i.e. even before the changes announced in *Finance Act* 2007);
- an election was necessary (but is now no longer generally possible) to secure a balancing allowance, or for a purchaser to obtain allowances on his expenditure; and
- allowances may be due on dwelling houses (such as farmhouses and cottages) and sometimes on shops.

Income Tax

Different rules applied to expenditure incurred before 1 April 1986 (or 1 April 1987 under certain transitional provisions).

Phasing out of ABAs

The Chancellor announced in the Budget of March 2007 that ABAs (and IBAs) were to be phased out over a four-year period. The phasing-out is put into effect in different ways:

- FA 2007 provides that no ABA balancing adjustment is to be made for balancing events occurring (broadly) from 21 March 2007.
- FA 2008 confirms that the annual ABA writing-down allowance is reduced to 3 per cent from April 2008 and by a further 1 per cent per year thereafter, until the allowances are finally withdrawn from 1 April 2011.

Section 84 of the *Finance Act* 2008 confirms that the ABA legislation ceases to apply in relation to expenditure incurred from 1 April 2011 (for corporation tax purposes) or 6 April 2011 (for income tax).

Law: FA 2008, s. 84–87; FA 2007, s. 36; CAA 2001, s. 361–393

See *British Tax Reporter* ¶253-000.

2394 Flat conversion allowance

The introduction of a 'flat conversion allowance' is part of a package of measures designed to encourage the regeneration of Britain's towns and cities and builds on recommendations made by the Urban Task Force, chaired by Lord Rogers, in its report *Towards an Urban Renaissance*. In particular, it is intended to encourage expenditure on the conversion of disused business property for residential use.

The rules for a flat conversion allowance follow basically those for industrial buildings allowances (CAA 2001, Pt. 3) but the flat conversion allowance is considerably simpler. In particular:

- 100 per cent initial allowances will generally be available;
- there will be no balancing charges for events more than seven years after the completion of the flat; and
- entitlement to allowances will not be transferable.

The flat conversion allowances will be available only to expenditure incurred after 11 May 2001 (date of Royal Assent for FA 2001).

Law: CAA 2001, Pt. 4A.

See *British Tax Reporter* ¶254-000.

2396 Mineral extraction allowances

The rules set out below govern the availability of capital allowances in respect of expenditure incurred on certain mineral extraction, often known as MEAs.

To obtain MEAs, the taxpayer must carry on a 'trade of mineral extraction', i.e. a trade which consists of or includes the working of a 'source of mineral deposits', including exploration and gaining access thereto or restoration within a three-year period thereafter. A 'source of mineral deposits' includes a mine, an oil well and a source of geothermal energy. Pre-trading expenditure is subject to special rules.

Further, 'qualifying expenditure' must have been incurred after 31 March 1986. 'Qualifying expenditure' is capital expenditure on:

- mineral exploration and access;
- the acquisition of a mineral asset;
- construction of works which, when the source is worked out, are likely to have little or no remaining value;
- construction of works in connection with a foreign concession, which are likely to have no value to the trader when the commission ends; and
- certain capital contributions to the cost of foreign works for the provision of utilities or facilities for employees and their dependants.

In order to be 'qualifying expenditure', the last-mentioned contributions must be incurred for the purposes of the claimant's trade of mineral extraction and the buildings, etc. must be likely to have little or no residual value for him.

Limitations on qualifying expenditure

Where an allowance is claimed in respect of a mineral asset and that expenditure includes expenditure on the acquisition of an interest in land, so much of the expenditure as represents 'undeveloped market value' of the interest in land does not constitute qualifying expenditure. Similar provisions apply to exclude the 'undeveloped market value' of the interest from disposal receipts.

The allowances available to the trader ('the buyer') are restricted where they are claimed in respect of assets previously owned by another trader, whether or not that trader was entitled to an allowance in respect of his qualifying expenditure. If the previous trader was entitled to an allowance, then the buyer's qualifying expenditure cannot exceed the residue of the previous trader's qualifying expenditure. If the previous trader was not entitled to an allowance or the previous owner did not carry on a mineral extraction trade, then the buyer's qualifying expenditure cannot exceed the amount of the previous trader's qualifying expenditure or the previous owner's overall expenditure.

Where a mineral asset is transferred from one company to another company within the same group, the transferee company's qualifying expenditure is limited to that of the transferor.

Income Tax

585

Specifically excluded from the definition of qualifying expenditure is the cost of certain land and expenditure ancillary to the mining function, except offices falling within a 10 per cent de minimis limit.

Allowances and charges

For the chargeable period in which the qualifying expenditure is incurred an allowance may be claimed equivalent to the 'appropriate percentage' of the excess of qualifying expenditure over disposal receipts required to be brought into account.

For any subsequent period the allowance which may be claimed is equivalent to the 'appropriate percentage' of the excess of qualifying expenditure over the aggregate of allowances already given in earlier periods together with any disposal receipts required to be brought into account.

The 'appropriate percentage' is 25 per cent, except in relation to:

- expenditure on the acquisition of a mineral asset; or
- pre-trading expenditure on machinery or plant which is sold; or
- pre-trading exploration expenditure.

In these three cases the 'appropriate percentage' is 10 per cent. Whatever the appropriate percentage, it is adjusted if the chargeable period is not one year in length.

The disposal value of any asset which ceases to be used for the purposes of the trade must be brought into account as a receipt.

Where disposal receipts and allowances previously given exceed qualifying expenditure (plus certain demolition costs) in any period a balancing charge will arise. Conversely, a balancing allowance equivalent to the whole expenditure outstanding may be applicable in the case of permanent discontinuance, loss, destruction or change of use.

Law: CAA 2001, s. 394–436

See *British Tax Reporter* ¶255-500.

2398   Dredging allowances

Where a person incurs capital expenditure on dredging for the purposes of any qualifying trade (maintaining or improving the navigation of a harbour, estuary or waterway, etc.), a writing-down allowance of 4 per cent of cost per annum is available.

Law: CAA 2001, s. 484–489

See *British Tax Reporter* ¶258-000.

2400   Films, tapes and discs

The tax treatment of film production was changed for films that commence principal photography from 1 January 2007. One effect of the special rules for films is that expenditure on creating a film is generally classed as revenue expenditure, if it would otherwise be treated as expenditure on the creation of an asset (i.e. the film). This treatment does not extend to the cost of capital items such as lighting equipment and cameras. Such items continue to attract capital allowances in the ordinary way.

Law: FA 2006, s. 37 and Sch. 4; *Ensign Tankers (Leasing) Ltd v Stokes* [1989] BTC 110

Website: www.hmrc.gov.uk/films/guidance/taxation.pdf

See *British Tax Reporter* ¶245-870.

2402   Know-how and patent right allowances

'Know-how' means any industrial information and techniques likely to assist in the manufacture or processing of goods or materials, or in the working of a mine, oil well or other source of mineral deposits or in the carrying out of any agricultural, forestry or fishing operation.

'Patent rights' means the right to do or authorise the doing of anything which would, but for that right, be an infringement of a patent.

In respect of expenditure incurred after 31 March 1986 expenditure on know-how or patent rights qualifies for an annual writing-down allowance of 25 per cent on a reducing balance basis, adjusted where the chargeable period is not one year in length; expenditure incurred before then is written off over their life, subject to a 17-year maximum.

Law: CAA 2001, s. 452–463, 464–483

See *British Tax Reporter* ¶257-000.

2404   Research and development allowances

Research and development allowances (RDAs) are available for certain capital expenditure on research and development. Separate relief, not under the capital allowances code, is available for qualifying revenue expenditure. Both the capital allowance relief and the revenue relief are generous compared to reliefs for other types of expenditure.

A 100 per cent capital allowance is available in the relevant chargeable period:

- for capital expenditure on scientific research related to a trade incurred whilst carrying on that trade; or

- for capital expenditure on research and development/scientific research where the person undertaking the research (or on whose behalf it was undertaken: see below) later commences a trade connected with that research.

There is a form of balancing adjustment where an asset ceases to belong to the trader – 'the relevant event' – by way of an additional trading deduction or receipt representing the difference between the disposal value and, effectively, the expenditure (including certain demolition costs) less the allowance.

For commentary on relief for revenue expenditure on research and development see 2251, and for the additional relief for companies see 4915.

Law: FA 2003, s. 168; CAA 2001, Pt. 6; *Gaspet Ltd v Elliss (HMIT)* [1987] BTC 218

See *British Tax Reporter* ¶256-000.

ASSESSMENT, RATES AND ENFORCEMENT

ADMINISTRATION GENERALLY

2500 Officers of 'the Board'

The *Taxes Management Act* 1970, which contains many of the provisions relating to the administrative and judicial machinery required to effectively collect tax, opens by stating that:

> 'Income tax, corporation tax and capital gains tax shall be under the care and management of the Commissioners of Inland Revenue (. . . "the Board") . . . '

The head office of the commissioners is at Somerset House, London WC2R 1LB. The officers of the Board are civil servants who are subject to the control of the Treasury. Certain assessments (in relation to certain foreign dividends) are made by the Board, and some claims for relief are also made to them. Claims by non-residents regarding entitlement to personal reliefs (see 1585) are made to the Board and are dealt with by Financial Intermediaries and Claims Office (FICO).

Many statutory powers and duties are entrusted to 'officers of the Board', rather than to inspectors.

> 'Officers of the Board include inspectors, collectors and people who hold office neither as inspector nor as collector, but who are of adequate seniority in the Inland Revenue to discharge those functions . . . the function set out in the statute . . . can be discharged by any adequately qualified person in HMRC.'

HMRC officers

The Board is empowered to appoint inspectors of taxes who act under the Board's direction. Each of the many tax districts into which the UK is divided is in the charge of an officer who may be assisted by other officers. In addition to obtaining returns, making assessments, etc. the officer conducts negotiations with members of the public. As a result, agreement with him is often reached regarding assessments, etc. thus making the hearing of formal appeals unnecessary. The Director-General of the Tax Inspectorate is also a member of the Board.

Collectors

Also under the control of the Board are the collectors of taxes, who are full-time civil servants. They are responsible for collecting the tax assessed. When tax becomes due and payable the collector issues a demand for the sum, which may be made on the person charged, or at the last place of abode, or on the premises in respect of which the tax is charged.

HM Revenue & Customs

The *Commissioners for Revenue and Customs Act* 2005 (CRCA 2005) received Royal Assent on 7 April 2005. The Act provides the legal basis for the integrated department, Her Majesty's Revenue & Customs (HMRC), and the new independent prosecutions office, Revenue and Customs Prosecutions Office. These departments were launched on 18 April 2005. Broadly, the Act gives the Commissioners the power to appoint staff, to be known as officers of Revenue and Customs, and through these officers, they are responsible for the collection and management of revenue for which the Commissioners of Inland Revenue were responsible before the commencement of the Acts; the collection and management of revenue for which the Commissioners of Customs and Excise were responsible before the commencement of the Acts; and the payment and management of tax credits for which the Commissioners of Inland Revenue were formerly responsible.

2504   Taxpayer's Charter

HMRC is now statutorily required to maintain a Charter. The Charter sets out standards of behaviours and values for HMRC to aim at when dealing with taxpayers and others. The legislation also requires the Commissioners for HMRC to report annually on how well HMRC is doing in meeting Charter standards.

Law: FA 2009, s. 92

Website: HMRC: *Your Charter*: www.hmrc.gov.uk/charter/

See *British Tax Reporter* ¶180-100.

Income Tax

2506 Ways of complaining about HMRC conduct

Most complaints about HMRC conduct are settled locally by the office concerned or, if agreement cannot be reached, the Controller of the Executive Office concerned or the Chief Executive of the Valuation Office Agency (for addresses, see www.hmrc.gov.uk). The matter can be taken further by applying to the HMRC Adjudicator (who considers complaints free of charge), or to a Member of Parliament or, through an MP, to the Ombudsman. The Adjudicator's Office has published a leaflet explaining generally which complaints will or will not be dealt with by the Adjudicator and the procedures which will be followed once a complaint has been accepted for consideration. The following points may be of interest:

- the Adjudicator may, in appropriate cases, consider complaints where the full HMRC complaints procedure has not been followed;
- the matters within the Adjudicator's jurisdiction include excessive delay, errors and discourtesy on the part of HMRC; they also include the way in which HMRC have exercised any discretion – including, it appears, a complaint that they have dealt unreasonably with a request for time to pay by a taxpayer short of money;
- the Adjudicator will attempt to persuade HMRC and the taxpayer to come to an agreement to settle the dispute; in the absence of such an agreement, she will make a formal recommendation to HMRC as to how she considers the complaint should be dealt with (a copy of the recommendation being sent to the taxpayer) and HMRC have undertaken to follow the Adjudicator's recommendations 'in all but exceptional circumstances'.

Copies of the leaflet are available from all HMRC and Valuation Agency Offices or direct from the HMRC Adjudicator's Office.

The taxpayer can, of course, seek to avoid later argument by confirming matters with HMRC in advance of the transaction in point. However, such clearance might well be withdrawn if it could be argued that full disclosure was not made to an official of an appropriate level. Hence, the House of Lords held in one case that there was no unfairness amounting to an abuse of HMRC's power in the withdrawal of an inspector's clearance of an investment scheme involving a enterprise zone property unit trust.

Various codes of practice support and amplify taxpayers' rights and relate to investigations, PAYE audits, mistakes by HMRC and inspection of the records of charities or financial intermediaries. For example, a HMRC booklet explains how complaints about HMRC error or delay can best be resolved. The code also sets out the circumstances in which HMRC will reimburse additional costs arising from their serious errors and delays, and the exceptional circumstances in which they will make consolatory payments for worry or distress. Leaflets explaining all these codes are available from local tax offices.

Regulations came into force on 5 August 2010 which update and consolidate the legislation relating to the handling of complaints and misconduct by the Independent Police Complaints Commission in so far as it applies to HMRC.

Law: *The Revenue and Customs (Complaints and Misconduct) Regulations* 2010 (SI 2010/1813); *R v IR Commrs, ex parte Matrix Securities Ltd* [1994] BTC 85

See *British Tax Reporter* ¶180-100.

2508   Confidentiality of information

Taxpayer information held by HMRC or certain other official bodies (such as an advisory commission established under the arbitration convention: see 1780) is treated on a strictly confidential basis.

However, there is provision for certain transfers of information for specified purposes, such as between HMRC departments, for statistical purposes, for double tax purposes or between EU member states.

Law: FA 1989, s. 182, 182A; ICTA 1988, s. 816; FA 1978, s. 77; FA 1972, s. 127; FA 1969, s. 58

See *British Tax Reporter* ¶180-550.

RETURNS AND INFORMATION GENERALLY

2550   Notice of liability to income tax

Every person who is chargeable to income tax (or CGT) for any tax year and who has not received a notice requiring a tax return (see 2564) must notify HMRC that he is chargeable within six months after that year if he has not already been requested to make a tax return. However, the penalty only becomes due to the extent that he does not settle the liability by the following 31 January: i.e. there is a four-month period in which HMRC might issue an assessment on which he could pay the tax and avoid penalties.

The above notice must specify each separate source of income except sources excluded, broadly, by reference to deduction of tax at source where no liability will arise to a rate other than basic or lower rate. The notice must be given to an officer of the Board, and failure to give notice will render that person liable to a penalty not exceeding the tax due under late assessments, i.e. the taxpayer may end up paying double the tax due on undisclosed income (see 2648).

A taxpayer will not generally be in a position to know by the end of the time-limit for notifying chargeability (5 October) whether a PAYE code change will be made to collect outstanding tax. HMRC will accept that an individual does not need to notify chargeability in respect of P11D items if he has received a copy of the P11D and is satisfied that it is correct and complete (and is not aware that it has not been submitted); he is not relieved of

Income Tax

his responsibility to notify chargeability in relation to other items even if he is aware that the employer has submitted information in some form to HMRC.

Law: TMA 1970, s. 7

Source: SP 1/96, *Notification of chargeability to income tax and capital gains tax years 1995–96 onwards*

See *British Tax Reporter* ¶180-700.

2551   Return forms

A 'return' includes any statement or declaration under the Taxes Acts, but is generally taken to refer to the response to a statutory request by an inspector (or the Board) for information. HMRC may prescribe the format in which returns must be made and often issue specific forms. Computer-produced returns may be approved by HMRC in certain cases following written application.

A tax return is the term generally used to refer to the document issued by the tax inspector, instructing the person who receives it to furnish him with information about his (or, in certain cases, other persons') income for that year. It is delivered to the usual or last-known address of that person. Those who have property income or income from a trade, profession or vocation will have to complete an income tax return each year.

A HMRC statement clarifies the position regarding the use of schedules in making personal tax returns. Schedules (i.e. unofficial statements or forms) have always been acceptable as documents supporting entries in an official return form. HMRC will also accept returns where the declaration of accuracy and completeness on the official form is signed but which is otherwise answered generally by overall reference to attached schedules.

A return must in HMRC's view strictly be signed by the person liable to make it (see 2554). Signature by an attorney is accepted in cases of illness or old age if a copy of the general or enduring power has been sent to HMRC. Following an agreement with the Court of Protection, repayment claims for amounts less than £1,600 may be signed by the next of kin, provided the incapacitated person's income is less than £800 for claims of more than that amount.

Law: FA 1999, s. 133; TMA 1970, s. 115A, Sch. 3A

Source: SP 5/83, *Use of schedules in making personal tax returns*; SP 5/87, *Tax returns: the use of substitute forms*; SP 1/97

Website: www.hmrc.gov.uk/bulletins/index.htm

See *British Tax Reporter* ¶184-250.

2552   Internet filing

Individuals are able to file self-assessment returns via the Internet. It is also possible to send attachments with online returns.

Employers have been able to submit certain PAYE forms and returns voluntarily via the Internet for some years. Electronic filing of PAYE returns will, however, be compulsory for all but certain employers by 2011. To encourage employers to switch to electronic filing sooner rather than later, HMRC have been offering financial incentives.

Electronic filing of PAYE returns became mandatory for large employers (i.e. businesses with 250 employees or more) from April 2004. Mandatory electronic filing of certain returns has been extended with effect from 13 August 2009, from those employing 50 or more employees to all employers (SI 2009/2029). For 2010–11 and subsequent years the provisions on e-payment notices have been amended so that large employers (except certain excluded employers) are required to make their monthly payments electronically in all cases.

From 2011–12 all but certain excluded employers are required to file in-year forms (P45 and P46) online.

Law: FA 2003, s. 204; FA 2002, s. 135, 136; FA 2000, s. 143 and Sch. 38; *Income Tax (Pay As You Earn) (Amendment) Regulations* 2010 (SI 2010/668); *Income Tax (Pay As You Earn) (Amendment No. 2) Regulations* 2009 (SI 2009/2029); *Income Tax (Pay As You Earn) Regulations* 2003 (SI 2003/2682), reg. 190, 209; *ZXCV Ltd v R & C Commrs*(2008) Sp C 706

Source: HMRC *Brief* 15/07: *PAYE Update*; *Tax Bulletin*, Issue 73 (October 2004); Inland Revenue press release, 16 February 2000

Website: www.hmrc.gov.uk/inyear/index.htm
www.hmrc.gov.uk/e-tax/index.htm
www.hmrc.gov.uk/employers/doitonline.pdf

See *British Tax Reporter* ¶185-950.

2554   Persons liable to make returns

If income is received in any tax year, the person receiving that income, whether on his own behalf (individuals) or on behalf of others (trustees), must make a return. The persons who must make the returns include:

- individuals (see 2564);
- partnerships (see 2582);
- trustees (see 2588);
- personal representatives, e.g. executors (see 2585);
- employers (see 2579);

- EEIGs (see 2589); and
- agents (see 2590).

2555 Informing the authorities of a new business

HM Revenue & Customs

Unlike some jurisdictions, an individual starting in business in the UK on their own account does not generally need permission to do so. Exceptions to this general principle apply when entry to the sector concerned is regulated, either by government (such as the medical profession) or by professional institutes.

When an individual begins to carry on a trade, he has a duty to inform HMRC that he is chargeable to income tax. Failure to do so will render him liable for a penalty of anything up to the amount of tax for which he is liable in respect of income from the relevant source for that year. This applies both where an assessment is made by an officer of HMRC and where there is a self-assessment, and is on the basis of the tax unpaid at the 31 January following the year of the failure.

Before the introduction by FA 2008, Sch. 41 of a new penalty regime for failure to notify, a self-employed person also had to register to pay Class 2 National Insurance contributions within three months of commencing in business or face a penalty of £100. With the introduction of the new penalty regime, the £100 fixed penalty for failing to notify liability for Class 2 National Insurance contributions was abolished.

Notification to HMRC will cover income tax, National Insurance contributions and VAT matters.

Law: TMA 1970, s. 7; FA 2008, Sch. 41; *Social Security (Contributions) Regulations* 2001 (SI 2001/1004), reg. 87

TYPES OF RETURN

2561 System of returns and payment under self-assessment

The system of self-assessment normally requires returns from individuals, trustees, partnerships etc., by 31 January following the tax year. Tax returns for 2007–08 onwards made on paper must be filed by 31 October. This date is the same for taxpayers who want HMRC to calculate their tax liability (30 September for earlier years). The present filing date of 31 January remains for returns filed online. HMRC have significant power to specify in the return form and in the accompanying guidance notes the necessary information, accounts and statements, which may need annual adjustment. They may also prescribe different return forms for different groups of taxpayers, and these may call for different information.

The return consists of a core section applying to all taxpayers, which is then customised by the addition of extra pages according to the taxpayer's known circumstances. It is up to the taxpayer to request supplementary pages if necessary.

For the requirement to maintain adequate records in support of a return, see 2657. For the system of automatic penalties for late filing of returns, see 2652.

Law: FA 2007, s. 88; TMA 1970, s. 8, 8A, 9, 12A, 113(1)

See *British Tax Reporter* ¶181-200.

2564 Personal returns

Individuals are to submit returns of income and capital gains when required by notice of an officer of the Board. This notice may also, within reason, require accounts, statements and documents relating to information contained in the return.

The self-assessment filing deadlines for 2007–08 and subsequent returns are 31 October for paper returns and 31 January for online returns.

The amounts to be returned are net amounts: i.e. the amounts chargeable to income tax and CGT must take into account any claim or relief claimed in the return. Similarly, the amount payable by way of income tax must take into account tax deducted at source and tax credits on distributions received.

An individual's return is to include his share of any partnership income, losses, tax (i.e. tax deducted at source), tax credit or charge. These figures will be derived from the relevant partnership statement. A partnership statement is relevant if it is for a period which includes all or part of the tax year or its basis period. The requirement for a partnership statement is discussed at 2582.

Every return must include a declaration that the return made by the person is 'to the best of his knowledge correct and complete'.

For penalties in relation to failure to make the return or for submitting an incorrect return, see 2648ff.

Provisional figures

A late filing penalty may be levied where a return contains provisional figures if the taxpayer fails to take 'reasonable care' or if the taxpayer could have supplied the correct figures.

Income Tax

Amendment of self-assessment

Except when HMRC are formally investigating a return, the taxpayer has 12 months in which to amend it; HMRC may amend obvious errors. Such amendments do not preclude penalties being imposed for the incorrect completion of the original return (see 2655).

Law: TMA 1970, s. 8(1)–(2), 9(4)–(6); *Steedon v Carver* (1999) Sp C 212

Website: www.hmrc.gov.uk/bulletins/index.htm

See *British Tax Reporter* ¶184-200.

2566 HMRC enquiries

For tax returns up to 2007–08, HMRC could give notice to the taxpayer at any time:

- within one year of the filing date, in respect of a return delivered on time (or amendment made within such time); or
- before the first quarter day (31 January, 30 April, 31 July or 31 October) falling more than 12 months after the return or amendment is made,

that they were investigating that return or amendment.

Budget 2007 announced certain changes to the HMRC enquiry windows that affect individuals, trustees and partnerships which complete income tax self-assessment tax returns. Broadly, the changes link the period during which HMRC can enquire into returns to the date the return is received by HMRC. Under the new rules the enquiry window will close one year after delivery of the return. So where a return is received before the filing deadline the enquiry window will close earlier than under previous legislation.

Following the completion of HMRC's enquiries, the officer of the Board will issue a closure notice. This will either make amendments to the return or state that no amendment is necessary. The taxpayer may appeal against any amendment the officer makes.

If a taxpayer wishes to end HMRC's enquiries, he can apply to the tribunal for a direction to that effect. The tribunal will direct that the enquiry be closed unless it is satisfied that there are reasonable grounds for pursuing it.

Law: FA 2007, s. 96; TMA 1970, s. 9A, s. 28A; *Gould & Anor (t/a Garry's Private Hire) v R & C Commrs* (2007) Sp C 604; *Wing Hung Lai v Bale (HMIT)* (1999) Sp C 203

See *British Tax Reporter* ¶183-000.

2573   Returns in respect of employees

Employees are taxed under the PAYE system by deduction at source (see 2784). Each employee is given a code by which the employer can determine how much tax to deduct. By this system the employer will collect tax on behalf of HMRC and must make a return at the end of each tax year of all the tax collected (see 2579).

An employer may be required to make returns relating to persons who have been employed by him up to six years before the tax year in which notice requiring a return is issued. The notice must specify the employees for whom a return is wanted and the tax years for which information is required and the names and addresses of employees to whom the notice relates. The return should include details of payments by the employer to the employee, including:

- expenses;
- payments on the employee's behalf which have not been repaid;
- payments for services rendered;
- any benefits in kind or in cash relating to the employment;
- the cost of providing the benefit to the employee;
- the name and business address of the person providing the benefit if it is someone other than the employer.

Code numbers are determined by HMRC from the taxpayer's claim for allowances in his annual tax returns. If there is a change in the employee's code number, the employee will be notified by HMRC (P2) as will the employer (P9). New employees whose code number has been changed from the last code number of the preceding tax year will have their new code number transmitted to their employer by P6.

When an employee leaves his job, P45 will be used to transfer information about the employee to his new employer and to HMRC.

A new employee without a P45 is put on an emergency code which generally means that he is given a single personal allowance and no additional allowances or reliefs. The employer must send to HMRC all the new employee's basic details on P46 so that the appropriate code may be determined for the employee.

Law: TMA 1970, s. 15

See *British Tax Reporter* ¶181-550.

2576   Reporting benefits of certain employees and directors

The P11D (or P9D for certain lower paid employees) is used to record the cash equivalents of benefits or expenses given to employees who are paid at a rate of £8,500 or more (including benefits, etc.) or to directors (see 382ff.). It is completed on a tax year basis

Income Tax

(6 April to 5 April). The employee or director may still claim that the benefit or expense was incurred wholly, exclusively and necessarily in the performance of his duties (see 1990).

Forms P9D and P11D must be submitted to HMRC, together with the employer's declaration and statutory Class 1A return, P11D(b), by 6 July after the end of the tax year to which they relate.

Under self-assessment, employees who are in employment on the last day of a tax year must be provided with a copy of the appropriate form by 6 July (i.e. within three months); employees who leave during the year can obtain a copy if they notify the employer.

Law: *Income Tax (Pay As You Earn) Regulations* 2003 (SI 2003/2682)

See *British Tax Reporter* ¶496-950.

2579 Employer's end-of-year return

An employer must account to HMRC for all PAYE deductions made during the tax year.

Employers are required to complete an end of year summary form (P14 (OCR)) for each employee for whom a deduction working sheet (P11) was completed during the year plus a summary return form (P35). The P14 and the P35 must be with HMRC by 19 May after the end of the tax year. Changes in code are notified to the employer by P9, otherwise he must use the same code each year for the same employee.

The return (P35) must include:

- details of all employee deduction cards;
- a certificate with details of the total net tax deducted from or repaid to each employee;
- a certificate with details of the total net tax deducted from or repaid to all the employees in the tax year;
- details of all National Insurance contributions deducted during the year.

The P35 must go to HMRC within 44 days of the end of each tax year together with P60 and must contain full details of pay and tax deductions for each employee for the whole tax year. However, by concession, no penalty will be charged if the return is received by HMRC within seven days of the statutory filing date.

For 2009–10 onwards employers and agents can use the HMRC online facility to declare that they have no PAYE Employer Annual Return (P35 and P14s) to make.

Form P14 (OCR)

The P14 (OCR) is a three-part form, the top two copies of which are sent to HMRC and the third copy is given to the employee, forming his certificate of pay and tax deducted (P60). The P60 should be given to each employee employed by the employer at the end of the tax year by 31 May after the tax year. The form details pay and tax and National Insurance deducted during the year. Employers are able to provide forms P60 to their employees electronically.

Law: *Income Tax (Pay As You Earn) Regulations* 2003 (SI 2003/2682); *Income Tax (Pay As You Earn) (Amendment) Regulations* 2010 (SI 2010/668)

Source: ESC B46, *Automatic penalties for late company and employers' and contractors end-of-year returns*; *Tax Bulletin*, Issue 73 (October 2004); *Tax Bulletin*, Issue 72 (August 2004)

Website: www.hmrc.gov.uk/paye/payroll/year-end/annual-return.htm#4

See *British Tax Reporter* ¶496-900

2580 Contractor's end-of-year return

Under the reformed CIS scheme, which came into effect from 6 April 2007, contractors are no longer required to submit annual return forms. For commentary on the CIS, see 2787.

See *British Tax Reporter* ¶283-900.

2582 Partnership return

Under self-assessment, a partnership return, made by a specified partner or his successor (or a person identified by a given rule), must include a statement of profits, the separate partners being treated as if their share of profits accrued directly to them from a sole trade. The partnership statement may be for the tax year as well as for the accounting period, and may include details of the allocation of consideration from the disposal of partnership property.

Under self-assessment, for 2006–07 and earlier years, the filing deadline is the later of the dates given by reference to individuals and companies, depending upon whether the partnership comprises solely individuals, solely companies or both; the dates are:

- individuals – later of 31 January following the tax year and three months after the issue of a notice requesting submission of a return;
- companies – later of 12 months after the end of the period for which the return is required and three months after the issue of a notice requesting submission of a return.

In July 2005 Lord Carter was asked to undertake a review of HMRC online services. Following the publication of the *Carter Report* the Government confirmed that it would accept Lord Carter's revised recommendations for self-assessment filing deadlines for 2007–08 and subsequent returns, namely 31 October for paper returns and 31 January for online returns.

Every partnership return must, under self-assessment, include a partnership statement, showing partnership income (and gains) less charges and allocating the resulting amounts between the partners. Except when HMRC is formally investigating a statement, the partnership has 12 months in which to amend it; HMRC may amend obvious errors. (Such amendments do not preclude penalty charges being imposed (see 2655) for the incorrect completion of the original return.) Any amendment of the partnership statement will be reflected by HMRC in each of the partners' self-assessments. For tax returns up to 2007–08, HMRC could give notice to the taxpayer at any time:

- within one year of the filing date, in respect of a return delivered on time (or amendment made within such time); or
- before the first quarter day (31 January, 30 April, 31 July or 31 October) falling more than 12 months after the return or amendment is made,

that the return or amendment is being investigated. This is also regarded as notice to each of the partners that their returns are being investigated.

Budget 2007 announced certain changes to the HMRC enquiry windows that affect individuals, trustees and partnerships which complete income tax self-assessment tax returns. Broadly, the changes link the period during which HMRC can enquire into returns to the date the return is received by HMRC. Under the new rules the enquiry window will close one year after delivery of the return. So where a return is received before the filing deadline the enquiry window will close earlier than under previous legislation.

Following the completion of HMRC's enquiries, the officer of the Board will issue a closure notice. This will either make amendments to the return or state that no amendment is necessary. The taxpayer may appeal against any amendment the officer makes.

For penalties for failure to make a return, see 2648.

See 2681 for details on time-limits for making assessments.

Law: TMA 1970, s. 12AA, 12AB, 12AC; former TMA 1970, s. 9

Website: www.hmrc.gov.uk/bulletins/index.htm

See *British Tax Reporter* ¶186-450.

2585 Personal representatives' return

Personal representatives (executors and administrators) of a deceased person are required to return estate income and gains on the trusts and estates return. They are also liable for the tax chargeable on the deceased at death. HMRC will, on request, issue a tax return before the end of the tax year in which death occurred and give early confirmation if they do not intend to enquire into that return. Personal representatives can also request such confirmation at any time before the expiry of the normal time-limit.

Source: Inland Revenue press release, 4 April 1996

See *British Tax Reporter* ¶186-400.

2588   Trustees' returns under self-assessment

The requirements for returns by trustees under self-assessment resemble those for individuals: the time-limit is the same, as is the requirement to return net amounts and to include a self-assessment based on those amounts (see 2564).

Notices are given, by an officer of the Board, for the purposes of establishing the amounts in which the following persons are chargeable to income tax and CGT, and the amount payable by them by way of income tax:

- the 'relevant trustees' (see below);
- the settlor or settlors; and
- the beneficiary or beneficiaries.

Notices may be given to any relevant trustee, or separate notices given to each relevant trustee, or to such of the relevant trustees as the officer thinks fit.

'Relevant trustees' are:

- for the purpose of trust income, any person who was a trustee at or after the time when the income arose;
- for the purpose of trust gains, any person who was a trustee during or after the tax year in which the gain accrued.

The relevant trustees are liable for any tax which falls due as a result of the self-assessment included in the return.

In the absence of a return, an officer of the Board may determine the amount of the relevant trustees' liability (see 2679). Similarly, an assessment may be made on the relevant trustees where a loss of tax is discovered (see 2680).

The usual penalties for failure to make a return, or for making an incorrect return, apply (see 2648, 2655).

Bare trusts under self-assessment

A 'bare trust' exists where the beneficial owner of the property held in trust is fully entitled to both the capital and the income from the property. Although the property is held in the trustee's name, the trustee has no discretion over what income to pay the beneficiary. The trustee is in effect a nominee in whose name the property is held. Trustees of such trusts are no longer expected to account for tax at the appropriate rate on income paid over to beneficiaries. Any income which is received gross by the trustees will be paid gross by them. In addition, trustees of bare trusts will not be required to complete self-assessment

Income Tax

returns or make payments on account. (However, they are entitled, if they so wish, to make a self-assessment return of income (not capital gains) and to account for tax on it at the appropriate rate.) Beneficiaries must include income and gains from these trusts in their returns.

Law: TMA 1970, s. 7(9), 8A(1), (5), 118(1)

Website: www.hmrc.gov.uk/bulletins/index.htm

See *British Tax Reporter* ¶185-700.

2589 EEIG's return

If a European Economic Interest Grouping is registered in Great Britain or Northern Ireland, an inspector may require an individual to make a return. The individual in point is the manager or any manager or, if the manager is not an individual, any individual designated as the representative of the manager.

If the grouping is not so registered, the inspector may require any UK-resident member(s) or, if none, any member(s) to make a return. The return must include a declaration that, to the best of the maker's knowledge it is correct and complete.

There are penalties on the grouping or members for failures to comply with the above.

Law: TMA 1970, s. 12A(8), 98B

See *British Tax Reporter* ¶596-200.

2590 Non-residents trading through UK representatives

In order to accommodate self-assessment, the regime for the taxation of non-residents trading through UK representatives (see 1672) was also modified for 1996–97 onwards (for corporation tax, from accounting periods beginning after 31 March 1996). In brief, the UK branch or agent is made jointly responsible with the non-resident trader for all that needs to be done in connection with self-assessment of the profits from or connected with the branch or agency.

Finance Act 2003 introduced a measure to change the term 'branch or agency' to 'permanent establishment' in relation to accounting periods beginning on or after 1 January 2003 (see 4500).

Law: FA 2003, s. 153; FA 1995, s. 126(9), 127(19)

See *British Tax Reporter* ¶765-100.

2591 Returns of tax deducted from annual payments

A person who is required to deduct basic rate income tax from a payment must account for it to HMRC (see 1372, 4954).

Where such a payment is made and tax is deducted from it, the person receiving the payment will need to show that the tax has been paid if he is not liable to tax and wishes to reclaim the tax deducted. The R185 provides the necessary evidence. The payments covered are:

- certain interest;
- annuities;
- rents;
- royalties;
- payments from a trust (if it is not a discretionary trust R185E should be used).

See *British Tax Reporter* ¶116-050.

2594 Returns by banks and other payers of interest

Any bank and every person carrying on a trade who receives or retains money on which interest becomes payable without deduction of tax must make a return of interest paid if so required by notice from an inspector. The return must include:

- the names and addresses of persons to whom the interest is paid or credited; and
- the amount of interest (if the interest did not exceed a given level it was ignored for this purpose during the existence of the arrangements before the basic rate of tax scheme: see 1372).

This only applies to money received or retained in the UK and, if the individual receiving the interest declares in writing that the person beneficially entitled to it is not ordinarily resident in the UK and asks for it to be left out of the return, then the person paying or crediting the interest will not be required to include it in any such return. A declaration of status to enable gross payment will often be sufficient as a declaration for this purpose also (see 1372).

Other payers

Similar provisions relate to the power of the inspector to call for information from other payers of interest without deduction of tax. This extends to individual payments rather than the more general requirement in relation to banks, etc.

Law: TMA 1970, s. 17, 18

See *British Tax Reporter* ¶181-750.

2597   Returns by persons of sundry payments

There are a number of returns which, albeit of a fairly rare nature, may be required by HMRC; these relate to the following:

(1)   persons in receipt of taxable income belonging to another, as respects income in the three years before the notice;

(2)   landlords in respect of the names and addresses of persons who have been lodgers or inmates;

(3)   persons paying non-employee' fees, commissions, etc. for services or in respect of copyrights, designs, etc.;

(4)   persons paying amounts for services of agency workers;

(5)   payments in respect of grants, subsidies, licences or approvals in relation to public funds and licences;

(6)   lessees, etc. in respect of lease terms;

(7)   issuing houses, stockbrokers, etc. in relation to chargeable gains from share transactions entered into with other parties (see 6431).

The Court of Appeal has held that auctioneers who received the proceeds of sale on behalf of farmers selling livestock were obliged to provide details of farmers selling livestock at auction, including amounts of money received by the auctioneers on their behalf, information requested by HMRC in notices under (1) above. The court rejected the auctioneers' argument that the gross sums received on behalf of the farmers could not properly be described as 'profits or gains' within the legislation as that phrase denoted a net amount after deduction of appropriate expenditure.

Law: TMA 1970, s. 13, 14, 16, 16A, 18A, 19; *Fawcett (HMIT) v Special Commrs and Lancaster Farmers Auction Mart Ltd* [1997] BTC 24

OTHER SOURCES OF INFORMATION

2621   Access to information generally

HMRC may require certain information from persons generally or from taxpayers in particular (see also 2624).

Under self-assessment, subject to appeal to the tribunal within 30 days, HMRC may call for 'documents' and such 'accounts' or 'particulars' as they may reasonably require (a provision bolstered by the penalties applicable for failure to keep certain records for a specified period: see 2657).

In relation to interest and other amounts paid and credited or received after 6 April 2001, HMRC's powers to request information about interest paid to or received from third parties are extended to apply to individuals who are not resident or ordinarily resident in the UK and to paying and collecting agents of quoted UK Eurobonds and foreign dividends. HMRC will have the power to audit the underlying documents that are used to provide the information so requested.

There are also certain restrictions in relation to permitting the taxpayer reasonable opportunity to deliver documents before reverting to third parties, to documents relating to the conduct of appeals, to notices to barristers and solicitors, etc. and as to time-limits. Barristers and solicitors, etc. may also be protected by the common law legal professional privilege (or, in Scotland, confidentiality). In one case a challenge to the validity of a notice requiring production of documents and particulars failed on the ground that it was not unreasonable for the inspector to suspect irregularities in a taxpayer's affairs if a close associate was known to have received undisclosed income (the burden was on the taxpayer to prove unreasonableness).

Even if 'public interest immunity' attaches to documents held by HMRC relating to a taxpayer's affairs, it does not, it seems, extend to tax documents held by a taxpayer who refuses to disclose them.

Orders for delivery of documents

As an alternative to a search warrant, from 28 July 2000 HMRC may issue an order for a delivery of documents. Such an order is intended to be used to obtain information from third parties who may have advised the individual or company suspected of fraud. The order must specify the documents to be supplied and can only cover documents that may be used in evidence in proceedings against the suspected offence.

HMRC are encouraged to use the orders in place of search warrants.

HMRC officers or officers of other government departments who carry out duties under the *National Minimum Wage Act* 1998, can use the information obtained for the assessment and collection of tax and the payment of tax credits.

It is a criminal offence intentionally to falsify or destroy documents called for by HMRC.

Law: FA 2008, s. 113–117 and Sch. 36–38; FA 2000, s. 148, 149, 150 and Sch. 39; TMA 1970, s. 17, 19A, 20, 20B, 20BA, 20BB, 20D, Sch. 1AA; *An Applicant v Inspector of Taxes* (1999) Sp C 189; *R v HMIT, ex parte Northern Bank Ltd* [1996] BTC 519; *Lonrho plc v Fayed* [1993] BTC 8,038; *Kempton (Executrix of J Kempton) v Special Commrs* [1992] BTC 553; *R v IR Commrs, ex parte T C Coombs & Co* [1991] BTC 89

See *British Tax Reporter* ¶180-500.

Income Tax

2624   Access to accountants' papers

Under normal circumstances, an auditor or tax adviser cannot be required to deliver or make available documents (see 2621) which are his property and relate to certain functions. This does not protect documents explaining information, returns, accounts or other documents assisting a client in preparing returns, etc.

HMRC's powers are wholly different where a tax accountant has committed a tax offence. In this case, an officer authorised by HMRC may require him to deliver 'documents' (other than 'personal records' or 'journalistic material') which may contain information relevant to any tax liability to which any client of his is or has been, or may be or may have been, subject. The officer must obtain consent from the 'appropriate judicial authority', e.g. a circuit judge.

HMRC have explained how they use their right of access to accountants' working papers.

It is a criminal offence intentionally to falsify or destroy documents called for by HMRC.

Law: FA 2008, s. 113–114 and Sch. 36; TMA 1970, s. 20A, 20B, 20BB

Source: SP 5/90, *Accountant's working papers*

See *British Tax Reporter* ¶181-200.

2627   Entry, search and seizure

HMRC can enter premises, by force if necessary, and search them where there is a serious case of suspected fraud. The Board must approve and the consent must be obtained of the 'appropriate judicial authority', e.g. a circuit judge.

In one case the Court of Appeal rejected a challenge to the validity of warrants issued under the above provision mounted on the ground (inter alia) that the officers authorised to enter premises were not named.

It is a criminal offence personally or by one's employee to obstruct or hinder the search.

Law: FA 2008, s. 113–114 and Sch. 36; TMA 1970, s. 20C

See *British Tax Reporter* ¶181-300.

2630   International exchange of information

HMRC have the power to exchange information with other countries under the mutual assistance directive, or with countries with whom the UK holds a double taxation agreement.

HMRC can also collect from and provide to other countries not covered by those agreements information on income tax, capital gains tax or corporation tax matters, provided the country in question is party to a tax information exchange agreement with the UK.

Law: FA 2000, s. 146; EC Directive 77/799 (mutual assistance directive)

See *British Tax Reporter* ¶170-000.

PENALTIES

2645   Penalties and determination thereof

There are a number of penalties which may be imposed under the Taxes Acts. The most common are penalties for failure to notify chargeability to tax and for failure to deliver a return (see 2648). There are also stringent penalties for careless or deliberate behaviour in submitting an incorrect return (see 2655).

Most penalties can be 'determined' by HMRC, subject to appeal to the tribunal; in other cases, the tribunal imposes any penalty on application from the Board of HM Revenue & Customs. Where a penalty is determined by HMRC, it becomes due 30 days from the issue of the appropriate notice; it is treated as tax and, if necessary, is a debt payable of a deceased person's estate. Where a penalty is imposed by the tribunal, any final assessment is evidence of the relevant liability in relation to which any offence has occurred. Penalties can only be imposed within a given time-limit specified within the legislation.

Penalties may be reduced from the maximum amounts according to the extent of co-operation and other factors, either by HMRC or on appeal; in this regard, the points set out below are relevant.

- In one case the High Court reduced the award of almost 100 per cent available penalties to 80 per cent. The court was concerned that the penalties imposed were out of line with those imposed by other panels of former general commissioners and the particular panel had not given reasons to support the high penalties.
- The courts have only limited discretion to alter penalties, so that where a taxpayer failed to appear at penalty proceedings because he did not appreciate that a document handed to him was a summons, the penalties had to stand.
- HMRC may legally (and often do in enquiry and investigation cases) enter into contract with taxpayers whereby potential liabilities for penalties, interest and outstanding tax are settled on payment of a specific sum. HMRC are prepared to apply error or mistake relief (see 2678) to such settlements even though there is no 'tax charged under an assessment' which is excessive, as demanded by the applicable legislation.

The taxpayer does not discharge his obligation to complete a return and is liable to a penalty if he inserts 'details to follow' or 'to be advised' against any entry.

Income Tax

Tax-geared penalties are not generally imposed in respect of the same amounts more than once.

Law: TMA 1970, s. 97A, 100–103; *IR Commrs v Nuttall* [1990] BTC 107; *Montague v General Commrs for Hampstead and IR Commrs* [1989] BTC 531; *Cox v General Commrs for Poole and IR Commrs* [1988] BTC 37; *Brodt v General Commrs for Wells and IR Commrs* [1987] BTC 186

See *British Tax Reporter* ¶194-000.

2646 Late payment of tax

From 6 April 2010 a new penalty regime applies for late payments of tax in the case of the following items:

- amounts payable under the PAYE regulations;
- construction industry scheme deductions; and
- tax charges payable by scheme administrators of registered pension schemes under FA 2004, Pt. 4.

Further instruments are expected in the future (expected to be from 1 April 2011) to make the penalties effective for late payments of other taxes and regimes.

Law: *Finance Act* 2009, Sch. 56; *Finance Act 2009, Schedule 56 (Appointed Day and Consequential Provisions) Order* 2010 (SI 2010/466)

2648 Failure to make returns on time

Under self-assessment, initial failure to comply with a notice to make a return (see 2564) attracts an automatic penalty of £100. The penalty increases to £200 if the failure continues for six months after the filing date. The penalty will be reduced to the amount of tax outstanding if the taxpayer can prove that it is less. At any time after the initial failure, HMRC may apply for a direction from the tribunal that the penalty should be anything up to £60 per day (displacing the further £100 above, if imposed within six months). If the tax remains outstanding for more than one year after the filing date, a further penalty may be imposed of an amount up to the outstanding tax.

The above penalties also extend to failures to make partnership returns. Failure of the representative partner generates the penalties, and each and every partner is liable for the penalties.

Reasonable excuse defence

The above penalty for failing to make a return (and the surcharge for late payment of tax: see 2764) can be avoided should the taxpayer have a 'reasonable excuse'. As a matter of law, inability to pay can never be regarded as a reasonable excuse for avoiding the surcharge for late payment. Apart from this, the only guidance on what may or may not constitute a reasonable excuse is found in HMRC self-assessment booklets. Each case, HMRC say, is considered on its own facts, and a strict view is taken, though appeal to the tribunal is possible. HMRC's general view is that a taxpayer only has a reasonable excuse where some exceptional event, beyond his control, prevents him from meeting the deadline in question.

The following are examples of what HMRC say they may accept as a reasonable excuse for missing the deadline for a return:

(1) where the deadline was not met because the taxpayer did not receive the return;

(2) where the return was posted in good time but an unforeseen event disrupted the postal service (e.g. prolonged industrial action within the Post Office) and led to the loss or delay of the return;

(3) where the taxpayer or tax adviser lost his records as a result of fire, flood or theft;

(4) where serious illness prevented the taxpayer from controlling his business and private affairs immediately before the deadline;

(5) where a close relative or domestic partner died shortly before the deadline, provided that the taxpayer had already taken any necessary steps to have the return ready on time;

(6) where the taxpayer's time and attention were preoccupied by the serious illness of a close relative or domestic partner during the period from the deadline to despatch of the return, provided that the taxpayer had already taken any necessary steps to have the return ready on time.

The following are examples of what HMRC say they will not accept as a reasonable excuse for missing the deadline for a return:

- the return is too difficult to complete;
- pressure of work;
- failure by the taxpayer's agent;
- the unavailability of certain information;
- absence of reminders from HMRC.

Law: FA 2009, s. 106–109, and Sch. 55–57; TMA 1970, s. 93A, 98A; *Frossell* [2010] TC 00392; *Chudusama* [2010] TC 00393; *Haque* [2010] TC 00394

See *British Tax Reporter* ¶194-150.

2652 End-of-year returns

Automatic penalties apply to delays by employers in sending end-of-year returns of pay, PAYE and National Insurance deductions in respect of employees (P14); the due date is 19 May (but see 2579 for a concession here). The penalty is £100 for every 50 persons whose particulars should be included on the return for each month of delay up to 12 months. If the number of employees is less than 50, the monthly penalty is £100.

> **Example**
>
> A P35 return covering 51 employees submitted on 20 June 200x attracts a penalty of
> £400: i.e. £100 for the first 50 employees, £100 for the further employee, £100 for one
> month's delay to 19 June and £100 for the further delay into the next month.

If the delay continues beyond 12 months, the penalty is up to 100 per cent of the tax unpaid
by 19 April after the end of the relevant tax year.

Where the automatic penalty would exceed the total tax and NICs due, it is normally
reduced to that amount or £100 if greater. This practice of mitigation is applied
automatically in appropriate cases, no application being needed by the employer.

For 2009–10 onwards employers and agents can use the HMRC online facility to declare
that they have no PAYE Employer Annual Return (P35 and P14s) to make.

Law: TMA 1970, s. 98A; *Income Tax (Pay As You Earn) Regulations* 2003 (SI 2003/2682)

Website: www.hmrc.gov.uk/paye/payroll/year-end/annual-return.htm#4

See *British Tax Reporter* ¶194-200.

2655 Incorrect returns

Finance Act 2007 contained provisions for a single new penalty regime for incorrect returns
for income tax, corporation tax, PAYE, NIC and VAT. Penalties are now determined by the
amount of tax understated, the nature of the behaviour giving rise to the understatement and
the extent of disclosure by the taxpayer. The new rules apply for errors made during
2008–09 and subsequent years.

The main concepts in the new provisions are as follows:

- the single penalty regime for incorrect returns replaces all existing penalty systems for
  incorrect returns for income tax, corporation tax, PAYE, the construction industry
  scheme, and VAT, as well as underpayments of NIC as a result of an error in one of
  those returns;
- the level of penalty will depend on the underlying behaviour of the taxpayer giving rise
  to the incorrect return, with a stepped and differentiated approach leading to a penalty
  from nil to 100 per cent. There will be statutory maximum and minimum penalties for
  each behaviour;
- all penalties are mitigable for disclosure, within a range. There is no provision for
  mitigation based on either co-operation or the seriousness of the offence;
- there is a new concept of 'suspended penalties' where the taxpayer can demonstrate that
  his compliance has improved over a specified period; and
- all penalties will be subject to the right of appeal.

Finance Act 2008 extended the new penalties for incorrect returns across most taxes, levies and duties, for incorrect returns for periods commencing from 1 April 2009 where the return is due to be filed from 1 April 2010.

Penalties are behaviour-related. Three categories are identified:

- careless (defined as failure to take reasonable care);
- deliberate, but not concealed; and
- deliberate and concealed.

The penalties have been designed so that people who take reasonable care when completing their returns will not be penalised. If they do not take reasonable care, errors will be penalised, and the penalties will be higher if the error is deliberate. Disclosing errors to HMRC early will substantially reduce any penalty due.

'Reasonable care' varies according to the person, the particular circumstances and their abilities. Every person is expected to make and keep sufficient records for them to provide a complete and accurate return. A person with simple, straightforward tax affairs needs only to keep a simple system of records, and these must be regularly and carefully updated. A person with larger and more complex financial tax affairs will need to put in place more sophisticated systems and maintain them equally carefully. HMRC believe it is reasonable to expect a person who encounters a transaction or other event with which he is not familiar, to take care to check the correct tax treatment, or to seek suitable advice. HMRC expect people to take their tax seriously.

FA 2007, Sch. 24, para. 4 sets out the maximum penalty payable for each type of behaviour, expressed as a percentage of the potential lost revenue. For the most serious category of 'deliberate understatement with concealment' the maximum penalty is in line with the current rate of 100 per cent. Penalties for the two less serious categories are lower – for behaviour which is deliberate but not concealed, the maximum is 70 per cent, and for 'careless' behaviour, the maximum is 30 per cent.

FA 2007, Sch. 24, paras 9 and 10 deal with the maximum reductions that may be obtained. These are summarised as follows:

Behaviour	Maximum penalty	Minimum penalty with unprompted disclosure	Minimum penalty with prompted disclosure
Careless	30%	0%	15%
Deliberate but not concealed	70%	20%	35%
Deliberate and concealed	100%	30%	50%

FA 2007, Sch. 24, para. 8 sets out provisions where an inaccuracy is one of timing rather than absolute tax loss. Where the payment has been delayed, e.g. as the result of an

611

inaccurate accounting adjustment, resulting in tax being paid in a later period, 5 per cent of the delayed tax is treated as lost revenue and is liable to the penalty. This is charged on an annual basis and pro-rated for part years.

Law: FA 2007, s. 97 and Sch. 24; TMA 1970, s. 95, 95A, 97, 98A(4), 99; *Rowland v Boyle (HMIT)*; *Stockler v R & C Commrs* [2009] EWHC 2306 (Ch)

See *British Tax Reporter* ¶194-250.

2657   Failure to maintain records

A person who may be required to submit a general return of income/gains, a trustee's return of income/gains or a partnership return of income/gains must, on penalty of an amount of up to £3,000, keep appropriate records; for a person carrying on a trade, profession or vocation or letting property, the records must be kept for some six years but otherwise the retention period is approximately two years, though this may be extended if enquiries are being made into a return or an amendment to a return.

The record-keeping requirement is normally satisfied by taking copies of the information or recording it in the business books, but vouchers, etc. showing that tax (domestic or foreign) has been suffered must be kept in their original form.

Record-keeping requirements currently vary from tax to tax. *Finance Act* 2008 contains provisions which pave the way for an aligned approach to record-keeping from a date to be announced.

Law: FA 2008, s. 115 and Sch. 37; TMA 1970, s. 12B; *Seafield General Store & Post Office v R & C Commrs* [2010] TC 00333

Website: HMRC Factsheet: www.hmrc.gov.uk/factsheet/record-keeping.pdf

See *British Tax Reporter* ¶194-250.

2658   Failure to comply with special return notice or produce documents

If a taxpayer fails to comply with a notice requiring him to make a return of particular income, he is liable to a penalty not greater than £300 plus £60 per day for each day the failure continues. If he delivers an incorrect return negligently or fraudulently, the penalty is up to £3,000.

Under self-assessment, HMRC have special powers to demand that the taxpayer produce certain documents to help with their enquiries into the taxpayer's self-assessment or amendments to it (see 2621). Failure to comply will result in an automatic penalty of £50 and, if the failure continues, HMRC may determine a further penalty or may apply to the tribunal to impose a stiffer penalty; the further penalty is of up to £30 per day if it is determined by HMRC or £150 per day if it is set by the tribunal (for determination, etc. see 2645).

Law: TMA 1970, s. 97AA, s. 98

See *British Tax Reporter* ¶194-250.

2659   Criminal offences

The various infringements attracting pecuniary penalties (see e.g. 2648–2658) should not be confused with criminal offences, which may result in public prosecutions, media publicity, fines or even imprisonment. The existence of the penalty provisions is no bar to criminal proceedings in respect of the same matter. In serious cases the criminal charge of 'cheating HMRC' may be brought. This is a wide common law offence which can carry a term of imprisonment or an unlimited fine on conviction.

Statutory criminal offences for which HMRC may prosecute include the following (see also 2624, 2627):

- making false returns;
- theft (e.g. of subcontractors certificates: see 2787);
- false accounting; and
- forgery.

A person who aids, abets, counsels or procures such an offence is liable to the same punishment as the person abetted, etc. Inciting, attempting or agreeing to commit such an offence is also punishable.

HMRC have issued a statement of their practice on seeking penalties where there is or might be a criminal prosecution of the offender.

HMRC have been given new powers to publish the names and details of people and businesses who are penalised for deliberately evading taxes in excess of £25,000. The change ensures consistency of treatment for tax fraud, whether investigated through civil or criminal proceedings.

Law: FA 2009, s. 94; *Forgery and Counterfeiting Act* 1981, s. 1, 3; TMA 1970, s. 104; *Theft Act* 1968, s. 1, 17; *Perjury Act* 1911, s. 5(b); *R v Dimsey & Allen* [1999] BTC 335; *R v Werner* [1998] BTC 202; *R v Mulligan* [1990] BTC 135; *R v Redford* [1988] BTC 5,252

Source: SP 2/88, *Civil penalties and criminal prosecution cases*

See *British Tax Reporter* ¶180-600.

Income Tax

ASSESSMENTS, DETERMINATIONS AND CLAIMS GENERALLY

2678   Nature of assessments and determinations

Assessments other than self-assessments are generally made by an 'officer of the Board' (see 2500) or, in some specialised circumstances, by the Board (for assessments relating to a return, see 2679; for those relating to discovery, see 2680). Determinations apply to income tax and CGT only under self-assessment and are made by an officer of the Board where a taxpayer fails to submit his return on time (see 2679).

An assessment is made when a certificate recording its entry in the assessment book is signed but may be properly made where an inspector, etc. exercises his discretion to make it and calculates the amount but leaves another person to complete the administration.

A notice of assessment must be served on the person assessed. This may be done by delivering it to him, usually by post, or sending it to his usual or last-known place of residence, his place of business or employment.

Once an assessment has been served it cannot be altered except on appeal. The burden is on the taxpayer to displace the assessment, not on the Crown to prove it.

The assessment becomes final unless an appeal is made in time (see 2846); but the Board can 'vacate' an assessment, upon a claim, if there has been a double charge to tax.

The Board may also give relief, upon a claim, where an assessment or self-assessment has been excessive due to some error or mistake in a return or, under self-assessment, a partnership statement; in practice such 'error or mistake' relief also applies to investigation settlements. HMRC will challenge an error or mistake claim where a substantive point was 'squarely in issue' when a taxpayer agreed a computation with HMRC. Appeals against the Board's decision on such a claim lies to the First-tier Tribunal. Further appeal (to the High Court or, in Scotland, the Court of Session) is only allowed in respect of a point of law arising in connection with the computation of income or chargeable gains.

Under 'equitable liability', HMRC will also refrain from collecting the full amount legally due where HMRC's status as a preferred creditor puts other creditors at a disadvantage; under self-assessment it will be rare that the taxpayer misses an opportunity to displace an officer's determination, but HMRC will still consider applying equitable liability.

An assessment (or determination: see 2679) is not void by reason of mistake, defect or omission where in substance and effect it conforms with the Taxes Acts. So if, for example, the taxpayer's second forename were misspelt the assessment would stand. However, this provision does not justify HMRC treating an assessment for one year as an assessment for a different year where an error in dates is made.

Cumulative assessments are void. However, in a case where HMRC had claimed a cumulative sum in respect of assessments which should have been in the alternative but had corrected the error by amending the writ to include one assessment for each year, the taxpayer had no arguable defence to a summary judgment order for recovery of tax due to the Crown.

Income tax chargeable in respect of income arising to the trustees of a settlement, or to the personal representatives of a deceased person may be assessed and charged on any one or more of the 'relevant' (see 2588) trustees or personal representatives.

Law: TMA 1970, s. 30A(3), (4), 32–33A, 114, 115; FA 1989, s. 151; former TMA 1970, s. 29(5), (6); *Honig v Sarsfield (HMIT)* [1986] BTC 205; *Brady (HMIT) v Group Lotus Car Companies plc* [1987] BTC 480; *Bird v IR Commrs; Breams Nominees Ltd v IR Commrs* [1988] BTC 164; *Baylis (HMIT) v Gregory* [1988] BTC 268; *Burford v Durkin (HMIT)* [1991] BTC 9; *IR Commrs v Wilkinson* [1992] BTC 297; *Eagerpath Ltd v Edwards (HMIT)* [1999] BTC 253

Source: HMRC *Brief* 16/10; Report of the Parliamentary Commissioner for Administration: 2nd report, Session 1989–90, Selected Cases 1990, vol. 1, HC 151 at pp. 51–62

Website: www.hmrc.gov.uk/bulletins/index.htm

See *British Tax Reporter* ¶185-450.

2679   Assessments and determinations relevant to returns

Apart from discovery assessments (see 2680), HMRC have powers to make estimated assessments or determinations by reference to the taxpayer's return (or his failure to make a return) or to adjust a taxpayer's self-assessment. For the nature of the assessment or determination, see 2678.

Self-assessment

Under self-assessment the duty of making assessments still generally falls on an officer of the Board of HM Revenue & Customs; however, the officer does not have to make an assessment if he accepts the taxpayer's own computation of his liability but, if he needs to do so, he can include income under every schedule in one assessment.

Enquiries
Indeed, the officer can enquire into aspects of the taxpayer's self-assessment and, if the taxpayer fails to amend the assessment to reflect the officer's opinion as to any discrepancy which will result in a loss of tax to the Crown, he can amend that assessment himself; on completion of his enquiries, the officer again has the chance to adjust the assessment to reflect final figures (see 2566). Similar rules apply to enquiries into a partnership statement (to be included with the partnership return: see 2582), amendments to which ripple through to the partners. If a taxpayer wishes to end the officer's enquiries, he can apply to the

Income Tax

tribunal for a direction to that effect; this will not necessarily prevent the officer later making a discovery of further profits (see 2680).

Determinations

Under self-assessment, an officer of the Board can also make a 'determination' of income or gains 'to the best of his information and belief' if the taxpayer fails to deliver the return on time; this does not relate to a partnership, since it is each partner who is responsible for the tax and the partnership return is entirely separate (for the filing date, see 2585, 2588). It is assumed that these determinations will have many of the characteristics of best-of-judgment assessments (see below).

Law: TMA 1970, s. 28A–28C, 30A(1), (2), (5); former TMA 1970, s. 29(1); *Blackpool Marton Rotary Club v Martin (HMIT)* [1990] BTC 3; *Billows v Robinson (HMIT)* [1990] BTC 95; *Bi-Flex Caribbean Ltd v Board of Inland Revenue (Trinidad and Tobago)* [1990] BTC 452

Source: HMRC *Brief* 16/10

See *British Tax Reporter* ¶185-450.

2680 Assessments where loss of tax discovered

Whether under self-assessment or otherwise, if an HMRC officer or the Board itself 'discovers' that:

- any profits have not been assessed which should have been assessed;
- an assessment is or has become insufficient; or
- any relief given is or has become excessive,

the officer, etc. or the Board may make an assessment of an amount which it is felt should be charged. However, under self-assessment, no such assessment will be made if the taxpayer acted honestly (i.e. there was no fraudulent or negligent conduct) and HMRC could reasonably have been expected to be aware of the deficiency when the officer concluded (or was treated as having concluded) his enquiries into the return nor if the return accorded with the basis prevailing at the time (or practice in relation thereto); notwithstanding the time-limit above, the assessment may be made at any time before HMRC's enquiries are treated as completed.

Under the self-assessment regime as it applies to partnerships, rules similar to those above apply in relation to a discovery in relation to the partnership statement (to be included with the partnership return: see 2582), amendments to which ripple through to the partners.

An officer who discovers an error of substance in an assessment can correct the error by a further assessment. In the past, the question of what is meant by 'discover' has been debated at length but it is now clearly established that the word in this context broadly means 'to find out'. A discovery may be made even where the taxpayer has made a full disclosure and the officer or inspector was originally in error. However, in some cases, HMRC do forgo arrears of tax due to official error (see 2758).

Once an assessment or additional assessment is made, either by agreement following an appeal or determined on appeal, the officer or inspector cannot make a new assessment on the same income for the same year even if he discovers a fresh point of law. In HMRC's view:

- if a point has been specifically agreed with HMRC or HMRC have agreed a computation containing a point which is both 'fundamental to the whole basis of the computation' and 'so fully described that its significance for the computation of the taxpayer's liability was clearly and immediately apparent', HMRC do not go back and raise a discovery assessment in respect of that point; by concession this extends to cases where, even though there is no determination of an appeal or decision on a claim, the point relates to agreement of the final figures for assessment purposes;
- otherwise, by concession, HMRC regard themselves as bound by their acceptance of a computation (as respects a claim or the proper amount of the assessment) if the view of the point implicit in the computation was based on a full and accurate disclosure of all the relevant facts and was a tenable view.

HMRC may, in particular, make a discovery assessment where:

'– profits or income have not earlier been charged to tax because of any form of fraudulent or negligent conduct;
– the inspector has been misled or misinformed in any way about the particular matter at issue;
– there is an arithmetical error in a computation which had not been spotted at the time agreement was reached, and which can be corrected by the making of an in date discovery assessment;
– an error is made in accounts and computations which it cannot reasonably be alleged was correct or intended, e.g. the double deduction from taxable profits of a particular item (say group relief).'

However, the CIOT and ICAEW have obtained the opinion of leading counsel that the point at issue does not have to be fundamental to the agreement of the relevant figures provided that all such facts as it is reasonable to regard as relevant to considering the point at issue were disclosed and either:

- the particular point had previously been raised expressly by the inspector, the taxpayer or the taxpayer's agent; or
- the point was so clearly presented that 'an ordinarily competent inspector' would have, or ought to have, taken it into account.

On 31 May 1996, HMRC published a paper containing guidance on the operation of discovery and disclosure under self-assessment. The paper makes it clear that where a taxpayer has made a self-assessment for the relevant chargeable period, HMRC can raise an assessment if there would otherwise be a loss of tax from the taxpayer's failure to make a complete disclosure of all the relevant facts relating to his liability to tax.

Income Tax

Statement of practice SP 01/06 sets out the circumstances in which HMRC will regard a taxpayer as having made full disclosure and gives assurance of finality in particular situations. The statement of practice confirms guidance issued to help taxpayers achieve finality when completing their returns and extends it to CTSA. The statement does not cover cases where a self assessment is insufficient due to fraud or negligent conduct by or on behalf of the taxpayer.

An additional assessment is not precluded by an agreement between a taxpayer and HMRC, settling a dispute in respect of an earlier assessment, if the information on which the agreement was based was misleading or incorrect.

A document entitled *Prosecution Policy of the Board of Inland Revenue* is available on HMRC's website.

Law: TMA 1970, s. 29, 30B; *Rouf v R & C Commrs* [2009] CSIH 6; *Cenlon Finance Co Ltd v Ellwood (HMIT)* [1962] AC 782; *Scorer (HMIT) v Olin Energy Systems Ltd* [1985] BTC 181; *R v IR Commrs, ex parte Preston* [1985] BTC 208; *Coy v Kime (HMIT)* [1987] BTC 66; *Gray (HMIT) v Matheson* [1993] BTC 76; *Momin & Ors v R & C Commrs* [2007] EWHC 1400 (Ch)

Source: SP 01/06; SP 8/91 *Discovery assessments*

Website: www.hmrc.gov.uk/prosecutions/prosecution-policy.htm

See *British Tax Reporter* ¶185-500.

2681   Time-limits for assessments

From 1 April 2010, the ordinary time-limit for making assessments reduced to four years after the end of the year of assessment. Prior to 1 April 2010, the latest date for making assessments was 31 January, which was five years and ten months after the end of the tax year; the date for amending a self-assessment was 31 January next following the tax year, almost 22 months after the end of the tax year.

There are a number of qualifications to the standard time-limit including:

(1) *Loss of tax brought about carelessly or deliberately.* Under self-assessment, an assessment on any person to make good loss of tax attributable to his careless or deliberate conduct or that of a person acting on his behalf may be made up to 31 January which is 20 years and ten months after the end of the tax year. In the case of partnerships, such an assessment may be made not only on the partner in default but on any of his individual co-partners. For the similar rules for corporation tax, see 4986. From 1 April 2010, the former concept of 'fraudulent or negligent conduct' was replaced with the concept of a loss of tax brought about carelessly or deliberately. The time-limits under the revised legislation however, remain as above.

(2) *Personal representatives.* Under self-assessment, assessments on personal

representatives in respect of income accruing to the deceased before his death cannot currently be made later than four years after the end of the year of assessment. See further 2585.

Law: FA 2008, s. 118 and Sch. 39, para 9; TMA 1970, s. 34, 36(1), (2), 40

Source: HMRC *Brief* 16/10

See *British Tax Reporter* ¶180-050.

2684   Nature of claims, elections and notices

Deductions are usually given automatically. Reliefs and allowances generally have to be claimed by the taxpayer in writing to HMRC; under self-assessment, most claims must, if possible, be made by way of inclusion in the tax return or an amendment to it and be quantified. Elections are generally treated in the same way but notices, originally within the scope of these provisions, are provided for in relation to each particular situation though notice generally means notice in writing.

Many of the rules relating to claims otherwise remain substantially the same under self-assessment:

- the claim may be made by a trustee, guardian, tutor or curator on behalf of an incapacitated taxpayer;
- if the claimant later discovers a mistake in his claim, a supplementary claim may be made within the time for making the original claim;
- where an assessment is adjusted in order to give effect to a claim, the assessment is not out of time if it is made within one year of the final determination of the claim.

Under self-assessment, claims for certain reliefs involving two or more years, for example loss carry-back, relief for fluctuating profits of farmers (see 942), carry-back of post-cessation receipts (see 662) and spreading back payments (see 592) – are effectively related to the later year so as to enable the earlier year's figures to be settled.

Those claims, elections and notices ('claims') which can be made under self-assessment otherwise than by way of the return and which do not relate to PAYE are subject to more stringent conditions than before that regime with regard to the matters set out below:

(1) Making of claims. The required form of claim will provide for the taxpayer to make a statutory declaration that it is correctly stated to the best of his information and belief. It may require a statement of the tax to be discharged or repaid (with documentary proof of payment in the latter case) and such information (being accounts, statements and documents) as is reasonably required to determine whether the claim is correct.

(2) Keeping and preserving records which may be required for the purposes of making a correct and complete claim.

(3) Amendment of claims. Except when HMRC are formally investigating a claim, the taxpayer has 12 months in which to amend it (HMRC may amend obvious errors).

(4) Power to enquire into claims. HMRC may give notice to the taxpayer at any time before the latest of the following:

    (a) the first quarter day falling more than 12 months after the claim is made (the quarter days are 31 January, 30 April, 31 July and 31 October);

    (b) where the claim or amendment relates to a tax year, the period ending with the first anniversary of 31 January next following that year; or

    (c) where the claim or amendment relates to a period other than a tax year, the period ending with the first anniversary of the end of that period.

(5) Power to call for documents for purposes of enquiries.

(6) Amendments of claims where enquiries made. Following the completion of HMRC's enquiries, the taxpayer has an opportunity to amend the claim within 30 days. HMRC have a further 30 days in which the claim can be amended. If a taxpayer wishes to end HMRC's enquiries, he can apply to the tribunal for a direction to that effect. HMRC have 30 days from any amendment to give effect to it and the taxpayer may, within that period, appeal against it. The tribunal may vary the amendment to the disadvantage of the taxpayer as well as to his advantage. HMRC again have 30 days in which to give effect to such variation.

However, various discretions have been removed. HMRC are no longer required to make a decision or take other action in relation to various provisions before an assessment can be made, the issues in point being reviewed in accordance with self-assessment procedures generally.

Law: ITTOIA 2005, s. 878(3); FA 1996, s. 130, 134; Sch. 20; ICTA 1988, s. 832(1); TMA 1970, s. 42(1)–(3), (5), 43A; Sch. 1A; *Savacentre Ltd v IR Commrs* [1995] BTC 365

See *British Tax Reporter* ¶184-200.

2687   Time-limits for claims

From 1 April 2010, the general time-limit for making claims is four years after the end of the year of assessment to which the claim relates.

For lists of time-limits for claims and elections, see 59 (income tax), 78 (corporation tax) and 86 (CGT).

Law: FA 2008, s. 118 and Sch. 39, para 12; TMA 1970, s. 43(1)

See *British Tax Reporter* ¶183-100.

PAYMENT AND INTEREST

2743 Procedure for paying tax

When tax becomes due and payable the collector (see 2500) issues a demand for the sum, which may be made on the person charged, or at the last place of abode, or on the premises in respect of which the tax is charged.

Payment can be made by cheque, it being generally considered propitious to include the taxpayer's reference number as part of the description of the payee (as regards the date of payment, see 2764).

Where credit cards payments are made to HMRC the fee payable is 1.25 per cent of the payment.

HMRC are able to offer the option of paying by direct debit for self-assessment tax payments, PAYE and corporation tax.

Many returns can now be filed over the Internet and tax paid electronically.

See *British Tax Reporter* ¶181-250.

Law: *Taxes, etc. (Fees for Payment by Telephone) Regulations* 2009 (SI 2009/3073); *Taxes (Fees for Payment by Internet) Regulations* 2008 (SI 2008/2991)

2748 Employers' payment of PAYE

In relation to PAYE, an employer is generally required to pay income tax deducted within 14 days of the end of every income tax month. However, where an employee receives a fixed salary or wage, HMRC can authorise the employer to deduct tax from each payment of emoluments by reference only to the amount of the payment (i.e. without regard to the cumulative emoluments and cumulative tax). In such a case, payment of tax deducted under PAYE is due quarterly (i.e. 19 July, 19 October, 19 January, 19 April).

Certain PAYE and other regular payments to HMRC may, if the employer so wishes, be made quarterly. The following conditions and procedures are relevant:

- the employer/contractor must reasonably believe that his average monthly payment due to HMRC for PAYE, NICs, and student loans recovered is £1,500;
- the decision to make quarterly payments can be made at any time in the year;
- any quarterly payments are for the quarters ending 5 July, 5 October, 5 January and 5 April and are payable within 14 days of the end of the quarter, i.e. by the nineteenth of these months;
- if the average monthly payments turn out to exceed the given limit in practice, the employer can continue to pay quarterly for the remainder of the tax year;
- a decision to pay quarterly only concerns the current tax year; a new decision must be

Income Tax

taken at the start of the next tax year, based on a reasonable estimate of the average monthly payment for that tax year;

- employers need not notify HMRC of their decision to pay quarterly, unless the collector of taxes issues a reminder or demand; the collector will normally only issue reminders or demands to employers, who can pay quarterly, if no payment has been made by a quarter payment date;

- the starter pack for new employers will ask them to notify the collector if they have chosen to pay quarterly; and

- the payment books will have monthly pay slips; employers paying quarterly should use the pay slip for the last month in the quarter.

HMRC are able to offer the option of paying by direct debit for self-assessment tax payments, PAYE and corporation tax.

Law: *Income Tax (Pay As You Earn) Regulations* 2003 (SI 2003/2682)

See *British Tax Reporter* ¶496-450.

2750   PAYE settlement agreements

PAYE settlement agreements (PSAs) allow employers to account for any tax liability in respect of their employees on benefits and expense payments that are minor or irregular, or that are shared benefits on which it would be impractical to determine individual liability, in one lump sum. A statement of practice (SP 5/96) explains how PAYE settlement agreements operate.

National Insurance due in relation to items included with a PSA can be settled in a similar way to the tax by means of Class 1B contributions.

For interest on late payments, see 2764.

Law: ITEPA 2003, s. 703–707; *Income Tax (Pay As You Earn) Regulations* 2003 (SI 2003/2682)

See *British Tax Reporter* ¶495-000.

2755   Postponement of tax pending appeal

Where HMRC make an assessment, tax generally becomes due and payable on the date shown in the table at 58 despite an appeal by the taxpayer. However, if an application to postpone tax is also made by the taxpayer, some deferment in the due date may be obtained. The general rule is that an application to postpone payment must be made by a taxpayer within 30 days after the date of the issue of the notice of assessment. That 30-day period is extended if there is a change in the circumstances of the case as a result of which the appellant has grounds for believing that he is overcharged to tax by the assessment.

In appealing from the determination of the tribunal to the courts, tax must first be paid in accordance with that determination.

Law: TMA 1970, s. 55, 56(9)

See *British Tax Reporter* ¶187-150.

2758   Arrears of tax due to official error

In certain circumstances, by concession, arrears of tax are wholly or partly waived if the arrears have arisen due to official error in utilising the information supplied by the taxpayer (or in certain circumstances by an employer).

Source: ESC A19, *Giving up tax where there are Revenue delays in using information*

See *British Tax Reporter* ¶181-200.

2761   Tax deposit certificates

A taxpayer may provide in advance for the payment of most taxes (except PAYE and corporation tax). This can be done by making deposits at any tax collecting office. The first payment must not be less than £2,000 and any subsequent deposit (which must not be less than £500) must maintain the total sum on deposit at or above £2,000.

The advantage in making such deposits lies partly in the fact that interest is paid by HMRC at attractive rates. (In fact two basic rates of interest apply: a lower rate applying where the deposit is withdrawn for cash and a higher rate applying where the sums are utilised in the payment of tax.) The rates of interest change regularly. Full details of current rates and information on how to use certificates of tax deposit are on the HMRC website at www.hmrc.gov.uk/payinghmrc/cert-tax-deposit.htm.

Rates of interest in force at the date of deposit apply to the amount deposited for the first two years. Thereafter, the rates of interest are those applicable on the second and fourth anniversaries of the deposit. Interest is paid for a maximum of six years.

Deposits may also be sent to the Bank of England (for the General Account of the Commissioners of Inland Revenue, No. 23411007) where the sum is not less than £100,000. The remittance should indicate that it is intended for a Certificate of Tax Deposit and a confirmatory letter should be sent to the Central Accounting Office stating the name and address of the depositor and the date and amount of the remittance.

Deposits may be withdrawn for cash at any time in such order as the depositor requires. Generally, requests for withdrawal should be made to the Central Accounting Office.

One spouse is not able to use a certificate to settle a tax liability of the other spouse.

Income Tax

Law: FA 1995, s. 157

Website: HMRC: www.hmrc.gov.uk/payinghmrc/cert-tax-deposit.htm

See *British Tax Reporter* ¶336-450.

2764   Interest on overdue tax

Interest is charged on income tax (and CGT) which is overdue for payment.

Where tax is paid by cheque, the effective date of payment is the day when HMRC receive it. (The exception to this is where the payment is received by post following a day when the tax office is closed (for whatever reason), in which case the effective date of payment is the day the office was first closed. This means that payments received on Monday are treated as being made the previous Saturday.)

Where payment is made by electronic funds transfer (EFT), BACS or CHAPS, payment is treated as made one working day immediately before the date the value is received. Where payment is by Bank Giro or Giro Bank, it is treated as made three working days prior to the date of processing by HMRC.

Adjustments of interest charged may be made where a relief from tax is subsequently agreed.

Interest is chargeable on unpaid PAYE; before that date interest could run only in respect of a formal determination on the employer.

For rates of interest and interest factor tables, see 15, 30.

When interest starts to run

Interest runs on amounts due and payable under self-assessment from the 'relevant date' until the actual date of payment as follows:

- on the two required payments on account based on the previous year's assessment (adjusted to take into account any overpayment and, to the extent that the taxpayer has claimed a reduction, any underpayment), from 31 January in the tax year and 31 July immediately after the end of that year – the date they become due and payable;
- on the balance of the liability shown by any self-assessment, from 31 January which is ten months after the end of the tax year (or, where the individual gave notice of his liability to tax by 5 October following the end of the tax year but was not asked to make a return until after 31 October, three months after receiving the request) – the date it becomes due and payable; and
- in respect of additional tax resulting from an amendment of a self-assessment (whether or not it becomes due following a postponement application), the same day as in respect

of the liability shown by the self-assessment (above) or, if later, 30 days after notice of the amendment is given (see 2679).

Surcharges

There is also a surcharge under self-assessment, which itself carries interest. Where tax is due in accordance with a person's self-assessment or an amendment to it – the second and third categories, above – there is a maximum surcharge of five per cent of the unpaid tax (less amounts instead attracting a penalty) if the amount remains outstanding for more than 28 days; this is increased to ten per cent in respect of any of the tax debt which becomes more than six months old. The surcharge attracts interest from 30 days after it is imposed. The taxpayer can appeal against the surcharge in the usual manner and the tribunal may set it aside if it appears to them that the taxpayer had a reasonable excuse throughout the period of default for not paying; inability to pay is not a reasonable excuse. Each case, HMRC say, is considered on its own facts, and a strict view is taken.

Discovery

If HMRC amend a return (see 2566, 2679) or discover further profits (see 2680), the increased amount is deemed always to have been the proper amount due, so interest will flow on that amount from the due date. Similar adjustments apply if the payments on account for the year affected by the discovery assessment also need adjustment: this will be the case where there has been a claim to reduce the amount of the payments on account.

Law: TMA 1970, s. 59C, 70A, 86, 91; *Income Tax (Sub-contractors in the Construction Industry) Regulations* 1993 (SI 1993/743), reg. 10(5); *Income Tax (Pay As You Earn) Regulations* 2003 (SI 2003/2682); *McMullan v R & C Commrs* (2009) TC 00305

Website: www.hmrc.gov.uk/sa/surcharges.htm

See *British Tax Reporter* ¶193-500.

2770 Interest on overpaid income tax: 'repayment supplement'

There is provision for the payment of interest (also called repayment supplement) on delayed tax repayments which is free of all forms of tax. An overpayment of £10 or less will be informally adjusted unless the taxpayer requests otherwise.

Under self-assessment, the date varies according to the nature of the payment: essentially this allows for different due dates in respect of payments on account, a penalty or surcharge and other income tax – broadly, it is the date the tax is actually paid, even if this is earlier than the due date. Where a repayment is due to the taxpayer but HMRC commence an enquiry (see 2566, 2679), repayment is deferred until the enquiries have been completed but may, before then, be made on a provisional basis to the extent that the officer sees fit.

Interest is receivable on overpaid PAYE in certain circumstances.

A supplement will be added to tax repayments made to an individual for a tax year in which he or she is resident in an EU member state, other than the UK, on the same basis as applies to UK residents.

For rates of interest and interest factor tables, see 15, 30. For when tax is paid, see 2764.

Law: ICTA 1988, s. 824; TMA 1970, s. 59B(4A); *Income Tax (Pay As You Earn) Regulations* 2003 (SI 2003/2682)

Source: SP 6/95, *Legal entitlement and administrative practices*

See *British Tax Reporter* ¶181-550.

COLLECTION

2775 Methods of collection

There are two basic methods of collecting tax:

- by direct assessment; and
- by deduction of tax at source.

Tax deduction at source is employed in relation to a number of sources of income, e.g. some annual payments (see 1368–1370), interest (see 1372), dividends, PAYE (see 2784), the subcontractors scheme (see 2787).

See *British Tax Reporter* ¶192-800.

2784 PAYE

The main method of collecting tax where emoluments are charged under the charge on income from employment provisions is by means of the pay as you earn ('PAYE') scheme. The scheme imposes upon the employer the duty to deduct tax from emoluments of his employees at the time when the emoluments are paid and to account for, and pay, the deductions to HMRC. The employer, in effect, acts as tax collector for HMRC. Failure to deduct tax may make the employer liable to pay the tax, and he may be subject to penalties. For the payment system, see 2748.

In future HMRC will be allowed to collect small debts owed through PAYE. This is likely to begin from April 2012.

For PAYE purposes, an 'employer' includes any person paying emoluments or controlling/managing the worker. This might bring agency workers within its scope (see 260) and, even if a taxpayer pays a worker, control and management by another person (the principal employer) might make that person the deemed employer.

If tax should have been deducted by the employer under PAYE, in certain cases, HMRC may be unable to impose a charge directly on the employee.

Employers are not obliged to operate PAYE on cash payments to employees in respect of qualifying removal expenses which are taxable only because they exceed the £8,000 exemption (see 298). Retirement benefit scheme annuities and personal pension annuities are subject to PAYE.

Various indirect arrangements are treated as within the scope of PAYE and these include payments made by an intermediary, income in the form of a 'readily convertible asset' (e.g. gold bars, coffee beans, etc.), non-cash vouchers which are either exchangeable for tradeable assets or are themselves tradeable assets, credit-tokens to obtain money or tradeable assets, cash vouchers and payments of shares to employees (but not payments under approved share schemes); regulations may govern how employers are to account for PAYE on certain notional payments.

Briefly, the system operates to take account of a proportion of the employee's entitlement to reliefs and allowances when tax is deducted. This is done by providing the employer with a series of tables and by notifying him of the relevant code number applying to a particular employee. The tables set out the cumulative allowances and the cumulative tax applying to the employee.

Negative (or 'K') codes are designed to enable income tax on benefits in kind, where the value of the benefits exceeds the employee's personal allowances, to be collected through the PAYE system, rather than by assessment at the end of the tax year. The system contains an overriding limit on the amount of tax which may be deducted from a payment of emoluments so as to ensure that the tax liability does not exceed 50 per cent of the employee's pay.

The system of coding is designed to allow to be taken into account the great variety of possible allowances and reliefs to which an employee might be entitled without actually informing the employer of the employee's reliefs' entitlement. Notice of the code determined by HMRC is given to the employer by a code authorisation and, if it differs from the code notified in the preceding year, the employee is also notified. The employee may appeal against such notice of coding.

The exact code depends on the employee's personal circumstances. Where these change during the year, the employee should inform HMRC so that his code can be altered accordingly.

The coding system can, of course, only approximate the tax position of each individual. An assessment might be used to make an adjustment at the end of the year (though in many cases there is no need for a formal assessment). If there has been an overpayment of tax, this is repaid by HMRC (subject to a de minimis limit: see 2770). Any underpayment of tax is usually taken into account in the following year's coding, a matter specifically incorporated into the self-assessment regime. Tax underpayments can be collected via the PAYE coding

Income Tax

system if the underpayments is less than £2,000 and the tax return is submitted by 31 October after the end of the tax year.

The code notified to the employer must be the one used by him. He must also keep records on a deductions working sheet regarding payments made to the employee, cumulative tax, etc. Where there is no code notification (e.g. in the case of a school-leaver who has not previously been employed) the emergency code must be used and HMRC informed (by making a return on P46) of the necessary particulars (see further 2573).

Joiners/leavers and casuals

When an employee leaves his employment he is given a P45 by his employer which will show, inter alia, the last entries on the deductions working sheet kept by him. The form is handed to the departing employee's new employer which will enable him to make the correct tax deductions. There is the amount of £200 which:

- an employer may repay to a new employee, when making the first wage/salary payment, without reference to HMRC, and
- must be notified by the Department of Work and Pensions to HMRC (and which must not be repaid without his authority) as a repayment due to an unemployed person in receipt of social security benefits, some of which are taxable.

In the case of casual employees, where the PAYE system cannot be operated, HMRC may make an estimated assessment on the employee or else he may issue a deductions working sheet to the employee who then deducts tax from his emoluments (and pays it to HMRC) as if he were his own employer. Certain overseas farm students can be supplied with a P38(S), which should be completed and handed to the farmer employing them; receipt of the P38(S), which the farmer should retain, will enable the farmer to pay students without deducting tax.

Troncs

Certain organised arrangements fall within the scope of the 'tronc' system which require PAYE to be deducted by the 'tronc master' (see 285). If the tronc master fails to do this, the responsibility falls on the principal employer. The Court of Appeal has held that the directors of a restaurant company who shared out the waiters' tips at the end of the week between themselves and the waiters were acting as officers of the company and the company was the person responsible for operating PAYE.

Note that in the case of Annabel's restaurant and nightclub, the Employment Appeal Tribunal held that tips and gratuities may not count towards a worker's earnings for the purposes of making wages meet the minimum wage payment requirement. Thus an employer must pay his staff the national minimum wage (NMW) regardless of the tips and gratuities they may receive. However, any tips paid through the employer's payroll will not be exempt and will count towards earnings for NMW purposes.

Student loans

From April 2000, employers have been responsible for collecting repayments of income contingent student loans through the PAYE system when notified by HMRC that repayments should be collected in respect of a particular employee. Broadly, deductions are made in respect of student loan repayment when a start notice (SL1) has been received from HMRC at the rate of nine per cent on income above £15,000 a year (£10,000 prior to 6 April 2005). The repayments are determined for each pay period on a non-cumulative basis. Tables are provided in the annual pack, which can be used to determine the amount of the repayment to be deducted. The repayments deducted are paid over to HMRC with PAYE tax and National Insurance.

Law: FA 2009, s. 110 and Sch. 58; ITEPA 2003, 684–707; TMA 1970, s. 59A(10), 59B(8); *Income Tax (Pay As You Earn) Regulations* 2003 (SI 2003/2682); *Andrews v King (HMIT)* [1991] BTC 338; *Figael Ltd v Fox (HMIT)* [1992] BTC 61; *Booth v Mirror Group Newspapers plc* [1992] BTC 455; *IR Commrs v Herd* [1993] BTC 245

Source: SP A21; CSL, *Collection of student loans, employer's guide*

See *British Tax Reporter* ¶493-000.

2787　Construction industry tax deduction scheme

The Construction Industry Scheme (CIS) first came into operation in 1971. However, extensive amendments were made in 1975 and full operation of the revised scheme commenced from 6 April 1977. Problems within the industry regarding the scheme continued to arise and led to certain changes contained in the Finance Acts 1995 and 1996.

A consultation paper was published in the 2002 Pre-Budget Report, proposing major reform of the scheme and the resulting legislation is now contained in the Finance Act 2004 and the regulations (SI 2005/2045). The proposals included replacing existing documentation with a verification service run by HMRC, periodic returns and a new employment status declaration. It was originally planned that the new scheme would come into effect from April 2006, but this was subsequently delayed until 6 April 2007.

Broadly, the CIS is a quasi PAYE system designed to counter tax evasion in the construction industry by imposing responsibility for making a deduction at source from payments made for labour services provided by self-employed building subcontractors and companies unless those persons have received prior certification from HMRC. The CIS, however, is not, and never has been, a system designed to replace the PAYE system with respect to the employees of firms in the construction industry. This is a common misconception brought about partly by the way in which HMRC have operated the scheme in practice. Nevertheless, since its inception, PAYE auditors have been charged with the responsibility for ensuring that the scheme is being operated properly by building contractors and many of the regulations providing the rules for operating the scheme have parallels within the PAYE regulations.

Income Tax

CIS from 6 April 2007

The main changes under the new CIS are as follows:

- CIS cards, certificates and vouchers no longer exist;
- contractors must check or 'verify' new subcontractors with HMRC;
- subcontractors are still to be paid either net or gross, depending on their own circumstances, but it is HMRC who tell the contractor which treatment to use during verification;
- there is a higher rate tax deduction if a subcontractor cannot be 'matched' on the HMRC system. This rate applies until the subcontractor contacts HMRC and registers or sorts out any matching problem;
- there are no CIS annual returns under the new scheme;
- contractors must make a return every month to HMRC, showing payments made to all subcontractors. Contractors must declare on their return that none of the workers listed on the return are employees. This is called a status declaration;
- Nil returns must be made when there are no payments in any month. These can be made over the telephone as well as via the Internet or on paper;
- the vast majority of subcontractors registered under the old CIS rules will be transferred over to the new system and will not have to re-register; and
- new subcontractors are required to register with HMRC.

Employment status

Under the CIS, contractors must check or 'verify' new subcontractors with HMRC. Broadly, this means that HMRC will check the employment status of the subcontractor and ensure that he is properly registered for income tax and National Insurance contributions (NICs) purposes.

A worker's employment status, that is whether they are employed or self-employed, is not a matter of choice. Whether someone is employed or self-employed depends upon the terms and conditions of the relevant engagement. The tax and NICs rules do, however, contain some special rules that apply to certain categories of worker in certain circumstances. A worker's employment status will determine the charge to tax on income from that employment or self-employment. It will also determine the class of NICs, which are to be paid.

HMRC provide an 'Employment Status Indicator (ESI) Tool' on their website. Employers and contractors may use the tool to obtain a HMRC 'view' of the employment status of their workers. It should be noted that the tool will provide a general guide only which would not be binding on HMRC. To obtain a written 'opinion' of employment status in the construction industry the contractor will need to telephone the New CIS Helpline on 0845 366 7899.

Payments to subcontractors

There are certain requirements that a contractor must fulfil before payments can be made to subcontractors.

Verification

Verification is the process HMRC use to make sure that subcontractors have the correct rate of deduction applied to their payments under the CIS. There are three main steps to the process:

- The contractor contacts HMRC with details of the subcontractor.
- HMRC check that the subcontractor is registered with them.
- HMRC tell the contractor what rate of deduction to apply, if any.

Before a contractor can make a payment for construction work to a subcontractor, they must decide whether they need to verify the subcontractor.

The general rule is that a contractor does not have to verify a subcontractor if they last included that subcontractor on a return in the current or two previous tax years.

If a contractor does not have to verify a subcontractor they must pay the subcontractor on the same basis as the last payment made to them. This means that if the subcontractor was last paid under the standard rate of deduction, the current payment must also be made under the standard rate of deduction. If the last payment was made gross, because a deduction was not required, the current payment must also be made gross.

Monthly returns

Each month, contractors must send HMRC a complete return of all payments made to all subcontractors within the CIS in the preceding tax month. This is regardless of whether the subcontractors were paid gross or net of either the standard or higher deduction. Monthly returns must reach HMRC within 14 days of the end of the tax month they are for. Returns may be made electronically or by post.

Contractors who have not paid any subcontractors in a particular month must submit a 'Nil return'.

It is possible to correct entries on a monthly return. Full details of how this may be done are set out in Chapter 4 of the HMRC booklet CIS340.

Contractors must pay the amount deductible from payments to subcontractors to HMRC Accounts Office monthly. They must pay deductions due to be made in each tax month within 14 days of the end of that month or within 17 days where payment is made electronically, whether or not these deductions have actually been made. This means that where a required deduction has not actually been made from the subcontractor's payment, for whatever reason, the contractor is still responsible for paying that amount over to HMRC.

There are no annual returns within the CIS. Contractors that are required to submit an Employer's Annual Return on form P35 should remember to include on that form the total amount of CIS deductions they are due to pay so they can reconcile the total payments made during the year.

Income Tax

Registration

Subcontractors who were registered under the previous CIS (before 6 April 2007) do not need to need to register for the new CIS if they, or their business, had one of the following:

- a tax certificate CIS5, CIS5(Partner) or CIS6; or
- a permanent registration card CIS4(P); or
- a temporary registration card CIS4(T) with an expiry date of 04/2007 or later.

New subcontractors starting working in the construction industry on a self-employed basis should register for new CIS if they do not want deductions at the higher rate made from their payments.

HMRC will only authorise a contractor to make gross payments to a subcontractor where the following conditions are satisfied.

Tax will be deducted at the rate of 20 per cent for registered subcontractors and at 30 per cent if the subcontractor is not registered.

The business test

To satisfy this condition, the subcontractor must provide evidence that he is carrying on a business in the United Kingdom which:

(a)   consists of or includes the carrying out of construction operations or the furnishing or arranging for the furnishing of labour in carrying out construction operations, and

(b)   is, to a substantial extent, carried on by means of an account with a bank.

Evidence prescribed to satisfy the business test is as follows:

- the business address;
- invoices, contracts or purchase orders for construction work carried out by the applicant;
- details of payments for construction work;
- the books and accounts of the business; and
- details of the business bank account, including bank statements.

The turnover test

The applicant must satisfy HMRC that in the year following the making of the application:

- as an individual, his net business turnover from construction work (that is, after the cost of any materials used to earn that income) is £30,000 a year or more; or
- as a partnership or company, the net business turnover from construction work (that is, after deducting the cost of any materials) is £30,000 a year or more multiplied by the number of partners or directors.

In the case of 'close companies' (broadly, companies controlled by five or fewer individuals), the figure will be multiplied by the number of individuals who are directors and/or shareholders. For a husband and wife team, for instance, it would be £60,000.

An alternative test for partnerships and companies is that the business has an annual net turnover from construction work (after deducting the cost of materials) of £200,000 or more.

The compliance test

The subcontractor must have kept all tax affairs up to date during the 'qualifying period' (the period of 12 months ending with the date of the application in question). This means he must have paid all tax liabilities, including any PAYE and subcontractor deductions, and submitted all tax returns on time. HMRC will not accept an application from a subcontractor who brings his tax affairs up to date just prior to submitting that application. Having said that, regulations do allow applicants to pass the compliance test even though they have failed to pay their tax bill, or have paid late, provided that amount is small.

CIS online

Contractors can file online using HMRC's CIS Online service. Contractors can use CIS Online to file monthly returns and perform verifications over the Internet. Agents that administer CIS payments on behalf of contractors can use the PAYE/CIS Online for Agents service.

Law: FA 2004, s. 70 and 71; *Finance Act 2004, Section 61(2), (Relevant Percentage) Order 2007* (SI 2007/46); *Finance Act 2004, Section 77(1) and (7), (Appointed Day) Order 2006* (SI 2006/3240); *Income Tax (Construction Industry Scheme) (Amendment) Regulations 2010* (SI 2010/717); *The Income Tax (Construction Industry Scheme) (Amendment) Regulations 2009* (SI 2009/2030); *The Income Tax (Construction Industry Scheme) Regulations 2005* (SI 2005/2045), reg. 7, 27, 28; *Enderbey Properties Ltd* [2010] TC 00396; *Leeds Lifts Ltd v R & C Commrs* (2009) TC 00231; *Jonathan David Ltd v R & C Commrs* (2009) TC 00233; *A Longworth & Sons Ltd v R & C Commrs* (2009) TC 00230; *Mutch v R & C Commrs* (2009) TC 00232; *Munns v R & C Commrs* (2009) TC 00234; *Strongwork Construction Ltd v R & C Commrs* (2009) TC 00236; *Prior Roofing Ltd v R & C Commrs* (2009) TC 00246; *Ductaire Fabrication Ltd v R & C Commrs* (2009) TC 00288; *Castle Construction (Chesterfield) Ltd v R & C Commrs* (2008) Sp C 723; *Oriel Support Ltd v R & C Commrs* (2007) Sp C 615; *R & C Commrs v Smith* [2007] EWHC 488 (Ch); *Neil Martin Ltd v R & C Commrs* [2007] EWCA Civ 1041

Website: www.hmrc.gov.uk/calcs/esi.htm;
www.hmrc.gov.uk/ebu/cis-online.htm

See *British Tax Reporter* ¶282-450.

RECOVERY

2801 Choice of recovery methods

Unpaid tax may be recovered by the Crown in the following ways:

- by levying distress upon the lands or goods of the person in default (see 2804);
- by action to recover the debt through court proceedings (see 2807);
- by bankruptcy proceedings (see 2822).

Any tax mistakenly repaid to a taxpayer may be recovered (together with any repayment supplement) by an assessment as if it were unpaid tax. The assessment must be made before the end of the chargeable period following that in which the amount assessed was repaid (except in the case of fraudulent or negligent conduct: see 2681). Such assessment will not be made if the taxpayer acted honestly (i.e. there was no fraudulent or negligent conduct) and HMRC could reasonably have been expected to be aware of the mistake when they concluded (or were deemed to have concluded) their enquiries, nor if the return accorded with the basis prevailing at the time (or practice in relation thereto); notwithstanding the time-limit above, the assessment may be made at any time before HMRC's enquiries (see 2566, 2679) are deemed to be completed.

Special provisions ensure that tax not deducted from certain payments (notably wages and salaries) made by government departments, and not otherwise recoverable, can be obtained from them.

HMRC will consider all reasonable offers of payment of tax in arrears, including payment in instalments.

Law: TMA 1970, s. 30

Source: Financial Secretary to the Treasury, *Hansard*, 8 February 1993

See *British Tax Reporter* ¶192-850.

2804 Distraint

The collector in England, Wales and Northern Ireland can distrain upon the land in respect of which tax is charged or upon the goods of any person charged where that person neglects or refuses to pay tax charged upon him and demanded from him. Interest on tax is treated as if it is tax charged, due and payable under the assessment; under self-assessment penalties and surcharges are also included. The distress levied by the collector may be sold by public auction and the costs and charges of distress may be retained by the collector from the proceeds.

The collector may break into premises in the daytime for the purpose of levying distress if he is in the possession of a warrant issued by a justice of the peace.

Similar provisions apply in Scotland as to recovering tax by poinding the goods of the defaulter.

Law: TMA 1970, s. 61, 63, 69

See *British Tax Reporter* ¶192-900.

2807 Court proceedings

Court proceedings to recover unpaid tax may be instituted in the magistrates' court (in England, Wales and Northern Ireland), the county court (or the sheriff court, in Scotland), or the High Court (the Court of Session sitting as the Court of Exchequer, in Scotland).

In certain cases an appeal can be lodged to the Court of Appeal in respect of county court proceedings for the recovery of tax. From 1 October 1991, leave of a Court of Appeal judge must be obtained if the value of the appeal is £5,000 or less.

Magistrates' court

Under self-assessment, tax which is due and payable and is less than £2,000 or, if payable by instalments or on account, where the sum due and payable in respect of any instalment or payment on account is less than £2,000, is recoverable summarily as a civil debt by proceedings in the magistrates' court commenced in the name of the collector.

Any tax due from one person to any one collector, and which is recoverable summarily, may be included in the same complaint, summons, order, warrant or other document required by law to be laid before the justices.

Under self-assessment, proceedings for the recovery of income tax charged may be brought in England and Wales at any time within one year from the time when the matter complained of arose (the usual time-limit for bringing summary proceedings is six months from the time that the tax became due).

County court and High Court

Where the amount of tax due and payable does not exceed the county court limit (or, in Scotland, the sheriff courts limit), it may be sued for as a debt due to the Crown. The action is brought in the name of the collector.

Tax may also be sued for and recovered in the High Court (or, in Scotland, the Court of Session) as a debt due to the Crown.

Proceedings for recovery of tax due to the Crown may be pursued under the Rules of the Supreme Court. In a case where HMRC had claimed a cumulative sum in respect of assessments which should have been in the alternative (see 2678) but had corrected the error by amending the writ to include one assessment for each year, the taxpayer had no arguable defence to such proceedings.

Law: TMA 1970, s. 65–68; *County Court Appeals Order* 1991 (SI 1991/1877); *Income Tax (Pay As You Earn) Regulations* 2003 (SI 2003/2682); *IR Commrs v Wilkinson* [1992] BTC 297

See *British Tax Reporter* ¶193-000.

2810 Evidence and pleadings

A written statement as to the wages, salaries, fees, and other earnings or amounts treated as earnings paid for any period to the person against whom proceedings are brought under TMA 1970, s. 65, 66 or 67, purporting to be signed by his employer for that period or by any responsible person in the employment of the employer, will be accepted prima facie as evidence that the wages, salaries, fees and other earnings or amounts treated as earnings therein stated to have been paid to the person charged have in fact been so paid.

Law: TMA 1970, s. 70; *Limitation Act* 1980, s. 37(2)(a); *Rules of the Supreme Court* 1965, O. 77, r. 6; *Lord Advocate v Hepburn* [1990] BTC 250

See *British Tax Reporter* ¶193-100.

2816 Recovery of tax from unincorporated company

Tax may be recovered from the proper officer (i.e. treasurer or person acting as treasurer) of any unincorporated company (or a body corporate not incorporated in accordance with the law of the UK). That officer may retain out of any money coming into his hands on behalf of the company sufficient sums to pay that tax and, so far as the sums are insufficient to meet the liability, he is entitled to be indemnified by the company.

Law: TMA 1970, s. 108

See *British Tax Reporter* ¶193-150.

2820 Recovery from employees

If the employer does not deduct the full amount of tax due under the PAYE system (see 2784) and HMRC is of the opinion that an employee received his emoluments knowing that the employer wilfully failed to deduct the due amount of tax, the tax due can be recovered from the employee.

Law: *Income Tax (Pay As You Earn) Regulations* 2003 (SI 2003/2682); *Pawlowski v Dunnington* [1999] BTC 175

See *British Tax Reporter* ¶192-800.

2821 Recovery from lessees and agents

Liability to tax under the property income business rules currently falls on the person or persons 'receiving or entitled to the income' (see 1205). In most cases the person entitled to the income will also receive it. A landlord who engages an agent to handle the rental business remains 'entitled to' the income in question and therefore liable to tax. Although provisions formerly giving the collector recourse to agents (and tenants) have been repealed for years after 1994–95, HMRC's power to charge persons 'receiving ... the income', without entitlement to it, should be noted.

For the collection of tax from agents or tenants where the landlord normally lives abroad, see 1671.

Law: Former ICTA 1988, s. 23

See *British Tax Reporter* ¶192-800.

2822 Crown priority on insolvency

On the insolvency of an individual or partnership, or when a company goes into receivership or liquidation, the Crown (among others) has priority with respect to the payment of certain 'preferential debts'. In the distribution of the insolvent's property, preferential debts rank ahead of other debts for payment (after the expenses of the bankruptcy or winding-up of a company). Preferential debts include money owed to HMRC at either the date of the making of the bankruptcy order or the date of the appointment of an interim receiver for income tax deducted at source:

- under PAYE in respect of emoluments paid in the 12-month period before the above dates; or
- under the deduction scheme for subcontractors in the construction industry.

Preferential debts also include certain debts due to Customs and Excise (e.g. VAT and insurance premium tax referable to the six months before the relevant date), sums on account of Class 1 and 2 NICs which became due within the 12 months before the relevant date, and sums that have been assessed and are due in respect of Class 4 NICs up to the 5 April before the relevant date, not exceeding any one year's assessment. Preferential debts rank equally between themselves and are paid in full unless the property is insufficient, in which case they abate in equal proportions.

HMRC's policy is to take bankruptcy proceedings as a last resort only when all other attempts to encourage payment of tax debts have failed.

Law: *Insolvency Act* 1986, s. 175, 386; Sch. 6

Source: *Hansard*, 10 December 1992

See *British Tax Reporter* ¶193-300.

Income Tax

Corporation Tax

CHARGEABLE GAINS – SPECIAL SITUATIONS

CLOSE COMPANIES

SPECIAL COMPANIES

PARTICULAR RELIEFS FOR COMPANIES

ADMINISTRATION AND COMPLIANCE

WHAT'S NEW

- For the financial year 2010 the main rate of corporation tax is 28 per cent (see 3092); the full or main rate applies if profits exceed the upper profits limit (namely £1,500,000). The main rate of corporation tax will reduce to 27 per cent for the financial year 2011. For North Sea Oil and Gas ring fence companies the 2010 main rate of corporation tax is 30 per cent.
- For the financial year 2010, the small profits rate (formerly, the small companies' rate) is unchanged at 21 per cent (see 3092). For North Sea Oil and Gas ring fence companies the 2010 small companies rate is 19 per cent.
- The new *Corporation Tax Act* 2010 which is the second of two corporation tax acts rewriting the corporation tax code became effective for accounting periods ending on or after 1 April 2010 (see 3001).
- The *Taxation (International and Other Provisions) Act* 2010 has been introduced with effect for accounting periods ending on or after 1 April 2010. This act rewrites the legislation, in particular, on transfer pricing, double tax relief and the 2009 worldwide debt cap provisions.
- The *Corporation Tax Act* 2010 has renamed 'small companies' rate' the 'small profits rate' (see 3092) and has rewritten the provisions on charges on income and renamed them 'charitable donations relief' (which, since 2005 was the last remaining category of expenditure that fell within the definition of 'charge on income') (see 3059).
- New provisions have been introduced to restrict the availability of capital allowances following, broadly, a change in ownership of a company (see 3034).
- New provisions have been introduced to prevent corporation tax relief where a loan made by a close company to a participator is written off (see 3036).
- Changes have been made to the conditions applying to the exemption from the loan relationship charge when an impaired debt becomes held by a connected company (see 3036).
- An extended definition of 'charity' has been introduced (see 3059).
- A new anti-avoidance provision restricting the relief available on gifts of shares to charities has been introduced (see 3059).
- The amount of the annual investment allowance has been increased from £50,000 to £100,000 with effect from 1 April 2010 (see 3034).
- A new penalty regime for failure to notify chargeability to corporation tax has been introduced (see 4952).
- HMRC have published their views on the inheritance tax consequences of company contributions to employee benefit trusts (see 4278).
- Various extra-statutory concessions have been enacted, including those allowing a negligible value claim where an asset is transferred between group companies on a no gain/no loss basis (see 3684), preventing a reduction in the base cost of a shares for CGT purposes where a transfer of an asset at an undervalue by a close company is taxable on the recipient as employment income or as a distribution (see 4278) and allowing the value of shares disposed of by a transferee company (who acquired them from another group company under a no gain/no loss transfer) to a third party to be the appropriate proportion of the value of any larger holding held by the transferor company at 31 March 1982 (see 3684).
- HMRC have published their views on the meaning of 'ordinary share capital' in the context of overseas companies following the decision in *Swift v HMRC* (see 3653).
- The dividend exemption for demergers has been extended to companies resident in EU member states (see 3200).
- HMRC have announced a delay in the introduction of managed payment plans (see 4966).
- The government has confirmed that distributions of a capital nature will be exempt

from corporation on income under the new distribution exemption that applies for distributions made on or after 1 July 2009 (see 3085).

- HMRC have published guidance on the form of accounts that need to be included with a corporation tax return (see 4952).
- An additional test for the extent that losses of a company owned by a consortium can be surrendered as group relief is to be introduced (see 3812).
- Electronic filing of corporation tax returns using XBRL will be compulsory where an accounting period ends after 31 March 2010 (see 4952).
- HMRC have published the most commonly asked questions and answers in relation to the Role of Senior Accounting Officer introduced for large companies and groups (see 4959).
- The following Court decisions have been reported:

  - The Upper Tribunal decision in *Dawsongroup Limited v R & C Commrs* on the meaning of 'investment business' and 'expenses of management' (see 4553).
  - The decision in *Laerstate BV v R & C Commrs* on the meaning of 'central management and control' for the purposes of determining whether a company is resident in the UK for UK tax purposes (see 3014).
  - The decision in *Research & Development Partnership Ltd v R & C Commrs* that under the pre-2009 penalty regime, reliance on another can in some situations be a reasonable excuse (see 4980).
  - The decision in *FCE Bank plc* that the non-discrimination clause of the UK–US double tax treaty enables group relief to be claimed under the pre-2000 group relief rules (see 3809).
  - The decision in *Philips Electronics UK Ltd v R & C Commrs* that the requirement for the consortium relief 'link company' to be UK resident is contrary to EU law and the subsequent announcement of correcting legislation (see 3809).
  - Two further decisions in the ongoing *Marks and Spencer plc v R & C Commrs* case concerning the availability of group relief on the overseas losses of foreign companies, this time in relation to the quantification of the amount of the losses and the time on which group relief claims are taken to be made when made in a series (see 3809).
  - The decision in *First Nationwide v R & C Commrs* concerning the criteria for determining whether a distribution received from a foreign company is of an income nature or capital nature (see 3085).

KEY POINTS

- Corporation tax is a tax on the profits of a company (see 3004 and 3008).
- The territorial scope of corporation tax extends to UK resident companies and companies carrying on a trade in the UK through a UK permanent establishment (see 3011).
- Corporation tax is an annual tax charged for financial years (see 3008) but by reference to the company's accounting periods (see 3009).
- A company's taxable profits comprise its income and chargeable gains (see 3027).
- Capital allowances are given for corporation tax purposes in respect of similar categories of expenditure to those available for individuals (see 3034).
- Double tax relief is available to give relief for foreign tax suffered (see 3097).
- A single set of rules (the 'loan relationships' regime) applies to all money debt (see 3036ff.).
- A company can incur losses, which may be trading losses or non-trading losses. Trading losses may be relieved in a variety of ways (see 3100).

- Companies are subject to the corporation tax self-assessment (CTSA) regime (see 4950ff.).
- Under CTSA corporation tax is due on the day following nine months after the end of the accounting period to which it relates. Large companies must pay their corporation tax in instalments (see 4964).
- Special rules apply to groups of companies allowing, for example, assets to be transferred between group members on a no gain/no loss basis and the surrender of losses for offset by another group member (see 3650ff.).
- Chargeable gains made by a company are subject to corporation tax (see 3050ff.)
- Special rules apply to particular types of companies, e.g. close companies (see 4250ff.), close investment holding companies (see 4280ff.), non-resident companies (see 4500ff.), companies with investment business (see 4550ff.), life assurance companies (see 4600ff.), local authorities (see 4630ff.), building societies (see 4650ff.), friendly societies (see 4658ff.), mutual companies (see 4680ff.), banks (see 4699ff.), controlled foreign companies (see 4713) and shipping companies (see 4730).
- HMRC have various powers to ensure compliance with the corporation tax regime and interest and penalties may be levied for overdue tax and non-compliance.

TAXATION OF COMPANIES: GENERAL FRAMEWORK

3000 Introduction and background to corporation tax

Introduction of company taxation

Corporation tax was first imposed by the *Finance Act* 1965 and for the first time separated the tax liabilities of a company and its shareholders. Prior to 1965 there was no general distinction between a company and any other person in so much that all persons were subject to income tax.

The corporation tax system introduced in 1965 was a 'classical system'. Under such a system tax is levied at the level of the business entity when profits are withdrawn from it, usually by deduction at source (withholding tax). Distributed profits are effectively taxed at a higher rate than retained profits to encourage the company to reinvest profits in the business.

Imputation system

Corporation tax was modified to the imputation system from 1 April 1973.

The salient features of the imputation system are that a company is charged to corporation tax on all its profits, distributed and undistributed, and income tax is not deducted at source from dividends paid to shareholders.

Prior to April 1999, when a company made a qualifying distribution (see 3076), it had to account to HMRC for advance corporation tax (ACT) of an amount equal to a fraction of the distribution. This fraction varied each year. The shareholder who received a distribution also had imputed to him part of the tax payable by the company; this represented a tax credit in his favour to satisfy his liability to income tax at the lower rate.

A company was able to set off its ACT payments, up to a certain limit, against its corporation tax bill and the resulting figure was payable by the company as an amount sometimes referred to as mainstream corporation tax (MCT).

Abolition of ACT

Advance corporation tax was abolished with effect for distributions made on or after 6 April 1999. A reduced imputation system remains with the continuation of a tax credit.

From 6 April 1999, the amount of the tax credit attaching to distributions is 10 per cent (matching the rate of tax on dividend income up to the basic rate limit).

Under the current system, trading income remains chargeable on a current year basis under an imputation system.

Law: F(No. 2)A 1997, s. 30–33, 35, Sch. 4 and 5

See *British Tax Reporter* ¶700-000.

3001 The corporation tax legislation

The Tax Law Rewrite Project

Following the introduction of corporation tax in 1965 the legislation relating to income tax and corporation tax was consolidated in the *Income Tax and Corporation Taxes Act* 1970 and then later into the *Income and Corporation Taxes Act* 1988. Concerns about the complexity of tax law and the way it was written in the legislation led to the establishment of the Tax Law Rewrite Project (TLR Project). The principal focus of the project has been to rewrite the direct tax legislation in a way which is clearer and easier to understand, without making major changes to the legislation. This is achieved by using a more logical structure, shorter sentences, clearer signposts and grouping of similar rules together. Only minor changes are made to legislation, the changes that are made are to improve the rewritten legislation.

As part of the TLR Project the provisions of the income tax code were rewritten in three acts: the *Income Tax (Earnings and Pensions) Act* 2003 (ITEPA 2003), the *Income Tax (Trading and Other Income) Act* 2005 (ITTOIA 2005) and the *Income Tax Act* 2007 (ITA 2007).

The separation of the income tax code and the corporation tax code began with ITTOIA 2005 and continued with ITA 2007.

This left two separate sets of legislation based on income tax principles; the legislation in the rewritten style applying for income tax purposes and the old style legislation applying for corporation tax purposes. The separation of the two codes were completed when the *Corporation Tax Act* 2009 (CTA 2009) and *Corporation Tax Act* 2010 (CTA 2010) were enacted. The *Taxation (International and other Provisions) Act* 2010 (TIOPA 2010) also has effect for accounting periods ending on or after 1 April 2010 and contains the rewritten legislation on, in particular, transfer pricing, double tax relief for companies and the 2009 worldwide debt cap rules.

Corporation Tax Act 2009

The *Corporation Tax Act* 2009 (CTA 2009), which received Royal Assent on 26 March 2009, was the first of two acts, which rewrite the provisions of the tax code which apply to companies. It is the longest single act to have been passed by Parliament and includes 1,330 sections and four schedules. The act applies to accounting periods ending on or after 1 April 2009. The second corporation tax act, the *Corporation Tax Act* 2010 applies for accounting periods ending on or after 1 April 2010. The provisions of the tax law relating to corporation tax self assessment are not going to be rewritten in the foreseeable future.

CTA 2009 rewrites the charge to corporation tax and the primary corporation tax code used to compute the income of companies for corporation tax. CTA 2009 removed the schedular system of taxing income and has replaced it with the following main heads of charge

- trading income;
- property income;
- loan relationships;
- intangible fixed assets;
- intellectual property; and
- miscellaneous income.

CTA 2009 is set out in 21 parts which cover the charge to corporation tax, accounting periods, residence of companies, as well as those provisions which relate to trading income and income from other sources. The Act also covers parts of the corporation tax code which are not relevant for income tax purposes, such as those provisions necessary to calculate income from loan relationships, derivative contracts and intangible fixed assets. Also included in the act are those provisions which cover particular categories of expenditure including expenditure on research and development as well as film expenditure and remediation of contaminated land.

In common with the other rewritten legislation, CTA 2009 has not generally changed the law as a result of the rewriting of the legislation. Though there are over 100 minor changes to the legislation, they are designed to clarify the predecessor legislation and bring it in line with well-established practice. Schedule 2 of the Act provides for the continuity of the corporation code by stating that the repeal of provisions and their enactment in a rewritten form by CTA 2009 does not affect the continuity of the law, unless a change is made to the effect of the law by the Act. References to the new legislation should also be taken as references to the source legislation.

Corporation Tax

Corporation Tax Act 2010

CTA 2010 is the second of two rewrite acts which address corporation tax. Whereas the first, CTA 2009, mainly rewrote the provisions dealing with the computation of a company's income, CTA 2010 is wider in application, rewriting the provisions dealing with:

- the calculation of corporation tax payable on a company's profits. This includes the renaming of the small companies' rate of corporation tax as the 'small profits rate' and the enactment of a number of extra statutory concessions concerning the former small companies' rate;
- losses and reliefs, including group relief and charitable donations relief (which replaces the term 'charges on income');
- special types of business and company, including close companies and charitable companies;
- distributions; and
- tax avoidance including the transactions in securities rules.

CTA 2010 has effect for accounting periods ending on or after 1 April 2010.

Election to use predecessor legislation

Because both CTA 2009 and CTA 2010 apply to corporation tax accounting periods that end on or after a date that was shortly after the acts were enacted the Acts could apply to transactions which took place before the Bills were even introduced into Parliament. As the changes in the Acts are minor, and will usually benefit companies, it is thought unlikely that a company could be adversely affected by any of these changes in the law for a transaction occurring before 1 April 2009 (for CTA 2009) or 1 April 2010 (for CTA 2010). To provide for such an adverse situation provision is made in each act which allows a company to elect for the consequences of a transaction for corporation tax purposes to be governed by the predecessor legislation. The election can only be made in respect of accounting periods which straddle 1 April 2009. Such an election must be made within two years of the accounting period concerned.

> ### Example
>
> R Beynon Builders Ltd makes up annual accounts to 30 April. The first accounting period which is effected by CTA 2009 is 30 April 2009. The company has a transaction which took place before 1 April 2009, which is treated differently by CTA 2009. The company can elect that the corporation tax consequences of the transaction are treated as if CTA 2009 had not been enacted. The company must make the election by 30 April 2011.

3004   Bodies liable to corporation tax

Corporation tax is charged on the profits of 'companies'.

A 'company' is any body corporate (e.g. a company incorporated under the *Companies Act* 2006 or predecessor Acts) or unincorporated association (e.g. a club or an authorised unit trust), but not a partnership, local authority or local authority association (see 4630). Health service bodies are exempt from corporation tax (see 4635).

There are three main types of incorporated company under the *Companies Act* 2006.

● A company formed so that, for example, a sole trader, family members or several partners can carry on a business and still retain control of its management and share any profits made, while separating the liability of the company from its members. The liability of such a 'private company' is limited by shares.

● A company formed to allow members of the public to invest in its profits without being involved in its management. The liability of such a 'public company' is limited by shares.

● A company formed for charitable, public or social purposes, which is limited by *guarantee*.

An incorporated company has a legal identity separate from that of its shareholders, with its own rights, powers, duties and liabilities, and is likewise a taxable entity distinct and separate from its shareholders.

Income tax and corporation tax cannot be charged on the same income or profits of a taxpayer. Any company paying corporation tax on its profits is not liable to suffer income tax on those profits.

Law: CTA 2009, s. 2, 3; CTA 2010, s. 1121

See *British Tax Reporter* ¶700-300.

3008 The charge to corporation tax

Corporation tax is an annual tax and is charged for each 'financial year'. A financial year is the period from 1 April to the following 31 March. Thus, the financial year 2009 started on 1 April 2009 and ends on 31 March 2010. Likewise, the financial year 2010 starts on 1 April 2010 and ends on 31 March 2011. Although corporation tax is charged for each financial year, it is computed and assessed by reference to a company's 'accounting periods' (see 3009 below) and then apportioned between the relevant financial years where the accounting period does not fall wholly within one financial year.

Corporation tax is charged on the profits of companies. The 'profits' means income and chargeable gains. For the rules for calculating income and chargeable gains see 3026ff.

Companies within the charge to corporation tax (see 3011 for the territorial scope of UK corporation tax) are not chargeable to income tax or capital gains tax. A company's chargeable gains are, however, calculated in much the same way as for capital gains tax purposes (see 3050) but they are then chargeable to corporation tax (subject to the territorial scope limitations below).

Corporation Tax

A body is within the corporation tax charge if it has a source of income within the corporation tax charge. A source of income is within the corporation tax charge if corporation tax is chargeable on the income arising from it, or would be were there any such income. However, a non-resident company is only within the corporation tax charge if it trades in the UK through UK permanent establishment (see 3011).

A company may come within the corporation tax charge if it:

- acquires an appropriate source of income, not previously having had one; or
- becomes UK-resident while having an appropriate source of income.

Conversely, a company may cease to be within the corporation tax charge if it:

- ceases to have an appropriate source of income; or
- being non-resident ceases trading in the UK through a UK permanent establishment.

Law: CTA 2009, s. 2, 3, 4 and 8

See *British Tax Reporter* ¶700-350.

3009 Accounting periods

Corporation tax is charged by reference to 'accounting periods'. Under the *Companies Act 2006*, a company is obliged to prepare accounts for each of its 'financial years', which are the periods between its accounting reference dates. A company's accounting financial years are normally 12 months in length but, confusingly, they are not always. Where a company changes its accounting reference date, the financial year can be as short as a few months or as long as 18 months. To prevent abuse and to create uniformity, tax legislation lays down certain rules to define what is an accounting period for tax purposes.

CTA 2009, s. 9 states that an accounting period for corporation tax begins on one of the following occasions.

(1)   Whenever the company first comes within the charge of UK corporation tax, perhaps by becoming UK resident, or by starting to trade, or acquiring a source of income.

(2)   When an accounting period ends without the company ceasing to be within the charge to corporation tax.

CTA 2009, s. 10 states that an accounting period ends on the earliest of the following occasions:

- 12 months after the accounting period started;
- an accounting date of the company (that is to say, the date to which the company makes up its accounts – which has been held to mean accounts made up on which the auditors have formally reported and which are laid before the company in general meeting – so, for example, drawing up management accounts will not bring the accounting period to an end);

- on the company beginning or ceasing to trade in respect of all of the trades carried on by it;
- the company beginning or ceasing to be resident in the UK;
- the company ceasing to be within the charge to corporation tax;
- on the company beginning or ceasing to be in administration, and
- the commencement of winding up of the company.

Law: CTA 2009, s. 9 and 10; CTA 2010, s. 1119(1)

See *British Tax Reporter* ¶700-800.

3011   Territorial scope of corporation tax

A UK resident company is chargeable to corporation tax on all its profits wherever arising.

A non-UK resident company is within the charge to corporation tax only if it carries on a trade in the UK through a UK permanent establishment. If a non-UK resident company does carry on a trade in the UK, it is chargeable to corporation tax on the profits attributable to the UK permanent establishment.

The concept of a 'permanent establishment' (PE) is much used in double taxation treaties. CTA 2010, Pt. 24, Ch. 2 provides a statutory definition for tax purposes which is intended to accord, in large part, with that in common use in the UK's tax treaties.

For corporation tax, a company has a PE in a territory if (and only if) either:

(1)   it carries on business (wholly or partly) through a 'fixed place of business' in that territory; or

(2)   there is an agent in the territory acting habitually on the company's behalf who is not acting in an independent capacity in the ordinary course of his own business.

However, it will not be treated as having a PE if the activities carried on are merely of a preparatory or auxiliary character (for example, storage, display, delivery operations or collecting information).

A 'fixed place of business' can include a number of possible types of establishment, but is not exclusively:

- a place of management;
- a branch;
- an office, factory or workshop;
- any project for construction or installation or building site;
- an installation or structure for the exploration of natural resources, as well as a mine, quarry, oil or gas well, or any other place where natural resources are extracted.

Case law has determined that a trade is carried on where its contracts are concluded (*Pommery & Greno v Apthope*) and 'where the operations take place from which the profits in substance arise' (*F L Smidth & Co v Greenwood*). In most cases, the substance of the business operations will be where the contracts are concluded.

The profits attributable to the PE comprise the following:

- trading income arising directly or indirectly through or from the permanent establishment;
- any income from property or rights used by, or held by or for the permanent establishment; and
- chargeable gains on the disposal of assets situated in the UK which are used for the purposes of the trade carried on though the permanent establishment.

For clarification, *Finance Act* 2003 inserted a new section and schedule which describe exactly what will be regarded as the chargeable profits of a PE of a non-resident company. Broadly, the profits attributable to the PE shall be those which it would have made had it been a separate entity dealing with the non-resident on arm's length terms – referred to as the 'separate enterprise principle'. Certain assumptions may be made in order to support this stand alone treatment, namely that:

- the PE shares the same credit rating as the non-resident company; and
- it has such equity and loan capital as would be expected given that treatment.

Expenses incurred, in the UK or elsewhere, for the purposes of the PE (whether reimbursed by the PE or not) will be allowable for corporation tax purposes on the same basis as a UK company. Certain costs are specifically disallowed or allowance for them is modified as follows:

(a) no relief is available for any payments akin to royalties made by the PE to another part of the non-resident for the use of intangible assets. However, a contribution towards the creation of such an asset may be deductible;

(b) unless the PE carries on a business as a bank, deposit-taker, money-lender, debt-factor or similar, or deals in commodity or financial futures, and pays interest, etc. in the ordinary course of that business, no deduction will be available for interest or other costs of finance made by the PE to another part of the non-resident; and

(c) where the non-resident provides goods or services to the PE, they will be dealt with as an expense incurred by it for the PE (and hence allowable in calculating the chargeable profits of the PE, see above), except where they are goods or services that the non-resident supplies in the normal course of its own business. In that latter case, the stand alone 'separate enterprise principle' will apply in order to determine the amount deductible.

Law: CTA 2009, s. 5, Pt. 2, Ch. 4; CTA 2010, Pt. 24, Ch. 2; *Pommery & Greno v Apthope* (1886) 2 TC 182;*F L Smidth & Co v Greenwood* (1922) 8 TC 193

3014 Residence and companies

There are two ways in which a company could be UK resident. Prior to the introduction of the legislative basis for UK residence, namely by incorporation in the UK, the courts had developed the test of UK management and control, which was the only way a company would be UK tax resident. Now it can be managed and controlled abroad but still be UK resident if incorporated in the UK.

Incorporation

With effect from 14 March 1988, a company incorporated in the UK will be regarded as resident here. This rule has effect for companies incorporated before that date, from 14 March 1988 onwards. Where a company is given a different place of residence by a rule of law it shall be ignored for the purpose of the incorporation rule.

This can clearly give rise to dual residence, as a company managed and controlled in another jurisdiction will also be UK resident if incorporated in the UK.

An important exception to the incorporation rule is provided by CTA 2009, s. 18 which was originally introduced in 1994. If a company is regarded as resident in another territory under the domestic law of that territory and also resident in the UK under UK tax legislation (e.g. by reason of being incorporated there) and there is a Double Taxation Agreement between the UK and the other territory that includes a 'tie breaker' test and under the tie breaker test, the company is regarded as resident in the other territory (typically, under DTAs following the OECD model, because the 'effective management' of the company is exercised from the other territory), then the company will not be regarded as UK resident for UK tax purposes.

Central management and control

Prior to the statutory deeming provisions previously enacted in *Finance Act* 1988 there was no statutory definition of residence for tax purposes. The test for residence developed by the courts and described below continues to apply where a company is incorporated outside the UK.

The courts determined in the early case of *Calcutta Jute Mills Co Ltd v Nicholson Ex D* that the test for residence was where the real business of the company is carried on, which is where its central management and control takes place. Several cases have been decided on this issue since then and the management and control criterion has stood the test of time.

The concept of central management and control is, in broad terms, directed at the highest level of control of the business of the company and can be distinguished from the place where the main operations of the business are to be found.

In the case of *De Beers Consolidated Mines Ltd v Howe* a South African company operating in South Africa but controlling its important affairs in the UK was held to be resident in the UK, where the Board meetings on important issues took place and where the majority of the Board were resident. Other decisions made in favour of HMRC on the same grounds include *New Zealand Shipping Co Ltd v Thew HL*; *American Thread Co v Joyce, HL*; *John Hood & Co Ltd v Magee KB*.

Corporation Tax

It is particularly difficult to apply the 'central management and control' test in the situation where a subsidiary company and its parent operate in different territories. In this situation, the parent will normally influence, to a greater or lesser extent, the actions of the subsidiary. Where that influence is exerted by the parent exercising the powers which a sole or majority shareholder has in general meetings of the subsidiary, for example to appoint and dismiss members of board of the subsidiary and to initiate or approve alterations to its financial structure, HMRC would not normally seek to argue that central management and control of the subsidiary is located where the parent company is resident. However, in cases where the parent usurps the functions of the board of the subsidiary or where that board merely rubber stamps the parent company's decisions without giving them any independent consideration of its own, HMRC draw the conclusion that the subsidiary has the same residence for tax purposes as its parent.

The case of *Wood and another v Holden* appeared in the Court of Appeal in January 2006. In this case HMRC contended that a Dutch company used as part of sophisticated capital gains tax planning scheme, was resident in the UK. The CA stressed that the burden of proof was on HMRC to show that a company was UK resident and that HMRC in this case had not done so. The court held that the company's decisions, which were influenced by UK accountants, were made by the trust which was set up by the managing director of the company in the Netherlands, and that without those decisions having been made by the trust, the agreements that were the subject of the decisions would not have been entered into. There was no evidence produced by HMRC to show that the company was controlled otherwise than by the trust in the Netherlands, and that the meetings in which the transactions were approved were mere formalities.

In the case of *News Datacom Ltd v HMIT* the special commissioners considered the existing line of authority and highlighted the tests distilled by Chadwick LJ in the Court of Appeal decision in *Wood v Holden*. No further tests were added to those that emerged from *Wood v Holden*, however, the special commissioners made it clear that in deciding where management and control is situated, there are two mutually exclusive categories to be considered.

Category 1

It must first be decided whether the functions of the constitutional organs have been usurped. If they have, then the case falls into the first category.

Category 2

Where this is not the case, i.e. where the functions are in fact carried out by those organs, it is essential to recognise the distinction between an outsider to those organs who influences the decisions of those organs, and one who dictates what those decisions should be.

In *News Datacom*, there was no usurpation of the Board of Directors and therefore the first category was not considered. In considering what the influence of outsiders to the constitutional organs were, the special commissioners found that any outside influence was exercised outside the UK, therefore the company could not be UK resident. Full consideration was found not to be required of the second category because the outside influence could only have made the company UK resident if it occurred in the UK.

It is therefore clear that the first thing to consider is whether the functions of the Board are actually carried out by the Board and not by some other person or persons. If some other person(s) carries out the functions of the Board then the company will be resident where those functions are carried out. Where the functions of the Board are indeed carried out by the Board, the company will be resident where the functions of the board are carried out. In this case however, the role of outsiders who influence the decisions of the Board will also be examined, and if it transpires that there are outsiders who influence the Board to such an extent that it could be said that the Board are merely 'rubber stamping' decisions that have already been made elsewhere and by other people then the company will be resident where the decisions are actually made.

In the more recent case of *Laerstate BV v R & C Commrs* the First-tier Tax Tribunal found that a company incorporated in the Netherlands was centrally managed and controlled by its sole shareholder, and sometime director, in the UK. This does not mean to say that the existence of a dominant shareholder will always determine the residence of a company; it is still necessary to establish who exercises central management and control of the company and from where. The Tribunal found that even where a majority shareholder instructs directors on how to act, and the directors consider those wishes and act on them, it will still be their decision: 'the borderline is between the directors making the decision and not making any decision at all'. Where directors engage in 'mindless signing' they can not be said to have made a decision and so can not be said to exercise central management and control.

SP 1/90 sets out the residence tests and HMRC's view of the test of management and control. In July 2010 HMRC published draft guidance on the circumstances in which they will not normally review residence (see the HMRC website at www.hmrc.gov.uk/international/intm120130-draft.pdf).
These include where a company incorporated outside the UK is managed and controlled, at least in part, by its directors in board meetings which take place outside the UK and in which UK directors, who do not represent the majority of board members, habitually participate by electronic link from the UK.

Law: CTA 2009, s. 14, 18, Sch. 2, Part 5; *Laerstate BV v R & C Commrs*[2009] TC 00162; *Wood & Anor v Holden (HMIT)* [2006] BTC 208; *News Datacom Ltd v HMIT* (2006) Sp C 561; *Calcutta Jute Mills Co Ltd v Nicholson Ex D* 1876, 1 TC 83; *New Zealand Shipping Co Ltd v Thew HL* 1922, 8 TC 208; *American Thread Co v Joyce, HL* 1913, 6 TC 163; *John Hood & Co Ltd v Magee KB* 1 1918, 7 TC 327; *Unit Construction v Bullock* (1958) 38 TC 712; *Esquire nominees Ltd v Commr of taxation* (1971) 129 CLR 177; *Re Little Olympian Each Ways Ltd* [1995] 1 WLR 560; *Untelrab Ltd v McGregor; Unigate Guernsey Ltd McGregor* (1995) Sp C 55

See *British Tax Reporter* ¶764-120.

3020 Companies and income tax

Non-resident companies are chargeable to corporation tax only on the profits of a trade in the UK carried on through a UK permanent establishment. However, they are chargeable to income tax at the basic rate on other UK source income.

Apart from this, companies do not pay income tax. But they do have to deduct income tax from certain payments, and pass this tax on to HMRC. The tax is accounted for under a system of quarterly returns (see 4954) where income tax due to HMRC is set off against income tax suffered at source by the company. If at the end of its accounting period the company has suffered more deduction of tax on its income than it has deducted on payments, then it may set the excess against corporation tax due (or get a repayment if there is no CT liability).

The impact of the rules relating to deduction of tax has diminished considerably since 1 April 2001. From that date the requirement to deduct tax on relevant payments between UK resident companies (or to non-UK companies carrying on a trade through a UK permanent establishment) is removed. For payments made after 30 September 2002, the list of recipients of gross payment is extended to include the manager of a personal equity plan or individual savings account; an institution which receives the payment in respect of a TESSA; and various tax-exempt bodies listed in ITA 2007, s. 936. From the same date, a company may pay royalties (but not interest) gross to a non-resident if it has a reasonable belief that the recipient is entitled to relief from UK tax on them under a double tax treaty. HMRC will collect the tax, plus interest, from the payer if this turns out to be incorrect.

In so far as they are not to other UK companies, payments from which tax must be deducted ('relevant payments') are:

(1) annuities and other annual payments (like deeds of covenant – although not those to charity after 1 April 2000, see 3059);

(2) patent royalties;

(3) annual interest paid (except to a bank carrying on business in the UK):

  (a) by a company; or
  (b) by a partnership which includes a company; or
  (c) to someone whose usual place of abode is outside the UK.

(4) copyright royalties paid to someone whose usual place of abode is outside the UK.

Tax is deducted at the basic rate apart from payments of interest before 6 April 2008, where tax is deducted at the lower rate. Where tax has been deducted from a payment, the recipient may demand a certificate of deduction of tax, showing the gross and net payment and the amount of tax deducted.

Tax deduction schemes also apply to the following in essentially the same way as for individuals:

- PAYE (see 2784);
- payments to subcontractors in the construction industry (see 2787);
- payments to non-UK resident entertainers and sportsmen (see 1673);
- public revenue dividends (see 1402, 1652);
- foreign dividends (see 1654).

Law: ICTA 1988, Sch. 16; ITA 2007, s. 930, 933–936; CTA 2009, s. 3

See *British Tax Reporter* ¶701-150.

CALCULATING PROFITS

COMPUTATION OF PROFITS CHARGEABLE TO CORPORATION TAX

3026 Profits chargeable to corporation tax

Corporation tax is chargeable on the profits of a 'company' (see 3008).

Profits comprise the company's income and chargeable gains.

Law: CTA 2009, s. 2(1)

See *British Tax Reporter* ¶700-550.

3027 Computation of company's taxable profits

A company's taxable profits comprise its income and chargeable gains.

A company's taxable income and chargeable gains are computed in much the same way as those of an individual, using income tax and capital gains tax principles.

Corporation tax is payable on the total profits of a company for each of its 'accounting periods' (see 3009 above). The tax is calculated by apportioning the profits of those accounting periods so as to apply the tax rate for the relevant financial year (see 3090). Deductions can only be made in accordance with the Corporation Tax Acts (see also below). The rules relating to accounting years and corresponding years for individuals do not apply to companies.

Total profits are profits accruing to the company plus profits accruing for the benefit of the company under a trust or partnership and profits arising when the company is wound up.

Corporation Tax

Tax is strictly chargeable on every fraction of a pound, but in practice amounts chargeable are rounded down while tax is calculated to the nearest penny. Of particular relevance to companies is the willingness of HMRC to accept tax computations rounded to the nearest £1,000 in most cases where turnover exceeds £5m.

A pro-forma corporation tax computation for accounting periods ending on or after 1 April 2009 would be as follows:

	£	£
Trading income		
Adjusted profits	X	
Less: capital allowances	(X)	
Net trading income		X
Property income		X
Net non-trading loan relationship credits	X	
Net non-trading credits under derivative contracts	X	
Net non-trading gains on intangible fixed assets	X	
Profits from disposal of know-how or patent rights	X	
Miscellaneous income	X	
Gains on disposal of chargeable assets	X	
	X	
Less: amounts relieved by set off against total profits (e.g. trading losses of current accounting period, group relief, charitable donations relief, etc.)	X	
Profits chargeable to corporation tax	X	

In the above pro-forma corporation tax computation it should be noted that credits arising on loan relationships or derivative contracts entered into by a company in the course of a trade continue to be brought into account for tax purposes as part of the trading profits. Similarly, credits arising under the intangible fixed asset code are brought into account as part of the trading profits to the extent that the intangible asset is held by the company for the purposes of its trade.

As implied above, the computation of trading profits for a company involves much the same principles as for an individual. The implications of receipt of certain foreign income and relief for unremittable foreign income are also relevant to companies in the same way as to individuals (see 1607, 1650ff.). Payments, etc. constituting distributions to shareholders (see 3065ff.) are not deductible in computing profits, and annual interest paid by companies is allowable, for accounting periods ending after 31 March 1996, in accordance with the rules for taxation of loan relationships (see 3036ff.).

If a corporate unit holder receives distributions from an authorised unit trust, various provisions govern the treatment of the distribution in the recipient's hands. The treatment broadly depends on the nature of the income (UK dividends, foreign income, or interest) out of which the distribution is made. Although a corporate unit holder will receive a single distribution, that distribution may consist of one or more elements of franked investment income (with a tax credit), unfranked income (with income tax deducted available for offset against corporation tax or repayment), a foreign income dividend (with a notional tax credit) or unfranked income (with notional income tax available for offset but not repayable). Alternatively, it might be received as interest under deduction of income tax.

Anti-avoidance rules generally apply irrespective of the nature of the taxpayer, though some measures are aimed purely at companies so that, for example, tax relief may be restricted where interest is paid by thinly capitalised companies, the profits of controlled foreign companies can in some situations be assessed on UK resident parent companies (see 4713) and certain tax regimes that apply only for corporation tax purposes (e.g. those relating to loan relationships, derivatives, intangible fixed assets, R&D tax credits, groups of companies, corporate capital gains, etc.) have their own anti-avoidance provisions. There are also transfer pricing rules for certain transactions between affiliated companies, and other special provisions can apply to payments of rent and interest between affiliated companies.

Special rules apply in certain situations. There are rules for the taxation of 'loan relationships', i.e. interest and movements in value of debt which now also incorporates the rules on foreign exchange gains and losses (see 3036ff.) applicable for accounting periods ending after 31 March 1996, intangible fixed assets (see 3042), reliefs for payments to employee share ownership trusts (see 4900) and rules giving a corporation tax deduction where shares are awarded to employees (see 4850). Special provisions apply to certain other types of company (see 4500ff.). Extensive provisions relating to the taxation of financial instruments held by companies for managing interest rate and currency risk apply in such a way that profits and losses on qualifying contracts are to be recognised for tax purposes as they accrue, and taxed or relieved as income receipts or deductions (see 3036).

Law: ICTA 1988, s. 9; FA 2004, s. 207; CTA 2009, s. 5–8; CTA 2010, s. 4; *Authorised Investment Funds (Tax) Regulations* 2006 (SI 2006/964)

See *British Tax Reporter* ¶700-550.

3028 Accounts or statements prepared in a foreign currency

The general rule is that a company's taxable profits and losses should be calculated in sterling. However, many companies have been required since the introduction of International Accounting Standards (IAS) on 1 January 2005 to prepare their accounts in a currency other than sterling and legislation now provides for companies in some circumstances to calculate their taxable profits and losses in a currency other than sterling. For accounting periods beginning after 31 December 2004, the position is as follows for companies who prepare their accounts in a currency other than sterling.

If the company is resident in the UK and in its accounts identifies sterling as its functional currency but (unusually) prepares its accounts in another currency, then the profits and losses of the company must be computed in sterling as if the company prepared its accounts in sterling. Situations like this are likely to be encountered rarely.

Corporation Tax

If the company is resident in the UK and prepares its accounts in one currency (other than sterling) and in those accounts it identifies another different currency (other than sterling) as its functional currency, then the profits and losses of the company must be computed in sterling by:

(a) computing those profits or losses in the functional currency as if the company prepared its accounts in that currency, and

(b) taking the sterling equivalent of those profits and losses by translating the amounts into sterling using the average exchange rate for the accounting period.

If the company, whether resident in the UK or not, prepares its accounts in accordance with generally accepted accounting practice in a currency other than sterling and neither of the two circumstances above apply, then the profits and losses of the company must be computed in sterling by:

(a) computing those profits and losses in the currency in which the accounts are prepared, and

(b) taking the sterling equivalent of those profits and losses by translating the amounts into sterling using the average exchange rate for the accounting period.

For the purposes of these rules the functional currency is the currency of the primary economic environment in which the company operates. The above rules apply to the profits or losses of the company other than chargeable gains or allowable capital losses. For the purposes of corporation tax on chargeable gains (or allowable losses) the profits or losses always have to be computed in sterling. If the sale proceeds or cost of the relevant asset were in a currency other than sterling they have to be translated into sterling using the spot rate on the date of the sale or purchase, as the case may be.

From January 2005, but with regard to accounting periods beginning before 29 December 2007 only, profits *and* losses calculations were always to be made using translation rates for the current period. This fixed the sterling amount of unutilised losses and other reliefs at that point (subject to a one-off adjustment to convert surplus management expenses, trading losses from an overseas property business and non-trading loan relationship deficits which were brought forward to the first period of account beginning after 31 December 2004).

For accounting periods beginning on or after 29 December 2007, subject to transitional arrangements, the general rule is that any losses carried forward to future accounting periods, or back to a previous accounting period, will be converted into sterling at the same exchange rates as the profits which they are offsetting. This removes significant exchange risk which all parties were exposed to under the previous rules. This was brought into sharp focus by the financial climate at the time and was of particular concern to foreign banks trading in the UK.

Companies can elect that the commencement date for the special rules applying to carried back and carried forward amounts is changed to 21 July 2009 (i.e. the new rules apply to accounting periods beginning on or after 21 July 2009). Such an election is irrevocable and must be made within 30 days of the beginning of the first accounting period beginning on or after 21 July 2009.

Law: CTA 2010, Pt. 2, Ch. 4

See *British Tax Reporter* ¶703-700ff.

CALCULATION OF INCOME – ISSUES FOR COMPANIES

3030 Introduction

The concept of income

Corporation tax is charged on the profits of companies, being their income and chargeable gains. It is therefore important to understand what constitutes income for these purposes.

Prior to the enactment of the *Corporation Tax Act* 2009, corporation tax was imposed on income computed according to income tax rules. For accounting periods ending on or after 1 April 2009, income is liable to corporation tax if it falls within one of the heads of charge laid out in CTA 2009 (see below). However, there is no general definition of 'income' in CTA 2009 or in any of the other Tax Acts. It is therefore necessary to rely on general principles. For example, the fundamental differences between income and capital have been much discussed by economists, capital often being likened to the tree or the land, and income to the fruit or the crop. There are also a number of things which are obviously income (e.g. business profits, interest and dividends), whilst there are also other things which are obviously not (e.g. a lump sum legacy and a prize).

In addition, there have been a large number of judicial decisions in regard to the question whether a particular item is 'income'. Although the courts have refrained from attempting to formulate any precise tests of general application, some general points arise. For example, income will usually have an element of periodicity, recurrence or regularity although it does not follow that an isolated payment could not be income. Also, the characterisation of a receipt or surplus as income is unaffected by the fact that the recipient is bound to use it in a particular way and cannot enjoy it as a profit in the ordinary sense.

In *Countrywide Estate Agents FS Ltd* an up-front payment of £25 million made in exchange for the company undertaking to use its position to introduce the third party's products to the customers of the group and held by the lower-tier tribunal to be revenue in nature and not, as the company had argued, a (capital) disposal of part of its goodwill.

As stated above, for accounting periods ending on or after 1 April 2009 income is liable to corporation tax if it falls within one of the heads of charge laid out in CTA 2009. This means that the charge to corporation tax on income is driven by the particular heads of the charge to corporation tax on income as set out in CTA 2009. The main heads of charge are as follows:

- trading income (see 3031);
- property income (see 3032);
- loan relationships (see 3036);

Corporation Tax

- intangible fixed assets (see 3042);
- intellectual property falling outside the intangible fixed asset regime; and
- miscellaneous income (e.g. past cessation receipts, non trading gains on intangible fixed assets, profits on disposal of know-how or patent rights, gains from artificial transactions in land etc.).

Law: *Countrywide Estate Agents FS Limited* [2010] TC 00557

Restriction on deductions – rules applying generally

Restrictions are imposed on certain deductions. The restrictions apply to all income charged to corporation tax, including trading and property income, and also to expenses of management and expenses of companies with investment business. The restriction applies to the following expenses:

(1) remuneration not paid, broadly, within nine months of the end of the accounting period;

(2) contributions to an employee benefit trust (but see 4900 for details of a specific corporation tax deduction when benefits are provided out of the trust);

(3) business entertainment and gifts;

(4) annual payments;

(5) social security contributions (except employers' National Insurance contributions);

(6) penalties, interest and VAT surcharges;

(7) crime-related payments; and

(8) dividends and other distributions.

Transfer of income streams

The legislation to prevent the conversion of income into capital where a person sold the right to income but kept the underlying asset generating the income was piecemeal and was the subject of schemes to exploit the inconsistencies and differences between the way the various provisions worked.

Legislation introduced in FA 2009, Sch. 25 is to ensure that receipts which would be taxable as income on the transferor continue to be taxable as such following a transfer of the rights to those receipts only. Consequently the legislation is not concerned with receipts which would not have been taxed as income in the hands of the transferor had the transfer not taken place, nor is it concerned with transfers which involve, or are deemed to involve, the transfer of the underlying asset (subject to exceptions for annual payments and transfers under sale and repurchase agreements).

Where, on or after 22 April 2009, a company within the charge to corporation tax transfers a right to relevant receipts to another person, but does not also transfer the asset from which the right arises, the charge to corporation tax on income applies to the relevant amount unless an exclusion applies.

The relevant amount is either:

- the amount received for the transfer of the right; or
- the market value of the right at the time of the transfer where no amount is received or the amount received is substantially less than the market value.

Tax is charged in the same way as it would have been had the relevant receipts not been transferred. For example, if the relevant receipts would have been included in calculating the transferor's trading profits, the amount taxable will be so included. If the relevant receipts would not have been wholly taxed as income, the charge to tax is limited to the relevant proportion of the amount received/market value.

Where the taxable amount under Sch. 25 does not exceed the consideration received, it is treated as arising when it is recognised in the transferor's profit or loss account or income statement in accordance with GAAP. Where the amount exceeds the consideration received, it is treated as arising at the same time as it would have been recognised, if it did not exceed the consideration received. Where the full amount taxable under Sch. 25 would not otherwise be recognised in an accounting period of the transferor, it is to be treated as arising immediately before the time it is reasonable to assume that this will be the case. This is to ensure that the taxable amount is always taxed in full.

If the amount is already taxable as income, or as part of the profits of the transferor, then no charge arises under Sch. 25. Similarly, Sch. 25 does not apply if the income is already brought into account by the *Capital Allowances Act* 2001 (e.g. as proceeds on the disposal of an asset qualifying for capital allowances).

Transactions treated as transfers of assets

In the following instances, the underlying asset is treated as transferred and so Sch. 25 does not apply:

- the reduction in the transferor's share in the profits or losses of a partnership where either there is a corresponding reduction in the transferor's share in the partnership property, or it is not the main purpose, or one of the main purposes, of the transfer to prevent the relevant receipts from being brought into account for tax purposes as income of any partner;
- the grant or surrender of a lease of land;
- the disposal of an interest in an oil licence;
- the grant or disposal of an interest in intellectual property which constitutes a pre-2002 asset.

The transfer of an asset under a sale and repurchase agreement is not regarded as the transfer of an asset for the purposes of Sch. 25 and so is within the scope of Sch. 25 (para. 1(3)).

Corporation Tax

The exception to the general rule

The general rule, that a transfer of a right to relevant receipts will not fall within Sch. 25 if the underlying asset is also transferred, is subject to one exception. Where all rights under an agreement for annual payments are transferred, Sch. 25 applies even though the underlying asset has been transferred.

Law: CTA 2009, Pt. 20, Ch. 1; FA 2009, s. 49, Sch. 25

See *British Tax Reporter* ¶701-200 and ¶809-000.

3031   Trading income

General Principles

The profits of a trade must be calculated for tax purposes in accordance with generally accepted accounting practice, subject to any adjustment required or authorised by law in calculating profits for corporation tax purposes. The starting point in calculating taxable business profit is therefore the profit and loss account. The profit and loss account and the balance sheet are part of the financial statements, or accounts that companies produce. The profit or loss of a trade consists of trading income less trading expenses.

The adjustments to the accounts profit (or loss) required or authorised by tax law typically include the following:

- a disallowance of expenses that are not incurred wholly and exclusively for the purposes of the trade (e.g. excessive director's remuneration, expenses incurred by one group company in respect of a trade carried on by another group company, expenses that have a dual purpose, payments made in connection with the discontinuance of the business, etc.);
- a disallowance of capital expenditure and the depreciation or amortisation of such expenditure (except in relation to certain intangible fixed assets – see 3042);
- a disallowance of the expenses for which a deduction is generally prohibited (see 3030 above – for example, business entertaining, dividends and other distributions, etc.);
- a disallowance of expenditure which is specifically disallowed in computing trading profits, for example, a proportion of the hire costs of cars, patent royalties, etc.;
- the removal of expenditure or income which is dealt with for tax purposes otherwise than as part of trading profits (e.g. net non trading credits or net non trading debits on loan relationship or derivative instruments);
- a deduction for expenditure for which a specific deduction is allowed, for example, capital allowances, awards of shares to employees (see 4850), debts proving irrecoverable after a business discontinuance, certain pre-trading expenditure, a proportion of the premium paid in respect of a lease of property occupied for the purposes of the trade, gifts of medical supplies and equipment for humanitarian purposes;
- exclusion of income which is non taxable, for example, most company distributions received after 1 July 2009, capital receipts; and

- exclusion of income or expenses that are brought into account for tax purposes in a different accounting period than the one in which they are reflected in the accounts, for example, contributions to a pension scheme not paid during the accounting period, a general provision for bad debts, etc.

Post cessation receipts carry back

ICTA 1988 contained an election which allowed a post cessation receipt to be carried back to the date trade ceased. Unfortunately this section was repealed by ITTOIA 2005. CTA 2009 now reinstates the rule for corporation tax and allows the company to carry back the post cessation receipt.

The election is available where a company receives a post cessation receipt in an accounting period beginning not later than six years after the company ceased to carry on the trade. The effect of the election is to allow the company to have post cessation receipt carried back so that it is taxed as though it was received in the accounting period in which trade ceases. The election must be made within two years of the period beginning immediately after the accounting period in which the receipt is received.

The election may be useful where there are unrelieved trading losses.

Law: CTA 2009, Pt. 3 and s. 198–200;

3032 Property income

Rental and other income from the letting of UK land and (furnished and unfurnished) property is taxed as a single UK property business for corporation tax purposes. However, any property business income will generally be recognised as an investment' activity – for example, for the purpose of determining whether a company is a trading company under the substantial shareholding exemption regime, see 4035. Capital allowances relating to the rental business are deducted as an allowable expense of the property business. Profits and losses from a property business are computed in the same way as for a trade. The results of the rental business are therefore calculated on an accruals basis in accordance with normal commercial accounting principles. Income from an overseas property is taxed as a single overseas property business on broadly the same basis as a UK property business (but separate from the single UK property letting business).

Under the quasi-trading basis, relief is available for all expenses incurred wholly and exclusively for the purposes of the letting business. Certain statutory trading profit rules, including the disallowance of business entertaining and the timing of relief for unpaid remuneration (see 3030 above) also apply for rental business purposes. Premiums received are dealt with separately under the special rules which treat a proportion of the premium as income and a proportion as capital. Relief for bad or doubtful rental debts is based on trading profit principles. Expenses of a capital nature are not allowed. Provisions for future repairs are also not allowed. Legal and other fees for granting leases exceeding one year are disallowed as capital expenditure. Interest relating to the letting business is deducted under the loan relationship rules as a non-trade deduction (see 3036 below).

Law: CTA 2009, Pt. 4

3034   Use of capital allowances by companies

Capital allowances are given for corporation tax in respect of similar categories of expenditure to those for individuals, (although obviously the part private use apportionment does not apply (see 2330ff.)). The methods of giving effect to allowances or taxing balancing charges are substantially the same as for income tax purposes (see 2324ff.). There are, though, special provisions for investment companies and in relation to the special leasing of plant and machinery.

The term 'special leasing' of plant and machinery refers to leasing other than in the course of a trade which consists of, or includes, leasing. The general rule is that a charge is treated as income from special leasing, and allowances are given by set off against income from special leasing. Any excess is carried forward to set against future income from special leasing. However, companies may claim to set the excess against current profits, or carry it back. The carry back period is limited to the length of the current accounting period. This claim must be made within two years of the end of the accounting period in which the excess arose.

Companies with investment business may deduct plant and machinery capital allowances from the income of the business. Any excess is added to the company's management expenses (see 4559). Charges are treated as income of the business.

Annual investment allowance

For many companies, capital allowances are from April 2008 given mainly by way of an annual investment allowance (AIA), allowing full relief for expenditure in the year of up to £100,000 (£50,000 before 1 April 2010). This figure is adjusted pro rata for accounting periods of less than 12 months. The AIA is available for 'special rate' items (for example, integral features and long life assets) as well as other expenditure on plant and machinery, but subject to certain exclusions, including cars. Where qualifying expenditure exceeds the maximum AIA figure, the excess may attract writing-down allowances in the same period. If a company spends £80,000 on plant, for example, in a 12-month accounting period ended 31 March 2009, it may obtain allowances of up to £56,000 in the year – £50,000 by way of AIA and £6,000 (20 per cent of the balance of £30,000) as a writing-down allowance.

Finance Act 2009 introduced a temporary measure providing for first-year allowances at the rate of 40 per cent on expenditure on plant and machinery in excess of the £50,000 annual investment allowance. The first year allowance is available for expenditure incurred in the 12-month period beginning on 1 April 2009. So, if a company spends £80,000 on plant in that 12-month period, it may obtain allowances of up to £62,000 in the year – £50,000 by way of AIA and £12,000 (40 per cent of the balance of £30,000) by way of first-year allowance.

Transitional measures apply as, for companies, the AIA applies, broadly, with the effect that entitlement to the AIA accrues on a daily basis from 1 April 2008. Where an accounting period spans that date, the amount of the AIA is therefore time-apportioned. For a company with a 31 December year-end, for example, the maximum AIA for the year to 31 December 2008 is calculated as £37,500. A company with a 30 June year-end will only obtain AIAs of up to £12,500 in the year to 30 June 2008, and so on. The same applies for accounting periods spanning 1 April 2010. So, for example, for a 12-month accounting period ended 31 December 2010, a company will be entitled to an AIA of £87,500 (although no more than £50,000 can claimed in respect of expenditure before 1 April 2010).

The following restrictions apply for companies:

(1)   A company that carries on more than one qualifying activity is only entitled to one AIA in respect of all its qualifying activities in the chargeable period.

(2)   A group of companies has to share a single AIA.

(3)   A third restriction applies, allowing just one AIA between the various companies, where – in a given financial year – two or more *groups of companies* are controlled by the same person and where they are related to one another.

(4)   A single amount of AIA is shared between the various companies, where – in a given financial year – two or more companies are controlled by the same person and where they are related to one another.

(5)   There is a restriction where, broadly, qualifying activities are under common control (not necessarily restricted to companies).

Finance Act 2010 introduced a restriction on the amount of relief available for losses from a UK or overseas property business where the loss is attributable to the AIA. This restriction only applies for income tax purposes, not for the purposes of corporation tax.

It was announced in the June 2010 Budget that it is intended to reduce the maximum amount of the AIA to £25,000 with effect from 1 April 2012.

Claims for capital allowances

A claim for capital allowances for an accounting period must be included in the company's tax return (see 4952), either as originally delivered, or via an amendment to the return submitted within the normal time-limit. The claim must specify the amount of the allowance. Claims for capital allowances, once made, can only be amended or withdrawn by amendment of the relevant return.

Consequential amendment of return for another accounting period

Where a claim for capital allowances in an accounting period affects the allowances otherwise due for a subsequent period for which a return has been submitted, the company

Corporation Tax

must amend the later period's return within 30 days. If the company fails to do this, HMRC may amend the return (by written notice). An appeal can be made against such a HMRC amendment in the normal way.

Time-limits for capital allowances claims

Subject to HMRC permitting an extension to the time-limit, claims for capital allowances must be made, amended or withdrawn by the *latest* of:

(1)   12 months after the claimant company's filing date for the return for the accounting period covered by the claim;

(2)   30 days after a closure notice is issued on the completion of an enquiry;

(3)   30 days after HMRC issue a notice of amendment to a return following the completion of an enquiry (issued where the company fails to amend the return itself); or

(4)   30 days after the determination of any appeal against a HMRC amendment (as in (3) above).

'Enquiry' in the above does not include a restricted enquiry into an amendment to a return (restricted because the time-limit for making an enquiry into the return itself has expired), where the amendment consists of making, amending or withdrawing a capital allowance claim.

The time-limits above have priority over any other general time-limits for amending returns.

Capital Allowance Buying

Where there is a change of ownership of a company, long standing legislation restricts or prohibits the carry forward (and carry back) of certain losses and other reliefs. For example, the carry forward and carry back of unutilised trading losses is restricted if there is within a 3 year period both a change in ownership of a company and a major change in the nature or conduct of its trade. Similarly, where there is a transfer of a trade between two companies under common ownership, there is a restriction on the ability of the successor to set off trading losses arising before the transfer of the trade (see 3143 below). However, up until 21 July 2009 there were no restrictions on the utilisation of capital allowances on a change in ownership of a company. Many companies were therefore disclaiming capital allowances, or not claiming them in the first place, prior to a change of ownership to avoid the restrictions on losses carried forward. With effect from 21 July 2009 (or 9 December 2009 in respect of the special rules for ships) new legislation restricts the use of capital allowances and the utilisation of losses attributable to capital allowances where there has been, broadly, a change in ownership of a company and there is a deferred tax asset (i.e. broadly, where the tax written down value of the assets exceeds their balance sheet value). The new rules do not just apply where there is a change in ownership of a company but also where there is an increase in the percentage of ownership of a jointly owned company and also where there is a decrease in the profit sharing ratio of a corporate partner in a trading partnership. However, in all cases, the new rules only apply where the main purpose or one of the main purposes of the transaction is to obtain a tax advantage.

The new legislation is consistent with the rules to deter loss buying transactions and will restrict the way in which capital allowances can be utilised following a transfer of entitlement to benefit from those capital allowances. Capital allowances or any loss attributable to a capital allowances claim will only be available to reduce the profits that they would have been able to reduce before the transaction took place.

There are three other conditions that must be met for the legislation to take effect (that is, in addition to the unallowable purpose test). A company must carry on a trade or carry on a trade in partnership with others, that company (or that partnership) must have an excess of capital allowances and there must be a qualifying change in relation to the company. Broadly, a qualifying change is either the sale or partial sale (to create a consortium) of a company, a change in the ownership proportions of a consortium company, a change in the profit sharing ratio of a partnership in which the company is a partner or a transfer of the trade (with the excess of allowances) in circumstances such that the transfers of a trade without a change of ownership provisions (see 3140) apply.

The amount by which the tax written down value of plant and machinery exceeds the balance sheet value is the excess of allowances. The legislation operates by allocating an amount of expenditure equal to the excess of allowances in each pool to a new separate pool of the same type (i.e. a new single asset, class or main pool). WDA are calculated on the old and the new pools separately but at the same rate. If, however, in respect of another pool the balance sheet value of plant and machinery is greater than its tax written down value, then this difference can be used to reduce the excess of allowances in a pool. To enable the excess of allowances to be calculated the company's (or the partnership's) accounting period is brought to an end on the day of a qualifying change and a new accounting period begins on the following day.

Capital allowances claimed in respect of expenditure in the new pools may only be used to reduce the profits (or increase the losses) from the trade as it was carried on, and to the extent that it was carried on, before the qualifying change. Any trading activities transferred in to the company or the partnership will be treated as a separate trade for these purposes. Any losses attributable to capital allowances on new pool expenditure may not be surrendered as group relief or set against other profits of the company for the year, unless they could have been used to reduce those profits before the qualifying change.

Example 1

A company C is a member of the X group of companies. It draws up its accounts to 31 December each year. On 31 December 2010 C is sold to the Y group. The X group and the Y group are independent of each other. On 31 December 2010 C's capital allowance pools have the following balances of unrelieved qualifying expenditure: main pool £150,000, short life asset single asset pool £15,000, special rate pool for high emission cars £50,000. The balance sheet value of the relevant assets are: short life asset £10,000, high emission cars £75,000 other plant and machinery (main pool) £50,000. The company has been loss making and is being sold primarily for the purpose of enabling Y group to benefit from the capital allowances. For the accounting period ended

31 December 2011 C incurs a trading loss of £100,000 (before the deduction for capital allowances).

The capital allowance pools in C on 1 January 2011 will be as follows:

- main pool: 'new' pool: £75,000; 'old' pool: £75,000 (assuming that the excess of the balance sheet value over the tax written down value of the high emission cars is set off against the main pool);
- special rate pool for high emission cars: 'old' pool: £50,000;
- short life single asset pool: 'new' pool: £5,000; 'old' pool: £10,000.

Assuming that there are no additions or disposal of qualifying assets in the year ended 31 December 2011, C's entitlement to capital allowances for that year will be:

- main pool: new pool £15,000, old pool £15,000;
- special rate pool: £5,000;
- short life asset pool: new pool £1,000, old pool £2,000.

The trading loss for the year ended 31 December 2011 after capital allowances will therefore be £138,000. £122,000 of the loss is unrestricted and can be set off against C's other income and gains in the year ended 31 December 2011, carried back against profits of earlier accounting periods in the normal way or surrendered as group relief to other members of the Y group. £16,000 of the loss is restricted under the new capital allowance buying provisions and can only be set off against income in the same or earlier accounting periods from qualifying activities (e.g. an ordinary property business, an overseas property business, managing the investments of a company with investment business, etc.) that were carried on by C prior to the change in ownership, or carried forward against future profits of the trade. It is worthy of note the restricted loss cannot be set off against capital gains in C in the accounting period ended 31 December 2011 or earlier years even if the relevant asset was owned by C prior to the change of ownership because a capital gain will not be a profit from a qualifying activity.

Example 2

Same facts as Example 1 above. Z, a company in the Y group carries on a similar trade to C and after the acquisition of C, the trade of Z is transferred to C so as to amount to an extension of C's trade. In the year ended 31 December 2011 the newly extended trade of C produces a profit, before capital allowances, of £50,000.

Only the capital allowances from the 'old' pools (i.e. £22,000) can be deducted in calculating the taxable trading profits of C. The profits of C after the change in ownership will need to be streamed and the capital allowances due on the 'new' pools will only be available to deduct in arriving at the taxable profits of the stream that relates to the part of the trade that was carried on by C before the change in ownership.

Example 3

Same facts as Example 1 but after acquisition of C, the Y group recapitalises C and the funds are utilised by C in repaying bank borrowings. As a result of the lower interest costs, the trade of C becomes profitable.

> In these circumstances, there is no restriction on the use of the capital allowances and the capital allowances in all the pools, totalling £38,000, can be deducted.

Tax credits

Loss-making companies that incur expenditure on certain 'green' technology from 1 April 2008 are able to surrender their losses in return for a cash payment from HMRC, but only if such companies are otherwise unable to use their losses against their own profits or those of a group member. The rules are directly linked to the first-year allowances that are given for expenditure on energy-saving plant and machinery or environmentally beneficial plant and machinery. In this way, companies can gain an immediate cash payment rather than carrying losses forward indefinitely in the hope of obtaining relief when profits start to be realised in the future.

The main features of the relief are as follows:

- relief may be given for expenditure incurred on technology currently qualifying for 100 per cent FYAs under either the 'energy-saving' plant and 'environmentally beneficial' plant provisions;
- the scheme is available to companies (small, medium or large) but not to excluded companies (e.g. charities, scientific research organisations, etc.), or to any sole traders, partnerships or other entities, and
- companies may surrender losses, to the extent that they are attributable to qualifying expenditure, so as to receive a percentage (currently, 19 per cent – but subject to a limit of £25,000 or, if higher, the amount of the company's PAYE and NIC liabilities for the period) of the surrendered loss as a tax-free cash payment from HMRC.

A payment in respect of a first-year tax credit is not treated as income of the company for any tax purpose.

Law: FA 1998, Sch. 18, Pt. IX; CAA 2001, Pt. 2, Ch. 16A (as inserted by FA 2010, Sch. 4); 262A and Sch. A1, para. 23

See *British Tax Reporter* ¶713-600 and ¶242-000ff.

3036   Loan relationships

All 'money debts' held and owed by companies which arise from the lending of money are known as 'loan relationships'. Profits and losses on such relationships are taxed or allowed, for corporation tax purposes, as income. Where the company is a party to the relationship for the purposes of its trade all profits, gains and losses are included in the calculation of its trading profit. In any other case, profits and gains are taxed as non-trading loan relationships and losses (called 'non-trading deficits') are set against non-trading loan relationship profits and gains in the same accounting period and any excess is relieved against specified profits of the company or of fellow group members. For accounting periods beginning on or after 1 October 2002 foreign exchange gains and losses on loan relationships and other

Corporation Tax

transactions are included within these rules. Previously, these items were dealt with under FA 1993 foreign exchange legislation, now largely repealed. Also from 1 October 2002, derivative contracts are included within their own new provisions – which are very similar to the overall thrust of the loan relationships legislation. Like trading loan relationships, debits and credits on derivative contracts to which a company is a party for the purposes of its trade are included in the overall trading income result, whilst non-trading debits and credits are dealt with in a similar manner to non-trading debits and credits on loan relationships.

Overview of regime for taxation of loan relationships

To a very great extent, the treatment of corporate and government debt for corporation tax purposes follows the accounting treatment. For the majority of companies which do not have complex borrowing or lending arrangements and are not attempting to exploit the loan relationship rules for tax avoidance, the legislation is simple to apply and is generally helpful. However, the rules behind the simple principle of taxing/relieving the profit and loss account entry are inevitably complex. They are found in CTA 2009, Pt. 5.

Money debts

'Money' is defined to include money expressed in a currency other than sterling. A money debt is a debt settled in money, or by the transfer of a right to settlement under a debt which is a money debt. 'Money', which is not defined further, must be taken to have its ordinary meaning. It would not, therefore, include physical commodities or a barter arrangement. 'Debt' includes a debt the amount of which falls to be ascertained by reference to matters which vary from time to time.

A transaction for the lending of money

The rules provide the following guidance on the meaning of this term:

- where an instrument is issued to evidence any money debt, the debt is taken to have arisen from a transaction for the lending of money. This is intended to catch a situation where the original transaction is not one for the lending of money so the debt would not otherwise be a money debt arising from a transaction for the lending of money and bring the debt into the loan relationship provisions by virtue of the issue of the security. The instrument must be issued for the purpose of representing a security, and not simply documenting a transaction (such as a contract for a monthly service charge payable in arrears). An example would be a sale of shares in a company where the vendor receives part of the consideration in loan note;
- a debt arising from rights conferred by shares in a company does not arise from a transaction for the lending of money;
- 'loan' includes any advance of money.

According to the Revenue press release announcing the publication of the original draft legislation (REV 21 of 28 November 1995), a loan relationship would arise from any debt 'which, under general law, is a loan'. So any transaction which would generally be regarded as lending would qualify, e.g. unsecured loans, overdrafts, drawn-down credit facilities, in addition to all securitised debts. Neither the duration of the financing, nor the form of payment for the loan – interest, discount, premium, or any combination – is relevant. Finance leases are excluded for, whatever their economic character, they are not loans for legal purposes.

From 6 April 2005, references to loan relationships include references to 'alternative finance arrangements' for the taxation of lending under Shari'a law.

HMRC have confirmed that straightforward commercial contracts and invoices do not represent a security, and therefore, not a transaction of lending money. However, it would seem possible for such a transaction to become a transaction of lending – for example, where a debtor is granted extended time to pay.

Any instrument which represents a pure equity interest in a company cannot be a loan relationship. The reference to 'shares in a company' is qualified by CTA 2009, s. 476, in that the term 'share' is deemed to mean any share under which entitlement to receive distributions may arise. It must therefore be taken to include preference shares. Building society shares are not shares for this purpose (CTA 2009, s. 476) so debits and credits on those shares are taken into account under the loan relationship rules. Equity instruments which have some debt-like characteristics, such as convertibles, may rank as loan relationships but are subject to special rules.

The special commissioners have decided that, on the proper construction of the FA 1996 basis for the taxation of profits or losses arising from loan relationships, receipts from the making of contracts for financial futures by a number of life insurance companies were not subject to the loan relationship regime. Although tax considerations played a decisive part in the choice of structures, the transactions were genuine and not shams and the deliberate tax-efficient structuring of the business did not affect the commercial and legal characterisation of what was done (*HSBC Life (UK) Ltd v Stubbs (HMIT)* and related appeals). The mere economic equivalence of a transaction to a loan did not show that it was a loan. The authorities showed that the concept of 'loan' or 'lending' might vary from statute to statute if a particular meaning was adopted. By specifically referring to the concept of 'a transaction for the lending of money', CTA 2009, s. 302(1)(b) intended to confine a concept whose extent might otherwise be uncertain within well-known and ascertainable bounds. It was impossible to conclude that any of the parties to the transactions thought that they were lenders or borrowers, or that they intended that to be the case. They plainly intended to enter into the legal relationships which the documentation showed that they established, and they took care to enter the relationship of buyer and seller of financial futures and not that of lender and borrower. The fact that, in doing so, they were clearly anxious to fall within one tax regime rather than another was beside the point.

Relevant non-lending relationships

The application of the loan relationship legislation is extended by CTA 2009, s. 481 to money debts not arising from a transaction for the lending of money where the debt is one on which interest is payable (or receivable), on which a foreign exchange gain or loss arises and, for creditor companies, where the debt is one in relation to which an impairment loss arises in respect of a business payment or a debt on which a discount arises to the company.

A business payment in this context means a payment which, if it were paid, would fall to be brought into account for tax purposes as a receipt of a trade, UK property business or overseas property business. For example, a provision against trade debtors would fall into this category.

The loan relationship rules are extended to these type of non-lending relationships only in respect of the following matters:

(1)   interest payable by or to the company;

(2)   exchange gains and losses;

(3)   for debts on which interest is payable to the company, profits on the sale of the right to the interest;

(4)   for creditor companies, an impairment loss in respect of a business payment;

(5)   for creditor companies, the discount on the debt or an impairment loss in respect of the discount, and

(6)   for creditor companies in relation to a debt from which a discount arises, the profit (but not the loss) on a disposal of the rights under the loan.

An example would be consideration outstanding on the purchase of an asset, e.g. Co A is in the business of selling properties. Co B buys a property and fails to pay the consideration due to Co A. The amount outstanding did not arise from a transaction for the lending of money therefore there is no loan relationship. If Co B pays Co A interest on the amount outstanding, or Co A makes an impairment adjustment in respect of any of the amount outstanding, those debits and credits will be treated as loan relationship debits and credits in Co A, and the interest would be a loan relationship debit for Co B. If A was not in the business of selling properties but was, for example, disposing of its business premises, the interest would be a loan relationship credit for A but the impairment would not be an allowable debit since the impairment loss would not be in respect of a business payment.

For accounting periods beginning before 1 April 2009 there was an anomaly arising from a mismatch in treatment between the debtor and creditor company where a trade debt owed by a connected company was written off. The creditor company's position was governed by the loan relationship rules and so no relief was available because of the connected party rules. However, nothing in the loan relationship rules bore on the debtor's position and so it would have been taxable under CTA 2009, s. 94 on the release of the debt. For accounting periods commencing on or after 1 April 2009, this anomaly has been removed by bringing the debtor company within the loan relationship rules in these circumstances so that the debtor does not need to bring in a taxable credit.

Common instances where the tax treatment of loan relationships differs from the accounting treatment

The overall purpose of the recasting of the tax legislation dealing with loan relationships was to align the tax treatment with the accounting treatment. However, there are specific situations where the amounts brought into account for tax purposes differ from the amounts recorded in the company's profit and loss account. These include the following.

Late paid interest

A special rule applied for accounting periods beginning after 30 September 2002 but before 1 April 2009 (see below for the position for accounting periods beginning on or after 1 April 2009) where:

- the payer and the recipient of interest were connected (determined by a control test); or
- the payer was a close company and the recipient was a participator, associate of a participator, or company controlled by a participator; or
- the payer company had a major interest (40 per cent or more) in the recipient company, or vice versa; or
- the recipient was a pension scheme and there was a connection between the paying company and the employer of the employees to whom the scheme related.

In these circumstances, if the creditor did not bring the corresponding credits for interest into account for corporation tax purposes, the debtor company's deduction for interest payable was deferred if it fails to pay the interest for more than 12 months after the end of the accounting period in which it accrued. The deduction was permitted only in the accounting period in which the company actually paid the interest. This applied, for example, where the connected lender was non-UK resident.

> ### Example
>
> Toad Rock Ltd owns High Rocks BV, a non-UK resident company. Toad Rock accrues interest annually on a loan from High Rocks in its accounting period ended 31 December 2005 but does not pay the interest until 28 February 2007. The deduction will be allowed in the period ended 31 December 2007.

Rulings of the European Court of Justice, however, raised concerns that this provision was not compatible with European law. To ensure that the law is compatible with European law *Finance Act* 2009 amended the rule so that the accruals basis will apply unless the connected creditor company is resident or effectively managed in a 'non-qualifying territory'. Then the paid basis will apply. A territory is a non-qualifying territory for these purposes if it does not have a double tax agreement with the UK that includes a non-discrimination clause. Most tax havens will be non-qualifying territories.

The changes have effect for accounting periods beginning on or after 1 April 2009. As a transitional measure a company may elect that the amendment is not to have effect for the first accounting period beginning after that date. The election must be made on the corporation tax return for the accounting period which the election applies to. No election can be made for an accounting period after 31 March 2011.

Connected parties

Where the debtor company and the creditor company are connected, that is to say, one has control of the other:

Corporation Tax

673

- debits and credits in respect of the loan relationships have to be accounted for on an amortised cost basis, and
- debits and credits in relation to loans written off or released and debits in respect of impairment losses are not taken into account for tax purposes.

For the purposes of these connected party rules 'control' is defined widely to include the power of a person to secure that the affairs of the company are conducted in accordance with his wishes. In *Fenlo Ltd v R & C Commrs* the Special Commissioner decided that the terms of a debenture given to the lender charging the undertaking and assets of the borrower by way of security for the loan did not give the lender the power to secure that the affairs of the borrower were conducted in accordance with the lender's wishes and that the two companies were not therefore connected parties.

Loan relationship for unallowable purposes

Debits on loan relationships which have an unallowable purpose are not recognised for corporation tax purposes. In addition, any exchange gains on a loan relationship which has an unallowable purpose will similarly not be recognised. Where a loan relationship has an unallowable purpose, so much of the debits, and foreign exchange credits, on that loan relationship for the accounting period as are attributable, on a just and reasonable apportionment, to the unallowable purpose are left out of account. Debits on loans for unallowable purposes which are not brought into account (and thus are already refused relief as loan relationship debits) are similarly denied relief under any other corporation tax provisions in CTA 2009.

The test, which must be carried out for every accounting period during which the company is party to the loan relationship in question, is whether the purpose for which the company is a party to the loan relationship or enters into a related transaction in respect of that loan relationship (such as the disposal or release of a loan) is one 'which is not amongst the business or other commercial purposes of the company'.

Credit not taxable on release of liability

In addition to the situation where the debtor and creditor are connected there are several circumstances listed at (1) to (4) below, where the release of a liability will not give rise to a taxable credit in the debtor company.

(1) The release is part of a statutory insolvency arrangement.

(2) The creditor company is in insolvent liquidation and immediately before it went into liquidation, the debtor and creditor were connected companies and they were not connected immediately after that time.

(3) The relationship is not with a connected company but the debtor company is in insolvent liquidation.

(4) The release is in consideration of, or of any entitlement to, shares forming part of the ordinary share capital of the debtor company.

Close company releasing loan to a participator

Where a close company makes a loan to an individual who is a participator and releases it, the recipient of the released loan is charged to income tax but is treated as having paid income tax at the dividend ordinary rate. As with the receipt of a dividend, there will be no further liability to income tax unless the participator is a higher rate taxpayer. The company will have a liability to corporation tax under CTA 2010, s. 455 at the time that the loan is made but this can be reclaimed once the loan is released or written off (or repaid). However, prior to 24 March 2010, for corporation tax purposes under the loan relationships rules a loan released will normally give rise to an expense recognised in the company's accounts and be allowable for corporation tax purposes (since, in particular, a participator who is an individual will not be a connected party for the purposes of determining whether an impairment loss is allowable). This position was changed with effect from 24 March 2010. Where a loan by a close company to a participator which gave rise to a charge to corporation tax under s. 455 is released or written off on or after 24 March 2010, the company is not entitled to a deduction under the loan relationship rules.

Deemed release where an impaired debt becomes held by connected party

There are two instances where there is a deemed release of a liability under a debtor loan relationship. Where these circumstances apply, the credit arising in the debtor company on the deemed release has to be brought into account for tax purposes.

The first instance applies where a company (C) acquires a debt from an unconnected creditor (T) and immediately after that acquisition C is connected with the debtor company (whether such connection arises by virtue of acquiring shares at the same time as the debt, or whether the debtor and C were previously connected) and the pre-acquisition carrying value of the debt (being the original amount of the liability in the accounts of the debtor due less any release by T) exceeds the consideration which C has paid for the debt. This would apply, for example, where a parent company acquires from a bank (for a consideration less than the face value of the loan) a loan made by the bank to a subsidiary company of the parent. In such circumstances, there is a deemed release of the debt in the amount of the excess, so that the difference between the face value of, and the amount actually paid for, the debt is treated as released and therefore constitutes a credit taxable on the debtor.

For acquisitions of debt after 14 October 2009, an exception to the deemed charge (referred to in the legislation as the 'corporate rescue exception') applies in the following circumstances:

- the acquisition by the new creditor is at arm's length;
- there has been a change in ownership of the debtor company in the period beginning one year before and ending 60 days after the acquisition of the debt;
- it is reasonable to assume that but for the change in ownership the debtor company would have become insolvent; and
- it is reasonable to assume that the new creditor would not have acquired the debt but for the change in ownership.

Corporation Tax

The second instance where a deemed release occurs is where the identity of the creditor remains the same, but the creditor changes from being unconnected to connected, in circumstances where the amount that would have been the carrying value of the loan relationship asset in the accounts of the creditor if a period of account had ended immediately prior to the companies becoming connected would have been adjusted for impairment. The deemed release is of an amount equal to the impairment adjustment that would have been made. This instance would occur, for example, if a parent company acquired the company that had previously made a loan to the parent company's subsidiary where the value of the debt had become impaired (for example, because the subsidiary was in financial difficulty).

Disguised interest

FA 2009 makes changes to the loan relationship rules introducing a new comprehensive principle to tackle disguised interest.

Where a company is party to an arrangement which produces for the company a return in relation to any amount which is economically equivalent to interest, then the loan relationship rules apply as if the return were a profit arising to the company from a loan relationship. For this purpose a return produced for a company by an arrangement in relation to any amount is 'economically equivalent to interest' if and only if:

(a) it is reasonable to assume that it is a return by reference to the time value of that amount of money;

(b) it is at a rate reasonably comparable to what is (in all the circumstances) a commercial rate of interest; and

(c) at the relevant time there is no practical likelihood that it will cease to be produced in accordance with the arrangement unless the person by whom it falls to be produced is prevented (by reason of insolvency or otherwise).

There are three exclusions:

(1) where the return is otherwise taxable such as trading income, or under the fixed asset rules or under the derivative contracts rules;

(2) where the arrangements have no tax avoidance motive; or

(3) where the arrangements involve excluded shares such as certain group companies or companies that would be controlled foreign companies (CFCs) (see 4713) but for an exemption.

Where there is no tax avoidance motive a company can elect for the exclusion not to apply. The election must be made no later than the time when the arrangement begins to produce a return for the company, and is irrevocable.

The amendments made have effect in relation to any arrangement which produces for a company a return which is economically equivalent to interest if the company becomes a party to the arrangement on or after 22 April 2009.

Transitional arrangements apply in respect of existing arrangements in force as at 22 April 2009.

Law: CTA 2009, Pt. 5 and 6, s. 94 and 481; *HSBC Life (UK) Ltd v Stubbs (HMIT)* (2001) Sp C 295; *Fenlo Ltd v R & C Commrs* (2008) Sp C 714

Source: HMRC Corporate Finance Manual (CFM13420)

See *British Tax Reporter* ¶717-000.

3037 Loan relationships – bringing amounts into account

For accounting periods beginning after 31 December 2004, debits and credits made in accordance with generally accepted accounting practice (GAAP) that are recognised in determining the company's profit or loss for the period are used to calculate a company's taxable income or deductions resulting from its loan relationships. For earlier accounting periods, the debits and credits were those made under 'authorised accounting methods'. Some debits and credits are disallowed, even though they fall to be made for the purposes of the company's accounts (see 3036 above for common examples of this).

Trading loan relationships

For any loan to which a company is a party for trading purposes:

- credits are treated as trading receipts; and
- debits are treated as deductible trading expenses.

The test of whether or not a company is party to a loan relationship for the purposes of its trade depends on whether the company is a creditor or debtor. As a debtor, it need only show that it took on the debt for the purposes of its trade: whether the loan represents a temporary facility or is part of the company's capital should be irrelevant. It should not matter whether the loan finances current or fixed assets.

A creditor, however, may only treat a loan as a trading loan if it made or acquired the loan 'in the course of activities forming an integral part of [its] trade'.

Non-trade loan relationships

Any loan which is not for a trading purpose will give rise to debits (i.e. losses) and credits (i.e. profits) which are called, respectively, 'non-trading debits' and 'non-trading credits'. In any accounting period the treatment of these is respectively:

- net non-trading credits (i.e. the aggregate of a company's non-trading credits, less the sum of all its non-trading debits, if any) are taxed as non-trading loan relationships; and
- net non-trading debits (i.e. the aggregate of a company's non-trading debits, less the sum of all its non-trading credits, if any) are relieved, as a 'non-trading deficit', under special rules outlined below.

Corporation Tax

Note that non-trading foreign exchange gains and losses are also dealt with under these loan relationship provisions for accounting periods ending after 31 March 1996.

Set off of non-trade deficits

To the extent that a non-trading deficit is not surrendered as group relief for a period it can be used in any of the following ways, in this order:

(1)   set against the company's total profits for the accounting period in which the deficit arises;

(2)   to the extent not group relieved or set against profits of the same period, carried back and set against profits arising in earlier periods, or

(3)   to the extent not used in any of the ways already mentioned, carried forward and set against non-trading profits arising in future periods to the extent that it is not used in any of the ways already mentioned.

Profits of the same period

Where a claim is made to set the deficit against profits arising in the same period, trading losses brought forward from earlier periods must be used in priority to the non-trading deficit. The non-trading deficits must be set off in priority to losses arising in that period from a UK property business, and in priority to losses arising from a trade in that period and in priority to non-trading deficits carried back from future accounting periods.

Example

For the two years ending 31 March 2010, S Ltd has the following results:

	2009	2010
	£	£
Trading profit/(loss)	80,000	(12,000)
Trading loss brought forward	(60,000)	–
Other income and gains	8,000	–
Loss on sale of fixed interest company debentures	(20,000)	–

A claim to set the entire non-trading deficit against trading profits for the deficit period would give rise to the following computation of profits for 2009:

	£	£
Trading	80,000	
Less: Trading loss brought forward	(60,000)	
Non-trading deficit	(20,000)	
		Nil
Other income and gains		8,000
Less: Trading loss carried back		(8,000)
Profits chargeable to corporation tax		Nil

Such a claim would leave the balance of the trading loss for the year to 31 March 2010 which could not be carried back – £4,000 – to be carried forward to later accounting

---

> periods. If the claim had been to set the non-trading deficit against other income and gains first, the result would have been the same.

Carry back claims

Where a carry back claim is made, the deficit can be set off against non-trading loan relationship profits arising in the period of 12 months preceding the beginning of the period in which the deficit arises. The non-trading loan relationship profits of the preceding period will first be reduced by the following in priority to the non-trading deficit carried back:

(1) relief in respect of losses or deficits incurred or treated as incurred in an accounting period before the period in which the deficit arose;

(2) charitable donations relief (previously charges on income) in relation to payments made wholly and exclusively for the purposes of the trade;

(3) where the company is a company with an investment business, priority will be given to capital allowances, management expenses, and charitable donations relief in relation to payments made wholly and exclusively for the purposes of the trade;

(4) trading losses of the same or a later period, and

(5) non-trading deficits of the preceding period.

Carry forward

To the extent not used in any of the ways already mentioned, excess non-trade deficits will be carried forward automatically and set against non-trading profits of future periods, however, the company can make a claim to exclude any amount of the deficits brought forward from being set off. Where such a claim is made, the deficit is treated as arising in the period in respect of which such a claim is made for the purpose of carry forward to the next period, such that a claim could be made for the deficit to be excluded from set off against non-trading profits in the following period, and so on, indefinitely.

Law: CTA 2009, s. 353, 471, 476 and 481; *Loan Relationships and Derivative Contracts (Exchange Gains and Losses using Fair Value Accounting) Regulations* 2005 (SI 2005/3422); *Nuclear Electric plc v Bradley* [1995] BTC 445

See *British Tax Reporter* ¶717-200, ¶717-600.

3038 Tax treatment of financing costs and income: debt cap

FA 2009, Sch. 15 has introduced legislation aimed at preventing the use of interest deductions from eroding the UK corporation tax base, and is particularly aimed at upstream loans where a large group has either a UK or foreign parent. Sch. 15 has been rewritten as Part 7 of *Taxation (International and other Provisions) Act* 2010 for accounting periods ending on or after 1 April 2010. The legislation itself applies to periods of account of a worldwide group that begin on or after 1 January 2010. A worldwide group is a large group which has at least one company which is UK tax resident. It includes a company which while not resident in the UK, carries on a trade in the UK through a permanent establishment. A group will be large where any member of the group has 250 or more employees or has both annual turnover of €50 million or more and a balance sheet total of €43 million or more (after aggregating the headcount, turnover and balance sheet totals of any partner or linked enterprises).

The broad effect of the new legislation is to restrict any tax deduction for inter group finance expenses to the external gross finance expense of the worldwide group. The Schedule applies if the UK net debt of the group exceeds 75 per cent of the 'worldwide gross debt of the group'. Where the UK net debt does not exceed 75 per cent of the worldwide gross debt of the group then the debt cap does not apply.

The legislation applies a reduction in the amount of interest which can be deducted where the tested expense amount exceeds the allowable amount. The tested expense amount is the total of the net amount of financing expenses payable by each relevant group company that has net financing expenses. The available amount is the external gross finance expense of the worldwide group of companies.

The excess is known as the total disallowed amount. If this is negative for an individual company then the net financing deduction for the company is nil. Where it is less than £500,000 for an individual company then it is treated as being nil.

The group is required to notify HMRC of the allocation of the disallowance between relevant group members by submitting an allocation statement to HMRC. This statement must be received by HMRC within 12 months of the end of the period of account. The statement must show the 'tested expense amount', 'available amount' and 'total disallowed amount' and must list companies that are allocated a disallowance, and identify the particular financing expense amount(s) that are to be disallowed for each such company. The statement must confirm that the total of the amounts specified must equal the total disallowed amount. The effect of the statement is that a financing expense amount of a company specified in a statement is not to be brought into account by the company for corporation tax purposes. Where a company has delivered a corporation tax return for a period and because of the revised statement either the amount of profits or any other information in the return changes then the company is treated as having amended its return.

A revised statement can be submitted to HMRC with subsequent revisions provided this is done within 36 months of the end of the accounting period. The revised statement must indicate the respects in which it differs from the previous and confirm that it supersedes the previous statement.

The statement must be given by a reporting body. The companies to which Part 7 apply may appoint one of their number to exercise functions conferred on the reporting body in relation to the relevant period of account. Such an appointment is of no effect unless it is signed on behalf of each company by the appropriate person. The appropriate person being the proper officer of the company, or such other person as may for the time being have the express, implied or apparent authority of the company to act on its behalf.

Where a disallowance has been made then an amount of financing income received by one or more UK members of a worldwide group is to be exempted from corporation tax. The total amount of financing income that can be disregarded in this way, is limited by reference to the tested expense amount for a period of account of the worldwide group which is the sum of the net financing deductions of each relevant group company and the available amount.

A statement of allocated exemptions must be made to HMRC within 12 months of the end of the relevant period of account. The format for reporting is similar to that for reporting disallowances, and similar provisions apply to reporting a revised statement of exemptions as that for reporting revised disallowances.

Law: TIOPA 2010, Pt. 7

3039   Derivative contracts

The derivative contracts legislation was introduced by the *Finance Act* 2002 and took effect for accounting periods beginning on or after 1 October 2002. The legislation applies to 'relevant contracts', which are defined as options, futures and contracts for differences, provided that such contracts would be treated as derivative financial instruments for the purposes of Financial Reporting Standard 25 (FRS 25) or for any successor standard thereto (such as the revised versions of IAS 32 'Financial Instruments: Disclosure and Presentation' and IAS 39 'Financial Instruments: Recognition and Measurement', both issued in December 2003 by the International Accounting Standards Board (IASB) and which apply to listed companies for annual periods beginning on or after 1 January 2005 (or earlier if international accounting standards are adopted by a company before then). The derivative contracts legislation also applies to certain options, futures or contracts for differences which are not treated as derivative financial instruments for the purposes of FRS, where such derivative contracts are treated as financial assets for the purposes of that standard, and such derivative contracts, or such contracts together with certain associated transactions, are designed to produce a guaranteed interest-type return, or to ensure that the amount payable in respect of the contract does not fall below a guaranteed minimum amount. Finally, the legislation applies to options, futures or contracts for differences which would not otherwise fall within its scope where the underlying subject matter of such derivatives is commodities and also to contracts for differences whose underlying subject matter is intangible fixed assets, weather conditions or creditworthiness (embedded derivatives).

The derivative contracts legislation provides definitions of an option, a future and a contract for differences.

An 'option' is defined as including a warrant. A 'warrant' is in turn defined as an instrument which entitles the holder to subscribe for shares in a company, or for assets representing a loan relationship of a company, whether or not the shares or assets to which the warrant relates exist or are identifiable.

Corporation Tax

681

A 'future' is defined as a contract for the sale of property under which delivery is to be made at a future date agreed when the contract is made, and at a price so agreed. The legislation provides that the price will be taken to have been agreed when the contract is made where the price is left to be determined by reference to the price at which a contract is to be entered into on a market or exchange, or could be entered into at a time and place specified in the contract, as well as cases where the price is expressed by reference to a standard lot and quality with provision for a variation in the price to take account of any variation in quantity or quality on delivery.

A 'contract for differences' is defined as a contract the purpose or pretended purpose of which is to make a profit or avoid a loss by reference to fluctuations in the value or price of property described in the contract, or an index or other factor designated in the contract. None of the following will be treated as a contract for differences: a future; an option; a contract of insurance; a capital redemption policy; a contract of indemnity; a guarantee; a warranty; and a loan relationship.

Where the terms of a future or option provide that it is to be settled by a cash payment and do not contain any provision for physical delivery then, except where the underlying subject matter is currency, that contract will be treated as a contract for differences and not as a future or option for the purposes of the derivative contracts legislation.

Debits and credits to be brought into account

Derivatives are taxable and relieved under the following two regimes:

(1)   an income regime, where the underlying subject matter is not a chargeable asset, and

(2)   a capital gains regime where the underlying subject matter is a chargeable asset which is not held by a bank, financial trader or a CIS.

The capital gains regime does not just apply in relation to disposals, but also to any other gains and losses recognised in the accounts.

The taxation of derivatives is closely aligned with the accounting treatment.

The general rule is that the amounts to be brought into account for tax purposes under the derivative contracts legislation (for both the income regime and the capital gains regime) are the amounts that are recognised in determining the company's profit or loss for the period in question in accordance with generally accepted accounting practice. The legislation also specifically provides that the debits and credits to be brought into account are those which fairly represent, for the accounting period in question:

(a)   all profits and losses of the company which (disregarding any charges or expenses) arise to a company from its derivative contracts and related transactions, and

(b)   all charges and expenses incurred by the company under or for the purposes of its derivative contracts and related transactions.

Profits and losses are therefore identified separately to charges and expense, which are only allowable if they are incurred directly –

(a)   in bringing any of the derivative contracts into existence;

(b)   in entering into or giving effect to any of the related transactions (see below);

(c)   in making payments under any of those contracts or as a result of any of the transactions (for example, bank charges for the transfer of the funds), or

(d)   in taking steps to ensure the receipt of payments under any of those contracts or in accordance with any of those transactions (e.g. legal fees).

Guidance can be found in relation to this in HMRC's Manuals at CFM13566.

For accounting periods beginning on or after 22 April 2009 (and treating an accounting period that spans that date as two separate accounting periods beginning, or ending as the case may be, on that date) full recognition of the profits and losses of a derivative contract is required for tax purposes even if the derivative contract is not fully recognised for accounting purposes. This provision was inserted by *Finance Act* 2009 in response to tax avoidance schemes that had been notified to HMRC under the avoidance disclosure rules. It applies where the company is party to a derivative contract in the period and either:

(a)   a capital contribution has at any time been made to the company which is not recognised for accounting purposes in determining its profit or loss for the period, or

(b)   the company has issued securities that form part of its capital for the period and an amount in respect of the securities is not recognised for accounting purposes in determining its profit and loss for the period.

A related transaction is defined as 'any disposal or acquisition (in whole or in part) of rights or liabilities under the derivative contract'. Disposal and acquisition for this purpose are extended to include the transfer of rights or liabilities under a derivative contract or their extinguishment by any sale, gift, surrender or release and any disposal which occurs where the contract is discharged by performance in accordance with its terms.

Novations are included. However, the closure of a contract by entering into an equal and opposite contract is not included. Instead, both contracts would be taxed separately, albeit the debits and credits should cancel each other out.

Treatment of profits and losses on derivative contracts

Where a company is party to a derivative contract for the purposes of a trade which it carries on and profits arising under the derivative contract are otherwise chargeable to corporation tax as income under the first general rule, the company will be required to bring credits and debits under that derivative contract into account as receipts and expenses of a company's trade.

Where a company is not party to a derivative contract for the purposes of its trade, and profits arising under the contract are chargeable to corporation tax as income, the company must bring such credits and debits into account as non-trading credits and debits under the loan relationship rules.

Corporation Tax

Accounting periods beginning on or after 22 April 2009

The *Loan Relationships and Derivative Contracts (Disregard and Bringing into Account of Profits and Losses) Regulations* 2006 (SI 2006/843) were aimed at two particular one-way exchange effect avoidance schemes. Because other schemes have circumvented the regulations, a new broader ranging Targeted Anti Avoidance Rule (TAAR) has been introduced in 2009, while the regulations in SI 2006/843 are revoked.

The TAAR will be relevant to two types of arrangement:

- arrangements having a 'one-way exchange effect' (broadly arrangements which aim to generate an exchange gain eligible for matching should an exchange rate move in one direction and an exchange loss attracting tax relief should the exchange rate move in the opposite direction); and
- arrangements under which a company seeks to match and therefore disregard an exchange gain that arises because of a fixed difference between exchange rates.

Where the TAAR applies, it will prevent exchange gains in relation to the first type of arrangement and certain exchange gains and losses in relation to the second from being matched and therefore disregarded for tax purposes.

The TAAR will apply to exchange gains and losses that arise in accounting periods beginning on or after 22 April 2009 and where an accounting period straddles this date, to exchange gains and losses that would arise between 22 April 2009 and the end of the accounting period if that second part of the accounting period and the earlier part were separate accounting periods.

Broadly speaking, however, arrangements will have a one-way exchange effect and the legislation will apply (assuming the arrangements give rise to a tax advantage and include options or 'relevant contingency contracts') where the net allowable exchange losses arising on loan relationships and derivative contracts that form part of the arrangements ('amount A') are different in amount than the taxable exchange gains that would have arisen under those instruments had the relevant exchange rate moved the other way ('amount B') and that difference would not be the same if the matching rules were ignored.

Although the first aspect of the TAAR has a potentially wide ambit, it also contains what might be described as avoidance filters. The arrangements must give rise to a tax advantage within the meaning of CTA 2009, s. 476 (other than a negligible tax advantage) in order for the provisions to be relevant in the first place). This allows for those situations where as a result of hedging arrangement a very small one way exchange effect results. It would also exclude any company whose foreign exchange arrangements operate in an asymmetric manner, but which pays more tax as a result. This guards against the possibility of companies that are not engaged in avoidance being caught by the legislation because, for whatever reason, their hedging arrangements produce a very small 'one-way exchange effect'.

The second target of the TAAR is whenever an exchange gain or loss arising under a derivative contract which would otherwise be matched is not calculated by reference to spot rates of exchange, the gain or loss must be split out into separate exchange gains or losses, namely, an exchange gain or loss calculated by reference to spot rates of exchange and a residual exchange gain or loss.

In turn, it is only the first exchange gain or loss that is eligible for matching.

Law: CTA 2009, Pt. 5, Ch. 3; FA 2009, s. 43 and Sch. 21; *The Loan Relationships and Derivative Contracts (Disregard and Bringing into Account of Profits and Losses) Regulations* 2006 (SI 2006/843)

See *British Tax Reporter* ¶719-200, ¶719-500 and ¶719-600.

3042   Intangible fixed assets – outline

Finance Act 2002 introduced a regime for the taxation of goodwill and other intangible fixed assets created or acquired after 31 March 2002. This applies only to companies. It follows UK accounting practice as closely as possible in both the scope and calculation methods. The regime should limit the need for adjustments between accounts and tax profits.

The legislation takes the accounting entries ('losses and gains') in relation to intangible fixed assets and allocates corresponding tax debits and tax credits. Some of these can arise throughout the ownership of the intangible asset, whilst others only arise on realisation.

The tax debits and credits are either trade debits and credits, which arise on assets used for the purposes of a trade and are treated as trading receipts and expenditure; or non-trading debits and credits. The non-trading debits and credits are amalgamated for an accounting period. Net credits are charged to corporation tax on income, whereas net debits can be offset against other profits of the company or the group, any excess being carried forward as a non-trading loss.

There is a form of roll-over relief, where a company realises an intangible fixed asset (the 'old asset') and incurs expenditure on other intangible fixed assets ('other assets').

In order to fall within the regime an intangible fixed asset must have been created or acquired after 1 April 2002. This means that some intangible assets (e.g. internally generated goodwill) may potentially remain outside the new rules for many years.

An intangible asset takes the meaning it has for accounts purposes, so long as the accounts are drawn up in accordance with generally accepted accounting practice. Intellectual property, (for example patents, trade marks and copyrights) is specifically included by the legislation.

An intangible fixed asset means an intangible asset that is used on a continuing basis in the course of the company's activities, whether or not it is capitalised in the balance sheet. This applies to assets acquired from another party and those created by the company itself. Options to acquire or dispose of intangible fixed assets are to be treated as intangible fixed

Corporation Tax

685

assets in their own right. The legislation includes goodwill (as defined for accounts purposes) as an intangible fixed asset.

Assets excluded by the legislation include:

- rights over intangible fixed assets;
- financial assets;
- rights in companies, trusts etc.;
- intangible fixed assets held for a non-commercial purpose.

Because companies have been taking a different view to HMRC on the meaning of certain rules relating to goodwill *Finance Act* 2009 amended the rules on goodwill, to ensure that the legislation operates as originally intended for the purposes of the corporate intangible asset regime. Goodwill includes 'internally-generated' goodwill, and that all goodwill is created in the course of the carrying on of a business and is subject to rules determining whether goodwill is treated as being created before or on or after 1 April 2002. The legislation applies for the purposes of accounting periods beginning on or after 22 April 2009, and the part of any accounting period straddling this date which falls on or after 22 April.

Law: CTA 2009, Pt. 8, s. 712(1), 715 and 883–885; FA 2009, s. 70

See *British Tax Reporter* ¶723-000.

3043 Debits for intangible fixed assets

Accounting losses relating to intangible fixed assets are not immediately deductible for tax purposes. Instead they give rise to deductions via the notion of a corresponding tax debit. As can be seen from the table below however, in many cases no adjustment to the accounting loss is necessary to arrive at the tax debit.

In order to get an accounting loss there must be expenditure on intangible fixed assets. This is defined as expenditure (including abortive expenditure):

- for the purpose of acquiring, creating, or establishing title to the asset; or
- incurred by way of royalty in respect of the use of the asset; or
- for the purpose of maintaining, preserving or enhancing, or defending title to the asset.

Accounting entries	**Tax debit**
Expenditure on intangible fixed assets, which is not capitalised but written off to, the profit and loss account incurred.	Company entitled to a tax debit equal to the amount written off, (subject to exclusions for some categories of expenditure not generally deductible for tax purposes, e.g. entertainment, fines and expensive hired cars). Royalties would generally fall within this category. For tax purposes these have traditionally been deductible when paid. In future they will follow the accounts treatment, i.e. the accrual basis.
Writing down of an intangible fixed asset capitalised for accounts purposes by way of amortisation or an impairment review.	Company entitled to a tax debit calculated as follows:

$$\text{Accounting loss} \times \frac{\text{Tax value}}{\text{Accounting value}}$$

Accounting entries	**Tax debit**
	Where: Accounting loss is the amount of the loss (write down) recognised for accounts purposes. Tax value is the tax written down value of the asset immediately before the amortisation or impairment is recognised. Accounting value is the value of the asset for accounting purposes immediately before the amortisation or impairment is recognised. *The tax written down value of an asset is the tax cost minus the total amounts of tax debits previously brought into account plus the total amounts of tax credits previously brought into account.* The legislation recognises that in most cases the tax debit will equal the accounting loss. This may not be the case however where reinvestment relief has been claimed for tax purposes. Example: Goodwill is acquired for £200,000. For accounts purposes it is written off over ten years on a straight-line basis. For tax purposes the cost is reduced by £50,000 as a result of a reinvestment claim. The tax debit in year 1 is £20,000 multiplied by £150,000/£200,000 or £15,000. The tax debit in year 2 is £20,000 multiplied by £135,000/£180,000 or £15,000.

Corporation Tax

Accounting entries

Intangible fixed asset capitalised for accounts purposes but not amortised.

Tax debit

Irrespective of the accounting treatment, a company may elect to write down the cost of the intangible fixed asset at a fixed rate for tax purposes. This will be particularly beneficial where the intangible asset is not amortised in the accounts. The election must be made in writing within two years after the end of the accounting period in which the asset is created or acquired.

The fixed rate tax deduction will be:

- 4% of the cost of the asset for tax purposes (reduced proportionately where the accounting treatment is less than 12 months), or
- if less the balance of the tax written down value.

Accounting entries

Reversal of accounting gain recognised in a prior period for tax purposes.

Tax debit

A tax debit is available calculated as follows:

$$\text{Accounting loss} \times \frac{\text{Previous credit}}{\text{Accounting gain}}$$

Where:

Accounting loss is the amount of the loss (write down) recognised for accounts purposes.

Previous credit is the amount of the credit previously brought into account for tax purposes. Accounting gain is the amount of the gain that is reversed (in whole or in part).

3044   Credits for intangible fixed assets

Accounting receipts and gains of a company relating to intangible fixed assets are again not automatically taxable. Instead they give rise to a series of tax credits.

Accounting entries

Receipts relating to intangible fixed assets recognised in the profit and loss account as they accrue.

Revaluations either above original cost or to restore past losses.

Tax credit

Company entitled to a tax debit on an accrual basis in accordance with the accounts.

The tax credit is restricted to the debits previously deducted by limiting the taxable amount to the lower of:

Accounting entries

Tax credit

- the increase in value for tax purposes, or
- the net aggregate amount of relevant tax debits previously brought into account.

The increase in value for tax purposes equals:

$$\text{Accounting adjustment} \times \frac{\text{Tax value}}{\text{Accounting value}}$$

Where:
Accounting adjustment is the amount of the increase in the accounting value of the asset.
Tax value is the tax written down value of the asset immediately before revaluation.
Accounting value is the accounting value of the asset immediately before revaluation.
The net aggregate amount of relevant tax debits equals the total amounts of previous debits brought into account for tax purposes less the total amounts of previous debits brought into account for tax purposes.
A tax credit in relation to a revaluation cannot apply where the asset is being written down on a fixed rate basis for tax purposes.

Accounting entries

Tax credit

Negative goodwill acquired on the acquisition of a business and written back to the profit and loss account.

Corresponding credit brought into taxable income.

Reversal of accounting loss recognised in a prior period for tax purposes.

The tax credit is calculated as follows:

$$\text{Accounting gain} \times \frac{\text{Tax debit}}{\text{Accounting loss}}$$

Where:
Accounting gain is the amount of the gain recognised for accounts purposes.
Tax debit is the amount of the debit previously brought into account for tax purposes.
Accounting loss is the amount of the loss that is reversed (in whole or in part).

3045   Realisation of intangible fixed assets

Additional debits and credits can arise on the realisation of intangible fixed assets. The proceeds of the realisation are defined as the amount recognised for accounts purposes reduced by any incidental costs of realisation. They are taxed as follows.

Corporation Tax

Realisation proceeds	Tax treatment
Assets previously written down for tax purposes.	If the proceeds of realisation exceed the tax written down value of the asset, a tax credit arises equal to the excess. If the proceeds are less than the tax written down value of the asset, a tax debit arises equal to the shortfall.
Assets shown in the balance sheet but not written down for tax purposes.	If the proceeds of realisation exceed the tax cost of the asset, a tax credit arises equal to the excess. If the proceeds are less than the tax cost of the assets, a tax debit arises equal to the shortfall. The cost for tax purposes should be the same as the amount capitalised for accounts purposes unless there are circumstances such as reinvestment relief.
Assets never shown in the balance sheet (e.g. if internally generated).	Tax credit is the realisation proceeds.
Abortive expenditure on a realisation.	A corresponding tax debit arises.

Where there is a part-realisation of an asset the tax debits and credits need to be calculated by reference to the percentage reduction in the accounting value of the asset as a result of the realisation. The tax written down value immediately after a part realisation is the previous value reduced in the ratio which the accounting value (i.e. net book value) of the asset in the accounts immediately after the realisation bears to the accounting value immediately before.

Example

Goodwill was acquired for £200,000 on 1 January 2005. For accounts purposes it is written off over ten years on a straight-line basis. For tax purposes the cost is reduced by £50,000 as a result of a reinvestment claim. On 1 January 2006 part of the goodwill was disposed of for £150,000. The value of the remaining asset for accounts purposes immediately after the disposal is £60,000.

Debit for year ended 31 December 2005

The accounting amortisation is £20,000 (£200,000/10). The tax debit for the year is £15,000 (£20,000 × £150,000/£200,000)).

Disposal

Immediately prior to the part disposal, the accounts value of the goodwill is £180,000 (£200,000 − £20,000). The tax written down value is £135,000 (£150,000 − £15,000).

The tax written down value of the part of the asset disposed of is calculated as £90,000 (£135,000 × (£180,000 − £60,000)/£180,000)). A tax credit therefore arises on realisation being £60,000 (£150,000 − £90,000).

Immediately after the part disposal, the accounts value of the goodwill is £60,000. The tax written down value is £45,000 (£135,000 × £60,000/£180,000).

Debit for year ended 31 December 2006

The accounting amortisation is £6,000 (£60,000/10). The tax debit for the year is £4,500 (£6,000 × £45,000/£60,000).

Roll-over relief

There is provision for a form of roll-over relief, modelled very closely on the capital gains tax rules (see 6305). Where a company realises an intangible fixed asset (the 'old asset') and incurs expenditure on other intangible fixed assets ('other assets'), the proceeds from the realisation of the old asset and the tax cost of the other assets are each reduced by the amount available for relief.

The amount available for relief is the amount by which the proceeds of realisation exceed the tax cost of the old asset. However, if the expenditure on replacement assets is less than the proceeds the amount of available for relief is the difference between the expenditure and the tax cost.

See *British Tax Reporter* ¶724-000.

3046   Interaction with other schemes

The rules relating to intangible assets interact with a number of other tax treatments.

Computer software

Software acquired with the related hardware often falls to be treated for accounting purposes as part of the cost of that hardware. If this is the case then the software is excluded from the new rules, except in relation to any royalties which may arise.

Software not acquired with hardware is an intangible asset, and the intangible assets rules override those in respect of capital allowances. This may not be desirable to a company, especially if it is entitled to first year allowances. It is therefore possible to make an election to disapply the intangible provisions. The election must be made in writing not more than two years after the end of the accounting period in which the expenditure was incurred. It is irrevocable.

Research and development expenditure

Expenditure on intangible fixed assets can take the form of research and development expenditure. The legislation effectively removes research and development expenditure from the intangible rules except in relation to:

- any receipts recognised as they accrue (e.g. royalties);

Corporation Tax

- any accounting loss resulting from an adjustment to the value of receipts recognised as they accrue.

Any debits or credits resulting from realisation must be calculated by excluding any research and development expenditure from the cost of the asset.

Transfer of business or trade

Rules exist to ensure continuity of treatment where intangible fixed assets change ownership in the course of a business reorganisation. They are broadly equivalent to those for capital gains tax purposes (see 4015 and 4024).

Transactions between related parties

Where there is a transfer of a chargeable intangible asset between a company and a related party then it is deemed to be transferred at market value, (i.e. the price at which the asset might reasonably be expected to fetch on a sale in the open market). This mirrors the rules for capital gains tax and hence the value is consistent for all parties even though one of the parties may still be under the old rules.

Where a royalty is payable by a company to a related party and for some reason it is not paid within 12 months of the end of the period of account in which it is charged, it does not give rise to a tax debit until such time as it is paid.

Roll-over relief may be restricted where related parties are involved in the transaction.

A related party of a company is defined widely and does not necessarily require control. Rather it relies on the concept of a 'major interest' in a company. Also a close company is connected with its participators and the associates of its participators.

Finance Act 2008 introduced anti-avoidance legislation to clarify that, for transactions from 12 March 2008, the effect of the 'related party' rules in the corporate intangible assets regime is unaffected by any administration, liquidation or other insolvency proceedings or equivalent arrangements in which any company or partnership may be involved.

Groups

For commentary on the rules on intangible assets relating to groups of companies, see 3715.

Law: CTA 2009, Pt. 8

Source: HMRC Manual: Corporate Intangibles Research and Development

See *British Tax Reporter* ¶715-600.

CHARGEABLE GAINS

3050   Treatment of companies' capital gains

Capital gains made by a company are not chargeable to capital gains tax. Rather, a company pays corporation tax on its chargeable gains; other capital gains are outside the scope of the UK tax net unless they are to be specifically taxed under income provisions.

It is important to make this distinction between companies and other persons because the general rules relating to capital gains will not necessarily apply to companies, although corporation tax does apply 'capital gains tax principles' (see 3027).

See *British Tax Reporter* ¶753-000.

3051   Calculation of chargeable gains of companies

Chargeable gains and allowable losses are calculated according to the normal capital gains tax rules (see 5221ff.) except that accounting periods are treated as if they are years of assessment. However, indexation (see 5286) continues to apply for the purposes of corporation tax on chargeable gains. Indexation allowance is not available to create or to augment a loss. The indexation allowance is limited to the amount of the unindexed gain.

The gains of a company to be included in total profits chargeable to corporation tax (see 3050) for an accounting period are calculated by setting off allowable losses suffered in the same and earlier accounting periods. There are special provisions for groups (see 3682ff.) and the loss offset may be restricted in the case of gains on assets transferred in to a company by a fellow group company to soak up allowable losses attributable to periods before the company joined the group (see 3684).

Example

Company Ltd prepares accounts annually to 30 June. In March 2006 (i.e. in the year to 30 June 2006), it sold a chargeable asset for £500,000. The asset was purchased in July 1996 for £200,000. The company also sold a chargeable asset in January 2006 for £100,000 that it had purchased in January 2003 for £120,000.

The company also made trading profits of £2,000,000 for the year to 30 June 2006.

The profits chargeable to corporation tax (PCTCT) are computed as follows.

Asset 1	£
Disposal proceeds	500,000
Less: acquisition cost	(200,000)
Unindexed gain	300,000
Less: indexation allowance say	
0.257 × £200,000	(51,400)
Chargeable gain	248,600

Corporation Tax

Asset 2		£
Disposal proceeds		100,000
Less: acquisition cost		(120,000)
Allowable loss		(20,000)
PCTCT – y/e 30/6/2006	£	£
Trading profits		2,000,000
Chargeable gain	248,600	
Less: allowable loss	(20,000)	
		228,600
PCTCT		2,228,600

Law: TCGA 1992, s. 8

CHARITABLE DONATIONS (FORMERLY CHARGES ON INCOME)

3055 Relief for 'charges on income' of company

Since 2005 and prior to the enactment of the *Corporation Tax Act* 2010, relief for charges on income was, in effect, restricted to qualifying donations to charity. Although the legislation applying to charges on income had formerly been of wide application, much of the substance of the relief was removed with the introduction of the loan relationships regime in 1996. Further rationalisation was made in 2002, with the removal of royalties from the charges on income regime, and again in 2005 with the removal of annuities and annual payments. With effect for accounting periods ending on or after 1 April 2010, the legislation relating to relief for charitable donations was rewritten, and renamed as charitable donations relief, by CTA 2010. As a result, the concept of 'charges on income' was consigned to history.

As the purpose behind the enactment of CTA 2010 was to change the way in which the law is expressed and arranged, and not the law itself, the commentary in 3059 below on the relief available for charitable donations also applies for accounting periods ended before 1 April 2010 unless otherwise indicated. The following commentary is therefore only applicable to annuities and annual payments made before 16 March 2005 (changes made more than six years ago being outside the scope of this commentary).

Payments which were charges on income (see below) were deductible for the accounting period in which they were paid. Charges on income were only deductible to the extent that they were paid out of the company's profits brought into charge to corporation tax, and were deducted after deductions for any other relief, such as loss relief, had been made from the profits of the accounting period, but before any allowance for group relief. Where charges on income paid in any accounting period exceeded the profits of that period, the excess may in certain cases have been treated as a trading expense in computing a loss to be carried forward or as an amount available for group relief.

Following changes made by *Finance Act* 2002, 'charges on income' meant (and only meant):

(a) a qualifying donation to a charity;
(b) an amount specifically designated as a charge in accordance with relief for gifts of shares to charities and gifts of interests in land to charities; and
(c) for payments made prior to 16 March 2005, an 'annuity' or other 'annual payment' – which were defined separately, but one of the key requirements was that they did not relate to a company's loan relationships. As indicated, this only applied for payments made before 16 March 2005. After that date, annuities and annual payments that are not trading deductions may only qualify for relief as expenses of management. Where a company's accounting period straddled 16 March 2005, there were provisions to prevent double relief (i.e. both as charges and expenses of management), or to avoid an item of expenditure dropping out of account altogether.

For commentary on amounts within (a) and (b) above, see 3059 below (and the explanation given above).

Law: Former ICTA 1988, s. 337A, 338; *Minsham Properties Ltd v Price (HMIT)* [1990] BTC 528; *MacArthur (HMIT) v Greycoat Estates Mayfair Ltd* [1996] BTC 13

See *British Tax Reporter* ¶716-680.

3059 Charitable donations relief

For accounting periods ending on or after 1 April 2010, relief for qualifying charitable donations is provided by CTA 2010, Pt. 6. For earlier periods, relief was available as a charge on income.

Where a company makes a qualifying charitable donation, a deduction is allowed against that company's total profits for the accounting period in which the donation is made. However, an exception is made where a donation is paid to a charity of which the company is a 100 per cent subsidiary (see below). The deduction is to be made after any other relief but before group relief. However, the amount of the deduction is limited to the amount which reduces the company's taxable total profits for the period to nil. Where this restriction applies, the excess amount can not be offset against the profits of earlier or later periods. Relief is only available for the excess amount by way of surrender as group relief and by set off against the apportioned profits of a CFC.

Example

A company (company A) which is a 100 per cent subsidiary of another company (company B) makes a qualifying charitable donation of £100,000 during its accounting period ended on 30 April 2010. Company A's total profits for that period, before

---

Corporation Tax

> deducting the charitable donations relief due, are £80,000. The amount of charitable donations relief which can be claimed by company A is limited to £80,000, being the amount which reduces its taxable total profits for that period to nil. Company A is unable to claim relief in respect of the excess amount of £20,000. However, it may be possible to surrender the excess amount as group relief to company B.

The relief is not available in respect of payments which are otherwise deductible (for example, gifts of trading stock by a trading company to charities and other bodies including designated educational establishments and gifts for humanitarian purposes of medical supplies and equipment where they are held as trading stock which, in either case, would be deductible for tax purposes in calculating the profits of the trade).

A payment to a charity will be a qualifying payment for charitable donations relief purposes if each of the following conditions are met:

(a) the payment must be a sum of money;

(b) it must not be subject to a condition as to repayment (except where the company is wholly-owned by the charity and both the charitable payment and the repayment are made in order to reduce the company's taxable profits to nil and the repayment is made within 12 months of the end of the accounting period);

(c) the company making the payment must not be a charity;

(d) the payment must not be disqualified on the basis that there is an associated acquisition (being, broadly, an acquisition of property by the charity from the company making the payment or a person associated with it);

(e) the payment must not be disqualified on the basis that it is regarded as a distribution. For payments made on or after 1 April 2006, a non-dividend payment made by a company which is wholly-owned by a charity is not regarded as a distribution for this purpose; and

(f) the payment must not be disqualified on the basis that benefits are associated with the payment unless the total value of the benefits associated with the payment are less than £500 and the total value of the benefits associated with the payment is less than the variable limit, which is, where the payment is £100 or less, 25 per cent of the amount of the payment, where the payment is between £101 and £1,000, £25; and where the payment is £1,001 or over, 5 per cent of the amount of the payment.

For payments made before 1 April 2006, conditions (b), (d) and (f) applied to payments made by close companies only.

Qualifying donations to charity

In addition, where a company makes a donation to a charity in the form of a qualifying investment, charitable donations relief will be available where the company is not itself a charity and where it makes a claim. For these purposes a 'qualifying investment' is defined as:

● shares or securities which are listed on a recognised stock exchange or dealt in on a designated market in the UK;

● units in an authorised unit trust scheme;

- shares in an open-ended investment company;
- an interest in an offshore fund; and
- a qualifying interest in land (being, broadly, a freehold interest in land in the UK and a leasehold interest in UK land which is a term of years absolute). In this situation relief is clawed back if the donor company becomes within six years entitled to an interest in all or part of the land concerned is party to an arrangement whereby it enjoys some right in relation to all or part of that land.

The amount of relief due in respect of the donation of a qualifying investment is to be determined in accordance with one of the two formulas at CTA 2010, s. 206 one applying where the disposal is a gift and the second applying where the disposal is at an undervalue. In both cases, if the amount given by the formula is a negative amount, the amount of the relief is nil.

Finance Act 2010 introduced new rules to block tax avoidance schemes that exploit the rules for tax relief on gifts of qualifying investments to charities. The legislation does not affect charities; it operates by restricting tax relief to a donor on gifts of qualifying investments to charities. The avoidance depends on the donor receiving tax relief at their marginal rate of tax on the full market value of the qualifying investments at the date of the gift where the donor acquired the investments at below market value as part of a scheme or arrangement or the market value of the investment is artificially inflated at the date of the gift to charity. The new anti avoidance provision adjusts the amount of relief to the donor to the economic cost of acquisition of the gift to the donor where the qualifying investment gifted to the charity (or anything from which the investment derives) was acquired within four years of the date of disposal and the main purpose, or one of the main purposes, of acquiring the qualifying investment was to dispose of it to a charity and claim the tax relief. One particular type of arrangement likely to be caught by this new anti avoidance provision is where a company (A) enters into an agreement with another company (X) to buy £200,000 of shares in a FTSE 100 company from X for £30,000. The shares come with an option attached for X to buy them back after three years for £1. Two days after purchasing the shares A donates them to a charity and claims under CTA 2010, Pt. 6 that this is a donation of £200,000 – the market value of the shares. The new anti avoidance provision applies in relation to any disposal made to a charity on or after 15 December 2009.

Law: CTA 2010, Pt. 6, FA 2010, Sch. 7

See *British Tax Reporter* ¶716-600.

Definition of charity

UK charitable tax reliefs are being extended to organisations equivalent to charities and Community Amateur Sports Clubs in the EU and in the European Economic Area (EEA) countries of Norway and Iceland following a judgment in the European Court of Justice (ECJ) in January 2009. *Finance Act* 2010 therefore introduces new statutory definition of a charity entitled to UK charity tax reliefs. The definition is based on that of a charity under the law of England and Wales which is already used for UK tax purposes.

Corporation Tax

The definition introduces a four-stage test to determine if an organisation is eligible for UK charity tax reliefs.

First, the organisation must be established for charitable purposes only. The definition of charitable purposes is that under the law of England and Wales and is found in s. 2 of the *Charities Act* 2006.

Second, the organisation must meet the jurisdiction condition. It must be located in the UK or a member state of the EU or a specified country. The Commissioners for HMRC will have the power to specify countries outside the EU by statutory instrument. The countries of Iceland and Norway will be specified as soon as practicable.

Third, the organisation must meet the registration condition. Where the organisation is required under the law of its home country to be registered with a charity regulator similar to the Charity Commission for England and Wales, it must be so registered. The purpose of this condition is to ensure that only organisations that comply with their charity obligations in their home country are eligible for UK charity tax reliefs.

Fourth, the organisation must meet the management condition. All persons in the organisation having control and management responsibilities must be 'fit and proper' persons. The term 'fit and proper' is not further defined. 'Persons' include corporate bodies and individuals who are trustees, directors, managers or any other officer of the organisation in a management position. While a properly run charity always seeks to appoint persons of integrity to key management positions there is always a chance that a charity may unknowingly appoint a person who is not fit and proper. In such a case, the charity would cease to meet the management condition and would no longer be eligible for charitable tax reliefs even where it meets all the other conditions. However the management condition is subject to the relaxation in certain circumstances where the manager is not in a position to prejudice the administration of the charity or where a person has been appointed to a management position within the charity and it is subsequently found that the person is not a fit and proper person. In such a case, where the charity has not colluded with the manager and works with HMRC to rectify the position, the Commissioners for HMRC may consider that the relaxation applies and the charity to have met the management condition throughout the period the person was in post. HMRC have stated that they will use its discretion under this paragraph to ensure this test does not impose an undue burden on existing charities. Whether either of the relaxations apply will depend upon the circumstances of each case. A charity may challenge a decision by the Commissioners for HMRC not to apply the relaxations by appealing against the refusal of a claim to a tax Tribunal.

Law: FA 2010, Sch. 6

PAYMENTS TO SHAREHOLDERS

DIVIDENDS AND DISTRIBUTIONS

3065   Dividends and other distributions to shareholders

A company does not exist in isolation and the shareholders who invest in it expect to get some financial benefit when the company makes a profit. A company confers some benefit on its shareholders in the form of distributions which it makes from time to time. The distribution will usually take the form of a dividend but there are other types of distribution. Not all distributions are 'distributions' for tax purposes (see 3067, 3069, 3071, 3072).

Following the abolition of ACT in 1999, the major tax implication of a payment made by a company being treated as a distribution is that the payment will not be deductible for corporation tax purposes.

The distributions a company makes are subject to special rules when calculating the tax payable on them by the recipient of the distribution.

Generally, the tax treatment of company distributions in the hands of the shareholder depends on whether it is a 'qualifying distribution', in which case there is an associated tax credit, or a non-qualifying distribution (see 3075ff).

Special provisions apply to stock dividends (see below).

Information relating to distributions

For dividends or payment of interest which are deemed to be distributions, payment must be accompanied by a statement from the company (and in the case of payments via nominees, by such nominees) showing, in the case of a qualifying distribution, the amount and accompanying tax credit or, in the case of interest which is not a qualifying distribution, the amount gross and net of any tax deducted at source. The penalty is £60 per offence, restricted to £600 per distribution. The recipient of a qualifying distribution may also call for a statement from the payer showing the amount and accompanying tax credit.

Returns relating to distributions

Electronic delivery of returns is possible provided the sender notified the recipient in advance that he intends to use electronic format, the recipient agrees, and the electronic format used is designed to prevent alteration of what is delivered.

Stock dividends

In general terms a stock dividend is share capital issued by a 'UK-resident' (see 3014) company either instead of a dividend or as a bonus issue to which there is a right under the

Corporation Tax

terms on which the original shares were issued. They are not regarded as distributions for tax purposes.

An individual is charged to higher rate tax in respect of the appropriate amount in cash, which is generally the amount foregone unless the market value is substantially different); HMRC regard 15 per cent as substantial. The charge is modified in relation to personal representatives and discretionary trustees, and a statement of practice has been published which sets out the tax treatment of enhanced stock dividends received by trustees of interest in possession trusts. Company recipients are generally treated as having received capital under general principles and so are not subject to corporation tax in respect of stock dividend.

For the chargeable gains position in respect of stock dividends, see 5915.

Law: CTA 2010, Pt. 23, Ch. 6, s. 104; ITTOIA 2005, Pt. 4, Ch. 5; *Income and Corporation Taxes (Electronic Certificates of Deduction of Tax and Tax Credit) Regulations* 2003 (SI 2003/3143); *IR Commrs v Blott* [1921] 2 AC 171

Source: SP A8, *Stock dividends*; SP 4/94, *Enhanced stock dividends received by trustees of interest in possession trusts*

See *British Tax Reporter* ¶743-100.

3067 What is a 'distribution' for tax purposes?

Although any detailed discussion of what is meant by a distribution would require an excursion into the world of company law, it is necessary to have, at least, a basic definition in order to understand their tax treatment. Distributions include those matters set out below.

(1)   Any dividend paid by the company, including a capital dividend.

(2)   Any other distribution out of assets of the company (whether in cash or otherwise) in respect of shares in the company, except any part of the distribution which:

    (a)   represents a repayment of capital (see below); or
    (b)   is equal to any new consideration received by the company for the distribution.
'Shares' include stock and any other interest of a member in the company. Something is done in respect of a share if it is done to a person as the current or former holder of a share, or because of a right granted or offer made with reference to the share. Anything done in respect of shares referring to a shareholding at a particular time is done to the then shareholder or to his personal representatives.
'New consideration' is consideration not provided directly or indirectly out of the assets of the company. It does not include amounts retained by the company by capitalising a distribution. So for example, a bonus issue of securities or redeemable shares will not be treated as issued for new consideration and so will be a distribution. A bonus issue of ordinary (non-redeemable) shares is also not for new consideration but it would not normally be out of assets of the company and so not a distribution. A

premium paid when shares are issued and later used to pay up share capital may be treated as new consideration. The making of a loan is generally matched by new consideration of the obligation to repay; if the obligation is released, this can result in a charge to tax if the loan is by a close company to its participators (see 4312).

A distribution is made out of assets of a company if the cost falls on the company.

(3) Any redeemable share capital or any security:

(a) issued by the company in respect of shares in the company; or

(b) issued by the company after 5 April 1972 in respect of securities in the company otherwise than for new consideration.

(4) Any interest or other distribution out of assets of the company in respect of 'non-commercial' securities of the company (but see also 3071). Securities issued by a company are 'non-commercial' if the consideration given by company for the use of the principal represents more than a reasonable commercial return.

(5) Any interest or other distribution out of assets of the company in respect of 'special securities'.

The following securities issued by a company are 'special securities' for these purposes:

(a) securities issued under (3) but not including those issued before 6 April 1965; or

(b) securities convertible directly or indirectly into shares in the company, or securities issued after 5 April 1972 with a right to receive shares in or securities of the company (unless the securities are listed or the terms are reasonably comparable with listed securities); or

(c) securities which have variable interest according to the results of the business of the company; or

(d) securities connected with shares in the company. 'Connected with' means that because of the terms, conditions or rights attached to the securities, it is necessary or advantageous for a person holding them to hold, dispose of or acquire a proportionate holding of the shares; or

(e) in respect of interest, etc. paid after 14 May 1992, 'equity notes' issued by the company and held by an associated company or a company funded in respect thereof by the issuer or an associated company; equity notes are broadly securities with a term of at least 50 years and companies are associated if they are under 75 per cent common control (normal inter-company indebtedness, bank overdrafts, bank deposits and demand loans are not equity notes).

(6) A transfer of assets between a company and its members if the benefit received by the member exceeds any new consideration given in return. The value of any benefit is decided according to its market value. The company is treated as making a distribution of an amount equal to the difference between the two figures. In HMRC's view, 'assets' for these purposes do not include cash.

(7) An issue of paid up share capital after a repayment of share capital. A distribution is treated as made in respect of bonus shares on the later issue. The amount of the distribution is limited to the difference between the total share capital repaid and any

Corporation Tax

amount treated previously as a distribution. Where the bonus share capital is issued after 5 April 1973, this provision is only applicable if:

(a) the issue is made within ten years of redeemable shares; and
(b) the issue is of redeemable share capital.

but the provision applies in full if:

(a) the company is under the control of five or fewer persons; or
(b) the company is unlisted; and
(c) where the company is controlled by another company, the controller fulfils these conditions.

Repayment of share capital

Where a company issues any share capital other than by the receipt of new consideration and any amount so paid is not a distribution, then any subsequent distributions within ten years of issue will not be treated as repayments of share capital, except to the extent that those distributions, together with any previous distributions, exceed the amounts so paid up on such shares after that date which are not qualifying distributions.

All shares of the same class are treated as representing the same share capital; and where shares are issued in respect of other shares, or converted into or exchanged for other shares, they are treated as representing the same share capital.

Where share capital is issued at a premium representing new consideration (see (3) above), the premium is part of the share capital to decide whether any repayment is a distribution. Otherwise, any premium paid on the redemption of share capital is not a repayment of share capital and consequently is a distribution.

Law: CTA 2010, Pt. 23, Ch. 2

Source: Law Society's *Gazette*, 24 February 1993; TAX 5/93

See *British Tax Reporter* ¶743-200.

3069   Payments not treated as distributions

If one company transfers assets or liabilities to another company it will not be treated as a distribution if both companies are resident in the UK and neither is a 51 per cent subsidiary of a foreign company and they are not under common control (see 3653) or if both companies are UK resident and one is a 51 per cent subsidiary of the other or both are 51 per cent subsidiaries of another UK resident company.

A distribution does not occur where fully paid preference shares are repaid and those shares existed on 6 April 1965 or were issued after that date for new consideration not derived from ordinary shares and remain fully paid until the date of repayment.

Law: CTA 2010, s. 1021

See *British Tax Reporter* ¶743-800.

3071 Limited meaning of distribution in respect of interest

The *Finance Act* 1982 introduced a limitation to the meaning of distribution in respect of interest payments falling within 3067(5)(a), (b), (c) and (d) above, with effect for payments after 8 March 1982.

The limitation was introduced to stop lenders, principally banks, from converting an interest receipt (taxable) into a non-taxable distribution by the simple expedient of linking part of the interest to the results of the borrower. It excludes such interest from being a distribution if it is paid out of the assets of the borrower to another company within the charge to corporation tax (see 3008) and it is not excessive.

A distribution is also still treated as occurring for corporation tax purposes if the company to which the interest or other distribution is paid is entitled to a tax exemption on that payment other than by virtue of the fact that UK company distributions are not chargeable to corporation tax.

3072 Non-distributions

In defining a distribution for tax purposes (see 3067), a further complication arises because, besides the specific distributions, etc. made by a company which are not treated as distributions for tax purposes (see 3069), there are also a number of general descriptions of transaction which are not regarded as distributions for tax purposes.

Company transactions which are not distributions for tax purposes include:

- distributions made in respect of share capital on a winding-up (see 4740);
- payments made to a charity under a covenant for annual payments over a period which may exceed three years;
- group relief payments (see 3809) or payments for the surrender of ACT (see 3662) (in this case, any excess over the amount surrendered is treated as a distribution);
- share or loan interest paid by a registered industrial and provident society;
- building society interest or dividends;
- dividends or bonuses deductible in calculating the tax chargeable on trading profits made by an industrial or provident society (see 4670);
- taxable stock dividends (see 3065);
- small distributions on the dissolution of an unincorporated association of a social or recreational nature which has not carried on a trade or investment business (see 4689);
- certain demergers (see 3200);
- certain purchases by a company of its own shares (see 3220).

Corporation Tax

Law: CTA 2010, Pt. 23, Ch. 3

See *British Tax Reporter* ¶743-800.

3073 Extraction of profits

The extraction of profits from a privately owned company can be done either by way of a dividend or additional salary/bonus. Salaries and bonuses attract National Insurance contributions. Dividends can push taxpayers into higher rates. Bonuses may take corporation tax rates down to lower levels. The most tax-efficient solution will always depend on the particular facts.

It is often convenient to consider the marginal rates of income tax, NIC and corporation tax in addressing this issue.

For the 2010 Financial Year, that is the year ended 31 March 2011, the marginal rates of corporation tax are as follows for a company with no associated companies:

On profits up to £300,000	21%
On profits between £300,000 and £1,500,000	29.75%
On profits above £1,500,000	28%

For the 2010/11 year of assessment the effective marginal rates of income tax on dividend income will be:

For basic rate taxpayers	0%
For higher rate taxpayers	25%
For additional rate taxpayers	36.11%

For the 2010/11 year of assessment the combined marginal rate of income tax and employers NIC on salary/bonuses will, very broadly, be as follows:

For basic rate taxpayers	31%
For higher rate taxpayers	41%
For additional rate taxpayers	51%

For 2010–11 the rate of employers NIC on salary/bonuses is 12.8 per cent.

Assuming that a company has 100 units of (pre-corporation tax) profits which are to be extracted either by way of bonus or dividend, the comparison of the marginal tax on the extracted profit is as follows:

Example 1

Additional rate taxpayer

Marginal small profits rate of corporation tax

	Dividend £	Bonus £
Profit	100.00	100.00
Bonus		(88.65)
Employer's NIC		(11.35)
	100.00	Nil
Corporation tax	(29.75)	
	70.25	
Dividend/bonus	70.25	88.65
Income tax	(25.37)	(44.33)
Employer's NIC		(0.89)
Net cash	44.88	43.44

Example 2

Higher rate taxpayer

Marginal small profits rate of corporation tax

	Dividend £	Bonus £
Profit	100.00	100.00
Bonus		(88.65)
Employer's NIC		(11.35)
	100.00	Nil
Corporation tax	(29.75)	
	70.25	
Dividend/bonus	70.25	88.65
Income tax	(17.56)	(35.46)
Employer's NIC		(0.89)
Net cash	52.69	52.30

Example 3

Basic rate taxpayer

Marginal small profits rate of corporation tax

	Dividend £	Bonus £
Profit	100.00	100.00
Bonus		(88.65)
Employer's NIC		(11.35)
	100.00	Nil
Corporation tax	(29.75)	
	70.25	
Dividend/bonus	70.25	88.65
Income tax	(0.00)	(17.73)
Employer's NIC		(9.75)
Net cash	70.25	61.17

These examples suggest that it will usually be more beneficial to extract profits by way of dividend rather than salary bonus for 2010/11 irrespective of the level of other income of the shareholder/director. For companies with a marginal rate of tax lower than 29.75 per cent (i.e. where profits exceed £1,500,000 or are less than £300,000) the tax savings by paying a dividend will be greater.

These results should however be taken with caution as the most tax efficient solution will depend on the particular facts. In particular, care should be taken when the income level of the shareholder/director are at the margin between the basic rate/higher rate or higher rate/ additional rate or at the margin between the primary threshold/upper earnings limit for NIC purposes since in those situations, the marginal rates of income tax and NIC may be higher than those used in the example. For example, for a taxpayer with earnings below the basic rate limit and dividend income which takes his total income over the basic rate limit, the marginal rate of income tax on additional salary or bonus is 45 per cent: 20 per cent tax on the bonus and an additional 25 per cent because an equivalent amount of dividend income moves out at the dividend basic rate (of 0 per cent) into the dividend higher rate (of, effectively, after tax credit, 25 per cent). There will also be employees NIC of 11 per cent on the bonus, giving a combined rate of income and NIC of 56 per cent in the margin.

Care also needs to be taken when the shareholder's/director's income is between £100,000 and approximately £113,000 since the marginal rates of income tax on dividend income and salary/bonuses will be higher because of the phased withdrawal of the benefit of the personal allowances.

Also, non tax factors might influence the decision between dividend and bonus, for example, pension planning, minority shareholder share valuation issues.

While some owner managers would consider that the payment of a large cash dividend could not be supported by the company's cash flow, the money could be lent back to the company via the owner manager's loan account. Care needs to be taken when paying such a dividend as the tax point for interim dividends is the date of payment. HMRC treat an interim dividend as paid when unreserved right to draw a dividend exists. This could be when such a dividend is credited to the owner manager's loan account. Problems can arise because many small companies do not make such an entry to the loan account until the annual audit takes place, after the end of the accounting period in which the directors resolved that an interim dividend be paid. Then the dividend is treated as being paid in the later accounting period. The most effective way of showing that the dividend has been paid is to pay the dividend by cheque, and loan the money back to the company by a cheque drawn on the owner manager's personal bank account.

QUALIFYING AND NON-QUALIFYING DISTRIBUTIONS

3075 Importance of qualifying nature of distribution

Once a company has decided that a transaction which it has made is a distribution for tax purposes (see 3067), it must perform yet another task before it can deal with and account for the payment. It must consider whether that distribution is a qualifying or a non-qualifying distribution. This will determine whether the person receiving the distribution is entitled to an associated tax credit.

A person receiving a non-qualifying distribution or not entitled to a tax credit may be liable to higher rate income tax on the amount or value of the distribution; there is relief for a subsequent repayment of share capital constituting a distribution.

Law: CTA 2010, s. 1109

See *British Tax Reporter* ¶743-200.

3076 What is a 'qualifying distribution'?

All distributions of a company are 'qualifying distributions' except:

- any bonus security or any bonus redeemable share capital issued by a company after 5 November 1972 in respect of securities of the company to the extent that it is not referable to new consideration;
- a distribution by company A of any bonus share capital or bonus security of company B received directly or indirectly by company A where the bonus security is a non-qualifying distribution of company B.

Law: CTA 2010, s. 1136

See *British Tax Reporter* ¶743-200.

Corporation Tax

3077 Treatment of qualifying distributions

From 6 April 1999, where a UK-resident company makes a distribution, and the person receiving the distribution is another UK-resident company or a UK-resident person other than a company, the recipient is entitled to a tax credit. The value of the tax credit is determined in accordance with the fraction in force at the time the distribution was made. Since 6 April 1999, the fraction has been one-ninth.

> ### Example
> Sharing Ltd pay a dividend of 90 pence per share in July 2008. In the hands of the recipient there is an associated tax credit of 10 pence per share (90 pence $\times$ $^1/_9$).

If a company makes a qualifying distribution (see 3076) to another UK-resident company, the company which receives the distribution is entitled to a tax credit. Following the abolition of ACT with effect from 6 April 1999, the tax credit is fixed at ten per cent of the dividend plus the tax credit.

A non-resident company may be entitled to an amount (often known as a 'tax credit') under the appropriate 'double tax treaty' (see 1780) calculated as a portion of the tax credit given to UK companies less a withholding of income tax.

An individual is treated as receiving an amount of income equal to the cash dividend and the tax credit (see 1350). That tax credit is only payable in limited circumstances after 5 April 1999.

The distribution plus the tax credit in the hands of a recipient company is called 'franked investment income'.

Franked investment income does not include group income, either:

- before 6 April 1999, where the group or consortium has elected to pay dividends within the group without ACT being paid (see 3665); or
- after 5 April 1999 and the abolition of ACT, where the distributions have been made by members of the same group.

Rectification of excessive

An inspector may make any necessary assessments to rectify an excessive offset or payment of tax credit, including interest thereon.

Law: CTA 2010, s. 1109, 1110, 1126

See *British Tax Reporter* ¶743-200.

3078 Qualifying distributions in the hands of a dealer

With effect for distributions and manufactured payments made after 1 July 1997, the legislation recognises the principle that where shares in UK companies are held as trading assets, rather than as investments, distributions relating to those shares should be treated as trading income. The rules ensure that *all* UK distributions (and manufactured payments representing such distributions) received by dealers are chargeable to corporation tax. (Prior to 6 April 1999, this was net of their tax credit, which was available to set against franked payments.)

Law: CTA 2009, s. 130

See *British Tax Reporter* ¶743-200.

3085 Distributions paid on or after 1 July 2009

A number of significant changes were made to the taxation of distributions received by UK companies by FA 2009. The changes were made as a result of the Government's review of the taxation of foreign profits. For most companies, the most important of these changes was the replacement of the exemption for UK distributions, and the credit system for the taxation of foreign dividends, with a broad exemption applying to UK and foreign dividends received by companies. The changes were introduced by Part 9A of CTA 2009 as inserted by FA 2009, s. 34 and Sch. 14, and apply to distributions received on or after 1 July 2009.

Although Part 9A has the effect of removing most distributions from the charge to corporation tax on income, it begins by applying that charge. Distributions are then removed from the charge to corporation tax if they are not of a capital nature and are exempt. This approach contrasts with that of former CTA 2009, s. 1285 which removed all non-capital UK company distributions from the charge to corporation tax on income without recourse to exemptions. Under the new approach the assumption is that all income distributions received will be subject to tax unless an exemption applies. This change in structure appears to have been made to ensure that Part 9A is compliant with EU law. The rules for distributions received by small companies are distinct from the rules for medium and large companies. The result in each case is that the great majority of distributions will be exempt from corporation tax.

Distributions of a capital nature do not fall within the scope of Part 9A and instead continue to be taxed according to the rules applying to chargeable gains. As Part 9A neither includes nor refers to a definition of 'distribution of a capital nature', there has been some concern as to how such distributions are to be identified, especially with regard to distributions paid by foreign companies.

Prior to the enactment of the *Income Tax (Trading and Other Income) Act* 2005, (ITTOIA 2005) it was generally accepted that all UK distributions were income in nature unless a specific rule said otherwise (e.g. distributions in respect of shares in a winding up). It has

Corporation Tax

been suggested that as a result of ITTOIA 2005, this previously accepted interpretation was no longer possible and that, as a result, more dividends might be regarded as capital distributions and so fall outside the new dividend exemption. An example might be dividends paid out of reserves created by a reduction of capital. In a Written Ministerial Statement made on 24 February 2010, the Financial Secretary to the Treasury, Stephen Timms, said that legislation would be included in the 2010 Finance Bill to clarify the corporation tax treatment of distributions. Mr Timms said that changes would now be made with 'a view to restoring previous expectations about the way that distributions are taxed'. Mr Timms said that the new rules would give companies certainty that distributions would be taxed in accordance with 'established expectations of HMRC practice'. The Statement can be found on the Parliament website at www.publications.parliament.uk/pa/cm200910/cmhansrd/cm100224/wmstext/100224m0001.htm. Due to the guillotining of most of the 2010 Finance Bill provisions as a result of the General Election the provisions referred to by Mr Timms were not included in the 2010 Finance Act. In June 2010 Budget the new Government announced the provisions would be included in the Autumn 2010 Finance Bill to remove the condition in the legislation that the distributions have to be of an income nature.

With regard to distributions paid by foreign companies HMRC practice is to treat distributions received by UK companies from foreign companies as capital distributions if they were treated as such under the company law in the jurisdiction under whose laws the foreign company was incorporated. In *First Nationwide v R & C Commrs* the First-tier Tax Tribunal found that dividends paid out of the share premium account of a company incorporated in the Cayman Islands were income and not capital. Once the changes announced in the June Budget are enacted, this case will only have relevance (for the purposes of corporation tax on income) for distributions made before 1 July 2009.

For some capital gains purposes, a capital distribution is defined as a distribution from a company which is not treated as income for income tax purposes.

Distribution received by a small company

For a distribution received by a small company to be exempt the following conditions must be met:

(a) the payer is a resident of (and only of) the UK or a qualifying territory at the time that the distribution is received;
(b) the distribution is not of a kind mentioned in paragraph (4) or (5) of 3067 above;
(c) no deduction is allowed to a resident of any territory outside the UK under the law of that territory in respect of the distribution; and
(d) the distribution is not made as part of a tax advantage scheme.

A qualifying territory is a territory with which the UK has a double taxation treaty that includes a non-discrimination provision in a standard form.

A company is defined as a 'small company' in an accounting period if it is in that period a micro or small enterprise, as defined in the Annex to Commission Recommendation 2003/361/EC of 6 May 2003. That is a company with less than 50 employees or has a turnover of balance sheet total not exceeding €10,000,000. But a company is not a 'small company' in an accounting period if it is at any time in that period an open-ended investment company, an authorised unit trust scheme, an insurance company, or a friendly society.

Distributions received by medium and large companies

A distribution received by a company which is not small will be exempt if:

- it is not of a kind mentioned in paragraph (4) or (5) of 3067 above.
- no deduction is allowed to a resident of any territory outside the UK under the laws of that territory; and
- it falls into an exempt class.

The exempt classes are:

- dividends or other distributions paid by the distributing company to the controlling company;
- distributions paid on non-redeemable preference shares;
- dividends from portfolio holdings where there is an interest of less than 10 per cent;
- dividends derived from transactions not designed to reduce tax, or if there is a reduction of tax, the reduction is minimal or not the main purpose of the transaction;
- dividends paid from shares which would be classified as debt under GAAP which means either International Accounting Standard (IAS) 32 or the UK equivalent Financial Reporting Standard (FRS) 25.

The exemptions are subject to a number of anti-avoidance provisions which largely apply where there is a tax avoidance motive.

A company can elect that a distribution which qualifies as exempt be treated as taxable. This would be advantageous where an exemption distribution would lead to a higher rate of withholding tax or where dividends can only be taken into account for the purposes of the CFC acceptable distribution policy (ADP) exemption if they are subject to tax. The election must be made within two years of the end of the accounting period in which the distribution is received.

Details of the ADP for controlled foreign companies which applied before 1 July 2009 and the transitional provisions designed to ensure that the ADP and associated rules continue to apply to profits which accrued before 1 July 2009 are set out at 4716.

Law: CTA 2009, Pt. 9A; FA 2009, s. 34, Sch. 14; *First Nationwide v R & C Commrs* [2010] TC 00339

See *British Tax Reporter* ¶745-300.

Corporation Tax

CALCULATING TAX DUE

3090 Rates of corporation tax

The full rate of corporation tax for the financial year 2010 (the year beginning on 1 April 2010) is 28 per cent, 30 per cent for North Sea Oil and Gas ring fence activities. The corresponding figures for the financial year 2009 are also 28 per cent and 30 per cent respectively. The full rate of corporation tax for the financial year 2011 will be 27 per cent.

The 'small profits rate (formerly small companies rate)' (see 3092) for the financial year 2010 is 21 per cent (19 per cent for North Sea Oil and Gas ring fence activities). The lower and upper limits for the financial year for the purposes of the small companies' rate are £300,000 and £1,500,000 respectively.

For a table of corporation tax rates and limits, see 70.

See *British Tax Reporter* ¶803-000.

3092 Small profits rate (formerly small companies' rate)

For accounting periods ending after 1 April 2010, CTA 2010 has renamed the small companies' rate 'small profits rate'. At the same time, a number of extra statutory concessions concerning small companies rate have been formally enacted.

The 'small profits rate' for the financial year 2010 is 21 per cent (19 per cent for North Sea Oil and Gas ring fence activities).

The rate applies to a company whose total profits are £300,000 or less; here profits are defined as profits chargeable to corporation tax, plus franked investment income. Certain close investment-holding companies are excluded from benefiting from the small companies' rate (see 4280).

See *British Tax Reporter* ¶803-150.

3094 Marginal relief

There is also marginal relief on the corporation tax payable by a company whose profits exceed £300,000 but are less than £1,500,000; though again certain close investment-holding companies are excluded (see 4280). In these circumstances, the corporation tax payable at the full rate is reduced by reference to the following formula:

$$F \times (U - A) \times \frac{N}{A}$$

where

F   is the standard fraction;
U   is the upper limit;
A   is the profits chargeable to corporation tax, plus franked investment income; and
N   represents the basic profits, i.e. the profits chargeable to corporation tax,

the 'standard fraction' being the fraction determined by Parliament from time to time – for the financial year 2010 it is $^7/_{400}$. The specified fraction for ring fenced companies is $^{11}/_{400}$.

The above profit limits are reduced for accounting periods of less than 12 months and by reference to the number of associated companies. In determining whether companies are controlled by the same persons so as to be associated the rights and powers of persons associated (being broadly, the person's relative, partners and the trustees of certain trusts connected with the person), HMRC will, by concession, often ignore rights of relatives other than a spouse and minor children, certain trustee holdings and fixed rate preference shares.

Associated companies which do not carry on any 'trade or business' in an accounting period are disregarded in calculating the above limits. It is also ignored if it is an associated company for only part of an accounting period, and it has not carried on any trade or business at any time in that part of the accounting period.

Business partners

From 1 April 2008, and for the purposes of the small profits rate only, the term 'associate' excludes a business partner except where 'relevant tax planning arrangements have at any time had effect in relation to the taxpayer company'. Prior to this change introduced in FA 2009 it was possible for two companies to be associated for small companies rate purposes, even though they operated independently of one another, merely because the controlling parties of each company were members of an otherwise unrelated partnership. For some time before, unofficial HMRC practice had been to not enforce the legislation in that way. Following concerns raised by the professional bodies about enquiries the CIOT published the following guidance to its members:

> 'In a recent meeting with HMRC/HM Treasury, we were advised that, whilst the legislation was not backdated, the practice regarding earlier years will, in most cases, be influenced by the new rules. HMRC will no longer look to establish evidence of associated companies where it would be unreasonable to expect an individual to be aware of the business interest of his partners.'

The upper and lower limits are calculated on a pro-rata basis. For example, nine months accounting period and three associated companies (i.e. four companies in total) gives:

$$M = £1,500,000 \times \frac{9}{12} \times \frac{1}{1+3}$$

$$= £281,250$$

The lower limit of £300,000 would similarly be reduced to £56,250.

713

Example

For the year ended 31 August 2010, Axyd Ltd, which has no associated companies, has the following results:

	£
Profits chargeable to corporation tax ('basic profits' – 'N')	1,129,000
Franked investment income (gross) from unrelated companies	161,000
Augmented profits ('A') for the purpose of small companies' rate	1,290,000

The corporation tax payable is calculated as follows:

		1/9/09 to 31/3/10 £	1/4/10 to 31/8/10 £
Upper profits limits:			
	£1,500,000 × 7/12	875,000	
	£1,500,000 × 5/12		625,000
Profits:			
	£1,290,000 × 7/12	752,500	
	£1,290,000 × 5/12		537,500
Corporation tax at full rate:			
	28% × £1,129,000 × 7/12	184,403	
	28% × £1,129,000 × 5/12		131,717
Deduct marginal relief:			
$(875,000 - 752,500) \times \dfrac{1,129,000}{1,290,000} \times \dfrac{7}{400}$		(1,876)	
$(625,000 - 537,500) \times \dfrac{1,129,000}{1,290,000} \times \dfrac{7}{400}$			(1,340)
		182,527	130,577
Corporation tax payable for year to 31/8/10		312,904	

If an accounting period straddles a change of tax rate at 31 March, profits must be apportioned between the financial years in order to apply the correct rate of tax. The relevant limits are time-apportioned as appropriate.

The effective rate of tax in the margin

In effect, each additional £1 of profit over the lower limit is taxed at a marginal rate, which for the financial year 2010 is 29.75 per cent until the upper limit for small companies marginal relief is reached. This is arrived at as follows:

	Profits	Tax
Lower limit when tax will be at 21% on	300,000	63,000
Upper limit for marginal relief £1,500,000 when tax will be at 28% on	1,500,000	420,000
Difference	1,200,000	397,000

As an extra £357,000 tax arises on an extra £1,200,000 of profit, the marginal rate is therefore:

$$\frac{357,000}{1,200,000} \times 100 = 29.75\%$$

For a list of marginal relief rates, see 70.

Law: CTA 2010, Pt. 3

Source: ESC C9, *Associated companies*

See *British Tax Reporter* ¶704-000.

3097 Double tax relief

If income and gains are not exempted from tax in the UK by either the new distribution exemption (see 3085) or by the operation of a double taxation agreement, relief for foreign tax (known as 'double tax relief' (DTR) is usually available in one of three forms:

(1) tax credit relief against UK foreign tax payable directly on profits, dividend, interest or other profits taxable in the UK. This can be by the operation of a double taxation agreement (known as 'treaty relief') or otherwise in the absence of any treaty (known as 'unilateral relief' (UL))

(2) credit relief against UK tax (either via a treaty or as unilateral relief) for tax suffered indirectly, usually on dividends from sizeable shareholdings (broadly, with ten per cent or more of the votes) taxable in the UK. The foreign tax suffered ('underlying tax') is either on profits out of which the dividend itself is payable or on the profits etc. of a company below the subsidiary; and

(3) relief by deduction from profits taxable in the UK where relief by credit is not available.

Various amendments to the double taxation provisions were introduced by the *Finance Act 2000*, aimed in the main at curtailing avoidance of tax via the use of 'mixer companies'.

As a result of the changes, the rate of foreign tax for which companies can claim relief in respect of dividends from overseas companies is capped at 28 per cent (the UK rate of corporation tax). However, underlying tax above the cap is, up to a maximum of 45 per cent, allowed against the UK tax payable on other dividends that have not themselves been subject to the cap or to another form of limitation of relief. Where the foreign tax cannot be relieved in the current accounting period it may be carried back three years or carried forward indefinitely to set against the UK tax payable on permitted dividends in other periods. Similarly, relief will be allowed for foreign underlying tax and withholding tax to a maximum of 45 per cent where UK companies receive dividends directly from foreign subsidiaries by setting tax against UK tax payable on dividends of the permitted type.

Corporation Tax

To facilitate the reliefs, it is possible to pool the dividends against which the UK tax on which the foreign tax up to 45 per cent can be set. A company may also surrender foreign tax to another company in the same group, provided that certain conditions are satisfied.

Mismatch in relation to tax suffered and double taxation relief on dividends

The reduction in the corporation tax rate from 30 per cent to 28 per cent with effect from 1 April 2008 meant that foreign dividends paid in an accounting period which straddled 1 April 2008, were apportioned between two financial years and taxed at a higher rate of corporation tax than 28 per cent. The legislative mixer cap formula acts with the effect of restricting the amount of double tax relief available to UK companies. This happens because the amount of double tax relief is calculated, by reference to the corporation tax rate in force on the dividend payment date. For dividends paid after the 1 April 2008 this is 28 per cent, as a result there is a mismatch between the tax rate and the amount of relief available.

The new measure introduced by FA 2009, s. 57 will, with retrospective effect from 1 April 2008, ensure that the amount of double taxation relief on foreign dividends will be calculated and based on the blended corporation tax rate actually suffered on the foreign dividend.

The provisions providing for double tax relief in respect of dividends received from non-UK resident companies now, generally, only apply to dividends received before 1 July 2009 and to dividends received after that date in respect of which an election is made to disapply the new distribution exemption. Most dividends received by UK resident companies after 1 July 2009 are now generally exempt from UK corporation tax (see 3085) above.

Law: TIOPA 2010, Pt. 2, Ch. 2

Source: ESC C1, *Credit for underlying tax: dividends from trade investments in overseas companies*; SP 12/93, *Double taxation: dividends income: tax credit relief*; SP 2/95, *Payment of tax credits to non-resident companies*

See *British Tax Reporter* ¶768-000.

SPECIAL SITUATIONS

LOSSES

3100 Types of company loss

The losses incurred by a company can be generally divided into two groups:

(1) trading losses (see 3103); and

(2) non-trading losses, such as capital losses (see 3131), property income losses (formerly Sch. A) (see 3133) and miscellaneous income (formerly Sch. D, Case VI) source losses (see 3136).

See *British Tax Reporter* ¶730-000.

3103   Meaning of trading losses for companies

A company's trading losses in any accounting period are losses arising from the company's trade in that period. They are determined after the deduction of capital allowances given in taxing the trade (see 3027).

Prior to 1 April 2010 charges on income were, in theory, treated as trading losses where those charges were greater than the profits of the same period (see 3055). The relief was, in theory, available for charges on income incurred by the company wholly and exclusively for the purposes of its trade. The difference between the company's profits and the total charges on income were in practice added to the company's trading losses for the accounting period. Relief was available up to the lower of:

- excess charges; or
- payments made wholly and exclusively for the purposes of the trade.

Consequently, for this purpose, non-trade charges were deemed to be used before trade charges.

Although that was the position in theory for accounting periods ending before 1 April 2010, in practice, due to the introduction of the loan relationship rules in 1996 and other changes to legislation in 2005, only donations and gifts to charities fell to be taken as charges on income. The provisions allowing for the carry forward of excess charges on income therefore had no application as it is difficult to imagine circumstances where a donation or gift to a charity (which is not deductible in computing trading profits) would have been incurred wholly and exclusively for the purposes of the company's trade. In recognition of this, the rewritten legislation in CTA 2010 has renamed 'charges on income' 'charitable donations relief' and has removed the provisions allowing for a carry forward of excess charges on income. For accounting periods ended on or after 1 April 2010, excess charitable donations made by a trading company (A) for an accounting period can only be relieved by being surrendered as group relief or set against the income of a controlled foreign company apportioned to A in the same accounting period.

The principal reliefs available for trading losses are current period relief (see 3106), preceding period's relief (see 3109) and future period's relief (see 3116).

Whilst losses on investments would, except in the case of dealing companies, be capital losses, special relief is given for investment companies (see 5265).

Corporation Tax

Special provisions may limit the amount effectively regarded as a trading loss of a company involved in a partnership or receiving first-year allowances from a leasing contract which it transfers to another person.

Law: CTA 2010, Pt. 4, Ch. 2

See *British Tax Reporter* ¶730-000.

3106   Company trading losses: offset against current profits

A company's 'trading losses' (see 3103) may be set off against total profits made in the same accounting period. A company wishing to set off losses in this way must make a claim within two years after the end of the accounting period in which the losses occur.

Example

A company makes a trading loss of £60,000. In the same accounting period it receives rents of £20,000 and bank interest of £15,000.

	£
Property income	20,000
Non-trading loan relationship credit	15,000
Total profits	35,000
Less: loss under CTA 2010, s. 37(3)(a)	(35,000)
Chargeable profits	Nil

Profits of an accounting period for the purpose of loss relief can include dividends on investments and interest which would fall to be taxed as trading receipts but for the fact that they have been taxed under other provisions. In the case of industrial and provident societies, this is extended by concession to amounts assessable under miscellaneous income (formerly Sch. D, Case IV and V) as well as most interest. A shipping company contended that interest it received on money invested to provide a fund to replace ships in its fleet was trading income eligible for loss relief. It was held that the interest was investment income and not trading income and that loss relief was not available.

For accounting periods ending before 1 April 2010 where it is not possible to deduct charges or income incurred wholly and exclusively for the purpose of the trade because of insufficient profits or loss claims, they may be carried forward to set-off against future trading income (see 3103, 3116).

If a company makes a loss in the trade of farming or market gardening it cannot claim relief against its other taxable income and gains when it has incurred a loss in carrying on that trade in each of the five years prior to the start of the accounting period when the loss is made. The company may still carry forward the trading loss against future trading income.

Relief may be denied in respect of certain losses from dealing in commodity futures or qualifying options.

Trading losses which had been set against assessments raised on a company that had been estimated but had become final could not be used again even though the Revenue admitted that the assessments had eventually been seen to be excessive (see 3116).

Law: CTA 2010, s. 37; *Bank Line Ltd v IR Commrs* (1974) 49 TC 307; *Auckland (HMIT) v PAVH (International) Ltd* [1992] BTC 518

Source: ESC C5

See *British Tax Reporter* ¶730-300.

3109   Company trading losses: offset against previous profits

A company's 'trading losses' (but including excess capital allowances given by discharge or repayment of tax, irrespective of whether a loss otherwise arises) can, to the extent that they cannot be used against the current period's profits (see 3106), also be carried back against profits arising in the previous 12 months, any necessary apportionment of the results of a previous accounting period being made to effect this. Terminal losses (see 3125) can be carried back for a period of three years.

There are certain trading losses to which relief does not apply. These are losses from foreign trading and from trades carried on on a non-commercial basis, without a view to realising a gain.

A company must make its claim for relief within two years of the end of the accounting period in which it made the loss, or within such further period as the Board may allow.

Relief is given against profits of a later accounting period before those of an earlier accounting period.

> ### Example
>
> H Ltd prepares accounts to 30 June each year. For the year to 30 June 2008, H Ltd made a trading profit of £20,000. For the year to 30 June 2009, H Ltd made a trading loss of £12,000. The company also had chargeable gains of £5,000 in the year to 30 June 2008 and £3,000 in the year to 30 June 2009.
>
> On a claim, the trading loss for the year to 30 June 2009 will first be set against the chargeable gains for that year (see 3106), the balance being set against the trading profit for the year to 30 June 2008 as follows:

Corporation Tax

	Year to 30 June 2008 £	Year to 30 June 2009 £
Trading profit	20,000	–
Less: loss carried back	(9,000)	
	11,000	–
Chargeable gains	5,000	3,000
Less: current year loss		(3,000)
Chargeable profits	16,000	Nil

The trading loss in the year to 30 June 2009 is thus utilised as follows:

	£
Trading loss y/e 30/6/2009	12,000
Set-off against chargeable gains of same period (CTA 2010, s. 37(3)(a))	(3,000)
	9,000
Set-off against profits of previous accounting period	(9,000)
Loss carried forward	–

For the purposes of the carry-back of losses, repayment interest is to be calculated by reference to the accounting period in which the loss is incurred rather than the period to which the loss is carried back except where this is wholly within the previous 12 months (see 4968).

Law: CTA 2010, s. 37

See *British Tax Reporter* ¶730-300.

3110 Temporary extension of carry back of losses

Legislation was introduced in FA 2009 to provide a temporary extension to the loss relief rules for trading losses. Where a trading loss arises in respect of an accounting period ended after 23 November 2008 but before 24 November 2010, the operation of CTA 2010, s. 37 is changed so that the company is able to set the loss against its profits of the same period and its profits for the preceding three years.

The loss must be carried back so that it is set against the profits of the most recent year first. The existing rules relating to the carry back of a loss to the preceding year also apply to the carry back of a loss to the second and third years with one exception. Where the amount of the loss that can be carried back one year is not subject to a cap, the amount of the loss which can be carried back to the second and third years is restricted to:

- £50,000 for losses incurred in accounting periods ending after 23 November 2008 and before 24 November 2009; and

- £50,000 for losses incurred in accounting periods ending after 23 November 2009 and before 24 November 2010.

If a company has a relevant accounting period which is less than 12 months long, the limit is reduced by reference to the following formula:

$$\frac{RAP}{Y}$$

Where:

RAP is the number of days in the relevant accounting period; and
Y is 365.

Example

Because of difficult trading conditions caused by unseasonable weather for the summers of 2008 and 2009 and general economic conditions, the Castle Beach Deckchair Company Limited has experienced the following losses:

P/E 31/10/2009	(90,000)
Y/E 30/06/2009	(150,000)
Y/E 30/06/2008	48,000
Y/E 30/06/2007	75,000
Y/E 30/06/2006	160,000

Because of the extended carry back of losses introduced by FA 2009, the company can carry back the losses for the year ended 30 June 2009 not only to the year ended 30 June 2008 but also to the year ended 30 June 2007. The loss relieved in this way will be £48,000 for the year ended 30 June 2008 and £50,000 for the year ended 30 June 2007.

The extended relief allows the loss incurred in the four-month period to 31 October 2009 to be carried back and relieved against the year to 30 June 2007. This carry back is limited to the lower of the profits for 2007 available for relief of £25,000 and a reduced cap of £16,849 calculated as follows:

$$50,000 \times \frac{123}{365} = 16,849$$

Loss utilisation

	Trading profit/ (loss)	Loss relief under s. 393A	Trading profit after relief	Loss c/fwd under s. 393
P/E 31/10/2009	(90,000)	16,849	–	(73,151)
Y/E 30/06/2009	(150,000)	98,000	–	(52,000)
Y/E 30/06/2008	48,000	(48,000)	–	–
Y/E 30/06/2007	75,000	(66,849)	8,151	–
Y/E 30/06/2006	160,000	–	160,000	–

This means that the company has been able to relieve losses of £66,849 earlier than it would have otherwise been able to do. The claim to carry back losses in this way must be made within two years of the end of the accounting period in which the loss arose.

Because the legislation was not enacted until July 2009, HMRC have made provision for companies to be able to claim repayments of corporation tax, under the extended carry back with effect from 24 November 2008 when the relief was first announced. Details are set out in HMRC's Technical Note *Extension of Loss-Relief Rules – Carry Back of Trading Losses* published on HMRC's website on 24 November 2008.

Law: FA 2009, s. 23 and Sch. 6

See *British Tax Reporter* ¶730-300.

3116 Company trading losses: offset against future profits

Any trading losses of a company which are not relieved by offset against current profits (see 3106) or previous profits (see 3109) are carried forward to be set off against the first available profits of the same trade for subsequent accounting periods. Relief is given automatically.

The loss can be carried forward indefinitely subject to provisions dealing with reconstructions and changes in company ownership (see 3140, 3143) or where a government investment in the company is written off.

Law: CTA 2010, s. 45 and 92; *Auckland (HMIT) v PAVH (International) Ltd* [1992] BTC 518

3125 Company terminal trading losses

When a company ceases trading, a trading loss incurred in the 12 months beforehand can be set off against the trading income of the company made in the three preceding years. If the final accounting period is less than 12 months, a proportionate part of the penultimate accounting period's loss can be used to produce a final 12-month loss.

As with the calculation of the final 12-month trading loss, if the final accounting period is less than 12 months (and ends before 1 April 2010) a proportionate part of the penultimate accounting period's excess trade charges on income can be used to calculate the amount available to increase the loss.

Where a trade is transferred between two companies there is a cessation of the trade in the hands of the transferring company. Where the companies are in common ownership, for certain aspects the trade is treated as continuing throughout (see 3140). This treatment is applied to what would otherwise be terminal losses of a transferring company. Thus losses accruing in the 12 months prior to the transfer of a trade to another company in common ownership will not qualify for the extended, three-year, carry-back.

With effect for cessations occurring on or after 21 May 2009, terminal loss relief is not available where a trade is transferred to a person outside the charge to corporation tax under a scheme or arrangement entered into to secure that relief. This amendment was made to counter a specific scheme notified to HMRC under the DOTAS rules.

Law: CTA 2010, s. 39, 41 and 944

See *British Tax Reporter* ¶730-300.

3126 Relief of losses determined in a foreign currency

A company can carry back losses for relief against the profits of a previous accounting period or carry forward those losses to set off against any future profits of the same trade. Where a company draws up accounts in a currency other than sterling, for an accounting period beginning before 29 December 2008, the rate of exchange used to convert the foreign currency is the rate of exchange for that period. Losses have to be converted into sterling at the rate of exchange for the accounting period when the losses were incurred.

In a period of exchange volatility the amount of profits which can be offset by losses will be partially determined by the movement in exchange rates. For accounting periods beginning on or after 29 December 2008, FA 2009 introduces amendments to FA 1993. The purpose of the amendments is to ensure that where a company calculates profits and or losses in a currency other than sterling, any losses carried forward to a future accounting period for relief will be translated into sterling at the same rate of exchange as the profits which are offset. Similarly where losses are carried back to a previous accounting period the losses carried back will be translated into sterling at the same rate of exchange as the profits offset. There are detailed rules dealing with losses calculated in one currency and offset against profits for an earlier or later accounting period computed in a different foreign currency.

The company may elect to defer the commencement date of these provisions as they apply to the company, to the beginning of the first accounting period which begins on or after the date of the Royal Assent of the Finance Act of 21 July 2009. The election must be made before the end of the 30-day period beginning with the first day of the accounting period of the company beginning on or after the date of the Royal Assent of the Finance Act of 21 July 2009. The election is irrevocable.

Law: CTA 2010, Pt. 2, Ch. 4

See *British Tax Reporter* ¶703-725

3131 Capital losses of companies

Allowable capital losses can only be set against chargeable gains of the same or subsequent accounting periods. Losses must be set against current period gains before future gains. The set-off is mandatory. Losses must be set against gains at the earliest opportunity.

Corporation Tax

> **Example**
>
> A company makes a chargeable gain of £100,000 and an allowable loss of £175,000 in the year to 31 March 2009. In the year to 31 March 2010, it makes a chargeable gain of £250,000.
>
> The allowable loss of £175,000 is first set against the gain of the same accounting period so as to reduce net gains to nil. The balance of £75,000 is then set against the gain for the year to 31 March 2010, leaving net gains of £175,000 to be included in the company's profits chargeable to corporation tax for that period.

Allowable capital losses cannot be set against trading profits.

Targeted Anti-Avoidance Rules (TAARs) were introduced with effect from 5 December 2005 to prevent the avoidance of tax through the creation and use of capital losses by companies. The legislation is targeted specifically at the following three areas of avoidance:

(1)   the contrived creation of capital losses;

(2)   the buying of capital gains and losses; and

(3)   the conversion of income to capital and using capital losses to create a deduction against income.

From 21 March 2007, new legislation prevents schemes that exploited an exception in existing anti-avoidance rules. Broadly, the new measures are intended to prevent groups of companies obtaining a tax advantage where a company changes ownership (see 3143) and one of the main purposes of the arrangements is for the new owners to gain access to the company's capital losses or gains.

HMRC have provided reassurance that the legislation will not apply where there is a genuine commercial transaction that gives rise to a real commercial loss as a result of a genuine commercial disposal.

Law: TCGA 1992, s. 8, 16A and 184A–184I

See *British Tax Reporter* ¶753-150.

3133   Losses from UK and overseas property businesses

CTA 2009 rewrites the former corporation tax charges on property income under:

- Sch. A ('a business carried on for the exploitation, as a source of rents or other receipts, of any estate, interest or rights in or over land in the United Kingdom' Sch. A, para. 1(1) at ICTA 1988, s. 15(1)); and
- Sch. D, Case V ('income arising from possessions out of the United Kingdom', ICTA 1988, s. 18(3)).

For corporation tax purposes, these charges ceased with effect for accounting periods ending on or after 1 April 2009 and are replaced by the charge under CTA 2009, Part 4 which deals with 'property income' under several discrete chapters of charge. The main property income charge is levied on the profits of a 'property business' which is subdivided into either a 'UK property business' or an 'overseas property business'.

Although the rules relating to property income were comprehensively rewritten with effect for accounting periods ending on or after 1 April 2009, this was done without major changes to the underlying detail. It was not the essence of the law that was changed by the enactment of CTA 2009 but the terms in which that law was expressed. Therefore, and in most instances, the charge to tax on property income will remain the same even though that income is now taxed under a different category.

Property income losses

Subject to transitional provisions (see below), from 1 April 1998, a UK property income business (formerly Sch. A) corporation tax loss is set against total profits (see 3027) in the accounting period. To the extent that the loss cannot be so set off, it is carried forward for set-off against future total profits, as long as the company continues to carry on the UK property business.

Companies with investment business ceasing UK property income business

Where a company with investment business with a UK property income business (formerly Sch. A) ceases to carry on the business, any unrelieved loss is treated as an expense of management of the succeeding accounting period.

See *British Tax Reporter* ¶730-650.

Restriction to UK property or overseas property business conducted on a commercial basis

Loss relief is only available for a UK or overseas property businesses conducted on a commercial basis or in the exercise of statutory functions. A business or part of a business is only conducted on a commercial basis if it is conducted with a view to making a profit, though it suffices that it is conducted so as to afford a reasonable expectation of profit. If a business, or part, begins or ceases to be conducted on a commercial basis, it is treated as conducted throughout the accounting period in the way in which it was being conducted by the end of the period. All this follows the treatment of trading losses for corporation tax purposes (see 3109).

Law: CTA 2009, Pt. 4; CTA 2010, Pt. 4, Ch. 4

See *British Tax Reporter* ¶730-700.

Corporation Tax

3136 Losses from company's miscellaneous income source

Losses made by a company from a miscellaneous income source charged under CTA 2009, Part 10 (formerly Sch. D, Case VI income) (essentially as for income tax: see 1452, 3027) can be set off against any other miscellaneous income received in the same accounting period; however, a company may also carry forward such losses and offset them against any future miscellaneous income. Relief may be extended to interest on money lent to certain financial institutions or interest on a certificate of deposit where a loss is made on exercise or disposal of the rights therein.

Law: ICTA 1988, s. 398; CTA 2010, s. 91

See *British Tax Reporter* ¶730-800.

3138 Pre-trading expenditure by company

Expenditure incurred by a company for the purposes of a trade before that trade commences may in some respects be regarded as a loss but is treated for corporation tax as trading expenditure incurred on the day trading starts. The expenditure must not be incurred more than seven years before trading commences and is allowable as a deduction in computing trading profits only if it would have been allowable had trading commenced (essentially as for income tax: see 2150ff.) at that time.

However, this does not apply to expenditure that would fall under the loan relationships provisions. A company may elect to delay accounting for what would be a non-trading debit until it begins trading. The expenditure will then be treated as a trading debit in the accounting period in which the trade began.

It is HMRC's view that pre-trading expenditure does not include costs incurred by persons other than the eventual trader: for example, where an individual incurs the expenditure but incorporates when trading begins; or where one company in a group incurs the expenditure and a fellow group member then starts to carry on the trade.

There are special rules for preparation of waste disposal sites, which apply to corporation tax in essentially the same way as to income tax (see 2152).

Law: CTA 2009, s. 61

See *British Tax Reporter* ¶707-410.

3140 Losses where company is reconstructed

If a company (C) stops trading and a second company (S) starts to carry on the same trade, and the shareholders who held 75 per cent (or more) of the ordinary share capital of C within one year before the change hold 75 per cent (or more) of the ordinary share capital of S within two years after the change, C and S are treated as one company when calculating the capital allowances and losses of the trade in so far as S is entitled to reliefs to which C would have been entitled.

It is the activity of C, rather than the trade as such, which must be carried on by S.

Loss relief is restricted where the predecessor company is insolvent at the time it ceases to carry on the trade or part of a trade. Where the predecessor company's 'relevant liabilities' exceed its 'relevant assets', the entitlement of the successor company to the predecessor company's losses is restricted to the excess of the losses over the amount by which relevant liabilities exceed relevant assets.

Example

Predecessor company has losses of £50,000, relevant liabilities of £250,000 and relevant assets of £230,000.

(1)   Excess of liabilities over assets = £250,000 − £230,000 = £20,000

(2)   Losses = £50,000

(3)   Excess of losses over the amount by which liabilities
       exceed assets = £50,000 − £20,000 = £30,000

'Relevant liabilities' are those outstanding and vested in the predecessor company immediately prior to cessation of trade and not transferred to the successor. A liability representing the predecessor's share capital, share premium account, reserves or relevant loan stock is not a relevant liability.

'Relevant assets' are all assets which were vested in the predecessor company immediately before its cessation of trade which were not transferred to the successor company.

If S only takes over part of the activities of C, that part is treated as a separate trade and a just apportionment of the income and expenses is made.

C and S are not treated as a single company when dealing with losses other than trading losses, i.e. allowable capital losses, nor in dealing with surplus franked investment income.

Law: CTA 2010, Pt. 22. Ch. 1; *Falmer Jeans Ltd v Rodin (HMIT)* [1990] BTC 193

See *British Tax Reporter* ¶731-050.

3143   Losses where a company changes ownership and change in trade or business

A company cannot carry forward losses arising in a period prior to a change in ownership to set off against the profits of an accounting period after a change of ownership if that change

Corporation Tax

and a major change in the nature or conduct of the company's trade occurred within three years of each other. Nor can a company carry back losses incurred after the change in ownership against profits before the change.

The company cannot carry forward losses if there is a change of ownership at any time after the activities in a trade carried on by a company have become small or negligible but before there is any considerable revival of trade.

When a company is calculating the losses which it cannot carry forward, the capital allowances for accounting periods before the change of ownership are treated as a first charge against the profits of those periods. This results in an increase in the trading losses which cannot be carried forward.

Similar provisions prevent a taxpayer using unrelieved management expenses (and similar reliefs available to companies with investment business), in respect of ownership changes occurring after 28 November 1994, unless in pursuance of a contract entered into before that date.

Rules also apply from 1 April 1998 to prevent a UK property income loss (formerly Sch. A) arising before a change of ownership of a company carrying on a UK property income (formerly Sch. A) business being relieved against profits of an accounting period after the change in ownership.

Major change in nature or conduct of trade

A statement of practice explains the basis on which HMRC interpret the term 'a major change in the nature or conduct of a trade'.

In addition to the qualitative issues included in statute (matters to be considered in determining whether something is a change), HMRC will also have regard, if appropriate, to changes in such other factors as the location of the company's business, the identity of its suppliers, management, or staff, its methods of manufacture, or its pricing or purchasing policies. With respect to the quantitative component (whether a change is a major change), HMRC will not regard as a major change those alterations made to increase efficiency, to keep pace with developing technology in the industry concerned or with developing management techniques. Similarly, a rationalisation of product range by withdrawal of unprofitable items and, possibly, replacement by items related to existing products will not amount to a major change.

The statement also refers to the position where a company carries on a trade (comprising activities A and B) and transfers part of the trade (comprising activity A) to another company under similar control (so as to treat losses as being carried over, etc. see 3140), such that the second company may carry on activity A as a separate trade or as part of a combined trade. The transfer will not, by itself, be regarded as a major change in any separate trade comprising activity A or any separate trade comprising activity B. However, activity A after the transfer (whether amounting to a separate trade or part of a combined trade) will be compared with activity A before the transfer and activity B after the transfer will be compared with activity B before the transfer. Also, where the transfer occurs after the change in ownership, in determining whether there has been a major change in respect of the original trade (activities A and B), HMRC will not contend that the transfer constitutes a major change if, within the relevant period, there is no other change in the original trade or, after the division, in activities A and B.

The statement also includes some examples to assist in showing where HMRC consider the borderline falls:

> **'Examples where a change would not of itself be regarded as a major change**
>
> a. A company manufacturing kitchen fitments in three obsolescent factories moves production to one new factory (increasing efficiency).
>
> b. A company manufacturing kitchen utensils replaces enamel by plastic, or a company manufacturing timepieces replaces mechanical by electronic components (keeping pace with developing technology).
>
> c. A company operating a dealership in one make of car switches to operating a dealership in another make of car satisfying the same market (not a major change in the type of property dealt in).
>
> d. A company manufacturing both filament and fluorescent lamps (of which filament lamps form the greater part of the output) concentrates solely on filament lamps (a rationalisation of product range without a major change in the type of property dealt in).
>
> e. A company whose business consists of making and holding investments in UK quoted shares and securities makes changes to its portfolio of quoted shares and securities (not a change in the nature of investments held).
>
> *Examples where a major change would be regarded as occurring*
>
> f. A company operating a dealership in saloon cars switches to operating a dealership in tractors (a major change in the type of property dealt in).
>
> g. A company owning a public house switches to operating a discotheque in the same, but converted, premises (a major change in the services or facilities provided).
>
> h. A company fattening pigs for their owners switches to buying pigs for fattening and resale (a major change in the nature of the trade, being a change from providing a service to being a primary producer).
>
> i. A company whose business consists of making and holding investments in UK quoted shares to investing in real property for rent (a change in the nature of investments held).'

Law: CTA 2010, Pt. 14; *Willis (HMIT) v Peeters Picture Frames Ltd* [1983] BTC 325

Source: SP 10/91

See *British Tax Reporter* ¶731-050.

3145   Change in ownership

A company has a change of ownership (see 3143) if one person acquires more than half of its ordinary share capital other than as an unsolicited gift or by succession on death.

There is a change of ownership also if two or more persons acquire more than half of the company's ordinary share capital and each acquires at least five per cent of that capital or has a holding of at least five per cent as a result of the acquisition.

Where a change in ownership would be treated as occurring after 13 March 1989, any actual change in ownership of a company will be taken as an acquisition by the person(s) involved of relevant shares owned by the company so as to bring about possible changes in ownership of companies in which those shares subsist. No deemed acquisition will take place if the change in ownership of the company can be disregarded because the company remains throughout a 75 per cent subsidiary of any company – with comparable entitlements to profits and assets available for distribution to equity holders (see 3812).

Law: CTA 2010, Pt. 14, Ch. 7

See *British Tax Reporter* ¶731-050.

DEMERGERS

3200   Demergers which are not distributions

A 'demerger' is a transaction whereby trading activities carried on by a single company or group are divided so that they are carried on by two or more companies not belonging to the same group or by two or more independent groups.

If a company makes a distribution to facilitate a demerger, that distribution is exempt from the usual tax treatment and it is an 'exempt distribution' (see 3072). However, this exemption is hedged by numerous conditions and exclusions which must be considered at some length to acquire a full understanding of its application. There is a corresponding chargeable gains deferral for the shareholders.

Conditions for exemption

A distribution will not qualify for exemption unless it is one of the following.

(1)   A distribution consisting of a transfer of shares by a company to all or any of its members of shares in one or more companies which are its 75 per cent subsidiaries. The shares must be irredeemable and constitute the whole or substantially the whole of the distributing company's holding of the ordinary share capital of the subsidiary. The distribution must confer the whole or substantially the whole of the distributing company's voting rights in the subsidiary. The distributing company must, after the

distribution, be either a trading company or the holding company of a trading group. The latter condition does not apply where the transfer relates to two or more 75 per cent subsidiaries of the distributing company and that company is dissolved without any net assets remaining after the distribution which are available for distribution in a winding-up.

(2) A distribution consisting of the transfer by the distributing company to one or more other companies of a trade or shares in one or more companies which are 75 per cent subsidiaries of the distributing company. Before this can apply:

(a) if a trade is transferred, the distributing company must either not retain any interest or retain only a minor interest in that trade;

(b) if shares in a subsidiary are transferred, they must constitute the whole or substantially the whole of the distributing company's voting rights in the subsidiary;

(c) the only or main activity of the transferee company after the distribution must be the carrying on of a trade or the holding of shares transferred to it;

(d) shares issued by the transferee company must not be redeemable, must constitute the whole of the issued ordinary share capital and must confer most of the voting rights in that company;

(e) the distributing company must, after the distribution, be either a trading company or the holding company of a trading group. This is not applicable if there are two or more transferee companies, each of which has shares in a separate 75 per cent subsidiary of the distributing company transferred to it and the distributing company is dissolved without any net assets available for distribution in a winding-up after the distribution.

Further conditions require the distributing company, its subsidiaries and the transferee companies to be 'UK-resident' (see 214) at the time of the distribution and a subsidiary whose shares are transferred to be either a trading company or the holding company of a trading group at that time.

For distributions made on or after 11 November 2009, this requirement is replaced with a requirement that the companies must be resident in an EU member state (*Corporation Tax (Implementation of the Mergers Directive) Regulations* 2009 (SI 2009/2797)).

The distribution must be made wholly or mainly for the purpose of benefiting some or all of the trading activities which before the distribution are carried on by a single company or group and after the distribution will be carried on by two or more companies or groups.

Ineligible distribution

A distribution will not be eligible for exemption if it forms part of a scheme or arrangement whose main purpose is:

● to avoid tax;

● to make a chargeable payment or what would be a chargeable payment if any company taking part were unquoted (i.e. not listed) (see 3205);

Corporation Tax

- for any person or persons other than members of the distributing company to acquire control of that company or another company in the same group; or
- to enable trading to cease or the business to be sold after the distribution.

75 per cent subsidiaries

If a company is a 75 per cent subsidiary of another company, the group to which the distributing company belongs when the distribution occurs must be a trading group. That distribution must be followed by one or more distributions which result in a member of the holding company of the group, to which the distributing company belonged at the time of the distribution, becoming a member of one of the following:

- the transferee company to which a trade was transferred by the distributing company; or
- the subsidiary whose shares were transferred by the distributing company; or
- a company of which the company is a 75 per cent subsidiary.

By concession, relief is still available if the company retains, after the distribution, sufficient funds to meet the cost of liquidation and to cover what will usually be the negligible amount of share capital remaining. The concession only applies where the company retains no more than a negligible amount of share capital.

Law: CTA 2010, Pt. 23, Ch. 5; TCGA 1992, s. 192

Source: SP 13/80

See *British Tax Reporter* ¶743-800.

3205 Chargeable payments made after an exempt distribution

Where, after a demerger, a chargeable payment is made less than five years after the exempt distribution is made (see 3200), the amount paid is treated as income chargeable to tax under miscellaneous income or an annual sum payable otherwise than out of profits or gains charged to income tax, except where the payment is a transfer of money's worth. Where appropriate, that amount is also treated as a distribution which is not deductible for corporation tax purposes. It may also be deemed to be a payment which cannot be a repayment of capital.

A 'chargeable payment' embraces the transfer of money's worth including the assumption of a liability and is any of the following:

- a payment which is not made for bona fide commercial reasons; or
- a payment which forms part of a scheme or arrangement whose main purpose is to avoid tax.

Any such payment must also be:

- a payment made by a company concerned in an exempt distribution directly or indirectly to a member of that company or of any other company concerned in the distribution;

- a payment connected with the shares of that company; or
- a payment which is not a distribution or an exempt distribution or made to any other company which belongs to the same group as the company making the payment.

Chargeable payments and unquoted companies

If an unquoted company (i.e. one which is not listed) is concerned with an exempt distribution, a chargeable payment will include any payment made by or to another person under a scheme or arrangement made with the unquoted company. This only applies if the unquoted company is under the control of no more than five persons and not under the sole control of a company which is not itself under the control of fewer than five persons.

Law: CTA 2010, s. 1088, 1089 and 1090

See *British Tax Reporter* ¶743-800.

PURCHASE OF OWN SHARES

3220 Purchase by an unquoted trading company of its shares

The *Companies Act* 2006, Part 18, provides a system whereby a limited company can buy back its own shares out of distributable profits or proceeds from a new share issue. A payment made to shareholders in this way would normally constitute a distribution (see 3065, 3067) but for a corporate vendor would still be taken into account in the capital gains calculation (see 3050, 5890).

Certain payments by a company on the redemption, repayment or purchase of its own shares are not treated as distributions by the company. The company must be an unquoted company (i.e. one which is neither listed, nor a 51 per cent subsidiary of a listed company) and a trading company or the holding company of a trading group.

There are two sets of circumstances in which the tax treatment following such purchase applies. Either the purchase, redemption or repayment is made wholly or mainly for the purpose of benefiting a trade carried on by the company or by any of its 75 per cent subsidiaries, or the whole of the payment is applied by the recipient in meeting an inheritance tax liability arising on death (see below).

Legal expenses incurred are not likely to be deductible (see 2242).

Payment for benefit of trade

The redemption, repayment or purchase must be made wholly or mainly to benefit the company's trade or that of any of its 75 per cent subsidiaries (see 3653).

Corporation Tax

It must not form part of a scheme or arrangement set up mainly to allow the share owner to participate in the company's profits without receiving a dividend or to avoid tax.

If the inspector has reason to believe that the payment by the company does form part of a scheme, he may require the company to supply him with a declaration in writing whether or not such a scheme exists. The company must also supply any other information the inspector may reasonably require to decide whether there is a scheme or arrangement and whether the payment is to benefit the trade of the company. The company has at least 60 days to comply with this requirement, or any longer time which the inspector specifies.

Discharge of inheritance tax liability

The whole or substantially the whole of the payment must be used by the person who receives it to discharge a liability for inheritance tax he has incurred on a death within two years after that death. The payment will still be treated as a distribution if the recipient could have settled the tax liability from some other source without undue hardship.

Other conditions

There are further rules (see 3223 and 3245) to be complied with before payments by a company to purchase its own shares can be exempted from treatment as a distribution.

Law: CTA 2010, s. 1033

Source: ICAEW Technical Release, TR 745, SP 2/82

See *British Tax Reporter* ¶744-550.

3223   Vendors qualifying for relief on buy-back of shares

In order for a purchase of its own shares by a company not to involve a distribution (see 3220), the person selling the shares or his nominee where applicable must be 'resident' (see 213, 214) and, in the case of an individual, etc. 'ordinarily resident' (see 216) in the UK in the year of assessment when the payment is made; if that person is a personal representative, his residence is taken as that of the deceased immediately before his death.

The vendor must also have owned the shares for five years prior to and ending with the date of sale.

Where the vendor acquired the shares as a beneficiary under a will, he must have owned the shares for a period of three years ending with the date of purchase; any period when the shares were owned by the deceased is treated as a period of ownership by the vendor.

If the vendor acquired shares of the same class at different times, the shares acquired earlier are taken into account before those acquired later; any previous disposal of shares of the same class is treated as a disposal of the later rather than the earlier acquired shares.

Law: CTA 2010, s. 1034–1036,

See *British Tax Reporter* ¶744-750.

3226 Required reduction of vendor's interest in company on buy-back

In relation to the vendor (see 3223) of shares in a company to that company, if the vendor owns shares in the company immediately after the repurchase, etc. is made, his interest (or the interest of his associates: see 3236) as a shareholder must be substantially reduced to qualify for relief from normal distribution treatment (see 3220); for group holdings see 3228.

A vendor's interest will only be treated as substantially reduced if the total nominal value of the shares owned by him immediately after the purchase expressed as a fraction of the issued share capital of the company at that time does not exceed 75 per cent of the same fraction prior to the purchase (see, however, 3230).

Law: CTA 2010, s. 1037

See *British Tax Reporter* ¶744-850.

3228 Required reduction of vendor's interest in group on buy-back

A company making a purchase may be a member of a group immediately before the purchase and then, immediately after the purchase, the vendor may own shares of one or more other group members, or alternatively, after the purchase, the vendor may own shares of the company making the purchase and immediately before he may have owned shares of other group members. In either of these circumstances, the vendor's interest as a shareholder in the group must be substantially reduced (or the interests of its associates: see 3236). For present purposes, a *group* means a company which has one or more 51 per cent subsidiaries, but is not itself a 51 per cent subsidiary of any other company, plus all its subsidiaries; there are certain rules to prevent a company leaving the group artificially.

Ascertainment of vendor's interest

The vendor's interest as a shareholder in a group is ascertained by the following steps.

(1) Express the total nominal value of the shares owned by him in each relevant company as a fraction of the issued share capital of the company.

(2) Add the fractions together.

(3) Divide the result by the total number of relevant companies including any in which he owns no shares.

Corporation Tax

Example

A group of companies is made up of five members.

Company A has issued share capital of 50,000 £1 shares

Company B has issued share capital of 100,000 £1 shares

Company C has issued share capital of 75,000 £1 shares

Company D has issued share capital of 60,000 £1 shares

Company E has issued share capital of 50,000 £1 shares

$$\text{V owns 20,000 shares in A} = \text{fraction} \quad \frac{20,000}{50,000} = \frac{2}{5}$$

$$\text{30,000 shares in B} = \text{fraction} \quad \frac{30,000}{100,000} = \frac{3}{10}$$

$$\text{6,000 shares in D} = \text{fraction} \quad \frac{6,000}{60,000} = \frac{1}{10}$$

$$\text{25,000 shares in E} = \text{fraction} \quad \frac{25,000}{50,000} = \frac{1}{2}$$

Add fractions together:

$$\frac{2}{5} + \frac{3}{10} + \frac{1}{10} + \frac{1}{2} = \frac{13}{10}$$

Divide by total group members:

$$\frac{13}{10} \div 5 = \frac{13}{50} = 26\% = \text{vendor's interest in group}$$

The vendor's interest as a shareholder in a group will be substantially reduced only if it does not exceed 75 per cent of the corresponding interest immediately before the purchase. In the last example this would mean that V's interest after a purchase by a group member must not exceed 75 per cent of 26 per cent, i.e. 19.5 per cent of his interest before purchase.

Law: CTA 2010, s. 1039 and 1040

See *British Tax Reporter* ¶744-850.

3230 Buy-back where continued economic ownership by vendor

A buy-back of shares will not qualify for non-distribution treatment (see 3220) if the vendor's interest in the group is not substantially reduced (see 3228) and it will not be considered to be so reduced where he would be entitled to a significant share of the profits if every company distributed all its profits available for distribution immediately after the purchase. To be significant that share, when expressed as a fraction of the total distributable profits, must exceed 75 per cent of the corresponding fraction immediately before the purchase. If a person is entitled to receive a fixed amount from the company making the purchase, he is treated as being entitled to that same amount if the company made a distribution immediately after the purchase.

Profits available for distribution

Profits available for distribution are a company's accumulated and realised profits not previously used in a distribution or capitalisation less its accumulated realised losses if they have not already been written off in a reduction or realisation of capital.

The amount of profits available for distribution is assumed for present purposes to be increased by £100 plus, where a person is entitled to a fixed periodic distribution (see 3067), a sum equal to the amount of that distribution.

Law: CTA 2010, s. 1038 and 1041

See *British Tax Reporter* ¶744-550.

3236 Buy-back where vendor's associates continue to hold shares

If a vendor's 'associate' (see 4268) owns shares of the company immediately after the purchase, their combined interests as shareholders must be substantially reduced to obtain non-distribution treatment on a buy-back (see 3220); the reduction is calculated as for the vendor (see 3226). This may be relaxed in relation to a vendor who agrees to the purchase in order for another vendor to satisfy the condition.

Law: CTA 2010, s. 1037(2), 1039(4) and 1043

See *British Tax Reporter* ¶744-850.

3240 Buy-back where vendor remains connected with company

A payment to purchase a company's own shares will not be exempt from treatment as a company distribution (see 3220) if it is only made as part of a scheme or arrangement designed to give, or which is likely to give, the vendor or his associate interests in the company which prevent him from satisfying the conditions for exemption or if the vendor remains 'connected with the company'.

Law: CTA 2010, s. 1042

See *British Tax Reporter* ¶744-900.

3245   HMRC approval in advance of buy-back

It is possible for a company wishing to redeem shares to apply in writing to the Board for its approval of the redemption. The application must give full details of the relevant transactions and the Board has 30 days after receiving the application to request further details. If the company does not provide these within 30 days, the Board need not go any further with the application. Otherwise, the Board has 30 days in which to give its decision whether the payment will be treated as exempt from being a distribution or not. This 30-day period runs from either the date of receipt of the application or the date the company complies with the Board's request for further details, whichever is applicable.

If the company fails to give all relevant details, the Board's decision may be void.

Law: CTA 2010, s. 1044 and 1045

See *British Tax Reporter* ¶744-950.

SELLING A BUSINESS

3300   Introduction

In this section the sale of a company by an owner-manager and, on occasion, of a subsidiary from a larger group is considered. Flotation of the company, in which the owner-manager commonly retains all or part of his shareholding is not covered. There is also an assumption that the business has been a commercial success and there will therefore be capital gains tax payable as a result of the sale.

The overriding objective of the owner is clearly to maximise the net after tax proceeds of sale. This may be achieved by a combination of optimising the company's value before sale and capital gains tax planning for the owner. The former, for example, may be influenced by the tax position of the company, and particularly what unrelieved tax losses it contains. The latter may be considered to have three elements, as follows:

(1)   minimise the overall chargeable gain payable;

(2)   where feasible defer as large a proportion of the tax bill as possible; and

(3)   maximise the amount of tax recoverable should any contingent consideration not be received.

Negotiating with the buyer

The extent of the negotiations with a buyer depends considerably on both the intrinsic complexity of the sale and the extent of pre-sale planning that the vendor has undertaken. Clearly if the company being sold is relatively small, does not belong to a group and has only one trade within it, the complexity of the sale is much reduced.

Pre-sale tax issues

The extent to which pre-sale tax planning is possible or effective depends to a significant extent on the time available for it. Clearly, much less can be achieved where the owners take advantage of a good 'out of the blue' offer than where they are planning their exit from the company over a period of years.

Within the context of the time available, the following aspects need to be considered.

Administration
Ensure that the company's 'housekeeping' is adequate. In particular, the company will need to ensure that all expenditure, probably going back over many years, is properly recorded so that, where assets are being sold, appropriate CGT calculations can be made.

In the light of the 'housekeeping' exercise mentioned above, the seller needs to make sure that the base costs are maximised for all chargeable assets being sold. For assets held since March 1982, this involves deciding whether or not a rebasing election to March 1982 value is or is not appropriate.

Use of losses
Losses, whether revenue or capital, are difficult to hand over to new owners. Anti-avoidance legislation allows HM Revenue & Customs (HMRC) to challenge the availability of losses in the hands of a 'new' owner, sometimes several years after the purchase transaction. Buyers are understandably reluctant to pay for losses where these might prove to be valueless several years later. It is thus better for both sides of the transaction if the 'old' owners can arrange for the losses to be used prior to the sale.

Capital losses may be set off only against capital gains of the same or later accounting periods. Thus the sellers should consider selling assets with unrealised gains so that realised capital losses can be absorbed. Trading losses also need to avoid being carried forward. If they have arisen in the current accounting period the main ways to relieve them are by carry back against total profits of the year before or, where applicable, by surrender as group relief. Where the losses have been brought forward from earlier accounting periods, they can be set off only against profits of the same trade. To avoid the potential problems in the hands of the new owner, where the losses are significant in terms of the overall transaction it may be preferable for the sellers to delay the sale if there is a likelihood that the company will generate taxable profits again in the near future.

Pre-sale dividends
The vendors' overall aim is to maximise the net after tax proceeds of the sale in their hands. They may therefore arrange for part of the value of their company to be paid to them before its sale, as a pre-sale dividend. The rationale for this tactic is to take advantage of a more favourable tax regime on dividends than on capital gains (which might be the case, for example, if entrepreneurs' relief is not available). Since dividends are paid net of a tax credit (one ninth of the net dividend) the tax on dividend income upper rate (formerly Sch. F)

Corporation Tax

739

ensures that higher rate taxpayers suffer an effective tax rate of 25 per cent on dividends they receive.

Whether a pre-sale dividend is worthwhile depends on the effective rate of CGT to be suffered on the eventual sale of their shares. This in turn depends principally on:

- the base cost of the shares vis-à-vis the disposal proceeds;
- the availability of reliefs from CGT, notably entrepreneurs' relief, and EIS reinvestment relief.

The same rationale determines whether owners selling shares rather than assets should attempt to make use of the 'purchase of own shares' provisions, which are reviewed below.

Some owners have their affairs arranged in the form of a holding company and one or more subsidiaries. Prior to the introduction of the substantial shareholding exemption (see 4035 below) pre-sale dividends were also a well-used technique when the company to be sold has a subsidiary being sold from a group. The dividend was used to reduce the undistributed profits of that subsidiary, which caused the value of the subsidiary to fall before it was sold. In effect, after the sale the parent company will have received value for the subsidiary partly as income (the pre-sale dividend) and partly capital (the sale of the shares).

This approach avoided double taxation because the undistributed profits of the subsidiary had already been subject to corporation tax. Leaving them in the subsidiary would increase the value of the subsidiary's shares and so lead to second corporation tax charge (on the chargeable gain). Following the introduction of the substantial shareholding exemption this technique is now only relevant in situations where the SSE does not apply.

It is important not to 'overdo' the pre-sale dividend. HMRC may seek to invoke anti-avoidance legislation, particularly where the dividend payment being made is out of pre-acquisition profits.

Pension planning

If the company being sold has a pension fund, its treatment in the sale transaction may well exert a significant influence on the agreed price, because a sizeable transfer out of the pension fund is likely to be needed. The seller needs to take specialist advice on pension arrangements at the earliest opportunity.

3310 What to sell: assets or shares

It is often the case that the sale route that best suits the vendors is inappropriate for the buyers, and vice versa. Thus whether the transaction ultimately concerns shares or assets is mostly a matter for negotiation between the seller and buyer and will reflect the relative strength of their negotiating positions. However, from the standpoint of the seller, the positive aspects of selling assets rather than shares are the following:

- the warranties that the seller will probably be obliged to give will be minimised, and so there will be less financial risk to the seller after the transaction is completed;

- where assets are sold at less than their tax written-down values, balancing allowances may accrue to the seller's company; and
- the seller can choose exactly what to sell and what to retain, selling sets of assets to more than one purchaser, if desired.

These advantages are balanced by a number of disadvantages, however:

- loss of exemptions and reliefs that might apply on the disposal of shares, for example, entrepreneurs' relief for individual vendors and the substantial shareholding exemption for corporate vendors;
- the consideration for the sale may be provided in a number of ways, typically cash, other assets or shares in another company. Where the vendor disposes of assets he cannot take advantage of the CGT deferral that is potentially available on a share for share exchange;
- sale of assets is likely to produce double taxation for the seller. The sale will generate chargeable gains in the seller's company and will subsequently increase the capital gain made by the seller on the sale or repayment of the company's share capital;
- selling assets, not the company, will ensure that the vendor will retain a contingent liability for claims made against the company; and
- there may be adverse corporation tax consequences in the seller's company if the sale of the assets has caused a cessation of trade.

In short, there is no 'correct answer' to whether a sale of assets or the company's share capital is more appropriate. Often a hive-down of certain assets and the associated trade provides a compromise solution that the buyer and seller both find acceptable. The advantages and mechanics of this method are reviewed earlier in this chapter.

3320   Types of sale consideration

In this part of the chapter we are considering normal sales – that is where (whether the sale is of assets or share capital) there is both a buyer and seller involved in the transaction. An alternative method of disposing of an interest in a company is for the company to repurchase the shares from the shareholder, which can be treated as an income distribution rather than as a capital disposal. This is dealt with separately above and is not considered further at this point. Thus, from the standpoint of the seller, it is the CGT implications that must be borne in mind.

Where the sale consideration is expressed as a precise amount of money (sterling rather than foreign currency), payable in full at the time of the sale, in principle the CGT position is fairly straightforward. However, other factors may complicate the position, notably:

- consideration is partly or wholly deferred, or is payable in instalments;
- variable consideration, dependent on future events (normally profitability); or
- consideration other than cash, in particular other assets or shares in another company.

Corporation Tax

Deferred consideration

Firstly we consider the position where the sale consideration is expressed in cash terms but the seller's right to receive all or part of the cash is deferred to some future date.

A CGT disposal occurs at the time at which the contract for sale becomes unconditional. That is the time at which the CGT calculation is made. The legislation expressly provides that the calculation should make no adjustment for:

- deferral of all or part of the consideration;
- the risk that all or part of the consideration proves to be irrecoverable; or
- the right to all or part of the consideration being contingent.

If any part of the consideration does prove to be irrecoverable the taxpayer is entitled to reperform the CGT calculation and to be repaid any tax overpaid. If the taxpayer considers that payment of the whole CGT liability would cause him hardship, where part of the consideration had been deferred for more than 18 months, he may request that HMRC permit payment in instalments. If HMRC are satisfied that hardship would result they may allow payment by instalments (over a period of up to eight years). This treatment affects when the tax liability is paid but not its calculation.

Consideration contingent but calculable

The *Marson v Marriage* case held that provided consideration on a share sale (or any other asset) can be calculated, it is brought into account at its full value at the time of disposal.

Example

Suppose that X is selling his shares in X Ltd. The buyer agrees that the sale price should be £1,000,000 plus a further £400,000 if X Ltd's profits exceed £300,000 for each of the two financial years following the sale. Clearly, at the time of sale, the £400,000 is contingent. However, the uncertainty is not in the amount of the extra consideration – only if it will be paid. Thus the sale consideration brought into the CGT computation is £1,400,000.

Incalculable consideration

The *Marren v Ingles* case established that contingent consideration was not brought into the original CGT calculation where its amount could not be calculated at the time of sale. In brief, the case involved the sale of shares. The sale price was set at £750 per share plus a further amount that depended on the quoted price of those shares when floated on a stock exchange. That further amount proved to be nearly £3,000 per share.

It was held that the taxpayer had acquired an asset (the right to the future contingent consideration) from which a capital sum was derived. There was thus a disposal when the capital sum was received (and would be more than one if the contingent consideration were to be received in stages).

Two awkward practical problems result from this treatment of unascertainable contingent consideration. First, the right to receive it, acquired when the original sale contract is made, has to be valued. This will inevitably entail detailed and probably prolonged negotiations with HMRC. If there are several receipts, the right will have to be revalued (for part disposal calculations) on each occasion. Secondly, the subsequent disposals are divorced from the original disposal, so any reliefs (for instance entrepreneurs' relief) to which the taxpayer was entitled on the original disposal will no longer apply on the disposal derived from the contingent consideration.

The only exception to the second problem, which is potentially very serious where the reliefs available to the taxpayer are significant in the context of the size of the gain, is if the contingent future consideration is expressed as an issue of shares or securities to which the 'paper for paper exchange' rules applied.

Paper for paper exchanges

Sometimes the vendor of a company will accept other shares as consideration for the sale of the shares in his company. Typically this occurs either where the buying company is a quoted company, or is expected to become one shortly. Otherwise this arrangement is very much to the seller's disadvantage; he would probably be left with a minority stake in another unquoted company.

Provided that various conditions are met, the seller is able to defer any CGT liability on the sale of the shares where the consideration is in the form of the shares or debentures of the purchasing company. The new shares are treated as having been acquired on the same date and at the same price as the original shares. There are several alternative tests that may be used to gain the benefit of this rule. However, the most important one in this context is that the purchaser holds, or will hold as a result of the exchange, more than one quarter of the ordinary share capital of the target.

No claim is required for the relief to apply, although it is subject to an anti-avoidance rule that precludes it unless the exchange:

- is made for genuine commercial reasons; and
- does not form part of a scheme or arrangement of which a main purpose is to avoid a CGT or corporation tax liability.

Example

X wishes to sell his shares in X Ltd. Y Ltd offers to purchase X's shares, in return for an issue of Y Ltd shares to X. The paper for paper exchange relief is available provided that, as a result of the transaction, Y Ltd will own more than one quarter of the ordinary share capital of X Ltd.

It was noted above that where unascertainable contingent consideration is paid in the form of shares or debentures, and the 'paper for paper exchange' relief applies, the additional

Corporation Tax

shares or debentures issued when the contingency is unwound may also benefit from the relief.

Law: TCGA 1992, s. 48, 135, 280 and 138A; *Marren (HMIT) v Ingles* (1979) 54 TC 76; *Marson (HMIT) v Marriage* (1980) 54 TC 59

INTERNATIONAL TRANSACTIONS REQUIRING TREASURY CONSENT

3400 International transaction before 1 July 2009 requiring Treasury consent

Except as noted below, it was unlawful for a company which is resident in the UK to carry out any of the following transactions prior to 1 July 2009 without obtaining the consent of the Treasury:

- to cause or permit a non-resident company over which it has control to issue shares or debentures;
- to transfer to any person or cause or permit to be transferred to any person shares or debentures in a non-resident company over which it has control (except for the purpose of enabling a person to be qualified to act as a director).

The Treasury issued certain 'general consents' which gave blanket permission for companies to carry out certain types of transaction within the categories set out in the legislation. Those companies whose intended activities did not fall within the scope of the 'general consents' had to apply for 'special consent' usually from HM Treasury. Copies of the 'general consents' were also available from the Treasury.

Capital movements within EU member states

In relation to transactions carried out from 1 July 1990 (and before 1 July 2009), the issue of shares or debentures by a company resident in the EU (to another company or person so resident) or the transfer of shares or debentures in a company between two or more persons each of whom is resident in the EU did not require consent. However, transactions, which would otherwise have required specific consent, had to be reported by the UK company within six months. Penalties applied in relation to the failure to furnish information and the provision of false information.

Law: ICTA 1988, s. 765 and 765A; TMA 1970, s. 98(5); *The Movements of Capital (Required Information) Regulations* 1990 (SI 1990/1671)

Source: SP 2/92

See *British Tax Reporter* ¶810-430.

3450 International transactions carried out on or after 1 July 2009

The requirement to seek Treasury consent to transactions involving the international movement of capital was regarded by businesses as an obstacle to commercial transactions. The *Finance Act* 2009 repeals the Treasury Consent legislation found in ICTA 1988, s. 765–767 removing the consent requirement. In place of the requirement for Treasury consent a post-transaction reporting requirement is introduced, targeted at transactions which HMRC consider carry a high risk of possible tax avoidance.

The new requirement has effect in relation to those transactions carried out on or after 1 July 2009. Where any UK body is a reporting body at the time a reportable transaction or event occurs, a report must be made to an officer of HMRC within six months of the transaction or event. Any reports in respect of events or transactions which occur before 1 October 2009 can be reported by 1 April 2010.

The reportable event must have a value exceeding £100m and must be:

- an issue of shares or debentures by a foreign subsidiary;
- a transfer by the reporting company or a transfer caused or permitted by the reporting body of shares or debentures in which the reporting body has an interest;
- any situation which results in a foreign subsidiary becoming or ceasing to be a controlling partner in a partnership; or
- of a description in regulations issued by HMRC.

Where an otherwise reportable transaction takes place that reporting requirement will be disapplied where the transactions are carried out in the ordinary course of business between residents of the same territory, or is the giving of any security by a foreign subsidiary to financial institution.

A reporting body is the parent company of a UK owned group, or a UK resident company which heads part of a foreign owned group. Where a group is structured for example as a parallel sub-group controlled by a foreign parent, then the UK resident parents of each sub-group are reporting bodies unless both make an election for one company to be the reporting body.

The initial penalty for failing to make a report will be a penalty levied under TMA 1970, s. 98, not exceeding £300 for the initial failure. An additional penalty not exceeding £60 for each day on which the failure continues after the initial penalty was imposed can be levied.

Law: FA 2009, s. 37 and Sch. 17

See *British Tax Reporter* ¶809-300.

GROUPS OF COMPANIES

NATURE OF TAX GROUPS OF COMPANIES

3650 Basis of group taxation

In general, the same rules relating to corporation tax apply to groups of companies as to individual companies: each company is taxed separately and there is no consolidated tax treatment. However, there are specific provisions which apply solely to a recognised 'group of companies' (see 3653).

These specific provisions deal mainly with the following:

- transfers of assets between members (see 3684);
- replacement of business assets by group members (see 3695);
- transfers to shareholders of shares in, or business of, subsidiary members on a demerger (see 3730);
- the surrender of losses for offset by another member (group relief: see 3809);
- the recovery from other members of the group of unpaid tax on chargeable gains (see 3698);
- the surrender of a tax refund, etc. (including, under self assessment, repayments of instalments paid by large companies) within a group (see 3710).

In order to understand these provisions it is necessary to consider a number of definitions in relation to the meaning of group (see 3653).

Law: CTA 2010, Pt. 5

See *British Tax Reporter* ¶735-000.

3651 Arrangements with respect to payment of corporation tax

Under its 'care and management' powers (see 168), the Board may enter into arrangements with a group of companies to allow one member to discharge the corporation tax liabilities of the group (effective from 31 July 1998). The arrangements aim to ease the transition to quarterly payments. 'Group' for these purposes is a company and all of its 51 per cent subsidiaries, any 51 per cent subsidiaries of those subsidiaries and so on. Any such payment will not have to be broken down between the respective group members at the time of payment, but will be allocated to them as their tax liabilities arise under self-assessment.

Such arrangements may include provision for, inter alia:

(a) companies joining or leaving a group;
(b) payment of interest and penalties on corporation tax;

(c)   amounts treated as corporation tax (i.e. liabilities under the provisions for loans to participators: see 4300 and controlled foreign companies: see 4713ff.);

(d)   ending the arrangements; and

(e)   any other necessary or expedient provision.

Arrangements entered into will not impact on the actual liability, or the duty to pay corporation tax of any company covered by the arrangements, or any other tax liabilities. Therefore, if a subsidiary's corporation tax is not paid under a group arrangement, that subsidiary is still liable to pay that tax and any collection, interest, etc. provisions of the legislation will continue to apply.

HMRC have published details of the way payment arrangements will operate for groups of companies liable to pay their corporation tax by quarterly instalments. The arrangements apply for accounting periods ending on or after 31 December 1998. They will allow groups of companies that wish to do so to account for corporation tax (including quarterly instalment payments) on a group basis, instead of by individual company. Companies which undertake to pay tax under the arrangements must make such payments by electronic funds transfer. Once in place, the arrangements will generally apply automatically to subsequent accounting periods, but there are procedures which cover changes in the members of the group or if it transpires that the conditions for the arrangements have been breached.

In addition to the points already made above it should be noted that:

- companies whose tax affairs are in arrears cannot apply,
- generally, the accounting period must be that of all the participating companies, but there will be adaptations for a company or companies joining a group and aligning their accounting period with that of the group,
- not all companies in the group need be UK resident, *but* the company nominated to pay on behalf of the companies covered by the arrangement must be resident,
- not all members of the group need be covered by the group payment arrangements, and
- there may be more than one arrangement for different sub-groups.

For further details and if groups wish to take advantage of these arrangements, companies should register their interest by contacting the group payment team at the HMRC Accounts Office to which their CT payments are normally made.

Law: TMA 1970, s. 59F

See *British Tax Reporter* ¶739-300.

3653   What is 'a group of companies'?

Basically, there is no single definition of a 'group of companies' since the meaning may vary for different purposes.

Provisions relating to groups generally apply by reference to 75 per cent subsidiaries and 51 per cent subsidiaries:

Corporation Tax

- a company is a **75 per cent subsidiary** of another company if, and so long as, not less than 75 per cent of the ordinary share capital is owned directly or indirectly by that other company (see below); and
- a company is a **51 per cent subsidiary** of another company if, and so long as, more than 50 per cent of its ordinary share capital is owned directly or indirectly by the other company (see below).

These requirements are further refined in relation to each specific relief. Ownership also generally requires rights to income and assets on a winding-up. Generally, holdings by share dealers are ignored.

In general terms the two types of company qualify the groups of which they are part for the following reliefs:

75 per cent subsidiary

- group relief for losses etc.,
- surrenders of repayments to another group company, and
- capital gains reliefs.

51 per cent subsidiary

- following the abolition of ACT and the need for group income elections in 1999 and 2001, the concept of 51 per cent subsidiary is now most relevant in the context of capital gains reliefs where, in additional to being a 75 per cent subsidiary, a subsidiary also has to be an effective 51 per cent subsidiary (see 3682 below).

Certain reliefs are also available for particular forms of shareholding arrangements known as consortia including certain reliefs by reference to 90 per cent subsidiaries. A company is a 90 per cent subsidiary of another company if, and so long as, not less than 90 per cent of the ordinary share capital is directly owned by that company.

Ownership of ordinary share capital

'Ordinary share capital' is all issued share capital of a company except that capital which carries a right to fixed rate dividend but with no other right to a share in the company's profits.

Such capital is owned directly or indirectly where it is held directly by the company itself, through another company or companies or partly directly and partly indirectly through another company.

Example

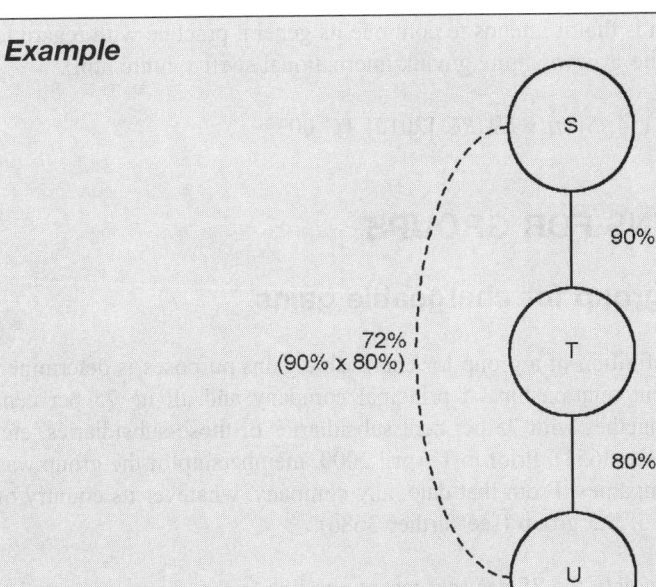

Company S owns 90 per cent of the ordinary share capital directly in company T.

Company T owns 80 per cent of the ordinary share capital directly in company U.

Therefore, S is treated as owning 72 per cent (90% × 80%) of the ordinary shares in U through T.

Thus, T is a 75 per cent subsidiary of S.

U is a 75 per cent subsidiary of T.

U is a 51 per cent subsidiary of S.

HMRC have set out in HMRC Brief 87/09 their views on the meaning of 'ordinary share capital' in the context of overseas companies. The Brief includes specific comments in relation to Delaware Limited Liability Companies (DLLCs) and German GmbH.

In relation to DLLCs, HMRC believe that there is legal authority for such entities to issue 'shares' under the Delaware Limited Liability Act, s. 18–702(c). Where 'shares' are issued in this way, HMRC will accept that they may be regarded as 'ordinary share capital' for the purpose of the definition of 'ordinary share capital' in CTA 2010, s. 1154. This means that such an LLC may be a '75% subsidiary'. It follows that it is possible for an LLC to:

● be a member of a capital gains group, and
● be a member of the same group as another company for the purposes of group relief.

This continues to be the case even though the First-tier Tribunal found that a member's interest in a particular Delaware LLC was 'not similar to share capital but something more similar to partnership capital of an English partnership' (*Swift v HMRC*). HMRC guidance

Corporation Tax

issued following the decision is that it intends to continue its general practice with regard to LLCs (see the HMRC website at www.hmrc.gov.uk/international/swift-v-hmrc.htm).

Law: CTA 2010, s. 1119, 1154; *Swift v HMRC* [2010] TC 00399

CHARGEABLE GAINS FOR GROUPS

3682   Definition of group for chargeable gains

From 14 March 1989, the definition of a group for chargeable gains purposes is determined by reference to a 75 per cent relationship. A principal company and all its 75 per cent subsidiaries form a group, together with 75 per cent subsidiaries of those subsidiaries, etc. (for the required ownership, see 3653). Prior to 1 April 2000, membership of the group was restricted to UK-resident companies. From that date, any company, whatever its country of residence, can be a member of the group (see further 3686).

However, companies which satisfy the 75 per cent test at any link in the chain are excluded if they are not 'effective 51 per cent subsidiaries' of the principal company.

A company is an effective 51 per cent subsidiary of its parent if:

- the parent is beneficially entitled to more than 50 per cent of any profits available for distribution to equity holders ('income'); and
- the parent would be beneficially entitled to more than 50 per cent of any assets available for distribution to equity holders on a winding-up ('assets').

Example

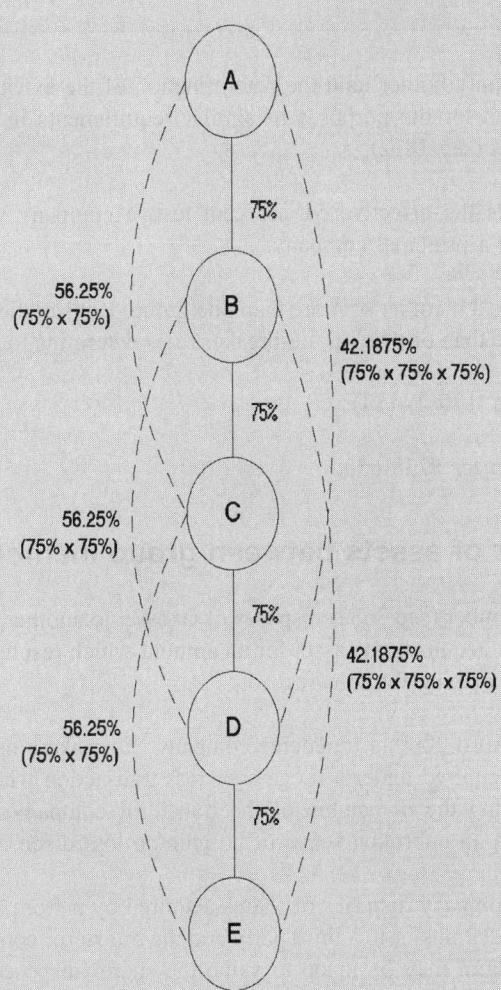

A is the principal company of a chargeable gains tax group comprising A, B and C. B is a 75 per cent subsidiary of A and C is a 75 per cent subsidiary of B, C is also an effective 51 per cent subsidiary of A, A being entitled to 56.25 per cent (75 per cent × 75 per cent) of its income or assets in a winding up. D is not a member of A's chargeable gains group. Although it is a 75 per cent subsidiary of A, it is not an effective 51 per cent subsidiary of A. A is only entitled to 42.1875 (75 per cent × 75 per cent × 75 per cent) of its income or assets in a winding up.

C, D and E cannot form a separate chargeable gains group because C is a 75 per cent subsidiary and as such cannot be a principal company. Similarly, B, C and D, cannot form separate chargeable gains group; B, being a 75 per cent subsidiary of A, cannot be a

> principal company. D is however a principal company of a separate chargeable gains group comprising D and E.

The definition of 'equity holder' and the determination of the extent of equity holdings are essentially those used for the purposes of similar requirements in relation to a group for group relief purposes (see 3812).

Except where it fails the effective 51 per cent test, a company which is a 75 per cent subsidiary cannot be a principal company.

A company cannot be a member of more than one group. If it satisfies all other conditions to be a member of more than one group, tie-breaker rules determine to which group it belongs.

Law: TCGA 1992, s. 170(2)–(14)

See *British Tax Reporter* ¶738-650.

3684 Transfer of assets between group members

Where one group member (see 3682) disposes of an asset to another, the company receiving the asset is treated as acquiring the asset for an amount which results in neither a gain nor a loss to the company making the transfer.

With effect from 6 April 2009, a transferee company can make a negligible value claim in relation to an asset acquired under a no gain/no loss transaction where the asset became of negligible value during the ownership of the transferor company or of an earlier owner where there has been an unbroken series of no gain/no loss disposals.

Where a transferee company disposes of shares acquired by it from another group company under a no gain/no loss transfer to a third party and the transferor company held the shares at 31 March 1982, a claim may be made to value the shares disposed of as the appropriate proportion of the value of any larger holding held by the transferor company at 31 March 1982.

From 1 April 2000, it is possible to utilise capital losses and benefit from the no gain/no loss provisions without the need to physically transfer the asset (see 3685).

The ability to transfer an asset tax-free to a fellow group company led to the practice of buying in capital losses, or more precisely buying and bringing into the group a company with unused allowable losses: assets pregnant with gain could be transferred to the loss company before realisation, thereby permitting any chargeable gain to be relieved by the allowable losses. The set-off of capital losses brought into a group of companies as a result of a company joining the group is restricted to certain permissible gains (and provided there is no major change in the nature of the company's trade, etc.) for losses set off against gains arising after 15 March 1993 where the losses came from a company which joined the group after 30 March 1987. This applies equally to the 'pre-entry proportion' of a loss on an asset held at the time of entry by the loss company or later transferred to it within the group without there having been a disposal outside the group since that date (a 'pre-entry asset'); the restriction applies essentially to a time-apportioned amount of the loss or, by election, to an amount calculated by reference to market value on entry to the group. These calculations are further affected, for disposals made after 29 November 1993, by the provisions ensuring that, subject to transitional relief in certain circumstances, indexation cannot be used to create or increase a loss (see 5280). There are special rules for pooled shares, etc. With effect from 5 December 2005 a more targeted anti-avoidance provision has been introduced to counteract the effect of arrangements that have as their main purpose, or one of their main purposes, the securing of a tax advantage and either involves a change of ownership of a company or converting income to capital or generating a deduction against income for an expense that would otherwise be relieved against chargeable gains.

If, within a group, a share exchange takes place, the provisions relating to tax-free transfers on reorganisation or company takeover (see 4024, 5900) take priority. The no gain/no loss rule is disapplied. Legislation was enacted to this effect to displace the decision to the contrary in the *Woolcombers* case.

HMRC published an interpretation clarifying the position where shares are exchanged within a group of companies in exchange for qualifying corporate bonds (QCBs) (see 5865). In these circumstances the legislation does not operate to cancel the no gain/no loss rule. However, HMRC's view is that such a transfer is still outside the no gain/no loss rule and that the acquisition cost is covered instead by the general capital gains tax acquisition rules. The following example is based upon HMRC's interpretation.

Example

Companies A and C are members of the same chargeable gains group. Company A holds shares in Company B which it transfers to C on 30 June 1997. The consideration for the transfer is not shares in C but consists entirely of a new issue by C of loan stocks which are QCBs. The transfer by A and acquisition by C of shares in B is not within the no gain/ no loss rule. Instead:

- C is treated as having acquired the shares in B for a consideration equal to their market value at 30 June 1997 with no addition for indexation which would have accrued over A's period of ownership;
- there is no disposal by A and A's holding of QCBs is outside the scope of capital gains tax altogether. Any future increases or decreases in value are taxable under the loan relationship rules instead;
- however, there is calculated the chargeable gain or allowable loss that would have accrued if A had disposed of its holding of shares in B for a consideration equal to its market value immediately before 30 June 1997. That chargeable gain or allowable loss is deemed to accrue on a subsequent disposal by A of the whole or part of the QCBs.

Corporation Tax

Exceptions

The no gain/no loss transfer rule does not apply to certain excluded disposals. In particular, the rule does not apply to a disposal of a debt owing by one member of a group when another member satisfies the whole or part of that debt. It does not apply on the redemption of redeemable shares in a company or to a disposal by or to an investment trust, or to a disposal to a dual resident investing company. Nor does it apply to disposals to a company which, at that time, would be exempt from tax under a double tax treaty on a notional gain in respect of the disposal of the assets in point.

Law: TCGA 1992, s. 171, 184A–184I and Sch. 7A; *Westcott (HMIT) v Woolcombers Ltd* [1987] BTC 493

See *British Tax Reporter* ¶735-800.

3685   Notional transfers within a group

Gains or losses accruing before 21 July 2009

In relation to disposals after 1 April 2000, it is possible to utilise capital losses in different group companies without an actual physical transfer of the asset involved on a no gain/no loss basis. Such an election saves the group incurring the compliance costs associated with an actual transfer.

Where two companies (A and B) are members of a group (see 3682) and one of those companies (A) disposes of an asset to a person who is not a member of a group (C), the two group companies (A and B) can jointly elect for the purposes of corporation tax on chargeable gains that the asset in question is treated as transferred from A to B on a no gain/no loss basis immediately prior to the transfer to C and that B disposed of the asset to C. Furthermore, the actual incidental costs of disposal by A are deemed to be the incidental costs of disposal by B; thus B can get a deduction in computing the chargeable gain on its disposal to C even though B did not actually incur these costs.

The deeming of incidental costs of disposal affects disposals made on or after 1 April 2000 (even though introduced by FA 2001).

The election must be made on or before the second anniversary of the end of the accounting period of A in which the disposal to C was made.

Gains or losses accruing on or after 21 July 2009

Following the enactment of FA 2009, it is now possible for chargeable gains and allowable losses to be transferred within a group. For gains and losses made before 21 July 2009, this result could only be achieved by electing for the notional transfer of an asset before its disposal to a third party (former TCGA 1992, s. 171A). However, as former TCGA 1992, s. 171A only applied where the asset was to be sold to a third party, an election could not be made where an asset was destroyed, where a group company was liquidated or on the making of a negligible value claim. Therefore, new s. 171A, as inserted by FA 2009, s. 31, Sch. 12, provides a simpler and more comprehensive means of transferring gains and losses within a group.

This election can only be made where:

(a) a chargeable gain or an allowable loss accrues on or after 21 July 2009 to a company (Company A) in respect of an asset;

(b) at that time, Company A and another company (Company B) are members of the same group; and

(c) had Company A transferred the asset to Company B immediately before the time of the accrual, the transfer would have taken place on a tax neutral basis under TCGA 1992, s. 171(1).

An election cannot be made where it relates to a degrouping charge.

There is provision to allow gains or losses to be transferred to a non-resident company provided that the company carries on a trade through a permanent establishment.

Where Company A and Company B have made such an election the effect is to treat the loss as accruing to company B. The election can be made for all or part of the gain, but cannot exceed the amount of the gain or loss. Where the election exceeds these amounts the election is ineffective, a parliamentary reply suggests that there is nothing to prevent a revised election being submitted.

Where Company A (the transferor) and Company B (the transferee) enter into an election, the effect of the election is that the gain or loss is treated as accruing to Company B and not Company A.

Law: TCGA 1992, s. 171A and 171B

See *British Tax Reporter* ¶753-925, ¶753-950.

3686 Non-UK residents

The ability of companies to transfer assets on a no gain/no loss basis across residence barriers was enhanced significantly from 1 April 2000, with associated anti-avoidance measures applying from 21 March 2000. From that date, membership of a chargeable gains group (see 3682) is not restricted to UK-resident companies. Transfers within the group can be made on a tax neutral basis if the asset remains within the UK tax net. So, for example, a transfer of an asset can be made on a tax neutral basis between a UK resident member of a group and a non-UK resident member of the group if the asset is used by the non resident member for the purposes of a trade carried on in the UK through a UK permanent establishment.

The change means, that for example, transfer of assets are possible between UK-resident subsidiaries with a non-resident parent on a no gain/no loss basis, where the subsidiaries and

Corporation Tax

parent are members of a chargeable gains group. Previously, the transfer between the subsidiaries would have been treated as if the subsidiary making the disposal has disposed of it at market value, irrespective of the actual consideration.

Also from 1 April 2000, the transfer of assets from one company to another company as part of a scheme of reconstruction or amalgamation will attract tax relief irrespective of where the participating companies are resident, provided the assets remain in the UK tax net.

Prior to 1 April 2000, companies which were not UK-resident could not generally benefit from the no gain/no loss provisions (see 3682). However, relief was available in the case of the transfer of a UK branch or agency to a UK-resident company. The transferor and transferee must be in a relationship such that if both were UK-resident they would essentially qualify for the general relief. A claim for the extension must be made by the two companies within two years of the end of transferee's accounting period (see 4080).

Further forms of relief applied in respect of the transfer by a UK-resident company to a company resident in another EU member state of a non-UK branch (see 4088) and in respect of the transfer between EU member states involving at least one non-resident company of a UK branch (see 4096).

If a company ceases to be resident it is normally required to notify HMRC and to pay tax on any capital gains which have accrued on assets which it holds. This requirement has been removed in the case of companies which cease to be UK-resident by virtue of the provisions that treat dual resident companies which are not treated as resident in the UK by virtue of a double taxation agreement as not resident for all tax purposes (see 3014). In these circumstances any tax on gains which accrued whilst the company was UK resident will be deferred until the assets are sold, but with a maximum deferral of six years.

Law: TCGA 1992, s. 25 and 171

See *British Tax Reporter* ¶735-800.

3687 Consequences when a member leaves a group

Where a company leaves a group after it has acquired an asset from another group member it is sometimes treated as if it had disposed of that asset as soon as it was acquired and then reacquired it at its market value for capital gains purposes (see 3050, 5130ff.). Any gain or loss so computed is treated as accruing on the later of the time of the deemed reacquisition and the beginning of the accounting period in which the company left the group (although this timing may be altered if the exemption for disposal of substantial shareholdings is in point – see 4035). For recovery from other group members where tax remains unpaid, see 3698.

For degrouping events taking place after 31 March 2002, the whole or a part of any gain or loss arising may be re-allocated to one or more members of the group. A joint election must be made within two years of the end of the accounting period in which the charge arises.

Any payment in respect of the re-allocation is ignored, provided it does not exceed the amount of gain or loss.

From the same time, it is also possible to roll-over any gain arising (including a re-allocated gain). The roll-over relief provisions (see 6305) are suitably modified for the purpose (see TCGA 1992, Sch. 7AB).

Except as noted below, the charge applies where the asset was acquired within six years ending on the date when the company ceases to be a group member.

Example

Company A acquires office premises in 1987 at the then market value of £250,000.

The premises were transferred to B, its 100 per cent owned subsidiary, when the market value of the premises was £300,000.

Within six years, B leaves the group and sells the offices for £400,000 one year later.

B is liable to pay any tax assessable on a capital gain arising at the date of transfer or at the beginning of the accounting period in which B leaves the group as applicable.

Deemed gain	£
Market value at transfer date	300,000
Cost to the group	(250,000)
Unindexed gain	50,000

Actual gain on disposal by B	£
On disposal, the offices were sold for	400,000
Notional cost to B	(300,000)
Unindexed gain	100,000

If a company would cease to be a member of a group by failing the effective 51 per cent subsidiary test when the principal company joins a new group, the deemed disposal is not triggered until the company also fails to meet the 75 per cent test with any company in the new group; the gain or loss then arises at the time of the original transfer.

Where a company left a group on 14 March 1989 purely as a result of the redefinition of the meaning of group (see 3682), the deemed disposal was deferred, and continues to be deferred until (if ever) it would have arisen under the former definitions.

The deemed disposal does not apply to:

- a company which ceases to be a member of a group on the winding-up or dissolution of itself or in consequence of another group member ceasing to exist;
- any asset acquired by one associated company from another if they leave a group at the same time (two or more companies are associated if together they would form a group of companies) (see below);
- any asset (or property to which a chargeable gain is carried forward from the asset on a

Corporation Tax

replacement of business assets: see 6305ff.), which is held as trading stock by the chargeable company or its associate which is also leaving the company.

The exception to the deemed disposal rules which applies where two or more associated companies together leave the group at the same time, could, before 29 November 1994, be exploited to enable an asset to leave the original group without a charge arising. However, where a company leaves a group after 28 November 1994, this device is countered by the effective re-imposition of the de-grouping charge where a company successively leaves two connected groups with an asset which it acquired in the first group, in circumstances in which the exception would otherwise apply. Furthermore (in a case decided upon the version of the rules which applied for periods before 1 October 1993), the exception to the deemed disposal rules has been held not to apply where the principal company of a group became non-resident after it had acquired shares in another company from a fellow group member, the gain on that earlier transfer having been deferred. The two could not be said to have left the group 'at the same time' because the group itself ceased to exist without its principal company. The Court of Appeal chose to adopt the purpose of the legislation in interpreting the legislation.

There is an exception for certain mergers so that the deemed disposal does not apply if the company leaves the group for bona fide commercial reasons (see 3730ff.).

Law: TCGA 1992, s. 179 and 179A; *Johnston Publishing (North) Ltd v R & C Commrs* [2008] BTC 443

See *British Tax Reporter* ¶737-600.

3689 Acquisition or disposal of trading stock within group

If one member of a 'group' (see 3682) acquires an asset as trading stock from another group member for which it was not trading stock, the acquirer is treated as acquiring it other than as trading stock and then immediately appropriating it to trading stock, so that a chargeable gain or allowable loss will result (see 5145).

Example ignoring indexation

Company A is a member of a group of companies.

A has a capital asset acquired in 1997 for £50,000. In 2002 it is worth £75,000.

A transfers the asset in 2002 to B, another group member as trading stock.

The capital asset is treated as sold by A to B for	£50,000

B's appropriation to trading stock is treated as a gain made by B of:	£
Market value	75,000
Deemed acquisition cost	(50,000)
	25,000

B is therefore liable to pay any tax assessed on that gain.

If a group member disposes of assets from trading stock to be used for some other purpose by the acquirer, the disponor is treated as appropriating that asset for that other purpose immediately before the disposal; this will effectively result in a market value transfer from revenue to capital account (see 636, 5145).

Law: TCGA 1992, s. 173(1) and (2); *Coates (HMIT) v Arndale Properties Ltd* [1984] BTC 438; *Reed (HMIT) v Nova Securities Ltd* [1985] BTC 121

See *British Tax Reporter* ¶736-850.

3692   Disposals to non-group members after intra-group transfer

Where one member of a 'group' (see 3682) acquires an asset from another member and then disposes of it outside the group, there may be a chargeable disposal on which a chargeable gain or allowable loss may arise which is subject to special provisions which take into account the ownership by any other group member.

Any allowable loss incurred is reduced by the amount of any capital allowances made in respect of it to any group member so far as not previously recovered (see 3815).

If the asset was acquired by the group before 1965, for the purposes of the rules that any gain may be time-apportioned, etc. (see 5380ff.), the members are treated as one person and the company is treated as if it acquired the asset at the time when it was originally acquired by a group member; these rules are relevant only in so far as they are not excluded in relation to assets held on 31 March 1982 (see 3050, 5060ff.). The pre-1965 rule does not apply to a disposal to or by an investment trust.

Law: TCGA 1992, s. 174

3695   Replacement of business assets by group members

All trades carried on by members of a 'group' (see 3682) are treated as a single trade for the purpose of applying the rules relating to the replacement of business assets. It has been Revenue practice to regard this as permitting a gain arising on an asset owned by one member to be rolled over into the cost of an asset acquired by another member. This extends to treating the members of a group as a single person.

However, this rule does not apply where the replacement is made by a dual resident investing company.

Corporation Tax

Although roll-over relief is denied for acquisitions of assets by group companies in a no gain/no loss transaction, roll-over relief for disposals of land under compulsory purchase orders is extended to those situations in which the disposal of the land and the acquisition of its replacement are made by different group companies.

The rules applicable to depreciating assets apply to the group members as if the group were one person and as if all trades were the same trade (see 6310).

Law: TCGA 1992, s. 175 and 247(5A)

Source: SP 8/81

3698 Recovery within group: failure to pay tax on chargeable gains

If a member of a 'group' (see 3682) makes a chargeable gain and fails to pay the tax assessed thereon within six months of it becoming payable, the inspector may recover that tax from the principal company in the group at the time of the gain, or from any company which was a member of the group within the two years before the date when the gain was made and which owned the whole or part of the asset disposed of or an interest in it.

The tax inspector has two years from the date when the tax became payable to make such an assessment. The assessment is in the name of the company which made the gain. The amount of tax charged must not exceed the corporation tax payable on the gain at the rate in force when that gain was made.

A company so charged may recover the tax (and any interest on overdue tax) from the company which made the gain or from the principal company of the group. If the principal company repays the tax then it may in turn recover the sum from the company which made the gain or from any other group member which owned the asset disposed of whilst it was a member of the group. The amount recoverable from such a company is in proportion to the value of the asset when that company disposed of it.

Similar provisions apply specifically in relation to tax charged when a company leaves a group with an asset transferred to it intra-group (see 3684).

Law: TCGA, 1992, s. 190

See *British Tax Reporter* ¶738-650.

3710 Surrender of tax refund within group

Companies in a group can effectively offset underpayments and overpayments within the group in calculating interest on overdue tax payable by any individual company. Under self-assessment (CTSA), the ability to surrender repayments of tax to other group members is extended to cover payments of corporation tax under self-assessment, i.e. including repayments of instalments paid by large companies.

The offset is treated as having been made for all purposes of the Tax Acts. A consequent adjustment will also be made in any tax-geared penalty arising as a result of failing to deliver a tax return on time.

Membership of a group for this purpose is essentially the same as for group relief, although the two (or more) companies involved must have coterminous accounting periods, and must also be members of the group throughout the period from the start of the relevant accounting period until the date on which the offset election is made (see 3809ff.).

Law: CTA 2010, s. 963

See *British Tax Reporter* ¶739-300.

3715   Intangible fixed assets

For the purposes of the rules relating to intangible fixed assets (see 3042) a group is defined in a similar way to that used for chargeable gains purposes (see 3682). The single company rules are extended in a number of group situations including:

- transfers of intangible fixed assets within a group;
- roll-over relief on reinvestment: application to group members;
- companies ceasing to be members of a group (degrouping);
- payments between group members in respect of reliefs.

Transfers of intangible fixed assets within a group

Where an intangible fixed asset is transferred between two companies which are members of the same group and the asset is a chargeable intangible asset immediately before and after the transfer, then the transfer is treated as being tax neutral. A tax-neutral transfer is not regarded as a realisation by the transferor. The transferee is treated as though it has held the asset for the same length of time as the transferor and has done all the things that the transferor did in relation to the asset.

Roll-over relief

The roll-over relief for reinvestment into intangible fixed assets is extended where a company is a member of a group. Where a company which is a member of the same group as the company realising the old assets incurs the expenditure on new assets the reinvestment relief can apply. The relief does not apply if the company incurring the expenditure is a dual resident investing company or if the expenditure on other assets relates to assets acquired from another member of the group by a tax-neutral transfer.

Reinvestment relief is also extended under certain circumstances to reinvestment in shares in a company where the assets of that company include chargeable intangible fixed assets.

Corporation Tax

Degrouping

The degrouping provisions apply if a company, which has acquired a chargeable intangible asset by way of a tax-neutral transfer, leaves a group within six years (see 3687). If the company leaving the group (or an associated company also leaving the group) still owns the intangible asset at the time then the provisions have effect. The transferee company is deemed to realise and immediately reacquire the asset immediately after the transfer at its market value at that time. The resulting amendments to the tax debits and credits are brought into the computation in the period in which the company leaves the group.

Under certain circumstances it may be possible:

- for the deemed realisation under the degrouping rules to be subject to a reinvestment relief claim;
- for a remaining member of a group to elect jointly that the degrouping tax credit be brought to account by them rather than the departing company;
- for the company which elects to take on the degrouping charge to make a claim for reinvestment relief in relation to the deemed realisation.

Payments between group companies in respect of reliefs

Where there are payments between group members for group roll-over relief or for the reallocation of a degrouping charge then the payments shall not be taken into account in computing profits or losses for corporation tax purposes.

Law: CTA 2009, Pt. 8

See *British Tax Reporter* ¶724-500.

COMPANY MERGERS

3730 Consequences of company mergers

A 'merger' is an arrangement between several parties, which may include a non-resident company, whereby the merging company acquires one or more interests in the whole or part of the business of the leaving company. The members of the group which that company has left then acquire an interest in the business carried on by either the merging company itself or its '90 per cent subsidiary' (see 3653) before the merger. In either case, the interest acquired must be at least 25 per cent of the ordinary share capital of the relevant company. The remaining interest may include shares and/or debentures. The interest must not be acquired with an intention to dispose of it.

If a company leaves a group as part of a 'merger' which is not taking place to avoid tax, the charge which arises in respect of assets transferred to that company intra-group (see 3684) is disapplied.

Law: TCGA 1992, s. 181

See *British Tax Reporter* ¶735-000.

GROUP RELIEF

3809 Nature of group relief

One advantage of being a member of a group is that it is possible to transfer the benefit of some corporation tax reliefs between members by way of group relief. Similar benefits apply as between consortium members and companies owned by the consortium.

Subject to certain restrictions (see 3826), this may be particularly useful where one company incurs large trading losses which it cannot expect to relieve against its own income in the foreseeable future but another company has income against which to set off the losses.

Prior to 1 April 2000, only UK-resident companies qualified for group relief, with holdings by non-UK resident companies or share dealers being ignored. However, following the principle established in *Imperial Chemical Industries plc v Colmner* [1999] BTC 440 in which the European Court of Justice held that the group relief provisions as they stood at the time were contrary to EC law in that companies in the EU were prevented from claiming consortium relief, the group relief provisions were extended from 1 April 2000, permitting groups and consortia to be established through the presence of non-resident companies in the ownership structure. In addition, group relief was extended from the same date to UK branches of overseas companies.

In a recent case (*FCE Bank plc*) now of mainly historical interest only it was held that, before the change in the law in 2000, the non-discrimination clause of the UK–US double tax treaty had the result that group relief was available between two UK resident directly-held 75 per cent subsidiaries of a US parent company in circumstances where it would have been available had the parent company been UK resident.

Despite the FA 2000 relaxation, the legislation did not, thus far, extend to allowing losses in overseas subsidiaries to be offset as group relief. A claim by a parent company *Marks and Spencer plc v Halsey (HMIT)* that it was entitled under European Community law to offset the losses of its indirectly held subsidiary companies incorporated and resident for tax purposes in other member states against its profits for purposes of UK group relief (the subsidiaries were resident in Belgium, France and Germany and were held via a UK incorporated and tax-resident subsidiary of the parent and then through a Dutch incorporated and tax-resident holding company) was ultimately accepted in the European Court of Justice (ECJ), albeit with the significant limitation that other possibilities for utilisation of the losses had to be exhausted first.

On 20 February 2006, the government announced that it would introduce legislation to reflect the ECJ ruling in the *Marks & Spencer* case. Accordingly, FA 2006, s. 27 and Sch. 1

Corporation Tax

763

extended the application of group relief to cases where a UK parent company has a foreign subsidiary with a foreign tax loss that is not otherwise relievable. The extension applies with effect from 1 April 2006, except for an anti-avoidance rule (the 'unallowable losses' rule), which applies from 20 February 2006. These rules apply to groups but not to consortia. They do not affect the operation of other kinds of group relief.

The foreign losses will be 'relievable in the UK' only where all possibilities of relief have been exhausted and future relief is unavailable in the country where they were incurred or in any other country. Where there is a foreign company in the ownership chain between the surrendering company and a UK parent, precedence rules will be used to determine whether relief will be available in the UK.

In order to obtain relief against UK profits the foreign tax loss will need to be recomputed under UK tax principles. This means that relief will only be available for losses or other amounts that may be surrendered under the existing UK rules. In addition, when calculating the amount of the relief, regard will be had to the overall amount of the unrelieved foreign loss. That is, relief will not be given for an amount that does not represent an unrelieved foreign tax loss.

All appropriate compliance obligations will be placed on the UK claimant company. Therefore, the claimant company will be responsible for demonstrating that the losses meet the relevant conditions. From 20 February 2006 loss relief is denied where there are arrangements which either result in losses becoming unrelievable outside the UK that might otherwise be relievable, or give rise to unrelievable losses which would not have arisen but for the availability of relief in the UK, if the main purpose or one of the main purposes of those arrangements is to obtain UK relief.

The *Marks and Spencer plc v Halsey (HMIT)* case returned to the High Court to be dealt with in the light of the ECJ judgment. The judge dismissed the company's appeal with regard to the losses of the French subsidiary and directed that to the extent the appeal related to the losses of the Belgium and German subsidiaries, the appeal be remitted to the special commissioners. Both HMRC and the company appealed. In the Court of Appeal, the judges said that following the ruling of the ECJ the losses of the non-resident subsidiaries should be treated, as far as possible, in the same way as losses of resident companies. Therefore, the decision of a non-resident company to surrender its losses, because they could not be used in its own state of residence, could be made at, or up to the time, when the company made its claim for group relief. There was no support in the reasoning that the conditions had to be satisfied at the end of the surrender period, as HMRC contended, rather than when the group relief claim was made. The judges also decided that the phrase 'no possibility' should be read as 'no real possibility' for utilisation of the losses in the company's own state of residence then fell to the Tribunal (formerly, the Special Commissioners) to determine if the claims made by Marks and Spencer in respect of the losses of its German and Belgium subsidiaries were valid in light of the earlier judgments. The Tribunal found that in applying the no-possibilities test, only 'recognised possibilities legally available given the objective facts of the company's situation at the relevant time' must be considered. In addition, and for the purpose of considering if losses are likely to be used in future periods, 'a real possibility is one which cannot be dismissed as fanciful'. The first group of claims was dismissed because at the relevant time there was nothing to prevent the companies continuing to trade, or to start another trade, and so use the losses in a later period. The second, third and fourth groups of claims, which were all made after liquidation proceedings had commenced, were allowed because at the relevant time no new activities could be started (the liquidator's functions merely being to pay the liabilities and distribute the assets) (para. 29 and 30). The Tribunal's decision also provides guidance on how to calculate the losses which can be claimed. Briefly, the no-possibilities test must be applied to losses computed under the company's local law. Those losses which satisfy the no-possibilities test must then be converted into sterling and recalculated in accordance with UK tax law.

In September 2008 the European Commission sent the UK a formal request to implement properly the ECJ judgment in *Marks & Spencer v Halsey*. In the legislation meant to implement the ruling, the UK imposes conditions on cross-border group relief which the Commission contends makes it virtually impossible for taxpayers to benefit from the relief.

The case returned to the First-tier tribunal again later in 2009 on a different point of law. The point at issue this time was whether relief should be given in the year in which the overseas loss fell for UK computational purposes, or the year in which the overseas loss would have been recognised under the tax law of the state in which it was resident. The commissioners decided that relief should be given in the year in which the loss fell for UK computational purposes.

The conclusions reached by the First-tier Tribunal with regard to the calculation of the losses and the manner in which relief is to be given were endorsed by the Upper Tribunal. However, the Upper Tribunal did find that the First-tier Tribunal had been wrong to set aside the normal time limits and allow a claim to be made after it became clear that, to be effective, the claim had to satisfy the no possibilities test. The Upper Tribunal also provided further guidance on the quantum of losses which can be claimed, finding that 'it is correct to cap the amount of group relief available by the amount of any local loss to the extent that the differential in the amount of the losses (UK and local) results from differences in principle between tax regimes, rather than from timing differences'.

Company simultaneously a member of a group and a consortium

Group relief is available where at the same time a company is in the same group (see 3812) as one or more other companies and is also either a company jointly owned by a consortium (see 3812) or one of the joint owners of a consortium company. In this situation it is possible for:

- a loss or other amount of the surrendering company to be claimed partly as group relief and partly as consortium relief; and
- for consortium relief to 'flow through' the consortium member to and from other companies in the consortium member's group.

Corporation Tax

The relaxations aim to give such companies greater flexibility in using group and consortium relief.

When extending the group and consortium relief provisions in 2000 to allow non-UK resident companies to be taken into account the draftsman overlooked the mechanics of the link company rules contained with the result that a member of a group of companies of which another member of that group (the 'link company') is a consortium member can only claim consortium relief from a consortium company where the link company is resident in the UK (or carrying on trade in the UK though a UK permanent establishment).

In *Philips Electronics UK Ltd v R & C Commrs* the First-tier tribunal held that this restriction (that a link company must be resident in the UK or carrying on a trade here through a permanent establishment) was contrary to the freedom of establishment principle of EU law, could not be justified and that therefore, consortium relief was available where, as in the *Philips* case, the link company was resident in another member state notwithstanding that UK tax legislation prohibited it. It was announced in the March 2010 Budget and reconfirmed in the June 2010 Budget that legislation will be introduced to amend the law to allow a company established within the European Economic Area to be a link company. It is anticipated that the changes to the legislation will have effect for accounting period ended after the date on which the legislation is published, likely to be in the autumn of 2010.

Law: CTA 2010, Pt. 5; *Marks and Spencer plc v Halsey (HMIT)* Case C-446/03 [2006] BTC 318; *Marks and Spencer plc v Halsey (HMIT)* [2006] BTC 346; *Marks and Spencer plc v Halsey (HMIT)* [2007] BTC 204; *Marks and Spencer plc v R & C Commrs* [2009] TC 181; *Marks and Spencer plc v R & C Commrs* [RDT 42]; decision released 22 June 2010; *Imperial Chemical Industries plc v Colmner* [1999] BTC 440; *Boake Allen Ltd & Ors (including NEC Semi-conductors Ltd) v R & C Commrs* [2007] BTC 414; *Pilkington Bros Ltd v IR Commrs* [1982] BTC 79; *Shepherd (HMIT) v Law Land plc* [1990] BTC 561; *Steele (HMIT) v EVC International NV* [1996] BTC 425; *Scottish and Universal Newspapers Ltd v Fisher (HMIT)* (1996) Sp C 87; *Philips Electronics UK Ltd v R & C Commrs* [2009] TC 176; *FCE Bank plc* [2010] TC 00445

Source: SP 3/93; ESC C10; Inland Revenue Tax Bulletin, Issue 26, December 1996, p. 372

See *British Tax Reporter* ¶736-150 and ¶736-550.

3812   Application of group relief

One company, the claimant company, may obtain relief against its profits (see 3821) for a trading loss or similar amount (see 3815), incurred by another company, the surrendering company, in the same accounting period. The surrendering company must agree to the arrangement.

This rule applies where either company is a '75 per cent subsidiary' (see 3653) of the other or they are both 75 per cent subsidiaries of a third company. Alternatively, either company must be a member of a consortium of 20 or fewer members and the other must be one of the following:

- a trading company owned by the consortium which is not a 75 per cent subsidiary of any company; or
- a trading company which is a '90 per cent subsidiary' (see 3653) of a holding company owned by the consortium and which is not a 75 per cent subsidiary of a company other than the holding company; or
- a holding company owned by the consortium which is not a 75 per cent subsidiary of any company.

A company is owned by a consortium if 75 per cent or more of its share capital is owned by companies, each owning at least five per cent of the total share capital.

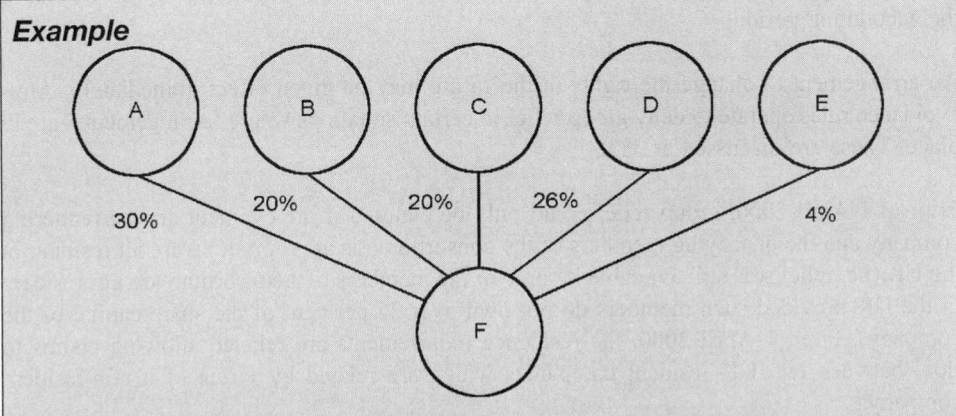

Example

A, B, C, D and F form a consortium. Collectively, A, B, C and D own 96 per cent of F, and each company individually owns more than 5 per cent of F. E is not a consortium member as it owns less than 5 per cent of F.

Prior to 1 April 2000, the application of group relief was limited to UK-resident companies. However, from 1 April 2000, this requirement was lifted.

A company will not be regarded as a 75 per cent subsidiary or a 90 per cent subsidiary unless:

- it is beneficially entitled to at least 75 per cent or, as the case may be, 90 per cent of the subsidiary's profits distributable to its equity holders (see below); and
- it is beneficially entitled to not less than 75 per cent or, as the case may be, 90 per cent of the subsidiary's assets distributable to its equity-holders (see below) on a winding-up.

For the purposes of group relief, a member's share in a consortium, in relation to an accounting period of the surrendering company (be it the consortium member or a company owned by the consortium) is the lowest of the following:

- the percentage of the ordinary share capital of the other company beneficially owned by that member; and

- the percentage of any profits distributable to equity holders (see below) of the other company to which the member is beneficially entitled; and
- the percentage of the other company's assets distributable to its equity holders (see below) on a winding-up to which the member company is beneficially entitled.

It was announced in the June 2010 Budget that an additional test based on the proportion of voting rights and the extent of control the member holds in the consortium will be introduced with effect for accounting periods ended after the date on which the legislation is published, likely to be in the autumn of 2010.

If there are any fluctuations in any of the percentages during the surrendering company's accounting period, the average percentage over the period is used. In determining the average percentage, HMRC apply a weighted average rather than a flat average, to prevent the percentage being manipulated by changes in shares for a short period towards the end of the accounting period.

An arrangement to change the rights in the future may be given effect immediately. Anti-avoidance rules operate to deny group relief in certain situations where 'arrangements' are in place. These are discussed at 3826.

Prior to 1 April 2000, group relief could only be claimed if the claimant and surrendering company and the qualifying members of the consortium (as appropriate) were all resident in the UK (i.e. relief was still available if some of the members of a consortium are not resident in the UK provided such members do not own over 25 per cent of the share capital of the company). From 1 April 2000, the residence requirements are relaxed allowing claims to flow between two UK resident companies which are related by virtue of a non-resident company.

In a recent case (*FCE Bank plc*) now of mainly historical interest only it was held that, before the change in the law in 2000, the non-discrimination clause of the UK–US double tax treaty had the result that group relief was available between two UK resident directly-held 75 per cent subsidiaries of a US parent company in circumstances where it would have been available had the parent company been UK resident.

If group relief is given, no further relief may be claimed for the same loss. No relief will be given if, in any accounting period, the share of the claimant, as a member of a consortium, in the surrendering company is nil or if any profit on the sale of the shares in the surrendering company is a trading profit of the claimant.

'Equity holder'

An 'equity holder of the company' is any person who:

- holds 'ordinary shares' in the company; or
- is a 'creditor' of the company for a loan which is not a 'normal commercial loan'.

'Ordinary shares' are all a company's shares except restricted preference shares. To qualify as restricted preference shares, shares must, in particular, not carry a right to a dividend other than a fixed amount or at a fixed percentage rate (or a fluctuating rate where the rate fluctuates in accordance with the RPI or other similar general index of prices issued by the government) of the nominal value of the shares and the company must not be entitled to reduce the amount of, or not pay, the dividends. However, this latter restriction (i.e. that the company must not be entitled to reduce the amount of the dividend) is removed for accounting periods beginning on or after 1 January 2008 where the company is only entitled to reduce the amount of the dividends in special circumstances, being when the company is in severe financial difficulties or when it is unable to pay all or part of a dividend because of a recommendation by the Financial Services Authority or a similar body. Non-cumulative preference shares are not therefore restricted preference shares (because the dividend is not fixed – depending on the level of reserves the dividend might be at a rate below the quoted coupon rate) and so would be regarded as ordinary shares which could lead to two companies which would otherwise have qualified for group relief ceasing to qualify.

In addition to these conditions on the restricted right to dividends, shares have to meet the following conditions in order to qualify as a restricted preference shares:

(a)   the shares were issued for a consideration which includes new consideration (so, for example, shares issued on a bonus issue can not be restricted preference shares);

(b)   the shares do not carry the right to conversion into other shares or securities (except into other restricted preference shares or shares or securities of the company's quoted parent company);

(c)   the shares do not carry any right to the acquisition of other shares and securities;

(d)   on repayment, the shares do not carry the right to an amount exceeding the new consideration given for the shares (except so far as those rights are reasonably comparable with those generally carried by listed fixed dividend shares); and

(e)   the rate of the dividends on the shares is no more than a reasonable commercial return on the new consideration given for the shares.

A 'loan creditor' of a company is a person to whom the company owes a debt for the following:

- money borrowed; or
- capital assets acquired; or
- any right of the company to receive income created in favour of the company; or
- consideration which, at the time the debt was incurred, was to the company substantially less than the amount of the debt (including any premium on the debt); or
- any redeemable loan capital issued by the company.

A 'normal commercial loan' is a loan:

- wholly or partly of new consideration; and
- which gives no right to conversion into, or acquisition of, additional shares or securities (except as mentioned below); and
- the interest on which is no more than a reasonable commercial return on the new consideration, and is not dependent on either the company's profitability or the value of its assets (except where the rate reduces, when the results of the debtor company's business improve or the value of its assets increase and except in respect of non-recourse

Corporation Tax

loans made on terms which restrict the security for the payment of interest or principal to non-dealing land); and

- which does not give a right to more than a reasonable commercial premium on redemption.

From 27 July 1989, subsidiary companies issuing certain types of convertible shares or securities will not be prevented from being members of groups. A share or loan may as a result be convertible into restricted preference shares or a normal commercial loan which do not themselves carry conversion or additional acquisition rights and would not be regarded as equity. They may also be convertible into shares or securities in the quoted parent company (i.e. one for which the subsidiary is a 75 per cent subsidiary, which is not itself a 75 per cent subsidiary of any company and whose shares are listed, including the USM) or into restricted preference shares or a normal commercial loan themselves convertible into such shares or securities.

From 21 March 2000, anti-avoidance provisions ensure that loans to companies where the rate of interest increases where the business results detiorate or, conversely, falls when the results improve (known as 'ratchet loans') are treated as ordinary commercial loans.

Law: CTA 2010, Pt. 5, Ch. 2 and 6; *J Sainsbury plc v O'Connor (HMIT)* [1991] BTC 181; *Imperial Chemical Industries plc v Colmer (HMIT)* [1999] BTC 440; *Imperial Chemical Industries plc (ICI) v Colmer (HM Inspector of Taxes) (Case C-264/96)* [1998] BTC 304; *Philips Electronics UK Ltd v R & C Commrs* [2009] TC 00176; *FCE Bank plc* [2010] TC 00445

See *British Tax Reporter* ¶736-650.

3815 Amounts available for group relief

The rules set out below apply from 1 April 1998.

The losses and other amounts which a company may be able to surrender as group relief are split into two categories:

(1)   trading losses, excess capital allowances, and a non-trading deficit on the company's loan relationships (see below for these); and

(2)   qualifying charitable donation – previously charges on income (see 3055), UK property business losses (see below) (but not losses carried forward from earlier periods, or a loss incurred in a Sch. A business not conducted on a commercial basis: see 3133), and management expenses (but not expenses of management or UK property business losses carried forward from earlier periods) which are available for group relief.

Subject to the detailed provisions in the rest of the group relief rules (see 3809ff.), the above amounts may be set off against the claimant company's total profits (see 3027) for its corresponding accounting period.

A deficit on a non-trading loan relationship can only be surrendered as group relief if a claim is made to treat it as eligible for group relief (see 3037).

Trading losses, excess capital allowances, non-trading deficits on loan relationships

Amounts in category (1) above (trading losses, excess capital allowances and non-trading deficits on loan relationships) may be surrendered as group relief even if the surrendering company has other profits in the same accounting period against which they could be set.

Charitable donations, UK property business losses, management expenses

Amounts in category (2) above (charitable donation, property losses and management expenses) may only be surrendered as group relief to the extent that in aggregate they exceed the surrendering company's 'gross profits' (see below) for the surrender period. Any excess surrendered is taken to consist first of charitable donations, then property losses, and finally management expenses.

The surrendering company's 'gross profits' comprise its profits for the period without deduction either for:

(1)   the losses, allowances or other amounts of the accounting period which are potentially available for surrender as group relief (see above); or

(2)   any other losses or allowances, etc. of any other accounting period, whether or not within that description.

Dual resident investing companies

The amounts which may be surrendered are subject to the restriction on group relief which can be surrendered by dual resident investing companies (see 3829).

Trading losses

The amount of the trading loss which a company can surrender as group relief is the amount of the loss which, if it had any, it could set off against its other profits under the current year set off rules (see 3106).

Exclusion of foreign and hobby trades

A company cannot surrender a trading loss as group relief if it would be unable to set it off against its own profits because it was incurred either:

(1)   in a trade carried on wholly outside the UK, or a trade which was not carried on for the purpose of making a commercial profit; or

(2)   in a farming or market gardening trade in which losses have been made in each of the chargeable periods comprised in the previous five years.

Corporation Tax

Companies owned by consortia

The amount of group relief which can be surrendered by a company owned by a consortium is restricted. Such a company is deemed to use up as much as possible of its trading losses by setting them off against its other profits of the same accounting period (see 3106) before it is allowed to surrender any of them as group relief. The restriction applies whether or not the company in fact makes a current period set-off claim. The restriction also applies before any reduction of the amount which can be claimed or surrendered by a company which is both a member of a group and of a consortium (see 3809).

Excess capital allowances

The excess capital allowances which can be surrendered as group relief are defined as the excess in an accounting period of a company's capital allowances which are to be given by discharge or repayment of tax over the income against which they are primarily available. Allowances carried forward from an earlier period do not affect this calculation. Allowances or losses of any other period cannot be deducted from the income against which the allowances above are primarily available.

Differing accounting periods

If the accounting periods of the claimant and the surrendering company do not coincide, apportionment of their respective profits and loss must be made.

Law: CTA 2010, Pt. 5, Ch. 2

See *British Tax Reporter* ¶736-850.

3821 Set-off of group relief

Group relief can be set off against the total profits of the claimant before they are reduced by any relief derived from a subsequent accounting period, but after all other reliefs are deducted. The claimant is assumed to set off all trading losses and capital allowances against total profits of the same accounting period, in so far as they exceed income from the same source.

Relief derived from a subsequent accounting period includes relief on trading losses given against profits of a preceding accounting period (see 3109) and relief on capital allowances given against profits of a preceding accounting period (see 3027). This also applied to 'terminal loss relief' (see 3125) on a loss incurred in an accounting period after the end of the accounting period in which the profits were being calculated.

Where the claimant is a member of a consortium, it can only set off a fraction of the surrendering company's loss equal to the percentage of the ordinary share capital of the surrendering company or its holding company held by it. Where the surrendering company is a member of a consortium, the loss cannot be set off against more than a fraction of the total profits of the claimant.

Differing accounting periods

If the accounting periods of the claimant and the surrendering company do not coincide, apportionment of their respective profits and loss must be made.

Example

Blue Ltd, Green Ltd and Red Ltd are trading companies in the same group for group relief purposes. Blue Ltd and Green Ltd make their accounts up to 31 December each year. For the accounting period ending 31 December 2010 their tax adjusted results are profits of £2,000,000 for Blue Ltd and £600,000 for Green Ltd. Red Ltd makes its annual accounts up to 30 September each year. Its tax adjusted result for the accounting period ending 30 September 2010 is a loss of £2,080,000. Blue Ltd claims the maximum possible group relief for Red Ltd's loss of the overlapping period. Subsequently Green Ltd also makes a maximum claim for group relief from Red Ltd. All necessary consents to surrender are given. All apportionments are on a time basis.

The overlapping period in this case is 9 months (from 1 January 2010 to 30 September 2010).

Blue Ltd's claim will be £1,500,000 since this is the lesser of:

- Blue Ltd's otherwise unrelieved profits for the overlapping period, £1,500,000 (£2,000,000 × $^9/_{12}$); and
- Red Ltd's otherwise unutilised loss for the overlapping period, £1,560,000 (£2,080,000 × $^9/_{12}$).

Blue Ltd's chargeable profit for the accounting period ending 31 December 2010 after group relief will be £500,000 (profit £2,000,000 less group relief £1,500,000). Blue Ltd will be unable to make any further group relief claims in respect of this overlap period since all of its apportioned profit has been relieved.

Green Ltd's later claim will be £60,000, since this is the lesser of:

- Green Ltd's otherwise unrelieved profits for the overlapping period, £450,000 (£600,000 × $^9/_{12}$); and
- Red Ltd's otherwise unutilised loss for the overlapping period, £60,000 (£2,080,000 × $^9/_{12}$ = £1,560,000 less £1,500,000) (being the relief already given).

Green Ltd could claim further losses (from other group companies) for this overlap period of £390,000 (£450,000 less £60,000 (losses already claimed)).

Red Ltd has obtained full relief for its group relievable losses, £1,560,00, of the period from 1 January 2010 to 30 September 2010 (£1,500,000 to Blue Ltd and £60,000 to Green Ltd). No further surrender of relief can be made in respect of this period. The loss for the period 1 October 2009 to 31 December 2009 cannot be used for any overlapping period beginning after 31 December 2009.

Law: CTA 2010, s. 138–142

See *British Tax Reporter* ¶736-650.

Corporation Tax

3825   Group relief claims under CTSA

Under corporation tax self-assessment (CTSA), a claim to group relief for any accounting period must be included in the claimant company's return (either as originally delivered, or via an amendment to the return submitted within the normal time-limit). The claim must specify the amount of relief and the surrendering company (or companies), which must provide a notice of consent to the surrender. However, the Treasury has the power to make regulations dispensing with the requirement for a company to file a copy of the notice of consent from the surrendering company with any group relief claim. The Treasury may also regulate that the dispensation is dependent on the agreement of the group company authorised to amend the returns for group purposes.

It is not necessary to claim all of the relief(s) available for surrender; a lesser amount of relief may be requested. However, if a claim exceeds the 'amount available for surrender', it will be ineffective. It seems that this may mean that the whole claim will be disregarded, not just the excess amount. Claims to group relief, once made, cannot be amended but may be withdrawn (by amendment to the relevant company tax return) and if necessary replaced by another claim.

All claims, surrenders of losses, etc. by companies in a group can be administered by one group company on behalf of all group members.

Amounts available for surrender

To determine the 'amount available for surrender':

(1)   on the basis of the company's tax return (see 4952), determine the total amount available for surrender according to 3815; then

(2)   deduct all amounts included in extant notices of consent.

In (1) above, any company's amendments to its return which are made during an enquiry into the return are disregarded.

Multiple claims

Where, in the case of multiple claims, some are withdrawn and some are made on the same day, the withdrawals are given effect to first. However, where multiple claims exceed the amount available for surrender, HMRC have the power to determine which claims will be ineffective, so as to bring the total claimed within the limit available.

Reduction in amount available for surrender

Where, after notice(s) of consent have been given, the amount available for surrender is reduced below the amount of relief consented to, the company must withdraw the notice(s) of consent to bring the amount surrendered to an acceptable level. If necessary, new notices can be issued, to ensure the surrender limit is not exceeded. All affected claimant companies, and HMRC, must be notified in writing of any consent withdrawals and reissues in different amounts. Where a surrendering company fails to withdraw consent, HMRC may by notice issue such directions as are necessary to prevent any over-surrender of reliefs. All parties affected by such a direction must receive notification in writing. Claimant companies must amend their self-assessments upon receiving details of any alterations to the amount(s) surrendered. Surrendering companies may appeal against any directions issued by HMRC regarding these matters.

Assessment to recover excessive group relief

If HMRC discover that excessive group relief has been given, they may recover the amount that they consider excessive by assessment, without prejudice to the general power to make discovery assessments (see 4990).

Legislation enables recovery from other specified beneficiaries of tax arising from an excessive claim to group relief. Where tax relating to the excessive claim remains unpaid six months after the expiry of the final time-limit for a claim for the period, HMRC can have recourse to other claimant companies which have benefited from the same surrender, subject to a maximum of the tax which those other companies have saved.

For accounting periods ending after 1 April 2000, in consequence of the extension of the group relief rules to encompass groups with non-resident members, the tax payable by the non-resident can be recovered from other members of the group in the event of default.

Joint amended returns

The Treasury may make regulations modifying, as they see fit, any of the provisions relating to making and withdrawing claims in order to facilitate arrangements whereby one person may be authorised to act on behalf of two or more companies (in the same group) as far as the amendment of returns to revise group relief claims is concerned.

Consent to surrender

All claims to group relief require the consent of the company surrendering relief. Where there is a consortium claim, each member of the consortium must also consent.

Any such consent(s) must be given in writing at or prior to the time that the corresponding claim is made, to the officer of the Board to whom the surrendering company renders returns. Failure to provide such a consent renders the claim ineffective, because all claims to group relief (and consortium relief) must be accompanied by a copy of the relevant consent(s) to be valid.

However, the Treasury has the power to make regulations dispensing with the requirement for a company to file a copy of the notice of consent from the surrendering company with any group relief claim. The Treasury may also regulate that the dispensation is dependent on the agreement of the group company authorised to amend the returns for group purposes.

Corporation Tax

Notice of consent by surrendering company

To be effective, a consent notice must include all of the following details:

- the name of the surrendering company and its tax district reference;
- the name of the claimant company and its tax district reference;
- the amount of relief being surrendered; and
- the accounting period of the surrendering company to which the surrender relates.

Once given, a notice of consent may not be amended but it may be withdrawn (by notice to HMRC) and a new notice issued. However, the withdrawal of a consent notice is not permitted without the permission of the claimant company, which must amend its return if such permission is given. An exception to the requirement of obtaining the claimant company's permission is when withdrawal of consent is required because the amount available for surrender is reduced.

Notice of consent requiring amendment of return

Where a notice of consent is given after the delivery of a surrendering company's tax return (see 4952), an amendment to that return must be made, fully reflecting the effect(s) of the surrender of relief(s). Failure to make such an amendment renders the notice of consent ineffective.

Time-limits for group relief claims

Subject to HMRC permitting an extension to the time-limit, claims to group relief must be made (or withdrawn) by the *latest* of:

(1)   12 months after the filing date for the claimant company's tax return for the accounting period covered by the claim;

(2)   30 days after the issue of a closure notice is issued on the completion of an enquiry;

(3)   30 days after HMRC issue a notice of amendment to a return following the completion of an enquiry (issued where the company fails to amend the return itself); or

(4)   30 days after the determination of any appeal against a HMRC amendment (as in (3) above).

'Enquiry' in the above does not include a restricted enquiry into an amendment to a return (restricted because the time-limit for making an enquiry into the return itself has expired), where the amendment consists of a group relief claim or withdrawal of claim.

The above time-limits have priority over any other general time-limits for amending returns.

Law: FA 1998, Sch. 18, para. 63–65 and Sch. 18, Pt. VIII; *Corporation Tax (Simplified Arrangements for Group Relief) Regulations* 1999 (SI 1999/2975)

See *British Tax Reporter* ¶738-350.

3826 Loss of group relief where arrangements are in existence

A group of companies may make relevant 'arrangements' to transfer available relief outside a group. Relevant arrangements include all kinds of arrangements whether oral or in writing.

If two companies (A and B) satisfy the criteria for being members of the same group in a particular accounting period but, during that period:

(1) A could cease to be a member of the same group as B and become a member of the same group as C; or

(2) any person or persons could obtain control of A but not of B; or

(3) C could begin to carry on a trade which is carried on by A, as A's successor or as the successor of another company which began to carry on the same trade during or after the accounting period,

then, for group relief purposes, A is not treated as a member of the same group as B. Group relief is not denied for the whole of the accounting period; the group relationship is only broken for the period from the beginning of the arrangements until their termination, apportionments of results being made as necessary.

Example

Company A is a parent company. Company S is its subsidiary. S purchases capital assets and is entitled to capital allowances which it cannot use. A is not in a position to use them if S surrenders the allowances to it (see 3815).

Therefore, A sells its equity in S to B. Subject to possible limitation (see 3830), B is then entitled to S's allowances which are surrendered as group relief.

However, if A had retained an option to buy back its equity (at a price taking into account the reliefs which B was given), B and S would not be treated as members of the same group, and the reliefs granted above would not apply.

If a company makes relevant arrangements in an accounting period, and it is a trading company, it loses any right to surrender available reliefs to a member of a consortium if any of the following circumstances exist:

(1) the trading company could become a '75 per cent subsidiary' (see 3653) of a third company; or

(2) the owner(s) of less than 50 per cent of the ordinary share capital of the trading company has or could obtain control of that company; or

(3) a person, other than a holding company of which the trading company is a '90 per cent subsidiary' (see 3653), holds or could hold or control alone or with 'connected persons' the exercise of at least 75 per cent of the casting votes on a poll taken at a general meeting of the trading company, in that or a later accounting period; or

(4)   a third company could begin to carry on the trade which, at any time in that accounting period, is carried on by the trading company, either as that company's successor or that of another company which has begun to carry on that trade during the same accounting period.

Definition of 'connected persons'

A 'person' is connected with his/her spouse, any of his/her relatives, i.e. brother, sister, ancestor or lineal descendant, and any such relative of his/her spouse.

A trustee of a 'settlement' is connected with the 'settlor' (see 1071), any person connected with the settlor and any company connected with the settlement. A company is connected with a settlement if:

(1)   it is a close company (see 4253) (or only not a close company because it is not resident in the UK) and the participators (see 4256) include the trustees of the settlement; or

(2)   it is under the control of a company within (1) above.

A company has control of another company if it can secure, by means of shares or voting power, or by virtue of articles of association or other document, that the company's affairs are conducted in accordance with its wishes.

A 'partner' is connected with any person with whom he is in partnership, his/her relatives and the relative of any partner.

A 'company' is connected with another company if they are both controlled (see above) by the same person, or one person controls it who also controls the other together with connected persons or where the other company is controlled by connected persons alone. Companies are also connected where they are both controlled by the same group of persons or are under the control of different groups but members of one group are connected with members of the other group.

Arrangements

HMRC have published a statement of practice concerning the terms 'arrangements' and 'option arrangements'; it includes the following views:

*   if an agreement provides for the creation of specified option rights exercisable at some future time, option arrangements come into existence when the agreement was entered into;
*   neither a public offer nor private negotiations for the disposal of shares, etc. will generally give rise to arrangements until an offer is accepted (usually subject to contract or some similar conditional basis) or, where required, shareholder approval is given (or effectively definite) or the parties come to an understanding in the nature of an option (e.g. an offer allowing the purchaser to choose the moment to create a bargain) – arrangements may exist between parties even though they are not enforceable.

Power of HMRC to request information

If HMRC have reason to believe that any 'relevant arrangements' may exist, they may serve notice in writing on the company requiring it to make a written declaration that those arrangements do or do not exist and/or any other information he may require. The company is given 30 days to supply that information.

Law: CTA 2010, s. 154–156; *Boake Allen Ltd & Ors (including NEC Semi-conductors Ltd) v R & C Commrs* [2007] BTC 414; *Marks & Spencer plc v Halsey (HMIT)* (Case C-446/03) [2006] BTC 318; *Pilkington Bros Ltd v IR Commrs* [1982] BTC 79; *Shepherd (HMIT) v Law Land plc* [1990] BTC 561; *Steele (HMIT) v EVC International NV* [1996] BTC 425; *Scottish and Universal Newspapers Ltd v Fisher (HMIT)* (1996) Sp C 87

Source: SP 3/93; ESC C10

See *British Tax Reporter* ¶736-000.

3827 Group relief: foreign and non-commercial trades

There are certain trading losses to which group relief does not apply. These are losses from foreign trading and from trades carried on on a non-commercial basis, without a view to realising a gain (see 3815).

Law: CTA 2010, s. 100(2)

3829 Group relief: dual resident companies

Losses made by dual resident companies are frequently available for worldwide tax relief twice. Many countries have provisions permitting the aggregation or consolidation of profits and losses within a group of resident companies. Some countries determine residence by reference to incorporation and some by other means, e.g. place of management, hence the concept of dual resident companies.

Provisions were enacted in 1987 to remove the tax advantage in the UK from the deliberate setting up of dual resident companies financed by borrowing, but not adversely to affect genuine trading companies.

Any loss or other amount is unavailable for set-off by way of group relief if the surrendering company is a dual resident investing company. A dual resident company is an investing company in any accounting period throughout which it is not a trading company or one of its main functions is to borrow money, pay interest or charges or to acquire shares.

Law: CTA 2010, s. 109

See *British Tax Reporter* ¶737-950.

Corporation Tax

3830 Group relief where a member joins or leaves a group

If a new company joins or an existing member leaves a group before the end of its accounting period that period comes to an end and another begins for purposes of group relief. The claimant and surrendering companies must be members of the same group in the surrendering company's accounting period and the corresponding period of the claimant.

> ### Example
>
> C owns 83 per cent of the ordinary share capital of S when S joins the group on 1 August 2009. S incurs losses of £20,000 for period 1 November 2008 to 31 October 2009. C makes a profit of £60,000 for period 1 May 2009 to 30 April 2010.
>
> S's accounting period for group relief: 1 August–31 October.
>
> C's accounting period for group relief: 1 August–30 April.
>
> S's loss apportioned: $^3/_{12} \times £20,000 = £5,000$.
>
> Profits of C available: $^9/_{12} \times £60,000 = £45,000$.
>
> C's profits must then be further adjusted to determine the profits of the period common to both companies ('corresponding accounting period', see 3815 and the example at 3821): $^3/_9 \times £45,000 = £15,000$.
>
> Therefore profits are still available to absorb the loss.

It has been held that if the surrendering company leaves the group after the end of the accounting period to which the claim relates, relief will still be available to the claimant company and may be claimed (within the appropriate time-limits) even though the surrendering company is not a member of the group at the time the claim is made.

Only one claim allowed

A group of companies may claim relief only once for the same loss. Where more than one company claims relief for one loss, they may obtain in total only the same relief which would be available to a single company whose corresponding period coincides with that of the surrendering company.

Law: CTA 2010, s. 137(7)

Source: *AW Chapman Ltd v Hennessey (HMIT)* [1982] BTC 44

See *British Tax Reporter* 735-737.

CHARGEABLE GAINS – SPECIAL SITUATIONS

RECONSTRUCTIONS AND REORGANISATIONS

4012   Shareholders liable to pay company's tax on capital gains

Shareholders connected with a UK-resident company may be liable to pay the tax on the capital gains made by that company where they receive a capital distribution; this does not apply where the distribution represents a reduction of capital.

A shareholder is connected with a company if he has control of it alone or together with other persons connected with him.

A person is connected with their spouse and other 'relatives' (or spouses thereof); that person is also connected with relatives of their spouse (or spouses of those relatives). 'Relative' includes brother, sister, ancestor and lineal descendant.

'Control' has the same meaning as applies to close companies (see 4250).

Circumstances in which shareholder liable

A shareholder who qualifies for liability to the tax will be held liable where the distribution is made after a disposal of assets which results in a capital gain by the company or where the distribution amounts to a disposal of assets.

When a shareholder becomes liable

If the corporation tax for the accounting period in which the capital gain is made is not paid by the company within six months from the date it became payable, a shareholder who has received a distribution may be assessed and charged to corporation tax; the assessment must be made within two years of the date when the tax became payable.

Limit on the amount of the liability

The amount of corporation tax charged on a shareholder must not exceed the amount of the capital distribution and a portion of the tax charged on the gain in proportion to the recipient's share of the distribution.

The shareholder so charged is entitled to reclaim the corporation tax paid and any interest on overdue tax from the company.

Capital distributions

Capital distributions are distributions which are not income in the hands of the recipient for income tax purposes (see 5890).

Corporation Tax

781

All distributions in a winding-up are capital distributions.

Most capital distributions to shareholders and debenture holders are treated as resulting from disposal of an interest in those shares and debentures, and the gains over the cost of acquisition are taxable.

This rule does not apply to the issue of shares and debentures. The shares resulting from a capital distribution are identified with the original holding and no acquisition or disposal is deemed to occur, e.g. when a company makes a bonus issue of shares or debentures to its shareholders or a rights issue in proportion to each holding, or alters rights attached to issued shares or reduces capital.

Law: TCGA 1992, s. 189 and 286; CTA 2010, s. 450

See *British Tax Reporter* ¶756-900.

4015 Company reconstruction or amalgamation

Where, under a scheme of reconstruction or amalgamation, one company transfers the whole or part of its business to another company it is treated as a transfer resulting in neither a gain nor a loss to the company making the transfer and the transferee will take over the assets as if it had acquired them on the same date as the person making the transfer.

Both companies must be resident in the UK at the time of the transfer and, from 19 March 1990, the transferee must not be exempt from tax under a double tax treaty on a notional gain in respect of the disposal of the assets in point. From 30 November 1993, any such company would, in any case, be regarded as resident outside the UK, and therefore outside the scope of these provisions (see 3014).

The transferor must receive no consideration for the company's business.

To be treated as a reconstruction, the transaction must be for bona fide commercial purposes so that there is no reconstruction where an arrangement is effected to avoid liability to corporation tax.

Once HMRC decides that the transaction is not bona fide and that the company would be assessed to tax if it were not in liquidation, it may charge tax on the company which receives the assets or its shareholders.

There is machinery for a prospective transferee to apply in writing to the Board for a ruling that HMRC is satisfied with the scheme before the transfer takes place. It must supply all material facts and details to the Board after which the Board has 30 days in which to ask for further information. It then has a further 30 days to give its decision. If the applicant wishes to challenge the finding, it may refer to the special commissioners. In cases of genuine urgency, a faxed copy of HMRC's response by the office in Solihull may be made available at Somerset House for collection; HMRC will also try to offer assistance in the case of applications from outside London including in some cases a fax direct to the applicant.

Reconstruction involving an issue of shares or securities

Where in a scheme of reconstruction or amalgamation, shareholders of a company receive shares in another company and the old shares are either retained or cancelled, they may in certain circumstances be treated as having exchanged their original holdings for the new holdings so as to obtain a tax deferral: provided the tax avoidance motive test is passed (or advance clearance obtained) as in relation to the relief for certain actual exchanges, that relief applies notwithstanding that there is no general offer or resultant substantial holding (for discussion of the exchange relief, see 4024). Where the new holding comprises debentures or gives right to the issue of debentures which, rarely, would not constitute a debt on a security they are treated as such; hence, unless they are qualifying corporate bonds they do not fall outside the chargeable gains net (see 6183). By virtue of an extra-statutory concession, published on 12 May 1995, costs incurred as part of a share exchange, company reconstruction or amalgamation treated as a share reorganisation under these provisions may be treated as an additional payment for the new shares or debentures and consequently treated as allowable expenditure when the shares are disposed of.

What is a reconstruction?

In the *South African Supply and Cold Storage* case Buckley J said at p. 286:

> 'What does "reconstruction" mean? ... It involves, I think, that substantially the same business shall be carried on and substantially the same persons shall carry it on. But it does not involve that all the assets shall pass to the new company or resuscitated company, or that all the shareholders of the old company shall be shareholders in the new company or resuscitated company. Substantially the business and the persons interested must be the same.'

As a general rule, therefore, a scheme of reconstruction is considered to entail the second company carrying on substantially the same business with the same members as the first. Therefore, the division of a company's undertaking into two or more companies owned by different sets of shareholders would not be a reconstruction. In practice, however, for capital gains purposes, HMRC do not insist upon identity of shareholdings in the old and new companies where a division of companies is carried out for bona fide commercial reasons.

A scheme whereby the shares are reorganised into separate classes under which new companies are formed to take over separate parts of the undertaking allocated to the different classes and each group of shareholders receives shares in a separate company, is treated as a scheme of reconstruction. This is so even though the new companies have no common shareholder provided that there is a segregation of businesses and not just assets. For this purpose it is enough that there are identifiable parts of a trade or business which can be carried on in their own right. A later chargeable disposal of shares in one or more of the newly created companies does not on its own prevent the division of the original company being recognised as a reconstruction. In the context of demergers, a shareholding in a company which is a 75 per cent subsidiary of the distributing company is treated as constituting an identifiable part of the trade or business of the distributing company.

Corporation Tax

Therefore, the division of a company involving the transfer of shares in a subsidiary to a newly formed company by way of a demerger is also regarded as a scheme of reconstruction.

HMRC have confirmed that, in their view, relief is available for a scheme of reconstruction which involves an arrangement under CA 2006, s. 899 where shares in a company (company A) are cancelled, new shares in company A are issued to a new company (company B) and company B issues its own shares to the former members of company A pro rata to their holdings in company A.

What is an amalgamation?

An amalgamation occurs when two or more businesses merge within one company. The resulting company must be one of the participating companies to which the business of another company is transferred. Alternatively, the company must have been formed specially to accommodate the enterprises.

The shareholders in the new company must be all the shareholders in the participating companies.

Again in the *South African Supply and Cold Storage* case Buckley J said at p. 287:

'The difference between reconstruction and amalgamation is that in the latter is involved the blending of two concerns one with the other, but not merely the continuance of one concern ... It is not necessary that you should have a new company. You may have a continuance of one of the two companies upon the terms that the undertakings of both corporations shall substantially be merged in one corporation only.'

It is possible for an amalgamation to take place within a series of arrangements which are not made primarily for purposes of amalgamation.

The position post-16 April 2002

The statute governing schemes of reconstruction and amalgamation was replaced by FA 2002 with effect from 17 April 2002. However, the effect of the legislation remains largely unchanged, except that it now contains practice previously outlined in Statement of Practice SP 5/85.

Law: TCGA 1992, s. 136–139 and Sch. 5AA; *Re South African Supply and Cold Storage Co* [1904] 2 Ch 268; *Crane Fruehauf Ltd v IR Commrs* [1975] 1 All ER 429

Source: ESC D52

See *British Tax Reporter* ¶756-900.

4024   Exchange of shares or securities

The provisions relating to the reorganisation of share capital which broadly defer chargeable gains by disregarding the disposal and treating the replacement securities as if they were the original shares (see 5900 to 5910) apply where:

(1)   company A issues shares or debentures to a person in exchange for shares or debentures of company B if:

    (a)   company A holds (or, because of the exchange, will hold) more than 25 per cent of company B's ordinary share capital; or

    (b)   company A issues the shares, etc. in exchange for shares as a result of a general offer which is made to shareholders of company B, and is made initially on a condition that, if satisfied, company A would have control of company B; and

(2)   the exchange is for bona fide commercial reasons and is not a tax avoidance manoeuvre). This condition is satisfied if advance clearance for the exchange of shares is obtained from HMRC (see below).

The ICAEW have published a guidance note containing the text of an exchange of letters between themselves and HMRC concerning the above clearance procedure – it sets out certain matters concerning the way in which a request should be drafted.

In cases of genuine urgency, a faxed copy of HMRC's response by the office in Solihull may be made available at Somerset House for collection; HMRC will also try to offer assistance in the case of applications from outside London including in some cases a fax direct to the applicant.

By virtue of an extra-statutory concession, published on 12 May 1995, costs incurred as part of a share exchange, company reconstruction or amalgamation treated as a share reorganisation under these provisions may be treated as an additional payment for the new shares or debentures and consequently treated as allowable expenditure when the shares are disposed of.

Where the new holding comprises debentures or gives right to the issue of debentures which, rarely, would not constitute a debt on a security they are treated as such; hence, unless they are qualifying corporate bonds they do not fall outside the chargeable gains net (see 6183).

The position post-16 April 2002

The statute governing exchanges of shares or securities was replaced by FA 2002 with effect from 17 April 2002. However, the effect of the legislation remains largely unchanged, except that it now applies in relation to companies without share capital.

Law: TCGA 1992, s. 135 and 137–139

Source: ICAEW Guidance Note, TR 657, ESC D52

See *British Tax Reporter* ¶757-400.

4027 Interest on capital not deductible for chargeable gains of companies

For accounting periods ending after 31 March 1996 the rules applicable to the taxation of loan relationships in the hands of companies apply (see 3036ff.). The assumption is that relief will be afforded for such interest under those rules and therefore relief against capital gains will be prevented from applying by the general prohibition against deductions in calculating chargeable gains for expenditure which is allowable in arriving at income. However, it is possible for a company to own a capital asset now in respect of which interest was incurred in accounting periods ended before 31 March 1996 which was capitalised (so as not to have been an allowable deduction against income for corporation tax purposes). In these circumstances, the capitalised interest will be an allowable deduction in calculating the chargeable gain on a disposal of the asset.

Law: TCGA 1992, s. 39 and 40

See *British Tax Reporter* ¶760-500.

Disposal of substantial shareholding

4035 Introduction

The *Finance Act* 2002 introduced an exemption for capital gains and losses on disposals by companies with substantial shareholdings in other companies. The exemption, which is effective from 1 April 2002, essentially applies where:

- an independent trading company or a company which is a member of a trading group disposes of a substantial shareholding in another company which is itself a trading company or the holding company of a trading group; and
- the investing company has held ten per cent or more of the ordinary shares of the company invested in for a period of at least 12 months in the two years before the share sale.

The rules apply equally whether the shares being disposed of are in a UK or overseas company. Where the exemption applies no claim is necessary. Any gain on the disposal of the shares is not chargeable to tax and any loss is not available to set against other gains.

The exemption will not apply where there is a major change in the trade of the company in between the acquisition and disposal of its shares.

In addition to the main exemption, other subsidiary exemptions apply (see 4039 below), being:

- the disposal of assets relating to shares; and
- disposals where the main exemption was previously met.

The rules regarding negligible value claims (see 5090) and degrouping charges (see 3687) are modified slightly in relation to disposals of substantial shareholdings (see below).

Law: TCGA 1992, s. 192A and Sch. 7AC

See *British Tax Reporter* ¶759-800.

4037   Conditions for exemption

In order to qualify for the main or subsidiary exemptions detailed conditions must be complied with. Care needs to be exercised to ensure that the favourable treatment will apply.

Substantial shareholding requirement

The investing company must have held a substantial shareholding in the company invested in throughout a 12-month period beginning not more than two years before the date on which the disposal took place. More complex rules cover situations involving reconstructions or reorganisations.

For the purposes of this legislation, a company has a substantial shareholding in another company if:

- it holds not less than ten per cent of the company's ordinary share capital, and
- it is beneficially entitled to not less than ten per cent of the profits available for distribution to equity holders of the company, and
- it would be beneficially entitled on a winding up to not less than ten per cent of the company available for distribution to shareholders.

It is possible therefore to hold ten per cent of the shares of a company but for the shareholding not to be a substantial shareholding. This may be the case if there are different classes of share, low profits available for distribution or a low asset value.

A company that is a member of a group is able to include shares (and interests in shares) held by any other member of the group in determining whether a substantial shareholding exists.

The investing company

The investing company must be:

- either a sole trading company or a member of a qualifying group throughout the qualifying period; and

- either a sole trading company or a member of a qualifying group immediately after the time of the disposal.

Broadly, a qualifying group is a trading group. There are careful definitions of what is meant by 'trading'.

The qualifying period begins with the start of the latest 12-month period by which the substantial shareholding requirement is met and ends at the time of disposal.

The company invested in

The company invested in must be both a qualifying company throughout the qualifying period and a qualifying company immediately after the time of the disposal.

A qualifying company is a:

- trading company; or
- the holding company of a trading group; or
- the holding company of a trading sub-group.

See *British Tax Reporter* ¶759-800.

4039 Subsidiary exemptions

There are two subsidiary exemptions available.

Assets related to shares

Where a company meets the conditions for the main exemption and it also owns 'assets related to shares' of the company invested in, it may also be possible to dispose of these assets without chargeable gain. Assets related to shares include for example, an option to acquire or dispose of shares or an interest in shares in that company.

Disposals where main exemption previously met

Special rules apply where a disposal of shares or assets related to shares is made at a time when the substantial shareholding requirement is met, but the other requirements are not. If it can be determined that a disposal at any time in the previous two years would have qualified for the exemptions, then generally the disposal can occur without any gain being chargeable to tax or any loss being available to set against other gains. The rules are complex and require careful consideration, but the intention is to bring within the exemption gains which would not otherwise qualify – e.g. gains made while the company invested in is in liquidation. It is also intended to preclude losses being made allowable that would previously have been within the exemption.

See *British Tax Reporter* ¶759-800.

4041 Modification of negligible value and degrouping rules

It is possible to backdate negligible value claims (see 5090). The operation of this rule is modified in relation to substantial shareholdings so that a loss which would otherwise fall within the exemption cannot be backdated to before the exemption was introduced.

If a company leaves a group ('degroups') within six years of acquiring an asset from another group company then it shall be treated as if it sold and immediately reacquired the asset at market value at the date of the initial transfer (see 3687). If the asset in question is a holding of ten per cent or more in a trading company or a holding company of a trading group then new rules could apply.

It is necessary to determine whether, at the time of the degrouping a disposal of the shares in question would give rise to a chargeable gain under the substantial shareholding rules. If a gain would not be chargeable at this time, then the degrouping charge is calculated by reference to the date of the degrouping.

See *British Tax Reporter* ¶759-800.

TRANSACTIONS INVOLVING A NON-RESIDENT COMPANY

4060 Transfer of assets to a non-resident company

If a company decides to transfer the business of a foreign branch to a company not 'resident in the UK' (see 214) any net chargeable gain made on the transfer can be rolled over for a potentially indefinite period to the extent that shares are received in return. The net chargeable gain is the aggregate of chargeable gains arising from the transfer after the deduction of allowable losses so arising.

This rule only applies if the transferor is a UK-resident company which carries on a trade through a foreign permanent establishment. The transferor must transfer the business and all its assets in the branch to a non-resident company and must hold not less than 25 per cent of the ordinary share capital of the transferee company after the transfer.

Where applicable the transferor can choose between this deferral and the relief by reference to notional tax in the home territory, if it is within the EU (see 4088).

Time when deferment ends

The deferment of tax will come to an end when the shares are disposed of or the assets transferred are disposed of (see 4063, 4066, 4069).

When there is a disposal of this kind, the deferred gain is chargeable to corporation tax along with the consideration for the disposal.

Portion of gain chargeable

If shares are received by the transferor as part consideration for the transfer, only a fraction of the gain is taken into account when the deferment comes to an end. The fraction is the proportion which the market value of the shares bears to the total consideration.

If the shares received by the transferor company represent the whole of the consideration for the transfer, the whole of the gain can be deferred.

Example

Company A merges its US branch with S Inc (incorporated in US) in 2007. Total consideration for transfer of assets in US branch (market value):

	£
£1 shares in the merged US company issued to A to value of	40,000
Cash payment	60,000
	100,000

Assume the net gain to A on transfer (ignore indexation) is £30,000. Shares form only part of the consideration.

Therefore, fraction of gain deferrable is

$$\frac{\text{market value of shares}}{\text{market value of total consideration}} = \frac{£40,000}{£100,000} = \frac{4}{10}$$

The gain deferred is £30,000 $\times$ $^4/_{10}$ = £12,000.

Law: TCGA 1992, s. 140(1)–(3)

See *British Tax Reporter* ¶758-850.

4063 Part disposal of foreign transferee's shares by transferor

If, following relief on the transfer of assets to a non-resident (see 4060), the transferor disposes of all or a part of the shares issued to him, the consideration he receives is increased by the whole or part of the deferred gain. The fraction of the gain brought into account on the part disposal is the proportion of the market value of the shares disposed of to the market value of the shares held immediately before the disposal.

Example

Assume the same facts as contained in the example in 4060.

In 2008 shares issued to A rose in value to £60,000. A decided to sell 15,000 at market value which is £22,500.

Fraction of capital gain brought into account:

$$\frac{\text{market value of shares disposed of}}{\text{market value of total shares prior to disposal}} = \frac{£22,500}{£60,000} = \frac{3}{8}$$

The gain crystallising is $^3/_8 \times £12,000 = £4,500$

	£
Total consideration on sale of 15,000 shares	22,500
Gain no longer deferred	4,500
	27,000
Base cost	(15,000)
Total gain on disposal (ignoring indexation)	12,000

Law: TCGA 1992, s. 140(4)–(8)

See *British Tax Reporter* ¶759-100.

4066 Disposal by foreign transferee of assets within six years of transfer

If, following relief on the transfer of assets to a non-resident (see 4060), the transferee disposes of the whole or part of the assets received within six years of the transfer the transferor is assumed to make a chargeable gain. The fraction of the deferred gain brought into account on a part disposal is the proportion of the capital gain deferred on the part disposed of to the total chargeable gain on the whole of the assets held immediately before the disposal (but see also 4069).

Example

Assume the same facts as contained in the example in 4060.

In 2008 S Inc disposes of the buildings, which it received on the merger, for £60,000.

Market value	2007	Gain on deferral	2008
	£	£	£
Building	40,000	15,000	60,000
Plant and machinery	25,000	4,000	30,000
Goodwill	35,000	11,000	50,000
Total market value	100,000	30,000	140,000

Fraction of deferred gain attributable to company A:

$$\frac{\text{capital gain deferred on building}}{\text{capital gain deferred on whole}} = \frac{£6,000}{£12,000} = \frac{1}{2}$$

Corporation Tax

> The gain crystallising is $^1/_2 \times £12,000 = £6,000$

See *British Tax Reporter* ¶764-750.

4069 Assets disposed of by foreign transferee after sale of shares by transferor

If, following relief on the transfer of assets to a non-resident (see 4060), a transferee disposes of the assets acquired after the shares held by the transferor have been sold, only the part of the deferred chargeable gain not dealt with in the earlier transaction is brought into account (see also 4063, 4066).

> ### Example
>
> (Applying the rule to the facts in the example in 4063 followed by that in 4066.) Fraction of chargeable gain brought into account on disposal by S Inc:
>
> $$\frac{\text{capital gain deferred on building}}{\text{capital gain deferred on whole}} = \frac{£6,000}{£12,000} = \frac{1}{2}$$
>
> The capital gain brought into account is calculated as follows:
>
> $^1/_2 \times$ (total capital gain − fraction already accounted for)
>
> $= ^1/_2 \times (£12,000 − £4,500)$
>
> $= ^1/_2 \times £7,500 = £3,750$
>
> In the reverse situation, where the transferee makes the first disposal, the fraction is calculated:
>
> $$\frac{\text{market value of shares disposed of}}{\text{market value of total shares prior to disposal}}$$
>
> $^3/_8 \times (£12,000 − £6,000)$
>
> $^3/_8 \times £6,000 = £2,250$

See *British Tax Reporter* ¶759-150.

4072 Transfer of company residence

A company ceasing to be 'UK-resident' (see 214) or becoming dual-resident may be subject to a charge to tax on chargeable gains (an 'exit charge'). This charge can be deferred if the company has ceased to be resident in the UK as a result of the operation of the provision which deems that any company which would be regarded as dual-resident, but is treated as not resident in the UK by virtue of a double taxation agreement, ceases to be resident in the UK on 30 November 1993 (see 3014).

When a company ceases to be resident in the UK, there is a deemed disposal of all chargeable assets, except those which relate to any UK branch and which are retained in the UK, on the date the transfer of residence takes place. Replacement roll-over relief is also denied where the emigration falls between the disposal and acquisition (see 6305ff.). There are provisions to ensure that payment of the tax occurs prior to the company becoming non-resident.

Where a UK-resident company became dual resident before 30 November 1993, enabling it to benefit from exemption from tax in respect of chargeable gains on such assets (under a double tax treaty) or if a company which was dual resident became subject to new treaty arrangements which took assets outside the UK tax net, a similar deemed disposal of assets took place.

The gain (net of any losses) can be postponed if the company is a '75 per cent subsidiary' (see 3653) of a UK-resident company after migration or becoming a dual resident. The two companies must elect for postponement within two years of migration. If the company disposes of its assets within six years the UK parent is deemed to incur the relevant part of the postponed gain. Similarly the postponed gain will crystallise if the 75 per cent relationship is broken or the parent becomes non-UK resident.

Example

S Ltd is a wholly-owned subsidiary of P Ltd, which is UK-resident. When S Ltd ceased to be UK-resident on 15 October 2008, the two companies elected to postpone the gain which was deemed to arise, as shown below.

	Asset A £	Asset B £	Asset C £	Asset D £	Total £
Deemed gains	50,000	30,000	80,000		160,000
Deemed losses				(40,000)	(40,000)
Postponed net gain					120,000

Within six years of ceasing to be resident in the UK, S Ltd disposes of asset A. At that time P Ltd (not S Ltd) is deemed to realise a gain of £37,500, which is calculated as follows:

$$\frac{50,000}{160,000} \times £120,000 = £37,500$$

At a later date, but still within the six-year period, S Ltd disposes of asset B.

At that time P Ltd is deemed to realise a gain of £22,500 being:

$$\frac{30,000}{110,000} \times (£120,000 - £37,500 \text{ already assessed})$$

At a later time P sells all of its shares in S Ltd and so P Ltd is deemed to realise at that time a gain of £60,000 (being the postponed gain of £120,000 less the previously assessed gains of £37,500 and £22,500).

Corporation Tax

Losses

If at any time the company, which ceases to be UK-resident or becomes dual resident, has allowable losses which have not been deducted from chargeable gains, but the principal company is assessed in the manner explained above, then the two companies can elect to deduct the loss in whole or part from the gain; the election needs to be made in writing to the inspector within two years of the gain arising.

Law: TCGA 1992, s. 185–188

See *British Tax Reporter* ¶764-400.

4080   Transfer of UK branch trade to UK company

For disposals made prior to 1 April 2000, a specific provision provided that a company which was not 'resident in the UK' (see 214) could transfer the business of a UK permanent establishment to a UK company without an immediate capital gains charge.

To qualify for relief, the transferor had to dispose of assets (after 19 March 1990) at a time when the two companies would have been members of the same group for chargeable gains purposes (see 3682) if the transferor were UK-resident; a claim had to be made by the two companies within two years of the end of the accounting period of the transferee company during which the disposal occured.

The transfer was treated as taking place on a no gain/no loss basis.

The assets must have been within the corporation tax net as regards the transferor (see 4500).

The relief did not apply where the transferee company was a dual resident investing company or an investment trust or (prior to 30 November 1993) a company which at that time would be exempt from tax under a double tax treaty on a notional gain in respect of the disposal of the assets in point.

For disposals of assets on or after 1 April 2000 an express provision is no longer required due to the removal of the UK residence requirement in the provisions dealing with the transfer of assets between group companies (see 3984).

See *British Tax Reporter* ¶764-400.

4088   Transfer of non-UK branch trade to company in another EU member state

In consequence of the EC mergers directive, the UK has provided for relief where a UK-resident company transfers a branch or agency situated in another EU member state to a company resident outside the UK (but within the EU). Any net gains can be taxed in the UK with relief for notional tax relevant in the state in which the branch or agency is situated. The provisions for taxing the net gains are set out below; the provisions for providing for the appropriate double tax relief are discussed at 1789 and 1792.

Where it is applicable, the taxpayer can choose between this treatment and the deferral for domestication of certain foreign branches (see 4060).

Except as noted below, a claim for this treatment may be made by the transferor in respect of the transfer of the whole of the trade assets (with the possible exception of cash) at least partly for securities.

The transfer of the trade (or part) must meet a tax avoidance motive test. The relief does not apply unless the transfer is effected for bona fide commercial reasons and does not form part of a scheme or arrangements of which the main purpose or one of the main purposes is avoidance of liability to income tax, corporation tax or capital gains tax. Advance clearance can be obtained from the Board. The test and clearance procedure are largely the same as in relation to company reconstructions, etc. (see 4024) and various administrative provisions are imported therefrom.

If a valid claim is made, chargeable gains and allowable losses arising on the transfer are aggregated so as to produce a single net chargeable gain. There are special rules for certain insurance business.

Law: TCGA 1992, s. 140(6A), 140C and 140D; EC Directive 90/434

See *British Tax Reporter* ¶764-400.

4096   Transfer of UK branch trade between companies in different EU member states

In consequence of the EC mergers directive, the UK has provided for relief where a company resident in one EU member state transfers all or part of its UK trading operations to a company resident in another member state in exchange for securities issued by the transferee company.

In the case of the domestication of a UK branch (i.e. the transfer of a UK branch of a non-resident company to a UK-resident company), a similar relief otherwise exists where the two companies would be part of the same chargeable gains group if the overseas company were incorporated under the Companies Acts and UK-resident – although there is no tax avoidance motive test and the issue of securities as consideration is not a necessary condition (see 4080).

A joint claim can be made by the transferor and transferee in respect of assets 'included in' the transfer of the whole or part of the trade; there must be no other consideration for the

Corporation Tax

transfer other than the issue of securities. The transferee must be exposed to UK tax in respect of the assets.

No claim can be made if the transfer fails a tax avoidance motive test. The relief does not apply unless the transfer is effected for bona fide commercial reasons and does not form part of a scheme or arrangements of which the main purpose or one of the main purposes is avoidance of liability to income tax, corporation tax or capital gains tax. Advance clearance can be obtained from the Board. The test and clearance procedure are largely the same as in relation to company reconstructions, etc. (see 4024) and various administrative provisions are imported therefrom.

If a valid claim is made, the transfers are treated on a no gain/no loss basis; if the occasion is one on which a non-resident ceases to carry on its branch activities, the general rule providing for a deemed market value disposal and reacquisition immediately before the transfer (see 5705) does not apply.

Consequential amendments are made to deny re-basing to 31 March 1982 on the transfer (see 5302), to extend deferral in respect of the replacement of a security by a qualifying corporate bond (see 5865), to extend the restriction of allowable losses by reference to capital allowances to those given to the transferor (see 5226), to extend the dividend stripping rules to losses avoided by such a transfer before ultimate disposal (see 4176) and to deny indexation allowance in respect of linked company shares by reference to the transferor rather than the transferee (see 5280).

Law: TCGA 1992, s. 140A and 140B; EC Directive 90/434

See *British Tax Reporter* ¶764-400.

'BED AND BREAKFAST' TRANSACTIONS

4150 Company bed and breakfasting shares

A 'bed and breakfast' transaction is a term commonly used where a person has losses on shares which are realised by a sale and immediate repurchase to avoid disposing of them permanently, and to crystallise the capital gains loss.

To control these transactions by companies, there are statutory provisions which govern the order in which shares so dealt with are identified with other shares acquired just before or after the transaction (see 4153). They apply where the company disposing of the shares holds at least two per cent of the total of shares in the same class at any time within six months prior to the disposal.

See *British Tax Reporter* ¶556-700.

4153   Order of identification of shares for bed and breakfasting

Shares disposed of by a company are identified where possible with shares which it acquires within six months before or after the disposal (or one month for quoted shares) as set out below. The shares are identified with shares acquired before rather than after the disposal and nearer to rather than further from the disposal date. They are also identified with disposals by the company acquiring them rather than with another group member. A disposal of acquired shares already identified with a disposal by another group member must be identified with shares acquired by that other member.

The rules which govern the acquisition or disposal of shares on the same day (see 5826) have priority over rules of identification except where there are more shares disposed of than are acquired.

See *British Tax Reporter* ¶556-700.

VALUE SHIFTING

4161   Introduction to value shifting by companies

Any chargeable gain (or allowable loss) made by a company may be subject to adjustment if it is materially reduced (or in the case of a loss materially increased) as a result of certain schemes or arrangements designed to avoid tax ('value shifting').

Reductions in gains caused by certain distributions (see 4164) and intra-group disposals (see 4167) are also within the value shifting net from that date (increased losses were previously, and still remain, caught by separate provisions dealing with 'depreciatory transactions' (see 4173) and 'dividend stripping' (see 4176) but will also be within the revised scope of the general provisions).

Certain tax-free reorganisations (see 5900ff.) may be adjusted by way of a deemed disposal, notwithstanding that any actual disposal is disregarded.

Law: TCGA 1992, s. 30, 33(1)–(7), (9) and (10) and 34

See *British Tax Reporter* ¶760-800.

4164   Dividends from artificial profits

An adjustment may be made to a chargeable gain or allowable loss on shares if the value of the shares has been reduced by a dividend paid (principally to the chargeable company or a fellow group company) out of artificial profits.

Such profits are:

- profits on certain intra-group disposals of capital assets which are for tax purposes on a no gain/no loss basis;
- profits on an exchange of shares or debentures in any company for shares or debentures in another company in the same group which is not regarded as a disposal for tax purposes;
- revaluation reserves (not generally distributable for UK companies anyway by virtue of Companies Acts restrictions);
- distributions from other companies out of similar profits.

Example

Company X wishes to dispose of its shares in its wholly-owned subsidiary, company Y, when its value is £2,500,000 in circumstances where the substantial shareholding exemption (see 4035 above) does not apply. The base cost to company X was £100. Company Y has no distributable reserves but owns an asset worth £1,110,000 for which its base cost (and carrying value in the accounts) was £700,000.

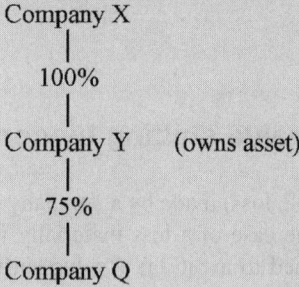

Company X

100%

Company Y   (owns asset)

75%

Company Q

A simple sale of its shares in company Y would result in a chargeable gain accruing to company X of £2,499,900 (ignoring indexation).

Instead, company X decides to reduce its exposure before the sale. Company Y disposes of the asset to its 75% subsidiary, company Q, for its full value. For tax purposes, this transaction takes place on a no gain, no loss basis. Company Y then distributes the accounting surplus of £410,000 to company X by way of dividend, reducing the value of company X's holding in company Y by a corresponding amount.

On the sale of its shares in company Y, there accrues to company X a chargeable gain of only £2,089,900 (ignoring indexation). This gain could be adjusted.

Law: TCGA 1992, s. 31, 33(1)–(6) and (8)

See *British Tax Reporter* ¶760-800.

4167   Disposals intra-group at an artificial discount

An adjustment may be made to a chargeable gain or allowable loss on shares if the value of the shares has been reduced by a transfer of an asset intra-group at a discount below both cost and market value.

The asset transfer must be one for which there is no gain/no loss for tax purposes by virtue of the transferor and transferee companies being members of the same group.

Law: TCGA 1992, s. 32

See *British Tax Reporter* ¶761-450.

4173   Consequences of a depreciatory transaction by a company

If a company sells shares at a loss and tries to claim an allowable loss on the transaction, the claim will be limited by the extent of any depreciatory transaction (see below). However, the provisions do not apply to increase a gain. Thus a transaction reducing a gain from £500,000 to £1, is not depreciatory within these rules so that, other things being equal, the gain will be £1.

If the company making the final disposal is not a member of the group when the shares are disposed of, the loss will not be reduced according to the depreciatory transaction which occurred when that company was not a member of the group.

However, allowance can be made for any other transaction by which the value of the company's assets is increased and the value of assets of any other group member is depreciated.

Where the allowable loss claimed is reduced and shares in any other company which was a party to the depreciatory transaction are (within six years of the depreciatory transaction) disposed of resulting in a chargeable gain, that gain will be reduced by the same amount as the reduction in the earlier loss.

What is a 'depreciatory transaction'?

A 'depreciatory transaction' is where one group member disposes of any assets to another group member for a consideration other than market value, or when the company whose shares are finally disposed of or its 75 per cent subsidiary was a party to the transaction and where the parties to the transaction include two or more companies which were members of the same group when the transaction took place.

Example

Company A purchases shares in company B so that B becomes a 75 per cent subsidiary of A. The purchase price reflects underlying assets held by B. B transfers assets to A at an undervalue.

Shares in B held by A lose their value and A sells those shares at a loss. A then claims a capital loss on the sale.

That loss is one created by a depreciatory transaction.

Corporation Tax

Law: TCGA 1992, s. 176

See *British Tax Reporter* ¶760-550.

4176   Dividend stripping

Dividend stripping is the practice of paying dividends out of a company so as to reduce the value of another person's holding in that company pending a disposal of that holding.

A capital loss on such a disposal may be disallowed where one company has a holding in another company which is the whole or part of ten per cent of all holdings of the same class in that other company. A company's holding of whatever size is treated as a ten per cent holding if the total of its holding together with those of any 'connected persons' (see 4012) amounts to ten per cent of all shares in that class.

The capital loss will only be disallowed if certain conditions also exist. The holding company must not be a 'dealing company' in relation to the holding. In other words, it must be a capital asset of that company. There must also have been a distribution in respect of that holding resulting in the net value of the holding being 'materially reduced'.

A company is a dealing company in relation to a holding if a profit on its sale would be taken into account in calculating the company's trading profits. All the company's holdings of the same class in another company are treated as a single holding.

There is no statutory indication of the meaning of 'materially reduced'. Although there are no decided cases on the point, each case will presumably depend on its particular facts and all the circumstances surrounding them.

The disallowance cannot be avoided by transfer of the shares to an affiliate, etc. under no gain/no loss provisions before ultimate disposal.

The primary purpose of this legislation is anti-avoidance. It aims to attack the sort of transaction where a company with a substantial cash surplus and distributable reserves is acquired and a large distribution made prior to resale at a reduced value. HMRC have confirmed that they will not generally treat as a depreciatory transaction a dividend paid out of post-acquisition reserves (commonly called a 'pre-sale' dividend); nor generally will they apply the principle of looking at the overall effect of certain composite transactions (see *Furniss v Dawson* and similar decisions) to the payment of dividends in order to reduce the value of shares before their sale.

Law: TCGA 1992, s. 177

See *British Tax Reporter* ¶761-250.

CLOSE COMPANIES

'CLOSE COMPANIES' AND THE PERSONS INVOLVED

4250   Introduction to close companies

Alongside the sometimes complex provisions which govern the taxation of companies generally, there are further special provisions which relate to the taxation of close companies.

When a company is closely controlled by a few persons, it is possible for them to reduce the tax payable on the profits made. The directors may be content to plough back the company's profits into the business, take some as directors' remuneration and make no distributions; alternatively they may take cash out of the company by way of loan or may receive non-cash benefits. Since 95 per cent of all companies in England are small private companies, the government takes the view that such artificial influences are unsatisfactory and the purpose of the legislation is to ensure that such persons do not gain a material advantage.

Certain investment-type close companies (close investment-holding companies) are prevented from using the small profits rate (formerly, small companies' rate) of corporation tax (see 4286).

There are also special rules governing the tax treatment of gains realised by non-resident close companies (see 5720).

Before setting out how the legislation applies, it is important to define certain terms which occur throughout the provisions so that they can be understood.

Law: CTA 2010, s. 34

See *British Tax Reporter* ¶776-000.

4253   What is a 'close company'?

A 'close company' is a company which is 'UK-resident' (see 3014) and not otherwise excluded (see 4270) which is controlled by five or fewer participators or by participators who are directors or a company over half of whose assets could be distributed on a notional winding-up between five or fewer participators or director participators (for the meaning of 'participator' and 'director', see 4256 and 4262).

Law: CTA 2010, s. 439

See *British Tax Reporter* ¶776-350.

4256   What is a 'participator' in a close company?

In relation to a 'close company' (see 4253), a 'participator' is any person who has, or is entitled to acquire, share capital or voting rights in the company, a person entitled to participate in distributions by the company, a person entitled to have income or assets of the company applied for his benefit or a 'loan creditor'.

A 'loan creditor' is a creditor in respect of any debt incurred by the company for money borrowed, or for capital assets purchased by the company, or for a right to receive income in favour of the company, or for consideration which was worth substantially less to the company than the amount of the debt. The definition also includes any person who is not a creditor but who has a beneficial interest in any loan capital or debt regarding which another person is a loan creditor.

A banker is not a loan creditor as regards any loan capital or debt issued or incurred by the company for money lent by him in the ordinary course of his business. A person who is not a creditor in respect of, but has a beneficial interest in, any debt or loan capital, is deemed to be a loan creditor to the extent of that interest.

Law: CTA 2010, s. 453 and 454

See *British Tax Reporter* ¶776-100.

4262   What is a 'director' of a close company?

In relation to a 'close company' (see 4253), a 'director' is any person who occupies the position of director whatever his title, and any person on whose instructions or directions the directors are accustomed to act, and the manager of a company if he holds or controls 20 per cent of its ordinary share capital either alone or with his associates.

A person is not a director where the company's articles of association allow the appointment of that person as a special, executive or assistant director on condition that such a person shall not be regarded as a member of the company's board or of any committee and shall only attend board meetings at the invitation of the board, and shall have no power to vote.

A person is not a director merely because the directors act upon his professional advice. He must be in the habit of directing company policy and company affairs and the directors should act frequently on those directions.

Law: CTA 2010, s. 452

See *British Tax Reporter* ¶776-250.

4265   What is 'control' of a close company?

The tests to determine control of a company so as to make it a close company refer to a single person; control by more than one person applies by aggregation. Except as noted below, a person controls a company if he directly or indirectly controls the company's policies and has power to appoint and dismiss the directors by ordinary resolution in general meeting.

A person is also in control of a company if he is entitled to acquire more than half of its nominal or issued share capital or voting power. Hence, if a person holds convertible debentures in a company he may have potential control if the majority of voting power were to rest in him if the debentures were turned into ordinary shares.

Example

A holds 100 convertible debentures in company X. Each debenture is convertible into five ordinary shares. A would therefore hold 500 ordinary shares if the debentures were converted.

Total ordinary share capital in X is 1,350 shares:

   B holds 200 ordinary shares

   C holds 100 ordinary shares

   D holds 150 ordinary shares

   E holds 150 ordinary shares

   F holds 50 ordinary shares

Other persons each with less than 50 shares hold the balance of 700 shares.

Therefore, company X is controlled by five or fewer participators.

A controller includes a person who holds or is entitled to acquire issued share capital with a right to receive more than half the company's income if it were all distributed. Amounts payable to loan creditors are not taken into account.

Any person entitled to more than half the company's net assets distributable amongst participators on a winding-up is also a controller.

In determining control, a person is treated as having the rights and powers of his associates.

Law: CTA 2010, s. 450

See *British Tax Reporter* ¶776-300.

4268   What is an 'associate' of a participator in a close company?

An 'associate' of a participator is:

- any relative or partner of the participator;
- a trustee of a settlement created by the participator or any relative of his;
- where the participator holds trust shares in the company, the trustee of the relevant settlement and, if the participator is a company, any other company interested in the trust; excluded from aggregation with the participator's shares are the personal shares of other beneficiaries of the trust.

Law: CTA 2010, s. 448 and 451; *Willingale (HMIT) v Islington Green Investment Co* (1972) 48 TC 547

See *British Tax Reporter* ¶776-150.

4270   Non-close companies: specific exemptions

A company cannot be a close company if it is not a UK resident (see 214).

If a company has allotted ordinary share capital to the public which carries 35 per cent of its total voting power, it will not be treated as a close company if those shares have been dealt in and listed by a recognised stock exchange (as defined) in the last 12 months. A stock exchange listing alone is not enough. The shares must be dealt in and held by the public. Despite this exception, a company will still be regarded as a close company if its principal members control more than 85 per cent of the voting power. Principal members of a company are the five persons who have individual control of the largest percentage of the voting power. Each person must control at least five per cent. The voting power exercisable by their nominees and associates and companies under their control is attributable to them.

A company is not deemed to be close if it fulfils the conditions only because it is controlled by or on behalf of the Crown.

A registered industrial and provident society and a building society are not close companies.

If the controlling shareholders of a company are one or more companies which are not close companies, and that company is only treated as a close company if a non-close company is included as one of its five or fewer controlling participators, it may be treated as a non-close company. This will occur if the company would not be a close company but for the fact that the participators include loan creditors which are companies other than close companies.

Where a non-resident company would be a close company if it were resident in the UK, any UK company which controls it is deemed to be a close company for the purposes of this rule.

Law: CTA 2010, s. 442–447 and 1137

See *British Tax Reporter* ¶776-550.

4271   What is an 'associated company' for close company purposes?

A company is associated with another at a particular time if, at that time or within the past year, one of the companies is or has been in control of the other or both are or have been under the control of the same persons, or where both together would form a group.

Two or more companies are not necessarily associated merely because they are controlled by the same 'loan creditor' (see 4256), provided that the loan creditor is a non-close company or some other bona fide loan creditor. There must be no other connection between the companies.

Law: CTA 2010, s. 449

See *British Tax Reporter* ¶776-200.

4277   Extended meaning of distribution for close companies

In addition to the normal payments which are treated as distributions by all companies (see 3067), there are additional payments which are artificially treated as distributions by close companies. Such payments cannot be deducted from the company's profits for corporation tax purposes. They are treated as the income of the recipient and subject to a charge to income tax at the appropriate rate (see 15).

The payments that are treated as distributions by a close company are any net expenses incurred by the company to provide its participators with accommodation, entertainment, domestic or other services, or other benefits or facilities of whatever nature. A participator includes an associate of a participator, and a participator in a company which controls the company making the payment.

There are certain exceptions to this rule, such as pensions, annuities, lump sum payments or gratuities paid to the spouses, children or dependants of a person which are payable on or as a result of that person's death or retirement, and certain transfers of assets or liabilities between companies which are UK-resident, and where one of the companies is a 51 per cent subsidiary of the other, or where both companies are 51 per cent subsidiaries of a third UK-resident company.

If there are reciprocal arrangements between unconnected close companies to attempt to circumvent a charge to tax, then any payments or facilities provided will be treated as provided to each participator by the close company in which he is himself a participator.

Corporation Tax

Law: CTA 2010, s. 1064

4278 Transfers of value by close companies

Capital gains implications

If a close company transfers an asset, otherwise than to a group member, for consideration less than its market value the difference between the market value and the consideration is apportioned between the shareholders and reduces the base cost of their shares in the company.

Where the transferee is a participator the transfer is instead treated as an income distribution or as a capital distribution. Where the transferee is an employee, that amount will be taxed as employment income.

If the transfer is to an employee benefit trust for the benefit of employees of the transferee company, the apportionment to shareholders is of an amount equal to the difference in the consideration paid by the EBT and either the market value of the asset, or, if lower, the acquisition cost of the asset.

Inheritance tax implications

When a transfer of value is made by a close company, the value transferred is apportioned amongst the company's participators although the actual IHT due is primarily payable by the company itself. IHT is charged as though each individual participator has made a transfer of value of the amount apportioned to him. Such transfers are not potentially exempt transfers and so are immediately chargeable to IHT.

In March 1975, HMRC issued a statement of practice in respect of certain close company transactions. This statement clarified the position concerning dividend payments and transfers of assets from a subsidiary company to a parent or sister company as appropriate. In HMRC's view, a dividend paid by a subsidiary company to its parent is not a transfer of value. Similarly HMRC do not feel that they can justifiably treat a transfer of assets between a wholly-owned subsidiary and its parent or between two wholly-owned subsidiaries as a transfer of value.

The value transferred by a close company will be apportioned amongst its participators according to their respective rights and interests in the company immediately before the transfer and, if one of those participators is itself a close company, that amount will be further sub-apportioned. Rights and interests in a company include rights and interests in the assets of the company available for distribution amongst the participators in the event of a winding up or in any other circumstances.

If a disposal of an asset by a close company (the transferor) to another member of the same 'group' gives rise to a transfer of value, then, provided the effect on the rights of the minority participators is small, no amount will be apportioned to those minority participators unless the transferor company is the principal member of the group. Group has the same definition as that for the purposes of chargeable gains (see 3682). A minority participator is a person who is not, and is not a person connected with, a participator of the principal member of the group or of any of the principal company's participators.

No apportionment will be made in the following instances:

(a) if the value transferred is liable to income tax or corporation tax;

(b) if the value is attributable to property outside the UK and the participator is domiciled outside the UK;

In addition, under normal inheritance tax principles, dispositions which are not intended to confer any gratuitous benefit on any person are not transfers of value and so would fall outside these close company provisions. This is likely to remove from the scope of these provisions most transactions undertaken by close companies in the normal course of their trade or business (but see below in relation to HMRC's views on contributions to employee benefit trusts). Similarly, any disposition that is an allowable deduction in computing the company's corporation tax liability is not a transfer of value.

In practice, potential IHT charges can arise in connection with contributions by close companies to employee benefit trusts. Under normal IHT principles, dispositions made by companies into trusts for the benefit of their employees are not transfers of value but this exemption does not apply if any participators owning 5 per cent or more of the share capital can benefit under the trust. Also, since November 2002, a contribution by a company into an employee benefit trust is not deductible for corporation tax purposes in the year in which it is made, but a deduction is often available later when the trust makes payments out to the employees. In HMRC's view relief from IHT is only available under (b) above to the extent that a deduction is allowable to the company for the accounting period in which the contribution is made. Also, in HMRC's view it will often be difficult for close companies to argue that there is no intention to confer any gratuitous benefit when making a contribution to an employee benefit trust because, for example, it is common for the beneficiaries of such trusts to include wives, husbands, children and stepchildren of the employee.

HMRC's views in relation to the IHT implications of contributions by close companies to employee benefit trusts is set out in HMRC Brief 49/09.

Law: TCGA 1992, s. 122, 125 and 239(3); CTA 2010, s. 1000(1) and 1020; IHTA 1984, s. 12

CLOSE INVESTMENT-HOLDING COMPANIES

4280   Introduction to close investment-holding companies

Certain close companies which are of an investment nature, close investment-holding companies (CICs), are, for accounting periods beginning after 31 March 1989, prevented from benefiting from the small profits rate (formerly, small companies' rate) of corporation tax or marginal relief (see 4286).

See *British Tax Reporter* ¶777-350.

4283   Definition of close investment-holding company

All close companies are close investment-holding companies (CICs) unless they satisfy certain requirements.

A company must satisfy any one requirement, although it may also satisfy more than one. In outline, they relate to the following types of company:

- trading companies;
- commercial property investment companies;
- group-holding or group-finance companies;
- administrative co-ordination companies;
- group-service (trade) companies;
- group-service (property investment) companies.

In more detail, to be excepted from being a CIC a close company must exist wholly or mainly for one or more of the required purposes. The test must be satisfied for each accounting period in point, and throughout the period.

A company in liquidation is normally a CIC, any trade or business which it continues to carry on during its winding-up is likely to be incidental to its main purpose of winding up its affairs although in such case its status would be continued for the first accounting period after commencement of the winding-up; if trade ceased before the winding-up, protected status is not generally applicable.

Law: CTA 2010, s. 34

See *British Tax Reporter* ¶777-450.

4286   Small profits rate unavailable to close investment-holding companies

For accounting periods beginning after 31 March 1989, there is a requirement that a company must not be a 'close investment-holding company' (CIC: see 4283) at the end of an accounting period for it to claim that its corporation tax liability should be calculated at the small profits rate for that period.

Because marginal relief, given between the lower and upper profits limits, refers back to such companies, the requirement also applies to such relief.

Law: CTA 2010, s.18(b)

See *British Tax Reporter* ¶777-400.

LOANS TO PARTICIPATORS BY CLOSE COMPANIES

4300   Charge on loans to participators by close companies

If a company makes a loan to one of its 'participators' (see 4256) or an 'associate' (see 4268) outside the ordinary course of its business, it is chargeable to tax for the accounting period when the advance was made. This rule applies even though the whole or any part of the loan or advance may have been repaid before the charge is raised. However, in such circumstances the company remains entitled to the proper measure of relief (see 4306).

The money-lending exemption is really two tests:

(1)   the company must carry on the business of lending money in general and not just to a single participator, and

(2)   the loan must be in the ordinary course of that business; HMRC's view is that this would not be the case where the size, terms or conditions of the loan differed from those which normally applied.

From 6 April 1999 the rate of charge is fixed at 25 per cent of loans or advances made on or after that date. Previously, the tax was linked to the rate of ACT in force for the financial year.

Close companies must notify HMRC of loans to participators, etc. and must notify both chargeability and liability to tax.

Law: CTA 2010, s. 455 and 456; *Steen v Law (Liquidator of International Vending Machines Pty Ltd)* [1964] AC 287; *Earlspring Properties Ltd v Guest (HMIT)* [1995] BTC 274

See *British Tax Reporter* ¶776-900.

4303   What is a 'loan' to a participator?

A close company is treated as making a loan to another person if that person incurs a debt to the company or assigns a debt owed to a third person to the company. The amount of the debt is treated as the loan.

Exception

A debt will not be treated as a loan to a participator if it is incurred for the supply of goods or services by the company in the ordinary course of its business. However, this will not apply where either more than six months' credit is given or if a longer credit period than that normally given to the company's customers is given.

Small loans

If the company makes a small loan to a restricted class of participators it is not chargeable to corporation tax, but there are some conditions which must be fulfilled. A company may make a loan to a director or an employee of up to £15,000 if that person is a full-time employee of the company or its associate who has no material interest in that company.

A person will have a material interest in a company if he or his associate is the beneficial owner of, or can control directly or indirectly, more than five per cent of its ordinary share capital or (for accounting periods beginning after 31 March 1989) if more than five per cent of the company's assets on a notional winding-up could be distributed to him and/or his 'associate' (see 4268).

Where the borrower acquires a material interest whilst there is still a loan outstanding which was made after 30 March 1971, the close company is treated as making, at the time of the acquisition of the material interest, a loan equal to that sum.

A loan made before 31 March 1971 so that the borrower can purchase his main or only dwelling house can only gain this exemption if it does not exceed £10,000.

Law: CTA 2010, s. 455(4), 456 and 457; *Grant v Watton (HMIT)* [1999] BTC 85

See *British Tax Reporter* ¶777-150.

4306   Payment of tax on loan to participator

The tax payable on loans to participators (see 4300) must be paid within nine months after the day after the end of the accounting period.

If the loan is wholly or partly repaid more than nine months after the end of the accounting period in which it was made, relief for the repayment is not given before nine months after the end of the accounting period in which the repayment occurred. However, if the loan is wholly or partly repaid within nine months after the end of the accounting period in which it was made, relief can take effect as soon as the tax falls due, the company having to make its claim within six years after the end of the financial year in which the loan was repaid.

Relief from a charge is extended to include circumstances where the debt in respect of the loan is released or written off, in addition to where it is repaid. Such an event could lead to a refund of any tax paid on the amount of the loan or advance repaid, released or written off. Interest on the refund of such a charge also applies where a loan debt is released or written off and not just when the loan is repaid. This brings the interest provisions into line with the tax repayment provisions.

Law: ICTA 1988, s. 826(4); CTA 2010, s. 455(3) and 458

See *British Tax Reporter* ¶776-950.

4309 Loans made indirectly to participator

If a close company makes a loan indirectly to one of its participators, it is treated as a loan subject to a corporation tax charge (see 4300).

Example

A close company lends money to a bank which would not normally be chargeable to corporation tax. The bank then makes a loan to one of the company's participators. The loan made by the close company to the bank is, in these circumstances, treated as a loan made directly to the participator.

Where a transaction which might amount to an indirect loan takes place in the ordinary course of the company's business, the rule now being considered does not apply. This is also the case where the loan is treated as part of the total income of the participator (see 4256).

For the purposes of this rule, a participator includes a company receiving a loan in a fiduciary capacity or as a representative, and a non-resident company.

See *British Tax Reporter* ¶777-200.

4312 Loans to participator written off by a close company

If a close company releases or writes off the whole or part of a debt created by a loan to a participator which is assessed to tax (see 4300), a tax charge may arise. The amount written off or released is grossed-up by reference to the dividend ordinary rate (10 per cent for 2010/11) and included in the participator's total income for the year.

Law: ITTOIA 2005, s. 416; *Collins v Addies (HMIT)* [1992] BTC 532

See *British Tax Reporter* ¶777-200.

4315 Loans to participator in close company by controlled company

Where a close company 'controls' another company (see 4265) and that other company makes a loan, that loan is treated as if the close company made it in relation to the charge to tax for loans to participators (see 4300).

If a company is controlled by a close company after it makes a loan, the close company is regarded as making the loan immediately after it acquires control.

If there are two or more close companies which control the company making the loan, they are both treated as making the loan in proportion to their interests in the company which they control.

The above rules do not apply where the company making the loan can show that there was no arrangement connecting the making of the loan and the close company acquiring control, or the close company providing funds for the company making the loan.

A close company is deemed to provide funds for a company if it directly or indirectly makes any payment or transfers any property to or releases or satisfies a liability of the company making the loan.

Law: CTA 2010, s. 460

See *British Tax Reporter* ¶777-200.

SPECIAL COMPANIES

COMPANIES WITH INVESTMENT BUSINESS

4550   Introduction to companies with investment business (prior to 1 April 2004, investment companies)

Generally, companies with investment business are taxed in the same way as any other company, with the exception that deductions available in computing the non-trading profits of such companies are subject to greater restrictions than is the case with a trade. Holding companies in a group will often be companies with investment business but need not necessarily be so.

The definition of 'company with investment business' (see 4553) does not preclude such a company from carrying on a trade. Commentary on trading companies generally applies equally to investment companies carrying on a trade.

See *British Tax Reporter* ¶713-000.

Open-ended investment companies

An open-ended investment company (OEIC) is a form of retail investment fund which could not be set up in the UK until 1997. Although an OEIC resembles an authorised unit trust, it is constituted as a company, issues shares rather than units, and has a board of directors. The tax rules relating to OEICs and their shareholders are broadly based on the principle of equivalence with provisions relating to authorised unit trusts and their unit holders (under regulations applying from 28 April 1997). In particular, the total amount shown in the 'distribution accounts' of an OEIC as available for distribution to the owners of its shares is treated for tax purposes as though it is distributed to them on the relevant distribution date, and the company has to issue tax vouchers accordingly.

Law: FA 1995, s. 152; *Open-ended Investment Companies (Tax) Regulations* 1997 (SI 1997/1154)

See *British Tax Reporter* ¶782-000.

4553   Definition of a company with investment business

Finance Act 2004 extended relief for expenses of management to companies with investment business. A company carries on an investment business if its 'business consists wholly or partly of making investments'. Prior to the changes made by the *Finance Act* 2004, relief for expenses of management could only be claimed by an investment company, being 'a company whose business consists wholly or mainly in the making of investments and the principal part of whose income is derived therefrom'. Although the term 'company with investment business' is more inclusive than the term 'investment company', extending relief to many companies which previously did not qualify for it, both phrases focus on the making of investments. Consequently, previous decisions in the courts and other interpretations relating to investment companies continue to be of valid application in the context of the definition, and understanding, of what constitutes a company with investment business. They are summarised below.

It is now well established that the making of investments will not also require that the investments be turned over and that making an investment is not of itself trading. It follows that a holding company can be an investment company or have investment business. Also, in principle, a company can carry on a business of investment even though its investments provide no income but whether it actually does so is a matter of fact in each case. It does not necessarily follow that, because a company's formal object was to carry on the business of an investment company, the company in fact carried on that business.

The parent company of a trading group, which also provided head office services to its subsidiaries, was found to be an investment company in *Dawsongroup Limited v R & C Commrs* (the Upper Tribunal overturning an earlier ruling by the First-tier Tribunal). Although the case is now mainly of historical interest only, in view of the widening in 2004 of the circumstances in which a company can claim a deduction for expenses of management, the Upper Tribunal Judge made some important observations. He ruled that it was incorrect to separate the holding of shares from the exercise of control which that holding enables the holder to do and that, therefore, exercising control by means of holding shares can be part of the investment activity and not necessarily a trading activity.

Residents' associations were found not to constitute investment companies (*Tintern Close Residents Society Ltd v Winter (HMIT)*). The businesses of the companies concerned did not consist wholly or mainly in the making of investments: further, the principal part of the companies' business was not derived from the making of investments. However, the High Court found that a housing society was an investment company. Although the object of the society was to acquire housing for renting with a social, rather than a profit, purpose, it did not follow that the houses were not investments. In fact, the houses were income-producing investments and the business of the society consisted in the making of investments (*Cook (HMIT) v Medway Housing Society Ltd*). It was also found to be irrelevant that the profit realised was to be used in furthering the objects of the society and not to be distributed to members.

Law: CTA 2009, s. 1218; *IR Commrs v Tyre Investment Trust Ltd* (1924) 12 TC 646; *Simpson (HMIT) v The Grange Trust Ltd* (1935) 19 TC 231; *Cook (HMIT) v Medway Housing Society Ltd* [1997] BTC 63; *Dawsongroup Limited v R & C Commrs* [2010] BTC 1528; *Tintern Close Residents Society Ltd v Winter (HMIT)* (1995) Sp C 7

See *British Tax Reporter* ¶713-100.

4556 Management expenses of an investment company

In computing the profits for an accounting period of a 'company with investment business' (see 4553) certain expenses commonly referred to as management expenses are deductible. The term 'management expenses' is also used in relation to life assurance companies (see 4606). Such expenses are deductible if they qualify as 'expenses of management', an expression which is not defined in relation to either investment companies or life assurance companies. Although the specific limitations on what may or may not be included in expenses of management differ for investment companies and life assurance companies the expression 'expenses of management' applies equally for both. Confusingly, qualifying (deductible) management expenses are often referred to as 'management expenses'.

For the means by which relief is obtained, see 4562.

Certain expenses are specifically excluded from inclusion in management expenses and some expenses are made specifically deductible. There is also judicial authority relating to whether certain items are or are not management expenses.

Law: CTA 2009, s. 1219

See *British Tax Reporter* ¶713-250.

4557 Management expenses: expenses not deductible

The rules governing management expenses remained largely unchanged until 2004 when changes were made to reflect a more modern business climate. Those changes included, amongst other things, an unallowable purpose rule.

Since the 2004 changes, various attempts have been made to circumvent the unallowable purpose rule and/or to create contrived expenses that could be deducted as expenses of management under ICTA 1988, s. 75 (see 4556). HMRC do not consider that these schemes succeed but their use has shown that the 'unallowable purpose' rule is not a sufficient deterrent. *Finance Act* 2007, s. 28, which received Royal Assent on 19 July 2007, therefore introduce a targeted anti-avoidance rule (TAAR) for management expenses. It also amended the existing unallowable purpose rule, so that similar provisions apply to both the purpose for which investments are held and the purpose for which management expenses are incurred. Both new provisions apply to expenses of management paid on or after 20 June 2007, the date the measure was announced.

The new TAAR will apply where the main purpose or one of the main purposes of arrangements is to seek to produce a wholly or partly contrived deduction for management expenses or other tax advantage. It is based upon the principle that relief for expenses of management should only be available where a company has genuinely incurred expenditure in the course of managing its investment business. Where the rule applies, its effect is to disallow relief for expenses of management where companies enter into arrangements where tax avoidance is the main purpose or one of the main purposes of the arrangements. The provisions are unlikely to affect the vast majority of companies, only those which have deliberately and knowingly entered into a scheme to avoid tax.

In addition the following expenses are not deductible management expenses (i.e. are not 'expenses of management'):

- any amount disbursed which is deductible in computing profits apart from as expenses of management;
- expenses of a capital nature unless falling within any of the categories in 4558 below or are employer contributions to a pension scheme;
- expenses for which there is a statutory prohibition on deduction (e.g. business entertaining and gifts, crime-related payments, remuneration not paid within nine months of the end of the accounting period, contributions to employee benefit trusts, penalties, interest and VAT surcharges, a proportion of the hire costs of cars costing more than £12,000, etc.);
- brokerage and stamp duty on the purchase and sale of investments;
- the costs of raising finance, such as the issue of the debentures;
- payments that are not wholly for the purposes of the company's business, such as excessive directors' fees or administrative expenses paid to a parent company otherwise than pursuant to an agreement;
- exchange losses on payment of interest on capital liability (in relation to exchange losses generally see SP 1/87 with particular reference to para. 31);
- premiums for insurance against war risk;
- certain payments for war injuries to employees;
- certain payments in respect of unapproved retirement benefits schemes (whether by contribution or pension, etc.) unless and until the recipient is charged to income tax on them; certain foreign arrangements are treated as approved;
- rent in excess of commercial amounts paid under lease-back arrangements;
- rent for leased-back assets to the extent of any capital sums received under a lease-back

Corporation Tax

arrangement, although strictly the deduction is not prevented, an equal amount being charged to corporation as miscellaneous income (formerly, under Sch. D, Case VI).

At first, the courts put a narrow interpretation on what constituted expenses of management. In *Capital and National Trust Ltd v Golder*, the Court of Appeal interpreted expenses of management as those involved in taking managerial decisions, but excluding expenses involved in carrying them out. This narrow interpretation was rejected by the House of Lords in *Sun Life Assurance v Davidson*, where the question at issue was whether the life assurance company could include, as expenses of management, sums representing brokerage and stamp duties incurred in connection with purchases and sales of investments made in the course of its business. Although the House found that the brokerage and stamp duties were not expenses of the management of the company's business, being too closely linked with the purchases and sales, it did reject the narrow construction put on 'expenses of management' adopted in *Capital and National Trust Ltd v Golder*. This wider interpretation of 'expenses of management' was also favoured by the Court of Appeal in *Hoechst Finance Ltd v Gumbrell*, where commission payments were considered.

The general principle established by this line of cases is that to be deductible, expenses of management have to be expenses of managing the investment business, rather than the investment themselves. So, expenses that relate to the purchase or sale of a particular investment will not generally be deductible as expenses of management.

Professional advisers' fees in connection with an aborted acquisition were held to be deductible expenses of management in *Atkinson v Camas plc* and professional advisers' fees in connection with an investigation into the affairs of a company in which an investment had previously been made were also held to be deductible expenses of management in *Holdings Ltd v IR Commrs*. Expenses incurred in 2000 (before the statutory prohibition on the deduction for expenses of management of capital nature was introduced) in connection with the delisting of a company's shares from the Stock Exchange were, unsurprisingly, held not to be deductible expenses of managing its investment business in *Dawsongroup Ltd v R & C Commrs*.

Law: CTA 2009, s. 1219 and Pt. 16, Ch. 4; CTA 2010, s. 838; *Bennet v Underground Electric Railways Co of London Ltd* (1918–1924) 8 TC 475; *London County Freehold and Leasehold Properties Ltd v Sweet (HMIT)* (1942) 24 TC 412; *Capital and National Trust Ltd v Golder (HMIT)* (1949) 31 TC 265; *Sun Life Assurance Society v Davidson (HMIT)* (1957) 37 TC 330; *LG Berry Investments Ltd v Attwooll (HMIT)* (1964) 41 TC 547; *Fragmap Developments Ltd v Cooper (HMIT)* (1967) 44 TC 366; *Hoechst Finance Ltd v Gumbrell* [1983] BTC 66; *Atkinson v Camas plc* [2004] BTC 190; *Holdings Ltd v IR Commrs* (1997) Sp C 117; *Dawsongroup Limited v R & C Commrs* [2010] BTC 1528

Source: SP 1/87

See *British Tax Reporter* ¶710-600.

4558 Management expenses: deductible expenses

Expenses of management (i.e. deductible management expenses) include certain expenses by operation of statute; this covers 'commissions' and the following expenses:

- any statutory redundancy payment and corresponding employer's other payments in excess of the recoverable rebate (including payments after discontinuance of trade);
- any payment which is made after discontinuance of trade in addition to a statutory redundancy payment or other employer's payment up to three times the redundancy payment or other employer's payment provided it would be deductible under general principles if made before discontinuance;
- costs of establishing share options and profit sharing schemes;
- contributions to certain profit-sharing schemes;
- contributions to an agent's expenses under a payroll deduction scheme (see 2240);
- outplacement counselling expenses (see 438);
- contributions to certain pension schemes;
- the costs of valuing the fixed assets of the company, where such valuation is necessary to comply with CA 2006, s. 461 which requires the reporting of significant changes in the company's fixed assets;
- any expenditure attributable to employing a person whose services are made available on a temporary basis either to a charity;
- any expenditure incurred by an employer in paying or reimbursing 'relevant expenses' in connection with a 'qualifying course of training' undertaken by an employee who holds or held an office or employment under the employer, with a view to 'retraining' the employee (see 2241);
- certain payments to the Export Credits Guarantee Department.

Expenditure incurred by an investment company on professional fees of accountants and solicitors in investigating the financial and legal affairs of a trading company in which it had a 50 per cent shareholding qualified as allowable 'expenses of management'.

Law: CTA 2009, s. 1219 and Pt. 16, Ch. 3; *Holdings Ltd v IR Commrs* (1997) Sp C 117

See *British Tax Reporter* ¶710-450.

4559 Capital allowances for investment companies

The management of an investment company is a qualifying activity for the purposes of claiming capital allowances on plant and machinery. Relief is given by deduction from the income of the accounting period.

Any capital allowances that cannot be given against the income of the period are added to the company's management expenses and may be carried forward to subsequent accounting periods.

Corporation Tax

Law: CAA 2001, s. 253

See *British Tax Reporter* ¶713-700.

4562　Method of relief for deductions of an investment company

In computing an investment company's profits for an accounting period, expenses of management (i.e. deductible management expenses: see 4556) are first deducted from income from sources not charged to tax (except franked investment income, group income (in relation to distributions made before 6 April 1999) and regional development grants) and next from the company's other income and gains in the period.

If in an accounting period the expenses of management together with qualifying charitable donations (for accounting period ended before 1 April 2010, charges on income) paid wholly and exclusively for purposes of the business exceed the profits for that period, the excess is carried forward to the next accounting period and treated as expenses of management of that period.

The excess expenses of management may alternatively be surrendered as group relief (see 3809ff.) to be set off against the profits of the claimant company's corresponding accounting period. Expenses of management brought forward from previous years cannot be surrendered. Group relief is available for expenses of management whether or not the claimant company is an investment company.

Detailed provisions apply to changes in ownership of investment companies which occur after 28 November 1994 (unless they are in pursuance of a contract entered into before that date) which seek to prevent exploitation of unrelieved management expenses and other similar reliefs available to investment companies.

Law: CTA 2009, s. 1219; CTA 2010, Pt. 14, Ch. 3

See *British Tax Reporter* ¶710-500.

4565　Approved investment trusts

An approved investment trust is not a trust but a UK-resident company which is not a close company (see 4250) and is approved as such for the accounting period in question. An approved investment trust is exempt from corporation tax on capital gains which accrue when it disposes of its investments in that period (see 5917). The requirements for approval must all be satisfied throughout each accounting period for which approval is sought.

The tests which an investment trust must satisfy to gain approval include a requirement that the bulk of its income be derived from shares and securities ('wholly or mainly' – interpreted by HMRC as 70 per cent of taxable income including franked investment income, 50 per cent for the first period for which approval is sought:). 'Shares and securities' implies investments with a degree of permanence. A company whose income consists wholly or mainly of 'eligible investment income' (which includes income from letting dwelling-houses as well as income from shares and securities) can qualify as an investment trust, and that part of an investment trust's activities which is attributable to its eligible letting activities is chargeable at the small companies' rate.

HMRC are given power by FA 2009, s. 45 to issue regulations which will give investment trust companies (ITCs) the option to treat dividends as distributions of interest, and to provide that such distributions will be treated as interest payments to their shareholders. This will move the point of taxation for income from interest bearing assets from the trust to the shareholder. The shareholder will effectively be treated for tax purposes as if they had owned the interest bearing asset direct.

Regulations can also be made so that the interest distribution is treated as a payment of yearly interest for an individual or as a loan relationship credit for a company. The purpose of the new legislation is to enable investment trust companies to invest in interest bearing assets tax efficiently.

For the transfer of assets to an investment trust, see 5917.

Law: FA 2009, s. 45; CTA 2010, Pt. 24, Ch. 4; *Investment Trust (Dividends) (etc.) Regulations* 2009 (SI 2009/2034)

See *British Tax Reporter* ¶782-850.

4580   Corporate members of Lloyd's

Since 1 January 1994, Lloyd's has admitted corporate members. Broadly, corporate membership is open to UK-resident companies, or companies incorporated in certain other specified jurisdictions. A UK-resident corporate member will be chargeable to corporation tax on the whole of its profits from its trade as an underwriter, and a non-resident corporate member which carries on its trade through a branch in the UK will be chargeable on the profits of the branch.

Where members significantly overestimate provision for unpaid claims or premiums for reinsurance to close, a tax charge will apply. The charge is intended to compensate for tax deferred as a result of the overprovision. The amount of any deductible provision is not restricted, but if it transpires that the provision deducted was excessive, an amount equivalent to an interest charge will be levied on the amount of the excess. A de minimus relief may be prescribed by regulations. The charge applies in respect to profits declared in periods of accounts beginning on or after 1 January 2000.

Two changes apply in connection with corporate members to distributions made after 1 July 1997 as part of the general restrictions on entitlement to tax credits:

Corporation Tax

- the entitlement to tax credits on distributions received in respect of assets held in the premiums trust fund (whether of corporate or non-corporate members) is withdrawn. Thus, credits will no longer be paid into the premiums trust fund; and
- distributions relating to assets held in a corporate member's ancillary trust fund, or employed by it in its underwriting business are to be included in its trading income profits, without taking into account the associated tax credit.

Law: FA 1994, s. 219–230; F(No. 2)A 1997, s. 22

See *British Tax Reporter* ¶802-900.

LIFE ASSURANCE COMPANIES

4600   Introduction to life assurance companies

Life assurance companies are taxed separately on profits from their life assurance business and on other classes of insurance business, e.g. accident, marine, etc. Only the life assurance business and, under corporation tax self-assessment, capital redemption business, are subject to special rules. Profits from other classes of business are taxed as trading profits.

Life assurance business includes life policies, which consist of whole life policies, endowment policies and term assurance, and pension annuity contracts which include employer/employee pension schemes and private annuity retirement plans. There are also purchased annuities which include immediate and deferred annuities. Capital redemption business is a form of long term insurance not made on human life but regulations apply life rules to such business (see 4606).

Each type of policy is treated differently for tax purposes.

Where it is necessary to match income and gains/losses from general funds with particular business, an allocation is made in accordance with the extent to which assets are 'linked' to particular business and the balance is apportioned. Since 1995, capital allowances on management assets have been similarly apportioned while relief for allowances on investment assets has been restricted.

In relation to accounting periods beginning on or after 1 January 2000 and ending on or after 21 March 2000, revised rules govern the allocation of interest payable between different categories of business. Where the business is all or largely linked business, debits and credits on debtor loan relationships are allocated on a statutory basis.

HMRC may choose to tax profits of life assurance business carried on by a proprietary life company as trading income (formerly as a trade under Sch. D, Case I) or as investments under miscellaneous income (formerly Sch. D, Case VI) less management expenses (see 4603, 4606). A mutual life company will only be taxed on its activities as investment income less management expenses. Investment income and gains on pension business are specifically exempt from tax, although any profits on pension business calculated on a trading basis are assessable under miscellaneous income. Losses on pension business activity calculated on the same basis are ring-fenced and are effectively not available for surrender as group relief.

As part of the general restrictions on the entitlement to tax credits included in F(No. 2)A 1997 (see 3000), two further restrictions apply specifically to life assurance contained in:

(1) provisions which deny payable tax credits to pension providers on investments referable to pension business and which mirror the denial of tax credits to pension funds. In effect, the exemption of investment income and gains of pension business from corporation tax provided by ICTA 1988, s. 438 is disregarded for the purpose of establishing the competence of a claim to payment of a tax credit. A consequence of this is that such franked investment income will be available to frank a proprietary company's own distributions in full. These changes apply to franked investment income consisting of distributions made after 1 July 1997; and

(2) provisions which include distributions as trading profits where shares are held as trading assets and which rationalise existing rules about bringing distributions into the calculation of profits for accounting periods beginning after 1 July 1997.

Loss relief and group relief is denied against the policy holders' share of profits.

There are special rules for overseas life companies (see 4503).

Equalisation reserves

Transfers into and out of equalisation reserves (or equivalent reserves) to cover certain lines of business are recognised for tax purposes, broadly, if the reserves are maintained in accordance with Department of Trade and Industry (DTI) rules.

Deemed annual disposal and reacquisition of investments

For chargeable gains purposes, there is a deemed market value disposal of certain assets held at the end of each accounting period. The assets involved are authorised unit trust units and comparable offshore fund interests, in so far as they are not linked solely to pension policies, life reinsurance business or business done through an overseas branch. A gain may be spread over a seven-year period subject to certain provisos.

Transfer of long term business to another company

The transfer of long term business from one insurance company to another does not prevent continuity of tax treatment of that business whilst associated assets will pass on a no gain/no loss basis). HMRC have also issued a statement of practice which confirms that the disposal of an asset which partly backs taxable life assurance business and partly exempt pension business as, for that reason alone, being disqualified from the provisions which defer a charge to corporation tax on chargeable gains when a life assurance business transfers all or part of its long term business to another company. Expenses of management (see 4606), losses and capital allowances continue after a transfer, essentially as if there had been no change, although there are technical details to consider. The chargeable gains, management expenses and loss reliefs only apply if the transfer is effected for bona fide commercial reasons and not to avoid tax – a clearance application may be made in advance to HMRC.

Investor protection schemes

Insurance companies may contribute to investor protection schemes. Relief is given for levies imposed under the Investor Compensation Scheme established by the SIB in accordance with the provisions of the *Financial Services Act* 1986. Payments imposed under other schemes may qualify for relief in accordance with specific regulations; regulations have been made which will allow relief for levies imposed under the LAUTRO indemnity scheme (which provides for the payment of compensation to investors for otherwise irrecoverable losses). Similar relief is to be permitted by extra-statutory concession in respect of levies imposed by the rules of LAUTRO for the purpose of meeting liabilities attributable to members of FIMBRA for the three years to 31 March 1993.

Law: ICTA 1988, s. 76(7) and Pt. XII, Ch. I; FA 1989, s. 84 and 89; TCGA 1992, s. 211 and 212–214A; *Income Tax (Insurance Companies) (Expenses of Management) Regulations* 1992 (SI 1992/2744)

See *British Tax Reporter* ¶780-150.

4603 Trading income (formerly Sch. D, Case I) basis of assessment of life assurance companies

If tax is charged on life assurance business under trading income (formerly Sch. D, Case I (see 4600)), it is on the net income of the business after expenses of earning that income have been deducted.

The franked investment income (see 3077) (and prior to 6 April 1999, the foreign income dividends (see 1350)) from the life assurance business where the company is resident in the UK may be treated as part of the profits of the business. Losses are also calculated on a similar basis but without reference to pension, reinsurance or overseas life business losses. The *Finance Act* 1995 also enacted a provision which reduced or extinguished a loss incurred by a life assurance company where there was in the same period an injection of cash or other assets into the long term business fund of the company. The government then accepted that this rule should be limited to cases where the transfer of funds arose in consequence of or as part of a transfer of business for accounting periods beginning after 31 December 1995.

As part of the changes to the tax credit regime introduced by F(No. 2)A 1997 (see 3000), the rules governing the inclusion of distributions in the trading income profits from total life assurance business, or any part of that business considered separately for tax, are both simplified and rationalised. The effect is that all distributions (generally ignoring the associated tax credit) are to be included in all circumstances. This applies to distributions made on or after 2 July 1997.

The ability to make a claim to set losses and other items against policy holders' share of franked investment income from investments held in connection with life assurance business is removed with effect for accounting periods beginning on or after 2 July 1997. Where an accounting period straddles 2 July 1997, claims can be made, but distributions made on or after that date must be ignored in the calculations. Franked investment income may not be 'double counted' both for these purposes, and for 'ordinary' claims against franked investment income for such an accounting period.

Investment income and any realised or unrealised surplus or deficit on assets of an insurance company's long term business fund are brought into the trading income computation. Where the business in question forms only a part of the business of the company it may be necessary to allocate/apportion profits – if the policy holders in point are entitled to a share of the profits this basis is used subject to a floor calculated by applying a specified rate of investment yield (see the applicable regulations) to the liabilities in point (see also 4600). With effect from 31 December 1998, no distinction will be made between stocks with high coupons and stock with other forms of coupon, for the purposes of the specified rate of yield.

Annual payments in satisfaction of policy claims and annuity payments are specifically deductible, notwithstanding the general restriction to this effect (see 3027 and 3055). Similar but slightly narrower relief was granted for accounting periods beginning in 1995.

Deductions are permitted for bonus payments made, reversionary bonuses declared, reductions in future premiums or tax paid on behalf of policyholders, etc. and also, where the life assurance fund is in surplus, for any amount provided as a result for future bonuses, etc. An amount so deducted as a provision is effectively reversed in the following period.

Law: FA 1989, s. 82, 83, 432B–432F, 434 and 434A; FA 1996, Sch. 31; *Insurance Companies (Corporation Tax Acts) (Amendment) (No. 2) Order* 2008 (SI 2008/3096); *Insurance Companies (Calculation of Profits: Policy Holders' Tax) Regulations* 2003 (SI 2003/2082); *Life Assurance (Apportionment of Receipts of Participating Funds) (Applicable Percentage) Order* 1990 (SI 1990/1541)

See *British Tax Reporter* ¶780-150.

4606　Income less expenditure basis of assessment for life assurance companies

'I–E basis': introduction

If HMRC choose to make an assessment on life assurance business on the income less expenditure (I–E) basis (see 4600), relief is given for 'expenses of management' (see below) and allowances in respect of capital expenditure. These reliefs are restricted for accounting periods beginning after 31 December 1995, in so far as they do not reduce the aggregate of the profits chargeable to corporation tax and franked investment income of the company to below the profits chargeable on a trading income (formerly Sch. D, Case I) assessment. For

Corporation Tax

earlier accounting periods the restriction was by reference to the amount of tax on a trading income assessment, rather than profits, requiring a more detailed calculation to establish the reliefs available.

In May 2006, HMRC published *Life Assurance Company Taxation: A Technical Consultative Document* to solicit views on how to simplify certain aspects of the tax law relating to life insurance companies. *Finance Act* 2007 subsequently contained the products of that consultation.

Broadly, the new legislation, which has effect for periods of account beginning on of after 1 January 2007, sets out the circumstances in which the profits of a life insurance company will be charged to corporation tax under trading income rather than under the 'I minus E' basis normally applying to such companies. New legislation also modifies the treatment of structural assets held by life insurance companies.

Categories of business

For the purposes of calculating tax payable on the I–E basis, life assurance business is divided into separate, ring fenced categories:

- pension business and overseas life assurance business (including, under self-assessment, overseas capital redemption business): each of which is distinct from the other, but both of which are taxable under miscellaneous income (formerly Sch. D, Case VI); and
- basic life assurance/general annuity business: which is taxed on investment income and gains less expenses.

Pension business is determined by reference to premiums from a specified source; overseas life assurance business (OLAB) is essentially business done through a non-UK branch or agency; basic life assurance/general annuity business is the remainder.

The actual computation of the amount of profits from each class of business which is taxed separately under miscellaneous income is made according to the trading income rules; profits are determined by reference to premium income, investment income and gains, less expenses and increases in liabilities (including certain reserves).

Pension business: exemption and charge on profits

Pension business investment income and chargeable gains are not chargeable to tax but this does not prevent pension business profits under miscellaneous income, *including* investment income and gains, being part of the overall profits subject to tax (see above). The miscellaneous income charge is done on a different basis.

As a result of the exemption, an insurance company may qualify for a repayment of tax deducted at source (but not, with effect from 2 July 1997, a repayment of tax credits; see 4600), which may be claimed in the year in which the income is received without waiting for the overall agreement of profits, under corporation tax self-assessment, according to the 'provisional fraction' shown in the latest return); the appropriate regulations provide that:

- repayments are to be reduced by a notional percentage set at–

  for accounting periods ending before 1 January 1994, by a notional percentage – 7.5 per cent,
  for accounting periods ending after 31 December 1993 and before 1 January 1995 – 12.5 per cent,
  for accounting periods ending after 31 December 1994 and before 1 January 1996 – 10 per cent, and
  for accounting periods ending after 31 December 1995 and before 1 January 1998 – 7.5 per cent,

- certain information must be included in a claim;
- interest may be charged when a provisional repayment proves to be excessive.

Where appropriate, a repayment claim may be reduced by any requirement under quarterly accounting arrangements (which largely disappeared after 5 April 1999) to account for tax due on interest on UK Government securities which have been paid gross in accordance with those arrangements.

A company cannot reclaim any tax by reference to receipts of foreign income dividends, including distributions treated as if they were foreign income distributions.

The repayment provisions described above also apply, with modifications (particularly as regards repayment of tax credits), to a friendly society with exempt life assurance business: see 4658.

Where a life insurance company is taxed on the I–E basis, and its capacity to set franked investment income against franked payments or against corporation tax is less than it would have been under trading income because of the exclusion of the policyholders' share, relief has hitherto been available by, inter alia, payment of tax credits. For accounting periods beginning after 31 December 1997, this method of relief is no longer be available. Relief will therefore only be available by set-off against, or repayment of, corporation tax.

Taxable profits and tax rate applicable

The offset of management expenses is restricted to general annuity/basic life assurance business (for accounting periods beginning before 1 January 1992, the restriction was to basic life assurance business alone). For accounting periods under self-assessment (CTSA – periods ending after 30 June 1999), a company's profits from capital redemption business will be worked out and taxed as if it were part of the company's life assurance business except where that capital redemption business was written before 1 January 1938 (in which case it will continue to be taxed as trading income).

There are several potential rates of corporation tax at which profits can be charged, depending on when profits are taxable, who is entitled to them, the nature of those profits and what type of company it is:

- from 1 January 1990 until 31 March 1996, the policyholders' share of life assurance business ('relevant') profits is taxed at a rate equal to the basic rate of income tax (for the year of assessment beginning in the financial year). Where the company is a mutual with no shareholders so that all profits are deemed to be held for policyholders, the whole of those profits are taxed at that rate. In a proprietary company the balance, being the shareholders' share, will be taxed at the full rate, marginal small companies' rate or small companies' rate as appropriate to the level of those profits; and

- with effect for the financial year 1996 onwards, in addition to the position described above, so much of the policyholders' share of the company's profits from basic life assurance/general annuity business as represents its 'lower rate income' will be subject to corporation tax at a rate equivalent to the lower rate of income tax (for the year of assessment beginning in the financial year). Where that basic life/general annuity business is mutual business (so that all profits are deemed to be held for policyholders) or, in a proprietary company, the policyholders' share is equal to relevant profits, or more than the profits from basic life assurance/general annuity business, then the investment income element of the whole of those profits is taxed at that rate. Otherwise, a further calculation must be made to determine the investment income (see further below).

Thus for example, a proprietary life assurance company is, on the I–E basis, potentially subject to three different rates of corporation tax:

- normal corporation tax on its shareholders' share of life assurance business profits and profits from non-life business – the actual rate applying being determined by the amount of those profits as with any company;
- a rate equivalent to the lower rate of income tax on the investment income element of its policyholders' share of profits from basic life/general annuity business; and
- a rate equivalent to the basic rate of income tax on the other policyholders' income and all policyholders' gains.

Neither the basic rate nor the lower rate apply to a proprietary company which is charged to tax under trading income (see 4603).

Establishing the amount of profits subject to reduced rates

For these purposes both 'relevant' and basic life assurance/general annuity profits are defined in a similar way as the income and gains of a company's life assurance business or basic life assurance and general annuity business respectively, reduced by the following items in so far as they are referable to that business:

- any non-trading deficit on the company's loan relationships;
- management expenses; and
- charges on income.

(Prior to 1995, this definition was not so clear cut so that a company was able to allocate charges against its shareholders' profits, taxable at a higher rate, to its advantage.)

Lower rate income

A company's 'lower rate income' is defined in similar terms to the savings income of individuals which is taxed at the lower rate, namely:

- income falling within non-trading loan relationship rules as it applies for corporation tax (profits or gains from loan relationships);
- distributions of a non-UK resident company which would be taxable under Sch. F had the company been UK-resident;
- the income element of purchased life annuities; and
- the element of any dividend and foreign income distributions from authorised unit trusts which is deemed to be an annual payment.

As described above, in order to determine the amount chargeable at the lower rate, a calculation must be made where an insurance company's basic life assurance and general annuity business is mutual business or the policyholder's share of the company's relevant profits is either the full amount of those profits or more than its profits from basic life and general annuity business. In these circumstances, the amount chargeable at the lower rate is calculated by multiplying the profits from basic life and general annuity business by the proportion which the 'lower rate income' bears to the total income and gains of that business ('the applicable proportion'). Where an insurance company's basic life assurance and general annuity business is *not* mutual business or the policyholder's share of the company's relevant profits is *less* than the full amount of those profits or its profits from basic life and general annuity business, the company's income chargeable at the lower rate is the 'applicable proportion' of the fraction obtained by dividing the policyholder's share of basic life and general annuity profits by the total such profits of the company.

The policyholders' share

In order to calculate the applicable rate of corporation tax, it is necessary to determine the policyholders' and shareholders' shares of profits respectively. This allocation is also important in the granting of reliefs as only shareholders' profits can benefit from set off of group relief or losses and, prior to 6 April 1999, only shareholders' franked investment income could frank the company's distributions and only tax on the shareholders' profits could be reduced by ACT paid.

As indicated above, in a mutual company all profits belong to policyholders by definition. No further apportionment is required to determine their share; all that is required is to calculate the amount of the savings income.

In a proprietary company however, profits must first be allocated between shareholders and policyholders. That is done by allocating to the policyholders the remainder of the profits after deduction of the trading income profits. The trading income profits used for these purposes were originally those after eliminating any pension business franked investment income on which payment of tax credits was claimed (see above), plus the shareholders' share (calculated by reference to a formula) of franked investment income and foreign income dividends. Following the withdrawal of the entitlement to payment of pension business tax credits, the adjustments for ascertaining the policyholders' share of relevant profits and franked investment income were amended. For these purposes, in arriving at the policyholders' share of relevant profits, the trading income profits are now only reduced by shareholders' franked investment income and (until abolition with effect from 6 April 1999) foreign income dividends, both of which are referable to the company's basic life assurance and general annuity business. This is effective for distributions made after 1 July 1997.

Where the deduction of the trading income profits from the life assurance profits produces a nil or negative figure, then all the profits are shareholders' profits and are taxed accordingly. Where there is still a balance of profits after deduction of the trading income profits, then that balance is the policyholders' share and should next be allocated between profits subject to corporation tax at rates equivalent to the basic and lower rate of income tax respectively (see above).

Overseas business

Special rules relate to overseas life assurance business including a wider tax base and a restriction of double tax credit relief. They apply generally for accounting periods beginning after 31 December 1989. Under self-assessment (CTSA – accounting periods ending after 30 June 1999), these rules also apply to capital redemption business where the policyholder is not resident in the UK. This is intended to remove an obstacle to UK-based companies selling capital redemption policies successfully in other European countries where this type of policy is more prevalent.

For overseas life assurance companies, see 4503.

Expenses of management for life assurance

There is no definition of 'expenses of management' in relation to life assurance companies (but see expenses of management generally: 4556) and judicial opinion is divided. The wider view is that expenses of management are those expenses normally deductible in calculating the liability of a life assurance business carried on by a life assurance company when the assessment is made on its profits as a trade. The narrower view holds that there should be a distinction between expenses *of* management, e.g. capital expenditure incurred in forming company policy, and expenses *by* management, e.g. expenses incurred in carrying out the day-to-day running of the company's business, (i.e. administration, maintenance, repairs, etc).

From 1 January 1990, expenses of management are subject to stricter rules. They are reduced by any refund, etc. of acquisition expenses (for which relief is separately permitted, below). They cannot include expenses referable to general annuity business, pension business or overseas life assurance business. Other reliefs and exemptions receive priority.

Acquisition expenses: spreading

From 1 January 1990, relief for 'acquisition expenses' is spread over a number of periods, spanning seven years, whilst reinsurance commissions are charged to tax in a similar manner – the net expenses are spread. 'Acquisition expenses' are defined as commissions, other expenses of management disbursed solely for the purpose of acquiring business, and so much of any other expenses of management as are disbursed partly for this purpose and partly for such other purpose as is properly attributable to it. From the total of such amounts there fall to be deducted repayments or refunds of such expenses. The acquisition of business includes the securing of the payment of increased or additional premiums in respect of existing policies.

The income element is the only amount in respect of annuities which is deductible as a charge on income. New mortality tables are to be used where the first payment falls after 30 March 1992.

The normal trading loss rules are used to determine whether a loss has been incurred and the way in which such a loss may be used notwithstanding that any profit would be aggregated with the return on the investment of premiums from policyholders. A number of proprietary companies had challenged this long-established interpretation.

Law: ICTA 1988, s. 76, 431(2)–(4), 434, 436, 437, 438, 438A, 441, 458A and Sch. 19AB; FA 1989, s. 85–89; F(No. 2)A 1992, s. 65; FA 1996, s. 164; F(No. 2)A 1997, Sch. 3, para. 3, 14; FA 2007, s. 38–42; *Insurance Companies (Pension Business) (Transitional Provisions) Regulations* 1992 (SI 1992/2326); *Insurance Companies (Capital Redemption Business) (Modification of the Corporation Taxes Acts) Regulations* 1999 (SI 1999/498); *Insurance Companies (Gilt-edged Securities) (Periodic Accounting for Tax on Interest) Regulations* 1999 (SI 1999/623); *Sun Life Assurance Society v Davidson (H.M. Inspector of Taxes) Phoenix Assurance Co., Ltd. v Logan (H.M. Inspector of Taxes)* (1954-1958) 37 TC 330; *Capital and National Trust Ltd v Golder (HMIT)* (1949) 31 TC 265; *Johnson (HMIT) v Prudential Assurance Co Ltd* [1998] BTC 112; *Prudential Assurance Co Ltd v Bibby (HMIT)* [1999] BTC 323

See *British Tax Reporter* ¶780-200.

LOCAL AUTHORITIES AND SIMILAR BODIES

4630   Tax exemptions for local authorities

Local authorities and local authority associations in the UK are exempt from all charges to income tax, corporation tax and CGT.

In England and Wales, a 'local authority' is any billing or precepting authority, a body which can issue a levy, an authority which can make or determine a rate, a combined police or fire authority, and a residuary body established under the *Local Government Act* 1992.

In Scotland, a local authority is any regional, islands, or district council (or any authority having power to requisition a sum from these councils) and any joint board or committee.

In Northern Ireland, a local authority is any authority with power to make or determine a rate or any authority with power to issue a precept, requisition or other demand for the payment of money to be raised out of a rate.

A rate is a rate whose proceeds are applicable for public local purposes and which is levied according to the value of land or other property.

Corporation Tax

Where a local authority issues securities to be expressed in a currency other than sterling, interest on those securities is paid without tax being deducted and is exempt from income tax if the beneficial owner is resident outside the UK. These rules only apply where the Treasury so directs. Corporation tax will still be payable.

Law: TCGA 1992, s. 271(3); CTA 2010, s. 984 and 1130

See *British Tax Reporter* ¶806-200.

4635　Health service bodies

'Health service bodies' enjoy exemption from income tax, corporation tax and capital gains tax. Gifts to such bodies are also exempt from capital gains tax (see 6189) and inheritance tax (see 7198).

A 'health service body' is a health authority or special health authority, a National Health Service trust, a Health Board or Special Health Board, the Common Services Agency for the Scottish Health Service, a State Hospital Management Committee in Scotland, the Dental Practice Board, the Scottish Dental Practice Board, and the Public Health Laboratory Service Board.

Law: TCGA 1992, s. 271(3); CTA 2010, s. 985 and 986

BUILDING SOCIETIES

4650　Charge to corporation tax

A building society is a 'company' for the purposes of the Taxes Acts and is therefore chargeable to corporation tax on its profits (see 3004). In the absence of specific provision, any dividends or interest paid by a building society on shares, etc. in the society would be a distribution for tax purposes; however special rules are applied.

For corporation tax purposes, dividends or interest payable in respect of shares in, or deposits with or loans to, a building society are dealt with as follows:

- liability to pay the dividends or interest are treated as arising under a loan relationship of the society (see 3036);
- dividends or interest payable to a company are treated as payable to the company in pursuance of a right arising under a loan relationship of the company;
- no part of such dividends or interest paid or credited is treated as a distribution of the society or as franked investment income of any company resident in the UK.

Building societies must deduct basic rate tax from dividends and interest on deposits: the detailed requirements are set out in regulations. The tax deducted is repayable where appropriate, though non-taxpayers can complete a certificate permitting gross payment, and certain other deposits are excluded by virtue of the nature of the investor. Companies generally receive interest gross from building societies, banks and other deposit takers (see 1372).

HMRC have access to information and inspection powers in respect of interest, etc. paid gross, though approved societies are excluded in respect of investments by persons not ordinarily resident in the UK.

Building societies must account quarterly for tax deducted on interest paid to investors. The quarterly periods end on the last day of May, August, November and February and tax is payable 14 days later.

Societies may be required to provide HMRC with information about interest payments or credits made to investors.

Law: CTA 2009, s. 498

See *British Tax Reporter* ¶805-850.

4652 Building societies: conversion to company status

Provisions were introduced in 1988 to cater for the transfer of the business of building societies to companies as provided for in the *Building Societies Act* 1986, s. 97.

The basic position is that the transfer can be effected without tax consequences (including exemption from stamp duty). Assets are transferred such that no tax charge arises.

Where a building society converts to company status, certificates of non-liability to tax and declarations by investors given or made before conversion which satisfy the building societies regulations (see 4650) are treated as having been given or made by the successor company.

Law: FA 1988, Sch. 12; *Income tax (Deposit-takers and Building Societies) (Interest Payments) Regulations* 2008 (SI 2008/2682), reg. 19

See *British Tax Reporter* ¶805-850.

4653 Building societies issuing permanent interest bearing shares

Building societies may issue a form of equity capital known as permanent interest bearing shares (PIBS). These are an additional form of core (Tier 1) capital. Special rules govern their tax treatment, largely as amendments to existing legislation.

Corporation Tax

Interest on PIBS is paid net of basic rate tax and societies do not obtain relief for interest in excess of a normal commercial rate.

Incidental costs of the issue of PIBS are allowable as loan relationship debits in the normal way for accounting periods beginning on or after 1 October 2002.

PIBS come within the accrued income scheme (see 1378).

There are exemptions from tax on capital gains in respect of sterling-denominated PIBS and the issue of PIBS to existing members on preferential terms.

Law: TCGA 1992, s. 117(4)–(6); ITA 2007, s. 619(1)(b)

See *British Tax Reporter* ¶806-860.

FRIENDLY SOCIETIES

4655   Unregistered friendly societies

An unregistered friendly society is an unincorporated mutual insurance association whose members subscribe for provident benefits on behalf of themselves and their families; it is a society which is neither an incorporated friendly society nor a registered friendly society (see 4658). If such a society has income of not more than £160 per year, it is exempt from income and corporation tax on either its income or its chargeable gains but must make a claim to be treated as exempt.

Law: ICTA 1988, s. 459

See *British Tax Reporter* ¶805-200.

4658   Incorporated or registered friendly societies

A friendly society may be incorporated or registered under the *Friendly Societies Act* 1992, although a society registered under the *Friendly Societies Act* 1974 is deemed to be registered under the 1992 Act. Incorporation of a society became available for the first time under the 1992 Act and there are provisions for assets to be transferred tax-free on incorporation and for the transferee to step into the shoes of the transferor.

Incorporated friendly societies and registered friendly societies are confusingly referred to as 'friendly societies', other societies being unregistered friendly societies (see 4655). If a 'friendly society' makes a claim it is exempt from income and corporation tax on its profits with certain exceptions: for life or endowment business the size of policies determines the extent of exemption while for other business the overall nature of its business is paramount;

for life or endowment business further conditions must also be met as to the types of policy made (see below).

As part of the general restrictions on the entitlement to tax credits included in *Finance (No. 2) Act* 1997 (see 3000), there are provisions which deny payable tax credits to pension providers which mirror the denial of tax credits to pension funds. However, unlike life assurance companies' pension business (see 4600, 4606), the entitlement to in-year payments of tax credits was preserved until 5 April 2004 in relation to friendly societies.

As a result of the exemption, a friendly society with exempt life assurance business may qualify for a repayment of tax deducted at source, which may be claimed in the year in which the income is received. The Treasury has made regulations providing for the tax attributable to a friendly society's tax-exempt business to be repaid at quarterly intervals in a similar manner to a life assurance company's exempt pension business (see 4606). The first accounting period to which the regulations apply is that commencing after 31 December 1993. If the life assurance business carried on by the friendly society is not subject to a tax exemption, its business and distributions are treated according to the same rules as apply to mutual life assurance companies, with minor modifications as noted below (see 4600ff., 4686).

Certain life assurance provisions relate primarily to the way in which income and gains are attributed or apportioned between different classes of business. These are modified so as to apply to friendly societies. The regulations (with effect from 1 January 1994 for registered friendly societies and from 19 February 1993 for incorporated friendly societies) provide for different rules for 'directive societies' and 'non-directive societies' – the directive in point is Directive 79/267 on the co-ordination of laws, regulations and administrative provisions relating to the taking up and pursuit of the business of direct life assurance, which applies to registered friendly societies with an annual contribution income of more than €500,000. The directive was implemented for these friendly societies by further regulations. Apart from applying 'linking provisions', etc. for matching income and gains with particular business similar to those which relate to insurance companies (see 4600), the regulations provide for relief for certain investor protection levies. These rules supplement previous modifications, largely treating as expenses of management Financial Services Act levies and referring to the Friendly Societies Act return.

Policies which are made on the basis that they will be non-exempt business generally remain so. For accounting periods ending after 24 July 1991, the exemption from tax does not apply to policies, etc. made after 19 March 1991 which are expressed at the outset not to be made in the course of tax exempt business, or on an election made before 1 August 1992, to similar policies made before then. Nor does it apply, on an election made before 1 August 1992, to policies made at any time if they are assumed to be non-exempt and conform with the standard form of policy.

Any payment made to a member of a friendly society, other than in the course of life or endowment business, is a qualifying distribution to the extent that it exceeds contributions or deposits made by the member to the society. This rule does not apply where the society's rules limit its business to providing benefits for or in respect of employees of a particular employer or another group of persons approved by the Registrar. The rule is not applicable where the society was registered before 27 March 1974 and its rules limit the aggregate amounts and deposits payable by members in contributions to no more than £1 per month.

There are some societies which are not eligible for relief at the direction of the Registrar of Friendly Societies or the Friendly Societies Commission.

The special rules relating to 'tax exempt' friendly societies (as opposed to tax exempt business) were withdrawn to bring them into line with 'mixed business' societies from 13 March 1984.

Transfers of business

Provisions preserve the continuity of taxation of life or endowment business following transfer to another friendly society so that the transferee essentially steps into the shoes of the transferor as regards losses, capital allowances, etc. However, if a society acquires any life or endowment business on a transfer after 31 December 1989 of long-term business of an insurance company as part of an approved reorganisation, the business acquired will not be regarded as tax exempt business.

Premium limits

The exemption from tax does not apply to profits from life or endowment business which consists of assurance of gross sums under contracts where total premiums payable in any 12-month period exceed £270 (lower limits applied prior to 1 May 1995) or the granting of annuities exceeds £156. Where premiums are payable more often than once a year, ten per cent of the premiums are disregarded in applying the limit.

Internal reorganisations

The status of particular business is preserved notwithstanding certain changes by societies with reference to size criteria (£2,000 gross assurance or £416 annuities limits within its rules). If the society changes its rules to restrict the amounts assured, its life or endowment business is exempt from tax only on contracts entered into after the change occurs. If restrictions already existing are removed, its life or endowment business is exempt on any contracts entered into before the change occurred. Where a society becomes incorporated, profits made before incorporation are still exempt and are treated as profits of a separate business. If a society acquires any life or endowment business on a transfer from, or amalgamation with, another society, the business acquired is treated in the same way as it was before the transfer.

Types of policy and benefits

The following conditions apply to insurance policies made or varied after 18 March 1985 in order for them to be qualifying policies (see below). Note that the ending of certification, announced by the *Finance Act* 1995, and due to take place with effect from 5 May 1996, has been deferred to a date to be appointed by the Board.

The policy issued by a friendly society claiming relief must satisfy certain conditions. In the case of a policy for the assurance of a gross sum or annuity, the term of the policy must last at least ten years unless it comes to an end on death or retirement due to ill-health. The premiums payable under the policy must be of equal or rateable amounts payable yearly or at more frequent intervals over the whole term of the policy or until the person making the payments or whose life is assured reaches a certain age. Where a policy satisfies these conditions, the society cannot vary the terms of that policy; this does not apply to certain changes between the passing of the *Finance Act* 1991 and 31 July 1992, nor to certain changes between 1 May 1995 and 31 March 1996.

Where the policy is to secure a gross sum which is a capital sum payable only on death occurring after an age not exceeding 16 is attained, that sum must not be less than 75 per cent of the total premiums payable (see below) if the beneficiary had died at 75. If the policy secures a capital sum payable only on survival for a specified term, that capital sum must be not less than 75 per cent of what the total premium would be if the policy ran for that term. When the policy secures a capital sum payable on survival for a specified term or earlier death or disability, the capital sum payable on death must be less than 75 per cent of the total premiums payable if the policy ran for its full term. However, if at the beginning of that term the beneficiary is over 55, the 75 per cent figure may be reduced for each year over that age by two per cent. If the policy does not secure a capital sum in the event of death before 16 or less, it must not provide for payment in that event of an amount exceeding the total premiums previously paid under it.

In determining the total premiums payable an amount of £10 (or ten per cent of the premiums if that is greater and the premiums are not annual premiums) may be ignored.

In respect of a policy which would otherwise be a qualifying policy, tax exemption will be denied if the benefits payable under all outstanding friendly society contracts with that policyholder exceed a given level. The level is calculated by reference to the total annual premiums payable – £270 (see above). Previously, the level was determined by reference to the gross sum assured.

In the case of a policy issued by a new society (i.e. a society registered after 3 May 1966) the contract for the insurance must be made by a member of the society over the age of 18. In respect of insurances made between 1 June 1984 and 19 March 1985, if any of the conditions for qualifying policies are infringed, the friendly society will not be entitled to a tax exemption on profits attributable to that policy.

From 19 March 1985, measures to relax the penalties against friendly society tax exempt life business which infringes the statutory requirements were introduced. Before the changes, a minor infringement by one policy could, in strictness, result in a pre-1966 society losing tax exempt status in respect of all its life business. If the Board so direct, such a defect will disqualify the offending policy but will not in general affect the tax exempt status of the society.

Corporation Tax

Law: ICTA 1988, s. 460–466 and Sch. 15; TCGA 1992, s. 217A and 217C; FA 1995, s. 55; FA 1998, s. 90(3); *Friendly Societies (Transfers of Other Business) (Modification of the Corporation Tax Acts) Regulations* 2008 (SI 2008/1942)

See *British Tax Reporter* ¶805-200.

4670 Industrial and provident societies

An industrial and provident society is a society registered under the *Industrial and Provident Societies Act* 1965. Any share or loan interest paid to its members is not treated as a distribution.

These payments are deductible in calculating the income from the society's trade. If the society does not carry on a trade, the payments are treated as charges on income.

Every society must make a return to HMRC within three months of the end of its accounting period and if it fails to do so, the share or loan interest paid by the society is not deductible in calculating the society's income nor can it be treated as a charge on income.

The same rules apply to co-operative associations which have as their object, or primary object, helping members to carry on agricultural, horticultural or fishery businesses (and, by concession, prior to 1 April 2010, one could look through second and third-tier agricultural associations). A 'co-operative association' means a body of persons with a written constitution from which the minister is satisfied that the body is a co-operative association in substance. The minister must take account of the way in which the income is to be applied for its members' benefit and to all relevant provisions.

The minister refers to the Minister for Agriculture, Fisheries and Food for England and Wales; the Secretary of State for Scotland; and the Minister of Agriculture for Northern Ireland.

Law: CTA 2009, s. 499 and 500

Source: ESC C13

See *British Tax Reporter* ¶805-450.

MUTUAL COMPANIES

4680 Introduction to mutual companies

A mutual business is one where the persons carrying on the business are customers as well as traders and are entitled to any profits made. The profits of such a company are not liable to a charge to tax.

The 'distributions' (see 3067) of companies carrying on mutual business or carrying on no business at all are subject to special rules.

Proceeds from investment income are taxable but distributions by a mutual company to its members are taxed as distributions (formerly, under Sch. F) if they are made out of profits subject to corporation tax or out of 'franked investment income' (see 3077). Where a club distributes any surplus from its mutual trading to its members, it is not charged to tax.

Law: CTA 2010, s. 1070

See *British Tax Reporter* ¶806-800.

4683 Building society interest received by mutual company

If a 'mutual company' (see 4680) receives building society interest it is treated as a net amount and grossed up. The amount grossed up is then taxed at the appropriate corporation tax rate and the income tax notionally deducted from the interest can be set off against the total corporation tax liability.

Law: CTA 2010, s. 1070

See *British Tax Reporter* ¶806-800.

4686 Mutual life assurance companies

If a mutual life assurance company makes distributions, they are not treated as distributions if the recipient took part in the mutual activities of the business resulting in the distribution. The person receiving the distribution is not affected by the fact that the company making it carries on a mutual business.

Law: CTA 2010, s. 1070

See *British Tax Reporter* ¶806-800.

4689 Non-trading companies

Where a company is not a trading company and does not hold investments and is not established to carry on a trade or investment business, its distributions are not treated as such except in so far as they are made out of the company's profits charged to corporation tax or out of franked investment income.

On dissolution, the members of an unincorporated association of a social or recreational nature which has not carried on a trade or investment business may opt to have distributions

Corporation Tax

to members treated as capital instead of income where the amount distributed to each member is not large.

Law: CTA 2010, s. 1070 and 1071

Source: ESC C15

See *British Tax Reporter* ¶806-950.

4692   Trade unions

Generally, a registered trade union is exempt from income and corporation tax in respect of non-trading income applicable to and applied for provident benefits. Provident benefits are any payment made to a member during sickness or incapacity from personal injury or while out of work. The payment must be authorised by the trade union's own rules. A special fund must be set up to make such payments.

Subject to certain conditions, a registered trade union is entitled to exemption from tax in respect of its income and capital gains which, as provided for under the rules of the union, are used for purposes of provident benefits.

The following expenses incurred by a registered trade union are regarded in a statement of practice as payments made for the purpose of provident benefits:

- legal expenses in representing members at industrial tribunal hearings of cases alleging unfair dismissal;
- legal expenses in connection with a member's claim in respect of an accident or injury he has suffered; and
- general administrative expenses of providing provident benefits.

HMRC take the view that any trade union which has not already made a claim for relief for expenses incurred before the issue of the statement referred to above may make a supplementary claim provided that that claim is made within the statutory time-limit (usually six years after the end of the relevant chargeable period).

To qualify for exemption, a trade union must be registered under the *Trade Union and Labour Relations Act* 1974. A special relief is available for any unions deregistered under the *Industrial Relations Act* 1971 or any trade unions formed after 1971, which have failed to register. For purposes of this rule, a registration under the 1974 Act is retrospective.

The exemption also applies to police federations and employer associations listed in the record of employer associations kept under the *Trade Union and Labour Relations Act* 1974.

The union will qualify for relief provided it is not authorised to assure the sum of more than £4,000 nor to grant an annuity of over £825 per year. To gain exemption, the union must make a claim to the inspector and any appeal from his decision must be made to the special commissioners.

Law: CTA 2010, s. 981–983

Source: SP 1/84

See *British Tax Reporter* ¶805-600.

BANKS AND SIMILAR DEPOSIT TAKERS

4699   Introduction to banks and similar deposit takers

Whilst banks and similar financial institutions are involved in a special type of business which is subject to various commercial controls, they are not generally distinguished from other taxpayers for tax purposes. They are, however, required to operate a special tax deduction scheme (see 4700).

Special provisions apply to savings banks (see 4707).

There is also a relief for deposit-takers which are wound up and which were insolvent when the winding-up commenced or which become insolvent within the following 12 months. Most income arising from the discontinued trade and not otherwise taxed is treated as chargeable as miscellaneous income (formerly, under Sch. D, Case VI) but with relief for expenses which would have been allowable had the trade continued and for trading losses unrelieved at the date of discontinuance. An election may be made to relate back the charge to the date of discontinuance.

Law: CTA 2010, Pt. 13, Ch. 6

4700   Deduction of tax by banks from relevant deposit interest

Banks and other deposit takers must deduct income tax from interest, etc. on many deposits. The rate of deduction is 20 per cent. The bank will account to HMRC for the tax deducted. The tax deducted will be repayable where appropriate, although non-taxpayers can complete a certificate permitting gross payment and interest on certain other deposits is payable gross (see 1372). The detailed requirements are set out in regulations. The amount received by the recipient is grossed up at the basic rate and used to calculate any higher rate tax which may be payable. Foreign currency deposits were brought into the scheme from 6 April 1986.

Such tax deduction applies to the Bank of England, any recognised bank, the post office, local authorities and any person who receives deposits in the course of his business and who is prescribed as a deposit taker. Such persons include the British Railways Board. Solicitors' and estate agents' undesignated client accounts and Lloyd's premium trust funds are excluded from the scheme.

Corporation Tax

The scheme does not apply to deposits of individuals who are not ordinarily resident in the UK nor to certain special deposits. HMRC have access to information and inspection powers in respect of interest paid gross, though approved banks are excluded in relation to investments by persons not ordinarily resident.

Law: ITA 2007, Pt. 15, Ch. 2

4707   Savings banks

Savings banks are divided into two categories:

- companies which are successors to the Trustee Savings Bank; and
- other savings banks.

Savings banks other than successors to trustee savings banks are 'investment companies' (see 4553) and therefore entitled to the same allowances and deductions for management expenses, etc. as any other investment company (see 4556).

Successors to the Trustee Savings Bank are treated as companies subject to general rules.

See *British Tax Reporter* ¶805-000.

CONTROLLED FOREIGN COMPANIES

4713   Scope of CFC legislation

Provisions were introduced in 1984 to prevent UK companies from avoiding UK tax by diverting income to subsidiaries in tax havens. The provisions apply to any 'controlled foreign company' (CFC), i.e. a company which:

(1)   is not resident in the UK (see 3014 regarding companies which cease to be UK-resident under the provisions applicable to dual resident companies), but which is controlled by individuals or companies that are UK-resident; and

(2)   is subject to a level of tax on income less than three-quarters of what it would have been had it been resident in the UK.

Note that the comparison between the tax which would have been paid in the UK and that which applies in the other country should be made by reference to the amount of tax actually *paid* and not the tax rate applying to the profits of the CFC (see example below).

Companies with foreign subsidiaries which are engaged in genuine trading activities in their country of residence, or which regularly distribute their profits back to the UK will be unlikely to be affected by the CFC regime.

From 22 March 2006 companies that became tax resident outside the UK before 1 April 2002 by operation of a double tax treaty are brought within the CFC rules.

Control and the '40 per cent' test

A new definition of 'control' for the purposes of determining whether a company was is within the CFC regimes was introduced by the *Finance Act* 2000. Broadly, with effect from 21 March 2000, 'control' is defined as the ability to secure that a company's affairs are conducted with the wishes of the person exercising the control, whether through share or votes or via the articles of association of other documents. In addition, a '40 per cent test', similar to that applying under the 'transfer pricing regime' is used to determine whether or not a CFC is under the control of two persons, at least one of whom is UK resident. The test is satisfied where each of the two persons, who together control the company, have at least 40 per cent of the interests, rights and powers. The test is of use to HMRC where one of the persons satisfying the 40 per cent test is non-resident. The effect is to extend control by UK residents to include the situation where:

- the company is controlled by two persons who together meet the new definition of control;
- each of them individually satisfies the 40 per cent test; and
- only one of them is UK resident.

The company is deemed to be controlled by the UK resident and is potentially a CFC.

Previously, control was determined in accordance with the meaning close companies definition (see 4250) but by reference to person resident in the UK rather than five or fewer participators.

The territory of residence

A company's residence is the territory in which it is liable to tax by reason of domicile (see 219), residence or place of management (see 214).

If there is more than one such territory, its residence is the place where it is effectively managed. After corporation tax self-assessment (which applies in respect of accounting periods ending after 30 June 1999), where the normal rules do not produce a single territory of residence, holders of a majority UK assessable interest in the CFC (see 4719) may elect for it to be treated as resident in a specific territory; if no election is made, HMRC may designate, on a just and reasonable basis, the territory of residence.

Excluded countries list

A company which is resident and carrying on business in a country appearing on a list (originally published by the Revenue on 5 October 1993) will be treated as meeting the statutory exclusion conditions, subject to any qualification set out in the list for the country concerned (see 4716).

Responsibility for establishing a charge

Prior to the introduction of self-assessment (CTSA), a charge to tax only arises if HMRC so direct. A direction will not be made unless the UK company, together with connected or

Corporation Tax

associated persons, has at least a ten per cent 'share' of the CFC's profits. For appeals against CFC directions, see 4722.

Under CTSA, this direction requirement is removed, so that the charge applies automatically if the necessary conditions are met. A charge will not apply unless the UK company, together with connected or associated persons, has at least a 25 per cent 'share' of the CFC's profits. The onus is on the UK company to include an apportionment of the profits of a CFC in its annual return. A special supplementary page is provided for this purpose. In the original consultation document announcing the CTSA proposals for CFCs it was stated:

> 'Penalties would not be charged where a company could demonstrate that it had made reasonable efforts to get its self assessment of its CFC liabilities right.'

The charge to tax

The charge is calculated by reference to the profits of the overseas company. For accounting periods beginning on or after 23 March 1995 (the appointed day for the FOREX provisions: see 4713) the home country currency (that in which the accounts are required) is to be used to compute the profits which are then translated on a closing rate basis.

Regulations dealing with various features specific to CFCs carrying on general insurance business have been published. In particular, the regulations will allow companies using a recognised form of non-annual accounting to benefit from the exemption for CFCs.

The following flowchart summarises the initial steps to take in ascertaining whether or not a company is a CFC:

For an accounting period is the company:

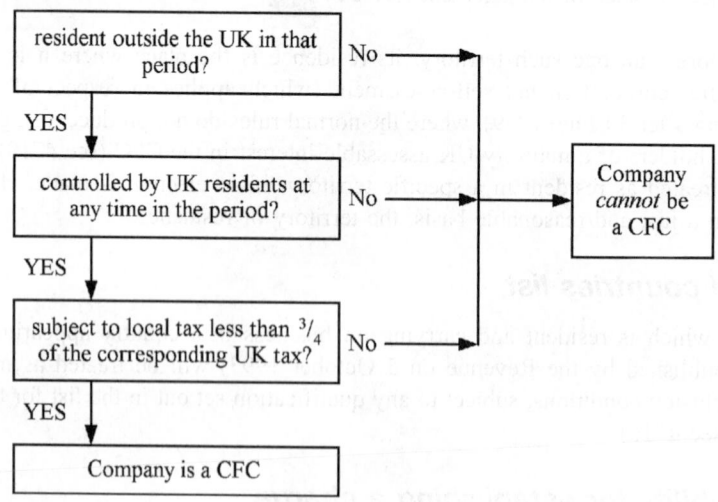

The following example illustrates the above points:

Example

Transalp Ltd is a company not resident in the UK but controlled by UK residents. It has income for an accounting period of £500,000 on which it has suffered tax in a third country, other than its country of residence, of £50,000. Assuming a rate of taxation in its own territory of 25 per cent and UK corporation tax of 33 per cent, the comparison is made as follows:

	Own territory		UK equivalent	
	%	£	%	£
Full rate of tax	25	125,000	33	165,000
Relief for foreign tax		(50,000)		(50,000)
Net tax payable		75,000		115,000
Total tax bill		125,000		165,000

Comparison – more than $^3/_4$ (75 per cent) of UK CT?

Tax rate:	$^{25}/_{33}$	= 75.76% not statutory test
Total tax:	$^{125,000}/_{165,000}$	= 75.76% not statutory test
Local/UK tax:	$^{75,000}/_{115,000}$	= 65.22% *statutory test*

Transalp Ltd is subject to a lower level of taxation and is therefore a CFC potentially subject to a charge unless it qualifies for one of the available exceptions (see 4716). In determining whether or not its overall tax burden is more than three-quarters of the total equivalent UK charge, tax in another territory is deducted.

Law: ICTA 1988, s. 747–756 and Sch. 25; *Vodafone 2 v R & C Commrs* (2007) Sp C 622

See *British Tax Reporter* ¶770-000.

4716 Companies excluded from CFC provisions

No charge is made on some CFCs' income because of a variety of exclusions in the legislation. There are five main ways in which CFCs may escape the charge to tax (see 4713). However, the Treasury has the power to specify in regulations jurisdictions where the exemptions will not apply. Thus, all CFCs in that jurisdiction would be within the charge to tax. The aim is to protect the UK against jurisdictions indulging in 'harmful tax practices'.

(1) The 'acceptable distribution policy' test (accounting periods beginning before 1 July 2009)

For accounting periods commencing prior to 1 July 2009, no charge will arise in respect of a CFC for an accounting period in which it pursued an 'acceptable distribution policy'. For the changes made by FA 2009, see 4720.

Corporation Tax

To satisfy this test, the CFC must have distributed at least 90 per cent of the company's available profits. For accounting periods ending after 29 November 1993 the 90 per cent test was quantified by reference to taxable profits less capital gains and tax suffered.

Dividends could have been channelled through intermediary non-resident companies. The test was satisfied if the dividend was paid within 18 months after the end of the accounting period to which it related.

The dividend must have been taken into account in computing the recipient's income for corporation tax. For accounting periods ending after 29 November 1993, the requirement that dividends be paid out of profits of the relevant period was relaxed for non-trading CFCs to allow distributions to be made out of profits from earlier periods. However, for distributions made on or after 9 March 1999, the test could not be satisfied to the extent that the CFC was effectively distributing franked investment income which it had received from a UK company.

(2) The 'exempt activities' test

No charge will arise in respect of a CFC for an accounting period throughout which it is engaged in 'exempt activities'. To meet this test the CFC must have a business establishment in the territory in which it is resident, and its business affairs must be effectively managed there. In addition, its main business must not consist of investment business or dealing in goods for delivery to or from the UK. The purpose of this test is to exclude automatically those CFCs which, because of the nature of their activities, can reasonably be assumed not to be being used to avoid UK tax.

The requirements for satisfaction of the test were tightened for accounting periods beginning after 20 March 2000. For such accounting periods the list of activities excluded from satisfying the exempt activities test is extended to include service companies.

For the changes made by FA 2009, see 4720.

Clearance procedure for non-trading CFCs

For non-trading CFCs, HMRC are prepared to confirm that, on the facts provided, a company will not be subject to the CFC charge because it satisfies either the exempt activities test (above) or the motive test (below). Details of how to make an application and guidance on the information which will need to be supplied can be obtained from International Division 412, Room 311, Melbourne House, Aldwych, London WC2B 4LL or tel: (020) 7438 6495.

Guidance notes on the application of the CFC rules under self-assessment (CTSA) have been published. These contain details of a new CFC clearance procedure which begins on 1 January 1999.

(3) The 'motive' test

No charge will arise if the CFC's transactions were carried out for bona fide commercial reasons, and it was not the main purpose of these transactions to achieve a significant reduction of UK tax, nor a main reason for the company's existence to divert profits from the UK. See above regarding HMRC clearance that a company satisfies the motive test.

In the earlier *Cadbury Schweppes* case, the ECJ found that the UK CFC rules would comply with EU law if only profits arising from 'wholly artificial arrangements' were taxable. It was left up to the UK courts to decide if the CFC rules, and in particular the motive test at ICTA 1988, s. 748(3), achieved this objective and this has been the subject of *Vodafone 2*. Vodafone contended that the UK CFC rules, and in particular s. 748(3), could not be interpreted in this way but the special commissioners found in favour of HMRC (*Vodafone 2 v R & C Commrs*), concluding that s. 748(3) was capable of being construed as being in conformity with the right of freedom of establishment under the *European Communities Act 1972*, s. 2, art. 43.

This judgment was overturned by the High Court in July 2008 (*Vodafone 2 v R & C Commrs*).

The case was subsequently heard by the Court of Appeal which found in favour of HMRC in a decision released in May 2009. Importantly, the Court of Appeal considered the CFC rules in their entirety and did not restrict itself to considering only the motive test at s. 748(3): 'the obligation of the national court is to examine the whole of the national law to consider how far it may be applied so as to conform to enforceable Community rights' (para. 34). In so doing, the Court of Appeal found that 'the grain or thrust of the legislation recognises that the wide net cast by s. 747(3) is intended to be narrowed by s. 748' (para. 44). Consequently, all that is required for the UK CFC rules to be compatible with EU law is for the following additional exemption to be read into the legislation at s. 748(1) or at s. 748(3) (para. 39): 'if it is, in that accounting period, actually established in another member state of the EEA and carries on genuine economic activities there'.

(4) Public quotation test

For accounting periods commencing before 6 December 2006, no charge will arise in respect of a CFC for an accounting period in which it fulfilled the 'public quotation' test.

(5) Small profits test

No charge will arise if the CFC's profits for a 12-month period do not exceed £50,000.

Note that profits apportioned to a UK shareholder in a CFC are not income from the non-resident company for the purposes of any double tax treaty. Thus, UK source income of a Netherlands company controlled by a UK company ('the taxpayer'), in this case interest paid by another UK company, was to be apportioned to the taxpayer, the Netherlands company's only shareholder. The terms of art. 11 of the UK–Netherlands double taxation

Corporation Tax

agreement did not exempt the shareholders of a CFC from a liability to UK tax under the CFC provisions.

'Excluded countries list'

The 'excluded countries list' may be referred to in order to establish whether or not a company located in a particular country can be regarded as prima facie outside the CFC provisions providing it is resident *and* carrying on business in that country. Originally the list was published as part of a Revenue press release although it has been updated since then. Under CTSA, regulations replace the non-statutory excluded countries list.

The list was first published as an indication that a company satisfied the motive test (see above) although it appears to be based on levels of taxation. It is in two parts:

Part I – companies resident in countries in this part will not be charged under the CFC provisions; and

Part II – companies resident in countries in this part will only be charged under the CFC provisions if they benefit from specified reliefs (which usually provide for a favourable tax rate or exemption from tax altogether).

The following flowchart summarises the available exclusions from a CFC charge:

Does the CFC:

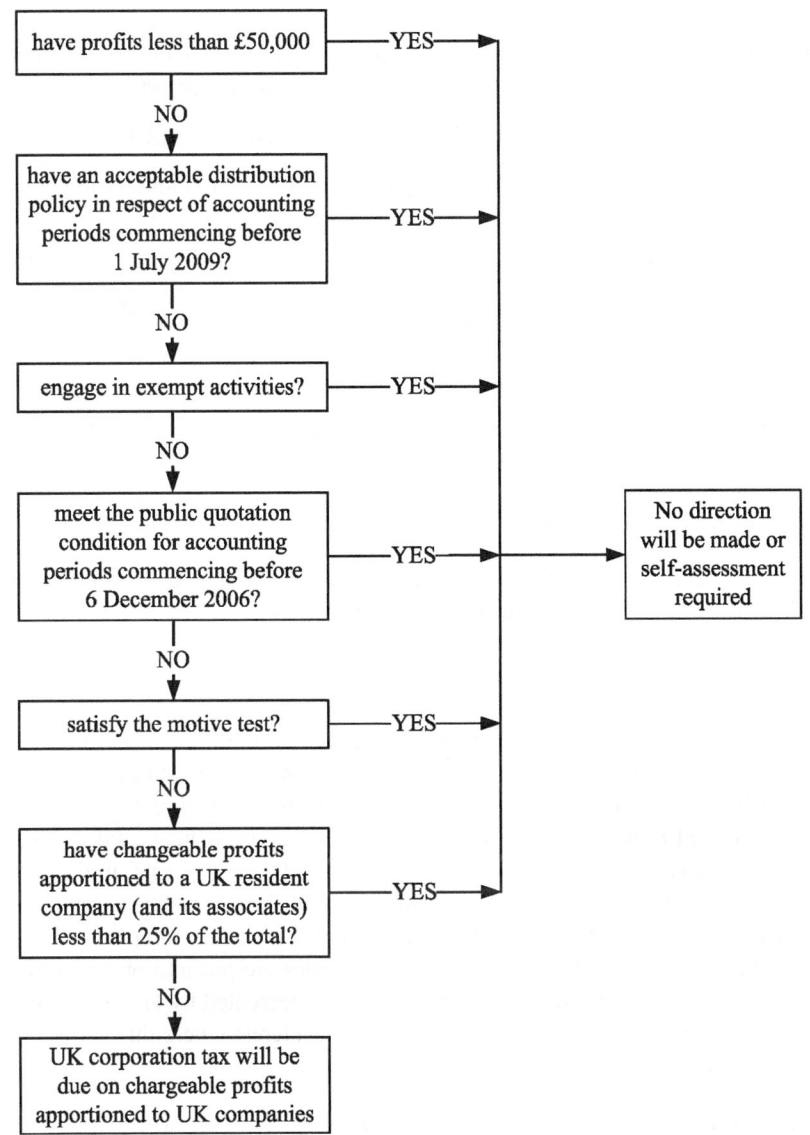

Law: ICTA 1988, s. 747, 748 748A and Sch. 25; FA 2000, s. 104 and Sch. 31; *Controlled Foreign Companies (Excluded Countries) Regulations* 1998 (SI 1998/3081); *Vodafone 2 v R&C Commrs* (2007) Sp C 622; *Vodafone 2 v R & C Commrs* [2008] BTC 526; *Bricom Holdings Ltd v IR Commrs* [1997] BTC 471

See *British Tax Reporter* ¶771-800.

4719   Apportionment of chargeable profits

Where a tax charge arises in respect of a CFC (see 4713), the notional UK tax is apportioned to persons with an interest in the CFC. An interested person is one who:

(1)   possesses or is entitled to acquire shares or voting rights in the CFC;

(2)   possesses, or is entitled to acquire, a right to receive distributions or any payment to loan creditors by way of premium on redemption;

(3)   is entitled to secure that income or assets of the company will be applied directly or indirectly for its benefit (unless the entitlement is contingent upon default of the company under any agreement and the default has not occurred);

(4)   has control of the CFC either alone or together with others.

Rights which a person has as a loan creditor do not constitute an interest in the company for the above purposes.

Method of apportionment

Once it has been decided who has an interest in the CFC, the next step is to determine the proportion in which the CFC's chargeable profits are to be allocated to those persons. The profits (and 'creditable tax') are apportioned according to the respective interests of the persons who at any time during the accounting period in question have had an interest.

The self-assessment rules enable a UK company to apportion to itself the appropriate amount of a CFC's chargeable profits and creditable tax. Where all holdings in a CFC are by means of ordinary shares, the apportionment will be made in direct proportion to the percentage of issued ordinary shares. In any other case, apportionment will be made on a just and reasonable basis among the persons who have 'relevant interests' in the CFC at any time in the relevant accounting period. A means of establishing which interests are relevant interests is provided, the aim being to identify the UK-resident company or companies which hold the most direct interest in the CFC. The rules are put into practical effect by a formula to establish the proportion of ordinary shares represented by an indirect holding of ordinary shares, and a formula to compute the relevant interest where this varies during the accounting period.

Law: ICTA 1988, s. 749(5)–(7), 749B, 752, 752A–752C and 756(3)

See *British Tax Reporter* ¶770-900.

4720   CFC transitional provisions following FA 2009

No apportionment may be made in respect of a CFC for an accounting period beginning before 1 July 2009 in which it pursues an 'acceptable distribution policy' (ADP), within the meaning of former ICTA 1988, Sch. 25, Part I (former ICTA 1988, s. 748(1)(a)). The ADP rules were repealed by FA 2009 with effect for accounting periods of CFCs beginning on or after 1 July 2009, subject to transitional provisions designed to ensure that the ADP and associated rules continue to apply to profits which accrued before 1 July 2009 (FA 2009, Sch. 16, para. 6–8).

Transitional provisions

Where the accounting period of a CFC straddles 1 July 2009 (i.e. begins before and ends after that date), the period to 30 June 2009 and the period from 1 July 2009 are to be treated as separate accounting periods for the purposes of ICTA 1988, Part 17, Ch. 4 (the CFC rules) and ICTA 1988, Part 18 (double tax relief). The CFC's chargeable profits and its creditable tax are to be apportioned between the two deemed periods on 'a just and reasonable basis' (FA 2009, Sch. 16, para. 7(2)(b)). Should a dividend be paid in the second of the two deemed periods (i.e. the part of the accounting period beginning on 1 July 2009), ICTA 1988, s. 799 has effect as if the reference to 'the last period for which accounts were made up which ended before the dividend became payable' (s. 799(3)(c)) was to the first of the deemed periods (i.e. the part of the accounting period ended on 30 June 2009).

It is made clear at FA 2009, Sch. 16, para. 8(1) that the amendments made by FA 2009 to the ADP rules do not affect the application of the ADP rules formerly at ICTA 1988, Sch. 25, Part 1, nor the application of ICTA 1988, s. 801, former s. 801C and 803A (underlying tax on ADP dividends), in relation to dividends paid on or after 1 July 2009 if they are paid for accounting periods beginning before that date.

Exempt activities test: holding companies

The exempt activities test has a number of conditions that have to be satisfied before the exemption is available. These include: the 'business establishment' and 'effective management' conditions. In addition, there is a third condition which relates to the nature and activities of the subsidiaries from which it derives the bulk of its income.

Significant changes were made to this third test by FA 2009 as part of the introduction of a revised regime for the taxation of the foreign profits of companies. Prior to the FA 2009 changes, exemption was available to local holding companies, non-local holding companies and superior holding companies. For CFCs which are not qualifying holding companies, only the local holding company exemption remains after 1 July 2009. For CFCs which are qualifying holding companies, the non-local holding companies and the superior holding companies exemptions remain, subject to additional conditions, but only until 1 July 2011.

Meaning of 'qualifying holding company'

As stated above, different rules apply to qualifying holding companies and to companies which are not qualifying holding companies after 1 July 2009. For the purposes of these rules (FA 2009, Sch. 16, Part 2), a CFC is a qualifying holding company if it is an exempt holding company in relation to the last accounting period to end before 1 July 2009. The deemed accounting periods created by FA 2009, Sch. 16, para. 14 and 15 are ignored for this purpose. A company is an 'exempt holding company' in respect of a period if it is engaged in exempt activities within the meaning of ICTA 1988, Sch. 25, Part 2 throughout that

Corporation Tax

849

period and if the special rules applying to non-local and superior holding companies (ICTA 1988, Sch. 25, para. 6(4), (4A)) apply to the company in relation to that period.

FA 2009 removes the non-local holding company exemptions and superior holding companies exemptions. For companies which are qualifying holding companies as defined at FA 2009, Sch. 16, para. 13, these changes are effective for accounting periods of the CFC beginning on or after 1 July 2011 and not 1 July 2009 as is the case for companies which are not qualifying holding companies. However, 1 July 2009 does mark the beginning of the two-year transitional period for qualifying holding companies during which the non-local holding company and superior holding company exemptions continue to be available subject to the conditions at FA 2009, Sch. 16, para. 17.

Two-year transitional period

The special rules at FA 2009, Sch. 16, para. 17 apply to relevant accounting periods, being accounting periods of qualifying holding companies which begin on or after 1 July 2009 and end on or before 1 July 2011. Where the provisions at FA 2009, Sch. 16, para. 17 apply, ICTA 1988, Sch. 25, para. 6(4) and (4A) (the exemptions for non-local holding companies and superior holding companies) have effect only if new conditions relating to ownership (Condition A) and non-qualifying gross income (Condition B) are met.

Condition A
To satisfy condition A, the CFC must be a member of a group with the same ultimate corporate parent at 9 December 2008 and at all times during the accounting period in question.

The ultimate corporate parent is the corporate member of the group which is not a subsidiary of another body corporate. The terms 'group' and 'subsidiary' have the meaning given by International Accounting Standards. A body corporate does not include:

- the Crown;
- a Minister of the Crown;
- a government department;
- a Northern Ireland department; or
- a foreign sovereign power.

Condition B
To satisfy condition B, the CFC's non-qualifying gross income in the accounting period in question (amount X in the legislation) must not exceed the highest amount of its non-qualifying gross income for any of up to three reference periods (amount Y in the legislation).

'Non-qualifying gross income' is income which does not satisfy the local holding company, the non-local holding company and the superior holding company tests at ICTA 1988, Sch. 25, para. 6(3), (4) and (5).

For a period to be a reference period it must be one of the last three accounting periods to have ended before 9 December 2008 and it must be a period in relation to which the company is an exempt holding company. Where there is no reference period, amount Y is the gross non-qualifying income for the 12 months ending with 9 December 2008.

An anti-avoidance provision applies where, on or after 9 December 2008, a company changes its accounting reference date so that a period (period A) which would otherwise have fallen in an accounting period ending on or after 9 December 2008 falls instead in an accounting period ending before that date. Where this provision applies, the definition of 'relevant period' is amended with the effect that only the last three accounting periods ended before the beginning of period A can be reference periods.

Accounting periods straddling 1 July 2011

Where an accounting period of a CFC straddles 1 July 2011 (i.e. begins before and ends after 1 July 2011), it is to be divided into two deemed accounting periods for the purposes of ICTA 1988, Pt. 17, Ch. 4 (rules applying to CFCs); the first being the period to 30 June and the second being the period from 1 July (FA 2009, Sch. 16, para. 15). The company's gross income, chargeable profits and creditable tax for the accounting period are to be divided between the two deemed accounting periods on a time basis.

A number of significant changes were made to the taxation of the foreign profits of companies by FA 2009. For most companies, the most important of these changes was the replacement of the exemption for UK distributions, and the credit system for the taxation of foreign dividends, with a broad exemption applying to UK and foreign dividends received by companies (Part 9A of CTA 2009).

The charge to tax on distributions received on or after 1 July 2009 is considered in 3085.

Law: FA 2009, Sch. 16

See *British Tax Reporter* ¶771-900, ¶772-900

4725   Designer rate regimes

Broadly, for accounting periods beginning on or after 6 October 1999, anti-avoidance rules apply to counter the use of so-called 'designer tax regimes'.

The legislation deems a company resident outside the UK, but subject to an effective rate of tax of 75 per cent or more of the UK equivalent tax on those profits, nevertheless to be subject to a lower level of taxation for CFC purposes in the accounting period concerned where the local tax is determined by 'designer rate' provisions. The legislation does not actually define 'designer rate' regimes beyond granting the power to name them in regulations. In practice, the provisions are directed towards territories that effectively permit a company resident there to choose its rate of tax to enable it to circumvent the three-quarters of UK tax rule.

Corporation Tax

The regimes already named in regulations are those which apply to the following bodies:

- Guernsey – bodies with international tax status;
- Jersey – international business companies;
- Isle of Man – international companies;
- Gibraltar – income tax qualifying companies; and
- Ireland – companies taxed in accordance with the *Irish Taxes Consolidation Act* 1997, s. 448(7).

Law: FA 2000, s. 104 and Sch. 31; ICTA 1988, s. 750A

See *British Tax Reporter* ¶773-450.

4730 Shipping companies

As an alternative to a corporation tax charge based on its shipping profits, a shipping company may elect to use the tonnage tax regime and instead pay corporation tax by reference to its tonnage tax profits. The tonnage tax profits are calculated by reference to a fixed profit table per 100 net tons as follows:

	£
For each 100 tons up to 1,000 tons	0.60
For each 100 tons between 1,000 and 10,000 tons	0.45
For each 100 tons between 10,000 and 25,000 tons	0.30
For each 100 tons over 25,000 tons	0.15

Where the company meets certain criteria and wishes to use the tonnage tax regime, an election must be made. Initially the election had to be made during the 12 months from 28 July 2000 and normally took place from the start of the next accounting period. The election had to be made before the end of the period of 12 months beginning with the day on which the company became a qualifying company. Further regulations published in June 2005 provide a further opportunity for shipping companies that previously chose not to make an election to now make that election at any time in the 18 months from 1 July 2005 to 31 December 2006.

For a company to be a qualifying company, it must be subject to corporation tax, operate qualifying ships and strategically and commercial manage those ships in the UK. A qualifying ship is one that is over 100 tons and which is used for the carriage of passengers or cargo or for towage, salvage or other marine assistance or transport of type necessarily provided at sea. Certain types of vessels, such as fishing vessels and pleasure craft, harbour ferries and offshore installations are specifically excluded from the tonnage tax regime.

Special rules exist to restrict a lessor's entitlement to capital allowances to most long-term leasing arrangements (see 1260), rather than just where the lease is a finance lease. There are exceptions for ordinary chartering arrangements made between shipping companies. *Finance Act* 2003 introduces provisions to extend the restrictions in certain cases. The new measures apply to leases entered into on or after 19 December 2002.

Law: FA 2000, s. 82 and Sch. 22; FA 2003, s. 169; *Tonnage Tax (Further Opportunity for Election) Order* 2005 (SI 2005/1449); *Tonnage Tax (Exception of Financial Year 2005) Order 2005* (SI 2005/1480); *Tonnage Tax (Training Requirement) Regulations* 2000 (SI 2000/2129)

See *British Tax Reporter* ¶790-000.

4740   Companies in liquidation or receivership

The position of the liquidator of a company in relation to that company differs from that of the receiver or administrator of the assets of the company whose powers are governed by the terms of his appointment.

Liquidation

On commencement of the winding-up of a company its accounting period comes to an end and a new one starts; thereafter, until the completion of the winding-up, each accounting period spans 12 months except that an accounting period ends if a date is agreed with HMRC as a likely completion date.

Where a company ceases to be in liquidation without actually being wound up then the fixed 12-month accounting period rule that is normal from the start of liquidation will cease to apply.

A company in liquidation may well be a close investment-holding company (see 4280ff.).

For the financial year in which the winding-up is completed special provisions may determine which rate of corporation tax or ACT is applicable. After corporation tax self-assessment, interest on overpaid tax will be taxable (see 4968). However, there will be no liability where such interest does not exceed £2,000.

Prior to abolition of ACT, no ACT liability arose in respect of a distribution made in respect of share capital on the winding-up as this is not treated as a distribution for tax purposes.

On its liquidation, the company ceases to be the beneficial owner of its assets and accordingly various reliefs applicable to groups may cease to be available (see 3650ff.); however, the capital gains group is preserved.

Receivership or administration

There are a variety of circumstances in which a receiver or administrator may be appointed to realise all or part of a company's assets or to run the company's business. The appointment does not affect the continuation of the company's trade in itself.

The commencement of administration will cause one accounting period to end and another to start, as will the date a company comes out of administration. In a parallel move to put administration on the same footing as liquidation, administrators will be able to calculate tax based on an earlier period's rates and to self-assess the compay's corporation tax liability early.

Law: TCGA 1992, s. 170(11); CTA 2009, s. 9–12; CTA 2010, Pt. 13, Ch. 5 and s. 1030

See *British Tax Reporter* ¶802-300.

PARTICULAR RELIEFS FOR COMPANIES

EMPLOYEE SHARE INCENTIVE SCHEMES

4850   Corporation tax deduction for employee share acquisitions

For the position where an employee acquires shares in pursuance of an option granted by the employer see 4860 below. This section deals with the corporation tax deduction available where an employee acquires shares in the employing company (and certain other companies) by reason of his employment otherwise than in pursuance of an option.

Share awards can take many different forms and there are several different approved share schemes still in existence. Unapproved schemes are also widely used by employers. Share schemes are usually considered to be an effective way of incentivising employees to contribute to the performance of the company as a whole and retaining them for a longer period of time. A corporation tax deduction is normally available to the employing company in respect of the award of shares to employees.

For accounting periods commencing on or after 1 January 2003, for the purpose of calculating the amount of the corporation tax deduction in respect of such awards, the amount charged to the profit and loss account of the company is generally ignored. The deduction is prescribed by statute at the time the employee acquires his shares. These statutory provisions, explained below, were originally contained in FA 2003, Sch. 23 but have now been rewritten as CTA 2009, Pt. 12. For accounting periods commencing prior to this date, there were no prescriptive provisions in relation to corporation tax deductions for share awards to employees. Companies would, generally, have been able to claim deductions in accordance with the amounts charged in their accounts in respect of the share awards.

A corporation tax deduction for an award of shares can now only be obtained where the conditions of CTA 2009, Part 12 are met (other than for Share Incentive Plans where relief is given under what is now CTA 2009, Pt. 11). Part 12 is exclusive and implicitly precludes any other deduction in any accounting period (commencing on or after 1 January 2003, deductions in previous years are not disrupted) in relation to the cost of shares, by the employing company or any other company. Transitional rules exist where costs of awarding shares have been deducted in accounting periods commencing prior to 1 January 2003, so that a deduction can be obtained under Part 12 in relation to costs to the extent that the market value of the shares at the time of relief under Part 12 exceeds the amounts previously deducted.

Where the conditions of Part 12 are met, corporation tax relief is given for the amount equal to the market value of the shares at the time of acquisition by the employee (or other person in relation to the employee's employment), less any consideration provided by anyone for the shares.

Relief can only be obtained by the legal employer of the employee who acquires the shares. There are also conditions to be met in relation to the business to which the award is made, the company whose shares are acquired, and the income tax position of the employee.

The business to which the award is made must be carried on by the employing company and be within the charge to corporation tax.

The company whose shares are acquired does not have to be the same company as the legal employer. For example, it is possible to have three different companies within the same group that play separate roles (e.g. legal employer, parent company (the shares in which are awarded to employees of the legal employer)), and a company carrying on a trade in which the employees are active. In this example, the legal employer (provided it is carrying on a trade of being a service company) would be the company which obtains the Part 12 deduction. It would be likely that in this example there would be recharges in relation to the cost of awarding the shares. Whichever company suffers the ultimate cost would have a corporate tax disallowance for the charge to the profit and loss account.

In order for the employing company to obtain relief, it must be the case that the employee for whose employment the shares are awarded is subject to income tax or would be subject to income tax if the employee were UK resident and ordinarily resident at all material times and the duties by reason of which the share award is made were performed in the UK at all material times.

The shares acquired by reason of the employment must be ordinary shares that are fully paid up and not redeemable, and must be shares in any one of the following categories:

- listed on a recognised stock exchange;
- shares in a company not controlled by any other company;
- shares in a company that is under the control of a listed company.

Furthermore, the shares must be shares in the employing company (i.e. the company which employs the employee in respect of whose employment the award is made), or a company that is the parent company of the employing company at the time the shares are acquired. Alternatively, the shares could be in:

- a company that is a member of a consortium that owns either the employing company or the parent company of the employing company, or

- where the employing company or its parent company is a member of a consortium, then shares in a company that is a member of that consortium or its parent company, or, shares in a company which is a member of the same commercial association of companies as the consortium company.

Law: CTA 2009, Pt. 12, Ch. 2

4860 Corporation tax deduction where employee obtains options to acquire shares

Corporation tax relief can be obtained under Part 12 where an employee or another person acquires shares pursuant to an option awarded as a result of employment.

In most circumstances, the relief is straightforward and is obtained at the time the shares are acquired (not the time that the option is granted). The amount of the corporation tax deduction is an amount equal to the market value of the shares less any consideration paid.

Conditions must be satisfied in relation to the company whose shares are acquired, which are broadly the same as where shares are acquired absent an option (see 4850 above), except the conditions must be met at the time of the grant of the option.

The acquisition of the shares must be an event that would give rise to a tax charge for the employee in respect of whose employment the option has been granted (see 326).

Where the event would have been a chargeable event had the employee been resident and ordinarily resident in the UK at all material times and had the duties of the employment by reason of which the shares were awarded been performed in the UK at all material times, then the condition in relation to income tax position of the employee will still be met. Similarly, corporation tax relief is preserved where the employee is exempt from income tax on the exercise of his share options under an approved share option scheme (e.g. an EMI Option scheme).

The amount of relief given in relation to shares acquired pursuant to an option is the difference between the market value of the shares at the time they are awarded and the consideration given in respect of the option or the shares.

Special rules apply if employees acquire qualifying shares which are:

- subject to a risk of being forfeited (forfeitable shares), or
- subject to other kinds of restrictions (other restricted shares), or
- convertible into other shares or securities (convertible shares).

From 1 September 2003, these special rules broadly align the timing and amount of deductions for the employer with the timing and amount of charge to tax on the employee as employment income in respect of:

- the acquisition of the shares, and

- subsequent post-acquisition events.

Law: CTA 2009, Pt. 12, Ch. 3

CONTRIBUTIONS TO EMPLOYEE BENEFIT TRUSTS

4900 Corporation tax deduction for contributions to employee benefit trusts

Prior to 23 November 2002, no specific tax provision applied to contributions to employee benefit trusts (EBTs): contributions were deductible for corporation tax purposes in accordance with normal corporation tax principles. This means that contributions prior to that date were normally deductible on being made (but subject to case law and accounting principles). Company contributions to an employee benefit trust after 23 November 2002 will now usually fall within CTA 2009, s. 1290. Under s. 1290, any act or omission by an employer (e.g. payment of a contribution to the EBT) which results in value being added to an employee benefit trust, will result in a disallowance for corporation tax purposes for the employer company. A deduction can be obtained subsequently where, broadly, remuneration is paid out of the EBT to an employee or, if the trust funds are applied in acquiring shares in the employing company (or certain other companies), under the rules described in 4850 and 4860 above when the shares are acquired from the trustees by employees. However, a corporation tax deduction is not obtainable where benefits in kind are provided out of the trust to an employee or anyone else, even where the benefits are taxable on the employee.

The Special Commissioners decided in *Sempra Metals Ltd v R & C Commrs* that the provisions of what was then FA 2003, Sch. 24 (now CTA 2009, s. 1290) applied to disallow a corporation tax deduction for a contribution to a trust where the beneficiaries were family members of the employees and not the employees themselves.

Legislation was introduced in 1989 providing for, in particular, corporation tax relief on contributions to a specific type of employee benefit trust, called a QUEST (Qualifying Employee Share Ownership Trust). QUESTs required, in particular, that all employees and directors were beneficiaries of the trust and that the majority of trustees were employees who were not directors. Contributions by a company into a QUEST prior to 31 December 2002 were deductible for corporation tax purposes. For accounting periods beginning on or after 1 January 2003, contributions to QUESTs are now longer specifically deductible for corporation tax purposes but fall within the general provisions outlined above.

Law: CTA 2009, s. 1290; *Sempra Metals Ltd v R & C Commrs* (2008) Sp C 698

Corporation Tax

RESEARCH AND DEVELOPMENT

4915   Relief for research and development expenditure

Small and medium-sized companies with accounting periods ending after 31 March 2000 may claim additional relief for qualifying research and development (R&D) expenditure. The additional relief enables an amount equal to 175 per cent of the qualifying expenditure for an accounting period to be deducted in computing profits, to create an allowable loss, or form the basis of a repayable tax credit (for expenditure incurred before 1 August 2008, the rate of relief is 150 per cent). The relief is available to trading companies and also companies that have not yet commenced trading.

Large companies are eligible to claim additional tax relief amounting to 30 per cent of the cost of qualifying R&D expenditure incurred after 31 March 2002 but are not entitled to the repayable tax credit. For expenditure incurred prior to 1 April 2008, additional relief of 25 per cent is due. The expenditure must be incurred on R&D directly undertaken by the company, or where the R&D work is subcontracted to an organisation that cannot claim relief under this scheme or the scheme for SMEs.

Where a company loses its SME status on or after 1 December 2008 as a result of being taken over by a large enterprise, HMRC will regard it as a large company for R&D and vaccine research relief purposes for the whole accounting period in which the change occurred. Former practice had been to allow the company to retain its SME status until the end of the accounting period concerned.

Qualifying R&D expenditure incurred by an SME during an accounting period which cannot be relieved because it is unrelated to the carrying on of a trade (perhaps because the company is not yet trading or the trade that is carried on is unrelated to the expenditure), but which would have been allowable as a deduction if the company had been carrying on trading activities that were relevant to the expenditure, may be subject to an election. The effect of the election is to treat the unrelieved qualifying R&D expenditure as if it were a trading loss of the accounting period, equal to 175 per cent (or 150 per cent, see above) of the expenditure. The normal rules giving relief for pre-trading expenditure (ICTA 1988, s. 401 – treating the loss as arising on the day that trading commences) are disapplied if this election is made. The election for pre-trading R&D tax relief must be made in writing, to HMRC, within two years of the end of the accounting period that is specified in the notice containing the election.

Finance Act 2006 made two minor changes to the rules governing R&D tax relief and vaccines research relief (see below). Broadly, these changes aligned the claims process and time-limits for claims to enhanced deductions with those for payable credits, and extended the categories of qualifying expenditure to include payments made to clinical trial volunteers. The changes to the claims process apply for accounting periods ending on or after 31 March 2006. Transitional rules apply in the case of accounting periods ending before that date.

For commentary on relief for capital expenditure on research and development, see 2404, and for ordinarily deductible revenue expenditure, see 2251.

Meaning of R&D

The term 'research and development' is defined at CTA 2010, s. 1138. The core of this definition is that activities will amount to 'research and development' if 'generally accepted accounting practice' classifies them as such. This is, however, subject to any regulations, made by the Treasury, which may prescribe certain activities as either being or not being 'research and development'.

Vaccine research

This scheme, introduced by *Finance Act* 2002, gives an additional 40 per cent tax relief for qualifying R&D expenditure incurred on projects relating to vaccines or medicines for use with humans to treat or prevent HIV/AIDs, malaria, tuberculosis or other diseases specified by regulation (for expenditure incurred before 1 August 2008, additional tax relief is given at the rate of 50 per cent). This tax relief is given in addition to the tax relief given to small and medium-sized companies or enterprises (SMEs) and large companies for the same qualifying R&D expenditure under the R&D scheme. If the R&D expenditure does not qualify under the SME R&D scheme or the large company R&D scheme, but does qualify under the vaccines scheme, the company can deduct 140 per cent (or 150 per cent, see above) of the qualifying costs from its taxable profits, giving it an additional 40 per cent (or 50 per cent) tax relief.

Small and medium-sized companies are eligible to claim pre-trading qualifying R&D expenditure as a trading loss and convert any loss created by the vaccines research relief into a tax credit in the same fashion as applies for R&D tax credits for SMEs (although restrictions apply for larger SMEs). Any election to treat the relief received under this scheme as a pre-trading loss must be made in writing to HMRC within two years of the end of the accounting period in which the expenditure was incurred. Large companies cannot claim the pre-trading relief or convert losses into a tax credit.

The relief applies to expenditure incurred from 22 April 2003.

Additional R&D relief

Small and medium-sized companies with accounting periods ending after 31 March 2000 may claim additional or enhanced relief for qualifying R&D expenditure. The additional or enhanced relief enables, with the ordinary relief, a total amount equal to 175 per cent of the qualifying expenditure for an accounting period to be deducted in computing profits, to create an allowable loss, or form the basis of a repayable tax credit (for expenditure incurred prior to 1 August 2008, the rate of relief is 150 per cent). The relief is available to trading companies and also companies that have not yet commenced trading. The R&D may be undertaken directly by a company, or be subcontracted out to another person.

Corporation Tax

The way the enhanced relief, with the ordinary relief, is given is by treating qualifying R&D expenditure 'as if it were an amount equal to 175% of the actual amount'.

In order to be qualifying R&D expenditure, the expenditure must meet the following conditions:

The expenditure must be:

- not capital;
- attributable to relevant R&D directly undertaken by the company or on its behalf, and
- incurred on any of the following:
    - staff costs;
    - software and consumables;
    - externally provided workers, or
    - subcontracted R&D.

Relief is not available directly to sole traders or partnerships (including Limited Liability Partnerships). However, both large and SME companies can obtain the benefit of the enhanced R&D tax reliefs when subcontracting R&D to partnerships and sole traders, who may therefore benefit indirectly. It is also open to a partnership or sole trader to create a wholly-owned special purpose company to enable it to obtain more direct benefit from the relief. The Government confirmed, in 'R&D tax credits: responses to "Defining Innovation" and Government proposals' that there is no intention to change the status quo in this respect.

Law: CTA 2009, Pt. 13; *BE Studios Ltd v Smith & Williamson Ltd* [2005] BTC 361

Source: HMRC Brief 55/08

See *British Tax Reporter* ¶714-200.

REMEDIATION OF CONTAMINATED AND DERELICT LAND

4916   Land remediation relief

Land remediation relief allows a company to claim relief for qualifying expenditure incurred on remedying contaminated land, and to claim an enhanced deduction for that expenditure. The land must have been acquired by the company for the purposes of a trade or UK property or business carried on by it. Land is in a contaminated state if it is in such a condition because of the substances in, on or under the land that harm is being caused or there is the possibility of harm being caused or pollution of controlled waters is being or is likely to be caused. Though for this purpose a nuclear site is not land in a contaminated state.

Relevant land remediation

Relevant land remediation in relation to the land means the doing of any works, carrying out of any operations or the taking of any steps in relation to the land in question, controlled waters affected by the land or any land adjacent or adjoining the land. The purpose of the activities must be to prevent, or minimise, or remedy or mitigate, the effects of any harm, pollution of controlled waters by which the land is in a contaminated state or to restore the land or waters to their former state. This would include any preparatory activities undertaken for the purpose of assessing the condition of the land or waters concerned.

Qualifying expenditure

For this purpose qualifying expenditure is expenditure on land in a contaminated state which would not have been incurred if the land was not in a contaminated state, the expenditure is on work undertaken by the company itself or on its behalf. The expenditure must be on staffing costs, materials or qualifying expenditure on sub-contracted remediation.

The relief

Providing all the conditions are met the company can claim that the qualifying capital expenditure on land remediation is to be allowed as a deduction, in calculating the profits of a UK property business or trade for the period in which the expenditure is incurred. The election to claim this relief must be made in writing to HMRC and must be given before the end of the period of two years, beginning immediately after the end of the accounting period to which the election relates. The company can claim an additional relief where expenditure on land remediation has been allowed as a deduction in calculating the profits of the business or trade for the period. The additional amount of the relief is 50 per cent of the expenditure allowed. Where a company has a qualifying land remediation loss for a period, the company is entitled to a land remediation tax credit for the period. The tax credit is 16 per cent of the land remediation loss.

Derelict land

Finance Act 2009 has made modifications to the rules on land remediation and in particular has brought land in a derelict state within the scope of the legislation. For this purpose derelict land is not in productive use, and cannot be put into productive use without the removal of buildings or other structures. In addition the land must have been in a derelict state throughout the period beginning with the earlier of 1 April 1998, and the date on which a major interest in the land was first acquired by the company or a person who was connected with the company.

The amended land remediation relief applies to expenditure incurred on or after 1 April 2009. It also excludes from the scope of the amended land remediation relief expenditure actually incurred before 1 April 2009, but deemed to have been incurred on or after 1 April 2009 under CTA 2009, s. 61 (pre-trading expenditure).

Law: CTA 2009, Pt. 14; FA 2009, s. 26 and Sch. 7

Corporation Tax

CORPORATE VENTURING SCHEME

4920 Corporate venturing scheme – introduction

The corporate venturing scheme is closely related to the enterprise investment scheme and the venture capital trust scheme that apply to individuals. The corporate venturing scheme enables companies that subscribe for ordinary shares in independent, unquoted trading companies to obtain:

- investment relief at 20 per cent of the amount subscribed, provided the shares are held for at least three years;
- loss relief against income for any allowable capital loss (net of corporation tax relief already obtained) arising on the disposal of the investment; and
- deferral relief, whereby one can defer any chargeable gain made on the disposal of the investment where the disposal proceeds are used to subscribe for other ordinary shares that qualify under the corporate venturing scheme.

The above tax reliefs are available in respect of shares issued after 31 March 2000 and before 1 April 2010, provided certain conditions are satisfied.

Law: FA 2000, Sch. 15

See *British Tax Reporter* ¶716-020.

4922 Qualifying investing company

A qualifying company is a company that subscribes for shares in the issuing company when all of the following requirements are fulfilled:

- it has no material interest (more than 30 per cent) in the issuing company;
- there are no reciprocal arrangements – i.e. the investing company must not subscribe for the relevant shares as part of any arrangements that provide for another person to subscribe for shares in another company in which the investing company, or any other party to the arrangements, has a material interest;
- the investing company must not control the issuing company;
- the investing company must exist wholly for the purpose of carrying on one or more non-financial trades;
- the relevant shares must be a chargeable asset of the investing company; and
- The investing company must subscribe for the relevant shares for commercial reasons, and not as part of a scheme or arrangements of which the main purpose, or one of the main purposes, is the avoidance of tax.

See *British Tax Reporter* ¶716-040.

4924   Qualifying issuing company

An issuing company is a qualifying issuing company when the following requirements are satisfied:

- it is unquoted;
- from 19 July 2007, has fewer than 50 full-time employees (or their equivalents) at the date on which the relevant shares or securities are issued;
- it is independent – i.e. not a 51 per cent subsidiary and not under the control of another company;
- at least 20 per cent of the ordinary share capital is owned by one or more independent individuals;
- it must be carrying on, or preparing to carry on, a qualifying trade (see below);
- any subsidiaries must be qualifying subsidiaries;
- special conditions relating to partnerships and joint ventures are satisfied; and
- its gross assets are within certain limits.

A 'qualifying trade' is a trade which:

- is carried on wholly or mainly in the UK;
- is carried on commercially with a view to making profits; and
- does not consist wholly or substantially of carrying on 'excluded activities'.

The following are excluded activities:

- dealing in land;
- dealing in commodities;
- dealing in shares, securities or other financial instruments;
- dealing in futures;
- dealing in goods not in the course of an ordinary trade of wholesale or retail distribution;
- banking, insurance, money-lending, debt-factoring, hire-purchase financing or other financial activities;
- leasing (including ships on charter or other assets on hire);
- receiving royalties or other licence fees (other than for intangible assets created by the company itself);
- providing legal or accountancy services;
- property development;
- farming or market gardening;
- holding, managing or occupying woodlands;
- carrying on forestry activities or timber production;
- operating or managing hotels or comparable establishments (where the person carrying on the particular activity has an estate or interest in the hotel or comparable establishment in question, or is in occupation of it);
- managing property used as a hotel or comparable establishment;
- operating or managing nursing homes or residential care homes;
- managing property used as a nursing home or residential care home;
- servicing another business which comprises substantially of excluded activities and where the same person has a controlling interest in both businesses;

Corporation Tax

- shipbuilding;
- producing coal; and
- producing steel

The last three items are included in *Finance Act* 2008, but are subject to EC state aid approval.

There is no requirement for the issuing company to be resident in the UK. However, the profits of the issuing company must, to some extent, be chargeable to UK corporation tax.

Ceasing to meet trading requirements because of administration, receivership, etc.

The fact that a company is, or any of its qualifying subsidiaries are, in administration or in receivership or dissolved with or without winding up will not cause that company to fail to meet the trading activities requirement, provided that everything done in consequence of the administration or receivership etc. is for commercial reasons and not part of a scheme or arrangement of which the main purpose, or one of the main purposes, is the avoidance of tax.

Qualifying subsidiaries requirement

If the issuing company has a subsidiary then that subsidiary must be a qualifying subsidiary.

A company is a qualifying subsidiary if the issuing company has a 75 per cent interest in:

- the issued share capital;
- the assets of the subsidiary if all of the assets were distributed to the subsidiary's shareholders;
- the profits that are available for distribution to the shareholders.

In addition, no other person must control the subsidiary. There must not be arrangements in place which would breach any of these conditions (unless this is a result of a sale or winding up of the subsidiary for commercial reasons).

Partnerships and joint ventures requirement

Throughout the qualification period relating to the relevant shares, the issuing company and any of its qualifying subsidiaries must not be a member of a partnership or a party to a joint venture where:

- that partnership or joint venture carries on any trade that is relevant to the issuing company meeting its trading activities requirement;
- that partnership or joint venture has at least one other company amongst its members or parties; and
- the same person or persons beneficially own more than 75 per cent of the issued share capital or the ordinary share capital of both the issuing company and one or more of the other members/parties of that partnership/joint venture.

Gross assets requirement

The value of the issuing company's (or group's) gross assets must not exceed:

- £7m (£15m prior to 6 April 2006) immediately before the shares are issued; and
- £8m (£16m prior to 6 April 2006) immediately afterwards.

HMRC's interpretation of the gross assets requirement is set out in SP 2/00 – Venture Capital Trusts, the Enterprise Investment Scheme, the Corporate Venturing Scheme and Enterprise Management Incentives: Value of 'gross assets' (3 August 2000).

Investment limit shares issued before 22 April 2009

For an investment to qualify for relief under the CVS, the company (or group of companies) must have raised no more than £2m under any or all of the schemes in the 12 months ending on the date of the relevant investment.

If the limit is exceeded, none of the shares or securities within the issue that causes the condition to be breached will qualify for relief under the CVS.

The limit applies to shares issued after 19 July 2007.

Investment limit shares issued on or after 22 April 2009

For shares issued on or after 22 April 2009, FA 2009, Sch. 8, para. 8 requires that all of the money raised by the share issue under the CVS, must be employed wholly for the purposes of the relevant trade within two years of the issue date. Where the issuing company, or a qualifying 90 per cent subsidiary of that company, did not carry on the relevant trade when the shares were issued, the time-limit is two years from the date the relevant trade began to be carried on. The FA 2009 amendment represents an easing of the pre-22 April 2009 requirement where at least 80 per cent of the money raised had be employed within 12 months, with the remaining 20 per cent being employed wholly for the purposes of the relevant trade within two years of the issue date. The 12 months was extended to run from the date trading commenced if the issuing company or its 90 per cent qualifying subsidiary had not begun to trade at the date the shares were issued.

Law: FA 2009, s. 27 and Sch. 8, para. 8; FA 2008, s. 32 and Sch. 11; FA 2007, s. 51 and Sch. 16; FA 2006, s. 91 and Sch. 14

See *British Tax Reporter* ¶716-020.

4926 Obtaining the relief

Before a company can receive relief for the amount it has subscribed for new ordinary shares under the corporate venturing scheme, the following four conditions must be met:

(1) The shares must be fully paid up ordinary shares subscribed for in cash. They must be

non-redeemable shares which do not have any present or future preferential rights to dividends or assets on a winding-up.

(2)   The money raised by the issue of shares under the corporate venturing scheme must be employed within two years (for issues before 22 April 2009, see 4924 above) wholly for the purposes of a relevant trade. The two years is extended to run from the date trading commences if the issuing company has not begun to trade at the date the shares were issued. The money may be used to prepare to carry on a trade, and the condition will not be broken if an insignificant amount is used for some other purpose.

(3)   There must be no arrangements made in connection with the issuing of the shares to allow the subscriber to protect or recover his investment.

(4)   The issue must not be part of a scheme or arrangement whose main purpose is the avoidance of tax.

No arrangements must be in place which would cause any of the conditions from (1) to (4) above not to be satisfied

In addition to these general requirements, the following steps need to be taken to allow the investing company to claim the relief:

*   the issuing company must submit a compliance statement to HMRC;
*   when HMRC have given their authority the issuing company must produce a compliance certificate to send to the investing company; and
*   when the investing company has received the compliance certificate and if the general requirements are still met, it is entitled to make a claim for the relief due to be given in respect of the accounting period in which the shares were issued.

Before the issuing company issues any shares under the corporate venturing scheme, it may wish to obtain an advance clearance from HMRC to confirm that the general requirements of the scheme and the specific requirement which apply to the issuing company have been met.

Advance clearance is not necessarily required for the scheme to move forward, but it would be advisable to obtain it.

Amount of relief

The relief given under the corporate venturing scheme is calculated as the lower of:

*   20 per cent of the amount subscribed for in the accounting period; and
*   the amount which will reduce the investing company's corporate tax liability for the accounting period to nil.

Withdrawal of investment relief

The investment relief can be withdrawn or reduced on the occasion of any of the following events:

- the investing company disposes of the relevant shares within the qualifying period (three years from issue, or the commencement of the trade if later);
- the investing company receives significant value from the issuing company;
- the investing company grants options over the relevant shares;
- the issuing company repays any of its share capital to any of its shareholders or pays them for giving up rights to share capital.

Disposal of shares

Relief will be withdrawn or reduced if the disposal does not fall under one of the four acceptable circumstances:

- as part of a distribution of assets from the issuing company undertaken as part if the winding up or dissolving of that company;
- by virtue of the total loss or destruction of the shares;
- by way of a negligible value claim; or
- by way of a bargain at arm's length for full consideration.

The investing company can dispose of the relevant shares at any time after the qualification period for any reason and any consideration without having the relief given under the corporate investment scheme withdrawn or reduced.

The company is treated as disposing of the relevant shares if they are exchanged for other shares as part of a reconstruction or amalgamation which is not a complete share for share exchange.

Amount of relief withdrawn or reduced

When the relevant shares are disposed of within three years, the investment relief is reduced rather than completely withdrawn if the shares are disposed of for less than the subscribed amount or the consideration received is less than the amount of investment relief originally given.

If the relief has already been withdrawn due to a triggering event, it cannot also be withdrawn due an event under another heading. For example relief may be withdrawn due to a disposal of the relevant shares within the qualification period it cannot also be reduced due to a significant value received from the issuing company.

Information to be provided

If the investing company breaches one of the requirements for the corporate venturing scheme, or it receives value from the issuing company, it must provide details of the event which breached the requirements to HMRC within 60 days of the event or its knowledge of the event.

If after the issuing company has provided a compliance statement, it breaches one of the requirements of the corporate venturing scheme, or value is received by the investing company or another shareholder which causes the investment relief to be withdrawn or reduced, details of the event must be provided to HMRC. Both the issuing company and any person connected with the company who has knowledge of the event which causes the

Corporation Tax

scheme requirements to be breached, or value to be transferred, must give notice to HMRC within 60 days of the event or within 60 days of coming to know of the event.

If HMRC suspect that they should have been provided with information by the issuing company, the investing company, or some other person, concerning an event which would trigger the withdrawal or reduction of investment relief, they can serve a notice on that person to demand details of the event. The recipient of the notice must provide such information that HMRC may reasonably require within a time period which must not be less than 60 days.

If information is not provided as required by HMRC, either on demand or within the 60-day period, the company may be subject to a penalty of up to £3,000.

Relief for losses on disposal of shares

If the investing company makes a loss on a disposal of CVS shares for which investment relief is attributed and not withdrawn in full by the disposal, the remaining investment relief must be taken into account in the calculation of the capital loss. The revised capital loss is calculated by deducting the investment relief which is attributable to the shares immediately after the disposal from the original cost of those shares. This calculation cannot produce a chargeable gain.

Eligibility for relief

If the investing company makes a loss on the disposal of relevant shares it can claim a capital loss to be set off against any capital gains it may make in the normal way. However, if it has held the relevant shares continuously since issue, and the investment relief given has not been withdrawn, it may claim loss relief to set against income. This income loss relief must be claimed within two years of end of the accounting period in which the loss was incurred and can be set against the profits of that accounting period and of any accounting periods ending in the previous 12 months.

Deferral relief

Deferral relief is designed for companies that catch the CVS habit. If an investing company makes a capital gain on the disposal of some relevant shares on which it has gained investment relief, it can reinvest the gain in relevant shares of another issuing company and defer the taxation of that gain until the second batch of shares are disposed of. The investing company can use deferral relief to disposal of relevant shares with the three-year qualification period while sheltering any gains made from tax. The investing company can also reinvest suitable chargeable gains in a serial fashion without limit.

When an event occurs that triggers the withdrawal or reduction of investment relief, and thus the withdrawal of deferral relief, the deferred gain is treated as crystallising at the time of that event. The amount of the gain that becomes chargeable is that which is attributed to each of the qualifying shares that are affected by the event.

Company restructuring

If the share capital of the issuing company is reorganised due to a takeover, a merger or simply a rights issue the investment relief and any deferral relief attributed to those shares may be affected. These are subject to detailed rules.

See *British Tax Reporter* ¶716-000.

4928 Advance clearance

Before the issuing company issues relevant shares under the corporate venturing scheme, it can apply to HMRC for an advance clearance notice in respect of that issue. The advance clearance is not a necessary condition to be met before the scheme proceeds, but it does provide some certainty for the issuing company that it meets the specific requirements of the scheme, and the general requirements of the corporate venturing scheme are also met.

Advance clearance notice

The application for the advance clearance notice must contain details of all the material facts and circumstances surrounding the proposed share issue.

HMRC have 30 days from receipt of the application for an advance clearance notice to respond. They must either issue an information notice which requests further information from the applicant, refuse the application or issue the advance clearance notice as requested. HMRC are not obliged to continue with the application if it is not provided with further information as requested, or the issuing company issues the shares in question before the clearance notice is given.

If more than one information notice has been issued in connect with the application, HMRC have 30 days from receipt of the information requested in the last issued notice to issue the advance clearance notice or refuse the application.

If the issuing company is not happy with HMRC's response, it can ask the special commissioners to examine the facts of the case. If the special commissioners are happy that the general requirements of the scheme and the specific requirements for the issuing company are met, then they can issue an advance clearance notice as if they stand in the shoes of HMRC.

The clearance is given on the basis that all facts and circumstances relating to the application for clearance have been disclosed. If it is discovered that the information given was not complete and correct, the clearance will be void. Similarly, if the issuing company or any of its subsidiaries fail to act in accordance with any declaration given as part of the application for the advance clearance, the clearance notice given is void.

On receipt of an application for an advance clearance notice, HMRC may issue an information notice to the applicant requesting such particulars as it may require to allow it to

Corporation Tax

come to a decision concerning the application. The notice must give the applicant at least 30 days to provide the information requested.

The information notice must be issued within 30 days of receipt of an application for an advance clearance notice, or within 30 days of receipt of further information provided in response to an earlier information notice.

See *British Tax Reporter* ¶713-250.

ADMINISTRATION AND COMPLIANCE

COMPANY RETURNS

4950   Introduction

The regime of corporation tax self-assessment, effective for accounting periods ending on or after 1 July 1999, preserves much of the old Pay and File system, particularly arrangements for filing returns. The self-assessment rules relating to assessments, determinations, appeals and enquiries into returns are enacted, as adapted, for corporation tax.

Corporation tax self-assessment applies to corporation tax payable as well as amounts chargeable as if they were corporation tax. This specifically includes:

- tax on close company loans to participators (see 4300ff.); and
- tax on controlled foreign company profits (see 4713ff.).

Capital allowances claims and claims for group relief under CTSA are dealt with at 3034 and 3825. For transfer pricing legislation under CTSA, see 3042.

Law: FA 1998, s. 117 and Sch. 18, para. 1

Website: www.hmrc.gov.uk/ctsa/index.htm

See *British Tax Reporter* ¶811-600.

4952   Corporation tax return

Duty to give notice of chargeability

For accounting periods ending on or after 1 July 1999 the duty to give notice in relation to a company coming within the charge to corporation tax is dealt with by FA 1998, Sch. 18, para. 2. In relation to such accounting periods, a company chargeable to corporation tax for an accounting period that has not received a notice to deliver a return is required to give notice within 12 months from the end of the accounting period that it was so chargeable.

Prior to 1 April 2010 tax-geared penalties applied for a failure to comply, where the tax due in relation to the accounting period in question remained unpaid 12 months after the end of the accounting period.

With effect from 1 April 2010 the old penalties for failure to comply are replaced by new penalties under FA 2008, Sch. 41. The new penalties, like the old ones, only apply where the corporation tax due in relation to the accounting period in question remains unpaid 12 months after the end of the accounting period but the amount of the penalty is now:

- for a deliberate and concealed act or failure, 100 per cent of the unpaid corporation tax (or a reduced percentage not below 50 per cent where the company has made a prompted disclosure or a lower percentage not below 30 per cent where the company has made an unprompted disclosure);
- for a deliberate but not concealed act or failure, 70 per cent of the unpaid corporation tax (or a reduced percentage not below 35 per cent where the company has made a prompted disclosure or a lower percentage not below 20 per cent where the company has made an unprompted disclosure); and
- for any other case 30 per cent of the unpaid corporation tax (or a lower percentage not below 10 per cent when the company has made a prompted disclosure or a lower percentage which may be 0 per cent where a company has made an unprompted disclosure).

FA 2004, s. 55 introduced an additional and more burdensome rule with effect for accounting periods beginning on or after 22 July 2004. After this date, a company is obliged to give notice to HMRC of its coming into charge to corporation tax. A company will come into charge to corporation tax either at the beginning of its first accounting period or at the beginning of any subsequent accounting period that does not immediately follow the end of a previous accounting period, for example when a company begins to trade after a period of dormancy. A company must notify HMRC of its chargeability to corporation tax within three months of the beginning of the relevant accounting period. The notice must be in writing, it must state the date that the accounting period began and it must also include within the notice the information as prescribed by *Corporation Tax (Notice of Coming within Charge – Information) Regulations* 2004 (SI 2004/2502), reg. 2.

Where a company has a reasonable excuse for not fulfilling its obligation to give notice to chargeability within the three months from the beginning of the accounting period, so long as the company gives notice as soon as the excuse has been resolved, then the company will not be regarded as having failed to comply with that obligation.

Prior to 1 April 2010, failure by a company to notify HMRC of its coming into charge to corporation tax could have resulted in penalties being levied against the company. An initial penalty of £300 could have been levied in the event of such a failure and a further £60 per day could have been levied for each day the failure continued after the day on which the initial £300 penalty has been levied. Where a company had notified HMRC of its chargeability to corporation tax but had done so in a way that was fraudulent or negligent thus resulting in incorrect information appearing on the notification, the above penalties of £300 and £60 were increased to £3,000 and £600 respectively.

Corporation Tax

FA 2008, Sch. 41 has removed with effect from 1 April 2010 the old penalty regime which applied where a company failed to notify its coming into charge to corporation tax under FA 2004, s. 55 but has not extended the new Sch. 41 penalty regime to such a failure. It is assumed that this is an oversight by the parliamentary draftsman.

Law: FA 1998, Sch. 18, para. 2; FA 2004, s. 55; *Corporation Tax (Notice of Coming within Charge – Information) Regulations* 2004 (SI 2004/2502), reg 2

See *British Tax Reporter* ¶811-300, ¶812-050.

Accounts required in case of Companies Act companies

Where a UK-resident company is required to prepare accounts for *Companies Act* 2006 purposes (or Northern Ireland equivalent Orders), a company tax return may only require such accounts (together with annexed documents and information) as are required to be prepared under the Act (or Order).

In June 2010 HMRC issued guidance on the form of accounts that need to be submitted with the company tax return. This is available on HMRC website at www.hmrc.gov.uk/ct/company-accounts.pdf.

Information about business carried on in partnership

If a company carries on any business in partnership, the company tax return must include details of its share of profits, losses, etc. as shown in the partnership return.

Information about chargeable gains

A notice to make a company tax return required details of chargeable assets acquired (including details of the person from whom acquired and the consideration). Exempt from this disclosure requirement are the following items normally outside or exempt from capital gains tax:

- trading stock (except where held by an insurance company for its long-term business),
- private passenger vehicles (see 6175),
- chattels acquired for less than the exemption limit (£6,000: see 6155), and
- some non-marketable government securities (see 5860).

For notices issued after 13 August 2009 the requirement to provide this information is removed.

Period for which return required

A notice to make a company tax return must specify a period to which it relates. If a company accounting period ends during, or at the end of, the specified period, a return must be made for that period. Separate returns are required for each such accounting period within the specified period. If no accounting period ends during a specified period, but one begins (e.g. where a company first becomes chargeable to UK corporation tax), a return is required for that part of the specified period immediately before the accounting period began. If a company is outside the scope of UK corporation tax throughout the period, a return for the whole period is required. In any other case, no return is needed.

Return to include a self-assessment

Any company tax return must include a self-assessment of corporation tax due based on the information, etc. in the return, taking into account any reliefs or allowances (and including amounts due on close company loans to participators (see 4300ff.) and on controlled foreign company profits (see 4713ff.) for the return period).

Notice relating to period beginning before self-assessment

Notices to make a company tax return under the self-assessment rules may be issued after 1 July 1999. Such notices may specify a period beginning prior to 1 July 1999 but where a company's accounting period ends prior to that date, the return is to be made under the old Pay and File rules.

Calculation of tax payable

An outline of the method for calculating the corporation tax payable is provided by the legislation. This follows the following approach:

Step 1

Take the amount of company's profits for the accounting period and apply the rate of corporation tax applicable for that accounting period.

Step 2

Give effect to any marginal small profits rate, any relief under the Corporate Venturing Scheme, any double tax relief and any relief for surplus ACT brought forward from 1999 and earlier periods.

Step 3

Add any amounts that are assessable as if they were corporation tax, e.g. tax on a loan made by a close company to a participator and tax on profit of a controlled foreign company.

Step 4

Deduct any amounts to be set off against the company's overall tax liability, e.g. income tax borne by deduction.

Filing date

The normal filing date, where a company produces annual accounts, is twelve months from the end of the company's accounting period. However, there are special rules to accommodate long periods of account (which include more than one accounting period) and for cases where the notice requiring a return is delayed. Thus, the filing date is the later of:

- twelve months from the end of the period to which the return relates;
- for long periods of account that are less than eighteen months long, twelve months from the end of the period of account;
- for long periods of account over eighteen months, 30 months from the start of the period of account; and
- three months from the date on which the notice requiring a return was served.

> **Example**
>
> A Ltd prepares accounts for the 12 months to 30 September 2009, and receives a notice to make a return for this period. If the notice was issued on 22 October 2009, the filing date would be 30 September 2010.

For the purposes of the three-month rule (above), HMRC assume that a notice which is served by post will be received four working days after it is issued.

> **Example**
>
> A Ltd prepares accounts for the 12 months to 30 September 2008, and receives a notice to make a return for this period. If the notice was issued on Friday 30 July 2010, it would be deemed to be received on Thursday 5 August 2009, and the filing date would be 5 November 2010.

Claims and elections to be included in returns

Generally, all elections and claims for relief or credit that can be made for a specified period must be made in the company tax return. (Time-limits for claims, elections, etc. are unaffected by this provision: see 4970.) This includes making a claim, election, etc. via an amendment to a return (see below). Certain claims can only be made by being included (via amendment, if necessary) in a return. These are claims:

(1) for group relief;

(2) for capital allowances;

(3) to repay income tax because a company is exempt or excluded from liability to income tax; and

(4) to tax credits (unless the company is exempt from corporation tax completely or exempt from corporation tax regarding everything bar trading profits).

In (4), tax credits subject to the payment on account rules for insurance companies carrying on pension business are excluded.

Amendment and correction of returns

A company may amend its tax return at any time within 12 months of the filing date. HMRC can specify the form that an amendment must take and can require any reasonable statement or information in support of the amendment to accompany it.

HMRC can, by notice, correct any 'obvious errors or omissions' in a return. These include errors of principle, arithmetic or otherwise. The normal time-limit for such corrections is nine months from the date the return is submitted; however, if a correction is needed following a company's amendment to a return, the time-limit is nine months from the date the amendment was made.

A company may amend a return that has been corrected by HMRC, within the normal time-limit for amending returns, so as to reject HMRC's correction. If this time-limit has expired, a HMRC correction can be rejected by the issue of a notice, to the officer who made the correction, within three months of date that the correction was made.

Conclusiveness of return

Once an amount in a return can no longer be altered, whether by the company itself or by HMRC, it is regarded as conclusive for the purposes of tax payable for another accounting period of that company, or the tax liability for any accounting period of another company.

See above and the ensuing paragraphs in this chapter for the various ways in which a company's return may be altered.

Penalties

For penalties in relation to returns, see 4980.

Return forms

The return form is made up of a basic 12 page form (CT600) with customised supplementary pages for:

- loans to participators;
- controlled foreign companies;
- group and consortium relief;
- insurance companies; and
- charity exemption.

Compulsory electronic filing of corporation tax returns

UK companies will need to submit both their corporation tax returns and company accounts on-line in an XBRL electronic format where an accounting period ends after 31 March 2010. iXBRL (inline eXtensible Business Reporting Language) is a web-based computer language written specifically for business reporting.

Corporation Tax

HMRC want accounts and returns to be in iXBRL because information can be stored in a database format. If the accounts and return are not in iXBRL format then they will be considered as rejected by HMRC. This is likely to be problem for the filing of company accounts as many companies produce their accounts using Microsoft Word or Excel or similar program. The requirement is thought to be a particular problem for large companies who will have to consider how they are going to prepare their accounts.

iXBRL has already been adopted by various regulatory bodies in the US, Japan, Australia, Belgium and the Netherlands. The aim is that all corporation tax return and company account numbers will be tagged within iXBRL using descriptions predefined by HMRC and by the UK GAAP/IFRS Taxonomy. The electronic file containing all the tags will need to be submitted through the Government Gateway.

Law: FA 2004, s. 55; FA 1998, Sch. 18, para. 2–16 and 88; *Corporation Tax (Notice of coming within charge – Information) Regulations* 2004 (SI 2004/2502)

Website: www.hmrc.gov.uk/ctsa/index.htm

See *British Tax Reporter* ¶804-050.

4954 Quarterly returns

Where a company has made a payment under deduction of tax, it must account to HMRC for the tax deducted. It does this through a system commonly known as the 'quarterly accounting' system.

Return periods

For this purpose the company's accounting period is divided into return periods, based the quarterly dates 31 March, 30 June, 30 September and 31 December. Where the accounting period does not end on one of these dates, there will be two short return periods. For instance, if a company produces accounts for the year to 31 July, its return periods will be:

- 1 August to 30 September;
- 1 October to 31 December;
- 1 January to 31 March;
- 1 April to 30 June; and
- 1 July to 31 July.

A return of relevant payments (i.e. those made under deduction of tax) is due within fourteen days of the end of the return period. The tax is paid at the same time.

Relief for tax suffered at source

Where a company has suffered income tax deducted at source, relief can be obtained through the quarterly accounting system. The tax suffered may be used to reduce the amount of tax owing in respect of relevant payments. It may also be used to obtain repayment of income tax paid in earlier return periods in the same accounting period.

Income tax suffered at source which is not relieved in this way may be set against corporation tax due for the accounting period. If the corporation tax liability is insufficient to cover this, then any remaining income tax is repaid.

Law: ITA 2007, Pt. 15, Ch. 15

See *British Tax Reporter* ¶804-150.

4956   PAYE obligations

As an employer, a company must file various returns in respect of PAYE in the same way as individuals (see 2573, 2576, 2579). Similar requirements apply to companies which are contractors (in the wide sense in which this term is used) using the services of construction industry subcontractors (see 2580).

Special return procedures apply to certain payers of interest, including banks (see 2594).

There are a number of sundry return requirements which may also apply to companies in the same way as for individuals (see 2597).

4958   Preservation of company records

The records that must be maintained and retained by a company in support of its company tax return (see 4952) are wide-ranging and extensive. Records (or the information contained within them) of the amounts and nature of receipts and expenses, including all purchases and sales of stock, where relevant, together with supporting documents in the form of receipts, vouchers, contracts, deeds, books and accounts, are included.

Before 1 April 2009, the records that are to be kept must be preserved for six years from the end of the period for which it may be required to make a return. If a notice to deliver a return is issued within the six-year period, the records must be preserved beyond the six-year period until either any enquiry into the return is completed or, in the absence of an enquiry, HMRC no longer have the power to make an enquiry into the return. If a notice to deliver a return is issued after the end of the six-year period, all extant records that would assist in the making of the return must be preserved, again, until either any HMRC enquiry is complete, or, in the absence of an enquiry, HMRC no longer have the power to make an enquiry into the return.

HMRC have set out their interpretation of these requirements in the *Tax Bulletin*.

'*Specifically*:

- information may be stored in alternative formats from the original, such as optical imaging,

Corporation Tax

so long as *all* the information needed to satisfy the statutory requirement is preserved and it can be retrieved in legible form. If that is the case, the originals may be destroyed;

- companies whose information storage complies with BSI 1996 DISC PD 0008 will automatically satisfy the tax requirements;
- however, the original records **must** be preserved where the information relates to:
  - written statements detailing qualifying distributions and tax credits, or the gross amount, tax deducted and net payment for payments made under deduction of tax,
  - certificates etc. of payments made to sub-contractors under deduction of tax, and
  - details of foreign tax paid (including certain foreign taxes which are not actually paid due to relief being given in the foreign territory), but
  - it should be noted that, whereas photocopies of foreign tax assessments *will* be acceptable for calculating underlying tax on dividends from abroad, copies of UK dividend or interest vouchers will *not*;
- the requirement to retain records when a notice to deliver a return is issued after the end of the six year period is likely, in the Revenue's view, to arise only on rare occasions.'

From 1 April 2009, the records that are to be kept must be preserved until the end of the relevant day. The relevant day is the sixth anniversary of the end of the period for which the company may be required to deliver a CTR, or an earlier day if specified by the Revenue Commissioners. If a notice to deliver a return is issued before the end of the relevant day, the records must be preserved beyond the relevant day until either any enquiry into the CTR is completed or, in the absence of an enquiry, HMRC no longer have the power to make an enquiry into the return. If a notice to deliver a CTR is issued after the end of the relevant day, all extant records that would assist in the making of the return must be preserved, again, until either any HMRC enquiry is complete, or, in the absence of an enquiry, HMRC no longer have the power to make an enquiry into the return. But in some cases the actual records must be preserved, such as certificates of dividend tax credits, statements of income tax deducted from payments, sub-contractors' certificates and tax records, and records of tax paid (or payable if there were no double tax agreements) under the law of another country.

Where a company fails to keep and preserve the records needed to enable it to deliver a correct and complete CTR for the requisite period, or fails to produce documents when required to do so, it may be liable to a penalty (see 4980).

For penalties in relation to records, see 4980.

Law: FA 2008, s. 115 and Sch. 37; FA 1998, Sch. 18, para. 21 and 22

Website: www.hmrc.gov.uk/ctsa/index.htm

See *British Tax Reporter* ¶812-100.

4959 Senior accounting officers

For financial years beginning on or after 21 July 2009 senior accounting officers of large qualifying companies are required to take reasonable steps to ensure that the company establishes and maintains appropriate tax accounting arrangements and must in particular, take reasonable steps:

(a) to monitor the accounting arrangements of the company; and
(b) to identify any respects in which those arrangements are not appropriate tax accounting arrangements.

The senior accounting officer must give a certificate for each financial year to HMRC stating whether the company had appropriate tax accounting arrangements throughout the financial year, and if it did not, give an explanation of the respects in which the accounting arrangements of the company were not appropriate tax accounting arrangements. This certificate must be given to HMRC no later than the end of the period for filing the companies accounts.

The senior accounting officer is liable to a penalty of £5,000 if he fails to provide a certificate to HMRC or provides a certificate that contains a careless or deliberate inaccuracy. An inaccuracy is careless if the inaccuracy is due to a failure by the senior accounting officer to take reasonable care. An inaccuracy in a certificate that was neither careless nor deliberate when the certificate was given is to be treated as careless if the senior accounting officer discovered the inaccuracy some time later, and did not take reasonable steps to inform HMRC.

Senior accounting officer, in relation to a company that is not a member of a group, means the director or officer who, in the company's reasonable opinion, has overall responsibility for the company's financial accounting arrangements. While senior accounting officer in relation to a company that is a member of a group, means the group director or officer who, in the company's reasonable opinion has overall responsibility for the company's financial accounting arrangements.

Appropriate tax accounting arrangements means accounting arrangements that enable the company's relevant liabilities, as follows, to be calculated accurately in all material respects as regards:

- corporation tax (including any amount assessable or chargeable as if it were corporation tax);
- value added tax;
- amounts for which the company is accountable under PAYE regulations;
- insurance premium tax;
- stamp duty land tax;
- stamp duty reserve tax;
- petroleum revenue tax;
- customs duties;
- excise duties.

A qualifying company is liable to a penalty of £5,000 if for a financial year, the Commissioners are not notified of the name or names of its senior accounting officer or officers.

A company is a qualifying company in relation to a financial year if the qualification test was satisfied in the previous financial year.

The qualification test is that the company or the company and its subsidiaries satisfied either or both of the following requirements:

(1)   relevant turnover more than £200m; and

(2)   relevant balance sheet total, being the aggregate of assets, more than 2 billion.

The legislation does not apply to non-resident companies, partnerships, charities, Crown Estates or public bodies.

Provision is made in the legislation for assessing and appealing any penalty levied.

In June 2010 HMRC published a list of the most commonly asked questions in relation to Senior Accounting Officer responsibilities. This can be found at www.hmrc.gov.uk/largecompanies/sao-large-companies.htm.

Law: FA 2009, s. 93 and Sch. 46

See *British Tax Reporter* 813-600.

PAYMENT OF CORPORATION TAX

4960   Due date for payments

Corporation tax is due on the day following nine months after the end of the accounting period to which it relates.

Example

A company prepares accounts to 30 September each year. In respect of its accounting period ending 30 September 2009, tax is payable by 1 July 2010.

If the 'tax payable' is then exceeded by the total of any 'relevant amounts previously paid' (as stated in the relevant company tax return), the tax will be repaid. The 'tax payable' is the amount computed in accordance with FA 1998, Sch. 18, para. 8 (see 4952).

'Relevant amounts previously paid' are any of the following, so far as relating to the accounting period in question:

- any amount of corporation tax paid by the company and not repaid;
- any corporation tax refund surrendered to the company by another group company;
- any excess of the amounts available for set off against overall tax liability under Step 4

of the calculation in FA 1998, Sch. 18, para. 8 (for example income tax borne by deduction see 4952 above);

- any deductions from payments to sub-contractors treated as corporation tax paid in respect of profits of the company.

The above is subject to the payment of corporation tax by instalments (see 4964).

HMRC are able to offer the option of paying by direct debit for self assessment tax payments, PAYE and corporation tax.

Law: TMA 1970, s. 59D, 59DA and 59E

Website: www.hmrc.gov.uk/ctsa/index.htm

See *British Tax Reporter* ¶811-000.

4961 Repayment claims

A company which has paid corporation tax for a period and which has, following a change in its circumstances, grounds for believing that the amount paid exceeds its probable tax liability for the period, may claim repayment of the excess. The claim must state the grounds for believing that the amount paid is excessive. Companies will either be able to claim repayment nine months after the end of the accounting period to which the overpayment relates or at the earlier date or dates provided by regulations where the corporation tax was paid by quarterly instalments (see 4964).

A company which has appealed against an assessment or an amendment to an assessment may apply to the commissioners who will hear the appeal to determine the amount that should be repaid. The application may be combined with an application to postpone payment of tax.

A claim (for repayment of the excess) or application (to the commissioners) can be heard and determined in the same way as an appeal.

A company that wishes to include amounts deducted under the subcontractor's scheme in its provisional repayment must have delivered a company tax return for the period.

The above is subject to the payment of corporation tax by instalments (see 4964).

Law: TMA 1970, s. 59D, 59DA and 59E

Website: www.hmrc.gov.uk/ctsa/index.htm

See *British Tax Reporter* ¶811-000.

Corporation Tax

4962 Recovery of excessive repayments

Where it appears that HMRC has paid, repaid or set-off against other liabilities:

- tax (including income tax and tax credits);
- repayment supplement; or
- interest on overpaid tax,

that appears to be excessive, an assessment may be issued to recover the excess amount(s). Interest may be charged on the excessive repayment, etc. from the date it was paid to the company to the date it was recovered. The normal four-year (six years prior to 1 April 2010) time-limit for making assessments (see 4986) is overridden where a recovery assessment is made either:

(a) before the end of the accounting period after the one in which the excess repayment was made, or
(b) if later, before the expiry of three months after the conclusion of an enquiry into the company's return.

(In order for this extension to apply there does not have to have been a loss of tax brought about carelessly or deliberately (or, prior to 1 April 2010, fraud or negligence on the part of the company). Where there *has* been a loss of tax brought about carelessly or deliberately, then the further extended six-year (for carelessness) or 20-year (otherwise) time-limit may be invoked by HMRC to recover the excess.)

Law: FA 1998, Sch. 18, para. 52, 53

Website: www.hmrc.gov.uk/ctsa/index.htm

4963 Recovery of overpaid tax

The error or mistake provisions allow a taxpayer to claim repayment of tax overpaid where there is an overpayment of tax as a result of a relevant mistake in a return.

Finance Act 2009 inserted a new para. 51 to FA 1998, Sch. 18, and allows a company to claim repayment of tax overpaid where a person has paid an amount by way of tax but believes that the tax was not due, or a person has been assessed as liable to pay an amount by way of tax, or there has been a determination or direction to that effect, but the person believes that the tax is not due.

The claim will only be possible where there is no other statutory route to recover the overpaid tax when a person first becomes aware, or might reasonably be expected to be aware, that they have overpaid. The person must also have used any appeal rights that were available and the claim will have to be made within time-limits. A claim under para. 52 may not be made more than four years after the end of the relevant accounting period.

Law: FA 1988, Sch. 18, para. 51

4964   Large companies: corporation tax payable in instalments

A quarterly instalment payment system applies to 'large' companies under CTSA. For these purposes, 'large' companies are companies with profits in excess of the upper relevant maximum amount for the purposes of small profits rate (including reductions in that amount to reflect associated companies and short accounting periods: see 3090). 'Profits' means chargeable profits shown in an assessment (or determination) plus franked investment income (excluding group income).

The arrangements for filing the tax returns under CTSA of large companies are the same as for other companies (see 4952).

For these purposes, 'corporation tax' includes any amounts due under the legislation applicable to loans to participators, etc. (4300) and controlled foreign companies (4713).

Outline of instalments regime

Large companies (broadly those with profits of more than £1.5m, or less if the company has other associated companies) have to pay their corporation tax in instalments starting during the accounting period for which the tax is payable, rather than in one lump sum nine months and one day after the end of the accounting period. For a normal 12-month accounting period this will result in quarterly instalments starting in month seven during the accounting period (therefore, two of which will be before the end of the accounting period).

The instalment regulations provide a de minimis limit to prevent companies in large groups having to make instalment payments of small liabilities. The limit is currently £10,000.

Where companies become large for the first time, they will be protected from any unanticipated liability to payment in instalments. Instalment payments will not be required if:

- the corporation tax profits for the accounting period do not exceed £10m (reduced where there are associated companies by reference to the number of associated companies at the end of the immediately preceding accounting period or, where there is no such period, at the beginning of the period concerned); and
- the company was not a large company for the previous year (either because it did not exist – or did exist but had no accounting period – or because it was not a large company for an accounting period ending in the preceding 12 months).

Pattern of instalments

A maximum of four instalments will be due six months and thirteen days after the beginning of an accounting period, carrying on, where the length of the period allows, at three-monthly intervals and ending three months and fourteen days (i.e. on the fourteenth day of the fourth month) after the end of the accounting period.

Corporation Tax

For a 12-month period, this simply translates into instalments being due quarterly on the fourteenth day of:

(1)   month 7 after the beginning of the accounting period;

(2)   month 10;

(3)   month 13; and

(4)   month 16 (the final instalment).

These are intended to reflect the dates which used to apply to most companies for the payment of any liability to advance corporation tax, prior to abolition, albeit starting later in the period.

Example 1

As an example, Gross plc is a large company which has a 12-month accounting period which ends on 31 December. Instalment payments will be due on:

- 14 July and 14 October in the course of the accounting period for which the corporation tax is due, and
- 14 January and 14 April in the following year.

One quarter of Gross plc's corporation tax liability for an accounting period will be payable on each of those dates.

If, in the calendar year 2009, Gross plc changed its accounting reference date to 30 September, it would have a nine-month accounting period ending on 30 September 2009. Its instalment dates for that accounting period would be 14 July 2009 and 14 October 2009 with a final instalment on 14 January 2010. There would only be three instalment dates for the short period. If Gross plc continues to use 30 September as its year-end after 2009, it would revert to a pattern of four instalments for each accounting period thereafter.

Amount of instalments

Instalment payments will be based on a large company's total liability for the accounting period. By the very nature of the system, this will have to be based on estimated figures, at least initially. For these purposes, the 'total liability' is:

(1)   corporation tax included in an assessment or a determination, less any subcontractors' tax deducted; and

(2)   the aggregate of any liabilities under the provisions for:

    (a)   close company loan to participators; and
    (b)   controlled foreign companies.

Instalments are intended to be in equal amounts: however, this will not always be the case. Accordingly, the amount of each instalment is calculated according to a formula:

$$\frac{3}{n} \times CTI$$

Where CTI is the amount of the company's total liability for the period and n is the length of the accounting period in months. The amount of tax due on the first instalment date will be the *smaller* of CTI and the amount produced by the above formula. For subsequent instalments, the amount due will be the smaller of the balance of tax left after the previous instalment and the amount produced by the formula. Thus there may not be the maximum number of instalments for the period where all the tax is payable in less than four instalments.

Example 2

From Example 1 above, Gross plc has a corporation tax liability for the nine-month accounting period ended 30 September 2009 of £2.5m. Its instalments are calculated as follows:

CTI = £2,500,000
n = 9 months

Cumulative
total of tax
paid

First instalment:

$$\frac{3}{9} \times 2,500,000$$

Lesser of CTI and formula = 833,333.33 due 14 July 2009   833,333.33

Second instalment:

$$\frac{3}{9} \times 2,500,000$$

= 833,333.33 A

Balance of tax after first
instalment   1,666,666.67 B

Lesser of A and B   833,333.33 due 14 October 2009 833,333.33

Third instalment:

$$\frac{3}{9} \times 2,500,000$$

= 833,333.33 C

Balance of tax after first and
second instalments   833,333.33 D

Lesser of C and D   833,333.33 due 14 January 2010 833,333.33

Total tax paid in instalments   2,500,000.00

If, using the same corporation tax liability, Gross plc instead ended its accounting period on 15 May 2009, its instalments would be reduced in number as follows:

CTI = £2,500,000
n = 4.5 months

Cumulative
total of tax
paid

First instalment:

$$\frac{3}{4.5} \times 2,500,000$$

Lesser of CTI and formula = 1,666,666.67 due 14 July 2009 1,666,666.67

Second instalment:

$$\frac{3}{4.5} \times 2,500,000$$

$$= 1,666,666.67 \quad \text{A}$$

Balance of tax after first instalment	833,333.33	B
Lesser of A and B	833,333.33	due 29 August 2009 833,333.33
Total tax paid in instalments		2,500,000.00

Repayments of excessive instalments

Any instalment payments already made will normally be repaid if a company decides on reflection that they ought not to have been paid and the aggregate amount already paid exceeds the aggregate amount which should have been paid using the revised total liability. A claim can be made for repayment of the excess amount. Such a claim must give the amount being reclaimed and the grounds for making the claim. The commissioners may determine the amount which should be repaid where an assessment is under appeal prior to determination of the final liability. An application to the commissioners for such a determination will be treated like an appeal.

Repayments will carry interest (see below). Repayments of excess instalments may also be surrendered within a group.

Miscellaneous requirements

The following matters are also covered by the regulations:

- HMRC's right to request such information, including copies of books, documents and other records, relating to the calculation of instalments as they may 'reasonably require'; and
- the right of inspection of any records so required.

For arrangements for groups of companies, including arrangements whereby one company will be able to make instalment payments on behalf of the group, see 3651.

Law: TMA 1970, s. 59D, 59DA, 59E and 87A; ICTA 1988, s. 826A; *Corporation Tax (Instalment Payments) Regulations* 1998 (SI 1998/3175)

Website: www.hmrc.gov.uk/ctsa/index.htm

See *British Tax Reporter* ¶811-050.

Corporation Tax

4965   Business Payment Support Service

From 24 November 2008 taxpayers having difficulty in meeting their tax liability can contact HMRC's Business Payment Support Service to see if a payment plan can be agreed to pay the tax. While any taxpayer can use the service it is primarily aimed at the business community. Taxes covered include corporation tax, income tax, VAT and PAYE.

The conditions which must be met for the taxpayer to use the service are:

- they must be in genuine difficulty;
- they must be unable to pay their tax on time; and
- they must be likely to be able to pay if allowed more time.

Interest will continue to be payable charged on any taxes which are subject to a payment plan, but HMRC will not charge additional late payment surcharges.

Information for agents

An agent can call the Business Payment Support line to discuss a client's affairs if they have authority to act on behalf of the client, either through a Form 64-8 or an online agent authorisation. HMRC can agree a payment arrangement with the agent but may have to contact the client to set up payments through direct debit. Further guidance is available on the HMRC website.

Reviewing or extending the arrangements

If the circumstances of the taxpayer change and they become unable to make the payments covered by the agreement they need to contact HMRC before they miss any payment. Provided HMRC are satisfied that the business continues to be viable, they will consider amending and extending the agreement.

Extension to the service announced on 22 April 2009

From 22 April 2009, extra help is available for businesses which have been profitable in recent years but which now expect to be loss-making. Businesses which qualify to use the service, those due to make an income tax or corporation tax payment in respect of the previous year's profits and expect to make a treading loss in the current year, will have this taken into account when a payment plan is offered. The business must be genuinely unable to pay immediately or enter into a reasonable Time to Pay arrangement.

A compliance officer will contact the taxpayer or agent to discuss why a loss for the current year is expected. It may also be necessary to submit supporting documentation.

It should be noted that:

- the loss can only be taken into account when considering Time to Pay for income tax or corporation tax liabilities and does not extend to VAT or PAYE;
- where a business has losses but is unable to enter into a Time to Pay arrangement,

HMRC will only defer collection of the tax until the normal filing date for the return in which the loss is expected;

- if the loss turns out to be less than anticipated, the balance of any debt suspended will become payable when the current year return is submitted and the loss claim finalised. It will carry interest from the date it should have originally been paid.

Further guidance and Q & As can be found on the HMRC website

Website: www.hmrc.gov.uk/pbr2008/business-payment.htm
www.hmrc.gov.uk/budget2009/bus-payment-support-582.htm

4966 Managed Payment Plan

The Managed Payment Plan is a voluntary plan under which companies may pay corporation tax by instalments balanced equally before or after the normal due date. While in the plan the company is protected from interest and penalties on payments made on or after the due date. A taxpayer who fails to make payments on time but remains in contact and discussions with HMRC about the debt will remain relieved of penalties. Due to a delay in updating HMRC's computer and accounting systems, the introduction of managed payments plans has been delayed until April 2011.

Law: FA 2009, s. 110

INTEREST

4967 Interest on overdue tax/underpaid tax by company

For accounting periods ending after 30 September 1993, unpaid or underpaid corporation tax carries interest (at rate prescribed by regulations – see 15 for the table of rates) from the due date, nine months after the end of the accounting period. Special provisions apply in relation to any corporation tax which becomes payable as a result of a company disposing of chargeable assets after it has ceased to be resident in the UK solely by virtue of the provisions (see 4072) treating dual resident companies as non-resident.

There are provisions which may preserve a charge to interest where a loss or non-trading loan relationship deficit is carried back to earlier accounting periods for which there is tax outstanding which, but for the carryback, would carry interest.

Changes on the introduction of self-assessment

Before corporation tax self-assessment (see 4986ff.), interest paid on overdue tax was not deductible in computing profits or losses. However, for accounting periods within self-assessment (periods ending after 30 June 1999), companies are able to obtain relief for such interest. This puts such interest on a par with other forms of interest for which relief is already available through the loan relationship regime (see 3037). This is matched by an

Corporation Tax

increase in rates of interest to a more commercial basis (see 15 for a list of rates). For the taxability of interest on overpaid tax after corporation tax self-assessment, see 4982.

Law: TMA 1970, s. 87 and 87A; FA 1989, s. 178

See *British Tax Reporter* ¶811-350.

4968 Interest on overpaid tax by company

HMRC must pay interest to a taxpayer company on certain refunds of tax. The refunds in question relate to the following:

- corporation tax, (including ACT);
- income tax deducted at source from amounts received by the company;
- tax credits on franked investment income (see 3077).

Interest on corporation tax is payable at a rate prescribed by regulations (see 15) and runs from the later of the date on which the tax is paid or nine months after the accounting period; for income tax and tax credits it runs from nine months after the accounting period in which the company receives the income.

There are provisions which restrict payment of interest where a loss or non-trading loan relationship deficit is carried back to earlier accounting periods.

Taxability of interest on overpaid tax

Companies are taxable on interest on overpaid tax. This is the converse of the relief for interest on overdue tax (see 4980).

Law: ICTA 1988, s. 826 and 826A; *Savacentre Ltd v IR Commrs* [1993] BTC 203; *R v IR Commrs, ex parte Commerzbank AG* [1993] BTC 299

See *British Tax Reporter* ¶811-350.

4970 Time-limits for claims and elections

For claims made before 1 April 2010, the claim had to be made within six years from the end of the accounting period to which it relates, unless a longer or shorter time-limit was given by a specific provision. If a mistake was discovered in any claim or election, a company could make a supplementary claim, etc. within the time-limit for making the original claim or election. All claims to reliefs, allowances or repayments had to be for specific quantified amounts.

For commentary on the special CTSA provisions relating to claims for capital allowance, see 3028 and, for group relief, see 3825.

Changes made by the Finance Act 2008

With effect from 1 April 2010, a claim must be made within four years from the end of the accounting period to which it relates, unless a longer or shorter time-limit is given by a specific provision (FA 1998, Sch. 18, para. 55 as amended by FA 2008, Sch. 39, para. 45 with effect from the day appointed by the *Finance Act 2008, Schedule 39 (Appointed Day, Transitional Provision and Savings) Order* 2009 (SI 2009/403)). This is illustrated as follows:

Example

A company makes up its accounts to 31 December. A claim is required in respect of the accounting period ended 31 December 2005. The claim can be made at any point up to 31 March 2010 as at that date a time-limit of six years applies and so the period during which the claim can be made has not elapsed. The claim cannot be made on or after 1 April 2010 as from that date the time-limit is four years and so the period during which the claim could be made ended on 31 December 2009.

Transitional rules are provided.

Claims or elections not included in returns

If a claim or election can be made without being included in a return (for example, because the time-limit for making an amendment to the return has expired), the administrative rules of TMA 1970, Sch. 1A apply (see 2684).

Consequential claims

Following the closure of a HMRC enquiry (see 2684) or the issue of an assessment that results in more tax being payable, it is possible to make further claims and elections (or revoke existing claims, etc.) to reduce the tax due to the amount originally returned. Such further claims must be made within 12 months of the end of the accounting period in which the closure notice or assessment is made. Claims that could affect the liability of other parties (e.g. companies in the same group) require their written approval. Where the assessment is made as a result of a loss of tax brought about carelessly or deliberately (or, for periods prior to 1 April 2010, as a result of fraudulent or negligent conduct of the company or its servants, etc.) (see 4990), the scope for making additional claims, etc. is restricted to those that could have been made within the normal time-limit for the accounting period concerned.

Late claims

Late claims for losses, capital allowances or group relief may be accepted, provided the delay was for reasons beyond the company's control. HMRC's approach is set out in SP 5/2001.

Law: FA 1998, Sch. 18, para. 54–65

Corporation Tax

Source: SP 5/2001

Website: www.hmrc.gov.uk/ctsa/index.htm

See *British Tax Reporter* ¶812-150.

4972   Relief where self-assessment excessive

Mistakes in returns

Under corporation tax self-assessment (CTSA, which applies in respect of accounting periods ending after 30 June 1999), where a company considers that it has paid tax under an assessment which is excessive due to some mistake in a return, it may claim relief by issuing a written notice to the Board within four years (six years for claims made prior to 1 April 2010) of the end of the accounting period concerned.

The Board has wide powers to review all the circumstances of the claim and may also examine other accounting periods as well as the one that is the subject of the claim. In particular, they are required to consider whether the granting of relief for the period in question might result in amounts being excluded from the charge to tax.

If the Board do decide to grant relief, it is given by way of repayment in such sum as is considered 'reasonable and just'.

No relief may be given where the methods or practices used to derive the tax liability were those generally prevailing and approved at the time the return was submitted, notwithstanding a subsequent change of view. Relief is also denied where the mistake relates to a claim or election included within the return.

Any appeal against the Board's decision on a claim lies to the special commissioners who, in hearing the appeal, must consider the same issues and principles as the Board is required to. An appeal against the commissioners' decision can only be on a point of law.

Double assessment

If a company considers that it has been taxed more than once in the same accounting period for the same matter, it may make a claim for relief to the Board. Where the Board agree that the claim is correct, relief can be given by any appropriate method to eliminate any over charge. An appeal may be brought against the Board's decision.

Law: FA 1998, Sch. 18, para. 50, 51

See *British Tax Reporter* ¶811-850.

4973 Agreement to forego tax reliefs

Where a government department or other public body provides financial support to a person including a company, either directly to the person who has given the undertaking or to another person, as part of the designated arrangement then as part of the arrangement that person may agree to forego tax relief or the right to tax relief.

Because some tax reliefs are automatic, express provision is made in FA 2009 to disable these automatic reliefs which are part of any such agreement. The legislation applies to arrangements entered into on or after 22 April 2009, but it may have effect in respect of tax reliefs that arise or would otherwise be effective in respect of periods before that date. The legislation was prompted by an Asset Protection Scheme introduced by the Government to restore confidence in the banks and other financial institutions and get credit flowing again, by dealing with the losses associated with impaired assets.

Law: FA 2009, s. 25

HMRC DETERMINATIONS AND DIRECTIONS

4975 Determinations and assessments by HMRC

If no return is delivered by a company following the issue of a notice, or if a notice to deliver a return is complied with only partially, HMRC may determine to the best of their information and belief the amount of tax payable by a company.

Determinations to have effect as self-assessments

Such determinations are treated as self-assessments for most practical purposes, including:

- payment of tax due;
- collection and recovery proceedings;
- interest on overdue tax;
- tax related penalties; and
- assessment of unpaid tax on other persons (to enable collection to be effected).

In the absence of adequate information regarding the matter, the period covered by the determination is to be treated as an accounting period of the company.

When return not delivered

A determination made in the absence of any return may be made after the filing date for that return has passed. If, for some reason (e.g. lack of information about the commencement of an accounting period) the filing date cannot be ascertained, the exercise of determination powers may be made after the later of 18 months from the end of the period specified in the notice to deliver the return and three months from the date the notice was served.

Corporation Tax

Determination of tax payable if notice complied with in part

A determination made because a return for only part of the period specified in the notice has been delivered may be made after the filing date for the outstanding return has passed. If for some reason the filing date cannot be ascertained, the exercise of determination powers may be made after the later of 30 months from the end of the period specified in the notice and three months from the date the notice to deliver a return was served.

Time-limit for determinations

No determination may be made more than three years (five years for determinations made prior to 1 April 2010) after the date that the power to make a determination first arose. If a company can show that a determination should not have been made (e.g. because it has actually delivered a return for the period, or that the period covered by the determination was not an accounting period, etc.) the determination will be treated as having no effect.

Determinations superseded by actual self-assessments

If, after a determination has been made (and within the later of five years of the date that the power to make a determination first became exercisable and 12 months from the date of the determination) a company delivers a return, the self-assessment in the return supersedes the determination. The delivery of a self-assessment in these circumstances does not delay or impede any tax recovery proceedings in relation to the determination. The period of five years was reduced to three years with effect from 1 April 2009.

Law: FA 1998, Sch. 18, para. 36–40

Website: www.hmrc.gov.uk/ctsa/index.htm

See *British Tax Reporter* ¶812-000.

4977 Priority of charge

Occasionally, there are difficulties in determining how and on what basis particular receipts are to be taxed. For accounting periods ended before 1 April 2009, HMRC had the power to direct what the basis of assessment should be in two sets of circumstances (former FA 1998, Sch. 18, para. 84):

- where amounts could be brought into charge either under Sch. D, Case I or alternatively Sch. D, Case III or Sch. D, Case V; and
- where amounts could be brought into charge either under the rules of Sch. D, Case I or under the 'I minus E basis' for companies carrying on life assurance (and annuity) business.

HMRC's determination on this matter was final and conclusive as regards the accounting period concerned.

For accounting periods ended on or after 1 April 2009, such issues are to be determined in accordance with the priority rules at CTA 2009, s. 287 and 982(1) (see Change 55 in the Explanatory Notes accompanying CTA 2009).

Law: FA 1998, Sch. 18, para. 84

Website: www.hmrc.gov.uk/ctsa/index.htm

See *British Tax Reporter* ¶812-000 and ¶700-275.

PENALTIES

4980   Penalties under CTSA

Failure to deliver a return within the time-limit

A company which has had a notice to make a tax return and fails to deliver it by the filing date (see 4952) may become liable to a flat-rate penalty of:

(1)   £100; if it is delivered within three months of the filing date; and

(2)   £200; if it is delivered after three months.

The penalty under (1) is increased to £500 and under (2) to £1,000 if the returns for the two immediately previous consecutive accounting periods were also late.

Excuse for late delivery of return

No flat-rate penalty is due if a company is required to deliver accounts under the *Companies Act* 2006 (or equivalent Northern Ireland Order) and submits its return within the time allowed for delivering the accounts to the Registrar of Companies.

Tax-geared penalty

Where a company tax return is delivered later than 18 months after the end of the accounting period (i.e. more than six months after the filing date, in the usual case of a company with a regular 12-month accounting period), a further tax-geared penalty will become due (in addition to the flat-rate penalties shown above). The tax-geared penalty is:

(1)   10 per cent of the unpaid tax, if it is delivered within two years of the end of the period for which the return is required (i.e. within 12 months of the filing date in the usual case of a company with a regular 12-month accounting period); or

(2)   20 per cent of the unpaid tax, if it is delivered after the two-year period in (1) above.

Corporation Tax

New penalty regime for late filing of CT returns

From a date yet to be announced, *Finance Act* 2009 introduced a new flat rate and tax-geared penalty regime for the late filing of corporation tax returns. Under the new regime, the following flat rate and tax-geared penalties will be payable:

(a) A flat-rate penalty of £100 if the return is filed after the filing date.

(b) A flat-rate penalty of the greater of £300 and 5 per cent of the amount of tax that is shown, or would be shown, by the return if it is filed more than six months after the filing date.

(c) A daily penalty of £10 (for a maximum of 90 days) if the return is filed more than three months after the filing date and HMRC have notified the company that the daily penalty is due. The daily penalty can be imposed from a date earlier than the HMRC notification, but not from a date earlier than three months after the filing date.

(d) If the return is more than 12 months late and the company has withheld information which would enable HMRC to assess the company's liability to tax, a penalty of the greater of 100 per cent of the tax and £300 if the withholding of information was deliberate and concealed, or the greater of 70 per cent of the tax and £300 if the withholding of the information was deliberate but not concealed.

(e) If the return is more than 12 months late and (d) does not apply, a penalty of the greater of 5 per cent of the tax and £300.

It should be noted that each of these penalties is additional to the others so that, for example, if a corporation tax return showing corporation due of £100,000 is filed nine months late, the penalty would be the sum of £100 under (a), £5,000 under (b) and, if HMRC notify the company that they intend to charge the daily penalty, £900 under (c). A total of £6,000.

The tax-geared penalties under (c) and (d) above (i.e. for returns filed more than 12 months late) can be reduced if disclosure is made. If the disclosure is unprompted, the 100 per cent penalty can be reduced to an amount not less than 30 per cent and the 70 per cent penalty to not less than 20 per cent – the amount of the reduction in both cases depending on the quality of the disclosure (i.e. the timing, nature and extent of the disclosure). If the disclosure is prompted, the 100 per cent penalty can be reduced to not less than 50 per cent and the 70 per cent penalty to not less than 35 per cent, again, depending on the quality of the disclosure.

Companies have a right of appeal against all penalties and no penalty can be charged if the company has reasonable excuse for its failure. The legislation makes it clear that the following are not reasonable excuses:

• an insufficiency of funds, unless attributable to events outside the control of the company, and

• reliance on another person to do anything, unless the company took reasonable care to avoid the failure by the other person

If the company had a reasonable excuse for the failure but the excuse has ceased, the company is treated as having continued to have the excuse if the failure is remedied without unreasonable delay after the excuse ceased.

Law: FA 2009, Sch. 55

Penalty for incorrect or uncorrected returns (returns required to be made before 1 April 2009)

A penalty of up to an amount equal to the tax understated may be charged if:

- an incorrect company tax return is fraudulently or negligently delivered; or
- a company discovers an 'innocent' error in a submitted return and fails to remedy the error without 'unreasonable delay'.

Incorrect accounts

A penalty of up to an amount equal to the tax understated may be charged if a company fraudulently or negligently:

- submits to HMRC incorrect accounts in connection with its tax liability; or
- makes any incorrect return, statement or declaration regarding a claim for any allowance, deduction or relief.

Accounts submitted on behalf of a company are regarded as submitted by the company unless it can be shown that they were submitted without its 'consent or connivance'.

Penalties for incorrect returns or accounts for returns made up after 1 April 2009

FA 2007 introduced a new regime for penalties in respect of incorrect documents submitted to HMRC for documents in respect of income tax, capital gains tax, corporation tax, PAYE, Class 1 and Class 4 NICs, Construction Industry Scheme and VAT. The new penalty regime applies for returns for periods commencing on or after 1 April 2008 and due on or after 1 April 2009.

FA 2008 extended this new regime to insurance premium tax, inheritance tax, stamp duty land tax, stamp duty reserve tax, petroleum revenue tax, excise duties including aggregates levy, climate change levy, landfill tax, air passenger duty, alcoholic liquor duties, tobacco product duty, hydrocarbon oil duties, general betting duty, pool betting duty, bingo duty, lottery duty, gaming duty and remote gaming duty, warehouse keepers, and registered excise dealers and shippers.

Document is defined in some detail for the various taxes and duties. For corporation tax a document includes a company tax return, accounts in connection with ascertaining the liability to tax, return statement or declaration in connection with a claim for an allowance, deduction or relief.

The definition is further widened to include:

'Any document which is likely to be relied upon by HMRC to determine, without further enquiry, a question about:

Corporation Tax

(a)   the person's liability to tax

(b)   payments by the person by way of or in connection with tax

(c)   any other payment by the person (including penalties), or

(d)   repayments, or any other kind of payment or credit to the person.'

Most companies will be potentially chargeable to a penalty in respect of other taxes and duties in addition to that for corporation tax. A company like other taxpayers can be subject to a tax geared penalty where an inaccurate assessment has been made, and the company has failed to take reasonable steps to notify HMRC.

The purpose of the new regime is to provide greater consistency in charging penalties, and to encourage taxpayers to take the steps necessary to ensure that the documents they submit to HMRC are correct. The regime differentiates between the seriousness of the underlying behaviour which led to the inaccuracy:

- careless inaccuracy without taking reasonable care;
- deliberate inaccuracy without concealment;
- deliberate inaccuracy with concealment.

There is no penalty for an inaccuracy despite taking reasonable care.

The penalties are levied on an increasing scale to reflect the severity of the inaccuracy:

- careless errors: 30 per cent of the potential lost revenue;
- deliberate but not concealed errors: 70 per cent of the potential lost revenue;
- deliberate and concealed errors: 100 per cent of the potential lost revenue.

Potential lost revenue is the amount of tax due or payable as a result of correcting the errors. Where a loss has been overstated and used to reduce the tax payable, the potential lost revenue will be calculated as on the amount of extra tax payable. Where the overstated loss has not been wholly used to reduce tax payable then the potential lost revenue will be calculated as 10 per cent of the loss. Where the inaccuracy results in tax being declared later than it should have been then the potential lost revenue is calculated at a rate of 5 per cent per annum of the delayed tax.

For companies which are members of groups the amount of potential lost revenue is calculated without adjustment for group relief. Under the pre-1 April 2008 regime group relief could be used to reduce the amount of penalty chargeable.

The new regime prescribes a penalty mitigation structure which differentiates between prompted and unprompted disclosure of inaccuracies.

HMRC advise officers that they should give a penalty reduction for taxpayers telling HMRC about the inaccuracy or failure, giving HMRC reasonable help in quantifying the inaccuracy or underassessment, and allowing HMRC access to records to ensure that the inaccuracy or underassessment is fully corrected. The weighting for these facts is 30 per cent, 40 per cent and 30 per cent respectively. This is then applied to the difference between the maximum and minimum penalty for a particular inaccuracy. This figure is then deducted from the maximum penalty to give the penalty percentage chargeable.

Type of inaccuracy	Maximum penalty %	Minimum penalty with unprompted disclosure %	Minimum penalty with prompted disclosure %
Careless	30	0	15
Deliberate but not concealed	70	20	35
Deliberate and concealed	100	30	50

HMRC are able to suspend all penalties or a penalty for careless inaccuracy without taking reasonable care, if conditions can be set that would help the taxpayer to avoid becoming liable to further penalties for careless inaccuracy. The conditions of suspension can specify the action to be taken, and the period within which the action or actions must be taken. This period cannot exceed two years. If at the end of the set period HMRC are satisfied that the conditions of suspension have been met the suspended element of the penalty is cancelled. If the conditions of suspension are not met, then the penalty becomes payable. If during the period of suspension the taxpayer becomes liable for a penalty for inaccuracy then the suspended penalty becomes payable.

Where a penalty is chargeable on a company as a result of a deliberate inaccuracy by an officer of the company, HMRC can pursue the officer as well as the company for the penalty. HMRC can pursue the officer for all or part of the penalty, though HMRC cannot recover more than 100 per cent of the penalty. Officer of a company is widely defined and includes shadow director, a secretary, director or manager or any other person managing or purporting to manage any of the company's affairs.

FA 2009 also introduces penalties where in complying with an information notice, a person provides inaccurate information or produces a document that contains an inaccuracy, and either the inaccuracy is careless or deliberate or that person discovers the inaccuracy some time later, and fails to take reasonable steps to inform HMRC.

Where an investigation discovers inaccuracies which arose both before and after the start of the new regime, any penalty will be calculated on the basis of the penalty regime which applied in the period for which the inaccuracy was made.

Failure to keep and preserve records

Where a company fails to keep and preserve the records needed to enable it to deliver a correct and complete tax return for the requisite period (broadly six years from the end of the period covered by the company tax return) it may be liable to a penalty of up to £3,000. There are four exclusions to this penalty:

(1)   where HMRC are satisfied that alternative documents, etc. provide an adequate replacement for the missing originals;

(2)   where the missing records would only have been used in a claim, election or notice that would *not* have been included in a company tax return;

(3)   copies of statements, counterfoils, etc. where the recipient of a qualifying distribution formally requests details of the distribution and any tax credit (see 3065); and

Corporation Tax

(4)   copies of statements, counterfoils, etc. where the recipient of a payment made under deduction of income tax formally requests details of the gross amount payable and the income tax deducted (see 1370).

There can be only one penalty for each accounting period, regardless of the number of offences or documents not retained. HMRC's stated intention is that penalties will only be sought 'in the more serious cases', such as where records have been destroyed deliberately to obstruct an enquiry.

Failure to produce documents

Prior to 1 April 2009 where a company failed to produce documents or information required in a formal notice, served during an enquiry into a return or amendment to a return, a penalty of £50 could have been charged. Where the failure continued daily penalties could have been imposed for each day of continued failure:

- £30 per day, if the daily penalty was determined by an officer of the Board under TMA 1970, s. 100 (see 2645); or
- £150 per day if the daily penalty was determined by the commissioners under TMA 1970, s. 100C (see 2645).

In *Research & Development Partnership Ltd v R & C Commrs* the First-tier Tribunal held that, for the penalty regime that applied up to 1 April 2009, reliance on a third party was capable of being a reasonable excuse and that in the circumstances of the case (because, for example, it was unreasonable to expect a company to be able to provide a detailed explanation of its R&D claim with reference to the relevant legislation without reference to professional advisers) it was reasonable for the company to rely on its agent to provide the information to HMRC. It should however be noted that the new penalty regime introduced with effect from 1 April 2009 (see above) specifically provides that reliance on another person to do anything is not a reasonable excuse unless the company took reasonable care to avoid the failure by the other person.

From 1 April 2009, the new information powers in FA 2008, Sch. 36 come into effect (see 4983). The new legislation gives HMRC wide-ranging powers to require the production of information, documents, and explanations from companies and others and to require the creation of schedules which do not already exist, and to enter business premises (used by the person whose liability is being checked) and inspect documents. So far as corporation tax is concerned, these powers to enter premises and inspect documents are new. Previously, without the consent of the occupier, there was no right to enter premises to inspect records in connection with corporation tax. Rights of appeal are given to the company and others on whom notice is served (unless the notice has been issued with the approval of the Tribunal, in which case no appeal is available) and documents covered by legal privilege, auditors papers and some tax advisory papers are excluded from the powers. From 1 April 2010 the new information powers are further extended to permit HMRC to enter any premises, not just business premises, for valuation purposes and to inspect business premises of 'involved third parties' (although in the context of corporation tax the definition of 'involved third party' only extends to Lloyds managing agents).

Multiple tax-geared penalties in respect of same accounting period

Where a company incurs more than one tax-geared penalty, the total penalty chargeable by reference to any particular portion of tax shall not exceed the largest of the individual penalties chargeable on that portion.

Where it is necessary to calculate the 'tax understated' for the purposes of a tax-geared penalty, no account is taken of any deferred relief for the repayment of loans made to participators in close companies where the repayment was made more than nine months after the end of the accounting period in which the loan was made (see 4306).

Law: FA 1988, Sch. 18, para 17–19, 23 and 90; FA 1998, Sch. 18, para. 2; FA 2007, s. 97 and Sch. 24; FA 2008, Sch. 36; FA 2009, s. 95 and Sch. 47, para. 40A; *Finance Act 2007, Schedule 24 (Commencement and Transitional Provisions) Order* 2008 (SI 2008/568); *Research & Development Partnership Ltd v R & C Commrs* [2010] TC 00271

Website: www.hmrc.gov.uk/ctsa/index.htm

See *British Tax Reporter* ¶812-050.

APPEALS

4982 Appeals

Appeals under the corporation tax self-assessment (CTSA) provisions (see 4952ff.) are subject to some general rules.

Notices of appeal

Notices of appeal should be made in writing, within the time limited (usually 30 days from the appealable event). Notices of appeal must generally be sent to the officer of the Board who initiated the appealable event, unless the Board itself initiated the event; in which case the appeal generally lies to it.

Notices of appeal should specify the grounds of appeal. If the appeal is eventually heard by the tribunal, further or different grounds not originally specified in the notice may be taken into consideration, provided that the tribunal is content that their omission was not wilful or unreasonable.

The appeals system was reformed for direct and indirect taxes from 1 April 2009. For further commentary on the new regime, see 235.

Corporation Tax

Appeal hearings

As part of the reform of the Tribunal system, the General and Special Commissioners of Income Tax were replaced by the Tax Chamber of the First-tier Tribunal. Accordingly appeals from decisions of HMRC will lie with the First-tier Tribunal Tax Chamber. There is a further right of appeal to the Upper Tribunal which replaces the jurisdiction of the High Court in tax but only on points of law. There is a right of appeal from the Upper Tribunal to the Court of Appeal and ultimately to the House of Lords.

The First-tier Tribunal can ask the Upper Tribunal to hear a case in the first instance.

Appeals for corporation tax must continue to be made to HMRC. Though a request by the appellant for a hearing before the Tribunal, is made by notifying an appeal to the Tribunal Service.

First-tier Tribunal hearings

In order to streamline the Tribunal's handling of cases, cases will be allocated to one of four categories when the Tribunal receives a notice of appeal, application notice or notice of reference:

- default paper cases;
- basic cases;
- standard cases; and
- complex cases.

The initial allocation of a case is not final. Either on its own initiative or upon an application of a party, the Tribunal may reallocate a case to a different category by giving a further direction.

Default paper cases

A default paper case will usually be disposed of without a hearing, though the appellant may request an actual hearing.

It is proposed that this category will generally apply to appeals against:

- fixed penalties for late filing of tax returns;
- fixed penalties for late filing of employer returns (P35s);
- fixed penalties for late filing of returns under the Construction Industry Scheme;
- Class 2 NICs late notification penalties;
- income tax surcharges (for late payment of tax under self-assessment); and
- applications by HMRC for the imposition of daily penalties in relation to late self-assessment tax returns.

Such cases may (upon request by any party) be dealt with at a hearing.

Basic cases

Basic cases are those which will usually be disposed of after a hearing, but with minimal exchange of documents beforehand. It is proposed that the basic case category will generally apply to appeals against:

- tax-geared penalties for late filing of tax returns;
- most tax-geared penalties for incorrect returns (but not where the penalty is for deliberate and concealed action, nor where there is also an appeal against the assessment itself);
- mitigation and reasonable excuse appeals against indirect tax penalties;
- appeals against CIS gross payment status decisions;
- appeals against information notices.

The basic case category is also expected to include:

- applications for permission to make a late appeal;
- postponement applications (where HMRC refuse);
- closure notice applications.

Standard cases

Standard cases are those which will usually be disposed of after a hearing, and subject to more detailed case management.

Complex cases

The Tribunal may not direct that a case be allocated as a complex case unless the Tribunal considers that the case:

- will require lengthy or complex evidence or a lengthy hearing;
- involves a complex or important principle; or
- involves a large financial sum

Statutory review procedure

As part of the reform of the tribunal system a new statutory review procedure was introduced. The purpose of the review procedure is to reduce the amount of appeals which will require a hearing before the Tribunal. The statutory review provisions have been inserted into the primary legislation by the *Transfer of Tribunal Functions and Revenue and Customs Appeals Order* 2009 (SI 2009/56), which came into effect on 1 April 2009.

The review procedure is not mandatory but triggered by either:

- the appellant requesting a review; or
- HMRC offering a review to the appellant.

The review officer must be somebody outside the direct line management of the case worker or decision maker, though for local compliance the review officer will be a member of the Regional Appeals Unit. The review officer will not be the advocate on the case where there is an appeal hearing. The review officer is tasked by HMRC to check whether the decision is in line with legal and technical guidance policy and practice, and must consider whether it is

Corporation Tax

a case HMRC would wish to defend before the tribunal. The review must take into account any representations made by the taxpayer, provided that they are made sufficiently early to give HMRC a reasonable opportunity to consider them.

Where the appellant has requested a review, HMRC has to issue a letter within 30 days of receiving the review request. The letter must set out HMRC's view of the matter. This letter is the trigger for the start of the review period, where the review has been requested by the appellant.

HMRC may want to offer a review where it is felt unlikely that further discussion will fail to reach agreement or is unlikely to settle the matters under appeal. Because HMRC cannot notify the Tribunal of the appeal, it is the only way HMRC can move things forward where there is such an impasse. The appellant has 30 days to accept the offer of the review or notify the appeal to the tribunal. If the appellant does not accept the offer of the review or notify the tribunal then the matter is settled on HMRC's view of the matter unless HMRC is willing to accept a late review application letter. The appellant accepting the offer letter is the trigger for the review period which is normally 45 days.

Where the review offer is accepted by the appellant, HMRC must within 30 days of the review issue a letter setting out HMRC's view of the matter, this is then the trigger for the review period for an offered review.

The review period is the period in which HMRC must complete the review and notify the outcome of the review to the appellant. Normally the review period is 45 days, though this is extended to 90 days where the appeal was made before HMRC and the review was requested or offered before 1 April 2010. A different review period can be agreed by HMRC and the appellant.

When HMRC has notified the appellant of the outcome of the review, the appellant can either accept the offer of the review conclusion or notify the appeal to the tribunal within 30 days of the review conclusion letter.

Where a review officer does not complete the review within the agreed period and has not agreed an extension of the review period, then the review is treated as being settled on HMRC's view of the matter. The review officer must notify the appellant of this as soon as possible, who then has 30 days to notify the appeal to the tribunal.

Where a review is undertaken it is important that the time-limits are monitored, as the tribunal may not be willing to favourably consider an application for late notification of an appeal.

Law: FA 1998, Sch. 18, para. 92; *Tribunals Courts and Enforcement Act* 2007; *Tribunal Procedure (First-tier Tribunal) (Tax Chamber) Rules* 2009 (SI 2009/273); *Transfer of Tribunal Functions and Revenue and Customs Appeals Order* 2009 (SI 2009/56)

Website: www.hmrc.gov.uk/ctsa/index.htm

See *British Tax Reporter* ¶812-000.

4983   Information and inspection powers

Historic legislation dealing with the provision of documentation and information in direct tax matters has been repealed from 1 April 2009 and replaced by FA 2008, Sch. 36.

Wide ranging new information powers introduced by FA 2008, Sch. 36 apply from 1 April 2009, and give HMRC power to obtain documents and information. The legislation applies initially to corporation tax, income tax, capital gains tax and VAT. Under the new powers there is no need for a return to have been submitted in order to carry out a compliance check, the legislation allows pre-return checks to be undertaken; information notices under Sch. 36 can be issued before tax returns have been filed; nor is there any requirement that a tax return has to have been issued.

It should be noted that there are no transitional provisions in respect of the new powers. However, HMRC have indicated that, where enquiries straddle 1 April 2009, they will voluntarily commit to restricting the use of the Sch. 36 powers, so that they do not seek information or documentation which they would not have been entitled to obtain under the previous regime.

The provisions at FA 2008, Sch. 36, para. 1 enable an officer of HMRC to require a person to provide information or documentation where that information is reasonably required for the purposes of checking that person's tax position. This is known as a taxpayer's information notice. A person's tax position is his position as regards certain taxes and includes any amount assessable or chargeable as corporation tax and includes past, present and future liability to pay taxes.

FA 2008, Sch. 36, para. 2 enables an officer to require a third party to provide information or documentation where that is reasonably required for the purposes of checking the tax position of a person whose identity the officer knows. Such a notice can only be issued if it has been approved by the First-tier Tribunal, or by an authorised officer (para. 3(1)).

FA 2008, Sch. 36, para. 5 extends this third party information power to enable an officer to obtain information or documentation reasonably required for checking the tax position of a person or a class of persons whose identity he does not know. A notice under para. 5 can only be issued with the approval of the First-tier Tribunal. It is necessary for the tribunal to be satisfied, amongst other things, that the person or persons to whom the notice relates have failed, or may fail, to comply with their obligations under the Taxes Acts or the *Value Added Tax Act* 1994, and that the failure is likely to have led to, or will be likely to lead to 'serious prejudice to the assessment and collection of tax' (para. 5(4)).

A taxpayer's information notice cannot be used where a corporation tax return has been made in respect of a chargeable period, unless a notice of enquiry has been given in respect of the return claim or election where the enquiry has not been concluded or HMRC are in a potential discovery position.

A 'document' is widely defined as anything in which information of any kind is recorded.

The recipient of a notice under FA 2008, Sch. 36, para. 1, a first party notice, is entitled to appeal against the notice or any requirement in it (para. 29(1)). An appeal against the notice is to the First-tier Tribunal. However, where HMRC have obtained the consent of the tribunal to the issuing of the notice, there is no right of appeal (para. 29(3)). Additionally, a taxpayer cannot appeal against a notice to provide statutory records (para. 29(2)).

Where a third party notice has been issued, the recipient may appeal to the First-tier Tribunal on the basis that compliance with the notice or any requirement of it would be unduly onerous (FA 2008, Sch. 36, para. 30(1)). However, where the notice is for statutory records or where the notice has been pre-approved by the First-tier Tribunal, there is no right of appeal (para. 30(2) and (3)).

The recipient of an identity unknown notice, under FA 2008, Sch. 36, para. 5 may appeal to the First-tier Tribunal on the grounds that the notice or any requirement of it is unduly onerous.

Where the recipient of a notice fails to comply with the notice, including concealing, destroying or disposing of documents a penalty of £300 is chargeable (FA 2008, Sch. 36, para. 39(2)). Following the imposition of an initial penalty, further daily penalties of up to £60 are chargeable for each day on which the failure to comply or obstruction continues (para. 40). Penalties are assessed by HMRC and an appeal can be lodged to the First-tier Tribunal in respect of either the imposition or the amount of a penalty.

A penalty will not be chargeable where the recipient of a notice, or person subject to an inspection, can demonstrate that they have a reasonable excuse for non-compliance or obstruction (FA 2008, Sch. 36, para. 45) or where the failure is a failure to comply within time-limits but compliance took place within further time allowed by an officer of HMRC (para. 44).

It is an offence to destroy, conceal or otherwise dispose of a document required to be produced in an information notice which has been authorised by the First-tier Tribunal. However, where a document has been produced to HMRC, it is possible to dispose of it unless an officer of HMRC has indicated in writing that the document must be retained. Additionally, it is possible to dispose of documents where the notice enabled production of copy documents, those copies have been produced, and a period of six months from the date of production of the copy has expired (FA 2008, Sch. 36, para. 53(2) and (3)).

FA 2008, Sch. 36 para. 54 states that where an officer of HMRC notifies a person in writing that a document is, or is likely to be, subject to an information notice, it is an offence to destroy, conceal or otherwise dispose of the document. Where a period of six months has expired since notification, or where an information notice is issued, no offence is committed under para. 54 if the document is disposed of.

Inspection powers

FA 2008 introduced an inspection power enabling officers of HMRC to inspect business premises, business assets that are on the premises and business documents that are on the premises. The inspection must be 'reasonably required for the purposes of checking that person's tax position'.

'Business assets' are defined as assets which an officer of HMRC 'has reason to believe are owned, leased or used in connection with the carrying on of a business by any person'. 'Business documents' are defined as documents or copies thereof which relate to the carrying on of a business by a person and which form part of any person's statutory records. A person's statutory records are those documents and information which a person is required to keep and preserve in order to comply with the requirements of the Taxes Act and the *Value Added Tax Act* 1994 or any associated enactment. Where documents or information are required to be kept under these provisions but do not relate to the carrying on of a business, these records are only regarded as statutory records following the end of the chargeable period to which they relate. Records cease to be statutory records once they are no longer required to be retained for either Taxes Acts or *Value Added Tax Act* 1994 purposes or any associated enactments.

Inspections can be carried out at a time that is agreed with the occupier of the premises or at any other reasonable time.

Officers can carry out inspections without the agreement of the occupier of the premises where either the occupier has been given at least seven days' notice or the inspection is carried out with the agreement of an authorised officer of Revenue and Customs. Where an authorised officer has given consent the inspection can be made without giving any notice. HMRC may want to obtain the approval of the First-tier Tribunal to carry out an inspection, where the visit is likely to be obstructed or refused, as a penalty can be charged if the visit is obstructed when it has been authorised by the Tribunal. In these circumstances, the notice must first be approved by an authorised officer and the Tribunal must be satisfied that the inspection is justified in the circumstances.

An occupant of business premises is not required to provide documents for inspection if, at the time of the inspection, an information notice under FA 2008, Sch. 36, para. 1, 2 or 5 could not have required their production.

The occupant of the premises can refuse the officer access to the premises or can ask the officer to leave at any time. The officer must comply with the occupant's wishes.

From 1 April 2010 the new information powers are further extended to permit HMRC to enter any premises, not just business premises, for valuation purposes and to inspect business premises of 'involved third parties' (although in the context of corporation tax the definition of 'involved third party' only extends to Lloyds managing agents).

Corporation Tax

Law: FA 2008, s. 113 and Sch. 36

See *British Tax Reporter* ¶184-900.

ENQUIRIES

4984   Enquiries into company tax returns

Opening enquiries

Changes implemented by *Finance Act* 2007 revised the period during which HMRC can give notice of enquiry into a company tax return (the 'enquiry window'). The rules apply for accounting periods ending after 31 March 2008. Broadly, the changes apply to most returns delivered to HMRC before the statutory filing date and link the end of the enquiry window to the date that a return is received by HMRC. The new rules reflect recommendations made by Lord Carter of Coles in his March 2006 'Review of HMRC Online Services' and are designed to give earlier certainty to companies that file early.

For accounting periods ending on or before 31 March 2008, the enquiry window for returns filed early closes 12 months from the statutory filing date, which is normally 12 months after the end of the accounting period.

For accounting periods ending after 31 March 2008, the enquiry window for most returns delivered by, or on, the filing date will close 12 months from the day on which HMRC receive the return. For example, if a return for an accounting period ended 30 June 2008 is received by HMRC on 26 January 2009, the enquiry window will close on 26 January 2010, i.e. 12 months after delivery.

The change applies to the majority of companies, including all those that are not members of any group, and also those in small groups as defined in the *Companies Act* 2006 (see below). However, there is no change for companies in groups that are not 'small' and the enquiry window for such companies still closes 12 months from the statutory filing date.

A parent company qualifies as a small company in relation to a financial year only if the group headed by it qualifies as a small group (CA 2006, s. 383). Broadly, the qualifying conditions are met by a group in a year in which it satisfies two or more of the following requirements:

(1)   aggregate turnover: not more than £5.6m net (or £6.72m gross);

(2)   aggregate balance sheet total: not more than £2.8m net (or £3.36m gross); and

(3)   aggregate number of employees: not more than 50.

Certain companies are excluded from the small companies regime (CA 2006, s. 384 and 474) including public companies, authorised insurance companies and banking companies.

Companies in groups that are not 'small' will need to declare themselves on their company tax return and HMRC have provided a new check box on the front page of the CT600 return form and a similar option for returns delivered electronically.

HMRC are keen to encourage companies that are members of a group that is not a 'small' group in *Companies Act* terms to file their company tax returns early where it is possible for them to do so. Although in general, early filing is now encouraged by amendments made to FA 1998, Sch. 18, para. 24 by *Finance Act* 2007, which ensure that the period within which HMRC can open an enquiry into a company's tax return will close sooner for early filers than was previously the case, these amendments do not apply to the members of such groups. HMRC have therefore published a note setting out an operational practice that they will adopt in relation to large and medium-sized groups.

Where a corporation tax return is delivered late, a notice of enquiry can be issued before the end of the quarter-day next following the first anniversary of the day on which the return was delivered. Similarly, where a company amends its CT return, a notice of enquiry can be issued before the end of the quarter-day next following the first anniversary of the day on which the return was amended. The quarter-days for these purposes are 31 January, 30 April, 31 July and 31 October.

Unless a company amends a corporation tax return, only one enquiry may be made into the return. Amendments to a return can be subject to separate enquiries.

Scope of enquiries

Enquiries into corporation tax returns can cover anything contained within the return, including claims and elections. Specific reference is made in this context to the power to extend the coverage of an enquiry into whether to give a notice to a medium-sized company revoking its exemption from the transfer pricing provisions (under TIOPA 2010, s. 168). Such a notice can only be given for a transaction giving rise to profits arising after 31 March 2004 if the return for the chargeable period is subject to a self-assessment enquiry. However, where a notice of enquiry is given following a company's amendment of its corporation tax return and the time-limit for issuing a notice on the original return has expired, the enquiry may only cover matters to which the amendment relates, or which are affected by the amendment.

Enquiries into returns for wrong period

If HMRC consider that a return has been made for the wrong period, an enquiry can be made into the period for which the return should have been made.

The conduct of enquiries

Once an enquiry notice has been issued, HMRC could, prior to 1 April 2009, also issue a notice requiring the company to produce such documents and information as HMRC might 'reasonably' require, except where the documents, etc. related to a pending appeal by the company. Any such notice could include a time-limit (not less than 30 days). Photographic copies of documents could be provided, though HMRC could (by notice) insist on inspecting and if necessary taking copies of the originals. For penalties for failing to produce documents, see 4980.

HMRC have published a code of practice relating to enquiries into CTSA returns.

Since 1 April 2009, new HMRC Information and Inspection powers have come into force (see 4983 above).

Appeals against notice to produce documents

Prior to 1 April 2009, a written appeal against a HMRC notice, to be heard by the tribunal in the same way as an appeal against an assessment, may be made within 30 days of the issue of the notice. The tribunal's decision is final and conclusive and may either wholly or partly confirm the notice, or set it aside. See further 4982.

After 1 April 2009, the new Information and Inspection powers described above in 4983 have effect and include rights of appeal for the taxpayer.

Amendment of self-assessment during enquiry to prevent tax loss

In order to prevent a loss of tax during an enquiry HMRC may, by notice, amend a company's self-assessment (contained within the tax return).

Any such amendment may be appealed by the company giving written notice to the officer who issued the amendment within 30 days of its receipt. However, any appeal thus made cannot be heard and determined before the enquiry is completed.

Amendment of return by company during enquiry

A company may amend a company tax return during the course of an enquiry into the return). If it does so, the amendment may form part of the enquiry. However, such an amendment has no effect on the amount of corporation tax payable by the company (or any other company) until the enquiry is completed.

Completion and closure of enquiries

When an enquiry ends, it is formally concluded by the issue of a 'closure notice' (which will confirm that the enquiry is complete and give HMRC's conclusions). If one conclusion is that the return was made for the wrong period, the closure notice will specify the correct period. This may necessitate the delivery of a company tax return for the correct period. The filing date for such a return is the later of:

- the normal filing date for a return covering the period; and
- 30 days after the date that the correct period was finally determined following the enquiry (generally likely to be the date that the closure notice is issued).

Amendments to the return after enquiry

Once an enquiry has been completed, the company has 30 days to make amendments to the return to give effect to the conclusions. This may require amendments to be made to returns other than the one subject to the enquiry. In all such cases, the normal time-limits for making amendments to returns do not apply.

If a company fails, wholly or partly, to make such amendments as HMRC consider necessary to give effect to an enquiry's conclusions within the period of 30 days and the return is not considered to be correct and complete, HMRC have 30 days to serve a notice on the company, making such amendments as they consider appropriate. The company may appeal, by a notice in writing given within 30 days of HMRC's determination, to the officer issuing the notice of amendment (see further 4982).

Direction to complete an enquiry

If a company wishes to bring a HMRC enquiry to an end, it may apply to the tribunal for a direction that HMRC should issue a closure notice within a specified period. The tribunal hears the application as if it were an appeal (see 4982) and is obliged to give the direction sought by the company, unless it is satisfied that HMRC has 'reasonable grounds' for not giving a closure notice within a specified period. In this instance, therefore, it would appear that the burden of proof lies with HMRC.

Law: FA 1988, Sch. 18, para. 24–26 and 30–35

Website: www.hmrc.gov.uk/ctsa/index.htm
www.hmrc.gov.uk/leaflets/c11.htm

See *British Tax Reporter* ¶812-900.

4986   Discovery, fraud and negligence

Discovery assessments

If for any accounting period HMRC discover that:

(a)   an amount which ought to be assessed has not been assessed; or
(b)   an assessment has become insufficient; or
(c)   excessive relief has been given,

they may make a 'discovery assessment' in such amount as they consider necessary to make good any loss of tax. This provision closely resembles previous statutory rules regarding 'discovery' (see 2680). The Board's sanction is needed when an officer proposes to include an adjustment in a discovery assessment (or discovery determination: see below).

Corporation Tax

Discovery determinations

Similarly, HMRC may make a 'discovery determination' where a company tax return (see 4952) for one period incorrectly states an amount that affects either the tax payable by the company for another accounting period, or the tax payable by another company.

Restrictions on power to make discovery assessment or determination

A discovery assessment or discovery determination can only be made:

(1) if the discovery indicates a loss of tax was brought about carelessly or deliberately (or prior to 1 April 2010, if it was attributable to 'fraudulent or negligent conduct' by the company, a person acting on its behalf or a partner of the company); or

(2) if HMRC could not reasonably have been expected, on the basis of information then 'available' (see below) to them, to be aware of the circumstances leading to a loss of tax, either at the time they completed an enquiry into a company tax return or at the time their right to enquire into a return expired.

In (1) above, an assessment or determination can be made at any time up to six years after the end of the accounting period to which it relates in the case of carelessness and up to 20 years after the end of the accounting period where the loss of tax has been brought about deliberately. In any other case, the normal time-limit is four years (six years for assessments issued prior to 1 April 2010) after the end of the accounting period to which the assessment or determination relates.

In (2) above, information is regarded as being 'available' to HMRC if it is:

(1) contained in the return (or any accompanying documents) for the period in question, or the previous two accounting periods; or

(2) contained in a claim (or any accompanying accounts, statements or documents) for the period in question; or

(3) contained in any documents, accounts or information produced or provided for the purposes of a HMRC enquiry; or

(4) information the existence and relevance of which:

   (a) were reasonably inferable from matters in (1)–(3) above, or
   (b) HMRC were notified of in writing by the company or its agent.

Returns made in accordance with prevailing practice

Discovery assessments or determinations may not be made if the loss of tax is attributable to a mistake regarding the basis of the computation of liability and the return was made in accordance with generally prevailing practices at the time it was made.

Law: FA 1998, s. 110(1)(c) and (9) and Sch. 18, para. 41–49

Website: www.hmrc.gov.uk/ctsa/index.htm

See *British Tax Reporter* ¶805-100.

COLLECTION AND RECOVERY FROM COMPANIES

4990   Collection from companies

Corporation tax is generally collected direct from the taxpayer, although there are certain amounts from which income tax will have been deducted at source (see 1370, 1402, 1652, 1654, 3020).

HMRC issue payslips and reminders as follows:

- a notice requiring a return to be made contains a payslip;
- about a month before the due date, a payment reminder and a further payslip will be sent;
- where appropriate, a further reminder and payslip will be sent about a month after the due date.

Payment is, of course, due without the need for any action on the part of HMRC.

PAYE procedures apply to companies largely as they apply to individuals (see 2748, 2784).

Collection of tax from UK paying or collecting agents in respect of certain foreign dividends receivable by non-residents is broadly the same as for individuals (see 1654).

See *British Tax Reporter* ¶805-100.

4991   Recovery from companies

Unpaid tax may be recovered by the Crown in the following ways:

- by levying distress upon the lands or goods of the person in default;
- by action to recover the debt through court proceedings;
- by bankruptcy proceedings.

These remedies apply in relation to corporation tax much as they apply in relation to income tax (see 2804ff.).

Company purchase and abandonment schemes

HMRC may, in certain circumstances, collect unpaid corporation tax from the previous owners of a company or from other companies previously under the same ownership, where the company is sold in circumstances intended to ensure that its corporation tax liabilities arising prior to the sale are likely to remain uncollected. These provisions apply to contracts

Corporation Tax

for sale entered into after 29 November 1993. Their scope has been extended to catch liabilities that are no more than potential liabilities at the time of a change in ownership after 1 July 1997, unless in pursuance of a contract made before that date. From the same date, HMRC may by notice require documents and particulars from any person in order to establish the incidence and extent of any possible liability under these provisions (although from 1 April 2009 these provisions have been replaced by the new Information and Inspection powers described in 4983 above). The interest rules apply to tax due under the 'potential liabilities' provision above as if the tax were payable by the defaulting company.

If HMRC need to apply the above legislation, tax will be sought first from those who previously controlled the company, and from any companies which can be charged and are still controlled by the vendor, before looking to companies which are no longer under the vendor's control. A payment made in respect of actual unpaid tax or potential tax under these provisions is not an allowable deduction for the payer. However, the company which has to make a payment under this legislation is entitled to recover the amount of that payment from the company whose liability it is in fact, or from an associate of that company. Where recovery of such an amount is received under an indemnity from the purchaser, or from the taxpayer company, it will not be charged to tax on the recipient.

Law: CTA 2010, s. 710 and 713

See *British Tax Reporter* ¶805-100.

Capital Gains Tax

TRUSTS AND SETTLEMENTS FOR CAPITAL GAINS TAX

CAPITAL GAINS OF ESTATES IN ADMINISTRATION

CAPITAL GAINS TAX: THE FOREIGN ELEMENT

PARTNERSHIP GAINS

GAINS OF SPECIAL TAXPAYERS

WHAT'S NEW

- For 2008–09 onwards the standard rate of capital gains tax is 18 per cent for individuals (see 5410).
- A higher rate of capital gains tax of 28 per cent is introduced in respect of disposals on or after 23 June 2010. The new rate replaces the 18 per cent rate in respect of trustees and personal representatives. For individuals, however, it applies in addition to the 18 per cent rate; the actual rate applicable will be determined by the aggregate of the individual's taxable income and chargeable gains (see 5410).
- The annual exemption is equal to £10,100 for 2009–10 and 2010–11 (see 6150).
- The annual exemption for most trusts is £5,050 for 2009–10 and 2010–11.
- For disposals occurring in the period 6 April 2010 to 22 June 2010, the limit for entrepreneurs' relief is £2m (£1m prior to 6 April 2010). For disposals occurring on or after 23 June 2010, the limit is £5m (see 5293).
- FA 2010 contained legislation relating to foreign currency bank accounts.
- The provisions of ESC D50, relating to compensation receipts, have been enacted from 6 April 2010 (see 5080).

KEY POINTS

- A charge to capital gains tax (CGT) arises where there is a chargeable person, a chargeable disposal of a chargeable asset and a chargeable gain (see 5001).
- A person who is resident or ordinarily resident in a tax year is liable to CGT on chargeable gains made in that year (see 5004).
- A disposal occurs when an asset is sold, given away or exchanged or when a capital sum is received as a result of the ownership of an asset (see 5060).
- In most cases, the disposal proceeds are the total proceeds received on disposal of the asset (see 5062).
- In certain situations the acquisition of the disposal of an asset is deemed to be at market value (see 5100ff.).
- In computing net gains on which CGT is charged, it is necessary to take account of allowable losses (see 5260ff.).
- For disposals after 5 April 2008 entrepreneurs' relief (which replaced taper relief) may be available (see 5293ff.).
- Indexation allowance, other than for companies, is frozen for periods after 6 April 1998 (see 5268ff.).
- Disposals after 5 April 1988 of asset held at 3 March 1982 are rebased to their 31 March 1982 values (see 5300ff.).
- Special rules apply to wasting assets (i.e. assets with a predictable useful life of less than 50 years) (see 5330).
- Disposals between husband and wife, and between civil partners, are on a no gain/ no loss basis (see 5500).
- The CGT treatment of trust property depends on the nature of the beneficial interest in the property (see 5550ff.).
- There is no CGT liability on death. The assets of a deceased person are deemed to be acquired by his personal representatives at the market value at the date of death, giving a tax-free uplift on death (see 5680).
- From 23 June 2010, disposals by personal representatives are charged at a rate of 28 per cent (see 5697).
- Partnership gains are assessed and charged on the partners separately and for CGT purposes partnership dealings are treated as dealing by the partner and not by the firm (see 5760).

- An individual has an annual exemption for each tax year and a liability to CGT only arises if net gains exceed this exempt amount (see 6150).
- Various miscellaneous exemptions exist to take certain assets outside the charge to CGT (see 6155ff.).
- Generally, a gain made by an individual on the whole or part of a dwelling-house which is his only or main residence is not liable to CGT, or if liable not wholly liable (see 6220ff.).
- In certain circumstances it is possible to roll over the gain on the disposal of an asset (see 6302ff.).
- Capital gains tax is normally due by 31 January after the end of the tax year (see 6470).
- Targeted anti-avoidance rules exist to prevent tax avoidance (see 6410).

INTRODUCTION TO CAPITAL GAINS TAX

5000 History of capital gains tax

Capital gains tax (CGT) was introduced by the *Finance Act* 1965. The object of the legislation was to tax gains made by individuals and companies on the disposal of assets, and it supplemented existing legislation introduced in 1962 which charged short-term gains to income tax. The latter charge was abolished in 1971.

The *Taxation of Chargeable Gains Act* 1992 (TCGA 1992) consolidated the chargeable gains provisions. The chargeable gains of companies are liable to corporation tax, not CGT, and are dealt with at 3050ff., but reference should also be made to the present division for special reliefs and the general principles which apply equally to companies. The previous consolidating Act was the *Capital Gains Tax Act* 1979 (CGTA 1979) which excluded provisions relating exclusively to companies.

Capital gains tax applies to disposals of assets after 6 April 1965, whenever the assets were acquired.

See further 152.

See *British Tax Reporter* ¶500-000.

5001 Scope of CGT

There is a charge to CGT where there is:

- a chargeable person (see 5004);
- a chargeable disposal of a chargeable asset (see 5007ff.); and
- a chargeable gain on the disposal (in accordance with the computation provisions and provided that there is no exemption: see 5220ff. and 6140).

Allowable losses follow in a similar manner (see 5260).

Of course, the distinction between a revenue gain (e.g. arising in the course of a trade) which may be liable to income tax, and a capital gain (which may be liable to CGT) must be borne in mind (see 186).

There are a large number of exemptions and reliefs applying to CGT (see 6150ff.).

For the rates of CGT, see 5410ff.

See *British Tax Reporter* ¶500-200.

5004 Who is liable to CGT?

Except as noted below, any person who is resident or ordinarily resident (see 213, 216) in the UK for all or any part of a tax year is liable to CGT on chargeable gains made in that year. For a discussion of CGT and the foreign element, see 5698ff.

Certain persons, such as charities, approved superannuation funds and foreign diplomats are generally exempt from CGT (see 5800ff.).

Companies are chargeable to corporation tax in respect of their chargeable gains (see 3050).

Law: TCGA 1992, s. 1(2)

See *British Tax Reporter* ¶500-200.

5007 What is chargeable to CGT?

Capital gains tax is charged on chargeable gains accruing on *disposals of assets*.

There is no general definition of 'disposal'. A disposal occurs whenever the ownership of an asset is transferred, whether by sale, exchange or gift. Further, certain events are deemed to be disposals, and disposal includes a part disposal (see 5060ff.).

Law: *Drummond v R & C Commrs*[2008] EWHC (Ch) 1758

See *British Tax Reporter* ¶500-300.

5008 Assets

'Assets' include all kinds of property, whether situated in the UK or not, including:

- stocks and shares;
- options, debts and incorporeal property;

- land and buildings;
- business assets (e.g. goodwill);
- any currency other than sterling; and
- any form of property created by the person disposing of it, or otherwise coming to be owned without being acquired.

Though options are specifically included as assets so that any sale of an option would be potentially chargeable, other special provisions apply to them (see 5980). For debts and CGT, see 6183ff.

A right to receive an unascertained sum sometime in the future upon the occurrence of a contingency is also an asset capable of being valued.

Difficulty is sometimes encountered in discerning the extent of any given asset and whether more than one asset exists, in particular in the case of land. Land and the buildings on it may be treated as separate assets so as to enable a negligible value claim or loss on destruction (see 5086, 5090). HMRC generally argue that goodwill is distinct from any land in respect of which it has been generated. HMRC also generally accept that assets such as milk and potato quotas are separate from the land to which they relate (see 6306).

Law: TCGA 1992, s. 21(1), 144; *Marren (HMIT) v Ingles* (1980) 54 TC 76

See *British Tax Reporter* ¶508-000.

5009   Exempt assets

The disposal of some assets does not give rise to a charge to CGT (or to an allowable loss). Such exempt assets include:

- private cars;
- personal effects and goods worth £6,000 or less when disposed of;
- savings certificates and premium bonds;
- gains made within an individual savings account;
- interest on Individual Savings Accounts (ISAs);
- Child Trust Funds;
- UK government stocks (gilts);
- foreign currency for personal use;
- life assurance policies and deferred annuity contracts, unless purchased from a third party;
- betting, lottery or pools winnings; and
- save as you earn (SAYE) terminal bonuses.

For further details of exemptions and reliefs, see 6140ff.

See *British Tax Reporter* ¶508-400.

5010   Gains chargeable to tax

Capital gains tax is charged in respect of the total amount of chargeable gains in point for any tax year, all 'gains' being 'chargeable gains' in the absence of express exemptions, etc. The appropriate total is the aggregate of those amounts which arise in the tax year after deducting the following:

- any allowable losses accruing in that tax year; and
- allowable losses of any previous year which have been brought forward.

For the computation of gains and losses, see 5220ff.

Law: TCGA 1992, s. 1(3), 2(2), 15(2)

See *British Tax Reporter* ¶508-000.

5013   Location of assets

Persons not resident or ordinarily resident in the UK, but who carry on a business here through a branch or agency, are generally liable to CGT in respect of those assets situated in the UK and used in the business or used or held for the purposes of the branch, etc. (see 5700). Persons who are not domiciled in the UK are only liable to CGT on assets situated outside the UK where the gains are remitted here (see 5698). (The 'UK' generally includes UK territorial waters.) For these and other reasons, rules are laid down to determine the country in which particular types of asset are situated.

For example, shares and securities, and intellectual property rights (patents, trade marks, etc.), are situated in the country where they are registered. Also, a debt which is owed by a bank and is not in sterling and is represented by a sum standing to the credit of an account in the bank of a non-UK domiciled individual is only treated as situated in the UK where that individual is resident in the UK. The branch of the bank at which the account is maintained must also be situated in the UK.

Law: TCGA 1992, s. 10(1), 12(1), 275, 276

See *British Tax Reporter* ¶591-000.

DISPOSALS

INTRODUCTION TO DISPOSALS

5060   Importance of 'disposal'

Capital gains tax (CGT) is charged on chargeable gains accruing on the disposal of assets.

A disposal occurs when an asset is sold, given away or exchanged or when a capital sum is received as a result of the ownership of an asset.

A 'disposal' includes a part disposal, a part disposal occurring where an interest or right in or over the asset is created by the disposal (e.g. the creation of a lease) and where any part of the asset remains undisposed of. For the computation, see 5229.

Deemed disposals

In some cases there may be a deemed disposal (e.g. when a person becomes absolutely entitled to trust property: see 5575); in others there may be an acquisition but no disposal (e.g. property passing to personal representatives: see 5680), or a disposal but no acquisition (as with sums derived from assets: see 5080).

Value shifting

Certain transactions involving value shifting are treated as disposals; these involve:

- sale and leaseback, where there is a subsequent adjustment of the rights in favour of the lessor;
- the extinction, etc. of rights subject to which an asset is held; and
- share transactions (see 5950 (shares generally) and 4161ff. (transactions involving companies and groups)).

The transfer, etc. of an asset by way of the giving of a mortgage or charge is not a disposal of the asset, and a person dealing with the asset so as to enforce the charge does so as nominee for the person who is the owner of the asset subject to the charge.

Law: TCGA 1992, s. 1(1), 15(1), 21(2), 26(1), (2), 29(4), 29(5)

Source: ESC D39

See *British Tax Reporter* ¶514-000.

5062　Disposal proceeds

In most cases, the disposal proceeds are the total proceeds received when the asset is disposed of. This may include cash that is payable at the time of the disposal or at a future date, the value of any asset received in exchange for the asset that is disposed of or the value of the right to receive future payments.

In some cases, the market value is used in the computation in place of the actual disposal proceeds. This will be the case when the disposal is made to a connected person or by way of a bargain not at arm's length. For further details, see 5100ff.

See *British Tax Reporter* ¶514-150.

5065   Exit charges where asset leaves UK tax net

There are various deemed disposals of assets when they leave the UK tax net by virtue of a person ceasing to be UK-resident, a person becoming exempt under a tax treaty, an asset of a non-resident becoming situated outside the UK, or a UK branch ceasing to trade in the UK (see 5705).

See *British Tax Reporter* ¶581-150.

5068   Date of disposal: acquisition under contract and hire-purchase transactions

Where an asset is disposed of and acquired under a contract, the time at which the disposal is made is the time the contract is made. However, if the contract is conditional (e.g. conditional on the exercise of an option), the time at which the disposal is made is the time when the condition is satisfied.

A hire-purchase transaction is treated as a disposal at the beginning of the hire period. This treatment extends to any transaction whereby the use and enjoyment of an asset is passed but transfer of title and consideration is deferred.

Law: TCGA 1992, s. 27, 28; *Lyon (HMIT) v Pettigrew* [1985] BTC 168

See *British Tax Reporter* ¶515-450.

LOSS OF ASSETS AND SUMS DERIVED FROM ASSETS

5080   Capital sums derived from assets

In general, there is a disposal of assets where any capital sum (i.e. money or money's worth) is derived from assets. This is irrespective of whether an asset is acquired by the person making the payment. In particular, there is, prima facie, a disposal (at the time of receipt) where such a capital sum is received:

- in compensation for damage or injury to assets or when an asset is lost, destroyed or dissipated, or in compensation for any depreciation or risk of depreciation (e.g. compensation for infringement of copyright);
- under an insurance policy against risk of damage or injury to, or the loss or depreciation of, an asset;
- in return for the forfeiture or surrender of rights, or for refraining from exercising rights (e.g. compensation for not enforcing a restrictive covenant);
- for the use or exploitation of an asset,

though relief is available where the ultimate benefit is minimal (see 5083). There are exemptions in respect of trees for the occupier of the woodlands on which they stand.

Cash received by depositors when a building society is taken over is not chargeable to CGT. However, members of a society (such as share account holders and other investors or borrowers with membership rights) who receive a cash bonus on the conversion of their account are liable to CGT.

The extinction of an asset is treated as a disposal for the purpose of creating an allowable loss. However, where a person exercises or abandons an option he holds, there is only a disposal for CGT purposes if there is consideration for the abandonment.

Where there is a statutory right to compensation for loss of or damage to an asset, the compensation will frequently not be liable to CGT.

Certain compensation receipts (made under the *Foreign Compensation Act* 1950) in respect of property which has been confiscated or destroyed are exempt. The exemption was formerly given by concession (ESC D50) but the concession has been enacted by TCGA 1992, s. 268B, with effect for capital sums received on or after 1 April 2010 (for corporation tax) or 6 April 2010 (for capital gains tax). The rules are aimed at situations where special legislative provision is made for compensation for losses arising in exceptional circumstances which involved the destruction or confiscation of property, and applies to compensation received after 18 December 1994, and to any case where compensation was received before then but where the liability of such compensation had not been finally determined by that date.

By concession (ESC D33), damages for any wrong or injury suffered by an individual in a personal or professional capacity are exempt from CGT (see 6164).

Law: TCGA 1992, s. 22, 144, 250, 268B; *Davis (HMIT) v Powell* (1976) 51 TC 492; *O'Brien (HMIT) v Benson's Hosiery (Holdings) Ltd* (1979) 53 TC 241; *Davenport (HMIT) v Chilver* [1983] BTC 223; *Drummond (HMIT) v Brown* [1984] BTC 142; *Zim Properties Ltd v Procter (HMIT)* [1985] BTC 42; *Golding (HMIT) v Kaufman* [1985] BTC 92; *Powlson (HMIT) v Welbeck Securities Ltd* [1987] BTC 316; *Kirby (HMIT) v Thorn EMI plc* [1987] BTC 462; *Davis v Henderson* (1995) Sp C 46; *Pritchard v Purves* (1995) Sp C 47; *Foster and Horan v IR Commrs* (1997) Sp C 113

Source: ESC D33

See *British Tax Reporter* ¶514-350.

5083 Compensation and insurance money: minimal benefit

Generally, there is no disposal if a capital sum is derived from an asset in the situation (see 5080) where:

- the sum is wholly applied in restoring the asset; or
- the sum is largely applied in restoring the asset (HMRC consider that at least 95 per cent of the sum should be so applied); or
- the sum is small (not more than five per cent) compared with the value of the asset,

provided that a claim is made by the recipient of the money, for the disposal to be ignored and for his allowable expenditure to be reduced by an equivalent amount.

Example 1

Sue owns an antique violin which she bought for £10,000. The violin is accidentally dropped and it costs £700 to repair it. Sue recovers £700 under her insurance policy. Ordinarily, Sue would be treated as making a disposal when she receives the money, but she makes an election for the disposal to be ignored. Sue's acquisition cost is reduced by £700 (£10,000 − £700 = £9,300). However, the £700 spent on the restoration is in itself allowable expenditure and so Sue's revised allowable expenditure is £9,300 + £700 = £10,000.

However, the relief does not strictly apply to an asset which is a wasting asset (see 5330) or one that is lost or destroyed (see 5086). Insurance proceeds used to restore damage to property held on a short lease are disregarded.

If the allowable expenditure is insufficient to absorb the whole of the reduction, the disposal cannot be ignored but rather than the usual proportion (see 5229), the whole of the allowable expenditure is deductible from the consideration for the part disposal.

Where the capital sum received is only partly used to restore an asset and the rest is not a relatively small amount the recipient may make a claim that the amount spent in restoration should not be treated as consideration for the disposal but instead should be deducted from allowable expenditure. However, a part disposal does take place. (For details of the part disposal calculation, see 5229.)

Example 2

John buys an asset for £20,000. It is later damaged and the cost of restoration is £5,000. However, John receives £7,000 under an insurance policy. The market value of the asset after restoration is £30,000. The part disposal is calculated as follows:

	£
Consideration received for part disposal	2,000.00
Less: allowable expenditure on part disposal	
$(£20,000 + £5,000) \times \dfrac{£2,000}{£2,000 + £30,000}$	(1,562.50)
	437.50

On an eventual disposal of the asset, the deductible expenditure carried forward from the part disposal is calculated as follows:

	£	£
Acquisition cost		20,000.00
Expenditure in restoring asset		5,000.00
		25,000.00
Less:		
(1) allowable expenditure on part disposal	1,562.50	
(2) amount not treated as consideration for part disposal	5,000.00	
		(6,562.50)
Deductible expenditure		18,437.50

Law: TCGA 1992, s. 23(1)–(3); (6)–(8)

See *British Tax Reporter* ¶514-600.

5086   Assets lost or destroyed

In general, on the entire loss, destruction, dissipation or extinction of an asset there is a deemed disposal irrespective of whether compensation is received. However, if the owner receives compensation which he applies in acquiring a replacement asset within one year of receipt (or longer, if HMRC allow), the charge to CGT is deferred if the relevant claim is made.

If only part of the proceeds is used to replace the asset, full deferral is not possible but the taxpayer may claim to deduct part of the replacement expenditure in the computation in respect of the old asset rather than on disposal of the replacement; the part deductible is determined so as to leave chargeable the gain which is not reinvested, the gain being the last part of the proceeds to be so reinvested.

Where a building is destroyed or irreparably damaged and a capital sum received by way of compensation is wholly or partly applied in constructing or otherwise acquiring a replacement building elsewhere, both the original and replacement buildings may be treated as distinct assets separate from the land on which they stand, for the purposes of a claim to defer the charge to CGT.

If the asset is tangible moveable property, see 6155.

Law: TCGA 1992, s. 23(4)–(6); 24(1)

See *British Tax Reporter* ¶515-100.

5090 Assets becoming of negligible value

The owner of an asset which has become of 'negligible value' (which HMRC view as an amount considerably less than five per cent of the value) may make a claim to treat the asset as if it had been sold and immediately reacquired at that negligible value at the time of the claim or at an earlier time specified in the claim. This allows the owner to establish an allowable loss.

The earlier time specified in the claim must be:

(1)   no more than two years before the beginning of the tax year in which the claim is made; or

(2)   (for corporation tax purposes) on or after the first day of the earliest accounting period ending not more than two years before the time of the claim.

However, for the purposes of the restriction on indexation losses (see 5280), indexation relief is calculated as if the sale and reacquisition took place at the time of the claim.

Land and buildings

A building may be treated as a separate asset from the land on which it is erected so as to enable a negligible value claim by reference to the value of the building alone or so that its destruction, etc. will be regarded as a chargeable event; however, the land must also be treated as disposed of, in its case for market value.

Law: TCGA 1992, s. 24(2), (3); *A Director v Inspector of Taxes* (1998) Sp C 161

Source: HMRC Manual, *Capital Gains*: CG13124

See *British Tax Reporter* ¶515-150.

MARKET VALUE

5100 Disposals deemed to be at market value

In general, any acquisition or disposal of an asset is deemed to be for market value if the transaction:

●   is not at arm's length, e.g. a gift, a transfer into a settlement by the settlor, a distribution from a company in respect of shares in the company, or a transaction between connected persons (see 5130); or

●   is wholly or partly for a consideration that cannot be valued; or

●   is in connection with the loss of an office or employment or diminution of emoluments; or

●   is in recognition of past, present or future services.

However, this does not apply to an acquisition unless there is a corresponding disposal, provided there is no consideration in money or money's worth (or the consideration is less than the market value).

Re-basing to 31 March 1982 involves a deemed disposal and reacquisition at market value on that date (see 5300).

Law: TCGA 1992, s. 17, 149A

See *British Tax Reporter* ¶514-150.

5103   What is 'market value'?

The 'market value' of an asset is generally the amount it might reasonably fetch on the open market. Regard is not taken for any reduction in the market value due to the whole of an asset being placed on the market at the same time, e.g. disposal of a large shareholding might lead to a reduced valuation for each share, but this is not taken into account. However, there is a concession for valuing shares at 31 March 1982 where they formed part of a larger holding of a spouse or fellow group company on that date (see 5300).

Where the market value of an asset forming part of a deceased's estate has been ascertained for determining the amount chargeable to inheritance tax, this value may be accepted for CGT purposes at the date of death.

Special provisions apply to the determination of market value for certain disposals between connected persons (see 5136).

The person having custody or possession of any property must permit an authorised Revenue officer to inspect that property in order to ascertain its value.

Law: TMA 1970, s. 111; TCGA 1992, s. 272(1), (2), 274, Sch. 11, para. 8

See *British Tax Reporter* ¶518-850.

5105   Quoted shares and securities

The market value of shares or securities quoted in the Stock Exchange Daily Official List is, in general, either:

- the lower of the two prices shown in the quotations for the shares or securities in the Stock Exchange Daily Official List for the relevant date plus one-quarter of the difference between the two prices ('quarter-up rule'); or
- half way between the highest and the lowest prices at which bargains were recorded on that date.

If the London trading floor is closed on the relevant date, the market value is calculated according to the latest previous date or the earliest subsequent date on which it is open. The figure taken is that which gives the lower value.

For valuing quoted shares and securities on 6 April 1965 a slightly different formula is used.

Law: TCGA 1992, s. 272(3), (4), (6), Sch. 11, para. 3, 6, 7

See *British Tax Reporter* ¶527-950.

5110   Unquoted shares and securities

For unquoted shares or securities disposed of, the market value at any time is the price they would fetch in the open market where the prospective purchaser has all the information that a prudent purchaser might reasonably require were he proposing to purchase the asset from a willing vendor by private treaty and at arm's length.

Securities which were dealt in on the Unlisted Securities Market (USM) or its successor, the Alternative Investment Market (AIM) are not listed in the Stock Exchange Daily Official List and so fall to be treated with other unquoted securities for this purpose. However, in practice, initial evidence of their value will be suggested by bargains done at or near the date in point, though other factors may be more important.

The HMRC Shares Valuation Division (SVD) makes special arrangements in relation to valuations of unquoted shares for CGT purposes at 31 March 1982. These are frequently needed so that CGT computations can take account of indexation and the re-basing of CGT to 1982 (see 5300ff.). Where such values are needed and shareholders with similar holdings agree, the SVD will begin negotiations in advance of a formal request to do so from the tax office. Taxpayers can approach the SVD before making their tax returns or before their tax offices have asked the SVD for assistance.

Law: TCGA 1992, s. 273

Source: SP 18/80, *Securities dealt on the Stock Exchange Unlisted Securities Market: status and valuation for tax purposes*

See *British Tax Reporter* ¶528-300.

5115   Unit holders in unit trusts

Where the managers of a unit trust regularly publish buying and selling prices, the market value of a unit holder's rights in the unit trust is the buying price on the relevant date.

Law: TCGA 1992, s. 272(5)

See *British Tax Reporter* ¶528-150.

DISPOSALS BETWEEN CONNECTED PERSONS

5130   Disposals between connected persons generally

Transactions between 'connected persons' (see 5142) are treated as made other than by way of bargain at arm's length and are therefore deemed to be for a consideration equal to market value (see 5100ff.).

If a loss is incurred when a disposal is made between connected persons, the disponor may not treat it as an allowable loss; the only exception to this rule is where a chargeable gain is made on a later disposal between the same connected persons while they are still connected.

Further, where the disponor grants an option to a connected person, a loss made by the acquirer when he disposes of the option is only an allowable loss if the disposal is on an arm's length basis to a person who is not connected with him.

For married couples, see 5460ff.

For same-sex couples, see 225.

Gifts in settlement

Transactions by trustees are generally subject to the same provisions as other transactions though, by virtue of the limited number of persons with whom they are connected, their application is restricted to transactions with the settlor or persons connected with the settlor (see 5142).

HMRC no longer consider the transfer of unused losses to beneficiaries to be prevented where they are connected with the trust (see 5575).

Disposals made as gifts in settlement are not subject to the rule regarding losses on a disposal to a connected person if the gift and the income from it is wholly or primarily applicable for educational, cultural or recreational purposes. The persons who benefit from it must be restricted to members of an association of persons for whose benefit the gift was made and all or most of whom are not connected.

Schemes which rely on the availability of gifts relief on the disposal of assets to the trustees of trusts which are settlements in which the settlor has an interest are subject to anti-avoidance provisions (see 5550ff. for further details).

Law: FA 2004, s. 116 and Sch. 21; TCGA 1992, s. 18(1)–(5); *Kellogg Brown & Root Holdings Ltd v R & C Commrs* (2008) Sp C 693

See *British Tax Reporter* ¶503-800.

5133 Additional charge on series of transactions

Separate disposals by a person within six years of each other to another person or persons connected with him (see 5142) are each treated as made for a consideration equal to a proportion of the aggregate market value of the assets disposed of, had they been the subject of a single transaction.

Not only may there be a greater CGT liability on a second or later transaction, by virtue of these provisions, but liability in respect of earlier transactions in a series may be increased.

Although the legislation is clearly aimed at the 'fragmentation' of majority shareholdings in companies, or of 'sets' of antiques, in theory it may also catch what at first sight appear to be totally unrelated transactions, since the only requirement for the provisions to apply is that the aggregate value if disposed of together is greater than the sum of the individual values.

There are detailed provisions for determining the original market value and the aggregate market value for this purpose.

Law: TCGA 1992, s. 19, 20

See *British Tax Reporter* ¶530-250.

5136 Disposals subject to right or restriction

Basically, if there is a disposal between connected persons (see 5142) and the person making the disposal, or a person connected with him, has any right or restriction over the asset, then the market value of that asset is calculated as the market value of the asset without the right or restriction, less the lower of the following:

- the market value of the right or restriction; and
- the amount by which the value of the asset would increase were the right or restriction extinguished.

Example

Andy gives as a wedding present to his daughter a plot of land which has planning permission for a house. The gift is subject to a restriction in favour of Andy that no building may be built on the land. His daughter accepted the gift knowing about the restriction.

Capital Gains Tax

The land is valued as follows:

	£
Land with planning permission	50,000
Land with restriction	(10,000)
Increase in value on extinction of restriction	40,000
Market value of restriction	£12,000

On making the gift, Andy is treated as making a disposal of £50,000 less the lower of:

(1)   £12,000 (market value of the restriction);

(2)   £40,000 (increase in value on extinction of restriction),

i.e. A is treated as making a disposal for £38,000.

Law: TCGA 1992, s. 18(6)

See *British Tax Reporter* ¶503-800.

5142   'Connected persons' for CGT

Individuals

A person is connected with an individual if he is:

(1)   the individual's spouse;

(2)   the individual's relative;

(3)   the spouse of a relative of the individual;

(4)   a relative of the individual's spouse;

(5)   the spouse of a relative of the individual's spouse.

'Relative' means brother, sister, ancestor or lineal descendant.

See also the impact of the *Civil Partnerships Act* 2004 on same-sex couples (225).

Example

The following is H's family tree:

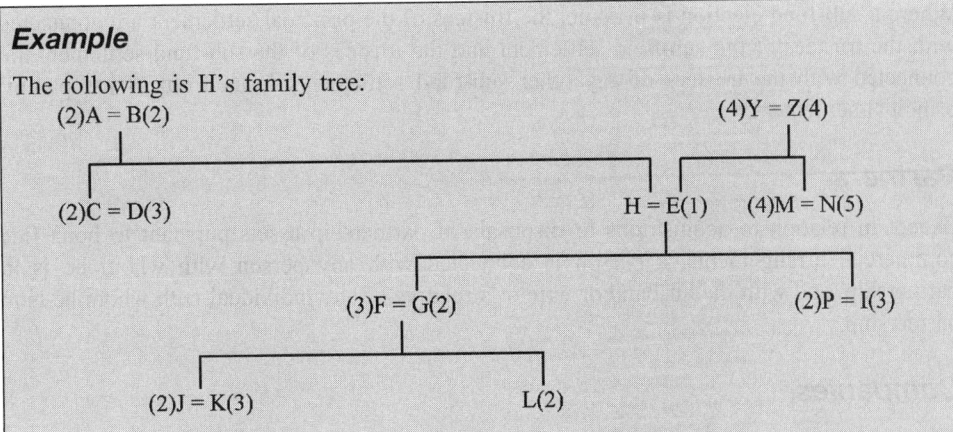

H is connected with all persons shown in this family tree in the manner indicated by the numbers which reflect his relationship with them as shown by (1)–(5) above.

Trustees

The settlor of a settlement and any trustee of the settlement are connected (TCGA 1992, s. 286(1), (3)). The terms 'settlement' and 'settlor' were originally imported from what is now ITTOIA 2005, s. 620. Thus a settlement is 'any disposition, trust, covenant, agreement, arrangement or transfer of assets' involving an element of bounty.

For periods prior to 6 April 2006, a settlor was 'any person by whom the settlement was made'. However, the Finance Act 2006 replaced that imported definition with a general definition applicable for most capital gains purposes. In essence, it still refers to a person who 'makes' a settlement, but expands to deem other actions to be making a settlement also.

Also with effect from 6 April 2006, a specific definition of 'trustee' is now provided for 'connected persons' purposes. Where there would otherwise be no trustee, any person in whom the settled property is vested or who is charged with the management of that property is to be treated as a trustee.

A trustee is also connected with any other person who is connected with the settlor, e.g. a fellow trustee in relation to the same trust, members of the settlor's family (see previous subheading), a person with whom the settlor is in partnership, a company controlled by the settlor (or by him/her and other persons connected with him/her) or any person with whom he/she acts to secure control of a company, etc.

A trustee is connected with any body corporate which is a close company (or a company which would be close, if UK-resident), and of which the trustees are participators or a body controlled (within the meaning of ITA 2007, s. 995; ICTA 1988, s. 840 for corporation tax) by a such a company.

Where a sub-fund election is in force, the trustees of the principal settlement are connected with the trustees of the sub-fund settlement and the trustees of the sub-fund settlement are connected with the trustees of any other sub-fund settlements formed out of its 'parent' principal settlement.

Partners

Except in relation to acquisitions or disposals of partnership assets pursuant to bona fide commercial arrangements, a person is connected with any person with whom he is in partnership, and with the husband or wife or a relative of any individual with whom he is in partnership.

Companies

A company is connected with another company:

- if the same person has control of both, or a person has control of one and persons connected with him, or he and persons connected with him, have control of the other, or
- if a group of two or more persons has control of each company, and the groups either consist of the same persons or could be regarded as consisting of the same persons by treating (in one or more cases) a member of either group as replaced by a person with whom he is connected.

A company is connected with another person, if that person has control of it or if that person and persons connected with him together have control of it.

Any two or more persons acting together to secure or exercise control of a company are to be treated in relation to that company as connected with one another and with any person acting on the directions of any of them to secure or exercise control of the company.

For the definition of 'control', see 4265. 'Company' includes unincorporated associations but excludes partnerships.

Example

(1) Alan has voting control of A Ltd. Alan's brother, Bertie, has voting control of B Ltd. A Ltd and B Ltd are connected. A Ltd is connected with Alan and B Ltd is connected with Bertie.

(2) Z Ltd possesses 51 per cent of the issued share capital in X Ltd and owns 49 per cent of Y Ltd's issued share capital and has an option to purchase a further 2 per cent. X Ltd, Y Ltd and Z Ltd are connected.

Law: TCGA 1992, s. 286, 288(1); *Foulser & Anor v MacDougall* (HMIT) [2007] BTC 95

See *British Tax Reporter* ¶527-750.

5145 Appropriations to and from trading stock

If an asset is not initially acquired as trading stock but is subsequently transferred or appropriated to a trade as trading stock there is a deemed disposal for CGT purposes at the asset's market value (see 5100ff.). The trade is then treated as if the asset was purchased for that value. An election can be made for income tax purposes to bring the asset into trading stock at its market value appropriately reduced (or increased) by the chargeable gain (or allowable loss). The otherwise chargeable gain is thus eliminated by the adjustment to the cost of the trading stock.

The election must be made within 12 months of the 31st January immediately following the end of the tax year during which the period of account in which the appropriation takes place ends.

If the trader appropriates an asset from his trading stock his acquisition cost for CGT purposes is the amount he brings into his trading accounts for tax purposes.

Law: TCGA 1992, s. 161

See *British Tax Reporter* ¶515-300.

COMPUTATION OF GAINS AND LOSSES

INTRODUCTION TO COMPUTATION OF GAINS AND LOSSES

5220 History of computational changes in gains and losses

The rules for computing chargeable gains have changed radically since the introduction of CGT in 1965. General principles on the deduction of allowable expenditure and the treatment of losses apply throughout the lifetime of CGT. Indexation allowance was introduced in 1982, amended in 1985 and potentially restricted with effect from November 1993. The basic rule after April 1988 is that only post-1982 gains and losses are taken into account.

See *British Tax Reporter* ¶518-000.

5221 Basic computation

Basically, CGT is computed by deducting 'allowable expenditure' from the 'disposal proceeds'. Expenditure which is allowable is generally limited by statute (see 5223) and there are specific disallowances (see 5226). Special rules apply to part disposals, contingent liabilities and deferred consideration (see 5229, 5232, 5235).

In its simplest form, the following proforma can be used to compute the gain.

	£	£
Disposal proceeds		x
Less: allowable expenditure		
Acquisition costs (A)	x	
Incidental costs of acquisition (B)	x	
Enhancement expenditure (C)	x	
Incidental disposal costs		(x)
Gain before indexation		x
Less: indexation allowance on A, B and C[1]		(x)
Gain before taper relief/entrepreneurs' relief[2]		x

Notes

[1] Indexation allowance is only available for period to 5 April 1998 (see 5280ff.).

[2] Taper relief, which reduces the amount of the chargeable gain, is available where the asset is held after 5 April 1998 (see 5268). Taper relief was abolished with effect from 5 April 2008 and replaced with entrepreneurs' relief (see 5293).

It has been held that, on general principles, there can be no allowance for inflation in the computation of chargeable gains and allowable losses. Hence, except to the extent to which indexation allowance for disposals on or before 5 April 2008 provided some degree of relief against the loss in purchasing power of the amounts spent on an asset, no account is taken of inflation.

In certain cases, exemptions and reliefs may be available to further reduce the gain. These are dealt with at 6150ff.

For specific provisions applying to shares and securities, see 5820ff.

Law: TCGA 1992, s. 26(3), 37, 52; *Secretan v Hart* [1969] 1 WLR 1159; *Drummond v R & C Commrs* (2007) Sp C 617; *Bentley v Pike (HMIT)* (1981) 53 TC 590; *Stanton (HMIT) v Drayton Commercial Investment Co Ltd* [1982] BTC 269; *Fielder (HMIT) v Vedlynn Ltd* [1992] BTC 347; *Capcount Trading v Evans (HMIT)* [1993] BTC 3

See *British Tax Reporter* ¶518-000.

5223 Allowable capital gains expenditure

In the calculation (see 5221), the following amounts are specifically deductible in calculating the amount of a chargeable gain (for limited exceptions, see 5226).

Acquisition cost

The acquisition cost is the cost of acquiring the asset. This will normally be the purchase price, though in some circumstances, for example if the asset was a gift, the acquisition cost is taken to be the market value at the date of acquisition (see 5100ff. for further examples of where the market value may be used instead).

Where the asset is one which the owner has created himself, the acquisition cost is the capital expenditure incurred wholly and exclusively in creating the asset. This may include, for example, the copyright or patent or the goodwill in a business.

Where the asset is inherited or the owner acquires it as a result of becoming absolutely entitled to settled property, the acquisition cost is the market value at the date of death, or the date on which the owner become absolutely entitled to the property, was appropriate, rather than the market value on the date on which the property was actually acquired.

As far as shares are concerned, the acquisition cost is generally the amount paid for the shares. However, special rules apply where shares of the same class in the same company have been acquired on different occasions. The special rules applying to shares and securities are dealt with at 5820ff.

Incidental costs of acquisition

Also allowable are any incidental costs of acquisition. These are costs incurred wholly and exclusively on the acquisition of the asset and include such costs as the fees, commission, etc. paid for the professional services of a surveyor, valuer, auctioneer, accountant, agent or legal adviser as well as the costs of transfer or conveyance (including stamp duty). However, the incidental expenses of valuation allowed extend only to the initial valuation made in order to comply with the requirements for making a return and not to expenditure incurred for pursuing a dispute with HMRC.

Enhancement expenditure

Enhancement expenditure is expenditure incurred wholly and exclusively in enhancing the value of the asset, and reflected in the asset at the time of sale (but which is more than simply expenditure on maintenance). This does not include the estimated cost of the taxpayer's own labour.

Incidental disposal costs

Incidental costs of disposal, as for incidental costs of acquisition, are allowable. These include the fees, commission, etc. paid for the professional services of a surveyor, valuer, auctioneer, accountant, agent or legal adviser as well as the costs of transfer or conveyance. Also included are the costs of advertising for a buyer and the costs of valuation, e.g. to ascertain market value, for the purposes of computing CGT liability. They do not, in HMRC's view, include the costs of negotiating the value with them.

Other allowable expenditure

Also allowable as a deduction in computing the chargeable gain is expenditure wholly and exclusively incurred by the taxpayer in establishing, preserving or defending his title to, or to a right over, the asset. The costs of personal representatives in establishing title to an asset are also deductible. A HMRC statement of practice sets out a scale of allowable expenditure regarding expenses incurred by personal representatives (see 5695).

As far as legatees and beneficiaries are concerned, a person who disposes of an asset to which he became absolutely entitled as a legatee or as against the trustees of settled property is entitled to deduct, as allowable expenditure, any expenses incurred by him and the personal representatives or trustees in transferring the asset to him (see 5690).

Where value added tax (VAT) suffered on the purchase of an asset is unavailable for set-off in the purchaser's VAT account, the cost for CGT purposes is inclusive of the VAT borne.

Example 1

Anthony buys a George III bureau for £7,000. It is restored at a cost of £3,000. Anthony sells the bureau at auction for £18,000. He pays ten per cent commission to the auctioneer. The chargeable gain is calculated as follows (ignoring indexation):

	£	£
Sale price		18,000
Less: cost of acquisition	7,000	
enhancement of value	3,000	
disposal costs: commission	1,800	
Total allowable expenditure		(11,800)
Chargeable gain		6,200

Example 2

Barry buys a small hotel for £200,000. The legal fees on acquisition were £1,200. A tennis court was added at a cost of £10,000. In order to provide space for a swimming pool the tennis court was dug out. The total cost of this was £30,000. Barry sells the hotel for £350,000. Agents commission and legal fees on sale are £3,500. The chargeable gain is calculated as follows (ignoring indexation, etc.):

	£	£
Sale price		350,000
Less: cost of acquisition	200,000	
legal fees on acquisition	1,200	
enhancement: swimming pool	30,000	
disposal costs: commission, etc.	3,500	
Total allowable expenditure		(234,700)
Chargeable gain		115,300

Capital Gains Tax

No relief is available for the cost of the tennis court because the expenditure is not 'reflected in the state of the asset at the time of disposal'.

Wasting assets

The acquisition cost is written off over the life of certain wasting assets, so that allowable expenditure is reduced (see 5330ff.).

Rebasing

Where the disponor did not hold the asset on 31 March 1982 but is treated for re-basing purposes as if he did so (see 5304), he is also treated as having incurred any enhancement expenditure which arose between that date and the time that he actually acquired it.

Law: TCGA 1992, s. 38(1), (2), (4), 43, 52(1); *IR Commrs v Richards' Exors* (1971) 46 TC 626; *Oram (HMIT) v Johnson* (1980) 53 TC 319; *Chaney v Watkis (HMIT)* [1986] BTC 44; *Couch (HMIT) v Caton's Administrators* [1997] BTC 360; VAT statement of practice D7; SP 2/04 (replacing SP 8/94 from 6 April 2004)

See *British Tax Reporter* ¶519-500.

5226 Expenditure statutorily disallowed in computing gains

The following items of expenditure are not generally deductible when computing the CGT liability:

- interest payments, except in relation to the financing of certain building work by companies (see 4027);
- expenditure allowable in computing the profits, etc. of a trade, profession or vocation for income tax purposes;
- expenditure to the extent that it is covered directly or indirectly by any central or local government or authority, in the UK or elsewhere, by way of a grant, reimbursement, etc. If the recipient of the grant has to repay it either directly or through a reduction in the amount of a later grant otherwise receivable, HMRC permit the consideration received for the asset in question to be reduced by the amount repaid;
- insurance premiums;
- where there is a loss on a disposal, any capital allowance or renewals allowance made in respect of that asset to the disponor or, in certain cases (see 3692, 4080, 4096), previous transferors.

Law: TCGA 1992, s. 38(3), 39, 41, 50, 52(5), 174, 205

Source: ESC D53, *Section 50 Taxation of Chargeable Gains Act 1992: grants repaid*

5229 Computation on part disposal

A part disposal occurs when some part of the asset remains undisposed of where a person disposes of an interest or right in or over an asset (see 5060).

Where a part disposal occurs the cost of the asset allowable as a deduction is apportioned between the part of the asset disposed of and the part remaining, according to the value of each part immediately after the disposal. The effect of the apportionment is to reduce the allowable expenditure on a later disposal of the remaining part of the asset. The following fraction is applied to allowable expenditure for the purpose of the apportionment:

$$\frac{A}{A + B}$$

where

A   is the consideration received for the part disposed of; and
B   is the market value of the property which remains undisposed of.

Example

Adam purchases a plot of land for £100,000. He splits it up into two equal plots. He then sells one plot to Bradley for £70,000.

Adam is treated as making a chargeable gain which is calculated as follows:

	£
Market value of part disposed of	70,000
Market value of part retained	70,000

Allowable expenditure on this disposal:

$$\frac{A}{A+B} \times \text{purchase price}$$

$$\frac{£70,000}{£140,000} \times 100,000 = £50,000$$

Chargeable gain: £70,000 − £50,000 = £20,000. (Incidental expenses and indexation, etc. have been disregarded for the purposes of this example.)

The allowable expenditure on a calculation of the gain or loss made when the land remaining is disposed of will also be £50,000.

Where the facts of a particular case show that any expenditure related wholly to the part disposed of, or to the remaining part, it will be treated as relating to that part alone and no apportionment takes place.

In the case of part disposals of land, HMRC allow an alternative basis of valuation for the part retained, i.e. the part disposed of is treated as a separate asset, and any fair and reasonable method of apportioning the allowable expenditure relating to both the part disposed of and the part retained is accepted (e.g. a reasonable valuation of the part disposed at the date of acquisition).

Example

Alastair buys 600 acres of farmland for £100,000 on 6 October 1981. He sells 150 acres for £50,000 on 4 May 2010. If Alastair elects for the alternative basis, he will not have to obtain a valuation of the part retained as at 4 May 2010. Instead, HMRC will accept an apportionment based on the value on 6 October 1981. Thus, the CGT payable is calculated on the price received on the sale less the valuation made of the part disposed:

$$£50,000 - £25,000 \text{ (i.e. } \frac{150}{600} \times £100,000\text{*)} = £25,000$$

*or March 1982 value, if greater

(Incidental costs of acquisition and disposal, indexation, taper relief, etc., have been ignored.)

The carry-forward of the part retained will be £100,000 − £25,000 = £75,000.

For certain small part disposals of a holding of land the transferor may make a claim for the transfer not to be treated as a disposal and the base cost of the total holding is reduced by the consideration received for the disposal. These rules apply where the amount or value of the consideration does not exceed the lower of one-fifth of the market value of the holding as it subsisted immediately before the transfer and £20,000, or if the land was compulsorily acquired or could have been so acquired by the transferee.

Example

Rupert buys Blackacre, a 100 acre farm, for £10,000. He sells five acres for £750 and makes the above claim. The remaining 95 acres will have a base value of (£10,000 − £750) = £9,250.

If the allowable expenditure is insufficient to absorb the whole of the reduction, the disposal cannot be ignored but, rather than the usual proportion, the whole of the allowable expenditure is deductible from the consideration for the part disposal. Similar rules apply to compensation for assets not lost or destroyed (see 5083), capital distributions (see 5890) and premiums on conversion of securities (see 5913).

Apportionment on a part disposal takes place before applying any rule which has the effect of producing neither a gain nor a loss on a disposal, for instance a disposal between a husband and a wife (see 5500) and replacement roll-over relief (see 6305ff.).

A reasonable rather than strict valuation is acceptable where a first or subsequent interim distribution is made during the course of the liquidation of an unquoted company. Shares and securities are dealt with at 5820ff.

There is also a simplified tax scheme for individuals investing regular sums in monthly savings schemes of authorised unit trusts and approved investment trusts.

Law: TCGA 1992, s. 23(6)–(8), 42, 242, 243, 244

See *British Tax Reporter* ¶520-050.

5232   Contingent liabilities

Contingent liabilities are not generally taken into account in initially determining CGT liability. If a contingent liability, such as a payment under a warranty has become enforceable, subsequent adjustments are made on a claim by discharge or repayment of tax.

Law: TCGA 1992, s. 49

5235   Deferred consideration

No allowance is made for delay in receipt of deferred consideration (e.g. a purchase price paid by instalments) in computing CGT liability; however, if the amount itself cannot be estimated at the outset (including reference to a maximum figure), it cannot form part of the 'consideration' (see 5221) but the right to it may be a separate asset acquired as part of the proceeds, at its value at that time, so that eventual receipt may constitute a disposal of the right and result in an additional CGT charge (see 5007).

The computation is based on the total amount of the consideration but, if there would otherwise be hardship, payment may be made by instalments.

Any part of the consideration which is subsequently shown to be irrecoverable is taken account of by later adjustments.

Law: TCGA 1992, s. 48, 280; *Goodbrand (HMIT) v Loffland Bros North Sea Inc* [1998] BTC 297; *Garner (HMIT) v Pounds Shipowners and Shipbreakers Ltd* [2000] BTC 190

See *British Tax Reporter* ¶508-100.

CAPITAL GAINS LOSSES

5260 Relevance of losses for CGT

Capital gains tax is charged on capital gains less 'allowable losses'. There are rules for establishing the amount of allowable losses (see 5263) and for determining the manner in which they are relieved (see 5265).

See *British Tax Reporter* ¶523-900.

5263 Establishing allowable losses

The following general rules apply to the calculation of losses for the purposes of tax on chargeable gains.

- *Computation:* losses arising on a disposal are computed in the same way as gains though, formerly indexation allowance and taper relief could not generally be used to create or increase a loss (see 5280). Losses must be set off against gains arising in the same tax year and only the excess of losses over gains may be carried forward.
- *Losses which are not allowable*: where if a gain arose on a disposal it would not be a chargeable gain, a loss arising on such a disposal cannot be an allowable loss.
- *Non-residents*: a loss accruing to a person in a tax year during which he is neither resident nor ordinarily resident in the UK is not an allowable loss. However, a non-resident trading through a branch or agency in the UK who is liable to CGT is entitled to relief for losses on those assets which, had there been a gain on disposal, would have given rise to a chargeable gain.
- *Non-domiciles*: losses accruing to an individual who is not domiciled in the UK on the disposal of foreign assets are not allowable losses.

A mechanism is provided for making a claim to a loss in a schedule to the tax return. This means that it is not necessary to wait until there are capital gains to offset before agreeing the amount of a loss. Losses claimed under these provisions take priority over losses brought forward from earlier tax years/accounting periods.

Law: FA 1995, s. 113(2); TCGA 1992, s. 16(1)

See *British Tax Reporter* ¶523-900.

5265 Relief for capital gains losses

The following rules relate to the use of 'allowable losses' (see 5260) for CGT purposes.

- *Losses and gains in the same year*: allowable losses must first be relieved against chargeable gains arising in the same tax year (see 5010) even if this has the effect of reducing total gains below the annual exemption.
- *Carry-back/carry-forward*: allowable losses cannot be carried back and relieved against

gains of earlier years, except on death (see 5685) or where the loss accrues in respect of a mineral lease or agreement. However, allowable losses can be carried forward indefinitely, but they must be set off against gains at the earliest opportunity (see 5010). However, losses brought forward from 1996–97 and later years must be used before losses brought forward from earlier years. Losses carried forward need only be used to reduce gains to the level of the 'annual exempt amount' (see 6150) for that year, and surplus losses may continue to be carried forward.

Finance Act 2003 introduced a rule to the effect that where a person disposes of an asset and incurs a liability to CGT on a gain on the disposal, and some or all of the consideration for the disposal of the original asset consists of a right to further payment (or series of further payments) whose amount or value cannot be established at the time the right is conferred, the person is treated as disposing of the right of an allowable loss for CGT purposes in a tax year which is later than the one in which the original asset was disposed of. In such circumstances, the person may elect to treat that loss as accruing in the year when the gain accrued.

- *Loss relief*: relief for losses can be given once only. No additional relief is available where relief has already been given under the Income Tax Acts.
- *Transactions between connected persons*: losses arising to a person on disposals between connected persons may not be relieved against chargeable gains except those arising to him on some other disposal to that same connected person (see 5130ff.).
- *Set-off against income*: capital losses cannot generally be set off against income. However, individuals and investment companies are entitled to relief from income tax and corporation tax for allowable losses accruing on disposing of shares in qualifying trading companies (see 5940).
- Whether a loss is an allowable loss is determined in the same way as for the ascertainment of whether a gain is a chargeable gain, but, from 6 December 2006, subject to anti-avoidance rules. Hence, there is a requirement that there is a chargeable asset on which the loss arises; this is sometimes sufficient to deny relief for a loss.
- *Finance Act* 2007 introduced a measure to stop groups of companies engaged in buying and selling companies, securing a tax advantage through gaining access to their capital losses and gains (see 3682).

Example 1

In 2010–11, Jake has chargeable gains of £15,000 and allowable losses for the year of £12,000. As the losses and gains arise in the same year, the allowable losses must be set in full against the gains, reducing the net chargeable gains to £3,000. As this is below the annual exemption, no CGT is payable. There are no losses to carry forward.

Example 2

Nigel has chargeable gains of £6,000 and allowable losses of £9,500 in 2010–11. The allowable losses are set against the gains so as to fully extinguish them, leaving allowable losses of £3,500 (£9,500 − £6,000) to be carried forward.

Example 3

In 2010–11, Emily realises chargeable gains of £14,000. She has losses brought forward of £10,000. The annual exemption is £10,100.

The losses brought forward are set against the gain so as to reduce it to the level of the annual exemption. Thus £3,900 of the brought forward loss is used in 2010–11, leaving allowable losses of £6,100 (£10,000 − £3,900) to be carried forward.

Where a company may set off trading losses against any of its profits liable to corporation tax, these include chargeable gains (see 3131).

Law: FA 2003, s. 162; TCGA 1992, s. 2(2), (3), 3(5)

See *British Tax Reporter* ¶523-900.

TAPER RELIEF (TO 5 APRIL 2008)

5268   Introduction

Taper relief applied from 6 April 1998 to 5 April 2008 in respect of disposals by individuals, trustees and personal representatives. It did not apply to companies, which generally continued to be subject to the indexation regime (see 5280).

Taper relief was also not available to set against chargeable gains which were treated as accruing to beneficiaries of an offshore trust under the anti-avoidance provisions in TCGA 1992, Sch. 4C, para. 11.

Any deferred gain brought into charge by TCGA 1992, s. 284A(3) was not eligible for taper relief.

Indexation relief was withdrawn for disposals after 5 April 1998 and replaced by taper relief which reduced the amount of the chargeable gain the longer the asset was held after 5 April 1998, with a greater reduction for business assets. However, the gain could not be reduced to nil; the maximum reduction, which applied after a qualifying holding period of four years (or ten years for non-business assets), was 75 per cent for business assets but only 40 per cent in other cases. Taper relief was based on the size of the gain and the length of time an asset had been held. The relief ignored the amount of the initial investment.

For assets acquired prior to 1 April 1998, indexation, from acquisition (or March 1982, if later) to April 1998, will be given in arriving at the chargeable gain, which will then be reduced by taper relief. In assessing the chargeable gain eligible for taper relief on a disposal after 5 April 1998, the cost taken is the indexed cost up to 1 April 1998.

In order to be eligible for taper relief, the asset either has to be a business asset owned for at least one complete year after 5 April 1998, or a non-business asset owned for at least three complete years after 5 April 1998. (This is subject to certain special provisions for assets owned prior to 17 March 1998.)

Law: FA 1998, Sch. 21, para. 8; TCGA 1992, s. 2A, 3(5)–(5C), Sch. A1

Source: CGT 1, *Capital gains tax: an introduction*

Website: www.hmrc.gov.uk/guidance/cgt1.pdf

See *British Tax Reporter* ¶521-050.

5269 Losses: calculation of the relief

For disposals prior to 6 April 2008, taper relief was applied after deducting allowable losses. The annual exemption was set against the net tapered gains (see 6150, 6152). Losses brought forward from an earlier year, or carried back from the year in which a person died (see 5685), need only be used to the extent to which it is necessary to reduce the untapered net gains to the level of the annual exemption (see 6150).

Law: FA 1998, Sch. 21, para. 8; TCGA 1992, s. 2A, 3(5)–(5C), Sch. A1

Source: CGT 1, *Capital gains tax: an introduction*

Website: www.hmrc.gov.uk/guidance/cgt1.pdf

See *British Tax Reporter* ¶521-100.

5270 Qualifying holding period

For disposals prior to 6 April 2008, the qualifying holding period is the time from 6 April 1998, or the date of acquisition of the asset if later, to the date the asset is disposed of.

The qualifying holding period of an asset is generally calculated on the basis of ownership of the asset after 5 April 1998 on the basis that before April 1998 indexation relief was available to reduce the chargeable gains.

Bonus year

However, in the case of non-business assets owned (for whatever period) before 17 March 1998, one year is automatically added to the qualifying holding period. Thus if a non-business asset is owned before that date, the disposal must occur after 5 April 2000 before any taper relief will apply.

As far as business assets are concerned the position is slightly more complicated. If the business asset is acquired before 17 March 1998 and the disposal takes place before 6 April 2000, the bonus year is available and the number of complete years that the asset is held after 6 April 1998 is increased by one.

However, in consequence of the introduction of a more generous taper for business assets disposed of after 6 April 2000, the bonus year does not apply if the business asset is disposed of after that date, irrespective of whether the asset was acquired before 17 March 1998.

Example 1

Matthew acquires a non-business asset on 22 May 1996. He disposes of it on 24 April 2007. For taper relief purposes, Matthew will have held the asset for nine complete years from April 1998 to the date of its disposal. However, as the asset was held on 17 March 1998, Matthew qualifies for the bonus year. Thus the taper relief will be calculated as if the asset had been held for ten years after April 1998 (nine years actual holding plus the bonus year). Indexation relief will be available for the period from acquisition in May 1995 to April 1998.

Example 2

Jackie acquires a non-business asset on 30 June 1998. She disposes of it on 27 August 2007. At the time of disposal, she has held the asset for nine complete years. As the asset was acquired after 17 March 1998, the bonus year is unavailable. Thus taper relief is based on the actual holding period of nine years.

Where the asset is acquired after 16 March 1998, the bonus year is not in point. Taper relief is based on the actual number of years for which the asset has been held at the date of its disposal.

For these purposes, a year is any continuous period of 12 months. A year does not have to coincide with a tax year (though it will do so for assets acquired before 6 April 1998 because of the deemed starting date). Fractions of years are ignored. If an asset is disposed of an the anniversary of its acquisition, HMRC accept that it has been held for a complete number of years.

Law: FA 1998, Sch. 21, para. 8; TCGA 1992, s. 2A, 3(5)–(5C), Sch. A1

Source: CGT 1, *Capital gains tax: an introduction*

Website: www.hmrc.gov.uk/guidance/cgt1.pdf

See *British Tax Reporter* ¶521-150.

5271 Percentage of gain chargeable

For disposals before 6 April 2008, taper relief operated in accordance with the tables at 84, which set out the reduction in the percentage of gain chargeable for business and non-business assets.

The period over which taper relief reduced the gain for business assets was decreased from four years to two years in respect of disposals after 5April 2002. However, the bonus year (see 5270) applying to assets held before 17 March 1998 is not in point where the disposal is after 6 April 2000.

Percentage of gain chargeable on non-business assets

The chargeable gain from a non-business asset reduced by 5 per cent per annum after a 'qualifying holding period' of at least three years. If the asset had a qualifying holding period of ten years or more, only 60 per cent of the gain will be chargeable.

Example 1

Penny acquires a non-business asset on 26 January 1998. She disposes of it on 3 May 2007. The gain (after indexation allowance) is £12,000.

At the date of disposal she has held the asset for nine complete years since 6 April 1998. As the asset was acquired before 17 March 1998, she qualifies for the bonus year. The taper relief is thus based on a holding period of ten years and thus 60 per cent of the gain (£7,200, i.e. £12,000 × 60 per cent) is chargeable.

Percentage of gain chargeable on business assets

For disposals after 5 April 2002 but before 6 April 2008, the chargeable gain reduced by 50 per cent after the first year, and by 25 per cent after the second year, so that after a two year qualifying holding period only 25 per cent of the gain was chargeable.

Example 2

Louise acquires a business asset on 5 May 2000 and sells it on 10 June 2002, realising a gain of £12,000. It was a business asset throughout her period of ownership.

Because it has been held for more than two whole years at the time of disposal, only 25 per cent of the gain is chargeable to tax (£3,000, i.e. £12,000 × 25 per cent).

For disposals between 6 April 2000 and 5 April 2002, the chargeable gain reduces by 12.5 per cent per annum for the first two years of the qualifying holding period then by 25 per cent per annum for the next two years, so that after four years only 25 per cent of the gain is chargeable. The bonus year does not apply if the disposal of the business asset is after 6 April 2000, even if it was acquired before 17 March 1998.

Example 3

Greg acquires a business asset on 24 July 1998. He sells it on 15 September 2001. At the time of disposal he has held the asset for three complete years. Taper relief, based on a qualifying holding period of three years, reduces the gain so that only 50 per cent of it is chargeable.

Law: FA 1998, Sch. 21, para. 8; TCGA 1992, s. 2A, 3(5)–(5C), Sch. A1

Source: CGT 1, *Capital gains tax: an introduction*

Website: www.hmrc.gov.uk/guidance/cgt1.pdf

See *British Tax Reporter* ¶521-200.

5272 Conditions for shares to qualify as business assets (pre-6 April 2008 disposals)

The following shares are treated as business assets if they are within the widened definition of a 'qualifying company'. Broadly, a 'qualifying company' is a trading company or the holding company of a trading group and one or more of the following conditions apply:

- the company was unlisted;
- the individual was an officer or employee of the company, or of a company having a relevant connection with it; or
- the individual was able to exercise not less than 5 per cent of the voting rights.

Business assets taper relief is available on the shares held by an officer or employee in a non-trading company, being the employing company or a company connected with the employing company, provided the officer or employee does not have a material interest in the company or a company controlling the company. The officer or employee has a material interest if he or she holds, or is entitled to hold, more than 10 per cent of: the voting rights, any shareholding, profit distribution rights, or asset distribution rights. It should be noted that the holdings, or entitlements, of persons connected with the officer or employee (e.g. a husband or wife, relatives, and certain trusts and companies) are taken into account for determining whether a material interest exists.

As far as trustees of a settlement are concerned, the company is a qualifying company if it is a trading company or a holding company of a trading group and the company is unlisted, either:

(i)   an eligible beneficiary is an officer or employee of the company, or of a company having a relevant connection with it, or
(ii) the trustees are able to exercise at least 5 per cent of the voting rights.

Business assets taper relief is also available on shares in a non-trading company, as applies to an officer or employee, for trustees where an eligible beneficiary is likewise an officer or employee. The trustees must not have a material interest, i.e. one which is determined in a similar way as that for officers or employees.

Where the disposal is made by the individual's personal representative, the company is a qualifying company provided that it is a trading company or a member of a trading group and the company is unlisted and/or the personal representatives are able to exercise at least 5 per cent of the voting rights in the company.

Law: FA 2001, s. 78, Sch. 26; FA 2000, s. 67; FA 1998, Sch. 21, para. 8; TCGA 1992, s. 2A, 3(5)–(5C), Sch. A1

Source: CGT 1, *Capital gains tax: an introduction*

Website: www.hmrc.gov.uk/guidance/cgt1.pdf

See *British Tax Reporter* ¶522-150.

5273 Conditions for other assets to qualify as business assets (pre-6 April 2008 disposals)

Individuals

An asset disposed of by an individual must satisfy one of the following conditions to qualify as a business asset (other than shares).

(1) It must be used for the purposes of a trade carried on by the individual or by a partnership of which he is a member. Alternatively, the asset owned by the individual can be used for the purposes of a trade carried on by a trading company or holding company of a trading group provided one of the following conditions is met:

    (a)   the company is unlisted;
    (b)   the individual works either part- or full-time for the company; or
    (c)   the individual holds five per cent or more of the voting shares.

(2) An asset qualifies as a business asset if it is owned by the individual and used for the purposes of a trade carried on by a subsidiary company of a trading group where the holding company is a qualifying company.

(3) An asset qualifies as a business asset if it is used for the purposes of an office or employment held by the individual with a person carrying on a trade.

Note that FA 2003 relaxed the condition that the individual works for the company. For periods of ownership from 6 April 2004, assets used for the purposes of the trade carried on by an individual, trustees of settlements, personal representatives or certain partnerships will qualify as business assets irrespective of whether the owner of the asset is involved in carrying on the trade concerned.

Trustees and personal representatives (pre-6 April 2008 disposals)

An asset owned by trustees qualifies as a business asset if it is used for the purposes of:

- a trade carried on by the trustees, by an eligible beneficiary (see above) or by a partnership in which either the beneficiary is a member or the trustees are a member; or
- a trade carried on by a trading company or member of a trading group where the group holding company or the trading company is unlisted or the trustees have five per cent or more of the voting rights or the beneficiary is an officer or employee of the company in which the asset is used.
- an office or employment held by an eligible beneficiary with a person carrying on a trade.

Broadly similar rules apply to assets used for the purposes of a trade carried on by personal representatives.

Note that FA 2003 relaxed the condition that trustees of settlements and personal representatives are involved in the company. For periods of ownership from 6 April 2004, assets used for the purposes of trades carried on by trustees of settlements or personal representatives will qualify as business assets irrespective of whether the owner of the asset is involved in carrying on the trade concerned.

Legatees (pre-6 April 2008 disposals)

An asset may qualify if acquired by a person as legatee (see 5690) who then disposes of it and it does not qualify as a business asset in the legatee's hands but did qualify as such in the personal representatives' hands.

Apportionment for non-business use (pre-6 April 2008 disposals)

Apportionments are made where assets have been business assets for only some of the relevant period of ownership, or are (in the case of assets apart from shares) used only partly for business purposes.

Law: FA 2003, s. 160; FA 1998, Sch. 21, para. 8; TCGA 1992, s. 2A, 3(5)–(5C), Sch. A1

Source: CGT 1, *Capital gains tax: an introduction*

Website: www.hmrc.gov.uk/guidance/cgt1.pdf

See *British Tax Reporter* ¶521-300.

5274   Taper relief: special cases (pre-6 April 2008 disposals)

Options

Where an asset is acquired by exercising an option, the taper period runs from the time of exercise. Whether the gain arising qualifies for business or non-business taper depends on the underlying asset.

Assets derived from other assets

Where assets have been merged or divided, the taper period can run from the earliest time when an interest was acquired in the original asset.

Assets transferred between spouses

Where an asset has been transferred between spouses who live together (see 5500) the taper relief on a subsequent disposal is based on the combined period of ownership of the spouses. Whether an asset was a business asset at any time in that period is determined by the use made of it by the spouse holding it at that time.

Held-over gains, rolled over gains and other deferred gains

For other no gain/no loss transfers and for gifts hold-over relief, the taper operates by reference to the holding period of the new holder. Where gains have been relieved under a provision which reduces the cost of a replacement asset (e.g. roll-over relief for business assets), the taper operates by reference to the holding period of the new asset. Where a relief defers the gain on a disposal until a later occasion, such as on the relief on reinvestment in a venture capital trust, the taper operates by reference to the holding period of the asset on which the deferred gain arose.

Anti-avoidance provisions

Anti-avoidance provisions aim to prevent persons claiming taper relief on an artificially extended qualifying holding period. Thus, for example, the taper period stops running at any time that the holder of an asset is not exposed to changes in the value of the asset.

Settled property originating from more than one settlor

Where settled property originates from more than one settlor, the property is treated as comprised in different settlements.

Law: TCGA 1992, s. 2A, 3(5)–(5C), Sch. A1; FA 1998, Sch. 21, para. 8

Source: CGT 1, *Capital gains tax: an introduction*

Website: www.hmrc.gov.uk/guidance/cgt1.pdf

See *British Tax Reporter* ¶522-700.

INDEXATION ALLOWANCE (TO 5 APRIL 2008)

5280 Introduction

Finance Act 2008 contained provisions for the withdrawal of indexation allowance in respect of disposals by individuals and trustees occurring on or after 6 April 2008. It remains available in respect of disposals by companies within the charge to corporation tax on chargeable gains. The commentary in the following paragraphs is therefore only applicable for periods up to 5 April 2008.

Since the introduction of CGT, the effect of inflation often meant that increases in the value of assets were much greater than otherwise might have been and that CGT was taxing gains due to inflation rather than real gains.

A measure of relief was introduced in 1982 by a complex system of indexing items of 'allowable expenditure' (see 5223). This is done by effectively adjusting allowable expenditure for increases in the Retail Prices Index (RPI), though the adjustment is a single item to be set against the gain; as before 6 April 1985, for disposals after 29 November 1993 this cannot generally create or increase a loss (see also 5283).

For individuals or trusts made before 30 November 1993, indexation effectively lost under the above rules in respect of disposals before 6 April 1995 gives rise to an 'indexation loss' which, in certain circumstances, can be relieved. Such indexation losses for 1993–94 reduce net gains otherwise brought into charge – 'relevant gains' – for that year, any excess being carried forward and added to indexation losses in 1994–95 for relief in that year; the maximum relief is generally £10,000. There are special rules for appropriations to/from trading stock and where the taxpayer also seeks income relief for a disposal of shares in a qualifying trading company.

Before the general restriction of indexation allowance from 30 November 1993 where it would create or increase a loss (see above), the allowance was removed or restricted to prevent losses in respect of the following:

- transfers of debts or redeemable preference shares between associated companies or companies within a group involving 'linked company financing' – aimed at preventing the artificial arrangement of a debt on a security between related companies which could be repaid in full but with an allowable loss equal to the indexation allowance;
- shares in a building society or registered industrial and provident society – aimed at preventing the former practice of closing share accounts in order to crystallise an allowable loss equal to the indexation allowance;
- deposit-based unit trust and offshore funds where at least 90 per cent of the market value of the investment property consists of non-chargeable assets and/or shares in building societies;
- certain oil-industry assets.

Replacement of indexation allowance by taper relief

For disposals after 5 April 1998 by individuals, trustees and personal representatives, indexation allowance has been replaced by a taper which reduces the amount of the chargeable gain the longer the asset is held after that date, with a greater reduction for business assets (see 5268).

Indexation allowance is only given in the months after April 1998 for companies within the charge to corporation tax. Indexation allowance is frozen for periods after April 1998 in respect of assets held by all other persons. Thus for individuals, trustees and personal representatives who hold assets acquired before 1 April 1998, indexation allowance is computed only up to April 1998. The withdrawal of the allowance is meant to be compensated for by the introduction of taper relief.

Law: TCGA 1992, s. 53(1)–(2A), (4)

Source: CGT 1, *Capital gains tax: an introduction*

Website: www.hmrc.gov.uk/guidance/cgt1.pdf

See *British Tax Reporter* ¶523-250.

5283 Description of indexation allowance

For the availability of indexation allowance on disposals after 5 April 1998, see 5268.

The indexation allowance applied to items of allowable expenditure, thereby adjusting for changes in the Retail Prices Index between acquisition (or 31 March 1982, if later) and disposal.

Where allowable expenditure is written down over the life of an asset (see 5330ff.) the written-down value is the value to which the indexation allowance applies.

Source: CGT 1, *Capital gains tax: an introduction*

Website: www.hmrc.gov.uk/guidance/cgt1.pdf

See *British Tax Reporter* ¶523-900.

5284 Substitution of March 1982 values

Where an asset was held on 31 March 1982, a gain may, since 1988, be re-based to that date (see 5300ff.); the manner in which this is effected brings about a deemed disposal and reacquisition at that date so that, in such cases, indexation allowance automatically becomes based on the 1982 value. Before re-basing was introduced, where a taxpayer held the asset on that date (or it existed on that date and had been the subject of only no gain/no loss transfers since then) he could nonetheless claim to have the indexation allowance based on the asset's market value (see 5103) at that date rather than on expenditure incurred before that date – this uplift continues to be relevant where re-basing does not apply, though no claim is required. If the disposal takes place after 29 November 1993, indexation allowance cannot create or increase a loss (see 5280); however, an exception is made where the disponor is treated as having held the asset on 31 March 1982 for indexation purposes following one or more no gain/no loss transfers – i.e. indexation allowance to the date of any transfer to him before 29 November 1993 can create or increase his loss. In practice, where re-basing is competent even though the disponor did not hold the asset on 31 March 1982, indexation applies to all enhancement expenditure incurred after that date, whether by the disponor or another person (see 5286).

The Shares Valuation Division may begin negotiations in respect of the value of unquoted shares before a referral from HMRC, usually for indexation allowance and re-basing purposes (see 5103).

Law: TCGA 1992, s. 53(3), 55

Source: CGT 1, *Capital gains tax: an introduction*

Website: www.hmrc.gov.uk/guidance/cgt1.pdf

See *British Tax Reporter* ¶523-450.

5286 Computation of indexation allowance

For the availability of indexation allowance on disposals after 5 April 1998, see 5268.

Although there are special rules for most shares (see 5826), the indexation allowance is generally calculated as follows.

Step 1

Identify each item of allowable expenditure.

Step 2

Calculate the indexed rise in that expenditure.

This is done by applying the following formula (expressed as a decimal and rounded to the nearest third decimal place) to each item of allowable expenditure:

$$\frac{RD - RI}{RI}$$

where

RD   is the RPI for the month of disposal; and
RI   is the RPI for the later of (a) March 1982, (b) the month of the expenditure (see 7 for monthly RPI figures).

The resultant figure is the indexed rise for that item of expenditure.

Step 3

Add together the indexed rise for each item of expenditure. The final total is the indexation allowance, subject to possible restriction where it would create or increase a loss (see 5280).

Expenditure on the enhancement, etc. of an asset is generally assumed to have been incurred when the expenditure became due and payable; where the disponor is treated as if he held the asset on 31 March 1982, this applies equally to enhancement or title expenditure which he is deemed to have incurred (see 5223). There are special provisions for certain call options.

Example

Toby buys a house in January 1987 which is not his sole or main residence (so not exempt from charge).

Step 1

He has the following items of allowable expenditure:

	£
(1) purchase price	50,000
(2) legal fees	400
(3) survey fees	150
(4) cost of extending central heating in October 1988	1,500

He sells the house in January 1997 for £92,000 incurring incidental costs of £500.

The RPI is 100.0 for January 1987
             109.5 for October 1988
             154.4 for January 1997

Step 2

Calculate indexation allowance for purchase price and incidental costs of acquisition:

$$£50,550 \times \frac{(154.4 - 100)}{100}$$

i.e. £50,550 × 0.544 = £27,499.

Calculate indexation allowance for enhancement expenditure:

$$£1,500 \times \frac{(154.4 - 109.5)}{109.5}$$

i.e. £1,500 × 0.410 = £615

Step 3

Add indexation allowances together:

£27,499 + £615 = £28,114 total indexation allowance.

Toby's chargeable gain is therefore:

	£	£
Sale price		92,000
Less: purchase price	50,000	
legal fees	400	
survey fees&	150	
central heating	1,500	
disposal costs	500	
		(52,550)
Unindexed gain		39,450
Less: indexation allowance		(28,114)
Chargeable gain		11,336

Where one asset is derived from another asset (perhaps rather than being acquired), expenditure on the original asset is apportioned between the two assets or, if the original asset ceases to exist, is attributed to the new asset (see 5223); by concession, HMRC will allow indexation allowance on the costs of acquisition of a lease to be calculated by reference to the date it was acquired, even though it ceased to exist on the acquisition of a superior interest in the property, such as the freehold reversion.

A gain realised on the disposal of assets acquired before the introduction of CGT in 1965, and to which the indexation allowance provisions apply, is computed by applying the time-apportionment rules after deduction of indexation allowance. This continues to be relevant where re-basing is excluded.

Law: TCGA 1992, s. 54, 114, 145; *Smith (HMIT) v Schofield* [1993] BTC 147

Source: ESC D42; CGT 1, *Capital gains tax: an introduction*

Website: www.hmrc.gov.uk/guidance/cgt1.pdf

See *British Tax Reporter* ¶523-350.

5289 Indexation allowance on part disposals

For the availability of indexation allowance on disposals after 5 April 1998, see 5268.

On a part disposal of an asset, allowable expenditure is apportioned between the part disposed of and the part retained (see 5229). This apportionment is to be made before the calculation of the indexation allowance; thus, the expenditure apportioned to the part retained is not taken into account in determining the indexation allowance.

In certain circumstances, the whole (or part) of the allowable expenditure may be taken into account in calculating the gain on the part disposed of with a corresponding reduction in the allowable expenditure on the part retained; in such cases as set out below, indexation allowance is calculated in respect of the subsequent disposal (of the part originally retained) on the amount without reduction and is then reduced by the amount of a notional indexed adjustment based on:

- the allowance already given against a receipt of compensation or insurance money (see 5083);
- the allowance already given against a capital distribution (see 5890);
- the allowance already given against a premium on conversion of securities (see 5913);
- the allowance already given against a gain from a small part disposal (see 5229).

Law: TCGA 1992, s. 56(1), 57

See *British Tax Reporter* ¶523-550.

5292   Indexation allowance: disposals on a 'no gain/no loss' basis

For the availability of indexation allowance on disposals after 5 April 1998, see 5268.

There are special rules for calculating indexation allowance in respect of disposals to which certain types of tax deferral apply, so that the transferor is treated as making neither a gain nor a loss on his disposal (e.g. the relief for the replacement of business assets, see 6305). Basically, the indexation allowance is calculated and is set off against a deemed gain of an equal amount so that there is no gain/no loss after indexation; any remaining gain is effectively rolled over to the transferee.

Example

Harry makes a gift of a non-business asset to his wife, Janet. Harry's acquisition cost was £13,000. At the date of disposal there was an accrued gain of £5,000 and, say, an indexation allowance of £3,000.

The disposal is regarded as being on a no gain/no loss basis, but only after the indexation allowance has been taken into account. Thus Janet is treated as having acquired the asset for £13,000 + £3,000 = £16,000.

Notwithstanding the above, where a person is deemed to have held an asset at 31 March 1982 following a no gain/no loss transfer of it to him, the acquisition cost may be reduced by an amount equivalent to the rolled-up indexation allowance to the date of transfer to accommodate the fact that indexation allowance is computed on market value at 31 March 1982 (see 5283).

Disposals after 29 November 1993

Where a disposal takes place after 29 November 1993, following a no gain/no loss transfer before that date, the indexation allowance to the date of transfer would be deducted from the base cost under the rule outlined in 5283. However, where a loss arises, with the result that some or all of the indexation allowance is wasted, indexation allowance up to the date of the no gain/no loss transfer may be preserved.

Law: TCGA 1992, s. 55(6)–(8), 56(2)

See *British Tax Reporter* ¶523-500.

ENTREPRENEURS' RELIEF

5293 Introduction

Entrepreneurs' relief was a hastily produced solution to a problem created by the Government's decision, announced in the 2007 Pre-Budget Report, to 'simplify' capital gains tax by abolishing taper relief and setting a single rate of tax at 18 per cent. The problem was that under the taper relief regime, most business owners were expecting to pay an effective rate of only 10 per cent on the disposal of their businesses. In order to placate the criticism which resulted, this new relief was proposed. It is largely based on the old retirement relief which was last available in 2002–03 and its effect is to preserve the effective 10 per cent rate for businesses which applied under taper relief.

The relief is to be given upon a claim being made in respect of 'qualifying business disposals', of which there are three:

(1)   a material disposal by an individual;

(2)   a disposal by an individual which is associated with a material disposal; and

(3)   a disposal by a trustee.

In contrast to both retirement relief, upon which it is based, and taper relief, which it replaced, entrepreneurs' relief must be claimed. That claim must be made by the first anniversary of 31 January following the year of the qualifying business disposal. In practice, however, the self-assessment return will include the facility to make a claim when returning the chargeable gains for the year.

'Relevant gains' arising on qualifying business disposals are to be aggregated with any 'relevant losses' arising on such disposals. The resulting net gains arising on disposals occurring on or after 23 June 2010 are charged to capital gains tax at a rate of 10 per cent. Where the net gains arose on disposals before that date, the resulting gains were to be reduced by $^4/_9$ths. Thus only $^5/_9$ths of the net relevant gains were chargeable gains and were charged at the 18 per cent capital gains tax rate then applicable, giving an effective rate of 10 per cent on the full amount of the gains.

Capital Gains Tax

If the result of the aggregation is a net loss, then obviously no relief is in point. To the extent that the relevant loss has not been set off against relevant gains of that year, it is allowed against any chargeable gains in the same or subsequent years. The rule requiring aggregation means that relevant losses arising in a year are to be set against relevant gains of that year in priority to any other losses of that or any previous year.

The relief is limited to the prevailing lifetime threshold of gains at the time of disposal, from which the amount of any net relevant gains on previous disposals is deducted. The threshold is as follows:

- £1m for disposals occurring in the period 6 April 2008 to 5 April 2010;
- £2m for disposals occurring in the period 6 April 2010 to 22 June 2010; and
- £5m for disposals occurring on or after 23 June 2010.

Relevant gains and losses

Where the disposal is of company shares or securities, the relevant gain or loss is that accruing on those shares, etc. as computed under normal capital gains rules and assuming, in the case of a loss, that a claim has been made. In other cases, the relevant gains or losses are those which arise on 'relevant business assets' similarly computed and, again in the case of losses, assuming that a claim has been made.

Earlier relevant qualifying business disposals

In the case of an individual, these are his previous qualifying disposals plus any previous qualifying disposals by the trustees of a settlement in respect of which he was the qualifying beneficiary. Similarly, in the case of trustees, these are their previous disposals which have qualified for relief plus any disposals made by the qualifying beneficiary in his own right.

Law: FA 2010, s. 4; TCGA 1992, s. 169M and 169N

5294 Restriction to relevant business assets

Where the qualifying business disposal is one comprising the disposal of the whole or part of a business, the 'relevant gains or losses' to be taken into account in computing relief are those which arise on 'relevant business assets'. These are defined as specifically including goodwill, and:

- in the case of the disposal of a business (or part of a business) carried on by the individual or by a partnership of which he was a member, the assets used for the purposes of that business;
- in the case of a trustees' disposal assets used for the purposes of a business carried on by a qualifying beneficiary either as a sole trader or in partnership with others;
- in the case of an associated disposal assets used for the purposes of a business carried on by the partnership or company concerned; and
- in all cases, excluding shares, securities and other assets held as investments.

Capital Gains Tax

Because the relief is given for the disposal of a business rather than individual assets, the intention behind this restriction is to deny relief to those assets forming part of the business which are held as investments or are otherwise not used for business purposes. To apply the restriction to associated disposals seems unnecessary as such a disposal can only occur if the asset is in use for the purposes of the business concerned.

There is no corresponding restriction where the business asset comprises of a holding of company shares; in such a case, relief is either due on the whole gain or it is not.

Law: TCGA 1992, s. 169L

5295 Personal company

Where a material disposal or a trustees disposal is one of company shares or securities, the company concerned must be the individual's (or, in the case of a trustees' disposal, the qualifying beneficiary's) 'personal company'.

In addition, in the case of an associated disposal, where the asset was being in a business carried on by a company, that company also has to be the individual's personal company.

The term 'personal company' is defined as a company in which the individual (or qualifying beneficiary, as the case may be) not only holds at least 5 per cent of the ordinary share capital but also is able to exercise at least 5 per cent of the voting power by virtue of that shareholding. Where the person concerned has a joint holding with another, only his proportionate share of that joint holding is taken into account for these purposes.

In the case of a trustees disposal of shares, those shares are ignored in determining whether the company concerned is the qualifying beneficiary's personal company; the beneficiary does not hold the shares, nor does he exercise voting power, those are the functions of the trustees. Therefore a trustee's disposal of shares can never qualify for relief unless the qualifying beneficiary already has beneficial ownership of at least 5 per cent of the company's ordinary share capital and voting power.

Law: TCGA 1992, s. 169S

5296 Trading company or holding company of a trading group

The definitions of 'trading company' and 'trading group' adopted are the same as those applying for the hold-over relief on gifts of business assets and which were also applicable for the now-abolished taper relief.

Trading company

A trading company is one 'carrying on trading activities whose activities do not include, to a substantial extent, activities other than trading activities'. It therefore follows that a company is either a trading company or it is not; there are no half measures. Where a company carries on non-trading activities, it may still qualify as trading provided those activities are not 'substantial'. The HMRC view on how this term was to be interpreted for taper relief purposes was provided in the Capital Gains Manual at CG17953p and this will remain relevant under the new relief. In essence, the HMRC view is that substantial means 20 per cent or more, measured in terms of income, asset value, costs and management time incurred or the company's recent history, whichever is appropriate.

Trading activities, apart from those undertaken for the trade currently being carried on, are defined as including those for the purposes of acquiring or setting up a proposed new trade, provided that where a new trade is acquired, the company starts to carry on that trade as soon as reasonably practical. Also included are activities undertaken with a view to acquiring a 'significant interest' in the ordinary share capital of another company which is itself a trading company or the holding company of a trading group and is not already a member of the same group of companies as the company concerned. Again, that acquisition must be made as soon as reasonably practical. A significant interest for these purposes means either more than 50 per cent or a qualifying interest in a joint venture company but without making the two companies members of the same group.

Holding company of a trading group

A holding company is one which holds more than 50 per cent of the ordinary share capital of one or more other companies.

A group of companies comprises the holding company and all the subsidiaries in which it holds at least 50 per cent of the ordinary share capital.

A trading group of companies is one where at least one of its members carries on trading activities and, if the activities of all of the group members are taken together, they do not include, to any substantial extent, any non-trading activities.

In a group context, the definition of trading activities is identical to that in respect of singleton companies, but modified to refer to activities carried on by a member of the group. The activities of all the members of the group are to be treated as one business and therefore intra-group activities are disregarded. Thus where one group member holds all the properties within a group and lets them out to other group members, those non-trading activities will fall to be disregarded in considering whether the group as a whole was a trading group.

Joint venture companies and qualifying shareholdings

A joint venture company is a trading company or the holding company of a trading group where more than 75 per cent of its ordinary share capital is held by five or fewer persons. For this purpose, shares held by members of the same group of companies are regarded as held by a single person.

A qualifying shareholding in a joint venture company is normally 10 per cent or more of the ordinary share capital but, in the case of a member of a group of companies, it is a holding which, when aggregated with those of other members of the same group, produces a holding of more than 10 per cent.

Law: TCGA 1992, s. 165A

5297 Material disposals by individuals

A 'material disposal' is one of business assets which have been owned for a minimum of one year and falls into one of three categories:

(1) the whole or part of a business;

(2) assets used in a business at the time it was discontinued; or

(3) shares in or securities of a 'personal company' (see 5295) which is either a trading company or the holding company of a trading group (see 5296) and the individual was an officer or employee of that company or another company in the same group.

For such a disposal to qualify as a material disposal, the business must have been owned by the individual throughout the period of one year ending with the disposal.

Relief is not confined to sole traders. In the case of a partnership business, it is treated as owned by each individual who is a member of the partnership at that particular time and the disposal by an individual of his interest in partnership assets is treated as the disposal of the whole or part of the business carried on by the partnership.

In addition, it is provided that a sole trader who takes another person into partnership, thus disposing of an interest in the assets of his business, is to be treated as disposing of a part of his business.

A business or part of a business

A business is something more than a mere collection of assets. For the purposes of entrepreneurs' relief, it is defined as a trade, profession or vocation which is conducted on a commercial basis with a view to profit (TCGA 1992, s. 169S(1)). Thus relief is not due where an individual or partnership sells one or more of its business assets whilst continuing with its business as before.

The requirement that there must be a disposal of a business or part of a business was also a feature of retirement relief and resulted in a string of cases before the court relating to farming, where the point at issue was whether a disposal of part of the farmland was the disposal of part of the farming business. The principles established by these cases will be relevant for entrepreneurs' relief.

Disposal of assets after business discontinued

To cater for situations where an outright sale of a business is not possible, relief is also available where business is discontinued and there are subsequent disposals of the individual assets which were used in that business at the time of its cessation.

The conditions to be satisfied are:

- the business must have been owned by the individual throughout the period of one year ending with the cessation of the business; and
- the date of the disposal must be within three years of that cessation.

A disposal of assets used in a partnership business which has been discontinued also qualifies as a material disposal subject to the same conditions.

Disposal of shares in a personal company

A disposal of shares or securities in a company is a material disposal where, throughout the period of one year ending with the disposal:

- the company is the individual's 'personal company';
- that company is a trading company or the holding company of a trading group; and
- the individual is an officer or employee of the company or of one or more companies in the same trading group.

Where the company ceases trading or ceases to be the holding company of a trading group before the disposal occurs, the conditions outlined above have only to be satisfied for an alternative qualifying period of one year ending with that event, provided that event occurs no more than three years before the disposal, and:

(1)   if the event is the company ceasing to trade, it is not thereafter a member of a trading group and does not become a member of such a group; or

(2)   if the event is the company ceasing to be a member of a trading group, it ceases to be a trading company and does not become one.

If a company falls within (1) above because it remains a member of a trading group despite having ceased to trade, then relief should still be available under TCGA 1992, s. 169I(6) if the company is the holding company of the group. HMRC take the view that the conditions in that subsection can be satisfied if throughout part of the qualifying period of one year ending with the disposal, the company was a trading company and throughout the remainder of the period was the holding company of a trading group (Capital Gains Manual CG 63097).

However, this will not apply where an individual holds shares in a trading subsidiary which is a member (but not the holding company) of a trading group. If, before the share disposal, that company ceases to trade but remains a member of that group, the conditions in TCGA 1992, s. 169I(6) will not be satisfied throughout the qualifying period ending with that disposal. The relaxation provided for in s. 169I(7) will not apply as the company has remained a member of the group following the cessation of trade.

There is no requirement that the individual, in his capacity as an officer or employee, must actually work for the company for any minimum number of hours per week. However, whilst it is possible to be a non-executive director, it is difficult to see how an individual could be an employee and yet perform no duties.

Law: TCGA 1992, s. 169I

5298 Associated disposals

Where an asset used in the business of a partnership or trading company is owned personally by a partner or director, relief is available for a disposal of these assets where they are associated with a material disposal.

There are three conditions to be satisfied for a disposal to qualify:

(1)   the individual must make a material disposal of either his interest in a partnership, or of shares/securities in a company;

(2)   he makes the associated disposal as part of a withdrawal from participation in the business carried on by the partnership or by the company (or a fellow member of a trading group; and

(3)   the asset which is the subject of the associated disposal has been in use for the purposes of that business throughout the one-year period ending with the material disposal, or, if earlier, the date on which the business was terminated.

The legislation, like that for retirement relief, does not actually specify that both the material and associated disposals should take place at the same time, or indeed, in any particular order. They must, however, share the same objective: that of enabling the individual to withdraw from the business concerned.

Under retirement relief, HMRC took the view that a withdrawal from the business required only that the individual should reduce his interest in the partnership or holding in the company. It did not mean that he should withdraw from working in the business concerned (see Capital Gains Manual CG 63729). There seems to be no reason why this view should not prevail for entrepreneurs' relief.

Relief may, however, be subject to a number of restrictions. Relief for associated disposals is restricted where:

●   the assets concerned have been used for the purposes of the business during only part of the individual's period of ownership;
●   only a part of the asset has been so used;
●   the individual was a partner, officer or employee for only part of the period in which the assets were used for business purposes; or
●   during any part of the period when the asset was in use for the purposes of the business, that use by the partnership or company was dependent upon the payment of rent (or any other form of consideration for its use: TCGA 1992, s. 169S(5)).

Where these conditions are satisfied, the relief is to be restricted to an amount which is 'just and reasonable'. In other words, only the just and reasonable part of the gain is to be reduced by the relief and the balance remains taxable in full.

In arriving at the relievable amount of the gain, consideration is to be given to the periods of time concerned in the situations in the first two bullet points, the proportion of the asset used in situations in the third and, in the final situation, the extent to which the rent paid was less than a commercial rent.

Similar restrictions were previously applicable for both retirement and taper relief. However, whilst retirement relief was restricted where rent was paid for the use of the asset, taper relief was not. The decision to reintroduce a restriction where rent is paid introduces a degree of retrospective taxation because it applies where rent has been charged at any time in the period of business use. This period, of course, will probably stretch back beyond April 2008 when rent may have been charged, because under the taper relief regime it was perfectly acceptable.

The expanded definition of rent to include other forms of consideration will also catch situations where an enhanced partnership profit share is received in recognition of the use of the asset or where the partnership pays the interest on a loan taken out by a partner to purchase the asset concerned.

5299   Disposals by trustees

Trustees are not entitled to an 'allowance' of entrepreneurs' relief in the same way as individuals. Any relief given to trustees is treated as having been given to the 'qualifying beneficiary' and serves to reduce his entitlement for future disposals.

Where there are two qualifying disposals made on the same day, one by the trustees and the other by an individual who is also a qualifying beneficiary of that trust, the trustees' disposal is to be treated as having occurred after the one made by the individual.

The effect of these provisions is to restrict an individual's relief threshold by the relief granted to trustees of a settlement of which he is a qualifying beneficiary.

A qualifying beneficiary is one who has an 'interest in possession' in that part of the settled property which includes the assets, shares or securities which are the subject of the disposal.

Law: TCGA 1992, s. 169J

RE-BASING TO 31 MARCH 1982

5300   Base date for disposals after 5 April 1988

For a post-5 April 1988 disposal of an asset held on 31 March 1982 the base value against which the chargeable gain is computed is the value on 31 March 1982 (for exceptions, see 5302). This is achieved by assuming that the asset was sold and immediately reacquired by the disponor on 31 March 1982 at market value. The indexation allowance continues against the March 1982 base value (see 5283).

Example

Tim bought a chargeable asset in 1975 for £10,000. He sells it in January 1997 for £25,000.

Value of asset on 31 March 1982 was £11,000.

	£
Disposal consideration	25,000
Allowable expenditure	(11,000)
Unindexed gain	14,000
Indexation allowance (£11,000 × 0.891)	(9,801)
Chargeable gain	4,199

Where an asset is acquired after 31 March 1982, the base cost is the cost of acquisition and indexation allowance is also based on acquisition cost, subject to certain exceptions (see 5292); however, relief may be provided in specific cases (see 5304). There is no re-basing in certain circumstances (see 5302).

For market value, see 5103ff.

Where shares formed part of a larger holding of a spouse or fellow group company on 31 March 1982 (but have been transferred to the taxpayer on a no gain/no loss basis), they may be valued by reference to the size of the larger holding if the taxpayer so claims; for disposals after 15 March 1993, a claim must be made within two years of the end of the tax year and, for disposals made before that date, a claim must be made before the liability in point is finally determined. This may raise the base cost of shares, particularly where a majority holding has been split to utilise reliefs, e.g. to use the annual exemptions of both husband and wife (see 6150).

The Shares Valuation Division agrees to certain approaches to value unquoted shares before a referral from HMRC, largely for indexation allowance and re-basing purposes (see 5103). For re-basing and shares generally, see 5826.

Law: TCGA 1992, s. 35(1), (2)

Source: ESC D44, *Rebasing and indexation: shares derived from larger holdings held at 31 March 1982*

See *British Tax Reporter* ¶520-350.

5302 Exceptions to re-basing

A simplified re-basing scheme can be applied by election (see below) but, otherwise, there is no re-basing to 1982 values in the following cases; unless special rules are given, where there is no deemed disposal on 31 March 1982, the prior acquisition of the asset remains critical subject to special rules for assets held on 6 April 1965 – referred to below, as a whole, as the 'pre-1988 rules'. This 'kink-test' comparison is after time apportionment, where appropriate.

- Where 1982 re-basing would produce a gain but a smaller gain would be produced without re-basing, the pre-1988 rules continue to apply. This exception ensures that the taxpayer is not worse off under the re-basing rules. See Example 1 below.
- Where 1982 re-basing would produce a loss but a smaller loss would be produced without re-basing, the pre-1988 rules continue to apply. This ensures that the taxpayer is not unjustifiably better off under the re-basing rules. See Example 2 below.
- Where 1982 re-basing turns what would be a gain without re-basing into a loss or what would be a loss without re-basing into gain. In either case the 1988 Act requires the disposal to be treated as producing neither loss nor gain, i.e. the chargeable gain/loss is nil. See Examples 3(a) and 3(b) below.
- If neither a gain nor a loss would occur without re-basing either on the facts of the case or under the special rules for pre-1965 assets, those pre-1988 rules (above) continue to apply. See Example 4 below.
- Where neither a gain nor a loss would accrue by virtue of certain specified provisions, re-basing does not override the existing no gain/no loss transfers.

Example 1

Sean bought a chargeable asset in 1975 for £10,000. He sells it in January 1997 for £25,000. The March 1982 value was £5,000.

With re-basing the chargeable gain would be:

£25,000 − £5,000 − (£10,000 × 0.944) = £10,560.

Without re-basing the chargeable gain would be:

£25,000 − £10,000 − (£10,000 × 0.944) = £5,560.

It is the smaller gain of £5,560 which is charged.

Example 2

William bought a chargeable asset in 1975 for £23,000. He sells it in January 1997 for £21,000. The March 1982 value was £25,000.

With re-basing the allowable loss would be:

 £21,000 − £25,000 = (£4,000).

Without re-basing the allowable loss would be:

 £21,000 − £23,000 = (£2,000).

The smaller loss of £2,000 is allowed.

Indexation allowance cannot be used to increase a loss.

Example 3(a)

Richard bought a chargeable asset in 1975 for £1,500. He sells it in January 1997 for £54,000. The market value in March 1982 was £55,000.

With re-basing the allowable loss would be:

 £54,000 − £55,000 = (£1,000).

Without re-basing the chargeable gain would be:

 £54,000 − £1,500 − (£55,000 × 0.944) = £580.

The disposal is treated as producing neither gain nor loss.

Example 3(b)

Gavin bought a chargeable asset in 1975 for £20,000. He sells it in January 1996 for £19,500. The March 1982 value was £500.

With re-basing the chargeable gain would be:

 £19,500 − £500 − (£20,000 × 0.944) = £200.

Without re-basing the allowable loss would be:

 £19,500 − £20,000 = (£500).

The disposal is treated as producing neither gain nor loss.

Example 4

Craig bought a chargeable asset in 1976 for £20,000. Its market value is £15,000 in March 1982. He sells for £34,000 in January 1997.

With re-basing the chargeable gain would be:

 £34,000 − £15,000 − (£20,000 × 0.944) = £200.

Without re-basing the result would be:

 £34,000 − £20,000 − (£20,000 × 0.944) = (£4,800), so no gain/no loss.

The disposal is still treated as producing neither gain nor loss.

Law: TCGA 1992, s. 35(3), (4), (10), Sch. 3, para. 6

See *British Tax Reporter* ¶520-500.

5303   Election for 1982 valuation on all assets

The examples set out in 5302 show the necessity for the retention by taxpayers of pre-1982 records and the complexity of tax computations made on alternative bases. However, taxpayers may elect that their capital gains and losses on all assets held as at 31 March 1982 be calculated by reference to March 1982 values. Such an election would displace the operation of the exceptions to 1982 re-basing. Special provisions determine the nature of the election for groups. Plant and machinery generally and certain mining or oil-related assets are excluded from the election.

An election made by a person in one capacity does not cover disposals made by him in another capacity. In this respect, HMRC have indicated that:

- a partner may make an election in respect of a disposal of his interest in partnership assets but it is not necessary for all partners to make elections; if an individual is a member of more than one partnership, a separate election is required for each; a separate election is required for assets held privately;
- where assets are otherwise held jointly, each individual's share or holding would be covered by an election made by him in his capacity as an individual;
- an election by a sole trader applies to business and private assets;
- an election by the single body formed by all the trustees of a settlement applies only to that one settlement.

Time-limit

Once made, an election is irrevocable and it has to be made by notice in writing to HMRC before 6 April 1990 or within two years after the end of the tax year within which the first relevant disposal was made or such later time as HMRC may allow. Simply submitting a computation which is based only on the 31 March 1982 value does not, in HMRC's view, in itself constitute a claim. For tax years after 1995–96, the time-limit is 12 months from the 31 January next following the tax year in which the disposal takes place; that is, approximately 22 months from the end of the tax year.

A Revenue statement of practice clarifies the operation of the time-limit for the re-basing election. The statement treats certain disposals which would not produce chargeable gains as not being 'relevant disposals' and accordingly such disposals can be left out of account in timing any election. Disposals included are of private cars; chattels below the value of the chattel exemption; chattels which are wasting assets; government non-marketable securities; gilt-edged securities and qualifying corporate bonds; rights to compensation for an injury or wrong suffered by an individual in his person, profession or vocation; shares held as part of a personal equity plan, etc.; life assurance policies, etc. unless purchased from a third party; foreign currency for personal expenditure; most debts held by the original creditor; BES shares in respect of which relief has been given and not withdrawn; gifts of works of art, etc.; decorations for valour, etc.; betting winnings and rights to certain superannuation allowances, annuities, etc.

In determining the time-limit for an election, HMRC will also omit those disposals which in practice do not give rise to a chargeable gain or allowable loss, the main examples being building society withdrawals, dwelling-houses where the whole gain qualifies for private residence relief, most no gain/no loss provisions. Discretion will also be exercised so as to ignore disposals where no election for the simplified re-basing scheme is possible. The statement also gives guidance for persons who become resident in the UK after 6 April 1988, for disposals of non-UK assets by individuals resident but not domiciled in the UK and for disposals by a UK resident during a period of non-residence.

Law: TCGA 1992, s. 35(5)–(8), Sch. 3, para. 7, 8

Source: SP 4/92

See *British Tax Reporter* ¶520-400.

WASTING ASSETS

5330 Importance of 'wasting assets'

A 'wasting asset' is an asset with a predictable useful life of no more than 50 years as ascertainable at the time of acquisition. Thus, a lease granted for a term of no more than 50 years is a wasting asset (see further 5333). The following general rules apply:

- plant and machinery (see 2360) are in all cases wasting assets (a Revenue interpretation gives a list of categories of assets which will be accepted as constituting machinery – this includes assets such as antique clocks and watches, motor vehicles that are not 'normal private passenger vehicles', and ships or boats propelled by engines);
- a life interest in settled property is a wasting asset where the life expectancy of the life tenant is 50 years or less (as ascertained from actuarial tables);
- freehold land is not a wasting asset.

The nature of wasting assets requires special rules of computation for CGT purposes. Since the owner will have had the use and enjoyment of the wasting asset, the basic rule is that the acquisition expenditure must be written off, save for a residual or scrap value. Any comparison of the price at which the asset is sold with the original purchase price is not a comparison of like with like, and any 'gains' or 'losses' arising would be an unsound basis for taxation.

The legislation deals with wasting assets in various ways.

- Wasting assets which are 'tangible moveable property' (chattels) are generally exempt from CGT unless they are used for a trade, profession or vocation as mentioned below.

This prevents claims for allowable losses on, e.g., household furniture. A tangible moveable asset sold for less than £6,000 is exempt from CGT irrespective of its trade use (see 6155).

- Wasting assets which have been used throughout the disponor's period of ownership for the purposes of a trade, profession or vocation and in respect of which the disponor was entitled to claim capital allowances (see 2360ff.) are liable to CGT to the extent so used; there is no writing-off of expenditure.
- Quoted options to subscribe for shares, traded options, commodity and financial futures involving certain approved financial institutions, etc. or a dealer on a recognised futures exchange and most options to acquire assets for trade purposes: there is no writing-off of expenditure (see 5980, 5985).
- Short leases of land: allowable expenditure is written off at a specified rate (see 5333).
- Other wasting assets: allowable expenditure is written off evenly over the life of the asset (see 5336).

Law: TCGA 1992, s. 44(1), (3), 45, 47

See *British Tax Reporter* ¶508-700.

5333   Short leases of land

Notwithstanding the general rules as to the meaning of wasting assets (which would apply by reference to the term of a lease: see 5330), leases with unexpired 'duration' of 50 years or less are, in general, wasting assets. A lease is widely defined and specific provisions determine the duration of a lease. The possibility of a claim for extending a lease by 50 years under the *Leasehold Reform Act* 1967 did not prevent a lease with 16 years to run from having a duration not exceeding 50 years, the High Court has held.

The allowable expenditure for CGT purposes is treated as wasting away over the length of the lease in accordance with calculations based on the following table:

Years	%	Years	%
		25	81.100
50 (or more)	100	24	79.622
49	99.657	23	78.055
48	99.289	22	76.399
47	98.902	21	74.635
46	98.490	20	72.770
45	98.059	19	70.791
44	97.595	18	68.697
43	97.107	17	66,470
42	96.593	16	64.116
41	96.041	15	61.617
40	95.457	14	58.971
39	94.842	13	56.167
38	94.189	12	53.191
37	93.197	11	50.038
36	92.761	10	46.695
35	91.981	9	43.154
34	91.156	8	39.399
33	90.280	7	35.414
32	89.345	6	31.195
31	88.371	5	26.722
30	87.330	4	21.983
29	86.226	3	16.959
28	85.053	2	11.629
27	83.816	1	5.983
26	82.496	0	0

The allowable expenditure can be calculated according to the formula:

$$\frac{X}{Y} \times Z$$

where

X   is the percentage (taken from the table) for the number of years remaining when the lease is disposed of;
Y   is the percentage for the number of years remaining when the lease was acquired; and
Z   is the cost at acquisition.

The resulting figure is subtracted from the consideration received on disposal to give the chargeable gain.

Example

Charlie acquired a 12-year lease for a sum the capital element of which (i.e. excluding any amount chargeable to income tax under the property income rules in ITTOIA 2005) was £10,000. Seven years later he assigned the lease to David for a premium the capital element of which was £7,000.

Chargeable gain	
	£
Price at disposal	7,000.00
Less: allowable amount:	
$\dfrac{26.722}{53.191} \times £10,000$	(5,023.78)*
Chargeable gain	1,976.22
* Subject to indexation, etc. (see ¶5286)	

Enhancement expenditure, if any, is discounted by applying the same formula:

$$\frac{X}{Y} \times Z$$

but now Y is the percentage for the number of years remaining when the enhancement expenditure is incurred and Z is the enhancement cost.

If the duration of the lease is not an exact number of years the percentage derived from the table is calculated using the lower of the nearest two exact year percentages plus one twelfth the difference between the two percentages for each odd month. In this context an incomplete month is counted if it comprises 14 days or more.

Special rules apply to subleases granted out of short leases.

Premiums for leases

A person who requires a premium under a lease of land is treated as making a part disposal, i.e. the premium is chargeable to CGT.

Any part of a premium for a lease which is liable to a charge to income tax under Sch. A (see 1260ff.) is deducted from the amount liable to CGT.

A number of amendments have been made to the tax treatment of certain sums treated as additional lease premiums. The sums in question are amounts received in lieu of rent or as consideration for the surrender of a lease, and amounts received as consideration for the variation or waiver of any of the terms of the lease.

Where such amounts are payable after 5 April 1996, the tax treatment is as described below.

A premium deemed to be received for the surrender of a lease is treated as a disposal by the landlord of his interest in the lease.

A premium deemed to be received in lieu of rent or as consideration for the variation or waiver of any of the terms of the lease is treated as a further part-disposal of the asset out of which the lease was granted, taking place on the date the premium is due.

Relief is allowed where the lessee of property on a lease which has 50 years or less to run receives insurance payments which are applied in discharging an obligation to restore any damage to the property (see 5083).

Law: TCGA 1992, s. 240, Sch. 8, para. 1, 3–6, 8, 10;

See *British Tax Reporter* ¶509-600.

5336   Wasting assets other than leases of land

Subject to special rules for tangible moveable property, assets used for a trade, short leases of land and various options or futures (see 5330), allowable expenditure attributable to wasting assets is written off evenly over the useful life of the asset so as to leave the residual or scrap value. The 'residual or scrap value' is the predictable value (as ascertainable at the time of acquisition) which the asset will have at the end of its predictable useful life, having regard to the purpose for which the asset was acquired.

The expenditure which is disallowed is calculated by using the following formulae:

(1)   *Expenditure on cost of acquisition:*

$$(A - S) \times \frac{O}{L} = \text{expenditure disallowed.}$$

(2)   *Expenditure on enhancing the value of the asset:*

$$E \times \frac{T}{L - (O - T)} = \text{expenditure disallowed.}$$

where

A   is the cost of acquisition.
E   is expenditure on enhancing the value of the asset.
L   is the predictable life of the asset as at the time of acquisition.
O   is the period of ownership.
S   is the residual or scrap value.
T   is the period during which E is reflected in the asset value.

Example

Peter buys a wasting asset with a predictable life of 20 years. The cost of acquisition is £10,500. Peter spends £5,000 on the asset after three years of ownership. He sells the asset after five years of ownership for £9,000. The scrap value of the asset is £500.

The calculation to ascertain CGT liability is as follows:

(1) $(£10,500 - £500) \times \dfrac{5}{20} = £2,500$

The acquisition cost (£10,500) is reduced by £2,500 to give allowable expenditure of £8,000.

---

(2) $£5,000 \times \dfrac{2}{20 - (5 - 2)} = £588.24$

The cost of enhancement (£5,000) is reduced by £588.24 to give allowable expenditure of £4,411.76.

The two resultant figures for allowable expenditure (£8,000 and £4,411.76) are added together, giving a total of £12,411.76. Thus, there is an allowable loss before indexation, etc. of £12,411.76 − £9,000 = £3,411.76.

Leases of property other than leases of land are subject to broadly similar provisions to those relating to leases of land (see 5333).

Law: TCGA 1992, s. 44(2), (3), 46, Sch. 8, para. 9

See *British Tax Reporter* ¶508-850.

ASSETS HELD ON 6 APRIL 1965

5380   Introduction to assets held on 6 April 1965

For disposals after 5 April 1988, chargeable gains or allowable losses are generally computed as if the asset in point had been disposed of and reacquired on 31 March 1982 at its market value at that time; however, such re-basing does not apply in certain cases where the former provisions would have dictated a result of a different nature. Hence, special rules applicable to assets held at 6 April 1965 continue to be relevant even after the introduction of re-basing to 31 March 1982.

Capital gains tax and corporation tax on chargeable gains were introduced in 1965. It was not intended that the charge should be retrospective and rules were provided with the broad objective of restricting any chargeable gain or allowable loss to that which had accrued after 6 April 1965.

It was considered administratively impossible and undesirable to require that all assets held on 6 April 1965 should be valued at that time. The rule for most assets is therefore that any gain or loss should be time-apportioned to determine the amount attributable to the post-6 April 1965 period which should be within the scope of the chargeable gains regime. However, an election is provided for taxpayers to choose instead to value an asset at its value on 6 April 1965. Special rules apply to quoted securities, where a market value at 6 April 1965 is readily available, and to land reflecting development value on that date, where such valuation was likely to have been available and where time apportionment would be wholly inappropriate.

The rules apply also to an asset held by a taxpayer's spouse at 6 April 1965 but later transferred on a no gain/no loss basis.

Law: TCGA 1992, s. 35(9), Sch. 2

Source: ESC D34; SP 5/89

See *British Tax Reporter* ¶520-750.

5383 Quoted securities held on 6 April 1965

Following the introduction of re-basing, special computational rules for assets held at 6 April 1965 are of limited but continuing relevance. For quoted shares or securities held at 6 April 1965, where there is a market value readily available, the asset is deemed to have been acquired on 6 April 1965 for its market value at that time, unless a smaller gain or loss would result from the use of actual costs; there is also the possibility of pooling shares or securities of the same class at their value at that date, so that gains or losses were calculated on the basis of the pool value irrespective of the actual cost position.

Law: TCGA 1992, Sch. 2, para. 1, 2(1), (2), 4–7

See *British Tax Reporter* ¶520-800.

5386 Land with development value at 6 April 1965

Following the introduction of re-basing, special computational rules for assets held at 6 April 1965 are of limited but continuing relevance. Where land had a potential development value at 6 April 1965, which was realised only after that date, it was considered inappropriate that the increase over its current use value should be spread evenly over the period since its acquisition. Hence, special rules were provided in place of the usual time apportionment formula.

On a disposal or part disposal of land to which these rules relate, it is generally treated as if it had been acquired at its market value at 6 April 1965. A similar exercise takes place each time there is a part disposal, so that additional considerations which have arisen can be taken into account in the valuation process; each earlier part disposal is then recalculated on the basis of the revised assumptions. This deemed acquisition does not apply where a smaller gain or loss would arise if the actual costs were used nor if a gain would be turned into a loss or vice versa, in which case there is deemed to be no gain/no loss.

Special provision is made for an allowance for betterment levy.

Land to which rules apply

These rules apply only to land situated in the UK.

Land which was acquired by gift prior to 6 April 1965 falls within these provisions in the same way as land acquired for consideration.

The disposal consideration must exceed the current use value at the time of the disposal or some material development of the land must have been carried out since the disponor acquired it.

Under TCGA 1992, Sch. 2, para. 9(5), 'land' includes buildings, and 'interest in land' means:

> '... any estate or interest in land, any right in or over land or affecting the use or disposition of land, any right to obtain such an estate, interest or right from another which is conditional on that other's ability to grant the estate, interest or right in question, except that it does not include the interest of a creditor (other than a creditor in respect of a rentcharge) whose debt is secured by way of a mortgage, an agreement for a mortgage or a charge of any kind over land, or, in Scotland, the interest of a creditor in a charge or security of any kind over land.'

'Current use value' is the market value, assuming that no material development was permissible or ever would be permissible. In *Morgan (HMIT) v Gibson* [1989] BTC 272, it was held that a finding by the commissioners that the consideration for the sale of a property included an element of 'hope value' was tantamount to a finding that it contained an element of anticipated development value. On a disposal resulting from the loss or destruction of the asset, the current use value ignores that event. The usual formula basis is generally applied to apportion such value on a part disposal. For leases, etc. any premium is ignored while, for leases which are wasting assets, the value is wasted in a similar manner to the base cost.

'Material development' in relation to any land means the making of change in the state, nature or use of the land (TCGA 1992, Sch. 2, para. 13(1), (4)). This is subject to para. 13(2), (3), which excludes certain matters such as maintenance, improvement or enlargement or alteration not increasing the cubic content of the building by more than one-tenth. Material development is generally taken to have begun on commencement of any specified operation.

Law: TCGA 1992, Sch. 2, para. 9–15; *Mashiter (HMIT) v Pearmain* [1985] BTC 105; *Morgan (HMIT) v Gibson* [1989] BTC 272

See *British Tax Reporter* ¶520-850.

5389 Time apportionment: pre-1965 gains or losses

Following the introduction of re-basing, special computational rules for assets held at 6 April 1965 are of limited but continuing relevance. For assets other than quoted shares or securities (including units in a unit trust scheme) and land reflecting development value, unless the taxpayer elects to apply the market value at 6 April 1965, the gain or loss is deemed to accrue on a straight-line basis over the period of ownership and only that part which is apportioned to the period after 6 April 1965 is a chargeable gain or allowable loss.

Where there has been no allowable expenditure on enhancement or establishing/defending title, etc. the apportionment is to be made by applying the following formula to the gain or loss otherwise arising:

$$\frac{T}{P + T}$$

where

T   is the period of ownership beginning on 6 April 1965; and

P   is the period of ownership from acquisition (or, if later, 6 April 1945).

Example

On 6 April 1960 Richard buys a house which is not his principal private residence. The purchase price is £10,000 and its value on 31 March 1982 is £9,000. He sells it on 5 January 1997 for £40,000. His chargeable gain is calculated as follows (ignoring incidental costs, etc.):

	£
Disposal consideration	40,000
Less: acquisition cost	(10,000)
Unindexed gain	30,000
Less: indexation (£10,000 × 0.944)	(9,440)
Indexed gain	20,560
Time apportioned gain ($^{31.75}/_{35.75}$)	18,260

The taxpayer may elect (subject to certain conditions) to have the 6 April 1965 value substituted as the base value. Under self-assessment, the election must be made within 12 months from 31 January following the tax year in which the disposal is made or, for corporation tax purposes, within two years from the end of the accounting period in which the disposal is made. (The previous time-limit was two years after the end of the tax year, or accounting period, in which the disposal was made, or a longer period if HMRC allowed.)

On certain reorganisations for which the new holding is equated with original shares held before 6 April 1965, the gain is limited to the actual gain arising notwithstanding the unusual effect of the 1965 rules.

Law: TCGA 1992, Sch. 2, para. 16, 17; *Smith (HMIT) v Schofield* [1993] BTC 147

Source: ESC D10

See *British Tax Reporter* ¶520-500.

RATES OF CAPITAL GAINS TAX

5410 Rate of capital gains tax for disposals from 23 June 2010

For the period 6 April 2008 to 22 June 2010, capital gains tax was charged at a single flat rate of 18 per cent, regardless of the person chargeable, the nature of the asset involved or the length of ownership of that asset.

In the June 2010 Budget, it was announced that a higher rate of tax was to be immediately introduced to reduce the gap between the existing 18 per cent rate and the higher rates of income tax. The new rate is 28 per cent and applies in respect of disposals on or after 23 June 2010. The new rate replaces the 18 per cent rate in respect of trustees and personal representatives. For individuals, however, it will apply in addition to the 18 per cent rate; the actual rate applicable will be determined by the aggregate of the individual's taxable income and chargeable gains. In addition, a special 10 per cent rate applies to gains eligible for entrepreneurs' relief (see 5293), whereas they were previously charged at the 18 per cent rate but after being reduced by 4/9ths to produce an effective 10 per cent rate.

Individuals

The rate of capital gains tax payable by individuals is determined as follows:

- if any of the gains are on qualifying business disposals which attract entrepreneurs' relief (see 5293), those gains will always be taxed at 10 per cent (TCGA 1992, s. 169N(3));
- where, for the tax year in which the gains arise, an individual is liable to pay income tax at the higher rate or dividend upper rate, chargeable gains (other than those eligible for entrepreneurs' relief) are taxed at 28 per cent (TCGA 1992, s. 4(4));
- where the individual is not liable to income tax at the higher rate or the dividend upper rate but the chargeable gains realised on or after 23 June 2010 exceed the unused part of the income tax basic rate band, that excess of the chargeable gains is charged at 28 per cent and the balance at 18 per cent (TCGA 1992, s. 4(5)). If the individual has gains which are eligible for entrepreneurs' relief, those gains are included in the total of chargeable gains for this purpose but are to be treated as being the lowest part that total (TCGA 1992, s. 4(6)). The effect in these cases is to push some or all of the non-business gains into the 28 per cent rate;
- if the aggregate of the chargeable gains and taxable income is less than the upper limit of the income tax basic rate band, the gains (other than those eligible for entrepreneurs' relief) are charged at 18 per cent (TCGA 1992, s. 4(2)).

For these purposes, an individual's taxable income is the figure calculated at Stage 3 of the prescribed method of calculating income tax liabilities and the unused part of his basic rate band is the excess of the basic rate limit over that taxable income.

The income calculated at Stage 3 is to be modified for these purposes by being:

(1) reduced by any deficiency relief due in respect of life insurance contracts;

(2) reduced by any reduction in residuary income as a result of inheritance tax being charged on accrued income; and

(3) reduced by the amount of any gains on life policies in excess of the annual equivalent of those gains.

(The reliefs at (1) and (2) above are normally given by means of a tax reduction at Step 6 of the income tax calculation, whilst the gains on life policies are included in total income in full but subject to top-slicing relief being given as a tax reduction at Step 6.)

Where 'top-slicing relief' has been given in respect of a gain on a life policy and the calculation of the individual's income tax liability on the gain does not involve higher rate income tax then he is to be treated as not having paid tax at that rate when it comes to determining the rate of capital gains tax applicable.

Trustees and personal representatives

All chargeable gains arising on disposals on or after 23 June 2010 are charged at 28 per cent, except where trustees' gains are eligible for entrepreneurs' relief, when the rate is 10 per cent.

Losses and annual exemption

Because it is possible for up to three rates of capital gains tax to be chargeable for the same year, the question arises as to how to allocate allowable losses and the annual exemption. It is specifically provided that losses and the annual exemption may be used in the way most beneficial to the taxpayer. Thus they should be set primarily against the gains bearing the highest rate of tax.

This provision does not, however, override any other provision which restricts the set-off of losses, such as losses arising on a connected persons transaction which can only be set against gains arising on a transaction with the same person.

Law: TCGA 1992, ss. 4, 4A; F(No. 2)A 2010, s. 2

See *British Tax Reporter* ¶5-000.

5415 CGT rates and annual exemption for trusts

For the years up to and including 2007-08 the rate of capital gains tax for trustees was the 'trust rate', which was a flat 40 per cent for 2007-08. For the period 6 April 2008 to 22 June 2010, capital gains tax was charged at a single flat rate of 18 per cent, regardless of the person chargeable, the nature of the asset involved or the length of ownership of that asset. All chargeable gains arising on disposals on or after 23 June 2010 are charged at 28 per cent, except where trustees' gains are eligible for entrepreneurs' relief, when the rate is 10 per cent.

The annual exemption for trusts continues and is in most cases one-half of that applying to individuals (but see 5595 concerning trusts for the disabled). However, where there is more than one settlement by the same settlor, that half is divided amongst them, but subject to a de minimis figure of ten per cent of the full exempt amount for each trust.

For a table of rates and thresholds, see 80.

Law: TCGA 1992, s. 4, Sch. 1, para. 2; F(No. 2)A 2010, s. 2

See *British Tax Reporter* ¶5-020.

5417 Capital gains tax and income tax rates unified but separate taxes

CGT and income tax remain separate and distinct. Income tax reliefs and allowances cannot generally be set against chargeable gains. Personal allowances against income tax which are unused in any year are lost (see 1840); they cannot be used to reduce liability to CGT. Neither can capital losses (generally) or the annual CGT exemption (see 6150) be set against taxable income.

See *British Tax Reporter* ¶5-000.

SPOUSES AND CIVIL PARTNERS: CAPITAL GAINS TAX

5460 Independent taxation for CGT

Spouses have been taxed independently of each other since 6 April 1990. The effect on CGT is that a wife's gains are not attributed to her husband, each spouse is entitled to a separate annual exemption (see 6150) and one spouse's unrelieved losses cannot be deducted from the other's gains. Disposals between husband and wife are on a no gain/no loss basis (see 5500).

The *Civil Partnership Act* 2004 took effect from 5 December 2005. Broadly, the Act allows registered same-sex couples the same legal rights and protections as married couples (see 225 for further commentary on this).

In the remainder of this Chapter, references to a spouse also apply equally to civil partners.

See *British Tax Reporter* ¶504-000.

5490 'Living together' for CGT

A married woman is treated as living with her husband unless:

- they are separated under a court order or deed of separation; or
- they are in fact separated in such circumstances that the separation is likely to be permanent.

Law: TCGA 1992, s. 288(3); *Holmes v Mitchell (HMIT)* [1991] BTC 28

See *British Tax Reporter* ¶504-000.

5500 Transfers between spouses and civil partners

Transfers of assets between husband and wife, or civil partners, 'living together' (see 5490) have always generally been on a no gain/no loss basis, the gain on the whole period of ownership being brought into charge when the asset is eventually disposed of.

Example

Hugh and Winnie are husband and wife living together. Hugh buys a painting for £15,000 in 1985. He gives the painting to Winnie in 1986 when it is worth £18,000. W sells it in 2010 for £22,000. Winnie is treated as having acquired the painting for £15,000. The gain attributable to Winnie is therefore (disregarding indexation allowance: 5286 and taper relief: see 5268) £7,000. No chargeable gain arises on Hugh's disposal to Winnie.

For the position if Hugh had bought the painting on or before 31 March 1982, see 5304.

There are a number of consequences of a transfer between spouses and civil partners. In particular, in place of re-basing on the transfer the acquiring spouse is treated as holding the asset on 31 March 1982 if the disposing spouse held it on that date: re-basing can apply to the ultimate disposal outside the union (see 5304). Where a shareholding is split between the couple after 31 March 1982, the market value on that date of the part holdings can be determined by reference to the larger holding (see 5304). The rules preventing indexation allowance from creating or increasing a loss on a disposal after 29 November 1993 sometimes permit relief for indexation to the date of any transfer before that time between spouses (see 5283, 5292).

Law: TCGA 1992, s. 58

See *British Tax Reporter* ¶504-050.

5502   Jointly held assets

For CGT purposes, the assets of each spouse are treated separately, with separate relief and exemptions (see 5460). HMRC have clarified that the CGT treatment of assets held jointly by husband and wife may be summarised as follows:

- gains are apportioned in accordance with beneficial interests at the time of the disposal;
- where the split of beneficial interests between them is clear, because, for example, they have a legal agreement between them, or where there is an agreement that one is merely a nominee and has no beneficial interest, gains should be apportioned on that basis;
- where the split of beneficial interests is unclear, HMRC will normally accept that the couple hold the asset in equal shares;
- for income tax purposes, despite the usual presumption that the couple are equally entitled to the income, where assets and the rights to income from them are held in the same unequal shares, the couple can declare this to HMRC and be charged to income tax (and CGT) according to that split. It is presumed that where a couple make a declaration for income tax purposes, the same split applies for CGT.

See *British Tax Reporter* ¶504-100.

5505   Sole or main residence for married couple

A husband and wife or civil partners 'living together' (see 5490) can have only one sole or main residence for the purpose of the principal private residence exemption (see 6233).

See *British Tax Reporter* ¶546-000.

TRUSTS AND SETTLEMENTS FOR CAPITAL GAINS TAX

TYPES OF TRUST FOR CGT

5550   General CGT considerations for settlements

Settlements are used for a number of different purposes; for example, to:

- put assets into the hands of trustees who are better able to administer the assets than the intended beneficiaries;
- separate the ownership of income and capital so that for the present income is employed for one person but the capital is held long-term for another;
- avoid the ownership of a particular asset having to be determined at a given time; and
- take advantage of tax planning opportunities.

Settlements do not exist wholly for tax planning purposes; it is the flexibility that can be achieved through the use of a settlement that most often makes them attractive. Successive governments have therefore accepted that the settlement vehicle should continue to exist but have repeatedly attempted to restrict the tax planning opportunities that it may offer.

The terms 'settlement' and 'trust' are often used interchangeably. However, in this division, the term 'settlement' is used to refer to the overall arrangement whereby property is held by a body of persons (the 'trustees') 'on trust' for the benefit of others (the 'beneficiaries').

A 'trust' is the obligation which binds the trustees to hold property and apply it or the income derived from it for the benefit of the beneficiaries. A trust is generally created by a person, known as the settlor, who transfers funds to the trustees directing the way in which the property transferred is to be held and administered. The trustees have a fiduciary duty to deal with the trust property according to the terms of the trust.

See *British Tax Reporter* ¶576-000.

5555 Nominees and bare trustees for CGT

Assets held for another by a nominee or bare trustee are treated as if they are vested in the person for whom the assets are held: the beneficiary. The acts of the nominee or trustee in relation to those assets are treated as the acts of the beneficiary.

A 'bare trustee' is a person who holds property for someone who is (or would be but for being an infant or mentally handicapped) absolutely entitled as against the trustee, i.e. he has exclusive right, subject to any outstanding charge, lien, etc. for the payment of taxes and the like, to direct the trustee how to deal with the asset. The same applies where two or more persons are, or would be, jointly entitled (see Examples 2 and 3 below). For the trustee to be a bare trustee, the beneficiary must have a vested and indefeasible interest.

Example 1

Trustees hold property in trust for such of the settlor's children as should attain 18 years or marry under that age. During the time that the children are unmarried infants, the trustees dispose of investments comprised in the trust fund and a gain accrues. The trustees are not bare trustees because it cannot be said that if the beneficiaries were not infants at the time of the sale they would be absolutely entitled to call for the money and be able to give a good receipt. The interests of the infants are contingent on their reaching 18 years. The gains, therefore, accrue to the trustees and not to the beneficiaries. (This example is based on *Tomlinson (HMIT) v Glyns Exor & Trustee Co* (1969) 45 TC 600.)

Example 2

Jack and Julie are trustees for sale of certain land for their own benefit as tenants in common. The land is sold and a gain accrues. Jack and Julie do not have interests in a

---

settlement but are bare trustees – a chargeable gain, therefore, accrues to each of them. The situation would be the same if Jack and Julie were joint tenants.

Example 3

Trustees are directed to hold a trust fund for Anita for life with remainder to Beatrice absolutely. Although Anita and Beatrice may join together to direct the trustees how to deal with the property, they are not 'jointly' entitled, i.e. they have successive rather than concurrent interests. The trustees are not bare trustees and so the property is settled property.

Funds in court are treated as bare trusts.

Law: TCGA 1992, s. 60, 61; *Kidson (HMIT) v MacDonald* (1973) 49 TC 503; *Jenkins (HMIT) v Brown; Warrington (HMIT) v Sterland* [1989] BTC 281

See *British Tax Reporter* ¶577-300.

5562 Settlor

From 6 April 2006 the defintion of 'settlor' is based on the wider definition in the settlements anti-avoidance legislation.

A person is a settlor in relation to a settlement if it was made (or treated as made) by that person directly or indirectly or if it arose on his or her death. A settlor of property means that which is settled or derived from settled property and a person is treated as having made a settlement if he or she has provided (or undertaken to do so) property directly or indirectly for the settlement. If A enters into a settlement where there are reciprocal arrangements with B, B is treated as the settlor for these purposes.

The legislation now identifies the settlor where there is a transfer of property between settlements made for no consideration or less than full consideration. Where property is disposed of from settlement 1 and acquired by settlement 2 (even if in a different form), the settlor(s) of settlement 1 will be treated as the settlor(s) of settlement 2 unless the transfer occurs because of a will variation.

The legislation also now identifies the settlor in relation to will and intestacy variations occurring on or after 6 April 2006 regardless of the deceased's date of death. The measure applies where there is a variation in accordance with TCGA 1992, s. 62(6) and property which was not settled property under the will becomes settled. In this case a person mentioned in the group below is treated as having made the settlement and providing the property for it:

- a person who immediately before the variation was entitled to the property, or to property from which it derives, absolutely as legatee (as defined);

- a person who would have become entitled to the property, or to property from which it derives, absolutely as legatee but for the variation;
- a person who immediately before the variation would have been entitled to the property, or to property from which it derives, absolutely as legatee but for being an infant or other person under a disability; and
- a person who would, but for the variation, have become entitled to the property, or to property from which it derives, absolutely as legatee if he had not been an infant or other person under a disability.

If property would have been comprised in a settlement as a result of the deceased's will but the effect of the variation is that it becomes comprised in another settlement, the deceased will be treated as the settlor. He or she will also be the settlor if an existing settlement of which the deceased was settlor becomes comprised in another settlement. In both cases the deceased is treated as having made the settlement immediately before his or her death unless the settlement arose on the person's death.

Law: *Finance Act* 2006, Sch. 12 and 13; TCGA 1992, s. 68A–D

5565   Trustees of a settlement

The trustees of a settlement are treated as a single and continuing body of persons, distinct from the persons who may from time to time be the trustees; thus, a change in the trustees of a settlement will not in itself give rise to a charge to CGT, whilst gains arising to the trust are dealt with separately from gains arising to trustees as individuals. See 5630ff. for non-resident trusts.

Where part of the settlement property is vested in one trustee and part in another, they are together treated as constituting a single body of trustees.

Trustees of a settlement and any settlor in relation to that settlement are connected persons and so any disposal or acquisition between trustee and settlor is at market value (see 5100ff.).

For the annual exemption for trustees, see 5415, 5595.

Law: TCGA 1992, s. 65(2), 69(1), (3)

See *British Tax Reporter* ¶578-850.

CHARGES TO CGT ON SETTLEMENT EVENTS

5570   Transfers into CGT settlement

A transfer of property into a 'settlement' (see 5560) is a disposal of the whole of that property, notwithstanding that the settlor might retain some interest as a beneficiary under the settlement or that he might be a trustee of the settlement. This provision, therefore, relates to what otherwise would be considered a part disposal.

The Court of Appeal has held that an allocation of trust funds to new settlements was not a disposal of property. The court found that the trustees had no power to dispose of the settled property, and the Crown's attempt to assess CGT on the 'disposal' failed.

Transfers into and out of a trust that come into the 'relevant property' rules for IHT are automatically eligible for holdover relief.

Law: TCGA 1992, s. 70, *Berry v Warnett (HMIT)* [1982] BTC 239 (at p. 240); *Bond (HMIT) v Pickford* [1983] BTC 313

See *British Tax Reporter* ¶577-700.

5575 Assets leaving CGT settlements

Where a person becomes absolutely entitled (see 5555) to any settled property as against the trustee (or would be so entitled had he not been an infant or mentally handicapped) all the assets forming part of the settled property to which the person becomes entitled are deemed to have been disposed of and immediately reacquired by the trustee as a bare trustee (see 5555) for a consideration equal to market value.

The deemed disposal and reacquisition applies but there is no charge to CGT if a person becomes absolutely entitled on the death of a person with an interest in possession or annuitant (see 5585). A claim is possible such that there should be no chargeable gain or allowable loss (or any gain would be restricted to the amount held over when that property is transferred to the trustees) if a person becomes absolutely entitled on the death of a person who had any other interest in possession (see 5585).

Example 1

Under the terms of a settlement, property is settled on Andrew for life, with remainder to Brian. On Andrew's death, Brian will become absolutely entitled against the trustees. Thus, if on Andrew's death, the market value of the trust fund is £20,000, the trustees are deemed to have disposed of those assets for £20,000 and to have reacquired them (as bare trustees) at the same value. (In this example there would be no charge to CGT though Brian's base value for CGT purposes will have been uplifted – see 5580.)

Example 2

Settled property is held in trust for Philip for life, with remainder to Catherine absolutely. Philip surrenders his interest. At that point there is a deemed disposal of the settled property at its market value. Philip becomes absolutely entitled as against the trustees and CGT liability arises on the trustees.

Allowable losses where beneficiary absolutely entitled

Where a person becomes absolutely entitled to settled property as against the trustees, any unused allowable losses accruing to the trustees in respect of that property are carried forward to the person becoming absolutely entitled to the extent that they cannot be set against chargeable gains accruing to the trustees of the settlement.

To counteract avoidance, in relation to an occasion after 15 June 1999 on which a person becomes entitled as above, a loss which arises on the actual disposal of an asset held by the trustees cannot be transferred as above. Where a person becomes absolutely entitled to an asset standing at a loss, the loss which is deemed to arise on that occasion is transferred as above if the trustees cannot set it against gains arising to them on the same occasion or earlier in the year. However, in such a case the loss may be used only to offset a subsequent gain arising to the person absolutely entitled on the disposal of that asset or any asset which is derived from it.

Law: FA 1999, s. 75; TCGA 1992, s. 71, 72, 75

See *British Tax Reporter* ¶579-850.

5580   Termination of life interests for CGT

There is no charge to CGT on the termination of a life interest where the assets forming part of the settled property continue to be settled property (but also no CGT uplift). Where the life interest is terminated by death (or where the life tenant dies but the interest does not terminate), there is a deemed disposal and reacquisition at market value (see 5100ff.) of the assets corresponding to the deceased's interest; thus, a new base value is established for CGT purposes, but there is no liability to CGT unless hold-over relief for gifts (see 6285, 6325ff.) was given on the transfer into settlement, in which case the chargeable gain is restricted to the gain held over. These provisions apply equally on the death of an annuitant.

> ### Example
>
> Settled property is held in trust for Adam for life, then Betty for life, then Christopher absolutely. The settled fund has a CGT base value of £20,000. On Adam's death the assets in the fund are deemed to have been sold and reacquired by the trustees at the then market value (say, £30,000). There is no liability to CGT at this point and £30,000 will be the new base value for CGT purposes.

Note that for disposals after 5 April 1988 of assets held on 31 March 1982, the 1982 value is likely to be the base value (see 5300ff.). Where the life tenant dies after 31 March 1982 a further re-basing will apply and computation of any gain will be made against the value of the property at that time.

'Life interest' includes a right to income of, or the use or occupation of, settled property for the life of another. However, a right which is contingent on the exercise of a discretion of the trustee or some other person is not a life interest. A right to an annuity payable out of settled property is only a life interest if part of the settled property is appropriated by the trustees as a fund out of which the annuity is payable.

A life interest 'in possession' is one which is not a reversionary interest, i.e. it is not expectant on the termination of a prior interest. However, the House of Lords has held (in a capital transfer tax case) that an 'interest in possession' exists where there is an immediate entitlement to income. A power of accumulation prevents there being an interest in possession.

A life interest which is a right to part of the income of settled property is treated as a life interest in a corresponding part of the settled property; a life interest in the income of part of the settled property (where there is no right of recourse to the remainder of the settled property) is treated as a life interest in a separate settlement consisting of the property in which the interest exists.

Law: TCGA 1992, s. 72, 74(1), (2), (4), 75; *Pearson v IR Commrs* [1981] AC 753

See *British Tax Reporter* ¶580-175.

5585   CGT on death of person with interest in possession

Interests in possession can be either life interests or other interests; a beneficiary with an interest in possession which will come to an end when he or she reaches a specified age is not a life interest (see 5580).

Where the death of a life tenant leads to the termination of a life interest and someone becoming absolutely entitled as against the trustee, the deemed market value disposal arising by virtue of the termination (see 5580) is subject to the following modifications:

- if the property reverts to the settlor, the trustee's disposal is deemed to be on a 'no gain/ no loss' basis;
- if the settlor has obtained hold-over relief for gifts (see 6285ff., 6325ff.) on the transfer into settlement, a chargeable gain arises of an amount which, unless the rule below applies, is equal to the gain held over;
- if the deceased life tenant's interest extended to only part of the settled property, the chargeable gain is reduced to the extent that the interest forms part of the whole property (though the reduction may be smaller where a clawback of the same proportion of any held over gain is necessary following gift relief, as above).

For the effect of 1982 re-basing and the charge on gains held over between 1982 and 1988, see 5304.

Other interests in possession

The treatment of the death of a person with an interest in possession other than a life interest has been brought into line with the treatment of life interests in possession.

Law: TCGA 1992, s. 73, 74

See *British Tax Reporter* ¶580-025.

5590 Disposals of interests in settlements for CGT

In general, no chargeable gain arises to a beneficiary where he disposes of an interest under a settlement (e.g. a life interest, an annuity, a reversionary interest), provided that he or someone before him did not acquire his interest for consideration in money or money's worth. The proviso does not apply to consideration consisting of another interest under the settlement.

From 6 March 1998, the exemption does not apply where the beneficiary's interest is in or originates from a trust which has at any time been an offshore trust. The aim is to clamp down on tax avoidance by trustees of an offshore trust which has realised substantial gains. The offshore trustees could pay the cash out to the UK-resident and domiciled beneficiary but this would trigger a CGT charge. Instead, the trustees would bring the trust into the UK and then the beneficiary would sell his interest under the trust to a third party for cash. (The third party might be exempt from tax and therefore the cash in the trust could later be appointed to that party by the trustees tax free.) No CGT was charged on the sale by the beneficiary.

Nor does the exemption apply where, at the time of the disposal, the trustees are neither resident nor ordinarily resident in the UK. For special provisions where the trustees become non-resident at some time after the person obtains the interest, see 5640.

From 21 March 2000, where an interest in a settlement in which the settlor has an interest is disposed of for a consideration, the assets to which the interest relates are deemed, for CGT purposes, to have been disposed of an reacquired by the trustees at their market value. Any resulting gains are chargeable on the settlor under normal provisions. Hold-over relief (see 6144) is unavailable in respect of gains arising on the disposal.

The rule also applies to any property that formed part of a settlement in which the settlor had an interest at any time in the two previous tax years, or at any time in the period beginning when the contract for sale of the interest is entered into and ending when the transaction is completed.

From 6 April 2006, the definition of a settlor-interested trust is extended to include accumulation and maintenance trusts set up by parents. The legislation provides that a settlor has an interest in a settlement where property is or may be comprised in a settlement, or may become payable for the benefit of the settlor's dependent child, or the child derives any benefit from it whatsoever either directly or indirectly.

Law: *Finance Act* 2006, Sch. 12; FA 1998, s. 128; TCGA 1992, s. 76, 76A, 77, 85(1), Sch. 4A

See *British Tax Reporter* ¶578-400.

5592 Transfers of value

Anti-avoidance measures were introduced, apply to transfers of value completed after 21 March 2000, to counter the use of loans taken out by trustees to enable gains to be extracted without a CGT liability, or with reduced CGT liability.

Broadly, if trustees transfer or lend property to another person, for example another trust, at a time when the trust's borrowed funds have not been used for regular trust purposes, the assets remaining in the trust are deemed to have been sold for their market value. Any resulting gain is chargeable on either any UK-resident settlor or any UK-resident beneficiaries who are to receive any capital payments.

Finance Act 2003 introduced measures to ensure that schemes designed to avoid a charge on UK beneficiaries receiving payments from trustees of offshore settlements who realise gains are subject to the anti-avoidance legislation contained in FA 2000. The rules bring the stranded gains into a pool so that they can be attributed to, and charged to CGT on, any beneficiary who receives capital payments from relevant trustees.

There is also a rule that requires payments to beneficiaries who are not domiciled and resident in the UK to be ignored in computing the amounts that may be charged on beneficiaries.

Law: FA 2003, s. 163; FA 2000, s. 92 and Sch. 25, 26; TCGA 1992, s. 76A, 85A, Sch. 4B

See *British Tax Reporter* ¶581-900.

5595 Trusts for the disabled and CGT

A trust for the benefit of the disabled must satisfy the following conditions before it is entitled to qualify for the full annual exemption (see 6150, 6152).

The exemption is available where the settled property is held on trusts which provide that during the lifetime of a mentally disabled person or a person in receipt of an attendance allowance:

- at least half of the property which is applied is applied for his benefit; and

- he is entitled to at least half of the income arising out of the property, or that no income arising from the property may be applied for the benefit of any other person.

More than one trust of this kind set up by a single person after 9 March 1981 will form a 'group'. The annual exemption allowed for each trust in the group is limited to the annual exempt amount divided by the total number of trusts in that group, except that the minimum for each trust is one-tenth of the annual exemption.

Trusts with vulnerable beneficiaries

New rules took effect from 6 April 2004 which create a new tax regime for certain trusts with vulnerable beneficiaries. Under the provisions, certain trusts and beneficiaries can elect into the regime and, where a claim for special tax treatment is made for a tax year, no more tax will be payable in respect of the relevant income and gains of the trust for that year than would be paid had the income and gains accrued directly to the beneficiary.

For CGT purposes, the special capital gains tax treatment will apply in relation to chargeable gains arising to the trustees of a settlement if the following conditions are met in relation to the tax year in question:

- chargeable gains ('qualifying trusts gains') arise in the tax year to the trustees on the disposal of settled property held on qualifying trusts for the benefit of a vulnerable person;
- the trustees would be chargeable to capital gains tax in respect of those gains were it not for the application of the new rules in FA 2005, Ch. 4;
- the trustees are resident or ordinarily resident in the UK during any part of the tax year; and
- the trustees make a claim for special tax treatment for the tax year.

Under the special regime, the trustees' liability to CGT for the tax year will be reduced by an amount determined by using a formula set out in the legislation. Broadly, the amount is equal to the difference between two quantities. The first quantity is the capital gains tax liability that the trustees would have in respect of the qualifying trusts gains were it not for the new regime contained in FA 2005. The second quantity is the amount of extra tax to which the vulnerable person would be liable to under the new rules, subject to making certain assumptions, in relation to the qualifying trusts gains.

Law: FA 2005, s. 23–45 and Sch. 1; TCGA 1992, Sch. 1, para. 1

See *British Tax Reporter* ¶579-450.

5600 Persons chargeable in respect of trustees' liability to CGT

Capital gains tax in respect of gains accruing to trustees may be charged on and in the name of one or more trustees; but where an assessment is not made on all the trustees the persons assessed cannot include a person who is not resident or ordinarily resident in the UK (see 213, 216).

With effect from 1996–97, a CGT assessment may be made on any one or more of the 'relevant trustees'. Trustees in the tax year in which the chargeable gains accrued, and any subsequent trustees are 'relevant trustees'.

If CGT assessed on any trustee is not paid within six months from the time it becomes payable and the asset (or the proceeds) in respect of which the gain accrued is transferred by the trustees to a person who is absolutely entitled, that person may instead be assessed (in the name of the trustees) at any time within two years from the time the tax became payable.

If the trustees of a UK-resident trust become neither resident nor ordinarily resident in the UK, they may be subject to an exit charge; if the tax is not paid within six months from the time it becomes payable, HMRC may in some cases have resort to a past trustee for payment (see 5640). With effect from 1996–97, there can be no assessment on a person who ceased to be a trustee before the migration of the trust, and who can show that, at the time of cessation, there was no proposal for the trust to migrate.

Law: TCGA 1992, s. 65

See *British Tax Reporter* ¶579-300.

5620   Sub-funds

From 6 April 2006, sub-funds are recognised for both capital gains and income tax purposes. The new provisions enable trustees to elect for a specified part of settled property (a sub-fund) to be treated as a separate settlement subject to various conditions being satisfied. One consequence of such an election is that the trustees of the principal settlement will also be a trustee of the sub-fund.

The election must be made by the first anniversary of the 31 January filing date for the tax year when it takes effect. The creation of a sub-fund will result in a capital gains tax disposal, so they are most likely to be of benefit when a new trust is created.

Law: *Finance Act* 2006, Sch. 12; TCGA 1992, Sch. 4ZA

NON-RESIDENT AND DUAL RESIDENT TRUSTS

5630   Residence of trusts

From 6 April 2007, common rules determine the residence of trustees and trusts. Trustees will together be treated as if they were a single person and the deemed person will be treated as resident and ordinarily resident in the UK when all of the trustees are resident; or at least one trustee is resident and at least one is not and the settlor is ordinarily resident or domiciled in the UK when the settlement was created.

Under the new rules, a non-resident trust must have all non-resident trustees if it has a UK resident or domiciled settlor. If the settlor is non-resident and non-domiciled there can be a majority of UK trustees provided that one of them is non-resident.

Where a settlement is made by a non-resident, person not ordinarily resident or non-domiciled, and where the trustees act as such in the course of a business which is carried on in the UK through a branch, agency or permanent establishment, and the trustees would be treated as resident under the new rules, they may elect to be treated as non-resident.

Law: *Finance Act* 2006, Sch. 12 and 13; TCGA 1992, s. 69(1), (2).

See *British Tax Reporter* ¶580-850.

5632   Settlements with foreign element: special returns

HMRC have extensive powers to obtain information in relation to non-resident or dual-resident settlements and the settlor, the trustees and persons who transfer property to the trustees must submit certain information to HMRC if the trust is, or becomes, non-resident; there are exclusions from the requirements to provide information where it has already been supplied as a result of some other provision. The relevant information should be sent to: Inland Revenue, Claims Branch (International).

Law: TCGA 1992, Sch. 5A.

See *British Tax Reporter* ¶580-925.

5635   Gains of offshore trusts apportioned to beneficiaries

In relation to any settlement where:

(1)   the trustees are not resident or ordinarily resident in the UK; and

(2)   for tax years before 1997–98, the settlor, or one of the settlors, was (or was when he made his settlement):

    (a)   domiciled (see 219) in the UK at any time during the tax year, and

    (b)   resident or ordinarily resident (see 213, 216) in the UK,

gains and losses accruing to trustees are, within certain limits, attributed to various beneficiaries (or from 1991–92 other persons) who receive capital payments from the trustees, etc. The removal of condition (2) above only affects gains, etc. accruing to the trustees, and capital payments received, after 16 March 1998.

For the meaning of 'settlor' and 'settlement', see 1070. In a case in which the beneficiary under a will entered into a deed of variation to redirect the property into a trust fund, it was held that the person who effected the variation (i.e., the beneficiary) was the settlor of the trust, rather than the deceased, since there was nothing in the legislation (see 5692) to deem anything to the contrary.

A capital payment is a transaction not at arm's length representing:

- any payment on which the beneficiary is not liable to pay income tax; or
- any payment received other than as income by a beneficiary who is resident or ordinarily resident outside the UK,

where 'payment' includes the transfer of an asset and any other benefit conferred on the beneficiary and also applies to any occasion on which a person becomes absolutely entitled to settled property. In order to put demand loans to offshore trustees on to a commercial footing, it may have been necessary for the trust to pay a sum in lieu of interest in respect of periods to 5 April 1992 (see 5637); HMRC have expressed the view that such payment would be a capital payment to the recipient for the purposes of potential apportionment.

Interest-free loans, repayable on demand, made by offshore trusts to UK-resident beneficiaries constitute a capital payment so long as the loan remains outstanding.

The gains of the non-resident trust are computed as if the trust were resident. Such gains arising in any tax year, in addition to such gains carried forward from earlier tax years but not previously attributed to beneficiaries under these provisions, are referred to as trust gains for the year.

Where the trustees, etc. make any capital payment in any tax year to a UK-domiciled beneficiary, the amount of the payment is treated as a chargeable gain made by the recipient up to the amount of trust gains for that year, but not exceeding the amount of the payment. In HMRC's view, gains which would otherwise be charged on UK charities under these provisions may attract the exemption discussed at 5800.

Payments received by close companies, or companies which would be close were they resident in the UK (see 4253), may be apportioned between their participators for tax years after 1990–91; a beneficiary of the trust is excluded from being automatically treated as a participator by concession. Any amount which would otherwise be charged on beneficiaries for a particular tax year is to be reduced by any amount chargeable on the settlor for the same year (see 5637).

Example 1

Non-resident trust set up in 1985

The trustees made the following gains:

	£
2005–06	10,000
2006–07	17,000
Total gains	27,000

Payments to beneficiaries 2007–08

A = £20,000

B = £40,000

Total gains for earlier years are apportioned between A and B in 2007–08 according to their receipts.

$$A = \frac{£20,000}{£60,000} \times £27,000 = £9,000$$

$$B = \frac{£40,000}{£60,000} \times £27,000 = £18,000$$

Example 2

X trust makes the following capital gains and capital payments to beneficiaries L and M (both domiciled in the UK).

Year	Gains	Capital payments to L	Capital payments to M
2004–05	£6,000		
2005–06		£5,000	
2006–07	£10,000	£7,000	£6,000
2007–08	£5,000		

The 'trust gains' for these years are therefore:

2004–05	£6,000
2005–06	£6,000 (carried forward from 2003–04)
2006–07	£11,000 (i.e. (£10,000 + £6,000 − £5,000)
2007–08	£5,000

As there was no capital payment in 2004–05, the trust gains of that year are carried forward. L is treated as having made chargeable gains of £5,000 in 2005–06.

For 2006–07, the trust gain of £11,000 is apportioned between L and M in proportion to the net capital payments received:

	£
Total capital payments received by L	
2005–06	5,000
2006–07	7,000
	12,000
Less: previous deemed gains	(5,000)
	7,000

999

	£
Total capital payments received by M	6,000
Less: previous deemed gains	–
	6,000

L's deemed gains for 2006–07 are:

$$\frac{£7,000}{£7,000 + £6,000} \times £11,000 = £5,923.08$$

M's gains for 2006–07 are:

$$\frac{£6,000}{£7,000 + £6,000} \times £11,000 = £5,076.92$$

The trust gain of £5,000 for 2007–08 would be similarly apportioned. However, the total of deemed gains cannot exceed the total of capital payments received. Thus L's deemed gain for 2007–08 is limited to £1,076.92 (i.e. total capital payments received less previous deemed gains) and M's deemed gain for 2007–08 is limited to £923.08. The balance of £3,000 (i.e. £5,000 − (£1,076.92 + £923.08)) is carried forward as a trust gain of succeeding years.

If property is transferred to the trustees out of another trust, otherwise than for money or money's worth, the unapportioned trust gains of the transferor trust are effectively transferred as well in such a way as to increase the amount to be apportioned to its beneficiaries under these provisions. If the transferee trust is not subject to apportionment for that tax year, the unapportioned trust gains of the transferor trust are effectively transferred in such a way as to be available for apportionment under the migrant settlement rules (see 5640), whether or not the transferee trust would otherwise be subject to these apportionment provisions.

Supplementary charge

For capital payments made after 5 April 1992 there is also a supplementary charge. Broadly, the effect of the provisions is to increase the CGT payable by beneficiaries by ten per cent for each complete tax year for which trust gains are not distributed to beneficiaries, though the period for which this additional charge may be levied is limited to six years. The CGT is not to be increased beyond the full amount of the payment made to a beneficiary; on the present CGT rate, and with a ten per cent additional levy, it could not do so of course, but power is given to the Treasury to vary the ten per cent charge, and the rate of CGT may change in the future.

For this purpose there are detailed rules to determine the amounts to be treated as available for distribution to the beneficiaries for any tax year (the 'qualifying amount') and the way in which payments are to be matched with those qualifying amounts; in particular, payments made to beneficiaries are to be matched with qualifying amounts on a first-in, first-out basis – i.e. they are to be matched with the earliest available qualifying amounts.

Where a capital payment has to be matched with more than one qualifying amount, for different tax years, the payment is treated as a number of different payments (applying the first-in, first-out principle) and the tax apportioned to them on a 'just and reasonable basis'. Similar apportionments are made when part of a payment only can be matched with qualifying amounts falling in years earlier than the one preceding that in which the payment is made.

Unmatched qualifying amounts may be transferred between settlements in parallel with transfers of trust property.

HMRC have detailed the practice they will follow in applying the rules in various different circumstances, in particular in relation to intra-group transfers.

Law: TCGA 1992, s. 2(4), (5), 87, 90–97; FA 1998, s. 130, Sch. 21, para. 2, 6; *Marshall (HMIT) v Kerr* [1994] BTC 258; *De Rothschild v Lawrenson (HMIT)* [1995] BTC 279; *Billingham (HMIT) v Cooper* [2000] BTC 28

Source: ESC D40; SP 5/92

See *British Tax Reporter* ¶581-325.

5637 Gains of offshore trusts treated as settlor's

Where a number of conditions are fulfilled, a charge to tax is levied on the settlor of a non-resident trust, the gains of the trust being treated as the highest part of his total chargeable gains for the year. Initially, the only trusts caught were either those created after 18 March 1991 or those to which, broadly, funds were added or the beneficiaries changed after that date. However, in relation to gains made after 5 April 1999 the date restriction has been lifted. A transitional period from the date this change was announced (17 March 1998) to 5 April 1999 could be used by those affected to reorganise their affairs if they so wished. The widened charge does not apply where the only members of the settlor's family who can benefit from the trust are children under 18, unborn children, or future spouses of the settlor or his children.

The other conditions are as follows:

- that the trustees are neither resident nor ordinarily resident in the UK, or are dual resident, at some time during the tax year;
- that the settlor (or one of the settlors if there were more than one in relation to the settlement) is domiciled in the UK at some time during the tax year and either resident for any part of or ordinarily resident for that year;
- that at some time during the year the settlor, members of his family (including, in relation to trust gains made on disposals after 16 March 1998, his grandchildren or their spouses if either the trust was created after that date or, broadly, funds are added or the trust migrates) or certain companies controlled by them have an interest in the settlement.

HMRC have confirmed that a settlor with a life interest in all the assets of a trust will not be regarded as adding funds to the trust if he fails to exercise a right to reimbursement out of trust income.

Note that, where the settlor is also a beneficiary under the trust, these rules do not operate to exempt the beneficiary from liability in respect of capital payments received (see 5635).

There are a number of exceptions to the charge including where the settlor, etc. dies in the year.

The settlor is entitled to recover any tax payable under these provisions from the trustees of the settlement, and for this purpose the inspector of taxes is obliged to provide a certificate showing the gains assessed and the tax paid.

Amounts subject to the charge

The charge is in respect of disposals of settled property originating from the settlor on which the trustees would be chargeable to CGT if they were resident or ordinarily resident in the UK throughout the tax year, and if no double taxation arrangements applied, but subject to the following:

- any annual exemption which would be due to the trustees is ignored;
- the provisions treating the settlor as entitled to the trust gains (see 5610) are also to be ignored;
- losses in the tax year, or brought forward (but not for years before the first where the conditions for the charge were fulfilled), in respect of disposals of any of the settled property originating from the settlor are allowable as deductions, but neither gains nor losses in respect of disposals before 19 March 1991 are to be taken into account;
- there are special provisions as to trust shareholdings in offshore companies and 'dual resident trustees' (see 5645).

Property put into the trust by a company may be treated as originating from the settlor if he controls it (with or without his associates, as in relation to close companies: see 4265). A concession excludes a beneficiary of the trust from being automatically treated as a participator in determining control of a company.

A statement details the practice HMRC will follow in applying the rules in various different circumstances; in particular, it includes transactions entered at arm's length, close companies, transactions with wholly-owned companies, loans made to settlements, loans made by trustees, failure to exercise rights to reimbursement, administrative expenses, life tenants, indemnities and guarantees, variations and ultra vires payments.

Interaction with other charges

Any amount which would otherwise be charged on beneficiaries (see 5635) for a particular tax year is reduced by any amount chargeable on the settlor under these rules for the same tax year.

Where an amount is chargeable on the settlor under anti-avoidance rate rules (see 5420), and an amount is also chargeable on him under these procedures for the same tax year, any tax recoverable by the settlor from the trustees under the provisions of the rate rules is to be calculated on the basis that gains under these procedures form the next highest part thereof.

Avoidance of double charge

A double charge to CGT is prevented on gains arising to the trustees of an offshore settlement as a result of the CGT charge imposed on non-residents. Non-resident settlors who return to the UK after a period of temporary residence abroad (less than five years) now suffer CGT in the year of return in respect of gains realised by offshore trusts during their period of non-residence (see 5702). However, UK-resident beneficiaries may have already paid tax on some of those gains if capital payments have been made to them while the settlor was abroad.

In these circumstances, the gains which would fall to be charged on the settlor on his return to the UK will be reduced by the amount of the gains which have been charged on UK-resident beneficiaries of the settlement during that period where the departure is in a year after 1996–97 (see 5635).

Law: TCGA 1992, s. 2(4), (5), (6), (7), (8) 86, 86A, Sch. 5; FA 1998, s. 131, 132, Sch. 22, 23

Source: ESC D40; SP 5/92

See *British Tax Reporter* ¶581-900.

5640   Migrant settlements

At the time ('the relevant time') when trustees of a UK-resident trust become neither resident nor ordinarily resident in the UK (after 18 March 1991), they are deemed for CGT purposes to have disposed of and reacquired, at market value at that time, 'the defined assets', i.e. all of the assets which constituted the property settled in the trust immediately before the relevant time other than:

- assets situated in the UK and used in or for the purposes of a trade which, immediately after the relevant time, the trustees carry on in the UK through a branch or agency, or
- assets which would not be regarded as liable to CGT, if they were disposed of immediately before the relevant time, by virtue of double taxation arrangements, thereby crystallising capital gains and losses in relation to those defined assets.

A former trustee may be required to pay the tax in some circumstances if it is unpaid.

The charge is limited where the change in residence status is caused by the death of a trustee and the former status is resumed within six months.

Roll-over relief on replacement of business assets (see 6305) is unavailable where the old assets are disposed of before the relevant time but the new assets are not acquired until after that time unless the new assets, at the time they are acquired, are situated in the UK and used in or for the purposes of a trade carried on by the trustees in the UK through a branch or agency, or used or held for the purposes of the branch or agency.

If resident trustees are replaced by non-resident trustees, any capital payment made to a beneficiary while the trustees were resident in the UK is ignored for the purposes of the apportionment to beneficiaries of non-resident trust gains (see 5635) if the payment was not made in anticipation of a disposal by the non-resident trustees.

In the opposite situation, where non-resident trustees are replaced by resident trustees, any gains of the non-resident trustees which have not been attributed to a beneficiary will be treated as chargeable gains made by the beneficiaries who later receive capital payments from the resident trustees. If property is transferred to the trustees out of another trust, otherwise than for money or money's worth, the unapportioned trust gains of the transferor trust are effectively transferred as well in such a way as to be available for apportionment to its beneficiaries, whether or not the transferee trust would otherwise be subject to these apportionment provisions.

Where trustees migrate so that the above provisions apply, and after the relevant time a person disposes of an interest in the settlement which was created for or acquired by him before that time, any chargeable gain on the disposal of the interest is to be calculated on the basis that the person disposing of it acquired it immediately before the migration of the trustees (any gain up to the date of migration would be exempt). These provisions do not apply if, before the interest disposed of was created for or acquired by the person disposing of it, the trustees had become dual resident giving rise to a charge to tax (see 5645).

Where the material date falls after 20 March 2000, there is no uplift in the beneficiary's interest to market value when a resident trust becomes non-resident if at the time of emigration, the trust had stockpiled gains which had not been attributed to the beneficiaries of the trust. This rule does not affect emigration trusts that do not have stockpiled gains.

Law: TCGA 1992, 80–82, s. 85(2)–(9), s. 89, s. 90; FA 2000, s. 95

See *British Tax Reporter* ¶580-950.

5645   Dual resident trusts

On a trust becoming dual resident, there is a deemed disposal and reacquisition, by the trustees, at market value at that time, of all their relevant assets. 'Relevant assets' means all those assets which are settled property and which are covered by the double taxation relief arrangements. This provision operates at the time, 'the time concerned' (being a date after 18 March 1991), that trustees of a settlement become dual resident (that is, even though they remain UK-resident for UK tax purposes generally, they become also resident in some other territory under the laws of that territory), and by virtue of double taxation relief arrangements they are consequently not liable to UK tax on gains.

Where dual resident trustees acquire 'new assets' after 18 March 1991 which would normally qualify for roll-over relief on replacement of business assets (see 6305), relief will not be allowed if those new assets are covered by double taxation relief arrangements (so that any gains on disposal by the trustees would not attract UK tax) at the time of acquisition.

There is a similar attribution of trust gains to beneficiaries as applies to non-resident trusts (see 5635); for this purpose the trust gains are the smaller of the total net gains on which the trustees would be chargeable if the double tax treaty did not apply and the net gains on assets 'protected' under the treaty on which they would be so chargeable if the treaty did not apply.

Law: TCGA 1992, s. 83, 84, 88; FA 1998, s. 130

See *British Tax Reporter* ¶581-200.

CAPITAL GAINS OF ESTATES IN ADMINISTRATION

5680 Death and the assets of the deceased

Assets of a deceased person are deemed to be acquired by his 'personal representatives' (see 5685) at the market value (see 5103) of the assets at the date of death; however, the assets are not deemed to be disposed of and, therefore, there is no CGT liability on death.

> **Example**
>
> Horace dies on 10 April 2010. His estate includes 10,000 XYZ Ltd shares which H purchased on 2 March 1990 for £20,000. The probate value of the shares is £25,500. The personal representatives sell the shares on 5 July 2010 and realise £30,000 from the sale. They are deemed to have acquired the shares for £25,500 and, therefore, are treated as having made a gain of £4,500 in 2010-11.

Assets of the deceased include a share in property to which he was beneficially entitled as joint tenant, e.g. a husband and wife owning a house as joint tenants are treated as having a half share each.

A notional market value gain held over where qualifying corporate bonds (QCBs) are issued in exchange for shares or securities which are not QCBs (see 5865) is in effect wiped out by the subsequent death of the holder.

Law: TCGA 1992, s. 62(1), (10)

See *British Tax Reporter* ¶584-000.

5685 Liability to CGT of personal representatives

Personal representatives are treated as a single and continuing body and not as individuals. Thus, any change in the personal representatives does not give rise to a gain or loss.

Personal representatives are treated as having the deceased's 'residence' (see 213), 'ordinary residence' (see 216) and 'domicile' (see 219) at the date of death. Thus, if the deceased were resident and ordinarily resident abroad, his personal representatives would be regarded as so resident and ordinarily resident even though some or all of them may in fact be resident, etc. in the UK. However, as personal representatives are not regarded as individuals, advantage cannot be taken of the provisions regarding the non-remittance of foreign gains by a non-domiciled individual who was resident or ordinarily resident at the date of death (see 5004, 1600ff.).

Example

Edward dies resident, ordinarily resident and domiciled in the Isle of Man. His estate has been left to his children who are all resident, ordinarily resident and domiciled in England. The personal representatives dispose of many of the estate assets at a substantial gain. This gain will not be subject to capital gains tax because the personal representatives are treated as being resident, ordinarily resident and domiciled in the Isle of Man.

Capital gains tax in respect of gains accruing to personal representatives may be charged on and in the name of one or more of them and not on anyone else; but where an assessment is not made on all of them, the persons assessed cannot include a person who is not resident or ordinarily resident in the UK (see 213, 216).

A CGT assessment may be made on any one or more of the 'relevant personal representatives'. Personal representatives in the tax year in which the chargeable gains accrued, and any subsequent personal representatives are 'relevant personal representatives'.

Personal representatives are liable for any CGT charged upon the deceased and still unpaid. Any allowable losses sustained by the deceased in the tax year of his death may be carried back and set against the gains of the three preceding tax years. The order in which losses are set off against gains is as follows:

- against gains made in the tax year of death;
- against gains made in a later year before gains made in an earlier year.

Example

Derek dies having made a chargeable gain of £10,000 in the year of death (2010–11). He also made an allowable loss of £19,000 in that year. £10,000 of the loss is set off against the 2010–11 gain. The remaining £9,000 of allowable losses may, similarly, be set against any unrelieved gains for 2009–10, 2008–09 and 2007–08 in that order (but so as not to reduce those gains below the annual exemption: see further 5697).

Carried back losses are taken into account in computing the excess of gains over losses for the purposes of computing taper relief (prior to 6 April 2008: see 5268).

Losses sustained by personal representatives cannot be passed on to beneficiaries and can only be relieved against chargeable gains accruing to the personal representatives in the usual manner (see 5260ff.).

Disposals of assets by personal representatives are only liable to CGT if the asset is not acquired by a legatee (see 5690). A notional market value gain held over where qualifying corporate bonds (QCBs) are issued to the personal representatives in exchange for shares or securities which are not QCBs (see 5865) crystallises on disposal of the QCBs or, if they transfer them to legatees, when the legatees dispose of them.

Law: TCGA 1992, s. 62(2)–(4), 65; FA 1998, Sch. 21, para. 5

See *British Tax Reporter* ¶585-750.

5690 Legatees and CGT

On a person acquiring an asset as a legatee, no chargeable gain accrues to the personal representatives and the legatee is treated as if the personal representative's acquisition of the asset had been his acquisition of it, i.e. the legatee's base cost for CGT purposes is the market value of the asset at the deceased's death.

Example

Bert dies on 21 January 2010. Alice is the residuary legatee. Bert's residuary estate consists of 10,000 quoted shares in ABC Ltd with a value of £20,000 at 21 January 2010. The shares are transferred to Alice on 24 February 2011 when the administration of the estate is completed. The shares are then worth £30,000. However, no gain accrues to the executors and Alice is regarded as having acquired the shares for £20,000 on 21 January 2010.

Where the legatee disposes of an asset held by him on 31 March 1982, the base value is likely to be the 1982 value (see 5300ff.).

> **Example**
>
> Will dies in February 1980 and Frank is legatee of property worth £20,000 at that time. The March 1982 value is £25,000. If Frank disposes of the property in January 2010 his base value is likely to be £25,000.

'Legatee' includes any person taking under a testamentary disposition or on an intestacy or partial intestacy. Whether he takes beneficially or as trustee, a person taking under a donatio mortis causa (a gift made in contemplation of death, i.e. before death but conditional upon it) is treated as a legatee and such gifts are specifically exempted from CGT.

A residuary legatee, of course, has no vested interest in the estate. Only when the personal representatives have ascertained the residue can the residuary legatee's interest be vested. Generally, at that stage, if the personal representatives have not distributed the estate, they are deemed to have absented themselves as trustees: as was said in one case, it 'is for the executors ... to determine what particular assets should be realised to enable them to satisfy prior purposes and vested rights antecedent to those of the residuary beneficiary', and thus any gains arising during the administration accrue to the personal representatives and not to the residuary legatee.

A legatee is entitled to deduct the cost of transferring assets to him from any gains made by him on a subsequent disposal of those assets.

A notional market value gain held over where qualifying corporate bonds (QCBs) are issued to the personal representatives in exchange for shares or securities which are not QCBs (see 5865) crystallises, if they transfer them to legatees, when the legatees dispose of them.

The provisions above apply equally in Scotland, subject to the fact that the next heir of entail or person entitled to possession is deemed to acquire property at market value on the death of an heir of entail or proper liferenter. Where an estate is administered under foreign law, the legatee's date of acquisition is governed by that foreign law.

Law: TCGA 1992, s. 62(4), (5), 63, 64; *Cochrane's Exors v IR Commrs* (1974) 49 TC 299; *Bentley v Pike (HMIT)* (1981) 53 TC 590; *Passant v Jackson (HMIT)* [1986] BTC 101

Website: www.hmrc.gov.uk

See *British Tax Reporter* ¶586-000.

5692 Instruments of variation

Whether or not administration is complete, the beneficiaries may effect an 'instrument of variation' (or deed of variation or of family arrangement) redirecting the deceased's property without tax penalty; provided certain conditions are met, any variation or disclaimer by a beneficiary does not constitute a disposal by him and the variation is treated as if made by the deceased or a disclaimed benefit is treated as it had never been conferred. The variation must be made within two years of the person's death. From 1 August 2002 the requirement to notify HMRC was removed, provided there is a statement in the instrument effecting the variation that it is intended to be effective for CGT purposes. There can be no consideration in money or money's worth other than a reciprocal variation.

The House of Lords has held that the rules deeming a variation to have been effected by the deceased do not apply for the purpose of determining the identity of the settlor of a trust created by a deed of variation. They apply only for the purposes of the present provisions.

Law: TCGA 1992, s. 62; *Marshall (HMIT) v Kerr* [1994] BTC 258

See *British Tax Reporter* ¶586-500.

5695 Personal representatives: allowable capital gains expenditure

A gain arising on a disposal by personal representatives is liable to CGT (unless the person acquiring the asset does so as legatee: see 5685). In computing their chargeable gains, the personal representatives may set off the costs of obtaining probate, etc. relating to that asset (i.e. expenditure incurred in 'establishing, preserving or defending' title to the asset concerned: see 5223). Thus, in one case, the personal representatives succeeded in a claim to set off against gains made on the disposal of stocks and shares a proportion of solicitor's fees incurred in obtaining probate.

As it is often difficult to establish the appropriate proportion relating to a particular asset, HMRC have issued a scale of expenses which are allowable as being the costs of establishing title. The scale is contained in a statement of practice and is set out below:

	Gross value of estate	*Allowable expenditure*
A	Not exceeding £50,000	1.8 per cent of the probate value of the assets sold by the personal representatives.
B	Over £50,000 but not exceeding £90,000	A fixed amount of £900, to be divided between all the assets in the estate in proportion to the probate values and allowed in those proportions on assets sold by the personal representative.
C	Over £90,000 but not exceeding £400,000	1 per cent of the probate value of the assets sold.
D	Over £400,000 but not exceeding £500,000	A fixed amount of £4,000 to be divided as at B above.
E	Over £500,000 but not exceeding £1,000,000	0.8 per cent of the probate value of the assets sold.
F	Over £1,000,000 but not exceeding £5,000,000	A fixed amount of £8,000, to be divided as at B above.

G   Over £5,000,000   0.16 per cent of the probate value of the assets sold, subject to a
                          maximum of £10,000.

These scales take effect where the death in question occurred on or after 6 April 2004.

HMRC generally accept computations based on the above scale or on actual expenditure
incurred.

For allowable expenditure generally, see 5223.

Law: *IR Commrs v Richards' Exors* (1971) 46 TC 626

Source: SP 2/04, *Allowable expenditure: expenses incurred by personal representatives and
corporate trustees* (replacing SP 8/94 from 6 April 2004)

See *British Tax Reporter* ¶585-450.

5697   Personal representatives: rate of tax and annual exemption

The Finance Act 1998 made significant changes to the rate of capital gains tax paid by
personal representatives. For 1998–99 and subsequent tax years, the personal representatives
of a deceased person (and the trustees of all other types of trust as well) are liable to capital
gains tax at the 'rate applicable to trusts'. The 'rate applicable to trusts' is 50 per cent from
6 April 2010 (40 per cent from 6 April 2004 to 5 April 2010). This rate is applied to the
chargeable gains of personal representatives irrespective of the status of either the deceased
person or the beneficiaries of the estate.

Tax is only due in respect of certain disposals, where the assets have risen in value from the
probate value at which the personal representatives acquired them to the date of disposal and
after losses and any annual exemption have been taken into account.

For a table of rates and thresholds, see 80.

Law: FA 1998, s. 120; TCGA 1992, s. 3(7), 4

See *British Tax Reporter* ¶586-950.

CAPITAL GAINS TAX: THE FOREIGN ELEMENT

5698   Introduction

The UK's power to tax capital gains depends primarily on the residence status of the person
making the gain and, in certain cases, the location of the asset concerned.

The territorial limits of the UK are therefore important for determining where taxpayers are resident and whether assets are located here. The UK consists of Great Britain (that is, England, Wales and Scotland) and Northern Ireland. It does not include the Channel Islands or the Isle of Man. The sea within a bay is brought 'onshore' if it lies on the landward side of a line not exceeding 24 miles in length which joins the low-water lines of the natural entrance points of the bay. The UK is further extended to 12 nautical miles from the coastline.

Dwellers on boats within UK coastal waters are thus within the scope of UK taxation.

Certain offshore oil and gas assets are also within the scope of the charge to tax, by virtue of being treated as either sited in the UK or used for the purposes of a trade carried on in the UK through a branch or agency.

Situs and territorial scope

The location of an asset is of relevance where:

- an individual making the disposal is not domiciled in the UK; in such a case, chargeable gains on assets sited abroad may, in certain circumstances, be taxable only to the extent that they are remitted to the UK; or
- a person who is neither resident nor ordinarily resident in the UK is carrying on a trade here, via a branch or agency. Chargeable gains only arise on the disposal of assets situated in the UK which were in use, or are intended for use, for the purposes of that trade.

Chargeable gains may also arise where an asset used for the purposes of a UK trade carried on by a non-resident becomes sited outside the UK, or where the trade is discontinued without an actual disposal of the assets.

Law: TCGA 1992, s. 276(1); *Territorial Sea Act* 1987, s. 1; *Davies (HMIT) v Hicks* [2005] EWHC 847 (Ch)

Source: SP D23, *Non-resident company: section 13 TCGA 1992 (section 15 CGTA 1979)*

See *British Tax Reporter* ¶591-000.

5700 Foreign assets: delayed remittances

If, in the case of any resident or ordinarily resident taxpayer, a chargeable gain cannot be remitted to the UK (where the assets are sited abroad), the taxpayer can defer the assessment of the gain, if:

(1) he or she makes a claim at any time before the fifth anniversary of the 31 January next following the end of the relevant tax year. In the case of a company, the claim must be made within six years of the end of the accounting period in which the gain accrues.

From 1 April 2010, the time limit for a claim, in all cases, is four years from the end of the tax year or accounting period;

(2)   he or she was unable to remit the gain to the UK because of the laws of the country where the asset was situated, or because of the executive action of its government, or because it was impossible to obtain foreign currency; and

(3)   his or her inability to remit the gain was not due to any want of reasonable endeavours on his or her part (TCGA 1992, s. 279(3)(c)); it is understood that HMRC have in the past interpreted 'reasonable endeavours' strictly.

The gain is deferred until the year of assessment in which the conditions set out in (2) above cease to be satisfied.

In the case of an individual who has died, his personal representatives may make any claim which the individual could have made.

Where any of the amount due is received by the taxpayer through a form of insurance cover arranged with the Export Credit Guarantee Department (ECGD), the amount cannot be treated at any time as unremitted.

Law: TCGA 1992, s. 279

See *British Tax Reporter* ¶591-050.

5702   Residence and ordinary residence – individuals

Subject to a few limited exceptions, an individual's capital gains for a tax year are subject to UK capital gains tax if he is:

(1)   resident in the UK for any part of the tax year; or

(2)   ordinarily resident for that year.

In order to be outside the scope of the tax, the person must be both not resident and not ordinarily resident.

'Residence' and 'ordinary residence' have the same meaning for capital gains tax (CGT) as for income tax. However, income tax legislation does not define either term.

The absence of a statutory test has led HMRC to publish its working interpretation of the law in HMRC booklet HMRC6: Residence, Domicile and the Remittance Basis (which replaced booklet IR20 Residents and Non-Residents: Liability to Tax in the UK from 6 April 2009). This is applied to CGT as it is to income tax.

Disputes as to an individual's ordinary residence are decided by the Board with an appeal to the special commissioners, in the same way as for certain income tax purposes.

An individual who, although resident, is in the UK for some temporary purpose and not with a view to establishing residence here, is not within the charge to capital gains tax for any year in which the total periods for which he or she is resident do not exceed six months. The question whether that individual is here for such a temporary purpose is to be determined without reference to any living accommodation he or she has available in the UK. Thus an individual who is only resident by virtue of having visits to the UK averaging more than 90 days over a four-year period will not be liable to capital gains tax.

Law: TCGA 1992, s. 9

Source: ESC D2, *Residence in the United Kingdom: year of commencement or cessation of residence: capital gains tax*

See *British Tax Reporter* ¶592–650.

5703   Partnerships

The residence of a partnership is not of importance: a partnership's capital gains are assessed separately on the partners, so any individual or corporate partner's liability to tax on the partnership's gains depends on that partner's residence status.

Law: TCGA 1992, s. 59(a)

5704   Companies

A UK-resident company is liable to tax in respect of its world-wide gains, while a non-resident company is only liable in respect of the gains of a permanent establishment in the UK. A company is resident in the UK if it is:

(1)   incorporated in the UK; or

(2)   'centrally managed and controlled' in the UK.

Consequently, there are exit charges where a company becomes non-resident, ceases to be chargeable to tax in respect of branch assets or becomes dual resident so as to shelter any gains under a double tax treaty.

Law: FA 1988, s. 66

5705   Non-residents trading in the UK

Gains on trading assets

Persons other than companies

The general rule is that if a person is not resident and not ordinarily resident in the UK but is carrying on a trade, profession or vocation in the UK through a UK branch or agency, then that person is liable to tax on gains arising from the disposal of those assets situated in the UK which are used for the purposes of the trade, etc. or used/held for the purposes of the branch or agency (TCGA 1992, s. 10(1), (5)). The term 'branch or agency' is defined in TCGA 1992, s. 10(6). A branch or agency means any factorship, agency, receivership, branch or management. However, general agents and brokers are not included as a branch or agency for this purpose of capital gains tax.

Law: Puddu v Doleman (HMIT) (1995) Sp C 38

Companies

In the case of a company, one looks at a permanent establishment instead of looking at a branch or agency which one did before the Finance Act 2003. Hence, this approach follows more closely the approach taken by double taxation agreements.

Under TCGA 1992, s. 10B(1), the profits chargeable to corporation of a company, which is not resident in the UK but which is carrying on a trade in the UK through a UK permanent establishment, include the chargeable gains accruing to the company on the disposal of:

(1)   assets situated in the UK and used in, or for the purposes of, the trade at or before the time the gain accrued; or

(2)   assets situated in the UK and used, or held, for the purposes of the UK permanent establishment at or before the time the gain accrued; or

(3)   assets situated in the UK and acquired for use by, or for the purposes of, the UK permanent establishment.

It is important, though, for the chargeable gains to be included in the profits chargeable to corporation tax; that the disposal, giving rise to the chargeable gains, is made when the company is carrying on a trade in the UK through the permanent establishment concerned.

Under TCGA 1992, s. 10B(3), the company's chargeable gains would not be included in its profits chargeable to corporation tax where it is exempt from corporation tax on the profits of the permanent establishment because of the use of double taxation relief rules.

Law: TCGA 1992, s. 10B(2)

See *British Tax Reporter* ¶592-500.

5710   Double taxation relief on gains

Many countries tax their residents (e.g. the UK) and/or their citizens (e.g. the US) on their world-wide income and gains. Most countries also tax, to some extent, income and gains arising within their jurisdictions. There is, accordingly, ample scope for double taxation. The UK is party to a large number of double tax treaties and is also a member of the Organisation for Economic Co-operation and Development (OECD). Most of the modern treaties to which the UK is party are based on OECD models, which aim to ensure that a resident of a territory which is party to a double tax treaty is only taxed in one state; persons who are resident in both territories are usually treated, for the purposes of applying the provisions of the treaty, as resident in the territory with which they are most closely related under a 'tie-breaker' clause.

There is considerable scope for income and gains to be taxed twice. Double taxation is generally seen as a clog on trade and international investment, and most countries give their taxpayers some form of relief for overseas taxes suffered.

Foreign tax can be relieved in three ways:

(1)   as a deduction from the amount on which tax is charged;

(2)   by offset against domestic tax; or

(3)   by exempting certain items of income or gains from taxation (tax sparing).

The UK gives relief for foreign tax by way of credit against domestic tax, either unilaterally or under an agreement with the other country. If the foreign tax is less than the corresponding UK tax, then relief is restricted to the foreign tax suffered; if the foreign tax exceeds the UK tax, then relief is restricted to the UK tax payable.

The legislation governing unilateral and bilateral relief for foreign income taxes is found in the Taxation (International and Other Provisions) Act 2010 ('TIOPA 2010').

A HMRC statement of practice deals with double taxation relief and CGT. The statement provides clarification, particularly in respect of situations where charges to foreign and UK tax on the same gain do not arise at the same time. It gives the following useful examples:

> 'HMRC's view is that the following sets of circumstances fall within the terms of the standard credit article and may therefore give rise to a credit for overseas tax against CGT or UK corporation tax on chargeable gains.
>
> (i)   The overseas tax charges capital gains as income.
>
> (ii)   Overseas tax is payable on a disposal falling within TCGA 1992, s. 170 (transfers within a group of companies treated as taking place on a no gain/no loss basis [see 3682]) and a liability to UK tax arises on a subsequent disposal.
>
> (iii) An overseas trade carried on through a branch or agency is domesticated (i.e. transferred to a local subsidiary) and relief is given under TCGA 1992, s. 140 [see 4060]. There is a subsequent disposal of the securities (or the subsidiary disposes of the assets within six years) giving rise to a liability to UK tax and overseas tax is charged in whole or in part by reference to the gain accruing at the date of domestication.

(iv) Overseas tax is payable by reference to increases in the value of assets although there has been no disposal. There is a subsequent disposal of the assets on which a liability to UK tax arises.'

Where gains of non-resident companies are apportioned to UK-resident or ordinarily resident shareholders, double tax relief extends in such cases to overseas tax paid by the company (see 5698).

Foreign tax for which no credit relief is available can be deducted in computing the income or gain.

Law: TCGA 1992, s. 277, 278

Source: SP 6/88, *Double taxation relief: chargeable gains*

See *British Tax Reporter* ¶593-300.

5720   Non-resident close companies

Special rules apply where chargeable gains accrue to a company which:

(1)   is not resident in the UK; and

(2)   would be a close company if it were resident in the UK. For discussion of the meaning of 'close company', see 4265.

In such a case chargeable gains accruing to the company may be apportioned to participators (in respect of gains accruing before 28 November 1995, shareholders) in proportion to their interest as a participator in the company. For discussion of the meaning of 'participator', see 4256.

Law: TCGA 1992, s. 13; FA 1998, s. 122(4), Sch. 21, para. 4

See *British Tax Reporter* ¶592-900.

PARTNERSHIP GAINS

5760   Introduction to partnership gains

Tax in respect of chargeable gains accruing on the disposal of chargeable assets is assessed and charged on the partners separately and partnership dealings are treated as dealings by the partners and not by the firm.

The practical application of CGT to partnership transactions is detailed in an important HMRC statement of practice. The following paragraphs outline the main points of that practice statement. However, the acquisition or disposal of an asset is deemed to be for a consideration equal to market value where the transaction is not made at arm's length (see 5100ff.) and a transaction is not at arm's length if it is made between connected persons (see 5130ff.), for which purpose a person is, inter alia, connected with:

- any person with whom he is in partnership (i.e. existing partners);
- the spouse or relative of any individual with whom he is in partnership.

Excepted from this definition of 'connected persons' is any acquisition or disposal of assets made pursuant to a bona fide commercial arrangement. In cases where the exception applies, market value is not substituted for actual consideration. However, strictly speaking, the exception does not apply where parties to the transaction are connected persons for reasons other than partnership, e.g. father and son.

Source: SP D12, *Partnerships*

See *British Tax Reporter* ¶504-350.

5765 Partnership assets

Chargeable gains accruing on the disposal of partnership assets are assessed separately on individual partners. Each partner is regarded as owning a share of the partnership assets. The size of that share is usually determined by the partnership agreement specifying the respective shares in asset surpluses. Where the agreement does not so specify, each partner's share will depend on the treatment of asset surpluses in the accounts. Where any surplus is not allocated among the partners, regard is had to the ordinary profit-sharing ratio.

Example

Annie, Bella and Chloe are partners. The profit-sharing ratios are 2:2:1 respectively. The partnership agreement does not deal with the division of surpluses arising from the disposal of assets. The partnership sells certain assets making a gain of £25,000. This surplus is not allocated among the partners but put into a common reserve. The gain apportioned to Annie and Bella is £10,000 each. £5,000 is apportioned to Chloe.

Expenditure on acquiring an asset is allocated similarly at the time of the acquisition.

See *British Tax Reporter* ¶504-350.

5770 Partnership assets received in kind

A partner receiving a partnership asset in kind is not regarded as disposing of his share in it. The asset is taken by the partner at its market value reduced by any gain attributed to his share. This will be his acquisition cost which he carries forward. Any gains attributed to the other partners are subject to CGT. The same principles apply where a loss results from the disposal.

> **Example**
>
> Alex, Brandon and Callum are partners, each having a one-third fractional share in asset surpluses. Alex and Brandon plan to retire soon and Callum agrees to take a heavier burden in the partnership business. The partnership premises, with a current market value of £50,000, are transferred to Callum. The premises were purchased for £44,000. At the time of distribution, a chargeable gain of £2,000 arises to each of Alex and Brandon. Callum is not regarded as making a chargeable gain. Instead, his base value for CGT purposes is reduced from £50,000 to £48,000 (i.e. by the gain attributed to him).
>
> If, instead of a gain, there had been an overall loss of, say, £6,000, C's share (£2,000) would have been added to the current market value to give a carry-forward value of £52,000.

See *British Tax Reporter* ¶504-650.

5775   Changes in partnership-sharing ratios and CGT

A change in partnership-sharing ratios (including changes made when a partner joins or leaves the firm), in general, gives rise to neither a chargeable gain nor an allowable loss. Where a partner reduces or gives up his share, he is treated as disposing of that fractional share for a consideration which gives rise to neither a gain nor a loss.

> **Example**
>
> Alice, Brenda, Christine and David are partners in a firm. Share ratios in asset surpluses are 3:1:1:1. The firm takes Emily on as a new partner. Emily is given a one-sixth share and Alice's share is reduced similarly. The current balance sheet value of the principal asset is £90,000, since the asset has not been revalued in the accounts since acquisition. The transaction takes place for a consideration calculated on the assumption that an unindexed gain accrues to the transferor equal to the indexation allowance, so that after taking account of the indexation allowance, neither a gain nor a loss arises. Thus, Alice is treated as disposing of a one-sixth share in the asset for consideration of £15,000, plus indexation allowance from the date of acquisition of the asset to the date of admission of Emily. This is also Emily's acquisition cost.

There are certain qualifications to this position, and these are dealt with at 5780 and 5785 below.

Where there has been a change in partnership-sharing ratios since 31 March 1982, and the partnership disposed of an asset after 5 April 1988, the question arose as to whether the benefit of re-basing and associated matters (see 5300ff.) could be applied to a partnership share in such circumstances. HMRC have announced that such benefit is available where appropriate. For detailed discussion of re-basing and partnerships, see 5300ff.

Source: SP D12, *Partnerships*; SP 1/89, *Partnerships: further extension of statement of practice D12*

See *British Tax Reporter* ¶504-500.

5780 Partnership accounting adjustments and CGT

In the case of partnership accounting adjustments, upward revaluations are not occasions of charge and, therefore, do not give rise to chargeable gains. However, if there is a subsequent reduction in the partner's sharing ratio, he is regarded as disposing of a fractional share of the partnership asset (i.e. the fractional difference between his old and new share). The deemed consideration is that fraction of the current book value. The partner with the increased share has a similarly increased acquisition cost to carry forward. The same principles apply to a downward revaluation.

Example

Alan, Brian, Charles and Daniel are partners in a firm. Each is entitled to a quarter share in capital profits from the disposal of Blackacre. Blackacre was acquired for £100,000 in January 1984 and is revalued in the partnership accounts from £100,000 to £240,000 in September 1999. Following the revaluation, the share ratios are altered in January 2002. Alan becomes entitled to a half share and Brian, Charles and Daniel have their shares reduced to one-sixth each.

There is no chargeable gain at the time of revaluation; but a gain arises to each of Brian, Charles and Daniel on the alteration of ratios. Each is treated as having disposed of a one-twelfth share (i.e. $\frac{1}{4} - \frac{1}{6}$) for a consideration of £20,000 (£240,000 $\times$ $\frac{1}{12}$). Alan is regarded as acquiring a quarter share in Blackacre for a consideration of £60,000. Alan's acquisition cost carried forward is £85,000 (i.e. £60,000 + £25,000 attributable to his original one-quarter share). Brian, Charles and Daniel have each made a gain of £11,667 before indexation and taper relief.

	£
Proceeds	20,000
Cost (£100,000 $\times$ $\frac{1}{12}$)	(8,333)
Gain	11,667

See *British Tax Reporter* ¶504-500.

5785 Payments by partners outside accounts for CGT

Payments made outside the partnership accounts upon the change of partnership sharing ratios are included as part of the consideration for the disposal of a partner's share. For example, such payments may be for goodwill not included in the balance sheet, in which case the partner receiving the consideration will have no acquisition cost to set off against his CGT liability (unless he himself made a payment for the share he is now disposing of, or where the value at 5 April 1965 (see 5380ff.) is applicable).

See *British Tax Reporter* ¶504-600.

5790 Transfers between partners not at arm's length

Changes in partnership sharing ratios do not in themselves normally give rise to chargeable gains or allowable losses (see 5775) unless payments are made outside the accounts (see 5785). However, there is a charge to tax when the transactions are not between persons at arm's length. Market value is substituted for any deemed or actual consideration for the disposal (see 5100ff.).

The transaction is not at arm's length if the parties are 'connected' (see 5130). Often transactions between existing partners will be bona fide commercial transactions and the market value rule will not apply. But market value is substituted where the partners are connected other than by partnership (e.g. father and son).

Market value is not substituted if nothing would have been paid if the parties had been at arm's length or if the sum paid would have been paid if the parties had been at arm's length.

See *British Tax Reporter* ¶504-450.

GAINS OF SPECIAL TAXPAYERS

5800 Charities, local authorities, health service bodies, public institutions

Gains accruing to charities are exempt from taxes on chargeable gains if they are applicable and applied for charitable purposes; in this regard, the exemption may be restricted to the extent that the charity incurs non-qualifying expenditure, as in relation to income tax. Gains accruing to trustees under a will have been held not to be exempt from CGT, although charities were among the residuary beneficiaries. However, donations from one charity to another (giving rise to capital gains) may be exempt from CGT although the recipient charity merely adds the donations to its general funds and does not distribute them.

If property ceases to be held for charitable purposes, there is a deemed market value disposal which is not exempt; further, if that property was acquired on a disposal of other assets held on charitable trusts the previous exemption for that disposal is lost. In certain circumstances a concession may remove any CGT charge which might otherwise occur during a temporary loss of charitable status.

There is no charge to CGT where a charity or any of a list of specified public benefit bodies becomes absolutely entitled to settled property as against the trustees (see 6189).

Local authorities, local authority associations and health service bodies are also exempt from tax on capital gains (see 4630, 4635).

There are also exemptions for the Crown, the Treasury, etc. various museums and other public institutions, for consular officials, and for the central banks of India and Pakistan.

Law: TCGA 1992, s. 256(1), 271(1)(a), (f), (5)–(8); *IR Commrs v Helen Slater Charitable Trust Ltd* (1981) 55 TC 230

Source: ESC D47, *Temporary loss of charitable status due to reverter of school and other sites*

See *British Tax Reporter* ¶589-100.

5803 Scientific research associations

Exemption from CGT is provided for scientific research associations approved by the Secretary of State.

Law: TCGA 1992, s. 271(6)(b)

See *British Tax Reporter* ¶589-650.

5810 Lloyd's underwriters

Gains or losses on assets forming part of a Lloyd's underwriter's premiums trust fund or special reserve fund are subject to income tax for years after 1991–92.

Other fund assets are subject to CGT in the usual manner, the member being treated as absolutely entitled to the assets.

For the premiums trust fund, gains or losses are calculated on the basis of the difference in values between the beginning and end of the accounting period and, until the underwriting year 1994, are allocated to the corresponding underwriting year together with indexation allowance thereon.

Individual members of Lloyd's who participate in syndicates through a Members' Agent Pooling Arrangement (MAPA) have been able, since 6 April 1999, to treat their share of the various syndicate capacities held through the MAPA as if it were a single direct holding of syndicate capacity, so reducing the number of CGT computations needed when the MAPA manager buys and sells syndicate capacity or when other members join or leave the MAPA. Further, all syndicate capacity, whether held directly or through a MAPA, is eligible for CGT roll-over relief on acquisitions or disposals after 5 April 1999.

Law: FA 1999, s. 82, 83; FA 1993, s. 176(1); TCGA 1992, s. 207–209

See *British Tax Reporter* ¶588-350.

5813 Pension funds

Gains accruing to a person on the disposal of investments held in registered pension schemes, personal pension schemes and most other types of superannuation fund are exempt.

The relief was extended with effect from 26 July 1990 to cover capital gains arising from options and futures contracts dealt in by occupational or personal pensions schemes, etc.

Law: TCGA 1992, s. 271(1)(b)–(e), (g)–(j), (2), (10), (11)

See *British Tax Reporter* ¶565-250.

5816 International organisations and officers

There are exemptions for various designated international organisations and for foreign diplomats, consular officials, etc.

Law: TCGA 1992, s. 11(2), (3), 265, 271(1)(f), (5)

See *British Tax Reporter* ¶589-200.

GAINS IN RESPECT OF SHARES AND SECURITIES

5818 Nature of CGT treatment of shares and securities

Incorporeal property is specifically included as an asset for the purposes of chargeable gains (see 5007). Two of the most important types of incorporeal property are shares and securities.

For capital gains purposes, the term 'securities' sometimes encompasses shares, although the most widely adopted treatment defines them separately.

There are special rules for identifying shares and securities involving, in some cases, the pooling of those of the same class in the same company (see 5820ff.).

There are a number of exemptions and reliefs which specifically involve the disposal and/or the acquisition of shares or securities (though others may do so). In particular, as well as various provisions of notable importance to companies (see 3682, 4012ff.), special rules apply to:

- government securities and qualifying corporate bonds (see 5860);
- reorganisations of share capital (see 5900);
- shares in special schemes, plans or arrangements (see 5923ff.);
- relief for losses on unquoted shares (see 5940);
- transfer of a business to a company in exchange for shares (see 6302);
- disposals of shares to qualifying employee share ownership trusts;
- gains which are reinvested in shares of qualifying unlisted trading companies, etc. (see 5923).

The House of Lords has held that, in order to determine the date on which shares are issued, the crucial date is the date of registration and not the date of allotment. The question arose in relation to the business expansion scheme but it appears to have wider implications.

Finance Act 2003 introduced a measure that reversed the elective provisions which enable the charge to CGT to be postponed in certain circumstances where a person sells company shares or debentures wholly or partly for the right to receive an uncertain amount of another company's shares or debentures at a later date. Such rights are known as 'earn-out rights' and they are sometimes used where a company is sold for amounts which depend on the future profitability of the company's business. Under the existing rules, the postponement of the tax charge can occur only if an election is made for the right to be treated as a security. The effect of the change made by FA 2003 is that this treatment as a security will apply for rights conferred on or after 10 April 2003 unless an election is made. The purposes of the change is to reduce the need for elections.

Law: FA 2003, s. 161

Source: *National Westminster Bank plc v IR Commrs; Barclays Bank plc v IR Commrs* [1994] BTC 236

See *British Tax Reporter* ¶555-000.

SHARE IDENTIFICATION

5820   Need for share identification rules

Where shares of the same class in the same company have been acquired at different times and at different prices, some form of identification rules are needed to establish which of those shares have been sold, where a sale takes place which is of less than the full amount of the total holding.

On the introduction of capital gains tax in 1965, the question was addressed by the introduction of the 'pooling' concept. Under this concept, all shares of the same class in the same company held by the same person in the same capacity were to be regarded as a single asset.

Shares held by an individual personally were not affected by disposals made by him in his capacity as trustee. Shares issued either to a person as employee, or to a person who is restricted from disposing of them, were treated as if held in a different capacity from other shares or securities for the purposes of pooling (TCGA 1992, s. 104(4) and Sch. 2, para. 4(6); in the case of such restrictions, this continues so long as those terms were in force).

The notional single asset increased or decreased as more shares of that class were acquired or sold. On the sale of shares, the cost to be taken into account in the computation of the gain was a proportionate part of the total cost of the pool at that point.

The pooling concept, under which shares lost their individual identity and date of acquisition, was incompatible with indexation relief, introduced in 1982, because the precise date of acquisition was a key factor in determining the relief due.

In 1985, it became possible to claim indexation relief based upon a notional acquisition at 31 March 1982 at the prevailing value at that date. Pooling once again became viable.

With the replacement of indexation relief by taper relief for individuals and trustees from April 1988, the date of acquisition once more became important, as taper relief depended upon the length of ownership. As a result, pooling was abolished from April 1998 for individuals and trustees, and new identification rules were introduced (but not for companies).

The Finance Act 2008 abolished taper relief in respect of disposals on or after 6 April 2008. As a consequence, there was no continuing need to identify the date of acquisition and pooling was re-introduced.

For all in-date years, therefore, there are three sets of identification rules applicable to:

(1) disposals from 6 April 2008 onwards by individuals and trustees;

(2) disposals in the years up to 5 April 2008 by individuals and trustees;

(3) disposals by companies.

Law: TCGA 1992, s. 288(1)

See *British Tax Reporter* ¶556-500.

5826 Identification rules for individuals and trustees: 2008–09 onwards

Disposals on or after 6 April 2008 are to be identified with acquisitions in the following order:

(1) same-day acquisitions;

(2) acquisitions within the following 30 days on the basis of earlier acquisitions in that period, rather than later ones (a FIFO basis); and

(3) securities within the expanded 's. 104 holding' (see below), which specifically does not include acquisitions under (1) and (2) above.

Where the number of securities which comprise the disposal exceed those identified under the above rules, that excess is identified with subsequent acquisitions beyond the 30-day period referred to above.

Same day transactions

Before a disposal is identified with any previous acquisition or pool, it is matched, as far as possible, with acquisitions on the same day which are made in the same capacity. For this purpose, all acquisitions on the same day are treated as if they were made by a single transaction and all disposals on that day are similarly treated as made by a single transaction.

A 'bear' transaction is one whereby the taxpayer disposes of shares or securities which he intends to acquire but does not hold at the time of the disposal. In such a case, unless the taxpayer is a company and the disposal is identified with acquisitions according to other 'prescribed period' anti-avoidance provisions, the disposal is matched with the first shares or securities of that type subsequently acquired by the taxpayer in the same capacity. If there remains a balance of unmatched shares or securities, they are identified with the next subsequent acquisition, and so on.

HMRC have confirmed (Tax Bulletin 52) that this same-day rule, which treats a disposal as being identified with an acquisition on the same day, does not serve to frustrate a 'negligible value' claim. Concern had been expressed that the interaction the same-day rule and such a claim, which deems there to be a disposal and an immediate re-acquisition, would mean that, on the deemed disposal, neither a gain nor a loss would arise because the securities disposed would be treated as being those deemed to have been re-acquired. It also follows that where a deemed disposal and re-acquisition would give rise to a gain, that gain cannot be avoided by relying on the same-day rule.

Alternative treatment of shares acquired on the same day

Because of the general identification rule, employees who acquired shares under an approved share option scheme at a low base cost and, on the same day, acquired other shares of the same class at a higher value, would find that the acquisition costs would be averaged.

Where an individual:

- has acquired two or more holdings shares on or after 6 April 2002 as a result of transactions on the same day and in the same capacity, referred to as the 'relevant shares';
- those shares are all of the same class; and
- some of those shares were acquired under an Enterprise Management Initiative or an approved share option scheme, without incurring a charge to income tax,

he may elect an alternative identification rule to apply on any subsequent disposal of any of the relevant shares.

The time limit for the election is the first anniversary of 31 January next following the end of the tax year in which the first disposal of any of the relevant shares is made; in other words, 22 months after the tax year concerned. Once made, the election will apply to that disposal and all subsequent disposals of the relevant shares.

Under the alternative identification rule, the approved scheme shares and the remaining shares are treated as acquired in separate single transactions. Subsequent disposals are then identified with the remaining shares in priority to the approved scheme shares. As the remaining shares can be expected to have a higher base cost for future disposal purposes than the approved scheme shares, the effect would be to produce a lower chargeable gain on the earlier disposals than would be the case otherwise. Clearly, for this election to be relevant, there needs to be only a part disposal of the relevant shares.

Where the shares in question attracted EIS income tax relief or capital gains deferral relief, the alternative identification rule is adapted to ensure that the existing identification rules for EIS shares are not displaced. The EIS rules provide for shares acquired on the same day to be put into different categories, but if any of the categories contains approved-scheme shares and remainder shares, the remaining shares are treated as disposed of before the approved-scheme shares. Thus, for EIS purposes, the alternative identification rule works within the existing categories for same-day acquisitions.

Where EIS shares are transferred between husband and wife, the person to whom the shares are transferred is treated as having acquired the shares on the date on which they were issued, ensuring consistency with existing EIS rules.

Acquisitions within 30 days of disposal – individuals and trustees

Under the capital gains rules as originally enacted, it was possible to realise a gain or loss for tax purposes, while effectively continuing to hold the asset after completion of the transaction. A 'bed and breakfast' transaction was a term commonly used where a person wishing to crystallise an allowable loss (to set against other chargeable gains in the period) or a chargeable gain (to utilise the annual exempt amount or other exemptions or reliefs) usually in respect of shares, without disposing of them permanently, sold the shares (e.g. at the close of business one day) and reacquired them (e.g. at the opening of business on the following day).

Under current legislation, where a person disposes of shares and then acquires shares of the same class in the same company within 30 days following that disposal, the shares disposed of are matched with the subsequent acquisitions in priority to any acquisition of such shares before the date of the disposal. Where there is more than one acquisition in that 30-day period, the earliest acquisition is matched first.

In Tax Bulletin 52, April 2001, HMRC confirmed that an acquisition on the same day as the disposal was not 'within the period of 30 days after the disposal' and therefore the 30-day rule would not frustrate a 'negligible value claim'. They also opined that the 30-day rule could not be used to nullify gains arising on a deemed disposal and re-acquisition as, for example, on a settlement becoming non-resident.

The situation put to them was a UK-resident settlement with a holding of shares whose market value was well in excess of original cost. The shares could be sold on Day 1, the UK-resident trustees replaced by non-resident trustees on Day 3 and an equal number of the same shares repurchased on Day 5. The suggestion was that the disposal on Day 1 would be matched under the 30-day rule with the re-purchase on Day 5 and little or no gain would arise. On Day 3, when the deemed disposal occurs on the emigration of the settlement, there would be no chargeable assets held by the trustees and so no gain could arise at that time. Thus the whole value of the shareholding would have escaped the UK CGT net.

The HMRC view was that the shares sold on Day 1 were regarded as the ones bought on Day 5. It must follow, they said, that the shares held before Day 1 had not been disposed of (again, for CGT purposes) by the time the settlement left the UK. Those shares still constitute settled property immediately before the emigration, and must be treated as disposed of and re-acquired at that time under TCGA 1992, s. 80(2).

However, that opinion was not upheld in the High Court. In Davies (HMIT) v Hicks [2005] BTC 331, the trustees of a UK-resident settlement sold a holding of shares in a quoted company and later that same day retired and were replaced by a Trust Company resident in Mauritius. The following day the Mauritian trustee (of the now non-resident settlement) purchased an almost identical holding in the same company. The arguments outlined in the Tax Bulletin article were rejected by both the special commissioners and the High Court. The purpose of s. 106A was simply to provide rules for the computation of a gain and when that computation has been performed, the purpose of the section is fulfilled. It did not have any extended effect to deem the trustees to have still held shares at a time when their only asset was in fact a debt due from the stockbrokers for the sales proceeds.

As a result of this decision and disclosures under the avoidance scheme disclosure regime an amendment was introduced by Finance Act 2006. The section is disapplied in respect of disposals on or after 22 March 2006 when the subsequent acquisition is at a time when the taxpayer is:

- neither resident nor ordinarily resident in the UK; or
- resident or ordinarily resident but treated as 'treaty non-resident'.

A person is treaty non-resident at any time when he is treated as resident in another territory under the terms of a double taxation agreement between the UK and that territory.

Acquisitions within 10 days of disposal – companies

Before a disposal is identified with any shares or securities, it is matched with acquisitions made on the same day and then with acquisitions in the previous ten days made in the same capacity, if both disposal and acquisition would otherwise fall within the 'new holding' or 's. 104 holding' provisions, being of the same class.

Where there is more than one such acquisition in the ten-day period, the disposal is matched with them on a first-in, first-out (FIFO) basis. If the shares or securities acquired in the matched acquisition exceed those similarly disposed of, any excess is subject to the normal 'new holding/s. 104 holding' rules, mentioned above. If the shares or securities disposed of exceed those acquired in any matched acquisition (i.e. one or more matched acquisitions), any excess is identified with other securities in the normal manner.

Even where, within the ten-day period, the acquisition and disposal straddle a month-end, the benefit of indexation allowance is withdrawn: such an acquisition is taken for indexation purposes to consist of 'relevant securities', so that no indexation allowance is available where a disposal of securities takes place within ten days of their acquisition.

If the taxpayer is a company and the company has a sufficiently large holding of the issued shares or securities of that class, this rule may be overridden by provisions matching the disposal with acquisitions made within a 'prescribed period' before or after the disposal.

The 's. 104 holding' from 6 April 2008 (individuals and trustees only)

Under the rules applying for years to 2007–08, two separate pools could be in existence: the '1982 holding' (comprising shares acquired in the period 6 April 1965 and 5 April 1982) and the 's. 104 holding' (comprising shares acquired in the period 6 April 1982 and 5 April 1998). The changes introduced by the Finance Act 2008 removed the provision which prevented securities acquired prior to 6 April 1982 from forming part of the s. 104 holding (TCGA 1992, s. 104(2)(a) prior to its omission by the Finance Act 2008). The effect was therefore to expand the s. 104 holding to include all acquisitions of securities of the same class held in the same capacity.

The s. 104 holding from 6 April 2008 therefore now includes:

- any securities remaining in the existing s. 104 holding at 6 April 2008;
- any securities remaining in the 1982 holding at that date;
- any securities acquired in the period 6 April 1998 to 5 April 2008 which had not already been identified with disposals in years prior to 2008–09; and
- any securities acquired prior to 6 April 1965 which also had not been previously identified with disposals.

The 's. 104 holding' for companies (and for individuals and trustees for years to 5 April 2008 only)

Shares or securities of the same class acquired by a person in the same capacity after the end of 1981–82 were pooled together, as a 's. 104 holding', except where a sub-fund election was in force.

Pooling is an arrangement for treating a person's holding of shares of the same class as a single asset which grows as further shares are acquired and diminishes when there is a disposal of part of the holding. Under this arrangement, when there is a disposal of only some of the shares in the holding, it is treated as a disposal of part of an asset and the acquisition cost of those shares for chargeable gains purposes is not their actual cost but a proportionate part of the cost of all shares in the holding.

Because pooling did not originally apply between the end of 1981–82 and the end of 1984–85, the pool was first created with those shares or securities, if any, which were acquired before 6 April 1982 and were still held at 6 April 1985 (or 1 April for companies) with indexation allowance calculated to that date; the pool was then indexed from that date to any following event which increased or decreased the size of the pool – an 'operative event' – and between successive events of that type. The allowance or indexed rise on the occasion of an operative event (there was no clawback or indexed fall) was expressed in similar terms to that which applied generally, though the statute did not, in this instance, provide for rounding of the figures to three decimal places. Strictly, the legislation required two separate pools – a pool of 'qualifying expenditure' and an 'indexed pool of expenditure'; however, the latter would provide a figure for allowable costs plus indexation and the former was required only in order to determine the split between costs and indexation – though this did not affect the manner in which market value was to be determined.

The value of shares depended upon the extent of the holding; for the purposes of determining the value of any holding at 31 March 1982, HMRC permitted all the shares or securities held to be considered together irrespective of whether they were to be pooled together or whether they were acquired subsequently on a no gain/no loss basis.

If a holding of shares treated as a single asset by way of the 's. 104 holding' pool was transferred in a no gain/no loss transaction after 29 November 1993, the recipient was treated as having acquired the shares for their original cost, and only this amount was added to the recipient's unindexed pool of expenditure. However, the indexed rise in the cost of the shares at the date of the transfer was added to the recipient's indexed pool of expenditure; this was an amount of indexation allowance in the hands of the transferee, which was therefore subject to the same use restrictions as other indexation allowance. The indexation allowance available on the disposal of any of the shares was the difference between the relevant proportions of the unindexed and indexed pools of expenditure. However, this allowance could only reduce a chargeable gain to £Nil.

Certain shares and securities did not fall to be pooled as part of the s. 104 holding:

Capital Gains Tax

- securities within the accrued income scheme;
- qualifying corporate bonds; and
- material interests in non-qualifying offshore funds.

For these securities, the special identification rules applied.

There were also special identification rules for certain shares or securities held by insurance companies or underwriters and a simplified regime was applied, in practice, for individuals investing regular sums in monthly savings schemes of authorised unit trusts and approved investment trusts.

The '1982 holding' for companies (also for individuals and trustees for years to 5 April 2008 only)

Shares or securities of the same class acquired by a person in the same capacity between 6 April 1965 and the end of 1981–82 were pooled together, as part of a '1982 holding', except when a sub-fund election was in effect.

The '1982 holding' pool treated a person's appropriate pre-1982 holding of shares or securities of the same class as a single asset which diminished when the disposal was only part of the holding; however, it could not grow by the addition of further shares or securities, though the value of the pool could be enhanced if there was a bonus or rights issue or other reconstruction involving the shares or securities.

Being a pool of shares or securities held at 31 March 1982, the 1982 holding was eligible for re-basing to the value at that date, in accordance with the usual rules. The value of shares depended upon the extent of the holding; for the purposes of determining the value at 31 March 1982, HMRC permitted all the shares or securities held to be considered together irrespective of whether they were to be pooled together or whether they were acquired subsequently on a no gain/no loss basis.

Law: *Finance Act* 2006, s. 74; TCGA 1992, s. 104, 105, 105A, 105B106A, 107, 109, 110(6A), 110A, 113, 288(7B); FA 1998, s. 123–125

See *British Tax Reporter* ¶556-500.

5830 Special rules for relevant securities

There are various securities ('relevant securities') which are excluded from the general pooling and identification provisions (see 5826), namely:

- securities falling within the accrued income scheme;
- for accounting periods ending after 31 March 1996, and for tax years after 1995–96, qualifying corporate bonds;
- for accounting periods ending on or before 31 March 1996, and for tax years before 1996–97 (the legislation having been repealed on the introduction of the loan relationship provisions, deep discount securities);

- material interests in non-qualifying offshore funds,

though the special rules do not apply to either quoted shares/securities unless an election has been for them to be pooled at their market value on 6 April 1965 or to unquoted shares/securities held at that date.

The general rule is that, notwithstanding any identification specified in transfer documents, as regards securities of the same class and disposals made in the same capacity, earlier disposals are to be considered before later ones. It should not be forgotten that, with an unconditional contract, a disposal takes place at the time of the contract and not the transfer or delivery date.

Securities acquired in or after 1982–83

Rules for the identification of 'relevant securities' held on, or acquired after, 5 April 1982 (31 March 1982 for companies) are subject to specific rules for 'bed and breakfast' transactions by companies (see 4150). Reference should also be made to 5865 for identification rules relating to gilt-edged securities.

Securities disposed of are identified as follows.

Rule 1: With securities acquired within 12 months before the disposal and with securities acquired on an earlier date rather than on a later date (first-in, first-out (FIFO)).

Rule 2: With securities acquired more than 12 months before the disposal, taking securities acquired on a later date rather than an earlier date first (last-in, first-out (LIFO)).

Rule 3: Where securities are acquired at different times in any one day, identification is as nearly as possible in equal proportions.

Special provisions exist to identify disposals of securities with acquisitions where a person, by a single bargain, acquires securities for transfer or delivery on a particular date (or in a particular period) and disposes of them for transfer or delivery on a later date (or in a later period).

Securities held at the end of 1981–82

Due to the introduction of the indexation allowance (see 5280ff.), all share pools held at the end of 1981–82 (i.e. on 31 March 1982 for companies and 5 April 1982 for other persons) were frozen: the holding continued thereafter to be regarded as a single asset but one which could not grow by adding further securities (as for 1982 holdings generally: see 5826).

> ### Example
>
> William conducts the following transactions in relevant securities of Y Ltd. The March 1982 value was £0.50 per security.
>
> (1) Buys 2,000 for £1,850 in May 1979.

(2)   Buys 2,000 for £1,750 in June 1979.

(3)   Sells 1,000 for £1,000 in August 1980.

(4)   Buys 2,000 for £1,500 in March 1981.

(5)   Sells 4,000 for £6,000 in April 1991.

(6)   Buys 2,000 for £2,000 in May 1997.

The securities held by William at the end of 1981–82 are (applying the pooling provisions) 5,000 securities acquired for £4,200 calculated as follows:

Transactions (1) and (2) are added together giving a total of 4,000 securities acquired for £3,600. Transaction (3) is a part disposal of this holding and the acquisition costs attributable to the securities disposed of are:

$$\frac{1,000}{4,000} \times £3,600 = £900$$

The costs attributable to the balance of the holding (3,000 securities) are, therefore £2,700 (£3,600 − £900).

Transaction (4) is pooled with the rest of the holding, i.e. the holding now stands at 5,000 securities with an acquisition cost of £4,200 (£2,700 + £1,500).

Transaction (5) qualifies for an indexation allowance. Four-fifths of the holding are being disposed of, therefore the acquisition cost attributable to the disposal is:

$$\frac{4}{5} \times £4,200 = £3,360$$

This is well above the 1982 value and re-basing will not apply.

The indexation allowance, given that the RPI for March 1982 is 79.44 and for April 1991 is 133.1, will be:

$$£3,360 \times 0.675 = £2,268$$

Transaction (6) is after 5 April 1982 and is not pooled with the 1,000 securities not yet disposed of.

Law: ICTA 1988, s. 763; TCGA 1992, s. 108, 118, 119

See *British Tax Reporter* ¶556-500.

GOVERNMENT SECURITIES AND QUALIFYING CORPORATE BONDS

5860   Non-marketable government securities

Savings certificates and non-marketable securities (i.e. non-transferable securities or securities transferable only with the appropriate official consent) are not chargeable assets and are exempt from CGT.

Law: TCGA 1992, s. 121

See *British Tax Reporter* ¶559-000.

5865   Gilt-edged securities and qualifying corporate bonds

Where gilt-edged securities or qualifying corporate bonds (or options on them) are disposed of after 1 July 1986, the gain on disposal is exempt from CGT. The closing out of an option by a person entering into a reciprocal option is a disposal for this purpose. In consequence, losses accruing on disposals after that date are not generally allowable, though a limited relief for loans may be available (see 6185).

'Gilt-edged securities' are, for this purpose, those government securities set out in a prescribed list and any additional securities which may be specified subsequently by statutory instrument.

Qualifying corporate bonds

A 'qualifying corporate bond' (QCB) is, broadly:

- (for corporation tax purposes in relation to accounting periods ending after 31 March 1996), any asset representing a 'loan relationship' of a company (see 3036–3038); or
- a security acquired after the above date without tax deferral and which represents a normal commercial loan (permitting conversion into another corporate bond but not into shares or securities of the issuing company's quoted parent), which is expressed in sterling with no provision for conversion into or redemption in another currency (for the date of issue of shares, see 5818); or
- (in relation to tax years after 1995–96), any asset which is a 'relevant discounted security', whatever its date of issue. Such a security is broadly one issued at a discount to its redemption value of greater than half of one per cent for each year of its projected life (see 1401). 'Excluded indexed securities' are not relevant discounted securities: these are securities for which the redemption value is found by increasing the issue price in the same proportion as the change in value of specified assets (or an index of them) over the life of the security bears to the value of those assets when the securities are issued; or
- before the tax year 1996–97 was a deep gain security or, from a specified date, a security which fell to be treated as a deep gain security after that date (see 1401).

For corporation tax purposes in relation to accounting periods ending after 31 March 1996, foreign currency loan relationships (see 3037ff.), unit trusts and offshore funds held in exempt circumstances are not QCBs.

Before 14 March 1989, there was a requirement that the securities must since their issue have been quoted on a UK stock exchange or dealt in on the Unlisted Securities Market (for the date of issue, see 5818).

Because of the exemption for QCBs, special provisions apply to reorganisations, conversions and reconstructions which would otherwise be treated as not involving a disposal or acquisition in such a way that the new holding is broadly treated as if it were the original shares (see 5900), if either the original shares or the new holding but not both include QCBs. The usual rules do not apply to the extent that QCBs are involved:

- if the QCBs represent the old asset, there is a disposal and acquisition at market value, as adjusted for the acquisition by other consideration passing;
- if the QCBs represent the new asset, a notional market value gain or loss is postponed until subsequent disposal of the new asset, unless other consideration also passes; if there is an exempt gift of the bonds to charity (see 6189), the deferred gain does not crystallise either on the donor or on the charity on a subsequent disposal.

In a reaction to a tax avoidance technique involving QCBs changes have been made to ensure that any gain on a non-QCB security, whilst it is chargeable to CGT, will remain chargeable. It was suggested that where the terms of such a security changed, converting it to a QCB, the security could move from being within the scope of CGT to outside it. Any deferred capital gains would then have been moved outside the scope of CGT. Such gains are now postponed until the disposal of the QCB. The changes apply to disposals occurring after 25 November 1996, regardless of when the conversion took place.

The notional market value gain is in effect wiped out by the subsequent death of the holder; if the shares or securities are held by personal representatives at the time of the reorganisation, the gain crystallises if the personal representatives dispose of the QCBs or, if they transfer them to legatees (see 5690), when the legatees dispose of them. If the consideration received on a share exchange is only partly in the form of QCBs, the shares inherit a just and reasonable proportion of the base cost while the remainder is used to calculate the notional market value gain deferred until disposal of the QCBs.

The reinvestment relief rules were changed in 1996 to ensure that, where a gain in respect of an asset exchanged for QCBs comes back into charge on disposal of those QCBs, the gain arising is eligible for reinvestment relief. Where shares are exchanged partly for cash and partly for QCBs, a claim to reinvestment relief may be made in respect of the chargeable gain arising attributable to the cash consideration.

Law: TCGA 1992, s. 115–117B, 132, Sch. 9; *Klincke v R & C Commrs* [2009] TC 00122; *Weston v Garnett (HMIT)*[2005] BTC 113, 342

See *British Tax Reporter* ¶559-000.

5890 Capital distributions

A capital distribution received from a company in respect of any shares in that company is treated as consideration for the disposal of an interest in the shares (unless the distribution is 'small'). A capital distribution is, generally, any distribution not subject to income tax in the hands of the recipient, but it also includes consideration for disposal of a member's right in respect of a provisional allotment of shares or debentures. Ordinarily, a distribution by a company by way of dividends of gains arising on the sale of capital assets is liable to income tax; however, a repayment of share capital on a dissolution or winding-up of the company will be a capital distribution. (See also 5905.)

If a capital distribution is small (less than five per cent) in relation to the value of the shares in respect of which the distribution is made, then, except as noted below, the distribution is not treated as a disposal but is deducted from allowable expenditure. However, in practice, HMRC have confirmed that a taxpayer can insist that a small capital distribution be treated as a part disposal and can ask HMRC not to make a direction ignoring the disposal.

If the allowable expenditure is less than the amount distributed, there is a part disposal but rather than the usual apportionment (see 5229) the taxpayer can elect to have the whole of the allowable expenditure deducted on the part disposal.

Where a company purchases its own shares from a corporate shareholder in circumstances that amount to a distribution, the amount of the distribution is nonetheless included in the consideration for chargeable gains purposes. HMRC's view is that the distribution does not suffer a charge to tax as income within the terms of TCGA 1992, s. 37(1) (see 5221). In the case of a corporate shareholder, it is not therefore excluded from the capital gains computation so as to escape tax altogether. This does not apply where the shareholder is an individual because the exemption for company distributions does not apply to the individual, i.e. the individual pays income tax on the amount of the distribution.

Law: TCGA 1992, s. 122, 123; *O'Rourke (HMIT) v Binks* [1992] BTC 460

Source: SP 4/89, *Company purchase of won shares: capital gains treatment of distribution received by corporate shareholder*

See *British Tax Reporter* ¶562-000.

REORGANISATION OF SHARE CAPITAL

5900   Importance of a 'reorganisation'

A 'reorganisation of share capital' is not exhaustively defined but specifically includes the case where persons are allotted shares in, or debentures of, a company in respect of and in proportion to their holdings of shares in that company or where there is more than one class of shares and rights attaching to a class of shares are altered – thus, a reorganisation of share capital occurs when there is a bonus issue, or a rights issue, of shares.

Except in certain cases involving qualifying corporate bonds (see 5865), a reorganisation is not treated as involving any disposal of shares held before the reorganisation ('the original shares') or any acquisition of new shares or debentures ('the new holding') which represent the original shares; the new holding is treated as having been acquired at the same cost and at the same time as the original shares and CGT will only apply on a disposal of the new holding.

If there is consideration received by the taxpayer other than the new holding, there is a part disposal of the original shares effectively before (or at the same time as) the equation of the old and new holdings; the apportionment of the cost of acquisition of the original shares is carried out not on the usual part disposal basis (see 5229) but by reference to market value on the date of disposal.

If there is additional consideration given by the taxpayer, it is treated as if it had been given for the original shares so that it forms part of the acquisition cost of the new holding treated as incurred as the original cost had been. Indexation allowance (see 5280) has complicated matters where consideration is given for any part of the new holding since, for that purpose, the actual date of the additional consideration is used to index that amount.

The CGT treatment of the reorganisation of share capital also applies to the conversion of securities (see 5913) and certain company takeovers and reconstructions (see 5920). If an open offer is made to shareholders, then HMRC will treat any subscription for shares which is equal to or less than the shareholder's minimum entitlement as a share reorganisation. Any shares subscribed for in excess of the minimum entitlement will be treated as a separate acquisition.

For the treatment of collective investment schemes, see 5917 below.

Law: TCGA 1992, s. 126–129, 131; *Dunstan (HMIT) v Young, Austen & Young Ltd* [1989] BTC 77

See *British Tax Reporter* ¶560-000.

5905 Bonus and rights issues

Bonus issues

Bonus issues are free distributions of shares (e.g. two new shares for each share already held), treated as a reorganisation (see 5900).

> ### Example
>
> In 2000, Richard purchased 300 ordinary shares in S Ltd at £3 per share, total cost £900 (ignoring expenses for the purposes of the example). In 2006, Richard received a bonus issue of 300 shares.
>
> He then held 600 shares at £1.50 per share. They are all treated as purchased in 2000.

Rights issues

Rights issues are treated in the same way as bonus issues except that any consideration given for the new holding (or any part of it) is added to the original acquisition cost and treated, for most purposes, as if incurred when the original expenditure was incurred. However for the purposes of the indexation allowance, the additional consideration for the new holding is treated as a separate item of allowable expenditure incurred when it was due and payable (see 5900).

Example 1

John owns 10,000 ordinary shares in H Ltd, which he bought in 1995 for £20,000 (including expenses). H Ltd makes a one for five rights issue in 2000 at £1 per share.

John's total acquisition cost for 12,000 shares is: £20,000 + £2,000 = £22,000

Example 2

The facts are the same as in Example 1.

John sells the shares at a gain in, say, 2005. His allowable expenditure will include not only the acquisition costs (£22,000) but also indexation calculated separately on:

- the original cost of £20,000;
- the additional cost of £2,000.

A disposal of rights to acquire shares is treated as if the consideration for the disposal were a capital distribution by the company (see 5890).

Example 3

The facts are the same as in Example 1, but John sells his rights for 150p per share (i.e. £3,000) when each share is worth 250p. John's gain is calculated as follows:

	£
Consideration for rights	3,000.00
Less: apportioned acquisition cost (below)	(2,142.86)
Gain	857.14

The acquisition cost attributable to the rights shares is calculated as with part disposals:

$$\text{Acquisition cost of shares} \times \frac{\text{Consideration for sale of rights}}{\text{Market value of original shares} + \text{Consideration for sale of rights}}$$

$$£20,000 \times \frac{£3,000}{£25,000 + £3,000} = £2,142.86$$

If the consideration for the rights had been less than five per cent of the market value of the original shares there would (if John had made a claim) have been no disposal at this

---

stage. Instead, the acquisition cost of John's original shares would have been reduced by the amount of the consideration (see 5890).

See *British Tax Reporter* ¶560-100.

5910 Composite new holdings

A reorganisation of share capital may result in the new holding consisting of more than one class of securities (e.g. shares and debentures). The apportionment of the acquisition cost between the different classes of securities must be made upon a part disposal of the new holding.

The rules of apportionment differ depending on whether the new holding includes any quoted securities.

Quoted securities

If at least one class of the securities in the new holding is quoted on a recognised stock exchange, the acquisition cost is apportioned among the various classes of securities by reference to the market value quoted for the securities in the new holding.

Example

In 1993, Jack buys 10,000 ordinary shares in Y Ltd for £20,000 (including expenses). In 1995 there is a bonus issue of one preference share for every five ordinary shares held. On the first day on which the shares in the new holdings are quoted, their values are:

	£
10,000 ordinary shares at 290p	29,000
2,000 preference shares at 110p	2,200
	31,200

The £20,000 acquisition cost is apportioned between the ordinary shares and the preference shares:

10,000 ordinary shares $\dfrac{£29,000}{£31,200} \times £20,000 = £18,589.74$

2,000 preference shares $\dfrac{£2,200}{£31,200} \times £20,000 = £1,410.26$

If Jack sells the preference shares at £2 per share, his unindexed gain will be £2,589.74 (£4,000 − £1,410.26).

Unquoted securities

Where none of the securities in the new holding are quoted, the apportionment is made by reference to their market value at the date of the disposal.

> **Example**
>
> In 1986 James buys 10,000 ordinary shares in Y Ltd for £10,000. In 1989 there is a rights issue of one preference share for every two ordinary shares at 150p per share (i.e. £7,500). James accepts the allotment in full. In 1997 James sells the preference shares when worth £2 per share, and when the ordinary shares are worth £3 per share. The acquisition cost (ignoring indexation) of the holding (£10,000 + £7,500) is apportioned as follows:
>
> | | *Value at disposal* |
> |---|---|
> | | £ |
> | 10,000 ordinary shares at £3 | 30,000 |
> | 5,000 preference shares at £2 | 10,000 |
> | | 40,000 |
>
> $$\frac{£10,000}{£40,000} \times £17,500 = £4,375 \text{ (acquisition cost of preference shares)}$$
>
> This leaves James with his £13,125 to set against an eventual disposal of the ordinary shares.

Law: TCGA 1992, s. 129, 130

See *British Tax Reporter* ¶560-100.

5913 Conversion of securities

The CGT treatment of the reorganisation of share capital (see 5900–5910) also applies to the conversion of securities, e.g. a conversion of loan stock of a company into shares in the company; 'security' means loan stock or similar security (whether secured or unsecured) of any government, or of any public or local authority, or any company. It also includes alternative finance arrangements such as alternative investment bonds.

If a sum of money or premium is received on the conversion, there is a part disposal of the original securities (see 5900) but if it is small (less than five per cent) in relation to the value of the securities in respect of which the premium is given, then, except as noted below, the receipt of the premium is not treated as a disposal but the amount is deducted from allowable expenditure. If the allowable expenditure is less than the premium, there is a part disposal but rather than the usual apportionment (see 5229) the taxpayer can elect to have the whole of the allowable expenditure deducted on the part disposal; it is likely that the considerations as to whether the premium must be small for this purpose apply in the same way as for capital distributions (see 5890).

Where gilt-edged securities are received in recompense for the compulsory acquisition of shares, this is not treated as a conversion because of the exemption for gilts (see 5865);

instead, a notional market value gain or loss is calculated but postponed until subsequent disposal of the gilts. For the effect on re-basing, see 5303.

In a reaction to a tax avoidance technique involving qualifying corporate bonds (QCBs) changes were introduced in relation to disposals occurring after 25 November 1996 (regardless of when the conversion took place) to ensure that any gain on a non-QCB security, whilst it is chargeable to CGT, will remain chargeable. It was suggested that where the terms of such a security changed, converting it to a QCB, the security could move from being within the scope of CGT to outside it. Any deferred capital gains would then have been moved outside the scope of CGT. Such gains are now postponed until the disposal of the QCB.

Law: TCGA 1992, s. 132–134; *Employment Income (Meaning of Securities) Order* 2007 (SI 2007/2130)

See *British Tax Reporter* ¶561-000.

5915 Stock dividends

A stock dividend is an issue of shares in lieu of a cash dividend. Stock dividends used normally to be treated as a reorganisation of the shares already held by the investor and therefore as having been acquired at the same time as the original shares. Under the taper relief provisions (see 5268), the taper period would therefore run from the time of acquisition of these original shares on both the original shares and the new shares. This would obviously be to the taxpayer's advantage under the new rules, since it would maximise the relief. However, stock dividends issued after 5 April 1998 are treated as free-standing acquisitions, rather than reorganisations of share capital. The taper period will therefore run from the time that the shares were acquired, rather than from the time of acquisition of the original shares.

Law: TCGA 1992, s. 142

See *British Tax Reporter* ¶563-950.

5917 Collective investment schemes

Unit trust schemes are collective investment schemes under which the property in question is held on trust for the participants (*Financial Services Act* 1986); they are treated as companies in which the participants' rights are shares but, to the limited extent that they are not exempt, are subject to CGT rather than corporation tax on chargeable gains.

Gains accruing to an authorised unit trust, an investment trust, a court investment fund, a venture capital trust or a unit trust wholly for exempt unitholders, are exempt. By concession, exemption is not withheld from a unit trust because of any temporary holding necessary under ordinary arrangements of the trust for the issue and redemption of units.

FA 2004 introduced provisions, essentially clarificatory, amending the legislation relating to authorised unit trusts (AUTs) to bring its treatment of 'umbrella schemes' strictly into line with HMRC's established interpretation of the current rules. The amendments take effect for chargeable periods beginning on or after 1 April 2004. The legislation treats a unit trust scheme as though it were a company and the units held by investors as though they were shares in that company. An 'umbrella scheme' is an AUT whose investments are split into a number of separate sub-funds, usually having different investment strategies. The holders of units in the scheme have rights over individual sub-funds, and are entitled to switch their entitlements between different sub-funds. The new provisions make explicit provision for each sub-fund of an umbrella scheme to be treated as though it were an AUT, and for the scheme itself not to be a unit trust scheme for such purposes.

Transfer of company's assets to investment trust

Where a company becomes an investment trust (see 4565) so as to benefit from the above exemption, there is a crystallisation by virtue of a deemed disposal and reacquisition at market value of assets transferred on a tax-free reconstruction (see 4015). After self-assessment for companies (i.e. for company accounting periods ending after 30 June 1999), the chargeable gain or allowable loss crystallises at the end of the accounting period before the one in which the company becomes an investment trust, rather than at the time of the transfer of all or part of its business.

Law: FA 2004, s. 118; TCGA 1992, s. 99–102

Source: ESC D17, *Unit trusts for exempt holder: section 100(2) TCGA 1992*

See *British Tax Reporter* ¶588-000.

5920 Company takeovers and reconstructions

The acquisition of a company (or at least 25 per cent of the ordinary share capital thereof) in exchange for shares or a reconstruction involving the issue of shares may, in some cases, be treated as a tax-free reorganisation. This can have an unfortunate side-effect; if the consideration for the whole transaction consists of a future allocation of shares contingent on some event, such as attainment of specified profit levels, rather than an immediate issue of shares-for-shares. On a strict interpretation of the reorganisation relief rules, no relief would be due in relation to the value of the new shares issued on the happening of the contingency, because the initial disposal would be in exchange for the right to the future, contingent issue, not for actual shares in the company. A concession prevents this loss of relief (see 4024).

Where consideration received on a share exchange is partly in the form of qualifying corporate bonds (QCBs), the shares inherit a just and reasonable proportion of the base cost while the remainder is used to calculate the notional market value gain deferred until disposal of the QCBs (see 5865).

Law: FA 1997, s. 89

See *British Tax Reporter* ¶555-600.

5923 EIS

With the abolition of re-investment relief for acquisitions after 5 April 1988, the features of that relief were incorporated into an expanded Enterprise Investment Scheme (EIS) which has three features:

- income tax relief on qualifying investments in eligible companies;
- capital gains tax exemption on disposals of qualifying investments, provided the income tax relief is not withdrawn; and
- capital gains tax deferral on the disposal of any asset where sales proceeds are re-invested in qualifying EIS investments.

EIS deferral relief is a hold-over relief, not a roll-over relief. In other words, the gain is simply held in suspense until the happening of a chargeable event. The consideration for the disposal of the original asset and for the acquisition of the relevant shares is not reduced as a consequence of relief. When the relevant shares are sold, the gain on those shares will be calculated on normal rules and will be chargeable in addition to any deferred gain which is deemed to accrue.

The deferred gain is the chargeable gain which would, in the absence of a claim, arise on the original disposal. It is therefore the gain after any of the following reliefs:

- business asset roll-over relief;
- incorporation relief; and
- business asset gift relief.

Where a claim for relief is made, an amount of qualifying expenditure is set against the gain concerned. A corresponding part of the gain is then treated as not having accrued on the date it would otherwise have accrued, but as accruing on the occurrence of a chargeable event in relation to the eligible shares. That part of the gain is deferred until the chargeable event occurs.

The amount of the deferred gain is determined by the claimant specifying the amount of the qualifying expenditure to be set against the gain, the only limitations being:

- the available qualifying expenditure is that part of the total expenditure on the relevant shares remaining after previous claims; and
- the claim cannot exceed the amount of the gain remaining after previous claims under these provisions and claims for the relief that used to be available for investment in Venture Capital Trusts.

Capital Gains Tax

Law: *Finance Act* 2006, s. 91 and Sch. 14; TCGA 1992, s. 150A, 150C, 150D, Sch. 5B, Sch. 5BA; FA 1998, s. 74, Sch. 13, para. 26–36; FA 1999, s. 72, 73, Sch. 7, 8; *Blackburn & Anor v R & C Commrs* [2008] EWCA Civ 1454; *Daniels v HMRC* (2005) Sp C 489

See *British Tax Reporter* ¶568-000.

5925   Venture capital trusts

If an individual disposes of shares in a venture capital trust (VCT) (see also 1950ff.) the gain will be exempt from CGT if the original acquisition cost of the shares did not exceed £400,000 (prior to 2006–07 this limit was £200,000) in any one year.

A disposal is a qualifying disposal for these purposes if it is made by an individual aged 18 or over, and is made of shares which were acquired for bona fide commercial purposes (i.e. not as part of a tax avoidance scheme). The shares disposed of must not have exceeded the permitted maximum in the tax year in which they were acquired, (with the definition of permitted maximum, and the rules for identifying those shares which exceed the permitted maximum being imported from ITA 2007, Pt. 6, Ch. 2 (see 1954) for this purpose.

Identification of shares disposed of

In addition to the rules imported from ITA 2007, Pt. 6, Ch. 2 (see above) regarding identification of shares disposed of, a further provision ensures that shares acquired when the company was not an approved VCT are assumed to be disposed of before shares acquired when the company was an approved VCT. Once this provision has been applied, any shares acquired on different days are deemed to be disposed of on a FIFO basis, and shares acquired on the same day are deemed to be disposed of with those shares (if any) which exceed the permitted maximum being disposed of first.

Withdrawal of approval

Where approval of a VCT is withdrawn, then an individual holding shares in the VCT is deemed to have disposed of those shares and immediately reacquired them for their market value. The disposal is deemed to take place whilst the VCT is still approved, so that no chargeable gain or allowable loss arises, but the reacquisition, for the purposes of the share pooling rules (see 5826), is deemed to take place immediately after the company ceases to be a VCT.

Supplementary provisions

Where shares which enjoy different tax reliefs (specified in TCGA 1992, s. 151B(3)) are involved in a reorganisation under TCGA 1992, s. 126, then the shares are treated as being different holdings according to the different tax reliefs they enjoy. If a reorganisation such as a rights issue affects an existing holding, and results in the individual holding shares in a VCT (as defined in TCGA 1992, s. 151B(3)(a)–(c)), then the reorganisation provisions contained in TCGA 1992, s. 127–130 will not apply to the existing holding.

On a reconstruction, the rules contained in TCGA 1992, s. 135, 136 are disapplied where a VCT acquires another company which is not a VCT, or is acquired by such a company.

Law: *Finance Act* 2006, s. 91 and Sch. 14; FA 2004, s. 89 and Sch. 19, TCGA 1992, s. 151A, 151B(6), (7), Sch. 5C

See *British Tax Reporter* ¶565-300.

5928 Share option scheme shares

There are certain provisions which apply to options generally (see 5980).

Except as noted below, where an income tax charge is made in respect of shares (or an option to acquire shares) under an employee share scheme, this is taken into account in computing chargeable gains so as not to charge the amount to tax more than once; the relevant amount is added to what would otherwise be the allowable acquisition cost.

Provisions introduced in 1996 ensure that the release of an employee share option by the option holder in return for a replacement option does not give rise to a capital gain for the option holder or the grantor of the new option on the occasion of a takeover of the employing company.

Law: TCGA 1992, s. 120, 238

See *British Tax Reporter* ¶565-050.

5930 Shares in close companies

A close company may be broadly described as one that is under the control of a small number of persons who can direct its affairs (see further 4250ff.).

Where such a person has been assessed to income tax on an amount apportioned to him in respect of the company's income for an accounting period commencing before 1 April 1989, that tax is deductible in computing the chargeable gain or allowable loss on disposal of his shares.

Where a close company disposes of an asset at less than market value, the undervalue will sometimes be apportioned among its shareholders and effectively brought into charge by reduction of the base cost of the shares. (Similar provisions apply for inheritance tax purposes, where participators who are only marginally affected by the transfer may be ignored in any apportionment of the value transferred: see 6555.) HMRC will not seek to make the above reduction if the transfer has already been taxed as income or a distribution, or where the transferee is an employee of the company and has already been taxed under ITEPA 2003 on the difference between the market value of the asset and the amount actually paid for it.

A chargeable gain of a company which is not a close company by virtue only of the fact that it is not resident in the UK may be apportioned to UK-resident shareholders (see 5698). The apportionment is based on the shareholder's interest as a participator in the company. Where a member has paid tax on an apportioned gain and within two years of the date the gain accrued to the company, the company distributes an amount in respect of that gain, the participator may offset the tax already paid against the tax liability on the distribution received. As a result, the existing provision allowing tax paid on an apportionment to be set against the CGT liability arising on the disposal of the shares causing the apportionment is revised.

Law: TCGA 1992, s. 13(3), (5A), 124, 125; SI 2009/730

See *British Tax Reporter* ¶555-750.

5950 Value shifting and shares

Provisions treat and tax as a disposal any transaction whereby control of a company is exercised so that value passes out of shares or rights owned by one person into other shares or rights in the same company. The provisions also apply where value is shifted so as to set up an otherwise allowable loss.

Where value of an asset is materially reduced and matched by a tax-free benefit, the chargeable gain or allowable loss on disposal of the asset may be adjusted so far as just and reasonable. The charge is discussed in greater detail to the extent that it specifically relates to companies, although in so far as it does so the adjustment is expanded so as to relate also to relevant assets (see 4161ff.).

Law: TCGA 1992, s. 29(1)–(3), 30

See *British Tax Reporter* ¶555-400.

GAINS ON FUTURES, OPTIONS AND OTHER DERIVATIVES

5980 CGT treatment of options

Though options are specifically included as assets (see 5008) so that any sale of an option would be potentially chargeable, the grant of an option is a separate disposal (of the option even though the grantor may have divested himself of part of the equitable interest in the underlying asset) unless and until the option is exercised, when it is merged with the resulting sale or acquisition for both parties. Consequently a charge may arise on the grant of an option even if the option is never exercised. Notwithstanding the merger of the transactions, where a person acquires an option binding the grantor to sell – a 'call option' – and subsequently exercises the option, indexation allowance applies to the amount paid for the option and the amount paid for the underlying asset from the dates those amounts are actually given.

On exercise, if the sole effect is monetary – a 'cash-settled option' – as well as a deemed disposal of an asset by the person receiving the payment there is a deemed disposal of an asset by the payee and the payment is treated as if it were an incidental cost of that disposal, so that he obtains CGT relief for the payment.

Traded options are not subject to the write-down in allowable expenditure (see 5336) associated with other wasting assets. Where a taxpayer closes out a traded option by acquiring a matching option, the costs of obtaining the match are allowable in computing the gain on the disposal which arises when he granted the first option.

There are certain other rules relevant to option arrangements:

- replacement roll-over relief may be available by reference to the underlying nature of the asset which is the subject of the option (see 6308);
- the amount chargeable on a company when it grants an option to an employee under a share scheme is limited to the sum paid by the individual;
- unlike other wasting assets (see 5336), there is no write-down in allowable expenditure on a quoted option to subscribe for shares; similarly there is no write-down in respect of an option to acquire assets for use in a trade, except on transfer of an option over quoted shares;
- a quoted option to subscribe for shares which is dealt in within three months of a reorganisation, etc. is equated with the original shares in the same way as would be the underlying shares.

Law: TCGA 1992, s. 144, 144A, 146–148; *Strange v Openshaw (HMIT)* [1983] BTC 209

See *British Tax Reporter* ¶563-000.

5985   CGT treatment of commodity and financial futures

Transactions in commodity and financial futures and traded options on recognised exchanges are treated as capital in nature unless they are regarded as profits or losses of a trade. HMRC have given guidance on those transactions in futures and options which would be treated as trading transactions and those which would be treated as capital transactions giving rise to capital gains or losses.

Where a futures contract entered into after 29 November 1993 is not closed out so that a person makes a payment in settlement, as well as a deemed disposal of an asset by the person receiving the payment there is a deemed disposal of an asset by the payee and the payment is treated as if it were an incidental cost of that disposal (so that he obtains CGT relief for the payment) but, unlike other wasting assets (see 5336), there is no write-down in allowable expenditure.

Law: TCGA 1992, s. 143

Source: SP 14/91, *Tax treatment of transactions in financial futures and options*

See *British Tax Reporter* ¶563-000.

5990 CGT treatment of derivatives other than options or futures

Apart from options and futures (see 5980, 5985), there are few specific provisions dealing with derivatives, so that general principles apply.

Often, many of the foreign exchange rules introduced in 1993 in relation to companies apply from an appointed date of 23 March 1995 to certain financial instruments held by companies (see 3035). These rules were broadened by provisions introduced in 1994 and 1995 in relation to financial instruments for managing interest rate and currency risk held by companies: in essence, from this appointed date, profits and losses on qualifying contracts are to be recognised for tax purposes as they accrue and taxed or relieved as income receipts or deductions (see 3035). However, these rules apply in relation to various amounts of an income nature or treated as of an income nature; there are no specific rules to deal with any balance of gains within the chargeable gains net.

Law: *Whittles (HMIT) v Uniholdings Ltd (No. 3)* [1996] BTC 399

See *British Tax Reporter* ¶563-000.

EXEMPTIONS AND RELIEFS

TYPES OF EXEMPTION AND RELIEF FROM TAX ON CAPITAL GAINS

6140 Circumstances in which there is no charge to tax on gains

There are a number of circumstances in which general rules would result in a charge to tax in respect of a capital gain but there is a fiscal desire to reduce, postpone or eliminate the liability. Although there is no hard and fast rule, the term 'exemption' is generally given to rules taking a matter outside the charge to tax while the term 'relief' is generally given to something which postpones or reduces the charge to tax.

An exemption might work by treating a person or an asset as exempt from tax (see 5004 and 5009) or by deeming a gain not to be a 'chargeable gain' (see 5010).

A relief might treat a gain as being a chargeable gain only to an extent specified or in so far as it exceeds a certain level. Alternatively, it might deem a disposal to be at such amount as produces neither a gain nor a loss (see 5292). Certain rules adopt a form of relief specific to taxes on chargeable gains (whether corporation tax or CGT): 'roll-over reliefs' or 'hold-over reliefs' provide a temporary (if sometimes lengthy) deferral (see 6144).

See *British Tax Reporter* ¶570-800.

6144 Concept of roll-over and hold-over reliefs

The general scheme of roll-over and hold-over reliefs is to give a measure of relief from CGT in a variety of circumstances where its charge might otherwise be unfairly onerous. This is done by deferring the CGT payable until some subsequent disposal or event: a roll-over defers tax until a subsequent disposal while a hold-over generally has some time limitation (though the legislation often refers to gains being 'held-over' in either case). Some roll-overs are given by deeming a disposal to take place at no gain/no loss for both transferor and transferee: this rolls over the gain to the transferee; some roll-overs are given by reducing the disposal consideration so that there is no gain/no loss in the hands of the transferor, with the acquisition cost of a replacement asset being reduced by a corresponding amount – the transferee's acquisition cost is not amended; further roll-overs deem there to have been no disposal and equate the replacement asset with the original asset.

Example

Harry enters into a transaction with Julie, disposing of an asset, for consideration of £40,000. Harry later acquires a replacement asset for £40,000. A roll-over relief is available on Harry's indexed gain of £10,000. Depending upon the nature of the deferral in point, the disposal by Harry may be ignored and the replacement asset treated as if it had been the original asset. Alternatively, Harry may be treated as having made neither a gain nor a loss and the base value for CGT purposes either of the replacement asset or of the original asset in the hands of Julie may be reduced by the amount of the indexed gain (i.e. £10,000); if, in either case, the asset is later sold for, say, £50,000, the gain would be calculated as follows:

	£	£
Sale proceeds		50,000
Acquisition cost	40,000	
Less: roll-over relief	(10,000)	
Base cost as reduced	30,000	
Indexation allowance at, say, 38%		
38% × £30,000	11,400	
Indexed base cost		(41,400)
Indexed gain		8,600

See *British Tax Reporter* ¶570-350.

6147 Incorporation using relief for gifts of business assets

Conditions to be met

As far as its application to business incorporation is concerned, the general scheme of TCGA 1992, s. 165 is uncomplicated. The first and overriding condition is that the relief applies to disposals 'otherwise than by way of bargains at arm's length'. Consequently it applies both to outright gifts and sales which occur at a value less than market value. There are then three other types of condition, which are:

(1) the transfer must be made by an individual;

(2) the transfer must be made to a person who is resident in the UK; and

(3) the assets transferred must be used in a trade, profession of vocation carried on by the transferor.

In the first condition the term individual includes partners (other than corporate partners). In some circumstances it also applies to trustees.

Except where there are restrictions because an asset has not always been used for trade purposes, if no payment is received for the disposal, the full amount of the gain may be held over that otherwise would have been chargeable. So, there is no chargeable gain at the time of the disposal, but the amount of the held over gain is deducted from the transferee company's base cost. The held over gain is therefore brought into the capital gains computation automatically on any subsequent disposal of the assets by the company.

Example

B, who is 45, has carried on a business trading in architectural reclamations for ten years. He wishes to transfer his business to a newly incorporated company, B Ltd. He has business assets, as follows:

	£
Freehold premises	470,000
Goodwill	200,000
Stocks	150,000
Debtors	90,000
Cash	25,000

B purchased the premises, when he set up the business, for £85,000. B is making a gift of his business assets to B Ltd.

	£	£
Disposal consideration – premises (market value)	470,000	
Less: cost	85,000	
Unindexed gain	385,000	
Less: indexation allowance to April 1998 (say)	44,000	
Indexed gain		341,000
Disposal consideration – goodwill (market value)	200,000	
Less: cost	0	
Unindexed gain	200,000	
Less: indexation allowance	0	
Indexed gain		200,000
Total indexed gains on transfer to company		541,000

Because B received no payment from B Ltd, he is entitled to claim holdover relief for the full amount of the gains. When B Ltd sells the assets its allowable expenditure is the amount it is deemed to have given for the assets (market value at the date of transfer) less the amount of the held over gain.

If the transferor does receive payment, but it does not exceed his or her allowable expenditure for capital gains tax purposes, the treatment for hold over relief is the same as though he or she received no payment at all. If, however, the transferor receives a payment that exceeds that allowable expenditure, there is a restriction on the amount of the gain that may be held over. In determining whether the payment does or does not exceed the assets' base cost, any indexation allowance (to April 1998) due to the transferor is not taken into account as allowable expenditure. The amount of the gain which may be held over is reduced by the amount by which the payment received exceeds the allowable expenditure.

Emigration of the donee

One of the conditions that must be satisfied for holdover relief to apply is that the donee must be UK resident. Should the transferee company become non-UK resident while still holding the assets gifted to it, the legislation imposes a deemed disposal of all assets. This takes effect immediately before the company moves its tax residence offshore. Where a capital distribution is received by a person connected with a company (still UK-resident), and the distribution derives from chargeable gains made by the company, HM Revenue & Customs (HMRC) may assess the recipient. In the case of a company which is already non-UK resident, but makes a chargeable gain, HMRC have the power to assess the controlling director.

Making the choice: transfer to a company relief or gift of business assets relief

Which of the two methods is preferable depends entirely on the circumstances of the case but, on balance, the gifts of business assets route is probably used more widely. Its relative popularity is due principally to the perceived defect in s. 162 that all assets (other than cash) have to be transferred to the company. This can involve considerable amounts of stamp duty being payable, although, in the case of debtors, the position can be mitigated by converting as much as possible to cash before the transfer. The increase in the top rate of stamp duty to 4 per cent for assets worth more than £500,000 increases this cost; i.e. 4 per cent applies to instruments executed after 27 March 2000.

However, the stamp duty problem is at least a 'one-off' at the time of the transfer. A much more significant problem arises, using s. 162, where the business is of a type that requires large premises that appreciate in value. In so far as it is commercially possible, it is good tax planning to keep such assets outside a company, to avoid the owner being exposed to a potential double capital gains charge (once when the company sells the premises) and again, indirectly, when the owner sells his or her shares in the company. Using the gifts of business assets rules selectively enables the business owner to keep such assets outside the company.

The taper relief rules contain problems for both types of transfer. In each case the gains are deferred, until either the assets or the shares in the company are sold. The taper relief rules do not (except in the context of reinvestment of gains on EIS shares) count the period of ownership of the asset before the deferral. Since from 6 April 2002 the maximum taper relief for business assets accrues after two years, the owner will wish to consider whether the chargeable assets transferred, or the shares, are most likely to accrue the maximum taper relief before disposal.

Law: TCGA 1992, s. 165

See *British Tax Reporter* ¶575-250.

ANNUAL EXEMPTION AND MISCELLANEOUS EXEMPT ASSETS

6150 Annual exemption

An individual is not liable to CGT if his taxable amount (i.e. net gains) for any tax year does not exceed 'the exempt amount' for the year. The exempt amount is linked to the Retail Prices Index (RPI), unless Parliament determines otherwise; the 'exempt amount' is £10,100 for 2009–10 and 2010–11. For a table of figures for earlier years, see 80.

Allowable losses carried forward or back which are available to be set off against chargeable gains need only be used to reduce the gains for the tax year to the exempt amount for that year. This leaves more losses to be carried forward to subsequent years.

Husband and wife, and civil partners, are each entitled to a separate annual exemption (see 5460). For the annual exempt amount for trustees and personal representatives, see 5415, 5595, 5697.

Law: TCGA 1992, s. 3(1)–(5); *Capital Gains Tax (Annual Exempt Amount) Order* 2010 (SI 2010/923)

See *British Tax Reporter* ¶535-100.

6152   Annual exemption and taper relief

The annual exemption is set against net tapered gains (for disposals made before 6 April 2008; see 5268). Losses brought forward from an earlier year, or carried back from the year in which a person dies, need only be used to the extent to which it is necessary to reduce the untapered net gains to the level of the annual exemption.

See *British Tax Reporter* ¶535-100.

6155   Chattels sold for £6,000 or less

An asset which is tangible moveable property (e.g. a painting, carpet, piece of furniture or jewellery) may, subject to limited exclusions, be disposed of without liability to CGT so long as the consideration for the disposal is not more than £6,000. See also 6158 (wasting assets).

If the consideration is greater than £6,000 the chargeable gain is either five-thirds of the difference between £6,000 and the value of the consideration, or the actual gain, whichever is the lesser amount.

Losses

Relief for losses is available in full except that if the consideration for the disposal is less than £6,000, the consideration is deemed to be £6,000 and allowable losses are restricted in this way.

> ### Example
>
> Freddy sells a painting in 2010 for £5,900. Allowable expenditure is £6,500. Ordinarily, his allowable loss would be £600 but this is restricted to £500 (£6,500 − £6,000).

Sets of articles

There are provisions to prevent avoidance of CGT by breaking up a set of articles (e.g. a set of antique chairs, an issue of postage stamps, a canteen of cutlery or a set of books) and selling the individual items by separate transactions, in order to take advantage of the relief for chattels.

Where:

- two or more assets which have formed part of a set of articles owned by the same person are disposed of by two or more transactions, which may take place at the same or different times; and

● the disposals are to the same person, or to persons acting together 'in concert', or to persons who are 'connected persons': see 5142,

then the transactions are treated as a single disposal of one asset.

Example

Janice buys a matched pair of antique duelling pistols for £5,400. She sells one to Emma in March 2006. In May 2010 Janice sells the other to Emma. On both occasions Emma pays Janice £3,500. Janice is treated as having made one disposal for £7,000 and hence not within the chattel exemption, although five-thirds of the difference between £6,000 and the value of the consideration may be substituted, if less than the actual gain.

In many cases, these special provisions will be subject also to the general anti-avoidance computational rules relating to series of transactions (see 5133). Thus, in the above example, the gain on each occasion would most likely be calculated on one-half the market value of *two pistols* – probably a much greater sum than £7,000.

Part disposals

If a person disposes of a right or interest in a chattel, for the purposes of the chattels' exemption, the consideration for the part disposed of is, in the first instance, regarded as being the aggregate of:

● the actual consideration received for the part disposed of; and
● the market value of the part retained.

If this total exceeds £6,000 then the *limit* of consideration liable to CGT is calculated by applying the following formula:

$$((A + B) - \pounds6,000) \times \frac{A}{A + B} \times \frac{5}{3}$$

where

A is the consideration received for the part disposal; and
B is the market value of the part retained by the disponor.

In the case of a loss, where the aggregate of:

(1) consideration for the part disposed; and

(2) market value of the part retained,

is less than £6,000, then any loss is restricted by deeming the consideration to be the amount arrived at by applying the following formula:

$$A + \frac{(£6,000 - (A + B)) \times A}{A + B}$$

where

A   is the consideration received for the part disposal; and
B   is the market value of the part retained by the disponor.

Example

Julia buys an article for £6,800. She sells an interest in it for £2,400. The value of the share retained is £2,600. Julia is deemed to have received an amount calculated as follows:

$$£2,400 + \frac{(£6,000 - (£2,400 + £2,600)) \times £2,400}{£2,400 + £2,600} = £2,880$$

The loss is therefore limited to:

		£
Deemed disposal proceeds		2,880
Cost: $\dfrac{2,400}{£2,400 + £2,600} \times £6,800 =$		(3,264)
Allowable loss		(384)

Special rules apply to small part disposals of land (see 5229).

Currency disposals and dealings in commodities

The chattel exemption does not apply to the disposal of currency (note: currency in sterling is not a chargeable asset) or to a disposal of commodities on a terminal market.

Law: TCGA 1992, s. 262

See *British Tax Reporter* ¶535-200.

6162   Winnings as capital gains

Winnings from betting, including pool betting, or lotteries or games with prizes, are not chargeable gains and, therefore, not liable to CGT. No chargeable gain or allowable loss can accrue on the disposal of rights to such winnings.

Law: TCGA 1992, s. 51(1)

See *British Tax Reporter* ¶535-000.

6169 Mortgages and charges for capital gains

The conveyance or transfer by way of security of an asset (or an interest in it or right over it) does not involve any acquisition or disposal for CGT purposes; if the person entitled to the benefit of the charge enforces the security he is treated as doing so as nominee for the person entitled to the asset (subject to the security) (see 5060).

See *British Tax Reporter* ¶535-000.

6170 Gains from life assurance and other insurance policies

The rights of an insurer under an insurance policy (other than a life assurance policy) do not constitute a chargeable asset; however, the rights of the insured do constitute a chargeable asset to the extent that those rights relate to assets on the disposal of which a gain may accrue (see 5080ff.).

> **Example**
>
> Duncan takes out a policy of insurance on a house against fire damage. The property suffers severe fire damage and the insurance company agrees to pay £75,000 under the policy. Duncan assigns his rights to receive the money to Claire. The money is paid to Claire. Duncan is regarded as having made a part-disposal of a chargeable asset (see 5229).

There is normally no chargeable gain (and, therefore, no liability to CGT) where a person disposes of an interest in, or rights under, a life assurance policy or a deferred annuity contract; however, there may be a liability to CGT where the disponor is not the original beneficial owner and he acquired the rights or interest for a consideration in money or money's worth. Rights under a policy or contract are regarded as disposed of if the policy is held to maturity (or in the case of a deferred annuity payment of the first instalment) or surrendered.

The transfer of investments direct to the policyholder is a disposal which is, in the case of a non-life policy, automatically at market value.

Sums received for loss or depreciation of assets are derived from the assets (see 5080).

For annuities other than deferred annuities and for amounts paid out of superannuation funds or schemes, see 6186.

Law: FA 2003, s. 157; TCGA 1992, s. 204, 210

See *British Tax Reporter* ¶535-000.

6175   Passenger vehicles are not chargeable assets

Motor cars and other road vehicles are not chargeable assets if the vehicle is constructed or adapted for the carriage of passengers and is of a type commonly used as a private vehicle. This provision is largely designed to prevent claims for losses on motor cars.

Other motor vehicles which do not meet the dual tests of being both passenger vehicles and commonly used as private vehicles may still be exempt as 'wasting assets' which are also chattels, provided the assets do not qualify for capital allowances (see 6158). HMRC accept that the following vehicles may qualify for exemption:

- taxi cabs;
- racing cars and single seat sports cars;
- commercial vehicles (vans lorries, etc.);
- motor cycles and scooters; and
- railway locomotives, tramway and traction engines.

Law: TCGA 1992, s. 263

See *British Tax Reporter* ¶536-000.

6178   Gains exempt if decorations for valour

No chargeable gain arises on the disposal of a decoration awarded for gallantry unless it was acquired for money or money's worth.

Law: TCGA 1992, s. 268

See *British Tax Reporter* ¶536-100.

6180   Gains on foreign currency for personal expenditure

No chargeable gain (or allowable loss) arises on the disposal of currency acquired by an individual for the personal expenditure outside the UK of himself or his family or dependants. This includes expenditure on providing or maintaining a residence outside the UK.

For foreign currency bank accounts, see 6183.

Law: TCGA 1992, s. 269

See *British Tax Reporter* ¶536-200.

6183 Debts and tax on capital gains

The basic rule is that a person who is owed money 'disposes' of an asset (the debt) whenever repayment or satisfaction of the debt is made, or when he assigns, etc. the debt to a third party. However, no chargeable gain or allowable loss accrues to the disponor (or his personal representative or legatee: see 5690) if the disponor was the original creditor.

> ### Example
> Edward makes an unsecured loan of £8,000 to his sister and later accepts £6,000 in full satisfaction. As Edward is the original creditor, no allowable loss arises.

The above rule does not apply to foreign currency bank accounts which do not represent amounts for personal expenditure (see also 6180) or to a 'debt on a security'. There is no definition of a 'debt on a security' only of 'security' for this purpose which means any loan stock or similar security of any government or any public or local authority or of any company, whether secured or unsecured. The courts have held that the fact that a debt is evidenced by some form of certificate, note, or similar document is insufficient of itself to make a loan a 'debt on a security'. The essential feature of such an asset has been held to be its genuine transferability and marketability. The case of *W T Ramsay Ltd v IR Commrs* contains a useful summary of the position, which was relied on in a special commissioners decision. In another decision, the fact that an intra-group loan, evidenced by a promissory note, had no fixed term and was repayable on demand led to the conclusion that it lacked the permanence to be truly marketable and was thus not a debt on a security.

There are various events which are treated as disposals of debts and which determine the extent of the gain or loss. These do not apply to debts which are debts on a security (Revenue correspondence with the Law Society's Revenue Law Committee). In other words, if there has been an intra-group transfer of a debt on a security (which is not a QCB) a loss realised on a disposal by a group transferee is capable of being an allowable loss.

In the case of debts which are settled property, a person becoming absolutely entitled as against the trustee is treated as the original creditor.

Law: TCGA 1992, s. 132(3)(b), 251(1)–(5), 252; *W T Ramsay Ltd v IR Commrs* [1982] AC 300; *Tarmac Roadstone Holdings Ltd v Williams (HMIT)* (1996) Sp C 95; *Taylor Clark International Ltd v Lewis (HMIT)* [1998] BTC 466; *Cann v Woods (HMIT)* (1999) Sp C 183

See *British Tax Reporter* ¶535-000.

6184 Loans for trade purposes

Relief for losses is available in respect of certain loans to traders. Relief is available for 'a qualifying loan', i.e. a loan in the case of which:

- the money lent is used by the borrower wholly for the purposes of a trade, profession or vocation (or for setting up such a trade, etc.) carried on by him (but which does not include the lending of money);
- the borrower is 'resident in the UK' (see 213); and
- the debt is not a debt on a security (a loss on which may be allowable under general rules: see 213).

The lender may make a claim for an allowable loss where any part of the loan becomes irrecoverable and relief is otherwise unavailable. A special commissioner has held that loans made by a taxpayer to a company which he controlled became irrecoverable when he sold its subsidiary, which he had for some years been supporting by making loans to keep it trading. The taxpayer could not have been expected to continue to support the company indefinitely. By the time of the sale, the company was insolvent. Unless the taxpayer provided further money, it would have had to cease trading.

The loss arises when the claim is made, though the claim may specify an earlier time, which must be:

(1) no more than two years before the beginning of the tax year in which the claim is made; or

(2) (for corporation tax purposes) on or after the first day of the earliest accounting period ending not more than two years before the time of the claim.

Relief is also available to a person who has given a guarantee in respect of a qualifying loan which has become irrecoverable from the borrower, under similar conditions. In neither case must the borrower and lender be spouses, or companies in the same 'group' (see 3682). It has been held that a payment made by a guarantor could only be relieved to the extent that it was not recoverable from co-guarantors. The time-limit for claims is five years from 31 January following the tax year in which the payment was made or, for corporation tax purposes (in respect of accounting periods ending after 30 June 1999), six years from the end of the accounting period in which the payment was made.

Where loss relief has been granted under these provisions there will be a clawback if there is a subsequent recovery of principal or interest by the lender or guarantor, who will be treated as making a chargeable gain, equal to the amount recovered, at the time of recovery.

Law: TCGA 1992, s. 253; *Leisureking Ltd v Cushing (HMIT)* [1993] BTC 22

See *British Tax Reporter* ¶535-000.

6186 Gains on disposal of annuities, annual payments

No chargeable gain arises on the disposal of a right to:

- any allowance, annuity or capital sum paid under a superannuation scheme established solely for persons (and their dependants) in a trade, profession or employment;
- an annuity which is not granted under a deferred annuity contract;

- unsecured annual payments due under a covenant.

For deferred annuities under life contracts, see 6170.

Law: TCGA 1992, s. 237

See *British Tax Reporter* ¶535-600.

6189 Gifts exempt from tax on capital gains

Gifts to charities, etc.

Since 6 April 2000 gift aid relief, which previously only benefited donors who paid a certain level of income tax (see 902), has extended to CGT payers.

Gifts or disposals where the consideration does not exceed the acquisition cost and other allowable expenditure of the person making the disposal are exempt from CGT if the disposal is to a charity or for national purposes, i.e. to one of the bodies or institutions set out in IHTA 1984, Sch. 3 (see 7198) (e.g. the National Gallery, the British Museum, museums or galleries maintained by local authorities or universities, etc., health service bodies, etc.). The exemption in relation to a gift to a charity does not apply if the disposal is one of shares previously held in a venture capital trust.

Gifts of national heritage property

Gifts of property (including works of art, scientific collections, etc. of national, scientific, historic or artistic interest) are exempt from CGT if also exempt from inheritance tax (see 7346ff.).

Gifts to housing associations

Where there is a disposal of an estate or interest in land in the UK otherwise than by arm's length bargain to a registered housing association, the transferor and the association may make a claim, of which the effect is to displace the normal rule where the consideration is deemed to be market value where the transaction is not at arm's length (see 5100). If the disposal is by way of gift or for a consideration not exceeding allowable deductions the disposal is treated as a no loss/no gain disposal and the association's base cost is treated as being the same as the transferor's base cost, i.e. the transferor's gain is held over.

There are also certain exemptions in respect of the transfer of assets between the Housing Corporation, Housing for Wales or Scottish Homes and housing associations or between housing associations (including those in Northern Ireland).

Law: TCGA 1992, s. 218–220, 257–259; FA 1990, s. 25; FA 2000, s. 39

See *British Tax Reporter* ¶535-800.

6197 Capital gains: employee trusts

Disposals by close companies or individuals to trustees of employee trusts which are not liable to inheritance tax are exempt from CGT. For the meaning of 'employee trust', see 7159.

A Revenue concession removes a CGT charge on the trustees of employee trusts where the employee is liable to income tax on the full market value of assets transferred to the trustees; it effectively displaces the normal market value rule (see 5100).

Law: TCGA 1992, s. 239

See *British Tax Reporter* ¶535-000.

PRIVATE RESIDENCE RELIEF

6220 Relief from CGT for private residences

The general rule is that a gain made on the disposal by an individual of the whole or part of a dwelling-house (or an interest in a dwelling-house) which is his only or main residence is not liable to CGT, or if liable not wholly liable (see 6244).

A 'dwelling-house' has been held to include a caravan raised up on bricks. However, a mobile caravan not connected to an electricity or a water supply has been held not to be included.

A 'dwelling-house' will not be a 'residence' in the context of this relief if the claimant cannot show that the occupation of the property has some degree of actual permanence and continuity, or some expectation of such continuity and as such is not merely a temporary accommodation.

Law: TCGA 1992, s. 222(1)(a), 223(1); *Makins v Elson (HMIT)* (1976) 51 TC 437; *Moore v Thompson (HMIT)* [1986] BTC 172; *Goodwin v Curtis (HMIT)* [1998] BTC 176

See *British Tax Reporter* ¶540-000.

6222 Garden or grounds

The garden or grounds of the dwelling-house up to half a hectare, inclusive of the site of the house – or such larger area as is required for the reasonable enjoyment of the house as a residence – may also be sold without liability to CGT if sold with the dwelling-house or at a time when the house is the main residence of the person making the disposal. This has been held not to apply to the sale of the garden of a house after the house itself had been sold). HMRC have confirmed that where a dwelling-house and garden are sold together, but after the taxpayer has ceased to occupy the property, they do not seek to charge the sale of the garden to CGT.

In one case, a special commissioner decided that a taxpayer was entitled to private residence relief on the sale of two building plots which comprised a field which she had, until the time of disposal, enjoyed with her residence. It did not matter that the field did not adjoin the residence. In the light of this decision, HMRC have set out their interpretation of the garden or grounds provisions. The relevant extract is reproduced below:

'HMRC does not accept that land is garden or grounds merely if it is in the same ownership as the residence and is used as a garden. However, land which can be shown objectively, on the facts, to be naturally and traditionally the garden of the residence, so that it would normally be offered to a prospective purchaser as part of the residence, will be accepted. An example of this is where, as in some villages, it is common for a garden to be across the street from the residence. The separation itself would not be regarded as a reason for denying relief.

It must be stressed that these cases will be rare and if land is separated from the residence by other land which is not in the same ownership as the residence, it will usually not be part of the garden or grounds. For example, land bought some distance from the residence due to an inadequate garden at the residence and which is cultivated and regarded as part of the garden will not qualify for relief.'

Law: TCGA 1992, s. 222(1)(b), (2)–(4); *Varty (HMIT) v Lynes* (1976) 51 TC 419; *Wakeling v Pearce* (1995) Sp C 32

See *British Tax Reporter* ¶545-600.

6224 More than one building

It is clear from the authorities that where there is more than one building in the same grounds, CGT private residence relief (see 6220) may extend to more than one of them. Buildings which form part of the dwelling-house are clearly eligible for relief (these may include garages and fuel stores); buildings which are ancillary to the garden or grounds (such as greenhouses, gazebos and sheds) only qualify for relief if they fall within the permitted area; other buildings do not qualify for relief.

A 'dwelling-house' can comprise several dwellings not physically joined: e.g. a separate garage, a studio, or a self-contained staff flat.

The following two conditions if satisfied are indicative that the buildings constitute a single dwelling-house:

- the occupation of the building in dispute must increase the taxpayer's enjoyment of the main house; and
- the disputed building must be very closely adjacent to the main house. In determining that, the scale of the buildings as a group must be considered.

The proximity test

However, whilst proximity or otherwise of the building is an important factor, it is insufficient in itself to conclude that two buildings constitute separate dwellings. It is important that all of the facts are considered.

The courts have also applied the test of whether a subsidiary dwelling-house was appurtenant to and within the curtilage of the main house (the 'proximity test'). This approach also avoided the difficulty that a second dwelling-house, used for the enjoyment of the main house, might otherwise qualify for relief even if it were outside the 'permitted area' of garden and grounds.

HMRC have indicated that they would draw a distinction between the curtilage of a main house and the curtilage of an estate as a whole, and that the fact that a whole estate may be contained within a single boundary does not mean that buildings on the estate should be regarded as being within the curtilage of the main house.

Law: *Batey (HMIT) v Wakefield* (1981) 55 TC 550; *Markey (HMIT) v Sanders* [1987] BTC 176; *Williams (HMIT) v Merrylees* [1987] BTC 393; *Lewis (HMIT) v Lady Rook* [1992] BTC 102; *Honour (HMIT) v Norris* [1992] BTC 153

See *British Tax Reporter* ¶545-100.

6226   Joint owner occupiers

Joint owner occupiers who are not husband and wife, or civil partners, may benefit from full CGT private residence relief (see 6220) if they have unrestricted access to the whole property, even though some areas are not actually used by both. Where such owners do not have access to the whole property, they may be able to exchange their interests so as to acquire sole ownership without tax penalty, providing relief similar to compulsory purchase (see 6300).

Source: ESC D26, *Relief for exchange of joint interest in land*

See *British Tax Reporter* ¶546-050.

6228   Purchase for gain

Private residence relief (see 6220) is unavailable where the residence was acquired in whole or in part to make a gain on its disposal, even if the taxpayer lives in the house for a time before he sells it.

Law: TCGA 1992, s. 224(3)

See *British Tax Reporter* ¶540-050.

6230   More than one residence

When a taxpayer has more than one residence, he may elect by notice in writing to treat one or other residence as his main residence for CGT purposes (see 6220). The election has to be made within two years of the time that the taxpayer first has an interest in two or more residences. An election may be varied subsequently, but not so as to take effect earlier than two years before the notice of variation.

This time-limit may be extended where a taxpayer was unaware of the need to nominate a main residence but where his interest in each of them (or each of them except one) has no more than a negligible capital value, e.g. a short-term rented flat.

Law: TCGA 1992, s. 222(5); *Griffin (HMIT) v Craig-Harvey* [1994] BTC 3

Source: ESC D21, *Private residence exemption: late claims in dual residence cases*

See *British Tax Reporter* ¶545-950.

6233   Private residence relief and spouses

In the case of a married couple, or civil partners, 'living together' (see 5490), there can be only one sole or main residence for the purposes of the CGT private residence exemption (see 6220) and, where an election is made as to which house this applies to (see 6230), such election must generally be made jointly.

If the conditions in relation to absence are satisfied by an individual so that the absence is treated as a period of residence (see 6247), they are treated as satisfied also in relation to that individual's spouse provided they are living together.

A HMRC interpretation refers to the various possibilities as regards elections by a newly-married couple, which depend upon the two individuals' previous ownership of property.

A spouse, or civil partner, who inherits a dwelling-house from the other spouse, or civil partner, also inherits the latter's period of ownership for private residence relief purposes. (This is not overridden by the rule that a legatee acquires an inherited asset for CGT purposes on the date of death: see 5690.) The result of this is that periods of ownership, before the death of the first spouse or civil partner, to die, also fall to be taken into account in determining qualifying 'periods of residence' (see 6244).

Law: TCGA 1992, s. 222(6), (7)(a)

Source: ESC D3, *Private residence exemption: periods of absence*

See *British Tax Reporter* ¶546-000.

6235   Private residence relief and trustees

The CGT private residence exemption (see 6220) applies to trustees where, during the period of ownership of the trustee, the house has been the only or main residence of a person entitled to occupy it under the terms of a settlement.

> ### *Example*
>
> A dwelling-house is vested in trustees on trust for sale and to pay the income of property, until sale, to Frank, with a power to let Frank into occupation pending a sale. Frank is let into occupation until sale. The house is treated as Frank's principal private residence and is not liable to CGT.

A 'person entitled' may include a discretionary beneficiary.

Extra-Statutory Concession D5, *Private residence exemption: property held by personal representatives*, extends this relief to personal representatives where the house disposed of has been the only or main residence, both before and after the deceased's death, of individuals who under the will or on intestacy are entitled to the whole or substantially the whole (which is interpreted by HMRC to mean 75 per cent or more of the proceeds of the house either absolutely or for life.

In making an election to determine which residence is the main residence of a person (see 6230), such notice of election must be given jointly by the trustees and the person entitled to occupy the house.

Finance Act 2004 introduced measures to prevent exploitation of the interaction between private residence relief and gifts relief to avoid capital gains tax. Their effect is that private residence relief will not be available in certain circumstances where a disposal is made on or after 10 December 2003 by an individual or the trustees of a settlement. These circumstances arise where the computation of the amount of any gain arising on the disposal has to take account of gifts relief obtained in respect of an earlier disposal. This is subject to a transitional provision which will restrict the amount of private residence relief available in respect of the disposal if there has been no 'earlier disposal' on or after 10 December 2003.

Law: FA 2004, s. 117 and Sch. 22; TCGA 1992, s. 225; *Sansom & Anor v Peay (HMIT)* (1976) 52 TC 1

See *British Tax Reporter* ¶579-750.

6238   Private residence relief and dependent relatives

For disposals after 5 April 1988, the relief available for a dependent relative's residence is abolished. However, transitional provisions preserve the relief where at 5 April 1988 or an earlier date during the taxpayer's ownership, the property was the sole residence of a dependent relative and was provided rent-free (i.e. existing rent-free arrangements will still qualify). If the property ever ceases to be the sole residence of the particular dependent relative it cannot requalify for relief.

A 'dependent relative' is:

- any relative of a taxpayer or of his or her spouse who is incapacitated by old age or infirmity from maintaining him or herself; or
- the mother of a husband or wife who is either widowed or living apart from her husband, or is a single woman because of the dissolution or annulment of marriage.

The conditions that it be 'rent-free' will be satisfied where the dependent relative pays all or part of the owner's council tax and the cost of repairs to the home attributable to normal wear and tear; further, the relief will not be lost where the relative makes other payments in respect of the property, provided no net income (calculated according to Sch. A rules) is receivable by the individual taking one year with another. If the dependent relative pays the mortgage, the dwelling ceases to qualify.

Law: TCGA 1992, s. 226(6), (7)

Source: ESC D20, *Private residence exemption: residence occupied by dependent relative*

See *British Tax Reporter* ¶546-800.

6241 Job-related accommodation and private residence relief

For private residence relief (see 6220), a house is treated as occupied by an individual as his residence where, at any time after 30 July 1978, during his ownership of the house, he resides in other accommodation which is 'job-related' and he intends in due course to occupy the house as his only or main residence.

The relief extends to self-employed people under a contractual requirement to live in accommodation provided as part of the terms of their trade, profession or vocation but who are buying a home of their own.

Law: TCGA 1992, s. 222(8), (9)

See *British Tax Reporter* ¶546-100.

6244 Extent of exemption under private residence relief

To obtain complete exemption from CGT under the private residence provisions (see 6220), the house must have been the individual's only or main residence throughout the period of ownership, except for the whole or any part of the last three years of ownership. 'Period of ownership' is determined by reference to the first interest obtained in the property and may include that of a spouse but does not include any period before 31 March 1982; an initial period after purchase of the land of up to one year, or, if good reasons exist, up to two years, is treated as a period of occupation where a new house is being built, an existing house is being altered/redecorated or where the individual completes the necessary steps for disposing of his previous residence.

Where the house has not been the only or main residence throughout the period of ownership (exclusive of the last three years), only a fraction of the gain is not liable to CGT. That fraction is:

$$\frac{A + B}{C}$$

where

A   is the period after 31 March 1982 during which the house was the individual's only or main residence (but not including the last 36 months of the period of ownership);
B   is the last 36 months of ownership (24 months); and
C   is the total period of ownership after 31 March 1982.

Example

Jack buys a house on 1 June 2003 for use as his only residence. He lives in the house for thirty months before moving out and immediately occupying a nearby flat which he also owns. He elects for the flat to be his only or main residence from 1 December 2005 (date of initial occupancy). Jack does not return to live in the house and it remains empty until he sells it on 31 May 2010, making a gain of £70,000. The chargeable gain covering Jack's seven years of ownership is calculated as follows:

	£
Indexed gain	70,000
Private residence exemption	
Using $\dfrac{A + B}{C}$ formula above	
A = 30 months	
B = 36 months	
C = 84 months (7×12)	
$\dfrac{30 + 36}{84} \times £70,000 =$	(55,000)
Chargeable gain	15,000

The gain is also apportioned where part of the dwelling-house is used exclusively for the purposes of a trade, business, profession or vocation and the consideration may be apportioned where otherwise necessary. HMRC no longer apply the rule-of-thumb that one-third of a farmhouse is used for business purposes – each case must be considered on its particular circumstances.

Relief may be adjusted where there is a change in the extent to which a property is used as an individual's residence, etc. There are also provisions relating to periods of absence which may be treated as periods in which the property was used as the individual's only or main residence (see 6247).

Any taper relief available applies to the resultant chargeable gain.

Law: TCGA 1992, s. 222(7), (10), 223(1), (2), (5)–(7), 224(1), (2)

Source: ESC D49, *Private residence relief: short delay by owner-occupier in taking up residence*

See *British Tax Reporter* ¶546-650.

6247 Private residence relief: periods of absence

Although the extent of exemption in respect of a private residence (see 6220) is determined by reference to that part of the period of ownership in which it is used as the only or main residence (see 6244), in some cases a period of absence from the dwelling-house is, nevertheless, treated as a period during which the house was the individual's only or main residence. This is so, if:

(1) both before and after the period there is a time when the dwelling-house was the individual's only or main residence, though the requirement to return is waived where an individual is unable to return to the residence because:

    (a) the absence is due to employment duties being overseas; or

    (b) the absence is due to the employer requiring the individual to reside elsewhere to perform the duties of the employment (in or out of the UK); and

    (c) the terms of the individuals employment require the individual to work elsewhere without taking up residence in the dwelling again; and

(2) during the period of absence he had no residence otherwise eligible for private residence relief.

If those two conditions are satisfied, the following periods of absence do not adversely affect the private residence relief:

(1) one or more periods of absence totalling not more than three years;

(2) any period of absence throughout which the individual:

    (a) worked in an office or employment; and

    (b) all the duties of that office, etc. were performed outside the UK;

(3) any periods of absence not exceeding four years in total throughout which the taxpayer could not live in his private residence because of the situation of his place of work, or conditions of his employment.

If the conditions are satisfied by an individual they are treated as satisfied also in relation to that individual's spouse provided they are living together (see 6233).

Law: TCGA 1992, s. 223(3), (7)

Source: ESC D4, *Private residence relief: periods of absence (B)*

See *British Tax Reporter* ¶546-200.

6250   Lettings relief: private residence relief

Individuals can let all or part of their homes to residential tenants without fear of losing any of the principal private residence exemption (see 6220). The dwelling-house house (or part of it) must have been the individual's only or main residence for some part, at least, of his ownership period.

Where a gain accrues on disposing of a dwelling-house which (or part of which) has been let as residential accommodation, then any gain which would have been chargeable because of the letting is exempt to the extent that it does not exceed the lesser of:

- £40,000; or
- such an amount as is exempt from CGT because of the private residence exemption (see 6220).

Example 1

Peter buys a house in 2000. He lets one of the three floors of the house. The remaining two-thirds of the house form his only residence. He sells the house in May 2010. He makes a gain of £10,500. Disregarding the lettings relief, £7,000 (i.e. £10,500 × ²/₃) of this gain would be exempt from CGT under the private residence exemption following apportionment of the gain.

However, because of the letting relief, the amount of the gain attributable to the letting (£10,500 × ¹/₃ = £3,500) is also wholly exempt because it does not exceed £7,000 or the absolute ceiling of £40,000.

Thus all of the gain is exempt.

Example 2

Polly bought a house on 1 June 2003 as her only or main residence. She lived there for 12 months after which she moved into a bungalow that she had inherited. She let the house as residential accommodation from 1 June 2004 to 31 May 2006, following which she reoccupied it as her only or main residence. She remained there for 4 years until 31 May 2010 when she sold the house, realising a gain of £56,000. The chargeable gain, taking into account private residence relief and lettings relief, is calculated as follows:

	£
Indexed gain	56,000

(a) Private residence relief

Using $\dfrac{A + B}{C}$ (see ¶6244)

A = 12 + 12
B = 36
C = 84

$\dfrac{24 + 36}{84} \times £56,000$	(40,000)

Gain after private residence relief, but
before lettings relief   16,000

(b) Lettings relief

Gain attributable to period of letting

$£56,000 \times \dfrac{24}{84} = £16,000$

Letting relief is the lower of:
- £16,000; and
- £40,000   (16,000)

Chargeable gain	Nil

A lodger living as a member of a person's family does not affect that person's private residence relief and the lettings relief provisions are, therefore, not relevant to such a situation.

Law: TCGA 1992, s. 223(4)

Source: SP 14/80, *Relief for owner occupiers*

See *British Tax Reporter* ¶546-850.

6255   Use of relocation business to sell private residence

Where work is being relocated and the employer sets up arm's length arrangements under which an employee, office holder or person sharing with them, moves home because of the relocation and sells his or her home to his employer or to a relocation business with a right to share in any later profit made on a subsequent sale, the right will generally be exempt to the same extent as the home itself is (see 6220ff.). Thus if, for example, the home was used partly for business purposes, or was not the main home throughout the employee's period of ownership, only a corresponding proportion of any gain relating to the right to later profits will also be exempt.

The concession does not apply when the right is held by the employee for more than three years.

Source: ESC D37, *Private residence relief: relocation arrangements*

See *British Tax Reporter* ¶547-000.

GENERAL GIFTS RELIEF

6285 Former general gift relief

There was a general CGT hold-over relief for gifts made before 14 March 1989. The principles of the relief may still be important in so far as they affect the transferee (see 6289).

The relief applied to a transfer with an element of gift if:

- it was between individuals resident or ordinarily resident in the UK (see 213, 216) and made after 5 April 1980 where both transferor and transferee claimed relief within six years from the end of the relevant tax year;
- it was made after 5 April 1981 by an individual to trustees of a settlement resident in the UK, where the transferor made a claim; or
- it was a distribution out of a trust made after 5 April 1982, where both transferor and transferee made a claim.

This general hold-over relief was withdrawn for disposals after 13 March 1989. The relief was introduced in 1980 to avoid double taxation because there was at that time a simultaneous charge to capital transfer tax on gifts. However, the charge to what became inheritance tax on lifetime giving was generally removed in 1986 and increasingly the CGT hold-over relief was being used as a simple form of tax avoidance. Accordingly, the relief was withdrawn in 1989. However, roll-over relief was preserved and extended for gifts of business assets (see 6325). A modified form of general gift relief is available for gifts after 13 March 1989 only in certain circumstances in which a lifetime inheritance tax charge arises (see 6287).

Computation of relief

Where the conditions for general gift relief were satisfied, relief was provided by reducing to nil the amount of the chargeable gain accruing to the transferor and reducing the transferee's deemed consideration (i.e. his allowable expenditure on a subsequent disposal) by the same amount (referred to as the held over gain; see 6144).

Law: Former FA 1980, s. 79

See *British Tax Reporter* ¶548-600.

6287 General gifts outside potentially exempt transfer regime

In certain circumstances (usually in the case of transfers to discretionary trusts) inheritance tax (IHT) is still charged on a lifetime transfer. Where that is so, there remains the spectre of double taxation so provision has been made for continuing the general hold-over relief for gifts (see 6285) in such circumstances where the recipient of the gift is an individual or the trustees of a settlement. The relief continues as for gifts before 14 March 1989 in respect of IHT chargeable transfers but not potentially exempt transfers (see 6610). Hold-over relief also continues for certain transfers which are exempt from IHT anyway (i.e. such transfers do not attract IHT or immediate CGT liability). Transfers included are those to political parties, for public benefit, transfers to maintenance funds for historic buildings and of property designated by the Treasury as conditionally exempt.

As for gifts before 14 March 1989 (see 6285), the hold-over relief does not apply where the transferee is neither resident nor ordinarily resident; nor does it apply where, though resident or ordinarily resident in the UK, the transferee would not be liable to CGT on any subsequent disposal by him because of double taxation treaty relief.

Where the general hold-over relief applies to gifts after 13 March 1989, the roll-over relief for gifts of business assets (see 6325) is not available as well. However, the general hold-over relief takes priority over the roll-over relief for gifts of business assets.

If a disposal to which the general gift relief applied before 14 March 1989 was a chargeable transfer for inheritance or capital transfer tax purposes (see 6285), the transferee, on an ultimate disposal by him, was entitled to deduct from any chargeable gain accruing to him, the lesser of:

- the amount of inheritance or capital transfer tax on the original transfer (whether paid by the transferor or transferee);
- the chargeable gain on the transferee's disposal.

This rule is equally applicable under the post 13 March 1989 regime. Where the original transfer was potentially exempt but subsequently proves to be chargeable, necessary adjustments must be made.

Further, the exemption is unavailable in respect of a disposal to a dual resident trust eligible for a treaty exemption, i.e. if:

- the trustees to whom the disposal was made were treated as UK-resident even though the general administration of the trust is ordinarily carried on outside the UK (see 5630); but
- the trustees would be exempt from tax in respect of any gains on the asset under a double tax treaty.

There are circumstances in which HMRC will not need to agree at the time of the gift the market value of assets for which relief is claimed, applicable as in relation to gifts of business assets (see 6325).

Capital Gains Tax

Law: TCGA 1992, s. 165(3)(d), (10), 169, 260, 261

See *British Tax Reporter* ¶548-700.

6289 Emigration of transferee following general gift relief

In general, where a gift was made to a UK resident or ordinarily resident person (see 213, 216) after 5 April 1981 and hold-over relief has applied (see 6285 or 6287), then a chargeable gain equal to the held over gain is deemed to accrue to the transferee if he becomes neither resident nor ordinarily resident in the UK within six years of the gift. If, however, the reason that the transferee becomes non-resident is that he works in an employment or office all the duties of which are performed outside the UK and he again becomes resident or ordinarily resident in the UK within three years, during which time he has not disposed of the asset, the held-over gain does not crystallise.

Law: TCGA 1992, s. 67, 168

See *British Tax Reporter* ¶548-700.

6300 Relief on compulsory purchase

A disposal of land to an authority having compulsory purchase powers may give rise to a CGT liability. The timing of any disposal not made under contract is determined by reference to the agreement of compensation or the date of seizure, etc. Roll-over relief may be claimed by the landowner where, in general:

- the landowner took no steps (e.g. by advertising) to dispose of the land or make known his willingness to dispose of it; and
- the consideration for the disposal is applied in acquiring other land which is not the sole or main residence of the landowner or will not be such a residence within six years of acquisition.

The landowner's gain is rolled over to the new land purchased by him.

Where the new land is a depreciating asset, the gain is held over until the earlier of:

- the date of disposal of the land acquired; or
- ten years from the date of acquisition of the land.

HMRC accept that roll-over relief is available where a tenant exercises the following rights to acquire an interest in the tenanted property from the landlord:

- the right to acquire the freehold reversion or an extension of the lease under the *Leasehold Reform Act* 1967 or the *Housing and Urban Development Act* 1993; or
- the right to buy or acquire the freehold or an extension of the lease under the *Housing Acts* 1985–96.

This effectively brings leasehold tenants within the scope of the meaning of a person or body of persons with compulsory purchase powers.

In order to facilitate the introduction of self-assessment, provisions were introduced in 1996 to allow provisional claims to be made, enabling roll-over relief to be given before the reinvestment is made.

Law: TCGA 1992, s. 243, 245–248; *Ahad v R & C Commrs* (2009) TC 00291

Source: SP 13/93 (revised June 2005)

See *British Tax Reporter* ¶547-050.

TRANSFER OF BUSINESS TO A COMPANY

6302 Conditions for relief on transfer of business to a company

For roll-over relief on the transfer of business assets to a company, etc. the following conditions must be satisfied:

- the transferor of the business must be a sole trader or a partnership;
- the transfer must be to a body corporate or unincorporated association;
- the transfer must be of the business as a going concern together with all assets of the business (though cash may be excluded); and
- the transfer must be wholly or partly in exchange for shares issued by the transferee to the transferor (if liabilities are taken over this is not regarded as consideration).

Law: TCGA 1992, s. 162(1), (5)

Source: ESC D32, *Transfer of a business to a company*

See *British Tax Reporter* ¶574-150.

6303 Amount of relief on transfer of business to a company

If the conditions for roll-over relief on transfer of a business to a company are satisfied (see 6302), the gain arising on the disposal to the company can be deferred or 'rolled over' (see 6144) until the eventual disposal of the shares.

Where the consideration for the transfer is wholly in the form of shares, there is no CGT liability at the time of the transfer. Instead, the cost price, or base value of the shares for CGT purposes, is reduced by the amount of the gain on the transfer.

If there is also cash (or other consideration) for the transfer, the gain is apportioned by applying the fraction:

$$\frac{A}{B}$$

where

A is the cost of the shares; and
B is the total consideration received by the transferor.

Example

Joel is a sole trader. He transfers his business to X Ltd in May 1993 in exchange for 10,000 ordinary shares in X Ltd and £9,000 cash. The value of the shares when allotted to Joel is £40,000. All the assets, which are liable to CGT, were acquired just before 1982 and for less than their 31 March 1982 market value. Details of Joel's business assets are as follows:

Assets	Market value at 31/3/82 plus any indexation allowance	Market value on transfer	Indexed gain
	£	£	£
Freehold property	10,000	30,000	20,000
Goodwill	–	5,000	5,000
Trading stock	2,000	7,000	–
Plant and machinery	5,000	3,000	–
Debtors	–	5,000	–
	17,000	50,000	25,000
Liabilities			
Trade creditors	–	(1,000)	–
	17,000	49,000	25,000

The rolled-over gain for Joel on the transfer is:

$$\frac{£40,000}{£49,000} \times £25,000 = £20,408$$

The assessable gain is, therefore, £4,592 (being £25,000 − £20,408). The balance of the gain (£20,408) is rolled over. On the sale of the 10,000 shares in X Ltd, Joel's base value for those shares will be reduced by £20,408. Thus, if he sold the shares for £50,000 in April 2000, Joel would be liable to CGT on a gain of £20,567, which is calculated as follows:

	£	£
Sale proceeds of shares		50,000
Market value on acquisition shares	40,000	
Less: rolled over gain	(20,408)	
		(19,592)
		30,408
Less: indexation allowance		
$\dfrac{162.6 - 141.1}{141.1} \times 19,592$	(2,985)	
Indexed gain		(27,423)

Taper relief, based on a qualifying holding period of two years reduces the gain to £20,567 (75% × £27,423).

Example

Suppose that B has a balance sheet as follows:

	£
Business assets – chargeable to CGT (eg land/buildings)	200,000
Business assets – non chargeable (eg trade debtors, cash)	50,000
	250,000
Less: trade creditors	20,000
	230,000
Capital and reserves	230,000

Of the non-chargeable assets, £15,000 is cash. The balance sheet amounts are stated at cost. The chargeable assets, purchased several years earlier, have a current market value of £500,000. The non-chargeable assets' value is as stated in the balance sheet. No individual asset is standing at a loss. The company, B Ltd, to which B is transferring his business is issuing B with ordinary shares. B Ltd is not taking over the liabilities, nor having the business' cash transferred to its account.

The calculation of the relief then proceeds as follows:

Calculate the gain on the chargeable assets.

	£
Market value of chargeable assets	500,000
Less: cost	200,000
Unindexed gain	300,000
Less: indexation allowance to April 1998 (say)	25,000
Indexed gain (the aggregate net gains since no losses)	275,000

Calculate the value of the shares.

The value of the shares issued as consideration by B Ltd is the net value of assets transferred. This is:

	£
Chargeable business assets	500,000
Non chargeable business assets (NB cash not transferred)	35,000
Total value	535,000

Since the value transferred to the company exceeds the gains on the chargeable business assets, the whole gain may be rolled over, and so none is immediately taxable. The cost of B's shares in B Ltd is then reduced by the gain:

	£
Consideration for shares	535,000
Less: rolled over gain, s. 162 relief	275,000
Revised acquisition cost carried forward	260,000

Note that, where any of the gain which is deducted from the base cost of the asset is attributable, whether directly or indirectly and whether in whole or in part, to a gain accruing on the disposal before 6 April 1988 of an asset acquired before 31 March 1982, a claim may be made within two years of the end of the tax year or accounting period in which the disposal in question is made, to deduct only 50 per cent of the gain.

Claiming the relief

There is no need to make a claim for relief on incorporation, because, provided the conditions are satisfied, it applies automatically.

For incorporations after 6 April 2002, it is possible to elect to disapply incorporation relief. This may be beneficial in a number of circumstance, but most obviously where there is a quick sale of the business following incorporation, so that taper relief (up to 5 April 2008) on the shares has not built up. The election must be made by the second anniversary of 31 January following the tax year of the incorporation. So if the incorporation took place in 2004–05, the election must be made by 31 January 2008. However, if all the shares acquired on incorporation are disposed of by the end of the tax year following incorporation, the election must be made by 31 January following that later tax year. So if the incorporation took place in 2004–05, and the shares were all sold by 5 April 2006, the election would have to be made by 31 January 2007.

Law: TCGA 1992, s. 36, 162(2)–(5), Sch. 4, para. 2, 9; *Colley v Clements* (HMIT) (2005) Sp C 483

See *British Tax Reporter* ¶574-200.

REPLACEMENT OF BUSINESS ASSETS

6305 Replacement roll-over relief in outline

Roll-over relief applies in certain instances where consideration received for the disposal of business assets is applied in acquiring new assets for the purposes of a business (see further 6306–6309). The relief is strictly limited to the specific categories of asset set out in the legislation (see 6306).

This form of roll-over relief only applies if the new assets are also chargeable, i.e. if the taxpayer is not resident or ordinarily resident (see 213, 216) immediately after acquisition or is so resident but not then chargeable because of double taxation treaty relief, the relief is unavailable. The same disqualification applies to dual resident companies which, from 30 November 1993, are deemed to be non-resident for tax purposes (see 4500); previously there was a specific exclusion. A further disqualification applies in relation to old assets disposed of before that event and new assets acquired after that event where a company ceases to be UK-resident or becomes dual-resident.

For the concept of relief by way of roll-over, see 6144.

Law: TCGA 1992, s. 152(1), 153A, 159, 185(3)

See *British Tax Reporter* ¶570-350.

6306 Assets to which replacement roll-over relief applies

'Replacement roll-over relief' (see 6305) applies only to the following classes of assets used only for the purposes of a trade.

- Buildings and land occupied for the purposes of the trade, provided the trade is not one of dealing in or developing land nor one of providing services for the occupier of land in which the trader has an interest or estate.
- Fixed plant or machinery which does not form part of a building. Movable plant or machinery is ineligible for roll-over relief for business assets.
- Ships, aircraft and hovercraft.
- Satellites, space stations and spacecraft (including launch vehicles).
- Goodwill.
- Milk quotas and potato quotas.
- Ewe and suckler cow premium quotas.
- Fish quota.

Both assets disposed of and assets acquired must be within one of these classes, but not necessarily the same class.

Law: TCGA 1992, s. 155, 156; *Finance Act 1993, Section 86(2), (Fish Quota) Order* 1999 (SI 1999/564); *Williams v Evans (HMIT)* [1982] BTC 155; *Cottle v Coldicott* (1995) Sp C 40

See *British Tax Reporter* ¶570-800.

6307 Businesses to which replacement roll-over relief applies

'Replacement roll-over relief' (see 6305) is available for the disposal of assets used by any of the following:

- trades, professions or vocations, including certain commercial letting of furnished holiday accommodation (see 1255) and partners (often extending to assets used by the partnership;
- offices and employments (often extending to assets used by the employer rent-free and without any formal tenancy, etc.);
- public authorities;
- commercial woodlands;
- a trade association which has activities directed to the protection or promotion of the interests of its members who carry on a trade;
- professional associations which are non-profit making;
- non-profit making unincorporated associations and other bodies chargeable to corporation tax, i.e. trade unions, sports clubs, etc. (including claims for assets held by a company owned by such association).

As a result of a 1999 change, the relief now applies for UK oil licence gains.

Law: TCGA 1992, s. 158, 193, 241(4), (5); former TCGA 1992, s. 193; FA 1999, s. 103

Source: ESC D15, *relief for the replacement of business assets: unincorporated associations*; SP 5/86, *Relief for replacement of business assets: employees and office holders*

See *British Tax Reporter* ¶570-800.

6308 Conditions for replacement roll-over relief to apply

In addition to the restriction of relief to certain businesses (see 6307) and to certain classes of assets (see 6306) certain other conditions must be met before the relief can be obtained, as set out below. If the disponor is an individual, the trade in point may be carried on by him or by his 'personal company'. HMRC's view is that the asset must be used by the same personal or family company and not, for example, by a subsidiary of the personal or family company.

(1) Except as noted below, the asset disposed of must have been used solely for the

Capital Gains Tax

purposes of the business throughout the period of ownership. For disposals after 6 April 1988, no period before 31 March 1982 is included in the period of ownership.

Apportionment takes place where the asset is not used for the business throughout the disponor's ownership or where the asset is not used only for the purposes of the trade; in HMRC's view, there is statutory authority for the manner in which the apportionment takes place. In one case, the taxpayer sold his accountancy business and invested the proceeds in a 75 per cent share of a property which was to be used as to 75 per cent for a hotel business and as to 25 per cent for private residential accommodation for himself and his wife. Although the partnership deed between the taxpayer and his wife purported to attribute the taxpayer's 75 per cent share of the property to business use and the remaining 25 per cent share to his wife for residential purposes, the trust deed did not partition the property but declared the taxpayer and his wife tenants in common in the proportion 75:25 per cent. The High Court held that since under the trust deed the taxpayer and his wife were entitled to an undivided share in the entirety of the property, roll-over relief was only available on 75 per cent of the taxpayer's 75 per cent share in the property.

(2)   The consideration for the disposal of the assets must be used to acquire new business assets within the specified classes; such consideration is determined after other reliefs and may be a just and reasonable portion of the proceeds of a larger disposal. The new asset may be used in any business carried on by the person acquiring the asset, i.e. it need not be used in the same business for which the old asset was used. All trades carried on by companies within a group are treated as a single trade (see 3695), though the disponor and acquiring company need not be members at the same time and the property holding company in a group is generally regarded as trading for this purpose. Special conditions apply where assets are only partly replaced.

Concessionary relief is also given where the proceeds of sale are used to enhance the value of other assets, to acquire a further interest in an asset already in use for the person's trade or, in purely commercial transactions where the same assets are repurchased. In HMRC's view, relief is applicable only to actual rather than deemed disposals. In principle, there is no reason why relief should not be available where the consideration for the acquisition is satisfied by the issue of shares.

It should be noted that a statutory charge to tax has been enacted where a taxpayer has taken advantage of a concession published before 9 March 1999 which allows gains to be relieved in an earlier period on the understanding that they are brought back into charge in a later period, and tax on the deferred capital gains is not then paid. The charge is based on the amount of the gains deferred under the concession from the earlier period and applies where those deferred gains subsequently arise after 8 March 1999, irrespective of when the relief was given.

(3)   The new assets must be acquired (or an unconditional contract for their acquisition entered into) within a four-year period beginning 12 months before the disposal of the old assets and ending three years after the disposal; HMRC (but not appeal commissioners, etc.) have a discretion to allow an extension, which they will use, inter alia where the intention to acquire assets is frustrated by matters outside the taxpayer's control and where following compulsory purchase land is leased back to the trader

until the authority is ready to build on it – relief may be given provisionally in the interim period where an unconditional contract has been entered into. In preparation for self-assessment, provisions were enacted to allow provisional claims to be made where there is an intention to reinvest (see below).

(4) The new assets must be acquired for use in the business and not wholly or partly for the purpose of realising a gain on the disposal of the new assets.

(5) The new asset(s) must be taken into use 'on' the acquisition. In one case, the taxpayer company's claim to roll-over relief failed because there was a delay of eight months between completion of the sale and occupation of the premises. A delay to enable capital expenditure to be used to enhance the property before use is often permitted, provided it is not let before use.

(6) Where part of a newly acquired asset is sold shortly after the purchase it is not possible to claim roll-over relief in respect of any gain arising by identifying the part sold as the 'old' asset and the original acquisition (within the prior 12 months) as the 'new' asset.

(7) The person carrying on the business must make a claim for the relief. Under self assessment, provisional claims for roll-over relief can be made where there is an intention to reinvest the proceeds in acquiring new assets and the taxpayer makes a declaration to that effect. Such declarations enable provisional relief to be given until the earliest of:

- the date the declaration is withdrawn;
- the date it is superseded by a valid roll-over relief claim;
- in the case of CGT, the third anniversary of 31 January following the tax year in which the disposal took place or, for corporation tax purposes, the fourth anniversary of the end of the accounting period in which the disposal took place.

Relief may be available in relation to the grant of an option over land if it would be due on the disposal of the underlying land.

Law: TCGA 1992, s. 23(6)–(8), s. 152, 153, 153A, 157, 175(2B); FA 1999, s. 76; *Tod (HMIT) v Mudd* [1987] BTC 57; *Campbell Connelly & Co Ltd v Barnett (HMIT)* [1994] BTC 12; *Watton (HMIT) v Tippett* [1997] BTC 338; *Steibelt (HMIT) v Paling* [1999] BTC 184

Source: ESC D16, *Relief for replacement of business assets: repurchase of the same asset*; ESC D22, *Relief for the replacement of business assets: expenditure on improvements to existing assets*; ESC D24, *Relief for the replacement of business assets: assets not immediately brought into trading use*; ESC D25, *Relief for the replacement of business assets: acquisition of an interest in an asset already used for the purposes of the trade*; SP D6, *Replacement of business assets: time limit*; 1991/26, Technical Information Release, October 1991; Technical Release TAX 15/92

See *British Tax Reporter* ¶570-500.

6309 Effect of claim for replacement roll-over relief

If all the conditions for 'replacement roll-over relief' are satisfied (see 6308), then the disposal of the old assets is deemed to be on a 'no gain/no loss' basis and the consideration for the new assets is reduced by the amount of the gain.

Example

In 1985, Z & Co purchased (for £70,000) a 99-year lease of offices for the purposes of its business of management consultants. The partnership occupied the premises until 1990 when it assigned the unexpired term of its lease for £100,000. In 1989, the partnership acquired new office premises in anticipation of the sale of its old offices. The new premises were acquired for £180,000. The new premises are sold in 2007 for £200,000 and the partnership dissolved. The disposal of the old assets is deemed to be made at neither a gain nor a loss. Thus Z & Co pay no CGT on the first disposal but, ignoring incidental expenditure and indexation, on the disposal of the new premises the partnership gain (before taper relief) is £50,000 (i.e. £200,000 − (£180,000 − £30,000)).

Note: The tax treatment of the other party to these transactions is unaffected by any claim made by Z & Co.

Order of reliefs

In HMRC's view, claims to roll-over relief take priority over the relief for the transfer of a business to a company rules (see 6302).

Law: TCGA 1992, s. 152(1), (2)

Source: Inland Revenue Manual *Capital Gains*, vol. VI, CG 61560

See *British Tax Reporter* ¶570-500.

6310 Replacement by depreciating assets

Where, in a claim for 'replacement roll-over relief' (see 6308), the new asset acquired is a 'depreciating asset' (basically, one with a predictable life of not more than 60 years from the date of acquisition) the gain on the disposal of the old asset is not so much rolled over as held over. HMRC consider that whether new constructions (or the addition of fixtures) on leasehold land are depreciating assets is determined by reference to the duration of the lease at that time.

In this case, instead of being deducted from the cost of the new assets (see 6309), the gain is deferred until the earliest of the following events:

- the claimant disposes of the new asset; or
- he ceases to use the asset for the purposes of his business (from 16 December 1993, otherwise than on death); or

- the expiry of ten years from the date of acquisition of the new asset.

If the claimant later acquires another asset ('asset No. 3') which is not a depreciating asset and the acquisition is made before any of these events occurs, the postponed gain from the old asset may be rolled over to asset No. 3.

Example

In 1987 X Ltd buys factory premises (freehold) for its business. The purchase price is £100,000. X Ltd sells the factory in 1989 for £150,000 and buys a second factory (35-year lease unexpired) in 1989 for £170,000. A claim is made for relief. The gain (£50,000) on the disposal of the first factory is postponed until one of the events above takes place.

In June 1997 X buys a third factory (freehold) for £180,000 and sells the second factory in December 2000. X Ltd may make a claim to roll over the postponed gain (on the sale of the first factory) to the third factory, i.e. the acquisition cost of the third factory will be £180,000 − £50,000 = £130,000.

Special provisions exist where only part of the postponed gain is carried forward.

Law: TCGA 1992, s. 154(6)

Source: ESC D45, *Rollover into depreciating assets*

See *British Tax Reporter* ¶572-000.

6314 Employee share ownership plans

Capital gains tax rollover relief is available to enable shares to be transferred to employee share ownership plans in a tax efficient manner. The relief, which operates in a similar fashion to that available in respect of transfer to employee share ownership trusts, operates so as to deem the consideration in respect of the disposal to be at such an amount as gives rise to neither a gain or a loss. Partial relief is available where not all the consideration is reinvested, provided that the amount not reinvested is less than the gain.

Conditions

For the relief to be available, the following conditions must be satisfied:

- at the time of the disposal the employee share ownership plan must be approved;
- the shares disposed of to the plan (the 'relevant shares') must be eligible shares for that purpose. However, for the relief to be in point, they must not be listed on a recognised stock exchange;
- during the entitlement period, the trustees must hold for the beneficiaries of the plan trust at least ten per cent of the ordinary share capital of the company and carry rights to at least ten per cent of the profits available for distribution to the shareholders and the

assets of the company available for distribution to its shareholder in the event of a winding up. Shares held within the plan on behalf of an individual are treated as being held by the trustees for the purposes of the calculation until such time as they cease to be subject to the plan. The entitlement period is 12 months from the date of the disposal; and

- during the prescribed period, there must be no unauthorised arrangement that would enable the claimant or a person connected with him to acquire from the trustees, directly or indirectly, shares (or an interest in or right deriving from them). The proscribed period is the period from the date of the disposal to the date of acquisition, or, if later, the date on which the trustees satisfy the ten per cent holding requirement.

Example 1

Pauline disposes of 1,000 shares in an unlisted company to the trustees of an approved employee share ownership plan. The shares are eligible shares. The consideration is £2.25 per share. Pauline makes a chargeable gain of £1,480. Three months later she invests all the proceeds in chargeable assets. She satisfies the conditions for roll-over relief, and within the time-limit makes a claim for relief.

The effect of such a claim is to treat the consideration received from the disposal as being £770 (the actual consideration of £2,250 less the gain of £1,480), being the sum that gives rise to neither a gain nor a loss. The gain is rolled-over into the replacement assets.

Example 2

Justin disposes of 200 shares to the trustees of an approved employee share ownership plan for £3.50 per share. The shares are eligible shares in an unlisted company. He realises a gain of £680. Two months later he reinvests £3,000 in chargeable assets. He makes a claim for partial relief.

The sum not reinvested was £500 and this was less than the gain of £680. As a result of the claim, the gain crystallising on the disposal is reduced to £500 (the amount not reinvested), a reduction of £180. The consideration for the replacement assets is deemed to be £2,820 (i.e. the actual consideration of £3,000 less the balance of the gain of £180). Consequently, £180 of the gain is rolled over.

Law: TCGA 1992, s. 236A; FA 2000, s. 48

See *British Tax Reporter* ¶582-950.

6316 Enterprise management incentives

The enterprise management incentives scheme is designed to help small potentially high risk companies to recruit and retain high calibre individuals. Where options are granted under the scheme, on the sale of the shares, taper relief (until 5 April 2008; see 5268ff.) will normally be available from the date on which the options were granted, rather than from the date of exercise.

Law: FA 2000, s. 62 and Sch. 17

See *British Tax Reporter* ¶564-000.

GIFTS OF BUSINESS ASSETS

6325 Gifts of business assets by individuals

Relief is provided for certain gifts of business assets. The relief is by way of 'hold-over' (see 6144) of the gain otherwise chargeable, i.e. CGT liability is postponed until the transferee subsequently makes a chargeable disposal and his base cost is taken to be the transferor's base cost.

For the relief to apply there must be a disposal of business assets otherwise than at arm's length bargain and the relief must be claimed within six years of the end of the relevant tax year by both transferor and transferee; where the transferees are trustees of a settlement, the claim for relief should be made by the transferor alone.

The relief applies to the following business assets:

- an asset, or an interest in an asset used for the purposes of a trade, profession or vocation carried on by the transferor, his personal company or a member of a trading group of which his personal company is the holding company (for disposals before 16 March 1993 the legislation referred to family companies); or
- shares or securities of a trading company or of the holding company of a trading group, where either the trading company or holding company is the transferor's personal company (or previously family company), or those shares or securities are neither quoted on a recognised stock exchange nor dealt in on the Unlisted Securities Market.

The relief in the first category above expressly includes assets used by a trading group held by the personal company (or, before 16 March 1993, family company). From 13 March 1989 it is possible to claim hold-over relief on any disposal of shares or securities in a private, unquoted, unlisted company (as in the second category); before then a disposal of shares would only qualify for relief if the company was the individual's family company, though general gift relief could apply (see 6285).

Personal company

This is a company in which the individual can exercise 5 per cent or more of the voting power (TCGA 1992, s. 165(8)(a)). (N.B. This differs from the definition of 'personal company' for entrepreneur's relief, which requires a minimum 5 per cent ordinary shareholding in addition to voting power.) The company may qualify as 'personal' even though its shares may be listed on a recognised stock exchange. However, in such a case, it will only be assets owned by the individual and used by the company for its trade which will be qualifying business assets; the shares in that company will not qualify.

Gains already subject to retirement relief or subject to possible hold-over on a gift chargeable to inheritance tax (see 6287) have always been excepted from business asset hold-over relief; from 14 March 1989 the following exceptions also apply.

- The relief does not apply to disposals of qualifying corporate bonds where a gain crystallises following a company reorganisation involving old assets which were not such bonds (see 5865) – this prevents a further hold-over relief for gifts of business assets on the subsequent disposal of the new securities.
- The relief does not apply where the transferee is neither resident nor ordinarily resident in the UK.
- The relief does not apply where the transferee is resident or ordinarily resident in the UK but is regarded as a resident outside the UK under any double taxation treaty and under that treaty would not be liable to tax on a gain; from 30 November 1993, if the transferee is a company, it is regarded as non-resident (see 4500) and so excluded, even if the treaty does not provide for effective chargeable gains exemption.
- The relief does not apply where the gift of business assets is to a foreign-controlled company (i.e. a company controlled by a person connected with the transferor who is neither resident nor ordinarily resident in the UK).

The last three exceptions are all there because the gain which would have been held over without them would never be brought into charge. In each case, the subsequent disposal by the transferee would be outside the UK CGT charge. It would not be a postponement of tax but an avoidance of tax.

Valuations

A HMRC statement of practice explains the circumstances in which they will not need to agree at the time of the gift the market value of assets for which relief is claimed. A valuation may be necessary at some point before disposal as a result of the interaction of the hold-over reliefs with other CGT reliefs, e.g. retirement relief, relief in respect of deferred charges on gains before 31 March 1982 and time apportionment for assets held on 6 April 1965.

The practice aims to reduce the compliance burden for taxpayers. Valuation negotiations, including those of unquoted shares and land – which can often be both expensive and complex – will be saved. The time it takes to settle hold-over relief claims will be reduced as a result. However, the new arrangements are voluntary: HMRC will still agree valuations and calculate the held over gain in any case where the taxpayer wishes it.

The transferor and transferee must both make a request that the valuation be avoided and must provide:

- full details of the asset transferred;
- its date of acquisition;
- its allowable expenditure;
- a statement that they have satisfied themselves that the value of the asset at the date of the transfer was in excess of the allowable expenditure plus indexation to that date.

HMRC stipulate that once a claim made on this basis has been accepted it may not be subsequently withdrawn.

Extension to agricultural property

The relief also extends to agricultural property which is disposed of, even though it does not satisfy the trade use condition; such property is defined by reference to property eligible for inheritance tax agricultural property relief. The relief is given by reference to the nature of the asset, though the inheritance tax relief ultimately depends upon the value of the asset (which excludes hope or development value: see 7292ff.); the relief is, in principle, available on the whole of the gain not just that part which reflects the agricultural value of the property.

Reduction of relief

The relief is reduced where the asset is not used for the purposes of a trade, profession or vocation throughout the transferor's ownership; there are also rules for apportioning the gain where the asset is a building or structure only part of which was used for the trade, profession or vocation. Hold-over relief is available only in respect of that part of the gain referable to the business user.

Where the chargeable assets of the company whose shares are being disposed of include assets which are not business assets, the amount of the held over gain allowed is the same proportion as the company's business assets at market value bear to the company's total chargeable assets at market value on the date of disposal. The reduction is not actually made after 13 March 1989 unless the transferor held at least 25 per cent of the voting rights in the company at some time within the 12 months preceding the disposal or the company is his personal company.

If a disposal is, or eventually proves to be, also a chargeable transfer, and a claim for business asset roll-over relief is made, the transferee can deduct in computing the chargeable gain accruing to him on a subsequent disposal the lesser of:

- the inheritance tax due on the original transfer, or
- the chargeable gain computed apart from this relief.

Law: TMA 1970, s. 42; TCGA 1992, s. 165, 166(1), (2), 167, 169, Sch. 7, para. 1, para. 4–8; FA 2000, s. 90

Source: SP 8/92

See *British Tax Reporter* ¶574-400.

6326   Gifts of business assets by trustees

Hold-over relief for gifts of business assets can be claimed by trustees, similar in nature to that applicable to individuals (see 6325). Assets included are those used for the purposes of a trade, profession or vocation carried on by the trustees making the disposal or a beneficiary having an interest in possession immediately before the disposal. Alternatively, shares or securities of a trading company are included if they are neither quoted nor dealt in on the Unlisted Securities Market or the trustees have at least 25 per cent of the voting rights in the company at the time of the disposal. A further category includes agricultural property.

Law: TCGA 1992, Sch. 7, para. 2, 3

See *British Tax Reporter* ¶574-650.

ADMINISTRATION OF CAPITAL GAINS TAX

6400   Care and management of taxes on capital gains

Most of the provisions dealing with the administration of direct UK taxes are to be found in the *Taxes Management Act* 1970 which, so far as it relates to chargeable gains, is construed as one with the *Taxation of Chargeable Gains Act* 1992. The 'care and management' of taxes on capital gains are entrusted to the Board of HM Revenue and Customs (see 2500).

Regulations have been made to supplement the *Taxes Management Act* 1970, many of whose provisions apply not only to CGT but to income tax and corporation tax as well (see 2500ff.).

Law: *Commissioners for Revenue and Customs Act* 2005; TMA 1970, s. 119(4)

See *British Tax Reporter* ¶595-000.

6410   Targeted anti-avoidance rules (TAARs)

Finance Act 2007 contained a targeted anti-avoidance rule (TAAR) to counter schemes to create and use artificial capital losses to avoid tax. The measure is designed to ensure that allowable capital losses are restricted to those arising from genuine commercial transactions. The changes took effect in relation to capital losses arising on disposals on or after 6 December 2006.

Where a person has entered into arrangements, and a main purpose of those arrangements is to gain a tax advantage by creating an artificial capital loss, any resulting loss will not be an allowable loss for the purposes of CGT, income tax or corporation tax.

Law: TCGA 1992, s 16A

RETURNS OF CAPITAL GAINS

6425 Returns in respect of charge to tax on gains

Various persons may be required to supply information to HM Revenue and Customs to enable tax to be properly collected in respect of capital gains. Since chargeable gains form part of the profits of a company which are subject to corporation tax, the returns applicable to corporation tax are relevant to companies (see 3200ff., 4986ff.). A person chargeable to CGT must notify HM Revenue and Customs of that fact and returns in respect of CGT may be required from the taxpayer or a third party (see 6427, 6429).

See *British Tax Reporter* ¶595-650.

6427 Notice of liability to CGT

Under self-assessment, the CGT notice of liability requirements are combined with those relating to income tax (see 2550). The time-limit for notification, if the taxpayer has not already been requested to make a tax return, has become six months from the end of the relevant tax year. Delay is allowed for if the taxpayer has reasonable grounds; the delay may continue so long as the reasonable excuse exists, and when it ceases to apply the taxpayer still has a 'reasonable time' within which to comply.

Law: TMA 1970, s. 118(2)

See *British Tax Reporter* ¶595-700.

6428 CGT returns by individuals and partnerships

Under self-assessment the taxpayer may choose to make a self-assessment of his gains; alternatively, HM Revenue and Customs (HMRC) will make an assessment on his behalf – without penalty – if he submits his return before 31 October following the end of the tax year or, if later, within two months of the issue of the notice requiring him to make a return for that year (see 2564). The filing deadline for the combined income tax and CGT return is the later of 31 January following the tax year and three months after the issue of a notice requesting submission of a return (see 2564).

If in a tax year:

- the 'taxable amount' does not exceed the 'exempt amount'; and
- the aggregate consideration on disposals on which chargeable gains accrued does not exceed twice the exempt amount,

then (unless HMRC otherwise require) a statement that the two conditions are fulfilled is sufficient for compliance with the requirement to make a return of gains.

Valuations

Individuals and trustees liable to CGT may submit draft valuations to their tax office, before they complete their self-assessment returns. Applications should be made on CG34 as soon as possible after the date of the disposal, to allow adequate time for consideration. However, submission of the relevant return should not be delayed if agreement on the valuation has not been reached by the filing date.

Where a self-assessment enquiry (see 2566, 2679) is held open pending agreement of a CGT valuation, HMRC will not take advantage of the open enquiry to raise new issues, unless new facts come to light.

Effect of delay

Delay in sending in a return of capital gains may expose a taxpayer to interest on overdue tax and, under self-assessment, a surcharge (see 2764). There are also penalties (see 2550, 2645ff.).

Partnerships

Although a partnership in English law is not a separate legal person and is not itself liable to CGT, the partner required to make a return in respect of the income of the partnership (see 2582) is to include in that return the notional gains of the partnership for tax purposes. This is to include details in respect of disposals of partnership property and particulars of acquisitions of partnership property, subject to the exclusions listed below. The filing deadline may differ for the partnership return (see 2582).

Law: FA 2003, s. 159; TCGA 1992, s. 3(6)

Source: SP 1/99

See *British Tax Reporter* ¶595-750.

6429   Information about chargeable gains

HM Revenue and Customs may by the notice requiring a return of income and gains, etc. (see 2564, 2588, 4960) demand particulars of any assets acquired by the person concerned. However, there are certain exclusions from this, namely where various exemptions apply as follows:

- rights to winnings from pool betting, lotteries or games with prizes (see 6162);
- government non-marketable securities (see 5860);
- passenger vehicles (see 6175);
- decorations for valour or gallant conduct (see 6178);
- foreign currency for personal expenditure (see 6180);
- unless the amount or value of the consideration for its acquisition exceeds £6,000 any

asset which is tangible movable property (except where excluded for terminal markets and currency: see 6155);

- any assets acquired as trading stock.

Law: TMA 1970, s. 12

See *British Tax Reporter* ¶595-650.

6431 Returns by third parties for CGT

Issuing houses, stockbrokers and auctioneers

For the purpose of obtaining particulars of chargeable gains, HMRC may require returns as to relevant information from issuing houses, stockbrokers and auctioneers and any person dealing in chattels (where the auction dealing consideration exceeds £6,000).

Any issuing house or other person carrying on a business of effecting public issue or placing of shares or securities in any company, either on behalf of the company or on behalf of holders of blocks of shares or securities which have not previously been the subject of a public issue or placing, may be required to make a return of the issues or placings.

United Kingdom stock exchange members, and other market makers, may be required to make a return giving particulars of transactions effected by them in the course of their business. Particulars must be given of parties to the transaction, the number or amount of the shares or securities and the amount or value of the consideration. Agents or brokers in shares and securities transactions (other than stock exchange members) may be required to make a return giving the same particulars for transactions effected. The same applies to the committee or other persons or body of persons responsible for managing a clearing house for any terminal market in commodities.

Nominee shareholders

HMRC may require information from nominee shareholders as to the beneficial ownership.

The section applies to shares, securities and loan capital.

Settled property

HMRC may, by notice in writing, require any party to a 'settlement' (see 1070) to furnish them, within a period of not less than 28 days, such particulars as HMRC think necessary for capital gains purposes. There are also certain general requirements for settlements with a foreign element (see 5632).

Non-resident trusts

HMRC may require any person to supply them, within a period of not less than 28 days, with such particulars as HMRC think necessary for the purposes of the exit charge on non-resident and migrant settlements (see 5635, 5640).

Power to require production of accounts, books and other information

HMRC's rights of access to accounts and information, etc. apply for CGT purposes as for liability for other taxes (see 2621ff.).

Law: FA 2008, s. 113 and Sch. 36; TCGA 1992, s. 98; TMA 1970, s. 25–27

See *British Tax Reporter* ¶595-950.

ASSESSMENTS, DETERMINATIONS AND CLAIMS FOR CGT

6437   Claims in respect of CGT

Claims in respect of reliefs from CGT are generally to be made in the same way and subject to the same time-limit rules as for income tax (see 2684, 2687).

See *British Tax Reporter* ¶596-500.

6440   Scope of assessments to CGT and determinations

The assessable amount for CGT is the taxable amount of chargeable gains less allowable losses and net of the exempt annual amount (see 6150, 6152). Under self-assessment, where a taxpayer fails to submit his return on time HMRC may determine income and gains (see 2679, 6429).

Apart from discovery assessments (see 2680), HMRC have powers to make estimated assessments or determinations by reference to the taxpayer's return (or his failure to make a return) or to adjust a taxpayer's self-assessment, depending upon whether the tax year is a self-assessment year. The rules apply in much the same way as for income tax (see 2679).

Capital gains tax assessments may be made on various persons chargeable in a representative capacity, as they can for income tax; this might apply to, for example, personal representatives, guardians and receivers, while there is statutory protection for certain trustees, agents and receivers.

Law: TMA 1970, s. 71–77

See *British Tax Reporter* ¶596-450.

6442 CGT assessments in respect of partnerships

Even though an individual partner makes a return of partnership gains (see 6429), the tax on chargeable gains is to be charged (and assessable) on the partners separately.

Law: TCGA 1992, s. 59

See *British Tax Reporter* ¶595-850.

6444 Assessment of non-residents' CGT

Non-residents (i.e. persons neither resident nor ordinarily resident: see 213, 216) are not normally within the charge to CGT. For the position of non-residents trading within the UK through a branch or agency, see 1672.

Law: *Morris & Anor v R & C Commrs* [2007] EWHC 1181(Ch)

See *British Tax Reporter* ¶596-300.

6446 Arrears of CGT due to official error

In some circumstances, arrears of CGT are wholly or partly waived by concession if they have arisen through failure by HMRC to make proper and timely use of information supplied by the taxpayer (see 2758).

See *British Tax Reporter* ¶597-650.

APPEALS IN RESPECT OF CAPITAL GAINS

6450 Scope of appeals in respect of capital gains

An appeal may be brought against a determination of the amount of any tax (or an assessment to tax) or against a decision on a claim by notice of appeal in writing, given within 30 days of the date of the notice of assessment or decision. Except as noted below, the rules are much the same as for income tax (see 235).

Land

Where an appeal against an assessment to tax (whether to CGT or corporation tax) on chargeable gains involves a question as to the value of any land or of a lease of land that question is to be determined by a special tribunal. If the land is in England or Wales the question is to be determined on a reference to the Lands Tribunal; if in Northern Ireland by the Lands Tribunal for Northern Ireland; if in Scotland by the Lands Tribunal for Scotland.

Unlisted securities

Where an appeal against an assessment on chargeable gains involves the question of the value of any shares or securities in a UK-resident company which are not dealt in on a stock exchange in the UK, up to 5 April 2009 the special commissioners, and from 6 April 2009, the tribunal, are to determine the question. Shares includes stock.

Law: TMA 1970, s. 46B(3), 46D

Source: HMRC: *Litigations and settlement strategy*

Website: www.hmrc.gov.uk/practitioners/lss.pdf

See *British Tax Reporter* ¶596-600.

COLLECTION OF CGT

6470   Collection of CGT generally

Capital gains tax is collected by the collector of taxes.

If the taxpayer does not make payment HMRC have a number of methods of recovery open to them.

Distraint may be levied by the collector for non-payment of tax charged.

Proceedings for recovery of tax on capital gains may be taken through the courts in the usual manner (see 2807).

Date of payment

Capital gains tax for any tax year is due (in accordance with a person's self-assessment or HMRC's calculation thereof on his behalf) on 31 January which is ten months after the end of the tax year or, if later (provided he notified HMRC of his chargeability within six months of the end of the year), three months from the issue of the notice requiring him to make a return of his income or gains. There is a surcharge for late payments, and interest runs on overpayments and underpayments from the due dates (see 2764, 6484). Additional tax payable as a result of an amendment to the self-assessment figure becomes due as above or, if later, 30 days from the notice of the amendment. Further tax payable if HMRC make a 'discovery assessment' (see 2680) is due 30 days from the notice of assessment.

Payment by instalments of CGT on gifts

Tax can be paid in instalments where there is a disposal by way of gift or a deemed disposal on a beneficiary becoming absolutely entitled against the trustees of a settlement, or a deemed disposal on the termination of a life interest on death. The disposal must also be one to which the relief for gifts of business assets or the relief accorded for gifts on which inheritance tax is chargeable in various circumstances does not apply, or would not apply were a claim made. The first instalment is due on the day on which, had the tax been payable normally, it would have been payable; however, tax payable by instalments carries interest, excluding the default interest provisions while interest on the unpaid portion of the tax is added to each instalment and is payable accordingly (a taxpayer wishing to pay off outstanding instalments not yet due may do so).

Law: TMA 1970, s. 59B; TCGA 1992, s. 281

See *British Tax Reporter* ¶597-600.

6474 Recovery of CGT from person not primarily liable

A number of provisions enable CGT to be collected from someone other than the person primarily liable for the tax (see below).

Settlements

If CGT assessed on the trustees of a settlement is not paid within six months of its becoming payable and before or after the six-month period the asset on which the gain arose or the proceeds of sale from it is transferred to someone, who is absolutely entitled to it as against the trustees, the recipient can be assessed to the tax, or a proportion of it, within two years of the tax becoming payable (see 5600).

Gifts

If a gain accrues on the disposal of an asset by way of gift or otherwise by way of a bargain at arm's length and the tax assessed on the donor is not paid within 12 months of its becoming payable, the donee may be assessed and charged within two years of the tax becoming payable in the name of the donor. The amount in respect of which the assessment is made is not to exceed the lesser of (a) the chargeable gain accruing on the disposal and (b) the amount of CGT unpaid grossed-up at the marginal rate; the donee is given a right of recovery against the donor.

Non-residents trading through a branch or agency

Where non-residents carry on a trade in the UK through a branch or agency, HM Revenue and Customs will, broadly, treat that branch or agency as the non-resident's 'UK representative', and look to it for the performance of various tax obligations (see further 1672).

Company reconstructions and amalgamations

Where neither of the roll-over reliefs on share exchanges and company reconstructions apply by virtue of failing the tax avoidance motive test (see 4015, 4024) and tax is payable but is not paid within six months of when it is payable, any person who has acquired the original taxpayer's holding on a no gain/no loss transfer between spouse or within groups may be assessed to the tax within two years of its becoming payable.

Law: TCGA 1992, s. 137(4), 282

See *British Tax Reporter* ¶597-700.

INTEREST ON OVERDUE AND OVERPAID CGT

6480 Interest on overdue CGT

For interest on overdue CGT, surcharges etc., see 2764.

See *British Tax Reporter* ¶597-200.

6484 Interest on overpaid CGT ('repayment supplement')

Where there has been an overpayment of CGT and repayment is made, in some circumstances it is to be made with a tax-free supplement.

Under self-assessment any repayment by HMRC of CGT, penalties, surcharges, etc. are to be increased by a repayment supplement, equal to interest at a rate fixed by the Treasury, between the date of payment of the tax, etc. and the date of repayment.

For rates of interest and interest factor tables, see 15.

Law: ICTA 1988, s. 824(8); TCGA 1992, s. 283

See *British Tax Reporter* ¶597-350.

6490 General penalties in relation to CGT

For the pecuniary penalties for fraud and negligence and failures in relation to compliance requirements, see 2550, 2645ff.

See *British Tax Reporter* ¶597-400.

Inheritance Tax

KEY POINTS

- Inheritance tax is a tax on the transfer of value by individuals, including executors and trustees (see 6525).
- Transfers of value may be chargeable transfers, exempt transfers or potentially exempt transfers (see 6525 and 6610ff.).
- As regards lifetime transfers, the value is determined by the reduction in the transferor's estate (see 6526).
- Property is generally valued for IHT purposes at the price that it would fetch in the open market (see 6570ff.).
- On death, there is a deemed transfer of value (see 6526).
- Higher rates of inheritance tax apply to transfers on death than apply to lifetime transfers (see 6526).
- Additional tax may be due on lifetime transfer if death occurs within seven years. Death within seven years of making a PET will bring the PET into charge (see 6800ff.).
- Taper relief may apply to reduce the charge where additional tax is due on a lifetime transfer because the donor dies within seven years of making the transfer (see 6801).
- As far as settled property is concerned, inheritance tax distinguishes between trusts where someone is beneficially entitled to an interest in possession (see 6526ff.), discretionary trusts and trusts with no qualifying interest in possession (see 6940ff.) and special trusts, such as employee trusts or protective trusts (see 6998).
- Most trusts are subject to an inheritance tax charge on each ten-year anniversary (see 6943ff.).
- An exit charge applies where property leaves most trusts (see 6962 and 6964).
- Anti-avoidance provisions exist regarding pre-owned assets (see 6725).
- Various exemptions and reliefs apply to remove or reduce any charge to inheritance tax (see 7150ff.).
- Various administrative requirements apply in relation to inheritance tax, including the delivery of accounts and the payment of the tax (see 7500ff.).

INTRODUCTION AND GENERAL FRAMEWORK TO INHERITANCE TAX

INHERITANCE TAX IN THE UK

6505 Estate duty, capital transfer tax and inheritance tax

In 1974 capital transfer tax (CTT) replaced estate duty, an eighty-year old duty which had been levied on all property passing on death. Capital transfer tax was a tax on inter vivos gifts and upon the estate of a deceased. In its short life as such, CTT was much amended. From 25 July 1986 CTT was renamed inheritance tax (IHT) and its operation was substantially modified so as to exclude many, though not all, charges on inter vivos transfers. Inheritance tax was in some ways a return to the old concept of estate duty, but the central idea of CTT, that a transfer of value was to be measured by the loss to the donor's estate, was retained (see 6525).

Source: *HMRC Inheritance Tax: Customer Guide*

Website: www.hmrc.gov.uk/cto/customerguide/page1.htm

See *British Tax Reporter* ¶600-100.

6507 Consolidation of IHT legislation

The provisions of the *Finance Acts* 1975–1984 concerning CTT were consolidated in the *Capital Transfer Tax Act* 1984. The consolidation Act is effective from 1 January 1985. Since the passing of the *Finance Act* 1986, the *Capital Transfer Tax Act* 1984 is cited as the *Inheritance Tax Act* 1984. Furthermore, after 25 July 1986 all references to capital transfer tax are construed as references to IHT where they appear:

- in any other enactment passed before or in the same session as the *Finance Act* 1986; or
- in any document executed, made, served or issued on or before the passing of the 1986 Act or at any time after its passing.

See *British Tax Reporter* ¶600-500.

6520 Interaction between IHT and other capital taxes

If there is a disposal by way of a *sale* at arm's length between unconnected persons, there may be a liability to CGT but not to IHT.

If there is a disposal by way of a *gift*, there may be a liability to both IHT and CGT, but CGT hold-over relief may be available where there is an immediate charge to IHT.

If there is a disposal *on death* there may be liability to IHT but not to CGT.

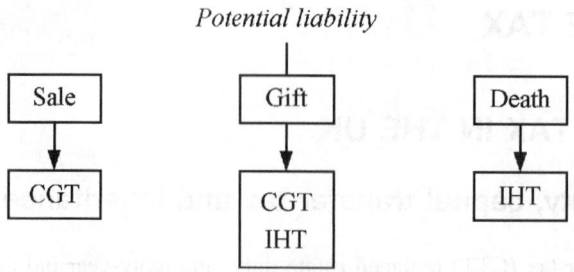

See *British Tax Reporter* ¶600-200.

AN OUTLINE OF IHT

6525 Persons and property chargeable to IHT

Inheritance tax is charged on individuals, including executors and trustees, but it does not apply to transfers of value by companies (other than close companies: see 6555).

All property is liable to be charged to IHT. However, there is no charge where an individual domiciled outside the UK transfers property 'situated outside the United Kingdom' (see 6550).

Transfer of value

Inheritance tax is charged on the value transferred by chargeable transfers. A transfer of value is determined by reference to a 'disposition' (see 6660) which results in a reduction in the value of the transferor's total property, i.e. his 'lifetime estate' (see 6630) (see further 6612). However, there is also a deemed transfer of value of the whole of a person's 'estate on death' (see 6780ff.). For these purposes transfers of value are of three kinds, namely, chargeable transfers, exempt transfers and potentially exempt transfers. There are also certain special charges in respect of settlements.

Chargeable transfer

A 'chargeable transfer' is any transfer of value other than an exempt transfer (see 7192ff.) or a potentially exempt transfer (see 6611).

Law: IHTA 1984, s. 1, 2, 3(1), 3A

Source: *HMRC Inheritance Tax: Customer Guide*

Website: www.hmrc.gov.uk/cto/customerguide/page1.htm

See *British Tax Reporter* ¶600-000.

6526 Scope of IHT charges

The deemed transfer of value made on death (see 6525) is liable to be charged to IHT. The tax also applies to potentially exempt lifetime transfers which are made less than seven years before the death of the transferor and to transfers inter vivos which do not qualify as 'potentially exempt transfers' (see 6611). The tax also applies to settled property.

Certain dispositions are not charged to IHT (see 6528).

Lifetime transfers

Inheritance tax is a cumulative tax (see 6527), charged on the value transferred by a chargeable transfer made inter vivos. It is charged by reference to the amount by which the transferor's estate has been reduced. It should be noted that the transferor's estate will be reduced by the IHT payable on the gift as well as by the gift itself (unless, of course, the transferee agrees to pay the tax). No other tax is taken into account when calculating the loss to the transferor's estate. Obviously if there is a 'disposition' (see 6660) for market value, there will be no diminution in the value of the transferor's estate.

There are two rates of inheritance tax: 0 per cent and 40 per cent (with tax on certain lifetime transfers chargeable at half rates).

The range of transfers made inter vivos which qualify as chargeable transfers is limited so as to exclude exempt transfers (see 7192ff.). 'Potentially exempt transfers' (PETs: see 6611) are treated as exempt transfers unless and until the transferor dies within seven years of making the transfer. Thus IHT is now largely a tax on transfers on or within a short time before death.

Death

When someone dies there is a deemed transfer of all the property to which he was beneficially entitled immediately before his death. The transfer on death is cumulated with previous chargeable lifetime transfers within the last seven years (see 6527). Higher rates of IHT apply to transfers on death.

Death may also bring about a tax charge or increased tax charge on transfers within seven years before death. If death occurs within seven years after making a chargeable transfer, additional tax may have to be paid by the transferee (see 6610). A potentially exempt transfer will also become chargeable if made within seven years of death and tax may become payable by the transferee as a result (see 6611).

Settled property

(1) Interest in possession
An interest in possession in settled property exists where the person having the interest has the immediate entitlement to any income produced by that property as the income arises. However, a discretion or power that can be exercised after the income arises which has the effect of withholding the income from that person, negates the existence of an interest in possession. A 'qualifying interest in possession' is an interest in possession to which an individual (or in certain circumstances a company) is beneficially entitled.

Example

Andrew transfers property to Brian and Claire on trust for Duncan for life with remainder to Emma for life and then Florence absolutely. Duncan has an interest in possession since

---

> he is entitled to the income from the property for his life. Emma does not have an interest in possession but will do so when Duncan dies.

For interests in possession, see 6903ff.

(2) No interest in possession

Under discretionary settlements there is no interest in possession since there is no interest until that discretion is exercised.

Example

Alan leaves property on trust to Bella and Charlie as trustees to appoint to such of his five children as they in their absolute discretion see fit. None of Alan's children at this stage has an interest in possession. As soon as Bella and Charlie appoint the property or part to one or all of Alan's children, an interest in possession will arise.

The principal charge to IHT occurs where, immediately before a ten-year anniversary, all or part of any property comprised in a settlement is 'relevant property' (see 6940). The ten-year anniversary occurs every ten years after the commencement of the settlement. However, no anniversary before 1 April 1983 was a chargeable event.

The charge at other times occurs when property ceases to be relevant property or where trustees dispose of property and thereby reduce the value of relevant property in the settlement.

The *Finance Act* 2006 made radical changes to the taxation of settled property. From 22 March 2006, only lifetime gifts to an individual, into a disabled trust, into a bereaved minor's trust on the coming to an end of an immediate post-death interest and on the creation of a transitional serial interest qualify for 'potential exemption'. Lifetime interest in possession trusts created on or after 22 March 2006, other than those mentioned above, are taxed under the 'discretionary tax regime' (see 6880ff.). Trusts created on or after 22 March 2006 no longer qualify as accumulation and maintenance trusts.

Law: *Finance Act* 2006, s. 157; IHTA 1984, s. 59(1); *Pearson v IR Commrs* [1981] AC 753

Source: *HMRC Inheritance Tax: Customer Guide*

Website: www.hmrc.gov.uk/cto/customerguide/page1.htm

See *British Tax Reporter* ¶600-700.

6527 Cumulation

The position used to be that all chargeable transfers made by a person during his lifetime would be cumulated. This meant that the rate of IHT payable on later transfers would be worked out by looking at the total of all previous chargeable transfers. The combination of a limitless cumulation period and graduated rates of tax would ensure a penal rate on later transfers. However, a ten-year maximum period on cumulations was introduced in 1981, and in respect of transfers after 17 March 1986 the cumulation period is reduced to seven years.

The deemed transfer on death is also cumulated with previous lifetime transfers within the last seven years.

For the effect on the calculation of tax, see 6614 and 6800.

Law: IHTA 1984, s. 7(1)

Source: *HMRC Inheritance Tax: Customer Guide*

Website: www.hmrc.gov.uk/cto/customerguide/page1.htm

See *British Tax Reporter* ¶604-150.

6528   Dispositions not charged to IHT

No liability to IHT will arise if the disposition is deemed not to be a transfer of value (see 7150ff.) or if the transfer is exempt (see 7192ff.) or potentially exempt (see 6611), or if the disposition is one of excluded property (see 7397). The legislation defines the circumstances in which the exceptions occur.

Reliefs are given in various ways:

- relief for transfers of business and agricultural property is given by reducing the value transferred (see 7253, 7292);
- relief for woodlands is given by leaving property out of account (see 7320);
- relief for successive transfers is given by quick succession relief which reduces the IHT chargeable on the second chargeable transfer.

Law: IHTA 1984, s. 3A, 10–42

Source: *HMRC Inheritance Tax: Customer Guide*

Website: www.hmrc.gov.uk/cto/customerguide/page1.htm

See *British Tax Reporter* ¶601-250.

6530   Crystallisation of IHT liability

The transferor, or trustees if settled property is involved, must, within 12 months of the lifetime transfer, deliver an account of the transfer to HMRC, or within three months of the beginning of the day on which the person who is to make the return becomes liable for the IHT if that date is later. However, the tax is due six months after the end of the month in which a chargeable transfer is made, except for transfers made between 5 April and 1 October in any year otherwise than on death, when the tax becomes due at the end of April in the next year.

Where the IHT charge occurs on death, an account of the deceased person's estate must be delivered to HMRC otherwise a grant of representation cannot be obtained. Delivery of the account must be within 12 months of the end of the month in which the transferor's death took place or within three months of the date when the personal representatives first act or have reason to believe that an account is required. Personal representatives must pay all the tax for which they are liable on delivery of their account. The 12-month time-limit after death also applies to tax on a potentially exempt transfer which becomes chargeable because of the donor's death within seven years.

Law: IHTA 1984, s. 216

Source: *HMRC Inheritance Tax: Customer Guide*

Website: www.hmrc.gov.uk/cto/customerguide/page1.htm

See *British Tax Reporter* ¶693-000.

6540   Domicile for IHT

The question of 'domicile' is important if the assets to be transferred are located outside the UK (see 6550). A person's domicile for tax purposes may be determined by general law (a domicile of origin or a domicile of choice: see 219) or it could be a fiscal domicile by operation of law (as for IHT, see below).

Domicile has an extended meaning for IHT purposes. A person who is not domiciled under the general law of the UK will be treated as domiciled in the UK at the relevant time:

- if he was domiciled in the UK within the three years immediately preceding the relevant time; or
- if he was resident in the UK in not less than 17 of the 20 tax years ending with the tax year in which the relevant time falls (though any dwelling-house available for use in the UK has always been ignored: see 213).

Exceptionally, the question of domicile for IHT is determined by reference to the UK, while for the purposes of the general law one is domiciled in one of the three jurisdictions within the UK (England and Wales, Scotland, or Northern Ireland).

Law: IHTA 1984, s. 267; *Allen (Executors of Johnson dec'd) v R & C Commrs* (2005) Sp C 481

Source: *HMRC Inheritance Tax: Customer Guide*

Website: www.hmrc.gov.uk/cto/customerguide/page1.htm

See *British Tax Reporter* ¶684-400.

6550 Location of assets for IHT

Property situated outside the UK is 'excluded property' (i.e. not within the charge to IHT: see 7397) if the person beneficially entitled to it is an individual domiciled (see 6540) outside the UK: in other words, for persons domiciled abroad, IHT generally applies only to their UK assets. (If an individual is domiciled in the UK, then any assets can be charged to tax regardless of their location.) It may therefore be important to know in what country certain property is located. Where there are no special rules governing the location of assets, the question is determined by the general law.

The potential charge to inheritance tax from holdings by foreign investors in UK-authorised funds was removed for transfers on or after 16 October 2002. The rules apply to the holding of non-UK domiciled investors or their trusts in authorised unit trusts and open-ended investment companies. IHT relief is also extended to losses on the sale of listed shares in open-ended investment companies.

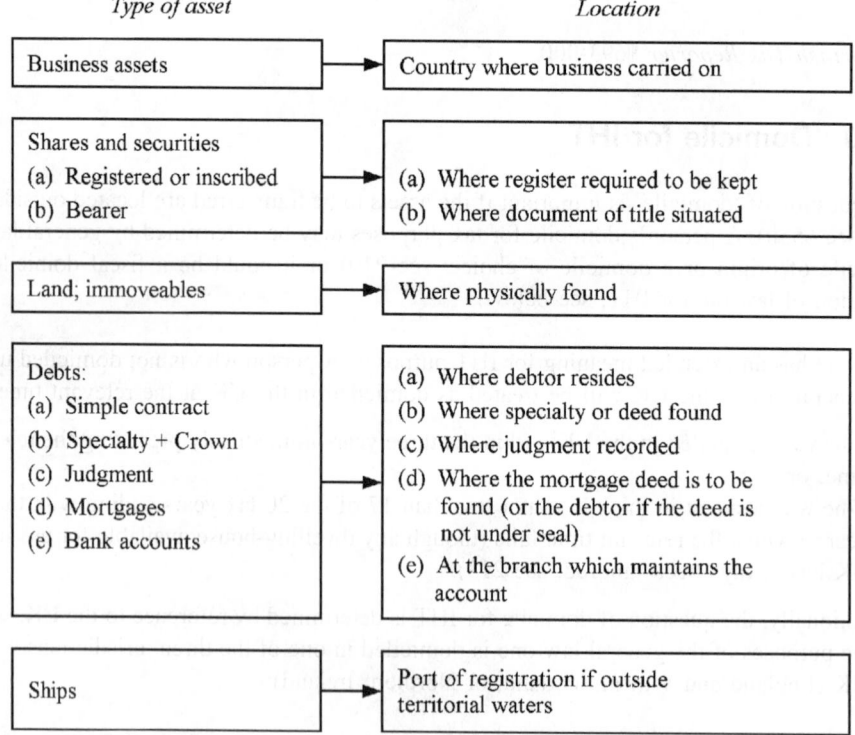

Type of asset	*Location*
Business assets	Country where business carried on
Shares and securities (a) Registered or inscribed (b) Bearer	(a) Where register required to be kept (b) Where document of title situated
Land; immoveables	Where physically found
Debts: (a) Simple contract (b) Specialty + Crown (c) Judgment (d) Mortgages (e) Bank accounts	(a) Where debtor resides (b) Where specialty or deed found (c) Where judgment recorded (d) Where the mortgage deed is to be found (or the debtor if the deed is not under seal) (e) At the branch which maintains the account
Ships	Port of registration if outside territorial waters

The Privy Council has held that the location of a non-negotiable promissory note is determined like that of most other debts (see above) and is accordingly located wherever it can be enforced (i.e. normally the country where the debtor resides). However, negotiable instruments are situated wherever there is an available market for their negotiation.

Where foreign works of art are normally kept outside the UK, they could be outside the scope of IHT as discussed above; if the owner dies while they are in the UK for exhibition, cleaning or restoration, any liability will be waived. Chattels are normally located where they are physically situated.

Law: FA 2003, s. 185; IHTA 1984, s. 3(2), 48, 82; *Kwok Chi Leung Karl (Exor of Lamson Kwok) v Commissioner of Estate Duty* [1988] BTC 8,073

Source: ESC F7, *Foreign owned works of art*; HMRC *Inheritance Tax: Customer Guide*

Website: www.hmrc.gov.uk/cto/customerguide/page1.htm

See *British Tax Reporter* ¶602-150.

6555 Close companies and IHT

Inheritance tax is chargeable only on individuals, except in relation to dealings in settled property. This means that companies are not liable to IHT when they make transfers of value. However, there are special provisions in the legislation which deal with close companies (for meaning of 'close companies', see 4253). A transfer of value by a close company is apportioned to the company's participators though the IHT is primarily payable by the company itself (for meaning of 'participators', see 4256). Such transfers are not PETs (see 6611).

Further, since (by virtue of the rules mentioned above) an interest in possession to which a close company is entitled is attributed to its participators, when a participator disposes of any part of his shareholding, in addition to any charge in respect of the actual shares, a charge can also arise in respect of the settled property (see 6909).

Neither a dividend paid by a subsidiary to its parent nor a transfer of assets between a wholly-owned subsidiary and its parent (nor between two wholly-owned subsidiaries) is a transfer of value.

Apportionment

The value transferred by a close company will be apportioned amongst its participators according to their respective rights and interests immediately before the transfer and, if one of those participators is a close company, that amount will be subapportioned.

If the value transferred is liable to income tax or if it is attributable to property outside the UK and the participator is domiciled outside the UK, no apportionment will be made. No apportionment is made if the value transferred is treated as franked investment income of the recipient. Neither the surrender of losses nor the surrender of ACT is a transfer of value. If a

Inheritance Tax

disposal (actual or notional) between companies in the same group gives rise to a transfer of value, then provided the effect on the rights of the minority participators is small, no amount will be apportioned to the minority participators unless the transferor company is the principal member of the group. The principal member of a group is the member of which all the other members are 75 per cent subsidiaries. A minority participator is a person not connected with a participator of the principal member of the group or any of the principal member's participators.

Alteration of share or loan capital

An alteration or extinguishment of a close company's 'unquoted' (see 6571) share or loan capital, or any 'rights' over that capital, is treated as a 'disposition' (see 6660) made by the participators. 'Rights' here include rights in the assets of the company available for distribution among the participators in a winding-up. Such alterations are not PETs (see 6611).

Liability for IHT

The company is primarily liable for IHT. However, if tax remains unpaid, the persons to whom any amounts in excess of five per cent have been apportioned and any individual whose estate has been increased by the transfer are liable for any unpaid tax.

An individual will only be liable for an amount of tax corresponding to the value apportioned to him or her or, in the case of an increase in his or her estate, will be liable only for the amount of the increase.

Law: IHTA 1984, s. 94–102, 202

See *British Tax Reporter* ¶603-700.

VALUATION RULES FOR IHT

6570   Valuation generally for IHT

The value of any property for IHT purposes is the price which the property might reasonably be expected to fetch if sold on the open market at that time. However, the price must not be assumed to be reduced merely because all the property is on the market at one time.

It must be assumed that there is both a willing buyer and a willing seller and that the asset is sold in the most advantageous way, e.g. well advertised, put into its most saleable form, etc.

There are a number of specific reliefs applicable on death (see 6810); subject to those, there are some specific rules which should be considered (see 6571 to 6573).

Law: IHTA 1984, s. 160

Source: Revenue Interpretation, 'Inheritance tax: valuation of assets at the date of death'

See *British Tax Reporter* ¶637-300.

6571 Valuation of quoted shares

Stocks and shares which are 'quoted' (i.e. listed on a recognised stock exchange) are valued at the lower of:

- the 'quarter up' value; and
- the mid-market value.

The quarter value is found by taking the lower of the selling price and buying price at close on the day of death, plus one-quarter of the difference between the two.

The mid-market value is the half-way price between the lowest and highest marked bargains for the day.

If the Stock Exchange is closed on the day in point, then the last previous quotation or the next quotation after that day may be taken. If the investment is quoted cum dividend, this means that the buyer will get the benefit of the next dividend and the price will, therefore, include that accrued net income. However, if the investment is quoted ex dividend, the dividend less any income tax must be brought into account since the price will not reflect the accrued net income.

Example

John dies on 18 July 2009. His net free personalty included:

	Investments	Quotation
(a)	5,000 10p ordinary shares in A plc	50–58p
(b)	2,000 £1 ordinary shares in B plc (dividend due on 19 August is 20p per share)	60–66 ex div.

	Valuation	£
(a)	5,000 10p ordinary shares in A plc at 52	2,600
(b)	2,000 ordinary shares in B plc at $61\frac{1}{2}$ ex div.	1,230
(c)	Dividend of 20p per share on (b)	400

Law: IHTA 1984, s. 160

Source: Revenue interpretation, 'Inheritance tax: valuation of assets at the date of death'

See *British Tax Reporter* ¶638-300.

6572 Valuation of unquoted shares

If stocks and shares are not 'quoted' on a stock exchange, etc. (see 6571), their market value must be estimated. The following matters will be considered, although they will not necessarily carry equal weight:

- the size of the hypothetical sale;
- dividend record;
- profit cover for dividends;
- earnings yield and price/earnings ratio;
- general economic climate;
- value of assets per share;
- comparisons with similar quoted companies;
- restrictions on transfer; and
- management.

Further, in arriving at a hypothetical open market value, evidence of open market sales of the same or similar property are particularly relevant and admissible, even if not conclusive. Similarly, the Court of Session has held that agreements between taxpayers and HMRC as to value are also relevant. The court said that the best evidence of open market value would be evidence of sales of the same or similar property, though if conditions had changed the evidence might have to be qualified by taking account of other evidence. It could not be said to follow from the fact that the value was to be ascertained on a hypothetical basis that any evidence of actual transactions should be ruled out. The same approach applied to agreements with HMRC, though the evidence might not carry much weight.

Law: IHTA 1984, s. 168

Source: Revenue interpretation, 'Inheritance tax: valuation of assets at the date of death'

See *British Tax Reporter* ¶638-450.

6573 Valuation of land

The valuation of land is negotiated between the representatives of the transferor and HMRC. HMRC usually refers the matter to the district valuer. In arriving at a value, recent sales of similar property in the area will be relevant although not conclusive. Also, if the property is subsequently sold, the actual sale price will not automatically upset the value placed on the property by HMRC or the district valuer. However, if land is sold less than three years after death for less than its valuation at death, the sale price may be substituted provided that it was the best reasonably obtainable in an arm's length transaction between unconnected persons (see 6810).

Where the transferor and HMRC cannot agree, a value will be placed on the land. The taxpayer can appeal against the valuation. Appeals may be made direct to the Upper Tribunal for England and Wales (prior to 1 April 2009, the Lands Tribunal for England), the

Lands Tribunal for Scotland or the Lands Tribunal for Northern Ireland, depending on where the land is situated.

Leased or tenanted property

A property that is subject to a lease is worth much less than if sold on the open market with vacant possession. The method of valuation will depend on the length of the unexpired lease. Where the lease is to expire in the reasonably foreseeable future, its value will be its vacant possession value reduced by an appropriate percentage. However, if the lease is a long one which is not due to come to an end in the foreseeable future, the value is determined by reference to the value of income (after deduction of reasonable outgoings) received from it.

Farm cottages

Farm cottages which are valued as part of an agricultural property and are occupied by persons employed solely for agricultural purposes are valued without regard to their value on the open market if they were not so occupied.

Law: IHTA 1984, s. 160, 169, 170; *Alexander v IR Commrs* [1991] BTC 8,024; *IR Commrs v Gray* [1994] BTC 8,034; *Walton (as surviving executor of Walton) v IR Commrs* [1996] BTC 8,015

Source: Revenue interpretation, 'Inheritance tax: valuation of assets at the date of death'

See *British Tax Reporter* ¶637-800.

6575   Related property

Where the value of any property comprised in the estate would be less than the appropriate portion of the aggregate value of that and any related property, IHT is charged on the appropriate portion of the aggregate value.

Property is related to the property comprised in a person's estate if:

(1)   it is comprised in the estate of the spouse; or

(2)   it is or has been within the preceding five years:

    (a)   the property of a charity, or held on trust for charitable purposes only; or

    (b)   the property of a body mentioned in IHTA 1984, s. 24, 24A, or 25 (see 7195ff.);

        and became so on a transfer of value which was made by him or his spouse or civil partner after 15 April 1976 and was exempt to the extent that the value transferred was attributable to the property.

With the exception of shares, the appropriate portion is the proportion that the property transferred bears to the sum of all items of related property if valued individually. This portion is then applied to the aggregate value.

Example

Jack owns one of a pair of Ming vases. His wife owns the other. Valued individually, the vases are worth £7,000 each. However, valued as a pair, they are worth £20,000.

On Jack's death, his vase is valued at £10,000. The appropriate portion is 50 per cent, and 50 per cent of the aggregate value is £10,000.

As far as shares are concerned, the appropriate portion is determined by reference to the numbers of shares held, rather than to their value.

Example

Hugo and Wendy, who are husband and wife, each own 49 per cent of the shares of their family company, HW Ltd. Each holding is 'related' to the other, therefore on a transfer of value each holding would be valued, not as a 49 per cent holding, but as one-half ('the appropriate portion') of the value of a 98 per cent holding ('the aggregate').

Where related property is sold within three years of death, and the sale price is less than the value determined on death in accordance with the related property provisions, the value at death may be recalculated ignoring any related property (see 6815).

Law: IHTA 1984, s. 161

Source: *HMRC Inheritance Tax: Customer Guide*; HMRC Brief 71/07: IHT and the valuation of property owned jointly by spouses or civil partners

Website: www.hmrc.gov.uk/cto/customerguide/page1.htm

See *British Tax Reporter* ¶637-450.

LIFETIME TRANSFERS

6610   IHT and lifetime transfers: IHT and PETs

Inheritance tax is charged on the value transferred by chargeable transfers of value made inter vivos after 26 March 1974 (see 6525). For these purposes, there are three kinds of transfer of value:

- chargeable transfers;
- exempt transfers; and
- potentially exempt transfers.

A 'chargeable transfer' is any transfer of value other than an exempt transfer or a potentially exempt transfer (see 6525).

An 'exempt transfer' is any transfer described as such in the IHT legislation (see 7192ff.).

A 'potentially exempt transfer' (PET) is described at 6611 below; a PET made seven years or more before the death of the transferor is an exempt transfer but if the transferor dies within seven years of making the PET the transfer becomes a chargeable transfer. Until it becomes clear that a PET is chargeable, the transfer is assumed to be exempt. The personal representatives may well be liable for the additional tax but there is limited relief where they have proceeded on the understanding that there were no appropriate transfers (see 7533).

Law: IHTA 1984, s. 2, 3A

Source: *HMRC Inheritance Tax: Customer Guide*

Website: www.hmrc.gov.uk/cto/customerguide/page1.htm

See *British Tax Reporter* ¶607-000.

6611   'Potentially exempt transfer'

A 'potentially exempt transfer' (PET) is a transfer of value:

- which is made by an individual after 17 March 1986; and
- which is a gift to another individual, or (prior to 22 March 2006 into an accumulation and maintenance settlement) a disabled person's trust; and
- which would otherwise be a chargeable transfer.

Further, if the transfer is a gift to another individual then it must be one whereby the property concerned becomes comprised in the estate of the transferee or whereby the estate of the transferee is increased even though the property in question does not become comprised in that estate. In the case of a gift subject to reservation of benefit by the donor, there is a PET at the time any reservation is released (see 6785). A PET may also take place where certain debts or encumbrances are discharged (see 6782).

There was considerable criticism that the definition of a PET did not include a transfer into settlement where there was an interest in possession or any disposition of the settled property by the tenant for life. Since the tenant for life of settled property is treated as though he were absolute owner for IHT purposes it was felt to be a startling anomaly that transfers by him or to him were not potentially exempt. That anomaly was corrected and potential exemption was extended to such transfers in 1987. The definition of a PET included any transfer after 16 March 1987 to 21 March 2006:

- which is attributable to property in which an individual becomes entitled to an interest in possession; or
- which increases the value of property in which an individual is entitled to an interest in possession.

Further, transfers by the tenant for life and the termination of his interest will be potentially exempt provided they satisfy the conditions for potential exemption generally, i.e. the

Inheritance Tax

transferee must be an individual, or (prior to 22 March 2006 an accumulation and maintenance trust) a trust for the disabled.

Until Budget Day 2006 (22 March 2006) gifts to either interest in possession or accumulation and maintenance trusts were regarded as PETs (see above). From that date this exemption no longer applies. In addition, the 10-year and exit charges, which previously only applied to discretionary trusts, now also apply to all trusts other than those which are specifically exempt.

For a further discussion of the rules and anti-avoidance provisions preventing property being transferred free of tax into discretionary trusts by means of short interests in possession, see 6909ff.

Deemed transfers of value, such as transfers on death, are not PETs.

Law: IHTA 1984, s. 3A; *Finance Act* 2006, s. 156 and Sch. 20

Source: *HMRC Inheritance Tax: Customer Guide*

Website: www.hmrc.gov.uk/cto/customerguide/page1.htm

See *British Tax Reporter* ¶607-100.

6612 Value transferred by lifetime transfer

A transfer of value is any disposition made by the transferor as a result of which the value of his estate immediately after the disposition is less than it would be but for the disposition. The amount by which it is less is the value transferred by the transfer – if the transferor pays any IHT due that is also a reduction in the estate and a grossing up process is necessary (see 6620).

Example

Albert transfers a two per cent shareholding in TPMC Ltd into a discretionary trust. Immediately before the transfer, he had a 51 per cent holding. There are 10,000 issued shares in the company. Values per share are as follows:

% holding	£ per share
51	12
49	7
2	2

The diminution in value of his estate is calculated as follows:

	£
Before	
5,100 shares at £12	61,200
After	
4,900 shares at £7	(34,300)
Diminution in value	26,900

If Albert pays any IHT due in consequence of the disposition, the above amount must be grossed up to give the diminution in value of his estate and hence the value transferred by the transfer of value (before business property relief if applicable; see 7253ff.).

No account is taken of the value of excluded property which ceases to form part of a person's estate as a result of a disposition (see 7394). Apportionment is made where the value has to be determined by reference to the value of other property. For detailed valuation rules, see 6570ff.

Usually, a chargeable disposition will involve the transfer of property to a donee, but a destruction, abandonment or omission which results in a loss to the estate of the transferor are all chargeable unless there is no gratuitous intent (see 7153).

Certain dispositions are treated as not involving transfers of value (see 7150ff.).

Law: IHTA 1984, s. 3(1); *Inheritance Tax (Indexation) Order* 2000 (SI 2000/803)

Source: *HMRC Inheritance Tax: Customer Guide*

Website: www.hmrc.gov.uk/cto/customerguide/page1.htm

See *British Tax Reporter* ¶607-300.

6614   IHT rates on lifetime transfers

Originally, there were two separate tables detailing the different rates of IHT applicable to transfers on or within three years of death and other transfers. Since 1986 there has only been one set of rates.

For tables of past and current IHT rates, see 90.

Law: IHTA 1984, s. 7, 8 and Sch. 1

Source: *HMRC Inheritance Tax: Customer Guide*

Website: www.hmrc.gov.uk/cto/customerguide/page1.htm

See *British Tax Reporter* ¶6-000.

6616　Seven-year rule

As originally formulated IHT, then known as capital transfer tax, was a lifetime cumulative tax, i.e. all inter vivos transfers were accumulated and aggregated with property passing on death. Tax was charged at the time of each transfer and the higher the cumulative total, the greater the tax rate. A ten-year cumulative period was introduced in 1981, and for transfers after 17 March 1986 the cumulation period is reduced to seven years.

To ascertain the amount of tax payable on a chargeable transfer, it is necessary to take into account the donor's chargeable transfers in the previous seven years.

The steps in the calculation are:

Step 1

Work out the value of the current transfer (i.e. work out the loss to the transferor as the result of the transfer, deduct reliefs and exemptions).

Step 2

Ascertain the transferor's total of chargeable transfers in the seven years before the current transfer.

Step 3

Add the values in Step 1 and Step 2 to create an 'aggregate chargeable transfer'.

Step 4

Deduct the tax threshold (the amount up to which tax is payable at 0% ascertained at the date of the current transfer) from the aggregate chargeable transfer. If the aggregate chargeable transfer is below the tax threshold there is no lifetime tax to pay.

Step 5

Work out the tax at half rate (i.e. 20%) on the value ascertained in Step 4 (i.e. the excess over the tax threshold).

Step 6

If the value in Step 2 (the previous lifetime transfers) exceeds the tax threshold, repeat Steps 4 and 5 with the value in Step 2. Deduct this notional tax from the tax on the aggregate chargeable transfer to calculate the tax on the current transfer.

Example

George makes the following chargeable lifetime transfers (after all reliefs and exemptions) into separate discretionary trusts:

5 December 2002	£200,000
11 May 2009	£180,000
12 January 2010	£160,000
14 March 2010	£50,000

The lifetime tax payable on the transfers is calculated as follows (assuming the tax is payable by the transferee i.e. the trustees):

Tax on transfer 5/12/02

Steps 1–3 £
Transfers in 7 years prior to this transfer Nil
Add: value of this transfer 200,000

Aggregate chargeable transfer 200,000

Step 4
Below tax threshold (£250,000) @ 5/12/02

Tax on transfer 11/5/09

Steps 1–3 £
Transfers in 7 years prior to this transfer 200,000
Add: value of this transfer 180,000

Aggregate chargeable transfer 380,000

Step 4
Deduct tax threshold @ 11/5/09
£(380,000 − 325,000) = £55,000

Step 5
Work out tax
£55,000 × 20% = £11,000

Step 6
Transfers in the 7 years before this transfer are below the tax threshold so no adjustment for tax on this value needs to be made.

Tax on transfer 12/1/10

Steps 1–3 £
Transfers in 7 years prior to this transfer 180,000
Add: value of this transfer 160,000

Aggregate chargeable transfer 340,000

Step 4
Deduct tax threshold @ 12/1/10
£(340,000 − 325,000) = £15,000

Step 5
Work out tax
£15,000 × 20% = £3,000

Step 6
Transfers in the 7 years before this transfer are below the tax threshold so no adjustment for tax on this value needs to be made.

Tax on transfer 14/3/10

Steps 1–3   £
Transfers in 7 years prior to this transfer   340,000
Add: value of this transfer   50,000

Aggregate chargeable transfer   390,000

Step 4
Deduct tax threshold @ 14/3/10
£(390,000 − 325,000) =   £65,000

Step 5
Work out tax
£65,000 × 20% =   £13,000

Step 6
Notional tax on previous transfers
£(340,000 − 325,000) =   £15,000

Work out tax
£15,000 × 20% =   £3,000

Tax on current transfer £(13,000 − 3,000) =   £10,000

You will see that the tax on the current transfer is £50,000 × 20% = £10,000 as all of the transfer is chargeable above the tax threshold.

For chargeable transfers followed by death within seven years, see 6803.

For PETs followed by death within seven years, see 6802.

Law: IHTA 1984, s. 7

Source: *HMRC Inheritance Tax: Customer Guide*

Website: www.hmrc.gov.uk/cto/customerguide/page1.htm

See *British Tax Reporter* ¶611-100.

6620 Reduction in value of estate: grossing-up

Inheritance tax is charged on the value transferred by a chargeable transfer. The value transferred is measured by reference to the diminution in the value of the transferor's estate. Where the transferor pays the IHT on the transfer, the diminution in the value of his estate will be twofold: the property or sum gifted and the tax paid. In order to find the IHT payable by a transferor in such circumstances the value of the gift must be grossed up at the appropriate rate and that rate should then be applied to the gross sum so found.

The calculation is performed as follows:

Step 1

Work out the value of the current transfer (i.e. work out the loss to the transferor as the result of the transfer, deduct reliefs and exemptions).

Step 2

Ascertain the transferor's total of chargeable transfers in the seven years before the current transfer. If this value exceeds the tax threshold (the amount up to which tax is payable at 0% ascertained at the date of the current transfer), deduct the tax threshold from it and then work out notional tax at half rate (i.e. 20%) on this value (i.e. the excess over the tax threshold). Deduct the notional tax from the total of transfers to give the net value of transfers b/f. If the value is below the tax threshold, the net and the gross values of the b/f transfers are the same.

Step 3

Add the values in Step 1 and Step 2 to create an 'aggregate net chargeable transfer'.

Step 4

Deduct the tax threshold from the aggregate net chargeable transfer. If the aggregate net chargeable transfer is below the tax threshold there is no lifetime tax to pay.

Step 5

Work out the tax on the value in Step 4 using the grossing up rate. This is found by dividing the lifetime rate by (100 minus the lifetime rate). Thus, where the lifetime rate is 20%, the grossed up rate is 1/4 (20/80) or 25%.

Step 6

Deduct any notional tax calculated in Step 2 from the tax on the aggregate net chargeable transfer to calculate the tax on the current transfer.

Step 7

Add the tax found after Step 6 to the current transfer to give the gross chargeable transfer to be carried forward in the cumulation.

> ### Example
>
> On 31 May 2010, Harry transferred £420,000 into a discretionary trust for the benefit of his children. Harry agreed to pay the lifetime tax due. Harry had made one chargeable transfer in the previous seven years, with a value of £150,000. For the purposes of this example the annual exemption is ignored.
>
> The tax payable on the transfer in May 2010 is calculated as follows:

Inheritance Tax

Step 1

Value of current transfer is £420,000.

Step 2

Transfers in 7 years prior to this transfer are £150,000 which is below tax threshold so gross and net value is £150,000.

Step 3	£
Net transfers in 7 years prior to this transfer	150,000
Add: value of this transfer	420,000
Aggregate net chargeable transfer	570,000

Step 4
Deduct tax threshold @ 31/5/10
£(570,000 − 325,000) =   £245,000

Step 5
Work out tax
£245,000 × 1/4 =   £61,250

Step 6
Transfers in the 7 years before this transfer are below the tax threshold so no adjustment for tax on this value needs to be made.

Step 7
Chargeable transfer to carry forward in cumulation is:
£(420,000 + 61,250) =   £481,250

Example

Assume in the above example that Harry had previously made a chargeable transfer of value of £350,000, instead of £150,000.

The tax payable on the transfer in May 2010 is calculated as follows:

Step 1
Value of current transfer is £420,000.

Step 2
Notional tax on previous transfers
£(350,000 − 325,000) =   £25,000

Work out tax
£25,000 × 20% =   £5,000

Net value of transfers b/f £(350,000 − 5,000)   £345,000

Step 3	£
Net transfers in 7 years prior to this transfer	345,000
Add: value of this transfer	420,000
Aggregate net chargeable transfer	765,000

Step 4
Deduct tax threshold @ 31.5.10
£(765,000 − 325,000) =   £440,000

Step 5
Work out tax
£440,000 × 1/4 =   £110,000

Step 6
Tax on current transfer £(110,000 − 5,000) =   £105,000

Step 7
Chargeable transfer to carry forward in cumulation is:
£(420,000 + 105,000) =   £525,000

Once again, you will see that the tax on the current transfer is £420,000 × 25% = £105,000 as all of the transfer is chargeable above the tax threshold.

Grossing-up does not apply where the transferee agrees to pay the tax.

Source: *HMRC Inheritance Tax: Customer Guide*

Website: www.hmrc.gov.uk/cto/customerguide/page1.htm

See *British Tax Reporter* ¶602-450.

6630   Meaning of lifetime 'estate'

A person's estate is the total of all the property to which he is beneficially entitled. 'Property' includes rights and interests of any description. A person who has a general power which enables him, or would if he were of full age, to dispose of any property other than settled property, or to charge money on any property other than settled property, will be treated as beneficially entitled to the property or money. 'General power' means a power or authority enabling the person by whom it is exercisable to appoint or dispose of property as he thinks fit. Therefore, property would include:

- houses, cars, land, caravans, any real property;
- shares, debentures, mortgages, insurance policies;
- options, rights, easements;
- businesses, woodlands, agricultural property;
- money whether in banks, building societies, or found at home;
- furniture, paintings, sculptures;
- beneficial interests in settled property.

Law: IHTA 1984, s. 5, 272

See *British Tax Reporter* ¶624-000.

6660 Meaning of 'disposition'

A transfer of value is any 'disposition' made by a person ('the transferor') as a result of which the value of his estate immediately after the disposition is less than it would be but for the disposition (see 6525). The word 'disposition' is not defined in the legislation, though it is stated that a disposition includes a disposition effected by 'associated operations' (see 6670). However, the word clearly has a very wide meaning.

Loans

There is an element of disposition where a person is allowed the use of money on soft terms or is allowed the use of property for less than full 'rent'; hence, exemptions apply as if it were an outright gift. The waiver of a loan would also appear to be a disposition, though HMRC only accepts that a loan made between individuals has been waived by the lender (so that the lender's estate is reduced for IHT purposes by the amount of the loan released) if the waiver is effected by deed.

Dispositions by omission

It is also provided in the legislation that where the value of a person's estate is diminished and that of another person's estate (or of settled property in which no interest in possession subsists) is increased by the omission to exercise a right, he will be treated as having made a disposition at the latest time when he could have exercised that right, unless he shows that the omission was not deliberate. Pension scheme benefits are often written into trust so that any pension is payable to the policyholder but if he dies before drawing the pension, a death benefit arises and is assigned directly to another individual rather than falling into his estate; where the policyholder is permitted to and does refrain from taking the pension with the intention of increasing the estate of such beneficiary then, if it is not clear that the policyholder's primary concern is to provide for his own retirement, HMRC may raise a claim under these provisions.

> ### Example
>
> Anthony owes Ben £150,000 for some capital equipment that he purchased. Anthony decides not to pay Ben and Ben decides not to take any action against Anthony. Ben has made a disposition in respect of the £150,000 debt that he has failed to claim from Anthony.

Non-resident trusts

If a settlor fails to exercise a right to recover CGT from a trustee of a non-resident trust where trust gains are treated as his (see 5637), this may fall to be regarded as a transfer of value.

Survivorship clauses

Dispositions made subject to a survivorship clause (whether on survival or death) are treated as effected when the potential entitlement arises. Dispositions which do not involve the transfer of property until a date more than 12 months thereafter do not give rise to a transfer until the later event.

Law: IHTA 1984, s. 3(3), 29, 92, 262; *Duke of Northumberland v A-G* [1905] AC 406

See *British Tax Reporter* ¶607-900.

6670   Associated operations

A 'transaction' includes a series of transactions and any associated operations. The statutory definition of 'associated operations' is any two or more operations of any kind being:

- operations affecting the same or related property or income arising from that property; or
- any two operations which are directly or indirectly related to each other,

whether those operations are effected by the same person or different persons, and whether or not they are simultaneous; and 'operation' includes an omission.

Example 1

William, who has already made previous chargeable transfers and is liable to IHT at the rate of 20 per cent, transfers property to his wife Betty who has made no previous chargeable transfers. This is an exempt transfer and, therefore, no tax is payable. However, before transferring the property, William obtains Betty's agreement to transfer it to certain discretionary trusts. When Betty transfers the property HMRC will treat William as the transferor since these are associated operations and William will be liable for any IHT.

It could be argued that if there is an obligation on Betty (wife) to pass on the property to Charlie, then Betty at no time becomes owner. If, however, William transfers to Betty property of which she becomes the owner with the option of either keeping the property or transferring it to Charlie or any other person, then it is argued this will not be viewed as an associated operation but good tax planning.

Example 2

Michael owns a set of four paintings worth £200,000, but individually only worth £25,000 each. He gives two of the paintings to Lynne in 2007. In 2010 he gives Lynne the other two in the set. Michael will be treated as having made a transfer of value of £200,000 by associated operations.

Where there are associated operations the transfer of value is treated as taking place at the time of the last of the operations. If the earlier operation is also a transfer of value it will

Inheritance Tax

reduce the value transferred by all the operations unless the earlier transfer is exempted as a transfer between spouses.

The House of Lords has held that to be chargeable, the associated operation must form part of, and contribute to, a scheme which confers a gratuitous benefit.

Grant of a lease

Leases granted for full consideration in money or money's worth are not associated with any operation effected more than three years after the grant, and no operation effected after 26 March 1974 will be taken to be associated with an operation effected before that date.

Law: IHTA 1984, s. 268; *Macpherson v IR Commrs* [1988] BTC 8,065

Source: *HMRC Inheritance Tax: Customer Guide*

Website: www.hmrc.gov.uk/cto/customerguide/page1.htm

See *British Tax Reporter* ¶608-150.

6675   Operation of the Ramsay principle

From the line of cases beginning with *W T Ramsay Ltd v IR Commrs* [1982] AC 300, it has been established that if a transaction or a series of transactions contains a step which has no commercial purpose apart from the avoidance or mitigation of tax, and at the time the step was taken the whole process was pre-ordained so as to produce a given result, the courts have power to ignore the inserted step and treat the series of transactions as one composite transaction for tax purposes.

On the face of it, this principle bears a certain resemblance to the associated operations rule for IHT discussed at 6670. Most of the cases through which the *Ramsay* principle evolved were concerned with CGT, but it is now clear that its scope is much wider. The first case in which the applicability of the rule to IHT was considered, albeit obiter, concerned an (unsuccessful) attempt to pass down property free of tax by means of two deeds executed on two consecutive days. The judge said that had he been asked to decide on the issue, he would have read the two deeds together on the basis that the parties never intended the situation brought about by the first deed to last more than one day.

On inter-spouse transfers, HMRC have said in a letter dated 20 September 1985 to the ICAEW that 'the circumstances of such transfers always need to be carefully examined to ensure, among other things, that the transaction has substance as well as form. For example, an understanding between the spouses on the ultimate destination of the assets would be important in this connection.'

In one case, HMRC chose to attack a scheme to avoid CTT on the basis of the *Ramsay* principle rather than the associated operations rule. Following the death of the tenth Earl

Fitzwilliam, the executors considered various proposals for mitigating CTT on the distribution of his large estate. The scheme finally adopted involved use of the surviving spouse exemption (the transitional relief retained after estate duty), the relief for distributions within two years of death out of a discretionary trust set up by will, the relief for mutual transfers, and the provisions then in force relating to the termination of an interest in possession and reverter to settlor. The taxpayers argued that by deft manipulation of these provisions they had achieved the appointment of some £3.8m out of the estate to one of the beneficiaries without incurring any liability to tax. HMRC issued notices of determination on the basis that the steps taken to mitigate tax constituted a single! composite transaction within the *Ramsay* principle. The House of Lords held that, on the evidence, the steps taken were not pre-ordained from the beginning, and did not fulfil the conditions previously laid down by the House: there was no person whose guiding will could procure that the scheme as planned would be carried out nor could it be said that there had been no practical or real likelihood that the scheme would not be completed.

Law: *Countess Fitzwilliam v IR Commrs* [1993] BTC 8,003

See *British Tax Reporter* ¶608-650.

6690 Voidable transfers

Where a chargeable transfer has been set aside as voidable through law, any IHT paid or payable will be repaid or not payable as the case may be. The transfer is treated as if it had never taken place for IHT purposes. The chargeable transfer may be set aside as voidable or otherwise defeasible by virtue of an enactment or rule of law.

Law: IHTA 1984, s. 150

See *British Tax Reporter* ¶615-000.

6710 Annuity purchased in conjunction with a life policy

Where a life insurance policy is issued, made, varied or substituted after 26 March 1974 and an annuity on the life of the insured is purchased and the benefit of the policy is vested in someone other than the person who purchased the annuity, then a transfer of value will be treated as having been made, unless it can be shown that the making of the insurance and the purchase of the annuity were not associated operations (see 6670). The person who purchased the annuity will be treated as having made the transfer of value by a disposition at the time the benefit of the policy became vested.

The value transferred is the lesser of:

(1) the total of:

   (a) the price of the annuity; and

(b) the premium paid or consideration given under the policy on or before the transfer; or

(2) the greatest value capable of being conferred at any time by the policy calculated as if that time were the date of the transfer.

Example

John, who expects to die shortly, buys an annuity for £1,500,000 which will give him £150,000 for the rest of his life, and concurrently John's daughter Molly assures her father's life for £1,450,000. The first premium payable is £150,000, and the annuity payments are set against this and subsequent premiums. If John then died Molly would receive £1,450,000. However, John is treated as having made a transfer of value to Molly when the benefit of the policy is vested in her. The value transferred is the lesser of:

(1) the price of the annuity (£1,500,000) plus any premium paid on or before the transfer (£175,000) which together make it £1,675,000; and

(2) the greatest value capable of being conferred at any time by the policy as if that time were the date of the transfer (£1,450,000).

Therefore, the value transferred is treated as being £1,450,000.

Law: IHTA 1984, s. 263

See *British Tax Reporter* ¶630-600.

6720 Timing and order of transfers

It is important to establish clearly the precise date of any lifetime transfers since reliefs (small gifts and annual exemptions) and any additional IHT charge on death may be affected. The most important rules are as follows.

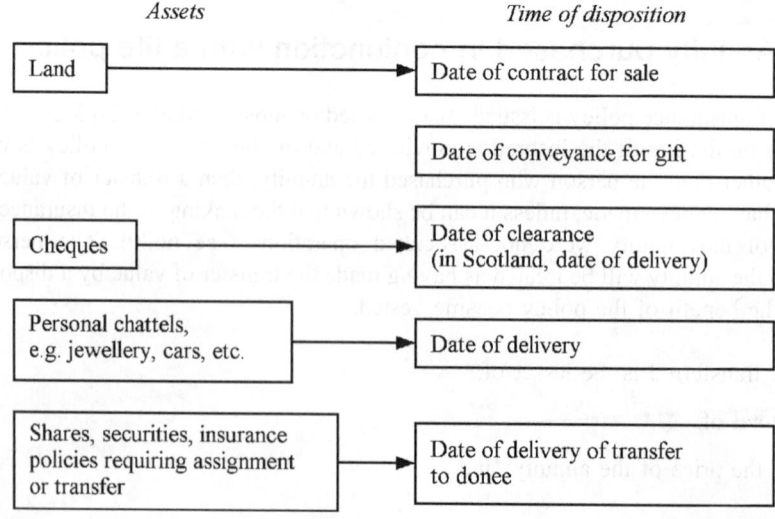

Assets	*Time of disposition*
Land	Date of contract for sale
	Date of conveyance for gift
Cheques	Date of clearance (in Scotland, date of delivery)
Personal chattels, e.g. jewellery, cars, etc.	Date of delivery
Shares, securities, insurance policies requiring assignment or transfer	Date of delivery of transfer to donee

Where the value transferred by more than one chargeable transfer made by the same person on the same day depends on the order in which the transfers are made, they will be treated as made in the order which results in the lowest value chargeable. The rate at which tax is charged on such transfers is the effective rate at which tax would have been charged if those transfers had been a single chargeable transfer of the same total value.

Example

Tim transfers £290,000 each to discretionary trusts A and B on the same day, 8 September 2009. The total IHT payable is £51,000 and each trust will bear half the charge. Had the transfers been on different days, the earlier transfer would not have incurred a tax charge and the later a charge to £51,000.

If a transferor makes two transfers on the same day, the earlier one not required to be grossed up and the later one requiring grossing up, then the total IHT is calculated by treating the later transfer as having been made first.

Law: IHTA 1984, s. 266

See *British Tax Reporter* ¶614-850.

PRE-OWNED ASSETS

6725 Overview

For 2005–06 onwards an income tax charge arises on benefits received by the former owners of property, referred to as pre-owned assets. Broadly, the charge applies to individuals (the chargeable person) who continue to receive benefits from certain types of property they once owned after 17 March 1986 but have since disposed of.

The property within the scope of the charge can be grouped into three headings:

- land;
- chattels; and
- intangible property.

If the chargeable person has either disposed of any property within these headings by way of gift or, in some circumstances, sale, or contributed towards the purchase of the property in question and they continue to receive some benefit from the property they are potentially liable to the charge. The benefit may be occupation of the land, use of the chattel or the ability to receive income or capital from a settlement holding intangible property.

Certain transactions are excluded from the charge (see below). There are also provisions exempting the relevant property from the charge where the property is subject to a charge to inheritance tax or where specific protection from inheritance tax is given by legislation.

Inheritance Tax

The conditions required for the charge to apply are virtually identical where the property in question is land or chattels but they differ slightly in respect of intangible property.

6730 Land and chattels

The charge applies where the chargeable person occupies any land or uses or possesses any chattels, either alone or with other persons, and either the 'disposal condition' or the 'contribution condition' is met.

Broadly, the disposal condition will apply if the chargeable person, at any time after 17 March 1986, owned relevant land or chattels, or other property whose disposal proceeds were directly or indirectly applied by another person towards the acquisition of the relevant land or chattels, and then disposed of all or part of their interest in the relevant land or chattels (or other property).

The contribution condition will apply if the chargeable person, at any time after 17 March 1986, provided any of the consideration given by another person for the acquisition of an interest in the relevant land or chattel, or for the acquisition of any other property, the proceeds of the disposal of which were directly or indirectly applied by another person towards an acquisition of an interest in the relevant land or chattel. As with the disposal condition, if the provision of the consideration qualifies as an excluded transaction, this condition will not apply.

Intangible property

The charge applies where the chargeable person settles intangible property or adds intangible property to a settlement after 17 March 1986 on terms that any income arising from the settled property would be treated under ITTOIA 2005, s. 624 (income arising under a settlement where the settlor retains an interest) as income of the chargeable person as settlor and any such income would be so treated even if s. 624(2) did not include any reference to the spouse of the settlor.

Excluded transactions

There are a number of situations where a charge to tax will not arise. Certain transactions are excluded from the charge and there are also exemptions from the charge where certain conditions are met. The concept of excluded transactions has no application to intangible property. They only serve to exclude from the income tax charge certain transactions relating to land and chattels.

For the purposes of the disposal conditions relating to land and chattels, the disposal of any property is an excluded transaction in relation to the chargeable person if:

- it was a disposal of their whole interest in the property, except for any right expressly reserved by them over the property, either by a transaction made at arm's length with a person not connected with them, or by a transaction such as might be expected to be made at arm's length between persons not connected with each other;

- the property was transferred to their spouse or civil partner, or former spouse or civil partner where the transfer has been ordered by a court;
- the disposal was by way of gift (or in accordance with a court order for the benefit of a former spouse or civil partner) by virtue of which the property became settled property in which his spouse or civil partner or former spouse or civil partner is beneficially entitled to an interest in possession. The spouse or civil partner must take an interest in possession from the outset. It is not an excluded transaction, however, if the interest in possession of the spouse or civil partner or former spouse or civil partner has come to an end other than on their death unless the spouse or civil partner or former spouse or civil partner has become absolutely entitled to the property in which case it would be accepted that the benefit of the exclusion is not lost;
- the disposal was a disposition falling within IHTA 1984, s. 11 (disposition for maintenance of family);
- the disposal is an outright gift to an individual and is wholly exempted from inheritance tax by either IHTA 1984, s. 19 (£3,000 annual exemption); or s. 20 (£250 small gifts exemption).

For the purposes of the contribution conditions relating to land and chattels, the provision by the chargeable person of consideration for another's acquisition of any property is an excluded transaction in relation to the chargeable person if:

- on its acquisition the property became settled property in which their spouse or civil partner or former spouse or civil partner is beneficially entitled to an interest in possession. The spouse or civil partner must take an interest in possession from the outset. It is not an excluded transaction, however, if the interest in possession of the spouse or civil partner or former spouse or civil partner has come to an end otherwise than on their death unless the spouse or civil partner or former spouse or civil partner has become absolutely entitled to the property; or the other person was their spouse or civil partner, or former spouse or civil partner where the transfer has been ordered by a court;
- the provision of the consideration constituted an outright gift of cash by the chargeable person to the other person and was made at least seven years before the earliest date on which the chargeable person occupied the land or had possession or use of the chattel;
- the provision of the consideration is a disposition falling within IHTA 1984, s. 11 (maintenance of family);
- the provision of the consideration is an outright gift to an individual and is for the purposes of IHTA 1984 a transfer of value that is wholly exempt by virtue of s. 19 (£3,000 annual exemption) or s. 20 (£250 small gifts exemption).

Gifts with reservation

The charging provisions also do not apply to a person at a time when, for IHT purposes, the relevant property or property deriving its value from relevant property falls within the Gifts with Reservation provisions set out in FA 1986 (FA 2004, Sch. 15, para 11(3)) See 6785.

De minimus

An exemption from charge applies where in relation to any person in a year of assessment, the aggregate of the amounts specified below in respect of that year do not exceed £5,000.

The tax charge

The approach to valuing property for the purpose of the pre-owned assets rules is generally the same as for IHT purposes (IHTA 1984, s. 160). In other words, it is the price that the property might reasonably be expected to fetch if sold in the open market at that time, without any scope for a reduction on the ground that the whole property is to be placed on the market at one and the same time.

The valuation date for property subject to the charge is 6 April in the relevant year of assessment or, if later, the first day of the taxable period.

When valuing relevant land or a chattel it is not necessary to make an annual revaluation of the property. The property should rather be valued on a five-year cycle. Before the first five-year anniversary the valuation of the property will be that set at the first valuation date. Thereafter the valuation at the latest five-year anniversary will apply.

6740 Land

The chargeable amount in relation to the relevant land is the appropriate rental value, less the amount of any payments which the chargeable person is legally obliged to make during the period to the owner of the relevant land in respect of their occupation.

The appropriate rental value is:

$$R \times \frac{DV}{V}$$

where

R is the rental value of the relevant land for the taxable period;
DV is:

- where the chargeable person owned an interest in the relevant land, the value as at the valuation date of the interest in the relevant land that was disposed of by the chargeable person or, where the disposal was a non-exempt sale, the 'appropriate portion' of that value;
- where the chargeable person owned an interest in other property, the proceeds of which were used to acquire an interest in relevant land, such part of the value of the relevant land at the valuation date as can reasonably be attributed to the property originally disposed of by the chargeable person or, where the original disposal was a non-exempt sale, to the appropriate portion of that property;
- if the contribution condition applies, such part of the value of the relevant land at the valuation date as can reasonably be attributed to the consideration provided by the chargeable person;

V   is the value of the relevant land at the valuation date.

The 'rental value' of the land for the taxable period is the rent which would have been payable for the period if the property had been let to the chargeable person at an annual rent equal to the annual value. The annual value is the rent that might reasonably be expected to be obtained on a letting from year to year if the tenant undertook to pay all taxes, rates and charges usually paid by a tenant, and the landlord undertook to bear the costs of the repairs and insurance and the other expenses, if any, necessary for maintaining the property in a state to command that rent.

FA 2004, Sch. 15, para. 4(4) introduces the concept of a 'non-exempt sale' for a disposal which is a sale of the chargeable person's whole interest in the property for cash, but which is not an excluded transaction as defined in para. 10. The 'appropriate proportion', which is relevant for ascertaining the appropriate rental value is calculated as follows:

$$M - \frac{P}{MV}$$

where

MV   is the value of the interest in land at the time of the sale; and
P   is the amount paid.

6750   Chattels

The chargeable amount in relation to any chattel is the appropriate amount, less the amount of any payments that the chargeable person is legally obliged to make during the period to the owner of the chattel for the possession or use of the chattel by the chargeable person.

The appropriate amount is:

$$N \times \frac{DV}{V}$$

where

N   is the amount of the interest that would be payable for the taxable period if interest were payable at the prescribed rate on an amount equal to the value of the chattel at the valuation date. The prescribed rate is the official rate of interest at the valuation date.

6755   Intangible property

The chargeable amount in relation to the relevant property is:

$$N - T$$

where

N   is the amount of the interest that would be payable for the taxable period if interest were payable at the prescribed rate on an amount equal to the value of the relevant property at

Inheritance Tax

the valuation date. The prescribed rate is the official rate of interest at the valuation date;

T   is the amount of any income tax or CGT payable by the chargeable person in respect of the taxable period by virtue of any of the following provisions: ITTOIA 2005, s. 624 or TCGA 1992, s. 86; so far as the tax is attributable to the relevant property.

IHT election

The provisions of the pre-owned assets legislation are optional. The reason for this is that the provisions are simply a device to prevent the avoidance of IHT by exploiting gaps in the gifts with reservation legislation. The legislation has therefore provided taxpayers the opportunity to opt back into the IHT rules. Such an option has to be made by the taxpayer in the form of an election.

There is a time-limit for making an election, which is the same as the self-assessment deadline for making a return for the tax year in which an individual is first liable for the pre-owned assets charge. From 21 March 2007 HMRC may accept late elections for IHT treatment that would otherwise be too late.

HMRC state that they will accept late elections where an event occurs which is 'beyond the chargeable person's control'. In general, HMRC will accept a late election if the chargeable person can show that an event beyond their control prevented them from sending the election by the relevant filing date. If the chargeable person was able to manage the rest of their private or business affairs during the period in question, HMRC are unlikely to accept that they were genuinely prevented from delivering the election on time. Examples of such circumstances include an unforeseen event disrupting the normal postal service; loss of records, etc. through fire, flood or theft; serious illness; or the death of a close relative or partner.

 In addition, there may be cases where, given the overall circumstances, HMRC will accept a late election even where the chargeable person cannot show that the reasons for the late election were beyond their control. Essentially, this will be where the chargeable person can show that they were unaware – and could not reasonably have been aware – that they were liable to an income tax charge under Sch. 15, and elected within a reasonable time of becoming so aware.

Law: *Finance Act 2007, s. 66; FA 2004, Sch. 15; Income Tax (Benefits Received by Former Owner of Property) (Election for Inheritance Tax Treatment) Regulations 2007 (SI 2007/3000); Charge to Income Tax by Reference to Enjoyment of Property Previously Owned Regulations 2005 (SI 2005/724)*

Website: www.hmrc.gov.uk/poa/poa_guidance.htm

Source: IHT500: *Election for inheritance tax to apply to asset previously owned*

TRANSFERS ON DEATH

6770 Charge to IHT on death

Where an individual dies, IHT is charged on his estate as if he had made a transfer of value of the whole of his estate immediately before his death (see 6525). This is a deemed transfer of value. The usual effect is that on death, one of the first jobs of the executor is to value the deceased's assets.

Law: IHTA 1984, s. 4(1)

Source: *HMRC Inheritance Tax: Customer Guide*

Website: www.hmrc.gov.uk/cto/customerguide/page1.htm

See *British Tax Reporter* ¶624-000.

MEANING OF 'ESTATE' ON DEATH

6780 Types of property included in death estate

A person's estate is the aggregate of all the property to which he is beneficially entitled, except that the estate of a person immediately before his death does not include 'excluded property' (see 7397). Included in the estate of the deceased would be:

- *real property* (land and interests in land), including any property over which he had a general power of appointment (unless that property over which he had a general power of appointment was settled property);
- *chattels* – cars, jewellery, furniture, boats, etc.;
- *insurance policies* where the deceased was entitled to be paid a sum of money;
- *a business or interest in a business*;
- *superannuation schemes' lump sums* payable by right to the deceased's personal representatives (but not generally annuities so payable but for which an option has been exercised for them to be paid to the former spouse or dependant: HMRC's views on benefits, the practice of not charging most death benefits and failure to exercise a power to nominate a beneficiary are set out in a statement of practice and notes issued by HMRC (see also 6660));
- *shares and securities*, either quoted or unquoted;
- *debts due* to the deceased (unless recovery is not reasonably practicable and has not been made so by the actions of the deceased);
- *settled property* in which the deceased had an interest in possession (or would have had if the administration of an estate had been completed). The estate of a deceased person does not include an interest in settled property where the person became beneficially entitled to the interest in possession on or after 22 March 2006, and the interest in

possession is not an immediate post-death interest, a disabled person's interest, and not a transitional interest;

- *the undivided share of a tenant in common*;
- *the undivided and severable share of a joint tenant*;
- *cash* in banks or building societies or in the deceased's possession;
- *property subject to a reservation in favour of the deceased* (see 6785).

Survivorship clauses

Dispositions made subject to a survivorship clause (whether on survival or death) are treated as effected when the potential entitlement arises.

For details of types of property specifically excluded from the estate at death, see 6790.

Law: IHTA 1984, s. 5(1), s. 5(1A), 91, 92, 152, 166; *Anand v IR Commrs* (1996) Sp C 107, *Marquess of Linlithgow & Anor v R & C Commrs* [2010] BTC 487

Source: SP E3, Superannuation schemes; SP 10/86, *Death benefits under superannuation arrangements*

See *British Tax Reporter* ¶624-250.

6782   Deductions from the estate on death

Liabilities may generally be offset only to the extent that reimbursement cannot reasonably be expected.

Allowance is made for reasonable funeral expenses, including the cost of mourning and a tombstone or gravestone.

Where property is situated outside the UK, an allowance may be made against the value of the property to be included in the estate for expenses incurred in administering or realising the property, where they are attributable to the situation of the property. This is subject to an upper limit of five per cent of the gross value of all foreign property in the estate.

Law: FA 1986, s. 103; IHTA 1984, s. 162, 172, 173

Source: ESC F1, *Mourning*; SP7/87, *Inheritance tax: reasonable deduction for funeral expenses*; HMRC Inheritance Tax: Customer Guide

Website: www.hmrc.gov.uk/cto/customerguide/page1.htm

See *British Tax Reporter* ¶625-450.

6785   Gifts with reservation: introduction

Where an individual dies and immediately before his death there is any property which in relation to him is property subject to a reservation, that property is treated for IHT purposes as property to which the individual was beneficially entitled before his death.

Where, after 17 March 1986, an individual disposes of property by way of gift, except for certain specified exempt transfers (see 6787), and either:

(1)   possession and enjoyment of the property is not bona fide assumed by the donee at or before the beginning of the 'relevant period' (see also substitutions and accretions at 6788); or

(2)   at any time in the relevant period the property is not enjoyed to the entire exclusion, or virtually to the entire exclusion, of the donor and of any benefit to him by contract or otherwise (see 6786),

the property concerned is referred to as 'property subject to a reservation'. For settled gifts, see 6789.

The 'relevant period' is a period ending with the individual's death and commencing seven years before or on the date of the gift, if it is later.

It is possible that the gifts-with-reservation rules result in a double charge. For example, a gift to discretionary trusts where the settlor is an object of the discretion would not be potentially exempt and would therefore be chargeable. The property would also fall into charge on the settlor's death under the gifts-with-reservation rules. Regulations eliminate such double charges (see 6830).

Where property ceases to be property within (1) or (2) above, the transferor is treated as making a 'potentially exempt transfer' (see 6610) at the date of such cessation.

Agricultural property and business property

Business and agricultural property reliefs (see 7253, 7292) are preserved in respect of property which is included in the transferor's estate because it was the subject of a gift with reservation. Special provision is necessary because ownership (and occupation, in the case of agricultural property) will usually have been assumed by the transferee, thus rendering it impossible for the transferor to meet the qualifying conditions in respect of the transfer immediately before death. Accordingly, in determining whether the property qualifies for relief, the transferee's occupation and ownership (taken in combination, where necessary, with the transferor's) is counted.

Law: FA 1999, s. 104; FA 1986, s. 102 and Sch. 20, para. 8; *Lyon's Personal Representatives & Ors v R & C Commrs* (2007) SpC 616

Source: *HMRC Inheritance Tax: Customer Guide*

Website: www.hmrc.gov.uk/cto/customerguide/page1.htm

See *British Tax Reporter* ¶625-350.

6786 Gifts with reservation: property not enjoyed to exclusion of donor

In determining whether any property falls to be regarded as disposed of by a gift with reservation as being property not enjoyed to the entire exclusion, or virtually the entire exclusion, of the donor and of any benefit to him by contract or otherwise (see 6785), the following points should be noted.

'Virtually' is not defined, though HMRC have expressed the view that property is enjoyed to 'virtually' the entire exclusion of a donor where the benefit to him is small.

A benefit received by the donor by virtue of 'associated operations' (see 6670) is treated as a benefit to him by contract or otherwise and there are specific rules for certain land, chattels and life policies. In particular, in the case of property which is an interest in land or a chattel, retention or assumption by the donor of actual occupation or actual enjoyment or actual possession of the property shall be disregarded if it is for 'full consideration in money or money's worth'. Further, in the case of an interest in land any occupation by the donor of the land or part is disregarded if:

- it results from an unforeseen change in the donor's circumstances not designed to exploit the provision; and
- it occurs when the donor has become unable to maintain himself through old age or infirmity; and
- it represents reasonable provision for the donor by the donee; and
- the donee is a relative of the donor or his spouse.

To determine whether the donor is entirely excluded from benefit, it is necessary to identify the subject-matter of the gift. There is a difference between giving away property and then retaining some interest (which would constitute reservation of a benefit) and carving out a lesser interest from that which is owned and giving away that lesser interest (no reservation of a benefit).

Some of the old estate duty cases give illustrations of this distinction. In one such case, the deceased gave away grazing land to his son and then later entered into partnership with his son, the grazing land being brought in as partnership property. It was held that the deceased was not excluded from benefit in respect of the land and it was dutiable on his death. However, in another case, the deceased agreed with his children that his business as grazier should be carried on by them as partners but with himself as manager. Ten years later he gave part of the grazing land to each child, subject to the partnership agreement. It was held that the subject-matter of each gift was the appropriate portion of the land subject to the partnership rights. In those circumstances there was no reservation of benefit and the land was not dutiable on the death of the deceased.

Applied to settled property, the reservation-of-benefit rules are not triggered if the donor retains a reversionary interest or if the reversion comes back to him by operation of law. The donor is treated as making a partial gift in those circumstances.

However, if the donor is an object of a discretionary trust, he is treated as not entirely excluded from benefit and the whole of the settled fund will be included in his estate on death. It is the HMRC view that if the donor can become eligible to benefit under a discretionary trust because of a power contained in the settlement, he will be treated as reserving a benefit. If the donor is trustee of a settled property, that, of itself, will not trigger the reservation-of-benefit/exclusion-from-property rules. The result is the same where there is entitlement to reasonable remuneration for acting as trustee. Where, however, the settlor can use his position as trustee to obtain a personal benefit, e.g. where trust shares give him majority voting rights in a company in which he owns shares beneficially, the result may be otherwise.

The original rules introduced in 1986 were intended to prevent the avoidance of the IHT charge on death through a lifetime gift aimed at reducing the value of the donor's estate for the purposes of the tax, without the donor having to give up enjoyment of the asset concerned. In *IR Commrs v Eversden*, the Court of Appeal held that the rules do not work when gifts made by a married person are routed through a trust for their spouse. Further to this, where gifts to a spouse are made on or after 20 June 2003:

- the property becomes settled property by virtue of the gift;
- the trusts of the settlement give an interest in possession to the donor's spouse, so that the gift is exempt from IHT by reason of the exemption for transfers between spouses and the rule which treats an interest in possession as equivalent to outright ownership;
- between the date of the gift and the donor's death the interest in possession comes to an end; and
- when that interest in possession comes to an end, the beneficiary does not become beneficially entitled to the settled property, or another interest in possession in it.

Gifts from 2005–06 onwards

Over recent years various schemes have been marketed which use artificial structures to avoid the existing rules about gifts made with reservation (see above). Broadly, such schemes enabled people to remove assets from their taxable estate but continue to enjoy all the benefits of ownership. *Finance Act* 2004 introduced a measure to block this sort of avoidance by implementing an income tax charge on this type of transaction from 2005–06 onwards (see 6725 above). The charge will not apply to the extent that:

- the property in question ceased to be owned before 18 March 1986;
- property formerly owned by a taxpayer is currently owned by their spouse or civil partner;
- the asset in question still counts as part of the taxpayer's estate for inheritance tax (IHT) purposes under the existing 'gift with reservation' (GWR) rules;
- the property was sold by the taxpayer at an arm's length price, paid in cash: this will not be restricted to sales between unconnected parties;

- the taxpayer was formerly the owner of an asset only by virtue of a will or intestacy which has subsequently been varied by agreement between the beneficiaries; or
- any enjoyment of the property is no more than incidental, including cases where an out-and-out gift to a family member comes to benefit the donor following a change in their circumstances.

There is a *de minimus* threshold of £5,000 per year.

Gifts of interests in land made after 8 March 1999

For gifts of interests in land made on or after 9 March 1999, the gift is treated as being a gift with reservation if there is some interest, right or arrangement which enables or entitles the donor to occupy the land concerned to a material degree without paying full consideration.

The change does not apply to a gift where:

- the right or interest concerned is negligible so that the donor is virtually entirely excluded from any enjoyment of the land;
- the donor may occupy the land or enjoy some right in relation to it only when the interest that he/she has given away comes to an end;
- the gift is made more than seven years after the right or interest concerned is granted or acquired;
- the gift is itself covered by the main exemptions from IHT, including transfers between spouses; or
- the donor is effectively forced to reoccupy the land concerned due to some unforeseen downturn in his/her financial circumstances.

The gift of an undivided share in land, which the donor occupies jointly with the other owner ('donee') will not be a gift with reservation, providing the donor receives no material benefit at the donee's expense in connection with the gift. This puts on a statutory footing the *Hansard* statement on joint occupation issued by the minister in 1986.

Law: FA 2004, s. 84 and Sch. 15; FA 2003, s. 185; FA 1999, s. 104; FA 1986, s. 102A–102C and Sch. 20, para. 6, 7; *IR Commrs v Eversden* [2003] EWCA Civ 668; *Chick v Commr of Stamp Duties* [1958] AC 435; *Commr for Stamp Duties of New South Wales v Perpetual Trustee Co Ltd* [1943] AC 425; *Munro v Commr of Stamp Duties* [1934] AC 61

Source: *HMRC Inheritance Tax: Customer Guide*

Website: www.hmrc.gov.uk/cto/customerguide/page1.htm

See *British Tax Reporter* ¶625-350.

6787 Gifts with reservation: exclusion of specified exempt transfers

The gifts-with-reservation rules (see 6785) do not apply if, or to the extent that, the gift is an exempt transfer of any of the following kinds:

- transfers between spouses or civil partners (see 7192);
- small gifts (see 7223);
- gifts in consideration of marriage or civil partnership (see 7229);
- gifts to charities (see 7195);
- gifts to political parties (see 7195);
- gifts to housing associations (see 7196);
- gifts for national purposes (see 7198);
- maintenance funds for historic buildings (see 7040);
- employee trusts (see 7005).

Law: FA 1986, s. 102(5)

See *British Tax Reporter* ¶614-350.

6788 Gifts with reservation: substitutions and accretions

If at any time before 'the material date' the donee ceases to have the possession and enjoyment of gifted property subject to a reservation or any part of it, the gifts-with-reservation rules (see 6785) apply instead to any property received by the donee in substitution for such property as he ceases to possess and enjoy, in addition to any gifted property retained by him.

The relevant rules prevent the avoidance of the gifts-with-reservation rules where the donee replaces property and allows the donor some benefit from the property substituted.

The 'material date' means the date of the donor's death, or any earlier date on which the property ceases to be subject to a reservation.

These rules do not apply to property which becomes settled by virtue of the original gift, or to sums of money in sterling or any other currency.

If the donee disposes of the gifted property for less than full consideration or for no consideration he is treated as continuing to have possession and enjoyment of it, unless the property has been returned to the donor.

Where the donee acquires a further interest in property in which he already has an interest resulting from a gift with reservation, the merger of the two interests will not prevent the transaction from being one whereby the donee voluntarily divests himself of property. He is therefore treated as continuing to have enjoyment and possession of the property subject to a reservation.

Bonus and rights issues

Where shares or debentures are comprised in a gift, and the donee receives a bonus issue or a rights issue in respect of those shares or debentures, the additional shares or debentures are treated as comprised in the original gift.

Donee predeceasing the material date

If the donee dies before the 'material date' (see above) the acts of the donee's personal representatives are deemed to be his acts and, consequently, his trustees are treated as continuing to have the possession and enjoyment of the property. He is treated as having voluntarily divested himself of the gifted property in favour of his legatees.

Law: FA 1986, Sch. 20, para. 1–4

See *British Tax Reporter* ¶614-600.

6789   Gifts with reservation: settled gifts

The rules relating to accretions and substitutions (see 6788) do not apply where the property subject to a reservation becomes settled as a result of the gift by the donor. However, the other rules relating to gifts with reservation (see 6785) still apply; as regards exclusion of benefit in relation to reversions to settlor and the settlor becoming an object of the trust, see 6786. Further, those rules apply to any property comprised in the settlement which consists of property originally settled by the donor or represents or is derived from such property.

If the settlor dies without having released his interest in the settled property, the property subject to a reservation and comprised in the original gift will be included in his estate on death for IHT purposes (see 6780).

If, however, the settlement terminates before the material date, i.e. before the release of the settlor's interest or his death, special tracing rules apply to determine which of the settled property is to be treated as comprised in the original gift. Where such a settlement terminates, in whole or in part, then the following are treated as comprised in the original gift:

- any property which, had the settlor died immediately before the termination, would have been treated as comprised in the gift, except any such property to which the settlor becomes absolutely and beneficially entitled, together with
- any consideration given by the settlor for any property to which he becomes absolutely and beneficially entitled.

Law: FA 1986, Sch. 20, para. 5

See *British Tax Reporter* ¶614-750.

6790 Exclusions from estates of deceased

Certain types of property are excluded when calculating the value of a person's estate on death. These are:

- 'excluded property' (see 7397);
- an interest in or under a registered pension scheme, a qualifying non-UK pension scheme or a section 615(3) scheme or by way of remuneration for acting as trustee, if it ends on that person's death;
- overseas pensions from certain former colonies that become payable on death (also excluded are returned contributions);
- reversion to settlor on death of an interest in possession in settled property, unless the settlor purchased that reversion;
- interest in possession passing to settlor's spouse or civil partner, on death of deceased, unless the spouse or civil partner was not domiciled in the UK at the time of death or the settlor or his spouse had purchased the reversion. A 'spouse' includes a widow or widower if the settlor dies less than two years before the deceased.
- certain payments received under schemes which provide compensation for wrongs suffered during the Second World War era are left out of account in determining the chargeable value of the estate for the purposes of IHT on death.

Foreign bank accounts of persons who were not domiciled in the UK and who were not resident or ordinarily resident there immediately before death, are left out of account in determining the value of the person's estate immediately before death.

Law: IHTA 1984, s. 54, 90, 151, 153, 157

Source: ESCF20 Late compensation for World War II claim schemes

See *British Tax Reporter* ¶625-850.

6800 IHT rates on death

Except as noted below, IHT is charged on a death at the full rates laid down in the Table in IHTA 1984, Sch. 1 as if the deceased had made a transfer of value immediately before death and the value transferred had been equal to the value of the estate at that time; unless Parliament specifically provides otherwise, the threshold(s) included in the Table are indexed. There is therefore in general no grossing-up on death and for 2010–11 a single rate of 40 per cent applies where the value of the estate together with other gross cumulative transfers exceeds £325,000. The steps in the calculation are:

Step 1

Work out the value of the chargeable estate (after reliefs and exemptions).

Step 2

Ascertain the transferor's total of chargeable transfers in the seven years before death.

Step 3

Add the values in Step 1 and Step 2 to create an 'aggregate chargeable transfer'.

Step 4

Deduct the tax threshold (the amount up to which tax is payable at 0% ascertained at the date of death) from the aggregate chargeable transfer. If the aggregate chargeable transfer is below the tax threshold there is no tax to pay on the death estate.

Step 5

Work out the tax at full rate (i.e. 40%) on the value ascertained in Step 4 (i.e. the excess over the tax threshold).

Step 6

If the value in Step 2 (the lifetime transfers) exceeds the tax threshold, repeat Steps 4 and 5 with the value in Step 2. Deduct this notional tax from the tax on the aggregate chargeable transfer to calculate the tax on the estate.

Example

Yvonne dies on 8 April 2010 leaving an estate of £330,000 which is chargeable to IHT, having made transfers amounting to £126,000 within the previous seven years.

The tax on the estate is calculated as follows:

Steps 1–3	£
Transfers in 7 years prior to death	126,000
Add: value of estate	330,000
Aggregate chargeable transfer	456,000

Step 4	
Deduct tax threshold @ 8/4/10	
£(456,000 − 325,000) =	£131,000

Step 5	
Work out tax	
£131,000 × 40% =	£52,400

Step 6
Transfers in the 7 years before death are below the tax threshold so no adjustment for tax on this value needs to be made.

Law: IHTA 1984, s. 7–9 and Sch.1

Source: *HMRC Inheritance Tax: Customer Guide*

Website: www.hmrc.gov.uk/cto/customerguide/page1.htm

See *British Tax Reporter* ¶6-020.

6801   Taper relief

Where tax, or additional tax, becomes due because the donor dies within seven years of making a lifetime gift, relief is available if more than three years have elapsed between the date of the gift and the date of the death. The amount of the charge is tapered as follows:

More than	But less than	Percentage of full rate
3 years	4 years	80
4 years	5 years	60
5 years	6 years	40
6 years	7 years	20

It should be noted that it is the rate of tax, rather than the value transferred, that is tapered.

For examples of the application of taper relief, see 6802.

Law: IHTA 1984, s. 7(4)

Source: *HMRC Inheritance Tax: Customer Guide*

Website: www.hmrc.gov.uk/cto/customerguide/page1.htm

See *British Tax Reporter* ¶611-400.

6802   PET becomes chargeable

No tax is due on a potentially exempt transfer (PET) at the time that it is made. If the donor survives seven years, the transfer becomes exempt, but if the donor dies within seven years of the date of the PET, then the transfer is brought into charge.

The steps in the calculation are:

Step 1

Work out the value of the PET (i.e. work out the loss to the transferor as the result of the transfer, deduct reliefs and exemptions).

Inheritance Tax

Step 2

Ascertain the transferor's total of chargeable transfers in the seven years before the PET. Remember that this will include both lifetime chargeable transfers and PETs – but only those made within the seven years before death.

Step 3

Add the values in Step 1 and Step 2 to create an 'aggregate chargeable transfer'.

Step 4

Deduct the tax threshold (the amount up to which tax is payable at 0% ascertained at the date of the death) from the aggregate chargeable transfer. If the aggregate chargeable transfer is below the tax threshold there is no tax to pay on the PET.

Step 5

Work out the tax at full rate (i.e. 40%) on the value ascertained in Step 4 (i.e. the excess over the tax threshold).

Step 6

If the value in Step 2 (the previous lifetime transfers) exceeds the tax threshold, repeat Steps 4 and 5 with the value in Step 2. Deduct this notional tax from the tax on the aggregate chargeable transfer to calculate the death tax on the PET.

Step 7

Check whether taper relief is available. If so, take the appropriate percentage of the death tax to arrive at the tax payable as a result of the PET coming into charge.

Example

Reginald dies on 22 May 2010. He had given his daughter Elinor a gift of £150,000 in September 2005 and his son Brian a gift of £150,000 in March 1999. He had also made a chargeable lifetime transfer of £200,000 in June 2004. For the purposes of this example, the annual exemption is ignored.

As a result of Reginald's death, IHT is payable on the gift to Elinor. The gift to Brian is exempt as it is a PET made more than 7 years before death.

The tax on the gift to Elinor is:

Step 1–3	£
Transfers in 7 years prior to PET	200,000
Add: value of PET	150,000
Aggregate chargeable transfer	350,000

Step 4
Deduct tax threshold @ 22/5/10
£(350,000 − 325,000) =   £25,000

Step 5
Work out tax
£25,000 × 40% =   £10,000

Step 6
Transfers in the 7 years before this transfer are below the tax threshold so no
adjustment for tax on this value needs to be made.

Step 7
Death occurred between 4 and 5 years after gift and taper relief applies, so that
60% of the death tax is payable.
Tax payable is £10,000 × 60% =   £6,000

Law: IHTA 1984, s. 7, 131–140, Sch. 2, para. 1A

Source: *HMRC Inheritance Tax: Customer Guide*

Website: www.hmrc.gov.uk/cto/customerguide/page1.htm

See *British Tax Reporter* ¶612-850.

6803 Death within seven years of a chargeable lifetime transfer

Where a donor dies within seven years of making a chargeable lifetime transfer, tax must be recalculated using the full rates applicable at death. If this amount, after any taper relief, exceeds the tax payable at the time of the transfer, additional tax is payable.

The steps in the calculation are:

Step 1

Write down the value of the chargeable lifetime transfer (already ascertained in lifetime).

Step 2

Calculate the transferor's total of chargeable transfers in the seven years before the lifetime transfer. Remember that this will include both lifetime chargeable transfers and also PETs made within seven years before death.

Step 3

Add the values in Step 1 and Step 2 to create an 'aggregate chargeable transfer'.

Step 4

Deduct the tax threshold (the amount up to which tax is payable at 0% ascertained at the date of the death) from the aggregate chargeable transfer. If the aggregate chargeable transfer is below the tax threshold there is no death tax to pay (see also Step 8).

Step 5

Work out the tax at full rate (i.e. 40%) on the value ascertained in Step 4 (i.e. the excess over the tax threshold).

Step 6

If the value in Step 2 (the previous lifetime transfers) exceeds the tax threshold, repeat Steps 4 and 5 with the value in Step 2. Deduct this notional tax from the tax on the aggregate chargeable transfer to calculate the death tax on the current transfer.

Step 7

Check whether taper relief is available. If so, take the appropriate percentage of the death tax to arrive at the adjusted death tax on the lifetime transfer.

Step 8

Deduct any lifetime tax already paid, to give the additional tax on the transfer as the result of death. If the lifetime tax is equal to or exceeds the adjusted death tax, there is no further tax to pay (but no repayment of lifetime tax).

Example

Peter dies on 2 June 2010. He made a gift into a discretionary trust on 2 April 2005 of £280,000 on which the trustees paid the lifetime tax of £3,400. He also made a gift to his sister of £110,000 in December 2004 and a previous gift to the trust in January 1999 of £38,000. For the purposes of this example, the annual exemption is ignored.

The death tax payable on the transfer to the trust in April 2005 is:

	£
Steps 1–3	
Transfers in 7 years prior to this transfer	148,000
Add: value of the current transfer	280,000
Aggregate chargeable transfer	428,000
Step 4	
Deduct tax threshold @ 2/6/10	
£(428,000 − 325,000) =	£103,000
Step 5	
Work out tax	
£103,000 × 40% =	£41,200

Step 6
Transfers in the 7 years before this transfer are below the tax threshold so no adjustment for tax on this value needs to be made.

Step 7
Death occurred between 5 and 6 years after gift and taper relief applies, so that the adjusted death tax is 40% of the death tax.

Adjusted death tax is £41,200 × 40% =   £16,480

Step 8
Additional tax payable on death is:

£16,480 − 3,400   £13,080

Law: IHTA 1984, s. 7 and Sch. 2, para. 2

Source: *HMRC Inheritance Tax: Customer Guide*

Website: www.hmrc.gov.uk/cto/customerguide/page1.htm

See *British Tax Reporter* ¶624-100.

6804   Transfers within seven years before death

Relief is available where a PET becomes chargeable or additional IHT becomes payable in respect of a transfer other than a PET, because of the death of the transferor within seven years, and either:

- there has in the intervening period been a fall in value of the gifted property in the transferee's hands; or
- the transferee has previously sold the property outright to an unconnected purchaser at arm's length for a price which is lower than its value at the date of the original transfer.

In these circumstances, unless the property is tangible moveable property which is a wasting asset, the transferee can elect to calculate any additional tax payable on the lower value or sale price. The market value for this purpose may be enhanced or reduced by reference to the difference brought about by any change in circumstances between the time of the transfer and the death/sale.

Law: IHTA 1984, 131–140

See *British Tax Reporter* ¶611-100.

Inheritance Tax

6805 Instruments of variation and disclaimers

If, within two years of death, a disposition is varied or disclaimed, the disclaimer or variation is treated as if made by the deceased and will not be a transfer of value by the beneficiary. It is possible to vary an inheritance under a will, the distribution of an estate on intestacy or the passing of an interest in property held as joint tenants by survivorship and to disclaim a gift. Tax will then be charged as though the deceased had left the estate as so varied, not as had originally passed on death. Accordingly, if tax has already been paid on the death estate, and less tax is due following the variation or disclaimer, the difference may be reclaimed from HMRC.

To qualify for this treatment, the variation or disclaimer must take place within two years after the death and must be made in writing by the original beneficiary or beneficiaries. In the case of a variation (not a disclaimer) written notice must be given to HMRC, within six months after the date of the variation, but for variations made after 31 July 2002 there is no longer any need to notify HMRC unless extra IHT results. Although execution of certain documents by deed is vital, it is not necessary for alterations of dispositions taking effect on death but, as a prudent precaution, a deed is normally used.

If one of the beneficiaries dies before a variation is made, HMRC take the view that the legal personal representatives of the deceased beneficiary may enter into a variation and sign an election.

When a variation results in more IHT being payable, the personal representatives must join in the notice to HMRC.

A second variation which alters the dispositions made by an earlier variation does not fall within the relief even if both are effected within the two-year period.

Variations and disclaimers do not affect the IHT due where a gift with reservation is brought into charge under the provisions discussed at 6785.

Rectification

The High Court has rectified deeds of variation to correct errors which, if left uncorrected, would have nullified the tax saving which the documents were intended to achieve.

However, rectification is likely to be refused where there is no adequate evidence of what the parties intended.

Applications to the court for family provision and 'legitim'

Where as a result of an application under the *Inheritance (Provision for Family and Dependants) Act* 1975 an order is made making reasonable financial provision for the applicant out of the deceased person's estate, IHT is payable on the estate as though the estate had been distributed ab initio subject to the provisions of the order. Thus, if the order has the effect of depriving a person of property received, either by gift or by bequest, on which tax may have been payable, the tax charge can be adjusted in consequence of the order.

In Scotland the surviving spouse and descendants of the deceased are entitled to claim a fixed share of the estate, called legal rights; the child's share is known as legitim. These rights may be renounced in favour of the provisions in the deceased's will. Where the estate is insufficient to meet claims for legitim on the basis of an intended disposition to the spouse, the executors or judicial factor of the testator may choose whether IHT should be charged on the basis that any disposition to the spouse is fully paid out or reduced by any legitim not renounced.

Distributions within two years of death out of discretionary trust set up by will

A similar relief is available where a distribution is made within two years of death out of a discretionary trust set up by the will of the deceased (see 7023).

Law: IHTA 1984, s. 142, 146, 147, 218A; *Racal Group Services Ltd v Ashmore* [1995] BTC 406; *Matthews v Martin* [1991] BTC 8,048; *Seymour v Seymour* [1989] BTC 8,043; *Lake v Lake* [1989] BTC 8,046; *Russell v IR Commrs* [1988] BTC 8,041; *Re Slocock's Will Trusts* [1979] 1 All ER 358

Source: Revenue interpretation, 'Inheritance tax: Variation of inheritance following a death', Inland Revenue, *Tax Bulletin*, February 1995, p. 194; Revenue interpretation, ' Post Death Variation of inheritance by survivorship', Inland Revenue, *Tax Bulletin*, October 1995, p. 254

6810 Value transferred on death and subsequent disposals

There is a deemed transfer of value immediately before death of the whole of the deceased's estate (see 6770). The value of any property for IHT purposes is generally the price it might reasonably be expected to fetch if sold in the open market at that time (see 6570), though there are certain reliefs and liabilities to be taken into account on death (see below).

If the deceased was a sole trader or a member of a partnership, the business assets (including goodwill) must be calculated and any liabilities deducted – the valuation will be on the basis that the business is a going concern unless more could be realised by discontinuing the business and selling the assets. Chattels, including cars, furniture, jewellery, collections, boats, etc. will generally be accepted at the executor's valuation, but professional valuations should be carried out for such things as antiques, etc. Debts owed to the deceased will form part of his estate at face value unless they are impracticable to recover. Life policies are valued as the amount assured, plus any bonus or share of profit.

Law: IHTA 1984, s. 5

See *British Tax Reporter* ¶602-400.

6815 Reliefs in relation to disposals shortly after death

Shares

If 'qualifying investments' are sold within 12 months of death at a lower value than at death or, in certain cases, it is otherwise recognised that they lose their value within that time frame, relief can be claimed.

'Qualifying investments' comprise 'quoted' (see 6571) investments, holdings in authorised unit trusts and shares in a common investment fund. The relief is calculated by adding together the price received from the sale of all qualifying investments within the 12-month period and subtracting this figure from the value as at the date of death. If shares or securities are bought within the period from the date of death and two months after the last sale within the 12 months after death, the relief may be wholly or partly lost.

Example

Personal representatives of Arnold sell shares quoted at £4,000 on his death for £3,000. Therefore, the value of shares on death will be reduced by £1,000. They purchase further shares for £2,000. Part of the relief of £1,000 will be lost, calculated as follows:

$$\frac{2,000}{3,000} \times £1,000 = £666.66$$

Thus, the value of shares on death will be treated as £3,333.34.

If a person other than a trustee or personal representative purchases further shares then they must be of the same description as those sold.

The relief also applies to loss in value recognised within the 12-month period by cancellation of the investments (a notional sale for £1 immediately before cancellation) or by suspension of 'listing' (a notional sale at market value at the 12-month date).

Land

If 'land' is sold within three years of death for less than its valuation at death, the sale price may be substituted, provided that the sale price was the best reasonably obtainable in an arm's length transaction between unconnected persons. Again, sales at a loss and sales at a profit in the three year period are netted off and the relief is restricted for purchases made within 4 months of the last sale in the three year period.

Sales in the fourth year after death at a loss are deemed to be made in the three year period. Sales at a profit in the fourth year are ignored. Fourth year sales do not affect the restriction for purchases.

'Land' is defined as including buildings and interests in land. Therefore a lease would be within the definition.

Related property

Where related property is sold within three years of death by the person in whom the property became vested on death or by the deceased's personal representatives, and the sale price is less than the value determined and the value is less than that determined in accordance with the related property provisions (see 6575), the value on death may be redetermined by ignoring the related property provisions and instead using the value that would have applied had the property in question been valued on its own.

Example

Mavis owns half an antique tea set. Her husband owns the other half. Individually, each half of the tea set is valued at £4,000. However, the complete set has a value of £20,000. Mavis dies. Under the related property provisions (see 6575), her property is valued as a 50 per cent share of the whole set, i.e. 50 per cent of £20,000 = £10,000.

However, six months after her death, Mavis's daughter, who was left her mother's half of the tea set on her death, sells it for £6,000. As the actual sale price is less than the value determined in accordance with the related property provisions of £10,000, the value at death is redetermined, ignoring the related property provisions. Taking the half-tea set alone, the value at death is revised to £4,000.

Law: IHTA 1984, s. 178–198

See *British Tax Reporter* ¶627-900.

Inheritance Tax

6818 Treatment of liabilities

Any liabilities due at death together with the interest thereon are deductible provided they were incurred for full consideration in money or money's worth.

However, no deduction is allowed in respect of the liabilities of the deceased to the extent that the creditor has received gifts from the deceased. If and to the extent that it is shown that the loan was not made to the deceased out of property derived from him or out of consideration provided by someone who had in his resources property derived from the deceased, the disallowance will not operate (see 6782).

In valuing the deceased's estate no account is taken of liabilities arising in connection with a policy of life assurance made after 30 June 1986 unless the sums assured form part of the deceased's estate immediately before death.

Reasonable funeral expenses are deductible, but executorship and administration costs are not. If the property is located outside the UK there is a special relief for the additional cost of administration arising through the location of the property, but the allowance cannot exceed five per cent of the gross value of all foreign property in the estate.

Law: IHTA 1984, s. 5(3)–(5)

See *British Tax Reporter* ¶617-400.

6820   Quick succession relief

Where the value of a person's estate was increased by a chargeable transfer made not more than five years before his death, the IHT chargeable on death is reduced by a percentage of the tax charged on so much of the value transferred by the first transfer as is attributable to the above increase. The relief applies only where there has been a transfer to the deceased within five years before his death and where the second occasion of charge is his death. The percentages are:

- 100 per cent if the first transfer is made within one year of death;
- 80 per cent if the first transfer is made within two years of death;
- 60 per cent if the first transfer is made within three years of death;
- 40 per cent if the first transfer is made within four years of death;
- 20 per cent if the first transfer is made within five years of death.

Relief is calculated using the formula:

$$\text{tax on gift} \times \frac{\text{increase in second transferor's estate}}{\text{value transferred}} \times \text{percentage}$$

If there is more than one later transfer, the reduction is only available in respect of the earliest of them. However, if the reduction is less than the whole of the IHT charged, a reduction may be made in respect of the later transfers (in chronological order) until reductions representing the whole of that tax have been made.

Any 'excluded property' (see 7397) consisting of a reversionary interest to which the transferor became entitled on the occasion of, or before, the chargeable transfer, will be disregarded in determining the increase in his estate from a chargeable transfer.

Relief is thus given by way of credit against the IHT bill attributable to the later transfer.

Example

Richard dies and as part of his will he makes a chargeable transfer of £140,000. It is assumed that tax of £10,000 was payable on the gift.

Eighteen months later, Anne dies. In calculating the tax payable on her estate, quick succession relief is available in respect of the bequest by Richard as follows:

$$£10,000 \times \frac{(£140,000 - £10,000)}{£140,000} \times 80\% = £7,428$$

Law: IHTA 1984, s. 141

See *British Tax Reporter* ¶627-400.

6830 Avoidance of double charge

Regulations eliminate a double charge to IHT by setting off the value transferred by one transfer against the value transferred by another or by setting the tax paid on one transfer against the tax paid on another or by both. The regulations deal with situations where, as a result of the provisions relating to PETs and gifts with reservations (see 6610, 6785ff.), the same property forms or is treated as forming part of one person's estate more than once for IHT purposes.

The regulations apply so as to charge whichever of the transfers produces the higher amount of tax. The transfer which produces the lower amount of tax is then ignored.

Law: FA 1986, s. 104; *Inheritance Tax (Double Charges Relief) Regulations* 1987 (SI 1987/1130)

See *British Tax Reporter* ¶614-300.

INHERITANCE TAX AND SETTLED PROPERTY

SCOPE OF IHT CHARGES ON SETTLED PROPERTY

6880 Types of settled property for IHT

The *Finance Act* 2006 introduced changes to the inheritance tax (IHT) treatment of trusts that are the most far-reaching reforms of capital taxation for some 20 years. The announcement of the changes in the March 2006 Budget led to widespread criticism from the professions and the financial press. The professions were particularly concerned that a consultation process on trusts had been ongoing for two years with no mention of the proposed reform to IHT. Whilst a number of amendments were made at Committee stage, the changes mean that the majority of trusts will now be subject to the 'relevant property' rules in IHTA 1984, Pt. III that were previously restricted to discretionary trusts.

Interest in possession trusts created before 22 March 2006 will continue to be taxed under the old rules as long as the interest of the life tenant benefiting at that date continues. If an interest in possession comes to an end during the life tenant's lifetime, the trust will fall within the discretionary trust regime subject to transitional rules for trusts created before 22 March 2006. Under the transitional rules, where the trust is replaced by a further interest in possession trust, the new interest in possession trust will be taxed under the old rules.

Accumulation and maintenance trusts created before 22 March 2006 continued to be taxed under the old regime to 6 April 2008. From 6 April 2008, accumulation and maintenance trusts created before 22 March 2006 continued to be taxed under the old rules if the beneficiaries have the right to capital on or before the age of 18. Where the beneficiary in an existing accumulation and maintenance trust will take the trust assets absolutely no later than age 25, the trust will be taxed under the provisions for the new age 18-to-25 trusts. New trusts created on or after 22 March 2006 no longer qualify as accumulation and maintenance trusts.

From 18 March 1986 to 21 March 2006, lifetime gifts into accumulation and maintenance trusts and disabled trusts qualified as potentially exempt transfers. Gifts into interest in possession trusts qualified as PETs from 17 March 1987 to 21 March 2006. If the settlor survived seven years from the date of the gift, no tax was payable.

Transfers into discretionary trusts give rise to an immediate tax charge, where the value of the gift to the trust and any chargeable transfers made by the settlor in the seven years prior to the creation of the trust exceed the level of the nil rate band, at half the rates set out in IHTA 1984, Sch. 1. If the settlor then dies within seven years, extra tax might be payable if the amount chargeable (at full rates) at the time of death, after taper relief, exceeded the amount paid when the transfer was made.

From 22 March 2006, only lifetime gifts to another individual, into a disabled trust (7011), into a bereaved minor's trust (7033) on the coming to an end of an immediate post-death interest and the creation of a transitional serial interest will qualify as PETs. If the settlor survives seven years from the date of the gift, no tax will be payable.

Lifetime gifts to other trusts are chargeable transfers and will give rise to an immediate tax charge where the value of the gift to the trust and any chargeable transfers made by the settlor in the seven years prior to the creation of the trust exceed the level of the nil rate band, and will be charged at half rates set out in IHTA 1984, Sch. 1. If the settlor then dies within seven years, extra tax might be payable if the amount chargeable (at full rates) at the time of death, after taper relief, exceeds the amount paid when the transfer was made.

Example

In May 2010, Robin created a trust, the assets of which amounted to £150,000, under which the income was payable to his daughter, Jenny, for life, with the remainder to Jenny's daughter, Emma. Chargeable transfers in the previous seven years amounted to £100,000. He has used his annual exemptions.

As the value of the gift to the trust and the chargeable transfers made in the previous seven years (ignoring annual exemptions) is below the nil rate band of £325,000, no tax is payable on the transfer to the trust.

> **Example**
>
> If Robin had made chargeable transfers of £200,000 in the previous seven years, an immediate tax charge would arise on the gift to the trust.
>
> £350,000 – £325,000 = £25,000 @ 20% = £5,000

If, in the second example above, Robin had created the trust in February 2006, the gift to the trust would have qualified as a PET. If he had survived seven years from the date of the gift, no tax would have been payable.

Law: FA 2006, s. 156 and Sch. 20; IHTA 1984, s. 43–93

Source: *HMRC Inheritance Tax: Customer Guide*

Website: www.hmrc.gov.uk/cto/customerguide/page1.htm

See *British Tax Reporter* ¶600-800.

6883 Creation of a settlement

The first occasion upon which most types of settlement are now penalised in comparison with transfers between individuals is when property is settled. If the trust is created on or after 22 March 2006 and is not a trust for the disabled, a transitional serial interest, or bereaved minor's trust on the coming to an end of an immediate post-death interest, the transfer is not a potentially exempt transfer. Tax is chargeable – at half rates – when the transfer is made where the transfer to the trust and any chargeable transfers made by the settlor in the seven years prior to the creation of the trust exceed the level of the nil rate band. If the settlor dies within seven years after making the transfer, extra tax may be payable to bring the total up to the full rates applicable at the time of the death.

Where a settlement terminates due to the impossibility of achieving its purposes, a charge to tax may arise.

> **Example**
>
> Charles creates a settlement for the benefit of his children, and transfers £100,000 into the settlement. Tax is payable on the creation of the settlement. Charles dies without having any children. The purposes of the settlement have failed and so the settlement terminates. A charge to tax will arise on the termination.

See *British Tax Reporter* ¶670-500.

6884 Variation of an existing settlement

It may be desirable for the trustees of an existing settlement to vary its purposes, either under a power given to them in the terms of the trust, or by application to the court under the *Variation of Trusts Act* 1958, s. 1 (or the *Trusts (Scotland) Act* 1961, s. 1). Such a variation could give rise to a charge to inheritance tax, depending on the effect which it has on the nature of the beneficiaries' interests. For example, if the variation involves property being made over to a beneficiary absolutely, a charge may arise. Likewise, the creation or termination of an interest in possession may have tax consequences.

> ### Example
>
> Trustees hold £500,000 in a settlement in which no interest in possession subsists. The trust is varied in such a way that a beneficiary becomes entitled to receive one-fifth of the income arising. Inheritance tax will be payable by the trustees on £100,000. If the tax is paid out of the £100,000, no grossing-up is required; if it is paid out of other trust funds, grossing-up is required.

6885 Distributions and appointments by trustees

Generally, any distribution to a beneficiary out of the trust fund is an event likely to give rise to a charge to tax. The same is true where an interest in possession is created in property in which no such interest previously subsisted.

The charge is not avoided by making dispositions to beneficiaries by indirect means, e.g. by an omission by the trustees to exercise a right, or by causing settled property to become 'excluded property'. Certain distributions/dispositions made by trustees are not chargeable to tax. These include:

(1)   costs and expenses of administration of the settlement;

(2)   payments of income to beneficiaries;

(3)   a grant of a tenancy of agricultural land for full consideration;

(4)   a commercial bad bargain which reduces the value of the settled fund but where there was no gratuitous intent;

(5)   gifts to charities, political parties and gifts for national purposes (provided certain conditions are fulfilled).

6886 Depreciatory transactions

Where the trustees of a settlement enter into an agreement with a beneficiary, potential beneficiary or a person connected with either, and because of the agreement the value of the settlement is reduced, then there is a charge to tax on that reduction. A commercial arrangement between the trustees and a beneficiary, where there is no gratuitous intent, is not a depreciatory transaction and will not give rise to a charge.

Examples of depreciatory transactions are the granting of a lease at less than the market rent; the granting of a loan of money at less than market rates; and a sale at an undervalue.

6887   Ten-yearly charge on 'discretionary' settlements

For trusts created before 22 March 2006, the ten-yearly or 'principal charge' only applied to discretionary trusts (i.e. settled property in which no interest in possession subsists). Following the changes in the *Finance Act* 2006, all new trusts created on or after 22 March 2006 during the lifetime of the settlor will be subject to the 'discretionary trust' regime, the only exceptions being trusts for the disabled and where new interest in possession trusts are created out of existing ones before 6 April 2006.

The principal charge arises on the tenth anniversary of the commencement of the settlement, and subsequent anniversaries at ten-yearly intervals. The rate of tax is 30 per cent of the appropriate lifetime rate.

> ### Example
>
> Alistair leaves property to Basil and Charles for those of his children (Wendy, Xavier, Yvonne and Zak) as Basil and Charles, in their absolute discretion, see fit. There is an interest in possession in the property for the first three years. Ten years after the discretionary trust has been set up, a charge to IHT arises on the value of 'relevant property' (see 6940) in the trust. The value of the property will be reduced by twelve-fortieths in arriving at the amount chargeable to tax (three years' interest in possession outside the discretionary trust).

6889   Meaning of settlement and settlor, etc.

The meaning of a settlement for inheritance tax purposes is in IHTA 1984, s. 43(2), which states that 'settlement' means any disposition or dispositions of property whether effected by instrument, by parol or by operation of law, or partly in one way and partly in another, whereby the property is for the time being:

(1)   held in trust for persons in succession or for any person subject to a contingency;

(2)   held by trustees on trust to accumulate the whole or part of any income of the property or with power to make payments out of that income at the discretion of the trustees or some other person with or without power to accumulate surplus income; or

(3)   charged or burdened (otherwise than for full consideration in money or money's worth paid for his own use or benefit to the person making the disposition) with the payment of any annuity or other periodical payment payable for a life or any other limited or terminable period.

or would be so held or charged or burdened if the disposition or dispositions were regulated by the law of any part of the UK; or whereby, under the law of any other country, the administration of the property is for the time being governed by provisions equivalent in effect to those which would apply if the property were so held, charged or burdened.

One settlement or more than one

It is important to identify in any disposition or dispositions whether one settlement or more than one settlement has been created. For example, every discretionary trust created before 27 March 1974 has its own inheritance tax rate scale. Also, when interests are appointed out of settled property, it is important to know how many settlements exist in order to determine the possibility of certain property qualifying for relief or becoming excluded.

Leases for life

A lease of property which is for life or lives, or for a period ascertainable only by reference to a death, or which is terminated on, or at a date ascertainable only by reference to a death, is treated as a settlement, and the property as settled property. Where a lease not granted as a lease at a rack rent is at any time to become a lease at an increased rent, it is treated as terminable at that time.

The exception is where the lease was granted for full consideration in money or money's worth; hence commercial transactions are not treated as giving rise to a settlement. A statutory tenancy is not a settlement.

Settlor

As a matter of general law, more than one person can be the settlor of the same settlement. The legislation defines 'settlor' in relation to a settlement to include any person by whom the settlement was made directly or indirectly, and in particular to include any person who has provided funds directly or indirectly for the purpose of or in connection with the settlement, or has made with any other person a reciprocal arrangement for that other person to make the settlement.

The legislation continues the definition in relation to multiple settlors, and states that where more than one person is a settlor in relation to a settlement and the circumstances so require, the settled property provisions of the Act shall apply in relation to it as if the settled property were comprised in separate settlements.

An example of a situation where the circumstances so require is where the trustees are resident abroad and tax must be recovered from the settlor. Thus, if A puts £20,000 into a settlement and B puts £40,000 into the same settlement, and the trustees are non-resident, the liability for tax due will be split between A and B in the ratio in which each put money into the trust. The trust itself will be held to be two trusts: A's trust and B's trust; and the tax will be due from each separately, not from both jointly.

It is important to identify the settlor or settlors because their identity and circumstances govern the rate of the ten-year charge for the discretionary trust regime; also, if the settlor is non-resident, then the settled property or part of it could be excluded property.

Trustee

From 6 April 2006, trustees of a settlement are treated as if they were a single person, distinct from the persons who are trustees of the settlement from time to time. Changes in the persona of the trustees have no effect on the trust as such, since the trustees are treated as a separate legal entity.

A bare trustee is not a trustee for inheritance tax purposes, because the property which he holds does not fall within the definition of settled property in IHTA 1984, s. 43(2) (see above). A 'bare' trustee means any person holding property to which another person is absolutely entitled (or would be so entitled if he were not an infant or under some other legal incapacity). Thus, for example, where a person entitled to an interest in possession in settled property becomes absolutely entitled to it, the property ceases at that moment to be settled property for tax purposes, and the person holding the legal title ceases to be a trustee.

Beneficiary

The term 'beneficiary' has no special meaning for inheritance tax. It includes an annuitant, a lessee for life, and (in Scotland) a proper liferenter. It includes anyone with either a present or a future right of enjoyment of settled property, including anyone with a contingent interest so long as the contingency is capable of being fulfilled.

The term also includes a person to whom the trustees have given a right of occupation of a dwelling-house comprised in the settled property, provided the rent paid is not a full market rent.

Law: TCGA 1992, s. 69(1); IHTA 1984, s. 43(2), (3), 44(1), (2); *Re Buttle's Will Trusts* [1977] 3 All ER 1039; *Re Ogle's Settled Estates* [1927] 1 Ch 22; *Vine v Raleigh* [1896] 1 Ch 37

INTEREST IN POSSESSION IN SETTLED PROPERTY

6903 Definition of 'interest in possession'

There is no statutory definition of 'interest in possession' in the legislation and, therefore, the ordinary rules of property law must be applied. References to an interest in possession include those to equivalent rights in Scotland. A reversionary interest is defined accordingly.

An interest in possession exists when the person having the interest has the immediate entitlement to any income produced by that property as the income arises. The Court of Session has held that an interest in possession was enjoyed where the settlor had an entitlement to income subject to the trustees' powers to appropriate income to meet capital depreciation or for any other reason they might deem necessary. It was held that on the true construction of the trust deed the trustees' powers were administrative only; they did not amount to a power to accumulate and did not prevent an interest in possession existing. Thus, an interest in reversion will not qualify as an interest in possession, whereas a life interest in property will so qualify.

> ### Example
>
> Anna leaves property to Bertie and Caroline upon trust for David for life with remainder to Edward. David has an interest in possession. Edward will acquire an interest in possession when David dies.

In HMRC's view, a discretion or power, in whatever form, which can be exercised after income arises so as to withhold it from that person, negates the existence of an interest in possession. For this purpose a power to accumulate income is regarded as a power to withhold it, unless any accumulations must be held solely for the person having the interest or his personal representatives. On the other hand, the existence of a mere power of revocation or appointment, the exercise of which would determine the interest wholly or in part (but which so long as it remains unexercised, does not affect the beneficiary's immediate entitlement to income) does not, in HMRC's view, prevent the interest from being an interest in possession. This broadly coincides with the House of Lords later decision in *Pearson v IR Commrs* [1981] AC 753.

Where there is no interest in possession in a dwelling-house, if the trustees permit a beneficiary to occupy it on a non-exclusive basis, this does not usually create an interest in possession. However, an interest in possession may be created indirectly by a direction not to sell the dwelling house. In one case, a testatrix (a tenant in common in the house) left her share of the house to her daughter. However, the executors of her will were directed not to enforce the sale of the house during the lifetime of the testatrix's spouse (the other tenant in common). On the death of the spouse, it was held that he had an interest in possession in the testatrix's share of the house. In another case concerning a trust for sale of a house, the settlor directed that the sale should be postponed for so long as any of the children desired to live there. One son lived in the house, the other did not. On the death of the son who lived in the house, it was held that both sons had an inter! est in possession and so only half of the value of the house was chargeable on the death.

Law: IHTA 1984, s. 46, 47; *Woodhall (as Personal Representatives of Woodhall dec'd) v IR Commrs* (2000) Sp C 261; *IR Commrs v Lloyd's Private Banking Ltd* [1998] BTC 8,020; *Pearson v IR Commrs* [1981] AC 753

Source: SP 10/79 *Power for a trustees to allow a beneficiary to occupy a dwelling-house*; IR press release 12 February 1976; *HMRC Inheritance Tax: Customer Guide*

Website: www.hmrc.gov.uk/cto/customerguide/page1.htm

See *British Tax Reporter* ¶671-900.

6906   Extent of interest in possession

A person beneficially entitled to an 'interest in possession' (see 6903) in settled property prior to 22 March 2006 is treated as beneficially entitled to the property in which the interest subsists, i.e. he is treated as owning it absolutely.

> ### Example
>
> Percy has a life interest in Whiteacre, the property passing to his two sons in equal shares on his death. Percy is treated as being beneficially entitled to the whole of Whiteacre. On Percy's death, the value of Whiteacre would be included in the value of his estate for IHT purposes.

Interest in part

If the person entitled to the interest in possession is entitled only to part of the income of the property, he is treated as being beneficially entitled to a proportionate share of that property.

> ### Example
>
> Jack is beneficially entitled to three-quarters of the income from Blackacre for the rest of his life. He is treated as being beneficially entitled to three-quarters of Blackacre.

If the beneficiary is entitled to a specific amount of income in a period, his interest is taken to subsist in such part of the property as produces that amount in that period.

A charge arising on the cessation of an annuity charged on property may be relieved by reference to the extent to which the value of the property in point reflects anticipated rent increases.

Where the person entitled to the interest is not entitled to any income of the property, but is entitled, jointly or in common with one or more other persons, to the use and enjoyment of the property, his interest is taken to subsist in such part of the property as corresponds to the proportion which the annual value of his interest bears to the aggregate of the annual values of his interest and that or those of the other or others.

From 22 March 2006, newly created interest in possession settlements are taxed under the discretionary trust (relevant property) regime unless the interest is an immediate post-death interest, transitional serial interest or a disabled person's interest.

Lease for life

Where a lease of property for life is treated as a settlement (see 6883), the lessee's interest in the property is taken to subsist in the whole of the property less such part of it as corresponds to the proportion which the value of the lessor's interest bears to the value of the property.

Law: IHTA 1984, s. 49(1), 50

Source: ESC F11, *Property chargeable on the ceasing of an annuity*; HMRC Inheritance Tax: Customer Guide

Website: www.hmrc.gov.uk/cto/customerguide/page1.htm

See *British Tax Reporter* ¶672-400.

6909   Charge to IHT on settled property where interest in possession

Consistent with the general rule that a tenant for life is treated as though he were beneficial owner of the settled property (see 6906), transactions involving the life interest are not actual transfers of value. However, subject to limited exceptions:

(1)   where a pre-22 March 2006 interest in possession comes to an end, otherwise than on the life-tenant's death, there is a deemed transfer of value equal to the value of the property in which the interest subsisted; this applies also for the purposes of certain exemptions if the transferor notifies the trustees of the availability thereof;

(2)   where the life tenant of a pre-22 March 2006 settlement disposes of his interest, the disposal is not an actual transfer of value, but is treated as the coming to an end of his interest, as above: there is a deemed transfer of value equal to the value of the property in which the interest subsisted, less any consideration received for the disposal.

It may therefore be seen that the usual method of valuing a disposition by reference to the fall in value of the transferor's estate (see 6612) is not applied in the case of deemed transfers of value by a life-tenant. Instead, the deemed transfer of value is measured by reference to the value of property in which the interest subsisted. Moreover, the value is measured in isolation, without reference to any similar property.

Example

Rupert owns 4,000 shares in S Ltd, an investment company, and is also the life-tenant of a settled fund which holds 2,000 shares. There are 10,000 issued shares. Values per share are agreed as follows:

% holding	£ per share
20	5
40	8
60	13

Clearly, if Rupert died, the value of the shares in both his free estate and in the settled fund of which he is a life-tenant would be valued at £13 per share as part of a 60 per cent holding (see 6906).

However, if Rupert assigns the whole of his life-interest, the value transferred will be measured as follows 2,000 shares × £5 = £10,000.

Where the interest is one to which the person became beneficially entitled on or after 22 March 2006, an actual or potential charge to tax will only arise in relation to the coming to an end of the interest only if the interest is an immediate post-death interest or a transitional serial interest and is not an interest in a bereaved minor's trust.

Prior to 22 March 2006, the rules governing PETs applied – whether or not that person was an individual – so that, provided the other conditions are satisfied, transfers or deemed transfers to or by a tenant for life were potentially exempt (see 6611).

> ## Example
>
> On 1 August 2004 Arnold settles £100,000 on trust for Billy for life, remainder to Cuthbert absolutely. Billy gives his interest to Diana on 1 December 2004. Both the August 2004 and December 2004 transactions are potentially exempt and there will be no IHT charge provided Arnold does not die before August 2011 and Billy before December 2011.

If Arnold had settled the property on trust on or after 22 March 2006 there would be an immediate charge to tax unless the interest is a transitional serial interest or a disabled person's interest.

An interest in possession to which a close company is entitled is attributed to its participators (see 6555); this applies for all IHT purposes, so that a charge can arise when a participator disposes of any part of his shareholding.

Where a close company became beneficially entitled on or after 22 March 2006 to an interest in possession, that interest will also include an immediate post-death interest or a transitional serial interest.

Trustees' annuities

An interest by way of annuity, etc. as commercial remuneration for a trustee's services is not subject to the charge.

Law: IHTA 1984, s. 51, 52, 57, 90

Source: *HMRC Inheritance Tax: Customer Guide*

Website: www.hmrc.gov.uk/cto/customerguide/page1.htm

See *British Tax Reporter* ¶672-400.

6910 Special rate of charge where property affected by PET

Anti-avoidance rules prevent property moving into discretionary trusts at reduced rates or free of IHT through the medium of short interests in possession. A special charge is imposed where:

(1) a PET is made after 16 March 1987 to an interest in possession settlement and within seven years the interest in possession comes to an end; and

(2) the settlor is alive when the interest in possession comes to an end; and

(3) any of the property in which that interest subsisted becomes settled property in which no qualifying interest in possession subsists.

> ### Example
>
> In October 2004, Alison settles £100,000 on Ben for life, remainder to discretionary trusts for Christopher and his issue. In December 2008, Ben surrenders his interest. But for the special rule, the £100,000 would pass to discretionary trusts free of IHT since both transfers would be potentially exempt.

A special rate of charge to IHT brings into the computation the settlor's cumulative total at the time of the creation of the settlement and the value of other property (if any) which passes at the termination of the life interest. That special rate of charge applies if it gives rise to a greater amount of tax than the tax that would otherwise be due.

> ### Example
>
> In July 2001, Annabel settles £130,000 on Bethany for life, remainder to discretionary trusts. Annabel had a cumulative total of £400,000 within the seven years before July 2003. Bethany dies in February 2002 when the settled property is worth £140,000. Bethany's free estate is worth £105,000.
>
> Special rate is:
>
> | | £ |
> |---|---|
> | £140,000 × 20% | 28,000 |
> | *Add*: tax attributable to Bethany's free estate | |
> | (see below: $^{105}/_{245}$ × £1,200) | 514 |
> | | 28,514 |

Tax on transfer of £140,000 by person with cumulative total of £400,000 at half 2001–02 rates.

	£
i.e. £140,000 × 20%	28,000
Add: tax attributable to Bethany's free estate (see below)	685
	28,685

The IHT that would have been paid on B's death, apart from the special charge is £245,000 at 2003–04 rates, i.e. £1,200 attributable $^{140}/_{245}$ free estate and $^{105}/_{245}$ settled property). The special rate therefore applies.

The special charge is recalculated if the settlor or life tenant subsequently dies.

Law: IHTA 1984, 54A, 54B

Source: *HMRC Inheritance Tax: Customer Guide*

Website: www.hmrc.gov.uk/cto/customerguide/page1.htm

See *British Tax Reporter* ¶674-200.

6912 Exceptions to deemed transfer of value rules

The deemed transfers of value mentioned at 6909 do not arise in various circumstances.

(1) If the person whose interest has come to an end becomes beneficially entitled to the property, or to another interest in possession in the property – unless the new interest is less valuable than the previous interest.

Example 1

Arthur transfers Whiteacre to Bertam and Christine upon trust for Daniel until he attains the age of 25 years and thereafter to Daniel absolutely. When Daniel attains the age of 25 years, his interest in possession in Whiteacre will end, but he will become absolutely entitled to the property so no IHT charge will arise.

Example 2

Arthur transfers Whiteacre and Blackacre to Bertram and Christine upon trust for Daniel until he attains the age of 25 years and, thereafter, Whiteacre is to be transferred to Daniel absolutely and Blackacre to Emily absolutely. Daniel will be treated as having made a transfer of value equal to the value of Blackacre and will be charged to IHT accordingly.

---

(2) If the settled property in question is 'excluded property' (see 7397).

(3)   If the interest comes to an end by being disposed of by the person beneficially entitled to it for a consideration in money or money's worth which is equal to or greater than the value of the interest disposed of. If the consideration for the interest is less than the value, there is a deemed transfer on the difference.

The value of any reversionary interest in the property, or of any interest in other property comprised in the same settlement, is left out of account.

(4)   Where the settlor becomes beneficially entitled to the property in which the interest in possession previously subsisted, provided that the settlor or his spouse had not acquired a reversionary interest in the property for a consideration in money or money's worth.

(5)   Where the interest in possession comes to an end and the settlor's spouse becomes beneficially entitled to the settled property in which the interest in possession previously subsisted, provided:

(a)   the settlor's spouse is then domiciled in the UK; and

(b)   neither the settlor nor the settlor's spouse had acquired a reversionary interest in the property for a consideration in money or money's worth.

Law: IHTA 1984, s. 52(2), 53, 54

Source: *HMRC Inheritance Tax: Customer Guide*

Website: www.hmrc.gov.uk/cto/customerguide/page1.htm

See *British Tax Reporter* ¶675-700.

6918   Transactions reducing the value of settled property

Where the value of settled property is reduced before the interest in possession comes to an end by a transaction between the trustees and a person connected with:

- the person beneficially entitled to an interest in the property; or
- a person beneficially entitled to any other interest in that property or to any interest in any other property comprised in the settlement; or
- a person for whose benefit any of the settled property may be applied,

then a corresponding part of the interest is treated as having come to an end. However, this is not so when, had the trustees been beneficially entitled to the property, the transaction would not have been a transfer of value.

Example

Mark transfers property worth £400,000 to James and Caroline upon trust for Thomas until he reaches the age of 25, and thereafter to Thomas absolutely. Shortly before Thomas reaches 25, James and Caroline sell him half of the settled property (worth

---

> £200,000) for one-quarter of its value (£50,000). Thus, the value of the settled property has been reduced by £150,000 which is three-eighths of the current value. Thomas's interest in three-eighths of the settled property is treated, for the purposes of the charge on termination of an interest in possession (see 6909), as having come to an end.

The House of Lords has held that an arrangement whereby certain paintings were taken out of the possession of the settlement for a specified period was a chargeable depreciatory transaction.

Where the interest is one to which the person became beneficially entitled on or after 22 March 2006, the above only apply where the interest is an immediate post-death interest, a disabled person's interest, or a transitional serial interest.

Law: IHTA 1984, s. 52(3); *Macpherson v IR Commrs* [1988] BTC 8,065

Source: *HMRC Inheritance Tax: Customer Guide*

Website: www.hmrc.gov.uk/cto/customerguide/page1.htm

See *British Tax Reporter* ¶673-150.

SETTLEMENTS WITH NO QUALIFYING INTEREST IN POSSESSION

6940 Types of settlement without qualifying interest in possession

There are special charges to IHT in respect of settlements with no qualifying interest in possession, other than 'privileged trusts' (see 6998). They are designed to ensure that there is a full charge to tax in respect of property held in such long-term trusts, once in every 30 years but spread over that time.

Relevant property

More specifically, the special rules apply in respect of relevant property. 'Relevant property' means settled property in which there is no qualifying interest in possession, other than certain types of property, e.g. property held for charitable purposes only. Property in a premiums trust fund or ancillary trust fund of a Lloyd's Name is not relevant property.

'Qualifying interest in possession' means an interest in possession to which an individual is beneficially entitled; it also applies to companies if their business consists wholly or mainly in the acquisition of interests in settled property, and the company has acquired the interest from an individual beneficially entitled to it for a full consideration in money or money's worth.

Property becoming settled on a death

For present purposes, will trusts, etc. are treated as if the property became comprised therein at the time of death.

Undistributed income

Undistributed income is taxed only if it is accumulated and from the date of accumulation.

Law: FA 1994, s. 248; IHTA 1984, s. 58, 59, 83, 84

Source: SP 8/86, *Inheritance tax: treatment of income of discretionary trusts*; *HMRC Inheritance Tax: Customer Guide*

Website: www.hmrc.gov.uk/cto/customerguide/page1.htm

See *British Tax Reporter* ¶674-050.

6943 The charge to IHT on settlements without a qualifying interest in possession

The principal charge to IHT on settlements without a qualifying interest in possession occurs immediately before a ten-year anniversary on the value of 'relevant property' (see 6940) in the settlement at that time. A 'ten-year anniversary' means the tenth anniversary of the date on which the settlement commenced and subsequent anniversaries at ten-yearly intervals; no date falling before 1 April 1983 can be a ten-year anniversary. The 'commencement of a settlement' is taken to be where property first becomes comprised in that settlement.

The other times at which tax will be charged are where property ceases to be relevant property, e.g. where someone obtains an interest in possession in that property, and where trustees make a disposition reducing the value of settled property which is not of the types mentioned below. Inheritance tax is charged on the reduction in value of the settled property or, if the tax is paid out of the relevant property, it will be charged on an amount which, after deducting tax, is equal to the amount by which the relevant property has been reduced.

From 22 March 2006, any new trust set up during lifetime or on death are subject to the relevant property regime unless it is:

- an immediate post-death interest;
- a transitional serial interest;
- an age 18–25 trust; or
- a trust set up for a disabled person.

Certain other trusts are excluded from the definition of 'relevant property', namely charitable trusts, maintenance funds for historic buildings, employee trusts and protective trusts.

No charge is incurred:

- where the event is within the first quarter after commencement of the trust or ten year anniversary; or
- on payments of costs or expenses (payment includes transfer of assets other than money); or
- where no gratuitous benefit was intended; or
- on property which becomes 'excluded property' (see 7397) by leaving the UK; or
- on property which becomes excluded property because it is invested in certain types of securities and the settlor (or in some cases a previous or subsequent settlor) was not domiciled in the UK at the time.

Law: IHTA 1984, s. 60, 61, 63–65, 82(2), (3)

Source: *HMRC Inheritance Tax: Customer Guide*

Website: www.hmrc.gov.uk/cto/customerguide/page1.htm

See *British Tax Reporter* ¶674–350.

6946   IHT on ten-year charge

Each period of ten years (see 6943) is divided into 40 quarters so that property is only charged to IHT for the period that the property is within the discretionary trust. Inheritance tax will be charged on the value of the property at the time of the charge, reduced by one-fortieth for each quarter that the property is outside the discretionary trust (a quarter being any period of three months).

> ### Example
>
> Alan transfers £500,000 into a discretionary trust in May 2000. In May 2010, the settlement fund is valued at £800,000. There have been no dispositions or distributions by the trustees in the ten-year period.
>
> Alan had made no transfers of value before setting up the settlement.
>
> | | £ |
> |---|---|
> | Value of relevant property | 800,000 |
> | Tax on transfer of £800,000 | 95,000 |
> | Effective rate $\dfrac{95,000}{800,000} \times 100\%$ | 11.88% |
> | Rate applicable is 30% × 11.885% = | 3.56% |
> | Tax payable £800,000 × 3.56% = | £28,480 |

The rules set out at 6950–6960 apply to settlements with a commencement date after 26 March 1974. Different rules apply in the case of settlements created before 27 March 1974.

Law: IHTA 1984, s. 63, 85

Source: *HMRC Inheritance Tax: Customer Guide*

Website: www.hmrc.gov.uk/cto/customerguide/page1.htm

See *British Tax Reporter* ¶674-350.

6950   Rate of ten-yearly charge

Inheritance tax is charged at 30 per cent of the half rates applicable to chargeable lifetime transfers (see 6614) which is determined by assuming that a chargeable transfer has been made on the following basis:

- that the value assumed to have been transferred is equal to the total, at the time of the charge, of all 'relevant property' (see 6940), non-relevant property which was not relevant property at the commencement of the trust and remained non-relevant property, and the value immediately after a 'related settlement' commenced of the property then comprised in it;
- that it is assumed to have been made immediately before the ten-year charge by an assumed transferor whose cumulative total value of previous chargeable transfers is assumed to be equal to the total of any chargeable transfers made by the settlor of the trust in the seven years before the settlement commenced and the value of any distributions made out of the trust in the ten years before the charge.

'Related settlements' are those where the settlor is the same in each case and they commenced on the same day, unless all the property held in one or both settlements is charitable property.

Added property

Where property is added to the settlement, if the total value of the settlor's chargeable transfers in the seven years preceding the addition is higher, that latter value will be substituted, in the calculation of the rate of IHT, for the total of his chargeable transfers in the seven years before the settlement commenced.

Law: IHTA 1984, s. 62, 66, 67

See *British Tax Reporter* ¶674-400.

6954   First ten-year charge

As regards settlements made on or after 27 March 1974, the following procedure is followed to calculate the first ten-year charge, where there have been no additions to the trust (see further below).

The steps in the calculation are:

Step 1

Work out the value of a hypothetical transfer which is the aggregate of:

(a)   the value of the relevant property in the settlement immediately before (i.e. day before) the anniversary date;

(b)   the value of any other property in the same settlement that is not relevant property (for example, property in which there is an interest in possession) at its value immediately after becoming comprised in the settlement; and

(c)   the value of any property comprised in a related settlement (i.e. made by the same settlor on the same day as this settlement, other than a non-temporary charitable settlement) at its value immediately after becoming comprised in the related settlement.

Step 2

Calculate the 'special cumulation' which is an imaginary cumulation total found by aggregating:

(a)   the settlor's total of chargeable transfers in the seven years before the commencement of the settlement; and

(b)   the amounts on which exit charges have been imposed in the last ten years.

Step 3

Add the values in Step 1 and Step 2 to create an 'aggregate chargeable transfer'.

Step 4

Deduct the tax threshold (the amount up to which tax is payable at 0% ascertained at the anniversary date) from the aggregate chargeable transfer. If the aggregate chargeable transfer is below the tax threshold there is no tax to pay.

Step 5

Work out the tax at half rate (i.e. 20%) on the value ascertained in Step 4 (i.e. the excess over the tax threshold).

Step 6

If the value in Step 2 (the special cumulation) exceeds the tax threshold, repeat Steps 4 and 5 with the value in Step 2. Deduct this notional tax from the tax on the aggregate chargeable transfer to calculate the tax on the hypothetical transfer.

Step 7

Calculate the effective rate by dividing the tax on the hypothetical transfer by that transfer and multiplying by 100.

Step 8

Calculate the actual rate of tax by taking 30% of the effective rate found in Step 7.

Step 9

Multiply the actual rate by the current value of relevant property in the trust (Step 1(a)) to obtain the tax payable by the trustees.

Example

Charles, who had made a chargeable transfer of £30,000 in 1994, creates a settlement on 8 May 2000, transferring property worth £300,000. Half of the fund is held on discretionary trusts, the other half being subject to an interest in possession for Charles' son. The trustees paid the lifetime tax amounting to £19,800 on the creation of the settlement. No exit charges occurred in the first ten years of the trust's life.

On 7 May 2010, the value of the whole trust fund is £800,000. The ten year charge is calculated as follows:

Step 1
Hypothetical transfer

	£
(a) current value of relevant property (1/2 × £800,000)	400,000
(b) value of other property in settlement immediately after commencement (1/2 × £(300,000 − 19,800))	140,100
(c) value of property in related settlement immediately after commencement	n/a
Hypothetical transfer	540,100

Step 2
Special cumulation

	£
(a) settlor's total of chargeable transfers in 7 years before the commencement of the settlement	30,000
(b) the amounts on which exit charges have been imposed in the last ten years	n/a
Special cumulation	30,000

	£
Step 3	
Special cumulation	30,000
Add: value of this transfer	540,100
Aggregate chargeable transfer	570,100
Step 4	
Deduct tax threshold @ 8/5/10	
£(570,100 − 325,000) =	£245,100
Step 5	
Work out tax on aggregate chargeable transfer	
£245,100 × 20% =	£49,020

Step 6

The special cumulation is below the tax threshold so no adjustment for tax on this value needs to be made.

Step 7

Effective rate

$$\frac{49,020 \times 100}{540,100} = 9.07610\%$$

Step 8
Actual rate
9.07610% × 30% = 2.72283%

Step 9	
Tax payable by trustees	
2.72283% × £400,000 =	£10,891

Where property has been added to the settlement which is relevant property at the anniversary date, an adjustment needs to be made to the actual rate of tax on such property. This is to ensure that the added property is not taxed for the period when it was not in the settlement.

Law: IHTA 1984, s. 64, 66

Source: *HMRC Inheritance Tax: Customer Guide*

Website: www.hmrc.gov.uk/cto/customerguide/page1.htm

See *British Tax Reporter* ¶674-650.

6960 Second and subsequent ten-year charge

As regards settlements made on or after 27 March 1974, the rules for computing the tax on the second and subsequent anniversaries are the same as for the first one. However, it should be remembered that only those existing charges within the ten years before each anniversary are taken into account.

Example

The facts are the same as in the example in 6954 above. In 2013, the trustees appoint £50,000 (gross) to Donald out of the discretionary part of the fund. In 2014, the interest in possession comes to an end and that half of the fund is made over to Eric (the beneficiary with the interest in possession) absolutely. If on 7 May 2020, the remaining fund is worth £900,000.

The ten year charge in 2020 will be calculated as follows (assuming threshold for 2010-11 applies):

Step 1
Hypothetical transfer £
(a) current value of relevant property 900,000
(b) value of other property in settlement
    immediately after commencement (as above) 140,100
(c) value of property in related settlement
    immediately after commencement n/a

Hypothetical transfer 1,040,100

Step 2
Special cumulation £
(c) settlor's total of chargeable transfers in
    7 years before the commencement of the
    settlement 30,000
(d) the amounts on which exit charges have
    been imposed in the last ten years 50,000

Special cumulation 80,000

Step 3 £
Special cumulation 80,000
Add: value of hypothetical transfer 1,040,100

Aggregate chargeable transfer 1,120,100

Step 4
Deduct tax threshold @ 8/5/20
£(1,120,100 − 325,000) = £795,100

Step 5
Work out tax on aggregate chargeable transfer
£795,100 × 20% = £159,020

Step 6
The special cumulation is below the tax threshold so no adjustment for tax on this value needs to be made.

Step 7
Effective rate
$$\frac{159,020}{1,040,100} \times 100 = 15.28892\%$$

Step 8
Actual rate
115.28892% × 30% = 4.58668%

Step 9
Tax payable by trustees on relevant property
4.58668% × £900,000 = £41,280

The example illustrates that it makes no difference that the interest in possession fund has ceased to exist: its original value continues to be aggregated when calculating the ten-year charge. It is therefore not advisable to set up 'mixed' settlements, or more than one settlement on the same day. Where possible, different settlements should be made on separate days.

Law: IHTA 1984, s. 64, 66

Source: *HMRC Inheritance Tax: Customer Guide*

Website: www.hmrc.gov.uk/cto/customerguide/page1.htm

See *British Tax Reporter* ¶674-500.

6962   Exit charge before the first ten-year anniversary

The rate of tax charged on an exit charge prior to the first ten-year anniversary is determined in accordance with the following procedure.

The steps in the calculation are:

Step 1

Work out the value of a hypothetical transfer which is the aggregate of:

(a)   the value of the settled property in the settlement at its value immediately after becoming comprised in the settlement (whether or not relevant property);

(b)   the value of any property comprised in a related settlement (i.e. made by the same settlor on the same day as this settlement, other than a non-temporary charitable settlement) at its value immediately after becoming comprised in the related settlement; and

(c)   the value of any property added to the settlement after commencement at its value immediately after becoming comprised in the settlement.

Step 2

Ascertain the value of the settlor's total of chargeable transfers in the seven years before the commencement of the settlement.

Step 3

Add the values in Step 1 and Step 2 to create an 'aggregate chargeable transfer'.

Step 4

Deduct the tax threshold (the amount up to which tax is payable at 0% ascertained at the exit charge date) from the aggregate chargeable transfer. If the aggregate chargeable transfer is below the tax threshold there is no tax to pay.

Step 5

Work out the tax at half rate (i.e. 20%) on the value ascertained in Step 4 (i.e. the excess over the tax threshold).

Step 6

If the value in Step 2 (the amount of the settlor's transfers in the seven years before commencement) exceeds the tax threshold, repeat Steps 4 and 5 with the value in Step 2. Deduct this notional tax from the tax on the aggregate chargeable transfer to calculate the tax on the hypothetical transfer.

Step 7

Calculate the effective rate by dividing the tax on the hypothetical transfer by that transfer and multiplying by 100.

Step 8

Calculate the actual rate of tax by taking 30% of the effective rate found in Step 7 and then multiply the result by the 'appropriate fraction'. If there have been no additions to the settlement, the 'appropriate fraction' is as many fortieths as there are complete successive quarters beginning with the day that the settlement commenced and ending with the day before the event causing the exit charge. For these purposes, 'quarter' means a period of three months.

Step 9

If the trustees pay the tax out of relevant property, a grossing up rate needs to be calculated by dividing the actual rate by (100 minus the actual rate). Otherwise, the actual rate is used. In both cases, charge is on the loss in value of relevant property as a result of the exit charge.

Example

On 1 February 2002, Paul, who had made a chargeable transfer of £82,000 on 1 May 1998, transferred £400,000 to a new discretionary trust. IHT of £48,000 was paid by the trustees.

On 1 November 2010 (35 complete quarters since commencement), the trustees make a capital payment to Sharon of £220,000. Sharon pays the tax due, which is calculated as follows:

Step 1

Hypothetical transfer   £

(a) the value of the settled property in the
    settlement at its value immediately after
    becoming comprised in the settlement
    (whether or not relevant property)
    £(400,000 – 48,000)   352,000

(b) the value of any property comprised in a
    related settlement at its value immediately
    after becoming comprised in the related
    settlement   n/a

(c) the value of any property added to the
    settlement after commencement at its value
    immediately after becoming comprised in
    the settlement   n/a

Hypothetical transfer   352,000

Step 2

Amount of settlor's total of chargeable transfers in 7 years
before the commencement of the settlement   82,000

Step 3   £

Transfers b/f   82,000
Add: value of hypothetical transfer   352,000

Aggregate chargeable transfer   434,000

Step 4

Deduct tax threshold @ 1/11/10
£(434,000 – 325,000) =   £109,000

Step 5

Work out tax on aggregate chargeable transfer
£109,000 × 20% =   £21,800

Step 6

The amount of the settlor's total of transfers is below the tax threshold so no
adjustment for tax on this value needs to be made.

Step 7

Effective rate

$$\frac{21,800}{352,000} \times 100 = 6.19318\%$$

Step 8

Actual rate

6.19318% × 30% x 35/40 = 1.625710%

Step 9

Tax payable by Sharon
1.625710% × £220,000 = £3,577

Law: IHTA 1984, s. 68

Source: *HMRC Inheritance Tax: Customer Guide*

Website: www.hmrc.gov.uk/cto/customerguide/page1.htm

See *British Tax Reporter* ¶674-850.

6964 Exit charge between ten-year anniversaries

After the first ten-year anniversary has passed, the exit charge rate is based on the rate of the most recent ten-year charge; a rate known as the 'anniversary rate'. The exit charge rate is calculated by multiplying the anniversary rate by the appropriate fraction, i.e. as many fortieths as there are complete successive quarters in the period beginning with the most recent anniversary and ending with the date before the event causing the exit charge.

Changes in rates of tax

Where rates change, the exit charge is calculated as if the new rate has applied at the time of the ten-year anniversary. This means recalculating a notional rate for the ten year charge.

Property added since last anniversary

The rate of the exit charge is reduced in respect of property that has entered the settlement, or has become relevant property since the most recent anniversary. The appropriate fraction relating to that property is calculated by omitting any quarter expiring before the day on which the property became (or last became) relevant property. If that day falls in the same quarter as the day before the event causing the exit charge the quarter will be counted, whether or not complete.

As the added property was not in the settlement at the last anniversary, it is given a hypothetical value at that date, so that the exit charge reflects the addition. This is done by recalculating the ten year charge as if the fund included the added property at the anniversary date. The added value is brought in at its value when it entered the settlement (or the date on which it became relevant property, if later).

The added property must be brought into account, even where the exit charge is on property comprised in the original fund and regardless of whether or not the added property is still in the settlement.

Law: IHTA 1984, s. 68, 69 and Sch. 2, para. 3

Source: *HMRC Inheritance Tax: Customer Guide*

Website: www.hmrc.gov.uk/cto/customerguide/page1.htm

See *British Tax Reporter* ¶675-400.

6966 Death of settlor

Where the settlor dies shortly after settling property on a discretionary trust, there are two main consequences.

(1) If the death is within seven years after the transfer into the trust, extra tax is payable in respect of that transfer. Liability for the extra tax falls on the trustees and on any person who has benefit out of the fund. However, it has no effect on the rate of tax chargeable on the ten-year and exit charges.

(2) If, within seven years before death and before the creation of the settlement, the settlor made any potentially exempt transfers (see 6611) which become chargeable, this will affect the special cumulation and is thus likely to affect the rate of tax chargeable on the ten-year and exit charges.

Law: IHTA 1984, s. 7, 64–69

Source: *HMRC Inheritance Tax: Customer Guide*

Website: www.hmrc.gov.uk/cto/customerguide/page1.htm

PRIVILEGED TRUSTS AND SPECIAL TRANSFERS

6998 Property leaving temporary charitable trusts

Where settled property is held temporarily for charitable purposes only, it will be charged to IHT:

● where it ceases to be held for charitable purposes, unless it is applied for charitable purposes; and
● in any other case, where the trustees make a disposition (otherwise than for charitable purposes) as a result of which the value of the settled property is reduced.

Payments of costs or expenses, or which are the income of any person, are excluded from the charge, as are payments which are dispositions not intended to confer gratuitous benefits.

Inheritance tax is charged on the reduction in value of the property comprised in the settlement. There will be grossing up where the tax is paid out of the settled property. The rate at which tax is charged is the total of the following percentages:

● 0.25 per cent for each of the first 40 complete successive quarters in the relevant period;
● 0.20 per cent for each of the next 40;
● 0.15 per cent for each of the next 40;

- 0.10 per cent for each of the next 40; and
- 0.05 per cent for each of the next 40.

The relevant period is the length of time the property has been held on charitable trust (or from 13 March 1975 until the chargeable event, if shorter). Where the property was 'relevant property' (see 6940) immediately before 10 December 1981, and became settled on charitable trusts after that date but before 9 March 1982, the relevant period will commence when the property last became relevant property before 10 December 1981.

Where the amount charged to tax is attributable to 'excluded property' (see 7397), no quarter throughout which that property was excluded property is taken into account in determining the rate of tax to be applied.

Law: IHTA 1984, s. 70

Source: *HMRC Inheritance Tax: Customer Guide*

Website: www.hmrc.gov.uk/cto/customerguide/page1.htm

See *British Tax Reporter* ¶678-250.

7002 Accumulation and maintenance trusts

Following changes made to the inheritance tax treatment of trusts in the *Finance Act* 2006, new trusts created on or after 22 March 2006 cannot qualify as accumulation and maintenance trusts. New concepts of 'a trust for a bereaved minor' (see 7003) and 'an age 18-to-25 trust' (see 7004) have been introduced but these are defined differently from the accumulation and maintenance trust.

Accumulation and maintenance trusts already in existence before 22 March 2006 will continue to be exempt from the 'relevant property' regime and will be treated under the old rules detailed below until 6 April 2008 unless, before then, the interest in possession vests or the trust is restructured so as to accelerate interest.

From 6 April 2008, existing accumulation and maintenance trusts must conform to the new rules that require beneficiaries to take the trusts assets absolutely on or before the age of 18 to continue to be taxed under the old regime in IHTA 1984, s. 71. Existing accumulation and maintenance trusts where the beneficiary will take the trust assets absolutely no later than 25 will be taxed under the new age 18-to-25 trust rules from 6 April 2008.

To qualify as an accumulation and maintenance settlement prior to 22 March 2006, the settlement must have one or more persons who will become beneficially entitled to the settled property, or to an interest in possession in it, on attaining a specified age not exceeding 25. Prior to that person or persons becoming so entitled, no interest in possession must subsist in the property, and the income arising must be accumulated so far as not applied for the maintenance, education or benefit of a beneficiary.

After 17 March 2006 but before 22 March 2006, a gift by an individual into an accumulation and maintenance trust is a potentially exempt transfer. After 21 March 2006, a gift by an individual into an accumulation and maintenance trust is no longer treated as a PET.

After 16 March 1987 but before 22 March 2006, a PET also occurs where an individual disposes of or terminates his beneficial interest in possession in settled property by gift and the property is settled on accumulation and maintenance trusts. Where an individual has an interest in possession in settled property which was in existence at 22 March 2006 and it terminates before 6 April 2008 with the property settled on accumulation and maintenance trusts then the new interest will come within the old taxing regime.

To qualify as an accumulation and maintenance trust before 22 March 2006, certain statutory requirements had to be met.

Law: IHTA 1984, s. 71; *Trustees of the Neil Roy Crawford Settlement v R & C Commrs* (2005) Sp C 473

Source: ESC F8, *Accumulation and maintenance settlements*; *HMRC Inheritance Tax: Customer Guide*

Website: www.hmrc.gov.uk/cto/customerguide/page1.htm

See *British Tax Reporter* ¶677-700.

7003 Trusts for bereaved minors

New trusts from 22 March 2006 will not qualify as an accumulation and maintenance trust (see 7002) but trusts for a bereaved minor created under a will or intestacy will not come within the relevant property regime.

A 'trust for a bereaved minor' applies to settled property (including property settled before 22 March 2006) held on trust for the benefit of a person under the age of 18, at least one of whose parents has died, where the trust is created in one of the following circumstances:

(1)   under the will of a deceased parent of the bereaved minor;

(2)   under a 'statutory trust' arising on an intestacy;

(3)   under the Criminal Injuries Compensation Scheme.

Where the trust arises under the intestacy rules, the terms of the trust are statutory and therefore invariable, and the trust will automatically qualify.

Where the trust arises under the will of a deceased parent of the minor, or under the Criminal Injuries Compensation Scheme, the trust will need to satisfy some further conditions.

A bereaved minor can be given an interest in possession in the trust (i.e. be entitled to all the income) and the trust will still qualify; unlike the old rules for accumulation and maintenance trusts where one of the conditions was that no interest in possession subsisted in the trust fund.

It should be noted that only will trusts arising on the death of a bereaved minor's parent (or step-parent or guardian) will qualify. Thus, trusts created under the will of a deceased grandparent in favour of a grandchild whose parents predeceased the grandparent will not qualify.

Where a trust qualifies as a trust for a bereaved minor it will be exempt from the relevant property regime, i.e. it will be exempt from the ten-yearly charge, and will be exempt from the exit charge on trust assets. The assets of the trust will also not be treated as part of the bereaved minor's estate (whether or not the bereaved minor has an interest in possession in it).

There will be no charge to tax where settled property ceases to be property to which s. 71A applies as a result of:

- a bereaved minor acquiring an absolute interest in the trust assets on or before the age of 18;
- the death of a beneficiary before attaining the specified age of 18; or
- being paid or applied for the advancement or benefit of the bereaved minor.

Where settled property on a bereaved minor's trust ceases to satisfy the necessary conditions set out in s. 71A (detailed above) then there will be a charge under the rates given at s. 70(6) (the temporary charitable trust exit rates – see 6998).

An example of where the charge may apply is where a bereaved minor dies before the age of 18 but the trust continues after his/her death.

A charge does not arise where settled property held on trust ceases to be so because the bereaved minor becomes absolutely entitled on or before the age of 18 or dies before the age of 18 or the property is applied or advanced to the bereaved minor before the age of 18.

If the trustees make a disposition which reduces the value of the settled property, a charge to tax arises. Tax will be calculated at half rates on the same basis as the mainstream exit charge for relevant property.

Law: IHTA 1984, s. 71A–71C

7004 Age 18-to-25 trusts

An age 18-to-25 trust is a trust for the benefit of a person under the age of 25, at least one of whose parents has died, where the trust is established:

- under the will of a deceased parent of the minor, or

- under the Criminal Injuries Compensation Scheme, and which satisfies certain conditions.

Existing accumulation and maintenance trusts which satisfy the conditions for age 18-to-25 trusts (above) by 6 April 2008 will be taxed as an 18-to-25 trust .

Where settled property ceases to satisfy the conditions above, or the trustees make a disposition which reduces the value of the settled property, tax will be charged under IHTA 1984, s. 71E.

The charge will not arise where:

- a beneficiary at or under age 18 becomes beneficially entitled to, or to an interest in possession in, settled property on or before attaining the specified age of 25;
- the beneficiary dies before attaining the age of 18;
- settled property becomes property held under trust for a bereaved minor while the beneficiary is living and under 18;
- settled property is paid or applied for the advancement or benefit of the beneficiary before attaining 18 but while the beneficiary is still living or on attaining 18;
- on the payment of costs or expenses attributable to the property; or
- where any payment is (or will be) income of any person for the purposes of income tax or would be if he were UK resident.

Where tax is calculated, the amount of tax is calculated by:

Chargeable amount $\times$ Relevant fraction $\times$ Settlement rate

The chargeable amount is the reduction in the value of the trust fund as a result of the transfer grossed-up where the settlement pays the tax.

The relevant fraction is 30 per cent of x/40 where x is the number of complete quarters from the time when the beneficiary attained 18 or, if later, on the day when the property became subject to the 18-to-25 trust to the day before the occasion of charge.

The settlement rate is the effective rate.

Example

A died on 20 June 2008 leaving all his assets valued at £500,000 in trust for his son, B. B is 25 on 20 May 2014 and on that date the trustees appoint the capital and any accumulated income to B. The capital and remainder of accumulated income at 20 May 2014 is £550,000. A made no previous chargeable transfers in the seven years prior to his death.

	£
Assumed chargeable transfer at 20 June 2014	
Value of relevant property on 20 June 2014	550,000
Less: nil rate band	325,000
	225,000
IHT at half rates (£225,000 at 20%)	£45,000

Effective rate

$$\frac{45,000}{550,000} = 8\%$$

Exit charge on B becoming 25 is:

3/10 × 8% = 2% × 21/40 × £550,000   £5,775

Law: IHTA 1984, s. 71D–71E

7005   Property becoming subject to employee trusts

Tax will not be charged in respect of shares or securities of a company which cease to be held in discretionary trust, etc. ('relevant property': see 6940) on becoming held on trusts for the benefit of employees, etc. provided that the following conditions are satisfied.

(1)   The persons for whose benefit the trusts permit the settled property to be applied include all or most of the persons employed by, or holding office with, the company.

(2)   Where the shares or securities cease to be relevant property, or not more than one year thereafter:

    (a)   the trustees hold more than one-half of the ordinary shares of the company and have powers of voting on all questions affecting the company as a whole which, if exercised, would yield a majority of the votes capable of being exercised; and

    (b)   there are no provisions in any agreement or instrument affecting the company's constitution or management or its shares or securities whereby the condition as to employee benefit above can cease to be satisfied without the consent of the trustees.

(3)   The trusts do not permit any of the settled property to be applied for the benefit of a participator in the company or in any close company that has made a disposition whereby property became comprised in the same settlement, or any person who has been such a participator at any time after, or ten years before, the transfer of value or to be applied for the benefit of any person connected with him.

Employee trusts also benefit from CGT exemptions in respect of transfers to the trustees (see 6197).

Property moving between employee trusts continues to be regarded as held in the original trust (see 7008).

Law: IHTA 1984, s. 28, 75

See *British Tax Reporter* ¶678-850.

7008   Property leaving employee trusts and newspaper trusts

Where property leaves a trust set up for the benefit of employees or newspaper publishing companies, or a payment is made to a 'qualifying person' or to a person who is connected with (see 7153) a qualifying person, or where the trustees make a disposition which reduces the value of settled property, an IHT charge will arise. The charge also applies to property leaving an employee share ownership plan.

Tax will be charged in the way described in 6998.

A 'qualifying person' is:

- one who has directly or indirectly provided any of the settled property otherwise than by additions not exceeding £1,000 in value in any one year;
- a participator, where the employment is by a close company, and is either beneficially entitled to not less than five per cent of its issued share capital or to at least five per cent of the assets on a winding up;
- one who has acquired an interest in the settled property for a consideration in money or money's worth.

Employee trusts also benefit from CGT exemptions in respect of transfers to the trustees (see 6197).

Property moving between employee trusts or newspaper trusts continues to be regarded as held in the original trust.

Law: IHTA 1984, s. 72, 86, 87

Source: *HMRC Inheritance Tax: Customer Guide*

Website: www.hmrc.gov.uk/cto/customerguide/page1.htm

See *British Tax Reporter* ¶679-050.

7011   Protective trusts and trusts for the disabled

Except as noted below, where property is held on protective trusts or trusts for the disabled, the principal beneficiary is treated as having an interest in possession in the settled property (potential charges in connection with such interests are set out at 6909).

Gifts into trusts for the disabled (though not protective trusts) are PETs, in respect of which no tax is chargeable if the donor survives for seven years after making the gift.

From 22 March 2006 the changes made to the IHT treatment of interest in possession trusts have required amendments to existing legislation to ensure that disabled person's trusts still continue to benefit from special treatment.

Law: IHTA 1984, s. 73, 74, 88, 89, *Pitt & Anor v Holt & Anor* ChD [2010] BTC 235

Source: *HMRC Inheritance Tax: Customer Guide*

Website: www.hmrc.gov.uk/cto/customerguide/page1.htm

See *British Tax Reporter* ¶678-650.

7014 Property becoming held for charitable purposes or by exempt bodies

Inheritance tax will not be charged on property which ceases to be 'relevant property' (see 6940), or ceases to be property to which the provisions for temporary charitable trusts (see 6998), accumulation and maintenance trusts (see 7002), employee or newspaper trusts (see 7008) or pre-1978 protective trusts or historic buildings funds (see 7371) applies, on becoming:

- property held for charitable purposes only without limit of time;
- the property of a political party qualifying for exemption (see 7195);
- the property of a body mentioned in 7198 (national purposes, etc.);
- the property of a body not established or conducted for profit.

Law: IHTA 1984, s. 76

Source: *HMRC Inheritance Tax: Customer Guide*

Website: www.hmrc.gov.uk/cto/customerguide/page1.htm

See *British Tax Reporter* ¶645-300.

7017 Initial interest of settlor, spouse or civil partner

If a settlor or his spouse, or civil partner, is beneficially entitled to an interest in possession in property immediately after it becomes comprised in the settlement, the property will be treated as not being comprised in the settlement on that occasion. However, where any of the same property becomes held on trusts under which neither of the spouses or partners is beneficially entitled to an interest in possession, that property will be treated as becoming comprised in a separate settlement.

A 'spouse of a settlor' includes a widow or widower of a settlor.

Law: IHTA 1984, s. 80

Source: *HMRC Inheritance Tax: Customer Guide*

Website: www.hmrc.gov.uk/cto/customerguide/page1.htm

7020   Property moving between settlements

Where property ceases to be comprised in one settlement and becomes comprised in another, it will be treated as remaining comprised in the first settlement unless any person has become beneficially entitled to that property and not merely to an interest in possession in it.

Law: IHTA 1984, s. 48(6), 81

Source: *HMRC Inheritance Tax: Customer Guide*

Website: www.hmrc.gov.uk/cto/customerguide/page1.htm

7023   Distributions within two years of death

Where property comprised in a person's estate immediately before his death is settled by his will and a chargeable event occurs within the period of three months to two years after his death, IHT will not be charged if no interest in possession has subsisted in the property. This is a relieving provision which disapplies the exit charge which would otherwise apply: it cannot apply during the first three months after the death as there would be no exit charge in any case during this time. In addition, the distribution will be treated as if it were made under the will and is thus effectively 'back-dated' to the date of the testator's death. This 'two-year discretionary trust' is a favoured tax planning device which may be employed to use up the nil-rate band available to the testator, while the residue of the estate is left to (e.g.) the testator's spouse. Alternatively, the will may create ! a discretionary trust over the whole estate, so that it can be distributed after the testator's death in the manner then considered to be the most tax-efficient.

Distributions out of a trust for a charity or other exempt body (see 7014), an employee trust (see 7005) or a national heritage maintenance fund (see 7371ff.) made within two years of the deceased's death are already exempt from any charge. Such distributions will be treated as taking place at the date of death so reducing the deceased's chargeable estate.

Law: IHTA 1984, s. 144

Source: *HMRC Inheritance Tax: Customer Guide*

Website: http://www.hmrc.gov.uk/cto/customerguide/page1.htm

See *British Tax Reporter* ¶676-900.

7040 Property becoming comprised in maintenance funds

The transfer into trust of various historic buildings or works of art, etc. is either exempt from IHT or conditionally exempt from IHT (see 7346ff., 7371ff.). There are special modifications to the trust regime to cater for these arrangements where other trusts are involved.

Maintenance funds

Where property leaves a discretionary trust to become comprised in a maintenance fund, the normal exit charge (see 6940ff.) does not apply except to the extent that the amount charged exceeds its value thereafter or the trustees are acquiring it for money or money's worth. Similarly no such exit charge arises if the property temporarily becomes subject to no settlement at all before being transferred by an individual as part of an exempt transfer (within 30 days or two years following death).

Where, within two years after the death of a person with an interest in possession, property becomes comprised in a maintenance fund, it is treated as if it had been settled by the deceased so that no intervening charges arise.

Trusts for works of art

Where property which is designated property has been within a discretionary settlement for six years, the provisions for conditionally exempt transfers of such property are modified so as to exclude the property from the normal exit charge (see 6940ff.) on leaving the trust. The usual loss of exemption where a condition is breached, etc. (see 7351) can thereafter apply by reference to the settlor.

Exemption from ten-yearly charge

Further, the ten-yearly charge on discretionary trusts (see 6940) does not apply to that property unless and until any conditions attaching to such property are broken; however, if such event occurs, a charge then arises on the value of the property at that time and the rate at which IHT is charged is the total of the relevant percentages set out at 6998.

Variation of undertakings

A procedure exists whereby if agreement to vary an undertaking cannot be reached, a special commissioner may direct that the variation should take effect if satisfied that it would be just and reasonable in all the circumstances. The procedure resembles that introduced for heritage property (see 7349).

Claims

In relation to transfers of property made, or other events occurring, after 16 March 1998, claims must be made within two years from the date of the transfer or other event in question, or such longer period as HMRC may allow. Previously, there was no time-limit.

Law: IHTA 1984, s. 57A, 77–79A and Sch. 4, para. 16

Source: *HMRC Inheritance Tax: Customer Guide*

Website: www.hmrc.gov.uk/cto/customerguide/page1.htm

See *British Tax Reporter* ¶651-900.

7055 Property leaving maintenance funds

Where property ceases to be held in a maintenance fund (and does not become part of another such fund) or where works of art, etc. leave a trust (and cease to be designated property), an IHT charge may arise. Further, a disposition by trustees reducing the value of property in a maintenance fund may also give rise to a charge to tax.

Maintenance funds

Where property ceases to be 'relevant property' (see 6940) comprised in a 'maintenance fund' (see 7040) or where trustees make a disposition reducing the value of property in the fund, IHT will be charged on the reduction in value of the settled property. However, tax will not be charged where the property is transferred into another maintenance fund by an individual within 30 days provided that individual did not acquire his interest for a consideration in money or money's worth. If the property which ceases to be comprised in the fund becomes property to which the settlor or his spouse is beneficially entitled or to which the settlor's widow or his spouse is beneficially entitled (if the settlor died within the preceding two years) there will be no charge to tax unless:

- the person acquired his or her beneficial interest for a consideration in money or money's worth; or
- the property was held on discretionary trusts, etc. before it became property comprised in the maintenance fund and tax was not chargeable when it ceased to be such 'relevant property' (see 6940); or
- the property was previously comprised in a maintenance fund and no tax was charged on becoming comprised in the present maintenance fund; or
- the person who becomes beneficially entitled to the property is domiciled in the UK at the time when he becomes so entitled.

Where property ceases to be part of a discretionary trust, etc. ('relevant property': see 6940) and no IHT is charged on it becoming comprised in a maintenance fund, then the tax to be charged when it leaves the maintenance fund will be the total of the relevant percentages as shown at 6998.

Where the above provision does not apply (i.e. the property was not previously part of a discretionary trust, etc. or tax was charged when it left such trust), the rate at which tax is charged will be the higher of:

- the total of similar percentages to those shown above (where the relevant period begins with the day the property became comprised in the maintenance fund);
- the effective rate at which tax would be charged if the amount were the value transferred

by a chargeable transfer (or if the settlor is dead if the amount were treated as the highest part of the value transferred on his death).

There are certain modifications where the property was previously subject to an interest in possession.

Trusts for works of art

The normal exit charge on discretionary trust property (see 6940ff.) will apply unless designated property has been within a discretionary settlement for six years before it ceases to be so held, as in relation to transfers into the trust from another settlement (see 7040); equally, if the property ceases to be designated on leaving the trust (if the appropriate conditions are breached), a charge may arise (see 7351).

Law: IHTA 1984, Sch. 4, para. 8–15A

Source: *HMRC Inheritance Tax: Customer Guide*

Website: www.hmrc.gov.uk/cto/customerguide/page1.htm

See *British Tax Reporter* ¶651-900.

EXEMPTIONS AND RELIEFS FROM INHERITANCE TAX

DISPOSITIONS WHICH ARE NOT TRANSFERS OF VALUE

7150 Introduction to dispositions which are not transfers of value

A transfer of value is any disposition made by a person (the transferor) as a result of which the value of his estate immediately after the disposition is less than it would be but for the disposition and the amount by which it is less is the value transferred by the transfer (see 6525). It is stated in statute that, notwithstanding the above definition, a disposition is not a transfer of value in several specific cases. If a disposition is not a transfer of value, no IHT is chargeable on the transfer.

Law: IHTA 1984, s. 1, 2

See *British Tax Reporter* ¶609-350.

7153   No gratuitous intent

A disposition is not a transfer of value (see 7150) if it is shown that it was not intended to confer any gratuitous benefit on any person and that it was made in an arm's length transaction between persons not 'connected with' each other, or that it was such as might have been expected to have been made in an arm's length transaction between persons not connected with each other. Thus, if there is no element of gift or giving away, there can be no transfer of value.

Reversionary interests, unquoted securities

The above rule is inapplicable where a person with an interest in possession acquires the reversion expectant on the interest; and it only applies to a sale of 'unquoted' (see 6572) shares or debentures if it is shown that the sale was at a price freely negotiated at the time of the sale, or at such a price as might be expected to have been freely negotiated at the time of the sale.

Example

Agatha transfers property to Beryl and Constance upon trust for Delia for life with remainder to Evelyn. The interest in remainder is valued at £50,000. Delia purchases Evelyn's reversion for £50,000. She is treated as having made a transfer of value of £50,000 since, for IHT purposes, she is treated as being already beneficially entitled to all the property so that the payment of £50,000 is treated as a gift for no consideration.

Connected persons

The following are connected persons.

Individuals
A person is connected with an individual if that person is the individual's husband or wife or civil partner, or a relative of the individual or of the individual's husband or wife or civil partner. For IHT purposes, a relative includes an uncle, aunt, nephew and niece.

Trustees
A person in his capacity as trustee of a settlement is connected with any individual who in relation to the settlement is a settlor, with any person who is connected with such an individual and with a body corporate which is deemed connected with the settlement.

Partners
A person is connected with any person with whom he is in partnership, and with the husband or wife or a relation of any individual with whom he is in partnership. This does not apply to the acquisition or disposal of partnership assets pursuant to genuine commercial arrangements.

Inheritance Tax

Companies

A person is connected with a company if that person has control of it or if that person and persons connected with him together have control of it. Any two or more persons acting together to secure or exercise control of a company will be treated in relation to that company as connected with one another and with any person acting on the direction of any of them to secure or exercise control of the company.

A company is connected with another company if:

- the same person has control of both, or a person has control of one and persons connected with him, or he and persons connected with him, have control of the other; or
- a group of two or more persons has control of each company and the groups either consist of the same persons or could be regarded as consisting of the same persons by treating (in one or more cases) a member of either group as replaced by a person with whom he is connected (see the similar rules for CGT: 5142).

'Control' is defined by reference to power over the majority of votes when taken together with related property and powers of trustees in relation to property to which the person in question has an interest in possession.

Law: IHTA 1984, s. 10, 55(2), 269, 270; *IR Commrs v Spencer-Nairn* [1991] BTC 8,003

See *British Tax Reporter* ¶609-350.

7156 Dispositions for maintenance of family

Dispositions for the maintenance of family are not transfers of value (see 7150) in certain circumstances.

Between spouses and civil partners, or to children

A disposition is not a transfer of value if it is made by one party to a marriage or civil partnership in favour of the other party for his or her maintenance. A disposition is not a transfer of value if made by one party to a marriage or civil partnership in favour of a child of either party for his or her maintenance, education or training, up to the age of 18 or until the time that the child ceases to undergo full-time education or training if later than 18. This will apply even if the disposition is in favour of a child who is not in the care of a parent of his or hers, but if the disposition is not to be a transfer of value after the child attains 18 years, the child must have been in the care of the person making the disposition for substantial periods before the child attains 18 years of age.

The provisions will apply to an illegitimate child if the disposition is made by the parent of that child.

A 'child' here includes a step-child and an adopted child and 'marriage' includes a former marriage in relation to a disposition made on the occasion of the dissolution or annulment of a marriage and in relation to a disposition varying a disposition so made. A 'year' means any period of 12 months ending with 5 April.

Dispositions to dependent relatives

A disposition is not a transfer of value if made in favour of a dependent relative of the person making the disposition and is a reasonable provision for his or her care or maintenance. A 'dependent relative' means a relation of a person or a relation of his or her spouse or civil partner, and one who is incapacitated by old age from maintaining himself, or the mother of that person or of his spouse or civil partner, if the mother is living apart from her husband or widowed, or is a single woman in consequence of dissolution or annulment of marriage. (The official view is that the exclusion does not apply to transfers on death.)

In practice, relief is permitted if an unmarried mother is not incapacitated but relies on the child making the disposition.

Law: *Civil Partnership Act* 2005; IHTA 1984, s. 11

Source: ESC F12, *Disposition for maintenance of a dependent relative*; *HMRC Inheritance Tax: Customer Guide*

Website: www.hmrc.gov.uk/cto/customerguide/page1.htm

See *British Tax Reporter* ¶610-200.

7159   Dispositions on trust for benefit of employees

Where a close company contributes to an employee trust, described at 7005 or an employee share ownership plan, there is not a transfer of value (see 7150) if the persons for whose benefit the trusts permit the property to be applied include all or most of the employees and office holders of the company and of subsidiary companies if their employees or office holders are also to benefit. Where a subsidiary is to be included, the employees and office holders of the two companies are taken as a single class, so that if the holding company's employees comprised only a minority of the total they could all be excluded.

This will not apply if the trusts allow any benefit to go to any of the following persons (apart from any benefit which would be income of the recipient for the purposes of income tax):

- a participator of the company making the disposition; or
- a participator of any close company making a disposition of property into the same settlement; or
- anyone who has been a participator in such a company as in the above categories at any time after, or ten years before, the disposition made by that company; or
- any person connected with a person in one of those three categories (see 7153).

'Close company' and 'participator' are explained at 6555. A participator for the above purposes will not include any participator entitled to less than five per cent of assets on a winding up of the company.

HMRC have set out their current view on the IHT position in relation to contributions to an employee benefit trust. An IHT charge arises on contributions made by a close company to an employee benefit trust where:

- the participators and any person connected with them are not excluded from benefit under the terms of the employee benefit trust; and
- the contributions are not allowable in computing the company's profits for corporation tax purposes and/or it is not shown that the contributions are made in arm's-length transactions not intended to confer a gratuitous benefit.

Where the trust deed specifically purports to exclude the participators from benefit but nevertheless the participators do in fact benefit, for example:

- by payment to them of loans; or
- by assigning funds from the employee benefit trust on sub-trusts for their benefit and that of their family,

then HMRC take the view that an IHT charge arises because the funds have been applied for the benefit of the participators.

Where a disposition is not prevented from being a transfer of value, a charge arises and the transfer of value is apportioned between the individual participators according to their respective rights and interest in the company immediately before the contribution to the employee benefit trust giving rise to the transfer of value.

Spotlight 5

In *Spotlight 5: Using trusts and similar entities to reward employees – PAYE (Pay As You Earn) and National Insurance contributions (NICs), Corporation tax and Inheritance tax*, HMRC state that they are aware that:

> '...companies have been seeking to reward their employees without operating PAYE/NICs by making payments through trusts and other intermediaries that favour the employees or their families. The arrangements usually seek to secure a Corporation Tax deduction, as if the amounts were earnings at the time they were allocated, and also defer PAYE/NICs altogether.'

HMRC's view in these circumstances is that:

> **'an Inheritance Tax charge may arise on the participators of a close company**. Unless the participators are excluded beneficiaries and have not had funds applied for their benefit, such as the receipt of a loan, a charge to Inheritance Tax arises on participators of close companies at the time the funds are paid to the trustee by the close company. Relief is only available to the extent that a deduction is allowable to the company for the year in which the contribution is made. Later payments of earnings out of the trust that may trigger a deduction to the company would not qualify for relief.'

Participators affected in this way may need to self-assess a liability to inheritance tax.

Law: IHTA 1984, s. 13

Source: SP E11, HMRC Brief 61/09, *Spotlight 5: Using trusts and similar entities to reward employees – PAYE (Pay As You Earn) and National Insurance contributions (NICs), Corporation tax and Inheritance tax*

See *British Tax Reporter* ¶610-700.

7162   Waiver of remuneration

The waiver or repayment of remuneration will not be a transfer of value (see 7150) if it would have been assessable to income tax under the charge on employment income provisions (see 250) but for the waiver or repayment.

If the amount of remuneration would have been allowed as a deduction in computing profits or gains or losses of the person by whom it is payable or paid, it will not be a transfer of value merely because the waiver or repayment means that it is not allowed as a deduction or is otherwise brought into charge in computing profits or gains or losses.

Law: IHTA 1984, s. 14

See *British Tax Reporter* ¶610-850.

7165   Waiver of dividends

A person who waives any dividend on shares of a company within 12 months before any right to the dividend has accrued is not treated as having made a transfer of value (see 7150) merely because of the waiver.

Law: IHTA 1984, s. 15

See *British Tax Reporter* ¶610-900.

7168   Dispositions conferring retirement benefits

A disposition made by any person is not a transfer of value (see 7150) if it is a contribution under a registered pension scheme, a qualifying non-UK pension scheme or ICTA 1988, s. 615(3) in respect of an employee of the person making the disposition.

Where the condition is satisfied only to a limited extent, the payment is treated as two separate dispositions: one of which is not a transfer of value, and the other that is.

Law: IHTA 1984, s. 12(2)–(5)

See *British Tax Reporter* ¶610-800.

7172   Dispositions allowable for income tax

A disposition made by any person will not be a transfer of value (see 7150) if it is allowable as a deduction in computing that person's profits or gains for income tax or corporation tax (see 2150ff.).

Law: IHTA 1984, s. 12(1), (5)

See *British Tax Reporter* ¶610-600.

7174   Grant of tenancies of agricultural property

Were it not specifically provided otherwise, the grant of an agricultural tenancy would result in a transfer of value because of the ensuing reduction in the value of the freehold. Accordingly, it is provided that the grant of a tenancy of agricultural property in the UK, the Channel Islands or the Isle of Man for use for agricultural purposes is not a transfer of value by the grantor (see 7150) if he makes it for full consideration in money or money's worth.

Law: IHTA 1984, s. 16

See *British Tax Reporter* ¶610-950.

7176   Changes in distribution of deceased's estate

Certain changes in the distribution of a deceased's estate are not transfers of value (see 7150):

- a variation or disclaimer made within two years of death (see 6805);
- the renunciation (in Scotland) to a claim to legitim within a specified period (see 6805);
- a transfer within two years of death in accordance with a testator's express wish (but not under the terms of his will) (see 7023); or
- an election by a surviving spouse to have his or her life interest redeemed where the deceased died intestate (the survivor thereafter being regarded as entitled to the capital value).

Law: IHTA 1984, s. 17, 145

Source: *HMRC Inheritance Tax: Customer Guide*

Website: www.hmrc.gov.uk/cto/customerguide/page1.htm

See *British Tax Reporter* ¶611-000.

TRANSFERS EXEMPT DURING LIFE AND ON DEATH

7192 Transfers between spouses and civil partners

Generally, transfers between spouses and civil partners are exempt without any limit, both during lifetime and on death, and this includes settled property. However, where the transferor is domiciled in the UK, but his or her spouse or civil partner is not, the exempt amount is restricted to £55,000.

> ### Example 1
>
> Andrew gives his wife, Beth, £500,000 in September 2009. They are both domiciled in the UK. There will be no IHT charge on this transfer of value.

> ### Example 2
>
> Christopher gives his wife, Jennifer, £500,000 in September 2010. Christopher is domiciled in the UK and Jennifer is domiciled in the USA. There will be a potential charge to tax on £445,000 since only £55,000 is exempt.

The exemption will not be given:

- if the gift or bequest is not immediately in favour of the other spouse or civil partner, unless the property is given to a spouse only if he survives the other spouse or civil partner for a specified period; or
- if the testamentary or other disposition depends on a condition which is not satisfied 12 months after the transfer; or
- if the property is given in consideration of the transfer of a reversionary interest, if that interest does not form part of the estate of the person acquiring it .

> ### Example 1
>
> Frank leaves property to his wife, Mavis, for life. This will be an exempt transfer since Mavis takes an immediate life interest.

Inheritance Tax

> **Example 2**
>
> Jeremy leaves property to Simon for life with remainder to his wife, Charlotte. The transfer to Simon would not be exempt since Charlotte (his wife) does not get an immediate interest in the property.

Law: IHTA 1984, s. 18, 56

Source: *HMRC Inheritance Tax: Customer Guide*

Website: www.hmrc.gov.uk/cto/customerguide/page1.htm

See *British Tax Reporter* ¶644-800.

7193   Transfer of unused nil-rate band between spouses and civil partners

Finance Act 2008 introduced legislation that allows a claim to be made to transfer any unused IHT nil-rate band on a person's death (no matter what the date of their death) to the estate of their surviving spouse or civil partner who dies on or after 9 October 2007. This applies where the IHT nil-rate band of the first deceased spouse or civil partner was not fully used in calculating the IHT liability of their estate. When the surviving spouse or civil partner dies, the unused amount may be added to their own nil-rate band.

The amount that can be transferred is based on the proportion of the nil-rate band that was unused when the first spouse or civil partner died, and applied in the same proportion to the nil rate band in force at the time of the second death.

> **Example 1**
>
> If on the first death none of the original nil-rate band was used because the entire estate was left to a surviving spouse, then if the nil-rate band when the surviving spouse dies is £325,000 that would be increased 100 per cent to £650,000.

> **Example 2**
>
> If on the first death the chargeable estate is £150,000 and the nil-rate band is £300,000, then 50 per cent of the original nil-rate band would be unused and is available for transfer. If the nil-rate band when the surviving spouse dies is £325,000, then the amount available for transfer would be 50 per cent of £325,000 or £162,500, giving the surviving spouse's estate a nil rate band of £325,000 + £162,500 = £487,500 in total.

The legislation does not require the first spouse to die domiciled or deemed domiciled in the UK.

Example 3

Anna and Adam had been domiciled for many years in Spain. However, on Adam's death Anna returned to the UK, resuming her domicile of origin. She died in 2008. Adam's unused nil-rate band is available for transfer.

The size of the estate of the first person to die is irrelevant. The question is what percentage of the nil-rate band did that person use up by making a chargeable transfer on death or by chargeable lifetime transfers that cumulated with his estate on death. So, if, for example, the first spouse's or civil partner's estate was worth only £100,000 and the entire estate was left to the surviving spouse or civil partner, 100 per cent of the nil-rate band is available for transfer when the surviving spouse or civil partner dies.

Example 4

Mr X died in 2000, having made no lifetime gifts, and leaving everything to his wife, Mrs X. Mrs X died at the beginning of 2008 and shortly before her death gave £600,000 to her son which qualified as a potentially exempt transfer (PET). As Mrs X died within seven years of making the gift, it is a failed PET which becomes chargeable on her death. Her remaining estate is worth £500,000.

There will be no IHT to pay on the lifetime gift as two nil-rate bands of £300,000 are allocated against it. The £500,000 left in her estate at death is fully chargeable at 40 per cent.

Example 5

If in the above example, Mrs X has settled property on her daughter instead of making an outright gift, this would have been an immediately chargeable transfer. Her nil-rate band of £300,000 would have been allocated against the £600,000 gift to the settlement which would have left tax a tax charge of £300,000 @ 20% = £60,000.

On her death within seven years of making the settlement, additional IHT is payable. However, Mr X's unused nil-rate band is available to allocate against it and no additional IHT is charged. It should be noted that there is no refund of the tax charged when the settlement was created.

The amount of additional nil-rate band that can be accumulated by any one surviving spouse or civil partner will be limited to the value of the nil-rate band in force at the time of their death. This may be relevant where a person dies having survived more than one spouse or civil partner, and therefore more than one unused nil-rate band could otherwise be transferred to them. This may also be relevant where a person dies having been married to, or the registered civil partner of, someone who had themselves survived one or more spouses or civil partners (see Frequently Asked Questions at www.hmrc.gov.uk/cto/iht/tnrb-faqs.pdf). Divorced couples cannot claim the nil-rate band when an ex-spouse dies.

Inheritance Tax

Where the new rules have effect, personal representatives will not have to claim for unused nil-rate band to be transferred at the time of the first death. Any claims for transfer of unused nil-rate band amounts will be made by the personal representatives of the estate of the second spouse or civil partner to die. The personal representatives will need to fill in a claim form that will show how much of the nil-rate band is available for transfer. They will also need to provide certain documents to support their claim including:

- the death certificate for the first person to die;
- the marriage certificate or civil partnership certificate for the couple;
- if the spouse or civil partner left a Will, a copy of it;
- a copy of the grant of probate or confirmation; and
- if there is a Deed of Variation, a copy of it.

The personal representatives should send the claim form and the supporting documents to HMRC when they send in the form IHT400 on the death of the surviving spouse or civil partner. The claim must be made within 24 months from the end of the month in which the surviving spouse or civil partner dies. For further information on the making of a claim, see Frequently Asked Questions at www.hmrc.gov.uk/cto/iht/tnrb-faqs.pdf.

The transfer of the unused nil-rate band would appear to negate the need for nil-rate band-planning debt or charge type trusts. However, these may still be good planning for some couples who:

- are not married;
- have more complex situations such as second marriages and stepchildren;
- have assets expected to grow faster than the likely increase in the nil-rate band; or
- have assets that are eligible for business property relief (see 7253) or agricultural property relief (see 7292) so that the relief is claimed before it is lost.

For those who died in the last two years the nil-rate band trust can be dismantled by an appointment by the trustees in favour of the spouse if it is thought no longer necessary under IHTA 1984, s. 144. However, if someone died more than two years ago, leaving assets into a nil-rate band trust, nothing can be done to take advantage of the new relief.

Law: FA 2008, s. 10 and Sch. 4; IHTA 1984, s. 8A–C

Website: www.hmrc.gov.uk/cto/iht/tnrb-faqs.pdf

7195 Gifts to charities and political parties

Transfers of property to charities and political parties are generally exempt from IHT.

A political party is one which before the gift is made had two members elected to the House of Commons or one member was elected and candidates, being members of that party, received at least 150,000 votes.

If the value of the property to the charity is less than the loss in value of the donor's estate, the exemption is not restricted.

Exceptions

The exemptions relating to charities and political parties will not apply to any property if:

- the disposition is not immediately in favour of the charity or political party; or
- the disposition depends on a condition which is not satisfied 12 months after the transfer; or
- the property is given on consideration of a reversionary interest if that interest does not form part of the estate of the person acquiring it; or
- the disposition is defeasible; or
- the property given is an interest in other property and that interest is less than the donor's full interest, or given only for a limited period; or
- the property is an interest in possession in settled property and the settlement does not come to an end in relation to that settled property on the making of the transfer; or
- the property is land or buildings and the donor has obtained the right of occupation for himself or others with whom he is connected at a rent less than market rent; or
- the property is not land or buildings and the donor has created or reserved an interest; unless that interest is for full consideration in money or money's worth, or the interest does not substantially affect the enjoyment of the property by the person or body to whom it is given; or
- the property or any part of it may be applied for purposes other than charitable, political, or national purposes.

These exceptions mean that the donor must part with his whole interest in the property transferred and must not affect the enjoyment of those to whom it is given.

Law: IHTA 1984, s. 23, 24, 56

Source: *HMRC Inheritance Tax: Customer Guide*

Website: www.hmrc.gov.uk/cto/customerguide/page1.htm

See *British Tax Reporter* ¶645-250.

7196   Gifts to housing associations

Gifts of land to registered housing associations are exempt. A 'registered housing association' is a non-profit making body established for the provision or encouragement of housing.

To be within the exemption, the gift must be immediate and not conditional, defeasible or limited, etc. (as in relation to gifts to charities: see 7195).

Law: IHTA 1984, s. 24A, 56

Source: *HMRC Inheritance Tax: Customer Guide*

Website: www.hmrc.gov.uk/cto/customerguide/page1.htm

See *British Tax Reporter* ¶645-900.

7198 Gifts for national purposes

Gifts for national purposes

Gifts for national purposes made to the following institutions are completely exempt from IHT:

- the National Gallery;
- the British Museum;
- the National Museums of Scotland;
- the National Museum of Wales;
- the Ulster Museum;
- any other similar national institution which exists wholly or mainly for the purpose of preserving for the public benefit a collection of scientific, historic or artistic interest and which is approved by HMRC;
- any museum or art gallery in the UK which exists wholly or mainly for that purpose and is maintained by a local authority or university in the UK;
- any library the main function of which is to serve the needs of teaching and research at a university in the UK;
- the Historic Buildings and Monuments Commission for England;
- the National Trust for Places of Historic Interest or Natural Beauty;
- the National Trust for Scotland for Places of Historic Interest or Natural Beauty;
- the National Art Collections Fund;
- the Trustees of the National Heritage Memorial Fund;
- the National Endowment for Science, Technology and the Arts;
- the Friends of the National Libraries;
- the Historic Churches Preservation Trust;
- Commission for Rural Communities;
- Natural England;
- Scottish Natural Heritage;
- the Countryside Council for Wales;
- any local authority;
- any government department (including the National Debt Commissioners);
- any university or university college in the UK;
- a 'health service body' (see 4635).

Law: IHTA 1984, s. 25, 26A, Sch. 3

Source: *HMRC Inheritance Tax: Customer Guide*

Website: www.hmrc.gov.uk/cto/customerguide/page1.htm

See *British Tax Reporter* ¶646-050.

TRANSFERS EXEMPT ONLY DURING LIFETIME

7210   Potentially exempt transfers as exempt transfers

Any PET made seven or more years before the death of the transferor is an exempt transfer. Any other PET is chargeable. During the period between the date of the PET and either seven years from that date or, if it is earlier, the date of the transferor's death the PET is assumed to be an exempt transfer (see 6611).

The nature of a PET is discussed at 6611.

Law: IHTA 1984, s. 3A

Source: *HMRC Inheritance Tax: Customer Guide*

Website: www.hmrc.gov.uk/cto/customerguide/page1.htm

See *British Tax Reporter* ¶643-200.

7220   Annual exemption

Transfers of value made by a transferor in any one year are exempt up to the value of £3,000. If the value transferred in any one year falls short of £3,000, the shortfall may be added to the £3,000 in the next following year. If the value transferred exceeds £3,000, the excess will be attributed to a later, rather than an earlier, transfer and, if the transfers are made in the same day, the excess will be attributed to them in proportion to the values transferred by them. A 'year' means any period of 12 months ending with 5 April.

Example 1

Margaret gives Lucy £2,800 in year 1 and £3,100 in year 2. The shortfall of £200 in year 1 may be carried forward to be used in year 2. There will be no chargeable (or potentially exempt) transfer in year 2, since £3,200 is available as an exemption, but the £100 left over cannot be carried forward any further. Since the gift in year 2 is over £3,000 there is no shortfall available for any gifts that may be made in year 3 that are over £3,000.

Example 2

Duncan gives Paul £2,000 in year 1 and £2,500 in year 2 and £3,750 in year 3. The gifts in years 1 and 2 are covered by the exemption since they are under £3,000, but the gift in

---

year 3 will be treated as a chargeable (or potentially exempt) transfer of £250 since only £500 was available as a carry forward from year 2.

The legislation states that, in a tax year where there are both PETs and chargeable transfers, when allocating the annual exemption the PETs are left out of account in the first instance. However, HMRC holds the view that this is inconsistent with other parts of the legislation and that the annual exemption should be allocated in chronological order, regardless of whether the transfer remaining after the exemption is a chargeable transfer or a PET. This is a more logical view since the question of whether a transfer is a PET or a chargeable lifetime transfer is determined after exemptions been taken into account. In practice the point is unlikely to be often encountered.

Law: IHTA 1984, s. 19

Source: *HMRC Inheritance Tax: Customer Guide*

Website: www.hmrc.gov.uk/cto/customerguide/page1.htm

See *British Tax Reporter* ¶643-200.

7223   Small gifts

Transfers of value made by a transferor in any one year by outright gifts to any one person are exempt if the values transferred by them do not exceed £250.

Law: IHTA 1984, s. 20

Source: *HMRC Inheritance Tax: Customer Guide*

Website: www.hmrc.gov.uk/cto/customerguide/page1.htm

See *British Tax Reporter* ¶643-700.

7226   Normal expenditure out of income

If the transfer of value is part of the 'normal expenditure' of the transferor and it came out of his income so that it left him with sufficient income to maintain his usual standard of living, then the transfer will be exempt from IHT.

Payment, whether directly or indirectly, of an insurance premium on the life of the transferor is not regarded as part of normal expenditure if an annuity has been purchased on his life at any time, unless it can be shown that the purchase of the insurance and annuity were not associated operations (see 6670).

The term 'normal expenditure' connotes expenditure which accorded with a settled pattern adopted by the transferor. While that pattern need not be immutable, it must have been intended to remain in place for more than a nominal period. 'Normal' refers to the type, not amount, of expenditure. The amount of the expenditure need not be fixed, nor need the individual recipients be the same (e.g. family members, needy friends). There is no fixed minimum period during which the expenditure has to be incurred. The expenditure need not be reasonable or such that an ordinary person would have incurred in similar circumstances. Nor does it matter that the object is to prevent accumulation of income in the transferor's hands, liable to IHT on his death.

Gifts made to relatives during the last few years of the donor's life were held by a special commissioner not to be 'normal expenditure' because they showed no regular pattern and no prior commitment.

Law: IHTA 1984, s. 21; *Nadin v IR Commrs* (1997) Sp C 112; *Bennett v IR Commrs* [1995] BTC 8,003

Source: *HMRC Inheritance Tax: Customer Guide*

Website: www.hmrc.gov.uk/cto/customerguide/page1.htm

See *British Tax Reporter* ¶643-950.

7229   Gifts in consideration of marriage

Gifts made in consideration of marriage are exempt to a certain extent, depending on the relationship of the transferor to the transferee. The limits are:

- £5,000 in the case of gifts by a parent of either party to the marriage;
- £2,500 in the case of gifts by more remote ancestors (e.g. grandparents) of either party to the marriage;
- £2,500 in the case of gifts by one party to the marriage to the other;
- £1,000 in any other case.

Both outright gifts and marriage settlements are included in the exemption, but if persons other than those being married, their issue, and the wife or husband of any issue are entitled to benefit, the marriage settlement would not normally qualify for exemption. The gifts must become fully effective on the marriage.

Example

Henry gives marriage gifts of £20,000 to his son and £5,000 to his son's fiancée in June 2010. He dies in December 2010. He has made no chargeable transfers for the year of the marriage. £4,000 of the gift to his son will be exempt and £1,000 to his bride. The actual calculation is as follows:

	£	£
Transfer	20,000	5,000
Less: exemption apportioned		
in ratio of £20,000 to £5,000 (IHTA 1984, s. 22(1))	(4,000)	(1,000)
	16,000	4,000
Less: £3,000 annual exemption apportioned		
in ratio of £16,000 to £4,000	(2,400)	(600)
	13,600	3,400

Henry has therefore made two PETs: one of £13,600 to his son, and one of £3,400 to his son's fiancée. (The annual exemption for 2010–11 has been allocated in accordance with HMRC's view (see 7220).) Both PETs become chargeable as a result of Henry's death in December 2010.

Law: IHTA 1984, s. 22

Source: *HMRC Inheritance Tax: Customer Guide*

Website: www.hmrc.gov.uk/cto/customerguide/page1.htm

See *British Tax Reporter* ¶644-450.

TRANSFERS EXEMPT ONLY ON DEATH

7250   Death on active service

Inheritance tax will not be charged if it is certified by the Defence Council or the Secretary of State that the deceased died from a wound inflicted, or an accident occurring when on active service against the enemy, or when on other service of a warlike nature. This will also apply if a disease was contracted at some previous time, the death being due to, or hastened by, the aggravation of the disease while on active service or on other service of a warlike nature.

The deceased must have been a member of any of the armed forces of the Crown (including women's services) or, by concession, a member of the Royal Ulster Constabulary.

Law: IHTA 1984, s. 154

Source: ESC F5, *Death of members of the Royal Ulster Constabulary*

See *British Tax Reporter* ¶646-950.

7252 Partial exemption where further transfer by exempt beneficiary

Where a transfer made on the death of any person is an exempt transfer to a spouse, civil partner, charity, political party, housing association, public body, maintenance fund or employee trust, and the exempt beneficiary, in whole or partial settlement of any claim against the deceased's estate, makes a disposition of property not derived from the transfer on death, the exemption on death is lost to the extent of the value transferred by the exempt beneficiary, i.e. there is a partial exemption.

Note that any order made by the court in recognition of a claim against the deceased's estate under the *Inheritance (Provision for Family and Dependants) Act* 1975 is treated as a disposition effected by the deceased (see 6805). That means that any transfer to give such an order effect is not taxable again but it does not necessarily enjoy exemption. The present provision seems to be an anti-avoidance measure aimed at the following situation.

Example

Thomas agrees with charity X (or any other exempt beneficiary) that he will leave charity X a bequest of £500,000 provided charity X transfers £200,000 of its own property to his mistress (or any other non-exempt beneficiary who may have a claim against the deceased's estate). The effect is that £200,000 passes to a non-exempt beneficiary free of tax. The exemption to the charity is abated to the extent of the charity's transfer, i.e. only £300,000 would enjoy exemption from IHT.

The 1984 Act already contains an 'associated operations' rule (see 6670) so it is arguable that the arrangement above would not have avoided IHT anyway. The provision enables HMRC more easily to charge such an arrangement.

Law: IHTA 1984, s. 29A

Source: *HMRC Inheritance Tax: Customer Guide*

Website: www.hmrc.gov.uk/cto/customerguide/page1.htm

See *British Tax Reporter* ¶646-950.

RELIEF FOR BUSINESS PROPERTY

7253 Introduction to business property relief

Where the value transferred in a transfer of value includes relevant business property, the value transferred may, in certain circumstances, be treated as reduced by:

(1)   100 per cent (50 per cent for transfers or as a result of death before 10 March 1992) if

the property consists of a business or interest in a business, or securities of an 'unquoted' company (see 6571) which, together with other securities owned by the transferor and any unquoted shares so owned, gave the transferor control of the company immediately before the transfer (before 6 April 1996, shares giving the transferor control of the company immediately before the transfer were also in this category); and

(2) 100 per cent for any unquoted shares in a company (before 6 April 1996, 100 per cent relief is only available where the transferor holds shares yielding more than 25 per cent of exercisable votes and has maintained such a holding during the preceding two years; where the transfer was made or death occurred before 10 March 1992, only 50 per cent relief was available in such circumstances);

(3) 50 per cent (30 per cent for transfers or as a result of death before 10 March 1992) if the property consisted of any land or building, machinery or plant which immediately before the transfer was used wholly or mainly for the purposes of a business carried on by a company which the transferor controlled, or by a partnership of which he was then a partner, or by the transferor, and was settled property in which he was then beneficially entitled to an interest in possession; and

(4) 50 per cent for a controlling shareholding in a quoted company.

There is a minimum period of ownership for relief to apply (see 7259) and additional conditions for transfers within seven years before death (see 7260). Certain property is excepted from relief (see 7265). If the property is subject to a contract for its ultimate sale at the time of the transfer, relief may be denied in certain circumstances; the HMRC view is that 'buy and sell agreements' whereby, on death, a person's interest must be acquired by his fellow partners or director shareholders, are sufficient to deny relief.

Where business property is disposed of by way of a gift with reservation, the availability of relief where the reservation is released, or when the donor dies, is determined by treating the shares or securities as having been owned by the donor since the disposal by way of gift, but otherwise determining entitlement to business property relief by reference to the donee (see 6785).

The Court of Appeal has held that settled property (settled land) used for the purposes of the life tenant's business qualified for relief under (1) above. HMRC accept that the higher rate relief is available provided the settled property is transferred along with the business; if the settled property is transferred alone, the lower rate applies.

Where there is a gift of cash which on the construction of a will can only be satisfied by resort to an asset which qualifies for business relief, the gift itself qualifies for business relief.

Law: IHTA 1984, s. 103–105, 109A, 113; *Inheritance Tax (Market Makers) Regulations 1992* (SI 1992/3181) (as amended by SI 2001/3629); *McCall & Anor (Personal representatives of McClean deceased) v R & C Commrs* [2009] BTC 8059, *McCall & Anor (Personal representatives of McClean, dec'd) v R & C Commrs* [2009] NICA 12; *Executors* *of Piercy (deceased) v R & C Commrs*; *Trustees of Nelson Dance Family Settlement v R & C Commrs* (2008) Sp C 682; *Russell v IR Commrs* [1988] BTC 8,041; *Fetherstonhaugh v IR Commrs* [1984] BTC 8,046

Source: SP 12/80, *Business relief from inheritance tax: buy and sell agreements*; HMRC *Inheritance Tax: Customer Guide*;

Website: www.hmrc.gov.uk/cto/customerguide/page1.htm

See *British Tax Reporter* ¶664-000.

7255 Excluded businesses

If the business concerned consists wholly or mainly of securities, stocks, shares, land, buildings, making investments, or holding investments, then relief will be denied unless the business is that of a market maker on The Stock Exchange (or a discount house) and is carried on in the UK, or unless that business is to act as a holding company for a company or companies whose business is not one of the above. Market makers on the London International Financial Futures and Options Exchange (LIFFE) are also excluded from the above restrictions.

In one case the High Court denied relief where the business of a caravan park was predominantly receiving rents and was therefore mainly the making or holding of investments.

The relief is also unavailable where the property is shares or securities of a company that is being wound up, unless the business of the company is to be continued after reconstruction or amalgamation, which must take place no later than one year after the transfer of value.

Law: IHTA 1984, s. 103–105, 109A, 113; *Inheritance Tax (Market Makers) Regulations* 1992 (SI 1992/3181) (as amended by SI 2001/3629); *Weston (Exor of the Will of Weston dec'd) v IR Commrs* [2000] BTC 8,041

Source: HMRC *Inheritance Tax: Customer Guide*

Website: www.hmrc.gov.uk/cto/customerguide/page1.htm

See *British Tax Reporter* ¶664-950.

7259 Minimum period of ownership for business property relief

To obtain 'business property relief' (see 7253), the property must have either been owned by the transferor for the two years immediately before the transfer, or must have replaced other property which was owned for two out of the five years immediately before the transfer. The value on which relief can be claimed is the lowest value during the five years. The property in either case must be one of the types set out at 7253 that qualify for business relief. If the transferor became entitled to any property on the death of another person, he is deemed to have owned it from that death and, if the deceased was his spouse or civil partner, then he is deemed to have owned it for any periods that the spouse or civil partner owned it.

Relief also will be granted, even though the property has not been owned for two years, if there have been two transfers of value, at least one being made as a transfer on death, and all or part of the earlier transfer qualified for relief; the property that qualified for relief must have become, on that earlier transfer, the property of the person making the later transfer or their spouse or civil partner. If only part of the earlier transfer was eligible for relief, then only a like part of the later transfer will be eligible for relief, and if the property is replacement property, the relief is not to exceed what it would have been had the property not been replaced.

HMRC take the view that where agricultural property is replaced by business property (or vice versa) shortly before the owner's death (see also 7297) the period of ownership of the original property will normally be relevant for applying the minimum ownership condition to the replacement property.

Law: IHTA 1984, s. 106–109

Source: Revenue interpretation, 'IHT: Business and Agricultural Property Relief', Inland Revenue, *Tax Bulletin*, December 1994, p. 182; *HMRC Inheritance Tax: Customer Guide*

Website: www.hmrc.gov.uk/cto/customerguide/page1.htm

See *British Tax Reporter* ¶665-500.

7260 Transfers within seven years before death and business property relief

Where because of the transferor's death within seven years a PET becomes chargeable or extra tax becomes payable in respect of a chargeable transfer (see 6800), additional conditions have to be met before business property relief (see 7253) is available. They are:

(1) the original transferee must retain ownership of the property originally transferred throughout the period from the original chargeable transfer to the death of the transferor;

(2) the original property must still fulfil the conditions and requirements of 'relevant business property' at the time of the transferor's death, except that it is not necessary for the transferee to have owned the property for two years if the original transfer was less than two years before the death.

The second condition above does not apply for shares which were 'quoted' (see 6571) at the time of the gift nor for shares which gave the donor control at the time of the gift and were unquoted throughout the period until death (this prevented relief from being lost if, for example, control passed from unquoted shares by virtue of a rights issue which is not taken up or the flotation of the company).

Business property relief is ignored in determining whether there has been a PET or a chargeable lifetime transfer. This is to avoid the argument that a transfer valued below £3,000 as a result of BPR, for example, could be an exempt transfer under the annual exemption provision.

Where the transferee dies before the transferor, the conditions set out above are treated as satisfied to the extent that they were satisfied at the transferee's death and the IHT payable on the transferor's death is to be reduced accordingly.

Replacement property

The relief is available where the original property is replaced by other qualifying property during the period in question provided that:

- the whole consideration received for any original property disposed of was applied in the acquisition of the replacement property;
- not more than 36 months elapsed between the conclusion of the contract for the disposal of the property sold and the conclusion of the contract for the acquisition of the new property (HMRC may permit a longer period);
- both the disposal and the acquisition were at arm's length;
- the transferee owned either the original property or the replacement property throughout the period from the date of the gift to the transferor's death;
- the replacement property qualifies as 'relevant business property' immediately before the transferor's death.

Law: IHTA 1984, s. 113A, 113B

Source: *HMRC Inheritance Tax: Customer Guide*

Website: www.hmrc.gov.uk/cto/customerguide/page1.htm

See *British Tax Reporter* ¶665-700.

7262   Valuation of business property eligible for relief

Business property relief (see 7253) is related to the value of the business transferred; the value of a business, or an interest in a business, is the value of the assets including goodwill, less any liabilities incurred for the purposes of the business. If a company is a member of a group and another company in the group deals in stocks or shares, etc. this company will be ignored when calculating the value of shares in the other companies of the group, unless that company is a discount house or a market maker or is a holding company.

Law: IHTA 1984, s. 110, 111

Source: *HMRC Inheritance Tax: Customer Guide*

Website: www.hmrc.gov.uk/cto/customerguide/page1.htm

See *British Tax Reporter* ¶664-150.

7265 Assets excepted from business property relief

Excepted assets are left out of account in the valuation of property which qualifies for relief (see 7262). An asset is excepted if it is not used wholly or mainly for the business for the two years immediately before the transfer, or 'required at the time of the transfer for future use for those purposes'. Cash held in a company's bank account at the date of the death of the holder of 50 per cent of the shares was excluded from relief in circumstances where the cash was not used for seven years. A special commissioner has held that at the time of the death, the money could not be said to be 'required ... for future use' if it was not in fact used for such a long period.

If a company is a member of a group, use of an asset by another company in the group will be treated as use for the business concerned, provided that immediately before the transfer and during use, the company is a member of the group and provided the company is not dealing in shares, securities, etc. However, this will not apply to any land or building, machinery or plant used immediately before the transfer, wholly or mainly for a business carried on by a company of which the transferor had control or a partnership of which he was a partner, unless it was so used for two years before the transfer or it replaced another asset so used and it and the other asset were so used for at least two out of the five years before the transfer. If the two-year ownership requirement is waived because of successive qualifying transfers (see 7259) and the asset is so used between the earlier and later transfer, the condition will be treated as satisfied.

Where only part of any land or buildings is used exclusively for business use, the value of the part so used will be such proportion of the whole as may be just.

Law: IHTA 1984, s. 112; *Barclays Bank Trust Co Ltd v IR Commrs* (1998) Sp C 158

Source: *HMRC Inheritance Tax: Customer Guide*

Website: www.hmrc.gov.uk/cto/customerguide/page1.htm

See *British Tax Reporter* ¶665-150.

7268 Interaction between business property relief and other reliefs

If 'agricultural relief' (see 7292ff.) or 'relief on the disposal of trees or underwood' (see 7320ff.) has already been obtained, then business property relief (see 7253) cannot also be claimed. If any value is included in the value of a person's estate immediately before his death, the value so included will not be reduced by these provisions.

Law: IHTA 1984, s. 114

Source: *HMRC Inheritance Tax: Customer Guide*

Website: www.hmrc.gov.uk/cto/customerguide/page1.htm

See *British Tax Reporter* ¶666-200.

RELIEF FOR AGRICULTURAL PROPERTY

7292 Introduction to agricultural property relief

The value of agricultural property in the UK or a qualifying EEA member state which is transferred will be reduced by 100 per cent (50 per cent for transfers or deaths before 10 March 1992) provided certain conditions are satisfied; there must be a right to vacant possession, or vacant possession must be obtainable within 12 months, otherwise the relief will be limited to 50 per cent (30 per cent). The condition as to vacant possession being obtained or obtainable within 12 months is regarded as satisfied where the transferor's interest in the property either:

- carries a right to vacant possession within 24 months of the transfer; or
- is, notwithstanding the terms of the tenancy, valued at an amount broadly equivalent to the vacant possession value of the property.

> ### Example
>
> Robert has owned and occupied a farm comprising agricultural land and buildings occupied for farming for ten years. He transfers the farm to his son in June 2010. There is a right to vacant possession of the farm. Since Robert is transferring agricultural property and has occupied it for at least two years before the transfer (see 7297) and since there is a right to vacant possession, the value of the property transferred will be reduced by 100 per cent, thereby effectively exempting it from IHT.

Where agricultural property is disposed of by way of gift with reservation, the availability of relief where the reservation is released, or when the donor dies, is determined by reference to the donee (see 6785).

If the property is subject to a contract for its ultimate sale at the time of the transfer, relief may be denied in certain circumstances.

Relief is given to those shareholders who control farming companies (see 7295).

The 100 per cent rate of relief is also available if the interest of the transferor in the property immediately before the transfer does not carry the rights referred to above where the property is let on a tenancy beginning after 31 August 1995 (or, in Scotland, a tenancy acquired after that date by right of succession). In HMRC's view, the 1995 amendments to the agricultural property relief regime applied to all tenancies commencing after 31 August 1995, provided other necessary conditions were satisfied, irrespective of whether the tenancy in question fell within the provisions of the *Agricultural Tenancies Act* 1995.

The availability of agricultural property relief at 100 per cent has been extended to circumstances where farmland subject to an agricultural tenancy is acquired as a result of the death of the previous tenant. This applies where the tenant's death or, in a case involving retirement, the landowner's death occurs after 31 August 1995.

Agricultural property relief has been extended to include land assets taken out of farming and dedicated under a habitat scheme (see 7310).

Law: IHTA 1984, s. 115(1), (5), 116, 124, FA 2009, s. 122

Source: ESC F17, *Relief for agricultural property*; Revenue interpretation, 'Relief for tenanted agricultural land'; *HMRC Inheritance Tax: Customer Guide*

Website: www.hmrc.gov.uk/cto/customerguide/page1.htm

See *British Tax Reporter* ¶658-000.

7295 Agricultural property and its value for relief

Agricultural property relief (see 7292) applies to agricultural property, which means agricultural land or pasture, including woodland and buildings occupied for farming. The value of such agricultural property is determined by treating the property as agricultural property for all time. A stud farm operation constitutes agriculture. Land used for short rotation coppice is also treated as agricultural land.

The Court of Appeal has held that the phrase 'agricultural land or pasture' means bare land or pasture and does not include buildings on the land. The inclusion of a reference to certain types of buildings later in the provision was intended to expand the availability of the relief to the categories of buildings mentioned rather than merely to clarify the meaning of the basic phrase 'agricultural land or pasture'.

Where there is a transfer of agricultural property which includes a cottage occupied by a retired farm employee or their widow(er), the requirement as to occupation for agricultural purposes is regarded as satisfied if the occupier is a statutorily protected tenant or the occupation is under a lease granted to the farm employee as part of the employee's contract of employment by the landlord for agricultural purposes.

Shares or securities giving the transferor control of a company can constitute agricultural property.

Law: FA 1995, s.154; IHTA 1984, s. 115(2)–(4), s. 122; *Starke & Anor (Exors of Brown dec'd) v IR Commrs* [1995] BTC 8,028

Source: ESC F16, *Relief for agricultural property and farm cottages*; HMRC *Inheritance Tax: Customer Guide*

Website: www.hmrc.gov.uk/cto/customerguide/page1.htm

See *British Tax Reporter* ¶658-250.

7297 Minimum period of occupation or ownership for agricultural property relief

Except as noted below, to obtain agricultural property relief (see 7292), the agricultural property must have been occupied by the transferor (or by a company he controls or by a Scottish partnership of which he is a partner) for two years immediately before the transfer, or owned by him for seven years and, during that time, must have been occupied by someone for the purposes of agriculture (which does not include the grazing of horses used for leisure purposes).

If the transferor became entitled to any property on the death of another person, he will be deemed to have owned it from that death and, if the deceased is his spouse, then he will be deemed to have owned it for any periods that the spouse owned it; this also extends to occupation by the other person but there are additional provisions determining the rate of relief in such cases.

Relief also will be granted, even though the property has not been owned for two years, if there have been two transfers of value, at least one being made as a transfer on death, and all or part of the earlier transfer qualified for relief; the property that qualified for relief must have become, on that earlier transfer, the property of the person making the later transfer or their spouse. If only part of the earlier transfer was eligible for relief, then only a like part of the later transfer will be eligible for relief, and if the property is replacement property, the relief is not to exceed what it would have been had the property not been replaced.

If the agricultural property replaced other agricultural property, relief may similarly be available, but together they must have been occupied for two out of five years or been owned for seven out of the ten years before the transfer. Changes resulting from the formation, alteration or dissolution of a partnership will be disregarded.

Inheritance Tax

See also 7259 regarding HMRC's view where agricultural property is replaced by business property (or vice versa) shortly before the owner's death.

Law: IHTA 1984, s. 117–121; *Exors of Wheatly (dec'd)* (1998) Sp C 149

Source: *HMRC Inheritance Tax: Customer Guide*

Website: www.hmrc.gov.uk/cto/customerguide/page1.htm

See *British Tax Reporter* ¶658-500.

7305 Transfers within seven years before death and agricultural property relief

Where a PET becomes chargeable or extra tax becomes payable in respect of a chargeable transfer other than a PET, by reason of the transferor's death within seven years (see 6800), and agricultural property relief (see 7292) is claimed, the following additional conditions must be met:

- the original transferee must retain ownership of the original property throughout the period from the original chargeable transfer to the death of the transferor ('the relevant period');
- the original property must still be agricultural property when the transferor dies and must have been occupied for the purposes of agriculture by the transferee or another, throughout the relevant period;
- where relief is claimed in respect of a controlling interest in a farming company, the property owned by the company must have been so owned by the company and occupied for the purposes of agriculture, whether by the company or another, throughout the relevant period.

Agricultural property relief is ignored in determining whether there has been a PET or a chargeable lifetime transfer. See further ¶7260.

Where the transferee has died within the period between the original transfer and the transferor's death, the conditions set out above will be treated as satisfied, and the tax or additional tax payable on the transferor's death reduced accordingly, to the extent that the conditions were so satisfied at the death of the transferee.

Agricultural relief remains available where, during the relevant period, the original property is replaced by other agricultural property, a farming business is incorporated or there is a reorganisation or reconstruction of shares.

Replacement property

If the original property has been replaced by other property, then the following further conditions must be met before the relief is available:

- the whole consideration received for any original property disposed of must be applied in acquiring the replacement property;
- not more than 36 months must elapse between the conclusion of a contract for the disposal and the conclusion of a contract for the acquisition (HMRC may permit a longer period);
- both transactions must be at arm's length;
- either the original property or the replacement property must have been owned by the transferee throughout the relevant period;
- the replacement property must be 'agricultural property' immediately before the transferor's death; and
- throughout the respective periods of ownership, the properties must have been occupied by the transferee or someone else for the purposes of agriculture.

Law: IHTA 1984, s. 124A, 124B

Source: *HMRC Inheritance Tax: Customer Guide*

Website: www.hmrc.gov.uk/cto/customerguide/page1.htm

See *British Tax Reporter* ¶658-850.

7310 Land in habitat schemes

Agricultural property relief (see 7292ff.) has been extended to include land in habitat schemes. All land in such schemes is treated as agricultural land, the management of such land to be agriculture and buildings used in carrying out that management to be farm buildings thus qualifying for relief. Land is treated as being in a habitat scheme for the purposes of relief if an application for aid under one of the enactments listed below has been made and is still in force.

The relevant statutory regulations (as long as the relevant undertaking has been given), which cover the habitat schemes that require land to be taken out of farming for 20 years and therefore come under the extended relief, are the:

- *Habitat (Former Set-Aside Land) Regulations* 1994 (SI 1994/1292);
- *Habitat (Salt-Marsh) Regulations* 1994 (SI 1994/1293);
- *Habitats (Scotland) Regulations* 1994 (SI 1994/2710); and
- *Habitat Improvement Regulations (Northern Ireland)* 1995 (SI 1995/134).

The above has effect in relation to any transfer of value made after 25 November 1996 and in relation to transfers on which IHT becomes chargeable due to events occurring after that date. This covers situations where a gift made before 26 November 1996 becomes chargeable to tax on or after that date due to the donor's death occurring within seven years of making that gift.

Law: IHTA 1984, s. 124C

Source: *HMRC Inheritance Tax: Customer Guide*

Website: www.hmrc.gov.uk/cto/customerguide/page1.htm

See *British Tax Reporter* ¶658-200.

RELIEF FOR WOODLANDS

7320 Introduction to relief for woodlands

The IHT which would normally be charged on death in relation to growing trees and underwood can be deferred until sale (see 7323), unless the land is the subject of agricultural relief (see 7292ff.).

Source: *HMRC Inheritance Tax: Customer Guide*

Website: www.hmrc.gov.uk/cto/customerguide/page1.htm

See *British Tax Reporter* ¶653-150.

7323 Deferral of IHT on woodlands until subsequent disposal

If the deceased was beneficially entitled to the land throughout the five years preceding his death, or became beneficially entitled to it for other than a consideration in money or money's worth (e.g. inherited it), and provided there are trees or underwood growing on the land, then the value of those trees or underwood may be left out of account in determining the value transferred on death An election so to do must be made within two years of the death. It should be noted that IHT will be charged on a subsequent disposal of the trees and underwood (unless the disposal is to a spouse) and the person entitled to the proceeds of sale will be liable to pay the tax (see 7326). *Finance Act* 2009 extended the relief to woodland located in a qualifying EEA member state.

Law: IHTA 1984, s. 125, FA 2009, s. 122

Source: *HMRC Inheritance Tax: Customer Guide*

Website: www.hmrc.gov.uk/cto/customerguide/page1.htm

See *British Tax Reporter* ¶653-650.

7326 Value and rate of IHT on disposal after woodlands deferral

If the value of trees has been left out of account on death (see 7323), and they have been subsequently disposed of, IHT will be charged on the net proceeds of the sale if it is a sale for full consideration in money or money's worth or, in any other case, on the net value of the trees or underwood at the time of the disposal. Tax is charged as if the trees or underwood had never been left out of account and had formed the highest part of the value of the deceased's estate on death.

If the property had not been left out of account, and if it would have been taken into account for the purposes of business relief, the amount on which tax is charged will be reduced by 50 per cent. This is an anomaly since the rate of business property relief has been increased to 100 per cent. In most cases, it will be advantageous simply to claim business property relief (if available at 100 per cent) rather than woodlands relief.

The expenses of disposal and replanting within three years of the disposal will be allowed as a deduction in arriving at the net proceeds of sale or the net value of the trees.

Example

Barry died in December 1996 leaving an estate of £650,000, including growing timber worth £85,000 which he had owned since 1965. He left it all to his son Thomas who elected to postpone payment of tax. Thomas died in May 2010 leaving an estate of £1,250,000 to his son Max. The growing timber is now worth £130,000. Max sells the timber in December 2010 for £165,000 net. No tax is chargeable on the value of the timber at Barry's death because the election was made to postpone payment of tax. If an election was also made on Thomas's death, no tax will be payable until the sale by Max. Assuming that Thomas made no chargeable lifetime transfers the tax payable will be on £1,250,000 less £130,000, i.e. on £1,120,000. The tax payable on the disposal of the timber by Max will be on the net sale price which is £165,000. The rate at which it will start is the point on the death scale where Thomas's estate finished. £165,000 will therefore be charged at 40 per cent. Therefore, total tax to be borne by Max is £66,000. Even though Thomas had not owned the timber for five years, the election to postpone could be made since the timber had been inherited.

Law: IHTA 1984, s. 126–130

Source: *HMRC Inheritance Tax: Customer Guide*

Website: www.hmrc.gov.uk/cto/customerguide/page1.htm

See *British Tax Reporter* ¶653-300.

RELIEF FOR WORKS OF ART AND HISTORIC BUILDINGS

7346 Introduction to relief for works of art and historic buildings

HMRC may designate certain types of property conditionally exempt from IHT. The property in point relates to artistic works and land or buildings of significant interest (see 7349).

An IHT charge may arise on the breach of any of the required undertakings or on death or disposal (see 7349, 7351).

There are similar provisions to disapply various discretionary trust charges where designated property is held in such a trust, with corresponding adjustments to the charge on breach of conditions (see 7040, 7055).

Law: IHTA 1984, s. 30, 31

See *British Tax Reporter* ¶650-300.

7349 Designated property and undertakings for conditional exemption

HMRC may designate any of the following property to be conditionally exempt (see 7346):

- any 'relevant object' which, or any collection or group of relevant objects which, taken as a whole, appears to HMRC to be pre-eminent for its national, scientific, historic or artistic interest;
  A 'relevant object' means a picture, print, book, manuscript, work of art or scientific object, or other things not yielding income; and in determining whether an object, etc. is 'pre-eminent', regard is had to any significant association of the object, etc. with a particular place;
  Before 31 July 1998, this first category comprised pictures, prints, books, manuscripts, works of art, scientific collections or other things not yielding income which appeared to HMRC to be of national, scientific, historic or artistic interest;
- any land which in HMRC's opinion is of outstanding scenic or historic or scientific interest;
- any building for the preservation of which special steps should in the opinion of the Board be taken by reason of its outstanding historic or architectural interest (or any land which adjoins it which in HMRC's opinion is essential for the protection of the character and amenities of the building or any object which in HMRC's opinion is historically associated with it).

A claim for the property to be so designated must be made. The provisions will only apply to a transfer of value on death, unless the transferor and/or his spouse have been beneficially entitled to the property for six years before the transfer, or unless the transferor acquired the property on a death which was the occasion of a transfer of value, which was itself conditionally exempt or left out of account. Conditional exemption may be obtained for designated property held in settlements for six years on the occasion of a ten-year charge or exit charge.

The rules relating to potentially exempt gifts are to be applied to national heritage property before the conditional exemption rules. If a PET becomes chargeable because of the donor's death within seven years (see 6800), it will then be possible to make a claim for conditional exemption. The claim may not extend to any property which has been sold by the donee during the period between the transfer and the donor's death. Further, in determining whether property is appropriate for designation, the circumstances prevailing at the time of death, rather than at the time of transfer, will be taken into account.

Undertakings

A person who HMRC consider to be appropriate, will be required to give an undertaking that the property will not leave the UK without HMRC's approval and that reasonable steps will be taken for the property's preservation and for securing reasonable public access. Before 31 July 1998, public access could be limited to those with a prior appointment. Owners may also now be required to publicise the terms of their undertakings and to disclose any other information relevant to public access: while this gives scope for agreeing terms for publishing certain types of confidential information, it operates subject to a claim to the Treasury not to grant access to such objects as manuscripts on grounds of confidentiality.

In the case of land and buildings, the undertaking will be for the maintenance of the land and preservation of its character or for the maintenance, repair and preservation of the property, as appropriate.

Variation of undertakings
Originally, an undertaking relating to conditionally exempt property could only be changed with the owner's consent. However, a procedure now exists for undertakings given after 30 July 1998 whereby if agreement to vary the undertaking cannot be reached with the owner, a special commissioner may direct that the variation should take effect if satisfied that it would be just and reasonable in all the circumstances. The same procedure may also be used to vary undertakings given before 31 July 1998, so as to secure extended access for the public where access is currently by appointment only, or to publish any terms of the undertaking.

Claims

In relation to transfers made, and other events occurring, after 16 March 1998, claims must be made within two years from the date of the transfer of value giving rise to the claim or, in the case of a PET, two years from the date of death which rendered the PET chargeable, or such longer period as HMRC may allow. Previously, there was no time-limit.

Inheritance Tax

A claim for exemption may be made on 700A. That form provides that an owner who does not live in a house which is or will be open to the public will be able to choose between:

- lending his objects for display in a house which is regularly open to the public;
- lending his objects to public collections on a long-term basis; or
- asking HMRC to arrange for details of the objects to be put on a register maintained by the National Art Library. That register will be available to museums, galleries and members of the public. Owners will be required, on request, to lend the objects for special exhibitions for up to six months in any two-year period and to make arrangements for members of the public to view the objects.

Law: IHTA 1984, s. 30(3BA), 35A

See *British Tax Reporter* ¶650-350.

7351   Amount of IHT charged where conditional exemption lifted

In relation to conditional exemption for works of art, historic buildings, etc. (see 7346), breach of an 'undertaking' (see 7349) is treated as a chargeable event, as are the death of the person beneficially entitled to the property and disposal of the property. If the property is sold or given to any of the bodies listed at 7195, or given to HMRC in satisfaction of the tax due, it will not be treated as a chargeable event.

A death or disposal other than by sale will also not be a chargeable event if similar undertakings are given. Undertakings given after 30 July 1998 must comply with the changed requirements outlined at 7349.

The persons liable for the IHT due are:

- in the case of death, the person entitled to the proceeds of sale if sold immediately after death; and
- in the case of a disposal, the person for whose benefit the property is disposed of.

Inheritance tax is charged on an amount equal to the value of the property at the time of the chargeable event. Death rates will apply if the relevant transferor (see below) is dead, as if the amount had been added to the value transferred on his death and had formed the highest part of that value.

The relevant transferor is usually the last person who made a conditionally exempt transfer. However, HMRC may select any person within the last 30 years before the event if there have been two or more such transfers within that period.

Example

Hugo has a very large estate, including valuable books, which are designated conditionally exempt on his death by HMRC. He leaves the books to Sophie and they are conditionally exempt from tax. Five years later Sophie gives the books to Annabel who gives fresh undertakings so that the conditional exemption is continued. Two years later Annabel sells the books so that tax becomes chargeable. Since the transfer by Hugo occurred within the 30-year period, HMRC can calculate the tax on the sale by Annabel by reference to Hugo's death. If so, the amount will be added to the value transferred on Hugo's death and tax will be charged as if that amount had formed the highest part of the value transferred on Hugo's death. This in effect prevents the use of Annabel as a middle man to escape tax at the high rates which are chargeable on Hugo's death.

The cumulative total of the last transferor will have to be altered if he is still alive. He will be treated as if he had made a gift of non-exempt property valued at the date of the chargeable event. If the transferor is dead his estate on death will be increased by the amount on which tax was charged on the chargeable event.

Law: IHTA 1984, s. 32–35 and Sch. 1

See *British Tax Reporter* ¶650-850.

MAINTENANCE FUNDS FOR HISTORIC BUILDINGS

7371   Maintenance of historic buildings

There will be no IHT liability where property is put into a settlement in order to repair, maintain or preserve historic buildings if HMRC give the necessary direction (see 7374). A direction may have effect at the time of the transfer or it may be given after that time. In the latter case, in relation to transfers of value made after 16 March 1998, a claim for the direction must be made within two years from the date of the transfer, or such longer period as HMRC may allow.

There may be a charge to tax where property ceases to be subject to maintenance funds or where the trustees make a disposition reducing the fund's value (see 7055).

Law: FA 1998, s. 144; IHTA 1984, s. 27, Sch. 4

See *British Tax Reporter* ¶651-900.

7374   Requirements for HMRC direction as to maintenance fund exemption

HMRC will give a direction for exemption in respect of donations to maintenance funds for historic buildings, etc. (see 7371) if the settlement meets certain requirements and the property being put into the settlement is of a character and amount appropriate for the purposes of the settlement. The trustees must be resident, must include a professional adviser, and they must be approved by HMRC.

Inheritance Tax

The requirements to be met are that:

- none of the property can, for six years, be used other than for the maintenance, repair or preservation of qualifying property (designated property for which undertakings have been given), or for defraying the expenses of the trustees or for the maintenance, repairs or preservation of property in the settlement; and
- none of the property can devolve, otherwise than on any body (see 7195) or charity, on ceasing to be comprised in the settlement; and
- none of the property can be applied at the end of the period except as mentioned above.

The first two requirements do not apply to property which was previously comprised in another settlement and became comprised in the current settlement in circumstances such that no IHT was charged (i.e. property which was exempt under another settlement and which within 30 days becomes comprised in the present settlement).

HMRC will give a direction that a fund qualifies, when a claim is made, if they are satisfied:

(1) that the property is of a character and amount appropriate for the purposes of those trusts and that the property can for six years from the date it became held on the trusts be applied only:

    (a) for the maintenance, repair or preservation of, or making provision for public access to, property which is for the time being qualifying property for the maintenance, repair or preservation of property held on the trusts or for such improvement of property so held as is reasonable having regard to the purposes of the trusts, or for defraying the expenses of the trustees in relation to the property so held; or

    (b) as respects income not so applied and not accumulated for the benefit of a body set up for national purposes or the public benefit (see 7198) or of a preservation charity; and

    (c) that none of the property can on ceasing to be held on the trusts at any time within that period, devolve otherwise than on such body or charity and that income arising from such property can only be applied as mentioned above; and

(2) that the trustees are approved by HMRC, include a trust corporation, solicitor, or accountant and are resident in the UK.

There are special provisions regarding property previously comprised in another settlement (see 7040, 7055).

HMRC may withdraw the direction by notice in writing to the trustees if the facts cease to warrant the continuance of the direction. Where a direction is in force the trustees must furnish such accounts and information relating to the property as HMRC may reasonably require.

Property is qualifying property for these purposes if it is land or a building of appropriate interest and has been designated as such.

Law: IHTA 1984, Sch. 4, para. 2(1)

See *British Tax Reporter* ¶652-000.

EXCLUDED PROPERTY

7394 Introduction to excluded property

No account is to be taken of the value of 'excluded property' (see 7397) which ceases to form part of a person's estate as a result of a disposition. A person's estate is the aggregate of all the property to which he is beneficially entitled, except that the estate of a person immediately before his death does not include excluded property.

However, an 'excluded' asset is not always completely irrelevant for IHT purposes. Thus:

- an excluded asset in a person's estate may still affect the valuation of another asset in the estate (e.g. an 'excluded' holding of shares in an unquoted company (see 6572) may affect the value of a similar holding in the estate which is not 'excluded');
- the value of an 'excluded' asset at the time the asset becomes comprised in a settlement may be relevant in determining the rate of any tax charge arising in respect of the settlement under the IHT rules concerning trusts without interests in possession (see 6950–6960).

Law: IHTA 1984, s. 3(2), 5(1)

See *British Tax Reporter* ¶602-150.

7397 Meaning of 'excluded property'

'Excluded property' (see 7394) is determined in accordance with the following rules.

Property 'situated outside the UK' (see 6550) is excluded property (i.e. not within the charge to IHT) if the person beneficially entitled to it is an individual domiciled (see 6540) outside the UK: in other words, for persons domiciled abroad, IHT generally applies only to their UK assets. Further, certain government securities (savings certificates, premium bonds, National Savings Bank deposits, etc.) are excluded property if the individual is domiciled in the Channel Islands or the Isle of Man.

By concession, decorations awarded for valour or gallant conduct are treated as excluded property if it is shown that they have never been transferred for consideration in money or money's worth.

Settled property

Slightly different rules apply to property held in a settlement. Property (but not a reversionary interest) comprised in a settlement and situated outside the UK when a chargeable event occurs is excluded property if the 'settlor' (see 6883) was 'domiciled' (see 6540) outside the UK at the time the settlement was made; for this purpose, property becomes comprised in a settlement when it, or other property which it represents, is introduced by the settlor. If the settlor or his or her spouse or civil partner was originally entitled to an interest in possession in the property, it is deemed to be comprised in a separate settlement when that interest ceases (see 7017) so that the settlor must, in addition, have been UK-domiciled when the original settlement was made. Similarly, if property moves between settlements without vesting in someone in between, it is deemed to continue to be held in the original settlement (see 7020), so that the settlor must, in addition, have been UK-domiciled when the second settlement was made.

Addition of assets to existing settlements

In the light of the definition of 'settlement' (see 6883), HMRC's view is that assets added to a settlor's own settlement made at an earlier time when the settlor was domiciled abroad are not 'excluded', wherever they may be situated, if the settlor has a UK domicile at the time of making the addition (see further 6883).

Reversionary interests

A reversionary interest is excluded property unless:

* it has at any time been acquired (whether by the person entitled to it or by a person previously entitled to it) for a consideration in money or money's worth; or
* it is one to which either the settlor or his spouse or civil partner is or has been beneficially entitled; or
* it is the interest expectant on the determination of a lease treated as a settlement (e.g. a lease for life: see 6883).

Visiting forces

Certain property of overseas forces visiting the UK is excluded property.

Law: IHTA 1984, s. 6, 48, 82, 155

Source: SP E9, *Excluded property*; ESC F19, *Decorations awarded for valour or gallant conduct*

See *British Tax Reporter* ¶602-200.

7410 Allocation of exemptions where transfer partly chargeable

A transfer of value (particularly a bequest under a will) may be chargeable or exempt; it may also be partly chargeable and partly exempt, e.g. where an exemption limit is exceeded. At the same time, a bequest may be stated to be free of tax or it may 'bear its own tax', i.e. the tax falls on the person who becomes entitled to the property given, etc. In combination, this variety of possibilities raises two separate problems:

- how to ascertain the value for tax of respective gifts and thus calculate the total tax payable on the transfer; and
- how the burden of tax, once calculated, is to be distributed among the donees or beneficiaries.

Specific rules apply where there is an exemption on transfer between spouses or civil partners or other transfers exempt during life and on death (see 7192ff.) or where there is a conditional exemption for the preservation of certain works of art and historical buildings, etc. (see 7346ff.).

Burden of tax

The 'burden of tax' is a term used to show the way in which the allocation of exemptions so as to produce the tax payable affects the distribution of the transfer after tax. This is clearly different from the 'incidence of tax' (see 7539) which refers to funds out of which the tax must be borne.

Notwithstanding the terms of any disposition, no tax is to fall on an exempt specific gift and no tax attributable to the residue is to fall on an exempt share of residue. This provision was considered in a case where a will which gave residue as to half to non-exempt individuals and half to exempt charities was construed, for IHT purposes, as giving the half-share of residue to the exempt beneficiaries after payment of debts, funeral and testamentary expenses, but before payment of IHT. Tax was to be borne by the non-exempt beneficiaries so that, in effect, the net amount which the non-exempt beneficiaries collectively received was less than the amount received collectively by the charities.

Attribution of value to gifts

Gifts are treated as reduced (or 'abated') for IHT purposes to the extent necessary to reduce their value to that of the assets available to meet them. Where gifts take effect out of different funds, the abatement is applied separately to each fund.

If there is a monetary limit on such exemption as is mentioned above, gifts bearing their own tax are covered by the exemption before other gifts; subject to that, the excess over the limit is apportioned rateably according to the amount of each gift.

The value attributed to residuary gifts is determined after value is attributed to specific gifts.

Inheritance Tax

If specific gifts bear their own tax, it makes no difference whether the residue is partly exempt since no tax on the specific gifts will fall on the residue and tax on the chargeable part of the residue cannot fall on any exempt part of it; the value transferred is attributed to any specific gifts according to their actual values, the balance to residue.

If there are specific gifts not bearing their own tax and other chargeable gifts, a specific method is applied involving the attribution of a hypothetical gross value to the tax-free gifts. This value is used to calculate the taxable estate and hence the effective gross value of the gifts.

If part of the value transferred is property eligible for business property relief (see 7253ff.) or agricultural property relief (see 7292), all specific gifts and any non-specific gifts out of the property in point are first reduced to reflect that relief.

Law: IHTA 1984, s. 36–42; *Re Benham's Will Trusts* [1996] BTC 8,008

See *British Tax Reporter* ¶602-250.

7450   Double tax relief for IHT

Where property suffers a charge to IHT and also to another similar tax in another territory, relief may be given in the UK either in accordance with a treaty between the UK and the other territory or unilaterally.

Treaties made by Order in Council are given effect for IHT purposes.

Unilateral relief is provided where there is no treaty in force. Where the property is situated in the overseas territory and not in the UK, the credit against IHT is equal to the whole of the foreign tax. Otherwise, a proportionate credit is given:

$$\frac{A + B}{A} \times C,$$

where

A   is the amount of IHT
B   is the overseas tax (or aggregate overseas tax), and
C   is the aggregate of all amounts included in A or B, except the largest.

Law: IHTA 1984, s. 158, 159

See *British Tax Reporter* ¶687-000.

ADMINISTRATION, LIABILITY AND INCIDENCE

ADMINISTRATION OF INHERITANCE TAX

7500 Scheme of administration of IHT

The management of IHT is carried out by HM Revenue and Customs (HMRC). HMRC are subject to the authority of the Treasury which is responsible for the imposition and collection of taxation. HMRC report to the Chancellor of the Exchequer. In practice IHT is administered by HMRC (Inheritance Tax). The scheme of administration and collection is laid down in IHTA 1984, Pt. VIII. In any correspondence between the transferor and HMRC, the transferor's official reference should always be quoted unless it is not known, in which case the name, date of birth, and if dead the date of death, of the transferor should be given.

See *British Tax Reporter* ¶693-000.

7503 Need to deliver IHT accounts

An account (or in Scotland an inventory or additional inventory) must be delivered to HMRC by:

- the transferor for a lifetime transfer chargeable when made (see 6610ff.);
- the trustees for chargeable transfers relating to settled property (see 6880ff.);
- the personal representatives for the estate of a deceased person (see 6770ff.); and
- by the transferee for lifetime transfers chargeable only by reason of the transferor's death within seven years and gifts with reservation (see 6610, 6785ff.),

specifying to the best of his or her knowledge and belief the value of all appropriate property. Personal representatives must include details of any chargeable transfers made by the deceased within seven years before death.

The form of account (or supporting papers) and exceptions, etc. are determined by HMRC.

Form IHT 400 is used for all estates (other than excepted estates). It comprises a 'core account' with a number of supplementary pages that only need to be completed if relevant to the estate. In certain circumstances (basically where the charity or spouse or civil partner exemption applies and the chargeable estate is below the tax threshold) a reduced account can be filed. In all cases, IHT 421 (Form C1 in Scotland) must be filled in, as this shows details of the estate relevant for the issue of a grant of representation (see below).

Providing additional information with the account may result in more focused questions or no question on that asset or deduction: for example, if a large debt owed to the deceased's son or other relative is to be deducted, where a deduction is claimed for a guarantee debt or if it is claimed that some person had an equitable interest in property held by the deceased as sole legal owner.

A person who delivers such an account and later discovers a material defect in it must, within six months of his discovery, deliver a corrective account.

Other than in the largest estates (and a small number of other exceptions), an IHT account will be required only where there is tax to pay. In other cases, contact with the Probate Service will cover both tax and probate formalities (in Scotland a Sheriff Court covers confirmation formalities).

The liability of trustees to deliver an account extends to foreign trustees of a settlement made outside the UK by a person domiciled in the UK, for the purpose of calculating the tax liability arising on the settlor's death.

Grants of representation

In order to obtain a grant of representation, the personal representatives must deliver the account and pay any tax due to HMRC. HMRC then fill in its part of the Form IHT 421 (or Form C1 in Scotland) and return it to the personal representatives. They then submit it with the other papers necessary to obtain the grant of representation from the probate registry (Sheriff Court in Scotland). If the personal representatives are unable to ascertain the exact value of any particular property, they must deliver a provisional first account and state it to be provisional and give an undertaking to deliver a further account as soon as its value is ascertained.

If no grant of representation has been obtained within 12 months of the deceased's death, any beneficiary, or any person for whom any of the property is applied, must deliver an account to HMRC of all property in which he has an interest, or which is applicable for his benefit, and the value of that property. This will not apply if HMRC are satisfied that an account will be delivered by the personal representatives in due course.

Excepted estates

Some estates are excepted from the requirement to make an IHT account. The principal criterion for exception is that for deaths on or after 1 September 2006 the gross value of the estate plus the chargeable value of any transfers in the seven years prior to death, does not exceed the nil rate band (see 98 for current thresholds), or £1 million and the net chargeable estate after deduction of the spouse or civil partner and, or, charity exemption only is less than the nil rate band. There are also additional limitations on the following property:

(i)   the limit for the value of foreign property is £100,000;
(ii)   the limit for the value of 'specified transfers' is £150,000;
(iii)   the limit for the value of settled property is £150,000; and
(iv)   the limit for the value of a non-domiciled individual's UK estate is £150,000.

Excepted terminations and chargeable events

Regulations, which apply for terminations or chargeable events arising under relevant property trusts (see 6940) made on or after 6 April 2007, have been made that mean the trustees do not need to deliver an IHT 100 in respect of those occasions of charge.

Law: IHTA 1984, s. 216, 217, 256, 257, 261

Source: *Inheritance Tax (Delivery of Accounts) (Excepted Estates) Regulations* 2004 (SI 2004/2543), *Inheritance Tax (Delivery of Accounts) (Excepted Estates) (Amendment) Regulations* 2006 (SI 2006/2141), *Inheritance Tax (Delivery of Accounts) (Excepted Transfers and Excepted Terminations) Regulations* 2008 (SI 2008/605), *Inheritance Tax (Delivery of Accounts) (Excepted Transfers and Excepted Terminations) Regulations* 2008 (SI 2008/606); SP 2/93, *Inheritance tax: the use of substitute forms*; HMRC *Inheritance Tax: Customer Guide*

Website: www.hmrc.gov.uk/cto/customerguide/page1.htm

See *British Tax Reporter* ¶693-800.

7506 Time for delivering IHT accounts

An IHT account (see 7503) must be delivered:

- in the case of transfers on death, or PETs which become chargeable, within 12 months after the end of the month in which the death occurred or, if later, three months from the date on which the personal representatives first acted as such;
- in the case of beneficiaries or any person for whom any of the property is applied, within three months of first realising that he must deliver an account; and
- in any other case, within 12 months of the transfer or, if later, three months from the date on which he becomes liable for tax.

There is no requirement to notify HMRC nor to deliver an account on the making of a PET. However, a PET may turn out to be chargeable so records should be kept. Also, the rate at which such a PET is chargeable depends on chargeable transfers made within the seven years before. Therefore, records back to 14 years before the deceased's death may be required by HMRC.

If a transfer is reported late and the tax on a later transfer has been miscalculated as a result, any additional tax may be collected with the tax on the earlier transfer.

See also 7503 above for *Finance Act* 2004 changes.

Law: IHTA 1984, s. 216(6), s. 264

Source: HMRC *Inheritance Tax: Customer Guide*

Website: www.hmrc.gov.uk/cto/customerguide/page1.htm

See *British Tax Reporter* ¶693-800.

7508 Power to require information

HMRC can call for IHT-relevant information, in not less than 30 days, from *any* person, whether or not he or she is liable to pay any IHT or deliver an IHT account. However, a barrister or solicitor cannot be required to give information without his client's consent, except that a solicitor may be obliged to disclose his client's name and address.

Additional powers

HMRC also have additional powers to call, in not less than 30 days, for documents, accounts or particulars from a more limited class of persons. The request can only be made for the purpose of inquiring into an account (see 7503), determining whether such an account is incorrect or incomplete or making a determination (see 7512).

The class of persons involved are those who have delivered or are liable to deliver an account (see 7503). Professional privilege in the conduct of any appeal is protected. There is a right of appeal.

Inspection powers for the purposes of valuation

From 1 April 2010, a HMRC officer or person accompanying the HMRC officer in assistance can enter and inspect premises and any other property on those premises in connection with checking a person's position with regard to inheritance tax. The valuation, measurement or determination of the premises or property must be 'reasonably required' by HMRC.

Law: IHTA 1984, s. 219, 219A, 219B, FA 2008, Sch. 36, para. 12A, 12B; FA 2009, s. 96 and Sch. 48, para. 5

Source: *HMRC Inheritance Tax: Customer Guide*

Website: www.hmrc.gov.uk/cto/customerguide/page1.htm

See *British Tax Reporter* ¶694-300, ¶694-450.

7509 Information as to settlements for IHT

If a person, other than a barrister, is concerned with the making of a settlement in the course of a trade or profession carried on by him, he must, within three months of the making of the settlement, make a return to HMRC stating names and addresses of the settlor and trustees if he knows, or has reason to believe, that the settlor was domiciled in the UK and the trustees are not or will not be resident in the UK.

Law: IHTA 1984, s. 218

Source: *HMRC Inheritance Tax: Customer Guide*

Website: www.hmrc.gov.uk/cto/customerguide/page1.htm

See *British Tax Reporter* ¶694-300.

7512   Determination of relevant IHT matters by HMRC

In relation to any transfer, HMRC may determine relevant IHT matters which are:

- the date of the transfer;
- the value transferred and the value of any property to which the value transferred is wholly or partly attributable;
- the transferor;
- the tax chargeable and the persons liable;
- the amount of any payment made in excess of the tax for which a person is liable and the rate at which tax or any repayment of tax overpaid carries interest; and
- any other matter which appears to be relevant to HMRC.

Law: IHTA 1984, s. 221

See *British Tax Reporter* ¶693-100.

LIABILITY AND INCIDENCE OF INHERITANCE TAX

7530   Importance of liability and incidence for IHT

Usually, more than one person is liable for the payment of tax and payment can be recovered from any one of them. Liability depends upon the nature of the transfer (see 7533), though there are certain rules to protect those persons who become liable for payment because of their access to the property but upon whom the burden should not fall.

The incidence of tax effectively refers to the person ultimately required to bear the burden of the tax (see 7539).

See *British Tax Reporter* ¶694-800.

7533   Persons liable for IHT

Subject to certain exceptions from liability and certain limitations on the extent of a person's liability for IHT (see 7536), the following rules apply. Generally, if more than one person is liable, each of them is liable for the whole amount.

Inheritance Tax

(1) Lifetime transfers

The person primarily liable is the transferor, unless it is agreed that the transferee will pay, in which case there will be no grossing up. The transferor's spouse or civil partner may also be liable if, after the transfer of value, all remaining assets are transferred to the spouse or civil partner. Then the spouse or civil partner would be liable for IHT to the extent of the value of the transfer to them. If payment of tax remains outstanding after the due date, the following persons are also liable:

- the transferee and any person the value of whose estate is increased by the transfer;
- any person who takes the property or a beneficial interest in possession in the property at any time after the transfer;
- in the case of property transferred into a settlement any person for whose benefit any of the property or its income is applied.

(2) Transfers within seven years before death

Where a PET becomes chargeable, or where additional tax becomes payable in respect of a chargeable transfer other than a PET, because of the transferor's death within seven years (see 6800), usually HMRC will look to the transferee to pay the tax due. However, the personal representatives of the transferor are also liable for the tax subject to the limitation on the extent of their liability discussed in 7536 below.

HMRC has given a limited assurance that where a lifetime transfer made by a deceased person in the seven years before death does not come to light until after a certificate of discharge has been obtained and the estate distributed, a personal representative who has made full and proper enquiries will not usually be pursued for IHT on the transfer.

(3) Transfers on death

The persons liable for the tax are:

- the personal representatives in respect of any property which they have collected, or would have collected but for their neglect or default (subject to special rules for Scotland);
- the trustees of settled property which passes on death;
- any person in whom property becomes vested on death;
- where the property was comprised in a settlement, the beneficiaries.

Where a person is entitled to part only of the income of property as a result of death, he will be treated as entitled to an interest in the whole of the property. All IHT on the property passing on death can, therefore, be recovered from any of the beneficiaries.

Law: IHTA 1984, s. 199, 200, 203, 205, 209

Source: *HMRC Inheritance Tax: Customer Guide*

Website: www.hmrc.gov.uk/cto/customerguide/page1.htm

See *British Tax Reporter* ¶694-900.

7536 Exceptions from and limitations of IHT liability

Where the transferor or trustees of a settlement leave tax unpaid then the other persons potentially liable in relation to that transfer (see 7533) become liable. Where the value transferred is partly attributable to the tax payable on it (i.e. the reduction in value of the person's estate is the value transferred plus the tax payable on it), then those other persons will be liable to no greater extent than they would have been had the value transferred been reduced by the tax remaining unpaid. Liability may also be restricted according to the nature of the person's interest therein as mentioned below.

> ### Example
>
> Ruby transfers £50,000 to Jacob. The tax for which Ruby is liable is £5,000 (assumed figures). Therefore Ruby's estate has been reduced by £55,000. If Ruby only pays £4,000 tax then Jacob's liability will be limited to the excess over £4,000 of tax which would have been payable on value transferred of £54,000 (value transferred £55,000 less tax unpaid £1,000).

Inheritance Tax

(1) Purchasers

A purchaser of property, and a person deriving title from him, will only be liable for IHT if the property is subject to a HMRC charge.

(2) Personal representatives

Personal representatives are only liable for assets that they received or might have received but for their own neglect or default. Where the tax is attributable to property which was comprised in a settlement immediately before death and consists of land in the UK, a personal representative's liability is limited to so much of that property as is at any time available in his hands for the payment of tax, or might have been available but for his neglect or default.

Personal representatives are liable for any tax payable on the transferor's death within seven years of a PET and for any additional tax payable in respect of a chargeable transfer, other than a PET, within seven years of death only to the extent that there is no recourse against donees, trustees, beneficiaries or nominees or to the extent that tax remains unpaid 12 months after the end of the month of death.

Personal representatives are liable for the tax due on property which is included in the deceased's estate because it was property which the deceased had transferred subject to a reservation (see 6785), to the extent that the tax remains unpaid 12 months after the end of the month of death.

Personal representatives may be liable in respect of pension rights, etc.

(3) Trustees

Trustees are only liable to the extent of property that they received or disposed of, or that they have become liable to account for to the persons beneficially entitled thereto, and any other property available in their hands for the payment of tax or property that might have been so available but for their neglect or default. Trustees of pension schemes are not liable in respect of pensions, annuity or death benefits.

(4) Life tenants and beneficiaries with an interest in property

A beneficiary is only liable to the extent of any property in which he has a beneficial interest.

(5) Beneficiaries with no interest in settled property

Beneficiaries of settled property are only liable to the extent of the amount of the property or income which is applied for their benefit.

(6) Designated property

Where a transfer is of designated property, such as a work of art, the person that is liable is determined according to the nature of the event which breaches the conditions (see 7346ff.); generally, it is the trustee, the person that would be entitled to receive the proceeds of sale or the person for whose benefit the property is disposed of.

Law: IHTA 1984, s. 204, 207, 210

Source: *HMRC Inheritance Tax: Customer Guide*

Website: www.hmrc.gov.uk/cto/customerguide/page1.htm

See *British Tax Reporter* ¶695-400.

7539 Incidence of IHT

The person liable to pay any IHT due is not always the person out of whose property it should be borne (see 7530). The person liable may apply to HMRC for a certificate showing the tax he has paid so as to be able to claim a refund from the ultimate payee, etc.

On a death, where a will contains no indications to the contrary, the tax attributable to non-settled property in the UK which vests in the executors will be treated as a testamentary expense, coming out of the estate as a whole.

If a person could have paid the tax by instalments (see 7596) and is entitled to recover that tax from another person, then that other person is entitled to refund the tax also by instalments.

Where a person, other than a transferor or the spouse of a transferor, is liable for IHT attributable to the value of any property he can raise the amount of tax by selling, mortgaging or creating a terminable charge on that property whether or not that property is vested in him; where a person has a limited interest in any property, and pays IHT on that property, he will be entitled to a charge on that property.

Inheritance tax on settled property may be paid out of any property comprised in the settlement and held on the same trusts.

An application may be made by the person paying the tax (if that person is not ultimately liable) for a certificate specifying the tax paid and the debts and encumbrances allowed in valuing the property. The certificate is conclusive between the person ultimately liable and the person who paid. Inheritance tax will be repaid to the person producing the certificate.

Inheritance tax here includes interest on the tax and costs properly incurred in respect of the tax.

Law: IHTA 1984, s. 211–214

Source: *HMRC Inheritance Tax: Customer Guide*

Website: www.hmrc.gov.uk/cto/customerguide/page1.htm

See *British Tax Reporter* ¶695-450.

PAYMENT AND RECOVERY OF INHERITANCE TAX

7590 Introduction to payment and recovery of IHT

There are various rules for determining the time for payment of IHT (see 7593), though in certain circumstances payment may be made by instalments (see 7596) or by way of the transfer of property to the Crown (see 7605).

HMRC have certain powers to recover unpaid tax (see 7611) with specific preference over other creditors in respect of the transferred property (see 7608). Interest may also be charged; conversely interest may be due to the taxpayer in respect of overpaid tax (see 7599).

Law: IHTA 1984, s. 226–244

Source: *HMRC Inheritance Tax: Customer Guide*

Website: www.hmrc.gov.uk/cto/customerguide/page1.htm

See *British Tax Reporter* ¶695-600.

7593 Time for payment of IHT

Unless it can be paid in instalments (see 7596), IHT is due in accordance with the following rules. Tax is due six months after the end of the month of the chargeable transfer. If the chargeable transfer is made between 5 April and 1 October in any year otherwise than on death, tax will be due at the end of April in the next year.

Personal representatives must pay the tax on delivering the account. If additional tax is due because the transferor dies within three years of making a lifetime chargeable transfer, tax will be due within six months of death.

The tax due on a PET which becomes chargeable because of the transferor's death within seven years should be paid six months after the end of the month in which death occurs.

Where foreign assets need to be transferred to the UK to meet the liabilities of the deceased, tax may be deferred for so long as they are unremittable.

From 5 November 2007, the provisions for paying IHT by cheque have changed. From that date, a bank approved payslip carrying an IHT reference must be sent with a cheque to the cashiers which from 16 March 2009 are the Banking Team in Cumbernauld. To coincide with the move to Cumbernauld, HMRC IHT will no longer be issuing receipts as a matter of course. You can apply for an IHT reference and payslip online at: www.hmrc.gov.uk/inheritancetax/online.htm.

Law: IHTA 1984, s. 226

Source: ESC F6, *Blocked foreign assets*, IHT and Trusts Newsletter December 2007, May 2009

See *British Tax Reporter* ¶695-600.

7596 Payment of IHT by instalments

Notwithstanding the general rules for payment of IHT (see 7593), tax may be paid in instalments if the tax payable on the value transferred by a chargeable transfer is attributable to the value of the following:

(1) land; or

(2) shares or securities of a company which gave the deceased control of that company before death; or

(3) 'unquoted' (see 6572) shares or securities if the tax on those shares amounts to at least 20 per cent of his liability on those chargeable transfers that may be paid by instalments, or if the payment of tax in one sum will, in HMRC's opinion, cause undue hardship; or

(4) unquoted shares if those shares exceed £20,000 in value and either –

    (a) the nominal value of the shares is at least ten per cent of the nominal value of all the shares in the company at the time of death; or

    (b) the shares are ordinary shares and their nominal value is not less than ten per cent of the nominal value of all ordinary shares of the company at the time of death; or

(5) a business or an interest in a business (otherwise than a business not carried on for gain) and the value here is the net value and is of the business as a whole and not individual assets; or

(6) timber.

The tax so attributable may be paid in ten equal yearly instalments, if the person paying the tax so elects by notice in writing to HMRC. The first instalment is due at the time the tax would have become due if it had not been for the election to pay by instalments (or six months after the transfer in the case of death or in relation to woodlands). Even if an election to pay by instalments has been made, all the tax may be paid in one sum with interest due to the date of payment if so desired.

If any of the property is sold, all or a proportionate part of the tax will become payable immediately unless the six-month period (see 7593) has not expired.

The above provisions will apply to lifetime transfers where the tax is borne by the person benefiting from the transfer or where there is a deemed capital distribution, or a principal charge to tax, or a charge under an accumulation and maintenance settlement.

For both potentially exempt and chargeable transfers which are brought into charge or extra tax is payable because of the death of the transferor within seven years, the option is available only if the same property is owned by the transferee throughout the period or if business or agricultural property has been replaced. For the option to apply to unquoted shares (see above), they must have remained unquoted throughout the period.

Law: IHTA 1984, s. 227–229

Source: *HMRC Inheritance Tax: Customer Guide*

Website: www.hmrc.gov.uk/cto/customerguide/page1.htm

See *British Tax Reporter* ¶695-650.

7599   Interest on overdue/overpaid IHT

(1) On overdue tax

If payment of IHT is overdue, it carries interest from the due date.

(2) On repayment of tax

Any repayment of an amount paid in excess of a liability for tax, or for interest on tax, will carry interest from the date on which the payment was made until the order for repayment is issued.

From 29 September 2009, interest charged on late payments of inheritance tax will be the Bank of England base rate plus 2.5 per cent. From the same date, the interest rate on overpayments is the Bank of England rate minus 1, subject to a minimum rate of 0.5 per cent on repayments.

(3) On payment by instalments

Where the tax payable on the value transferred by a chargeable transfer is payable by instalments, then interest on the unpaid portion of the tax will be added to each instalment and paid accordingly. This does not apply to dealers in land, buildings or securities, etc. unless the business is that of a market maker on The Stock Exchange (or a discount house) and is carried on in the UK, or unless that business is to act as a holding company for a company or companies whose business is not one of dealing. Market makers on the merged London International Financial Futures and Options Exchange (LIFFE) also fall within the exclusion from the above restriction.

(4) Interest-free instalments

Where the tax is attributable to the value of any shares, securities, business or interest in a business, or to the value treated as reduced in agricultural relief (see 7292) or to timber, it will, for the purposes of any interest to be added to each instalment, be treated as carrying interest from the date at which the instalment is payable.

This means that if each instalment is paid as it becomes due it will not carry interest. This will not apply to shares or securities of a company whose business consists wholly or mainly of dealing in securities, etc. land or buildings, or making or holding investments, unless its business is that of a holding company of one or more companies whose business is not dealing in securities, etc. or unless it is a market maker or discount house and its business is carried on in the UK.

Law: IHTA 1984, s. 233–236; *Taxes (Interest Rate) Regulations* 1989 (SI 1989/1297); *Inheritance Tax (Market Makers) Regulations* 1992 (SI 1992/3181); *Richardson v R & C Commrs* (2009) Sp C 730

Source: *HMRC Inheritance Tax: Customer Guide*

Website: www.hmrc.gov.uk/cto/customerguide/page1.htm

See *British Tax Reporter* ¶695-900.

7605 Acceptance of property in satisfaction of tax

HMRC may accept certain types of property in satisfaction of tax. These include:

(1)   land;

(2)   objects which are, or have been, kept in a building if the building:

    (a)   has been accepted in payment or part payment of tax or estate duty; or

    (b)   belongs to Her Majesty in right of the Crown or of the Duchy of Lancaster, or belongs to the Duchy of Cornwall, or belongs to a government department, or is held for the purposes of a government department; or

    (c)   is one of which the Secretary of State is guardian under the *Ancient Monuments and Archaeological Areas Act* 1979; or

    (d)   belongs to any body specified at 7195;

    (in all such cases it must appear desirable to the Secretary of State that the objects should remain associated with the building);

(3)   works of art, etc. (works by living artists have been accepted).

HMRC may waive interest charges where property is accepted in satisfaction of tax at a valuation date earlier than that on which the property is actually accepted.

The basis for negotiations is set out in a statement of practice.

Property otherwise used to pay tax

A person with the power to sell property to raise money to pay tax or interest may, instead, agree that the property be accepted in lieu of tax, as described above.

Where an administration action is pending as regards property to which a disposition relates, the court may provide that it should be used in payment of outstanding tax thereon.

Law: IHTA 1984, s. 230–232, 233(1A)

Source: SP 6/87, *Acceptance of property in lieu of inheritance tax, capital transfer tax and estate duty*, IR 67: National Heritage booklet: 'Capital Taxation and the National Heritage'

See *British Tax Reporter* ¶696-050.

7608 HMRC charge for unpaid IHT

Where IHT or interest remains unpaid, a protective charge will be imposed for the amount unpaid on any property to which the tax is attributable, or on any property comprised in a settlement. However, the charge will be subject to any encumbrance which is allowable as a deduction when valuing the property for tax.

Where the chargeable transfer is made on death, any personal or movable property of the deceased will be exempt from the charge. However, for deaths occurring after 8 March 1999, the charge can include leasehold interests. Any outstanding tax, charged after that date, in respect of assets previously benefiting from relief for heritage assets has also been brought within the charge.

Heritable property in Scotland is not subject to the charge.

A disposition of property subject to a HMRC charge will take effect subject to that charge. However, if the charge was not registered or protected by a notice in the case of land, or the purchaser had no notice in the case of movables, or a certificate of discharge had been given in the case of any property, then that property will no longer be subject to the charge, but any property representing it will be subject to the charge. Where property is disposed of and it does not cease to be subject to the charge, it will cease to be subject to the charge within six years from the later of the date when the tax becomes due or the date on which a full and proper account of the property was first delivered to HMRC.

Where property has been transferred by a PET which proves to be a chargeable transfer and is sold to a purchaser before the transferor's death, it is not subject to the charge, but any property representing it (e.g. the sale proceeds, or anything bought with them) is subject to the charge. Further, the charge applies to property which has been disposed of before the transferor's death otherwise than to a purchaser.

Law: FA 1999, s. 107; IHTA 1984, s. 237, 238

See *British Tax Reporter* ¶695-950.

7611 Recovery of unpaid IHT

As announced in the Pre-Budget Report 2009, HMRC will now normally require payment of tax even though a case may be under further appeal. This has effect in relation to all decisions made by the Tribunals or Courts on or after 1 April 2010. Thus, on an appeal to the Upper Tribunal, the tax in dispute must be paid. If the appellant is successful, the amount will be repaid.

HMRC have stated, however, that they will not enforce payment in cases where an agreement not to do so had been made with the appellant before 9 December 2009. Also, HMRC will not enforce payment in cases where to do so would be likely to drive the taxpayer into liquidation or bankruptcy.

Where there is a judgment in favour of a taxpayer, HMRC must repay overpaid tax, even if that judgment is subject to appeal.

Where HMRC accept the payment of tax in full satisfaction, no proceedings can be brought for the recovery of any additional tax after the expiration of six years beginning with the later of the following dates, namely:

- the date on which the payment (or in the case of tax paid by instalments the last payment) was made and accepted; and
- the date on which the tax or the last instalment became due.

On the expiration of this period any liability for the additional tax and any charge for that tax will be extinguished. However, if there is fraud, wilful default or neglect the date will start from the discovery of that fraud, wilful default or neglect by HMRC. Tax miscalculated as a result of the failure to report an earlier transfer on a timely basis can be recovered as if it related to the earlier transfer (see 7506).

In Scotland, tax and interest on tax may, without prejudice to any other remedy, and if the amount of the tax and interest does not exceed the sum for the time being specified in the *Sheriff Courts (Scotland) Act* 1971, s. 35(1)(a), be sued for and recovered in the sheriff court.

An authorised officer of the Board may address the court in any sheriff court proceedings for the recovery of tax or interest on tax.

In proceedings for recovery, a certificate by an officer of the Board that the tax or interest is due, or that, to the best of his knowledge and belief, it has not been paid, is sufficient evidence that the sum is due or unpaid as appropriate.

Where too little tax has been paid, the amount underpaid will be payable with interest even if the amount paid was stated in a notice of determination, but subject to the six-year limitation rule set out above.

Where too much tax has been paid, HMRC must repay the excess, again subject to the six-year limitation rule set out above.

Time-limit for fraud

In any case of fraud, wilful default or neglect by a person liable for the tax or the person who is the settlor in relation to a settlement, the time-limit for bringing proceedings for recovery of additional tax is six years from the date when the fraud, etc. comes to HMRC's knowledge.

Finance Act 2009 introduced legislation to align the time limits for changing the amount of tax due by assessment to four years. Time limits for taxpayers' claims will also be aligned at four years. The new time limits for making IHT assessments and claims come into force on 1 April 2011.

With effect from 1 April 2011, proceedings in a case involving loss of tax where the loss of tax has been careless may be brought within six years from the later of:

Inheritance Tax

(1)   the date on which the payment (or in the case of tax paid by instalments, the last payment) was made and accepted; and

(2)   the date on which the tax or the last instalment became due.

Where the loss of tax has been brought about deliberately, proceedings may be brought within 20 years from the later of the dates in (1) and (2) above.

Transitional provisions provide that, where:

(1)   the chargeable transfer took place before 31 March 2011; and

(2)   a loss of tax is brought about deliberately,

the period within which proceedings may be brought is the earliest of six years beginning when the deliberate conduct comes to HMRC's knowledge, or 20 years from (1) or (2) above.

A new subsection will apply to any case where too little tax has been paid, provided that case does not involve a loss of tax brought about deliberately. Where this subsection applies:

(1)   no proceedings are to be brought for the recovery of tax after the end of the period of 20 years beginning with the date on which the chargeable transfer was made; and

(2)   at the end of that period any liability for the tax and any Inland Revenue Charge for that tax is extinguished.

From 1 April 2011, if tax has been overpaid the Board will repay the excess tax paid (with interest, if appropriate) if the claim for repayment is made within four years of the date of the last payment of tax.

With effect from 1 April 2011, a new section will apply where:

(1)   information is provided to HMRC;

(2)   the person who provided the information, or the person on whose behalf the information was provided, discovers some time later that the information was inaccurate; and

(3)   that person fails to take reasonable steps to inform HMRC.

Any loss of tax brought about by the inaccuracy is to be treated as having been brought about carelessly by that person.

Law: IHTA 1984, s. 240–244, FA 2009, s. 99 and Sch. 51, para. 11, *the Finance Act 2009, Sch. 51 (Time Limits for Assessments, Claims, etc.) (Appointed Days and Transitional Provisions) Order* 2010 (SI 2010/867)

See *British Tax Reporter* ¶696-400, ¶696-600.

7617 Certificates of discharge

A person liable for tax may apply for a certificate of discharge (IHT 30) which will be granted if the tax has been paid, or HMRC are satisfied that it will be paid. Such a certificate need not be issued unless the transfer is on death. Where a PET becomes chargeable because of the donor's death within seven years, a certificate need not be issued until two years after the death. The certificate will discharge the property from any HMRC charge or all persons from any further claim for the tax, unless there is fraud or failure to disclose material facts.

Law: IHTA 1984, s. 239

Website: www.hmrc.gov.uk/cto/forms5.htm

See *British Tax Reporter* ¶696-450.

PENALTIES

7620 Incorrect returns of inheritance tax

FA 2008 extended the penalty provisions in FA 2007 which created a single penalty regime to incorrect returns of inheritance tax. The legislation covers errors for periods commencing on or after 1 April 2009 where documents are due to be filed on or after 1 April 2010. Penalties are based on taxpayer behaviour. There is no penalty where a taxpayer makes a mistake, but there will be a maximum penalty of:

- 30 per cent for careless behaviour (defined as failure to take reasonable care);
- 70 per cent for a deliberate understatement; and
- 100 per cent for a deliberate understatement with concealment.

In considering the penalty position with regard to careless, deliberate or deliberate and concealed, HMRC will consider whether the disclosure of an inaccuracy was prompted or unprompted. An unprompted disclosure means that the person has no reason to believe that HMRC IHT have discovered or are about to discover the failure to pay the required contributions. Prompted disclosure is likely to apply in all other cases.

The table below sets out the maximum reductions that can apply to each level of penalty for a prompted or unprompted disclosure. The reduction can never reduce the penalty below a statutory minimum.

Type of behaviour	Statutory maximum penalty	Statutory minimum penalty with unprompted disclosure	Statutory minimum penalty with prompted disclosure
Careless	30%	0%	15%
Deliberate but not concealed	70%	20%	35%
Deliberate and concealed	100%	30%	50%

The new regime also contains a provision that allows a tax-geared penalty to be charged where an inaccuracy in the liable person's document was attributable to another person. This is particularly relevant to IHT, where the personal representatives will inevitably be relying on other people to provide them with information about the deceased's estate

Where it can be shown that the other person deliberately withheld information or supplied false information to the liable person, with the intention that the IHT account or return would contain an inaccuracy, a penalty may be charged on that other person. But that will not necessarily mean that the personal representatives themselves may not also be chargeable to a penalty. If the withheld or false information gave rise to inconsistencies in the information they had received about the estate and they did not question those inconsistencies, the liable person might still be charged a penalty for failing to take reasonable care as well.

Law: FA 2008, Sch. 40; FA 2007, Sch. 24

Source: IHT and Trusts Newsletter April 2009

See *British Tax Reporter* ¶696-700.

7625   Failure to deliver an account

Failure to deliver an account attracts a penalty of £100, plus a further penalty not exceeding £60 per day after the day on which the failure is declared by a court or by the tribunal until the account is delivered. Where six months have elapsed since the date when the account ought to have been delivered, and the taxpayer still has not delivered the account at the end of that six-month period, but proceedings in which the failure could be declared have not been commenced (so that the daily penalty cannot be charged), a further penalty of £100 may be imposed. If, however, the tax due is less than any penalties due (i.e. the two penalties of £100), these penalties are limited to the amount of the tax. For other possible mitigations, see below.

Where 12 months have passed since the account ought to have been delivered, the taxpayer will be liable to a penalty of an amount not exceeding £3,000.

Finance Act 2009 has introduced a new penalty regime from a date to be appointed. The new regime will treat late filing and late payment (see below) separately. Failure to deliver an account will attract a penalty of £100. Where a penalty has been assessed as payable, and failure continues after three months beginning with the penalty date, a penalty of £10 for each day is charged whilst the failure continues during the period of 90 days beginning with the date specified in the penalty notice given by HMRC. If the failure to pay the penalty continues after the end of the period of six months beginning with the penalty date, then there is a further penalty of five per cent of any liability to tax which would have been shown in the return in question or £300, whichever is the greater.

Where the failure to pay the penalty continues after the end of the period of 12 months beginning with the penalty date, there will be a further penalty. That penalty will depend on whether the original inaccuracy was deliberate but not concealed, in which case the penalty will be the greater of 70 per cent of any liability to tax which would have been shown in the return in question, and £300. Where the original inaccuracy was deliberate and concealed then the further penalty will be the greater of 100 per cent of any liability to tax which would have been shown in the return in question and £300. In all other cases, there is a further penalty of the greater of five per cent of any liability to tax which would have been shown in the return in question and £300.

A new penalty regime for the late payment of IHT has also been introduced by *Finance Act 2009* from a date to be appointed. A taxpayer is liable to pay a penalty of five per cent of the unpaid tax. If this is still unpaid at the end of five months beginning with the penalty date then the taxpayer is liable to a penalty of five per cent of that amount. Further, if any of that tax is still unpaid after the end of 11 months beginning with the penalty date, a further five per cent is payable.

HMRC IHT may reduce a penalty in special circumstances. However, the inability to pay or the existence of an overpayment will not be classed as special circumstances.

Law: IHTA 1984, s. 216, 217, 245, FA 2009, Sch. 55, Sch. 56

See *British Tax Reporter* ¶696-700.

7630 Failure to make a return disclosing an overseas trust

Failure to provide information as to the making of an overseas trust attracts a penalty not exceeding £300, plus a further penalty not exceeding £60 per day after the day on which the failure is declared by a court or by the tribunal until the return is made.

Law: IHTA 1984, s. 218, 245A(1)

See *British Tax Reporter* ¶696-700.

7635 Failure to provide information or produce documents

Failure to comply with a notice to provide information attracts a penalty not exceeding £300, plus a further penalty not exceeding £60 per day after the day on which the failure is declared by a court or by the tribunal until the return is made.

Failure to comply with a notice to produce documents (or make originals available for inspection) attracts a penalty not exceeding £50, plus a further penalty not exceeding £30 per day after the day on which the failure is declared by a court or the tribunal until the return is made.

Law: IHTA 1984, s. 219, 219A, 245A(2) and (3)

See *British Tax Reporter* ¶696-700.

7640 Mitigating provisions

There are certain mitigating provisions which apply to penalties which may be imposed under s. 245 or s. 245A. Firstly, the daily penalty of up to £60 or £30 per day (as the case may be) is not due if the account is delivered before commencement of proceedings in which the failure could be declared. Secondly, a person who has a reasonable excuse for the failure in question is not liable for a penalty unless the failure continues after the excuse has ceased.

Law: IHTA 1984, s. 245(6), (7), 245A(4), (5)

See *British Tax Reporter* ¶696-700.

7645 Provision of incorrect information

Any person not liable for tax on the value transferred by a chargeable transfer who fraudulently or negligently furnishes or produces to the Board any incorrect account, information or document in connection with the transfer shall be liable to a penalty not exceeding £3,000.

Further, any person who assists in or induces the delivery, furnishing or production of any account, information or document which he knows is incorrect is liable to a penalty not exceeding £3,000.

If after any information or document has been furnished or produced by any person without fraud or negligence it comes to his notice that it was incorrect in any material respect, then it is treated as negligently furnished or produced unless the error is remedied without unreasonable delay.

Law: IHTA 1984, s. 247(3), (4); *Cairns (personal representative of Webb, deceased) v R & C Commrs* (2009) TC 00008

See *British Tax Reporter* ¶696-750.

7650 Criminal proceedings

It is open to the Board to initiate criminal proceedings instead of, or in addition to, proceedings under the revenue legislation. There have been prosecutions for fraud, although these are unusual and would generally occur in respect of large-scale evasion or persistent non-cooperation. In such cases it is, of course, possible that an offender would be sentenced to imprisonment.

See *British Tax Reporter* ¶696-850.

Value Added Tax

Value Added Tax

WHAT'S NEW

- The standard rate of VAT is due to rise from 17.5% to 20% on 4 January 2011.
- VAT registration limits increased from 1 April 2010 (see 8256).
- The new VAT and services rules came into effect on 1 January 2010 (aka the new VAT package); this extends the scope of the reverse charge (see 7820).
- Revised car fuel scale charges for VAT come into force with effect from 1 May 2010 (see 7762).
- The concession that allows employment businesses supplying temporary staff to choose whether to charge VAT on the staff costs charged to their clients was withdrawn from 1 April 2009.
- From 1 August 2009, it is possible to revoke options to tax made on the introduction of the legislation. Revised legislation sets out procedures to be followed if an election is revoked (see 8230).
- A new regime for charging penalties for errors came into effect on 1 April 2009 (see 8520).
- From 1 April 2010, VAT returns that are paper filed must be accompanied by cleared funds by the due date and not just an uncleared cheque.
- From April 2010 all businesses with taxable turnover above £100,000 and all newly registered businesses must file their VAT returns online. Online filers must also pay online.

KEY POINTS

- Value added tax (VAT) is an indirect tax, charged on taxable supplies of goods and services made in the course of business in the UK, on imports of goods into the UK from outside the EC, and on the acquisition of goods from elsewhere in the EC. VAT is also due on some imports of services (see 7822).
- The tax is borne by the final consumer and partially exempt traders within the supply chain.
- Traders must keep records of input and output tax and complete periodic VAT returns (see 8430ff.).
- VAT is primarily a tax on supplies (see 7758ff.).
- VAT is only due if the supply is made by a taxable person is the course of furtherance of his business (see 7792ff.).
- A supply may be a supply of goods or a supply of services (see 7804ff.).
- UK VAT is charge on supplies that are deemed to occur in the UK (see 7816ff.).
- The time of supply (or tax point) is important in that it determines the period for which the supplier must account for tax and therefore the date by which it must be paid over to HMRC (see 7830ff.).
- Importation of goods from outside the EC constitutes a chargeable event and triggers liability to both HMRC duties and import VAT (see 7880ff.).
- Special rules apply to acquisitions of goods from elsewhere in the EC (see 7972).
- Traders are obliged to account for VAT on taxable supplies and they can recover VAT on supplies made to them according to the normal VAT recovery rules (see 8034ff.).
- A business making both taxable and exempt supplies can, in principle, only recover input tax that relates to the making of the taxable supplies (see 8110ff.).
- Supplies may be taxable or exempt (see 8210ff.).
- Taxable supplies may be taxable at the standard rate, the reduced rate or the zero rate (see 8210 and 8216).
- Exempt supplies fall in to one of 15 groups (see 8228ff.).

Value Added Tax

- Businesses making taxable supplies in the UK above the registration limit are normally obliged to register with HM Revenue and Customs (HMRC) (see 8250ff.).
- A number of special VAT schemes exist, including retail schemes, flat rate scheme for farmers, the tour operators' margin scheme, second-hand goods schemes and special schemes for small businesses (see 8365 and 8410).
- VAT returns must be submitted to HMRC by the end of the month following the period to which it relates and any tax due paid by the same date (see 8430ff.).
- A penalty regime provides sanction against offences such as late submission of returns and payments (see 8480ff.).

OUTLINE OF VALUE ADDED TAX

7700 Application of VAT

Value added tax (VAT) was introduced in the UK on 1 April 1973 shortly after the UK joined what was then the European Economic Community (EEC), now the European Community (EC) or European Union (EU). VAT is the common value added tax of the EC.

Value added tax is charged on taxable supplies of goods and services made in the UK, where these are made in the course of business (see 7798ff.). It is also charged on imports of goods into the UK from outside the EC, on the acquisition of goods from elsewhere in the EC and on many imports of services (see 7880ff., 7972ff.).

Businesses which make taxable supplies are obliged to register with HM Revenue and Customs (HMRC), the government department which controls the tax (see 8250ff.). Registered businesses are often referred to as 'traders' by HMRC, and more recently as 'customers', although the term 'trader' includes businesses that would not generally be regarded as trades (e.g. a practising solicitor is normally regarded as being engaged in a profession rather than a trade, but in VAT terms would be called a trader).

Source: Notice 700, *The VAT guide*

Website: www.hmrc.gov.uk

See *British VAT Reporter* ¶1-100.

7706 VAT records and returns

Each registered trader is obliged to keep a record of the supplies which he makes in the course of any business carried on by him, and of the tax due on them. He must also keep a record of tax incurred on supplies to him, and on his imports and acquisitions.

He must then complete a periodical VAT return, and submit this to HMRC with a remittance for any tax due for the period. Returns are normally due quarterly, although some traders complete monthly or annual returns.

The trader must enter on his VAT return the totals of supplies made by him and of supplies (and imports and acquisitions) which he has obtained for the purposes of his business. He must also enter on it the total tax due on the supplies and acquisitions which he has made, and the amount suffered on supplies to him and on imports and acquisitions. He may set the tax incurred by him against the tax due on his own supplies. The tax which he is due to pay to HMRC is the difference between the two. If the tax due on his own supplies is less than the tax which he has suffered, he receives a repayment from HMRC.

Primary legislation requires records to be kept which enable a trader to make accurate returns.

Further details of accounting requirements are given at 8430ff.

Law: VAT Regulations 1995, Part V

Source: Notice 700, *The VAT guide*; Notice 700/21, *Keeping records and accounts*

Website: www.hmrc.gov.uk

See *British VAT Reporter* ¶4-620.

7712   Exemption and partial exemption

Certain supplies are exempt from VAT, so no tax is charged on them. A trader who makes only exempt supplies cannot register for VAT, and so cannot obtain credit for input tax suffered on his business expenses. A trader who makes only taxable supplies can reclaim all of his input tax (except that suffered on certain purchases of motor cars, etc.).

Special rules are needed in the case of a trader who makes both taxable supplies and exempt supplies (referred to as a partially exempt trader), in order to secure a fair and reasonable attribution of input tax.

In principle, a partially exempt trader can reclaim in full any input tax suffered in relation to the making of taxable supplies, and cannot reclaim any input tax suffered in relation to the making of his exempt supplies. Input tax suffered on supplies used both for the purposes of his taxable supplies and for the purposes of his exempt supplies must be apportioned between the two activities, and only the part relating to the taxable supplies made can be reclaimed.

The initial input tax deduction for certain expenditure on land and buildings and on computer equipment must be reviewed by reference to the use of the assets over a review period of five or ten years (see 8182). This is the Capital Goods Scheme.

Value Added Tax

The detailed application of these general rules, and the different ways of apportioning input tax between the types of activity, is a complex area (see 8034ff.).

Source: Leaflet 706, *Partial exemption*

Website: www.hmrc.gov.uk

See *British VAT Reporter* ¶3-130.

7718   Review of the system for control and enforcement of VAT

Value added tax is administered by HM Revenue & Customs (HMRC). They have a headquarters in London, a VAT Central Unit in Southend, and local VAT offices throughout the UK.

Traders making taxable supplies who are above the registration threshold, must normally register for VAT by submitting a form to one of the registration units. When this is processed the trader's details are entered on the register of taxable traders, and the VAT Central Unit at Southend will periodically issue VAT returns to the trader.

The VAT returns, with the related tax, must be submitted to HMRC by the end of the month following the accounting period concerned; the trader is responsible for completing his own VAT returns correctly (see 8454). Failure to submit returns (or any related payments) on time can expose the trader to a penalty (see 8480ff.).

Periodic checks are made on traders by officers from the local VAT office or from one of the large business groups (LBGs). These officers visit the trader's premises to inspect the VAT records to satisfy themselves that VAT is being accounted for correctly. Such visits are referred to as assurance visits (formerly, and still colloquially, control visits). The intervals between visits vary considerably, depending upon the size and type of business and the trader's own record of compliance (or non-compliance) with the VAT accounting requirements. Very large businesses are likely to have frequent control visits, and they will have their own 'customer relationship manager', while smaller businesses may be visited only at intervals of several years. Visits can also be triggered by changes of pattern becoming apparent from the VAT returns submitted by the trader.

If a visit reveals that the trader has underdeclared his VAT liabilities, an assessment will normally be issued to collect the tax. The trader may also become liable to pay interest and penalties in respect of the underdeclaration. Where underdeclarations arise because of dishonesty on the part of the trader, rather than because of errors, penalties may be due either under the civil law or under criminal law. In the latter case, a dishonest trader may also be imprisoned.

Law: VATA 1994, Pt. IV; FA 2007, Sch. 24

Source: Public Notice 989, *Visits by Customs and Excise officers*

Website: www.hmrc.gov.uk

See *British VAT Reporter* ¶3-500.

CHARGEABLE EVENTS – VAT ON SUPPLIES BY THE BUSINESS

7740   Liability to VAT: general

As VAT is in principle a tax on supplies, this generally means that a person has to account for VAT when he makes supplies. There are other occasions when VAT becomes due (see 7880ff, 7972ff.).

Law: VATA 1994, s. 1

7746   When VAT is chargeable

UK VAT is intended to be charged on the consumption of goods or of services within the UK, but is generally levied on the supplier of those goods or services rather than directly on the consumer. Because the tax is generally accounted for by suppliers, rather than the consumers who are ultimately intended to bear it, there are several occasions of charge. This is to prevent consumers from avoiding the tax by, for instance, obtaining taxable supplies from overseas suppliers.

The principal charge is on supplies of goods or of services made within the UK (including certain imports of services). The charge on imports of goods into the UK from outside the EC is covered at 7880ff. and the charge on acquisitions of goods from elsewhere in the EC is dealt with at 7972ff.

Some businesses may become liable to account for VAT on supplies which they are deemed to make to themselves (see 7766).

Law: VATA 1994, Pt. I; *Hutchison 3G UK Ltd & Ors v C & E Commrs* (Case C-369/04)

Source: Notice 700, *The VAT guide*

Website: www.hmrc.gov.uk

See *British VAT Reporter* ¶1-100.

Value Added Tax

7752   VAT on UK supplies

The main charge to VAT in the UK is on supplies made in the UK. As far as the law is concerned, this charging of VAT arises from a single section in the VAT Act and all of the other complexities of VAT flow from this one sentence. This particular provision is so important that it is well worth looking at the words used in the law. The charging provision concerned is VATA 1994, s. 4(1), and it reads as follows:

> 'VAT shall be charged on any supply of goods or services made in the United Kingdom, where it is a taxable supply made by a taxable person in the course or furtherance of any business carried on by him.'

Close examination of this provision reveals that there are five aspects to consider:

(1)   there must be a supply, either of goods or of services (see 7758ff., 7804ff.);

(2)   the supply must be made in the UK rather than elsewhere;

(3)   the supply must be a taxable supply;

(4)   the supply must be made by a taxable person, rather than by some other kind of person (see 7792ff.); and

(5)   the supply must be made in the course or furtherance of a business carried on by the taxable person who makes the supply (see 7798).

Law: VATA 1994, s. 4(1)

Source: Notice 700, *The VAT guide*

Website: www.hmrc.gov.uk

See *British VAT Reporter* ¶10-000.

SUPPLY

7758   The meaning of supply

Primarily, VAT is a tax on supplies (see 7752).

The UK law does not give a precise definition of the term 'supply' but states that it includes all forms of supply. Things done for no consideration are not supplies, unless there is specific provision within the law to class them as supplies. Anything done for consideration constitutes a supply.

It is apparent from this that:

• anything which is done for a consideration is a supply for VAT purposes; and

- anything which is not done for a consideration is not a supply unless the law specifically states that it is a supply.

In fact, the law does specify that a transfer of the property in goods, or of their possession, constitutes a supply. It follows that, where goods are provided, a supply arises whether or not there is consideration; only services can be provided for no consideration without a supply arising.

There are other occasions when a supply is deemed to arise, e.g. deregistration and certain self-supplies (see 7762, 7766).

Law: VATA 1994, s. 5(2)(a), (b), Sch. 4, para. 1

Source: Notice 700, *The VAT guide*

See *British VAT Reporter* ¶10-000.

7760   Consideration for VAT purposes

The term 'consideration' has long been used in UK law, particularly with reference to contract law. However, the UK law on VAT derives from EC law, and particularly the VAT Directive 2006/112 (this is the recast sixth directive on VAT). The UK courts are, therefore, obliged to construe the UK legislation so as to give effect to the directive.

Although 'consideration' is not defined in the VAT directive, a definition was given in Directive 67/228 (the second VAT directive) as follows:

> 'The expression "consideration" means everything received in return for the supply of goods or the provision of services, including incidental expenses (packing, transport, insurance etc.) that is to say not only the cash amounts charged, but also, for example, the value of the goods received in exchange or, in the case of goods or services supplied by order of a public authority, the amount of the compensation received.'

In *Apple and Pear Development Council v C & E Commrs* (Case 102/86) (1988) 3 BVC 274, the House of Lords considered that the intended scope of VAT was set by the then sixth directive but that there was no clear authority in European law on the meaning of consideration, and reference was made to the European Court of Justice for guidance on this point. The House of Lords noted the definition of consideration given in the second directive, and presumed that the term had the same meaning when used in the sixth directive. The Advocate General also made reference to the second directive in analysing the meaning of consideration for VAT purposes. The European Court considered that there must be a direct link between the supply made and the consideration received if there is to be consideration in the VAT sense. It has also been held that consideration for VAT purposes must be capable of being expressed in money (*Staatssecretaris van Financiën v Coöperatieve Aardappelenbewaarplaats GA* [1981] ECR 445).

A good rule of thumb is to regard 'consideration' as meaning anything (not only money) provided in exchange for something else, where the one is conditional on the other.

> ### Example
>
> John is a window cleaner. He cleans Emma's windows for £5. He cleans George's windows on condition that George (who is a carpenter) repairs his ladder. He cleans Linda's windows free of charge, because Linda is unwell and John wants to help out. Linda is grateful for John's help and gives him a new sponge.
>
> Clearly John cleaned Emma's windows for consideration, being the fee of £5.
>
> He cleaned George's windows for consideration too, the consideration being George's work on John's ladder. By the same token, George mended John's ladder for consideration in the form of John cleaning George's windows. Thus, there are two supplies for consideration in this instance, one by John and one by George.
>
> John did not receive any consideration for cleaning Linda's windows. Although Linda gave him a sponge (and presumably regarded it as a quid pro quo for the cleaning of the windows), she was under no obligation to do this. The cleaning of the windows in this case was done freely, as was the giving of the sponge. Since John was providing services, rather than goods, and there was no consideration, his action did not amount to a supply for VAT purposes.

It should be noted that in practice, where something is done freely but a quid pro quo is received, it may often be difficult to prove that the one is not consideration for the other.

It is also interesting to note that in the above example, while John has not made a supply to Linda, Linda has made a supply to John in giving him the sponge, since the transfer of the property in goods (in this case, the sponge) is a supply. In practice it is likely that no VAT will be due, either because her supply is not made in the course of a business or because it falls into the exclusion for small business gifts. Both of these aspects are covered later in this section.

While the 'anything in exchange' concept gives a good rule of thumb, it cannot be regarded as a complete expression of the law. The exact meaning of consideration is not entirely clear, and continues to be a matter of debate. In one case it was held that the act of arranging promotional parties constituted additional consideration for the supply of cosmetic cream at a reduced price (*Naturally Yours Cosmetics Limited v C & E Commrs* (1988) 3 BVC 428). In another, the handing in of a voucher in exchange for goods was held not to form part of the consideration for the supply of those goods. The voucher was no more than evidence of entitlement to a discount (*Boots Co plc v C & E Commrs* (1990) 5 BVC 21).

The European Court of Justice has held that the payment of a grant by the EC to compensate a farmer who undertook to discontinue milk production did not amount to consideration for a supply, on the ground that VAT was intended to be a tax on consumption and, in these circumstances, there was no consumption by the EC, which was merely acting in the common interest (*Mohr v Finanzamt Bad Segeberg* (Case C-215/94) [1996] BVC 293). Similar treatment will apply to most government grants.

The main thing which the business manager who is not a VAT specialist needs to bear in mind is the potentially wide meaning of 'consideration'. It is often assumed that any VAT liability will be picked up by the ordinary accounting systems of the business. This may often be the case; however, it can be seen that transactions which might not ordinarily enter the accounting systems (as no invoice would be generated) can readily give rise to VAT liability. Managers need to be aware of 'hidden' consideration, and preferably to take account of it when projects are being planned.

Particular care needs to be taken where commercial terminology is used which conceals the true nature of what is happening. This applies particularly where marketing activities are carried on which involve offers of 'gifts' or 'prizes' which are not really free, but have to be earned in some way. Frequently there is consideration for the provision of the 'gift' or 'prize', and this can affect the VAT position.

The 'anything in exchange' concept referred to above will provide a useful way of spotting potential supplies. As indicated, it should not be relied upon to produce an infallible answer in all cases. The best plan is to use it to spot transactions which might give problems, and to seek expert advice on borderline cases.

Another point worthy of note is that, while the receipt of money will often indicate that consideration is being received for a supply made, there are a number of occasions when money may be received without being consideration, and without there being a supply. A number of these are considered at 7776.

Law: The VAT Directive 2006/112; EC Directive 67/228 (the second directive); EC Directive 77/388 (the sixth directive); *Mohr v Finanzamt Bad Segeberg* (Case C-215/94) [1996] BVC 293; *Apple and Pear Development Council v C & E Commrs* (Case 102/86) (1988) 3 BVC 274; *Naturally Yours Cosmetics Limited v C & E Commrs* (1988) 3 BVC 428; *Staatssecretaris van Financiën v Coöperatieve Aardappelenbewaarplaats GA* [1981] ECR 445

Source: Notice 700, *The VAT guide*

Website: www.hmrc.gov.uk

See *British VAT Reporter* ¶10-985.

7762 Deemed supplies

The law specifically states that some transactions are to be treated as supplies for VAT purposes, whether or not there is consideration present. These are:

● the transfer or disposal of goods which are business assets (done under the directions of the person carrying on that business) so that they are no longer assets of the business. They may be excepted from this as small business gifts or gifts of industrial samples (see below). This includes, in the case of a sole trader business, the transfer of the goods to the sole proprietor in his personal capacity. However, there is no deemed supply unless the trader has been entitled to some input tax credit in respect of the goods;

- fuel for private use is also regarded as a deemed supply and if a trader recovers all of the input tax on fuel (both business and non-business element) then there is a deemed supply for the private element and output tax is due under the fuel scale charge tables. These are amended on 1 May each year (VATA 1994, s. 56 and 57);
- the use for non-business purposes of goods which are business assets and in respect of which input tax has previously been recovered. In the case of a sole trader business, this includes use for the personal purposes of the sole proprietor;
- when a person ceases to be registered for VAT, any goods remaining on hand are deemed to be supplied at that point unless it can be shown that tax has not been reclaimed on their purchase, or that the total tax involved is below £1,000.

It should be noted that, in applying these rules, land is specifically treated as being goods. This becomes especially important when the option for taxation has been exercised (see 8230).

The gift or private use of goods only gives rise to a supply if some part of the VAT on the goods concerned (or component parts) was deductible by the supplier (or some predecessor in the case of goods obtained under a transfer of a going concern).

Exceptions to deemed supply on gift of goods

(1) Small gifts

Although there is normally a supply of goods where business assets are transferred so as no longer to form part of the assets of the business, this does not apply if a gift is made in the course of the business and the cost of the goods to the business does not exceed £50. If the gift forms part of a series of gifts to the same person there is no supply unless the cumulative cost of the gifts in a 12-month period exceeds £50.

Where gift goods have been obtained under a transfer of a going concern, the cost for this purpose is the cost to the transferor (or, in the case of a series of such transfers, the first transferor), not the price attributed to them under the transfer.

It should be noted that this relief only applies to genuine gifts. As indicated earlier, there are many occasions where items are described as gifts but, in fact, they are provided in return for consideration.

(2) Gifts of samples

A gift of a sample is not treated as a supply. However, if more than one identical item is given to the same recipient, the relief is restricted to the first item.

Law: VATA 1994, Sch. 4, para. 5(2), (3); *Value Added Tax (Refund of Tax) Order* 2006 (SI 2006/1793); EC VAT Directive 2006/112

Source: Notice 700/35, *Business gifts and samples*

Website: www.hmrc.gov.uk

See *British VAT Reporter* ¶10-988.

7764 Supplies by a receiver

There is another occasion when a person can be treated as making a supply, without actually making a supply. If a receiver is appointed over assets of a business, then any supplies of goods made by the receiver are treated as if they had been made by the person carrying on the business. In this case, the receiver is liable to account directly to HMRC for the tax due, although the VAT continues to be shown on the trader's return.

This is in contrast to the position where a receiver is appointed over the whole of a company's assets. In this case the company is regarded as having become incapacitated, and it is for the receiver to make returns and payments of tax currently due on behalf of the company.

Law: VATA 1994, Sch. 4, para. 7; *Value Added Tax Regulations* 1995 (SI 1995/2518), reg. 9, 27, 30

Source: Notice 700, *The VAT guide*

Website: www.hmrc.gov.uk

7766 Self-supplies

In some circumstances a business can be treated as making supplies to itself. This arises in certain cases specified in statutory instruments, in certain cases relating to land, and in other instances covered below. In these cases the business must account for tax on the self-supply, but can then treat it as input tax as if the supply had been obtained from another trader. This might seem self-defeating, in that the tax would simply appear on both sides of the VAT return and cancel out, but the effect would be felt by partially exempt businesses that can't recover all the input tax charged to it.

(1) Self-supply of motor car

VAT suffered on the purchase of a motor car cannot be recovered if the car is to be put to any non-business use (such as private mileage, including home to work travel by an employee). Input tax on car purchase is recoverable if the car is to be used wholly for business purposes. However, if VAT is recovered on this basis and the car is subsequently put to non-business use, a self-supply arises.

(2) 'Self-supply' of residential or charitable building (a change of use charge)

A charge to VAT occurs when zero-rating under VATA 1994, Sch. 8, Grp. 5 has been obtained on the purchase or construction of a building for relevant residential or charitable use and, within ten years, the building is put to a non-qualifying use. These provisions are in VATA 1994, Sch. 10, para. 36.

(3) Self-supply of construction services

A self-supply arises if certain works of construction are carried out by a business without using outside contractors. If the value of the works is £100,000 or more, and they would have been positive-rated if bought in, a self-supply arises.

(4) Self-supply on acquisition of business by group

A self-supply arises where a business is transferred, as a going concern, to a VAT group of companies. This is intended to counter certain planning techniques which were previously available. The relevant provisions are in VATA 1994, s. 44.

If the group is partially exempt either during the prescribed accounting period (i.e. VAT return period) in which the supply takes place, or in the 'longer period' (see 8110ff.) which includes it, then a self-supply takes place. However, there is no self-supply if it can be shown that all of the assets transferred were acquired by the transferor more than three years before the transfer.

Law: VATA 1994, Sch. 10, para. 36; *Value Added Tax (Self-supply of Construction Services) Order* 1989 (SI 1989/472); *Value Added Tax (Cars) Order* 1992 (SI 1992/3122), art. 5

Website: www.hmrc.gov.uk

See *British VAT Reporter* ¶12-795.

7768   Reverse charge supplies

In some instances where a supply is made, it is treated as if it had been made by the customer rather than by the person who made the supply (the 'reverse charge'). This is relevant where the supply is made across an international boundary (see 7822).

The effect is that the customer (if registrable for VAT somewhere in the EC and this includes the UK) must account for output tax on the supply and can treat the same amount as potentially recoverable input tax. The input tax may, or may not, be deductible in full depending on the use to which the supplies are put (i.e. the normal VAT rules apply).

The reverse charge has become particularly important since 1 January 2010 under the new VAT package (see 7822).

Reverse charge supplies also count when considering whether the taxable turnover of the person carrying on the business exceeds the VAT turnover limits, making registration necessary (see 7792ff.).

See also 8492 in respect of the introduction of reverse charge accounting in relation to the supply of certain goods of a kind used in missing trader intra-Community fraud (MTIC).

Law: VATA 1994, s. 8, s. 7A and s. 4A

See *British VAT Reporter* ¶13-350.

7770   Imports and acquisitions

Value added tax arises, not only on supplies, but also on the importation of goods from outside the EC, and on their acquisition from elsewhere in the EC. These chargeable events are covered at 7880ff., 7972ff.

See *British VAT Reporter* ¶13-470.

NON-SUPPLIES (OUTSIDE THE SCOPE SUPPLIES)

7776   Receipt of money which is not consideration

When something is done for consideration there is a supply for VAT purposes (see 7758). It is therefore normal to conclude that, whenever a business receives money, it is likely to be consideration for something so it is likely that there is a supply. However, it is possible to receive money without that money being consideration for anything. Examples of this include:

- receipt of dividends;
- supplies in a warehouse (other than the last supply of certain goods before removal from the warehouse);
- compensation payments (in most cases, except certain payments which are expressed as compensation but are, in reality, consideration for permission to continue the actions giving rise to compensation ;
- disbursements, where these represent the recovery of amounts expended which were the liability of the person from whom they are claimed. Recovery of one's own expenses in making supplies represents consideration for those supplies;
- internal payments (i.e. payments flowing within the same legal entity);

Value Added Tax

- capital introduced into a business (corporate or non-corporate);
- loan repayments;
- gifts of money – provided that they are genuine gifts;
- grants, provided that these amount to no more than deficit funding and do not involve the body making the grant receiving any benefit;
- payments within a group of companies for group relief, provided that the payment is not expressed as encompassing anything other than the group relief (*C & E Commrs v Tilling Management Services Ltd* (1978) 1 BVC 185);
- payments under a contract of indemnity (such as the payment of a claim by an insurance company).

Law: VATA 1994, s. 18; *C & E Commrs v Tilling Management Services Ltd* (1978) 1 BVC 185

Source: Public Notice 701/1

See *British VAT Reporter* ¶10-988.

7778 Sale of a business as a going concern

If a business is sold as a going concern, and certain conditions are met, the transaction is treated as not being a supply (although a 'self-supply' charge may arise for a purchaser which is a member of a VAT group).

This non-supply treatment applies where:

- a business, or part of a business, is transferred as a going concern;
- the transfer is part of a business and that part is capable of separate operation;
- the assets transferred are to be used by the transferee in carrying on the same kind of business as that carried on by the transferor; and,
- if the transferor is a taxable person, the transferee is also a taxable person (or becomes one as a result of the transfer).

However, extra care is needed if the assets transferred include 'VATed' land or buildings (the supply of which is standard-rated, either because the supplier has waived exemption or because they consist of new freehold non-residential buildings). In this case the supply of the land and buildings remains standard-rated unless the transferee opts to tax (OTT) the land or buildings, and notifies this to HMRC, before the occurrence of the first tax point in respect of the transfer. It is also necessary that the transferee warrants that the OTT will not be disapplied because of the anti-avoidance provisions in VATA 1994, Sch. 10, para. 12.

Source: Public Notice 700/9, *Transfer of a business as a going concern*

See *British VAT Reporter* ¶54-150.

7780   Supplies made outside the UK

United Kingdom VAT is charged only on supplies made within the UK. It is perfectly possible for a business which is established in the UK to make a supply which, although taxed in the UK for other purposes, is regarded as made outside the UK for VAT purposes and so does not attract UK VAT.

The rules for determining whether a supply is made in the UK are quite technical, and are covered at 7816ff.

See *British VAT Reporter* ¶10-000.

7782   Repossessed goods

Certain disposals of goods repossessed by insurance and finance companies, etc. are treated as not being supplies, if their supply by the previous owner would not have attracted VAT, or attracted it on some amount less than the total proceeds.

The transactions affected are:

- the disposal of goods falling within a second-hand goods scheme, or of a used motor car, by a person who repossessed them under a finance agreement, or an insurer who acquired them as part of the settlement of an insurance claim;
- the disposal of a boat by a mortgagee who has taken possession of it under a marine mortgage; and
- the disposal of an aircraft by a mortgagee who has taken possession of it under an aircraft mortgage.

In each case the relief is denied if the goods have previously been relieved of VAT, as being exported, and have been reimported, or to goods which have been imported into the UK free of VAT. Also, the goods must be resold in the same condition as that in which the person making the disposal acquired them.

Law: *Value Added Tax (Cars) Order* 1992 (SI 1992/3122), art. 4

See *British VAT Reporter* ¶420.

7784   Gift of motor car

The gift of a motor car is treated as not being a supply if the tax on its acquisition or importation was non-deductible.

Law: *Value Added Tax (Special Provisions) Order* 1995 (SI 1995/1268), art. 4(1); *Value Added Tax (Cars) Order* 1992 (SI 1992/3122), art. 4(1)(c)

See *British VAT Reporter* ¶140.

Value Added Tax

It also has implications when there are other business activities which give rise to exempt supplies. This can result in unfavourable consequences, of which the businessman needs to be warned, if the exempt supplies cause him to be treated as partially exempt for VAT purposes. In this instance, he will be prevented from recovering part of the VAT input tax arising on his expenses. Unless proper steps are taken, the input tax lost can exceed that relating strictly to the exempt activity. If the main business giving rise to VAT registration includes some exempt supplies, but not enough to lead to partial exemption, an exempt sideline activity can tip the balance and cause significant loss of input tax recovery.

There can also be favourable implications, which may not be immediately obvious. If there is an exempt sideline activity, but the scale of it is too small for the partial exemption rules to apply, then the businessman may find himself with an unexpected bonus. In this case he will be able to reclaim tax on expenses relating to the exempt sideline business, which he could not have done before.

Example

An individual sets up a new business, and his accountant advises him that he is obliged to register for VAT. The annual taxable turnover of the business is likely to be in the region of £110,000 p.a.

The accountant notices from his client's tax return that he owns three houses, which are rented out and produce gross rentals totalling £8,500 p.a.

The property-letting activity is a business for VAT purposes. It seems likely that the input tax relating to the exempt activity will be sufficiently low compared with the scale of the new business that the businessman can recover the tax on expenses incurred in relation to the property business. This would include VAT on estate agents' fees for managing the properties as well as on repairs, refurbishment expenses, etc.

Note that the VAT position could alter significantly in a year in which input tax relating to the exempt activity exceeded the partial exemption de-minimis limits (see 8110ff.).

This interaction of different activities for VAT purposes affects partnerships and companies just as much as individuals. In these cases it is usually more obvious that there may be an interaction, since the accounts of a company or partnership are more likely to include all business activities.

7798 VAT only on business activities

Value added tax affects supplies only when they are made in the course or furtherance of a business. So when a VAT registered parent sells a child's old bicycle, no VAT is due since the transaction is a personal one, not done in the course of a business.

Value Added Tax

(1) Whether a business carried on

It is easy to assume that the term 'business' for VAT is synonymous with the term 'trade' used in income tax law. Indeed, the term 'business' does include a trade, profession or vocation. But the VAT term goes far wider than this, and covers many activities which would be regarded for income tax purposes as generating investment income. For instance, the letting of property is regarded as a business for VAT purposes.

Specific activities treated as business

The following activities are regarded as done in the course of a business by definition:

- the carrying on of a trade, profession or vocation;
- the admission of persons to premises for consideration; and
- the provision by a club or association of benefits to its members for consideration (including subscriptions).

General meaning of business

The list of activities treated as business activities which is given in the *Value Added Tax Act* 1994 (in Section 94) is not complete. The statute merely states that the term includes these activities. Each case has to be looked at on the basis of its facts, to see whether the activities carried on should be regarded as business activities within the ordinary meaning of that term. Furthermore, because VAT stems from European law, it is necessary to bear in mind the terms of the EC VAT Directive 2006/112 when construing the UK law. The directive does not use the term business, but refers to a taxable person as one who 'independently' carries on certain 'economic activities'. The economic activities concerned are those of (Directive 2006/112, art. 9):

> 'producers, traders and persons supplying services including mining and agricultural activities and activities of the professions. The exploitation of tangible or intangible property for the purpose of obtaining income therefrom on a continuing basis shall also be considered an economic activity.'

(2) Whether supply is made in the course or furtherance of business

Once it is established that a business is being carried on it is necessary, in order to establish whether a particular supply may be liable to VAT, to establish whether it is done in the course or furtherance of the business.

The legislation provides that a number of things which might not be seen as done in the course of a business or in its furtherance, such as closing it down, are brought within the meaning of the term by statute. Things which will be seen as done in the course or furtherance of a business are as follows:

- the supply of a business asset or a supply made for business purposes – this is not a specific statutory addition, but a general inference from the legislation and cases;
- *things done in connection with* closing a business down, such as selling the remaining business assets;

- transferring a business as a going concern; and
- supplies made as the holder of an office by a person carrying on a trade, profession or vocation if he accepted that office in the course of his trade, profession or vocation. An example of this would be a lawyer who accepts office as a director of a company in the course of carrying on his profession.

Law: VATA 1994, s. 94

Source: Notice 700, *The VAT guide*

Website: www.hmrc.gov.uk

See *British VAT Reporter* ¶18-090.

GOODS AND SERVICES

7804   Whether supply is of goods or services

VAT is charged on supplies of goods and supplies of services. There are many detailed rules covering such matters as whether a supply is regarded as made in the UK or elsewhere, the time when the supply is regarded as taking place (and so when the tax on it falls due), and even the amount taxable and the rate of tax applicable, which vary depending on whether the supply is of goods or of services. It is therefore important to distinguish between the two.

The legislation specifies a number of supplies which are to be treated either as supplies of goods or as supplies of services such as electricity (which is deemed to be a supply of goods). Any supply which is not a supply of goods and is done for a consideration, is deemed to be a supply of services.

Law: VATA 1994, s. 5(2)(b); Sch. 4

Source: Notice 700, *The VAT guide*

Website: www.hmrc.gov.uk

See *British VAT Reporter* ¶10-455.

7806   Composite (or compound) and multiple supplies

Before a supply can be classified as being of goods or of services, its real nature must be established. Often this is straightforward. For instance, if a person sells a van for a sum of money, there is clearly a supply of the van. However, if the van which is sold contains a load of carrots, and these pass to the purchaser as well, there may well be two supplies, one of the

Value Added Tax

van and the other of the carrots. So, sometimes what appears to be a single transaction can be made of more than one supply.

There are two possibilities:

- A multiple supply – where the different elements each have their own identity and each has its own VAT treatment; and
- A compound (or composite) supply – where the different elements have one VAT treatment overall and this follows the VAT treatment of the main element, so the other elements lose their VAT identity.

Example

The sale of a calculator with an instruction manual might be looked at as two supplies, one of the calculator (standard-rated) and the other of the manual (zero-rated). In all probability, though, it would be regarded as a single supply of a calculator, the manual being seen as merely incidental to the supply.

However, consider the position if the manual went beyond the operation of that particular calculator, and covered, for instance, mathematical techniques and number games. If the manual were sufficiently valuable in comparison with the calculator, and was of utility in its own right, the transaction might be regarded as a multiple supply. This would be even more likely if the manual were also available separately to people who did not wish to buy a calculator.

As can be seen, this is an area where great care needs to be exercised. The managers of the business need to be wary of transactions which might be seen in different ways, and take advice on them. It should be noted that HMRC are very much aware of the differences of treatment which can arise depending on how such supplies are viewed .

A line of cases suggests a general principle that, where a transaction includes a number of components, some of which are liable to VAT and some of which are not, it should be seen as involving a number of separate supplies and dissected accordingly if it is practical and realistic to do so. For example, a day excursion with a five-course lunch or dinner on the Orient Express was held to be two separate supplies of transport (zero-rated) and catering (standard-rated). This approach is based on the notion that the exemptions and zero-ratings are a fundamental part of the tax, and that the courts should give effect to the intentions of the legislators. It appears that a major factor in deciding, in borderline cases, whether it is practical and realistic to split the transaction is if the parties have found it possible to apportion the consideration, either in their agreement or when invoicing. Indeed, the Court of Appeal indicated that, while HMRC could seek to split into its components that which the contracting parties had sought to treat as a single supply, they could not join together elements that the parties had themselves split in the contractual arrangements.

Further general guidance was given by the seminal decision of the European Court of Justice in the *Card Protection Plan* case (although the court left it to the national court to apply these principles to the specific facts of the case before it) on the following lines:

(1) where the transaction involves a bundle of features, regard must be had to all of the circumstances in which the supply takes place;

(2) every supply of a service must normally be regarded as distinct and independent, but a supply which comprises a single service from an economic point of view should not be artificially split, as this would be distortive;

(3) there is a single supply if one or more elements are to be regarded as constituting the principal service, while other elements are merely ancillary and so share the same tax treatment as the principal service. A service is ancillary to the principal service if it does not constitute, for customers, an aim in itself, but provides a means of better enjoying the principal service supplied; and

(4) the fact that a single price is charged suggests that there is a single service, but is not decisive. If the circumstances suggested that customers intended to purchase two or more separate services liable at different rates, then the consideration must be apportioned. The simplest method of calculation or assessment should be used for this.

There have been many cases concerned with the fundamental question of what it is that is being supplied. This is ultimately an area for subjective judgment, and cannot readily be codified. It is important to consider the possible different views which might be taken of a particular transaction and, where different tax results might otherwise arise, to take all possible steps to document the true nature of the transaction (e.g. by means of formal contracts).

Example

A business sells a package which is made up of a book, a DVD and a customer support helpline. The sale price of the package is £250. The book and the DVD can be purchased separately for £120 each. Customers can subscribe to the helpline alone for £75 per annum. They can also subscribe to the helpline and take either the book or DVD for £150 per annum.

The helpline and the DVD are standard-rated for VAT, but the supply of the book is zero-rated.

The price of £250 therefore needs to be apportioned. The VAT at 17.5% is found by applying the fraction 7/47 to the amount relating to the standard-rated supply.

$$£250 \times \frac{75 + 120}{75 + 120 + 120} \times \frac{7}{47} = £23.05$$

Law: *Sea Containers Services Ltd v C & E Commrs*[2000] BVC 60; *C & E Commrs v Lloyds TSB Group Ltd* [1998] BVC 173; *C & E Commrs v Wellington Private Hospital Ltd* [1997] BVC 251; *Bophuthatswana National Commercial Corporation Ltd v C & E Commrs* [1993] BVC 194; *C & E Commrs v Bushby* (1978) 1 BVC 158; *Card Protection Plan Ltd v C & E Commrs* (Case C-349/96)

Value Added Tax

VAT Information Sheet 02/01 – *Single or multiple supplies – how to decide*; Business Brief 02/2001

See *British VAT Reporter* ¶10-000.

7808 Supplies of goods

The following are specified as being supplies of goods:

- the transfer of the whole property in goods;
- the transfer of possession of goods under an agreement for the sale of the goods, or under an agreement which expressly contemplates that the property in the goods will also pass at some ascertainable future date;
- the supply of power, heat, refrigeration or ventilation;
- the granting, assignment or surrender of a 'major interest' in land. A 'major interest in land' is the freehold or a leasehold interest having a term certain greater than 21 years; and
- the transfer or disposal of goods which are business assets so that they no longer form part of the business assets is treated as a supply of goods, even if no consideration passes. In view of the first two items above, this last provision seems redundant in the context of distinguishing between supplies of goods and of services. It is presumably included to put it beyond doubt that a gift of goods constitutes a supply, rather than to indicate the classification of the supply.

Law: VATA 1994, s. 96(1), Sch. 4, para. 1(1), 3, 4, 5

Source: Notice 700, *The VAT guide*

Website: www.hmrc.gov.uk

See *British VAT Reporter* ¶10-455.

7810 Supplies of services

The following are specified as being supplies of services:

- the transfer of an undivided share of the property in goods, or a transfer of the possession of goods except under a contract for their sale, etc. An example of the former would be the sale of a half-share in goods; and
- the use of goods which are business assets, under the directions of the person carrying on the business, for a private or non-business purpose, whether or not there is any consideration.

Anything else which is a supply, but is not specifically stated to be a supply of goods, will be a supply of services.

There is a deemed supply of services where input tax is reclaimed on the obtaining of services and these are subsequently put to non-business use for no consideration.

However, this deemed supply does not apply:

- if any part of the tax charged on the original supply of the services was disallowed as not being input tax (i.e. was apportioned as not being used for business purposes); or
- to services of car hire where 50 per cent of the input tax has been excluded from credit; or
- to services used for the provision of catering or accommodation for employees falling within VATA 1994, Sch. 6, para. 10 (see 7860).

Law: VATA 1994, s. 5(2)(b), Sch. 4, para. 1, 5(4), Sch. 6, para. 10; *Value Added Tax (Supply of Services) Order* 1993 (SI 1993/1507), art. 6A

See *British VAT Reporter* ¶10-455.

PLACE OF SUPPLY

7816   Determining where supplies are made

VAT in the UK is charged on supplies which are deemed to occur in the UK, but not on supplies made outside of the UK. It is important, therefore, to be able to tell where supplies are made.

The determination of the place of supply is done separately for each supply made. This is in contrast with other taxes where the determination of tax jurisdiction is generally carried out for the person concerned, rather than for individual transactions. The rules for determining the place of supply fall into two quite distinct sets, one for supplies of goods and the other for supplies of services.

See *British VAT Reporter* ¶13-350.

7818   The place of supply of goods

The UK law on the place of supply of goods is contained in VATA 1994, s. 7, while the equivalent EC provisions are in VAT Directive, art. 31 onwards.

(1) Place of supply of goods: basic rule

The rules governing the place of supply of goods are markedly different from the rules for liability to other taxes, in that they entirely ignore the locations of the parties to the transactions.

The basic rule is that goods are treated as supplied at the place where they are when their dispatch or transport to the customer begins, or the place where they are when the supply takes place if they are not to be dispatched or transported. Effectively, therefore, they are supplied at the place where they are when allocated to the supply in question. The location of the person making the supply does not have any effect on the place of supply of the goods, nor does the place where the goods are at the time when title in them passes. The place of supply is the place where they are when they first become identified with the particular supply.

Example

Terry sells a lathe and a computer to Ben. The lathe is in the US and the computer is in Huddersfield. Both are shipped to Ben's premises in Australia.

The lathe is treated as supplied outside of the UK, since it was outside of the UK when allocated to the supply.

The computer, on the other hand, was in the UK when allocated to the supply, and so is treated as supplied in the UK (this does not necessarily mean that standard-rated VAT will be charged on the supply – in all probability it will be zero-rated as an export of goods).

Terry also sells Ben a printer to go with the computer. Terry is awaiting a consignment of printers from Japan, and when they arrive he will forward one of these to Ben in fulfilment of the contract.

The supply of the printer is treated as made in the UK.

---

(2) Place of supply of installed goods

There is a special rule if the goods are to be installed or assembled by the supplier, or by some other person acting on his behalf (e.g. a sub-contractor). In this case the goods are treated as supplied at the place where installation or assembly takes place.

As a simplification measure, when installed goods are supplied by a supplier registered for VAT in another Member State but not in the UK and they are installed in the UK, instead of the supplier being required to register for VAT in the UK, to deal with the installation, his supply is ignored and the customer is treated as making an acquisition in the UK, provided that appropriate formalities are followed.

(3) Supplies on intra-EC journeys

Where goods are supplied during passenger transport within the EC, the supply is treated as made in the Member State of departure. For return trips, the outward and return stages are treated separately.

(4) Distance selling

The broad aim of the distance selling provisions is to prevent consumers in different Member States from using the internet, mail order, etc. to obtain goods at lower rates of

VAT (they are perfectly at liberty to achieve this end by travelling, and buying in person). They apply where a business in one Member State takes orders from an unregistered customer in another Member State, and delivers goods to that customer in that other Member State.

To prevent market distortion, a person selling significant quantities of goods to unregistered persons in a particular Member State must register there, and charge that state's VAT on these sales. These supplies are deemed to take place in the destination state.

These rules do not apply to the supply of a new means of transport, nor do they apply where there is a deemed supply on a movement of the trader's own goods from one EC location to another, without any actual supply.

(5) Supplies by importers

Where goods are imported into the UK from outside the EC, the supply of the goods by the importer, and any subsequent supplies, are treated as made in the UK.

UK businesses supplying customers elsewhere in the EC should note that other Member States are bound by the same VAT directive as the UK. Thus, the place of allocation of goods, the question of installation, and the mechanics selected for importation into the other state must all be considered to determine whether the UK business has an obligation to register for VAT in the other Member State.

(6) Intra-EC supplies of goods

The position for a supply of goods by a trader registered in one Member State to a trader registered in another is straightforward:

- the supplier must obtain the customer's VAT registration number and show it on the tax invoice (provided that he holds satisfactory evidence of departure from the UK he can then zero rate the supply: see 8220); and
- the customer is liable to pay VAT in his own state on his 'acquisition' of the goods. This VAT is also input tax in his hands (see 7972ff.).

If the customer cannot produce a valid VAT registration number the supplier must charge his own VAT on the supply. However, if his sales to unregistered persons in the Member State concerned exceed the relevant threshold, the supplier must register for VAT in that country and his supplies to such unregistered customers are deemed to take place there (see the distance selling arrangements above).

7820 The place of supply of services

The rules that determine where a supply of services is made have been modified from 1 January 2010 and are very important where services cross country boundaries. The status of the customer is essential.

Value Added Tax

The basic rules from 1 January 2010 are as follows:

If the customer is a business customer, the service is therefore a B2B (business to business) service and the place of supply is where the customer belongs. If the customer is in the EC, then that customer will have to bring the VAT to account using the reverse charge mechanism (see below).

If the customer is NOT a business customer, so the supply is B2C (business to customer), then the new rules provide that the place where the service is supplied is the place where the supplier belongs (this is, in effect, a default). There is, however, an override where the B2C customer is outside the EC (see below).

(1) The place where customers and suppliers belong

It is necessary to be able to tell where the customer or supplier belongs in respect of B2B and B2C services. The UK rules follow the EC VAT Directive and are as follows:

For a B2B supply, a business customer belongs in a country if the person has a business establishment or some other fixed establishment there and if there is more than one such country, the country most directly concerned with the supply.

If the supply is a B2C customer, then that person belongs in a country where that person's usual place of residence is.

Law: VATA 1994, s. 7A and s. 9; EC Directive 2006/112, art. 43 onwards

Source: Notice 741A (from 1 January 2010), *Place of supply of services*

Website: www.hmrc.gov.uk

See *British VAT Reporter* ¶13-470.

7824 Place of supply of services – special rules

The new VAT package, like its predecessor, has special rules in some circumstances.

There are some general exceptions, and these include:

1 services connected with land are treated as supplied where the land is located;

2 passenger transport is treated as taking place where the transport takes place (this could be in more than one Member State;

3 cultural, educational and entertainment services are treated as taking place in the country where they are physically carried out (these are due for revision in 2011);

4 restaurant and catering services on boats, planes and trains are treated as taking place in the country where the departure point is.

There are also some exceptions that apply only to B2C services:

1   transport of goods – the place of supply is where the transportation takes place (this could be in more than one Member State);

2   valuation and repair services – the place of supply is where the service takes place;

3   electronic services (such as website provision and software downloads) take place where the non-business customer belongs. There is, however, a simplified registration facility to save multiple registrations in the EC;

4   intellectual services supplied to non-business customers outside the EC (such as accountancy services) – these are supplied where the customer belongs, so no VAT needs to be charged by the EC supplier and the service is outside the scope of their local VAT;

5   intermediary services (i.e. agents) which are deemed to be supplied in the country in which the underlying principal's service takes place.

The effective use and enjoyment rules

There is a further layer of rules – 'the effective use and enjoyment rules' that modify the rules above. These rules, and the services subject to them, are covered in the EC VAT Directive (art. 43 onwards) and have been adopted by the UK law.

In summary, they say that where the services listed below are supplied to a customer that is in the UK and the services are effectively used and enjoyed outside the EC, then they will not be charged to VAT in the UK.

The reverse also applies; if the service is made by a UK supplier to a customer outside the EC and the customer effectively uses them in the UK, then they will be subject to UK VAT.

The services include:

1   the hiring of goods;

2   telecoms and broadcasting services;

3   electronically supplied services to business customers (i.e. B2B).

The reverse charge

Given that the B2B rules make the place of supply generally where the customer belongs, the mechanism by which the VAT is brought to account is the reverse charge and this only happens where the customer is in the EC. If the customer is outside the EC, then there is no VAT to bring to account. There may, however, be local tax implications.

In both cases, the supply is outside the scope of the supplier's Member State.

Value Added Tax

The reverse charge will also be imposed on UK traders that receive supplies of services (other than exempt supplies) from either another EC Member State or from a place outside the EC (see s. 8, VATA 1994).

The reverse charge mechanism is similar to the acquisition process for goods. The customer charges himself local VAT and puts this to output tax in his VAT return and then tries to recover as much as possible of this self-charged VAT under the normal VAT recovery rules.

The result of this (like the acquisition process) is that it is neutral whether the customer buys in his own Member State or in another Member State. The system is therefore anti-market distortion.

The EC Sales List

The EC Sales List is a method of auditing the reverse charge and acquisition process and to allow the tax authorities of the Member States to check that it is being done.

From 1 January 2010, the EC Sales List applies to services as well as goods. Prior to 1 January 2010, it applied to goods only.

Law: VATA 1994, s. 7A, 8, Sch 4A; VAT Dirctive 2006/112, art 43 onwards

Source: Notice 741A, *Place of supply of services*

Website: www.hmrc.gov.uk

See *British VAT Reporter* ¶13-470.

TIME OF SUPPLY

7830   Importance of time of supply

The time when a supply is deemed to occur for VAT purposes is important for a number of reasons. First and foremost, it determines the period for which the supplier must account for the tax, and so the date by which it must be paid over to HMRC. It also determines the period for which a VAT-registered customer can reclaim the tax.

When there are changes in the rate of tax, or in the classification of supplies which are exempt or zero-rated, the precise time of supply can be of crucial importance in determining the rate which attaches to supplies made around the time of the change.

The time of supply is also important in ascertaining the calculations of turnover for registration purposes, and partial exemption calculations.

There are slightly different rules for goods and for services, and special rules for a number of specified supplies.

In principle, the time of supply (or 'tax point') is the earlier of:

- the date when the supply is 'really' made, referred to by HMRC as the basic tax point (see 7832);
- the date when a tax invoice is issued in respect of the supply (see 7834); and
- the date when payment is received for the supply (see 7836).

There are a number of refinements to be borne in mind in applying this basic rule and there are also special rules for certain kinds of supply (see 7838).

Source: Notice 700, *The VAT guide*

Website: www.hmrc.gov.uk

See *British VAT Reporter* ¶11-700.

7832 Time of supply: the basic tax point

Identification of the 'basic tax point' (or the time when the supply actually takes place) is based on different rules depending on whether the supply is of goods or of services. This is yet another area where the VAT law distinguishes between goods and services, and treats them differently.

Example

Alfred dispatches goods to Bert on 15 September. This is the basic tax point. Bert paid for the goods on 25 August, and this is the actual tax point.

If Alfred issued an invoice on 20 September this further tax point would override the basic tax point, but not the earlier actual tax point.

In this example the goods are deemed to have been supplied on 25 August.

---

(1) Basic tax point: goods

In the case of goods which are to be delivered to the customer, or collected by the customer, the basic tax point is the date when delivery commences. If the supply does not involve movement of the goods (e.g. a supply of land, or of goods which are erected on the customer's premises), the basic tax point is the date when the goods are made available to the customer. In the case of supplies of land, the basic tax point is normally the date of completion rather than the date when contracts are exchanged (although the date of exchange of contracts can be important in Transfers of Going Concerns (TOGCs)).

It is possible for goods to be delivered to a potential customer without a supply yet having taken place. This would happen, for instance, if they were sent on approval or on sale or

Value Added Tax

return terms. If goods are delivered on such terms, so that it is uncertain whether there will in fact be a supply of them, the basic tax point does not arise until the supply becomes certain (e.g. by the customer adopting the goods, or the expiry of an agreed period within which they may be returned). However, the basic tax point will in any case arise if the customer holds the goods for 12 months without returning them, even if he still has the right to return them.

(2) Basic tax point: services

The basic tax point for a supply of services arises when the services are performed. HMRC generally take this to be the date when the performance of the service is completed.

Law: VATA 1994, s. 6(2)(a), (b), (c), (3)

Source: Notice 700, *The VAT guide*

Website: www.hmrc.gov.uk

See *British VAT Reporter* ¶11-750.

7834   Time of supply: issue of a tax invoice

The tax invoice is the formal document which a VAT-registered trader must issue to another VAT-registered trader or to a customer in another Member State (and may issue to anyone) in respect of a taxable supply other than a zero-rated supply (in the case of a customer elsewhere in the EC the issuing of the invoice is compulsory for a zero-rated supply also). It provides the evidence which enables another taxable trader to reclaim tax on the supply. For obvious reasons, HMRC does not wish to refund tax in respect of such an invoice unless the supplier has become liable to pay the tax to them, and so the issue of a tax invoice creates a time of supply, even if it occurs before the supply is actually made.

(1) Pro-forma invoices

Often payment is requested by issuing a document similar in appearance to a tax invoice, but which does not have the characteristics of one (e.g. a pro-forma invoice). In such cases great care should be exercised to ensure that the document cannot be treated as a tax invoice.

No VAT registration number should be quoted, and ideally no separate amount should be shown in respect of VAT. The document should be clearly marked to the effect that it is not a tax invoice. If such documents are to be used with any frequency, or for large amounts, it would be wise to agree the exact form of them with HMRC.

Example of a completed VAT invoice

Sales invoice No. 174

From: Foundation Trading (UK) Ltd   VAT Reg. No. 987 6543 21
                Bowman Street, Chester

To: A. N. Other Ltd
                57 North Road, London N12 5NA

                Sale: Time of supply 16/09/10   Date of Issue: 19/09/10

Quantity	Description and Price	Amount exclusive of VAT	VAT rate	VAT Net
6	Radios, SW 15 @ £25.20	151.20		
4	Record Players @ £23.60	94.40		
6	Lamps T77 @ £15.55	93.30	17.5	56.34*
		338.90		
	Delivery (strictly Net)	9.00	17.5	1.58
	Terms: Cash discount of 5% if paid within 30 days	347.90		57.92
	VAT	57.92		
	Total	405.82		

* calculated on the discounted price

(2) The 14-day rule

If a tax invoice is issued within 14 days after the basic tax point, then the basic tax point can be ignored in fixing the time of supply and the date when the invoice is issued is used instead. This can simplify VAT accounting in practice, as it is often easier to set up systems which operate by reference to the date of the invoice than it is to use the basic tax point.

There is no obligation to use the 14-day rule, and accounting can be done by reference to the basic tax point if this is more convenient. However, a trader who does not wish to use the 14-day rule must notify HMRC of this in writing. This notification will then effectively cancel the 14-day rule for all supplies made by that trader. It is possible to use the 14-day rule for some supplies, but not for others, but in practice this should be agreed with HMRC.

If required, the 14-day rule can be extended. Many businesses with monthly invoicing runs find it convenient to use a 31-day rule. If a longer period than 14 days is required, the trader must ask HMRC to make a direction to that effect. Often, a longer period is used without the issuing of a formal direction. This is unwise, because it will expose the trader to possible penalties and interest for incorrect returns and late payments of tax (8480ff.).

It should also be noted that the 14-day rule only overrides the basic tax point. The issue of an invoice cannot override an earlier tax point triggered by the receipt of payment for a supply (see below).

Value Added Tax

(3) On-account invoicing

If a tax invoice is issued for only a part of the total price of the supply, this will trigger the tax point only for that part of the supply. The tax point for the remainder of the supply, and the date when the tax on it becomes accountable to HMRC, will be determined separately.

Law: VATA 1994, s. 6(5)

Source: Notice 700, *The VAT guide*

Website: www.hmrc.gov.uk

See *British VAT Reporter* ¶11-765.

7836 Time of supply: date payment received

The date when a payment is received by the supplier triggers the tax point to the extent of the payment, if the tax point has not already arisen by reference to the basic tax point or the issue of a tax invoice.

If a deposit is received from the customer, the precise terms on which it is held need to be considered to decide whether it amounts to payment. Usually a deposit will amount to advance payment for a supply, in which case it gives rise to a tax point. However, a deposit which is merely security for, say, the return of goods which are let on hire, is not payment for a supply (even if forfeited) and so does not give rise to a tax point.

Most advance payments in respect of a supply will bring about a tax point, even if the money is refundable should the supply not proceed.

If a deposit is received for a supply, and represents payment for the supply, then it will be necessary to account for VAT on the amount of the deposit. If the supply is then cancelled by the customer, and the terms are such that the deposit is forfeited, it no longer represents consideration for a supply of any sort. The tax already accounted for can be claimed back on the next VAT return. However, care is needed if the deposit might be seen as consideration for some supply other than the one originally contemplated. In *C & E Commrs v Bass plc* [1993] BVC 34 the court held that a 'no show' fee, chargeable when a hotel customer failed to turn up having made a booking under a guaranteed reservation scheme, amounted to consideration for a supply of holding the room available for use.

Overpayments by customers, retained by the supplier and set against subsequent bills, were held not to give rise to a tax point until applied against those later bills.

Law: *C & E Commrs v Bass plc* [1993] BVC 34

See *British VAT Reporter* ¶11-900.

7838   Special time of supply rules

There are a number of instances in which the normal time of supply rules are overridden and special rules are used instead. These generally operate by ignoring the basic tax point, and using the earlier of the date when an invoice is issued and the date when payment is received as the tax point

The main occasions when the special rules apply are, briefly:

- deemed supply when goods or services are put to non-business use;
- deemed supply on import of services;
- compulsory purchase of land, or supply of it when amount of consideration undetermined;
- supply under a major interest lease;
- supply of power, heat, etc.;
- supply involving retention payments;
- continuous supplies of services;
- royalty payments, etc.;
- certain supplies in the construction industry;
- deemed supply on transfer of a going concern to partially exempt group;
- self-supplies.

Change in rate of tax: consequences

If there is a change in tax rate, or in the liability status of a supply, and the basic tax point falls under one set of rules while the tax point finally determined falls under the other set of rules, the supplier may elect to treat the supply as taking place at the basic tax point. This applies only for determining the rate of tax for the supply. The ordinary tax point is used for all other purposes, such as determining when the tax is payable to HMRC.

If, as a result, it transpires that a tax invoice already issued now bears an excessive amount of tax, the supplier must issue a credit note to reduce the tax within 45 days after the change.

The option to elect for the most favourable tax point does not apply in the case of self-supplies of cars, or in the case of goods sold by a receiver.

The ability to select the most favourable tax point, and therefore rate of VAT, applies to users of the cash accounting scheme as well as to other traders. The cash accounting scheme only affects the date when tax is paid to, or reclaimed from, HMRC, not the underlying tax point.

Law: VATA 1994, s. 88, s. 88(6); *Value Added Tax Regulations* 1995 (SI 1995/2518), reg. 81–93

Source: Notice 700, *The VAT Guide*

See *British VAT Reporter* ¶11-700, ¶12-305, and ¶12-500.

VALUE OF SUPPLY

7844 Introduction to value of supply

The value of a supply, as determined for VAT purposes, is the amount on which VAT is charged. Clearly it is important to understand the rules for determining the value of a supply (or the 'taxable amount', as it is called in the EC legislation), since this directly affects the amount of tax chargeable.

As is the case with the law governing the time of supply, there are some basic rules which cover most transactions, and then a set of special rules which apply in specified circumstances.

Law: VATA 1994, s. 19(1)

Source: Notice 700, *The VAT guide*

Website: www.hmrc.gov.uk

See *British VAT Reporter* ¶14-200.

7846 Consideration in money

If a supply is made for consideration, and the consideration is wholly in money, the value of the supply (or taxable amount) is taken to be the amount which, with the addition of the tax chargeable, is equal to the consideration. In other words, if a supply is made for money, the price charged includes the VAT due.

So:

VALUE PLUS VAT = CONSIDERATION

From the supplier's point of view it is therefore desirable to express the price as being a VAT exclusive amount, with VAT to be added as appropriate.

> ### Example
>
> Alfred sells standard-rated goods to Bert for £3,000.
>
> If the contract price is stated as being VAT-inclusive, the VAT is £446.81 (7/47 × £3,000).
>
> The value if the supply is £2,553.19.
>
> If the contract price is stated as being excluding VAT, the taxable value of the supply is £3,000 and the VAT is £525.00 (£3,000 × 17.5 per cent).

Law: VATA 1994, s. 19(2)

See *British VAT Reporter* ¶14-200.

7848 Change in value of supply

Although not specifically implemented in the UK legislation, the EC VAT Directive, art. 90, provides for the value of supply (or taxable amount) to be changed in certain circumstances. Its terms are as follows:

> 'In the case of cancellation, refusal or total or partial non-payment, or where the price is reduced after the supply takes place, the taxable amount shall be reduced accordingly under conditions which shall be determined by the Member States.

> However, in the case of total or partial non-payment, Member States may derogate from this rule.'

This provision has direct effect in the UK (except in the case of non-payment, where Member States may derogate) and, since the UK government has not taken advantage of its right to impose conditions, it has unconditional effect.

Law: EC VAT Directive 2006/211, art. 90

See *British VAT Reporter* ¶14-200.

7850 More than one supply: effect on value of supply

If a consideration in money relates to several items, then it must be split between those so that each supply is treated as made for a monetary consideration equal to the amount of the total consideration which is properly attributable to it.

Law: VATA 1994, s. 19(4)

See *British VAT Reporter* ¶14-200.

7852 Change in rate of tax: effect on value of supply

If there is a change in the rate of tax attaching to a supply (including a change in classification of the supply as between standard-rated, zero-rated or exempt) then the consideration due under a pre-existing contract for the supply is automatically adjusted to take account of the change, unless the contract provides to the contrary. The value of the supply remains the same, but the total consideration alters.

Value Added Tax

> **Example**
>
> Beryl contracts to sell goods to Claire for £5,875. Before the tax point arises, the standard rate of VAT changes from 17.5 per cent to 20 per cent.
>
> The value of the supply, or taxable amount, is £5,000 (£5,750 × $7/47$). This amount, with the addition of tax at 17.5 per cent, comes to £5,875.
>
> On the change in rate, the taxable amount remains the same. The tax chargeable becomes £1000 (£5,000 × 20 per cent), so the consideration under the contract is increased to £6000.

The exercising of the option to tax by a supplier of land, etc. is treated as a change of rate for this purpose.

However, a term under a lease or tenancy disapplying this rule is ineffective (so that s. 89 applies to vary the consideration) unless the term specifically refers either to VAT or to VATA 1994, s. 89 (VATA 1994, s. 89(2)).

Law: VATA 1994, s. 89, 89(2)

See *British VAT Reporter* ¶14-200.

7854 Non-monetary consideration

If a supply is made for a consideration which is not in money, or is not wholly in money, then under UK law the value of the supply is taken as being the amount of money which, with the addition of the VAT due, is equal to the value of the consideration.

The incidence of VAT on non-monetary consideration gives rise to an important planning point when framing contracts which is frequently overlooked. As indicated at 7846, it is important (from the supplier's point of view) to state that amounts of monetary consideration mentioned in the agreement do not include any VAT which may be due, and that VAT is to be added as appropriate. However, this is not sufficient if there is also non-monetary consideration. Unless there is specific provision in the contract requiring the customer to pay over any VAT arising on supplies made wholly or partly for non-monetary consideration, the supplier will be left to bear the VAT (although the customer may still be able to recover it as input tax).

Law: VATA 1994, s. 19(3)

See *British VAT Reporter* ¶11-295.

7856   Discounts

If a trader offers a discount for prompt payment, and assuming that the terms of supply do not allow payment by instalments, the value of supply is determined as if the supply were made for the sale price as reduced by the discount. This applies whether or not the discount is, in fact, taken.

Example

Jackie sells goods to Pauline for £1,000, subject to a 5 per cent discount for payment within 30 days.

The value of the supply is determined as if she sold the goods for £950 (£1,000 − 5 per cent). The taxable amount is therefore £808.51 (£950 × $^{40}/_{47}$) and the tax due is £141.49. This is so whether Pauline pays £950 within the 30-day period, or £1,000 thereafter.

If a discount is contingent upon another event occurring (for example 10 per cent discount if another order is placed within 30 days), the value of the supply is the amount actually paid. If the discount is taken up, a credit note may be issued and the appropriate adjustments made to the VAT account.

Example

Alfred makes a standard-rated supply of goods to Bert for £5,875 including VAT. If Bert places a second order within one month, he will be entitled to a 5 per cent discount on all those supplies.

At the time of the original supply, the value of the supply is £5,000 and the VAT is £875.00.

If Bert meets the discount criteria, the value of the supply will be reduced to £4,750 and the VAT due will be £831.25.

Law: VATA 1994, Sch. 6, para. 4

See *British VAT Reporter* ¶14-400.

7858   Consideration in foreign currency

If a supply is made for a consideration expressed in a foreign currency, certain values must be converted into sterling by reference to the market rate at the time of supply, unless the trader opts to use an exchange rate published by HMRC.

Law: VATA 1994, Sch. 6, para. 11; *Willis Pension Trustees Ltd* [2006] BVC 2,045

See *British VAT Reporter* ¶14-750.

Value Added Tax

7860 Special value of supply rules

There are a number of modifications to the basic rules as to the value of supply:

- HMRC can direct that certain supplies between connected persons be treated as taking place at market value;
- HMRC can direct that certain 'party plan' type supplies be treated as taking place at retail value;
- the sale of a token, stamp or voucher which carries a right to obtain goods or services is treated as taking place at a value limited to any excess of the consideration payable over the face value of the token;
- where there is a deemed supply on a self-supply of a motor car (see 7766), or where goods which are business assets cease to be such, or when a person ceases to be registered for VAT, the value of the supply is deemed to be equivalent to the current value of the goods, taking into account the age and condition of the goods concerned. If this cannot be ascertained then the value is taken to be equal to that of similar goods or, failing that, the current cost of production of such goods;
- a deemed supply arises when goods which are business assets are put to non-business use for no consideration. The VAT value of such a deemed supply is the full cost to the trader of making the goods available;
- there is a reduction in value for certain supplies of long stay hotel accommodation;
- in the case of the supply to employees of food or beverages (supplied in the course of catering) or of accommodation in a hotel, inn, boarding house, or similar establishment, the value of the supply is restricted to the amount of any money consideration;
- where goods are sold under a second-hand goods scheme (see 8392ff.), the consideration for which they are sold is regarded as limited to any excess of the actual consideration over the cost of the goods to the supplier;
- if a business provides car fuel to an employee, partner, proprietor or director for use for non-business purposes (including home-to-work travelling) free or for less than cost, the supply is treated as being made for a consideration calculated by reference to the cylinder capacity of the vehicle. The value is to be found in a table contained in VATA 1994, s. 57, as amended from time to time.

Law: VATA 1994, s. 56, 57, Sch. 6, para. 1, 2, 6, 7, 9, 10

CHARGEABLE EVENTS – VAT ON IMPORTS FROM OUTSIDE THE EC

7880 Introduction – imports

The general rule is that the importation of goods from outside the EC is a chargeable event, and VAT is due on the goods, regardless of whether the person importing the goods does so in the course of a business. Only imports from 'third countries' (i.e. non-EC countries) are covered by this charge – 'imports' from elsewhere in the EC are covered by the 'acquisition' rules reviewed at 7972ff. The tax is chargeable as if it were a duty of HMRC, and is payable at the same time as any HMRC duty arising.

There are a number of reliefs, and suspensions of liability, available, including some which also apply for customs duty purposes and some which are peculiar to VAT. It is important to appreciate that a customs duty relief will not automatically mean that a VAT relief will follow.

As a general rule VAT on importation is payable when the goods enter the country (or during the month following, under duty deferment arrangements), although in some limited circumstances involving low value goods a registered trader may account for the tax via his VAT return.

This section provides a general outline of the system for applying VAT to imports of goods from countries outside the EC, and of the main reliefs and suspensions available.

In most instances the mechanics of these rules will be handled for traders by freight forwarders, etc. The important points for traders to bear in mind are to ensure that the right person is named as importer, that the place of supply provisions are properly recognised for any supply by the importer, and that appropriate evidence is held for recovery of input tax.

Law: VATA 1994, s. 1

Source: HMRC Notice 702, *Imports*

Website: www.hmrc.gov.uk

See *British VAT Reporter* ¶63-710.

7886　The charge to VAT on imports – general

The basic charging provision for VAT on importation is VATA 1994, s. 1(4).

Tax is due when goods are imported into the EC from a place outside the EC. This is deemed to arise where:

- the goods are removed from a place outside the EC and enter the territory of the EC;
- they either enter the UK directly or enter it via another Member State; and
- the circumstances are such that it is on entry into the UK that any liability to customs duty arises (or would arise if the goods were dutiable).

Usually the charge will arise in the ordinary way, on a direct importation into the UK, at the time when the goods are entered. However, if on arrival in the UK, the goods are entered for some customs duty suspension regime (e.g. warehousing, etc.) the liability arises when they are removed into free circulation.

Value Added Tax

If goods first arrive in some other Member State and are entered into a customs duty suspension arrangement, and are in the UK when removed from this and entered for home use, the VAT charge on importation arises in the UK.

(1) Import by a business

Most imports are carried out by businesses. Any VAT due on importation will also rank as input tax in the hands of the importer, so is usually recoverable from HMRC via the importer's VAT returns (subject to the usual VAT recovery rules – see 8034ff., 8110ff.).

(2) Import by a private individual, etc.

Import VAT is due on importation regardless of the status of the importer. If the importation is by a private individual, or some other entity not carrying on a business, import VAT is due in the ordinary way. In this case there is, of course, no question of recovering a similar amount as input tax. Thus, a non-taxable person who buys goods from outside the EC, and imports them, is put in the same VAT position as a person who buys from a taxable business.

(3) Zero-rated goods

If the imported goods fall into a zero-rated category, there is no VAT liability on the importation of them, unless the zero-rating provisions in VATA 1994, Sch. 8 provide to the contrary (VATA 1994, s. 30(3)).

Goods excluded from this relief on importation include:

- building materials, etc. (VATA 1994, Sch. 8, Grp. 5, Note 24);
- gold (VATA 1994, Sch. 8, Grp. 10, Note 2); and
- certain drugs and other aids for handicapped persons, unless imported by a handicapped person for his own domestic or personal use, or by a charity for making available to handicapped persons for their own domestic or personal use (VATA 1994, Sch. 8, Grp. 12, Note 1).

(4) Exempt goods

There is no equivalent provision excluding from the charge on importation goods which would be exempt from VAT if supplied in the UK. This is presumably because, to the extent that the UK exemptions apply to goods, they only apply when the goods are supplied in particular circumstances or by particular persons. The supplier will in each case have suffered irrecoverable input tax on the acquisition or manufacture of the goods, and will normally pass this on in the price of the goods. Relieving from import VAT non-EC goods which do not bear such an underlying VAT burden would create a distortion of competition in favour of non-EC suppliers.

Law: VATA 1994, s. 1(4), 30(3), Sch. 8; *Premier Foods (Holding) Ltd v R & C Commrs*

Source: Notice 702, *Imports*

Website: www.hmrc.gov.uk

See *British VAT Reporter* ¶63-710.

7892 Procedure on importation – general

Goods entering the UK may only be landed at a Customs control area, such as a customs port or airport (CEMA 1979, Pt. III), and a vehicle arriving at such an area is obliged to report to HMRC. The importer of goods must enter them, by presenting C88 (the Single Administrative Document, or SAD).

The SAD gives details of the goods being imported, their value for customs and VAT purposes, the name of the importer, etc. Unless the goods are entered for a special regime, such as warehousing (see below), VAT (and any duty) payable on the importation is due at the time of importation (but see 7904), and the goods will not normally be released until payment has been made.

The SAD is submitted electronically by direct trader input, or by their agent. In some circumstances HMRC will complete the SAD for the trader.

For alternative entry procedures, see 7898.

Law: CEMA 1979, Pt. III; EC Regulation 2913/92, art. 40 et seq

Source: Notice 702, *Imports*

Website: www.hmrc.gov.uk

See *British VAT Reporter* ¶63-710.

7898 Alternative entry procedures

There are alternatives to the basic entry procedure (7892), the main ones being:

- bulked entry – this allows a person importing several consignments for different consignees to make a single declaration for all of the consignments;
- period entry – this allows a regular importer using computers for accounting and stock control purposes to use a simplified Single Administrative Document (SAD) at the point of entry and provide the detailed information to HMRC periodically, post-importation, on computer media;
- simplified procedure for import clearance – this is a simplified procedure for certain low value goods permitting a single form to be used for up to six consignments; and
- postal imports – in this case, where the value of the goods is less than £2,000 and appropriate procedures are followed, the VAT-registered importer can account for the VAT on importation via his VAT return. However, for Datapost packets the Post Office

Value Added Tax

will collect the VAT at the time of delivery. For consignments whose value exceeds £2,000 a declaration must be made and returned to HMRC with payment of the VAT on importation.

It is also possible to arrange to have goods entered and cleared at a trader's own premises, rather than at the port of arrival.

Details of the various entry procedures are contained in vol. 3 of the Customs Tariff.

See *British VAT Reporter* ¶63-760.

7904 Payment of VAT

Value added tax on importation is, in principle, due for payment at the time of importation.

It is also possible to enter into an arrangement whereby VAT on importation is collected by HMRC, by direct debit, on the fifteenth day of the month following importation. This involves providing HMRC with suitable security to cover deferrable charges (VAT, customs duty, etc.) each month and obtaining their approval. The amount of the guarantee can be topped up occasionally to cover unusually high levels of imports. Approved traders may be able to lower their guarantee through the Simplified Import VAT Accounting (SIVA).

Law: SI 1973/1223 the Customs Duties (Deferred Payment) Regulations

See *British VAT Reporter* ¶63-780.

7910 Identity of importer

The 'importer' of goods from the time of importation to the time when they are delivered out of charge is defined as including:

'any owner or other person for the time being possessed of or beneficially interested in the goods.'

There is therefore an element of choice as to the identity of the importer in relation to any particular transaction.

In practice the importer is generally taken as being the person named as such on the Single Administrative Document (SAD). Care needs to be taken in selecting the importer, to ensure that it is someone capable of recovering the tax concerned as input tax (i.e. someone involved in the supply chain, not a mere carrier, etc.), and to avoid any unintended side effects in relation to the place of supply (see 7916).

Law: CEMA 1979, s. 1(1)

Source: Notice 702, *Imports*

Website: www.hmrc.gov.uk

See *British VAT Reporter* ¶63-760.

7916   Interaction with place of supply rules

A supply of the imported goods by the importer of them into the UK is treated as made in the UK, even if delivery in respect of the supply commenced outside the UK.

7922   Value on importation

The value of imported goods for VAT purposes is generally the same as the value for customs duty purposes plus (if not already included) taxes, duties, etc. arising prior to or because of the importation, and all commission, packing, insurance, transport, etc. costs up to the place of importation. If a further destination of the goods within the EC is known at the time of importation, the value for VAT purposes includes the further transport, etc. costs in so far as they result from the transfer of the goods to that further destination. If the value is based on the price at which they are supplied, this is generally reduced to take account of any prompt payment discount.

The value for customs duty purposes is generally based on the price at which the transaction is taking place. Where this is inappropriate there are other possible bases, such as the transaction value of identical or similar goods, or a computed value based on cost (see Regulation 2913/92 on the valuation of goods for customs duties purposes).

Law: FA 2006, s. 18; FA 1996, s. 27; VATA 1994, s. 21, 21(3)

See *British VAT Reporter* ¶14-250.

7928   Reliefs – general

There are three main kinds of relief from VAT on the importation of goods from outside the EC.

(1) Suspension of the charge – the charge is not removed, but is suspended while the goods are in some kind of suspension regime (such as warehousing). The liability crystallises, and VAT becomes payable, as and when the goods are removed from the suspension regime for free circulation in the UK.

(2) Temporary import reliefs – under these certain goods brought temporarily to the UK escape the liability to VAT on importation altogether, provided that all appropriate conditions are met and the goods are subsequently re-exported. If the goods remain in the UK beyond the permitted period, a UK VAT liability then arises.

(3) Absolute reliefs – in some cases there is no liability to VAT on the importation.

Value Added Tax

The reliefs available are mentioned in 7934ff. Detailed coverage of these reliefs is beyond the scope of this work.

Source: Notice 702/8: *Fiscal warehousing;* Public Notice 232 *Customs Warehousing*

See *British VAT Reporter* ¶63-800.

7934   Reliefs – suspension

VAT on importation of goods from outside the EC into the UK is suspended in the following main cases:

- importation into a free zone – in this instance the import VAT is due only when the goods are removed from the free zone for home use or when they are consumed within the freezone;.
- importation into a customs warehouse, excise warehouse or a fiscal warehouse – in these cases, importation VAT becomes payable, if at all, when the goods are removed from the warehouse for home use;
- inward processing relief (IPR); and
- transit and transhipment.

Law: VATA 1994, s. 17–18F; Regulation 2913/92, art 98 onwards

Source: Public Notice 334: *Free Zones;* Public Notice 232 *Customs Warehousing*

7940   Reliefs – temporary import (TI) relief

Relief is available for various goods temporarily imported into the UK, including:

- certain personal effects temporarily imported;
- commercial vehicles and aircraft;
- goods for removal to another Member State;
- containers and pallets; and
- various goods specified in the legislation.

In each case there are a number of conditions to be met – security may be required, and VAT becomes due if the goods remain in the UK beyond a specified period or the conditions for relief are otherwise breached. TI is essentially a customs duty relief, but the import VAT follows the duty treatment. On importation, security may well be required for the customs duty and the import VAT and will be released when the goods are subsequently re-exported.

7946   Reliefs – absolute reliefs

There are a number of absolute reliefs from VAT on importation from outside the EC, including the following:

- reimportation by a person who is not a taxable person and who previously exported the goods, without having been altered, where they have previously borne VAT (which has not been repaid) within the EC and various detailed conditions are met;
- a similar relief for taxable persons (again conditional on any VAT suffered previously not having been reclaimed);
- a further similar relief for reimported motor cars;
- certain second-hand works of art, collectors' pieces, etc. are liable to import VAT at an effective rate of 5 per cent;
- goods specified in the *Value Added Tax (Imported Goods) Relief Order* 1984 (SI 1984/746);
- certain personal property imported by persons entering the UK to take up permanent residence;
- certain goods, such as labels, imported free of charge for incorporation in UK manufactured goods which are to be exported from the EC;
- certain trade samples; and
- imported legacies, awards for distinction, etc.

In each case detailed conditions must be met, and appropriate documentation completed, in order to qualify for relief. In addition, no VAT is payable on imported goods falling within travellers' duty free allowances.

Law: VATA 1994, s. 21(4)–(7); *Value Added Tax (Imported Goods) Relief Order* 1984 (SI 1984/746); EC Regulation 918/83

7952 Removal from warehouse, etc.

Import VAT on UK goods placed in a warehouse is due on their removal for home use. Any sales which have taken place in the warehouse are ignored.

However, if the goods are processed in the warehouse so as to lose their character, or mixed with UK-produced goods so that they are no longer identifiable, the position is different. In this case, import VAT is no longer due on their removal from the warehouse. However, if they are supplied while in the warehouse, VAT is due on the last such supply to take place, and is payable by the person removing the goods for home use.

Law: VATA 1994, s. 18

Source: Public Notice 200 – *Temporary Importations*; Public Notice 232 *Customs Warehousing*

See *British VAT Reporter* ¶63-875.

Value Added Tax

CHARGEABLE EVENTS – VAT ON ACQUISITIONS FROM ELSEWHERE IN THE EC

7972 Introduction to VAT on acquisitions

There are particular rules on the acquisition of goods from elsewhere in the EC. There are also special registration requirements for unregistered businesses and other entities acquiring goods in the UK from elsewhere in the EC.

The general rule for goods supplied within the EC is that they are taxed in the Member State to which they are dispatched:

- the supplier in the Member State of dispatch can zero-rate his supply, but only if he is supplying to a VAT-registered customer and quotes the customer's VAT registration number on his invoice (see 7818);
- the customer is liable to account for VAT in the Member State of arrival on his 'acquisition' of the goods;
- to enable the authorities to verify that acquisition tax is properly accounted for, the supplier must submit periodic EC sales listings to which the authorities in the Member State of arrival have access (see 8460);
- a supplier dispatching significant quantities of goods to unregistered persons in another Member State may become liable to register for VAT there, and account for that Member State's VAT on these supplies (see 7818). In such a case he is relieved of the liability to account for output tax in his own Member State; and
- some unregistered entities acquiring significant quantities of goods from suppliers in other Member States may become liable to register for VAT in respect of these acquisitions. They are then liable to account for their own country's VAT on the acquisitions and their suppliers can zero-rate their supplies in the Member State of dispatch.

See *British VAT Reporter* ¶64-220.

7978 Acquisition – normal procedure

The most common case involving acquisitions from elsewhere in the EC (see 7972) is where a UK business purchases goods from a supplier elsewhere in the EC, who ships the goods to the UK customer. The liability to pay acquisition VAT arises when:

- there is an acquisition of goods in the UK (see 7984, 8002);
- the acquisition does not involve the supplier in making a UK supply (i.e. it is not caught by the UK's distance selling rules or by the rules for supplies of installed goods – see 7818);
- the person making the acquisition does so in the course of a business, or in the course of a non-business activity of a company, club, etc.;
- the person making the acquisition is a taxable person (i.e. someone who is already

registered for VAT, or is liable to be registered, whether under the ordinary VAT system or under the rules for registration of persons making significant UK acquisitions); and
- the acquisition is not exempt or zero-rated.

Law: VATA 1994, s. 10; *JP Commodities v R & C Commrs*

See *British VAT Reporter* ¶64-210.

7984   Meaning of acquisition

The term 'acquisition of goods' is defined in the EC VAT Directive 2006/112, art. 20 and, in the UK, in VATA 1994, s. 11. An acquisition arises where goods are removed from one Member State to another and:
- the movement involves a supply by the person dispatching the goods; or
- the person is moving his own goods from one Member State to another.

A taxable person moving his own goods from one Member State to another is deemed to make a supply in the Member State of dispatch and an acquisition in the Member State of arrival.

However, a movement of own goods to another Member State for processing and return is not treated as involving a supply.

Law: VATA 1994, s. 11; EC VAT Directive 2006/112, art. 20

See *British VAT Reporter* ¶64-240.

7990   Exceptions from normal procedure on acquisition

The basic definition of an acquisition would cover any movement of goods within the EC (see 7984). However, where there would be relief from VAT on import from outside the EC under the *Value Added Tax (Imported Goods) Relief Order* 1984 (SI 1984/746) (see 7946) there is a parallel relief from VAT on acquisition from another Member State.

Similarly, no liability arises where the goods are transferred by a private individual, subject to the exceptions covered below.

(1) New means of transport

A new means of transport delivered from one Member State to another bears VAT in the Member State in which it is registered, even if the person to whom it is delivered is not a taxable person. Where the customer is a taxable person, the normal rules apply. Where the customer is not a taxable person, he is liable to account for VAT in the state of registration of the means of transport (*Value Added Tax Regulations* 1995 (SI 1995/2518), reg. 148).

Value Added Tax

The person making the acquisition must notify HMRC within seven days of their arrival, and pay the tax due within 30 days of receiving a demand for it.

The supplier of the goods must hold appropriate evidence that tax has been accounted for in the other Member State (where the acquirer is not a taxable person) in order to zero-rate the supply.

A UK supplier of a new means of transport for acquisition in another Member State may need to charge UK VAT in the first instance, pending receipt of evidence that acquisition tax has been accounted for in the other Member State. HMRC can refund the tax at a later date, on receipt of a claim accompanied by suitable evidence.

A 'new means of transport' is, broadly, a new ship, aircraft or land vehicle. Excluded from the definition are ships less than 7.5 metres long, aircraft less than 1,550 kilograms in take-off weight, and land vehicles of less than 48cc (or electric vehicles using less than 7.2 kilowatts). A means of transport is new until at least three months have elapsed from its entry into service (six months for a land vehicle) or it has had a specified amount of use.

(2) *Excise goods*

As a general rule, when goods liable to excise duty (such as tobacco products, alcohol, etc.) are delivered by a supplier in another Member State to a UK customer, this will involve a taxable supply in the UK under the distance selling rules (see 7818). This is because no turnover limit applies for the distance selling of excise goods (VATA 1994, Sch. 2, para. 1(3)).

In the rare case where the seller is not making the supply by way of business (or is otherwise not registrable in the UK) the customer (including a private individual) is obliged to notify the acquisition and account for VAT on it (*Value Added Tax Regulations* 1995 (SI 1995/2518), reg. 36).

It follows that the only way in which excise goods can enter the UK from elsewhere in the EC without payment of UK VAT (and duty) is if a private individual collects them personally from elsewhere in the EC and brings them back for his own private use. These excise rules require that VAT and excise duty is paid in the Member State in which they were purchased (say in a supermarket).

Law: VATA 1994, s. 40, s. 95; Sch. 2, para. 1(3), s. 36A; *Value Added Tax Regulations* 1995 (SI 1995/2518), reg. 36, 148; EC Directive 92/12, art. 8 and 9; HMWR 1992

See *British VAT Reporter* ¶64-360.

7996 Registration in respect of acquisitions

A person in business in the UK, and certain other persons, can become liable to register for VAT in the UK if acquisitions from other Member States exceed a certain threshold (measured from 1 January in the year concerned).

This liability to register affects all businesses, and also any body corporate, club, association, organisation or other unincorporated body carrying on non-business activities.

The liability to register in respect of acquisitions is covered in more detail at 8280ff.

Law: VATA 1994, s. 10(3)

See *British VAT Reporter* ¶64-300.

8002 Place of acquisition

If the goods are removed to the UK (the normal case), then the acquisition takes place in the UK.

The other instance where an acquisition might be deemed to take place in the UK arises where a person accepts an intra-EC delivery of goods in another Member State, but quotes his UK VAT registration number to enable his supplier to zero-rate the supply (referred to in the legislation as 'making use of a VAT number'). In this instance an acquisition is deemed to take place in the UK unless the acquirer can show that he has actually paid acquisition tax in the Member State of delivery. This facilitates the policing of the system, since the supplier will have included the UK registration number on his EC sales listing (8460).

Law: VATA 1994, s. 13

8008 Time of acquisition

An acquisition is deemed to take place on the earlier of the date when the supplier issues an invoice and the 15th day of the month following the date when the goods are removed. The date of payment for the supply is ignored.

Law: VATA 1994, s. 12

See *British VAT Reporter* ¶64-320.

8014 Value of acquisition

The value of an acquisition is the value of the transaction under which it takes place. This will normally be the value of the consideration, whether monetary or non-monetary.

Value Added Tax

There are special provisions to cover special cases (gifts, connected persons, etc.) on similar lines to those relating to supplies of goods.

Law: VATA 1994, s. 20, Sch. 7

See *British VAT Reporter* ¶64-340.

8016 Call-off stocks, consignment stocks and sale or return goods

It is the view of HMRC that if a trader ships goods to another Member State and holds them as stock under his control, this gives rise to a deemed supply. This is consignment stock. The subsequent supply of the goods to a customer in that other state is a supply made there. The normal EC movement rules apply. The trader will need to have a VAT number in the Member State where the goods will be stored and then the trader can zero-rate his supply as a dispatch into the other Member State.

However, if goods are shipped to another Member State and held under the control of a specific customer there, who can then 'call off' the goods for use as and when required, this is still regarded as a zero-rated supply to the customer (if VAT registered) and an acquisition by the customer in the other Member State, both arising at the time of the movement of the goods.

There is no distinction between the two for VAT purposes; both are treated as dispatches and acquisitions. However, there are major contractual and commercial differences. In call-off stock the title does not pass until the customer calls the stock off.

Goods sent to an overseas customer on sale or return are treated in the same way as consignment stocks.

The same treatment applies to goods shipped to the UK by a supplier in another Member State.

Care should be taken in dealings with other Member States, as not all of them accept these treatments.

Source: Notice 725

INPUTS AND INPUT TAX RECOVERY – GENERAL

8034 Overview of input tax recovery

Traders are obliged to account for VAT on taxable supplies which they make. They can also recover VAT charged to them on supplies which they obtain, and on imports of goods from outside the EC and acquisitions of goods from within the EC. The net effect of this is that the tax ultimately collected on taxable supplies is directly proportional to the price paid for those supplies by consumers. Zero-rated supplies bear no effective VAT, while exempt supplies are, in effect, subject to VAT to the extent that suppliers bear VAT on their costs.

A number of further complexities arise for businesses which make both taxable supplies and exempt supplies (even occasional exempt supplies), see 8110ff.

See *British VAT Reporter* ¶19-000.

8040   Definition of input tax

The only tax which may be recovered by a taxable trader is that which falls within the definition of input tax. 'Input tax' is defined as follows:

'... "input tax", in relation to a taxable person, means the following tax, that is to say–

(a)   VAT on the supply to him of any goods or services;
(b)   VAT on the acquisition by him from another Member State of any goods; and
(c)   VAT paid or payable by him on the importation of any goods from a place outside the Member States,

being (in each case) goods or services used or to be used for the purpose of any business carried on or to be carried on by him.'

It follows from this definition that a number of conditions must be met before a person can treat VAT as input tax. Even where these conditions are met, so that the tax ranks as input tax, some or all of it may still be non-deductible, and this aspect will be considered later. However, there is no possibility of tax being deductible unless it meets the basic criteria set out above.

(1) Taxable person requirement

A UK 'taxable person' is a person who is registered for VAT in the UK, or is required to be registered (VATA 1994, s. 3(1)). Value added tax in the UK is also deductible by a non-UK taxable person if, broadly, that input tax would have been recoverable if that trader was established in the UK (see 8080). Similarly, a UK taxable person can recover certain VAT suffered in other Member States (see 8082).

(2) Supply, acquisition or importation

It is implicit in the definition of input tax that a supply, acquisition or importation must actually take place for any 'tax' which is sought to be reclaimed to be input tax.

Transactions which do not amount to supplies are covered at 7776ff.

Value Added Tax

(3) Supply to or acquisition/importation by taxable person

Where an input tax refund is sought in respect of a supply, it is essential that the supply is made to the taxable person rather than to some other person. This does not necessarily mean that the supply must be paid for by the taxable person, or that all supplies for which a person pays rank as supplies made to that person.

The *Redrow* case concerned a business promotion scheme operated by a housebuilder. The builder would engage estate agents to sell the existing houses of potential customers. Provided the customers then bought new houses from Redrow, it would pay the estate agents' fees. The estate agents contracted separately with the customers for payment of the fees, in the event that the customers did not buy from Redrow. The court held that the estate agents supplied services to Redrow, so that the VAT on their fees was input tax in Redrow's hands.

The outcome of the *Redrow* case depended upon the contractual relationship between Redrow and the estate agents. It should be contrasted with the position where, for instance, a tenant is obliged to pay a landlord's professional costs in connection with a lease variation. In this instance, the tenant has no contractual relationship with the landlord's professional advisers, and the supplies by those advisers are made to the landlord, and not to the tenant. The right to input tax recovery (if any) rests with the landlord and not with the tenant.

In order to recover input tax on an importation of goods from outside the EC, or an acquisition from within the EC, the importation or acquisition must have been made by the claimant.

(4) Legal services relating to insurance claims

When claims are made against people who have insured against such claims, and the claims are resisted, lawyers are often engaged to handle the matter. It is accepted by HMRC that the supply by the lawyer, in this instance, is made to the policyholder rather than to the insurance company, even though the insurance company instructs the lawyer on behalf of the policyholder and the insurance company is ultimately responsible for the lawyer's fees.

(5) Supplies obtained by employees

As a rule, when supplies are ordered by employees of a taxable person for that person's business, it will be clear that the supplies are obtained on behalf of the employer and so no difficulty should arise over the deduction of related input tax. For instance, if a buyer for XYZ Ltd orders 200,000 printed circuit boards from a supplier, no one will be in any doubt that the contract is really between XYZ Ltd and the supplier, and the transaction will proceed accordingly.

There are occasions when employees may obtain supplies in their own right and recharge them to the employer. The most common of these are dealt with on a concessionary basis.

If an employee on a business trip obtains accommodation and meals for business reasons and the business bears the full cost, the tax can be treated as input tax even if the supply was made, in the first instance, to the employee. This will not enable tax to be recovered for business entertaining as such tax is specifically treated as non-deductible, but it does prevent tax on ordinary subsistence expenses from being disallowed on a technicality.

A special provision applies where employees buy petrol for business journeys, and the business reimburses the actual expenditure. In addition, tax can be reclaimed on a reasonable petrol element of mileage allowances paid to employees in respect of business mileage.

(6) Importation by taxable person

Value added tax on the importation of goods from outside the EC ranks as input tax in the hands of the taxable person concerned if it is paid or payable by the taxable person.

Value added tax on importation is payable as if it were a duty of customs (VATA 1994, s. 1(4)). It is therefore payable by the importer. The term 'importer' is defined, in CEMA 1979, s. 1(1), as follows:

> '"importer", in relation to any goods at any time between their importation and the time when they are delivered out of charge, includes any owner or other person for the time being possessed of or beneficially interested in the goods and, in relation to goods imported by means of a pipe-line, includes the owner of the pipe-line.'

It follows that, in relation to any particular importation, a number of different persons may each be entitled to act as importer. As some of these (such as the carrier of the goods) will usually not be in a position to reclaim the VAT, it is important to ensure that care is taken in deciding who is to act as importer for VAT purposes.

HMRC will regard as the importer for VAT purposes the person named on the import entry documentation as such. Since this documentation must be completed and passed to HMRC before the goods can enter the UK, the decision needs to be taken in advance.

(7) Tax properly chargeable

The tax which can be treated as input tax is the tax properly due on the supply, acquisition or importation concerned. While this seems straightforward, it gives rise to problems in practice.

It is not uncommon for VAT to be charged on transactions where it is not due, usually because of difficulties in understanding the law and a desire by the supplier to 'play safe' in cases where the customer can recover any tax due. In such instances, the tax cannot be treated as input tax in the hands of the customer, as it is not properly chargeable on the transaction .

(8) Domestic accommodation for directors

Tax on supplies, etc. used in providing domestic accommodation for directors is deemed not to be input tax, and so cannot be reclaimed. This rule applies where:

Value Added Tax

- supplies, acquisitions or imports are to be used by a company in connection with the provision of accommodation by the company; and
- the accommodation is used or to be used for the domestic purposes of a director of the company, or of a person connected with a director.

A 'director' includes an owner/manager who is not formally a director and, in the case of a company managed by its members rather than by a board of directors, a member of the company; a person connected with a director is a director's spouse, and a relative or the spouse of a relative of the director or the director's spouse.

This exclusion from the definition of input tax appears to apply even if the company receives consideration for the provision of accommodation, although its validity in that case appears questionable.

(9) Business use

Tax on supplies obtained by (or importations or acquisitions by) a taxable person cannot rank as input tax unless the goods or services concerned are used, or to be used, for the purposes of a business carried on or to be carried on by that person.

The concept of 'business' is considered at 7798.

It should be noted that the supplies concerned do not have to be put to business use immediately, provided that they are intended for business use and business use ultimately occurs.

Tax on supplies to be used for the purposes of a business not yet operating ranks as input tax. Thus, a taxable person with an existing business ought to have little difficulty in recovering tax on preparatory expenses of a new business not yet commenced, but to be operated by the same person. This view is supported by both UK and EC case law. More difficulty may be encountered where no supplies are yet being made, and HMRC will need to be satisfied that there is a genuine business activity before allowing registration.

It has also been established that input tax recovered in respect of preparatory activities may be retained by the trader, even if the activity proves abortive and no taxable supplies are actually made.

Law: VATA 1994, s. 1(4), 3(1), 24(1), (3), (7); CEMA 1979, s. 1(1); *Value Added Tax (Input Tax) (Reimbursement by Employers of Employees' Business Use of Road Fuel) Regulations* 2005 (SI 2005/3290); *C & E Commrs v Redrow Group plc* (1999) BVC 96; *Rompelman v Minister van Financiën* (Case 268/83) (1985) 2 BVC 200,157; *Belgian State v Ghent Coal Terminal NV* (Case C-37/95) [1998] BVC 139

Source: Leaflet 701/36; Notice 700, *The VAT guide*

See *British VAT Reporter* ¶19-000.

8046 Apportionment of tax

If tax arises on a supply, acquisition or importation used partly for business purposes and partly for other purposes, the taxpayer now has a choice: either to adopt an up-front apportionment (VATA 1994, s. 24(5)) or recover all the input tax up-front and pay the private element back each VAT quarter using the Lennartz principle over the tax life of the asset (120 months for land and buildings and 60 months for other assets).

Law: VATA 1994, s. 24(5); *Value Added Tax Regulations* 1995 (SI 1995/2518), Part 15A; *Finanzamt Uelzen v Armbrecht* (Case C-291/92) [1996] BVC 50; *Lennartz v Finanzamt München III* (Case C-97/90) [1993] BVC 202

See *British VAT Reporter* ¶19-040.

INPUT TAX WHICH CANNOT BE DEDUCTED

8058 Supplies on which tax is non-deductible

Although the general rule is that input tax is, in principle, deductible by a taxable person when making his VAT returns, there are a number of occasions when the tax cannot be deducted. In particular, there are a number of categories of supply (or importation) the tax on which is specifically treated as non-deductible:

(1) Purchase of a motor car for use in the business, unless:

    (a) the person to whom it is supplied intends to use it primarily:

        (i) to let with a driver, as passenger transport (e.g. as a taxi),

        (ii) to provide as 'self-drive hire', or

        (iii) to provide driving instruction;

    (b) the purchaser is a motor manufacturer or dealer for whom the vehicle is to be stock in trade; or

    (c) it is a 'qualifying car', namely where the purchaser has no intention of making it available for any form of private use (a hard test to fulfil, meaning that VAT should not be recovered without proper consideration of the rules).

(2) Leasing or contract hire of a motor car, to the tune of 50 per cent of the input tax incurred. The VAT may be recovered in full if the car falls into the categories identified at (a) to (c) of item (1) above and on any separately identified element of the leasing or contract hire charges relating to maintenance.

(3) Business entertainment. This means, broadly, input tax on supplies used in the gratuitous provision of hospitality of any kind, including expenses relating to staff acting as hosts, but does not include input tax relating to staff entertainment.

(4) Certain fittings acquired by the builder of a new dwelling. These are goods to be incorporated in the building by a person intending to grant a major interest in it other

than materials, builder's hardware, sanitary ware, or other items of a kind normally installed by builders as fixtures. Items specifically excluded from recovery are:

(a)   finished or prefabricated furniture, other than furniture designed to be fitted in kitchens (this prevents the builder from deducting input tax in respect of fitted wardrobes, etc.; note, however, that many built-in wardrobes making use of alcoves, etc. inherent in the design of the building are not regarded as 'furniture' so no blocking of input tax arises);

(b)   materials for the construction of fitted furniture, other than kitchen furniture;

(c)   domestic electrical or gas appliances, other than those designed to provide space heating and/or water heating, or such items as ventilation equipment and air-cooling equipment which is now commonly installed in buildings as a requirement of building regulations. The blocking applies, from 1 March 1995, to goods installed in buildings for relevant residential or charitable use as well as to dwellings.

(5)   Goods acquired under a second-hand goods scheme.

(6)   Certain imports of goods partly owned by another.

Input tax made non-deductible in this way is colloquially referred to as having been 'blocked'.

Law: *Value Added Tax (Input Tax) Order* 1992 (SI 1992/3222), art. 6, 7; *McLean Homes Midland Ltd v C & E Commrs* [1993] BVC 99; *Midlands Co-operative Society Ltd v R & C Commrs* [2007] EWHC 1432

Source: *Business Brief* 16/04, 9 June 2004, 'VAT – definition of a motorcar'; *Business Brief* 06/04, 27 February 2004, 'VAT avoidance: demonstrator cars'

See *British VAT Reporter* ¶29-500.

8060   Use to which supplies are put

Even where the basic rules relating to input tax are met (see 8040, 8058), the trader may be prevented from deducting some or all of the input tax arising on supplies to him and importations or acquisitions of goods by him.

The right to deduct input tax is restricted so that, broadly, only tax on supplies and importations used in making taxable supplies may be deducted. Input tax on supplies used in making exempt supplies is, in principle, non-deductible (see 8110ff.).

Law: VATA 1994, s. 26(2)

See *British VAT Reporter* ¶19-000.

8062 Evidence for deduction of input tax

Before a trader may deduct tax as input tax, he must hold evidence in support of the claim. Furthermore, the evidence must take a specified form which varies depending upon the manner in which the input tax arose. For instance, if the input tax arises on a supply, the evidence required is a valid tax invoice addressed to the claimant.

HMRC has power to accept other evidence for the deduction of tax. This power has been exercised as follows:

- an invoice made out to an employee is acceptable evidence in the case of subsistence expenses and petrol; and
- a tax invoice is not required for expenditure below £25 on telephone calls from public or private telephones, purchases through coin operated machines, car park charges, or privately operated road tolls.

HMRC can be asked to accept alternative evidence in particular cases, and they must act reasonably in the exercise of their discretion.

Law: *Chavda t/a Hare Wines* [1993] BVC 1,515

Source: Notice 700, *The VAT guide*

See *British VAT Reporter* ¶63-790.

8063 Repayment of input tax on non-payment

Where input tax has been claimed on a supply received by a taxable person and he has not made payment for that supply by the time six months have elapsed from the due date for payment of the supply (or the date of supply itself, if later), the input tax must be repaid to HMRC on the person's VAT return.

Law: VATA 1994, s. 26A

See *British VAT Reporter* ¶19-010.

PRE-REGISTRATION AND PRE-INCORPORATION SUPPLIES/POST-DE-REGISTRATION SUPPLIES

8068 Relief available pre-registration and post-de-registration

Relief is available for certain input tax incurred prior to registration (or, in the case of a limited company, prior to incorporation) and after de-registration. This tax would not, in principle, be deductible as the trader will not have been a registered taxable person at the time when the tax arose. Consequently, there are special provisions to give effect to the relief.

In each case, there are a number of conditions to be met and, even if these are met, the relief remains at the discretion of HMRC (see 8070, 8072, 8074).

Law: *Value Added Tax Regulations* 1995 (SI 1995/2518), reg. 111

See *British VAT Reporter* ¶43-050.

8070 Pre-registration supplies

Relief is available for certain input tax incurred prior to registration (see 8068). The tax which can be reclaimed is:

- tax on supplies of goods obtained within three years before registration, if the goods are still on hand at the date of registration, either in their original state or incorporated into other goods; and
- tax on supplies of services obtained within six months before the registration date and not disposed of before registration.

In order to reclaim the tax, the trader must hold ordinary evidence for deduction of input tax. In addition, the trader must make a list of all the services in respect of which a claim is made, showing their description, date of purchase and (if appropriate) the date of their disposal. A service would be disposed of if it consisted of work done on goods which were then sold.

Where a claim includes input tax relating to supplies of goods obtained before registration, the trader must compile a stock account showing quantities purchased, quantities used in making other goods, date of purchase and date of disposal (either of original goods or of goods made from them).

See *British VAT Reporter* ¶43-000.

8072 Pre-incorporation supplies

A company can reclaim input tax on supplies obtained on its behalf prior to its incorporation (see 8068). The tax covered is the same as that for pre-registration supplies, and the same time-limits apply (see 8070).

In order to qualify for this relief, certain extra conditions need to be met. The supplies must have been obtained for the benefit of the company or in connection with its incorporation. The person who obtained the supply must have become a member, officer or employee of the company, and must not have been a taxable person at the time of the supply or importation. The company must have reimbursed the person who acquired the supplies, or given an undertaking to do so. The goods or services must have been obtained for the purposes of a business to be carried on by the company, and must not have been used (even temporarily) for any other purpose.

The evidence required is as for pre-registration inputs (i.e. normal input tax evidence plus a list of services and/or a stock account).

See *British VAT Reporter* ¶43-050.

8074   De-registration: relief in respect of services

HMRC also have power to refund tax incurred after de-registration has taken place where this relates to services (but not goods) obtained for the purposes of the business which the person carried on while registered (see 8068). Relief for such input tax is at the complete discretion of HMRC.

Typically, relief is given in respect of services such as those of accountants and lawyers involved in closing the business down, or disposing of it. Normal evidence for input tax deduction must be held.

If possible, the claim should be made by including the tax as input tax on the trader's final VAT return. If this is not possible (e.g. because the work is not done, or a tax invoice is not received, until later), the trader should make a separate claim on form VAT 427. This must be done within four years of the supply.

Law: The VAT Regulations 1995, reg 111

Source: Notice 700/11

MISCELLANEOUS INPUT TAX MATTERS

8080   Repayments to non-UK traders – 8th and 13th Directive claims

There are provisions permitting repayments of input tax to traders established elsewhere in the EC and to traders established outside the EC.

A claim can be made if the claimant:

- is not registered, liable or eligible to be registered in the UK;
- has no UK business establishment; and
- does not make supplies in the UK, other than certain supplies connected with international freight transport or supplies of services treated as made in the UK merely because that is where the recipient belongs.

No input tax will be repaid under these provisions if the claimant intends to use the inputs in making a UK supply, or to export them from the UK (in either of these cases UK VAT registration is the proper mechanism to obtain a refund). Input tax will only be repaid if it would have been repaid to a similar trader registered for VAT in the UK.

From 1 January 2010, a claim must be made to HMRC via the website.

Details of the procedures are given in Notice 723A.

Anti-avoidance provisions – MTIC fraud

To prevent goods being sold VAT-free in the UK, a registration requirement applies to businesses that are not registered for VAT and are selling goods in the UK and, either:

- they are overseas businesses (with no business establishment in the UK); or
- they obtained the goods via a VAT-free transfer of a business as a going concern (or a chain of such transfers) from an overseas business.

The provisions were introduced in FA 2000 to counter a scheme known as Missing Trader Inter Community (MTIC) (aka carousel fraud) whereby overseas business claim back VAT brought in the UK and later sell them on in the UK VAT-free.

Law: *Value Added Tax Regulations* 1995 (SI 1995/2518), Pt. XX, XXI

Source: Notice 723A, *Refunds of VAT in the European Community for EC and non-EC businesses*

See *British VAT Reporter* ¶55-420.

8082 Repayment of input tax to UK traders by other Member States

There are equivalent provisions in other Member States to the UK provisions discussed at 8080, whereby UK traders can obtain input tax refunds from those states.

Source: Notice 723A

8084 Tax repayments to DIY builders

There are special rules enabling recovery of VAT on goods (but not on services) by persons building certain buildings (dwellings or buildings for relevant residential or charitable use), or on goods or services by persons converting certain non-residential buildings for residential use, otherwise than in the course of a business.

Law: VATA 1994, s. 35; *Value Added Tax Regulations* 1995 (SI 1995/2518), Part XXIII

See *British VAT Reporter* ¶37-000.

8090   Manner of claim for input tax deduction

As a general rule, deduction of input tax is claimed by including the tax on the periodic VAT return form for the period in which the claimed tax arises. In some cases of difficulty, and if authorised by HMRC, an estimated claim may be made and then rectified on a subsequent return. Input tax deduction cannot be claimed more than four years after the due date for submission of the return for the period in which the input tax arose.

In the case of pre-registration or pre-incorporation input tax, the tax should be included on the trader's first VAT return. For tax on supplies of services obtained after deregistration, the tax should be included on the final VAT return if possible, or otherwise claimed separately using VAT 427.

In no case may input tax be reclaimed unless the necessary evidence is held to support the refund. If the evidence is not to hand at the time when the relevant return has to be submitted, it should in strictness be notified separately to HMRC (either by letter or using VAT 652). In practice it will often be included as input tax on a later return, and HMRC has indicated that it will not normally see this as giving rise to a penalty. Such late input tax claims have been implicitly approved of in a number of tribunal decisions.

Law: *Value Added Tax Regulations* 1995 (SI 1995/2518), reg. 29(1A), (3)

Source: Form VAT 427, 652

INPUTS AND INPUT TAX RECOVERY – PARTIAL EXEMPTION

8110   Introduction – partial exemption

A trader that makes both taxable and exempt supplies must analyse its input tax, recovering only that which relates to the making of taxable supplies. Input tax related to making exempt supplies is, in principle, non-deductible.

While this is a simple enough idea, its practical implementation is a notoriously complex area.

Partial exemption is widespread. Most traders make exempt supplies at one time or another, and some such supplies can be substantial in relation to the size of the business. Typical exempt supplies which can give rise to partial exemption problems include sale of business

Value Added Tax

premises or land, sale and leaseback of business premises or land, sub-letting of business premises, and issues of shares.

Source: Notice 706, *Partial exemption*

Website: www.hmrc.gov.uk

See *British VAT Reporter* ¶19-400.

8116   Partial exemption legislation

The UK legislation on partial exemption is rooted in VATA 1994, s. 26, which establishes the basic principle that the input tax which is recoverable by a trader is that which relates to the making of taxable supplies. It also provides power for HMRC to make regulations setting out detailed rules to give effect to this principle. These detailed rules are contained in the *Value Added Tax Regulations* 1995 (SI 1995/2518), Pt. XIV and XV. The equivalent EC legislation is in the EC VAT Directive 2006/112, art. 167 onwards.

Law: VATA 1994, s. 26; *Value Added Tax Regulations* 1995 (SI 1995/2518), Pt. XIV, XV; EC VAT Directive 2006/112, art. 167; *DCM (Optical Holdings) Ltd v R & C Commrs* [2007] CSIH 58

Source: Notice 706, *Partial exemption*

Website: www.hmrc.gov.uk

See *British VAT Reporter* ¶19-420.

8122   Overview of the partial exemption rules

The general principle is that the input tax for which a trader may obtain credit is that which is attributable to the making of:

- taxable supplies; or
- supplies treated as made outside the UK which would be taxable if made inside the UK (this heading includes certain supplies made in warehouse) (these are referred to as 'foreign supplies'); or
- other supplies made outside the UK and certain exempt supplies designated by the Treasury (these are referred to as 'specified supplies').

Specified supplies for the third category above include certain insurance and financial transactions, and the making of arrangements therefor, supplied to persons outside the EC or in connection with the export of goods from the EC, if these supplies are exempt or would be if made in the UK.

Any other input tax is, in principle, non-deductible.

The regulations provide that this basic rule is to be implemented by analysing input tax according to the use to which the related supplies or importations are put. Tax on supplies used solely in making taxable supplies is deductible, while that on supplies used solely in making exempt supplies or for a separable business activity which does not involve the making of supplies is, in principle, non-deductible.

Some supplies obtained will inevitably not fall into one category or the other, being used in support of the business activities generally. The tax on such supplies is referred to colloquially as overhead input tax, or the 'pot', or as 'residual input tax'. This is input tax which cannot be directly attributed either to the making of taxable supplies or the making of exempt supplies. The relative use of supplies used in making both taxable and exempt supplies must be ascertained, and the pot must then be allocated between making taxable supplies and making exempt supplies in the proportion arrived at.

In principle, the input tax attributed to the making of taxable supplies, either directly or indirectly, is deductible while that attributed to making exempt supplies (referred to as exempt input tax) is non-deductible. However, if the exempt input tax falls below the de minimis limit, it too may be deducted.

Example

To summarise the points above, each trader is obliged to analyse input tax as far as possible according to the use to which the related supplies are put, then to reallocate the pot between taxable and exempt input tax as follows:

	Total input tax	Taxable input tax	Exempt input tax	The pot
Primary attribution	X	X	X	X
Secondary attribution of the pot, according to relative taxable and exempt use	–	X	X	(X)
Final attribution	X	X	X	X

If the exempt input tax so calculated is sufficiently small, the whole of the input tax for the period can be recovered. Otherwise, only the taxable input tax can be recovered and the exempt input tax is non-deductible.

This calculation must provisionally be done for each VAT return period, although from 1 April 2009, for each VAT quarter in a partial exemption year, for extra simplicity the trader may use the final figure from the previous year (see 8145). At the end of the trader's VAT year, the calculation must be reworked for the year as a whole to calculate the amount of input tax finally deductible. This is done to remove any seasonal distortion. Any under or overpayment arising from the calculations for the return periods is adjusted on the first return of the next period. However, from 1 April 2009, this annual adjustment may be done at the year-end, thus achieving certainty earlier (see 8145).

Law: VATA 1994, s. 26; *Value Added Tax (Input Tax) (Specified Supplies) Order* 1992 (SI 1992/3123)

Source: Notice 706, *Partial exemptions*

Website: www.hmrc.gov.uk

8126 Ignoring partial exemption: de minimis limit

If a trader incurs exempt input tax, that input tax is non-deductible in principle. However, if the exempt input tax falls below the de minimis limit, then the trader's input tax for the period concerned is treated as being wholly attributable to the making of taxable supplies, and therefore deductible.

The exempt input tax falls below the de minimis limit if it does not exceed:

- £625 per month (£7,500 p.a.); and
- 50 per cent of total input tax.

Exempt input tax for this purpose is the aggregate of:

- input tax directly attributed to exempt supplies; and
- the portion of the pot attributed to exempt supplies (*Value Added Tax Regulations* 1995 (SI 1995/2518), reg. 99(1)(a)).

Law: *Value Added Tax Regulations* 1995 (SI 1995/2518), reg. 99(1)(a), 106

Source: Notice 706, Partial exemption

See *British VAT Reporter* ¶19-430.

8127 Final attribution of input tax for a tax year or longer period

A trader is normally required to make a provisional attribution of input tax for each prescribed accounting period (or VAT return period) and then review this for a 'longer period'. A business which regularly incurs exempt input tax will almost always have a longer period which is the same as its VAT tax year.

The tax year is a period of 12 months ending on 31 March, 30 April or 31 May, depending upon the business's VAT accounting period. For a business making monthly returns, the tax year will normally end on 31 March.

A trader's first tax year is the first 'full' tax year (the part year from the date of registration to the normal tax year end being known as the 'registration period'). HMRC have power to approve or direct a different first tax year.

A different tax year is sometimes used in order to have a tax year which corresponds with the business's financial year. In the normal course of events, a trader's longer period is the same as the tax year. However, a different longer period may be used by mutual consent of the trader and HMRC.

There are special rules for businesses incurring exempt input tax for the first time, for new businesses, and for businesses ceasing to be registered for VAT.

A different longer period from those set out above can be used if this is approved by HMRC. However, they do not have the power to direct that a different longer period be used against the trader's will.

Law: *Value Added Tax Regulations* 1995 (SI 1995/2518), reg. 99(1)(d), (3)(a), (7), 107

Source: Notice 706, Partial exemption

See *British VAT Reporter* ¶19-520.

8128 Concept of attribution rules

On the face of it there is little conceptual difficulty in identifying supplies used only in making taxable supplies, or in making exempt supplies (although there may be considerable administrative difficulty). On closer examination, however, there are a number of areas which can give rise to difficulty, such as:

- the treatment of tax on supplies which, while not contributing directly to the making of supplies, are done in the course of the general business activity of making supplies rather than some separate and distinct non-supply activity – this is treated as part of the 'pot' of residual input tax;
- the treatment of tax on supplies obtained in connection with an exempt supply, where that exempt supply is itself undertaken in support of the general business activity rather than for its own sake.

Importance of intention

A point worth noting is that the attribution of input tax is based on intended future use of the inputs concerned and not simply on the status of the first supply made. It was held in these cases that where inputs were used in making an exempt supply, but there was an intention to make a subsequent taxable supply, the input tax must be apportioned. It was not to be attributed wholly to the first exempt supply.

Law: *C & E Commrs v Briararch Ltd; C & E Commrs v Curtis Henderson Ltd* [1992] BVC 118

See *British VAT Reporter* ¶19-405.

Value Added Tax

ATTRIBUTION OF THE PARTIAL EXEMPTION POT (OVERHEAD INPUT TAX)

8144 The standard partial exemption method

Once the primary attribution of input tax has been made, there will almost certainly remain input tax which has not been allocated specifically to the taxable input tax or exempt input tax categories, but is assigned to the pot as relating to both types of supply. It is then necessary to make a secondary analysis to allocate the pot between the making of taxable and exempt supplies.

The method by which this apportionment is normally carried out is 'the standard method' – is set out in the *Value Added Tax Regulations* 1995 (SI 1995/2518), reg. 101(2). The proportion of the pot attributed to taxable supplies, and hence regarded as deductible, is the proportion which taxable turnover bears to total turnover. This is calculated as a percentage, and may be rounded up to the next whole number if the overhead input tax does not exceed £400,000 per month on average. Otherwise it should be rounded up to two decimal places.

The sum of the input tax directly attributed to exempt supplies, and the exempt proportion of the pot, is referred to as 'exempt input tax'.

Exclusions from turnover under standard method

Certain potentially distortive amounts of turnover are to be excluded from the formula for the apportionment of the pot under the standard method. These are amounts resulting from:

* supplies of capital goods used for business purposes;
* non-taxable amounts relating to the supply of goods on which input tax deduction was blocked (e.g. sale of a business car);
* self-supplies;
* certain financial and property supplies which are incidental to the trader's business, such as land sales (if they are incidental to the trader's business rather than main business activities).

Following the important House of Lords decision in *C & E v Liverpool Institute for Performing Arts* [2001] BTC 5,258, certain supplies made outside the UK must also be excluded from the computation (see *Business Brief* 12/2001).

8145 The new 2009 changes to the standard method

The new partial exemption rules from 1 April 2009, need to considered.

For all accounting periods commencing on or after the 1 April 2009, the standard method is changed as follows:

(1) in-year provisional recovery rate;

(2)   early annual adjustment;

(3)   use-based option for newly partially exempt businesses;

(4)   widening the scope of the standard method.

The first three of these changes are optional. The fourth is mandatory.

In-year provisional recovery rate

Prior to 1 April 2009, all businesses using the standard method were required to make a provisional claim of input tax each quarter, based on sales, and then to do the annual adjustment after the end of each year to firm up the claim.

Businesses now have the option of using last year's recovery rate as a provisional basis for all quarters and then to adjust as normal after the year end. They are not obliged to do this. They can do each quarter as normal on the sales basis if they wish.

Early annual adjustment

The pre-April 2009 position is that all businesses using the standard method, were required to perform an annual adjustment under the *VAT Regulations* 1995, reg. 107, and to firm up on their provisional claims made in-year. This was done in the first VAT return after the year end.

The new rules allow businesses that wish to, to bring forward the annual adjustment and to do it in the last quarter of the year.

Use-based option for new partially exempt businesses

This measure allows newly partly exempt businesses to adopt a use-based recovery of input tax in their first year, to avoid unfair recovery.

Widening the scope of the standard method

Prior to 1 April 2009, the standard method only dealt with the recovery of input tax relating to supplies made in the UK. Businesses that made supplies outside the UK had to recover input tax on a use basis under the *VAT Regulations* 1995, reg. 103.

This new measure widens the scope of the standard method, so that it now deals with input tax on all supplies made by the business.

Such businesses will still need to perform the annual adjustment.

Standard method override

In order to ensure that taxpayers do not take advantage of the partial exemption rules, it is necessary to substitute a use-based attribution (i.e. based on the use of purchases) if this gives 'substantially' different results from the standard method. 'Substantially' means:

Value Added Tax

- more than £50,000; or
- more than 50 per cent of the residual input tax (but not less than £25,000).

The effect of this is that no over-ride calculation is necessary if residual input tax is less than £50,000 per year (although this is reduced to £25,000 for group undertakings other than VAT groups).

The need to carry out two calculations inevitably complicates matters for partially exempt businesses that fall above this threshold.

Law: *Value Added Tax Regulations* 1995 (SI 1995/2518), reg. 101(2), (3), (4), (5); 105(4), 106A, 107A to E;

Source: Notice 706, *Partial exemption*

Website: www.hmrc.gov.uk

See *British VAT Reporter* ¶19-400.

8146 Use of special partial exemption methods

HMRC may approve or direct the use of a partial exemption method other than the standard method. As a general rule, direct attribution will still be required where possible, and the variation of method will relate to the way in which the pot is apportioned. However, different methods may also be approved for the apportionment of the whole of the input tax.

If a non-standard method is required, written approval should always be obtained.

Law: *Value Added Tax Regulations* 1995 (SI 1995/2518), reg. 102(1)

Source: Notice 706, *Partial exemption*

Website: www.hmrc.gov.uk

See *British VAT Reporter* ¶19-480.

8148 Imposition of a partial exemption method

HMRC has the power to impose a partial exemption method. If HMRC seeks to use this power, the trader has a right of appeal to a VAT tribunal.

A method cannot be imposed retrospectively if the trader has been using a method which complies with the law.

Law: VATA 1994, s. 83(e); *Value Added Tax Regulations* 1995 (SI 1995/2518), reg. 102(2), (4)

Source: Notice 706, *Partial exemption*

Website: www.hmrc.gov.uk

See *British VAT Reporter* ¶19-405.

8150   Agreement of partial exemption method

The precise method used by a business to determine the extent to which input tax is recoverable is crucial, and so it is very important to make sure that entitlement to use a particular method is documented. If a special method is to be used, its terms must be considered carefully and documented.

Taxpayers who apply for a special method under reg. 102 will be required to make a formal declaration to the effect that, to the best of their knowledge and belief, the method requested is fair and reasonable. If it transpires that this was not the case, HMRC will be entitled to recoup any VAT that has been incorrectly claimed.

Law: *Value Added Tax Regulations* 1995 (SI 1995/2518), reg. 102(9)

Source: Notice 706, *Partial exemption*

Website: www.hmrc.gov.uk

See *British VAT Reporter* ¶19-495.

8154   The special method override

In parallel with the standard method, the legislation provides for a special method override, such that if the partial exemption method does not fairly and reasonably represent the extent to which goods and services are used in making taxable supplies, then HMRC can impose a notice on the taxpayer, such that he will be required to adjust the attribution and account for the difference.

Law: *Value Added Tax Regulations* 1995 (SI 1995/2158), reg 102(A) and 102(B)

Source: Notice 706, *Partial exemption*

See *British VAT Reporter* ¶19-430.

PARTIAL EXEMPTION: CHANGE OF USE

8158   Special partial exemption provisions for changes of use

There are special provisions to cover the position where input tax is attributed to an intended taxable supply but, in the event, the supply or importation on which the tax arose is actually used in respect of an exempt supply. There are similar provisions to deal with input tax attributed to an intended exempt supply if the supply, etc. is then used in respect of a taxable supply.

These rules are colloquially known as the claw-back and pay-back provisions.

Law: *Value Added Tax Regulations* 1995 (SI 1995/2518), reg. 108, 109

Source: Notice 706, *Partial exemption*

Website: www.hmrc.gov.uk

See *British VAT Reporter* ¶19-550.

PARTIAL EXEMPTION: NON-SUPPLY ACTIVITIES AND SELF-SUPPLIES

8174   Partial exemption: non-supply activities

It is possible to incur input tax in respect of activities that are outside the scope of VAT. How are these dealt with for partial exemption purposes? Examples include: sales of assets that are sold as a going concern and the issue (as opposed to the supply) of shares.

In a leading EC judgment, it was held that these inputs can be attributed to the pot, if they cannot be put elsewhere (the *Kretztechnic* case). Where they are directly linked to taxable supplies then they will be attributed there (*Abbey National* case).

Law: *Kretztechnic* and *Abbey National* cases

Source: Notice 706, *Partial exemption*

Website: www.hmrc.gov.uk

See *British VAT Reporter* ¶19-600.

8176 Self-supplies

It should be borne in mind that input tax arising on self-supplies must be brought into the partial exemption calculations (although the self-supplies themselves are excluded from turnover under the standard method: see 8144).

Input tax on a self-supply cannot be attributed to the self-supply itself.

Law: *Value Added Tax Regulations* 1995 (SI 1995/2518), reg. 104

See *British VAT Reporter* ¶19-670.

CAPITAL GOODS SCHEME

8182 Nature of the capital goods scheme

The original purpose of the capital goods scheme was to prevent partially exempt traders from making full recovery of input tax on major acquisitions of computers and buildings by putting them wholly to taxable use in the period of acquisition, then switching them to exempt use. Although such planning would now be caught by more recently implemented partial exemption rules, the scheme has remained in place.

The scheme allows an initial deduction (or disallowance) to be made in the ordinary way on acquisition, but to review this in later periods and make adjustments to the initial deduction in the light of subsequent taxable use.

The details of the scheme are set out in the *Value Added Tax Regulations* 1995 (SI 1995/2518), reg. 112–116, and the views of HMRC are set out in Public Notice 706/2.

Adjustments under the capital goods scheme may give rise to the need for adjustments to the accounts, and to capital allowances computations.

Although the capital goods scheme affects partially exempt traders, this does not mean that fully taxable businesses can ignore it. A person who is fully taxable when the input tax arises but becomes partially exempt during the adjustment period must also apply the scheme. A particular danger is that a fully taxable trader may buy a new building, and then sell it within the adjustment period by way of exempt supply. The remaining intervals will be attributed to exempt use, with significant loss of input tax.

Law: *Value Added Tax Regulations* 1995 (SI 1995/2518), reg. 112–116

Source: Public Notice 706/2, *Capital goods scheme*

Value Added Tax

Website: www.hmrc.gov.uk

See *British VAT Reporter* ¶19-800.

8184   Input tax affected by capital goods scheme

The capital goods scheme applies to input tax arising on the supply or importation of:

- computer equipment costing £50,000 or more. The £50,000 limit is applied to each item of equipment separately. A system consisting of a number of items each costing less than £50,000 is not affected, even though the total system cost may exceed £50,000;
- land, buildings, parts of buildings, and certain extensions or alterations, costing £250,000 or more. The scheme potentially applies to both freehold and leasehold acquisitions, and to self-supplies. The extensions and alterations affected are those which increase the floor area of the building by ten per cent or more; and
- civil engineering works costing more than £250,000 and to building refurbishments or fitting out with a capital cost over £250,000 (regardless of any change in floor area).

Law: *Value Added Tax Regulations* 1995 (SI 1995/2518), reg. 113(a), (b–f), (g), (h)

Source: Public Notice 706/2, *Capital goods scheme*

Website: www.hmrc.gov.uk

See *British VAT Reporter* ¶19-810.

8186   Capital goods scheme: period and manner of adjustment

For the purposes of the capital goods scheme (see 8182), the adjustment period is five years (strictly periods) for computer equipment (and for leases with less than ten years to run), and ten years for other property.

The initial deduction is made in the ordinary way, but must then be reviewed in each of the remaining years (four for computer equipment or an interest in land having less than ten years to run when acquired, nine for other land) of the adjustment period.

In each year (strictly period) the taxable use to which the item is put is calculated (using the current year partial exemption recovery percentage) and compared to the original year 1 recovery. If the taxable use has gone up in the year in question, then a bit more input tax may be claimed. If the taxable use has gone down, then a bit of input tax must be repaid.

This adjustment is made on the second VAT return after the end of the period to which it relates (*Value Added Tax Regulations* 1995 (SI 1995/2518), reg. 115(6)).

> ### Example
>
> Kelly Ltd acquires a new building for £1m plus £175,000 VAT. In the year of acquisition its partial exemption method enables it to recover 60% of the VAT on the building. In the next year the recovery percentage increases to 70% and in the following year it drops to 55%.
>
> In the first year Kelly Ltd recovers £105,000 of the VAT on the building.
>
> In the next year it must review the position. The taxable use of the asset has gone up by 10%, so there is an adjustment in respect of $^1/_{10}$ of the total input tax (£17,500). The current amount recoverable is £12,250, compared with £10,500 originally recovered, so an extra £1,750 can be reclaimed.
>
> In the following year the amount recoverable falls to £9,625, so Kelly Ltd must repay £875 of the £10,500 originally recovered.

Law: *Value Added Tax Regulations* 1995 (SI 1995/2518), reg. 114(3), 115(1), (2), (6)

Source: Public Notice 706/2, *Capital goods scheme*

Website: www.hmrc.gov.uk

See *British VAT Reporter* ¶19-830.

8188   Disposals within the adjustment period

If an asset to which the capital goods scheme applies is disposed of within the adjustment period (see 8186), use for the remaining complete intervals of the adjustment period is deemed to be taxable or exempt according to the status of the supply made on disposal of the asset. Computer equipment will always be taxable, so the taxable use for the remaining complete years will be 100%. This may result in repayments of input tax. Land may either be taxable or exempt, depending on circumstances, so a sale within the adjustment period could either be exempt (which could well result in input tax being repaid to HMRC) or taxable which could result in further input tax reclaims. The appropriate adjustment is made at the same time as the adjustment for the period of disposal.

Capping – basic rule

There is special provision that any additional input tax recoverable on disposal must not exceed the output tax due on the disposal (*Value Added Tax Regulations* 1995 (SI 1995/2518), reg. 115(3) proviso). This is intended to prevent recovery where, for instance, a computer system which has fallen rapidly in value is sold for a nominal sum. Without such a provision the owner might be able to recover the whole of the input tax for the remainder of the adjustment period, even if the bulk of the value of the asset had been exhausted in making, say, exempt supplies.

Value Added Tax

Capping – special disposal rule

These capping provisions are more stringent where the taxpayer seeks to obtain a tax advantage. The total recovery of input tax over the period of ownership must be compared with the output tax on disposal and (save as the Commissioners otherwise allow) an adjustment must be made to ensure that the *total* recovery does not exceed the output tax. Applied strictly this would result in a restriction on input tax recovery, even in the case of a fully taxable business, in all cases where the asset had diminished in value between purchase and disposal (very likely in the case of computer equipment).

However, HMRC has said that it will not normally require this special disposal rule to be applied in the following circumstances:

(a)   sales of computer equipment;
(b)   where an owner disposes of an asset at a loss due to market conditions (such as a general downturn in property prices);
(c)   where the value of the asset has depreciated;
(d)   where the value of the asset is reduced for other legitimate reasons (such as accepting a lower price to effect a quick sale);
(e)   where the amount of output tax on disposal is less than the input tax claimed only due to a reduction in the VAT rate;
(f)   where the asset is used only for taxable purposes throughout the adjustment period (including the final disposal).

They also say that, where capping does apply, they will not necessarily require it to be fully applied, but only to the extent needed to cancel any 'unjustified tax advantage'.

If an asset is supplied as part of a transfer of a going concern, the new owner takes over the obligation to make adjustments under the capital goods scheme (*Value Added Tax Regulations* 1995 (SI 1995/2518), reg. 114(7)).

If an asset is lost, stolen, or destroyed (or a short lease expires) no further adjustments are made (*Value Added Tax Regulations* 1995 (SI 1995/2518), reg. 115(4)).

Law: *Value Added Tax Regulations* 1995 (SI 1995/2518), reg. 114(7), 115(3), (4)

Source: Business Brief 30/97, 19 December 1997; Public Notice 706/2, *Capital goods scheme*

Website: www.hmrc.gov.uk

See *British VAT Reporter* ¶19-884.

RATES OF VAT

8210   Standard rate and other rates of VAT

The legislation does not provide a list of standard rated supplies. Instead, it works by exception. The legislation lists zero-rated supplies (in Schedule 8, VATA 1994), reduced rate supplies (in Schedule 7A, VATA 1994) and exempt supplies (in Schedule 9, VATA 1994). Thus, any supplies not within these schedules but within the scope of VAT MUST be standard rated (an example is goodwill).

The standard rate

The standard rate is currently 17.5% but is due to go up to 20% on 4 January 2011.

The reduced rate

In the UK there is also a reduced or lower rate of five per cent which applies to VAT on certain supplies and may be seen in VATA 1994, Sch. 7A.

It should be borne in mind that the Chancellor uses the 5 per cent rate for socially desirable matters – it is not open to him to use the 0 per cent rate as the Member States have agreed that no more zero-rates will be applied. The reduced rate includes:

- domestic and charity fuel and power supplies;
- installation of central heating systems and home security goods provided under grants to pensioners and grant-funded heating measures for the less well off;
- women's sanitary products;
- supply of children's car seats;
- cost of renovating dwellings that have been empty for at least two years (three years prior to 1 January 2008);
- cost of converting a residential property into a different number of dwellings (e.g. converting a house into flats);
- cost of converting a non-residential property into one or more dwellings, and converting a dwelling into a care home (or for other qualifying relevant residential use), or into a house for multiple occupation (e.g. bed-sit accommodation);
- converting a non-residential property into a care home (or other 'relevant residential' purpose);
- converting a non-residential property into a multiple occupancy dwelling, such as bed-sit accommodation;
- converting a building used for a 'relevant residential' purpose into a multiple occupancy dwelling;
- renovating or altering a care home that has not been lived in for three years or more;
- renovating or altering a multiple occupancy dwelling that has not been lived in for three years or more;
- constructing, renovating or converting a building into a garage as part of the renovation of a property that qualifies for the reduced rate;
- the installation of factory-insulated hot water tanks, micro-combined heat and power

Value Added Tax

systems, and heating systems that use renewable energy, to the extent that the costs of installation are funded by government grants and equivalent local authority schemes;

- the installation of ground source heat pumps;
- air-source heat pumps and micro-combined heat and power units;
- contraceptive products, including 'morning after' contraception (contraceptives which currently qualify for zero-rating are not affected by this provision); and
- mobility aids for the elderly and smoking cessation products. In the case of smoking cessation products, the reduced rate initially applied only for a limited period from 1 July 2007 to 30 June 2008, but this has subsequently been extended.

The zero rate

The other main rate of VAT in the UK is the zero rate. Supplies which are zero-rated attract VAT at the rate of zero per cent. The distinction between zero-rated supplies and exempt supplies is that the makers of zero-rated supplies can (indeed, must) register for VAT if they exceed the VAT registration limit and can recover tax on their expenses. As with exempt supplies, the legislation provides a list of supplies qualifying for zero-rating and there is also a general zero-rating which applies to exports of goods from the EC and to certain deliveries of goods to other EC Member States (see 8216ff.).

It is possible for a supply to fall within the list of exempt supplies, and also within the list of zero-rated supplies. In this case the zero-rating takes priority, so the supply is treated as zero-rated.

Law: VATA 1994, s. 30(1), 31, Sch. 7A

See *British VAT Reporter* ¶3-130.

ZERO-RATED SUPPLIES

8216 Meaning of zero-rating

If a supply falls into a zero-rated category, then it is treated as a taxable supply, but the VAT due is calculated at a rate of 0%. Thus, the supplier does not have to account for any effective VAT on the supply. However, since it is a taxable supply, the supplier can register for VAT (indeed must, if taxable turnover exceeds the registration limits) and so can recover input tax incurred on supplies obtained for the business.

The effect of this is that zero-rated supplies reach the consumer free of VAT, except to the extent that the supplier's costs include items on which the deduction of input tax is specifically blocked. This is in contrast with exempt supplies, where there is always a hidden VAT cost, being the irrecoverable VAT element of underlying costs.

Law: VATA 1994, s. 30, Sch. 8

See *British VAT Reporter* ¶20-000.

8220   Zero-rating of exports and dispatches

There is a general zero-rating whereby, if a person supplies goods by way of export from the EC (or by delivery to a taxable person elsewhere in the EC who makes an acquisition of the goods), that supply is zero-rated. However, the form of words used in granting the zero-rating is such that it is not sufficient merely to export the goods in order to qualify for zero-rating. The zero-rating only applies if HMRC 'is satisfied' that the supplier has exported the goods.

Supplies of goods can also be zero-rated if the goods are shipped for use as stores on a ship or aircraft with a non-UK destination, provided that certain conditions are fulfilled.

It should be noted that the zero-rating for exports applies only to supplies of goods. There is no general zero-rating for 'exports' of services, although some international supplies of services are relieved from UK VAT by being treated as made outside the UK (see 7816ff.). A supply of services consisting of work on another person's goods to produce goods which are then delivered outside the UK is zero-rated if a supply of the goods themselves would be zero-rated.

Law: VATA 1994, s. 30(2A), (8), Gp 7, Sch 8

Evidence of export

HMRC is generally only prepared to be satisfied that the goods have been exported if the supplier retains evidence of this in a form specified by them. Evidence which might be sufficient to satisfy a court that the goods have been exported is insufficient to ensure zero-rating, if it does not take the form specified by HMRC.

The type of evidence required by HMRC varies according to the manner in which the goods are exported. Details of the necessary proof of export are set out in Notice 703.

A common feature of the various proofs of export required is that they are generally obtainable only at the time when the export takes place. For instance, if the export is a postal export of goods requiring a customs declaration, the evidence required is a certificate of posting. The Post Office is scarcely likely to issue such a certificate at some later date.

Any trader who exports goods will therefore be well advised to make a careful study of Notice 703, as it relates to the particular form of export, and ensure that arrangements are in hand to ensure that proper evidence of export is obtained, and retained. Evidence of export must be obtained within three months of the date of the supply to justify the zero-rating.

Value Added Tax

For dispatches to other EC countries, zero-rating is only available if the customer is a taxable person. This must be evidenced by stating the customer's VAT registration number on the tax invoice.

- the exporter keeps a separate record of the transaction including evidence (such as the order) that the supply is made to an overseas trader;
- the goods are exported within three months of the time of supply;
- valid proof of export (see above) is obtained within three months of the export; and
- the goods are not used in the UK between leaving the exporter's premises and exportation taking place.

Law: VATA 1994, s. 30(2A), (8), (10)

Source: Notice 703, *Exports and the removal of goods from the UK*

See *British VAT Reporter* ¶20-125.

8222   Zero-rating groups in VATA 1994, Sch. 8

There is a statutory list of items to be zero-rated (see 8218); it consists of a series of 'groups' each of which contains a number of 'items' specifying supplies which are to be zero-rated. The groups are structured so as to contain items which are linked in some general way. For instance, the group headed 'Books, etc.' provides zero-rating for supplies of books and also for supplies of newspapers: essentially, the zero-ratings for supplies of published material are contained in this group.

Although each zero-rating group has a heading, these headings are of no legal force. The headings are there merely to assist in identifying which groups may provide zero-rating for a particular supply. In order to determine whether a zero-rating does, in fact, exist it is necessary to study the items within the groups, to see whether the supply fits precisely into one or other of the descriptions.

Furthermore, there are notes to each group which amplify or modify the meanings of the zero-ratings contained in the items, and these must be studied as well to see whether zero-rating is available.

The zero-rating groups, and a brief description of the supplies zero-rated by them, are set out below.

Group 1 – food (Notice 701/14)

Group 1 zero-rates many supplies of food for human consumption, animal food, seeds for food plants, and live animals used for food purposes. Certain supplies are excluded, particularly supplies in the course of catering (including supplies of hot take-away food) and confectionery.

Group 2 – sewerage services and water (Notice 701/16)

Group 2 zero-rates supplies relating to the bulk treatment of sewage, emptying cess pools, etc. and most supplies of water for non-industrial purposes.

Group 3 – books, etc. (Notice 701/10)

Most books, booklets, leaflets, pamphlets, newspapers and periodicals, printed music, maps, etc. are zero-rated, as are ancillary objects such as covers included in the price. The zero-rating does not extend to stationery.

Group 4 – talking books for the blind and handicapped and wireless sets for the blind (Notice 701/1)

Group 4 zero-rating covers supplies (including hire) of certain goods to the Royal National Institute for the Blind, the National Listening Library and similar charities. It also covers supplies (including hire) to any charity of certain equipment which is to be lent, free of charge, to blind persons.

Group 5 – construction of buildings, etc. (Notice 708)

Group 5 zero-rating relates only to dwellings and certain buildings for communal residential use, non-business use by charities, or use by a charity as a village hall or similarly in providing social and recreational facilities.

Zero-rating is provided for:

- supplies in the course of constructing the building;
- the sale of the freehold or long lease of the building by the person constructing it (or, in some instances, the person who created it by converting a non-residential building); and
- the sale of renovated houses that have been empty for ten years or more.

In addition, services in the course of construction of a civil engineering work necessary for the development of a permanent park for residential caravans are zero-rated. However, the sale of such a caravan park does not qualify for zero-rating.

Mains electrical wiring and lighting systems are part of the fabric of the building when determining whether the work qualifies for zero-rating. In the course of a new development, HMRC accepts that soft landscaping qualifies for zero-rating. Following the decision in *Rialto Homes plc* [2000] BVC 2,161 HMRC now accepts that soft landscaping can extend to planting other than turf, the zero-rating applying to both the labour element and the cost of the plants.

A number of conditions must be met to secure zero-rating.

Group 6 – protected buildings (Notice 708)

A further zero-rating is available for certain protected buildings, if they are qualifying buildings (see above), relieving from tax some alteration works. As with the construction zero-rating, there is one relief for supplies for such buildings by their owners, and a separate one for the supplies made to their owners by contractors. The buildings to which the reliefs apply are qualifying buildings which are also:

- buildings which are listed buildings under the *Planning (Listed Buildings and Conservation Areas) Act* 1990, or its Scottish or Northern Irish equivalents; or
- scheduled monuments within the meaning in the *Ancient Monuments and Archaeological Areas Act* 1979 or the *Historic Monuments (Northern Ireland) Act* 1971.

HMRC *Business Brief* 11/05 provides a definition of garages within Group 6.

Group 7 – international services (Notice 741A)

Most supplies of services across national boundaries are dealt with under the 'International services' heading.

There are however two zero-ratings for work carried out on goods for export from the EC, and for the making of arrangements for such a supply, for an export of goods from the EC, or for a supply of services made outside the EC.

Group 8 – transport (Notice 744A, B and C)

Group 8 provides zero-rating for supplies of ships and aircraft, for the public transport of passengers, for the international transport of goods and passengers, and for international freight handling and storage facilities.

The zero-ratings fall into five main categories:

(1)   supplies of ships and of aircraft, including repair, maintenance, hire, etc.;

(2)   supplies of lifeboats and certain ancillary equipment to charities;

(3)   supplies of passenger transport and public transport services;

(4)   supplies of freight transport and related supplies; and

(5)   certain supplies by tour operators outside the EC.

Zero-rating applies to passenger transport in vehicles, ships and aircraft which are designed or adapted to carry not less than ten passengers (including the driver).

Also, zero-rating applies to passenger transport in vehicles which are designed or constructed to carry more than ten passengers, but which carry less than ten passengers solely because they are equipped with facilities for persons in wheelchairs.

Group 9 – caravans and houseboats (Notice 701/20)

Group 9 provides zero-rating, broadly, for supplies of caravans and houseboats likely to be used as private residences, putting these on the same basis for VAT as private houses.

Group 10 – gold (Notice 701/21)

Group 10 is of little general interest, and zero-rates supplies of gold held in the UK between Central Banks and members of the London Gold Market.

Group 11 – bank notes

Group 11 is of interest mainly to the Bank of England and the Scottish banks, and zero-rates the issue of bank notes by banks.

Group 12 – drugs, medicines, aids for the handicapped, etc. (Notice 701/7)

The zero-ratings provided by Group 12 are tightly defined, and highly specialised.

The group zero-rates a number of supplies of goods and services for use by people who are handicapped. The supply must be made to the handicapped person or to a charity which makes it available to the handicapped person.

The supplies which can qualify for zero-rating are tightly defined, but include items such as specialised equipment, modifications to buildings, adapted vehicles etc.

Details are set out in Notice 701/7, which should be studied in detail by anyone making (or receiving) supplies which might be covered.

It should be noted that, to the extent that zero-rating is given for supplies of goods designed or adapted for use by handicapped persons, the tribunals have tended to take a narrow view and deny zero-rating where items have been of particular use to handicapped persons but also of use to the population generally (see, for instance, *Portland College* [1993] BVC 827).

The group also zero-rates the supply of drugs and medicines on prescription.

Group 13 – imports, exports, etc.

Group 13 provides certain peripheral zero-ratings in relation to international trade.

Group 14 – tax-free shops

Now repealed.

Group 15 – charities, etc. (Notice 701/1)

Group 15 zero-rates a number of supplies to or by charities and related bodies. However, it should be noted that it does not provide any general zero-rating for matters relating to charities. In the main, charities are subject to exactly the same VAT rules as other entities.

Value Added Tax

The zero-ratings cover some supplies by charities and some supplies to charities. In all cases there are a number of conditions to be met.

The zero rate is available for the sale of donated goods that are offered to sale only to disabled people or people receiving means-tested benefits. From the same date, the zero rate is extended to all supplies of charity advertising in all media.

Group 16 – clothing and footwear (Leaflet 701/23)

Group 16 zero-rates supplies of children's clothing, of protective boots and helmets for industrial use, and of pedal cycle helmets and motor cycle helmets.

Law: VATA 1994, s. 96(9), (10); Sch. 8; *Procter & Gamble (UK) Ltd v R & C Commrs*[2008] EWHC 1558 (Ch); *Rialto Homes plc* [2000] BVC 2,161; *Portland College* [1993] BVC 827; *C & E Commrs v Link Housing Association Ltd* [1992] BVC 113

Website: www.hmrc.gov.uk

See *British VAT Reporter* ¶20-200ff.

EXEMPT SUPPLIES

8228   Nature of VAT exempt supplies

The exemption schedule (Sch. 9) operates on similar lines to the zero-rating schedule (see 8222). If a supply falls within one of the categories listed in the groups (but not in their headings, which are merely to help in identification of potential exemptions), then the supply is exempted.

If a supply falls within an exemption category and also within a zero-rating category, then it is treated as zero-rated rather than exempt, since a supply falling within a zero-rated category is treated as zero-rated whether or not tax would otherwise be chargeable on it.

If a supply is exempt from VAT, no VAT is chargeable on it. However, the supplier is not entitled to deduct input tax incurred in connection with an exempt supply (subject to the partial exemption rules – see 8110ff.), so this input tax forms part of the costs of the business.

A person whose only supplies are exempt is not entitled to register for VAT.

Law: VATA 1994, s. 26, 30(1), Sch. 9

See *British VAT Reporter* ¶26-990.

8230   Sch. 9 – the exemptions

The groups contained in the statutory list of exempt supplies (see 8228) and a brief description of the supplies exempted by them, are set out below.

Group 1 – land (Notice 742, Notice 742A)

Group 1 exemption covers the grant or assignment of:

- any interest in land;
- any right over land; or
- any licence to occupy land.

As a matter of principle, a right to call for or be granted such an interest, right or licence is itself an interest in land, and so capable of falling within the exemption. However, in Scotland such a personal right is not considered to be a right over land, and the legislation therefore makes specific provision bringing such a right within the exemption.

Some supplies falling within these categories, such as holiday lettings, supplies of sporting rights, etc. are excluded from the exemption.

It is possible to opt to tax. The effect of this is to make taxable those supplies which would otherwise be exempt. The election is irrevocable (except for a statutory 6-month cooling off period and with the consent of HMRC, after 20 years have passed) so, once made, all future supplies of the land concerned by the elector are standard-rated. The operation and scope of the election to waive exemption are complex. From 1 August 2009 it will be possible to revoke the first options to tax made on the introduction of the 'option to tax' legislation.

Supplies in respect of land also extend to:

- surrenders;
- reverse surrenders;
- premiums;
- reverse premiums;
- assignments;
- reverse assignments.

Group 2 – insurance (Notice 701/36)

The Group 2 exemption covers the provision of insurance or reinsurance. This is generally, but not always by recognised insurance companies, it can also include provision such as credit card protection and funeral plans. It also includes the provision of various intermediary services.

Most intermediary services provided by insurance brokers or insurance agents are covered, but not market research, promotional activities, etc., valuation or inspection services, or supplies of loss adjusters, etc. (except where handling a claim with full written authority to conclude it).

Value Added Tax

Group 3 – postal services

Group 3 exemption covers supplies of the conveyance of postal packets by the Post Office, and the supply by the Post Office of services in connection with the conveyance of postal packets (other than the hire of goods).

Group 4 – betting, gaming and lotteries (Notices 701/13, 701/26, 701/27, 701/28)

Group 4 exemption applies to supplies of:

- the provision of facilities for placing bets;
- the provision of facilities for playing games of chance;
- the granting of a right to take part in a lottery.

However, excluded from the exemption are admission charges and gaming machines (fruit machines).

The VAT aspects of gambling are inextricably bound up with excise duty and it is not possible to understand the full picture without both.

Group 5 – finance (Notice 701/49)

Group 5 provides exemption for a wide range of financial transactions, including loans, dealings in money, the sale of stocks and shares (but not the issue of shares – which is outside the scope of VAT), management of special investment funds, etc.

The exemption applies to supplies made in the UK. As a general rule the place of supply will be outside the UK if there is a non-EC customer or an EC customer receiving the supply in a business capacity (see 7824). Where the customer is based outside the EC, related input tax will be recoverable for a supply which would be exempt under this head if made in the UK (*Value Added Tax (Input Tax) (Specified Supplies) Order* 1999 (SI 1999/3121); see 8060).

Group 6 – education (Notice 701/30)

Group 6 provides exemption, in broad terms, for the provision of education or vocational training by private schools (but not state schools), universities, and other 'eligible bodies'. Supplies of research by an eligible body to another eligible body are exempted. Supplies of examination services are exempt if the supply is either by or to an eligible body, and also if supplied to a person receiving exempt education or training.

All persons teaching English as a foreign language are regarded as being eligible bodies in respect of these supplies, but this does not necessarily mean that they are eligible bodies in respect of other supplies of education.

Group 6 also exempts certain ancillary supplies, and also the provision of facilities by youth clubs to their members.

Group 7 – health and welfare (Notice 701/57)

Group 7 provides exemption for a number of supplies connected with the provision of health and welfare services, and related goods. The views of HMRC on its application are set out in Notice 701/57. It covers supplies by doctors and other qualified health workers, the provision of care in hospitals and other approved institutions, and various related services. See also HMRC *Brief* 06/07: *Changes to medical services exemption from 1 May 2007.*

Group 8 – burial and cremation (Notice 701/32)

Group 8 exempts supplies of the disposal of the remains of the human dead, and the making of arrangements for and in connection with such disposal.

Group 9 – trade unions and professional bodies

Exemption is provided for supplies made in return for subscriptions by:

- trade unions;
- professional associations;
- learned societies and the like;
- certain trade associations;
- bodies which are made up of the exempt bodies above and which have the same objectives.

In each case, the body seeking exemption must be non-profit making.

The exemption also covers supplies received for payment of membership subscriptions to non-profit making organisations with aims of a political, religious, patriotic, philosophical, philanthropic or civic nature.

Group 10 – sport, sports competitions and physical education (Notice 701/45)

Group 10 exemption applies to the right to enter a sporting competition where all entry fees are returned as prizes, and also the right to enter a sporting competition promoted by a non-profit making body established for the purposes of sport or physical recreation. However, the latter exemption does not apply if the competition involves the free use of facilities for the use of which the body normally makes a charge.

Exemption also applies to supplies of sporting and physical education services to individuals by non-profit making bodies (such as many sports clubs). If the non-profit making body operates a membership scheme exemption only applies to supplies made to members.

At the time of writing, changes are awaited setting out detailed conditions for the recognition of a body as being non-profit making.

Value Added Tax

Group 11 – works of art, etc. (Notice 701/12)

Group 11 applies to the disposal of certain works of art, etc. exempted from capital taxes when disposed of by private treaty sale, or by way of acceptance in lieu of tax, under the douceur arrangements.

Group 12 – fund-raising events by charities and other qualifying bodies (Notice 701/1)

Group 12 exempts the supply of goods or services in connection with a one-off fund-raising event (such as a fete, performance, etc.) by:

- a charity, if the event is organised for charitable purposes by one or more charities; or
- a trade union or professional body within Grp. 9 above, or certain bodies with objects of a 'public' nature (VATA 1994, s. 94(3)), if the event is organised solely for the benefit of the body concerned.

In the case of a charity, relief is also available for supplies by a wholly owned subsidiary which covenants the whole of its profits to the charity.

Group 13 – Cultural services (Notice 701/47)

Group 13 provides exemption for supplies by public bodies and eligible bodies of admission to museums, galleries, art exhibitions and zoos, and theatrical, musical, etc. performances of a cultural nature.

Public bodies are local authorities, government departments, and other bodies listed as such by the Office of Public Service. Eligible bodies are non-profit making bodies managed on a voluntary basis by persons with no financial interest in their activities.

The exemption for supplies by public bodies only applies where it is not likely to cause distortions of competition with taxable persons.

Group 14 – Supplies of goods where input tax cannot be recovered

Group 14 provides exemption for goods where input tax cannot be recovered. The exemption prevents the double taxation on the supply of goods where no tax is deductible on the purchase, acquisition, importation or production of the goods because they are used for making exempt transactions or because the tax is blocked by a specific exclusion.

An example would be the sale of an input tax blocked car.

Law: VATA 1994, Sch. 9

Website: www.hmrc.gov.uk

See *British VAT Reporter* ¶27-000ff.

REGISTRATION AND DE-REGISTRATION

8250 Importance of registration

Businesses making UK supplies

Persons carrying on businesses of making taxable supplies in the UK (often referred to as traders) are generally obliged to register with HMRC However, not everyone who makes taxable supplies by way of business is forced to register. If the volume of taxable supplies is below certain registration limits, set out at 8256, then the trader is not obliged to register for VAT.

A trader who wishes to register, but is not obliged to register, can voluntarily apply for registration. If HMRC (or, on appeal, a VAT tribunal) is satisfied that the trader is carrying on a business and either makes taxable supplies already or intends to do so in the future, then the trader is entitled to registration. Similarly, registration can also be obtained by a person with a UK business establishment who makes (or intends to make) supplies overseas which would be taxable if made in the UK.

Intra-EC acquisitions of goods and distance selling

There are special rules requiring registration of UK businesses and other organisations making acquisitions of goods from elsewhere in the EC, and of EC businesses making distance sales of goods to UK customers who are not taxable persons (see 8280, 8294).

Disposals of assets for which a VAT repayment is claimed

To prevent avoidance of VAT by overseas businesses, overseas businesses will need to register for VAT in the UK where they are not currently registered, but are making supplies in the UK and, either:

- they are overseas businesses with no business establishment in the UK; or
- they obtained goods via a VAT-free transfer of a business as a going concern (or a chain of such transfers) from an overseas business.

Law: VATA 1994, Sch. 1, 2, 3, 3A

Source: Notice 700/1, *Should I be registered for VAT?*

Website: www.hmrc.gov.uk

See *British VAT Reporter* ¶5-050.

Value Added Tax

REGISTRATION – UK SUPPLIES

8256   Taxable turnover limits

The rules for determining whether a trader's business is sufficiently large to make registration mandatory are based upon the trader's taxable turnover. This refers to the amount of the trader's taxable supplies (including zero-rated supplies) in a given period (£70,000 from 1 April 2010). Consequently, it is not a measure of the size of the trader's business in terms of the net income which can be derived from it, but a measure of the value of supplies which are made to others.

Turnover for VAT includes all taxable supplies made in the course of a business, except that supplies of goods which are capital assets of the business may be ignored in determining whether the turnover limits have been reached. However, capital supplies of land which are taxable at the standard rate may not be ignored (VATA 1994, Sch. 1, para. 1(8)).

These turnover limits are based on the actual value of taxable supplies made, whether standard-rated or zero-rated. It is not permissible to reduce the turnover for any notional figure of VAT included in it. In allocating supplies to particular periods the ordinary VAT time of supply rules apply. However, a person who is not registered for VAT cannot issue an invoice which meets the technical definition of a tax invoice, so the date of invoicing does not affect the time of supply. In general, a supply is treated as made at the earlier of the date when the supply is actually made and the date when the payment is received for it.

When certain services, listed in VATA 1994, s. 8 (see 7824), are acquired from overseas by a person carrying on a business in the UK, they are treated as supplies made both by and to the importer (VATA 1994, s. 8). Thus they add to the importer's taxable turnover. These supplies count when checking whether the registration limits have been exceeded.

The rules for determining whether a person is liable to register for VAT in respect of UK supplies made are covered in VATA 1994, Sch. 1. Broadly speaking, a person is liable to register for VAT if he makes taxable supplies and his taxable turnover has exceeded the historic turnover limit, or there are reasonable grounds for believing that it will exceed the future turnover limit.

Annual turnover limit: historic

The historic turnover limit must be considered at the end of each calendar month, and is based on taxable turnover for the 12 months then ending. If the trader's turnover for the 12 months has exceeded the annual turnover limit , then registration is generally required; however, the trader need not be registered if he can satisfy HMRC that his turnover for the forthcoming 12 months will not exceed the de-registration annual turnover limit (see 8274). There are tables of registration and de-registration limits at 102 and 104 respectively.

Where a trader has become liable to register for VAT because of the historic turnover limit, he must notify HMRC of this within 30 days from the end of the calendar month for which the relevant turnover limit was exceeded. HMRC will then register him with effect from the end of the month following that in which the turnover limit was exceeded. However, registration can take effect from an earlier date if HMRC and the trader jointly agree to this (VATA 1994, Sch. 1, para. 5).

Example

On 30 June, John calculates that his taxable supplies for the previous 12 months have exceeded the registration threshold. John is liable to be registered for VAT from 30 June and must notify HMRC by 31 July. During July, John makes sales of £15,000. HMRC will register John from 1 August, unless an earlier date is agreed. John is not required to charge VAT on his supplies in July.

Turnover limit: future

The future turnover limit applies where there are reasonable grounds for supposing that the trader's taxable turnover within the next 30 days will exceed the annual turnover limit. There is a table of limits at 102.

A person who becomes liable to register for VAT because of anticipated turnover for a future period of 30 days, must notify HMRC of this by, at latest, the end of the 30-day period. HMRC will then register him from the start of the 30 days or, if agreed by HMRC and by the trader, from some earlier date.

In practice this may often mean that almost immediate notification is necessary. It is likely that a very small period of grace will be allowed before penalties are imposed for late registration, but this should not be reckoned as being any more than is necessary to allow for ordinary postal delay (i.e. one or two days). If notification is made by post, this should be followed up by telephone to ensure that the notification has arrived. Ideally the form should be sent by recorded delivery and HMRC should be told of its dispatch by telephone.

Example

On 12 May, James expects his taxable supplies in the next 30 days to exceed the current registration threshold. He is therefore liable to register for VAT from 12 May and must notify HMRC by 12 June. The effective date of registration will be 12 May.

Law: VATA 1994, s. 8, 7, Sch. 1, para. 1, 5, 6, Sch. 5

Source: Notice 700/1, *Should I be registered for VAT?*

Website: www.hmrc.gov.uk

See *British VAT Reporter* ¶43-025.

Value Added Tax

8258 Registration procedure

When a person becomes liable to register for VAT, he must notify HMRC. In doing this he is obliged to use the VAT registration form VAT 1. This may be downloaded from the HMRC website or completed online by himself or his agent. In addition, if the trader is a partnership, VAT 2 must be completed. This gives details of all of the partners.

Law: *Value Added Tax Regulations* 1995 (SI 1995/2518), reg. 5(1)

Source: Form VAT 2; Notice 700/1, *Should I be registered for VAT?*

Website: www.hmrc.gov.uk

See *British VAT Reporter* ¶43-000.

8260 Voluntary registration: supplies

A trader who already makes taxable supplies, but is not obliged to register for VAT by reason of either the historic or future turnover limits, can still seek registration if he wishes to do so. Provided that the trader can satisfy HMRC that taxable supplies are being made in the course of business, they are obliged to make the registration.

The application for registration by a trader seeking voluntary registration should be made on VAT 1, as for a trader who is obliged to register (see 8258).

Example

Nicky intends to open a corporate flower supply business. She estimates that her turnover in the first year will be £50,000, which is below the VAT registration threshold. However, she will suffer input tax on her direct costs and expenses. She intends to charge her customers an additional £5,000 to compensate for the VAT she will have to incur.

If Nicky registers for VAT, she will charge output tax of £8,750 (£50,000 × 17.5 per cent). If her customers are VAT registered, they will be able to reclaim this VAT, so the overall cost to the customers is £50,000. This enables Nicky to be more competitive than if she went ahead and charged the £55,000 she planned.

Nicky can also recover all her input tax, so she will be no worse off because of the VAT registration.

Source: Form VAT 1; Notice 700/1, *Should I be registered for VAT?*

Website: www.hmrc.gov.uk

See *British VAT Reporter* ¶43-000.

8262   Intending trader registration

A person who does not yet make taxable supplies, but intends to do so, can also apply to be registered for VAT. Such a person will typically have started business already but still be at the stage of developing products or markets, so that taxable supplies have yet to be made.

If HMRC (or a VAT tribunal) is satisfied that taxable supplies are intended to be made, they must allow such a registration. If the business fails before taxable supplies are made, the intending trader remains entitled to retain input tax recovered in anticipation of making taxable supplies.

Law: *Merseyside Cablevision Ltd* (1987) 3 BVC 596; *Rompelman v Minister van Financiën* (Case 268/83) (1985) 2 BVC 200,157

Source: Notice 700/1, *Should I be registered for VAT?*

Website: www.hmrc.gov.uk

See *British VAT Reporter* ¶43-000.

8264   Exemption from registration

A trader who makes mostly zero-rated supplies can, if he wishes, apply to be exempted from registration even though his taxable turnover exceeds the registration limits. This allows a trader who would only be reclaiming tax from HMRC, not paying tax into it, to escape from the administrative requirements of VAT registration. The cost to him is the input tax which he would otherwise be able to reclaim.

Law: VATA 1994, Sch. 1, para. 14(1)

Source: Notice 700/1, *Should I be registered for VAT?*

Website: www.hmrc.gov.uk

See *British VAT Reporter* ¶43-000.

8266   Registration by reference to overseas supplies

A trader established in the UK can be registered for VAT without making any UK taxable supplies. This applies if the trader:

- makes supplies outside of the UK which would be taxable if made within the UK; or
- makes supplies in a bonded warehouse which would otherwise be taxable (since these supplies are deemed to take place outside the UK, and so fall within the category above).

Such a trader can apply to HMRC to be registered for VAT (but is not obliged to register).

A business will also need to register if it is not already registered for UK VAT and they are selling goods in the UK and either:

* it is an overseas business with no business establishment in the UK; or
* it obtained the goods via a VAT-free transfer of a business as a going concern (or a chain of such transfers) from such an overseas business.

The purpose of this requirement is to prevent the avoidance schemes whereby overseas businesses claim back VAT on assets bought in the UK and later sell them in the UK VAT-free.

Law: VATA 1994, Sch. 1, para. 10, Sch. 3A

See *British VAT Reporter* ¶43-045.

8268 Registration by reference to previous owner's turnover

There is a special rule for determining taxable turnover for the purposes of the registration limits where a business has been taken over as a going concern. In determining whether the new owner is liable to be registered for VAT, he is deemed to have made the taxable supplies of that business before the transfer as well as after it. Thus, he has to count the previous owner's turnover as well as his own in checking whether he has reached the turnover limits.

This rule applies only if the person who previously carried on the business was himself a taxable person.

Law: VATA 1994, s. 49(1)(a)

Source: Notice 700/1, *Should I be registered for VAT?*

Website: www.hmrc.gov.uk

See *British VAT Reporter* ¶43-000.

8270 Effective date of late registration

A person who becomes liable to register for VAT may not realise this until some time later (in some cases, years later). Where this happens, the liability to be registered will still have existed from the proper time. Furthermore, the trader will (unknowingly) have been a taxable person throughout, since a taxable person is defined as one who makes taxable supplies and either is or is required to be registered.

In order to reflect this position, the registration of such a person will be made with retrospective effect to the proper registration date. He will be required to account for any output tax which has become due from that effective registration date. By the same token, he can reclaim input tax arising from then, provided that he holds the necessary evidence for reclaim.

Apart from the tax itself, a person registering late may be liable to a penalty for late registration. It should also be noted that there is no relief from the tax liability merely because customers would have been able to reclaim any tax charged to them.

Law: VATA 1994, s. 3(1); s. 67, Reg 25(1)(b), VAT Regulations

Source: Notice 700/1, *Should I be registered for VAT?*

Website: www.hmrc.gov.uk

See *British VAT Reporter* ¶43-149.

8272   HMRC may require security

Although it is not strictly a registration matter, it is worth noting that HMRC has the power to require security from a taxable person. Making taxable supplies without providing the security required under this provision is a criminal offence punishable by a fine at level 5 on the standard scale contained in the *Criminal Justice Act* 1982.

Law: VATA 1994, s. 72(11), Sch. 11, para. 4(2)

See *British VAT Reporter* ¶3-750.

8274   De-registration: supplies

A person who ceases to make taxable supplies is no longer a taxable person, and must notify HMRC that supplies are no longer being made within 30 days.

A trader who carries on making taxable supplies can also apply to be de-registered on the basis of reduced turnover. If HMRC is satisfied that turnover for the next 12 months will be below the de-registration limit (see 104), the trader ceases to be liable to be registered and so can be removed from the register. However, this does not apply if the reason for the drop in turnover is that the trader is about to cease trading, or intends to suspend the making of supplies for a period of 30 days or more.

A deemed supply of goods on hand arises on de-registration (see 7762). There are special arrangements permitting a refund of input tax on services (but not goods) arising after de-registration (8074).

Law: VATA 1994, Sch. 1, para. 3, 4(2), 11, 12

Value Added Tax

Source: Notice 700/11

See *British VAT Reporter* ¶510.

REGISTRATION – ACQUISITIONS OF GOODS FROM OTHER EC COUNTRIES

8280   EC acquisitions and registration

There is a possible liability to register by an organisation which acquires goods from EC suppliers not registered for VAT in the UK. The effect of registration is to bring these acquisitions into the UK VAT net, instead of that of the other EC countries concerned, and prevents substantial 'VAT rate shopping' between Member States.

This provision applies not only to (exempt) businesses, but also to clubs, associations, bodies corporate and unincorporated associations acquiring goods for non-business activities.

This provision does not apply to businesses that are otherwise registered for VAT in the UK; they will account for VAT on acquisitions in the normal way (see 7972).

If the value (net of VAT) of intra-EC acquisitions by a person since 1 January of a calendar year exceeds the acquisitions limit (see 8284) that person becomes liable to register for VAT.

The effects of registration are:

- the overseas supplier can zero-rate its supplies, quoting the organisation's (new) UK VAT registration number on its invoice; and
- the UK organisation becomes liable to account for UK VAT on its acquisitions from elsewhere in the EC.

Source: Notice 700/1

Website: www.hmrc.gov.uk

See *British VAT Reporter* ¶45-100.

8282   Persons affected by acquisitions registration requirement

Obviously, businesses which are already registered for VAT, or already liable to be registered in respect of supplies made, can ignore the provisions requiring registration by reference to the level of EC acquisitions (see 8280). They are already obliged to account for VAT on acquisitions of goods from elsewhere in the EC.

The liability to register in respect of acquisitions is therefore of importance to persons not already registered, or liable to be registered, for UK VAT. The liability to register arises under VATA 1994, s. 10 and Sch. 3, and applies to:

- any person carrying on a business; and
- a body corporate, club, association, organisation or unincorporated body carrying on a non-business activity.

Where such a person acquires goods from a taxable person in another Member State, and the place of acquisition is the UK, the transaction counts for acquisition tax purposes.

Law: VATA 1994, s. 10, Sch. 3

Source: Notice 700/1

Website: www.hmrc.gov.uk

See *British VAT Reporter* ¶45-100.

8284   Acquisitions limit for VAT registration

A person may be affected by VAT registration rules dependent upon the level of acquisitions from elsewhere in the EC (see 8282). The level of such acquisitions is generally changed by statutory instrument and might require him to be registered if:

- at the end of any month, the value of acquisitions from the previous 1 January to the month end exceeds the annual turnover limit (see 102); or
- at any time, there are reasonable grounds for believing that the value of acquisitions in the following 30 days will exceed the annual turnover limit (see 102).

The value of acquisitions for this purpose is reckoned exclusive of any overseas VAT charged. Acquisitions of new means of transport, and of excise goods, are ignored as there are alternative provisions rendering these liable to UK VAT (see 7990).

A person who becomes liable to register because of past acquisitions has 30 days from the end of the month in which the limit was exceeded in which to notify HMRC, and the Commissioners must register him from the end of the month following that in which the limit was exceeded (or a mutually agreed earlier date).

A person who becomes liable to register because of anticipated acquisitions must notify HMRC of this before the end of the 30-day period concerned, and they must register him from the beginning of that period (or a mutually agreed earlier date).

Where a taxable person becomes liable to register in respect of zero-rated acquisitions, he may apply for exemption from registration.

Value Added Tax

Law: VATA 1994, Sch. 3, para. 8

Source: Notice 700/1

Website: www.hmrc.gov.uk

See *British VAT Reporter* ¶45-100.

8286   Voluntary registration: acquisitions

It is also possible to register voluntarily in respect of EC acquisitions (see 8280), or intended acquisitions, regardless of the amounts involved. This may be advantageous either because the rates of VAT are higher in the supplier countries, or as a matter of administrative convenience where it is expected that the registration thresholds will in any case be exceeded before long.

HMRC may impose conditions on such a voluntary registration.

Law: VATA 1994, Sch. 3, para. 4

Source: Notice 700/1, *Should I be registered for VAT?*

Website: www.hmrc.gov.uk

8288   EC acquisitions: ceasing registration

As a general rule, a person who voluntarily becomes registered in respect of acquisitions (see 8280) must remain registered for at least two years. Where a registration is cancelled it will normally be from 1 January on, or following, the effective registration date.

However, if the person was never, in fact, registrable, or was in breach of a condition for voluntary registration, deregistration may take place from some earlier date.

Law: VATA 1994, Sch. 3, para. 7(3)

Source: Notice 700/1

Website: www.hmrc.gov.uk

See *British VAT Reporter* ¶45-100.

REGISTRATION – DISTANCE SELLING TO THE UK

8294 Distance selling and required registration generally

A trader established elsewhere in the EC can become liable to register for VAT in the UK in respect of sales of goods to UK customers who are not registered for VAT (see 7818). The place where such supplies are deemed to be made is then the UK, and the overseas supplier must account for VAT accordingly.

The distance selling registration provisions apply to a person who makes 'relevant supplies', being supplies of goods which involve the removal of the goods to the UK from another Member State, and their acquisition in the UK by a person who is not a taxable person.

Law: VATA 1994, Sch. 2, para. 10

Source: Notice 700/1

Website: www.hmrc.gov.uk

See *British VAT Reporter* ¶63-240.

8296 Distance selling registration limit

A person who makes relevant supplies (see 8294) of excise goods – goods liable to a duty of excise, such as tobacco products, alcoholic beverage, petrol, etc. – becomes liable to register as soon as such supplies are made; there is no turnover limit. A person who is not otherwise liable to register for VAT becomes liable to register on a day when the total value of his other relevant supplies to the UK since the previous 1 January exceed the distance selling threshold. There is a table of limits at 102.

The value of relevant supplies for this purpose is reckoned exclusive of any overseas VAT charged.

Notification must be made to HMRC within 30 days from the time when the liability to register arose, and they must register him with effect from the day when the liability arose (or from a mutually agreed earlier date).

The same notification and registration rules apply as for registration when the turnover limit is exceeded.

Law: VATA 1994, Sch. 2, para. 1(1), (3), 3

Source: Notice 700/1

Website: www.hmrc.gov.uk

See *British VAT Reporter* ¶63-240.

8298 Voluntary registration: distance selling

A person belonging in another Member State who has elected to treat his UK distance sales (see 8294) as taking place outside that state becomes liable to register in the UK when he makes such a supply.

The same notification and registration rules apply as for the other categories of distance selling registration (see 8296).

A person intending to make an election to treat his UK distance sales as made outside his own Member State, or who has made such an election, and intending to make distance sales to the UK, may request registration as a distance seller, and HMRC may impose conditions on such a registration (VATA 1994, Sch. 2, para. 4). However, if the person also qualifies for voluntary registration as a UK intending trader or as a person making supplies outside the UK and having a business establishment in the UK, he will be registered under those rules rather than the distance selling rules.

A person who has registered on the basis of an intended election, or intended distance sales to the UK, must notify HMRC within 30 days of the intended election or sales taking place.

Law: VATA 1994, Sch. 2, para. 1(2), 4(3), 5(2)

Source: Notice 700/1

Website: www.hmrc.gov.uk

8300 Distance selling: ceasing registration

A person registered under the distance selling rules (see 8294) ceases to be registrable if a position arises where he is neither obliged, nor able, to register under any of the UK VAT provisions, taking each separately. He must notify HMRC of this within 30 days of ceasing to be registrable (VATA 1994, Sch. 2, para. 5(1)).

A person who ceases to be liable to be registered may have his registration cancelled, provided he is not liable to be registered under other provisions (VATA 1994, Sch. 2, para. 6(1), 7(1)). Also, HMRC may cancel the registration of a person who has registered voluntarily, and who has failed to make the intended election or supplies, or has breached any conditions imposed (VATA 1994, Sch. 2, para. 6, 7).

Law: VATA 1994, Sch. 2, para. 5(1), 5(4), 6, 7

Source: Notice 700/1

Website: www.hmrc.gov.uk

See *British VAT Reporter* ¶43-030.

8306 Registration of UK suppliers in other Member States

A UK trader making distance sales to other Member States, but not compulsorily registered there, can make elections similar to those mentioned in 8298; distance sales to the other Member States concerned are then treated as made in those Member States and not in the UK.

Such an election must be notified to HMRC within 30 days before the date on which the first supply under it is to be made, and the trader must within 30 days of making that first supply provide documentary evidence of having notified the other Member State of the election. If the election is subsequently withdrawn, the trader must notify HMRC of this within 30 days before the first supply intended following such withdrawal. However, the withdrawal cannot take effect before 1 January which is, or follows, the second anniversary of making the first supply under the election.

A trader voluntarily electing to treat distance sales to another Member State as being made in that state is, therefore, bound by that election for a period of two to three years.

Law: VATA 1994, s. 7(5); *Value Added Tax Regulations* 1995 (SI 1995/2518), reg. 98

Source: Notice 700/1

Website: www.hmrc.gov.uk

See *British VAT Reporter* ¶43-030.

OTHER MATTERS RELATING TO REGISTRATION

8312 Tax representatives

A person who is liable to be registered for VAT in the UK, but who has no UK business establishment, may be required by HMRC to appoint a UK VAT representative. Such a VAT representative is responsible for his principal's compliance with UK VAT requirements, and is jointly and severally liable for any tax and penalties due.

A person who fails to appoint a VAT representative when so directed may be required to provide such security as HMRC thinks fit.

However, a non-established person in a Member State of the EC or in countries that have a suitable mutual assistance arrangement with HMRC cannot be forced to appoint a UK VAT representative.

Law: VATA 1994, s. 48

See *British VAT Reporter* ¶63000.

8314 Changes in circumstances

A person who is registered for VAT is obliged to notify HMRC of such changes as changes of name, constitution or ownership of the business, and any other changes which may necessitate the variation of the register or cancellation of the registration. Notification must be made within 30 days after the change.

Law: *Value Added Tax Regulations* 1995 (SI 1995/2518), reg. 5(2)

8316 Scope of registration and person registered

When a person is registered for VAT the registration covers all of that person's business activities and, in the case of a partnership, covers activities of other partnerships having the same partners. This is because it is the partners themselves who are registered for VAT rather than the partnership as such.

Although a change in partners does not trigger a new registration, merely an amendment to the register, a change from a partnership to a sole trader, or vice versa, does involve a new registration and all of the formalities of deregistration and notification of liability to register must be observed.

Joint owners of property, even though not in partnership, can be registered jointly on similar lines to a partnership.

In the case of a group of companies for which group treatment has been obtained, the registration of the representative member of the group covers the activities of all of the companies within the group. In effect the companies are treated as if they were a single taxable person. There are complex provisions covering the formation, variation and dissolution of VAT groups, and preventing their use for tax avoidance purposes.

Under the current rules, two or more bodies corporate are eligible to be treated as members of a VAT group if each is established or has a fixed establishment in the UK and they are under common 'control'. The present definition of control is taken from UK company law and is wide in scope. The group registration rules were amended from 1 August 2004 in order to counter VAT avoidance. The existing eligibility rules for VAT grouping were retained but two additional tests now apply where:

(1)   a jointly owned company, or a wholly owned subsidiary run by a third party, makes or intends to make positive-rated supplies to a member of the VAT group which it wants to join (other than supplies which are incidental or ancillary to its business activities); and

(2)   the VAT group would be unable to recover VAT on such supplies in full.

Limited partnerships will be subjected to these additional tests too. These partnerships can join a VAT group because for VAT purposes they are identified with the general partner of the partnership.

The two additional tests in these limited circumstances will be based on economic benefits and on consolidation in group accounts. The first test will not allow grouping where the majority of the economic benefits from the entity in question go to a third party. The second test will be that under generally accepted accounting practice, the entity's accounts are consolidated in the group accounts for the person controlling the VAT group (or would be so consolidated if that person prepared group accounts). Both of these tests will have to be satisfied.

Example

P Ltd makes taxable supplies to the New Group, which cannot recover all the VAT charged by P Ltd. P Ltd is jointly owned by O Ltd and Q Ltd, a third party. Q Ltd has the right to more than 50 per cent of the dividends from P Ltd. P Ltd is not consolidated into the group accounts.

P Ltd is not eligible to join the New Group's VAT registration.

In the case of a company organised in divisions, it is possible to arrange for each division to be entered in the register so that separate returns can be submitted but there is still, in principle, a single registration covering all of the divisions.

Example

A garage has the following departments:

- Car sales;
- Servicing; and
- Petrol sales.

Each department has its own accounting records, and the supplies are taxable.

The garage would satisfy the requirements for divisional registration.

A club, association, etc. is registered in its own name. Responsibility for meeting VAT obligations rests with its president, chairman, treasurer, etc. or, if none, its committee or, if none, with every member.

Value Added Tax

Law: VATA 1994, s. 43–46(1), Sch. 9A; *Value Added Tax Regulations* 1995 (SI 1995/2518), reg. 8

See *British VAT Reporter* ¶43-000.

8318 Splitting a business to avoid registration – anti-avoidance

There is a special provision to counter attempts to avoid registration by splitting a business activity among several legal entities, each with turnover below the VAT registration threshold. This entitles HMRC to make a direction treating the persons named in it as being one person for VAT purposes, and so liable to be registered with effect from the date of direction. Further persons can, if necessary, be added to the direction and such additions to an existing direction can have retrospective effect.

HMRC is entitled to make a direction under this provision if they are satisfied that:

- each person named therein makes taxable supplies; and
- the activities in the course of which the supplies are made form part of a business described in the direction, the remaining activities of that business being carried on by the other persons named in the direction; and
- when the whole of the activities of the business are considered together the person carrying it on is liable to be registered for VAT.

Example

Terry and June run a bar and restaurant. Terry runs the bar, whilst June serves all the meals in the restaurant. They maintain separate records of their takings, which are as follows:

Bar £62,000
Restaurant £14,000
Total £76,000

Terry and June share a business bank account. No rent is paid to either party for use of equipment or premises.

HMRC are likely to consider this situation to be an artificial separation of activities.

Law: VATA 1994, Sch. 1, para. 1A, 2

Website: www.hmrc.gov.uk

See *British VAT Reporter* ¶43-710.

8320 Transfer of registration number

Where a business is transferred as a going concern (TOGC) and the transferor ceases to be registered for VAT, it is possible for the registration number to be transferred to the transferee by mutual consent of the parties. In such a case the transferee takes over any VAT liabilities of the transferor. It is generally considered to be good practice to drop the old VAT registration number on a TOGC.

Law: *Value Added Tax Regulations* 1995 (SI 1995/2518), reg. 6

See *British VAT Reporter* ¶43-775.

8322 Supplies contracted before registration

It should be noted that, once registered, a trader is liable to account for VAT on all supplies whose tax point arises on or after the effective date of the registration. This has been thought to mean that liability can arise in respect of supplies contracted for (and even performed) before registration. It is therefore important, if registration is a possibility, to ensure that contracts and terms of trading provide for the addition of VAT if applicable. However, in the case of *BJ Rice & Associates v C & E Commrs* [1996] BVC 211 the Court of Appeal held that VAT was not due on a supply made before registration and having a payment tax point after registration.

Law: *BJ Rice & Associates v C & E Commrs* [1996] BVC 211; *Madisons* (1987) 3 BVC 638

Source: Notice 700/41, *Late registration penalty*

See *British VAT Reporter* ¶43-150.

8324 Penalties for late registration

A person who is late in notifying liability to register can incur a civil penalty of up to 15 per cent of the net VAT liability from the date when he should have been registered to the date when HMRC become aware of the need for registration (see 8480ff.).

Law: VATA 1994, s. 67(4)

See *British VAT Reporter* ¶43-000.

SPECIAL VAT SCHEMES

AGENTS AND VAT

8350   Areas of difficulty for agents

Two areas of difficulty arise in respect of agents, or persons describing themselves as such. The first is that of determining whether there is in fact an agent/principal relationship. If there is, the further difficulty arises in applying the special rules for agents.

A person who is an agent is one empowered to act on behalf of his principal in some matter. The concept does not extend, say, to a motor distributor who describes himself as an agent for a manufacturer, but in fact buys and sells as principal. The importance of the legal arrangements between the parties, and of recording these, is emphasised by the case of *C & E Commrs v Music and Video Exchange Ltd* [1992] BVC 30.

The basic rule is that the supplies arranged by an agent for his principal are supplies to or by the principal, and do not affect the agent's VAT position in any way. The agent is making a separate supply of agency services to the principal, for a fee or commission, and this will normally be taxable at the standard rate (although it may sometimes be exempt or zero-rated or outside the scope of UK VAT if it is made across national boundaries – see 7824).

Source: *C & E Commrs v Music and Video Exchange Ltd* [1992] BVC 30

8352   Agent acting in own name

In some cases an agent may appear to act in his own name, so that the parties with whom he deals are not aware that they are really dealing with the principal. Supplies of goods through such an agency arrangement are treated as supplied both to and by the agent. HMRC has the power to extend this treatment to supplies of services through an agent acting in his own name. This enables a selling agent to issue tax invoices to third parties, and receive equivalent tax invoices from the principal, so that the agent takes part in the underlying supply chain. Similarly, a buying agent can obtain tax invoices from the third parties, reclaiming the VAT as input tax, while passing on similar invoices (and accounting for output tax).

Such an agent must still account for VAT in the ordinary way on his agency fee or commission.

Law: VATA 1994, s. 47(2A), (3)

See *British VAT Reporter* ¶54-100.

8354 Agent for non-resident importer

If goods are imported into the UK from outside the EC (or acquired from another Member State) by a taxable person, and supplied by him as agent for a person who is not a taxable person, he is treated as having imported (or acquired) the goods, and supplied them, as principal. Consequently, he is liable to account for any tax due on the supply, and can also recover the VAT on the importation (or acquisition).

In applying this provision, if the principal is non-resident and has his principal place of business outside the UK, he can be treated as not being a taxable person in respect of the transaction (even though he is really a taxable person) if he is not registrable by reference to some other activity.

Law: VATA 1994, s. 47(1), (2)

See *British VAT Reporter* ¶54-050.

8360 Bad debt relief

A special relief is available to a supplier who is not on cash accounting and who makes a taxable supply (and so becomes liable to pay the tax on it) but does not receive payment from his customer. Relief is available when:

- at least six months have elapsed from the due date for payment of the supply (or the date of supply itself, if later);
- the supplier has formally written the debt off for VAT purposes; and
- the supplier holds the necessary records.

When these conditions are met, the supplier can recover from HMRC the VAT originally accounted for on the supply, by including an equivalent amount in the input tax box of the VAT return. If payments are subsequently received in respect of the debt, the VAT element must be repaid to HMRC.

The claim must be made within three years and six months of the due date for payment of the supply (or the actual date of supply if later).

VAT: refunds for bad debts account

A claimant under these provisions is required to maintain a record, known as the 'refunds for bad debts account' containing details of supplies in respect of which bad debt relief is claimed. There is no requirement that this forms part of the claimant's ordinary accounting system, so it can be maintained as a separate schedule in the VAT working papers.

The information to be recorded in respect of each claim made is:

(1) for each taxable supply on which the claim is based:

(a) the amount of tax chargeable;

Value Added Tax

(b) the period in which the tax was accounted for and paid to HMRC;

(c) the date and number of the related tax invoice, or other information showing the time, nature and purchaser of the supply;

(d) any payment received for the supply;

(2) the outstanding amount to which the claim relates;

(3) the amount of the claim; and

(4) the period in which the claim is made.

All relevant records must be preserved for a period of four years from the date of the claim (*Value Added Tax Regulations* 1995 (SI 1995/2518), reg. 169).

Effect of claim on customer

If the customer does not pay the invoice, then he must automatically repay input tax to HMRC where payment has not been made within six months of the supply (or the date on which payment is due, if this is later). This is done by adjusting the input tax claim for the period in which the end of the six months falls.

Amount of relief

The amount of bad debt relief available is generally the VAT fraction of the outstanding debt. In the case of supplies under the second-hand goods scheme or the tour operators margin scheme, the relief due is the VAT fraction of the margin for the supply or the VAT fraction of the outstanding debt, whichever is less.

Law: VATA 1994, s. 26A, 36; *Value Added Tax Regulations* 1999 (SI 1999/3029); *Value Added Tax Regulations* 1995 (SI 1995/2518), reg 165 onwards

See *British VAT Reporter* ¶18-900.

8365   Flat-rate scheme for small businesses

Some small businesses may be eligible for the flat-rate scheme (FRS), which can confer administrative and cash-flow savings on the taxpayer.

Conditions for FRS authorisation

The conditions for a person being eligible to be authorised to use the FRS include:

(1) there are reasonable grounds for believing that the VAT-exclusive annual taxable (being zero and positive-rated) turnover will not exceed £150,000. A supply is disregarded if it is a capital asset of the business or a reverse charge on a supply from abroad.

Future turnover may reasonably be forecast from past results and projections which supported applications for loans. The calculation of future turnover should be in writing and retained in case HMRC query the matter using hindsight;

(2)   the person is not a tour operator;

(3)   the person is not required to adjust input tax under the capital goods scheme;

(4)   the person does not intend to use a margin scheme;

(5)   in the previous year, the person has not operated the FRS and has a satisfactory compliance record; and

(6)   in the previous 24 months, the person has not been part of a group, or 'associated' with another person unless HMRC are satisfied that authorisation poses no risk to the revenue. The FRS is to help those who run a stand-alone business, i.e. the business is not part of a larger undertaking.

Repayment traders

Persons who usually receive VAT repayments from HMRC cannot use the FRS because the FRS calculates VAT due to HMRC and is unsuitable for regular repayment traders.

Calculation of VAT due to HMRC

FRS users avoid accounting internally for VAT on all their purchases and sales. They calculate the VAT due to HMRC by applying the appropriate flat-rate percentage for their trade category to the VAT-inclusive turnover, including all reduced-rated, zero-rated and exempt supplies. These trade categories are available on the HMRC website and cover the change of rate from 17.5% to 20% in January 2011 (see Budget 2010 – BN45).

Persons using the FRS can choose:

(1)   whether to account for VAT on a quarterly basis; and

(2)   whether to combine the FRS with the annual accounting scheme.

The record of turnover is based on:

(1)   cash receipts (i.e. similarly to the cash accounting scheme);

(2)   daily gross takings (i.e. similar to a retail scheme); or

(3)   invoices issued.

Users of the FRS:

(1)   still issue VAT invoices where the customer is VAT-registered, showing VAT at the normal rate for the supply (i.e. not at a flat rate). Such customers treat these as normal VAT invoices and so they are unaffected by whether they deal with an FRS user; and

(2)   still retain all sales and purchase invoices for six years.

Input tax and FRS users

Generally, no claim for input tax or for VAT on imports or acquisitions is due because the flat-rate percentage takes account of normal background input tax. However, subject to the usual conditions, an FRS user can claim input tax outside the FRS in respect of:

(1)   capital expenditure on goods with a value exceeding £2,000 including VAT; and

(2)   goods-on-hand at registration.

However, where capital purchases are dealt with outside the FRS, output tax on their disposal (or deemed disposal for assets held at de-registration) is also dealt with outside the FRS.

An FRS user is treated as fully taxable and need not consider partial exemption calculations: the flat-rate calculation takes irrecoverable VAT into account.

Record keeping

The FRS should simplify VAT accounting, because there is no need to identify VAT and value separately in the sales and purchase records. However, FRS users must keep a record of the flat-rate calculation showing:

(1)   the flat-rate turnover for the period;

(2)   the flat-rate percentage used; and

(3)   the VAT calculated as due.

Leaving the FRS

Generally, a person ceases to be authorised to use the FRS if:

(1)   at any anniversary of his start date, his income in the one year then ending totals more than £225,000, unless HMRC is satisfied that the total value of his taxable supplies in the one year then beginning will not exceed £150,000;

(2)   there are reasonable grounds to believe that the total value of his income in the 30 days then beginning will exceed £225,000;

(3)   he becomes a tour operator;

(4)   he intends to acquire, construct or otherwise obtain a capital item which requires an adjustment under the capital goods scheme;

(5)   he opts to use a margin scheme;

(6)   he becomes part of a group, or becomes associated with another person;

(7)   he notifies HMRC in writing that he wishes voluntarily to withdraw from the FRS. A person cannot rejoin the FRS for at least one year, so persons cannot decide whether to use the FRS on a return-by-return basis; or

(8)   HMRC terminates his authorisation to protect the revenue or because a false statement was made in relation to the application for authorisation.

Law: VATA 1994, s. 26B; *Value Added Tax Regulations* 1995 (SI 1995/2518), reg. 55A onwards

Source: Notice 733, *Flat rate scheme for small businesses*

See *British VAT Reporter* ¶55-350.

8366 Farmers' flat-rate scheme

A flat-rate scheme is available for farmers. This is based on the provisions of the EC VAT Directive 2006/211.

A farmer who chooses to use the scheme ceases to be registered for VAT in respect of his farming activities, and so ceases to be able to recover input tax. However, he is able to charge a 'flat-rate addition' (FRA) at a special rate of four per cent on supplies to taxable persons (and not to unregistered persons). These customers can recover the FRA as input tax, but the flat-rate scheme farmer is allowed to retain the money instead of paying it over to HMRC.

Law: VATA 1994, s. 54; *VAT (Flat-rate Scheme for Farmers) (Designated Activities) Order* 1992 (SI 1992/3220); *VAT (Flat-rate Scheme for Farmers) (Percentage Addition) Order* 1992 (SI 1992/3221); *Value Added Tax Regulations* 1995 (SI 1995/2518), reg. 202–211; EC VAT Directive 2006/211, art. 295 et seq.

Source: Notice 700/46, *Agricultural flat-rate scheme*

Website: www.hmrc.gov.uk

See *British VAT Reporter* ¶53-500.

8374 Monthly payments on account by large traders

There are provisions under which certain businesses have to make monthly payments on account of their VAT liability during a prescribed accounting period, any underpayment or overpayment being settled when the return for the period is submitted.

Broadly speaking, this requirement affects businesses whose net VAT payments exceed £2m p.a. A first payment on account is required by the end of the month following the first month of a period, a second one a month later, the balance being cleared by submission of the return at the end of the month following the period end. The amount of each interim payment on account is one twenty-fourth of the estimated annual liability.

There is provision for escaping this requirement where, in a subsequent 12-month period, the net VAT liability falls below £1.6m.

Law: VATA 1994, s. 28; *Value Added Tax (Payments on Account) Order* 1993 (SI 1993/2001)

Value Added Tax

Source: Notice 700/60, *Payments on account*

Website: www.hmrc.gov.uk

See *British VAT Reporter* ¶55-410.

8380 Local authorities, government departments and similar entities

Local authorities are liable to be registered in respect of taxable business activities, whatever their level of turnover. Business activities of local authorities are taxed in the ordinary way, and input tax blocked in respect of exempt business activities.

As far as non-business activities of local authorities, and certain similar entities, are concerned no output tax is chargeable, but the local authority, etc. is entitled to reclaim input tax (VATA 1994, s. 33(1)).

The bodies to which this relief applies include such entities as local authorities, water authorities, port health authorities, police authorities, the BBC, etc. and any body specified in a suitable Treasury order. Local authorities include the council of a city, district, London borough, parish or group of parishes, etc.

Government departments are treated slightly differently. They too will be bound by the normal VAT rules and may have to charge VAT on their non-statutory activities (their statutory activities are outside the scope of VAT). VAT charged to them may be recoverable under a special Treasury scheme under s. 41, VATA 1994.

Certain museums and galleries, which do not charge members of the public for admission, can claim a refund of input tax.

The input tax must be in respect of those supplies made to an applicable body that are attributable to the provision by that body of free rights of admission to a relevant museum or gallery. The Treasury may, by order, list applicable bodies and relevant museums and galleries for this purpose. Furthermore, HMRC will apportion the input tax where the bought-in supplies are attributable to both free admissions and other supplies.

Law: VATA 1994, s. 33(1), (3), 41, 42

See *British VAT Reporter* ¶51-000.

8386 Retail schemes

In principle, VAT is due on each supply made, and should be computed separately for each supply. In order to save retailers from having to keep a detailed record of each sale made, retail schemes are available to them. Under these a record is kept of daily gross takings (which includes credit sales). The output tax due is then calculated by estimating the proportion of takings which represent standard-rated sales and applying the VAT fraction ($^7/_{47}$ until 3 January 2011) to arrive at the VAT element contained therein.

Retailers with a turnover exceeding £10m p.a. cannot use a retail scheme without the specific agreement of HMRC, and other retailers may be refused the use of the scheme where it is practicable to account for VAT according to the normal rules.

Source: Notice 727, *Retail schemes*; Notice 727/2, *Bespoke retail schemes*; Notice 727/3, *Retail schemes: How to work the point of sale schemes*; Notice 727/4, *Retail schemes: How to work the apportionment schemes*; Notice 727/5, *Retail schemes: How to work the direct calculation schemes*

Website: www.hmrc.gov.uk

See *British VAT Reporter* ¶45-000.

8392 Second-hand goods schemes

Value added tax is intended ultimately to be collected at the retail stage of the supply chain. When a taxable supply is made by a trader to a final consumer, tax is accountable on the supply but cannot be recovered by the consumer. This works well for goods and services which are fully consumed by the consumer, but difficulties arise in the case of certain more durable goods which may pass back into the business system.

Under the basic VAT rules, if goods which have borne tax are sold by the consumer back into the business sector, then supplied again to another consumer, tax will arise on this new transfer into the non-business sector. As a result, the same article will be subjected to VAT twice.

In order to provide some measure of relief from this double taxation, the Treasury has power to make orders reducing the tax due on such transactions. This is the margin scheme.

The margin scheme is available for most supplies of second-hand goods, and can also be applied by an agent selling any goods in his own name.

The basic idea of the second-hand goods schemes is to restrict the amount of tax due on goods sold under them to tax on the trader's margin, rather than on the entire amount charged on reselling the goods. The trader must calculate the difference between the price at which he buys the goods and that at which he sells them, and account for tax out of the gross profit.

Where goods have been obtained under a transfer of a going concern their cost for margin scheme purposes is the cost to the transferor (or, if there have been two or more going concern transfers, the original transferor).

Value Added Tax

As a general rule the margin calculation must be made for each item separately. However, a global scheme can be used for goods costing £500 or less.

8398   Self-billing

It is sometimes desirable that a customer generates the tax invoice for a supply. This is appropriate where the customer controls or wishes to control events

These arrangements are particularly useful where it is the supplier who calculates the amount of the consideration for the supply, under a pre-agreed formula (such as royalties due under a publishing contract, where it is the publisher who has the information on sales made, and advises the author of the amount of the royalties due).

Where a trader (usually the customer) wishes to use self-billing, he must comply with the rules set out in a notice and obtain written approval of this from HMRC. In order to obtain this he must ensure that all of the suppliers concerned agree to the arrangement, and that they undertake not to issue tax invoices themselves for the transactions covered by it. The normal requirements for the contents of tax invoices apply, so the customer must satisfy himself that he has all relevant information.

The normal procedure is then that the customer generates the tax invoices, retains a copy for himself to act as evidence for his claim for input tax, and provides a copy to his supplier to enable him to account for output tax.

There is a special provision whereby, if a customer using a self-billing arrangement generates a self-billing invoice which understates the tax due, HMRC may elect to recover this from the customer rather than from the supplier.

Law: VATA 1994, s. 29; *Value Added Tax Regulations* 1995 (SI 1995/2518), reg. 13(3)

Source: Notice 700/62, *Self Billing*

See *British VAT Reporter* ¶56-200.

8404   Tour operators

A special tour operators' margin scheme (TOMS) applies to businesses who make supplies which include 'designated travel services'. These are known as 'tour operators'.

A supply of designated travel services is a supply of goods or services which the tour operator obtains, and resupplies without material alteration or further processing.

The broad basis of the scheme is that the tour operator cannot recover input tax on designated travel services, but the tax on his onward supplies to travellers is due only on his margin. The margin is calculated for the tour operator's supplies as a whole, the calculation being based on his financial accounts.

Law: VATA 1994, s. 53; *Value Added Tax (Tour Operators) Order* 1987 (SI 1987/1806); *R & C Commrs v Dunwood Travel Ltd* [2007] EWHC 319 (Ch)

Source: Notice 709/5, *Tour operator's margin scheme*

See *British VAT Reporter* ¶54-450.

8410 Special schemes for small businesses

In addition to the Flat Rate Scheme and the Flat Rate Farmers' Scheme, two other special schemes are available to businesses with relatively low turnover. These are the cash accounting scheme and the annual accounting scheme.

Cash accounting

The cash accounting scheme is intended to permit small businesses to account for VAT by reference to payments made and received, rather than the time when supplies are made and received. It is available to businesses with annual taxable turnover up to £1.35m. Once in the scheme, businesses can continue to use the scheme until their annual taxable turnover exceeds £1.6m. It is not necessary for businesses to have been trading before applying to join the cash accounting scheme. It is possible for businesses to be in both schemes at the same time, provided they satisfy both schemes' conditions.

Details of the scheme are contained in Notice 731, and the relevant legislation is in the *Value Added Tax Regulations* 1995 (SI 1995/2518), Pt. VIII.

Businesses that operate the cash accounting scheme do not have to claim bad debt relief for output tax paid on sale proceeds not received (see 8360). Conversely, such businesses cannot deduct input tax on purchases from their output tax in their VAT returns until payment has been made for those purchases.

See *British VAT Reporter* ¶55-450.

Annual accounting

The annual accounting scheme is available only to businesses which regularly pay tax to HMRC and not to repayment traders. Its use is optional, so businesses which prefer to account for tax quarterly (or monthly) can continue to do this.

The turnover figure below which a business is eligible to use the annual accounting scheme is £1,350,000. The turnover figure above which a business must leave the Scheme is £1,600,000.

Value Added Tax

Businesses opting for annual accounting make VAT returns only once a year. However, they are obliged to make payments on account (POAs) of the ultimate liability.

The POAs are set at either:

- a 'quarterly sum', payable on the last day of months four, seven and ten of the year; or
- a 'monthly sum' in nine equal instalments, starting on the last day of month four.

At the end of the year the trader makes a return for the whole year, and this is due (with any final balancing payment) two months after the end of the year.

Law: *Value Added Tax Regulations* 1995 (SI 1995/2518), Pt. VII, VIII

Source: Notice 731, *Cash accounting*; Notice 732, *Annual accounting*

See *British VAT Reporter* ¶55-300.

VAT PAYMENT AND ACCOUNTING REQUIREMENTS

8430   VAT payment dates

The VAT return must be submitted by the end of the month following the period to which it relates, and any tax shown on it as due to HMRC must be paid to them by the same date.

Failure to pay on time any VAT shown as due on a return can give rise to a liability to a surcharge (see 8516).

Taxpayers with problems paying should contact HMRC as soon as possible. Assistance under the Business Payment Support Service may be available.

Law: VATA 1994, s. 59; *Value Added Tax Regulations* 1995 (SI 1995/2518), reg. 25, 40

8436   Importance of VAT records

Because VAT is ultimately collected at the level of individual supplies, it is important that records should exist of all transactions. This becomes even more important given the provisions for refund of tax, so that one trader may be seeking repayment from HMRC of tax which should have been paid to them by another trader. Not surprisingly, HMRC is anxious to be able to verify that the tax has in fact been paid.

In order to meet this need, HMRC has a general power to require traders to keep such records as they may require. Their general requirements are set out in the *Value Added Tax Regulations* 1995 (SI 1995/2518), Pt. V.

From the trader's point of view, proper records are important in order to prevent HMRC from making assessments for tax which they might reasonably deduce to be due, but which is not in fact due when the full information is examined. The trader also needs to hold evidence when reliefs from tax are sought. Examples include the refund of input tax, and claiming zero-rating for a supply.

Law: VATA 1994, Sch. 11, para. 6(1); *Value Added Tax Regulations* 1995 (SI 1995/2518), Pt. V

Source: Notice 700, *The VAT guide*; Notice 700/21, *Keeping records and accounts*

Website: www.hmrc.gov.uk

See *British VAT Reporter* ¶58-800.

8442   General VAT accounting requirements

The general requirements as to record keeping for VAT are set out in the *Value Added Tax Regulations* 1995 (SI 1995/2518), reg. 31. Each taxable person has an obligation to keep and preserve his business and accounting records, copies of all tax invoices issued by him, tax invoices received by him, documentation relating to his imports and exports, and to his intra-EC acquisitions and dispatches of goods, credit notes, debit notes or other documents received which evidence changes in the consideration for supplies made or received, copies of such documents which he issues, and a value added tax account containing information specified in the regulations.

Such records must be preserved for a period of six years, unless HMRC allows a shorter period.

Law: *Value Added Tax Regulations* 1995 (SI 1995/2518), reg. 31

Source: Notice 700/21, *Keeping records and accounts*

Website: www.hmrc.gov.uk

See *British VAT Reporter* ¶58-800.

8448   Special VAT record-keeping requirements

Apart from the records needed by traders generally, it should be borne in mind that traders operating special schemes are usually subject to special record-keeping requirements (for special schemes and general records, see 8350ff., 8442). These may be specified by HMRC in Notices, which have the force of law for this purpose. For instance, a car dealer who wishes to use the second-hand goods scheme for second-hand cars has no legal entitlement

Value Added Tax

to do this unless records are kept in accordance with the scheme rules, providing acquisition and disposal details for each car dealt with under the scheme.

Other areas where special record-keeping requirements arise include retail schemes, retail export schemes, reclaim of pre-registration input tax, bad debt relief claims, and the cash accounting scheme.

Law: *Value Added Tax Regulations* 1995 (SI 1995/2518), reg. 31(2)

Source: Notice 700/21, *Keeping records and accounts*

Website: www.hmrc.gov.uk

See *British VAT Reporter* ¶58-800.

8454 VAT returns

Each trader must make a periodical VAT return to HMRC, showing amounts of output tax to be accounted for and of deductible input tax. The return also gives statistical information on the value of supplies made and received and intra-EC imports and exports of goods. The requirements of HMRC as to the way in which the amounts for supplies made and received are to be arrived at are set out in *Filling in your VAT return* – Notice 700/12.

The VAT return period differs between traders. Generally, returns are submitted quarterly, the quarter end to be used being notified to the trader by HMRC. Traders who regularly receive repayments of VAT (i.e. those who normally make zero-rated supplies) usually make a return each month, rather than each quarter. In some cases, notably when a business starts or finishes, it may be necessary to submit a return for a non-standard period.

The VAT return must be submitted by the end of the month following the period to which it relates, and any tax shown on it as due to HMRC must be paid to them by the same date. Failure to pay on time any VAT shown as due on a return can give rise to a liability to a surcharge (8516).

HMRC have been encouraging traders to file online and offer encouragement for this. Online filers must also pay online, but they have an extra 7 days in which to pay. As a disincentive to paper filers, from April 2010, the return must be accompanied by cleared funds rather than by a cheque by the due date.

Correction of errors

There is specific provision that, if an error is made in a return, it is to be corrected in such manner and at such time as HMRC may require.

The general requirements for the correction of errors are set out in Notice 700/45. In addition, there are special provisions allowing current period adjustment of earlier errors discovered. For accounting periods beginning after 1 July 2008, traders will only be required to disclose errors where they exceed the greater of £10,000; or one per cent of quarterly turnover up to a limit of £50,000. Under this limit, a taxpayer may self-correct the error. There are also special provisions for reclaiming tax incorrectly paid over to HMRC. Errors cannot be corrected if they are over four years old (from 1 April 2009).

Source: Notice 700/12, *Filling in your VAT return*; Notice 700/45, *How to correct errors you find on your VAT return*

Website: www.bsi-global.com/ICT/SoftwareQuality/PAS76.xalter

See *British VAT Reporter* ¶55-200.

8460   Additional returns for intra-EC trade

Apart from the VAT return itself (see 8454), further returns must be made by traders engaged in intra-EC movements of goods and services. The returns are:

- quarterly or monthly 'EC sales listings' (ESLs) required of all traders; and
- monthly 'Supplementary Statistical Declarations' (SSDs), more commonly known as Intrastat returns, are required of all but the smallest traders.

EC sales list

The EC Sales list (ESL) must be produced for each calendar quarter or month, as appropriate, and must be submitted to HMRC within 14 days of the reporting period for paper returns and 21 days for electronic submission.

The ESL is submitted on form VAT 101, and consists of a list of all customers elsewhere in the EC to whom supplies of goods (and from 1 January 2010, services as well) have been made in the period, their VAT registration numbers (including country prefixes) and the value of supplies of goods to them during the period. It is also possible to submit the information by way of plain paper reports or by electronic transmission.

The transactions which figure on the ESL are, broadly, supplies of goods delivered to other Member States for acquisition by taxable persons. In general the values and timing of supplies for ESL purposes are as for VAT return purposes. The value includes freight, etc. costs charged by the supplier to the customer. There are some transactions with special treatment for ESL purposes.

From 1 January 2010 businesses have to submit ESLs for taxable supplies of services made to business customers in other EU countries where the customer is required to account for VAT under the reverse charge procedure.

Value Added Tax

Supplementary Statistical Declarations (Intrastat)

The Supplementary Statistical Declaration (SSD) is a monthly return detailing all movements of goods between the UK and other Member States. It covers transfers between branches of the same business as well as purchases and sales of goods, and provides the information needed for the trade statistics. The obligation to submit SSDs arises under the *Statistics of Trade (Customs and Excise) Regulations* 1992 (SI 1992/2790).

The obligation to submit SSDs arises separately for imports and exports and depends on the value of the movements. The threshold is £600,000 p.a. from 1 January 2010 for arrivals and £250,000 for dispatches (see Revenue and Customs Brief 69/09).

The SSD must give details of each shipment, including such matters as the detailed trade classification of the goods, quantities, shipping costs, countries of departure and arrival, etc.

The SSD must be submitted within ten days of the month end.

Movements of goods excluded from SSDs

The following movements of goods should not be included on the SSD:

- goods dispatched to another EC country for a period of less than two years, if they would qualify for temporary importation relief if arriving from outside the EC (e.g. exhibition goods);
- goods transferred temporarily for hire, lease or loan, or for use in carrying out a service in another Member State;
- industrial or commercial samples sent to actual or potential customers free of charge;
- goods sent to another Member State for examination, analysis or testing followed by return or destruction, or the return of such goods after testing, etc.;
- dispatches of goods (other than excise goods or new means of transport) to unregistered customers.

Electronic submission of returns

Because of the large amounts of detailed information required in these statistical returns, arrangements are available whereby they can be submitted electronically. Possible means of submission include magnetic media, such as disks and tapes, and direct transmission of information to HMRC's computer.

Register of temporary movements of goods

The movement of a business's own goods from one Member State to another generally gives rise to a deemed supply in the state of departure and an acquisition in the state of arrival. However, certain temporary movements of goods are excepted from this procedure.

In order that such temporary movements can be controlled it is a requirement that the taxable person keeps a register of them, giving dates of removal and return, details of the goods, and of processing of them, etc.

Law: *Statistics of Trade (HMRC and Excise) (Amendment) (No. 2) Regulations* 2008 (SI 2008/2487)

Source: Notice 60, *The intrastat general guide*; *Revenue and Customs Brief* 69/09

Website: www.hmrc.gov.uk

See *British VAT Reporter* ¶64-600.

VAT ENFORCEMENT – THE PENALTY REGIME

8480   Nature of VAT penalties

A revised civil penalty regime for errors has been introduced across all the major taxes, including VAT, for return periods starting on or after 1 April 2008 that are filed on or after 1 April 2009. See 8520 for further details.

Law: FA 2007, Sch 24

8486   Late notification of liability to register for VAT

A trader who makes taxable supplies is obliged to notify HMRC if these supplies exceed the registration limits, so that a VAT registration can be effected (see 8256). Also, a trader who is exempted from registration by HMRC must notify a change in the nature of supplies made. There is a penalty for failure to make these notifications to HMRC by the proper date. The penalty is the greater of:

- £50; and
- a percentage of the tax due from the date when the trader should have been registered to the date when proper notification is made (or, if earlier, the date when HMRC becomes aware of the liability to be registered by some other means).

The percentage rate for this purpose depends on the length of the delay in notification, as follows:

Length of delay	Percentage
9 months or less	5
9–18 months	10
over 18 months	15

The penalty is based on the net tax due for the penalty period (i.e. output tax less input tax), not on the total output tax due. It applies, not only to 'black economy' traders who are discovered by HMRC, but also to traders who register in the ordinary way but are late in doing this.

Value Added Tax

The late registration penalty is not due if the trader can satisfy HMRC or, on appeal, a VAT tribunal, that there is a reasonable excuse for the failure (see 8556). The reasonable excuse defence also applies to several of the civil penalties.

The penalty can also be mitigated by up to 100 per cent by HMRC or, on appeal, the tribunal (for details of mitigation, see 8562).

Law: VATA 1994, s. 67, 70, 71

Source: Notice 700/41, *Late registration penalty*

Website: www.hmrc.gov.uk

8492 Criminal fraud: VAT

Criminal fraud arises, broadly, where a person knowingly takes steps to evade tax, or to enable another person to do so.

The penalties for criminal fraud apply, not only to the concealment of liability to account for tax, but also to such matters as the overstatement of claims for the repayment of input tax.

A criminal fraud penalty can only arise as a result of criminal proceedings, in which case the level of penalty depends whether the conviction secured is a summary conviction (i.e. before magistrates) or a conviction on indictment (i.e. before a jury). In either case, the penalty consists of a fine and/or imprisonment.

On conviction on indictment the maximum term of imprisonment is seven years, while the level of fines is unlimited; summary conviction also carries a possible prison term or a fine.

The following measures apply in an effort to combat missing trader fraud:

- HMRC officers have specific powers to enter premises, to inspect and mark goods with a date stamp and to record details of the goods by any means, including the electronic scanning of barcodes;
- HMRC may also give directions to businesses to require them to keep specified records relating to certain goods that they have traded (such as unique reference numbers for mobile phones). Failure to comply with such a direction will give rise to specified penalties.

The Missing Trader Intra-Community (MTIC) reverse charge accounting requirement was introduced from 1 June 2007. The main features of the scheme are:

- it applies to mobile telephones and integrated circuit devices, such as microprocessors and control processing units, in a state prior to integration into end-user products (note that this is a less extensive list than earlier published, but HMRC has confirmed that communication devices such as Blackberrys will come within the scope of the reverse charge);

- mobile phones supplied with an airtime contract are outside the scope of the reverse charge but 'pay as you go' ('prepay') phones are within the scope of the reverse charge;
- a 'de minimis' limit of £5,000 applies to the total value of goods subject to the reverse charge supplied together and detailed on a single invoice;
- businesses on the Payments on Account (POA) scheme affected by reverse charge accounting will be entitled to base their eligibility to POA and payments due thereunder on their notional liability excluding the reverse charge VAT;
- suppliers of goods subject to reverse charge accounting are required to submit web-based Reverse Charge Sales Lists giving information on their sales, in addition to their normal VAT returns;
- suppliers of goods subject to reverse charge accounting will be required to include a specific annotation on their invoices.

Law: VATA 1994, s. 55A; *Value Added Tax (Section 55A) (Specified Goods and Excepted Supplies) Order* 2007 (SI 2007/1417)

Source: HMRC Info Sheet 06/07

Website: http://ec.europa.eu/taxation_customs/taxation/tax_cooperation/reports/index_en.htm

See *British VAT Reporter* ¶60-715.

8498   Civil fraud: VAT

Civil fraud arises where a person takes steps, or omits to take steps, in order to evade tax. This is now dealt with under the new penalty regime (see 8520).

8500   Disclosure

Businesses with supplies of £600,000 or more are required to disclose the use of specific avoidance schemes that are included in HMRC's published list. This must be done within 30 days of the date when the first return affected by the scheme becomes due after 'listing'. Failure to disclose will incur a penalty of 15 per cent of the tax avoided. Businesses with supplies exceeding £10m a year are required to disclose the use of schemes that have certain hallmarks of avoidance. This must be done within 30 days of the date when the first return affected by the scheme becomes due. There is a voluntary facility for those who devise and market VAT avoidance schemes (promoters) to register schemes that have the hallmarks of avoidance with HMRC. A business using a scheme registered by a promoter will not have to make a separate disclosure of its use. Failure to disclose will incur a flat rate penalty of £5,000.

Value Added Tax

Law: *The Value Added Tax (Disclosure of Avoidance Schemes) Regulations* 2004 (SI 2004/1929); *The VAT (Disclosure of Avoidance Schemes) (Designations) Order* 2004 (SI 2004/1933)

See *British VAT Reporter* ¶60-850.

8504 Unauthorised issue of VAT invoices

Where a person who is not registered for VAT, or otherwise authorised to issue tax invoices (e.g. a receiver selling business assets owned by a taxable person can validly issue a tax invoice), issues an invoice which purports to include VAT, he is liable to a penalty of the greater of £50, or 15 per cent of the purported tax, whether or not the amount of 'tax' is shown separately.

The penalty will not be due if it can be shown that there is a reasonable excuse (see 8556), and the amount of the penalty may be mitigated by HMRC or, on appeal, by the VAT tribunal.

Law: VATA 1994, s. 67

See *British VAT Reporter* ¶18-043.

8510 Breaches of VAT regulations: records and payments

There are penalties for breaches of VAT regulations of any kind.

The amount of penalty varies with the type and frequency of the breach concerned. The basic penalty is at a rate of £5 per day while the breach continues. This is increased to £10 per day if there has been an earlier breach of the same regulation within the previous two years, and £15 per day if there has been more than one such earlier breach.

In some cases, this basic daily penalty is increased to a daily percentage of the tax involved, if this is greater. The percentage rises in line with the number of previous breaches, in exactly the same way as the basic daily penalty. The possible percentages are $\frac{1}{6}$ per cent, $\frac{1}{3}$ per cent and $\frac{1}{2}$ per cent. The equivalent annual rates are approximately 61 per cent, 122 per cent and 183 per cent.

The offence of failing to preserve records for the required period gives rise to a fixed penalty of £500.

An assessment for a daily penalty is subject to a maximum of 100 times the daily amount.

No penalty can be imposed under this provision, other than for failure to keep records or failure to notify end of liability or entitlement to be registered, unless HMRC has given the trader written warning concerning compliance with the requirement concerned within two years preceding the assessment.

An offence which has given rise to a criminal conviction, or a penalty for civil fraud or serious misdeclaration, cannot also be treated as a breach of regulations.

The following table shows the types of regulatory breach and the penalties which attach to them.

Breach	*Penalty*
Failure to notify cessation of taxable supplies	Fixed daily rate
Failure to make records	Fixed daily rate
Failure to retain records for six years	£500
Failure to furnish information and documents	Fixed daily rate
Failure to make a VAT return by the due date	Greater of fixed daily rate and tax-geared percentage rate
Failure to pay the tax due on a VAT return by the due date	Greater of fixed daily rate and tax-geared percentage rate
Any other breach of regulations	Fixed daily rate

The amount of tax on which the tax-geared percentages are to be based is the tax shown as due on the return for the period concerned. If no return has been made, it is the amount assessed as due for the period by HMRC.

The levels of penalties can be altered by statutory instrument, to take account of inflation.

A statutory defence is provided whereby no penalty is due if the trader can satisfy HMRC (or a VAT tribunal) that there is a reasonable excuse for the breach (see 8556). No mitigation is available for these penalties.

Law: VATA 1994, s. 69, 76(2)

See *British VAT Reporter* ¶850.

8516   Default surcharge

The default surcharge penalises traders who submit their VAT returns late, or submit the returns on time but defer payment of the related tax. The amount of the surcharge can range from a minimum of £30 to a maximum of 15 per cent of the tax due for the period depending on the frequency of late submission. The mechanics for fixing liability to surcharge, and its amount, are complex and are set out below.

If a return (or the payment due with it) is late in arriving with HMRC, the trader concerned is 'in default'. This does not, of itself, give rise to liability for default surcharge.

A surcharge liability notice is issued following a single default. This will specify a surcharge liability period beginning with the date the notice is issued and ending one year after the end of the period for which the trader is in default. Further defaults for return periods ending within the surcharge liability period may then attract a penalty.

A second default then attracts a surcharge liability of two per cent of the tax, a third and fourth are liable at five per cent and ten per cent respectively, while a fifth or later default is liable at 15 per cent. On a second or subsequent default within a surcharge period, the period is extended.

However, late returns do not attract a penalty in themselves, unless some or all of the tax due is paid late. Nil or repayment returns attract no penalty. Such a late return will still enable HMRC to extend the surcharge liability period, but will not attract a penalty itself, nor lead to an escalation in the rate of penalty for a subsequent default. The default surcharge system also applies to payments on account by larger traders (see 8374).

A trader who is late submitting a return is not liable to a default surcharge (and the late submission does not count in terms of a notice, etc.) if one of two defences can be substantiated to HMRC, or to a VAT tribunal:

- the trader can show that the return (or payment) was sent at such a time, and in such a manner, that it was reasonable to expect that HMRC would receive it by the due date; or
- there is a reasonable excuse for the late submission or payment (see 8556).

No mitigation is available for default surcharge.

Law: FA 1996, s. 35; VATA 1994, s. 59, 59A

Source: Notice 700/50, *Default surcharge*

Website: www.hmrc.gov.uk

See *British VAT Reporter* ¶60-450.

8520 New penalty regime for errors from 1 April 2009

HMRC has introduced a new penalty regime for errors, which applies across all the major taxes including VAT. Penalties are linked to the behaviour that gives rise to the error. People who take reasonable care when completing their returns will not be penalised. If they do not take reasonable care, errors will be penalised, and the penalties will be higher if the error is deliberate. Disclosing errors to HMRC early will substantially reduce any penalty due.

'Reasonable care' varies according to the person, the particular circumstances and their abilities. Every person is expected to make and keep sufficient records for them to provide a complete and accurate return. A person with simple, straightforward tax affairs needs only keep a simple system of records, which are regularly and carefully updated. A person with larger and more complex financial tax affairs will need to put in place more sophisticated systems and maintain them equally carefully. HMRC believe it is reasonable to expect a person who encounters a transaction or other event with which he is not familiar, to take care to check the correct tax treatment, or to seek suitable advice. HMRC expect people to take their tax seriously.

The new penalties, which will apply for errors made during 2008–09 and later years, are initially for errors on returns and documents for VAT, PAYE, National Insurance, capital gains tax, income tax, corporation tax and the construction industry scheme (CIS).

For these taxes, the penalties apply to returns or other documents for return periods starting on or after 1 April 2008 that are due to be filed on or after 1 April 2009.

The penalty charged will be a percentage of the extra tax due. The rate depends on the behaviour that gave rise to the error. The less serious the behaviour, the smaller the penalty will be. The charges are as follows:

- Reasonable care: no penalty
- Careless: minimum penalty 0% up to maximum of 30%
- Deliberate: minimum penalty 20% up to maximum 70%
- Deliberate and concealed: minimum penalty 30% up to maximum 100%

The *Finance Act* 2008 extended the new penalties for incorrect returns across most taxes, levies and duties, for incorrect returns for periods commencing from 1 April 2009 where the return is due to be filed from 1 April 2010.

Law: FA 2007, Sch 24

8522   Repayment supplement

A repayment supplement is added to certain late repayments of VAT shown as repayable on a VAT return. The terms of the supplement were revised in 1988; under the revised regime, any overpayment may often be offset against any underpayment by the taxpayer of tax, penalty, interest or surcharge.

In order to qualify for such a supplement, the return or, as regards local authority, etc. refunds, claim must have reached HMRC by the proper due date for its submission.

Repayment supplement is then due if HMRC fail to issue the written instruction directing the making of the repayment within 30 days of the later of:

- the end of the period concerned; and
- the date when HMRC received the return.

In determining whether the instruction is issued within the 30-day period, certain periods are ignored. These periods are those taken in making reasonable enquiries about the return, or correcting errors in the return, and periods in which the trader has failed to submit other returns, or pay the tax due on them or on assessments issued by HMRC, or comply with the conditions concerned with the production of documents or the giving of security.

Value Added Tax

If the return overstates the amount of the repayment due by more than the greater of five per cent and £250, no supplement is payable.

The supplement is the greater of five per cent of the repayment due or £50. There is a table of rates at 15.

Law: VATA 1994, s. 79

See *British VAT Reporter* ¶60-650.

THE MISDECLARATION PENALTY REGIME

8528 The misdeclaration penalty

This has now been replaced by the new penalty regime (see 8520 above) from 1 April 2009.

8544 Interest on underpaid VAT

The legislation provides for charging 'default interest' on assessable VAT paid late.

These provisions do not apply to tax properly shown on a VAT return, but paid over late, such late payments being covered by the default surcharge provisions (see 8516ff.) or dealt with as a breach of regulations (see 8510).

They apply, broadly, to tax which is recovered by way of assessment, or which could have been so assessed but is collected via a return instead.

Interest will arise in cases where:

(1) an assessment is made to recover extra tax for a period for which a return has already been made, or an assessment in lieu of a return issued;

(2) such an assessment could be made, but the tax is recovered on a later return instead;

(3) a person has failed to notify liability to register, or made late notification, and an assessment covering a period longer than three months is made to recover the tax;

(4) such an assessment could be made, but the tax is recovered by means of a 'long' first return period;

(5) a person exempted from registration has failed to notify a change in circumstances which makes him registrable, and the tax is recovered by way of a 'long period' assessment or return; or

(6) an invoice purporting to include VAT has been issued by a person not authorised to issue tax invoices.

In practice, default interest will only be due from a person who has registered late if he fails to pay the tax by the due date for the long first return period. Even then, it only runs from the due date, not from the dates when the tax would have been payable if he had registered at the proper time.

As a general rule, default interest runs from the due date for the submission of the VAT return for the period concerned until the date when the person pays the tax. However, if the assessment is to recover tax which has been incorrectly repaid by HMRC, interest runs from seven days after the date when HMRC issued a written instruction authorising the repayment. In the case of the issue of an invoice by an unauthorised person, interest runs from the date of the invoice.

The rate of interest is fixed by Treasury order, and is intended to reflect commercial rates of interest (there is a table of rates at 15). Default interest does not rank as an allowable expense for income tax and corporation tax purposes (see 2174, 3027).

Default interest is capped, so that it only runs for the last three years of the period. However, if the trader then fails to pay the assessment on time, interest will continue to run.

In practice, HMRC does not assess for default interest in cases where there has been no commercial loss to them, as when a trader has failed to charge output tax but, if tax had been charged, it would have been recoverable in the hands of the customer.

Also, interest is not charged in respect of net errors below £10,000, which could be adjusted on a subsequent return.

The practice of not charging default interest on net errors of £10,000 or less separately notified to HMRC ceased with effect from 1 September 2008. The decision in *Wilkinson v IR Commrs* deemed this practice to be unlawful. All error notifications (previously known as voluntary disclosures) requiring an assessment may be subject to a default interest charge, irrespective of the amount involved. However, as before, de minimis net errors can continue to be corrected on a VAT return and will not attract interest.

Law: VATA 1994, s. 74; *C & E Commrs v Peninsular and Oriental Steam Navigation Co* [1994] BVC 57; *C & E Commrs v Peninsular and Oriental Steam Navigation Co* [1992] BVC 170

Source: HMRC Brief 38/08; Notice 700/43, *Default interest*

See *British VAT Reporter* ¶60-680.

8550 Incorrect certificates

Certain zero-ratings (particularly in connection with property) depend upon the supplier obtaining a certificate of use from the customer. If an incorrect certificate is issued, HMRC may assess the customer for a penalty of 100 per cent of the tax 'saved' by the issue of the certificate.

The usual statutory defence of reasonable excuse applies for this penalty (see 8556), but there is no provision for mitigation.

Law: VATA 1994, s. 62

See *British VAT Reporter* ¶60-200.

8556   Reasonable excuse: VAT

There are a number of VAT penalties which are remitted if the taxpayer has reasonable excuse.

The term 'reasonable excuse' has not been defined in the legislation. However, the legislation does specify that the following are not to give rise to a reasonable excuse:

• an insufficiency of funds to pay any tax due; and
• the fact of reliance on another to perform any task, or dilatoriness or inaccuracy on the part of the person relied upon.

Law: VATA 1994, s. 71(1)

See *British VAT Reporter* ¶60-037.

8562   Mitigation of VAT penalties

Mitigation of VAT penalties is available in respect of the following:

• Penalty for late registration and unauthorised issue of invoice (see 8504, 8510).

Mitigation can be up to 100 per cent, and is exercisable by HMRC or, on appeal, the tribunal; the tribunal has power to reduce the mitigation allowed by HMRC as well as to increase it.

No account is to be taken of the following in considering mitigation (VATA 1994, s. 70(4)):

• insufficiency of funds to pay either tax or a penalty;
• the fact that there has been no significant loss of tax;
• the fact that the trader (or his representative) has acted in good faith.

Law: VATA 1994, s. 70, 70(4)

See *British VAT Reporter* ¶59-730.

8574 Failure to submit EC sales list

Failure to submit an EC sales list (ESL) by the due date can give rise to a civil penalty at a daily rate.

If an ESL is not submitted by the due date, HMRC may issue a notice. If the ESL is not submitted within a further 14 days then a penalty will be due. Penalties can also be levied (regardless of whether the first late ESL attracts a penalty) for any further late ESLs until 12 months have elapsed without an ESL being submitted late.

The penalty is at a rate of £5 per day for the first default, £10 per day for the second, and £15 per day for any subsequent default.

Law: VATA 1994, s. 66

See *British VAT Reporter* ¶64-920.

8580 Interaction of VAT penalties

In some cases, the same act or omission is capable of attracting more than one of the penalties available to HMRC.

For instance, an underdeclaration of VAT on a return might, depending upon the circumstances (and available evidence), be regarded as representing criminal fraud, or an error that would be dealt with under the new error regime (from April 2009).

The general principle of the various penalties (except for default interest on tax) is that they are mutually exclusive. It is up to HMRC to decide which kind of penalty they will seek. In some instances, a 'lesser' offence might give rise to a higher penalty. For instance, late submission of a return might attract higher penalties as a regulatory breach than under the default surcharge provisions. For a 'first' offence, the default surcharge penalty would be five per cent of the tax. If the return was more than 30 days late the penalty as a regulatory breach, at $^{1}/_{6}$ per cent per day (or £10 per day) would exceed this. The difference could be of particular significance to small concerns, where tax-geared penalties might be relatively low.

It seems that, in practice, HMRC normally seeks to use the penalty provision most closely suited to the nature of the offence, rather than that which involves the highest amount of penalties. However, it should not be presumed that this will always be the case, as there would then be no purpose in the degree of overlap provided in the law.

8586 Assessment of penalties

HMRC has the power under VATA 1994, s. 76 to assess amounts due by way of default surcharge or default interest (see 8516, 8544).

Law: VATA 1994, s. 76

VAT ASSESSMENTS, APPEALS AND DISPUTES

8606 VAT assessment powers

In the ordinary course of events the amount of VAT due is established by reference to returns submitted by the taxable person. Where this procedure breaks down, liability to tax is established by means of an assessment issued by HMRC.

HMRC has the power to assess tax due where:

- a person has failed to submit returns, or it appears that the returns are incomplete or incorrect;
- an incorrect credit or refund of input tax has been made for a period;
- a person has acquired, imported or been supplied with goods and is unable to account for those goods;
- a non-taxable person has acquired goods subject to excise duty, or a new means of transport, from another Member State and has failed to account for the VAT due on the acquisition.

They also have power to assess amounts due by way of penalties and interest.

The making of an assessment, and its due notification to the person concerned, establishes (subject to any appeal) the person's liability to pay the amount assessed.

Law: VATA 1994, s. 73(1), (2), (7), 75, 76

See *British VAT Reporter* ¶58-520.

8612 Time-limits and notification of VAT assessment

Except in cases involving fraud or dishonesty, there is an overall time-limit for the making of an assessment of four years from the end of the prescribed accounting period to which it relates (VATA 1994, s. 77(1)). In cases of fraud this time-limit is extended to 20 years (VATA 1994, s. 77(4)). In the case of a deceased trader there is a further overriding time-limit of four years from the date of death (VATA 1994, s. 77(5)).

Apart from these overriding time-limits, an assessment must be made by the later of:

- two years from the end of the prescribed accounting period concerned; and
- one year after evidence of facts, sufficient in the opinion of HMRC to justify the making of the assessment, comes to their knowledge (VATA 1994, s. 73(6)).

If further information subsequently becomes available HMRC can issue a further assessment. Even if no further information comes to light, HMRC can still make a supplementary assessment provided that this is done within the relevant time-limit (VATA 1994, s. 73(6)).

If an assessment is made after the time-limit for making it has expired, it is invalid. If a global assessment is made (i.e. a single assessment covering a number of periods, rather than breaking the tax down between the different prescribed accounting periods), and it is out of time as regards one of the prescribed accounting periods included in it, then the whole assessment falls. Provided that a breakdown is given, the mere fact that assessments for a number of periods are listed in a single notification does not in itself mean that a global assessment has been made.

However, the High Court has held that HMRC was entitled to delay making a 'best judgment' assessment until they had not only material justifying the making of an assessment but also material on which to calculate the amount of the liability.

In order for an assessment to be valid it must not only be made on time, but also be correctly notified. There is no specifically prescribed form for notification, but the courts have held that the person assessed is entitled to be notified, in reasonably clear terms, of the identity of the person assessed, the amount of the assessment, the reasons for it, and the period or periods to which it relates (see, for example, *House t/a P & J Autos v C & E Commrs*). If the notification is deficient in any of these respects it may be possible to overturn the assessment.

As stated above, under current law, HMRC can only issue an assessment to recover VAT from a taxpayer within one year of the full facts coming to their attention. This has caused problems where the facts have remained constant but a change in the interpretation of the VAT law has led to a different outcome.

Law: VATA 1994, s. 73(6), 77(1), (4), (5); *BUPA Purchasing Ltd & Ors v R & C Commrs* [2007] EWCA Civ 542; *House t/a P & J Autos v C & E Commrs* [1996] BVC 116

See *British VAT Reporter* ¶58-205.

8618 Matters which may invalidate a VAT assessment

When HMRC exercises its power to assess, the Commissioners must do so to the best of their judgment. This means that they must consider fairly the material before them, taking account of all matters which are relevant and ignoring matters which are not. They do not have to make exhaustive enquiries provided that they have some material on which they can form a judgment, but will generally be acting unreasonably if they ignore information provided to them by the trader.

Frequently, it is necessary to carry out some degree of estimation in order to arrive at the amount of an assessment, if exact figures are not readily available. In such cases it is permissible to use observations made for a sample period to estimate the amount of tax due for a longer period.

The main grounds on which an assessment may be invalid, and on which an appeal may therefore be successful, may be summarised as follows:

- the assessment is wrongly based in law (for example, it is based on the notion that a supply is a standard-rated one and it is, in fact, zero-rated);
- the assessment has been made out of time (see 8612);
- the notification of the assessment is procedurally incorrect (see 8612);
- the assessment has not been made to the best of HMRC's judgment; or
- although the assessment is procedurally and legally correct, and has been made to the best of HMRC's judgment, the appellant is able to bring evidence which convinces the tribunal not only that the amount of it is wrong but also what amount is to be preferred.

Law: VATA 1994, s. 73

See *British VAT Reporter* ¶58-300.

8620 Reviews and appeals

The whole process of reviews and appeals has changed as a result of the Tribunals, Courts and Enforcement Act 2007 (TCEA 2007) and the statutory instruments that give effect to the detail. The whole system changed on 1 April 2009.

The TCEA replaces the old tribunal structure with a new lower tax tribunal, called a First-tier Tribunal that hears basic VAT appeals and an Upper Tribunal that hears appeals from the lower tribunal and, in the first instance, more complex cases.

The appellate structure in the UK has also been modified, such that an appeal from the First-tier Tribunal will normally be heard in the Upper Tribunal, so in effect, this replaces the High Court. Appeals beyond this are as before: to the Court of Appeal and the Supreme Court (which replaces the House of Lords Appellate Committee).

When there is a dispute between a taxpayer and HMRC, the new process is as follows:

The taxpayer is notified of the decision (this could be, say, an assessment) and at that point HMRC must offer the taxpayer a review of the decision under VATA 1994, s. 83A.

If the taxpayer accepts the offer of a review within the statutory 30 days, then HMRC is bound to review the decision under s. 83C and notify the results of the review to the taxpayer.

The taxpayer may choose not to request a review and instead go straight to an appeal under s. 83G. This must be done within 30 days of the disputed decision. It is not possible to request a review and go to an appeal at the same time (s. 83C).

The review must be conducted and the results notified to the taxpayer within 45 days of the relevant date (normally the date of acceptance of the offer of the review).

The review will either confirm, vary or cancel the decision. The taxpayer can still appeal the review decision within 30 days of the conclusions of the review.

Law: VATA 1994, s. 82 onwards; Tribunal Procedures (First-tier Tribunal) etc 2009, SI 2009/273; Tribunal Procedure (Upper Tribunal) Rules 2008, SI 2008/2698

8624   Appealable matters: VAT

The matters on which an appeal lies to a VAT tribunal are listed in VATA 1994, s. 83, being decisions of HMRC with respect to various things such as an assessment, the registration of a person, the tax chargeable on a supply, the amount of input tax which may be credited, etc. This is a complete list, and anything which does not appear in it is not appealable to the tribunal (although there may be an alternative remedy by way of judicial review).

For the role of VAT tribunals, see 177.

Law: TCEA 2007; VATA 1994, s. 83 onwards; *R & C Commrs v Church of Scientology Religious College Inc* [2007] EWHC 1329 (Ch)

See *British VAT Reporter* ¶61-400.

8630   Time-limit for VAT appeal and local review

As a general rule, notice of appeal against an assessment or other decision must be lodged with the Tribunal Centre within 30 days of the disputed decision or the conclusions of a review (see 8620).

See *British VAT Reporter* ¶61-410.

8636   VAT appeal procedures

The procedures governing appeals to the VAT tribunals are set out in the *Value Added Tax Tribunals Rules* 1986 (SI 1986/590) and the *Tribunal Procedure (First Tier Tribunal) (Tax Chamber) Rules* 2009 (SI 2009/273) and the Tribunal procedure (Upper Tribunal) Rules 2008 (SI 2008/2698).

A tribunal may, in particular, require the taxpayer:

- to deliver to them such particulars as they may require for the purpose of determining the appeal; and
- to make various documents available for inspection.

Any party to an appeal may adduce lawful evidence and may call witnesses. A tribunal has the power to summon any person (other than the appellant) to appear before them and give evidence. Witnesses may be examined on oath.

Value Added Tax

Professional advisers (e.g. barristers, solicitors or accountants) may appear on behalf of any party to the appeal.

A tribunal has the power to award costs, although in the new system these are uncommon.

Law: *Tribunal Procedure (First Tier Tribunal) (Tax Chamber) Rules* 2009 (SI 2009/273) and the *Tribunal procedure (Upper Tribunal) Rules* 2008 (SI 2008/2698)

See *British VAT Reporter* ¶61-140.

National Insurance Contributions

National Insurance Contributions

National Insurance Contributions

1,391

- The lower earnings limit for Class 1 NIC is increased to £97 a week for 2010–11 (see 110 for tables).
- The upper earnings limit for Class 1 NIC is £844 a week for 2010–11.
- The primary threshold for Class 1 NICs for 2010–11 is £110 per week.
- Class 2 NICs for 2010–11 are £2.40 per week (£3.05 for share fishermen).
- The Class 2 NIC small earnings exemption limit is £5,075 for 2010–11.
- The Class 3 NIC rate is £12.05 per week for 2010–11.
- The Class 4 NIC lower and upper earnings limits for 2010–11 are £5,715 and £43,875 respectively.
- From 6 April 2010 expenses payments to ministers of religion in respect of heating, lighting, cleaning and gardening in connection with living accommodation provided with the employment will not attract NICs (see 8780 for tables).
- HMRC are consolidating their PAYE databases into one, which will mean that an individual's total employment position can be accessed by staff on one screen

KEY POINTS

- National Insurance is administered by HM Revenue & Customs (see 8700).
- There are six classes of Contributions – Class 1, Class 1A, Class 1B, Class 2, Class 3 and Class 4 (see 8710).
- Earners paying contributions may be employed or self-employed (see 8710).
- Employed earners pay primary Class 1 contributions, with secondary contributions payable by their employer (see 9100ff.).
- Class 1A and Class 1B contributions are secondary-only (i.e. employer-only) contributions (see 9120ff. and 9140).
- Class 1A contributions are payable on the provision of most taxable benefits (see 9100ff.).
- Class 1B contributions are payable in respect of items included within a PAYE settlement agreement that would otherwise attract a liability to Class 1 or Class 1A (see 9140).
- The self-employed pay Class 2 and Class 4 contributions. Class 2 contributions are flat rate contributions and Class 4 contributions are profit-related (see 9150ff. and 9240ff.).
- Class 3 contributions are voluntary contributions, which may be paid to preserve benefit entitlement (see 9210).
- Class 1 contributions are collected via the PAYE system (see 9354).
- Class 4 contributions are collected as for tax through the self-assessment system (see 9362).
- Class 2 and Class 3 contributions are usually paid by direct debit (see 9358 and 9360).
- Interest and penalties may be levied in respect of later paid contributions and returns (see 9386ff.).

National Insurance Contributions

1,393

INTRODUCTION TO NICs

8700   The National Insurance scheme

The aim of the UK's National Insurance scheme is to protect members of the population of the nation who fall upon hard times. However, its resemblance to commercially-based insurance is limited in that only in part does it involve the payment of compulsory and voluntary contributions by people with some link to the UK (e.g. residence, presence, or habitual residence in the UK) to provide for certain state benefits. It is in reality a system of social insurance.

Social security forms represents the largest single class of government expenditure each year, but only around one-half of social security expenditure is financed by National Insurance contributions (NICs), the remainder being funded from general tax revenues.

National Insurance Fund

In reality, there is no insurance scheme in the accepted sense. There is a National Insurance Fund as a notionally separate entity within the government accounts, but it only ever contains enough money at any point to pay out benefits derived from it for between two and four months. In the main, it is a system of cross-generational transfer, in that contributions of the current working population are used mainly to pay current state pensions, the balance being used to fund other current benefits. The term contribution is, in effect, a euphemism for tax.

National Insurance contributions are thought by many to provide entitlement to care under the National Health Service (NHS), but in reality only a small proportion of National Insurance Fund income is transferred to the NHS. Most NHS funding comes from general taxation, and entitlement to health care does not depend on contributions paid.

National Insurance Contributions Office

As part of HM Revenue & Customs' (HMRC's) wider Service Delivery Team, NICO work closely with HMRC Local Services, Large Business Office, Share Pensions Savings Schemes Office and all the National Business Streams. It also has strong links with the Department for Work and Pensions (DWP). NICO maintains over 65 million NIC accounts; updates over 40 million individual NI accounts; processes more than 53 million end of year notifications; deals with 1.4 million employers, 3 million self-employed and 5.7 million personal pension accounts; collects £3.5 billion in NICs each year; and employs over 4,600 staff.

Governing legislation

The Acts
The law governing NICs is mainly contained in the *Social Security Contributions and Benefits Act* 1992 (SSCBA 1992), while provisions on the running of the scheme are set out

in the *Social Security Administration Act* 1992 (SSAA 1992). Both of these Acts consolidate earlier legislation.

The *National Insurance Contributions Act* 2002 predominantly deals with increases in contributions applicable from 6 April 2003 to both primary and secondary Class 1 contributions and to Class 4 contribution levels.

The *National Insurance Contributions Act* 2006 received Royal Assent on 30 March 2006. The Act contains measures which aim to ensure that all employers and employees pay the correct amount of tax and NICs, particularly in relation to schemes involving shares and securities.

The regulations

Numerous regulations have also been made under the two consolidation Acts and their predecessors to govern the payment of contributions and entitlement to benefits. The most important are the *Social Security (Contributions) Regulations* 2001 (SI 2001/1004) and the *Social Security (Categorisation of Earners) Regulations* 1978 (SI 1978/1689).

The *Civil Partnerships Act* 2004 came into effect from 5 December 2005, the main purpose of which is to give legal status to same-sex couples. As a result of this legislation, various statutory instruments have been laid for social security and National Insurance contributions purposes, so that same-sex couples are now treated as husband and wife couples for benefits and NIC purposes.

Cases

There are few judicial decisions dealing with the interpretation of the legislation governing NICs. However, some decided cases are of assistance in clarifying particular issues.

Official publications

In the commentary that follows, references are made to several official explanatory publications. Particularly frequent references are made to booklet CWG2 *Employer's Further Guide to PAYE and NICs* (available from the employer's orderline (0845 7 643 643) or to download from the employer's download page of the Revenue's website (www.hmrc.gov.uk)).

Separate scheme for Northern Ireland

The Social Security Acts and regulations often refer to 'Great Britain'. A separate social security scheme exists for Northern Ireland, although following the consolidation of the Social Security regulations, the consolidated regulations (the *Social Security (Contributions) Regulations* 2001 (SI 2001/1004)) apply to both Great Britain and Northern Ireland but its rules on contribution liability are effectively identical to those in the rest of the UK.

Law: *Social Security Contributions (Transfer of Functions etc.) Act* 1999; *Social Security Contributions (Transfer of Functions etc.) Act 1999 (Commencement No. 1 and Transitional Provisions) Order* 1999 (SI 1999/527)

National Insurance Contributions

LIABILITY TO NICs

8705   Charge to NIC

Liability to National Insurance contributions (NICs) depends on the class of contributor into which the individual falls, i.e. whether an individual is employed or self-employed (see 253). In many cases this will be obvious. At the margin it is a question of law and is not determined merely from a job description or contract.

8710   Categorisation of National Insurance contributors

The National Insurance Fund (see 8700) exists to pay the benefits specified under the *Social Security Contributions and Benefits Act* 1992, Pt. II and to pay contributions towards the National Health Service. To enable the Fund to pay benefits, contributions are paid by earners, employers and others.

Those paying contributions are further identified as being:

- employed earners;
- employers and other persons paying earnings;
- self-employed earners; and
- others paying voluntarily in order to provide or make up benefit entitlement.

An 'earner' may be employed or self-employed, since the term must be construed according to the definition of earnings, which includes any 'remuneration or profit derived from an employment' (see 8750ff.).

The term 'employment' includes any trade, business, profession, office or vocation, so contributions are potentially due in connection with any income derived from working, be it as an employee or as a self-employed person.

In order to establish whether a liability to NICs arises and, if so, to calculate that liability, it is first necessary to be able to determine the group or category into which an earner falls.

Classes of contributions

As noted above, liability depends on the class into which the individual falls. The classes are:

Class 1: earnings-related, primary contributions being payable by employed earners and secondary contributions being payable by employers and others paying earnings (see 9000ff.);

Class 1A: contributions payable annually by secondary contributors only, based from 6 April 2000 on the cash equivalent value of taxable benefits in kind. Previously, the charge only applied in respect of employer-provided car and car fuel (see 9100ff.);

Class 1B (from April 1999): contributions paid by employers on the extension of PAYE settlement agreement principles to NICs (see 9140);

Class 2: flat rate, payable by self-employed earners (see 9150ff.);

Class 3: flat rate, payable voluntarily (to satisfy contribution requirements to certain long-term benefits) (see 9210ff.); and

Class 4: earnings-related, payable by self-employed earners (see 9240ff.).

An individual may be liable or entitled to pay more than one class of contribution. Various reliefs are also available where contributions are payable under certain combinations of classes (see 8756ff.).

Law: SSCBA 1992, s. 1(1), (2), (5), 2, 122

8712   The employed earner

Class 1 contributions are levied on the earnings of 'employed earners': i.e. persons gainfully employed in Great Britain either under a contract of service, or in an office with emoluments chargeable to income tax under the charge on employment income provisions of ITEPA 2003 (see 250ff.).

Remember that use of part-time labour can keep employees below lower earnings limits (LELs) so both employer and employee pay no NICs.

Law: SSCBA 1992, s. 2(1)(a)

8714   Office holders

The distinction between employment under a contract of service and employment in an office (see 8712) can be important. For example, certain company directors may receive fees as emoluments of the office but at the same time may be employees under a contract of service with an associated company, and since special rules apply to the calculation of the contribution liabilities of company directors (see 9026) it is important to know the true source of the individual's income.

An office has an existence independent of that of the person who occupies it at any particular time (see 252). No earnings-related contribution liability arises if the payment made to the office holder does not fall within the charge on employment income provisions of ITEPA 2003: for example, where the payment is made to a company director who is neither resident nor ordinarily resident in the UK and is paid only in respect of duties performed outside the UK.

The contributions legislation refers to *chargeable* emoluments, rather than simply charged under the provisions of the employment tax law. However, although a company auditor holds an office in relation to the company, for the sake of administrative convenience the strict legal position is not followed in relation either to income tax or NICs and, in practice, income tax under ITTOIA 2005 is charged on the profits of the profession and an auditor is treated as a self-employed earner for NIC purposes.

National Insurance Contributions

8716   Employed or self-employed?

Of vital significance to NICs is the distinction between a contract of service and a contract *for services*. While the former connotes an employer/employee relationship and, for NIC purposes, points clearly towards the existence of an employed earner, the latter is the legal relationship between an independent contractor and his customers.

The definition of 'contract of service', central to the distinction between employed and self-employed earners, is:

> 'any contract of service or apprenticeship whether written or oral and whether expressed or implied.'

This definition is equivalent to that used in employment protection law for the term 'contract of employment'. However, there are a number of situations in which a person is deemed by NIC regulations to fall into a category other than that into which he would normally fall, but it is generally the case that a person who falls to be treated as an employee for the purposes of NICs will equally be treated as an employee for the purposes of employment protection law, income tax law, and value added tax law.

The general discussion on employed or self-employed for income tax purposes is therefore also relevant to NICs (see 253).

Law: SSCBA 1992, s. 122

Website: www.hmrc.gov.uk/leaflets/es-fs1.pdf

8718   The self-employed earner

A self-employed earner is any person who is gainfully employed in Great Britain other than in employed earner's employment.

There are a series of tests used to differentiate between employed and self-employed earners (see 8716). This does not, of course, mean that a particular individual may not be simultaneously employed and self-employed.

However, what is clear is that a self-employed individual can only be self-employed once. As an independent contractor, he may provide his services to numerous customers and the services provided need not be the same in each case. The only requirement of contribution law is that he be gainfully employed in Great Britain.

A person will fit these criteria if he holds himself out as being anxious to be employed for the purposes of gain, although until he in fact commences his trade, profession or vocation, he cannot be gainfully employed.

Whilst the charge to Class 2 contributions arises on a weekly basis in respect of any self-employed earner, it is insufficient to test the status of any particular individual on the basis of one week's activity or lack of activity. Inevitably, there are certain situations in which the motive and opportunity for gain are difficult to determine.

Although the individual concerned may not have a motive of gain in entering into an arrangement to provide services, nevertheless, where actual gain arises, he will be gainfully employed and will fall to be treated as a self-employed earner.

Equally, someone in a business may be a partner simply because he has made an investment but takes no part in the managing, or working in the business. He therefore has a motive of gain but is not in fact employed in performing services. Such a sleeping partner falls outside the definition of a self-employed earner.

Law: SSCBA 1992, s. 2(1)(b); *Vandyk v Minister of Pensions and National Insurance* [1955] 1 QB 29; Decision M36 1953

8720   Decisions on status

Where persons paying or in receipt of earnings are in doubt about the class of National Insurance contributions (NICs) which they should be paying, they are advised to contact their local National Insurance Contributions Office (NICO) (see 8700) for advice. Such contact should be able to produce a firm decision, which will be binding in respect of both income tax and NICs, provided all relevant facts are disclosed.

Appeals against decisions

An appeal against a decision of the Revenue (after 31 March 1999) as to whether a person is or was an earner and, if so, the category into which he is or was to be included, lies to the tribunal (see 235ff.).

Law: *Social Security Contributions (Transfer of Functions etc.) Act* 1999, s. 11; *Social Security Contributions (Transfer of Functions etc.) Act 1999 (Commencement No. 1 and Transitional Provisions) Order* 1999 (SI 1999/527)

Website: www.hmrc.gov.uk/leaflets/es-fs1.pdf

8722   Retrospective recategorisation

The National Insurance Contributions Office (NICO) (see 8700) will usually consider any categorisation question whenever an individual applies for Class 2 registration. Difficulties can arise where the individual's status is not clear-cut, since NICO must then make enquiry in an attempt to establish the facts of the employment relationship in question in order to collect the correct class of contribution. Such enquiries provide NICO with the opportunity to recategorise as employees other contributors in a similar relationship to the alleged employer.

Where incorrect categorisation is established, NICO insists on an immediate change to the correct class of contribution being implemented. The date of change could be effective from an earlier date. While the tax authorities, in the absence of fraud, are allowed to look back no more than six years, NICO is not subject to similar time limits.

The official practice in cases of retrospective recategorisation to Class 1 is as follows: any Class 2 contributions which the contributor has paid erroneously as a result of the change of status from self-employed to employed earner are reallocated as employee (primary) Class 1 contributions. Any balance of employee contributions due and any arrears of employer (secondary) contributions are generally requested from the employer. If the erroneous Class 2 contributions amount to more than the employee Class 1 contributions due the excess is refundable. HMRC refund Class 4 contributions overpaid as a result of a change of status. Any Class 2 contributions paid in error may be reallocated as employee Class 1 contributions, but this is at the discretion of NICO.

On general principles, NICO cannot enforce collection for debts over six years old if they have not been deliberately concealed and are not acknowledged by the debtor.

All liabilities (after the set-off of any Class 2 contributions) fall to the account of the employer, since the regulations operate to prevent any recovery by the employer of employee (primary) contributions in respect of earlier tax years in this situation. The employer is made primarily liable whenever earnings are paid for the payment of Class 1 contributions, but is given a limited right of recovery against his employees in respect of the primary liability. Late recovery is allowed, but only:

- in respect of under-deductions in the current tax year;
- if those under-deductions were made by reason of an error made in good faith; *and*
- to the extent that the extra deduction in any earnings period does not exceed the employee contributions otherwise deductible.

Where recategorisation has taken place and the individual concerned has thereby been transferred into the category of self-employed earner after having paid Class 1 contributions, NICO's usual practice is to treat such recategorisation as having effect only from the date of the relevant decision. This effectively prevents any repayment claim in respect of Class 1 contributions paid, despite the fact that the individual has been found to have been self-employed during the period in question. However, the choice to make the change only prospectively rather than retrospectively may be challenged on those very grounds, and the question may even be taken as far as a decision by the Secretary of State under the procedure for the determination of questions (see 9380).

There are special procedures when a formal decision is made by the Secretary of State resulting in the recategorisation of a contributor or when the High Court overturns such a status decision.

1998 changes

Where an individual's status changes from employed to self-employed but Class 1, Class 1A or Class 1B NICs continue to be paid on the basis that the individual is an employed earner, adjustments to NICs are made not (as previously) for the preceding six years, but only for the tax year in which the error came to light and the preceding year. This means that for all earlier periods the individual's contributions and contributory benefits position, and entitlement to statutory sick pay and statutory maternity pay, are unaffected by the change in status. Conversely, employers will receive no refund of secondary contributions paid in error in earlier years. The above changes apply to contributions paid in a period falling in a year after 1997–98.

Law: SSA 1998, s. 54; SSCBA 1992, s. 19A; *Limitation Act 1980*; *Social Security (Contributions) Regulations 2001* (SI 2001/1004), reg. 17, 51; *Social Security (Categorisation of Earners) Regulations 1978* (SI 1978/1689), reg. 4

8724   Categorisation regulations

The basics of identifying the employed earner and the self-employed earner are irrelevant where regulations specifically provide for earners to be put into one category. A number of specific types of employment (i.e. in the sense of employment both as an employed earner and as a self-employed earner) have been identified as causing particular problems or administrative difficulties. Regulations therefore change or fix the status of earners in each of the specified types of employment or even, in specified circumstances, provide that the employment in question shall be entirely disregarded (see 8726ff.).

Law: *Social Security (Categorisation of Earners) Regulations 1978* (SI 1978/1689)

8726   Deemed employed earners

Earners in employments categorised as employed earners include the following:

- office cleaners, or those working in a similar capacity in any premises other than those used as a private dwelling-house;
- telephone kiosk cleaners, again excluding any who work on apparatus in premises used as a private dwelling-house;
- employment of a person by his or her spouse for the purposes of the spouse's employment (which includes self-employment);
- employment as a lecturer, teacher, instructor or in any similar capacity in an educational establishment by a person providing education. The deemed employee must give the instruction in the presence of the persons to whom the instruction is given, and the earnings must be paid by or on behalf of the person providing the education. The rule does not apply where the lecturer, etc. has agreed in advance that he will not give instruction on more than three days in three consecutive months or the instruction is given as public lectures;
- employment as a minister of religion, not being employment under a contract of service

National Insurance Contributions

or in an office within the charge on employment income provisions of ITEPA 2003. This rule is not applicable to ministers whose remuneration is not wholly or mainly stipend or salary, which means that, e.g. a Roman Catholic priest is not an employed earner, because his stipend is minimal; and

- employment via the agency of a third party. An employment is deemed to be employed earner's employment if the person concerned renders, or is obliged to render personal service and is subject to supervision, direction or control, or to the right of supervision, etc. as to the manner of the rendering of such service and he is supplied by or through some third person. Furthermore, for this rule to apply, the earnings paid must be paid by or through, or on the basis of accounts submitted by, the third person or in accordance with arrangements made with him, or payments other than to the person employed must be made by way of fees, commission, etc. which relate to the continued employment in that employment of the person in question. This rule specifically includes the possibility of a partnership supplying the services of one of its members, in which case the member concerned would be treated as an employed earner in relation to that employment. The deeming rule is expressed not to operate in respect of homeworkers or outworkers supplied through a third party, nor does it extend to persons employed as actors, singers, musicians or other entertainers, or as fashion, photographic or artists' models.

Regulations provide for the identification of the secondary contributor in relation to deemed Class 1 employments.

Actors and musicians

Entertainers have generally been treated as employees for NIC purposes but as self-employed for income tax purposes (see 253). Having been advised that the NIC treatment was unsustainable and that entertainers should generally be regarded as self-employed, the DSS made regulations, operative from 17 July 1998, that again required the majority of performers to be treated as employees for NIC purposes, whose earnings are liable to Class 1 contributions. Those who believe they have incorrectly paid contributions in the previous six years can seek refunds of contributions.

Law: *Social Security (Categorisation of Earners) Regulations* 1978 (SI 1978/1689)

Source: Guidelines on the special NIC rules for entertainers (Inland Revenue, 1 October 2004)

8728 Deemed self-employment

The only persons who would normally be employed earners but who fall into the self-employed bracket are those employed other than through the agency of another as an examiner, moderator, or invigilator, etc., under a contract which is to be completed in less than 12 months, where the examination leads to a certificate, diploma, degree or professional qualification. (See further 9294.)

Law: *Social Security (Categorisation of Earners) Regulations* 1978 (SI 1978/1689), reg. 2(3)

8730 Deemed non-employment

Several types of employment are disregarded for NIC purposes. These include:

(1) employment by a close member of the family in a private dwelling house other than for the purposes of that family member's business;

(2) any employment by a spouse otherwise than for the purposes of the spouse's employment;

(3) any employment as a self-employed earner (including examiners, etc. deemed to be so: see 8728) where the earner is not ordinarily employed in such employment or employments. In practice this is mainly taken to apply to those in an employed earner's employment who earn less than £800 per year from part-time self-employment but the limit has not been set by regulation, has remained unchanged since 1981–82 and as such is potentially open to challenge;

(4) employment for the purposes of any statutory election as a returning officer, etc. or any person employed by him;

(5) employment by visiting military forces, either as a member of those forces or as a civilian employee, except for civilians who are ordinarily resident (see 8760) in the UK; and

(6) employment as a member of any duly designated international headquarters or defence organisation, other than in the case of serving members of HM Forces or civilians ordinarily resident in the UK who are not members of the organisation's retirement scheme.

Law: *Social Security (Categorisation of Earners) Regulations* 1978 (SI 1978/1689)

8732 Personal service companies

In a bid to remove opportunities for the avoidance of Class 1 National Insurance contributions (NICs) by the use of intermediaries, such as service companies or partnerships, in circumstances where the worker would otherwise be an employee of the client, or the income would be the income from an office held by the worker, provisions were introduced that conferred wide ranging powers to make regulations to treat all money received by the intermediary in respect of a certain engagement, less certain deductions, as paid to the worker in a form subject to Class 1 NICs. The proposals, which are generally known as 'IR 35', came into force on 6 April 2000.

Broadly, the regulations provide that:

(1) where an individual ('the worker') personally performs, or has an obligation personally

to perform, services for the purposes of a business carried on by another person ('the client');

(2) the performance of those services by the workers is referable to arrangements involving a third party, rather than referable to a contract between the client and the worker; and

(3) the circumstances are such that, were the services to be performed by the worker under a contract between him and the client, he would be regarded as employed in the employed earner's employment by the client,

then the relevant payments and benefits are treated as earnings paid to the worker in respect of the employed earner's employment. These rules apply irrespective of whether the client is a person with whom the worker holds any office or employment.

The effect is that the worker is treated as being employed by the intermediary in the employed earner's employed employment. He is deemed to have received a payment of his 'attributable earnings' (as calculated in accordance with the regulations) from the intermediary on 5 April in the tax year concerned. The worker's attributable earnings are aggregated with any other earnings paid to or for the benefit of him or her by the intermediary in the year concerned. The amount of earnings-related contributions is determined on the aggregate amount according to normal rules. The intermediary is be treated for those purposes as the secondary contributor.

Regulations (SI 2003/2079) were brought into force with effect from 1 September 2003, which remove the requirement that a worker performs services for the purposes of a business, thereby extending the scope of the principal regulations (SI 2000/727) to all workers providing services through an intermediary.

Domestic workers

In his 2003 Budget, the Chancellor announced changes to the intermediate legislation affecting domestic workers, such as nannies or butlers, who provide services through an intermediary (usually a service company). The measure closes an avoidance device whereby domestic workers, who would otherwise be directly employed by the person to whom they provide their services, operate instead through an intermediary, such as a company. For income tax purposes, the changes took effect for income received in respect of services provided after 9 April 2003. The NIC changes apply to income received by the intermediary for services provided on or after 8 August 2003.

Law: *Welfare Reform and Pensions Act* 1999, s. 75; *Social Security Contributions and Benefits Act 1992 (Modification of Section 4A) Order* 2003 (SI 2003/1874); *Social Security Contributions (Intermediaries) Regulations* 2000 (SI 2000/727); *Welfare Reform and Pensions Act 1999 (Commencement No. 2) Order* 1999 (SI 1999/3420)

Source: Inland Revenue 2003 Budget press release – REV BN9

Website: www.hmrc.gov.uk/ir35/index.htm

SOCIAL SECURITY BENEFITS

8734   Types of social security benefit

Non-contributory benefits

National Insurance contributions (NICs) pay for only certain state benefits (see 8700). Many benefits are based on need or circumstantial conditions, with no link to past contributions paid. Instead they are based on some other link to the system, such as residence, and they are often subject to income limits or means testing. These non-contributory benefits are funded from general taxation and include:

- Attendance Allowance
- Back to Work Bonus
- Carer's Allowance (formerly Invalid Care Allowance)
- Child Benefit
- Child Tax Credit
- Christmas Bonus for pensioners
- Cold Weather Payments
- Community Care Grants
- Council Tax Benefit
- Disability Living Allowance
- Funeral Payment
- Guardian's Allowance
- Housing Benefit
- Income Support
- Industrial Injuries Benefits
- Jobseeker's Allowance (income-based)
- New Deal Payments
- Pension Credit
- Reduced Earnings Allowance
- Retirement Pension – Category D (paid to over-80s with inadequate contributory pensions)
- Severe Disablement Allowance
- Social Fund (grants, loans, payments)
- Vaccine Damage Payments
- War Pensions
- Winter Fuel payment and 80+ Annual Payment
- Working Tax Credit

A 'Category C' retirement pension is still on the statute book but now obsolete, as all beneficiaries retired before 5 July 1948.

Contributory benefits

The contributions paid by employees and their employers, the self-employed and voluntary contributors are used to pay for a series of short- and long-term benefits which are generally

National Insurance Contributions

payable as of right to anyone with a qualifying contribution record. However, a number of extra qualifying circumstantial conditions limit entitlements in some cases even for those with full records.

Contributions, and earnings subject to contributions, are recorded on HMRC's National Insurance Recording System, Mark 2 (NIRS2) computer each year. In some circumstances, contributions or earnings are credited to a contributor's record. The amounts for each year are converted into an 'earnings factor', which forms the basis of entitlement to the following contributory benefits:

(1)   Jobseeker's Allowance (contributions-based) (short-term);

(2)   Incapacity Benefit:

    (a)   short-term;
    (b)   long-term;

(3)   Maternity Allowance (a short-term benefit);

(4)   Bereavement Benefits (long-term);

(5)   Bereavement Payment (formerly Widow's Payment);

(6)   Widowed Parent's (formerly Mother's) Allowance;

(7)   Bereavement Allowance;

(8)   Widow's Pension (or pension to surviving civil partner);

(9)   Basic State Retirement Pension (a long-term benefit):

    (a)   Category A, paid by virtue of the claimant's own contributions, and subject to additions;
    (b)   Category B, paid by virtue of the contributions of a spouse or civil partner; and

(10) Child's Special Allowance (now obsolescent and paid only to existing claimants).

Note that contributions paid by employers (Class 1 secondary, Class 1A, Class 1B) and Class 4 contributions paid by the self-employed are irrelevant to benefit entitlements. Only Class 1 primary (main rate), Class 2 and Class 3 contributions count towards contribution records.

Law: EA 2002; SSCBA 1992, s. 20

Website: www.dwp.gov.uk/index.asp

8736 The link between contribution classes and benefits

National Insurance contributions (NICs) are payable by the individuals who (or whose dependants) are to benefit and by employers. There are currently six classes of contribution, though Class 1 is split between employees (Class 1 primary) and employers (Class 1 secondary). The type of contribution payable (and the benefit entitlement available) depends on whether the contributor is in employment or is self-employed, or is contributing voluntarily:

- Class 1 secondary contributions and Class 1A contributions are payable by employers and certain others paying earnings to employees. They carry no benefit entitlement and could justifiably be described as payroll taxes to fund social security expenditure;
- Class 1B contributions (see 9150) give no entitlement to benefit, though it is understood there are plans to protect the position of those who may fail to qualify for statutory sick pay or statutory maternity pay as a result of their payment; and
- Class 4 contributions are payable by self-employed individuals on their trading profits taxable under ITTOIA 2005. They also carry no benefit entitlement.

The link between contributions and contributory benefits is based entirely on the other classes of contribution paid by individuals:

- Class 1 employee (primary) contributions at varying appropriate levels and for appropriate periods, can qualify the contributor for all contributory benefits (unless the contributor is a married woman or widow who decided before 11 May 1977 to forgo future benefit entitlement by electing to pay a reduced rate of contribution) and, indirectly, for SSP and SMP. Incapacity benefit does not depend solely on contribution conditions being satisfied. Long-term incapacity benefit becomes payable when entitlement to sickness benefit, or short-term incapacity benefit expires, which themselves may derive from contributions of this class on the expiry of entitlement to SSP. Importantly, employees who pay Class 1 contributions on earnings between set limits automatically qualify for the earnings-related component of the state pension, known as SERPS (the state earnings-related pension scheme), unless they choose to make private provision for an earnings-related pension and contract out of SERPS. In return for paying lower contributions they receive only the basic state pension;
- Class 2 contributions can qualify the self-employed contributor for all contributory benefits except contribution-based jobseeker's allowance and SERPS pension (though the basic state pension is still available). Class 2 contributions are also irrelevant to entitlement to SSP and SMP, as self-employed contributors claim instead incapacity benefit and maternity allowance; and
- Class 3 contributions can be paid voluntarily by certain individuals to enable them and their dependants to qualify for the basic long-term benefits (category A and B pensions, widow's payment, widowed mother's allowance, widow's pension), but nothing else.

Contribution records

Contributory benefits are payable on the basis of the claimant having paid sufficient contributions in the relevant period, i.e. having a qualifying contribution record. For the long-term benefits, the claimant must have a qualifying contribution record for nine-tenths of his or her working life in order to obtain maximum entitlement. For short-term benefits, the period of qualification is limited to recent tax years.

The basic building blocks of the record are the contribution week and the lower earnings limit (LEL; see 9000). If an employed earner is paid earnings above the LEL in a week, he is liable to pay Class 1 contributions on those earnings and the week becomes a qualifying

National Insurance Contributions

week. Following the introduction, from April 2000, of the threshold below which no primary Class 1 contributions are payable, an employee's entitlement to contributory benefits is maintained in respect of earnings from the LEL to the primary threshold by means of notional contributions at a zero-rate. If a Class 2 or Class 3 contribution is paid in respect of a week, it becomes a qualifying week and the earner is, broadly, treated as having paid contributions on earnings equal to the LEL. Similarly, certain individuals who do not actually pay contributions may in appropriate circumstances be credited with contributions or earnings to protect their future benefit entitlements (e.g. an unemployed person will pay no contributions during the period of interruption of employment, so his contribution record is generally protected for pension purposes by a credit). Such credits are also equivalent to Class 2 or Class 3 contributions in that they are deemed to represent contributions paid on earnings at the LEL.

Law: SSCBA 1992, s. 21

8738 Earnings factors

It is necessary to have a common unit of measure because NICs are paid at a number of rates and on different bases. They must therefore be converted to some common factor for comparison with the requirements for benefit entitlement. The common factor is the earnings factor, expressed as an amount of notional earnings for a tax year.

Law: SSCBA 1992, s. 22; *Social Security Revaluation of Earnings Factors Order* 2010 (SI 2010/470)

8740 Recording of contributions

Contributions are recorded against the contributor's computer record, using his or her National Insurance number as the key. They are recorded for tax years, and as it is the practice to update contribution rates with effect from 6 April each year, all contributions paid in any one year are calculated on the same basis.

Benefit years

Benefits are payable on the basis of benefit years rather than tax years. The benefit year runs from the first Sunday in January in any calendar year and ends with the Saturday before the same Sunday in the following year. The contribution conditions for benefits claimed or due in any particular benefit year refer to past tax years rather than benefit years. This has sound practical grounds, since the processing of contributions paid inevitably takes time. There is therefore a period of around nine months between the end of the tax year and the start of the next benefit year in which contribution returns can be collected, collated and processed into contribution records.

Law: SSCBA 1992, s. 21(6)

EARNINGS

8750   Definition of 'earnings' for NICs

Liability for National Insurance contributions (NICs) rests on the existence of an earner, who contributes to the National Insurance Fund an amount which is determined, directly or indirectly, by reference to his earnings.

For National Insurance purposes, 'earnings' include any remuneration or profit derived from an employment, while 'employment' includes any trade, business, profession, office or vocation, subject to a proviso that regulations may make exceptions to this definition in appropriate circumstances; for discussion of the terms remuneration and profit, see 8754. While the term is in principle all-embracing, regulations made under the 1992 Act make numerous amendments to the definition in specified circumstances with the result that the rules for employed and self-employed earners are very different.

Law: SSCBA 1992, s. 3, 122

8752   Earnings from self-employment

Earnings of individuals who are self-employed are relevant to Class 2 and Class 4 contributions. Earnings for Class 2 are accounts profits whilst earnings for Class 4 correspond closely with taxable profits: they determine the amount (within given limits) to which the appropriate percentage rate is applied for Class 4 purposes and the availability of an exception from the flat-rate Class 2 contributions.

Law: SSCBA 1992, s. 3, 122

8754   Remuneration or profit?

Earnings on which National Insurance contributions (NICs) are payable are defined by reference to remuneration or profit (see 8750). There is, in National Insurance law, no further general definition of 'remuneration' or 'profit', which therefore take their ordinary meaning.

When seeking to establish earnings for National Insurance purposes, it is necessary to consider the rewards paid for services under a contract of employment. The meaning of the term 'remuneration' was considered in a 1974 employment law case concerning redundancy pay. Although not directly relevant to NIC, the comments of sir John Donaldson are of persuasive authority in a NIC context. In that case, 'remuneration' was held to include any wage or salary, but to exclude any benefit in kind or amount paid by someone other than the employer. Additionally, expenses paid to the employee should be considered, with any payment which was a profit to the employee rather than reimbursement of an expense being included as remuneration.

National Insurance Contributions

The income tax equivalent of earnings is emoluments, which include 'all salaries, fees, wages, perquisites and profits whatsoever' (see 274) and which must be from the employment (see 273) before they may be taxed under the charge on employment income provisions of ITEPA 2003. There is clearly much in common between the two terms, but only the term emoluments has been subject to detailed judicial scrutiny.

Cash emoluments are taxable under the charge on employment income provisions of ITEPA 2003 and subject to the PAYE system of deduction at source. The equivalent collection mechanism is imported into Class 1 National Insurance law. However, this clearly does not extend to non-cash rewards. Where income tax law provides for non-cash items to be subject to PAYE, the terms are set out in primary legislation.

There are National Insurance provisions which specifically bring into charge certain payments which might be thought not to be earnings on basic principles, together with numerous further provisions to exclude from the definition other payments which would otherwise be caught as remuneration or profit.

Law: *Social Security (Contributions) Regulations* 2001 (SI 2001/1004); *S & U Stores Ltd v Wilkes* [1974] ICR 645

8756   Dividends

Unless NIC law specifically provides otherwise, basic principles of law will apply to determine whether a payment represents earnings for contribution purposes. The question is whether the payment under consideration is derived from an employment. Dividend income is, of course, derived not from employment but from the ownership of shares in a company and as such is free of NIC liability.

If a company declares a dividend to director-shareholders which is illegal (e.g. because there are insufficient distributable profits) or outside the terms of its articles of association, it may be officially argued that the payment must be derived from the employment and is therefore earnings. The validity of this argument is questionable.

8758   Rents

Where a director owns property used by the company, it is possible for the company to pay him a commercial rent for the use of that property. The income is derived not from the office or employment but from the ownership of the asset that the company uses, so the rents are not earnings for NIC purposes. However, tax complications (e.g. loss of CGT retirement relief if rents have been drawn) must be borne in mind.

8760 Interest on directors' accounts NICs

A situation similar to that in relation to dividends (see 8756) occurs in respect of interest on current account balances. Because interest credited to a director on any balance standing to his credit in the company's books is derived from the lending of money rather than from the employment, such income is free of NIC liability.

8762 Calculation of earnings

Subject to exceptions outlined below, the amount of a person's earnings for Class 1 contribution purposes is to be calculated on the basis of his or her gross earnings from the employment or employments concerned. This is underlined in the official guidance, which devotes several pages to itemising for employers, whose responsibility it is to operate the Class 1 collection system, what is and is not included in 'gross pay', the term used in the guidance notes as a synonym for earnings. The term highlights the fact that employees' Class 1 contributions are, with only one exception (see 8800), collected at source from employees' pay by employers.

Furthermore, not all payments are automatically earnings for the purposes of NICs. Payments must be derived from the employment before they attract a Class 1 liability.

Unless contribution law dictates specifically how a particular type of payment is to be treated, it is necessary to examine the nature of the payment to an employee and ask whether it fits the criterion stated. Furthermore, it is important to note that the judicial definition (see 273) offers two alternatives, bringing into earnings not merely payments received by an employee in return for his acting as an employee, but also payments in return for his being an employee. While the first leg of this definition covers the common sense view of an employee being rewarded for services rendered or to be rendered, the second covers the less obvious position of employees who receive payments from their employer unrelated to the services they perform but which they would not have received had they not been employees.

Using the above principles, earnings will include the following items:

- wages, salaries, fees, overtime pay, bonuses, commission and so on;
- holiday pay;
- inducement payments (e.g. most 'golden hellos' or 'golden handcuffs');
- contractual maternity pay;
- statutory sick pay, statutory maternity pay, statutory paternity pay and statutory adoption pay.

For details of the treatment of specific payments that may be made to an employee, see 8780.

Law: *Social Security (Contributions) (Amendment No. 5) Regulations* 2006 (SI 2006/2829); *Social Security (Contributions) Regulations* 2001/1004 (SI 2001/1004), reg. 24; *Social*

National Insurance Contributions

Security (Contributions and Credits) (Miscellaneous Amendments) Regulations 1999 (SI 1999/568)

Source: Booklet CWG2, *Employer's further guide to PAYE and NICs*

8764 Timing of payment

Where in any tax week earnings are paid to or for the benefit of an earner in respect of any one employment of his which is employed earner's employment, a primary and secondary Class 1 contribution is payable (see 9000).

Payments made in advance

The most frequent problems with timing arise from payment in advance. The key factor to be considered is the unreserved entitlement to a payment. Where an employer takes on an employee on the basis that his salary will be paid monthly in arrears, but at the end of the first week lends the employee part of his first month's salary to tide him over until the first payroll run, no payment of earnings takes place, as the payment made is a loan. Until the employee has an unreserved entitlement to the first month's salary, the money in his hands is owed to the employer. Until it becomes his own money at the end of the month, it cannot be earnings for contribution purposes.

The position is, of course, the same in principle but quite different in effect if it is agreed between the employer and employee that salary will regularly be paid in advance: such advance payments are generally treated as normal pay.

8766 Apportionment of payments made for more than one earner

From 8 September 1998, payments made to or for the benefit of two or more earners may be apportioned, the aim being to strengthen provisions capturing vouchers (and certain payments into funded unapproved retirement benefit schemes (FURBS)).

Law: SSA 1998, s. 48

8768 Company directors

Special rules identify the earnings of company directors. Any payment made by a company to, or for the benefit of, any of its directors is treated as earnings if it is paid on account of or by way of an advance.

A company director is not usually entitled to remuneration until it has been voted to him by the members of the company. Such voting may, of course, take place in advance, or the director may be given a service contract which sets out a basis for his regular remuneration.

This would mean that any amounts paid to him under normal circumstances would indeed be earnings for contribution purposes. However, where a company director draws cash from his business without the benefit of an agreed service contract or the advance voting of fees, he will effectively take a loan, albeit technically unauthorised, until such time as the members vote his remuneration.

For these purposes, directors include shadow directors, though a person is not to be treated as such by reason only that the directors act on advice given by him in his professional capacity.

It should be noted that no Class 1 liability arises on overdrawn accounts unless payments which caused the account to become overdrawn were made in anticipation of earnings. A liability would still arise:

- where payments are made on which PAYE tax has been assessed;
- where an agreement between the employer and the employee is in force providing for the payments to be made in anticipation of remuneration becoming due; or
- where shareholders have agreed that the director can make withdrawals from the account in anticipation of the voting of fees or remuneration.

Source: CWG2, *Employer's further guide to PAYE and NICs*

8770 Settlement of pecuniary liability

Where an employee incurs a personal liability to a supplier of goods or services, his liability to that supplier is usually measured in terms of money. For National Insurance contributions (NIC) purposes, as with income tax (292), if the employer pays the amount due by the employee to the creditor, the employer is effectively doing no more than give the employee cash with which he settles his debt. Where an employer contracts with a provider of goods and services, there is no Class 1 NIC liability (although a Class 1A liability may arise from 6 April 2000). However, if the contract is between the employee and the provider, a Class 1 NIC liability arises if the payment is made direct to the provider or payment is made or reimbursed direct to the employee.

In a typical small family company, the directors may routinely settle personal bills with a company cheque and charge the amount in question to a current or loan account. This should not present any difficulty if the account is in credit (i.e. the director has previously lent amounts to the company and has not at that point withdrawn them), but a liability to Class 1 contributions may well arise if the account is, or by virtue of the payment becomes, overdrawn.

The correct identification of earnings is perhaps best seen from an example.

Example

Chris is a director of and majority shareholder in his family company, Driver Ltd. He votes himself fees at the annual general meeting of the company, but does not draw a regular salary, preferring instead to take cash from his current account with the company as and when he needs it. It is understood by all the other directors and shareholders that this is the normal practice. Whatever is outstanding at the time of the annual general meeting is cleared by the annual voting of fees. At 6 April 2010, the balance on his current account stands at £1,000 in his favour.

On 1 May 2010 he asks the cashier to give him £5,000 in cash for personal expenditure and instructs him to charge it to his director's current account.

The first £1,000 drawn is, of course, no more than a withdrawal of money invested in the company by Chris. He probably does not regard the balance on his account as an investment as such, but the fact remains that the last fee-voting resolution led to a large credit (after deduction of PAYE and NICs) to Chris's current account and he chose at the time not to draw the cash to which he was entitled.

The balance of the withdrawal on 1 May is clearly an advance on fees to be voted at the next annual general meeting, so the payment of £4,000 represents a payment of earnings for NIC purposes (see 8768). The cashier must therefore account for Class 1 contributions on this sum in accordance with the normal rules for company directors.

When Chris books his summer holiday, he gives the bill he has received to the cashier with the usual instruction to pay it and charge the amount to his current account. By this time, of course, his account is already overdrawn and the settlement of his personal pecuniary liability by the company simply increases the debit balance on his account. Once more, a payment of earnings has taken place which will lead to a Class 1 contribution liability.

Law: SSCBA 1992, s. 3(1), 6(1)

Source: CWG2, *Employer's further guide to PAYE and NICs*

8772   Waiver of earnings: NICs

The amount of a person's earnings are calculated on the basis of that person's gross earnings from the employment, unless specific provision is made to the contrary.

Hence, once earnings have been paid (i.e. actually paid by a transfer of cash or credited unconditionally to an account on which the director is free to draw), they remain earnings and any subsequent waiver or refund is not officially recognised. However, it is now fairly common for employees to make charitable donations via payroll giving schemes attracting income tax relief (see 904). However, there is no corresponding NIC relief. Consequently, the amount of the donation should be excluded from gross pay for PAYE purposes but not for NIC purposes.

However, as earnings do not arise until the earner becomes unconditionally entitled to them, if an employee agrees with his employer, *before* such unconditional entitlement arises, to waive any or all of his prospective earnings, it would seem that the creation of earnings liable to NIC liability is avoided.

Source: CWG2, *Employer's further guide to PAYE and NICs*

8780   Gross pay for NIC purposes

The following chart, based on the one that appears in CWG2, *Employer's further guide to PAYE and NICs*, indicates what should be included in gross pay for NIC purposes. It should be noted, however, where an item is not included in gross pay because it constitutes a payment in kind, although no Class 1 liability arises, from 6 April 2000 there may be a Class 1A liability (see further 9100ff.). Where the position is particularly complex, a cross-reference is given to more detailed information included in the following paragraphs.

Type of payment	Include in gross pay for NIC purposes?
Car/van fuel supplied for private motoring when the fuel is supplied using your credit card, or garage account or an agency card	No, if the conditions outlined below for credit cards, charge cards and so on are satisfied, but there may be Class 1A liability – see 9100ff.
Car parking fees for **business related journeys** paid or reimbursed to employees	No
Cars or vans made available for private use	No but there may be Class 1A liability, see 9100ff.
Childcare vouchers provided for the cost of childcare for children up to age 16	No
• up to £55 a week where the qualifying conditions are met	No
• over £55 a week where the qualifying conditions are met	Yes (excess over £55 per week)
• any amount not meeting the qualifying conditions	Yes
Christmas boxes in cash	Yes
Clothing or uniforms	
• clothing or uniforms provided by you	No but there may be a liability for Class 1A, see 9100ff.
• payments to employees for non-durable items such as tights or stockings	No but there may be a liability for Class 1A, see 9100ff.
• other payments to employees to purchase clothing or uniforms which can be worn at any time	Yes
• other payments to employees to purchase clothing or uniforms which can be worn only at work	No
Council tax on employee's living accommodation	

National Insurance Contributions

Type of payment	Include in gross pay for NIC purposes?
• employee provided with accommodation and the accommodation is within one of the categories where the value does not have to be included for tax purposes on form P9D or P11D	No
• all other circumstances	Yes
Credit card, charge cards and so on – employees use your card to purchase **goods or services bought on your behalf**	
• prior authority given by you to make the purchase **and** the employee explained in advance of the contract being made **and** the supplier accepted that the purchase was made on your behalf	No, but there may be a liability for Class 1A, see 9100ff.
• above condition not **fully** satisfied	Yes
Credit card, charge card and so on – employees use your card for expenditure **other than** goods or services bought on your behalf	
• payments relating to business expenses actually incurred	No
• readily convertible assets	See ¶8782
• any other payments not reimbursed to you	Yes at the date you decide not to seek reimbursement
Damages or similar payment made to an employee injured at work	
• there is a contractual liability to make it	Yes
• all other circumstances	No
Director's personal bills charged to loan account and so on	
• the transaction makes the account overdrawn (or more overdrawn) **and** it is normal practice for you to pay the director's earnings into the same account	Yes on the overdrawn (or additional overdrawn) amount
• all other circumstances	No
Director's remuneration, salary, bonuses, fees and so on, including any advance or anticipatory payments paid, voted or credited	Yes
Dividends from shares	No
Employee liability insurance – reimbursements of payments made by employees for insurance cover or uninsured liabilities (such as legal costs) for claims against the employee arising out of his or her work	No
Employment Retention and Advancement Scheme	No, with effect from 1 October 2003
Employment Tribunal Awards	See ¶8790
Expenses payments or reimbursements covered by a dispensation	See ¶8792

Type of payment	Include in gross pay for NIC purposes?

Eyecare vouchers to obtain:
• an eyesight test
• corrective appliance (for example, glasses or contact lenses) which the test shows are necessary where
   – the eyesight test is required under Health and Safety at Work Regulations and
   – the eyesight test and corrective appliance are available generally to employees
	No

Guarantee payments under the *Employment Rights Act* 1996	Yes
Holiday pay	See ¶8794
Honoraria	Yes
Incentive Awards	See ¶8802
Inducement payment such as 'golden hello' to recruit or retain employees	Yes
Insurance premiums for pension, annuities, or health cover and so on, **paid or reimbursed by you** where contract is between • you and the insurance provider	No, but there may be a liability for Class 1A, see ¶9100ff.
• employee and the insurance provider	Yes, see ¶8770
Loans	No, but there may be a liability for Class 1A, see ¶9100ff.
Loans written off	Yes at time of write off
Long service awards • Awards in the form of cash or cash vouchers • Other awards	Yes No, if they satisfy certain conditions
Lost time payments • payments made by a third party or by you on behalf of a third party • all other circumstances	No Yes
Maternity suspension payments made under the *Employment Rights Act* 1996 to an employee suspended from work on maternity grounds	Yes
Meal allowances and vouchers • cash payments for meals • vouchers redeemable for food and drink or a cash alternative • vouchers provided for food and drink provided on your business premises or any canteen where meals are generally provided for your staff • vouchers redeemable for meals only which cannot be transferred to another person, and	Yes Yes (see ¶8796) No

Type of payment	Include in gross pay for NIC purposes?
– are worth no more than 15p per working day	No
– are worth more than 15p per working day	Yes (on the excess amount – see ¶8796)
Medical suspension payments made under the *Employment Rights Act* 1996 to an employee suspended from work on medical grounds	Yes
Mobile phone vouchers to obtain one mobile phone for private use	No
Mortgage payments met directly by you for employees	
• mortgage provided by you or mortgage contract is between you and mortgagee	No, but there may be a liability for Class 1A, see ¶9100ff.
• mortgage contract is between employee and mortgagee	Yes
Parking fees at the normal place of employment paid for or reimbursed to employees	No
Payments in kind (but not readily convertible assets – see ¶8782)	
• which can be turned into cash **by surrender** such as Premium Bonds, and so on	Yes
• which can be turned into cash only **by sale** such as furniture, kitchen appliances, holidays and so on	No, but there may be a liability for Class 1A, see ¶9100ff.
Payments you make to an employee whilst he or she pursues a claim for **damages against a third party** for loss of earnings following an accident	
• employee must repay you, even if the claim for damages is unsuccessful	No
• employee not required to repay you	Yes, but if the employee later receives damages and repays you, NICs can be refunded
Pensions	No
Personal bills paid for goods and services supplied to employees, club memberships and so on	
• contract to supply goods and services is between you and the provider	No, but there may be a liability for Class 1A, see ¶9100ff.
• contract to supply goods and services is between the employee and the provider	
– payment made direct to the provider	Yes
– payment made or reimbursed direct to the employee	Yes
Personal incidental expenses (PIEs)	See ¶8800

Type of payment	Include in gross pay for NIC purposes?
Premiums for health cover, pensions, annuities and so on	See 'Insurance premiums' above
Prize money paid in cash to employees for competitions you run in connection with your business, which are not open to the public	Yes
Readily convertible assets: remuneration provided in non-cash form such as stocks and shares, gold bullion, commodities, fine wine and so on.	See ¶8782
Redundancy payments	See ¶8806
Relocation payments	See ¶8808
Retirement benefits schemes – payments you make into such schemes	
● Registered pension schemes	No
● Employer-financed schemes	No
Retirement benefits schemes – lump sum payments out of such schemes	
● Registered pension schemes	No
● Employer-financed retirement benefit schemes	No (provided certain conditions satisfied)
Round sum allowances	See ¶8810
Sickness, maternity and other absence from work payments	Yes
Statutory sick pay (SSP), statutory maternity pay (SMP), statutory adoption pay (SAP) and statutory paternity pay (SPP)	Yes
Stocks and shares	See ¶8782, ¶8784, ¶8786, ¶8788
Subscriptions or fees to professional bodies paid or reimbursed by you	No
Suggestions schemes awards to employees	No, if the award meets the criteria of Extra Statutory Concession A57. If you make awards in the form of benefits see ¶9100ff.
Telephone calls and/or rental cost Employer is the subscriber	No Class 1 liability, but there may be a liability for Class 1A NICs – see ¶9100ff.
Employee is the subscriber *but* **employer meets the cost of calls and/or rental**	
● telephone used exclusively for business use	No
● telephone used exclusively for private use	Yes
● telephone used for both business and private use	Rental: Yes – on the full amount of the rental. Calls: Yes – on the full amount of the cost of private calls. Any amount in respect of business calls, supported by appropriate evidence, can be excluded

National Insurance Contributions

Type of payment	Include in gross pay for NIC purposes?
Third party payments made to your employees	See ¶8796, ¶8802
Tips and service charges	See ¶8812
Training – payments for such things as course fees, books and so on	
• training is work related or is encouraged or required by you in connection with the employment	No
• all other circumstances	Yes
Transport vouchers, such as season tickets and so on, provided for	
• employees of a passenger transport undertaking under arrangements in operation on 25 March 1982 where the employee is earning less than £8,500 per year	No
• any other employee	Yes, see ¶8796
Travelling time payments	Yes
Vouchers which can be redeemed or exchanged for	
• both goods and cash or cash alone	Yes, see ¶8796
• goods alone (but not readily convertible assets)	Yes, see ¶8796
• use of sporting or recreational facilities	No
• readily convertible assets	See ¶8782
Wages, salaries, fees, overtime, bonuses, commission and so on	Yes

From 6 April 2010 there is no liability to NICs for expenses paid for or reimbursed to ministers of religion in respect of heating, lighting, cleaning and gardening in connection with living accommodation provided with the employment.

Law: *Social Security (Contributions) Regulations* 2001 (SI 2001/1004), reg. 24, 25; *Social Security (Contributions) (Amendment No. 2) Regulations* 2010 (SI 2010/188)

Source: Booklet CWG2, *Employer's further guide to PAYE and NICs*

Website: www.hmrc.gov.uk/leaflets/index.htm

8782 Readily convertible assets

Since 1 October 1998, payments in the form of readily convertible assets must be included in gross pay for NIC purposes.

A 'readily convertible asset' is one which:

- is capable of being sold on a recognised investment exchange or London Bullion market (e.g. stocks, shares and other financial instruments, gold bullion, other precious metals, etc.);
- is a right over a money debt (e.g. trade debts assigned by an employer to an employee);

- is subject to a fiscal warehousing regime, such as a bonded warehouse;
- gives rise to a right to enable an employee to obtain money (e.g. an interest in a trust which comes to an end shortly after being assigned to an employee, resulting in an automatic right to cash);
- subject to trading arrangements, either at the time that the asset is provided or that come into existence shortly afterwards as a result of an arrangement or understanding (e.g. jewellery that can be sold either at the time of its provision or shortly afterwards in consequence of an arrangement or understanding existing at the time the jewellery was provided);
- is already owned by the employee and whose value is enhanced by the employer (e.g. the payment by the employer of an additional premium to an employee's life assurance policy, thereby greatly increasing its value).

The value that is included in gross pay is the 'best estimate' at the time the payment is paid or treated as paid. The payment is added to other payments made in the relevant earnings period and NIC worked out on the total in the normal way. The NIC liability arises at the same time as income tax is due under PAYE.

Law: *R & C Commrs v Hyde Industrial Holdings Ltd* [2006] BTC 8,025; *EDI Services Ltd & Ors v R & C Commrs* (2006) Sp C 539

Source: Booklet CWG2, *Employer's further guide to PAYE and NICs*

Website: www.hmrc.gov.uk/leaflets/index.htm

8784   Share options

Since 6 April 1999 National Insurance has been payable by both employer and employee on the gains arising when share options granted after 5 April 1999 are exercised outside a HMRC approved scheme (or are cancelled or assigned) and where the shares or the options are readily convertible into cash. Before then, NICs were payable when share options were granted, but only if the options were granted at a discount and any charge was limited to the amount of this discount. The rules were changed because the charge at grant reflected neither the gain that the employee made when the option was exercised nor the fact that the option might not be exercised. The old rules were also deliberately used by some companies to pay large bonuses to directors and top-paid employees free of national insurance.

Legislation introduced by the *Child Support, Pensions and Social Security Act* 2000, and the *Finance Act* 2000, both of which received Royal Assent on 28 July 2000 and now contained within SSCBA 1992, Sch. 1, para. 3A, 3B, allows the employee to bear the employer's NIC on share option gains. Any employer's NIC paid by employees qualifies for relief against the share option. This may be achived in one of two ways:

- the employer and employee agree that the employee bears some or all of the secondary NIC, the legal liability remaining with the employer and the employer recovering the sum from the employee; or
- the employer and employee jointly elect for some or all of the secondary NIC liability to

National Insurance Contributions

be transferred to the employee, the employee assuming legal liability for NIC so transferred.

These changes however, continued to cause problems for some companies due to difficulties in predicting NIC liabilities arising on share options because gains are dependent upon the share price on the day that the option is exercised, assigned or released and the employer's liability is uncapped. Although the provisions enabled companies to enter into joint agreements with employees, so that the employee would pay the NIC liability arising, some companies felt that they were unable to make such agreements where the options were awarded before that flexibility was introduced on 19 May 2000. Consequently, a limited relief was introduced by the *Social Security Contributions (Share Options) Act* 2001, which allowed companies to settle the NIC liability arising on options granted between 6 April 1999 and 19 May 2000 (which remained unexercised on 8 November 2000).

The *National Insurance Contributions Act* 2006 came into force on 30 March 2006. Broadly, the Act contains measures which aim to ensure that all employers and employees pay the correct amount of tax and NICs but it also takes forward the announcement made on 2 December 2004 that where HMRC became aware of tax and NICs avoidance schemes, the Government would legislate to close them down, where necessary, from that date. The Act is not intended to have an effect on employers and employees who organise their affairs properly. In particular, genuine employee share schemes and share option plans will not be affected.

The Act provides the power to make regulations in respect of NICs on backdated anti-avoidance tax changes that take effect on or after 2 December 2004. These tax avoidance payments may be outside the scope of existing NICs legislation. The power will allow for NICs liability to be applied on these avoidance payments going back to 2 December 2004, if necessary.

The Act also allows for the extension of the avoidance disclosure rules that currently apply to tax to NICs. It will prevent the use of NIC elections and agreements over securities in avoidance schemes that have been targeted by any backdated NICs regulations so that employers cannot pass on the secondary NICs liability that they have tried to avoid to their employees.

HMRC have published a statement describing the elements that must be contained in an election before it can be approved. The statement warns that from 1 December 2008, where draft elections are presented for approval that include additional elements not required by the legislation nor essential for the implementation of the election, approval will not be given.

Law: *National Insurance Contributions Act* 2006; *Social Security Contributions (Share Options) Act* 2001; SSCBA 1992, Sch. 1, para. 3A, 3B; *Social Security Contributions (Share Options) Regulations* 2001 (SI 2001/1817)

Source: HMRC press release 10 November 2008; Inland Revenue press release 21 December 2000; Booklet CWG2, *Employer's further guide to PAYE and NICs*; *Tax Bulletin*, Special Edition (May 2005)

Website: www.hmrc.gov.uk/leaflets/index.htm

8786   Shares subject to forfeiture

Many companies offer their employees shares in the company they work for as part of their earnings. These shares often form part of a long-term investment plan (LTIP) and unconditional ownership of the shares is based on the employee satisfying relevant conditions (e.g. meeting performance targets).

With retrospective effect from 9 April 1998, if the shares are readily convertible assets and are not issued via a Revenue-approved scheme:

- there will normally be no National Insurance Contribution (NIC) liability when shares subject to forfeiture are first awarded; but
- there will be a liability based on the market value of the shares at the time when the risk of forfeiture is lifted, or, if sooner, when the shares are sold, less any consideration previously paid.

There will also be an NIC liability if the shares can still be subject to risk of forfeiture more than five years after they are first awarded. This is intended to stop NIC liability being postponed indefinitely but as most LTIPs run for five years or less, few employees will actually pay NICs when the shares are first awarded.

Law: *Social Security (Contributions) Regulations* 2001 (SI 2001/1004), reg. 22

Source: Booklet CWG2, *Employer's further guide to PAYE and NICs*

Website: www.hmrc.gov.uk/leaflets/index.htm

8788   Convertible shares

Convertible shares are shares of a certain class which can subsequently convert into another class. For example, some have different voting or dividend rights. An employer may grant one class of share, which can then be converted to a more valuable class.

With retrospective effect from 9 April 1998, if such shares are not issued via an approved scheme and are readily-convertible assets, a NIC liability will arise on the gain from the conversion. Generally, the gain is the market value of the converted share less any consideration previously paid, and any NICs paid when the shares were first awarded.

These changes generally mirror tax changes introduced in 1998 (see 327) and have the effect that the amount on which NICs are due is the same as the amount on which tax is due.

National Insurance Contributions

Employees may be entitled to income tax relief where they agree to meet some or all of their employer's secondary National Insurance liability arising from restricted or convertible employment-related securities (see 324).

Law: FA 2004, s. 85 and Sch. 16; *Social Security (Contributions) Regulations* 2001 (SI 2001/1004)

Source: CWG2, *Employer's further guide to PAYE and NICs*

Website: www.hmrc.gov.uk/leaflets/index.htm

8790 Employment tribunal awards

Where an NIC liability arises in respect of protective awards, an order for re-instatement or re-engagement or an order for continuation of employment required by an employment tribunal, the NIC liability should be based on the gross amount of the award, not the net amount payable.

If the tribunal decides that an employee was unfairly dismissed and the employer is ordered to re-employ the employee and pay arrears of pay, the award is liable to NIC. For NIC purposes, the payment of arrears is treated separately from other payments made at the same time. Where payment is made in a lump sum, the earnings period is the period covered by the award. If payment is made in instalments, the instalments must be added together and the NIC liability computed on the total amount. Again, the earnings period is the period of the award.

Where an employment tribunal orders that employment continues while a complaint of unfair dismissal is dealt with, the award attracts NIC. The earnings period is the period for which each payment which must be made under the order relates, or a week, if longer.

The tribunal may order the employer to pay wages for a certain time if it decides that the employer has broken some rules when making the employee redundant. This is known as a protective award, and is liable to NICs. Such payments are treated separately from other payments. The earnings period is the longer of the protected period, the part of the protected period to which the payment relates or a week.

Source: CWG2, *Employer's further guide to PAYE and NICs*

Website: www.hmrc.gov.uk/leaflets/index.htm

8792 Payments or expenses covered by a dispensation

A dispensation is a notice sent by the inspector of taxes authorising the employer not to report on forms P11D the expenses and benefits specifically covered by the dispensation. Provided that the conditions under which the dispensation was granted are still valid, NICO accepts a dispensation as evidence that the payments which it covers are expenses incurred in carrying out employment and are not to be included in gross pay for NIC purposes.

Source: CWG2, *Employer's further guide to PAYE and NICs*

Website: www.hmrc.gov.uk/leaflets/index.htm

8794 Holiday pay

From 30 October 2007, the provision which allowed employers to pay employees' holiday pay without having to pay NICs was withdrawn. However, the construction sector will be allowed a further five years before the exemption is withdrawn completely.

Source: CWG2, *Employer's further guide to PAYE and NICs*

Website: www.hmrc.gov.uk/leaflets/index.htm

8796 Non-cash vouchers

Since April 1999, the computation of an employed earner's earnings for Class 1 NIC purposes includes payment made by non-cash vouchers, unless the vouchers are of a type specifically excluded by the legislation. The value of the voucher is the cost to the employer of providing that voucher.

Exemptions

The following types of vouchers are specifically exempt:

- transport vouchers provided for the employee of a passenger transport undertaking under arrangements in operation on 25 March 1982 where the employee is earning less than £8,500 a year;
- vouchers for leave travel facilities for members of the armed forces;
- vouchers for sporting and recreational facilities (subject to the same conditions applying for income tax exemption);
- vouchers for long service awards, provided that the cost of providing the voucher does not exceed £50 for each year of service and there has been no similar award in the previous ten years;
- vouchers for social functions organised for employees, provided that the cost of providing vouchers does not exceed £150 per head and the function is open to employees generally;
- vouchers for travel between home and work provided to a person with a severe and permanent disability who is unable to travel on public transport;
- childcare vouchers;
- from 6 April 2006, employees may receive up to £55 a week (£50 per week between 6 April 2005 and 5 April 2006) of childcare, tax and National Insurance free, where their

National Insurance Contributions

1,425

employers contract with an approved childcarer or provide childcare vouchers for the purpose of paying an approved childcarer;

- meal vouchers for meals provided on the employer's premises or in a canteen where meals are provided for staff generally;
- luncheon vouchers to a maximum of 15 pence per day and £1.05 per week;
- a voucher provided by a donor who is not the employer and is unconnected with allowing the employee to obtain goods, provided that the total of this and other vouchers provided by the donor does not exceed £150 per year and the voucher is not given in recognition of past or future services;
- from 6 April 2000, the provision of a non-cash voucher in respect of the private use of a car where such provision attracts a Class 1A liability;
- from 14 August 2006, non-cash vouchers for mobile phones;
- from 14 August 2006, non-cash vouchers for eye tests and also special corrective appliances such as glasses; and
- non-cash vouchers that can be used to obtain health screening or a medical check-up.

Voucher provided by third parties

From 6 April 2000, non-cash vouchers provided by a third party are removed from the Class 1 charge and brought within the scope of Class 1A. During the tax year 1999–2000, non-cash vouchers provided by a third party attracted a Class 1 liability.

Non-cash vouchers provided by employers remain within the scope of Class 1.

Law: FA 2004, s. 78 and Sch. 13; *Social Security (Contributions) (Amendment No. 6) Regulations* 2007 (SI 2007/2091); *Social Security (Contributions) Regulations* 2001 (SI 2001/1004), reg. 24, 25, Sch. 3, Pt. V

Source: CWG2, *Employer's further guide to PAYE and NICs*

Website: www.hmrc.gov.uk/leaflets/index.htm

8798 Retirement benefit schemes

No NIC liability arises in respect of an employer's contribution to a HMRC-registered retirement benefit scheme. Generally speaking, no NIC liability arises if there is no income tax liability.

However, contributions to a funded unapproved retirement benefits scheme (FURBS) attract NIC. Where there is a separate trust for each employee, the full amount paid into the FURBS on behalf of the employee must be included in his or her gross pay for NIC purposes.

In the event that there is a single trust fund, but each employee has a distinct and separate benefit share, the amount paid to secure the employee's separate benefit share should be included in his or her gross pay.

However, if there is a single trust fund and at the time payments into the fund are made, the trustees have no indication of the benefit to be received by each employee, the amount of the payment must be apportioned equally between the employees who are members of the scheme, the sum apportioned in this way being included in each employee's gross pay for NIC purposes.

Law: SSA 1998, s. 48; SSCBA 1992, s. 3(1), (2A), 6(1); *Social Security (Contributions) Regulations* 2001 (SI 2001/1004), reg. 25

Source: CWG2, *Employer's further guide to PAYE and NICs*

Website: www.hmrc.gov.uk/leaflets/index.htm

8800 Personal incidental expenses

No Class 1 NIC liability arises where an employer pays for personal incidental expenses relating to a qualifying absence up to a maximum of £5 per night for stays within the UK and £10 per night for overnight stays outside of the UK. The NIC exemption mirrors that available for income tax purposes. Sums paid in excess of the tax-free limits must be included in gross pay.

Source: Booklet 480, *Expenses and benefits, a tax guide*, app. 8

Website: www.hmrc.gov.uk/leaflets/index.htm

8802 Prize incentive schemes

A prize incentive scheme is one where employees receive prizes or awards from either the employer or a third party. The awards may be made in cash or may be in the form of holidays, goods, voucher's, etc.

The extent to which an NIC liability exist depends on the nature of the award (see 8780). However, where the award is in a non-cash form, it should be noted that although a Class 1 liability may not arise, from 6 April 2000 there may be a liability to Class 1A (see 9100ff.).

Where the award is made by way of a non-cash voucher, the rules described at 8796 are in point.

Source: CWG2, *Employer's further guide to PAYE and NICs*

Website: www.hmrc.gov.uk/leaflets/index.htm

National Insurance Contributions

8806   Redundancy payments

No liability arises in respect of redundancy payments. The regulation does not specify that it covers only statutory redundancy pay. Since redundancy payments are really little more than compensation for the loss of rights in the employment, it would seem that any amount paid in excess of the statutory entitlement would also fall to be excluded from earnings. Before a payment is officially accepted as a redundancy payment, the following conditions must be met:

- the employee's contract has been terminated;
- the termination has occurred because of redundancy; and
- the payment is not being made for any reason other than redundancy.

For the redundancy to be officially regarded as a genuine redundancy, it must have arisen either because the employer ceased, or intends to cease, carrying on the business for the purpose of which, or the place in which, the employee was employed, or the requirements of the business have changed such that the employee's job is no longer needed.

Source: CWG2, *Employer's further guide to PAYE and NICs*

Website: www.hmrc.gov.uk/leaflets/index.htm

8808   Relocation payments

Changes were made from 6 April 1998 to the NIC treatment of the payment of relocation expenses and allowances to or for employees who have to move residence as a result of being relocated in the UK. Before that date NICs were not collected on relocation allowances, but now may be if they do not qualify for income tax relief (see 298).

Employee starts work at new location on or after 6 April 1998

In connection with employees who start work at a new location after 5 April 1998, all relocation allowances paid which qualify for income tax relief are excluded from gross pay, even if they exceed the £8,000 cap for tax. For NIC purposes there is no time limit within which the payment of qualifying allowances must start being paid.

Council tax

Where an employer pays an employee's council tax (e.g. because his old home stands empty for some time after he has relocated), this has traditionally been accepted as a business expense, though official guidance simply enjoins employers to seek advice on the Employer's Helpline (tel: 0345 143 143).

Relocation allowances taxed through PAYE settlement agreements

Relocation allowances which are taxed through PAYE settlement agreements (see 2750) continue to be excluded from NIC liability for 1998–99, as thereafter the NIC treatment of items included in such agreements has been aligned with the tax treatment (see 9150).

Source: CWG2, *Employer's further guide to PAYE and NICs*

Website: www.hmrc.gov.uk/leaflets/index.htm

8810   Round sum allowances

An employer who pays a round sum allowance to an employee and who can identify specific and distinct business expenses can exclude these from gross pay for NIC purposes. If the employer cannot identify the business expense, the whole allowance is included in gross pay, regardless of whether an expense is actually incurred.

Law: *Social Security (Contributions) Regulations* 1979 (SI 2001/1004), reg. 25

Source: CWG2, *Employer's further guide to PAYE and NICs*

Website: www.hmrc.gov.uk/leaflets/index.htm

8812   Tips and service charges

The NIC position depends on the arrangements under which payments in respect of tips and service charges are made.

Tips and gratuities

The following flowchart taken from the *Employer's further guide to PAYE and NICs* (CWG2) summarises the NIC position as regards tips and gratuities.

National Insurance Contributions

1,429

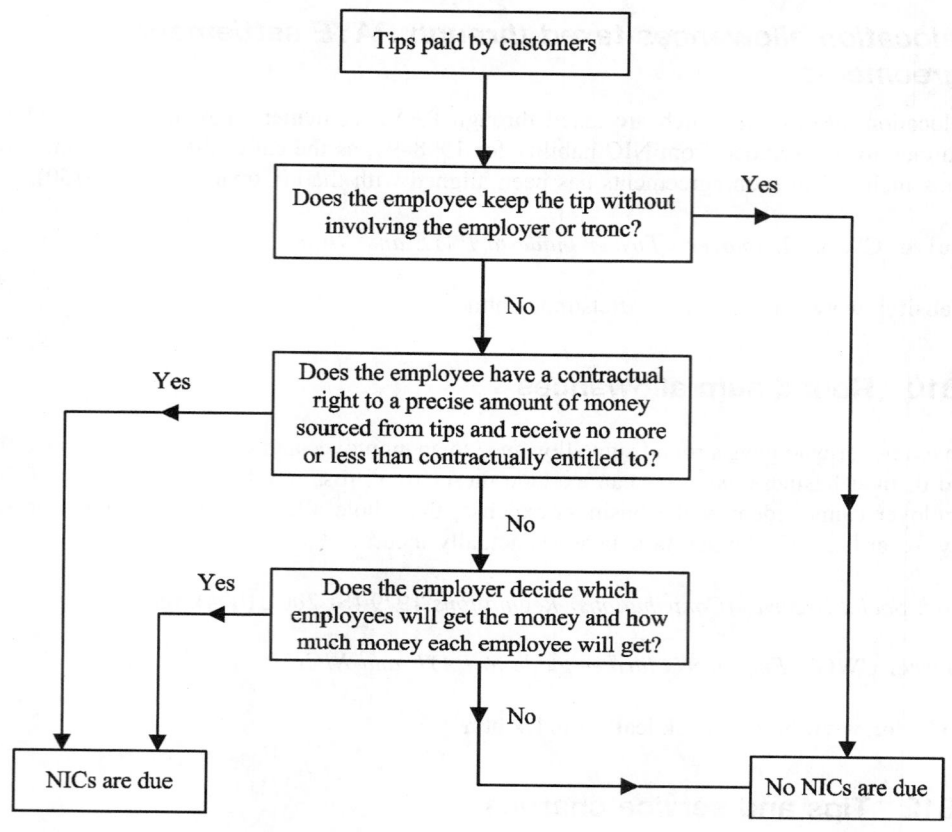

Service charges

For NIC purposes, a service charge is any sum that a customer is required by management to pay for services. Where service charges are levied and the money is paid out to the employees, a Class 1 NIC liability arises, irrespective of who shares out the money. Payments in respect of service charges should be included in gross pay for NIC purposes.

Troncs

A tronc is a special arrangement used to pool and distribute tips. It is usually run by one of the employees referred to as a troncmaster and is generally run independently of the employer's influence.

HMRC Booklet E24: *Tips, Gratuities, Service Charges and Troncs* provides guidance for employers and troncmasters in the catering and service industries. It covers the treatment of tips and service charges for income tax, NICs, National Minimum Wage (NMW) and VAT purposes. The booklet was revised in February 2005 to clarify some aspects of the guidance but following legal advice HMRC found it necessary to withdraw that edition. The February 2005 Booklet E24 advised that where payments of gratuities form part of contractual pay or are used to meet obligations under NMW legislation, they are liable for NICs and fall outside the NICs disregard for gratuities even if they are allocated to employees by a tronc run independently of the employer. HMRC, having decided to accept the further legal advice referred to above, have, accordingly, decided that the E24 had to be changed.

Payments of tips to the employee are liable for NICs if the employer makes the payment directly, or indirectly to the employee from sums previously paid to him; or allocates the tips directly or indirectly to his employees. Liability for NICs will always depend on the specific arrangements regarding the distribution of tips that are operated by individual employers. As regards NMW, provided the employer is not making the payment directly or indirectly to the employee from sums previously paid to him, or allocating the tips directly or indirectly to his employees, the tips are not liable for NICs. HMRC guidance advises that if the contract of employment indicates that the employee will be able to participate in the tronc, any payments made by the tronc are liable for NICs because they are contractual payments and therefore not gratuitous. HMRC now accept that these sorts of payments also fall to be disregarded from earnings and so are not liable for Class 1 NICs to the extent that the employer is not allocating, directly or indirectly, the tips.

Source: HMRC *Tax Bulletin*, Issue 82, April 2006; CWG2, *Employer's further guide to PAYE and NICs*; E24: *Tips, Gratuities, Service Charges and Troncs*

Website: www.hmrc.gov.uk/leaflets/index.htm

8814   Travel and subsistence

The changes to the income tax rules on employee travel and subsistence which apply from 6 April 1998 (see 1994) are also applicable to NICs from the same date. Broadly, in relation to business journeys made after 5 April 1998, reasonable travel and subsistence allowances paid to employees are excluded from 'earnings' attracting NICs.

Site-based employees

Before 6 April 1998, amounts paid by employers towards the costs of travel and/or subsistence of employees with no permanent workplace who worked for a short period at one place before moving on to another, were treated as 'earnings' attracting NICs. From that date reasonable costs are excluded from gross pay.

Triangular travel

Where an employee with a normal, permanent place of work travels directly from his home to another temporary place of work, after 5 April 1998 reasonable travel and subsistence expenses paid by the employer can be excluded in calculating gross pay for NIC purposes. Previously, the amount normally excluded from gross pay was the lesser of:

- the cost of travelling from the normal, permanent place of work to the temporary workplace; or
- the actual amounts of travelling costs incurred.

National Insurance Contributions

Home-to-work travel

The basic rule is that any reimbursement by an employer of home-to-work travel expenses to an employee is a payment of earnings for Class 1 purposes, though the rule is qualified in a number of respects.

Unexpected call-outs

If an employee is recalled to work unexpectedly (e.g. in the evening) reimbursement of the travelling expenses incurred is only a payment of earnings if the employee's conditions of service or employment require him to be on call.

Disabled employees

If the reimbursed employee is a disabled employee or trainee within the terms of the *Disabled Persons (Employment) Act* 1944, s. 15, or is a severely disabled person who cannot use public transport, travelling costs are NIC-free.

Temporary postings away from a permanent workplace

If an employee is temporarily sent to work somewhere other than his usual place of work for a period expected from the outset to be 24 months or less (12 months or less before 6 April 1998), the employer may pay travelling expenses free of contribution liability. If the absence lasts longer than 24 months, contributions should be paid once payments have been made for more than two years. If the posting is expected from the outset to last more than two years, all payments are liable to contributions from the start.

Employer contracts for the transport to be provided

If the employer contracts for the transport to be provided, the payment-in-kind rules exclude the payments made from earnings. This applies equally to, for example, season ticket purchases. However, from 6 April 2000, a Class 1A liability may arise (see 9100ff.).

Payments to employees travelling abroad

Where employers pay the travelling expenses of employees travelling between the UK and an overseas employment, or mariners who work outside UK territorial waters, the payments may be excluded from earnings if those expenses are not taxable under the charge on employment income provisions of ITEPA 2003.

Armed forces operational allowance

From 1 April 2006 a non-taxable operational bonus may be paid to eligible service personnel deployed to specified operational locations. From 14 November 2006 regulations ensure that the operational allowance can also be paid to service personnel free of Class 1 NICs.

Late-night transport home

Late-night taxi, etc. fares home which are reimbursed rather than paid direct to the taxi company may be excluded from earnings (see further 1994).

Disruption of public transport

If public transport is disrupted by a strike or other industrial action, and employers reimburse employees with the cost of taxi or other fares or overnight accommodation near the place of work, such reimbursements are excluded from earnings.

Allowances for carrying passengers and equipment

Allowances paid to cover the additional expense of carrying passengers and/or equipment specifically related to the employment are excluded from gross pay.

Car parking costs and fines

Car parking costs may be excluded from earnings either entirely, if the employer contracts directly with the provider of the parking space, or at least in part if the employer reimburses parking fees incurred for business purposes. A record should be kept of individual items of expenditure. Parking fines paid for employees are stated specifically to constitute earnings to be included in gross pay.

Employers paying insurance

Where road fund licence, insurance premium, car servicing and AA/RAC, etc. membership are paid directly by the employer in respect of a vehicle which he owns, the payment-in-kind rule would normally operate to exclude payments from earnings for Class 1 purposes (although from 6 April 2000, a Class 1A liability may arise). However, where the employer pays for these items in respect of the employee's own vehicle, the payments for these items must be included in the gross pay.

Law: *Social Security (Contributions) (Amendment No. 6) Regulations* 2006 (SI 2006/2924); *Social Security (Contributions) Regulations* 2001 (SI 2001/1004), Sch. 3

Source: Booklet 490, *Employee travel – a tax and NICs guide for employers*; CWG2, *Employer's further guide to PAYE and NICs*

Website: www.hmrc.gov.uk/leaflets/index.htm

8816   Pay in lieu of notice or remuneration

Pay in lieu of notice (PILON) and pay in lieu of remuneration (PILOR) are compensation payments made to employees whose contracts are terminated (i.e. breached) early or without notice, which covers three of the categories mentioned in the official guidance. Golden handshakes, etc. are no more than colloquial terms applied to any mixture of payments covering the termination of an employment, including redundancy, compensation and ex gratia elements. Since they derive from the termination of the employment rather than from the employee's acting as or being an employee, they could in principle be outside the definition of earnings. However, some contracts of employment make specific provision for such payments to be made. Where it is known from the commencement of an employment

National Insurance Contributions

relationship that compensation will be paid to the employee in the event of breach by the employer, the contingent right to such compensation may form part of the consideration given by the employer as his half of the employment bargain. It is therefore quite clearly a payment of earnings when made.

Law: *Hochstrasser v Mayes* [1960] AC 376; *Du Cross v Ryall (HMIT)* (1935) 19 TC 444; *Dale v De Soissons* (1950) 32 TC 126; *Delaney v Staples* [1992] 1 AC 687

Source: CWG2, *Employer's further guide to PAYE and NICs*

Website: www.hmrc.gov.uk/leaflets/index.htm

CLASS 1 CONTRIBUTIONS

CLASS 1: INTRODUCTION AND RATES

9000   Nature of Class 1

Class 1 contributions are earnings-related and based on an employed earner's employment (see 8712). They are payable in two parts:

(1)   *primary* contributions, payable by employed earners; and

(2)   *secondary* contributions, payable by the employers of employed earners or, in certain circumstances, other persons paying earnings.

The structure of Class 1 National Insurance was radically reformed from April 1999, with the introduction of a secondary earnings threshold, aligned to the personal allowance for tax purposes, below which no secondary contributions are payable. This was followed in April 2000 with the introduction of a primary threshold, which is aligned with the personal allowance from 2001. The 2008–09 year was, however, an exception. The personal allowance was originally announced as £5,435, the same as the primary threshold. However, in a move to compensate for the abolition of the ten per cent income tax rate, the Chancellor subsequently raised the personal allowance for 2008–09 to £6,035.

A primary Class 1 liability arises where in any tax week earnings are paid to or for the benefit of an earner in respect of any one employment of his which is employed earner's employment, and:

- he is over the age of 16; and
- the amount paid exceeds the primary threshold (£110 per week in 2009–10 and 2010–11) for Class 1 contributions (or the prescribed equivalent in the case of earners paid otherwise than weekly).

A secondary Class 1 contribution is payable if the amount paid exceeds the secondary threshold.

The primary threshold was introduced from 6 April 2000. Previously, a liability to primary Class 1 contributions arose if earning equalled or exceeded the lower earnings limit.

The secondary earnings threshold was introduced from 6 April 1999. Prior to this date, a secondary liability arose if earnings equalled or exceeded the lower earnings threshold.

For a full table of rates and limits, see 110.

The earnings on which contributions are payable are calculated or estimated in accordance with regulations, some of which provide for particular types of payment to be excluded from earnings in calculating liabilities (see 8750ff.).

The NIC enforcement procedure is more draconian and less sophisticated than the income tax system. If a 'back duty' investigation starts there is no time-limit but liabilities may be covered by the *Limitation Act* 1980 and the *Prescription and Limitation (Scotland) Act* 1973.

Law: SSCBA 1992, s. 1(2), 5(1), 6(1); *Social Security (Contributions) (Amendment) Regulations* 2010 (SI 2010/834); *Social Security (Contributions) Regulations* 2001 (SI 2001/1004), reg. 11

Source: CA 01, *National Insurance contributions for employees*

Website: www.hmrc.gov.uk/leaflets/nic.htm

9002   Primary (employee) Class 1 rate

From 6 April 2003, primary contributions at the rate of 11 per cent are payable on earnings between the primary threshold and the upper earnings limit (UEL). A national zero-rate of contribution is payable on earnings that equal or exceed the lower earnings limit (LEL) but that do not reach the primary threshold. This is to preserve benefit entitlement for employees earning in excess of the LEL.

Employees contracting out of SERPS effectively pay a lower primary rate as a result of the contracting-out rebate (see 9006).

From 6 April 2003, an additional one per cent Class 1 NIC contribution was introduced on earnings above the upper earnings limit. The NIC system has historically worked on annual maximum amounts so that employees did not pay more than the overall contribution limit based on the UEL. The legislation introduced in February 2003 mimics this principle, but allows for a charge of one per cent on all earnings, without limit. Maximum NICs payable annually are therefore calculated with respect to a certain amount of earnings rather than an absolute maximum.

National Insurance Contributions

> **Example**
>
> With bonuses and commissions, Susan is paid £1,000 in a tax week. In 2010–11 she pays £82.30 ((11% × (£844 – £110))+(1% × (£1,000 – £844)) and her employer pays £113.92 (12.8% × (£1,000 – £110)).

For a table of Class 1 rates, see 110.

Law: *National Insurance Contributions Act* 2002, s. 1; *Welfare Reform and Pensions Act* 1999, s. 73 and Sch. 9, para. 4; SSCBA 1992, s. 8(1), (2); *Social Security (Contributions) (Amendment) Regulations* 2003 (SI 2003/193); *Social Security Contributions (Notional Payment of Primary Class 1 Contribution) Regulations* 2000 (SI 2000/747)

Source: Treasury press release, 9 March 1999

Website: www.hmrc.gov.uk/leaflets/nic.htm

9004 Secondary (employer) Class 1 rate

The starting point for employer (secondary) Class 1 NICs is the secondary threshold which is aligned with the personal allowance for income tax. Since 6 April 1999, employers of employees whose weekly earnings do not exceed the current 'earnings threshold' pay no (secondary) Class 1 NICs. Above that threshold, from 6 April 2003 they pay NICs at 12.8 per cent (if the employee is not contracted out). There is no upper earnings limit for secondary Class 1 purposes.

For tables of secondary rates, see 110.

Law: *Social Security (Contributions) (Amendment) Regulations* 2010 (SI 2010/834); *National Insurance Contributions Act* 2002, s. 2; SSCBA 1992, s. 9

Source: Treasury press release, 9 March 1999

Website: www.hmrc.gov.uk/leaflets/nic.htm

9006 Contracting-out

A person who contributes at the standard rate to the National Insurance scheme will eventually (assuming certain conditions are met) receive from the state both a basic and an additional pension. Class 1 contributions (including 'notional' contributions payable from 6 April 2000 (see 9002)) on earnings at the lower earnings limit (LEL) buy the right to the basic pension and all other contributory benefits, while contributions on earnings above the LEL and below the upper earnings limit (UEL) (known as band earnings) buy the additional pension, also known as SERPS (the state earnings-related pension scheme).

However, it is possible for an individual to contract out of SERPS. He may instead join a registered occupational pension scheme that will provide the equivalent of the SERPS pension on retirement, or he may take out an appropriate personal pension policy with a life assurance company to provide similar benefits. Occupational pension schemes may be either final salary schemes (i.e. the emerging pension is based on earnings at or near the time of retirement, also known as a defined benefit scheme) or money purchase schemes (i.e. the emerging pension is based on the value of the accumulated fund at retirement, also known as defined contribution schemes).

If a person is contracted out of the state pension scheme he will receive only a basic pension from the state but will receive an additional pension from the private scheme. Because the state is thus relieved of the responsibility of funding the additional pension, the Class 1 contribution rates on band earnings are reduced.

The contracted-out rebate

The rates so reduced are known as the contracted-out rates and the reduction is known as the contracted-out rebate. It is accounted for in one of two ways. In occupational schemes, both employer and employee are allowed to deduct the rebate from the contributions paid to HMRC each month, thus enabling them to pay the amount saved directly into the occupational scheme. Holders of personal pensions and their employers continue to pay the full not contracted-out rate of contribution, receiving the rebate directly into their policy by means of a payment from the National Insurance Contributions Office (see 8700) once year-end returns have been processed.

The rebate is 1.6 per cent for employees for both COSR (salary related) and COMP (money purchase) schemes. As regards employers, the rebate is 3.7 per cent (3.5 per cent prior to 2007–08) for COSR schemes and 1.4 per cent (one per cent prior to 2007–08) plus an age-related rebate for COMP schemes. The age-related rebate, introduced from April 1997, ranges from 2.2 per cent at age 15 to nine per cent at age 63; the appropriate age-related percentage is applied to the part of earnings exceeding the lower earnings limit but not the upper earnings limit.

For a table of rates, see 110.

The rebate applies only to band earnings, since contributions on earnings up to the LEL count towards only the basic state retirement pension. Employers' contributions on earnings below the LEL and above the UEL are therefore due at the full rate.

Following the changes introduced from 6 April 1999, employers pay secondary contributions only on the earnings above the secondary (or employer's) threshold (see 9004). However, the NI rebate is still available in respect of all earnings between the lower earnings limit and the upper earnings limit, including those between the lower earnings limit and the secondary threshold on which no employer's NICs are payable. Since April 1999, employers operating contracted-out schemes have been able to reduce their overall NIC liability to reflect the rebate applicable to the employer's contributions on earnings above the lower earnings limit and up to and including the secondary threshold.

National Insurance Contributions

The introduction of the primary threshold from 6 April 2000 (see 9002) introduces a further complication. As noted above, from April, employees will not pay primary Class 1 contributions until their earnings reach the primary threshold. However, the employee's NI rebate remains payable in respect of earnings between the lower earnings limit and the upper earnings limit, including those above the lower earnings limit and up to an including the primary threshold. In the first instance, the rebate reduces total NICs payable by the employee. However, if the NIC payable by the employee is reduced to nil, the excess rebate is available for the employer to offset against his overall NIC bill. This is best illustrated by the following examples.

Example 1

From April 2010, Rupert earns £117 per week. He has contracted out of SERPS and is a member of his employer's COSR scheme. Rupert pays no primary contributions on earnings below £110 per week. On earnings between £110 and £117 he pays at the contracted-out rate of 9.4 per cent, i.e. 56 pence per week (£6 × 9.4%). However, this is reduced by the rebate payable on earnings payable between the lower earnings limit and the primary threshold of 24 pence (£15 × 1.6%). Thus Rupert's weekly NIC contributions are £0.32.

Example 2

Zak earns £107 per week from April 2010. He is a member of his employer's COSR scheme. As his earnings are below the primary threshold, Zak pays no primary NIC contributions. However, the NI rebate is available for earnings above the lower earnings limit (£97 for 2010–11) at Zak's actual earnings of £107 per week, amounting to 16 pence per week (£10 × 1.6%). As Zak's contributions are nil, this is available to reduce his employer's overall NIC bill.

Law: PSA 1993, s. 41; *Social Security (Reduced Rates of Class 1 Contributions, Rebates and Minimum Contributions) Order* 2006 (SI 2006/1009)

EARNINGS PERIODS FOR CLASS 1

9016   Earnings period basis

An 'earnings period' is a period to which earnings paid to or for the benefit of an employed earner are deemed to relate, irrespective of the period over which they were earned. Class 1 liability is calculated on the basis of the earnings paid in the earnings period and the limits applicable to that earnings period. No person may have more than one earnings period in respect of a single employment.

Employees paid at regular intervals

The majority of employees are paid a wage or salary at regular intervals of a week or a month. Where only a single regular payment pattern exists, except in the case of company directors in respect of whom special rules apply (see 9026), the earnings period equates with the pay interval, provided the interval is seven days or more (i.e. an employee who receives a weekly wage will have a weekly earnings period). The regular intervals need not be exactly equal, so payment on the last working day of each calendar month will satisfy this test, despite the fact that some months contain five weeks.

Where an employee (again, other than a company director) has more than one regular pay interval, special rules apply to identify the single earnings period on which liability is based. The earnings period is the *shorter* or *shortest* of those intervals, unless that interval is less than seven days. An employee in receipt of monthly salary, quarterly commission and annual bonus would therefore normally have a monthly earnings period, unless a written direction to the contrary is made by the National Insurance Contributions Office (NICO) (see 8700 and below).

An earnings period cannot be less than seven days in length and, if there is more than one such interval of less than seven days, the earnings period is set at a week. The same rule applies if there is more than one regular pay interval, one or more of which is less than seven days.

The first earnings period of the tax year

The first earnings period of the tax year begins on the first day of that year. For weekly-paid employees, the year may therefore contain *53* earnings weeks if they are paid on the first and last day of the year (or one of the last two days in a leap year). Similarly, an employee paid every four weeks may pay contributions on 56 weeks' earnings depending on how the payment dates fall. In such circumstances NICO (see 8700) argues that no overpayment arises.

Payment intervals other than a week or month

If the regular payment interval is other than a week or month, the regular interval becomes the earnings period. The exact percentage method of calculation must also be used (see 9056).

> ### Example
>
> Nigel is paid every ten days.
>
> Nigel has 37 earnings periods in a year (36 of ten days, one of five days), although he might be paid only 36 times.

Earnings limits and brackets are adjusted to match the length of the period by dividing each weekly bracket by seven and multiplying by the number of days in the regular interval.

1,439

Unusual circumstances

There are special rules for certain employment rights payments (see 9018). Official guidance sets out the earnings period rules in a number of unusual circumstances. NICO (see 8700) may sometimes direct that a particular earnings period should be used (see 9020).

Bonuses and commissions

Bonuses, commissions and suchlike are treated as part of the total pay at the time they are paid. If extra payments are made at a regular interval shorter than that for basic pay, the shorter period becomes the earnings period, but NICO (see 8700) can direct that the longer or longest interval be used if the greater part of earnings is paid at that interval, even if the structure of pay intervals was not intended as a method of avoiding contributions. If a second one-off payment is made after the normal rules have been applied to a first payment, the two payments must be aggregated within the earnings period to calculate the contribution rate. The deductions working sheet must be amended.

Law: *Social Security (Contributions) Regulations* 2001 (SI 2001/1004), reg. 1(2), 2, 3

Source: CWG2, *Employer's further guide to PAYE and NICs*

9018 Earnings periods for employment rights payments

Payments made by employers to employees (other than directors) under the *Employment Rights Act* 1996, where the payments represent earnings, may have their own earnings period and are not in that case added to other payments of earnings made at the same time. These payments include:

- guarantee payments paid for weeks when there is no work – the normal earnings period rule applies;
- medical suspension payments paid for weeks when an employee is suspended on medical grounds – the normal earnings period rule applies;
- awards of arrears in cases of orders for reinstatement or re-engagement – the earnings period is the period for which arrears have to be paid under the order made by the industrial tribunal, or a week if longer;
- pay due following an order for the continuation of employment – the earnings period is the period covered by the order, or a week if longer; and
- pay due following a protective award – the earnings period is the longest of the protected periods stated in the award, the part of the protected period the sum is paid for, or a week.

Source: CWG2, *Employer's further guide to PAYE and NICs*

9020 Official directions as to earnings periods

Manipulation of the earnings period rules (see 9016) by employers may lead to an official direction that a different earnings period should be used. Further, where the incidence of earnings-related contributions is avoided or reduced by means of irregular or unequal payments, counteracting directions may be given. However, any direction given may not be retrospective.

Law: *Social Security (Contributions) Regulations* 2001 (SI 2001/1004), reg. 3(2), 31

9022 Changes in normal pay days

Where a payment is not made on the usual day, it is treated as falling in the earnings period in which the usual day falls, unless that day falls in another tax year, in which case it is treated as made on the last day of the regular interval at which it is treated as paid in the same tax year. Thus a payment of salary always made on the last Friday in the month attracts a monthly earnings period. If the payment is exceptionally made on Thursday (e.g. before Good Friday), the change of pay day is irrelevant. If two weeks' wages are paid together because an employee will be away on the next pay day, two earnings periods of a week are used. If the second of those weeks falls in the next tax year the earlier year's rates are used for that week but it is not aggregated with the payment in the last earnings period of the old year.

Two payments received in an earnings period

If an employee receives two payments in an earnings period because for example, the pay day is changed permanently or there is a change in week-in-hand arrangements, each payment has its own earnings period based on the regular interval.

Employer changes the earnings period

Where an employer changes the earnings period, the treatment depends on whether the new interval is shorter or longer:

* shorter interval (e.g. monthly paid becomes weekly paid) – contributions are worked out on payments made after the change completely separately using the new earnings period, even if the two earnings periods overlap; or
* longer interval (e.g. weekly paid becomes monthly paid) – contributions are worked out as above, unless payment has already been made at the old short interval in the first longer period, in which case all earnings are aggregated in the new period and the total contributions adjusted to take account of those already deducted.

Such a change from weekly to monthly pay often involves entry into a contracted-out occupational pension scheme. All payments made in the new earnings period are charged at the contracted-out rate.

National Insurance Contributions

Arrears of pay

Where arrears of pay are paid, the rates and limits applied are those of the earnings period in which payment takes place, not those of the period when earnings were earned.

Supplementary payments

Sometimes an employer makes a supplementary payment after the regular payment of wages or salary has been made but within the same earnings period. Contributions must be calculated on the total payment made in the period and the payroll records amended to show the increased contributions.

Law: *Social Security (Contributions) Regulations* 2001 (SI 2001/1004), reg. 7(1)–(3)

Source: CWG2, *Employer's further guide to PAYE and NICs*

Website: www.hmrc.gov.uk/employers/emp-form.htm

9024 Earnings periods for new and leaving employees

Difficulty or uncertainty is often caused when employments begin or end.

New employee

The first payment above the lower earnings limit (see 9000) gives rise to a contribution liability in respect of a new employee, but the earnings period is that which will apply for the future (e.g. a week or month), not the length of time between the date on which the employee joins and the date of payment, which may be only a few days.

Employee leaves

When an employee leaves, he may receive two or more payments together which would normally have been made at the regular interval. The normal earnings period applies to each such payment separately. Whether the earnings period rules apply to both employer and employee contributions, or to employer contributions only, usually depends on whether the employee who leaves is over pensionable age, since an individual over that age pays no primary contributions (see 9066).

Holiday pay

If holiday pay is paid with the last payment of wages or salary, the treatment depends on when the contract of service ends. If it ends on the day the employee leaves, both amounts are added together and treated as paid in one earnings period. In contrast, if the employee simply takes holiday while serving his notice, the whole amount is treated as holiday pay and effectively spread over the period of holiday.

Regular payments after leaving

If an employee continues to receive regular payments after leaving, contributions are due in the normal way, unless the payment is of a type specifically excluded from earnings (e.g. a pension).

One-off payments after leaving

Where an employee receives irregular or one-off payments after leaving, such as back-dated pay awards, holiday pay for a holiday not taken, or a retrospective bonus, a weekly earnings period applies.

Statutory maternity pay

Statutory maternity pay is often paid after an employee's contract of service has ended, since an employer usually has to pay the benefit even if the employee will not return to work for him after her maternity leave. If SMP is paid *in a lump sum*, the weekly earnings period applies to the payment, unless it is made with the last regular payment of wages, in which case the two sums are aggregated and the normal earnings period applied. If it is paid *at the same regular interval as were the earnings before the employee left*, the earnings period used during the period of employment applies. If payment is made *at different intervals from regular earnings*, the interval between payments is used.

Employee dies

No contribution liability arises in respect of payments made after the employee's death.

Source: CWG2, *Employer's further guide to PAYE and NICs*

Website: www.hmrc.gov.uk/leaflets/index.htm

9026 Directors

For ordinary employees, the earnings period is usually set by a person's regular pay interval or intervals (see 9016). Company directors are generally in a position to decide when and how they receive a payment of earnings, which potentially gives them the ability to avoid primary Class 1 contribution liability by astute use of the earnings period rules. For this reason, a director's earnings period is a tax year, even if he is paid, say, monthly or leaves during the year.

Newly-appointed directors

The only exception to the above rule is where a director is first appointed during the course of a tax year. In such an event the earnings period is the period from the date of appointment to the end of the tax year, measured in weeks. The calculation of the earnings period includes the tax week of appointment, plus all remaining complete weeks in the tax year (i.e. week 53 is ignored for this purpose). This is known as the pro-rata earnings period.

National Insurance Contributions

Payments on account

From 6 April 1999, companies can save time and money by calculating directors' NICs in a similar way to other employees. Under the change, instead of paying very high levels of NICs on a short-term basis, directors who are paid regularly (e.g. directors who have contracts of service with their companies) can spread their contributions evenly throughout the tax year. The earnings period remains an annual earnings period, but contributions are made on account throughout the tax year.

Payments made in unusual circumstances

There are special earnings period rules where payments are made to directors in unusual circumstances:

Payments under the *Employment Rights Act* 1996	add any payments to other earnings from the company in the tax year of payment.
Payment to director for the period before appointment (i.e. for work as an employee)	use the earnings period which applies when the earnings are paid (i.e. the annual or pro-rata period).
Payment after resignation in respect of office previously held (even if the person is still an employee):	
● the same year	use annual or pro-rata earnings period for the year, adding payments to other earnings already paid.
● later tax year	separate from other earnings in the year, apply a separate annual earnings period and limits.

Directors include shadow directors, though a person is not to be treated as such by reason only that the directors act on advice given by him in his professional capacity.

Law: SSCBA 1992, s. 3(4), (5), 6A(2), (3), (6)

Website: www.hmrc.gov.uk/leaflets/nic.htm

9028   COMPS and COSRS

Where earnings fall to be aggregated (see 9036ff.), the shortest earnings period in relation to a contracted-out money purchase (COMP) scheme employment takes priority over any relating to a contracted-out salary related (COSR) scheme. This benefits members of COMP schemes by maximising their potential benefits from both COMP schemes and COSR schemes.

Law: *Social Security (Contributions) Regulations* 2001 (SI 2001/1004), reg. 6(2)(b), (c)

Website: www.hmrc.gov.uk/nic/referenceguide.pdf

AGGREGATION OF EARNINGS

9036 Aggregation: employees with more than one job

If an employee or director concurrently has more than one employment, it is a fundamental principle that contributions must be calculated separately for each.

The aggregation provisions

However, regulations contain aggregation provisions which lead in prescribed circumstances to different earnings being added together before contribution liabilities are calculated. The situations envisaged by the regulations are where earnings are paid in respect of different employments:

- under the same employer;
- with employers carrying on business in association (see below);
- with employers of whom only one is deemed by regulation to be the secondary contributor; or
- with employers of whom none is the secondary contributor because some other person is deemed by regulation to be the secondary contributor.

The main exception to these rules applies where it is not reasonably practicable to aggregate the earnings.

When employers are 'associated'

Employers are associated (see above) if they are carrying on business in association, which involves sharing profits or losses, or to a large extent sharing resources such as accommodation, equipment, personnel and customers, such that their fortunes are to some extent interdependent. Mere constitutional links between two companies (e.g. a parent/subsidiary relationship) are irrelevant for this purpose unless the companies also fulfil the above criteria.

Class 1 maximum

Prior to 2003–04 there was no annual maximum liability for contributions for a secondary contributor (i.e. usually an employer) but an annual maximum contribution liability was set by law for any employed earner (see 9302). From 6 April 2003 the maximum amount that an employee is liable to pay in Class 1 contributions is equal to 53 weeks full contributions at the main rate of 11 per cent, plus one per cent on all earnings above this sum. Where multiple jobs are held the primary threshold applies to each employment. There continues to be no limit for the secondary contributor.

Deferment

If an employee receives two or more salaries or wages which are not aggregated he may be eligible for deferment of contributions in one or more jobs (see 9310ff.).

National Insurance Contributions

9038   Not contracted out in all jobs

The following table summarises NICO's guidance on aggregation as set out in CWG2, *Employer's further guide to PAYE and NICs.*

Circumstances	Treatment
One payment of earnings for separate jobs with two or more employers.	If the employers are associated, the employer who pays the earnings accounts for contributions on all earnings and completes one P11 (Deductions Working Sheet); if the employers are independent, both account separately for contributions on earnings they pay and each completes a P11.
Employees with two or more jobs with the same employer (e.g. accounts clerk on the staff payroll but also weekly paid safety officer).	The employer must add all earnings together and use the shortest earnings period to calculate liability, keeping only one P11. If it is impracticable to do this, contributions are calculated and recorded separately.
Employees with two or more jobs with different employers.	The normal rules apply to each employment separately, unless the employers trade in association. In that case, only one overall liability is calculated and recorded. The employers agree how their share of contributions is to be borne. Again, the impracticability exception may apply. If one of the employers is overseas and has no UK place of business, only employee contributions are due on any earnings from that employment. If the overseas employer has a UK place of business, aggregation may be necessary if two employers trade in association).

Law: SSCBA 1992, s. 6(4); *Social Security (Contributions) Regulations* 2001 (SI 2001/1004), reg. 15

Source: CWG2, *Employer's further guide to PAYE and NICs*

Website: www.hmrc.gov.uk/leaflet/index.htm

9040   Mixed employment

If all the employments of an earner are contracted-out, the normal aggregation rules as set out above apply. If, on the other hand, the employments under consideration are mixed, i.e. not-contracted-out and contracted-out, the earnings must be kept separate for the purposes of calculating liability. In the case of mixed employments, the procedure that is to be followed depends on whether or not the employee has an appropriate personal pension arrangement. Further refinements apply where the earnings relate to employments with mixed occupational pension schemes, where some may be salary-related and others money purchase.

The basic rule is that contributions are calculated by adding all earnings together and establishing the earnings limits for the common or shortest earnings period to establish whether contributions are due. Priority is given to the earnings period for the contracted-out earnings, but the procedure depends on the value of the contracted-out earnings. Detail guidance is given in Booklet CWG2, *Employer's further guide to PAYE and NICs* and on CWG1, *Employer's quick guide to PAYE and NICs.*

Law: SSCBA 1992, s. 6(4); *Social Security (Contributions) Regulations* 2001 (SI 2001/1004), reg. 15

Source: CWG2, *Employer's further guide to PAYE and NICs*; CWG1, *Employer's quick guide to PAYE and NICs*, cards 11 and 12

Website: www.hmrc.gov.uk/leaflets/index.htm

9056   Class 1 calculation methods

The rates for calculating Class 1 liability are described at 9000ff. and a table of rates appears at 110.

There are two methods of calculating Class 1 liabilities, the exact percentage method and the tables method. Either may be used, but only one may be used in any single tax year in respect of any single employee, unless the National Insurance Contributions Office (see 8700) expressly permits a change. Permission is not required for a change resulting from a switch from a manual to a computerised payroll or vice versa.

Example

The employee contributions due on weekly earnings of £124.20 are, on the exact basis, £1.56. Table A gives £1.59, because it is based on earnings of £124.50.

9058   Exact percentage method

The exact percentage method is the more accurate and is generally used by payroll software. It is provided that contributions are to be calculated separately at the appropriate rate and rounded to the nearest penny. This method *must* be used in certain specified circumstances, e.g. where earnings from two employments are aggregated and one of those employments is contracted-out while the other is not (see 9038).

National Insurance Contributions

Example 1

Ellen is paid weekly. She has not contracted out of SERPS. For a particular week in 2010–11 her earnings are £1,000.

Primary contributions are payable on earnings between the primary threshold (£110 per week) and the upper earnings limit (£844 per week) at 11 per cent, and on the excess over the upper earnings limit at one per cent. Ellen thus pays primary contributions in respect of the week's earnings of £82.30.

Her employer pays secondary contributions on all earnings in excess of the secondary threshold (£110 per week), i.e. on earnings of £890, at a rate of 12.8 per cent. The secondary liability is thus £113.92.

Example 2

Milo is paid monthly. He has not contracted out of SERPS. For a particular week in 2010–11, he earns £2,000. His earnings do not exceed the upper earnings limit (£3,656 per month) and thus he pays primary contributions on all his earnings in excess of the primary threshold (£476 per month), i.e. £1,524 (£2,000 − £476), at a rate of 11 per cent. His primary liability for that month's earnings is thus £167.64.

His employer pays secondary contributions on all his earnings above the earnings threshold (£476 per month), i.e. on earnings of £1,524. The secondary liability is thus £195.07 (£1,524 × 12.8%).

Example 3

Patricia is paid weekly. She has contracted out of SERPS and joined a contracted-out salary-related (COSR) pension scheme operated by her employer. For a particular week in 2010–11, her earnings are £1,000.

Primary contributions are payable at the contracted-out rate of 9.4 per cent on earnings between the primary threshold (£110 per week) and the upper earnings limit (£844 per week), and at one per cent on the excess earnings above the upper earnings limit. Patricia therefore pays primary contributions of £70.56 ((£734 × 9.4%) + (£156 × 1%)) in respect of the week's earnings.

Secondary contributions are payable at the rate of 9.1 per cent (12.8 per cent less the rebate of 3.7 per cent applying to COSR schemes) on earnings between the earnings threshold (£110 per week) and the upper earnings limit (£844 per week) and at a rate of 12.8 per cent on earnings above the upper earnings limit. The secondary contributions payable are thus £86.76 ((£734 × 9.1%) + (£156 × 12.8%)).

Example 4

Ali was born on 26 April 1961. He is paid monthly. He has contracted out of SERPS and joined a contracted-out money purchase (COMP) scheme operated by his employer. For a particular month in 2010–11, his earnings are £4,000.

Primary contributions are payable at the contracted-out rate of 9.4 per cent on earnings between the primary threshold (£476 per month) and the upper earnings limit (£3,656 per month) and at the additional rate of one per cent on the excess over the upper earnings limit. Ali therefore pays primary contributions of £302.36 ((£3,656 − 476 × 9.4%) + (£344 × 1%)).

Secondary contributions are payable at the rate of 11.4 per cent (12.8 per cent less the rebate of 1.4 cent applying to COMP schemes) on earnings between the earnings threshold (£476 per month) and the upper earnings limit (£3,656 per month) and at a rate of 12.8 per cent on earnings above the upper earnings limit. The secondary contributions payable by Ali's employer are thus £406.55 ((£3,180 × 11.4%) + (£344 × 12.8%)).

Furthermore, an age-related rebate is paid by the National Insurance Contributions Office (NICO) directly to the COMP scheme. For the table showing the NICO payments to COMP schemes (see 110). The appropriate age-related percentage, found from the table, is applied to earnings exceeding the lower earnings limit but not exceeding the upper earnings limit.

9060 Tables method

The alternative method is the tables method, which relies on ready-reckoner tables in booklets prepared and distributed by HMRC (see 8700) each time rates change. The tables are issued as part of the employee's annual pack and can also be obtained from the employer's orderline (0845 7 646 646) or downloaded from the employers' orderline download page of HMRC's website.

The contribution tables are divided into sections identified by letter. HMRC generally refers to these letters in order to identify the category of Class 1 contribution payable by an earner and his employer.

Table A

Table A, which appears in Booklet CA38 and covers not contracted-out full rate contributions, is used for:

- all male employees aged 16 to 64 and in not contracted-out employment;
- all female employees aged 16 to 59 who are in not contracted-out employment and paying standard rate employee's NICs; and
- any employee with an appropriate personal pension or appropriate personal stakeholder pension.

Table B

Table B, which appears in CA41 and covers not contracted-out reduced rate contributions, is used for married women and widows who are:

- aged under 60 in not contracted-out employment; and
- who are entitled to pay employee's contributions at the reduced rate (see 9076).

National Insurance Contributions

The employer must have a valid certificate of election (CA4139 or CF383) or a valid certificate of reduced liability (CF380A) in respect of these women.

Table C

Table C, which appears in CA41 and covers employees over pensionable age or whose liabilities are deferred, is used for:

- men aged 65 and over and women aged 60 and over for whom a valid certificate CA41410 or CF384 is held; and
- employees who are in not contracted-out employment for whom a form CA2700 is held allowing them to defer paying employee's contributions; and
- employees in COSR schemes or the salary-related part of a contracted-out mixed benefit scheme for whom a form CA2700 is held authorising deferment of employee's contributions.

Table D

Table D, which appears in CA39 and covers contracted-out full rate contributions in respect of COSR schemes, is used for:

- all male employees aged 16 to 64 in a COSR scheme or the salary-related part of a contracted-out mixed benefit scheme; and
- all female employees aged 16 to 59 who are in a COSR scheme or the salary related part of a contracted-out mixed benefit scheme and paying standard rate employee's contributions.

Table E

Table E, which appears in CA 39 and covers contracted-out reduced rate contributions in respect of COSR schemes, is used for married women and widows:

- aged under 60 and in a COSR scheme or the salary-related part of a contracted-out mixed benefits scheme; and
- who are entitled to pay employee's contributions at the reduced rate (see 9076).

A valid certificate of election (form CA4139 or CF383) or a valid certificate of reduced liability (form CF380A) must be held in respect of such women.

Table F

Table F, which appears in CA43 and covers contracted-out full rate contributions in respect of COMP schemes, is used for:

- all male employees aged 16 to 64 in a COMP scheme or contracted-out money purchase stakeholder pension scheme, or the money purchase part of a contracted-out mixed benefits scheme; and
- all female employees aged 16 to 59 who are in a COMP scheme or contracted-out money purchase stakeholder pension scheme, or the money purchase part of a

contracted-out mixed benefits scheme and who are paying standard rate employee's contributions.

Table G

Table G, which appears in CA43 and covers contracted-out reduced rate contributions for COMP schemes, is used for married women and widows:

- aged under 60 in a COMP scheme or contracted-out money purchase stakeholder pension scheme, or the money purchase part of a contracted-out mixed benefits scheme; and
- who are entitled to pay employee's contributions at the reduced rate (see 9076).

A valid certificate of election (form CA4139 or CF383) or a valid certificate of reduced liability (form CF380A) must be held in respect of such women.

Table J

Table J, which appears in CA38, is used for all employees who are not in contracted-out employment, for whom a form CA2700 is held allowing them to defer payment of employee contributions at the full main percentage rate.

Table L

Table L, which appears in CA39, is used for employees in a COSR scheme or the salary related part of a contracted-out mixed benefit scheme for whom a valid form CA2700 is held authorising deferment of the employee's contributions at the full main percentage rate.

Table S

Table S, which appears in CA43, is used for employees in COMP schemes or contracted-out money purchase stakeholder pension schemes, or the money purchase part of contracted-out mixed benefit schemes and for whom form CA2700 is held authorising deferment of employee's contributions.

The letter X signifies that no contributions have been collected, for example earnings are below the LEL limit or because the employee has a certificate of coverage under a foreign social security scheme.

Website: www.hmrc.gov.uk/leaflets/index.htm

9062   Company directors

HMRC allow alternative arrangements for the assessment and payment of NICs for company directors. Liability to NICs for company directors is calculated using an annual earnings basis. However, subject to the qualifying conditions set out below, payments on account of directors' NICs may be made during the year based on the actual intervals of payment, usually weekly or monthly, in the same way as for other employees.

National Insurance Contributions

The calculation

The following procedure can be applied to determine the contributions payable in respect of a director's earnings each time a payment is made.

Step 1
Use an annual or pro-rata annual earnings period to calculate NICs.

Step 2
Calculate NICs on total earnings paid to the director each time that a payments of earnings is made. When performing the calculation all the director's earnings, including fees and bonuses, should be included.

Step 3
Deduct the NICs already paid in the year, if any, to arrive at the contributions now due.

The calculation can be performed using the exact percentage method (see 9058 or by adapting the tables method (see 9060) as set out on CWG1 (*Employer's quick guide to PAYE and NICs*), card 13 and described below.

Using the monthly tables, the procedure is as follows:

Step 1
Divide the total earnings by 12. This gives average monthly earnings to date.

Step 2
Look at the relevant monthly table for the average monthly earnings.

Step 3
If the average monthly earnings are less than or equal to the primary threshold, no primary contributions are due. If it is more than the primary threshold, multiply the NICs figure given in the table by 12 to give the NICs due to date.

Step 4
Deduct NICs already paid, if any. This gives the NICs now payable.

Secondary contributions are calculated in a similar fashion, but with reference to the earnings threshold.

If the weekly tables are used, the same procedure is followed, except that in step 1 the earnings are divided by 52 not 12, in step 2, the relevant weekly table rather than the relevant monthly table is used and in step 3, the NICs figure taken from the table is multiplied by 52 not 12.

The tables method can also be adapted for a pro-rata annual earnings period.

> ### Example
>
> Chris is appointed to the board of Teachers Ltd in week 44 of the tax year. The primary threshold and upper earnings limit are calculated by multiplying the weekly values by nine, because the earnings period starts with the week of appointment.
>
> In 2010–11, Chris will pay NIC at the main rate of 11 per cent on his director's earnings between £990 (9 × £110) and £7,596 (9 × £844) and at the additional one per cent rate on all earnings above £7,596 paid up to 5 April.

Alternative method

As noted at 8768 company directors may, from 6 April 1999, use the alternative arrangements to make payments on account of the annual liability based on the actual payment interval, as for other employees. Where the alternative arrangements are adopted, the directors contributions are calculated as for other employees, using either the exact percentage method (see 9058) or the tables method (see 9060). However, in month 12 it is necessary to compute the contributions for the year using and annual earnings period and deduct contributions paid on account to arrive at the month 12 figure.

Law: *Social Security (Contributions) Regulations* 2001 (SI 2001/1004), reg. 12(1), 12(2), 12(5)

Source: CWG1, *Employer's Help cards*

Website: www.hmrc.gov.uk/leaflets/index.htm

9066   Class 1 age limits

Class 1 liability does not begin to arise until the employed earner in question is over the age of 16. This is apparently linked to the statutory school leaving age, but it should be noted that children who stay on at school after that age are not automatically exempted from liability in respect of any earnings from weekend or evening employment.

Persons over pensionable age

Liability for primary (but not secondary) contributions ceases, in principle, and subject to certain exceptions, when an employed earner reaches pensionable age (65 for men, 60 for women). The liability rule applies where a payment of earnings takes place after the relevant birthday and is made on its normal due date. SSP paid to a woman over 60 constitutes earnings, but there is no primary contribution liability. To provide employers with the certainty that an employee is of pensionable age and that there is no requirement to deduct primary contributions, NICO will issue a certificate of age exemption (form CF4140 or form CF384) on application by the employee on form CF13.

National Insurance Contributions

It should be noted that employers remain liable for secondary contributions in respect of employees who continue to work beyond pensionable age.

Law: SSCBA 1992, s. 6(1), (2), 122; *Social Security (Contributions) Regulations* 2001 (SI 2001/1004), reg. 7(1)(a), 28, 29

Website: www.hmrc.gov.uk/leaflets/nic.htm

9076 Married women and widows: reduced rate elections

Prior to 12 May 1977, married women and widows were able to elect to pay reduced Class 1 contributions. Similarly, if self-employed they could elect to pay no Class 2 contributions (although Class 4 contributions remained payable).

Married women and widows who had reduced liability on 12 May 1977 can keep it unless:

- in the case of a married women, the marriage ends in divorce or is annulled;
- the marriage ends because the woman is widowed and she does not qualify for widow's benefits;
- widow's benefit ends, other than on re-marriage; or
- there has been no liability to pay NICs for two consecutive tax years after 5 April 1978 and the woman was not self-employed in those tax years.

Alternatively, a woman may decide to give up the right to reduced rate liability while reduced rate contributions are payable, the woman has no right to:

- retirement pension or other contributory benefits in respect of reduced Class 1 contributions;
- home protection responsibilities;
- pay voluntary contributions; and
- credits (except in the case of widows with reduced liability).

Employers should only deduct reduced rate contributions if the woman holds a certificate of election (form CA4139 or CF 383).

Law: *Social Security (Contributions) Regulations* 2001 (SI 2001/1004), reg. 128(1), (2), reg. 131–133

Source: CWG2, *Employer's further guide to PAYE and NICs*

Website: www.hmrc.gov.uk/leaflets/nic.htm

CLASS 1A CONTRIBUTIONS

9100 Nature of Class 1A contributions

Class 1A contributions were introduced with effect from 6 April 1991, the charge originally applying only where an income tax benefit arises (or, but for allowable deductions, would arise) on a director or P11D employee (see 386) in respect of private use of an employer-provided car and, where appropriate, fuel. However, from 6 April 2000, the Class 1A charge is widened to include most taxable benefits in kind (unless specifically exempted from the charge by the regulations). The liability for Class 1A contributions arises only in respect of the secondary contributor (i.e. the employer); there are no primary (employee) Class 1A contributions. The charge, based on the cash equivalent value of the benefit as calculated for tax purposes, is charged at the main secondary contributor rate (see 110).

The Class 1A contribution is based on tax years and is payable once annually after the end of the relevant tax year, on the basis of the cash equivalent value of the benefits as calculated for P11D purposes (see 9356).

Law: SSCBA 1992, s. 10

Source: CWG5, *Class 1A National Insurance Contributions on Benefits in Kind*; CA 33, *Cars and Car Fuel Manual*

Website: www.hmrc.gov.uk/employers/emp-form.htm
www.hmrc.leaflets/nic.htm

9110 Liability for Class 1A contributions

Class 1A contributions are payable only by secondary contributors (usually employers), whereas the income tax charge on which they are based results in a liability only for the director or employee personally.

As far as benefits in kind are concerned, the liability from 6 April 2000 applies in respect of benefits provided:

- to directors and other persons in controlling positions irrespective of the level of their earnings, unless the director does not have a material interest in the company and he or she is full-time working director and the company is a charity or non-profit making concern; and
- to employees and directors excluded above earning at the rate of at least £8,500 per annum, including expenses and benefits.

No Class 1A liability arises in respect of benefits and expenses provided to employees earning at a rate of less than £8,500 per annum, even if a P9D is required for tax purposes.

Similarly, no Class 1A liability arises if any benefit arising for tax purposes is offset by a corresponding deduction, for example, if the benefit was provided for use by the employee wholly, exclusively and necessarily in the performance of the duties of his employment or in the course of qualifying business travel.

Where a benefit attracts a liability to Class 1 (see 9000) or, because it has been included in a PAYE settlement agreement, to Class 1B (see 9140), no Class 1A charge will arise.

Employers may deduct Class 1A NICs when computing their taxable profits (see 2240).

For details of information requirements made of employers in relation to Class 1A, see 9338.

Law: SSCBA 1992, s. 10 (as substituted by the *Child Support, Social Security and Pensions Act* 2000, s. 75)

Source: CWG5, *Class 1A National Insurance Contributions on Benefits in Kind*; CA 33, *Cars and Car Fuel Manual*

Website: www.hmrc.gov.uk/employers/emp-form.htm
www.hmrc.leaflets/nic.htm

9112　Benefits in kind

The following table, which is adapted from CWG5, *Class 1A National Insurance Contributions on Benefits in Kind* summarises the liability arising in respect of the provision of benefits in kind.

Type of expense or benefit provided	Circumstances	Class 1 NICs due (include in gross pay)	Class 1A NICs due
Assets placed at the employee's disposal	provided for business use, and private use is insignificant	No	No
	provided for mixed business and private use	No	Yes
Assets transferred to the employee but not readily convertible assets	can be turned into cash only by sale, such as furniture, kitchen appliances, property and clothes	No	Yes
Car fuel for private motoring in a company car	Any means of supply or purchase – see booklet CA33 for exceptions	No	Yes
Car/van fuel for private motoring in a privately owned car/van	supplied using a company credit card or garage account or agency card and the conditions described in booklet *CWG2* apply	No[1]	Yes

Type of expense or benefit provided	Circumstances	Class 1 NICs due (include in gross pay)	Class 1A NICs due
	from your own fuel pump	No	Yes
	Any other circumstances	Yes	No
Car parking facilities including motorcycles	at or near place of work	No	No
	elsewhere – unless the parking is part of a journey which is qualifying business travel	No	Yes
Car parking fees paid for or reimbursed to employee	at or near place of work[3]	No	No
	for business-related journeys	No	No
	in all other circumstances	Yes	No
Cars made available for private use	See booklet CA33	No	Yes
Childcare help for children up to the age of 16	You provide nursery at the workplace (or in a facility managed and financed by you)	No	No
	You reimburse the employee or provide additional salary to meet the cost of childcare	Yes	No
Christmas boxes	in cash	Yes	No
	in goods	No	Yes
Clothing (protective) or uniforms (may have a logo) which are necessary for work	all circumstances	No	No
Clothing or uniforms which can be worn at any time	provided by you see ¶8780	No	Yes
	employee contracts[2][3]	Yes	No
Council tax	see ¶8780	No	No
	all other circumstances	Yes	No
Credit cards, charge cards, employee uses your card to purchase	goods or services bought on your behalf and the conditions described in booklet CWG2 apply	No	No[1]

Type of expense or benefit provided	Circumstances	Class 1 NICs due (include in gross pay)	Class 1A NICs due
	items for the personal use of the employee	Yes	No
	items relating to specific and distinct business expenses actually incurred by the employee	No	No
Employee's liability insurance	see ¶8780 for conditions	No	No
Entertaining clients expenses/allowances	employer contracts[2]	No	No
Entertaining staff expenses/allowances	employer contracts[2]	No	Yes
	employee contracts[3]	Yes	No
Expenses not covered by a dispensation	specific and distinct business expenses included in the payment	No	No
	any profit element in the payment	Yes	No
Expenses and benefits covered by a dispensation		No	No
Eyecare test, or corrective appliance (e.g. glasses or contact lenses)	employer makes available generally to employees for whom tests and appliances are necessary under regulations made under the Health and Safety at Work etc. Act 1974	No	No
Eyecare voucher to obtain test or corrective appliance (e.g. glasses or contact lenses)	employer makes available generally to employees for whom tests and appliances are necessary under regulations made under the Health and Safety at Work etc. Act 1974	No	No
Food, groceries, farm produce	employer contracts[2]	No	Yes
	employee contracts[3]	Yes	No
Goods, such as TV, Furniture, etc. transferred to employee	employer contracts[2]	No	Yes
	employee contracts[3]	Yes	No
Holidays	employer contracts[2]	No	Yes
	holiday vouchers	Yes	No

Type of expense or benefit provided	Circumstances	Class 1 NICs due (include in gross pay)	Class 1A NICs due
	employee contracts[3]	Yes	No
Incidental overnight expenses	See booklet *480* for special conditions	No	No
Income tax paid	but not deducted from employee	Yes	No
	on notional payments not borne by employee within 90 days of receipt of each notional payment	Yes	No
Insurance premiums for pensions, annuities, etc. on the employee's death or retirement. See *CWG2* for exceptions	employee contracts[3]	Yes	No
Living accommodation provided by you	see booklet *CWG2* for special conditions	No	No
	in all other circumstances	No	Yes
Loans, beneficial arrangements	qualifying loans	No	No
	non-qualifying loans	No	Yes
Loans written off	at time you decide not to seek repayment	Yes	No
Long service Award	Conditions of s. 323, ITEPA 2003 met	No	No
	above conditions not fully met	For the treatment applicable to NICs see the instructions under 'Staff suggestions', which apply similarly for long service awards	
Meal vouchers	15p a day of the value of vouchers which cannot be transferred to another person and can be used only for meals	No	No
	in any other circumstances	Yes	No

Type of expense or benefit provided	Circumstances	Class 1 NICs due (include in gross pay)	Class 1A NICs due
Meals provided by you	at canteen open to your staff generally or on your business premises on a reasonable scale and all employees may obtain free or subsidised meals	No	No
	in any other circumstances	No	Yes
Medical, dental, etc. treatment or insurance to cover such treatment	employer contracts[2]	No	Yes
	employee contracts[3]	Yes	No
	outside the UK where the need for treatment arises while the employee is outside the UK working for you	No	No
Mobile phones provided by you		No	No
Mobile phones costs of private calls	employer contracts[2]	No	No
	employee contracts[3]	Yes	No
Office accommodation, supplies/services used by employee in doing his/her work		No	No
Personal bills of the employee paid by you	employee contracts[3]	Yes	No
Readily convertible assets, remuneration provided in non-cash form such as shares, share options, bullion and other commodities	see *CWG2* for detailed information	Yes	No
Relocation expenses/benefits	expenses which are not exempt[4]	Yes	No
	benefits which are not exempt and exempt expenses paid after the relevant day	No	Yes
	exempt expenses/benefits of £8,000 or less[5]	No	No

Type of expense or benefit provided	Circumstances	Class 1 NICs due (include in gross pay)	Class 1A NICs due
	exempt expenses/benefits in excess of £8,000[5]	No	Yes
Retirement benefit schemes either registered schemes or employer-financed schemes	payments employer makes into such schemes	No	No
Round sum allowances	specific and distinct business expense identified	No	No
	profit element	Yes	No
Scholarships awarded to students because of their parent's employment	employer contracts[2]	No	Yes
	employee contracts[3]	Yes	No
School fees	employer contracts[2]	No	Yes
	employee contracts[3]	Yes	No
Social functions	conditions of s. 264, ITEPA 2003 are met	No	No
	any other type of function	No	Yes
Sporting or recreational facilities provided by you, for example, fishing, horse racing	conditions of s. 261, ITEPA 2003 are satisfied	No	No
	all other circumstances	No	Yes
Shares and share options	see **Readily convertible assets (RCA)**	–	–
Shares and share options (not RCA)		No	No

Type of expense or benefit provided	Circumstances	Class 1 NICs due (include in gross pay)	Class 1A NICs due
Subscriptions, professional & fees which are allowable tax deductions under s. 343 & 344, ITEPA 2003	any circumstances	No	No
Subscriptions, professional & fees which are **not** allowable tax deductions under s. 343 & 344, ITEPA 2003	employer contracts[2]	No	Yes
	employee contracts[3]	Yes	No
Suggestion schemes awards to employees	conditions of s. 321, ITEPA 2003 met	No	No
	above conditions not fully met	See paragraph 35 of CWG5	
Telephones You are the subscriber	cost of rental, unless private use is insignificant	No	Yes
	cost of calls, unless private use is insignificant	No	Yes
	cost of all private calls is reimbursed by the employee	No	No
Telephones Your employee is the subscriber, and you meet the costs of calls and/or rental	Phone used exclusively for business	No	No
	Phone exclusively for private use	Yes	No

Type of expense or benefit provided	Circumstances	Class 1 NICs due (include in gross pay)	Class 1A NICs due
	Phone used for both business and private purposes	Rental – Yes on full amount of the rental	No
		Calls – Yes on the full amount of the calls, *but any amount for business calls, supported by evidence, can be excluded*	No
Third party benefits/payments		See ¶8780	
Training payments for course fees, books and so on	training is work-related or encouraged or required by you in connection with the employment	No	No
	all other circumstances and employer contracts[2]	No	Yes
	all other circumstances and employee contracts[3]	Yes	No
Vans available for private use		No	Yes
Vouchers	see booklet *CWG2* for exceptions	Yes	No

Notes

[1] Where an employee purchases goods or services including car fuels on your behalf, and later ownership of these is transferred to the employee, Class 1A NICs will be due.

[2] Contract is between the employer and the provider of the benefit.

[3] Contract is between the employee and provider and the employer pays the provider or reimburses the employee.

[4] Expenses which are not exempt are any expenses not included in the list at Appendix 7 of booklet *480, Expenses and Benefits – A tax guide.*

[5] Details of what constitutes exempt expenses and benefits is described in booklet *480*.

Source: CWG5, *Class 1A National Insurance Contributions on Benefits in Kind*

Website: www.hmrc.gov.uk/employers/emp-form.htm

National Insurance Contributions

9116 Cars

A car provided by reason of employment to a director or an employee earning at the rate of at least £8,500 per annum, which is available for private use, attracts a Class 1A liability, as does the provision of any fuel for private use in such cars. There are special rules for Class 1A NICs for cars provided in unusual circumstances.

Detailed guidance on the Class 1A liability arising in respect of company cars and car fuel is given in HMRC booklet CA33, *Cars and Car Fuel Manual*, available from the employers orderline (0856 7 646 646) or to download from the HMRC website.

More than one employment

A person may have two or more concurrent but independent employments: e.g. working four days per week for company C and one day per week for company D. If both C and D make available a company car *and* pay earnings, both have a Class 1A liability if the employee is a P11D employee (see 403). However, if C were to pay earnings but not provide a company car, while D paid no earnings whatsoever but made available a company car for private use, neither would have a Class 1A liability, provided it could be shown that the car was not made available by D by reason of the employment with C, and that the payment of salary by C was unconnected with the employment by D. However, it should be noted that a payment of £1 of earnings by D would make D liable to Class 1A contributions.

The key questions in identifying the person liable to pay the Class 1A contribution are:

- to which job does the provision of the car relate?
- who uses the car?
- who made the last payment of earnings to that person in the tax year in question?
- who was liable to pay the secondary Class 1 contribution on those earnings (or who would have been liable had they exceeded the primary threshold: see 9000)?

Where a person holds two or more employments and is provided with one car by virtue of both employments, whether under the same employer or different employers, the Class 1A charge is shared equally between the employers involved. It is irrelevant that the employee may cover 10,000 business miles on behalf of the first employer and only 5,000 on behalf of the second.

Shared cars

A shared car can be:

(1) a car made available for concurrent use by two or more employees by reason of their employment and available for use by both; or

(2) a car which is made available for private use to one employee by reason of two or more employed earners' employments with the same or different employers.

For (1) a Class 1A NIC liability arises in respect of each employee. For (2) each employment attracts a Class 1A NIC liability. If the two employments are with the same employer, the calculation will need to take into account any differences in the employee's conditions of employment in the separate employments.

Pooled cars

There is no tax charge on the benefit of a car if it is a pooled car used only for business purposes. Similarly, there is no liability to Class 1A NICs for that car or for fuel supplied for that car. There may however, be a liability for Class 1 NICs if a lump sum or mileage allowance is paid.

Law: *Social Security (Contributions) Regulations* 2001 (SI 2001/1004), reg. 34, reg. 36

Source: CA 33, *Cars and Car Fuel Manual*

Website: www.hmrc.gov.uk/leaflets/nic.htm

9118 Fuel provided for private purposes: Class 1A

Where in any tax year fuel is provided for private use by a director or P11D employee (see 403), for Class 1A purposes, the amount of any cash equivalent taxable on the employee (see 60) is added to the cash equivalent of the benefit of the car. The contribution is calculated by applying the Class 1A percentage (see 9120) for the year of provision of the benefit to the total of the two figures).

If the full cost of private fuel is reimbursed by the employee, no Class 1A NICs are payable.

If the employer simply pays a round sum allowance which bears no relation to the actual expense incurred by the employee, the allowance should be included in gross pay and subjected to Class 1 contributions in the same way as a payment of wages or salary. In such a case, the employer does not provide free fuel for private motoring: the employee purchases the fuel personally out of net income. There is, accordingly, no liability to Class 1A contributions in respect of that employee.

Similarly, there is no question of a Class 1A liability arising in respect of fuel provided for private motoring in an employee's own car or in a van, lorry, etc., irrespective of the owner of the vehicle.

Law: SSCBA 1992, s. 10

Source: CA 33, *Cars and Car Fuel Manual*

Website: www.hmrc.gov.uk/leaflets/nic.htm

National Insurance Contributions

9120 Calculating the Class 1A charge

Class 1A NICs are payable at a single rate applied to the cash equivalent of the benefit as calculated for income tax purposes. The single rate applicable is known as the Class 1A percentage and is equal to the main secondary contributor rate for Class 1 purposes (for a table of rates, see 110).

No reduction of the rate applies where the employment is contracted-out, or a reduced rate of Class 1 contribution applies for some other reason (e.g. where a married woman or widow pays at the reduced rate, or where the foreign-going rebate applies to a mariner's earnings).

Example 1

George's employer provides private medical insurance cover for George and his family. The contract is between the employer and the insurance company. For 2010–11, the cash equivalent of the benefit as calculated for income tax purposes is £900. A liability to Class 1A National Insurance arises in respect of the provision of the benefit. The liability, payable by the employer only, is £115.20 (£900 × 12.8%).

It should be noted, however, that if the contract had been between the employee and the insurer, and the employer had either made the payment on the employee's behalf or reimbursed the employee, the liability would have been to Class 1 rather than to Class 1A.

Example 2

Ruby is provided with a car by reason of her employment. The car is available for her private use throughout the tax year 2010–11. Ruby is a P11D employee.

The cash equivalent value of the benefit as calculated for income tax purposes (see 402) is £4,500. Class 1A contributions payable by Ruby's employer are £576 (£4,500 × 12.8%).

Example 3

Nigel is provided with fuel for private use in a company car provided by his employer. The fuel benefit for income tax purposes for 2010–11 is £2,592. Class 1A contributions payable by Nigel's employer are thus £331.77 (£2,592 × 12.8%).

Law: SSCBA 1992, s. 10

Source: CWG5, *Class 1A National Insurance Contributions on Benefits in Kind*; CA 33, *Cars and Car Fuel Manual*

Website: www.hmrc.gov.uk/employers/emp-form.htm
www.hmrc.gov.uk/leaflets/nic.htm

CLASS 1B CONTRIBUTIONS

9140 Nature of Class 1B contributions

PAYE settlement agreements (PSAs) allow employers to account for any tax liability in respect of their employees on payments that are minor or irregular, or that are shared benefits on which it would be impractical to determine individual liability, in one lump sum (see 2750). From 6 April 1999, the principle was extended to NICs through a new contribution class: Class 1B. Where an employer has a PSA with HMRC, he will be liable to Class 1B contributions (at the secondary rate – see 110) on the amount of the emoluments in the agreement that are chargeable to Class 1 or Class 1A contributions, together with the total amount of income tax payable under the agreement.

When Class 1B was introduced, ministers were concerned to ensure that the transfer of earnings out of Class 1 did not result in any loss of benefit entitlement for the workers concerned.

If the use of a PAYE Settlement Agreement (PSA) means that earnings drop below the LEL it is possible that an employee could lose entitlement to SMP, SAP, SPP or SSP. Employers are required in such circumstances to recalculate earnings to include amounts in the PSA in respect of that employee. Where an amount is in the PSA because it is difficult to identify the recipients of the benefit, this will clearly be almost impossible to achieve. However, if the amount increases earnings to a level at which benefits become payable, the employee is treated as qualifying.

> ### Example
>
> Anna is a part-time barmaid. She earns £94 per week but the landlord also pays for a taxi home each night at a cost of £20 per week. He has several staff in this position and accounts for the tax through a PSA. Ignoring the PSA, Anna's earnings fall below the LEL so she would not qualify for SSP when she is unable to work through sickness. However, the landlord must include the amount paid for her taxis in assessing her average earnings for SSP, SMP and SAP purposes.

Law: SSA 1998, s. 53; *Social Security Act 1998 (Commencement No. 4) Regulations* 1999 (SI 1999/526)

Source: *PAYE Settlement Agreements*

Website: www.hmrc.gov.uk/employers/emp-form.htm;
www.hmrc.gov.uk/guidance/paye-settlements.htm

National Insurance Contributions

9142   Calculating Class 1B contributions

Class 1B contributions are calculated on the value of the items included with the PAYE settlement agreement (PSA) that would otherwise have attracted a liability for Class 1 or Class 1A NICs and the total tax payable under the PSA. The Class 1B contributions due are at the secondary rate (see 110).

From 2011–12 the Class 1 employer rate of NICs will be increased by 0.5 per cent to 13.3 per cent. The increased rate will also apply to Class 1B.

Example

Sunshine Ltd has a PSA in force for 2010–11. Tax payable under the agreement is £15,000. Included within the PSA are items to the value of £12,000 that would normally attract a Class 1 liability and items to the value of £30,000 that would normally attract a Class 1A liability.

The Class 1B liability is calculated as follows:

	£
Value of items that would normally attract a Class 1 liability	12,000
Add: value of items that would normally attract a Class 1A liability	30,000
Add: tax payable under the PSA	15,000
Value on which Class 1B contributions payable	57,000

Class 1B contributions payable are thus £7,296 (£57,000 × 12.8%).

CLASS 2 CONTRIBUTIONS

9150   Nature of Class 2 contributions

Class 2 contributions are payable at a flat weekly rate by every 'self-employed earner' (see 8718, 8728) over the age of 16 and under pensionable age (i.e. currently age 60 for a woman, age 65 for a man) for any week during which he or she is such an earner. Special rates apply to share fishermen and volunteer development workers (see 9160). For a table of rates of Class 2 contributions, see 110.

A self-employed person who does not earn any income in any particular week (e.g. due to holidays) does not thereby cease to be self-employed, but a person who is not ordinarily self-employed will have no Class 2 liability provided his earnings from self-employment do not exceed an annual amount (see 9180).

For the methods of paying Class 2 contributions, see 9358.

Law: SSCBA 1992, s. 1(2); *Social Security (Contributions) (Re-rating) Order* 2009 (SI 2009/593)

Source: CWL 1, *Starting your own business*; CF 10, *Self-employed people with small earnings*

Website: www.hmrc.gov.uk/forms/cf10.pdf

9160   Calculation of Class 2 contributions

Class 2 contributions are payable at a flat weekly rate (if profits exceed the small earnings exemption – see 9180). Therefore, no calculations need to be performed in arriving at the value of a contribution, though the level of total earnings in a tax year is used to determine whether a Class 2 contribution need be paid in respect of each week of self-employment in that particular year, since self-employed earners with small earnings may claim exception from liability in certain circumstances (see 9180).

A week is treated as falling wholly within the year in which it begins. In the past, if payment of Class 2 contributions was made at regular weekly intervals, it was possible in some years that 53 weekly contributions would be paid, since each year consists of 52 weeks and one or, in leap years, two days. If a year has 53 contribution weeks, this will be reflected in the quarterly bills.

Class 2 and benefit claims

A Class 2 contribution paid will count towards the benefit entitlement of the individual concerned, but the benefits covered do not include contribution-based jobseeker's allowance or the earnings-related component of the state pension scheme (see 8736).

Share fishermen and volunteer development workers

Notwithstanding the above, regulations have been made to allow share fishermen and certain volunteer development workers to qualify for contribution-based jobseeker's allowance on the basis of Class 2 contributions payable at special rates (see 110 for a table of rates).

Residence conditions for Class 2 liability

No person is liable or entitled to pay contributions of any class unless he fulfils prescribed conditions of residence or presence in Great Britain (see 9452). Before a person may become liable to pay Class 2 contributions in respect of any particular week, he must be ordinarily resident (see 9456) in the UK or, if he is not so ordinarily resident, he must have been resident in the UK for at least 26 out of the preceding 52 contribution weeks. Before entitlement to pay a Class 2 contribution can arise for a self-employed earner, the earner in question must have been present in the UK in the week in respect of which the contribution is to be paid.

National Insurance Contributions

Law: SSCBA 1992, s. 11(1); *Social Security (Contributions) (Re-rating) Order* 2009 (SI 2009/593); *Social Security (Contributions) Regulations* 2001 (SI 2001/1004), reg. 125(c), 145(1)(c), (d), 149, 150;

Source: CWL 1, *Starting your own business*; CF 10, *Self-employed people with small earnings*

Website: www.hmrc.gov.uk/leaflets/nic.htm

9170 Incapacity: automatic exception from Class 2 liability

Automatic exception from Class 2 liability is granted to a self-employed earner for a week where certain conditions are fulfilled, though he may, if he wishes, pay the contribution, subject to certain restrictions, if he so wishes. Exception is mandatory in respect of a contribution week where the earner is:

- in receipt of sickness benefit, invalidity benefit or incapacity benefit in respect of the whole week;
- incapable of work throughout the whole week;
- in receipt of maternity allowance;
- detained in legal custody or imprisoned during the whole week; or
- in receipt of unemployability supplement or invalid care allowance.

Those provisions which refer to a whole contribution week mean a week which excludes Sunday or some other day which is excluded on religious grounds from the working week.

Law: *Social Security (Contributions) Regulations* 2001 (SI 2001/1004), reg. 43

9180 Small earnings exception from Class 2 liability

A self-employed person may, on application and subject to conditions, be excepted from an otherwise unavoidable Class 2 liability for any period in which his earnings from self-employment are (or are treated as being) less than a specified amount. See 110 for a table of specified amounts.

Approval of claim for small earnings exception

If the National Insurance Contributions Office (NICO) approves the application, it issues a certificate of exception, CF17, which states the period of coverage, normally a tax year, or a period ending on 5 April if application is not made before the start of a tax year. The earner must produce the certificate to any official on request.

If any of the conditions for the granting of exception is not, or ceases to be, fulfilled (e.g. the earner ceases to be a self-employed earner), the certificate becomes invalid at that time and the earner must notify NICO of the fact, which is achieved by completing a declaration on the certificate and returning it to NICO. Similarly, the earner must notify NICO in writing (in practice also by completing a declaration on the certificate itself) if he wishes the certificate to be cancelled for whatever reason and the certificate ceases to have effect from a date specified by NICO.

Certificates may be renewed if the conditions of issue are still fulfilled and, indeed, NICO prompts any earner in possession of a certificate by forwarding a copy of booklet CA02 shortly before the old certificate expires. Certificates can cover three years from issue.

The granting of exception and the consequent non-payment of contributions may prejudice the earner's future benefit entitlement, which depends on the individual's contribution record.

Earnings for the purpose of small earnings exception

The key criterion for the availability of exception is the level of earnings. Earnings, in the context of the self-employed earner, means net earnings from employment as a self-employed earner, which is officially interpreted as meaning profits calculated according to normal commercial accountancy principles such as would be shown in a profit and loss account, time apportioned to the relevant tax year. Total net earnings are to be arrived at by deducting from income business expenses incurred in the course of the self-employed activity, e.g. rent and rates, insurance, employees' wages, printing and stationery, repairs and postage. Furthermore, official guidance states that the earner should make an allowance for depreciation of equipment such as a vehicle, if it is used for the business, and any stock taken for the earner's own use is to be taken into account as income. However, the guidance makes it clear that no deduction is available in respect of income tax or Class 2 or Class 4 contribution liabilities.

Earnings from all sources as a self-employed earner must be aggregated in arriving at a total to compare with the exception limit.

In looking at the likely level of earnings, NICO usually accepts the evidence of an income tax assessment, or the accounts for a period not yet agreed with the Revenue, or if neither is available, any evidence which the earner has to support his application, such as a record of business receipts and expenditure for the year.

Earnings which suffer Class 1 contributions, but are included in business profits (e.g. for sub-postmasters) may be excluded from the calculation of profit for the purposes of the small earnings exception.

Retrospective exception

Claims for retrospection may be made, in writing and with supporting evidence, for periods which commenced after 6 April 1988. Any application for exception must be made between 6 April following the end of the tax year and the following 31 December. As earnings are officially defined as profits as shown in the accounts for the year in question and expects those profits to be calculated on an actual basis (i.e. time-apportioned if the accounting year does not end on 5 April), many self-employed earners whose accounting year ends other

National Insurance Contributions

than on 5 April find it impossible to make an application for a certificate. It is understood that local offices have been instructed to accept any reasonable evidence of profits in the period from the accounting year end to the following 5 April.

A retrospective claim may involve the contributor repaying benefits already claimed on the basis of those contributions. The repayment automatically excepts the earner from liability for the period covered by the repayment if the earner is not already excepted, and NICO must issue the appropriate certificate to that effect.

Law: SSCBA 1992, s. 11(4); *Social Security (Contributions) (Re-rating) Order* 2009 (SI 2009/593); *Social Security (Contributions) Regulations* 2001 (SI 2001/1004), reg. 44(4)–(6), 45(2), 46

Source: CF 10, *Self-employed people with small earnings*

Website: www.hmrc.gov.uk/forms/cf10.pdf

9190   Married women and widows: Class 2

There is no separate rate or type of Class 2 contributions payable by married women or widows. However, where such earners are entitled by virtue of a reduced rate election made before 12 May 1977 (see 9076) not to participate in the NIC scheme, it is currently possible for them to elect not to pay Class 2 contributions.

Law: SSCBA 1992, s. 19(4); *Social Security (Contributions) Regulations* 2001 (SI 2001/1004), reg. 127(1)(b)

CLASS 3 CONTRIBUTIONS

9210   Nature of Class 3 (voluntary) contributions

Class 3 contributions are voluntary contributions. A person is never *liable* to pay Class 3 contributions, but he may be entitled to pay, to protect entitlement to widows' benefits and the basic retirement pension (see 8736). In certain limited cases involving overseas employment, voluntary Class 2 contributions may be paid as an alternative to Class 3 in order to protect entitlement to incapacity benefit and maternity allowance on the employee's return to the UK.

Class 3 contributions are flat-rate contributions. See 110 for a table of the rates applying.

Law: SSCBA 1992, s. 13(1), 14(1); *Social Security (Contributions) (Re-rating) Order* 2009 (SI 2009/593); *Social Security (Additional Class 3 National Insurance Contributions) (Amendment) Regulations* 2009 (SI 2009/659); *Social Security (Contributions) (Amendment*

No. 2) Regulations 2008 (SI 2008/607); *Social Security (Contributions) Regulations* 2001 (SI 2001/1004), reg. 49, 126–139, 145

Source: CA 5603, *To pay voluntary National Insurance contributions*

Website: www.hmrc.gov.uk/nic/ca5603.pdf

9220   Eligibility for Class 3 (voluntary) contributions

Class 3 contributions may be made by men between the ages of 16 and 65 years and by women between the ages of 16 and 60 years who satisfy the following conditions in respect of any tax year:

- the person is resident in the UK throughout the year;
- the person has arrived in the UK during the year and has been or is liable to pay Class 1 or Class 2 contributions in respect of an earlier period during that year;
- the person has arrived in the UK during the year and was either ordinarily resident (see 9456) in the UK throughout the year or became ordinarily resident during the course of it; and
- the person not being ordinarily resident in the UK has arrived during the year or the previous year and has been continuously present in the UK for 26 complete contribution weeks, entitlement where the arrival has been in the previous year arising only in respect of the next year.

No Class 3 contributions may be paid in respect of a contribution year if the individual has in any case satisfied certain contribution conditions by reference to Class 1 or Class 2.

Married women and widows with certificates of reduced liability following an election before 12 May 1977 (see 9076) (or under transitional provisions) cannot pay Class 3 contributions.

Law: SSCBA 1992, s. 13(1), 14(1); *Social Security (Contributions) Regulations* 2001 (SI 2001/1004), reg. 49, 126–139, 145(1)(e)

Source: CA 5603, *To pay voluntary National Insurance contributions*

Website: www.hmrc.gov.uk/nic/ca5603.pdf

9225   Is payment worthwhile?

The value of voluntary contributions will depend on a contributor's personal circumstances and attitude to investment return and risk.

With the basic state pension worth £95.25 per week in 2009–10 and pro-rata reductions for years with inadequate contribution records, the arithmetic for a single person should be fairly straightforward on one level.

National Insurance Contributions

A man needs 44 qualifying years if he is to receive the full basic pension, so each deficient year will reduce the basic pension by around $1/44$, or £2.16 per week (or £112.32 per annum) at state retirement age in current money terms.

A married male contributor will of course also qualify for an additional amount of Category B pension for a qualifying spouse of £57.05 (for 2009–10), if the spouse does not already qualify for her own Category A pension on the basis of her own contributions. A deficient or 'blank' year will then cost £3.46 per week or £179.92 per year in state pension. These provisions are also as relevant for registered civil partners as they are to married couples.

The actual figure will of course depend on the level of the basic state pension at the time (it is currently uprated each year in line with the Retail Price Index, unless the Government chooses to award a bigger increase (as was the case in April 2002 and 2003)), the rounding rules applied at the time and any changes in the state pension system introduced in the interim. It is possible that the Pension Credit will mean that blank years are in effect meaningless. A judgment will also need to be made about whether it is financially more sensible to 'invest' in extra state pension contributions, for extra pension from age 65, or in an alternative private pension fund. This decision may well be influenced by the age and health of the voluntary contributor and his or her attitude to both investment risk and political commitment to the state pension system.

The position is more complex for women than men because many of them will qualify for Home Responsibilities Protection (HRP) as a result of having caring responsibilities (e.g. being eligible for child benefit for a child under 16). HRP can reduce the number of qualifying years needed for a full basic pension from 39 to as few as 20 (22 after 2020 when state pension age is fully equalised for men and women). If a blank year reduces the number of qualifying years below 20 for a woman with maximum HRP, it may cost $1/20$ of the full pension rather than $1/39$. If the blank year has no effect, because there are already 20 qualifying years, there is little point in paying Class 3 contributions voluntarily. If the woman will receive more on the basis of her husband's contribution record (up to 60 per cent of his basic pension) than she can earn in her own right by paying voluntarily, there is again little reason to pay.

If the current year shows no contributions on the record, it can be brought up to the qualifying level with a Class 3 payment of £626.60 (for 2009–10) or, where possible, a Class 2 payment of £124.80 (for 2009–10). Whether it is worth paying this amount will depend on how far the contributor is away from state retirement age, and how much RPI-linked pension from state retirement age could be bought from a commercial insurer for the same price.

Example

Maggie is aged 51. She is married with two student children and she took most of 2000 and 2001 off as a career break. She now works part-time again as a teacher. In the years to 5 April 2000 and 5 April 2002 she paid enough Class 1 contributions to make the years qualify, but 2000–01 is a 'blank year'. If she wants to pay Class 3 contributions for the year, it will cost her £340.60 (52 × £6.55). Is it worth her while to pay?

> Leaving aside the uncertainty over the potential future political changes to the state pension scheme, and the fact that she is a member of an occupational pension scheme in her current job, it is possible to assess roughly what the contribution might earn.
>
> She has worked and paid adequate contributions for more than 24 years after 1978, and she has 20 years of HRP. She therefore already has the necessary 20 qualifying years to get a full basic pension in her own right, and should not pay voluntarily to make up the blank year.
>
> If she had had no children, and no HRP entitlement, she would have needed 39 qualifying years. The blank year would therefore cost her $1/39$ of £84.25 in today's terms, or £112.32 per year in pension when she retires. As her birthday was in early 1954, she has a state retirement date of 6 January 2018. If she pays £340.60 just before 5 April 2010, as she is entitled to do, it will return £112.32 (plus index-linking) per year for life from January 2018. If she lives 10 years after retirement, the return is around 8.9 per cent before tax, and it is indexed to retail prices as the rules currently stand.

In May 2006 the Government set out proposals to reduce the number of qualifying contribution years needed to qualify for a full basic state pension (*Security in retirement*: www.dwp.gov.uk/pensionsreform). HMRC followed this up with information on how the proposal may impact on the decision to pay voluntary NICs.

Broadly, someone reaching state pension age before 6 April 2010 should be unaffected by the proposed changes. They may wish to pay voluntary Class 3 contributions to increase entitlement to the basic state pension if they are not currently entitled to the full amount or will not be by the time they reach state pension age. However the new proposals will mean that they may not need to pay voluntary contributions if they are due to reach state pension age on or after 6 April 2010 and they:

- have already paid enough contributions to qualify for a full basic state pension under the proposed new rules; and
- anticipate working and paying enough contributions to qualify for a full basic state pension under the proposed new rules.

Law: *Clements v R & C Commrs*(2008) Sp C 677

Website: www.dwp.gov.uk/pensionsreform

CLASS 4 CONTRIBUTIONS

9240   Class 4 contributions liability

Class 4 contributions are profit-related and are payable by self-employed earners in addition to any Class 2 contribution liability (see 9150ff.). The Class 4 contribution liability arises in respect of tax years and is based on the earner's annual profits or gains immediately derived from the carrying on or exercise of one or more trades, professions or vocations, being profits or gains chargeable to tax under ITTOIA 2005 for the year of assessment corresponding to the tax year. Class 4 contributions do not count towards benefit entitlement (see 8736) but are nevertheless income of the National Insurance Fund used for the payment of benefits (see 8710).

Law: SSCBA 1992, s. 15(1)

Source: CWL 1, *Starting your own business*

Website: www.hmrc.gov.uk/leaflets/nic.htm

9244 Exceptions from Class 4

The following categories of person may, on application, be excepted from Class 4 contributions:

- men aged 65 or over and women aged 60 or over at the beginning of the tax year (including people whose sixtieth/sixty-fifth birthday falls on 6 April). However, a person reaching 65/60 during the tax year is liable for Class 4 contributions up to the following 5 April;
- those who are non-resident in the UK for tax purposes during the tax year;
- in some cases, a trustee, executor or administrator;
- a sleeping partner (i.e. someone who supplies capital and takes a share of the profits but takes no active part in running the trade);
- a diver or diving supervisor working in connection with exploration or exploitation activities on the UK continental shelf or in the UK territorial waters and whose earnings are taxed under ITTOIA 2005. (Such divers pay Class 1 contributions.)

It should be noted that exception is not automatic and must be applied for. The certificate should be requested before the start of the year to which it relates, but the National Insurance Contributions Office (see 8700) may accept a later application.

Law: SSCBA 1992, s. 1(6), Sch. 2, para. 5; *Social Security (Contributions) Regulations 2001* (SI 2001/1004), reg. 91(b), 92, 94, 97(5), 65

9250 Earnings for Class 4 purposes

The profits to which the specified percentage rate for Class 4 NICs is applied are closely related to the taxable profits.

The 'earnings' for Class 4 contributions purposes are defined as the profits or gains immediately derived from the carrying on of one or more trades, professions or vocations, being profits or gains chargeable to income tax under ITTOIA 2005 (for the income tax charge, see 550ff.). Furthermore, the charge is based on the full amount of such profits or gains, subject to deductions for allowances for capital expenditure (whether given by way of deduction from trading profits or by discharge or repayment of tax) available in respect of the activities of the trade, profession or vocation and to additions for any balancing charges arising. There is some relief for losses (see 9252).

'Immediately derived'

The term 'immediately derived' means that a contributor will not be liable to pay Class 4 contributions on profits or gains in the earning of which he was not personally involved. This covers the position of a sleeping partner, who is in reality no more than an investor in the business, supplying capital but taking no active part in the running of the business. Payment of a share of profits to a retired partner who provides no services, and the income of non-working Names at Lloyd's should also be covered by this rule.

Application of income tax basis of assessment

The basis of assessment adopted for income tax – including, before the introduction of self-assessment, opening and closing year rules – automatically applies for contribution purposes. It is also possible that the profits liable to Class 4 contributions will be affected by the use of the rule which allows farmers to average their year-on-year profits or by a change of accounting date, which allows HMRC to adjust the trading profits for more than one year.

Inapplicable income tax rules

Although, in principle, Class 4 contributions are levied on the taxable profits or gains from a trade, etc., it is important to distinguish those rules which apply for tax purposes but do not apply for Class 4 contribution purposes. The following are not deductible for Class 4 purposes:

- any personal allowance (see 1850ff.);
- deductions for personal pension premiums or retirement annuity premiums, etc.;
- interest paid in any tax year which falls under ICTA 1988, s. 353 (see 1884);
- where a business charge exceeds available income in a year and an assessment has been raised on the person who paid the charge to collect the tax which he deducted at source in making the payment, such that the surplus is carried forward against the profits of a later year from the same trade as if it were a trading loss (though relief may be given differently: see 9254);
- relief for excess interest payments laid out wholly and exclusively for the purposes of a trade, etc. by means of treating the excess as a loss available for carry-forward or carry-back under the terminal loss provisions (though relief may be given differently: see 9254); and

The concessionary relief for self-employed doctors and dentists to qualify for relief in respect of contributions to the NHS superannuation scheme does not extend to Class 4 contributions, a special commissioner has held.

Partnerships

Partnerships present potential difficulties in the context of Class 4 contributions and specific provision is made in respect of the earnings of partners. Where a trade or profession is carried on by two or more persons jointly, the liability of any one of them in respect of Class

National Insurance Contributions

4 contributions is based on his share of the profits or gains of that trade or profession (bearing in mind that such profits must be immediately derived from that trade or profession) together with his share of the profits or gains of any other trade, etc. which he carries on.

Law: SSCBA 1992, s. 15(1), Sch. 2; *Maher v IR Commrs* (1997) Sp C 111

9252 Loss relief

For the purposes of calculating the amount of profits or gains in respect of which Class 4 contributions are payable, relief is available under, and in the manner provided by, a number of provisions of the Taxes Acts, including the extension of offset to capital allowances:

- the set-off of trading losses against general income (see 2296; though relief is restricted for Class 4 contribution liability to losses arising from activities the profits or gains of which would be brought into computation for the purposes of Class 4 contributions);
- the carry-forward of losses from trading not utilised under the aforementioned rules against future profits from the same trade (see 2292); and
- terminal loss relief (see 2304).

The rules of Class 4 loss relief are extended beyond certain of the restrictions imposed by income tax law. Where losses are carried forward for income tax purposes, they reduce profits from the same trade in a later period, thereby automatically reducing Class 4 profits in that same period. Similarly, where the terminal loss provisions apply, the relief is restricted for income tax purposes to a reduction in taxable profits from the same trade, which has retrospective effect on the assessment for the tax year affected and, again, automatically reduces the Class 4 profits for that year.

Where a trading loss is relieved by a claim to set it off against income other than that derived from a trade, for income tax purposes, the trading profits of other years would be unaffected and there would, in the absence of special provision, be no reduction in Class 4 contribution liabilities. Where a person claims and is allowed relief in respect of a loss in any relevant trade, profession or vocation against total income, rather than against the profits of the same trade, the deduction granted is to be treated as far as possible as reducing the profits or gains for that year of any relevant trade, profession or vocation.

Any excess of loss in that year is carried forward to reduce the first available profits or gains for later years, again from any relevant trade, etc., irrespective of whether a claim for a current year loss exists in those years.

Whether a trading loss is time-apportioned to tax years on the statutory basis or is claimed in full in the year in which the period-end falls on the concessionary basis, any amount which is set against non-trading income must be separately identified and claimed against other trading income in the same or a later year for Class 4 contribution purposes.

Law: SSCBA 1992, Sch. 2, para. 3

9254   Interest and annuity payments

Profits for Class 4 contribution purposes may be reduced by certain payments of interest for which income tax relief is, or can be, given (see 1884ff.). The deduction is available in the year in which payment is made to the extent that such interest has been paid and incurred wholly or exclusively for the purposes of any relevant trade, profession or vocation. Where the profits or gains of the tax year of payment are insufficient to allow relief in full, the payments are carried forward and deducted from, or set off against, the first available profits or gains of any subsequent year:

- it is irrelevant that the payment of interest may not be deductible for income tax purposes in that later year. The fact that the interest was incurred in respect of a relevant trade, profession or vocation is sufficient to create a deduction, which is carried forward until it has been fully utilised against profits.
- the deduction need not be given against the later income from the *same* trade, profession or vocation, since the Act refers to deduction from the profits or gains of any relevant trade, etc.; and
- relief is not lost if the trade in which the loss arose ceases, provided there are earnings at some later point from some relevant trade, etc., since relief is carried forward without limit until it can be deducted.

Relief is also granted on the same basis as that applied to interest in respect of annuities (e.g. to retired partners) and other annual payments made under deduction of tax and wholly or exclusively for the purposes of the business.

Law: SSCBA 1992, Sch. 2, para. 3(5)

9270   Calculation of Class 4 liability

The calculation of liability to Class 4 contributions is based on limits and rates amended annually by statutory instrument, applied to a profit figure based closely, but not exactly, on that arrived at by applying the rules of ITTOIA 2005 income tax. Contributions are payable at a prescribed rate on so much of the relevant profits or gains as exceeds a specified lower annual limit. For a table of rates and limits, see 110.

Contributions are payable on earnings between the lower and upper limits and there is an extra one per cent contribution on profits above the upper limit. Both the lower and upper limits for Class 4 purposes apply on an annual basis and are not time-apportioned if the trade is not carried on for a full year.

Example 1

Peter has earnings as calculated for Class 4 purposes of £18,000 in 2010–11. He is liable to pay Class 4 contributions on so much of his earnings as exceed the lower profit limit of £5,715 (i.e. £12,285 (£18,000 − £5,715) at a rate of 8 per cent. His Class 4 liability for 2010–11 is thus £982.80.

National Insurance Contributions

> ### Example 2
>
> Jerry has earnings as computed for Class 4 purposes of £47,000 in 2010–11. He is liable to pay Class 4 contributions in respect of those earnings falling between the lower and upper earnings limits, i.e. £38,160 (£43,875 − £5,715) at 8 per cent, and at the rate of one per cent of those earnings exceeding the upper earnings limit, i.e. £3,125 (£47,000 − £43,875). His Class 4 liability for 2010–11 is thus £3,084.05.

Law: SSCBA 1992, s. 15(3); SSAA 1992, s. 141(1), 143(1), (3), (4)(b)

9284 Deferment and annual maximum

Where the National Insurance Contributions Office is satisfied that there is doubt as to the extent, if any, of an earner's liability to pay Class 4 contributions for a particular tax year (e.g. because of Class 1 liabilities) a certificate of deferment may be issued which defers the collection of the Class 4 liability until a later date.

9294 Special Class 4 contributions

An examiner, moderator, invigilator, etc. (employed other than through the agency of another) who would normally be an employed earner is treated as a self-employed earner (see 8728). Such a person is liable to pay a 'special Class 4 contribution' where, in any tax year:

- he has earnings (disregarding the amount) which would otherwise be Class 1 earnings;
- the earnings are taxable (but not necessarily taxed) under ITEPA 2003; and
- his total earnings exceed a lower annual limit (which is in practice usually set at the same level as the limit for ordinary Class 4 purposes: see 9240).

The special contribution is calculated using the same basis as ordinary Class 4 contributions (see 9240) applied to the earnings calculated as if they were Class 1 earnings and rounded down to the nearest pound.

Although such special contributions resemble ordinary Class 4 contributions, they are collected directly by the National Insurance Contributions Office (NICO) (see 8700). NICO notifies the earner of the amount of special contributions due for any year and payment is due within 28 days from the receipt of the notice, unless a question is raised under the procedure outlined at 9380.

The employer of the contributor must record the earnings, category letter and the contributor's National Insurance number (which the contributor must disclose) on the deductions working sheet.

Law: SSCBA 1992, s. 18(1)(c); *Social Security (Contributions) Regulations* 2001/1004 (SI 2001/1004), reg. 103–106

INTERACTION OF NIC CLASSES AND ANNUAL MAXIMA

9300 Need for NIC interaction rules

An individual can be liable to pay contributions in any year of Class 1, 2 and 4, e.g. because he has a job and also a part-time self-employed activity. He may also make voluntary contributions if necessary to make the year a qualifying year for benefit purposes. The rate of payment of each contribution is calculated initially without reference to any other class payable.

9302 Annual maximum amounts

Historically, the National Insurance system has worked on annual maximum amounts so that no employee ever paid more than the overall contribution limit based on the upper earnings limit. Legislation, which came into force on 6 April 2003, mimics this principle, but also provides for a charge of one per cent on all earnings without limit. The maximum contributions payable is now therefore a maximum with respect to a certain amount of earnings rather than an absolute maximum.

From 6 April 2003, the maximum amount anyone is liable to pay in Class 1 contributions is equal to 53 weeks full contributions at the main rate of 11 per cent, plus one per cent on all earnings above this sum. However, where multiple jobs are held a primary weekly threshold will apply to each.

Law: *Social Security (Contributions) (Amendment) Regulations* 2003 (SI 2003/193).

NATIONAL INSURANCE: DEFERMENT

9310 Class 1 deferment

From 6 April 2003, employees with more than one employment, who anticipate earning in excess of the upper earnings limit (UEL) in one, or in a number of employments, may apply to the National Insurance Contributions Office (NICO) for deferment of some of their contributions liability. Where permission is obtained, the employee will pay a reduced main employee rate of one per cent on all earnings from the earnings threshold to the UEL and the additional employee rate of one per cent on all earnings above the UEL in the deferred employments.

Where deferment is obtained, form CA2700 will be sent to the employers concerned authorising them to deduct primary NICs at a rate of one per cent on all earnings above the earnings threshold. Employer's contributions will remain payable at the full standard rate.

National Insurance Contributions

Where there is a choice, standard rate employee Class 1 contribution liability will always be deferred, rather than contracted-out liability.

Any application for deferment should be made before the beginning of the tax year for which it is sought. An application form for deferment is contained within leaflet CA 72A, *Deferring employee Class 1 National Insurance contributions (NICs)*.

Any employee Class 1 contributions which should have been paid but which, as a result of deferment, have not been paid, will be collected by direct assessment of the employed earner.

Law: SSCBA 1992, s. 19(1), (2); *Social Security (Contributions) Regulations 2001 (SI 2001/1004),* reg. 84, 85

Source: CA 72A, *Deferring employee Class 1 National Insurance contributions (NICs)*

Website: www.hmrc.gov.uk/leaflets/ca72a.pdf

9320 Repayment

Where an individual has overpaid contributions, the order of repayment is:

(1) Class 4, both ordinary and special (see 9240, 9294);

(2) primary Class 1 at married women's rate;

(3) Class 2;

(4) primary Class 1 at standard not-contracted-out rate; and

(5) primary Class 1 at contracted-out rate.

However, this order is changed if the contributor concerned has a contracted-out personal pension plan or stakeholder personal pension plan, such that the order of the fourth and fifth items is reversed.

Law: *Social Security (Contributions) (Amendment No. 3) Regulations 2010 (SI 2010/646); Social Security (Contributions) Regulations 2001 (SI 2001/1004),* reg. 52(2), 100(1), 110(1)

ADMINISTRATION AND PAYMENT OF NICs

NATIONAL INSURANCE RETURNS AND RECORDS

9336 Class 1 returns

Monthly recording

An employer must keep a P11 deductions working sheet (or computer equivalent) for each employee and record on it various information about the employee and the payments made.

Year-end reporting

At the end of the tax year, the employer must submit forms P14 for all employees, summarised on P35, on or before 19 May, together with any outstanding remittance of PAYE and contributions. Special rules apply to employers of mariners, who are subject to unusual rules on earnings periods and apportionment of earnings.

All but certain excluded employers are required to deliver the NICs end of year return electronically irrespective of whether the employer is also required to deliver a return electronically under the PAYE regulations (see 2552).

From 2010–11 all large employers are required to make specified payments by electronic means (see 2552).

An employer must produce and give to his employee a paper copy of the P14, known as P60, if the employee is in his employment on the last day of the year.

The contents of the P14/P60 in relation to contributions (which must be issued for contribution purposes even if not required under the PAYE regulations) for the year in question are specified in regulations.

The P35 is an employer's annual statement and declaration containing a list of all deductions working sheets which the employer was obliged to keep. The employer uses the standard form to summarise the total contributions due (after netting off SSP and SMP recoveries) on the basis of the deductions working sheets and compare them to the total amounts remitted to HMRC in respect of the year, thereby identifying any over or underpayment for the year. The P35 must be signed in the case of a company by the secretary or a director.

Disclosure of NIC schemes

Regulations came into force on 1 May 2007, which require certain NIC arrangements to be notified to HMRC. Broadly, the provisions for NICs now correspond to the disclosure of information requirements for income tax purposes (see 230).

National Insurance Contributions

Law: *Social Security Administration Act* 1992, s. 132A; *Social Security (Contributions) (Amendment No. 4) Regulations* 2010 (SI 2010/721); *Social Security (Contributions) (Amendment No. 4) Regulations* 2009 (SI 2009/2028); *National Insurance Contributions (Application of Part 7 of the Finance Act 2004) Regulations* 2007 (SI 2007/785); *Social Security (Contributions) Regulations* 2001 (SI 2001/1004), Sch. 4, para. 6; Sch. 4, para. 22; *Income Tax (Employments) Regulations* 1993 (SI 1993/744), reg. 43(1)

Source: *Disclosure of National Insurance Avoidance Schemes* (www.hmrc.gov.uk/aiu/avoidance-scheme.pdf)

9338   Class 1A information requirements

From 2000–01, the Class 1A charge was widened to include most taxable benefits in kind (see 9100ff.). In consequence, the employer will need to know the cash equivalent value of benefits provided, as calculated for income tax purposes and returned on forms P11D, to enable him to calculate the Class 1A liability. The revised P11D applying from 2000–01 includes Class 1A indicators and coloured boxes to make it easier to identify those figures required for the Class 1A return.

Form P11D(b) is the statutory Class 1A return. It is due to HMRC no later than 6 July after the end of the tax year. The form contains boxes for the calculation of Class 1A NICs due and any adjustments which may be necessary to the total benefits figure shown as liable to Class 1A on the P11D.

As far as company cars are concerned, there is an onus of proof on the employer, as the contribution is his liability.

Law: SSCBA 1992, s. 10

Source: CWG5, *Class 1A National Insurance Contributions on Benefits in Kind*

Website: www.hmrc.gov.uk/leaflets/nic.htm

9339   Class 1B reporting requirements

To calculate the amount of Class 1B contributions due in respect of a PAYE settlement agreement (PSA), records will need to be kept of:

- the overall cost of providing the benefits in question;
- the number of employees who received them;
- an indication of what rate of tax they pay;
- an indication which benefits and expenses give rise to a Class 1 or Class 1A liability; and
- the total tax payable under the PSA.

Source: *PAYE settlement agreements*

Website: www.hmrc.gov.uk/guidance/paye-settlements.htm

9340   Class 2 reporting requirements

Every person liable to pay a Class 2 contribution, or not liable but entitled and intending to do so, who has not made special direct debit arrangements with the National Insurance Contributions Office (NICO) (see 8700) or been granted a certificate of exception (see 9180), must notify NICO immediately in writing of the commencement or cessation of his liability or entitlement to pay a contribution. A penalty may be imposed for failing to notify HMRC when Class 2 NICs become payable. There is also a requirement that every person liable to pay a Class 2 contribution or paying voluntarily must immediately notify NICO in writing of any change of address.

Persons who have not previously notified NICO of their self-employment should complete and return to NICO CWF1.

Law: *Social Security (Contributions) Regulations* 2001 (SI 2001/1004), reg. 87, 88; *Social Security (Contributions) (Amendment No. 3) Regulations* 2009 (SI 2009/600)

9342   Class 3 reporting requirements

Since Class 3 contributions are voluntary contributions, there are no reporting requirements.

9344   Class 4 reporting requirements

Income tax information reporting requirements apply to anyone who is liable for Class 4 contributions (see 2550ff.).

PAYMENT AND COLLECTION OF NICs

9354   Class 1 payment and collection

The secondary contributor (usually the employer: see 9000), as well as being liable for his own contributions, is liable, in the first instance, for the employee's primary contributions, on behalf of and to the exclusion of the earner. Any primary contributions paid by the secondary contributor are deemed to have been paid by the earner. However, the secondary contributor may recover the primary contributions by deduction from the earnings paid to the employed earner and in no other way, subject to conditions laid down by regulations.

Where earnings are subject to the aggregation rules, the secondary contributor may deduct primary contributions from any part or parts of those earnings.

National Insurance Contributions

When an employer makes an error in good faith which results in the under-deduction of primary contributions when earnings are paid, he is given a limited right to recoup that under-deduction from later payments of earnings within the same tax year. The maximum supplementary amount which may be deducted in each later period is an amount equal to the primary contributions otherwise due in respect of that later payment of earnings. Correction of past errors may not cross tax year-ends.

Collection of Class 1 contributions with PAYE

The secondary contributor (i.e. usually the employer) is to pay, account for and recover Class 1 contributions in the same way as he pays, accounts for and recovers income tax deducted from emoluments under PAYE.

Payment of Class 1 contributions

Remittances of contributions, net of SSP and SMP recoveries, are generally made each month at the same time as any PAYE is remitted to the collector (i.e. within 14 days of the end of the tax period). Small employers can remit quarterly on or before 19 July, 19 October, 19 January and 19 April in respect of deductions in the quarter ended on the preceding fifth of the month. To qualify for this system, employers' average monthly remittances in the current year in respect of total deductions of PAYE, NICs and tax under the construction industry tax deduction scheme have to be less than £1,500 for periods beginning after 6 April 2000. Quarterly payment may be chosen where the employer has reasonable grounds for believing that the £1,500 per month condition is met, or in the case of an employee who receives a fixed salary or wage, where the inspector of taxes has issued a week 1 or month 1 PAYE code.

Payment by cheque is treated as made on the day on which the cheque is received by the collector.

Law: SSCBA 1992, Sch. 1, para. 3, 6(1); *Social Security (Contributions) (Amendment No. 4) Regulations* 2010 (SI 2010/721); *Social Security (Contributions) Regulations* 2001 (SI 2001/1004), reg. 67, 70, 86 and Sch. 4, para. 6–7, 10–11, 27–29

9356   Class 1A payment and collection

Class 1A contributions are payable by the secondary contributor to his or her PAYE reference at the Accounts Office by 19 July following the end of the tax year. Where payment is made other than by direct debit, a special Class 1A pay slip should be used.

Source: CA33, *Cars and Car Fuel Manual*; CWG5, *Class 1A National Insurance Contributions on Benefits in Kind*

9358   Class 2 payment and collection

Direct debit and quarterly billing are, in general, the only approved methods of paying Class 2 contributions. A third method of payment officially sanctioned by social security law is the deduction of contributions at source from certain state benefits at the time of payment.

Direct debit

Direct debit mandate is a payment system which is officially encouraged. Payments under this arrangement will normally be made by debit to the contributor's bank or building society account on the second Friday in every month covering each of the contribution weeks in the preceding tax month. This may cover four or five weeks' contributions (the exact number is based on the number of Sundays in the preceding tax month), or less if the earner is incapable of work throughout a particular week and HMRC are made aware of the fact (e.g. by the making of a claim to incapacity benefit).

Quarterly billing

Where Class 2 contributions are not payable as above, the contributor should receive within 14 days of the end of the 'contribution quarter' a written notice setting out the number of weeks of liability in that quarter (as reduced for any weeks when benefit was claimed or the liability did not otherwise arise, e.g. where self-employment commenced or ceased), the weekly rate and the formal date of notification. He must then pay the amount due for the quarter within 28 days of the formal date of notification. If the notice is not received, or is lost, defaced or destroyed, or the amount of the notice is disputed, NICO may issue or reissue the notice, giving a new date of notification. The notice must include a bank giro credit form in order that payment may be made at a bank or Post Office. The term 'contribution quarter' means one of the four periods of not less than 13 contribution weeks commencing on the first day of the first, fourteenth, twenty-seventh or fortieth contribution week in any year.

Deduction at source

Deduction of contributions at source from certain state benefits is sometimes possible. The benefits in point include war disablement pension.

Law: SSCBA 1992, Sch. 1, para. 10; *Social Security (Contributions) Regulations* 2001 (SI 2001/1004), reg. 89, 90; *Social Security (Crediting and Treatment of Contributions, and National Insurance Number) Regulations* 2001 (SI 2001/769), reg. 10

Website: www.hmrc.gov.uk/leaflets.htm

National Insurance Contributions

9360   Class 3 payment and collection

Since Class 3 contributions are voluntary contributions, there are less strict requirements for payment. The options are the quarterly bill or monthly direct debit (as with Class 2 contributions: see 9358), or single annual cheque.

Payment of Class 3 contributions is normally due on or before 5 April following the tax year in which the deficiency occurred, though six years may be allowed.

Law: *Social Security (Contributions) Regulations* 2001 (SI 2001/1004), reg. 89, 90(1)

Source: CA 5603, *To pay voluntary National Insurance contributions*

9362   Class 4 payment and collection

Most Class 4 contributions are self-assessed in the same way as tax and collected by HMRC, together with income tax. Subject to specific exceptions, provisions as to assessment (see 2500ff.), collection (see 2775ff.), repayment (see 2770, 8810), recovery (see 2801ff.) and penalties (see 2645ff.) apply as they do to income tax.

Appeals

The appeals system applicable to income tax assessments now also extends to Class 4 contributions assessments, though the provisions of income tax law have no effect on determinations of questions arising in relation to certificates of exception or deferment, or in relation to special Class 4 contributions.

Partnership assessments

Where two or more persons are carrying on business in partnership, the assessment to both tax and NICs will usually be made as a joint assessment in the name of the partnership, though it is possible for each partner to be assessed separately.

Construction industry tax deduction scheme

Deductions of income tax at source under the construction industry tax deduction scheme (see 2787) may exceed the subcontractor's final liability to income tax for a year (e.g. because of interest on borrowings or personal allowances). In such circumstances, the excess may be set off by HMRC against the subcontractor's liability for Class 4 contributions, up to the total of that liability for that year.

Law: SSCBA 1992, s. 15(2), 16(1), Sch. 2, para. 4(2), 8

9364 Repayment of Class 4 contributions

Excessive Class 4 contributions paid may be reallocated by the National Insurance Contributions Office as being on account of other contributions properly payable by the earner but they are otherwise repayable, provided they exceed the true liability by at least £0.50. The repayment must be claimed in the approved manner within:

(1) six years beginning with 6 April in the tax year following that in respect of which the payment was made where the application is in respect of any tax year ending before 6 April 1996;

(2) five years beginning with 1 February in the tax year following that in respect of which the payment was made where the application is in respect of any tax year beginning after 5 April 1996; or

(3) if later than (1) or (2), two years beginning with 6 April in the tax year following that in which the payment was made. The calculation is unaffected by a reduced rate election, even though no Class 2 contributions would in fact be payable. For the annual maximum, see 8790.

Refunds of Class 4 contributions are not made automatically where they are due and a claim must be made by the taxpayer or his agent.

For the circumstances in which repayments will be made to subcontractors before the end of the tax year, see 2787.

Repayment supplement

Repayment supplement has applied to refunds of Class 4 contributions since 19 April 1993 at the same rate as applies to income tax refunds (see 2770).

Law: SSCBA 1992, Sch. 2, para. 6(1); SS(CP)A 1992, Sch. 4, para. 8; *Social Security (Contributions) Regulations* 2001 (SI 2001/1004), reg. 101–103

9368 Compliance checks

A new framework for compliance checks was introduced from 1 April 2009 which changed the way that HMRC conduct enquiries, visits and inspections. Significant changes have been made to the HMRC management of compliance checks across most taxes including income tax, capital gains tax, VAT, PAYE, the construction industry scheme and corporation tax. See 229 for commentary on the compliance regime.

National Insurance Contributions

NIC ENFORCEMENT, PENALTIES AND INTEREST

9386 Enforcement: Class 1 contributions

When a person fails to pay a contribution which he or she is liable to pay, and is found guilty of a criminal offence, such a person shall be liable, on conviction on indictment, to imprisonment for a term not exceeding seven years or a fine, or both, or a summary conviction to a fine not exceeding the statutory maximum.

The collector of taxes, whose responsibilities include the collection of Class 1 contributions, may visit the employer's premises to inspect the records, in order to establish whether an underpayment has occurred. If the collector is not satisfied that the employer has paid the correct contributions due, he may notify the employer of his best estimate of the liability and request a return in respect thereof, to be made within 14 days. In certain circumstances, the contributions so specified will be certified as the amount of the true liability.

Evidence of non-payment of contributions

The collector's certificate thus issued is sufficient evidence of non-payment of contributions (or, from 6 April 1999, of interest on or penalties in respect of contributions), until the contrary is proven, in any court proceedings. Any document which purports to be such a certificate of non-payment is deemed to be such, until it is proven otherwise.

No time limit is placed on the period covered by the certificate which the collector issues, except that it covers the years or income tax months or quarters covered by the inspection.

Where a secondary contributor claims that a contribution has been paid but is unable to produce evidence of the fact, a statutory declaration by the officer dealing with the case to the effect that no record of the contribution has been found will be admissible in evidence in criminal proceedings against the secondary contributor, provided it has been served on the person charged with the offence at least seven full days before any hearing or trial of the offence. The declaration must be served in the same way as a summons or citation. However, the accused may give notice to the court, not less than three days before the due date of the hearing, requiring the person who made the declaration to attend the hearing. in such a case, the statutory declaration may not be admitted in evidence.

Recovering Class 1 contributions and tax

In most cases, if earnings have not been subjected to contribution liability, they have also escaped PAYE deduction. It is therefore specifically provided that proceedings may (but need not be) be brought for the recovery of the total amount of contributions and tax.

Conduct of proceedings

Criminal proceedings for non-payment of contributions (see above) may be brought at any time within three months from the date on which evidence sufficient to justify them comes to the attention of the Secretary of State (i.e. the collector, or the National Insurance

Contributions Office (NICO)), or within 12 months of the commission of the offence, whichever is later.

An employer compliance officer or any other person authorised to do so may conduct proceedings before a magistrates' court for such an offence. He need not be legally qualified.

Offences by companies

Where a company commits an offence of failure to pay a contribution, NICO may also proceed against any director, manager, secretary or other similar officer of the company if the offence has been committed with his consent or connivance, or is attributable to his neglect. The fact that a person is not formally a director is irrelevant if he is a member of a company that is managed by its members.

Such an offending director, etc. may have his personal assets frozen by High Court order until a confiscation order is paid.

Law: *Criminal Justice Act* 1988, Sch. 4, Pt. I; *SSAA* 1992, s. 115, 116(1), (2), 118; *SSA* 1998, s. 61, 62(1); *Social Security (Contributions) Regulations* 2001 (SI 2001/1004), Sch. 4, para. 14, 15, 16, 26; *Social Security Act 1998 (Commencement No. 4) Regulations* 1999 (SI 1999/526)

9388   Liability of directors for company's contributions

Where a company fails to pay contributions (or interest or penalties in respect of contributions) within the prescribed time, due to the fraud or neglect of a director, manager or secretary, etc., a 'personal liability notice' may be served on the culpable person, requiring him to pay some or all of the contributions, etc. Where there is more than one culpable person, the amount between them may be apportioned in the proportion which each person's culpability bears to that of all the culpable persons taken as a whole. In assessing such individual culpability, regard may be had regard both to the gravity of the person's fraud or neglect, and to the consequences of it. Any amount paid will be deducted from the company's liability. These measures are intended to deal with 'phoenix directors'.

There is a right of appeal against the issue or contents of a personal liability notice, but only on the ground that:

- the failure to pay the contributions due was not attributable to any fraud or neglect on the part of the individual concerned;
- the individual was not a director, manager or secretary, etc. of the company at the time of the alleged fraud or neglect; or
- the opinion formed by the Secretary of State as to the degree of culpability of the individual was unreasonable.

National Insurance Contributions

Law: SSAA 1992, s. 121C, 121D; SSA 1998, s. 64; *Social Security Contributions (Transfer of Functions etc.) Act* 1999, s. 11(4); *Social Security Act 1998 (Commencement No. 4) Regulations* 1999 (SI 1999/526); *Social Security Contributions (Transfer of Functions etc.) Act 1999 (Commencement No. 1 and Transitional Provisions) Order* 1999 (SI 1999/527)

9389   Enforcement of Class 2

Before 6 April 1999, it was an offence if a person failed to pay any contribution which he or she was liable to pay, at or within the time prescribed. In the case of a Class 2 liability, this was by the end of the 28-day period allowed from the end of each contribution quarter in respect of which the liability arose (see 9358). The offence has been replaced by one of fraudulently evading contributions (see further 9386).

Conviction on such a charge of failing to pay a contribution which remains unpaid at the time of the conviction leads to a liability to pay to the Secretary of State a sum equal to the amount of the contribution which the contributor failed to pay. The amount so due is recoverable as a penalty but counts as a Class 2 contribution if that is indeed what it represents.

Failure to pay a Class 2 contribution rarely leads to court proceedings, especially if arrears of contributions are paid by the contributor. A ministerial statement on 24 February 1978 disclosed that what is now the National Insurance Contributions Office (see 8700) waives arrears, by unpublished concession, in various cases (col. 836). The examples mentioned are where the contributor would have been entitled to small earnings exception for the year in question had it been claimed and where the contributor's financial circumstances would make recovery impracticable. The statement disclosed also that this practice extends to many thousands of cases each year.

Where Class 2 contributions are paid late, they may have to be paid at a higher rate and they may not count for benefit purposes. Where a contribution is paid in the year in which the liability arises or in the next year, the rate is that which applied on the normal due date. If payment is more than 12 months after the end of the year in which the contribution week in question fell, it must be paid at the highest of all rates which have applied in any of the years between the year of liability and the year of payment. In limited circumstances, another rate may apply.

Law: SSCBA 1992, s. 12(3); SSAA 1992, s. 114(1), 119(1), 121(4), (5); *Social Security (Contributions) Regulations* 2001 (SI 2001/1004), 63, 64, 65

9390   Enforcement of Class 3 contributions

Class 3 contributions are voluntary, and as such there is no enforcement procedure.

9391   Enforcement of Class 4 contributions

The enforcement provisions applying to income tax on trading profits apply to Class 4 contributions.

9392   NIC penalties

For 2010–11 onwards the penalty regime contained in *Finance Act* 2009, Sch. 56 applies to late payments of Class 1, 1A and 1B NICs (see 2646).

For 2010–11 and subsequent years, the penalty regime contained in *Finance Act* 2007, Sch. 24 applies for inaccuracies and other documents to returns of Class 1A NICs (see 2655).

Penalties: Class 2 contributions

A penalty of £100 may be levied where a person liable to Class 2 contributions fails to notify HMRC of his liability within three calendar months of starting in business.

Law: *Social Security (Contributions) (Amendment No. 4) Regulations* 2010 (SI 2010/721); *Social Security (Contributions) Regulations* 2001 (SI 2001/1004), reg. 87.

Penalties: Class 4 contributions

The penalty regime for Class 4 contributions is that for income tax on trading profits (see 2645ff.).

Law: FA 2007, Sch. 24; SSCBA 1992, Sch. 1, para. 7; SSAA 1992, s. 119(1), 121(4)–(6); SSA 1998, s. 61

9394   Interest on underpaid/overdue NICs

Interest is chargeable on Class 1 (and Class 1A) contributions not paid by the due date. The rate of interest is the same as for late-paid income tax or repayment supplement (see 15) and is non-deductible in the employer's tax computation. For Class 1, the reckonable date for interest is 19 April following the end of the year in which the earnings are paid (i.e. as for PAYE). For Class 1A, the reckonable date is now 19 July after the tax year.

Such interest may also be charged on Class 4 contributions collected by assessment. The statutory provisions relating to the final and conclusive nature of an assessment are extended to the Class 4 contribution liability and the Class 4 assessment may only be adjusted in accordance with the rules for income tax assessments, subject to an extension to allow relief for annuities, interest and other annual payments.

National Insurance Contributions

Law: TMA 1970, s. 30A(4), 31(1), 86, 118(4); SSCBA 1992, Sch. 2, para. 7; *Social Security (Contributions) Regulations* 2001 (SI 2001/1004), Sch. 4, para. 17–20

9396 Interest on delayed NIC refunds

Where Class 1 or Class 1A NICs are repaid after the 'relevant date', repayment supplement is now payable. The relevant date is:

- for NICs overpaid more than 12 months after the end of the year in respect of which the payment was made, the last day of the year in which they were paid; or
- for any other case, the last day of the year after the year in respect of which the NICs in question were paid.

Law: *Social Security (Contributions) Regulations* 2001 (SI 2001/1004), Sch. 4, para. 18

9400 Repayment of interest

Where an employer has paid interest on a Class 1 or Class 1A contribution which is subsequently found not to have been due (whether this was simply because interest was not due or because the contributions in question were returned or repaid to the employer under the provisions outlined at 9320, 9356), the interest is to be repaid.

Law: *Social Security (Contributions) Regulations* 2001 (SI 2001/1004), Sch. 4, para. 19

9404 Remission of interest

Interest may be remitted in cases of official error or omission, where the employer or his agent did not cause or materially contribute to the error or omission. Instead of running from the normal relevant date, interest does not begin to run until 14 days after the official error is rectified and the employer is advised of the rectification.

If a dispute over Class 1 contribution liability arises which leads to a question being put to the Secretary of State (see 9380) or a referral to the High Court (or Court of Session in Scotland), it is provided that the interest is still chargeable (on the amount ultimately due) but not actually payable until the question has been formally and finally determined. However, it does not run for the period from the date the question is put to the Secretary of State or the referral to the court is made until 14 days after the final determination of the question.

Law: SSCBA 1992, Sch. 1, para. 6(4); *Social Security (Contributions) Regulations* 2001 (SI 2001/1004), Sch. 4, para. 20

9406 Distraint: NICs

HMRC powers to take distraint, etc. action in respect of unpaid tax, etc. (see 2804) are to be extended to unpaid NICs, etc. where any such debt has not been paid within 30 days of service of the certificate of unpaid contributions, etc. (see 9386).

Law: SSA 1998, s. 63

NATIONAL INSURANCE: FOREIGN ELEMENT

9450 Territorial scope of NICs and benefits

For the employee working overseas it is important to know whether, if he is involved in an industrial accident while carrying out overseas duties, he is covered on repatriation to the UK or hospitalisation overseas for industrial injuries and invalidity benefits. By the same token, the responsible employer will wish to ensure that such cover is maintained. The employee who spends much of his working life overseas, but nevertheless intends throughout to retire to the UK, will wish to ensure that his retirement pension cover is being adequately maintained during his absence abroad.

For both employer and employee, it is obviously also very important to know how much continued social security cover is going to cost. For example:

- Is it necessary for the payment of Class 1 contributions to continue when an employee is sent to work overseas?
- Is there a liability to social security contributions or equivalent taxes in the host state?
- If overseas contributions are payable, what relief (if any) is available against UK liability? After all, income and corporation tax law provide for unilateral relief to prevent double taxation, so why should social security law be different?
- Are there any options as to the amount of cover which may be purchased?

other important questions to consider are:

- Are there any steps which may be taken to mitigate liability, either in the host state or in the UK, or in both?
- If such steps are taken, what is the effect on benefit entitlement for the employees involved?

Given the wide range of types of social security provision around the world, it is critically important for an employer to be able to establish before posting an employee exactly how much will be payable in contributions and how much could potentially be received by his employees in benefits, both in the UK and overseas.

For these purposes, it is convenient to divide the nations of the world into three groups which match the three broad sets of rules which may apply to situations involving international movements of staff. These groups are, in suggested order of importance to UK employers:

- EEA member states;
- states with which the UK has concluded a reciprocal agreement on social security; and
- the rest of the world.

HMRC have put together a webpage (www.hmrc.gov.uk/nic/work/new-rules.htm) to help employers prepare for the new EU Regulation 883/2004 (amended by Regulation 988/2009) and Implementing Regulation 987/2009. The regulations change some of the UK's National Insurance contributions rules for people moving around the EU and their employers. The rules apply from 1 May 2010.

Law: *Recovery of Social Security Contributions Due in Other Member States Regulations 2010 (SI 2010/926)*

Source: *National Insurance for employers of people working abroad*; NI 38, *Social Security abroad – National Insurance contributions; Social security benefits, Health care in certain overseas countries*

Website: www.hmrc.gov.uk/pdfs/nico/ni132/ni132.htm

9452 National Insurance: cross-border implications generally

An understanding of the basic rules of the UK system as they apply in connection with most countries is fundamental. However, there are reliefs available under EEA provisions and reciprocal agreements (see 8754, 9460).

Provision is made for exempting from paying UK contributions those persons who could make no call on the state for benefit.

An employed earner (i.e. potentially subject to Class 1 liability) is anyone who is gainfully employed *in Great Britain* (equivalent provisions apply in Northern Ireland) either under a contract of service, or in an office (including elective office) with emoluments chargeable to tax under the charge on employment income provisions of ITEPA 2003 (see 8712). However, no person is liable or entitled to pay contributions of any class on earnings of any kind unless he fulfils prescribed conditions of *residence* or *presence* in Great Britain. This applies to both employers and employees.

Anyone who falls to be categorised as an employed earner by reason of being gainfully employed in Great Britain is liable for employee Class 1 contributions in respect of the earnings from his employment if, at the time of his employment, he is:

- resident in Great Britain;
- present (or but for any temporary absence would be present) in Great Britain; or
- ordinarily resident in Great Britain (see 9464).

A person is employed in Great Britain if he works in Great Britain, irrespective of where he signed or otherwise entered into his contract of employment.

Law: SSCBA 1992, s. 1(6); *Social Security (Contributions) Regulations* 2001 (SI 2001/1004), reg. 145, 146

9454 Persons sent from abroad to work in the UK

Under the rule in 9452, an employee who visits the UK in the course of his employment potentially faces a contribution liability, however short the visit. Overseas directors of UK companies may, in certain cases, escape liability in respect of short visits, despite the fact that the board meets in the UK. Contributions may be avoided simply by ensuring that they fail to fulfil the specified conditions as to residence and presence. The directors in question are those UK company directors who are not ordinarily UK-resident.

The official view is as follows:

'At present, when a director is neither resident nor ordinarily resident in the United Kingdom, the Contributions Agency does not seek payment of Class 1 National Insurance contributions for employment in the United Kingdom as a director if;

(1)   the only work they do in the UK is to attend board meetings; *and*

(2)   either

   (a)   they attend no more than 10 board meetings in a tax year, none of which lasts more than two days *or*

   (b)   there is only one board meeting in a tax year and that meeting does not last more than two weeks.'

The rule may be automatically overridden by EEA regulations where they apply (e.g. where a French non-executive director attends four one-day quarterly board meetings of a UK company in the UK) or a reciprocal agreement applies.

Where an *employee* is not ordinarily resident (see 9464) in the UK, no Class 1 liability arises until a continuous period of 52 weeks of residence has elapsed beginning with the contribution week following the date of last entry into the UK. The conditions are that the employee:

● is not ordinarily employed in Great Britain, and
● the employment is mainly employment outside the UK by an employer whose place of business is outside the UK (whether or not he also has a place of business in the UK).

A 'place of business' is officially regarded as being any place from which a person can, as of right, conduct his business, or from which his agent has power to conduct business on his behalf. The premises of a UK subsidiary of an overseas parent company are not automatically a place of business of that parent. An employer who has no presence or place of business in the UK has no secondary Class 1 liability at any time, even when the initial period of 52 weeks has expired and the employee has become liable to primary contributions.

National Insurance Contributions

From 6 April 1994, a secondary liability has been imposed on UK host employers to which employees are seconded by overseas businesses with no UK presence, unless they are protected by treaty provisions.

Example

A Japanese employer seconds a member of staff to its UK subsidiary without his becoming an employee of the UK company. The UK subsidiary is responsible for secondary contributions in respect of the earnings of the employee, though only after the employee has lived in the UK for 52 continuous weeks.

Source: *Tax Bulletin*, Issue 79, October 2005 (Employees sent from abroad to work in the UK – time apportionment of earnings for Class 1 National Insurance); *National Insurance for employers of people working abroad*; NI 138, *Social Security abroad – National Insurance contributions; Social security benefits, Health care in certain overseas countries*

Website: www.hmrc.gov.uk/nic/work/abroad-index.htm

9456   Persons sent from the UK to work abroad

Where a UK employer sends an employee to work overseas, UK Class 1 liability does not automatically cease immediately. Contributions continue to be due for 52 weeks on all of the employee's earnings from the employment if:

- the employer has a place of business in Great Britain (see 9454);
- the earner is ordinarily resident in Great Britain; and
- immediately before starting the employment abroad the employee was resident in Great Britain.

Ordinary residence

Official guidance is that a person is ordinarily resident in a particular country if he:

- normally lives there, apart from temporary or occasional absences; *and*
- has a settled and regular mode of life there.

It is also stated that a person may be ordinarily resident in:

- a place from which he is temporarily absent, *or*
- in some circumstances, two places at once.

Some of the factors which are considered in deciding whether a person is ordinarily resident in Great Britain are listed as follows:

Factor	Indication that you are
You return to the UK from time to time during the period of employment abroad.	Continued ordinary residence. The more frequent or the longer the returns, the stronger the indication that you are.
Visits to your family who have remained at your home in GB, or holidays spent at your home in GB.	Ordinarily resident.
Visits in connection with the overseas work, e.g. for briefing or training or to make a report.	Not such a strong indication that you are.
Partner and/or children are with you during your overseas employment.	Not ordinarily resident especially if you do not retain a home in GB or only make occasional visits to GB.
You maintain a home in GB during your absence.	Ordinarily resident.
Your home in GB is available for your use on your return.	Ordinarily resident, but if your house has been rented on a long let it is not a strong indication of ordinary residence.
You have lived in GB for a substantial period.	The longer the period, the stronger the indication that you are despite the period of employment abroad.
You will return to GB at the end of your employment abroad.	The earlier the return, the stronger the indication that you are.

Postings to associated companies

Where the person sent overseas is placed under contract to an overseas company, UK liability ceases at once, except on earnings paid under any continuing UK contract. Whether the UK contract ceases will depend on a number of factors:

- which company has the right to control the employee's work while he is overseas;
- which company has the right to suspend or dismiss the employee;
- whether the UK company is able to recall the employee at any time; and
- which company funds the employee's earnings.

Regard may also be had to continued membership of the employer's UK pension scheme, though this is not a decisive factor.

If an employee sent overseas in continuation of a UK employment and covered by the 52-week rule is transferred to another offshore posting with the same employer within the 52-week period, the Class 1 liability ceases, because the condition that the employee must be UK-resident immediately before starting the employment abroad (see above) is no longer fulfilled.

From 6 April 2010, NIC credits may be provided for the accompanying spouse or civil partner of a member of HM forces who is on an assignment outside the UK.

Law: *Social Security (Credits) (Amendment) Regulations* 2010 (SI 2010/385)

National Insurance Contributions

Source: *National Insurance for employers of people working abroad*; NI 38, *Social Security abroad – National Insurance contributions; Social security benefits, Health care in certain overseas countries*

Website: www.hmrc.gov.uk/nic/work/abroad-index.htm

9458 EEA regulations: National Insurance

General UK cross-border National Insurance rules (see 9452) may automatically be overridden in the case of EEA nationals transferred between member states, as they are subject to regulations on social security for migrant workers. These regulations have direct effect in all member states. The European Economic Area came into being on 1 January 1994, extending EU regulations on social security for migrant workers to the then EFTA countries which acceded to the EEA agreement (see below). For transfers before that date between the UK and non-EU states, the existing reciprocal agreements apply. The remaining notes below relate to transfers between EU/EEA states from 1 January 1994.

Employers must be aware that the definition of the territory of each state within the EEA may not be exactly as expected. For example, the UK excludes the Isle of Man and the Channel Islands, but includes Gibraltar. France includes its overseas departments but excludes Monaco, while Spain includes the Canary and Balearic Islands and two territories in North Africa, but excludes Andorra.

The reciprocal agreements on social security between the UK and Iceland, Norway, Sweden, Finland and Austria (these last three becoming members of the EU in any case on 1 January 1995) were superseded on 1 January 1994 by the EU regulations as a result of the European Economic Area Treaty. Liechtenstein also became a member of the EEA upon ratification, but it will not become party to the social security arrangements for some time, as it must first disentangle itself from the Swiss economy. Switzerland, the only EFTA country to vote against ratification of the EEA Treaty, will remain covered by a reciprocal agreement with the UK.

The regulations apply only to EU/EEA nationals, and each member state defines its nationals in its own terms. Some Channel Islanders and Manxmen with links to the UK are deemed to be EU nationals, but they are only affected by the EU regulations when moving between member states, not when moving to and from their home islands.

The basic premise of EEA law is that a worker pays social security contributions in the state in which he works. However, there are exceptions for temporary duties in other member states.

Short-term postings

Where an EU/EEA national employed in the UK by an undertaking to which he is normally attached is sent by the employer to work in, e.g. Germany, he may remain in the UK contribution scheme if:

- the period of employment in Germany is expected to be less than 12 months; and
- he is not being sent to replace another person whose tour of duty has ended.

This rule applies to any short-term secondment of an EU/EEA national between two member states. As a result of Decision 128 of the EU Administrative Commission on Social Security for Migrant Workers, it may even apply to staff recruited in one state for immediate posting to a second member state, provided the posting employer normally operates at least part of his business in the home state.

The competent authority in the state in which the transfer originates will issue a standard certificate (E101) which proves to the host country authorities that no contributions need be deducted there.

Where a person is recruited by a UK company in, for example Spain, for work in that country, the short-term secondment rule cannot apply and Spanish contributions will be due from the outset.

Similarly, where a person is transferred to another EU/EEA member state to work there for more than 12 months, liability will arise in the host state (unless the extension of postings or longer postings rules, below, apply) from the outset.

Extension of postings

The initial period of 12 months may be extended with the agreement of the host country's authorities by up to 12 further months provided that the extension beyond 12 months was genuinely a result of unexpected circumstances. The further certificate is the E102. Application is made by completing the E102 in quadruplicate and submitting it to the authorities.

Longer postings

In certain exceptional cases, it is possible to obtain the agreement of the authorities to an extension of a E101 certificate for up to five years or, even more exceptionally, longer. No time limit is specified, but a maximum of five years has become a de facto standard. The conditions are laid down in Decision 16 of the EU Administrative Commission on Social Security for Migrant Workers:

- the employee must have special knowledge or skills not available in the local labour market; and
- the employer must have specific objectives in the other member state with which the employee is familiar; or
- remaining in the home scheme is in the employee's best interests.

The individual's explicit consent is required before an extension may be issued.

The contractual link between posting employer and posted employee must be maintained throughout the secondment period, as specified in Decision 128.

National Insurance Contributions

Construction workers

From 2 January 1998, self-employed British construction workers have only been eligible for E101 certificates (see above) if they have been self-employed in the UK for the majority of the 24 months before the E101 application. (Previously, such workers would be regarded as normally self-employed where they had a minimum of 12 weeks' self-employment within the last two tax years.) Employees who are sent to work abroad by a UK company are unaffected by the change.

Concurrent work in different member states

A person who is concurrently employed in two member states is subject to the legislation of the state in which he is habitually resident, if he carries out some of his duties there or he is attached to several undertakings or employers who have their registered offices or places of business in different member states. If he does no work in the state where he is habitually resident, he is subject to the legislation of the member state in whose territory is situated the registered office or place of business of his employer. If he has employers in different member states in these circumstances, there is no tie-breaker to settle where liability arises.

If a person is employed in one member state and self-employed in a second member state, he is generally subject to the legislation of the state in which he is in paid employment, though there are a number of exceptions.

Special provisions apply to mariners, staff engaged in international transport, civil servants and members of the armed forces.

Law: EC Regulation 1408/71 and 574/72

9460 Reciprocal agreements: National Insurance

The UK has entered into reciprocal agreements with many non-EEA states. Certain of those agreements deal only with reciprocity in benefit matters (e.g. Australia, New Zealand, Canada), though most deal also with the avoidance of dual liability for contributions. Some contribution arrangements cover only pension benefits (e.g. the UK–US agreement). Certain of the agreements cover only nationals of the contracting states while others cover any insured person.

In outline, the contributions articles of the agreements in force allow a similar form of temporary transfer relief to the EU regulations discussed above, though the 12-month limit varies. In the case of the UK–US agreement, for example, the period is five years, which may be extended for up to one further year. Again, standard certificates of coverage are issued to enable the host authorities to be satisfied that there is no host state liability.

9462   Overseas earnings

Two very important points must be made about the earnings of employees moving around the world with a continuing UK liability.

(1)   As 'earnings' attracting Class 1 NICs include all remuneration or profit derived from the employment (see 8750ff.), any overseas allowances, educational allowances, disturbance payments, etc. must be treated as gross pay and NICs calculated.

(2)   Nevertheless, certain allowances, etc. may be paid free of NIC liability. For example:

   (a)   where it can be shown that a business expense has actually been incurred in the course of the employment;

   (b)   in the case of income tax-free relocation allowances for employees moving abroad (see 298); or

   (c)   (since 6 April 1998) in the case of payments towards medical costs and expenses incurred by employees when carrying out overseas duties, and insurance against such costs.

9464   Cross-border movements: NI benefit entitlements

Absence from the UK need not necessarily prejudice future benefit entitlement, though this is a possibility about which employees should be warned. Benefit entitlement rests on the payment or credit of sufficient Class 1, Class 2 and/or Class 3 contributions in the relevant contribution year or years.

An employee may continue to pay Class 1 contributions while abroad. Short absences under a UK-based contract will generally lead to a liability under the 52-week rule, or the EU regulations may operate to create a liability. A reciprocal agreement may also permit the worker to be subject to a certificate of continuing liability in the UK while working abroad. UK benefit entitlement is maintained while Class 1 contributions are paid.

Where an employee pays overseas contributions, UK benefit cover may also be maintained by virtue of a reciprocal agreement or the EU regulations. Where no such cover is available, it is often possible for the employee to pay voluntary contributions in order to maintain UK coverage (see 9466).

9466   Voluntary contributions

If the employee is liable to pay UK contributions for the first 52 weeks of absence and then ceases to pay, his rights to all *short-term* benefits will be restored on his return to UK employment (provided that he remains with the same employer without a break in the employer-employee relationship). In that case, only Class 3 contributions may need to be paid in order to maintain entitlement to the UK basic state pension and widow's pension, i.e. the *long-term* contributory benefits.

National Insurance Contributions

If the employee is not abroad under the 52-week rule or covered by a treaty, he may lose both long *and* short-term benefit entitlement and should consider paying voluntary *Class 2* contributions during the last two complete tax years of his absence. These count for both basic state pension and all short-term contributory benefits except contribution-based jobseeker's allowance. However, the payment of such contributions is subject to certain restrictions.

If, upon being posted an employee has no 52-week continuing liability for UK Class 1 contributions, his benefit protection will cease on the date of his departure. If there is a possibility of UK benefits being needed in the future, he should be encouraged to obtain contribution protection by (where possible) voluntarily paying Class 2 or Class 3 contributions for the years he spends abroad.

The conditions for the voluntary payment of Class 2 contributions are that the employee concerned:

- was, immediately before he last left the UK, an employed or self-employed earner;
- has at some time in the past been resident in the UK for three continuous tax years or has paid contributions at basic level for each of any three past tax years; and
- is working overseas but had no continuing UK Class 1 liability on being posted there.

In November 2009, HMRC advised that non-residents whose previous application to pay voluntary Class 2 NICs was rejected because of their not being employed/self-employed 'immediately' before leaving the UK have a chance, if they wish, to resubmit their application for review. See the HMRC press release dated 25 November 2009 for further details.

The first condition need not be satisfied if an employee wishes to pay only voluntary Class 3 contributions, but that employee must still satisfy the second and third conditions.

The easiest way to pay voluntary contributions is by monthly direct debit (guidance and an application form are provided in leaflet CA04), but arrangements can be made for annual bills to be issued to employers who may pay as agents for their employees.

Most employees leave the UK in mid-year rather than on 6 April. If the employee pays Class 1 contributions for the part of the year before departure, there may be no need for voluntary contributions for the remainder of the year, as the Class 1 contributions paid for the part-year may make the year a qualifying year for benefit purposes. Similar considerations apply to the year of return. If the employee pays some, but insufficient, Class 1 contributions in a year, a deficiency notice is automatically issued after the end of the year, inviting payment of voluntary contributions by cheque. The employee needs therefore only to consider voluntary contributions for complete years of non-liability.

Law: *Social Security (Contributions) Regulations* 2001 (SI 2001/1004), reg. 146, 147

9468   SSP and SMP for posted workers

Because of regulations on benefits, employees working in EEA territories are entitled to statutory sick pay (SSP) and statutory maternity pay (SMP) on the same basis as if they were in the UK. With the abolition of the employers' SSP recovery from 6 April 1994, the SSP rule has become academic for those large employers who pay occupational sick pay at least equivalent to the SSP rate.

9470   Gurkhas

The earnings of members of the Brigade of Gurkhas from their duties performed overseas, which were previously exempt, are subject to UK income tax and NICs from 16 June 2006.

Law: ITEPA 2003, s. 28(5); *Social Security (Categorisation of Earners) (Amendment) Regulations* 2006 (SI 2006/1530)

Indirect Taxes

LORRY ROAD-USER CHARGE

Indirect Taxes

WHAT'S NEW

- A new electronic customs project aims to replace existing hybrid paper/electronic format transactions with EC-wide electronic ones. A modernised Customs Code has been adopted by the EC Commission (see 9510).
- The rate of Bingo duty was reduced from 22% to 20% on 29 March 2010 (see 9680).
- Cider duty rates which were increased in the March 2010 Budget were reduced in the emergency Budget in June 2010 (see 9710).
- The tobacco duty regime has been slightly amended for long cigarettes. From 1 January 2011, cigarettes longer than 8cm will be treated as two cigarettes for duty purposes (see 9720).
- In excise duties, the old paper-based system of controlling goods moving duty-free between EC Member States has gone from 1 April 2010. It has been replaced with an electronic system – the EMCS (see 9740).
- In excise duties, the REDS has gone from April 2010. The regime has been replaced with a new person, the 'Registered Consignee' (see 9750).
- The standard rate of IPT is due to rise to 6% and the selected higher rate is due to rise to 20% on 4 January 2011 (see 9800).
- Stamp duty land tax relief was extended to cover new zero carbon flats from 1 October 2007. The relief is time-limited and will expire on 30 September 2012 (see 10216).
- The Government is developing a new duty on aviation which is plane-based rather than passenger-based (see 9760).
- The standard rate of landfill tax for active waste has been increased to £48 per tonne from 1 April 2010. It is expected to rise to £56 per tonne in April 2011. The lower rate for inactive waste remains at £2.50 per tonne (see 9950).
- Rates of climate change levy are increasing from 1 April 2011 (see 10025).
- The standard rate for aggregates levy is £2.20 per tonne from 1 April 2011 (see 10040).

KEY POINTS

- Customs duty is a tax levied on goods imported into the European Community from outside. 'Free circulation' goods may move around EC countries without a liability to further customs charges (see 9500).
- Excise duties are generally charged on the production, rather than the sale, of a wide range of goods and services including alcohol (see 9710), betting and gaming (see 9660 and 9690), tobacco (see 9720) and mineral oils (see 9730).
- Air passenger duty (APD) was introduced with effect from 1 November 1994. A lower rate applies for departures on flights to destinations in the EU. Passengers arriving in UK airports to change planes are exempt. Air passenger duty is to be replaced with a new aviation duty (see 9760).
- Insurance premium tax (IPT) is charged on all risks in the UK, except those falling within certain specified exemptions (see 9800).
- Landfill tax is charged on 'taxable disposals' of waste made at landfill sites (see 9950).
- Climate change levy (CCL) is levied on supplies of electricity, gas and coal ('taxable commodities') to industry, commerce, agriculture and the public sector for their business use. CCL is not levied on supplies of taxable commodities for domestic or charity use (see 10020).
- Aggregates levy is charged per tonne of taxable aggregate that is subject to commercial exploitation (see 10040).

1,511

- Council tax is a property tax payable in respect of residential property (see 10050).
- Stamp duty is a charge on documents, not on transactions. It is now only charged on instruments relating to stock or marketable securities (see 10100).
- Stamp duty reserve tax (SDRT) applies to trading on the London Stock Exchange (see 10150).
- Stamp Duty Land Tax (SDLT) covers transactions involving any estate, interest, right or power in or over land in the UK (subject to certain exclusions) (see 10210).
- *Finance Act* 2002 introduced a lorry road-user charge which may be implemented in the life of the current Parliament (see 10250).

CUSTOMS DUTIES

9500 Introduction to customs duties

Customs duty is a tax levied on goods imported into the European Community (EC) from third countries, i.e. those outside the EC. The EC is a customs union, which means that the countries in full membership have no customs duty barriers between them, but have a common customs duty tariff against goods from outside the EC. This is to protect EC traders against foreign competition as well as being a producer of tax revenue.

If goods are in 'free circulation', they are free to circulate within the EC without any liability to pay further customs charges when they move from one Member State to the other. The term 'free circulation' means that either:

- the goods originate in the EC; or
- if imported from outside the EC, that all customs duties and similar charges have been paid and have not been refunded.

These goods are referred to as 'community goods' in the EC legislation.

The EC's common external tariff ensures that goods imported from non-EC countries are subject to the same customs duties wherever they arrive in the EC. The goods will also be subject to import VAT, but the rate of VAT will vary depending upon which Member State the goods arrive in.

The main legal provisions for the customs union are in the Community Customs Code (Code) and the Commission Regulation implementing the Code. This is known as the Implementing provisions (IP) or Implementing Regulations.

Law: EC Regulation 2913/92; EC Regulation 2454/93

The customs territory of the EC

The Member States and territories of the customs territory of the European Community are listed below:

(1)   the Republic of Austria;

(2)   the Kingdom of Belgium;

(3)   the Kingdom of Denmark;

(4)   the Republic of Finland;

(5)   the French Republic;

(6)   the Federal Republic of Germany;

(7)   the Hellenic Republic (Greece);

(8)   the Republic of Ireland;

(9)   the Italian Republic;

(10)   the Grand Duchy of Luxembourg;

(11)   the Kingdom of the Netherlands in Europe;

(12)   the Republic of Portugal;

(13)   the Kingdom of Sweden;

(14)   the Kingdom of Spain;

(15)   the United Kingdom of Great Britain and Northern Ireland;

(16)   Cyprus;

(17)   Czech Republic;

(18)   Estonia;

(19)   Hungary;

(20)   Latvia;

(21)   Lithuania;

(22)   Malta;

(23)   Poland;

(24)   Slovakia;

(25)   Slovenia;

(26)   Romania;

(27)   Bulgaria.

Included are:

(1)   the Isle of Man;

(2)   the Austrian territories of Jungholz and Mittelberg, and the territories of the Principality of Monaco;

(3)   the Portuguese Islands of Azores and Madeira.

(4) the following special territories of the EC, although included in the Customs territory, are excluded from the fiscal territory (i.e. the VAT territory) of the Community:

(a) Canary Islands (Spain);

(b) Channel Islands;

(c) French Overseas Departments of Guadeloupe, French Guiana, Martinique, and Reunion;

(d) Mount Athos – also known as Agion Poros (Greece);

Excluded from the customs territory are:

(1) the Faroe Islands and Greenland;

(2) the French overseas territories;

(3) the Islands of Heligoland and the territory of Büsingen;

(4) the Italian communes of Livigno and Campione d'Italia;

(5) the territory of the Republic of San Marino and the national waters of Lake Lugano which are between the bank and the political frontier of the area between the Ponte Tresa and Porto Ceresio;

(6) the North African enclaves of Ceuta and Melilla;

(7) the Principality of Andorra.

There is a customs union between the Republic of San Marino and the EC.

There is a customs union between the Principality of Andorra and the EC for certain goods.

There is a customs union covering most goods between the EC and Turkey.

The Channel Islands

Although the Channel Islands (the islands of Jersey, Guernsey, Alderney, Sark and their respective dependencies) are included in the customs territory of the EC they are excluded from the fiscal (VAT) territory of the Community.

Under the VAT Directive (Directive 2006/112) all goods from the Channel Islands must be declared to Customs. For goods imported from the Channel Islands which are subject to customs charges, including excise duty and/or import VAT with a value in excess of £600, a full 'single administrative document' (SAD) declaration is required (see 9510). For goods which are not subject to customs charges and are not restricted nor prohibited, no import SAD is required and commercial documents may be used to constitute the declaration. For consignments below a value of £600 subject to customs charges, a simplified import declaration can be made.

For goods exported from the UK to the Channel Islands a non-statistical export declaration is required. However, for consignments from certain South Coast ports a combined 'consignment note and customs declaration' (CNCD) can be used.

When Community goods move direct between the Channel Islands and the UK (in either direction), no 'Community transit' (CT) or status documents are needed, provided that the movement is cleared at the frontier.

The Isle of Man

As a general rule, goods moving between the Isle of Man and the UK, including any goods previously imported from non-EC countries on which the proper duty and tax have been paid, are considered not to be imported into, or exported from, either the Isle of Man or the UK, as the case may be. Such goods are not subject to customs control other than controls applicable to similar goods moving on the British mainland, e.g. for warehouse goods. There are restrictions on the movement of explosives.

Law: EC Regulation 2913/92, Arts. 3, 91, 163

Controls in intra-EC trade

There are no controls on the vast majority of EC goods moving within the Community. However, as non-EC goods can be in transit in the Community without payment of duty and Common Agricultural Policy (CAP) charges due on them, some controls remain on these goods moving within the Community – although these controls are now mainly documentary (see 'Community transit' below).

Prohibitions and restrictions

Despite the free movement of goods in free circulation within the Community, the Member States can impose restrictions or prohibitions for certain reasons such as health, public morality and security etc. In addition, there are provisions under Art. 115 of the Treaty of Rome and the Treaty of Paris to restrict the importation via another Member State of certain non-EC goods in special circumstances, even if those goods are in free circulation.

Law: Treaty of Rome, Art. 115

Anti-dumping duty

Anti-dumping duty (ADD) is an additional duty on imports providing protection against the dumping of goods in the EC at prices substantially lower than the normal value. In most cases, the normal value is the price which the foreign producer charges for comparable sales in his own country. Each anti-dumping duty covers specified goods originating in, or exported from, named countries or exporters. ADD is chargeable in addition to, and is independent of, any other duty to which the imported goods are liable. Whether ADD applies to particular goods at a particular time will be shown in the tariff. The indicator ADD and the country code will be shown on column 3 of the schedule in volume 2, against the commodity code of the goods in question. Where necessary, more detailed information is given as footnotes, or notes at the end of the relevant chapter in the tariff. The principal law relating to ADD is contained in Council Regulation 384/96.

In the UK, the overall responsibility for policy matters surrounding ADD rests with the Department for Business, Innovation and Skills. HMRC is responsible for the collection of the duty.

An investigation into an alleged dumping can be triggered by any business or representative body in the EC, which must present proof that the dumping of certain goods has, or will, cause real economic hardship or injury in the Community. The commission will then investigate the case, at which point a provisional ADD may be imposed for a period of up to nine months. At the end of the investigation, the provisional ADD may be made definitive or may lapse or be cancelled. Provisional ADD must be secured by either a cash deposit or guarantee. Deposits will be refunded without the need for prior application if the provisional ADD is cancelled, lapses or is not replaced in full by a definitive duty.

Anti-dumping duties imposed pursuant to the above regulation may be extended to imports of like products from third-world countries, or parts thereof, when circumvention of the measure in force is taking place. A Commission regulation will instruct EC customs authorities to make these imports subject to registration, or to request security by guarantee. Products will not be subject to registration where they are accompanied by a customs certificate declaring that the importation of the goods does not constitute circumvention.

Where an importer can show that the products imported were not dumped, or that the margin of dumping was less than that on which anti-dumping measures were based, the anti-dumping duties already collected may be partially or fully repaid.

Where goods are exported from a country against which an ADD measure applies and exemption from ADD is claimed on the grounds that the goods did not originate in that country, a 'certificate of origin' will need to be presented when the goods are declared.

Law: EC Regulation 384/96 (OJ 1996 L56/1)

Community transit

The majority of goods moving within the EC do not require transit documents or evidence of Community status. Goods arriving in one Member State from another are almost automatically regarded as Community goods in the absence of evidence to the contrary.

Community goods means:

- goods which originate in the Community; or
- goods which are imported from a non-Community country which have been put into free circulation in the Community; or
- goods which have been manufactured in the Community, wholly or partly from materials or parts imported from a non-Community country, provided that the imported materials or parts are in free circulation.

If goods have Community status they can normally be moved to any destination in the Community without becoming liable to customs duty and similar charges.

Law: EC Regulation 2913/92 , Art. 4(7)

9510   Import procedures

All goods exported from, or imported into, the EC from outside the Member States must be declared to the customs authorities ('customs'). In the UK the customs authority is HM Revenue and Customs (HMRC). Goods moving to or through other Member States and EFTA countries are controlled under the Community transit (CT) procedure (see 9500). Where necessary, declarations for all three purposes are made in all EC and EFTA countries using a standard form called the 'single administrative document' (SAD).

Declarations may be made by any person who is able to present the goods in question, or to have them presented, with all the documents that are required to be produced.

Any person may appoint a representative to perform the formalities laid down by customs, and this can be by way of direct or indirect representation. Direct representatives act in the name of, and on behalf of, another person. Indirect representatives act in their own name, but on behalf of another person. A representative must:

- state that he is acting on behalf of the person he is representing;
- specify whether the representation is direct or indirect; and
- be empowered to act as a representative.

If the representative does not do any of the above properly, he will be deemed to be acting in his own name and on his own behalf.

Representation is important both for the principals and their agents such as freight forwarders. For direct representation, only the principal is liable for duties. In indirect representation, both the principal and the agent are liable.

Whoever signs a declaration attests to the accuracy of the information being given, the authenticity of the documents attached and compliance with all the obligations relating to the goods in question under the procedure concerned.

Presentation

When the goods are imported they must be 'presented' to customs by the person who brought them into the EC, or the person who has responsibility for their onward carriage, such as freight haulage companies and shipping and aircraft lines etc.

Goods may be presented by using an approved computerised trade inventory system linked to HMRC's system or by lodging a form (C1600A) at a designated HMRC office. All goods must be presented within three hours of their arrival at the place of unloading. If the HMRC office is closed, presentation must be made within an hour of its reopening.

Electronic customs

The EC Commission is committed to implementing electronic customs in the EU and to replace the current hybrid system of part-paper and part-electronic systems with a totally electronic customs regime.

To this end a modernised Community Customs Code (Reg 2008/450) has been adopted, but not yet implemented. It aims to simplify legislation and to streamline customs processes.

Its principal features are:

- the introduction of electronic lodgement of customs declarations and accompanying documents;
- centralised clearance where traders can deal with customs matters in their home Member State, irrespective of where the goods arrive;
- a 'one-stop-shop' for entry into customs computer systems (i.e. a single entry point).

The Implementing Provisions for the modernised Code are currently in draft form.

Summary declarations

After presentation, the goods must be covered by a summary declaration containing all the information needed to identify the goods. The declaration is made by the person who conveyed the goods to the EC, or the person who assumes responsibility for their onward carriage, or a shipping, airline or haulage company, or the representative of any of the above. HMRC may accept commercial documents, such as bills, of lading or airway bills in place of C1600.

Following the summary declaration, which must be made within the laws of presentation (see above), the goods may be put to a prescribed procedure, for example entry to free circulation, the transit procedure, or warehousing regime etc.

Import declaration (aka the SAD or C88)

An import declaration is only required for the following categories of goods on arrival into the EC. That is:

- goods arriving direct from a non-EC country;
- goods arriving from a non-EC country via another EC country which have not already been cleared into free circulation;
- goods from the following special territories of the EC, namely the Channel Islands, French Overseas Department (for example, Martinique), the Canary Islands, Mount Athos and the Vatican City.

When the goods are imported into the EC, it is the responsibility of the importer or his authorised agent to declare them to customs. In most cases a SAD is used for this purpose. In the UK, the import declaration is then usually entered on to HMRC's entry processing computer which in the UK is known as 'CHIEF'. The input of data to CHIEF by traders direct is known as 'direct trader input' (DTI).

In signing an import declaration the signatory accepts full legal responsibility for all the information it contains, including that which was provided in the country of export. Any inaccuracies must be corrected, and these corrections must be drawn to HMRC's attention when the declaration is presented. If necessary, a fresh import declaration should be completed.

Customs clearance

Customs clearance is normally carried out at the port or airport of importation, but clearance facilities for goods transported in secure vehicles or containers are, with some exceptions, provided at specified inland depots.

All imported goods are liable to be examined by customs and this is normally carried out at the place where they are declared for importation.

Customs duties, and other charges that are due, must be paid, deferred or secured before the goods are cleared by customs. The deferred payment of customs duties and other charges is subject to the provision of adequate security and to other conditions of the 'duty deferment scheme'.

When the precise amount of duty etc. cannot be assessed at the time, the declaration is presented, clearance can usually be allowed on payment of a deposit, or provision of security to cover the element of duty in dispute. This may be equal to the full duty amount or the difference between the two potential duty amounts. For non-VAT-registered traders, the amount of VAT consequently in dispute must be secured. For VAT-registered traders, VAT is normally paid outright based on the value, which includes the highest potential duty regardless of whether this is secured by cash or cash less security.

Law: *Customs Controls on Importation of Goods Regulations* 1991 (SI 1991/2724), reg. 3, 4 and 5; EC Regulation 2913/92, Art. 5; EC Regulation 2008/450

9520 Valuation for customs duty

The majority of goods imported into the EC are subject to an ad valorem, rather than a specific duty. While the *rate* of customs duty payable is determined by the tariff heading under which the goods are classified and, consequently, by the commodity code given, the actual amount on which duty is payable is determined by the value placed on goods as importation.

The General Agreement on Tariffs and Trade (GATT) agreed a valuation code which was adopted by the EC in 1980. The GATT lays down six methods under which imported goods must be valued for duty purposes. With one exception, the methods must be used in strict hierarchical order, i.e. if Method 1 is not applicable, Method 2 must be considered and so on. The exception is that Method 4 does not have to be tried before Method 5. They can be swapped.

Indirect Taxes

Valuation for customs duty purposes is a complex area, and even when using the most usual method, Method 1, detailed negotiation with HMRC may be required to reach an appropriate value. The six methods are as follows:

(1)   the transaction value (i.e. sale) method (Method 1);

(2)   the sale value of identical goods method (Method 2);

(3)   the sale value of similar goods method (Method 3);

(4)   the deductive method (Method 4);

(5)   the computed value method (Method 5); and

(6)   the 'fall-back' method (Method 6).

Nearly all goods arriving into the EC are sold into the EC, so Method 1 is by far the most common method. Under Method 1, the value of the goods will need to be adjusted in accordance with the rules in the Customs Code, for example adding in the insurance and freight costs up to the place of introduction into the community.

The other valuation methods are only used when Method 1 can't be used; i.e. when there is no sale. So goods imported under a lease or goods given free, for example, cannot use Method 1.

Law: EC Regulation 2913/92, Art. 29–36

9530   Tariff classification procedure

The integrated tariff

Customs duty is charged according to the Community code shown in the tariff. Both the UK tariff and the combined nomenclature of the EC are based on the internationally agreed system of classification known as the 'Harmonised System'. This nomenclature provides a systematic classification procedure for all goods in international trade, designed to ensure, with the aid of the 'general rules for the interpretation of the nomenclature' and notes to the sections, chapters and subheadings, that any product or article falls to be classified in one place and one place only.

As a result, it should be possible to accurately (if laboriously) identify the amount of duty payable.

The tariff consists of three volumes:

(1)   general information;

(2)   the schedule, which gives the description, commodity code and full rates of duty, preferential duty rates, tariff quotas and ceilings, duty suspensions and anti dumping duties;

(3) detailed directions for completing the SAD and related documentation and import procedures and requirements.

Classification

In order to determine the proper classification within the Tariff for any goods imported into the EC, the appropriate heading for those goods (i.e. the appropriate four-digit heading printed in bold capitals in the schedule) must first be established. It may be helpful to refer to the list of section and chapter titles immediately before the schedule in Volume 2 of the Tariff which, in many cases, will immediately indicate the chapter or chapters in which the appropriate Tariff heading will be found. However, these titles are only provided for reference purposes. They have no legal force and it is essential that reference is made to any relevant section or chapter notes since these may define the scope of the relevant heading.

Source: The principal legal basis for the Volume 2 information is the Combined Nomenclature Regulation 2658/97.

The Government's Business Link website has Volume 2 available in the International Trade section so importers can classify their own import goods if they wish.

9540   EC preferences

The EC has a number of preferential trade arrangements with certain individual countries or groups of countries outside the EC. These provide for particular goods originating in the countries concerned to be imported and entered to free circulation at nil or reduced rates of customs duty. Details of these rates are shown in column 6 of the Schedule in Volume 2 of the tariff.

The different countries and groups of countries are referred to at the head of column 6 or in the footnotes to the schedule. An alphabetical list of countries and specific information concerning country codes and preference types is in Part 7 of Volume 1 of the tariff.

To be admissible to a preference, imported goods must:

(1) be of a description shown in the schedule as being eligible for the preference;

(2) qualify as 'originating' in the preference country in accordance with the origin rules for that preference; and

(3) have been transported direct from the preference country or groups of countries to the EC.

For some goods, the availability of preferential rates is restricted by tariff quota or ceilings, or is limited to a certain period of the year. If these restrictions apply, further information will be found in the tariff and from HMRC either at the port of entry or from the CHIEF Notice Boards.

Some countries are eligible for preferential treatment under two separate arrangements. Other non-preferential duty reliefs may also be available, for example 'customs duty suspensions'. Importers are entitled to enter the goods at the most advantageous rate for which they are eligible and for which appropriate valid documents are held.

Preferential arrangements do not affect the liability to anti-dumping duties.

The customs authorities may check goods which are imported under preference. Where any of these checks fail to show that the goods qualified for the preference claimed, the importer is required to pay duty at the full non-preferential rate, and Community legislation allows for the collection of back-duty (but not interest) for a period of up to three years after the goods have been imported. To ensure against the possibility, many importers now include a clause in the contracts with the supplier allowing them to recover duty from the supplier if it transpires that the goods that they bought in good faith did not comply with the origin rules for which a certificate has been granted.

Law: Reg 2913/92, Arts. 22–27, 220

9550   Licences

Most goods can be imported into the EC without the need for a specific import licence and are covered by the 'open general import licence' (OGIL). However, for certain imports, a licence must be applied for to a competent EC authority. In the UK this is the Department for Business, Innovation and Skills (BIS). In most cases restricted goods already in free circulation within the EC do not require a further licence to import into the UK.

Import licences are required for various reasons. These are mainly:

(1)   to protect certain UK or EC industries;

(2)   to implement internationally agreed policies designed to stabilise markets and encourage the practice of free trade;

(3)   for surveillance purposes, i.e. to provide information about trends in imports of sensitive goods; and

(4)   in the interests of public health and safety.

9560   Tariff Quotas (TQs)

Tariff quotas are a form of EC preference under which limited amounts of certain goods may be admitted to free circulation at a reduced or nil rate of customs duty, and/or charges under the Common Agricultural Policy (CAP) of the EC. The limit can be expressed in units of rate, volume, quantity or value.

Quotas are set for the whole of the EC and claims are granted on a first come, first served basis. Quotas are controlled entirely by the European Commission.

Quotas that are not expected to exhaust quickly are termed 'open' and valid claims to quota relief can be accepted without security for duty.

New quotas are ones which are likely to be exhausted within a short period of time and are termed 'critical' status.

Goods eligible for quotas that have become critical, or for open quotas which have been taken up to the extent that they become critical, may be released only against security for full duty. When a quota is exhausted, that information is sent electronically to the customs authorities, after which the full rate of duty must be paid.

Some quotas are restricted to goods from particular countries or groups of countries. In this case, importers must produce the appropriate certificate of origin or movement certificate to qualify and benefit from the nil or reduced rate.

Certain quotas can be expected to exhaust within a few days of opening, and these are called 'banded' quotas. To give fair and equal treatment, all valid claims lodged before a deadline previously announced by the EC are considered to have been presented simultaneously. If the volume of claims made within that banding period exceeds the quota available, allocation of the relief is then made on a pro rata basis.

Quota relief must be formally claimed and belated claims against a quota that has been exhausted, will not be entertained by HMRC.

Goods eligible for quota relief are individually described and coded in the tariff and can be identified by the abbreviation 'TQ' in column 3 of the schedule. Even if all initial indications of availability are there, the importer must still make further enquiries with HMRC immediately prior to actual import to ensure that the quota is still open.

9570 The Common Agricultural Policy of the EC

Certain basic and processed products in the agricultural sector are subject, not only to customs duties, but also to other charges under the Common Agricultural Policy (CAP) of the EC. The purpose of CAP charges is to protect EC produced goods by increasing entry prices, so that non-EC goods come in line with the generally higher prices in the EC. The rates are changed annually and are published in the tariff. Additional safeguard measures and charges may also be imposed in exceptional circumstances to give extra protection to EC production.

The CAP charge regime is administered by the Intervention Board.

9580   Duty reliefs

Customs duty suspensions

'Customs duty suspensions' are temporary duty suspensions available in certain circumstances. The Commission's objectives for allowing temporary suspensions of duty include the stimulation of incoming activity within the EC, an increase in EC industrial competitiveness, a reduction of consumer prices, the creation of employment and structural modernisation of industry within the EC. Suspensions of duty are granted to stimulate EC processing and manufacturing industries where it is found that no EC industry is prejudiced. Consequently, suspensions will only be granted for components undergoing further process or manufacture where there is no EC manufacturer that can supply identical or equivalent products, although a suspension subject to quota may be granted where merely insufficient EC supply is proved.

As a result of the processing criterion, most current suspensions relate to the chemical, pharmaceutical and the micro-electronic sectors. Consumer products are not covered as they are finished products not subject to further process.

Temporary Admission (formerly known as Temporary Importation)

Certain goods may be imported into the Community without payment of import duty or VAT, provided they are exported after only a temporary period of use in the EC (usually up to 24 months).

The Implementing Provisions contain a list of items that can be imported under this relief.

These include:

- goods for art exhibitions;
- personal goods;
- means of transport (lorries).

Source: Public Notice 200 (September 2009 edition)

Inward processing relief

Inward processing relief (IPR) is a widely used trade facilitation regime under which goods imported from outside the EC for repair or process and subsequent re-export outside the EC, may be relieved of customs duty, agricultural levies, other CAP charges and anti-dumping duty. It can also remove the need to pay VAT. The allowable processes range from simple inspection and re-packing through to more complex manufacture. IPR does not give relief from excise duty. Businesses can also obtain relief from the above taxes if they buy IPR goods from other traders in the UK or other Member States of the EC.

The relevant legislation is Council Regulation 2913/92, Art. 114–129 and Regulation 2454/93.

There are two methods of obtaining the relief.

IPR suspension

Under this method, the duties above are not paid at importation and remain suspended provided that the goods imported under IPR, or the products made from them (which are known as 'compensating products'), are actually re-exported to a non-EC country or put to another allowable use or are sold to another IPR trader.

This is obviously the most advantageous method for cash-flow purposes and is most suitable where the intention to re-export outside the EC is known at the time of import. However, if the business only sells a percentage of the products imported from non-EC countries, IPR suspension can also be used for that percentage of imports based on a reasonable estimate, and customs duty and VAT can be paid on the remainder. If a business imports to IPR suspension more goods than are needed for re-export and sales to other IPR traders, the surplus goods must be diverted to free circulation and the suspended Customs duty paid. It is important to note that any IPR suspension goods diverted to free circulation will be charged with compensatory interest.

Certain goods, such as agricultural goods, some licensable goods (mostly textiles) and goods which are intended for processing under IPR which are physically in a customs warehouse or free zone, must be imported under IPR suspension rather than IPR drawback described below.

Drawback

Under this method, the customs duty and other taxes due on non-EC goods are paid at the time of importation and claimed back from HMRC after process and subsequent re-export to a non-EC country, or other allowable disposal, or are sold to another IPR trader.

Businesses using IPR drawback cannot reclaim duty on goods destroyed even under HMRC's supervision, or on waste and scrap which results from that destruction.

The drawback method cannot be used for any of the following types of goods:

(1)   goods subject to the CAP of the EC;

(2)   goods subject to quantitative import restrictions; and

(3)   goods that might qualify for preferential arrangements within tariff quotas or allocated ceilings.

It is a condition of using IPR drawback that duty must be reclaimed from HMRC within six months of the date of export of the processed goods. HMRC do not allow retrospection.

IPR drawback is being withdrawn as part of HMRC's review of simplification of customs duties. Drawback is not commonly used in the UK.

Business must be authorised to claim IPR relief. There are five types of authorisation:

(1) simplified authorisation;

(2) full UK authorisation (using form C&E810);

(3) specific authorisations (for CAP goods);

(4) community authorisations; and

(5) integrated authorisation.

A business must be properly authorised to use IPR and IPR procedures must be correctly used at import (e.g. the correct customs procedure code (CPC)), otherwise the duty relief is lost. There is no retrospection.

Law: EC Regulation 2913/92, Arts. 114 et seq.; EC Regulation 2454/93, Arts. 356 et seq

Source: Public Notice 221

Outward processing relief (OPR)

Normally, when goods are exported outside the EC they lose 'Community status', and duty must be paid on their full value at re-importation. 'Outward processing relief' (OPR) is a trade facilitation measure available for the re-importation of Community goods which have been exported outside the EC for process (very often to take advantage of lower labour rates) or repair.

The amount of duty relief available on the re-imported product or 'compensating product' will depend on the type of process the goods underwent while outside the EC, and the duty rate applicable to the goods originally exported outside the Community.

A similar relief called the 'standard exchange system' (SES) is available for goods sent to the EC as replacements for faulty goods sent outside the EC.

If goods are repaired or replaced free of charge, there is total relief from import duties provided that evidence is submitted to HMRC to support this claim, for example, a guarantee or warranty document.

If goods are repaired or replaced in return for payment, the import duties are calculated on the cost of the repair or replacement plus any freight and insurance charges made for the return of the repaired goods or replacements. However, this is conditional on the cost not being influenced by any relationship between the exporter and the processor.

For all other processes the duty relief is calculated by deducting the import duty, which would have been payable on the exported goods if they had been imported at the same time and from the same country as the compensating product, from the import duty due on the full customs value of the compensating product. This is known as the duty differential method (Art 151, Code).

There is an alternative 'cost of operations method' which normally gives the importer a better result (Art. 591, IP).

With the exception of goods held under IPR, exported goods must be Community goods, that is, they must have originated in the Community or if originally imported from outside the Member States, all customs duty must have been paid. Their export must not result in any refund or remission of import duties or refunds or other financial benefits under the CAP.

Except for replacements imported under the SES, it must be possible to identify the exported goods in the imported compensating products. The compensating products must also be re-imported within time limits specified in the authorisation granted by Customs.

Law: EC Regulation 2913/92, Art. 145–160; IP, Art. 585 et seq

Source: Public Notice 235

Returned goods relief (RGR)

Goods exported from the EC can, in certain circumstances, be re-imported with total or partial relief from import duty, charges under the CAP, excise duty and VAT. The rules for the relief vary according to the category of tax involved. Where relief is sought for more than one category, the rules applicable to each must be satisfied.

This commonly used relief is used for goods exported outside the EC which are rejected by the buyer and it is also used for goods such as cranes, which are used outside the EC on construction projects and then reimported afterwards.

There is a general three-year time-limit on the goods being re-imported.

Returned goods relief (RGR) does not apply to goods temporarily exported outside the EC for process. Outward Processing Relief (OPR) should be used instead. However, if goods are exported for the process or repair and this does not take place, RGR can be used on re-import if the goods return unaltered.

Law: EC Regulation 2913/92, Art. 185–187; EC Regulation 2454/93, Art. 844–856

Source: Public Notice 236

End-use relief

End-use relief is designed to assist certain industries and trades in the EC by allowing a nil or reduced rate of duty on goods imported from non-EC countries provided those goods are put to a prescribed use. The relief is common to all EC Member States.

There are a number of areas of the economy that benefit from end-use relief. These include:

Indirect Taxes

- shipwork goods;
- continental shelf relief (oil rigs and parts);
- military aircraft;
- civil aircraft.

Law: Regulation 2658/87

Source: Public Notice 770

Personal reliefs

There are a number of personal reliefs that are available to individuals in certain circumstances which allow relief from duty and/or VAT.

These include:

(1) relief for persons entering the EC from a third country for their personal property. The property can be imported duty free provided the person has been normally resident in a third country for at least 12 months, and the property has been in the person's possession for at least six months. The property may not be alcohol or tobacco products;

(2) relief on wedding gifts under £800 in value;

(3) relief for honorary decorations and awards.

There are also personal reliefs for special visitors. These are designed to give relief from customs and excise duty to goods imported by either:

(1) diplomats; or

(2) serving members of visiting forces.

The reliefs cover motor vehicles, alcohol and tobacco products.

Law: For customs duties relief: Regulation 918/83; for import VAT: *Customs and Excise (Personal Reliefs for Special Visitors) Order* 1992 (SI 1992/3156), art. 14 and 18; *Customs and Excise Duties (Personal Reliefs for Goods Permanently Imported) Order* 1992 (SI 1992/3193), art. 11(1)(c), 14, 17

9590 Duty-free ships and aircraft stores in the single market

Duty-free stores sell goods which will be used, consumed or sold on ships and aircraft leaving the UK for third country destinations. These goods include, fuel, foodstuffs and spare parts.

These goods are stored under a modified form of customs warehousing, the details of which are in the relevant customs notice.

The ship or aircraft must be 'entitled' to this procedure.

For an aircraft, this means it must be departing on a flight to a country outside the UK.

For a ship, this means that it must be:

(1)   at least 40 tons net registered tonnage and departing on a voyage outside the UK; or

(2)   at least 40 tons departing to certain sea areas; or

(3)   yachts less than 40 tons departing on a voyage to a destination south of Brest or north of the Eider.

A warehouse keeper must not allow goods to be removed from the warehouse unless the ship or aircraft is entitled to receive them.

The shipper or agent ordering the goods must give a written statement to confirm entitlement.

Source: Customs Notice 232, para. 8.20

9610   Free zones

A free zone is an enclosed area in which non-Community goods are treated for the purposes of import duties as being outside the Customs territory of the Community. The administration of free zones is governed by EC regulations. They are rarely used in the EC.

In the UK, the detailed rules which govern the operation of free zones are in the *Free Zone Regulations* 1984.

Customs duty, import VAT and other import charges are not due until the goods are released for free circulation. This allows goods to be handled or processed without payment of duty or VAT.

Free zones are operated by free zone managers and not HMRC, but HMRC's approval is still required to operate within a free zone. The current locations are:

(1)   Liverpool;

(2)   Prestwick Airport;

(3)   Port of Sheerness;

(4)   Southampton;

(5)   Tilbury.

Law: Reg 2913/92 Reg 166 et seq; Reg 2454/93, Reg 799 et seq.; *Free Zone Regulations 1984* (SI 1984/1177); *Free Zone (Liverpool) Designation Order* 1991 (SI 1991/1738); *Free Zone (Prestwick Airport) Designation Order* 1991 (SI 1991/1739); *Free Zone*

Indirect Taxes

(Southampton) Designation Order 1991 (SI 1991/1740); *Free Zone (Port of Tilbury) Designation Order* 1992 (SI 1992/1282); *Free Zone (Port of Sheerness) Designation Order* 1994 (SI 1994/2898)

9615   Authorised Economic Operators (AEOs)

Following the 9/11 attacks, the USA brought pressure on other trading blocks to police the supply chains of goods moving round the world.

As a result, the EC has implemented the concept of the Authorised Economic Operator (AEO), which gives a certain status and credibility to importers and exporters in the EC.

The advantages to taxpayers who adopt these provisions are: increased security and safety and the benefit of simplifications.

Some taxpayers are embracing this as a 'kite mark' and some are adopting this under pressure, arguing that the AEO status does not confer any more advantages than they have already.

Law: Regulation 2913/92, Art. 5a; Regulation 2454/93, Art. 14a et seq

Website: www.hmrc.gov.uk – AEO FAQs

EXCISE DUTIES

9650   Introduction to excise duties

Historically, excise duties have been charged on certain home produced goods, such as beer duty which is the oldest excise duty. Excise duties are now charged on a wide range of goods and services. Unlike VAT, excise duty is chargeable on the production or importation, rather than sale. Excise duty falls into the following categories:

- *Alcohol*: beer and spirits are taxed according to their alcoholic content, whereas wine, made wine, cider and perry are all subject to specific (i.e. by volume) taxes;
- *Gambling*: Amusement Machine Licence Duty is levied on machines provided for play. Bingo Duty, Lottery, General Betting and Pools duties are ad valorem taxes. Gaming duty is a banded, premises based tax on casino profits;
- *Tobacco*: duties on tobacco are aimed at both raising revenue and to support the government's health objective. The duty is charged on the finished product, for cigars, hand-rolling tobacco and other smoking and chewing tobacco, the charge is specific (per kg) whereas for cigarettes there is an additional ad valorem component; and
- *Mineral and Heating Oils (Fuels duties)*: duties are levied for the purpose of revenue-raising, and protecting the environment with a particular focus on reducing emissions of greenhouse gases.

The holding and movement of excise goods within the EC by the use of excise warehousing is dealt with at 9740.

9660   General betting duty (GBD)

Scope of the duty

General betting duty is an excise duty and is levied on all:

- off-course bets made with a UK bookmaker (for example in a high street bookmaker);
- financial and other spread bets made with a UK bookmaker; and
- pool betting on horse and dog races.

On-course bets are not subject to general betting duty on horse and dog races. All other on-course bets are subject to GBD.

Rates of duty

The rate of general betting duty depends on the type of bet and is applied to the bookmaker's net stake receipts. The net stake receipts represent the difference between the total amount of money received (i.e. stake receipt) and the total amount paid out (i.e. winnings) in an accounting period (i.e. in effect gross profits). An accounting period is normally a calendar month but HMRC may designate another period.

GBD is charged at 15 per cent of the net stake receipts for that period.

For spread bets made with a bookmaker, the amount of general betting duty charged in an accounting period will be:

- in respect of financial spread bets, three per cent of the net stake receipts from those bets for that period, and
- in respect of other spread bets, ten per cent of the net stake receipts from those bets for that period.

Spread betting involves betting on the outcome of an event based on a points spread. Gamblers can buy at the top or sell at the bottom of the spread, with winnings or losses calculated by multiplying the unit staked by the difference between the actual result and the buying or selling price.

Internet betting has become very popular and attempts have been made by HMRC to raise revenue from the activities. One of these is through person to person (P2P) betting websites, where a person can bet with another. This is known in BGDA 1981 as a betting exchange.

Law: BGDA 1981, s. 1 et seq; *General Betting Duty Regulations* 1987 (SI 1987/1963)

Source: Public Notice 451 (April 2010 edition)

9670 Pool betting duty

Scope of the duty

Pool betting duty applies to bets made by pool betting with a UK-based promoter. This duty classically covers the 'Pools'. Most pool betting is liable to pool betting duty, but certain types of pool betting are currently liable to general betting duty, for example, any pool betting through the Tote's facilities and pool betting through a totalisator on an event that is taking place on that day at the track where the totalisator is situated (see 9660 above). This means that pool betting on horseracing or dog racing that is not made through the facilities described above, is liable to pool betting duty. All pool betting on dog racing or horseracing falls within the general betting duty provisions when the promoter or the totalisator is based in the UK. All other pool betting, where the promoter or totalisator is based in the UK, falls within the pool betting duty provisions.

Registration

A permit issued by HMRC is required to carry on a pool betting or fixed odds coupon betting business.

Rates of duty

The current rate of pool betting duty is 15 per cent of gross profits (also known as net pool betting receipts) calculated as stakes plus expenses and profits less winnings paid out. It is payable by the promoter of the betting.

Record-keeping requirements

Pools promoters are required to keep records to enable the calculation of the duty, in particular an excise duty account must be maintained. Agents for fixed odds coupon bookmakers are required to keep a record of the money collected and copies of returns and other information given to the bookmaker. Coupons must be retained for at least two months and other records for at least two years.

Law: *Betting and Gaming Duties Act* 1981, s. 6 et seq

Source: Public Notice 147 (April 2010 edition)

9680 Bingo duty

Scope of the duty

Bingo duty is levied on the playing of bingo in the UK, unless it is subject to one or more of the exemptions in BGDA 1981, Sch. 3.

These exemptions are: domestic bingo, small scale bingo and non-profit making bingo.

Bingo duty is charged on a person's bingo profits. The rate of duty is 20 per cent (from 29 March 2010 – reduced from 22%) of a person's profits derived from providing bingo in an accounting period. The legislation defines a person's bingo promotion profits as the difference between the amount he receives from providing bingo and the amount he pays out as prizes in any accounting period.

An accounting period runs from the first Monday of a calendar month until midnight of the Sunday before the first Monday of the next calendar month. Where payments that allow players to play bingo fall due to a person in an accounting period, for the purposes of bingo duty, he has bingo receipts for that period. These payments would include bingo card fees, but not admission fees (unless they carry a right to play).

Registration

Commercial bingo promoters must give their local HMRC advice centre at least 14 days' notice of their intention to operate a bingo club and complete a duty registration form.

Record-keeping requirements

Commercial records must be kept, including a bingo duty account, a summary account for use in completing the return and a stock account of bingo cards and tickets. Entries must be made in the accounting records within 48 hours of the end of the week. All records must be retained for at least two years.

Enforcement

HMRC officers have powers to enter premises where bingo is played or on which they have reasonable cause to suspect it has been or will be played. Officers may remain on those premises when they are being used for bingo or there is reasonable cause to suspect they will be used. They may:

- require information to be provided by any manager, promoter or player and for any card or document used in playing the game to be produced;
- direct which books, records and accounts shall be kept;
- require the production of any books, records and accounts including business bank accounts and trading accounts which relate to or appear to relate to the business;
- specify any other information which they require, and estimate the amount of duty due where books, records and accounts are not kept or are incomplete or inaccurate.

Law: FA 2009; *Betting and Gaming Duties Act* 1981, s. 17 et seq; *Bingo Duty Regulations* 2003 (SI 2003/2503)

Source: Public Notice 457 (April 2010 edition)

9690 Gaming duty

Scope of the duty

Gaming duty is levied on casino games and equal chance gaming. The games are not specifically listed but they will include roulette, blackjack and various forms of poker.

Any person who is:

- the holder of a gaming licence;
- a provider of premises used for dutiable gaming; or
- concerned on the management or organisation of a dutiable gaming on unlicensed premises,

must register, account for pay over gaming duty.

Rates of duty

The duty is based on the 'gross gaming yield' (GGY) (essentially gross profits). This consists of the total value of the value of the stakes, minus players' winnings, on games in which the house is banker, and participation charges, or 'table money', exclusive of VAT, on games in which the bank is shared by players.

It is accounted for in six month periods, usually beginning on 1 April and 1 October. Two returns are made in each six month periods:

After the first three months a return is completed and a payment on account made.

At the end of the six month accounting period, the gaming duty for the whole six month period is calculated. The amount of any payment made on account for the first three months of the period should be deducted from the total amount due and any balance paid. Current rates for accounting periods starting on or after 1 April 2010 are as follows:

Part of gross gaming yield	*Rate (%)*
Payment on account from 1/4/2010	
The first £1,975,000	15
The next £1,361,500	20
The next £2,385,000	30
The next £5,033,500	40
The remainder	50

Record keeping requirements

The gaming Board of Great Britain has produced a booklet *The Accounting Guide for Gaming Clubs* which provides guidance regarding accounts, procedures and documentation.

Law: FA 1997, s. 10 et seq; *Gaming Duty Regulations* 1997 (SI 1997/2196)

Source: Public Notice 453 (September 2009 edition)

9695   Remote Gaming Duty

Remote Gaming Duty attempts to levy duty on playing a game of chance for a prize by the use of remote communication – for example, the Internet, telephone or television.

Some of the leading players are established in places like Gibraltar, so they may or may not co-operate with this duty.

The rate of duty is 15 per cent of a persons remote gaming profits (in effect, gross profits).

Law: BGDA 1981, s. 26A et seq; *The Remote Gaming Regulations* 2007 (SI 2007/2192)

9700   Amusement machine licence duty

Scope of the duty

Most amusement machines provided for play on UK premises, with certain specific exceptions, require a licence and are subject to duty.

Amendments to the legislation apply from 1 August 2006 to more closely align excise and VAT definitions of a gaming machine with the *Gambling Act* 2005 and remove any amusement machine that is not a gaming machine (e.g. video or pinball machine) from the scope of amusement machine licence duty (AMLD).

VAT is chargeable on the profits of the machine.

Registration

Unless they are used in a fete or similar, each machine provided for play in the UK will need a licence. Some machines are, however, excepted machines and these will also not need licences.

The following are excepted machines (from 1 June 2009):

- machines that are not gaming machines;
- a gaming machine in respect of which:
  - the cost of a single game does not exceed 30 pence,
  - the maximum value of the prize for winning a single game does not exceed £8, and
  - the maximum cash component of the prize for winning a single game does not exceed £5;
- a gaming machine in respect of which:
  - the cost of a single game does not exceed 10 pence, and

- the maximum value of the prize for winning a single game does not exceed £15 (with the cash element not exceeding £8);

• a gaming machine in respect of which:

- the cost of a single game does not exceed £1, and
- a non-cash prize not exceeding £50 in value; and

• 'two-penny machines'.

Rates of duty

The rates of duty depend on the category of the machine and are as follows:

(1) category A – a gaming machine which is not within another category;

(2) category B1 – a gaming machine which is not within a lower category and in respect of which the cost of a single game does not exceed £2, and the maximum value of the prize for winning a single game does not exceed £4,000;

(3) category B2 – a gaming machine which is not within a lower category and in respect of which the cost of a single game does not exceed £100, and the maximum value of the prize for winning a single game does not exceed £500;

(4) category B3 – a gaming machine which is not within a lower category and in respect of which the cost of a single game does not exceed £1, and the maximum value of the prize for winning a single game does not exceed £500;

(5) category B4 – a gaming machine which is not within a lower category and in respect of which the cost of a single game does not exceed £1, and the maximum value of the prize for winning a single game does not exceed £250;

(6) category C – a gaming machine in respect of which the cost of a single game does not exceed 5 pence, and a gaming machine in respect of which:

(a) the cost of a single game does not exceed £1, and
(b) the maximum value of the prize for winning a single game does not, from 1 June 2009, exceed £70.

Rates from 26 March 2010 are as follows:

(1) Months for which licence granted	*(2)* Category A	*(3)* Category B1	*(4)* Category B2	*(5)* Category B3	*(6)* Category B4	*(7)* Category C
1	£520	£265	£210	£210	£190	£85
2	£1015	£505	£395	£395	£360	£150
3	£1,520	£760	£605	£605	£545	£225
4	£2,025	£1,015	£800	£800	£725	£300
5	£2,540	£1,270	£1,000	£1,000	£900	£375
6	£3,050	£1,520	£1,195	£1,195	£1,085	£450
7	£3,555	£1,775	£1,395	£1,395	£1,265	£520
8	£4,060	£2,025	£1,600	£1,600	£1,450	£600
9	£4,570	£2,285	£1,800	£1,800	£1,630	£675

(1) Months for which licence granted	(2) Category A	(3) Category B1	(4) Category B2	(5) Category B3	(6) Category B4	(7) Category C
10	£5,075	£2,540	£1,995	£1,995	£1,810	£750
11	£5,580	£2,795	£2,195	£2,195	£1,990	£820
12	£5,805	£2,905	£2,285	£2,285	£2,075	£860

Indirect Taxes

Enforcement

HMRC officers have powers to enter premises where an amusement machine is being, or is suspected as being, provided for play, inspect those premises and require any valid licence to be produced, or information in respect to the premises or any amusement machine thereon to be provided. HMRC officers also have the power to seize any unlicensed amusement machines. Anyone providing an unlicensed amusement machine for play may also be liable to a civil penalty. They may, as an alternative, use the default licence procedure in BGDA 1981, Sch. 4A.

Law: *Betting and Gaming Duties Act* 1981, s. 21 et seq; *Amusement Machine Licence Duty Regulations* 1995 (SI 1995/2631)

Source: Public Notice 454 (April 2010 edition).

9710   Alcoholic liquor duties

Scope of the duties

Alcoholic liquors comprise:

- Spirits;
- Beer;
- Wine;
- Made-wine; and
- Cider.

Spirits

Before producing spirits, application for approval of the plant and process to be used must be made to HMRC and a distiller's licence must be obtained from HMRC. In general, HMRC will not license manufacturers with stills of less than 1,800 litres capacity, although smaller stills may be allowed for, say, heritage centres and universities for research.

Spirits are made from ethyl alcohol and ethyl alcohol is produced in the EC for many purposes. It is only when it is drinkable (potable) that it is dutied as an alcoholic liquor.

Registration

All manufacturing operations must be approved by HMRC and carried out in distillation periods agreed with them. At the end of each quarter, a return for each class of spirit produced must be submitted to HMRC.

Rates of duty

The rates from 29 March 2010 are as follows:

Description	Rate from 29 March 2010
Spirits[1]	£23.80 per litre of pure alcohol @ temperature of 20°C
Beer[2]	£17.32 per hectolitre for every 1% of alcohol by volume and in proportion for any smaller quantity
Fortified wine and made-wine[3][4] (sparkling or still) of an alcoholic strength >22%	£23.80 per litre of pure alcohol
Spirits-based 'coolers'[6]	£23.80 per litre of pure alcohol
Fortified wine and made-wine[3][4] (sparkling or still) of an alcoholic strength >15% and not >22%	£299.97 per hectolitre
Sparkling wine and made-wine[3][4] of an alcoholic strength 8.5% and above, but not >15%	£288.20 per hectolitre
Sparkling wine and made-wine[3][4] of an alcoholic strength of >5.5% and <8.5%	£217.83 per hectolitre
Still wine and made-wine[3][4] of an alcoholic strength >5.5% and not >15%	£225.00 per hectolitre
Wine, made wine, spiritous and mixed drinks made from cider/perry base >4% and not >5.5%	£95.33 per hectolitre
Wine, made wine, spiritous and mixed drinks made from cider/perry base >1.2% and not >4%	£69.32 per hectolitre
Sparkling cider[5] or perry of an alcoholic strength >5.5% and <8.5%	£217.83 per hectolitre
Still cider[5] or perry of an alcoholic strength of >7.5% and <8.5%	£54.04 per hectolitre
Still cider[5] or perry of an alcoholic strength >1.2% and not >7.5%	£33.46 per hectolitre (from 29/06/10)

Notes

[1] 'Spirits' means spirits of any description which are of a strength exceeding 1.2%, any such mixture, compound or preparation made with spirits as is of a strength exceeding 1.2% or liquors contained with any spirits, in any mixture which is of a strength exceeding 1.2%, but does not include methylated spirits.

Indirect Taxes

(2) 'Beer' includes ale, porter, stout and any other description of beer and any liquor which is sold as beer or as a substitute for beer, and which is of an alcoholic strength exceeding 0.5% but does not include black beer, the worts of which before fermentation were of a specific gravity of 1200° or more.

(3) 'Wine' means any liquor obtained from the alcoholic fermentation of fresh grapes or the must of fresh grapes, whether or not the liquor is fortified with spirits or flavoured with aromatic extracts.

(4) 'Made-wine' means any liquor obtained from the alcoholic fermentation of any substance, but does not include wine, beer, black beer, spirits or cider.

(5) 'Cider' means cider (or perry) of a strength of less than 8.5% of alcohol by volume at 20°C, obtained from the fermentation of apple or pear juice without the addition at any time of any alcoholic liquor or of any liquor or substance which communicates colour or flavour other than such as the commissioners may allow as appearing to them to be necessary to make cider (or perry).

(6) Spirits-based drinks not exceeding 5.5% alcohol by volume ('coolers') used to be taxed as made-wine. From 28 April 2002 they are taxed as spirits.

Inward Processing Relief (IPR)

Individual grain whisky distillers may apply for approval under IPR to allow the levy-free importation of maize, high diastatic barley and high diastatic malted barley for use in the production of grain whisky and spirits for re-exportation as such or as blended whisky. HMRC's authorisation is required and certain conditions in respect of importation and exportation procedures and reporting requirements must be met. Such cereals for use in the production of gin or vodka for export may also qualify for IPR relief.

Record-keeping requirements

Records of spirit producing activities, including details of fermentations, distillations and deliveries to warehouse must be maintained. Also, all business records relating to stock, handling, purchases, sales, imports and exports must be maintained.

Any taking of account of spirits must be entered into the distiller's business records immediately before the account is taken. HMRC may require notice to be given of an intention to take the account.

Spirits must be removed to an approved warehouse immediately after details of the spirits account have been entered in the business records, or any standing time imposed by HMRC has elapsed.

Beer

Beer includes ale, porter, stout and any liquor which is branded or sold as a beer.

Reduced rate for small breweries

There is a reduced rate of beer duty for small breweries. The reduction is 50 per cent where production is less than 5,000 hectolitres per year. Where production is between 5,000 and 30,000 hectolitres per year the rate is found by applying the formula:

$$\% \text{ of duty payable} = \frac{\text{annual production} - 2,500}{\text{annual production}}$$

There is a detailed regime surrounding this relief. It can be found in the *Alcoholic Liquor Duties Act* 1979 sections 36A to 36H.

Wine and made-wine

Wine is made from the alcoholic fermentation of fresh grapes and made-wine is made from the alcoholic fermentation of any substance other than fresh grapes (for example country wines made from damsons, etc.). The duty rates for wine are in Sch. 1, ALDA 1979 and are amended as appropriate by the Finance Act each year.

Cider

Cider (which includes perry) is made from fermenting apples (or pears). To be cider, the alcoholic strength (ABV) must be between 1.2% and 8.5%. Any fermented apple juice with an ABV outside this range will not be dutied as cider.

The expected duty rise in cider duty (10% above the rate of inflation) announced in the March 2010 Budget was reversed in the emergency Budget in June 2010.

Law: *Alcoholic Liquor Duties Act* 1979; *The Spirits Regulations* 1991; *The Beer Regulations* 1993; *The Wine and Made Wine Regulations* 1989; *The Cider and Perry Regulations* 1989

9720 Tobacco products

Scope of the duty

The following are all liable to tobacco products duty if manufactured wholly or partly from tobacco or any substance used as a substitute for tobacco, but does not include herbal smoking products:

* cigarettes;
* cigars;
* hand-rolling tobacco;
* other smoking tobacco (pipe tobacco); and
* chewing tobacco.

Registration

Any premises in which tobacco products are manufactured must be registered. Application for registration must be made to the local HMRC advice centre. HMRC will also register stores adjoining factories to enable duty-free storage of products, as well as remote storage premises, subject to certain conditions being met.

Removals and warehousing

All tobacco products manufactured in the registered factory must normally be removed to the registered store immediately after manufacture. They cannot be removed from the registered store before duty has been accounted for or secured and removal documentation has been prepared and issued or deposited.

Tobacco products can be removed to home use in the UK on payment of the duty.

They can also be removed free of duty for certain specified purposes, including, exportation, consignment to another EU Member State, sale in duty-free shops, transfer to other registered stores, transfer to other registered factories for further manufacture or transfer to a UK excise warehouse. HMRC requires documentary procedures to be followed and all tobacco products will remain potentially liable to tobacco products duty until HMRC is satisfied that the products have been satisfactorily accounted for, supported by documentary evidence.

Importation

Imported tobacco products can be removed either in a finished state or for further manufacture to registered premises direct from the place of importation or via an excise warehouse, without payment of tobacco products duty subject to meeting HMRC's requirements. Any customs duty, payable on the imported product will need to be paid, unless customs warehouse approval is held in respect of the registered premises.

Rates of duty

The current rates of duty from 24 March 2010 are as follows:

Description	Current rate (24 March 2010)
cigarettes[1]	24% of the retail price[2] plus £119.03 per thousand cigarettes
cigars[3]	£180.28 per kg[4]
hand-rolling tobacco[5]	£129.59 per kg
other smoking tobacco	£79.26 per kg
chewing tobacco	£79.26 per kg

Notes

[1] 'Cigarette' means any roll of tobacco capable of being smoked as it is and not falling within any of the descriptions of a cigar. Any cigarette more than 9cm long (excluding any filter or mouthpiece) will be treated as if each 9cm or part thereof were a separate cigarette.

(2) The retail price is defined as the higher of,

(i) the recommended retail selling price in the UK of cigarettes of that description, and
(ii) the highest retail price shown at that time on the packaging of the cigarettes in question.

Where there is no such price recommended or shown, the retail price will be taken as the highest price at which cigarettes of that brand are normally sold by retail at that time in the UK.

(3) 'Cigar' means any cigar capable of being smoked as it is and which is either:

(a) a roll of tobacco with an outer wrapper of natural tobacco; or
(b) a roll of tobacco containing predominantly broken or threshed leaf, with a binder of reconstituted tobacco and with an outer wrapper which is of reconstituted tobacco having the normal colour of a cigar and which is fitted spirally; or
(c) a roll of tobacco containing predominantly broken or threshed leaf with an outer wrapper of reconstituted tobacco having the normal colour of a cigar; and having a weight exclusive of any detachable filter or mouthpiece, of not less than 2.3g; and having a circumference over at least one-third of its length of not less than 34mm.

(4) The weight for duty is the total weight of the cigar, which may however, exclude any detachable filter or mouthpiece.

(5) 'Hand-rolling tobacco' means tobacco which is sold or advertised by the importer or manufacturer as suitable for making into cigarettes; or which is of a kind used for making into cigarettes; or of which more than 25% by weight of the tobacco particles have a width of less than 1mm.

In the emergency Budget in June 2010, the Chancellor announced that the law on long cigarettes would be slightly amended, so that from 1 January 2011, cigarettes longer than 8cm will be treated as two cigarettes (down from 9cm) (TPDA 1979, s. 4).

Credits

A duty credit on products returned from UK customers to registered tobacco premises will be allowed if the products have been recycled, repackaged, or destroyed by a method acceptable to HMRC and are of a net weight of at least 1kg. Credit will also be allowed on products previously removed to duty-paid storage but not delivered to customers, provided they are returned to the registered premises for recycling, repackaging, or destruction. The terms 'recycling' and 'repackaging' are specifically defined by HMRC.

Duty can be reclaimed on imported tobacco products returned by an overseas supplier for recycling or repackaging, or disposal by a method acceptable to HMRC, providing the claim is made by the person who imported or removed the products from warehouse and paid the duty, the products were imported for sale and their net weight is at least 1kg.

Record-keeping requirements

A high standard of control on goods, persons and vehicles entering and leaving the registered premises must be maintained.

Records of all materials received, used in manufacture and disposed of, and resulting refuse and its disposal, giving details of quantity, description and date, must be maintained.

A production account of the products made in the factory must be raised as soon as the products are put in a state suitable for removal from the factory or are packed for delivery. For each tobacco product, the production account must show the quantity produced, the type, size and brand of the retail pack and the date of production and entry into the account.

A daily declaration of the total quantity of products manufactured (the production return) must be completed and submitted to HMRC, usually by noon of the following day.

A materials reconciliation account must be maintained to reconcile materials received against products manufactured.

A stock account must be maintained for products received into the registered store, operated on therein and removed.

Enforcement

Failure to comply with HMRC's requirements could result in civil penalties being imposed and cancellation of the registration.

Law: *Tobacco Products Duty Act* 1979; *Revenue Traders (Accounts and Records) Regulations* 1992 (SI 1992/3150); *Tobacco Products Regulations* 2001 (SI 2001/1712); *Tobacco Products (Description of Products) Order* 2003 (SI 2003/1471)

9730   Hydrocarbon oil duties

Scope of the duty

Historically, excise duties were charged on hydrocarbon oils, but times have changed and new forms of energy are now on the market. There is a European framework for this and generically, the products are referred to as 'energy products'. These include biofuels and electricity. In the UK, the law in the *Hydrocarbon Oils Duties Act* 1979, still taxes oils and biofuels, but the tax on electricity is Climate Change Levy (CCL) (see 10020).

All hydrocarbon oil is liable to excise duty at a full or rebated (i.e. reduced) rate. Hydrocarbon Oil means petroleum oils, coal tar, and oils produced from coal, shale, peat or any other bituminous substance, and all liquid hydrocarbons, but does not include such hydrocarbons as bituminous or asphaltic substances as are:

(1)   solid or semi-solid at a temperature of 15°C; or

(2)   gaseous at a temperature of 15°C and under a pressure of 1013.25 millibars.

Rates of duty

Excise duty rates on hydrocarbon oils are specific, and calculated per standard litre, that is litres at 15°C.

Legislation is contained in FA 2008 (with further provisions in Finance Act 2009 and 2010) to amend the duty rates for hydrocarbon oils and reduce the number of rates for heavy oils and light oils.

From 1 April 2010, the categories and rates are:

Duty rate per litre (£)

	On and after 1 April 2010	On and after 1 Oct 2010	On and after 1 Jan 2011
Unleaded petrol	0.5719	0.5819	0.5895
Heavy Oil	0.5719	0.5819	0.5895

Duty rate per litre (£)

	On and after 1 April 2010	On and after 1 Oct 2010	On and after 1 Jan 2011
Light oil (other than unleaded petrol or aviation gasoline)	0.6691	0.6791	0.6867

Duty rate per litre (£)

	On and after 1 April 2010
Aviation gasoline (Avgas)	0.3835

Duty rate per litre (£)

	On and after 1 April 2010	On and after 1 Oct 2010	On and after 1 Jan 2011
Light oil delivered to an approved person for use as furnace fuel	0.1055	0.1074	0.1088
Marked gas oil	0.1099	0.1118	0.1133
Fuel oil	0.1055	0.1074	0.1088
Heavy oil other than fuel oil, gas oil or kerosene used as fuel	0.1055	0.1074	0.1088
Kerosene to be used as motor fuel off-road or in an excepted vehicle	0.1099	0.1118	0.1133
Biodiesel for non-road use	0.1099	0.1118	0.1133
Biodiesel blended with gas oil	0.1099	0.1118	0.1133

Duty rate per litre (£)

	On and after 1 April 2010	On and after 1 Oct 2010	On and after 1 Jan 2011
Biodiesel	0.5719	0.5819	0.5895
Bioethanol	0.5719	0.5819	0.5895

	Duty rate per kg (£)		
	On and after 1 April 2010	**On and after 1 Oct 2010**	**On and after 1 Jan 2011**
Road fuel natural gas (NG), including biogas	0.2360	0.2505	0.2615
Road fuel gas other than NG – e.g. liquefied petroleum gas (LPG)	0.3053	0.3195	0.3304

Law: The Energy Products Directive (2003/96); *Hydrocarbon Oil Duties Act* 1979, s. 6 et seq; FA 2010

9740   Excise warehousing

Overview

Excise warehousing is quite different to customs warehousing. They both do different things: customs warehousing shelters goods against customs duties and import VAT; and excise warehousing shelters goods against excise duties and import VAT. It is possible to have a single building that can be both a customs warehouse and an excise warehouse.

Excise warehousing is central to the EC Holding and Movements regime, by which excise goods such as wine and spirits can move in duty suspension across EC boundaries. Duty only becomes due when the goods are removed from the regime.

There are three types of excise warehouse:

- general storage and distribution warehouses (GSD);
- trade facility warehouses; and
- distillers' warehouses (ALDA 1979, s. 15).

This distinction between GSDs and trade facility warehouses is not in the law, but is in one of the main public notices (Public Notice 196).

Approval of warehouses

To obtain HMRC's approval to operate an excise warehouse certain conditions must be met. Furthermore, each type has its own additional qualifying criteria. The most common type of warehouse in use is the general storage and distribution warehouse. To qualify for approval for such, there must be either a minimum potential duty liability of £500,000 on average stockholdings, or a minimum potential duty liability of £2m on annual throughput.

A computerised list of all UK authorised warehousekeepers, tax warehouses and REDS (see 9750) is available from HMRC. They are also able to confirm details of such traders operating in other EC Member States.

Access and security

Access to any part of the warehouse must be offered to HMRC officers at all reasonable times.

Financial guarantees are required to cover intra-EC movements of excise goods. Financial security may also be required as a condition of the warehouse approval or for UK movements. Premises must be physically secure.

What goods can be warehoused

Goods liable to excise duty can be warehoused, subject to meeting any additional conditions in respect of particular products, such as hydrocarbon oil or tobacco products.

UK-manufactured tobacco products can only be stored in an excise warehouse if they are intended for export, shipment as stores, or for visiting forces, embassies or duty-free shops, unless it also has approval as registered tobacco premises.

Record-keeping requirements

Stock accounts are required to be maintained in respect of all receipts into and deliveries from the warehouse. Computer records may be used, providing hard copy or visual interrogation facilities are available to HMRC. All information in stock accounts must be permanent and legible. They must provide:

- a full description of the goods;
- their location within the warehouse;
- their duty status and evidence of duty payment;
- details of the owner of the goods and whether they have been sold whilst in the warehouse; and
- the means to identify all goods by reference to their stock number.

A certified summary stock return may be required by HMRC on either a monthly or quarterly basis. Separate returns are required for:

- UK-produced whisky and plain spirits;
- other spirits;
- wine, made-wine, cider/perry and beer; and
- tobacco products.

An annual return of all whisky movements is also required by HMRC.

Receipts of goods

On receipt of goods into the warehouse, the warehousekeeper must carry out physical checks on the load and issue a certificate of receipt. HMRC require certain documentary procedures to be followed depending on the location from which the goods have been consigned.

All goods received must be recorded in the warehouse stock account.

Goods may be delivered duty-free from a warehouse for use as ship's stores by following HMRC's documentary procedures.

Movement of goods in the warehouse

All goods must be marked and stored in clearly identified locations in the warehouse in order that they can be readily identified from the stock account.

Any movements of goods within the warehouse must be recorded on the stock account.

A satisfactory inventory checking system, agreed by HMRC, must be in place to enable stock verifications. Stocktaking must take place annually for all goods other than bulk, which must be verified monthly.

Processing allowable in the warehouse

In contrast to customs warehouses, where only low-level operations are permitted, a wide range of operations are permitted in excise warehouses.

Operations necessary for the preservation, sale, shipment or disposal of the goods are normally allowed.

Furthermore, other operations are allowed, depending on the specific type of goods concerned. For example, bottled goods can be relabelled and repacked, whilst goods in casks, drums or vats can be bottled. The only operation allowed on tobacco products is repacking of retail packs.

All operations must be monitored and account taken immediately prior to and after each operation, as well as meeting other HMRC requirements.

Removal of goods from warehouses

Home use (i.e. to the UK market)

In order to remove goods from the warehouse to home use, the warehouse keeper must first write them off from the stock account. Commercial documents are required to identify the goods, their stock rotation number, the consignee and the type of transaction. A list of all home-use deliveries must be completed daily and show details of each delivery.

Excise duty is paid either by cash, banker's draft or guaranteed cheque before the goods leave the warehouse, or under duty deferment arrangements.

Rather than accounting for removals on a daily basis, warehouse keepers can apply to schedule their removals whereby they can submit twice-monthly schedules.

UK inter-warehouse removals

Excise goods can be removed to another excise warehouse without payment of the duty. HMRC requires certain procedures to be followed to ensure that properly endorsed certificates of receipt are obtained from the warehouse to which the goods are consigned (see .Public Notice 197).

Intra-EC movements

In order to transfer excise goods between approved warehouses in different EU Member States, a guarantee needs to be provided to cover the suspended excise duty.

From 1 April 2010, a new paperless control system (The Excise Movement and Control System (EMCS)) replaces the old paper-based AAD system for intra Member State movement.

Export

Excise duty is not liable on goods exported from the EC. However, commercial evidence of export must be held by the warehouse keeper in order to discharge his duty liability.

Ship's stores

Goods may be delivered duty free from the warehouse for use as ship's stores by following HMRC's documentary procedures.

Losses and deficiencies

Losses and deficiencies of warehoused goods are not chargeable with duty, providing it can be proved that they were due to natural causes or accidents. All losses must be recorded in the appropriate stock account and investigated. Losses can sometimes be offset against surpluses, providing they can be shown to be related and the offset can be justified.

Law: CEMA 1979, s. 92 and 94; ALDA 1979, s. 15; *Excise Warehousing (Etc) Regulations 1988* (SI 1988/809); *Excise Duties (Deferred Payment) Regulations* 1992 (SI 1992/3152); *Beer Regulations* 1993 (SI 1993/1228); *Excise Goods (Holding, Movement, Warehousing and REDs) Regulations* 1992 (SI 1992/3135)

9750   Registered consignees (formerly registered excise dealers (REDs))

From 1 April 2010 the concept of the REDs is gone. Instead, a new person is created – a 'Registered Consignee', who still has some of the characteristics of the REDs, but the regime has been modified.

Registered consignees are revenue traders who are approved by HMRC to obtain excise goods commercially from other EC Member States duty free. A registered consignee is an alternative procedure to the full excise warehousing procedure.

The difference is that a registered consignee may not hold or consign excise goods received in duty suspension, so duty (subject to deferment) is triggered on arrival.

Like excise warehouse keepers, the new registered consignor/consignee system will need to use the EMCS (Excise Movement and Control System).

Source: Public Notice 203A (April 2010)

AIR PASSENGER DUTY

9760   Introduction to air passenger duty

APD is a specific duty of excise, under the care and management of HMRC, levied on civil airlines and other aircraft operators on their carriage of passengers on flights from airports in the UK. The airlines invariably pass on the duty to the passengers.

For APD purposes, destinations are categorised into four geographical bands based on the distance from London to the capital city of the destination state (with the exception of Russia, which is split into two zones – east and west of the Urals).

Each band has two rates: one for standard class and one for other classes.

The bands are as follows from 1 November 2010. The numbers in brackets are the figures from 1 November 2009.

Band and distance in miles from London	In the lowest class £	Other classes £
Band A (0–2000)	12 (11)	24 (22)
Band B (2001–4000)	60 (45)	120 (90)
Band C (4001–6000)	75 (50)	150 (100)
Band D (over 6000)	85 (55)	170 (110)

Law: s. 30, FA 1994; FA 2009 and FA 2010

In the emergency budget on 22 June 2010, the Chancellor announced that HMRC would be consulting on a new plane-based rather than a passenger-based duty.

Law: FA 1994, s. 28 et seq; *APD Regulations* 1994 (SI 1994/1738)

Source: Public Notice 550: *Air Passenger Duty (December 2009 edition)*

9770   Persons liable for the duty

Aircraft operators are required to register for the tax with HMRC. Aircraft operators without permanent establishments in the UK are required to appoint a UK fiscal representative to ensure the principal's compliance, and to stand jointly and severally liable with them in regard to the tax.

The *Finance Act* 1998, s. 15 introduced a measure to address problems faced by foreign airlines looking for fiscal representation in the UK. Airlines are able to appoint a representative whose sole responsibility is to keep tax records and accounts, without being liable for duty debts. Airlines using this facility need to provide security to HMRC to cover any duty they have to pay.

HMRC have the power, after reasonable notice, to require that an aircraft operator or fiscal representative provide appropriate security for the payment of the duty. Additionally, after the service of notice, a non-resident aircraft operator's handling agent can be made jointly and severally liable in regard to the tax due from the aircraft operator.

Law: *Air Passenger Duty Regulations* 1994 (SI 1994/1738)

Source: HMRC Notice 550: *Air Passenger Duty*

9780 Administration

Aircraft operators registered for APD, or their fiscal representatives, are required to keep the duty accounts.

The *Aircraft Operators (Accounts and Records) Regulations* 1994 require that every operator keeps and retains an APD account which includes for each accounting period:

(a) the amount of duty payable;
(b) any adjustment;
(c) the adjusted duty payable;
(d) amounts paid, date and means of payment;
(e) the numbers of passengers carried at the lower rate and at the higher rate of APD;
(f) the numbers of passengers not chargeable by category for each of the exemptions; and
(g) Isle of Man passengers exempted.

Operators using a special accounting scheme (see below) are required instead of (e) above to record their calculation of the amount due, and additionally they are required to keep a copy of the scheme they are using, and any surveys necessary in establishing their calculations.

Returns and payment of the duty

Aircraft operators are required to file monthly returns with HMRC by the 22nd of the following month. The return shows the total number of passengers carried from UK airports, the number chargeable at the lower rate and the number chargeable at the higher rate. Then, by use of the appropriate rates, the duty is calculated and reported on the return.

Payment of the duty must be made either by the 29th of the following month when payment is by direct debit/credit transfer, or otherwise by the 22nd of the following month.

Special accounting schemes

HMRC have the discretion to prepare a scheme for an aircraft operator to calculate the extent of the connected flight, return journey, and any other of the exemptions from duty and of any consequent adjustments between the rates of APD to be applied, where there are, or would be, difficulties in obtaining or recording the information otherwise required in regard to the duty. At the heart of the complexity in determining APD liabilities for passengers is the connected-flights feature in the tax.

Connected flights

Many air passengers reach their destinations after a series of two or more flights in which they may have had to get from one intermediate airport to another, as well as having had to change aircraft. If such carriage is not to be taxed differently from single non-stop carriage from origin to destination, then mechanisms to connect separate intermediate flights in a journey are required.

Two rules are set out in the regulations by which successive flights can be connected so as to provide exemption for passengers transferring between flights within certain specified time-limits, and to identify, within these same limits, each passenger's final place of destination for determining which APD rate should apply.

The 'Case A rule' (domestic connections)

The Case A rule requires that the scheduled departure time of a UK domestic flight must be within six hours of the scheduled time of arrival of the preceding flight (extended for flights arriving after 1700 hours overnight, or for early morning arrivals before 0400 hours, to a departure time no later than 1000 hours) for the two flights to be treated as connected.

A flight from a particular airport cannot be connected using the Case A rule to a flight destined for this same (domestic) airport.

The 'Case B rule' (international connections)

The Case B rule requires that the scheduled departure time of an international flight must be within 24 hours of the scheduled time of arrival of the preceding flight for the two flights to be treated as connected.

A flight from an airport in a particular country cannot be connected using the Case B rule to a flight destined for an airport in this same country. This latter sustains the charging of APD on passengers, mainly businessmen and women, who are flying into the UK and returning all within 24 hours.

Worked examples

The following examples show how the tax works differently for three different passengers sitting on the single class morning flight from London's Gatwick airport to Newcastle.

Indirect Taxes

Example – Passenger one

The first passenger has boarded this flight after arriving at London's Heathrow airport at the scheduled arrival time of 0645 on a flight from New York. His ticket shows Newcastle as his final destination on a trip from the USA. No APD is due on his departure from Gatwick since the connected flight exemption applies. The requirements of the Case A rule are met, since they do not demand that the connection is made at the same airport.

Example – Passenger two

The second passenger is returning home to Newcastle after a trip to London. She flew down on a flight to Heathrow airport two days earlier. Even though she has a 'return' ticket, APD will be due at the lower rate of £11 on her departure from Gatwick (up to 31 October 2010) and £12 thereafter.

Remembering that in each of these cases two or more aircraft operators may be involved in 'connected' flying, then if one of them does not recognise the connection through an oversight, inevitably the tax will be over-charged.

Upgrades

If passengers are upgraded from one class of travel to another and:

- the upgrade has been provided at no extra cost to the passenger;
- the agreement for carriage does not include the possibility of an upgrade; and
- there has been no change in the agreement for carriage,

a reduced rate of APD applies to those passengers.

If the possibility of an upgrade at no extra cost has not been previously advertised or offered to the passenger prior to the decision to upgrade them, HMRC would not consider the agreement for carriage to have been changed.

Example

If passengers are upgraded because they:

- buy additional services on board unconnected with premium seats, for example, book an emergency exit seat or buy a bottle of champagne;
- were the earliest to book; or
- are on a package holiday,

then they will still be liable to a reduced rate of APD providing the conditions set out above are met.

The class of travel in a seat with a seat pitch in excess of 1.016 metres (40 inches) is regarded as standard class travel.

Law: *Aircraft Operators (Accounts and Records) Regulations* 1994 (SI 1994/1737); *Air Passenger Duty Regulations* 1994 (SI 1994/1738); *Air Passenger Duty (Connected Flights) Order* 1994 (SI 1994/1824)

Source: HMRC Notice 550: *Air Passenger Duty*

INSURANCE PREMIUM TAX

9800   Introduction to insurance premium tax

IPT is a tax on premiums where the risk covered is in the UK, unless the risk is on one of the excepted items.

It is a tax payable by the insurers on gross premiums, although clearly the insurer will seek to pass it on to the insured.

In common with VAT, insurers account to HMRC on a quarterly basis for all tax charged, which is either on a 'cash receipts' basis or as an alternative, a 'written premium' basis. There is no right of recovery of the tax by either the insurer or the insured.

There are two rates of IPT: the standard rate of 5 per cent on 'normal' insurance such as car and home insurance and a higher rate of 17.5 per cent on certain insurance such as car insurance sold with cars and insurance sold with white goods such as refrigerators.

These rates are due to rise to 6% and 20% respectively on 4 January 2011.

Example

Motor premium liable to the higher rate

A motor dealer has an associated insurance agent. Insurance is promoted as an optional add-on with every vehicle sold, and customers are encouraged to take out policies with the dealer's associated company. The majority of the agent's business is made up of such sales. This motor insurance arranged by the insurance agent would be regarded as 'connected' to the sale of the motor vehicles by the associated dealer and would be liable to the higher rate.

Example

Motor premium not liable to the higher rate

A motor dealer has an associated insurance agent, but this agent operates completely independently and from a different site. No attempt is made by the motor dealer to promote the insurance arranged by this agent, and the car dealer's customers buy their insurance from a range of outlets. The insurance agent is under no obligation to ask customers where they purchased the vehicle that they are insuring, in order to identify

---

those purchased from the associated dealer. The motor insurance arranged by the insurance agent is not liable to the higher rate of IPT even if, coincidentally, it should occasionally be sold to customers of the associated motor dealer.

Example

Examples of premiums liable to the higher rate

- Someone buys an extended warranty from an electrical retailer for a washing machine that they already own.
- Someone renews their extended warranty for a washing machine directly with the insurer and the insurer passes a commission to the store that sold the original policy.
- A customer buying a video player via mail order completes an application form which was enclosed with the equipment by the manufacturer; the form is sent back direct to the insurer who passes a commission back to the manufacturer.

Example

Some roadside assistance insurance (for example AA, RAC cover) is supplied to travellers who intend to take their vehicle with them. This is regarded as insurance relating to a motor vehicle risk, not to a travel risk, so it will generally not be liable to the higher rate of IPT (although higher rate would apply if supplied by a 'motor dealer').

Law: FA 1994, s. 48 et seq; *Insurance Premium Tax Regulations* 1994 (SI 1994/1774)

Source: HMRC Reference: Notice IPT 1: *Insurance Premium Tax*

9810 The scope of the tax

The essential point of the IPT legislation is that all insurance contracts which cover UK risks are taxable, except those falling within certain specified exemptions.

These exemptions are within FA 1994, Sch. 7A and include:

- reinsurance;
- the motorbility scheme;
- commercial ships and aircraft;
- risks outside the UK.

Thus, if a business is receiving insurance premiums in relation to taxable insurance contracts, then that business is engaged in a taxable business for IPT purposes.

IPT is therefore due on premiums received under taxable insurance contracts. IPT does not apply to contracts which are entered into by insurers which are not contracts of insurance. In this regard, some contracts are treated as insurance business for regulatory purposes but these are outside the scope of IPT. These include contracts for fidelity, performance, administration, bail or customs' bonds.

The IPT definition of 'premium' includes payments received by, or on behalf of, an insurer for a right to require the insurer to provide cover under a taxable contract of insurance.

Law: FA 1994, Sch. 7A

Source: Public Notice IPT1

9820 Apportionment

The Finance Act 1994, s. 70(1) says that all insurance contracts are prima facie taxable, unless they are specifically exempt under Sch. 7A.

If a contract contains both taxable and exempt portions, then the insurer is required to apportion that contract on a just and reasonable basis.

This is an important issue, especially as FA 1997 introduced 'higher rate' as well as 'standard rate' levels of IPT.

If the insurance cover is split into separate policies to avoid the need to apportion, each separate policy must be valued on an open market value basis and must ignore the inter-related nature of the two policies.

Where more than one insurer is involved in providing cover under a co-insurance arrangement, then it is the lead insurer who will normally decide on the apportionment and, having done so, must retain records on how the apportionment was done, for inspection by Customs.

Law: FA 1994, s. 69, Sch. 7A

9830 Registration

Liability to register

A person who receives, as insurer, premiums (and in some limited cases this can include fees) in the course of a taxable business and is not already registered for IPT, is liable to be registered. There is no minimum registration threshold as there is for VAT (FA 1994 s. 53(1)).

Additionally, anyone forming the intention of receiving premiums in the course of a taxable business must register such intention with HMRC (s. 53(2)).

Where a person is liable to be registered by virtue of s. 53(1) above, the Commissioners can register them with effect from the time when they begin to receive premiums in the course of the business concerned.

A person who is under an obligation to notify HMRC is required to do so in writing within 30 days.

Taxable intermediaries

The *Finance Act* 1997 introduced some anti-avoidance measures for IPT in areas where insurance was provided with goods and services subject to VAT. This was to prevent 'value shifting' from goods or services with a 17.5 per cent rate of VAT to insurance which was exempt for VAT purposes and had only a (then) 2.5 per cent rate of IPT thereon.

This is discussed in detail below (see 9850) but for the purposes of this section, FA 1997 introduced the concept of a 'taxable intermediary' (see 9860). From Royal Assent of FA 1997 (19 March 1997) anyone falling within this concept is required to register and account for IPT on the charging of an insurance fee with certain goods and services set out in FA 1994, Sch. 6A.

Thus a person who is a taxable intermediary and is not registered for IPT is liable to be registered (FA 1994, s. 53AA(1)).

A person who becomes liable to be registered under FA 1994, s. 53AA(1) above, will be registered from the time he begins to charge taxable intermediary's fees in the course of the business concerned.

Failure to notify liability to register

A person who forms the intention of either receiving premiums as an insurer or charging taxable intermediary's fees and fails to inform HMRC, may be liable to a penalty of five per cent of the relevant tax (subject to a minimum penalty of £250).

This is subject to a defence of a reasonable excuse for the failure to notify.

If a person is convicted of an offence or is charged with a penalty in respect of dishonesty, a penalty under Sch. 7, para. 14 will not arise.

Law: FA 1994, s. 53(1), (2), 53AA(1), Sch. 6A, Sch. 7, para. 14, FA 2010

9840   Method of accounting

Accounting periods

The *Finance Act* 1994 provides that a registrable person must account for IPT by reference to accounting periods determined under the regulations.

A normal accounting period is three months, as it is for VAT, although the regulations provide for non-standard accounting periods if that is helpful to the registrable person.

At the end of each accounting period, the registrable person completes an IPT return and returns it to HMRC by the due date, which is the last day of the next month following the end of the accounting period.

Tax points

Like VAT, the tax point is the date which triggers the liability to IPT and determines the accounting period in respect of which the tax must be paid. The tax point will depend on which accounting method is used.

Accounting methods

There are two methods of accounting for IPT, and the registrable person may choose which method he wishes to adopt.

They are:

(1) the 'cash receipt' method; and

(2) the optional special 'written premium' basis.

The 'cash receipt' method

Like cash accounting for VAT, this is based on the receipt of cash. A tax point is triggered when taxable premiums or insurance based fees by taxable intermediaries are received, or received on their behalf.

The 'written premium' basis

Under this accounting method, the tax point is the date that an entry is made in the accounts showing the premium or fee due (this is the written premium date). A registrable person must use this method for at least 12 months.

Under the written premium scheme there is a choice of tax points and a registrable person may choose which best suits him.

(1) The registrable person may account for IPT on the date on which the premium is due to him. For example, an entry in the registrable person's books on 18 November showing a premium due on 31 October will give rise to a tax point on 31 October.

(2) The registrable person may, as an alternative, account for IPT by using the date he enters the premium in his books.

So using the example above, the entry on 18 November will trigger a tax point on 18 November.

Whichever method is adopted, there are anti-avoidance rules for preventing unnecessary delay in bringing the tax to account.

Anti-avoidance

HMRC normally expect to see a premium written within 90 days of the tax point that would apply under the cash receipt method. HMRC will apply a number of tests and would expect to see a premium written in the same accounting period on the earliest of:

(1)   14 days of notification of receipt of premium by the broker or other intermediary;

(2)   14 days of notification by the broker or other intermediary of commencement of cover;

(3)   14 days of receipt of the premium by the insurer;

(4)   30 days of commencement of cover.

Law: FA 1994, s. 54; *Insurance Premium Tax Regulations* 1994 (SI 1994/1774), reg. 2, 12, 23, 26

Source: Public Notice IPT 1: *Insurance Premium Tax*

9850   The selective higher rate of IPT

The *Finance Act* 1997 introduced a selective higher rate of IPT to attack VAT planning schemes which indulged in 'value shifting' from goods and services subject to the standard rate of 17.5 per cent VAT to associated insurance which is exempt for VAT purposes.

Thus the sales price of the standard rated VAT goods and services was artificially lowered, and the price of the exempt insurance element was artificially raised, leading to a 'leakage' of VAT revenue for the Treasury.

Accordingly FA 1994 now provides that a premium received under a taxable insurance contract by an insurer is liable to tax at the higher rate if it falls within one or more of the paragraphs in FA 1994, Pt. II of Sch. 6A.

These are essentially:

●   Extended warranties insurance sold with cars and motorbikes (unless it's given free to the insured person);
●   Extended warranty insurance sold with household goods (unless it's given free to the insured person);
●   Travel insurance.

The higher rate of IPT is due to rise to 20% on 4 January 2011.

Law: FA 1994, Sch. 6A

9860   Taxable intermediaries

Having introduced the selective higher rate, discussed in 9850 above, HMRC then deemed it necessary to plan for avoidance and introduced advance anti-avoidance measures in FA 1997.

These were designed to beat planning schemes by which the value of the insurance itself is artificially lowered (thus lowering the exposure to 17.5 per cent IPT) and instead charge a 'fee' to arrange the insurance which avoids IPT. These fees are liable to IPT at the higher rate when they are charged in connection with a higher rate insurance contract.

9870   Administration

Record keeping

As with VAT there is a general duty on registrable persons to keep records. Regulation 16 of the IPT Regulations requires every registrable person to keep the following records:

(1)   his business and accounting records;

(2)   policy documents cover notes, endorsements and similar documents and copies of such documents that are issued by him;

(3)   copies of all invoices, renewal notices and similar documents issued by him;

(4)   all credit or debit notes or other documents received by him which show an increase or decrease in the amount of any premium and copies of such documents that are issued by him; and

(5)   such other records as the commissioners may specify in a notice published by them and not withdrawn by them.

Every registrable person must keep the above records for six years.

Records may be kept in hard copy, microfilm or microfiche, providing that copies can be easily produced and there are adequate facilities for HMRC to view them when required.

Records may also be kept on magnetic tape or disc, providing they can readily be accessed and understood by HMRC. The registrable persons should obtain agreement before starting to use any method of information storage other than hard copy.

Law: FA 1994, Sch. 7, para. 1; *Insurance Premium Tax Regulations* 1994 (SI 1994/1774) reg. 16

Source: HMRC Notice IPT 1: *Insurance Premium Tax*

9880   Tax representatives

Appointing a tax representative

If an insurer, or a taxable intermediary, has no fixed establishment in the UK, but nevertheless covers risks (or intends to cover risks) sited in the UK, then that person is still liable to account for IPT.

Until FA 2008, *Finance Act* 1994, s. 57 provided that such a person must appoint a tax representative in the UK and request HMRC approval of the same. The representative could be a company or an individual.

Rights and duties of a tax representative

The *Finance Act* 1994, s. 58 set out the rights and duties of a tax representative.

The representative was entitled to act on the insurers' or taxable intermediary's behalf for the purpose of IPT.

The representative secured the insurer's or taxable intermediary's compliance with the IPT legislation and was jointly and severally liable.

Finance Act 2008 repealed these provisions, so now an overseas insurer will not have to have a tax representative in the UK and if they do, the representative will not be jointly and severally liable for any debt.

Law: FA 2008; FA 1994; *Insurance Companies Act* 1982, s. 10; *Insurance Premium Tax Regulations* 1994 (SI 1994/1774), reg. 34, 35, 36, 38

Source: HMRC Notice IPT1 (2002 edition – now out of date and doesn't reflect the FA 2008 changes)

9890   Penalties

The IPT legislation provides for two avenues to punish wrongdoing in IPT, criminal proceedings and civil penalties. By far the majority of penalties will be civil penalties and are in FA 1994, Sch. 7. The law follows the VAT legislation in its shape.

9900   Effects of IPT: practical situations

Arrangements for brokers and agents

The main issues arising in relation to brokers and agents regarding IPT are:

- how to deal with policies sold through an intermediary where the insurer does not know the final selling price of that policy;

- whether amounts received by the intermediary as remuneration are part of the chargeable amount upon which insurers must account for IPT; and
- whether amounts received by intermediaries as remuneration are part of the chargeable amount upon which the intermediary must account for IPT at the higher rate.

Fees and commissions

Whether or not amounts received by a broker or intermediary for arranging taxable insurance contracts are included in the sum upon which the insurer accounts for IPT, depends upon the contract under which payment is received and the rate at which IPT applies to the contract of insurance.

Net premiums for contracts liable to IPT at the standard rate

Where an intermediary makes any additional charge in relation to an insurance contract that is taxable at the normal rate of IPT and this is done under a separate contract to the contract of insurance, these charges are not liable to IPT and should not be included in the intermediary's notification of the premium to the insurer for the purposes of IPT.

The main principle is that IPT is chargeable on the premium, which is defined as any payment under the insurance contract between the insurer(s) and the insured(s). The amount on which the insurer accounts for IPT includes commission paid to or retained by the broker, if the commission is part of the payment due to the insurer under the contract of insurance. The following examples assume that any commission paid to or retained by the broker is due to the insurer under the contract of insurance and also that the contract is taxable at the standard rather than the higher rate of IPT:

- The broker retains all commission due to him from the insurer and also charges the insured a fee, under a separate contract to the contract of insurance. The existence of both the fee contract and fee is disclosed in writing to the insured. The insurer accounts for IPT on the gross premium, inclusive of commission. The fee (because it is charged under a different contract) is not liable to IPT.
- The broker pays over to the insured a share of the broker's commission (thus indirectly reducing the cost of the insurance for the insured party). IPT remains due on the gross premium, which includes the entire amount of the commission.
- The broker pays over to the insured all of the commission due to the broker, thus heavily discounting the insurance. IPT is due on the gross premium, which includes the entire amount of commission.
- The broker pays over to the insured all of the commission due to the broker, and charges the insured a smaller fee under a separate contract the existence of both contract and fee being disclosed in writing to the insured. IPT is due on the gross premium, which includes the entire amount of the commission. The fee is not liable to IPT.

The above arrangements reflect the underlying contracts and are not, in any way, affected by the name given to any charges made (for example, 'fee', 'commission', and 'discount').

Indirect Taxes

Net premium for contracts liable to IPT at the higher rate

Where a taxable intermediary makes any additional charge in relation to an insurance contract that is liable to IPT at the higher rate, this additional charge forms part of the premium for IPT purposes. This is still the case even if this additional charge is not due under the contract of insurance. The taxable intermediary must account for the IPT based on this separate chargeable amount, which is separate to the chargeable amount on which the insurer must account for IPT.

Estimated premiums

If a taxable insurance contract is sold through a broker or intermediary and the final selling price of the insurance is unknown, the gross premium may be estimated. Estimation should be based on a representative sample of the final selling prices charged by the intermediary.

Arrangements for Lloyd's

Lloyd's is a very old and established insurance market and it has its own special working practices.

Registration

The IPT Regulations allow that where taxable business is carried out by underwriting members of Lloyd's, the syndicate rather than the individual members may be registered for IPT.

Any change in syndicate members will not affect the registration.

Responsibility for IPT

The regulations provide that compliance for IPT is the joint and several responsibility of both the underwriting members and the managing agent.

Lloyd's acting as representative

Where a syndicate which is registered for IPT has elected to account for IPT under the special accounting scheme (the written premium scheme), then the syndicate may make an election in writing that Lloyd's shall act as its representative in accounting for IPT.

In these circumstances, Lloyd's is also jointly and severally liable for the IPT with the syndicate and the managing agent.

Groups of companies

The IPT legislation provides for companies which satisfy the 'control' requirements to be treated as a group for IPT purposes.

The legislation is virtually a mirror of the VAT group legislation, and provides that the group of companies may make an application to be treated as a group for IPT purposes.

The group may only consist of companies, and each member must have an established place of business in the UK or be resident in the UK.

Two or more companies are eligible to be a group if one of them controls the other, or one person or partnership controls them both. Control means effectively 51 per cent of the votes.

A group is treated as being in existence from the beginning of an agreed IPT accounting period. One group member is treated as being the representative member.

HMRC may not refuse an application unless it appears necessary for the protection of the revenue.

The representative member is the group member whose name is on the IPT return.

In law, all the business of the group is treated as being carried out by the representative member, which is treated as either the insurer or a taxable intermediary. All members of the group are jointly and severally liable for tax due from the representative member. However, unlike in the case of VAT grouping, supplies of insurance between members of an IPT group are subject to IPT.

Warranties and extended warranties

A warranty is commonly given by a manufacturer or vendor of goods. The warranty is an undertaking that if the goods are faulty the provider of the goods will replace them without charge.

This type of warranty is not insurance and is not therefore subject to IPT.

If, however, the supplier takes out insurance cover against this replacement, the related premium is taxable but not at the higher rate.

If the warranty is an extended warranty (often called mechanical breakdown insurance (MBI)), and, in return for a premium, the insurer will replace the goods in the event of breakdown that premium is subject to IPT and may be caught by the selective higher rate rules.

Law: FA 1994, s. 63, 64; *Insurance Premium Tax Regulations* 1994 (SI 1994/1774), reg. 8 and 9(3)

LANDFILL TAX

9950 Introduction to landfill tax

Landfill tax is designed as a tax on waste disposal at landfill sites, in part, at least, as an incentive to reduce waste and to encourage alternative methods of dealing with waste such as recycling it. Thus in part it was billed, on introduction, as an environmentally friendly tax that would help protect the environment.

Landfill tax is charged on disposal of waste made at landfill sites and the time at which the waste is landfilled is the basic tax point for the tax.

The tax is chargeable by weight and there are two rates (as at 1 April 2010):

- a lower rate of £2.50 per tonne for inert waste (such as rocks and soil); and
- a standard rate of £48 per tonne for all other taxable waste from 1 April 2010 (£40 per tonne from 1 April 2009).

It is expected to rise to £56 per tonne in April 2011.

The tax falls on the landfill site operator who becomes liable to pay the tax, although where possible the operator will clearly seek to pass the tax on to people using the landfill site.

Where a disposal to landfill contains both active and inactive materials, tax is due on the whole load at the standard rate. However, as long as it does not lead to any potential for pollution, you may ignore the presence of an incidental amount of active waste in a mainly inactive load, and treat the whole load as taxable at the lower rate.

Example

HMRC would accept the following as qualifying for the lower rate:

- a load of bricks, stone and concrete from the demolition of a building that has small pieces of wood in it and small quantities of plaster attached to bricks as it would have not been feasible for a contractor to separate them;
- a load of soil that contains small quantities of grass;
- inactive waste such as mineral dust packaged in polythene bags for disposal; and
- a load of soil and stone from street works containing tarmac would qualify but a load of tarmac containing soil and stone would not.

Previously, waste from cleaning up contaminated land disposed of by landfill was exempt from landfill tax. However, this exemption is being phased out and applications for landfill tax exemption certificates will not be accepted by HMRC on or after 1 December 2008. Anyone in possession of a valid exemption certificate will have until 31 March 2012 to dispose of their waste if they wish to benefit from the exemption. All certificates issued under the scheme will cease to be valid on or after 1 April 2012 and disposals to landfill of waste from cleaning up contaminated land made on or after that date will be liable to landfill tax at the appropriate rate.

Liability is extended to landfill tax operators who are not the holders of the waste management licence for their sites. Such an operator will become liable with the licence holder for any landfill tax incurred on waste disposals at the site.

HMRC guidance on landfill tax is contained in public notice LFT 1 (June 2010 edition).

Law: FA 1996, s. 39–71, Sch. 5; FA 2010; *Landfill Tax (Material From Contaminated Land) (Phasing Out of Exemption) Order* 2008 (SI 2008/2669); *Landfill Tax Regulations 1996* (SI 1996/1527); *Landfill Tax (Qualifying Material) Order* 1996 (SI 1996/1528); *Landfill Tax (Contaminated Land) Order* 1996 (SI 1996/1529)

Source: HMRC Reference: Notice LFT1 (July 2010 edition)

9960 Scope of the tax

Landfill tax is charged on a 'taxable disposal'. A disposal is a 'taxable disposal' if:

(a) it is a disposal of material as waste;
(b) it is made by way of landfill;
(c) it is made at a landfill site; and
(d) it is made on or after 1 October 1996.

The *Landfill Tax (Prescribed Landfill Site Activities) Order* 2009 (SI 2009/1929) took effect from 1 September 2009. The Order prescribes seven uses of material on a landfill site which will be subject to landfill tax. It also provides that material is taxable if certain requirements for notification, designation of information areas, provision of information or keeping of records are not complied with.

This change in the legislation took place because of the defeat in the Court of Appeal of HMRC in the Waste Recycling Group Limited case in 2008 which rules that material received and used on a landfill site is not taxable. HMRC changed the law to ensure that material used (for example in building cells to contain waste) is now taxable.

Law: FA 1996, s. 40(1), s. 65A

Source: Public Notice LFT1 (June 2010 edition)

9970 Registration

A person who carries out taxable activities and is not registered for LFT is liable to be registered.

Additionally, a person who at any time forms the intention of carrying out taxable activities and is not registered must notify the commissioners of his intention.

Where a person ceases to have the intention of carrying out taxable activities he is required to notify the commissioners of that fact.

Taxable activities are the making of taxable disposals in respect of which he is liable to pay tax. Taxable disposals are defined in FA 1996, s. 40 (see 9960).

A person liable to be registered shall notify the commissioners within 30 days of either forming, or continuing to have, the intention of carrying out taxable activities. Notification shall be on the form(s) specified in reg. 4 of the *Landfill Tax Regulations* 1996 (SI 1996/1527).

Changes in registration particulars shall be notified to the commissioners within 30 days of the change. This is designed to help HMRC keep its records up to date.

Law: FA 1996, s. 47 and 69; *Landfill Tax Regulations* 1996 (SI 1996/1527), reg. 4 and 5

9980 Accounting for the tax

The landfill tax return

Once registered, a registrable person is required to submit a landfill tax return (form LT 100). This will normally be for three months and it is due by the last day of the month following the end of the accounting period.

Tax point

The tax point is the time at which the liability to account for the tax falls. There are two tax points:

(1) the disposal tax point – this is the date on which the waste was disposed of to landfill; and

(2) the invoice date tax point.

The legislation concerning landfill tax provides that if a landfill operator wishes, he can use as an alternative to the disposal tax point, the date on which a landfill tax invoice is issued. This must normally be within 14 days of the disposal tax point although a longer period (to allow for monthly invoicing) may be negotiated with HMRC.

If a landfill site operator chooses the invoice date tax point, then he must issue a landfill invoice, which must contain the details laid out in *Landfill Tax Regulations* 1996 (SI 1996/1527), reg. 37.

These include:

- an identifying number;
- invoice date;
- date of disposal;
- name, address and landfill tax registration number of the operator;
- weight and description of waste disposed of;
- the rate of tax applied to each disposal; and
- the total amount payable on the invoice.

It is not necessary to show the amount of landfill tax on the disposal but if it is shown, then the invoice must also contain a statement that the amount is not recoverable as VAT input tax.

If the operator wishes, he may issue a combined VAT and LFT tax invoice. The VAT must be applied to the full invoiced amount including LFT.

It is important to note that a tax point is NOT created (as it is in VAT) by the earlier issue of an invoice or the receipt of payment. A tax point can never arise before the date of disposal.

Correction of errors

In common with VAT and insurance premium tax, LFT contains a mechanism by which errors below a de minimis threshold may be corrected on the next LFT return. This threshold is £2,000. Errors above that amount are treated on a 'voluntary disclosure' basis.

Records

The LFT legislation requires a registrable person to keep records to provide an audit trail for Customs to follow. The records which a landfill operator must keep are:

(1)   the landfill tax account;

(2)   invoices;

(3)   credit and debit notes;

(4)   bad debt relief account; and

(5)   other records such as business and accounting records including analyses of waste.

These records must normally be kept for six years. However, bad debt records only need to be kept for five years.

Law: *Landfill Tax Regulations* 1996 (SI 1996/1527), reg. 16, 37; *Landfill Tax (amendment) Regulations* 2009 (SI 2009/1930)

9990   Credit

There are conditions under which a landfill site operator has accounted for LFT and then because of a change in circumstances needs to claim credit in respect of the LFT already paid. There are three circumstances in which this can happen:

(1)   permanent removal;

(2)   bad debt relief; and

(3)   environmental bodies credit scheme.

The maximum credit that landfill site operators may claim against their annual landfill tax liability, for contributions made to bodies with objects concerned with the environment, is 6 per cent of his relevant tax liability.

Law: *Landfill Tax Regulations* 1996 (SI 1996/1527); *Waste Recycling Group Ltd v R & C Commrs* [2008] EWCA Civ 849

10000   Assessments, penalties and interest

Power to assess

The LFT legislation provides that where a person has failed to make LFT returns, or failed to keep documents necessary to verify returns, or failed to afford facilities necessary to verify returns, or it appears to the commissioners that its submitted returns are incorrect or incomplete, then they may assess the amount of tax due from him to the best of their judgment and notify him accordingly.

There are two types of assessment arising from the legislation:

(1)   an assessment in respect of the tax itself; and

(2)   an assessment in respect of interest and penalties.

An assessment shall not be made more than two years after the end of the relevant accounting period, or one year after 'evidence of facts', sufficient in the commissioner's opinion to justify the making of the assessment, comes to their knowledge. In any event is subject to an overall time-limit of four years from 1 April 2010 (for careless behaviour) and 20 years for deliberate behaviour.

Interest

Interest on under-declared tax

Where an assessment has been raised for under-declared tax, the commissioners may also assess for interest which runs from the due date (one month after the end of an accounting period) to the day before 'the relevant day'.

The relevant day is the earlier of:

(a)   the day on which the assessment is notified to the person; or
(b)   the day on which the additional amount is paid.

The rate of interest is set by the *Air Passenger Duty and Other Indirect Taxes (Interest Rate) Regulations* 1998 (SI 1998/1461).

Interest on unpaid tax

The LFT legislation also provides for interest to run on unpaid tax on LFT returns. This interest runs from the due date until the date before that on which the tax is paid.

The interest charge is subject to mitigation by either the commissioners or, on appeal by a tribunal. A 'reasonable excuse' is a factor which may well influence the amount of mitigation.

Interest payable by the commissioners

Where, due to an error on the part of the commissioners, LFT is overpaid by a registrable person, interest will lie in favour of the 'taxpayer'.

Penalties

The LFT legislation provides (in common with the VAT and IPT legislation) two ways of punishing 'wrongdoing':

(1) criminal penalties; or

(2) civil penalties.

Criminal penalties

If a person is found guilty of an offence, he will be subject to the criminal penalties laid out in FA 1996, Sch. 5, Pt. IV.

These are:

(a) on summary conviction (in a magistrates' court) a fine of £5,000 or of three times the amount of tax, whichever is the greater and/or up to six months in prison; and

(b) on conviction on indictment, an unlimited fine and/or up to seven years in prison.

Criminal penalties are only likely to be sought in extreme cases and/or for habitual offenders.

Civil penalties

Most offences will be dealt with under the civil procedures.

The main civil penalties are as follows.

(a) *Evasion*

The civil evasion penalty regime has been repealed and landfill tax is now under the general penalties for errors regime introduced in April 2009 and extended to environmental taxes in 2010.

(b) *Registration*

A person who fails to notify the commissioners of his liability to register is liable to a penalty of five per cent of the tax (subject to a £250 minimum).

(c) *Breach of regulations*

Where the legislation requires compliance and that person fails to comply (such as a duty to produce records) that person will be liable to a fine of £250.

In the case of documents further non-compliance can result in a further fine of £20 per day for each day of non-compliance.

Indirect Taxes

Mitigation and reasonable excuse

Where a person is liable to a civil penalty, the commissioners, or on appeal a tribunal, can reduce the penalty as they think fit (including reducing it to nil).

Where a person satisfies the commissioners, or on an appeal a tribunal, that a 'reasonable excuse' exists, that may be taken into account in determining the level of mitigation. It is important to note that there is one major difference in this area between LFT and VAT. In VAT all of the civil penalties are subject to a 'reasonable excuse' which is an all or nothing defence but only certain penalties are subject to mitigation. In the LFT legislation, the draftsman has taken a different approach which is outlined above.

Law: FA 1996, s. 50 and Sch. 5, para. 33, Pt. V, VI

Source: Public Notice LFT 1

10010   Review and appeals

A review and appeal procedure for LFT is available to taxpayers who are in dispute with HMRC.

LFT is now subject to the revised review and appeal procedures form 1 April 2009.

If HMRC issues a 'decision' (often an assessment), HMRC is bound to tell the taxpayer that he has the following choice:

* have the decision reviewed; or
* appeal the decision.

If the taxpayer accepts the offer of a review within 30 days then HMRC will be bound to review it and inform the taxpayer within 45 days of the conclusions of the review.

The review will either:

* uphold;
* vary; or
* cancel the decision.

After the conclusions of the review have been notified to the taxpayer, the taxpayer will still have 30 days to appeal.

If the taxpayer does not wish to have the decision reviewed, then he may go straight to an appeal within 30 days, providing the matter is an appealable matter under s. 54, FA 1996 (most matters are appealable).

Law: FA 1996, s. 54–57

CLIMATE CHANGE LEVY

10020   Climate change levy: supplies

As part of its liabilities toward the Kyoto agreement and the Copenhagen Climate Summit, climate change levy (CCL) is levied on supplies of electricity, gas and coal to industry, commerce, agriculture and the public sector for their business use of light, heat and power. In other words, the CCL is levied on supplies of 'taxable commodities' for business use. The CCL is not levied on supplies of taxable commodities for non-business use, such as domestic use or use by a charity to the extent it is for non-business purposes.

Supplies by utilities and producers of taxable commodities for their own use and not for production are deemed to be self-supplies for CCL purposes. However, in general, no CCL is levied on taxable supplies made by a utility or producer of taxable commodities to another utility or other such producer; the aim is to prevent CCL being charged twice on the same commodity.

Generally, the CCL will be added to the consumer's energy costs by inclusion on the invoice issued by the supplier. Due to the exemption for non-business use, residential consumers should not see the CCL on their energy bills.

Climate change levy is levied on taxable supplies of taxable commodities. These are supplies of taxable commodities that are not *excluded*, *exempt* or *outside the scope* of CCL.

Taxable commodities comprise:

- electricity;
- gas that is in a gaseous state and is of a kind normally supplied by a gas utility;
- petroleum gas, or other gaseous hydrocarbon, in a liquid state; coal and lignite; and
- coke, semi-coke, of coal or lignite; petroleum coke.

Taxable commodities do not include hydrocarbon oils, steam, heat, road fuel gases and any waste containing taxable commodities.

An *excluded* supply is a supply for domestic use, or for non-business use by a charity. Where a supply is for domestic use and business use, or for business and non-business use by a charity, then an apportionment of the mixed supply is required. If the percentage attributable to non-business use is 60 per cent or more then the whole of the mixed supply shall be deemed to be an excluded supply; accordingly CCL is not then charged on any part of the mixed supply.

Certain small supplies are deemed to be always for domestic use. For example:

- supplies of coal or coke not exceeding one tonne when held out for sale as domestic fuel;
- supplies of gas or petroleum gas, in a gaseous state, through pipelines to the buildings concerned at a rate not exceeding 4397 kWh per month;

- supplies of liquid petroleum gas in cylinders weighing less than 50 kg each, either made through the delivery of 20 or less cylinders, or, where in excess of this number, the liquid petroleum gas is not intended for resale;
- supplies of liquid petroleum gas made other than by delivering cylinders where the recipient does not have the capacity to store more than two tonnes;
- metered supplies of electricity where the supply to the building was not exceeding the rate of 1,000 kWh per month in total; and
- unmetered supplies of electricity where the supply to the building was not exceeding the rate of 1,000 kWh per month in total.

The following are *exempt* supplies:

(a)   supplies of taxable commodities, other than electricity and gas in a gaseous state, for burning outside of the UK (i.e., mainly LPG and solid fuels);
(b)   supplies of gas by a gas utility for burning in the province of Northern Ireland;
(c)   supplies of taxable commodities for burning (or consuming in the case of electricity) to propel:

    (i)   a train for transporting passengers or freight, or
    (ii)   other vehicles for transporting passengers,
or to provide light and heat in:

    (i)   a train and railway carriages for transporting passengers and freight,
    (ii)   other vehicles for transporting passengers, or
    (iii)   a ship for transporting freight when part of its journey entails going outside of the UK territorial waters;

(d)   supplies to produce taxable commodities other than electricity;
(e)   certain supplies, other than self-supplies, to produce electricity in a generating station which is neither a fully exempt nor a partly exempt combined heat and power (CHP) station;
(f)   supplies, other than self-supplies, from a partly exempt CHP;
(g)   self-supplies by electricity producers;
(h)   supplies not used as fuel;
(i)   electricity generated from renewable sources; and
(j)   electricity generated from good quality combined heat and power.

Law: FA 2000, Part II

Source: Public Notice CCL1 (July 2010 edition)

10025   Rates of CCL

From 1 April 2009, the rates of CCL are as follows:

- £0.00470 for electricity;
- £0.00164 for gas supplied by a gas utility or any gas supplied in a gaseous state that is of a kind supplied by a gas utility;

- £0.01050 for any petroleum gas, or other gaseous hydrocarbon, supplied in a liquid state; and
- £0.01281 for any other taxable commodity.

From 1 April 2011, the rates are expected to be as follows:

- £0.00485 for electricity;
- £0.00169 for gas supplied by a gas utility or any gas supplied in a gaseous state that is of a kind supplied by a gas utility;
- £0.01083 for any petroleum gas, or other gaseous hydrocarbon, supplied in a liquid state; and
- £0.01321 for any other taxable commodity.

A reduced rate levy, which, in circumstances where the taxable commodities are used efficiently and in an environment-friendly way, may be as low as 20 per cent of the above full rates. For the reduced rate to apply, a Climate Change Agreement (CCA) with the Secretary of State for Energy and Climate Change needs to be in place.

These agreements, which are negotiated at sector level, will set targets for energy efficiency and milestone targets will be set every two years.

Law: FA 2000, Sch. 6, para. 42; FA 2008; *Climate Change Levy (General) Regulations* 2001 (SI 2001/838); FA 2010

Source: Public Notice CCL 1 (July 2010 edition); Public Notice CCL1/3 (July 2010 edition)

AGGREGATES LEVY

10040   Aggregates levy: general

The aggregates levy was introduced to combat the environmental damage done by quarrying operations, many of which take place in the most beautiful parts of the UK. The aggregates levy is administered by HMRC.

A standard charge of £2.00 per tonne of taxable material currently applies to the commercial extraction or importation of taxable aggregate in the UK or its territorial waters. This rate is due to rise to £2.10 per tonne from 1 April 2011.

There are a number of events that have to occur before a charge to aggregates levy arises. The type of aggregate and its intended usage are the main factors. It is 'commercial exploitation' which renders the aggregate liable to the levy. There are, to all intents and purposes, four limbs to the definition:

(1)   if the aggregate is removed from a site;

(2)   if the aggregate becomes the subject of a contract;

(3)   if it is used for construction services; and

(4) if it is mixed with another substance other than water.

Aggregate for the purposes of the levy means rock, gravel or sand, and substances that are incorporated in the rock, gravel or sand or are naturally mixed with it. The definition includes rock that has not been through an industrial crushing process. However, not all of this material is taxable. All commercially exploited aggregate is taxable unless exempted. Consistent with the aim of reflecting the environmental cost of quarrying and mining, recycled aggregate is exempted from aggregates levy. Aggregate that is, or is derived from, material which has already been subjected to the levy is not taxable (thereby avoiding double taxation). Aggregate commercially exploited before the commencement date is outside the scope of the levy.

All commercially exploited aggregate is deemed to be taxable unless specifically exempted. The exemptions are conferred on the grounds of 'quality' or the primary purpose for its extraction. For example, aggregate will be exempt if it is extracted as a by-product of another venture. Such by-products may arise from excavating the foundations of any building site, dredging a watercourse or maintaining a road. There is also a 'china and ball clay exemption', whereby the waste or spoil of the processes of extracting or separating such materials is exempt (but not any aggregate contained in the overburden).

In addition to extraction being exempt under these headings, aggregate may also be exempt if:

- it has at any time been used for construction purposes – i.e., it is recycled rubble;
- it is, or it is from, aggregate which has already been subjected to the aggregates levy; or
- it was removed from the originating site before the commencement date of the aggregates levy.

The levy does not apply to other quarried or mined products such as coal, clay, shale and slate, metals and metal ores, gemstones or semi-precious stones and industrial minerals.

Aggregate may also be exempt from the levy as a result of processes which are applied to it. The method of exploiting the aggregate may fall into the relevant definition of 'commercial exploitation' and the aggregate may fail to fall into an exempted type; nonetheless a process applied to the aggregate may allow it to qualify for an exemption. In this regard it should be noted that an intention to perform this process is insufficient. It is the process itself not the connection with a particular industry which gains the exception. So, aggregate may be exempt if it is produced from the cutting of any rock to produce dimension stone ('stone with one or more flat surfaces'), or is produced by a relevant substance having been extracted or separated, or alternatively if it is from the production of lime or cement from limestone or a similar substance.

In addition, if aggregate is exploited in order to extract certain, specified substances then it is also exempt. The substances include flint, gypsum, potash, metals and ores of metals, gems and semi-precious stones and the clay mentioned above. The list is clearly intended to be exhaustive as it fails to include a term such as 'and any other such substance', and variation of the list is stated to be by statutory order.

Aggregate removed from the ground along the line, or proposed line, of any railway, tramway or monorail for the purposes of improving, maintaining or constructing it, is exempt from the levy, providing the aggregate was not removed for the purpose of extracting the aggregate.

In *C&E Commrs v East Midlands Aggregates Ltd*[2004] EWHC 856 (Ch) , the High Court upheld a decision of the VAT and Duties Tribunal that the removal of certain aggregate in order to lay the foundations for a lorry park and the drainage system servicing a new warehouse would be exempt from aggregates levy.

The levy is administered by the creation of a register to be kept by HMRC of all those liable to account for aggregates levy. The returns and payments are to be filed periodically, and HMRC has the powers to make regulations governing factors such as the frequency of return periods.

Non-resident taxpayers (essentially importers) are mandated to appoint tax representatives for the purposes of provisions under the Act. Powers for security for the levy, recovery and interest are also available to HMRC. Credits and repayments of any overpaid levy are dealt with in essentially the same way as other indirect taxes, while the criminal and civil penalties and remedies laid down are based on existing provisions. Also akin to the landfill tax and climate change levy legislation, provision is made for aggregates levy groups, whereby members are jointly and severally liable for aggregates levy due from other group members in the same way as for VAT grouping.

The review and appeal procedure for aggregates levy is essentially the same for the other indirect taxes from 1 April 2009.

For rates of aggregates levy and associated interest rates, see 118.

Law: FA 2001, Pt. 2;

Source: Public Notice AGL 1 (July 2010 edition)

COUNCIL TAX AND BUSINESS RATES

10050   Council tax (domestic rates)

Council tax is a property tax. It is payable in respect of residential (i.e. domestic) property. Council tax was introduced on 1 April 1993. It is a local tax insofar as the tax is collected and retained by local authorities and the rate is fixed by them. However, it is not a true local tax as local authorities have no control over the structure of the tax or the detailed rules which impose liabilities – although they do have limited discretion in some areas. Furthermore, in recent years the government has imposed a cap or limitation on the level of council tax imposed by some local authorities.

Local authority spending is largely financed by grants from the central government. These are, however, largely earmarked to cover the provision of specific services, in particular education and housing which, together with social services, make up the bulk of local authority expenditure. Council tax and business rates are the main source of finance for the provision of discretionary local authority services.

Example

As an illustration, the London Borough of Brent's budgets for a particular year showed the following income:

	£ million	%
Government grants (£136.1m specific)	287.5	69.3
Business rates	56.3	13.6
Council tax	53.2	12.8
Charges for services	17.7	4.3
	414.7	100.0

These figures exclude council house rents as local authorities are required to fix such rents to cover their expenditure on such housing. These percentages vary from year to year and from council to council, but the contribution from council tax and business rates will normally account for roughly 25 per cent of a local authority's total income.

Law: *Local Government Finance Act* 1992

10060   Business rates (non-domestic rates)

Business rating is similar to a property tax. It is payable on non-domestic property (and some mixed use property). The tax payable in respect of an individual property is based on its rateable value and this is given by the Valuation Office Agency (VOA). This is, broadly speaking, its rental value on a letting from year to year, on the assumption that the tenant is responsible for all usual tenant's rates and tax and the cost of repairs and insurance and any other expenses necessary to maintain the building in a state to command that rent.

Rateable values are updated every five years. The most recent revaluation was in 2010 and some transitional arrangements were implemented in order to help small properties (those with a rateable value below £25,500 in London and £18,000 elsewhere).

Business rates are charged by using a multiplier on the rateable value. In England (outside of London), the multiplier for 2010–11 is 41.4 pence.

Example

If the rateable value of a property is £10,000, the local authority would multiply it by 41.4 pence to get a total for the year of £4,140, before any rate relief is applied.

STAMP DUTY

10100 Introduction to stamp duty

Stamp duties are imposed by Act of Parliament on certain documents (or technically 'instruments'). Historically they have been very important, but the FA 2003 changes essentially reduce them to charges on instruments relating to share transfers.

The rate of stamp duty charged on instruments relating to stocks and securities is 0.5 per cent.

Law: FA 1999, Sch. 13, para. 3

Legal background

Stamp duty is in the main governed by the *Stamp Duties Management Act* 1891 (SDMA 1891) (which is mainly administrative) and the *Stamp Act* 1891 (SA 1891) (which imposes the charges). Both these Acts have been amended by subsequent Finance Acts ('FAs') and in particular by FA 1999 which modernised the basis of the charge and the interest and penalty regime. *Finance Act* 2003 completely overhauled the legislation and introduced Stamp Duty Land Tax (SDLT) for land transactions, with effect from 1 December 2003.

Jurisdiction

The *Stamp Act* 1891, s. 14(4) is regarded as laying down the jurisdiction rule for stamp duty. It covers documents:

- executed in the UK; or
- not executed in the UK, but relating to any property situated in or to any matter or thing done or to be done in the UK.

United Kingdom means England, Wales, Scotland and Northern Ireland. It excludes the Channel Islands and the Isle of Man.

Scope of stamp duty prior to 1 December 2003

Stamp duty is paid by paying for a stamp, and affixing the stamp to the document. It follows that stamp duty is a tax on documents, not on transactions (e.g. unlike VAT). Consequently, if a transaction can be carried out orally, or by conduct, there is no duty.

However, 'instrument', the technical word for document, is very widely defined in SA 1891, as including 'every written document'. For example, an oral contract for the sale of goods, followed by the physical transfer of the goods by delivery attracts no duty. But if the parties effected the transfer of goods by means of an instrument, the same transaction would be chargeable to duty.

Indirect Taxes

Documents will attract stamp duty if they fall under the heads of charge, and may attract ad valorem or fixed amounts of duty. In addition, there are special charging rules relating to bearer instruments and to unit trusts and open-ended investment companies. There are, though, numerous exemptions and reliefs.

Stamp Duty is abolished except on instruments relating to stock or marketable securities with effect from 1 December 2003. So, effectively, it is only chargeable on paper transactions of share transfers at 0.5% of the value. Most shares are traded electronically and stamp duty is not chargeable.

Law: FA 2003, s. 125; FA 1999; SDMA 1891; SA 1891

STAMP DUTY RESERVE TAX

10150   Introduction to stamp duty reserve tax

Stamp duty reserve tax (SDRT) is a tax of relatively recent origin. In essence, it taxes transactions on the London Stock Exchange, that are not subject to the 0.5 per cent stamp tax, because they are not stampable at that stage to stamp duty. SDRT is, in effect, a substitute stamp duty to capture tax on these transactions.

It was introduced by FA 1986. SDRT is allied to, but is not part of, stamp duty. It is a separate tax enforceable by assessment and not by stamping of instruments. SDRT is not concerned with instruments as such, but rather with agreements to transfer chargeable securities for a consideration in money, or money's worth.

It was introduced to cover circumstances where shares were sold but no stamp duty was payable, as there was no instrument of transfer which could be charged to stamp duty. For example, the purchase and resale of securities within a stock exchange account period, the purchase of renounceable letters of allotment or the purchase of shares registered in the name of a nominee acting for the seller and purchaser. Such cases are, of course, outside the *Stamp Act* 1891, s. 59, which charges certain contracts as if they were conveyances on sale, since it excepts ' . . . agreement(s) for the sale of . . . marketable securities . . . '

Law: SA 1891, s. 59; FA 1986, s. 86

10160   The principal charge

Chargeable transactions

The principal charge is found in FA 1986, s. 87. Subsection (1) provides that:

'This section applies where a person (A) agrees with another person (B) to transfer chargeable securities (whether or not to B) for consideration in money or money's worth.'

Accordingly, for a charge to SDRT to arise there must be:

(1) an agreement between A and B;

(2) a transfer (whether to B or not);

(3) chargeable securities; and

(4) consideration in money or money's worth,

unless either stamp duty is paid or the instrument would be exempt from stamp duty.

By FA 1986, s. 91, the person liable for SDRT charged under s. 87, is the transferee (B). However, it is usually collected and paid, not by B, but by intermediaries in the securities market, called 'accountable persons'. The collection and administration of the tax is discussed in more detail below.

The rate of tax is 0.5 per cent (FA 1986, s. 87(6)), although a special rate of 1.5 per cent may apply where 'deposits' are involved or shares are put into a 'clearance service system' (see s. 93 and s. 96).

The principal charge gives rise to certain questions of definition which are considered below.

What constitutes an 'agreement'?

For a charge to SDRT to arise, the legislation requires (inter alia) an ' . . . agreement between A and B'. The identity of B is important since B is liable for the tax. However, the legislation provides only that A and B must be persons. This can result in theoretical difficulties, especially where there are intermediaries.

An 'agreement' would certainly include a contract (i.e. an agreement enforceable at law). However, it is not clear whether the agreement *must* be enforceable at law. The agreement does not need to be in writing, so it may be an oral agreement. It may be constituted under UK law or the law of a country other than the UK. The charge can arise even if the agreement has not been completed. The making of the agreement can be sufficient for a charge to arise. The agreement may be conditional. If it is, the charge does not arise until the day on which the condition is satisfied or, if there is more than one condition, when the final condition is satisfied (FA 1986, s. 87(3)(a)).

What kinds of transactions represent a 'transfer'?

General

The agreement must be one to 'transfer' chargeable securities. This presupposes that the chargeable securities are in issue, and so can be assigned or transferred. Accordingly, an agreement to issue shares would not fall within the principal charge under FA 1986, s. 87 since it is not an agreement to transfer chargeable securities.

Transactions involving onward sales of chargeable securities (sub-sales)

A charge can arise in the situation where A agrees to sell to B, and B agrees to sell on to C. Normally, the transfer would be direct from A to C. Thus, C pays stamps duty on the transfer to C. However, this only franks the transfer to C. The agreement to sell, i.e. transfer between A and B, is not franked and a SDRT charge arises. Careful analysis is needed where such a transaction is envisaged.

Definition of chargeable securities

The Stamp Office comments that in broad terms:

'Chargeable securities include stocks, shares and rights to stocks and shares in a UK company or in those shares of a foreign company which are kept on a register in the UK. Most categories of loan stock are not chargeable securities.'

This is a very helpful starting point, but the position needs to be considered in greater detail in the light of the legislation. Chargeable securities are defined in FA 1986, s. 99(3) as follows:

'... "chargeable securities" means:

(a) stocks, shares or loan capital;
(b) interests in, or in dividends or other rights arising out of stocks, shares or loan capital;
(c) rights to allotments of, or to subscribe for, or options to acquire, stocks, shares or loan capital; and
(d) units under a unit trust scheme.'

This is a wide definition, but is subject to the exceptions below:

(1) *Securities of foreign incorporated corporations with no UK register.*

By FA 1986, s. 99(4) 'chargeable securities' does not include securities issued or raised by a body corporate which is not incorporated in the UK unless:

(a) they are registered in a register kept in the UK by, or on behalf of, the body corporate by which they are issued or raised; or
(b) in the case of shares, they are paired with shares issued by a body corporate incorporated in the UK; or
(c) in the case of rights and options, the stocks, shares or loan capital to which they relate are either registered on a UK register or are 'paired shares' (see FA 1986, s. 99(6A)).

(2) *Securities exempt from stamp duty on transfer.*

By FA 1986, s. 99(5) 'chargeable securities' does not include ' ... securities the transfer of which is exempt from all stamp duties ... '. Securities exempt from stamp duties would include gilt-edged stock.

(3) *Rights etc. to securities exempt from stamp duty on transfer.*

By FA 1986, s. 99(5)(b) 'chargeable securities' does not include:

' . . . securities falling within paragraph (b) or (c) of subsection (3) above [i.e. rights and options] which relate to stocks, shares or loan capital the transfer of which is exempt from all stamp duties.'

(4) *Depositary receipts.*

The Finance Act 1986, s. 99(6) provides that 'chargeable securities' does not include interests in depositary receipts for stocks or shares (see FA 1986, s. 99).

These regulations extend the existing exemptions from stamp duty reserve tax that already apply to certain transactions on the exchange operated by virt-x Exchange Limited.

The *Stamp Duty and Stamp Duty Reserve Tax (Extension of Exceptions relating to Recognised Exchanges) Regulations* 2004 (SI 2004/2421) came into effect on 12 October 2004 and extend the exemptions for sales of stock to intermediaries and for repurchases and stock lending to the Alternative Investment Market (AIM).

What is meant by the term 'for consideration in money or money's worth'?

Broadly, the first question is what is the *quid pro quo* for the securities? The second question is whether it constitutes 'consideration in money or money's worth'. This expression is not defined by the FA 1986 but it is clearly wider than its stamp duty equivalent. It has been described 'as being a way of expressing the price or consideration given for property where property is acquired in return for something other than money, such as services or other property where the price or consideration which the acquirer gives for the property has got to be turned into money before it can be expressed in terms of money' (*Secretan v Hart* (1969) 45 TC 701 at p. 705H per Buckley J).

It is important to identify the whole consideration given for the securities. This is not always easy where collateral contracts form part of the consideration. Identification of the consideration is of practical significance for B who is liable for the tax.

Once the consideration is ascertained, s. 87(7) makes provision for its valuation.

Law: FA 1986, s. 84, 87, 91, 93, 96, 97B, 99; *IR Commrs v Ufitec* [1977] 3 All ER 924; *Eastham (HMIT)v Leigh London & Provincial Properties Ltd* (1971) 46 TC 687; *Secretan v Hart* (1969) 45 TC 701

10170 Other charges

Stamp duty reserve tax also applies to depositary receipts and clearance services.

Law: FA 1986, s. 93–97

10180 Repayment of SDRT and cancellation of the charge to SDRT

The following discussion applies only to SDRT charged under s. 87. It does not apply to SDRT charged under the rules for depositaries or clearance services.

The s. 87 charge to SDRT is relieved by s. 92 if an instrument is executed and duly stamped within six years, and the instrument transfers to B, or his nominee, all the chargeable securities to which the agreement relates (s. 92(1A), (1B)). The effect of s. 92 is to cancel the charge to SDRT, or if the tax has been paid, to provide for its repayment with interest if a repayment claim is made within six years of the date the charge to tax arose (see s. 87(3)).

A further effect of s. 92 is that if an instrument is exempt from stamp duty, the execution and stamping of an instrument may mean that the agreement will be at least partly exempt from SDRT, even though the agreement to transfer is not within a specific SDRT exemption. However, the benefits to be obtained by this strategy are limited by s. 88, which sets out special cases in which instruments within s. 92(1A) and (1B) are disregarded when determining whether s. 92 relief applies.

Law: FA 1986, s. 87, 87(7A), 88, 92 and 92(1A), (1B)

10190 Administration

The Finance Act 1986, s. 98 permits the Treasury to make regulations as to the administration, assessment, collection and recovery of SDRT. The Treasury is also given power to apply provisions of the *Taxes Management Act* 1970, with such modifications as they think fit.

STAMP DUTY LAND TAX

10210 Background

SDLT was introduced with effect on 1 December 2003 and replaced the existing stamp duty regime on UK land and buildings. Details of the current rates of stamp duty and stamp duty land tax are at 89.

Law: *Finance Act* 2003

10212 Outline

Taxpayers who take part in 'land transactions' will generally be required to report those land transactions to HMRC on a land transaction return and send it to HMRC, together with any tax payable within 30 days of completion, to HMRC's central processing centre in

Netherton. Taxpayers are then sent a stamp duty land tax certificate, which they, or their agent, need to submit to land registries in order to register ownership of land or to record a deed, as appropriate. Under this 'process now, check later' system, HMRC have a period of nine months from filing in which to open an enquiry for all transactions (see below).

As a result of FA 2008, many transactions are no longer notifiable and therefore do not need a return. Only the following are now notifiable:

- an acquisition of a major interest in land (i.e. a freehold or leasehold);
- an acquisition of a chargeable interest other than a major interest, but only where there is actual tax to pay;
- certain sub-sale transactions;
- some transactions that have been entered into for tax planning purposes.

There are some exceptions for the acquisition of a major interest in land, for example for acquisitions under £40,000. These are in s. 77A, FA 2003.

Law: FA 2008, s. 94; FA 2003, s. 76 and 77, 77A

10214 Details

Broadly, the scope of SDLT covers transactions involving any estate, interest, right or power in or over land in the UK. There are a number of exclusions, which are as follows:

- mortgages and similar security interests;
- licences to use or occupy land;
- transactions for no chargeable consideration; and
- zero-carbon homes and flats, for a limited period until 30 September 2012.

The charge includes:

- completions of transfers of freehold property and leases;
- grants of leases (including, in Scotland, missives of let);
- contracts for land transactions which are substantially performed before completion;
- transfers of such contracts; and
- options and rights of pre-emption in respect of land transactions.

Tax is due 30 days after the effective date, which is normally the date of completion or the date substantial performance occurs, if before completion.

Law: FA 2003, s. 58B and 58C; FA 2008, s. 93; *Stamp Duty Land Tax (Zero-Carbon Home) Regulations* 2007 (SI 2007/3437)

10216 Chargeable consideration

The rate of charge for all transactions other than the grant of leases depends on the amount paid for the transaction (this includes 'any payment or consideration' for linked transactions).

'Chargeable consideration' is money or money's worth. Where a single bargain includes more than one interest in land, or an interest in land and another interest or asset, the amount paid should be apportioned between the interests. Anything paid for goodwill that cannot be sold separately from the land is part of chargeable consideration. VAT is included in chargeable consideration only where it is paid as part of the transaction, or where a landlord has elected on or before the grant of a new lease to charge VAT on the rents under that lease.

Arrangements for certain transactions may provide for consideration to be paid in one or more instalments after the effective date of the transaction. Where:

- there is uncertainty about whether anything more will be paid, and/or about the amount of additional consideration due; and
- at least one instalment might be more than 18 months after the effective date,

it is possible to apply to HMRC to defer payment of tax until the amount to be paid is determined. If there is no application to HMRC for deferred payment, or an application is refused, payment should be made by the due date based on an estimate of the consideration that will be paid. This amount may then be adjusted once the final amount to be paid is confirmed. This provision would be useful, where a person buys land with planning permission and will pay 'overage' on the basis that a certain number of units will be given planning permission. If there is uncertainty, then deferment would provide cash-flow advantages to the buyer (as the buyer always pays SDLT).

Where an exchange of property takes place, there are two chargeable legs and both will be subject to SDLT.

The 'linked transaction' rules do not apply, so the two legs are charged without reference to each other.

Temporary exemption for residential property

From 3 September 2008 to 31 December 2009 a temporary exemption from SDLT applied for acquisitions of residential property worth not more than £175,000. The exemption was available for the acquisition of major interests in land (other than grants of leases for less than 21 years or the assignment of leases with less than 21 years to run). In order for the exemption to apply the acquisition must have consisted entirely of residential property; and be for a chargeable consideration of not more than £175,000.

Law: FA 2003, s. 55

10218   Relief from charge

Some transactions are relieved from charge, even though they may still need to be reported to HMRC. These include:

- acquisitions by a charity;

- transfers between group companies (subject to certain anti-avoidance criteria);
- transfers arising from company reconstructions;
- certain purchases by registered social landlords;
- crown exemption;
- acquisitions of dwellings by house-building companies in part-exchange for the sale of a new home;
- acquisition of dwellings by relocation companies;
- acquisitions by local authorities or other public bodies under compulsory purchase orders; and
- acquisitions by local authorities or other public bodies under the terms of planning arrangements.

Law: FA 2003

10222 Penalties

Returns submitted after the due date, or containing incorrect information or omissions may be subject to penalties. Late payment of tax is subject to interest. The penalty and interest regimes are similar to those for other Revenue taxes, and may be subject to mitigation.

Law: FA 2003, Sch. 14

10226 Leases

SDLT also applies to leases. When a lease is granted and the lessee pays the landlord consideration (rent and/or a premium), the lessee will have to complete a return in the same way as a purchaser of property (unless the lease is not notifiable (see 10212 above)).

The charge will depend on the consideration. Where the consideration is just rent, then the lessee will have to calculate the Net Present Value (NPV) of the rental stream and SDLT will be charged at 1 per cent of the NPV to the extent that the NPV is above £150,000 for commercial or mixed buildings and (after 31 December 2009) £125,000 for domestic dwellings (these would be very rare).

If the consideration is a premium (in whole or in part), then the premium is charged to the normal SDLT rates in FA 2003, s. 55.

LORRY ROAD-USER CHARGE

10250 Introduction of the lorry road-user charge

Finance Act 2002 introduced a tax to be known as the lorry road-user charge. It charges the use of roads by lorries. However, the persons who will pay the charge, the rate of the charge, and the lorries and roads that will be affected are yet to be determined.

What is known is that the charge will be calculated by reference to distance travelled, although the details of this calculation are also yet to be determined.

The coalition government has said that it is committed to introducing the lorry road user charge during the current term of Parliament, although no date has yet been fixed.

The care and management of the new charge will fall to HMRC.

Law: FA 2005, s. 100; FA 2004, s. 292; FA 2002, s. 137

The UK law is based on the EC legislation for energy products: Dir 2003/96

Overseas Aspects

Overseas Aspects

WHAT'S NEW

- Finance Act 2010 contains legislation to clarify that the definition of a 'relevant person' for remittance basis purposes includes subsidiaries of non-resident companies which would be close companies if they were resident in the UK. The change took effect from 6 April 2010.
- To ensure compliance with certain aspects of the *Human Rights Act* 1998, legislation was introduced by *Finance Act* 2009, which took effect from 6 April 2010, to withdraw the entitlement for non-resident individuals who previously qualified for UK personal tax allowances and reliefs solely by virtue of being a Commonwealth citizen (see 11700).

KEY POINTS

- Where activities or transactions involve more than one country, the tax rules of each country must be considered (see 10500 and 10950).
- A UK-resident individual is taxable on worldwide income. A non-resident is taxable only on income arising in the UK (see 10560).
- For individuals, a liability to tax will depend on residence (see 10570), ordinary residence (see 10580) and/or domicile (see 10590).
- Non-UK domiciled individuals who are resident in the UK can elect to use the remittance basis, subject to payment of an annual charge (see 11350).
- A UK-resident company is liable to UK corporation tax on its worldwide income, profits and chargeable gains. A non-resident company is not liable to UK tax on its foreign income and capital gains (see 10650).
- Provisions were introduced in 1984 to prevent UK companies from avoiding UK tax by diverting income to subsidiaries in tax havens. The provisions apply to any 'controlled foreign company' (CFC) (see 10670).
- There are complex rules regarding the taxation of overseas trusts and settlements, most notably because certain trusts may be exempt from UK CGT by virtue of being non-resident but may be resident for income tax purposes (see 10800 and 11600).
- There are fundamental differences in the tax legislation governing trade in the UK and trading *with* the UK (see 10830).
- 'Transfer pricing' describes the process by which associated bodies transfer goods, services, etc. between one another (see 10860).
- The tax treatment of employment income of individuals domiciled outside the UK depends on whether the employee is resident in the UK, and if so whether ordinarily resident; the duties are performed wholly abroad or wholly or partly in the UK; and remuneration is foreign emoluments (see 11000).
- UK source income is usually liable to UK tax, even in the hands of a non-resident individual (see 11150).
- Employers are obliged to operate PAYE, even if both employer and employees are non-UK resident, provided the employer has a trading presence in the UK and the remuneration is liable to UK income tax (see 11400).
- The UK has entered into numerous double tax treaties with other countries. The treaties are designed to eliminate the effect of a liability to tax arising in more than one country (see 11550).

Overseas Aspects

OVERVIEW

10500   Introduction to overseas aspects

A person, including a company, whose investment or business activities involve operations in more than one country will have to consider the tax rules of each country. .

Although there is a tendency to think of international tax as one topic, the criteria by which each country levies taxes differ.

The UK levies income tax and capital gains tax (CGT) by reference to residence, ordinary residence or domicile for individuals. Residence and ordinary residence are not defined in the Taxes Acts. The meanings of these two terms are largely based on rulings of the courts. The meaning of 'residence' for tax purposes is the same as that which is found in the *Oxford English Dictionary*, where the word 'reside' has been defined as:

> 'to dwell permanently or for a considerable time, to have one's settled or usual abode, to live in or at a particular place.'

For companies, there is a statutory test of residence. If a company is incorporated in the UK it is resident here. However, even if a company is not incorporated in the UK it may still be resident in the UK by reference to older rules. These rules are also based on rulings of the courts. The court-based rules show that a company is resident where its central management and control are situated and, if this is the UK, the company will be resident in the UK for UK tax purposes.

Liability to inheritance tax (IHT) depends upon domicile. Even then there is a separate understanding of domicile for IHT and income tax or CGT. It is important to note that, although a person can be resident in the UK, an individual will have a domicile in one of its constituent countries, that is, England (meaning England and Wales), Scotland or Northern Ireland.

Furthermore, some countries have a different understanding of residence for both companies and individuals. Because of the different rules, it is possible for a person, including a company, to be resident in more than one country. Similarly, it is possible for a person to be resident in no country for taxation purposes.

In addition to any tax implications, there are some other, non-tax, implications. For example, Dubai has no tax system to speak of but there are restrictions on who can trade in that country. Most Dubai partnerships need a Dubai national as one of the partners. There are also restrictions on buying property in Jersey. The list could continue.

A person whose investment or business activities involve operations in a number of countries may be liable to tax in more than one of them. On the other hand, it may be possible to avoid tax in some of the countries concerned.

The criteria by which each country seeks to levy taxes are varied and will not necessarily correspond in any given case with the criteria used by another country. The UK levies tax by reference to residence and, for individuals, ordinary residence and domicile, and by reference to the location of the source of income. Its policy is broadly to tax the income and capital of persons domiciled and resident in the UK, regardless of the locality of their income or assets, but only to tax the UK income and capital of non-domiciled and non-resident persons.

Some countries tax their citizens, wherever resident; others levy taxes only on local income and capital, regardless of the owner's status. Others deliberately create tax-free statuses, such as offshore trading or exempt holding companies.

See *British Tax Reporter* ¶370-000.

INDIVIDUALS

10550   Main terms and concepts

For taxation purposes, the UK comprises England, Scotland, Northern Ireland and Wales but excludes the Channel Islands and the Isle of Man.

An individual's liability to UK tax is determined by whether the individual is 'resident' or 'ordinarily resident' in the UK and by whether the individual is 'domiciled' in one of its constituent countries. An individual's 'nationality' is normally irrelevant, except for the purpose of double tax treaties in some instances. Residence is not essential to establish liability to UK tax. For example, an individual who is not resident or ordinarily resident in the UK may be liable to tax on remuneration for duties performed in the UK. The residence status will however affect the basis of assessment.

If a person's 'usual place of abode' is overseas, UK payments to that person may suffer withholding tax.

The location of a source of income, whether it is in the UK or not, is relevant and so is the location of an asset. The place where the duties of an employment are performed is also relevant.

See *British Tax Reporter* ¶111-350.

10560   UK taxes

Income tax

A UK-resident individual is taxable on world-wide income. A non-resident is taxable only on income with a UK source.

Exceptions are as follows:

(1)   Up until 5 April 2008 a resident but non-domiciled individual was taxable on income if the source was located abroad only if and to the extent that it was 'remitted' to the UK. From 6 April 2008, non-UK domiciled individuals who have been resident in the UK for more than seven out of the past 10 years, and who have unremitted foreign income and gains in excess of £2,000, can only use the remittance basis on payment of an annual £30,000 charge. The definition of a remittance is wider for individuals who are also ordinarily resident.

(2)   The rules for employment income are dealt with at 1560.

The complex rules for employment are covered in free HMRC booklet HMRC6 *Residence, Domicile and the Remittance Basis*.

Capital gains tax

A UK-resident or ordinarily resident individual is taxable on world-wide capital gains. If that individual is not domiciled in one of the constituent countries of the UK there may be some scope to delay paying tax on realised gains. Until 5 April 2008, a non-domiciled individual was taxable only on capital gains arising from disposals of assets located abroad if and to the extent they were 'remitted' to the UK. From 6 April 2008, non-UK domiciled individuals who have been resident in the UK for more than seven out of the past 10 years, and who have unremitted foreign income and gains in excess of £2,000, can only use the remittance basis on payment of an annual £30,000 charge.

Inheritance tax

An individual domiciled in one of the constituent countries of the UK is taxable on all assets, wherever located. A non-domiciled individual is not taxable on assets located outside the UK. See 6790 for a special rule relating to inheritance tax. An individual not domiciled in one of the constituent parts of the UK will only be liable on UK situated assets.

Law: FA 2008, s. 25 and Sch. 7

Source: HMRC booklet HMRC6 *Residence, Domicile and the Remittance Basis*

See *British Tax Reporter* ¶111-200.

10570   Residence

Basic rules

There is no statutory definition and the law is based on court decisions and HMRC practice. This practice tries to follow the court decisions closely. Whether or not a person is resident in the UK is a question of fact and degree.

Physical presence is normally a necessary but not sufficient condition. Conversely, physical absence is essential for loss of residence but is not conclusive in itself.

An individual is resident in the UK in any tax year (ended 5 April) if he or she spends in the UK:

(1) 183 days or more. There is no exception to this rule. It does not matter whether that is one period of 183 days or several periods making up 183 days. From 6 April 2008, UK residence is determined by reference to the number of days that the individual is present in the UK at midnight (the 'midnight test'), rather than counting the days of arrival and departure; or

(2) 91 days on average per year, over any four consecutive tax years. Any days spent in the UK due to exceptional circumstances, such as illness, will not be counted.

There used to be a test that depended on the individual having a place of abode available and spending just one day in the UK. Although this test was abolished as from 6 April 1993, it cannot be ignored completely because the special rules about domicile for inheritance tax also depend upon residence.

It was a question of fact whether any given accommodation was available. Ownership was irrelevant. A home owned or rented by one spouse was normally regarded as available to the other. If the home was let on a long lease that prevented use by the individual, the home was not counted as available for residence purposes.

Furnished accommodation rented for less than two years during a temporary stay (unfurnished, one year) was ignored. Staying in hotels did not normally count as having available accommodation unless a room was held available for use at any time. Staying in a hotel, however, could count for the other tests.

A UK place of abode was not regarded as being available if the individual worked abroad full-time in a trade, profession or vocation, office or employment, and:

(1) no part of the trade, etc. was carried on in the UK (e.g. there was no UK branch, even if he did not himself work in it); or

(2) no duties of the office or employment were carried on in the UK, other than incidental duties.

Finance Act 1998 introduced a test that an individual who is normally resident in the UK but is a temporary non-resident has to be non-resident for five complete tax years to avoid a charge to CGT on returning to the UK.

Visitors to the UK

Individuals will come to the UK for a variety of reasons. Some may be coming here for a temporary visit, to obtain temporary work or to move to the UK permanently. There are differing rules for short-term visitors, visitors coming to take up employment and longer-term visitors. The special rules for capital gains are dealt with at 5698. Residence usually applies for the entire tax year from 6 April to the following 5 April.

A person who visits the UK for any reason and is present for 183 days will be resident for the *entire* tax year. There is a concession to split the year of arrival or departure into two so that income or gains arising before arrival or after departure are treated as arising in a period of non-residence.

Anyone who visits the UK regularly and consistently will be treated as resident. For these purposes, regular visits will exist if they are for an average of 91 days per year. The individual will be treated as resident after the fourth year. However, if it is clear from the outset that such visits are planned, the individual will be resident from the first 6 April. If the decision is made part way through the four tax years, the individual will be resident from 6 April of the tax year in which the decision to visit regularly is made.

A person who visits the UK to take up employment will be treated as resident from the day of arrival if the period of work is planned to be at least two years. If the visit is planned to be for less than two years or the period of stay is not known, the rules for residence are as set out above.

A person who intends to stay in the UK for at least three years will be resident from the day of arrival if it is clear that there is an intention to stay. If the planned stay is to be less than three years but is later extended, the individual will be treated as resident in the UK from the beginning of the tax year after the third anniversary of the arrival.

Leaving the UK

The basic rules operate in reverse (e.g. return visits must average less than three months per year over four tax years). The important point is that, where an individual has been ordinarily resident and goes abroad for occasional residence, the person will remain ordinarily resident in the UK. On leaving the UK it may sometimes be difficult to show that the residence abroad will be more than temporary. There are special rules when an individual leaves to take up employment abroad and these are discussed below.

If evidence can be shown from the outset that a person intends to become non-resident, a claim to be non-resident is usually admitted provisionally and confirmed or revoked by reference to the facts after three years. The types of evidence that the individual intends to become non-resident can include sale of one home and purchase of another abroad. In other cases, the person is treated as remaining resident for three years with retrospective adjustment to non-resident status if the facts justify this.

If a person goes abroad for full-time service under a contract of employment, and all duties of the employment are to be performed abroad, the individual will normally be treated as non-resident from the day after departure until the day preceding the date of his return. This will be the case if the absence will include a complete tax year. On return, the individual will be treated as a new permanent resident. All duties, except incidental duties must be performed abroad. HMRC take a narrow view of what duties may be considered 'incidental'. The courts have decided, for example, that a pilot employed by a foreign airline who occasionally landed in, and took off from, the UK was carrying out duties which were more than incidental.

By concession, the effects of non-residence commence from the date of departure, although there have been changes here for capital gains.

Double residence

It is possible to be resident in more than one country at the same time under their respective domestic tax systems but double tax treaties may treat a person, for the purposes of the treaty, as resident in only one of the countries concerned.

The family

Husband, wife, civil partners and children are treated separately for residence purposes.

Children, even minors, physically present in the UK (e.g. for education) may be resident while one or both of their parents are non-resident.

Law: FA 2008, s. 24; *R (on the application of Davies & Anor) v R & C Commrs; R (on the application of Gaines-Cooper) v R & C Commrs* [2010] EWCA Civ 83; *Gaines-Cooper v R & C Commrs*[2007] EWHC 2617 (Ch)

Source: ESC A11, *Residence in the United Kingdom: year of commencement or cessation of residence*; *Tax Bulletin* (Issue 68, December 2003) – article: *non-residents working in the UK for short periods: the '60–day' rule*; HMRC *Brief*: 01/07: *Residence Gaines-Cooper*

See *British Tax Reporter* ¶111-350.

10580   Ordinary residence

Broadly this means habitual residence. It is possible to be resident but not ordinarily resident, and to be ordinarily resident in more than one country at a time (subject to double tax treaties). Some advisers question whether it is possible to be non-resident but still ordinarily resident in a year. HMRC believe it is possible even though it would seem that being non-resident should mean that the individual is not resident at all.

Strictly, ordinary residence cannot be for part only of a tax year but by concession its effects are limited to commence after arrival or to cease with effect from departure. See also 5698 for the restriction on capital gains.

Ordinary residence does not necessarily involve permanent or indefinite residence. Residence can be habitual (i.e. ordinary) even if it is essentially temporary, e.g. because the stay is for a particular purpose which, in due course, will be accomplished.

An individual who comes to the UK for education originally intending to stay for not more than four years will not be ordinarily resident. The individual may become ordinarily resident in the fifth year if the visit is extended. Someone who comes for employment will become ordinarily resident in the fourth tax year after the individual has been in the UK for three years. Ordinary residence will occur from the moment of arrival if an intention to stay is clear at the outset. Other individuals arriving in the UK may be treated as ordinarily resident on arrival if they clearly intend to come for three years. If intent is imprecise a person will become ordinarily resident from the beginning of the tax year in which the third anniversary of arrival falls. As with other tests, the residence position will be decided upon earlier if there is a clear decision to stay for that length of time before the end of the third year.

It is not easy to shed UK ordinary residence once acquired, as a temporary absence may create non-residence but the individual may remain habitually resident in the UK. The rules follow closely those for loss of residence.

Family members are treated separately.

See *British Tax Reporter* ¶111-400.

10590   Domicile

If it is difficult to change residence status, it is even more difficult to change domicile. The term 'domicile' signifies connection with a territory subject to a single system of law and is the place where an individual has a permanent home. Usually, an individual's domicile will be in a particular country. In the UK, this will be England (meaning England and Wales), Scotland or Northern Ireland. Where there is a federal system and legislative power is given to both the state and federal legislatures the individual is domiciled in the particular state, etc. and not the country. Examples of this situation are Australia, the US and Switzerland.

Although it is possible to be non-resident in any country for taxation, an individual cannot be without a domicile. Equally, although tax rules might mean that an individual is resident in more than one territory, it is not possible to have more than one domicile at a time.

Under English law, a person has either a domicile of origin, a domicile of dependency, or a domicile of choice. Until 1 January 1974, the domicile of a married woman was dependent on her husband; thereafter, a married woman is capable of having a separate domicile.

Domicile of origin is the domicile at birth. A child will take the domicile of the father unless the mother and father are not married. The child will then take the domicile of the mother. The place of birth is not usually significant when looking at domicile of origin.

A domicile of choice may be acquired by leaving a country and taking up residence in another country. Usually, only an adult can obtain a domicile of choice. The significant point is that the change of domicile must be with a permanent change of country. Planning to leave for a long period until retirement but to return to the original place of domicile will not effect a change from a domicile of origin to a domicile of choice. A domicile of choice requires the combination of residence and intention. If a domicile of choice is lost because, for example, the intended place of domicile proves to be unsatisfactory for some reason, the original domicile of origin is obtained again unless another domicile of choice is obtained.

Prior to 1 January 1974, a married woman acquired the domicile of her husband. Where the marriage took place before 1 January 1974, the wife's domicile followed her husband's throughout their married life. Even though the rules have changed, if she was married on 1 January 1974, she will retain her husband's domicile until she takes positive action and adopts the requisite intention to alter it.

Women marrying after 1 January 1974 can take a separate domicile. A woman leaving her native country to marry will not necessarily lose her domicile of origin or choice. If the matrimonial home is to be in another country and her husband is domiciled there, it will be difficult, but not impossible, to refute the inference that she has obtained a domicile overseas. All women who marry can, in theory, have a domicile different from their husband's but while the marriage is stable and the spouses live together it will be unusual. Where ages differ widely, it may be easier for the younger spouse to demonstrate an intention to return to another country if the other spouse dies first. However, since 1974 the theory should be that it is as easy for a husband to adopt his wife's domicile as for the wife to adopt his. The significance of the husband and wife having different domiciles is that the child will take the father's domicile as a domicile of origin.

The implication frequently is that it is the wife who follows the husband, even if this is not always the case. It may be necessary to undertake an investigation of a person's life to analyse whether a change of domicile has occurred. It is possible to live in the UK for a very long period without acquiring a domicile of choice. It is also possible to live abroad for many years without abandoning UK domicile of origin for a domicile of choice. A decision cannot simply be made because an individual has said that they have a feeling that 'they have made the right decision this time'. Intentions to leave or return will not be given weight if they are vague hopes and aspirations. The older a person becomes, the more difficult it is to show an intention to disturb a settled pattern of lifestyle.

From 1 January 1974, a minor child may acquire a separate domicile at age 16. Between the time of birth and attaining the age of 16, an unmarried child is incapable of acquiring a domicile of choice but may acquire a new domicile if the person upon whom the child is dependent does so. However, until the child can acquire an independent domicile of choice, the domicile of dependency will be retained. On the death of the father, a legitimate child's domicile follows his mother's, changing at that point if appropriate. On remarriage of parents, minor children do not necessarily acquire the domicile of the second husband. The position where spouses are separated or divorced now is that the child's domicile follows the mother's if the child has never had a home with the father even if the mother is dead. In other cases where the child has had a home with each, or with the father alone, domicile follows the father's.

The change in the law at 1 January 1974 also means that a married person under the age of 16 is capable of acquiring an independent domicile. Whilst children domiciled in England and Wales are incapable of contracting marriage below this age, the provision will be important in relation to a child whose foreign marriage is recognised here.

Overseas Aspects

In Scotland, a minor with legal capacity, i.e. a girl of 12 years or over or a boy of 14 years or over, is capable of acquiring an independent domicile. These rules apply for all tax purposes. However there is an additional rule for inheritance tax. This rule means that there might be a deemed domicile in the UK even though the individual retains a domicile of choice or of origin outside the UK. The deemed domicile will arise as a result of long residence in the UK. The deemed domicile arises where there has been residence for 17 years out of 20 income tax years. This deemed domicile and a domicile of origin or of choice is not lost for inheritance tax purposes until three years have elapsed after the loss of UK domicile for other legal purposes. The extended meaning of domicile for inheritance tax is determined by reference to the UK and not to the constituent parts as would a domicile of origin or of choice.

See *British Tax Reporter* ¶113-550.

10600   Working abroad

Very large numbers of British citizens go to live abroad for a substantial period of time, usually either at work or in retirement. Since tax is territorial there will inevitably be tax considerations; as always, it is best to plan well in advance of departure.

The basis of liability to UK income tax and CGT is residence. As is so often the case with key words in legislation, there is no statutory definition. The result is a mixture of case law and HMRC practice. Although many tax professionals do not agree with all the assertions made by HMRC in successive editions of their former booklet IR20 on HMRC6, for practical purposes it would be foolish to ignore it.

The obligation to file a self assessment return on individuals with small amounts of income from overseas employment has been removed with effect from 6 April 2008 where the overseas income is less than £10,000, and overseas bank interest is less than £100 in any tax year, all of which is subject to a foreign tax.

Income tax

General
There is no substitute for detailed local advice on the tax system of the host country, and careful consideration of the double taxation agreement. Many countries have more burdensome tax regimes than the UK. The traditional approach of UK tax advisers was to minimise the incidence of UK taxation. Given the relatively low income tax rates in the UK, advisers should always consider whether they might devote some of their energies to maximising that proportion of their clients' income over which the UK has sole taxing rights.

Leaving the UK
In outline, anyone who is physically in this country for 183 days or more in any tax year is resident here for the whole of that tax year. There is a further concept of 'ordinary residence'

– broadly, habitual residence over a period of several years – which is sometimes relevant. The tax year is split by HMRC concession when an individual goes abroad under a contract of employment. The conditions are:

- the individual must be absent from the UK for an entire tax year;
- the employment must extend over an entire tax year;
- the individual must not spend more than 182 days in the UK in any tax year; and
- he must not spend 91 days or more in a tax year in the UK on average, over a period up to four years.

In these circumstances the person is treated as neither resident nor ordinarily resident with effect from the date of his departure.

Example

Alfred, who has lived in Winchester all his life, goes to Germany on 31 March 2010 to take up a job. His job comes to an end and he returns to England on 31 March 2011. He has spent all the intervening time in Germany. Alfred is both resident and ordinarily resident in the UK for 2010–11.

If his job had continued until 6 April 2011, Alfred would have been regarded as neither resident nor ordinarily resident in the UK from 31 March 2010 to 7 April 2011.

Overseas Aspects

The taxation of the income of people who are domiciled in, but not resident in the UK (the normal case with those who go to work abroad for limited periods) is as follows:

Employment income	
– overseas duties	no liability
– UK duties	liable in respect of UK duties
Rent from UK property	taxable
UK source taxed investment income	no further liability
FOTRA securities	no further liability

On leaving the UK, employees should complete Form P85. The form asks questions about the intended length of stay overseas, whether the departure is permanent, what continuing UK source income is expected.

With the exception of the Republic of Ireland, other countries' fiscal years do not end on 5 April. It is possible to be resident in more than one country and in some cases there will be actual or potential double taxation of the same income. The UK has double taxation treaties with most countries and in most cases relief will be available; either the treaty will give one country the right to tax a particular type of income (for example, rent from property located in that country) or it will provide for credit relief (i.e. one jurisdiction will permit the set-off of tax paid in the other country).

The main income tax considerations for the ordinary British short-to-medium term expatriate are to do with timing. After the date of his going abroad he will only be liable as indicated in the table above. It is quite easy to work abroad for nearly two years and remain within the UK income tax net.

It is worth remembering that employees are generally taxed on amounts received in a tax year. However, the employee's tax liability is determined by his residence status during the tax year when the remuneration was earned.

The position for the self-employed is quite different. The split year treatment will only apply to the self-employed if they are going abroad for at least three years *and* will be not ordinarily resident in the UK following their departure. They will remain liable to UK tax to the extent that any part of the business is carried on in the UK. If the overseas country has a significantly more favourable tax regime it may be worthwhile incorporating an offshore company with non-resident directors so that the exposure to UK tax is limited to the profits of the UK branch.

With regard to partnerships, there is no joint assessment on the partnership and each partner is responsible for the tax on his share of the firm's profits. Where the partnership carries on business partly in the UK and partly abroad, the non-resident partner's taxable share in the UK is limited to his share of the profits of the trade carried on in the UK.

Returning to the UK
Normally those who return to the UK from overseas postings will be resident and ordinarily resident in the UK from the date of return. Income tax planning will usually involve maximising pre-return income. As a matter of course all offshore accounts paying gross interest should be closed before return. There is a danger of double taxation and complex fractional calculations based on the amount of time spent between the date of return and the end of the tax year.

Capital gains tax

General
The CGT regime differs so strongly from the income tax position that advice on the mitigation of one tax may conflict with advice about the other tax. A year's absence may be enough to avoid UK income tax; for CGT this is now usually five years (see also *Temporary non-residents* below).

An individual falls into the UK tax net if chargeable gains accrue to him:

'in a year of assessment *during any part of which* he is resident in the United Kingdom, or during which he is resident in the United Kingdom'.

Under the terms of HMRC extra statutory concession A11, the tax year can be split for CGT purposes if the individual was neither resident nor ordinarily resident in the UK for at least four out of the seven tax years preceding the year of departure. The concession thus will help temporary visitors to the UK but it is of absolutely no use to the ordinary person going to work abroad. The first planning point, therefore, for those going to work in a country with a generous CGT regime, is to defer capital gains as far as possible until after the next 5 April.

The basis of charge on short-term emigrants was greatly extended by the 1998 Budget. While this section seeks to avoid too detailed a discussion of the boundaries of residence and ordinary residence, absence from the UK for three whole tax years will always make an individual neither resident nor ordinarily resident. Dave Clark famously went to make his home and place of business in Los Angeles on 3 April, stayed there for a complete tax year, and escaped tax on a $450,000 sale of recording rights; the case established that one year might be enough to establish non-residence. The Revenue believed that successful entrepreneurs were arranging employments, or merely going to live in countries such as Germany, where most long-term gains are tax-free, and selling their companies from the safety of their absence. Non-resident trustees were also, under the old regime, able to distribute capital to non-resident beneficiaries and no CGT would be due. Besides, the concession was used to exempt from UK tax profits on disposals made after departure but in the same tax year by those who went to live abroad for three whole tax years.

The rules apply to an individual who was resident in the UK for at least four of the seven tax years preceding his departure. This catches most UK expatriates and spares most foreign visitors. The rules only apply to gains on assets acquired before the taxpayer's departure, and only apply if there are fewer than five whole tax years between departure and return. Their effect is to bring into the CGT charge for the year of the taxpayer's return all gains (less allowable losses) realised in the interval.

Example

Alistair has spent all his life in Edinburgh. On 1 November 2008 he goes to work in Saudi Arabia under a three-year contract, and returns on 1 December 2011. He realises two capital gains: one of £10,000 on 1 December 2008 and one of £200,000 on 1 June 2010.

He is resident in the UK for part of 2008–09 and so the £10,000 gain is taxable for that year. He is not saved by the concession, as he has been resident in the UK for at least four of the seven preceding tax years.

The £200,000 gain is also taxable, this time in 2010–11, because his absence has not covered five complete tax years.

Temporary non-residents

Individuals who return to the UK having been temporarily neither resident nor ordinarily resident in the UK, or are resident or ordinarily resident in the UK but have been temporarily treated for tax treaty purposes as resident in a territory outside the UK, are not able to exploit the terms of any double taxation agreement (DTA) to secure that capital gains arising to them while they are temporarily outside the charge to UK tax escape being charged to CGT under the rules for temporary non-residents (see 10500ff.).

Overseas Aspects

Planning

There is a proviso in the legislation which expressly makes it subject to the provisions of DTAs. Most agreements contain a clause giving each country the sole taxing rights over its residents, with exceptions relating to business assets. The DTA with Ireland contains a further clause permitting the UK to levy CGT on gains realised by an Irish resident individual who was resident in the UK at any time in the three years preceding the sale. Many modern agreements contain similar clauses.

Example

Chris has lived in London all his life. He wants to sell his family company and the buyer is prepared to wait. He moves to Dublin on 1 December 2008. He will be liable to UK CGT if he sells the company before 1 December 2011.

Before seeking to take advantage of a DTA, the taxpayer would be well advised to investigate the CGT regime of the country to which he hopes to emigrate.

Inheritance tax

Domicile is the main determinant of liability to inheritance tax (IHT). It is a common law concept, without statutory definition. The country where an individual has his permanent home may be an adequate definition for these purposes. Everyone has a domicile. At birth a child acquires a domicile of origin, usually that of the father. If the father, mother, or person on whom the child is legally dependent, changes his or her domicile, the child acquires a new domicile of dependency. Since 1974 married women have been able to change domicile without reference to their husbands' domicile. At age 16 a person obtains the legal capacity to acquire a new domicile of choice.

It is difficult to displace domicile. There are scores of cases which underline the gap between going to live in another country and becoming a permanent dweller in it.

The general law of domicile recognises the different jurisdictions within the UK. An individual can therefore be domiciled in England and Wales, in Scotland, or in Northern Ireland. But for IHT purposes, the concept of a UK domicile is used. A person domiciled in the UK is liable to IHT on all assets which he owns anywhere. In two cases a non-domiciled person's estate is brought into the IHT net:

(1) an individual who was domiciled in the UK within the three years preceding the transfer will be deemed to be domiciled in the UK at the time of the transfer; and

(2) a person who has been resident in the UK for at least 17 out of the 20 income tax years ending with the year of the transfer is also deemed to be domiciled at the time of the transfer.

Example 1

Robert, who had an English domicile, closes down his Oxford house, his London bank account, resigns from his London clubs, buys a grave plot on the Mount of Olives and

---

goes to live in Israel on 4 November 2006. HMRC agree that he is no longer domiciled in the UK. He dies on 31 October 2009. Robert's worldwide estate is subject to IHT.

Example 2

Helga arrived in England with the intention of residing there permanently on 31 March 1993. She carries out her intention. On 10 April 2009 she makes a chargeable gift, a PET. She has been resident for each tax year from 1992–93 to 2008–09 inclusive, 17 tax years. She is domiciled for IHT purposes at the time of the transfer. She needs to live a further seven years in order for the PET to fall completely out of her estate.

Law: ITTOIA 2005, Pt 9; FA 2005, s. 30–33; TCGA 1992, s. 2, 10A; *Reed (HMIT) v Clark* [1985] BTC 224; ESC A11, *Residence in the United Kingdom: year of commencement or cessation of residence*; ESC D2, *Residence in the United Kingdom: year of commencement or cessation of residence*

Source: HMRC6 *Residence, Domicile and the Remittance Basis*; Form P85: http://www.hmrc.gov.uk/cnr/p85.pdf

See *British Tax Reporter* ¶170-050.

COMPANIES

10650   Residence

A UK-resident company is liable to UK corporation tax on its world-wide income, profits and chargeable gains.

A non-resident company is not liable to any UK tax on its foreign income and capital gains. It is liable to UK tax on UK source income. It is outside the scope of the special rules taxing exchange gains.

A non-resident company is liable to UK corporation tax on trading income from a UK permanent establishment and on capital gains from disposals of assets held for the purposes of, or used in, the business of the UK branch, etc. Double tax treaties sometimes refer to a permanent establishment. This is often the same as a branch or agency but the terms of the double tax treaty will need to be checked to see what that particular treaty means by the phrase 'permanent establishment'. A non-resident company may be subject to income tax on UK source income other than trading income.

A company incorporated in the UK is regarded as resident in the UK for tax purposes. The residence of a company is determined by the location of its central management and control. This is a case law test and can mean that a company not incorporated in the UK is nonetheless resident in the UK. Normally central management will be exercised where the company holds its board meetings but it is always a question of fact and degree. Even where board meetings are formally held abroad (or in the UK) a company may be resident in the UK (or abroad) if control of its affairs is in practice exercised by or delegated to persons present in the UK (or abroad). In looking at control at board level, it is important to look at control of the company's affairs generally and not simply control of its business operations. The latter might be important for double tax treaties. However, whether an independent board of directors truly exercises control of a subsidiary where the parent company directs many policy matters is often a complex question.

It is possible for a company to be resident in the UK under UK tax law and also in another country under its tax system. Such a company is known as a dual-resident company. This is more common now that UK-incorporated companies are automatically UK-resident. A double tax treaty will often state which jurisdiction, the UK or overseas, has the power to tax. If a dual-resident company is treated as UK-resident under a double tax treaty with the UK, it is resident there for all UK tax purposes. A company ceasing to be UK-resident or on becoming dual-resident is subject to an 'exit charge'. This is a charge on any potential chargeable gain on assets held by the company. However, if the exit charge arises because the company becomes dual-resident but is regarded as not resident under a double tax treaty, there is a deferral for a company that is a 75 per cent subsidiary of a UK-resident parent. Where the exit charge falls on any other company the deemed gain is deferred until the earlier of 30 November 1999 or actual disposal.

A company resident in the UK may not carry out certain transactions without Treasury consent. The sanction can be imprisonment. Except as noted below, it is unlawful for a company which is resident in the UK to carry out any of the following transactions without obtaining the consent of the Treasury:

● to cause or permit a non-resident company over which it has control to issue shares or debentures; or
● to transfer to any person or cause or permit to be transferred to any person shares or debentures in a non-resident company over which it has control (except for the purpose of enabling a person to be qualified to act as a director).

There are a number of general consents. A general consent is given in advance to all companies carrying out that type of transaction. Furthermore, specific consent has been easier to obtain since the relaxation of exchange control. Consent is not necessary for a change of residence or transfer of business to a place outside the UK. However, a company cannot change its residence after that date without notifying HMRC and making approved arrangements for meeting its outstanding tax liabilities. There are penalties for failure to comply, in addition to the company remaining UK-resident and provisions enabling HMRC to recover unpaid tax from a fellow group member or a controlling director. Dividends, interest and royalties, etc. received from, or capital gains arising on the disposal of shares in foreign subsidiaries are liable to UK corporation tax in the hands of the UK parent. Consent is also unnecessary for certain movements of capital between residents of EC member states under EC directive. An Inland Revenue statement of practice explains its view of transactions and details information requirements. The *Finance (No. 2) Act* 1992 made changes (deemed always to have had effect) to the tax consequences of the transfer of a trade falling within the EC mergers directive.

Law: F(No. 2)A 1992; *De Beers Consolidated Mines Ltd v Howe* (1906) 5 TC 213; *Bullock v Unit Construction Co Ltd* (1959) 38 TC 712

Source: SP 2/92

See *British Tax Reporter* ¶764-000.

10660   Income tax

A company not resident in the UK is not chargeable to corporation tax unless trading through a branch or agency. It is, however, liable to income tax on income from a UK source.

In theory, if a company is carrying on a trade in the UK not through a branch or agency, the company may be subject to income tax. It is difficult, however, to see how a company could be trading in the UK otherwise than through a branch or agency unless the transaction is a short-term assignment. In that case, there may be no liability to corporation tax because relief under a double tax treaty may be due. In practice, a non-resident company will therefore be liable to income tax on rent from property in the UK. It will also be subject to the deduction of income tax from payments of rents to foreign landlords. However, a non-resident company could also be liable to income tax on dividends from UK-resident companies, as would an individual, most double tax treaties give some relief.

See *British Tax Reporter* ¶764-750.

10670   Controlled foreign companies

Provisions were introduced in 1984 to prevent UK companies from avoiding UK tax by diverting income to subsidiaries in tax havens. The provisions apply to any 'controlled foreign company' (CFC), i.e. a company which:

(1)   is not resident in the UK, but which is controlled by individuals or companies that are UK-resident; and

(2)   is subject to a level of tax on income less than three-quarters of what it would have been had it been resident in the UK.

Note that the comparison between tax which would have been paid in the UK and that which applies in the other country should be made by reference to the amount of tax actually *paid* and not the tax rate applying to the profits of the CFC.

The charge to tax on a CFC is only made on a UK-resident company and not a UK-resident individual, although shareholdings of individuals are taken into account when deciding whether the foreign company is controlled by UK-resident shareholders.

There have been significant developments from an EU perspective in the light of the European Court of Justice ruling in the *Cadbury Schweppes* case (Case C-196/04). In July 2007, HMRC issued a discussion document on the taxation of foreign profits in which it was recognised that the CFC rules were in need of change. This was followed by the inclusion in the *Finance Act* 2009 of a broad exemption from tax for all dividends, and the accompanying repeal of the acceptable distribution policy and the partial repeal of the exempt activities holding company exemptions. A period of consultation on the remaining CFC rules followed with a view to amendment in the Finance Bill 2011.

For further commentary on CFCs, see 4713.

Law: FA 2009, s. 36 and Sch. 16; FA 2006, s. 78; FA 2005, s. 89, 90; TIOPA 2010, ss. 63, 71; *Cadbury Schweppes*[2008] BTC 52

See *British Tax Reporter* ¶770-000.

PARTNERSHIPS

10750   Residence

A partnership, in English law, is not an entity distinct and separate from its members. Partnerships constituted under foreign law may be separate entities and in that case are likely to be taxed like companies.

If the control and management of a partnership business is located outside the UK it is treated for income tax and CGT purposes as a business carried on by non-residents, even though some of the partners are UK residents. The partnership is then also treated as being itself non-resident. Profits are taxed as if the firm was a non-resident individual, so a non-resident partner is only liable to tax on a share of the profits from the trade carried on in the UK. The remittance basis remains an option for a resident non-domiciled partner.

By implication, therefore, if the control and management of a partnership business is located in the UK it will be treated for income tax and CGT purposes as being subject to tax wherever profits arise. This will be so even though some of the members of the partnership are non-resident. Non-resident partners may escape tax if they only share in overseas profits.

Equivalent provisions for non-resident companies which are members of partnerships ensure that corporate partners only pay UK tax on their share of partnership profits arising in the

UK. The non-resident company's share is treated as arising from a trade carried on by it through a UK branch or agency.

See *British Tax Reporter* ¶288-500.

TRUSTS AND SETTLEMENTS

10800   Introduction

The rules regarding settlements are complex. The situation is further complicated because certain trusts which are exempt from UK CGT by virtue of being non-resident, may be resident for income tax.

Common rules determine the residence of trustees and trusts from 6 April 2007. Individual trusts are together treated as if they were a single person and the deemed person is treated as resident and ordinarily resident in the UK when all of the trustees are resident; or at least one trustee is resident and at least one is not and the settlor is ordinarily resident or domiciled in the UK when the settlement was created.

Under these rules, a non-resident trust must have all non-resident trustees if it has a UK resident or domiciled settlor. If the settlor is non-resident and non-domiciled there can be a majority of UK trustees provided that one of them is non-resident.

Where a settlement is made by a non-resident, person not ordinarily resident or non-domiciled, and where the trustees act as such in the course of a business which is carried on in the UK through a branch, agency or permanent establishment, and the trustees would be treated as resident under these rules, they may elect to be treated as non-resident.

Law: *Finance Act* 2006, Sch. 12 and 13; TCGA 1992, s. 69(1), (2)

See *British Tax Reporter* ¶350-800.

10810   Income tax

Where the trust is an interest in possession trust, the residence of the trustees will not affect the income tax treatment. This is because it is the beneficiary's residence status that is relevant. The residence of trustees is significant in deciding UK tax liability for discretionary trusts.

Trustees' residence status is determined by looking at the residence position of the individual trustees. The residence status of trustees, however, is looked at for the trustees as one body. Consequently, the trustees are not UK-resident where every trustee is not resident in the UK. However, where one of the trustees is resident in the UK the trustees will be UK-resident for income tax purposes. This provision will not apply where the settlor was not

Overseas Aspects

resident or ordinarily resident or domiciled in the UK when providing funds for the settlement.

The HMRC concession (ESC A11) that splits a year of arrival or departure into a period of residence and non-residence does not apply for trustees.

See *British Tax Reporter* ¶350-100.

10820   Capital gains tax

For CGT purposes, the trust is treated as being resident and ordinarily resident in the UK unless the administration of the trust is carried on outside the UK and a majority of the trustees are not resident or ordinarily resident in the UK. Care must be taken to ensure that the residence status of the trust is not jeopardised by undertaking activities in the UK. Where the trust is not resident it will generally be outside the charge to CGT, although there are special rules to tax beneficiaries and settlors of offshore trusts where they retain an interest in the trust or receive a capital payment.

The test for residence for CGT is different from that applied for income tax and it is possible for a trust to be resident for income tax purposes but not resident for the purposes of CGT. One important difference involves a professional trustee. Where the business of a professional trustee is that of managing trusts or acting as trustee, the professional trustee will be regarded as not resident in the UK if the whole of the trust property consists of property from a person who is not resident, ordinarily resident or domiciled in the UK when the property is provided. It follows that where a professional trustee is treated as resident outside the UK, any trust administration undertaken by that trustee would be treated as undertaken overseas even if undertaken in the UK.

The CGT regime for non-resident trusts is subject to the *Finance Act* 2008 changes (see 10560), with non-domiciled beneficiaries of non-resident trusts who claim the remittance basis being taxed on all UK and offshore assets from 6 April 2008. An irrevocable election may be made by the trustees to rebase assets held in an offshore trust at 6 April 2008 to exclude non-domiciled beneficiaries from being taxed on a chargeable gain that accrued prior to that date.

See *British Tax Reporter* ¶350-100.

NON-RESIDENTS DOING BUSINESS IN THE UK

10830   Trading in and with the UK

This is a fundamental distinction. A person who trades in the UK may be liable to UK tax but not a person who merely trades with the UK. There are two tests. The more traditional test looks at where the contract is made. If a UK customer places an order the contract is made outside the UK if accepted by a letter from abroad. Acceptance by telex is treated as taking place where it is received. The more modern test looks at where, as a matter of substance, profits are really made. HMRC are consulting on the impact of electronic commerce.

A UK agent who has authority to conclude contracts on behalf of his foreign principal can cause the principal to be treated as carrying on a trade in the UK. A general commission agent, who acts in the course of business on behalf of many principals, will not bring this about.

If the activity conducted in the UK is exclusively that of purchasing or procuring services it will not constitute the carrying on of a trade in the UK.

See *British Tax Reporter* ¶293-350.

10840   Self-employed persons

A non-resident individual, or partnership, carrying on business in the UK, is liable to income tax on trading income from any UK permanent establishment. Capital gains tax will be payable on any capital gains from disposals of assets used in the UK business or held for the purpose of that permanent establishment.

Many such persons will often choose to operate in the UK through the medium of a company or through an entirely separate and distinct partnership. In this way, profits and gains attributable to the UK activities can be clearly segregated because separate charges will be rendered to third parties by the UK operations. Transactions between the UK and the foreign operations must take place at arm's length prices.

See *British Tax Reporter* ¶293-400.

10850   Companies

A non-resident company is liable to corporation tax on trading income and capital gains from carrying on a trade through a UK permanent establishment and to income tax on its other UK-source income. Such a company may choose to conduct its UK business through a UK-resident subsidiary rather than a branch or agent.

Whether it is better to operate through a branch or a UK-resident subsidiary or one resident in a third country depends on a number of commercial and tax factors which in turn are related to the precise circumstances of each case. For example:

(1)   if losses are expected, at least initially, they may be capable of being offset against tax in the foreign country as well as in the UK if a branch is used;

(2)   branch profits always attract the full rate of corporation tax, never the small profits rate;

(3)   the deductibility of interest on local and foreign borrowing needs to be considered;

(4)   a tax treaty may change the balance of any advantage or disadvantage otherwise prevailing;

(5)   conversion of a branch to a subsidiary requires no consent but may give rise to a tax charge or other disadvantage in the UK or abroad, whereas conversion of a subsidiary to a branch (by its selling its business to a non-resident or transferring its residence abroad) requires consent as well as possibly involving a tax charge or other tax disadvantage. A form of roll-over relief is available where a UK branch is incorporated by means of a transfer of a business between two companies in the same world-wide group. Relief can be claimed where a UK-resident company transfers a trade (UK or non-UK) to a non-resident in an EC member state in exchange for shares or securities.

A company may open a representative office to show the flag, collect information, advertise, and so on and will not be treated as trading in the UK at all. The representative office must supply goods and services only to its head office and not to third parties, not even group companies or associated companies.

A UK-resident company ceasing to be UK-resident is deemed to dispose of and re-acquire its assets at market value. The rule also applies to a company continuing to be UK-resident but becoming resident elsewhere under a double tax treaty as regards assets relevant to that treaty. Roll-over relief is not available but an election for postponement of the charge may be made where the migrating company is a 75 per cent subsidiary of a UK-resident company.

See *British Tax Reporter* ¶293-400.

10860   Transfer pricing

A new regime for the tax treatment for transfer pricing issues was introduced by the *Finance Act* 1998. The changes were designed to accomplish two main aims. First, the transfer pricing legislation was made compatible with self-assessment. This means that the self-assessment compliance regime, including information powers and penalties, applies to transfer pricing. Secondly, the legislation was aligned with the OECD guidelines on transfer pricing, which is seen as representing international best practice.

A further, more wide-reaching change appeared in 2004, namely the general application of transfer pricing to large UK businesses, regardless of the nature of the transaction. This was coupled with the repeal, for all intents and purposes, of the old thin capitalisation regime linked to distributions and its absorption into ICTA 1988, Sch. 28AA. The legislation governing transfer pricing has been rewritten by the Tax Law Rewrite project and is now contained in TIOPA 2010, Pt. 4.

The arm's length principle is the most widely accepted basis upon which transfer pricing for tax purposes is determined.

Transfer pricing is the generally accepted term for pricing business transactions between related or associated persons. It means the determination of prices for property of all kinds sold, and for services or business facilities of whatever kind (including the provision of finance at low or nil rates of interest) supplied, by one person to another associated with him. Persons are related or associated for this purpose in terms of a significant degree of ownership or control by one person of another, or of common ownership or control.

Transfer pricing largely concerns businesses carried on internationally by companies in groups. It is not, however, confined to bodies corporate, nor to instances of total ownership or control, nor to transactions across national frontiers. This last point especially was further eroded by changes introduced for calculating profits arising after 31 March 2004.

When goods or services pass between associated persons, the profits of each depend upon the level of prices set.

When a manufacturing company sells its products to a subsidiary or fellow subsidiary company for onward sale, their respective results will depend upon the price set on transfer from manufacturer to sales company. The consolidated profit of both companies will reflect the profit on the whole operation from manufacture through to end sale to third parties. It is this consolidated profit with which the ultimate shareholders will be primarily concerned, rather than the respective proportions derived from manufacture and selling.

Law: TIOPA 2010, Pt. 4

See *British Tax Reporter* ¶790-100.

10870   Factors affecting transfer pricing

The prices set for goods or services between associated persons may be determined in the same way as they are between any two unrelated persons. For example, the manufacturing company and the sales company mentioned above might agree a price for the product by bargaining as unrelated companies, without regard to their common group interest. This could be the case particularly where the group product is one of many comparable products on the market. However, the price on transfer between companies within the same group may equally be determined on some special basis, having regard to the overall group interest.

> ### Example
>
> A manufacturing company in the UK buys in nuts, bolts and other fastenings used in its product. These are available from independent suppliers in the UK at £50 per gross. A fellow subsidiary company in Sweden manufactures fastenings for which the cost, delivered to the UK, is £52 per gross. It may be that the profit made in Sweden on each gross of additional output is greater than the £2 price differential in the UK, and the

> group policy is accordingly to use the group supplier, unless fastenings become available from independent suppliers at a price at least 10 per cent below that of the group supplier.

Another example of a particular group interest is where there is an outside minority shareholding in the group sales company while the manufacturing company is wholly-owned.

Associated companies often operate under differing conditions whilst transacting business with each other. One company may be subject to governmental price controls, or eligible for certain grants or subsidies based upon turnover, which do not apply to the associate. Associated persons doing business together may be in different jurisdictions for functional currency, exchange control, or customs duties. The political, economic, and legal systems and conditions applying to associated persons differ greatly so there are many factors which can affect the prices of goods and services across national frontiers.

One of the most important of these factors is the nature of the tax regimes applying to associated persons. This is most obviously so where associated persons operate in different countries and conduct their business across national frontiers. Important differences may still exist, however, within the same tax jurisdiction. For example, the tax treatment of the sale of property may depend upon whether the vendor and related purchaser are both treated as trading in the property on revenue account, or one is treated as an investment company buying or selling on capital account.

Whenever the aggregate tax liability of associated persons, in respect of the overall profit on transactions to which they have been a party, depends upon how that profit is reflected in their separate tax returns, there is a potential transfer pricing issue. Furthermore, multinational businesses do not simply have to react to different conditions applying to their individual members; they may create and exploit such differences by fragmenting their business and changing their corporate structure.

Example

An international group of companies manufacturing the group product in one country, may market it through local distributors in each country in which the product is sold. The group parent company may then establish, in a tax haven, a master or super distributor, interposed between the manufacturing company and each local national distributor, to co-ordinate all export sales.

See *British Tax Reporter* ¶790-100.

10890　Double tax treaties

These generally limit the right of the UK to tax business profits to those derived from the operation of a permanent establishment. A permanent establishment is more comprehensively defined than a branch or agency and may be narrower or wider than that definition, depending on the circumstances and the treaty.

See *British Tax Reporter* ¶170-050.

UK RESIDENTS DOING BUSINESS ABROAD

10950   Criteria for local taxation

The domestic tax rules of the local country determine whether the precise method of operation results in local tax liabilities. It should not be assumed that another country will employ tests similar to those used in the UK. If a double tax treaty is in force, the treaty is likely to use the concept of a permanent establishment.

See *British Tax Reporter* ¶293-000.

10960   Self-employed

Liability will depend upon whether the UK-resident individual or partnership is trading wholly overseas or is trading from the UK and selling into an overseas country.

The degree of physical presence in the UK required for residence usually means that at least part of the trade (or profession) will be conducted from the UK. The use of a partnership or company to conduct foreign operations will segregate them from UK activities.

Excess allowances and losses can only be offset against other income from foreign possessions or by carry forward against future profits from the same trade.

Where the business is carried on wholly abroad, relief is available for travel expenses incurred on business between the UK and overseas locations and between the locations of different such businesses.

Prior to 6 April 2008 a non-UK domiciled individual was taxable on the remittance basis on trading profits. From 6 April 2008, individuals can opt to use the remittance basis on payment of a £30,000 annual charge (see 10560).

See *British Tax Reporter* ¶293-050.

10970   Companies

A UK-resident company will have to choose between conducting its overseas operations through a branch or a subsidiary. The subsidiary might be UK-resident or resident overseas either in the country of trading or a third country.

Overseas Aspects

One factor will be the overseas country's laws about who may or may not trade in the country. Some countries have restrictions on the ownership of businesses by non-residents. Another factor will be the overseas country's domestic tax rules as modified by any available double tax treaty with the UK or the third country. The relevant considerations are comparable to those which have to be taken into account in the reverse situation.

For UK tax purposes, the main difference is that a branch's profits will be liable to UK corporation tax. Local tax may also be payable and double tax relief may be available. Transfer pricing rules apply between the UK company and the overseas company. Under CTSA, the transfer pricing rules also apply to transactions between the UK company and the overseas branch.

The undistributed profits of a non-UK resident subsidiary or associated company can be liable to UK tax if it is a controlled foreign company. Dividends will be taxed under the tax on foreign possessions rules, subject to double tax relief for any withholding tax levied by the foreign country and any underlying tax on the profits from which the dividend is distributed.

Double tax relief cannot be carried forward.

A foreign branch can be incorporated but this may involve local tax charges or disadvantages. Tax in the UK on any capital gain can be deferred by a claim for roll-over relief. The reverse procedure may involve UK and foreign tax but would not require Treasury consent.

See *British Tax Reporter* ¶764-000.

10990   Anti-avoidance

Provided a bona fide trade is carried on, the anti-avoidance provisions in ITA 2007, Pt. 13, Ch. 2 (Transfer of assets abroad) should not apply, even though they can apply to trading income.

The rules for taxing undistributed capital gains of non-resident companies do not apply to gains from the disposal of tangible property or foreign currency in bank accounts used wholly for trading purposes. A residual problem is that this exemption does not cover a non-resident holding company disposing of shares in trading subsidiaries.

Interest receivable by UK-resident companies on certain loans to non-UK-resident affiliates can be taxed on an accruals rather than arising basis under the foreign exchange rules.

Law:ITA 2007, Pt. 13, Ch. 2

EMPLOYEES IN THE UK

11000   Introduction

The tax treatment of employment income of individuals domiciled outside the UK depends on whether:

(1)   the employee is resident in the UK or not, and if so whether also ordinarily resident;

(2)   the duties are performed wholly abroad or wholly or partly in the UK;

(3)   remuneration is foreign emoluments.

Foreign emoluments are amounts paid by a non-resident employer (which includes a branch of a non-resident company or partnership) to a non-domiciled employee. An employer resident in the Republic of Ireland, or in the UK and abroad, cannot pay foreign emoluments.

The rules concerning residence and ordinary residence of a person coming to the UK for employment are discussed at 10570. An employee acquiring a UK domicile of choice will thereafter be treated in the same way as any other UK domiciled individual as regards emoluments for working in the UK or for working abroad.

See *British Tax Reporter* ¶406-050.

11010   The basic rules

The main points to note are:

(1)   a non-resident is liable on emoluments for duties in the UK;

(2)   a resident who is not ordinarily resident is liable on the same basis but, in addition, is liable on the remittance basis on emoluments for non-UK duties of that or other employments; and

(3)   a resident who is also ordinarily resident is taxed on all emoluments for duties within and outside the UK; if the remuneration consists of foreign emoluments, the liability may be on the remittance basis if the duties are performed wholly abroad.

It used to be possible for a UK-resident individual to obtain a deduction of 100 per cent against earnings from abroad if they related to a period of absence of 365 days even if those days did not include one complete income tax year. The deduction has been abolished for all qualifying periods beginning after 17 March 1998 except for seafarers. An individual who is abroad for one complete tax year will, of course, not be resident.

Where there is a difference in treatment between UK earnings and overseas earnings two separate contracts, one for UK and the other for foreign duties, are desirable. The contracts must be with separate employers as it is not possible to have two contracts of employment

Overseas Aspects

with the same employer. The use of two contracts allows the employer to specify that the foreign duties attract a higher rate of remuneration.

Incidental duties performed in the UK can be regarded as performed abroad. Directorships of UK-resident companies will normally involve more than incidental duties in the UK.

HMRC Statement of Practice (SoP) 1/09 sets out how HMRC will treat transfers made from an offshore account which contains only the income relating to a single employment contract, and how earnings should be apportioned between UK and non-UK employment where an employee is taxed on the remittance basis. HMRC previously stated that SoP 1/09 would be put on a statutory footing in the *Finance Act* 2010 but in March 2010 they confirmed that it would continue to apply for a further year.

Source: HMRC6: *Residents and non-residents. Liability to tax in the United Kingdom* (http://www.hmrc.gov.uk/cnr/hmrc6.pdf)

See *British Tax Reporter* ¶406-050.

11020   Travel expenditure

No taxable benefit usually arises for travel expenses paid or reimbursed by the employer for the employee between the UK and an overseas home.

Allowable expenses are travel to take up a foreign employment with duties wholly overseas, returning to the UK at the end of that employment, board and lodging while there or in travelling between an employment whose duties are at least partly overseas and any other employment. A deduction will be given if the employee is resident and ordinarily resident in the UK and the earnings are not foreign emoluments. Expenses are apportioned where travel is partly for another purpose. The employee is entitled to a deduction for these expenses whether or not the employer reimburses the expenditure.

In addition, where an employer provides travel facilities or reimburses the cost of travel, the employee will not suffer a tax liability. This rule applies to travel between any place in the UK and the place of performance of duties outside the UK and any return journey by the spouse or any child of the employee. The rule also applies to travel from the UK to the overseas place of duty by an employee whose duties are performed partly outside the UK and can only be performed outside the UK. Similarly, travel from the place of performance of the overseas duties to any place in the UK will be covered. The relief applies to the return journey as much as the original journey.

There are additional conditions for the travelling expenses of a spouse and children to qualify. The employee must be resident and ordinarily resident and absent from the UK for a continuous period of at least 60 days for the purpose of performing the duties the employment. The child must be aged under 18 at the beginning of the outward journey. The relief extends to a maximum of two outward and two return journeys by the same person in any tax year.

Source: HMRC6: *Residents and non-residents. Liability to tax in the United Kingdom* (http://www.hmrc.gov.uk/cnr/hmrc6.pdf)

See *British Tax Reporter* ¶455-600.

11030 Emoluments

Emoluments are calculated under the normal tax rules, including benefits in kind. Apart from the travelling expense rules already mentioned, expenses are deductible only according to the normal test of being wholly, exclusively and necessarily incurred in the performance of the duty of the employment. Pension contributions to a registered scheme are deductible within limits, but the pension will be taxed when received, and, being UK source income, will remain permanently liable to UK income tax. Pensions paid on behalf of a foreign employer are not liable to UK tax.

Many international employers operate tax equalisation schemes, also known as tax protected pay or net pay. It is an arrangement that ensures that an employee has the same take home pay wherever employed. Payments under these schemes are taxable. Golden handshakes are also taxable but, in addition to the general £30,000 allowance (see 440, substantial foreign service may give a full or further partial exemption.

From 6 April 2008, employees who are resident but not ordinarily resident in the UK, and who receive employment-related securities (ERS), are brought within the income tax provisions and associated tax charges of ITEPA 2003, Part 7. These provisions previously only applied to resident and ordinarily resident employees. Where gains on ERS are partly derived from employment duties in the UK, and partly from duties outside the UK, they will be apportioned appropriately, with gains from ERS related to duties outside the UK being subject to UK income tax to the extent that they are remitted. A similar apportionment will be available to individuals who are not domiciled in the UK in certain circumstances.

Corresponding payments will be permitted as deductions from foreign emoluments if they are paid out of them and there is insufficient overseas income not liable to UK tax to meet those obligations. Such a payment is one that would qualify for relief under UK tax rules if it were not paid under a foreign obligation (e.g. interest on a loan to buy a principal private residence, alimony and pension contributions). Pension contributions are deductible regardless of other income.

It is necessary to consider the status of an employee in a tax year to determine whether earnings are taxable in principle. If they are, they are actually taxed when received, even if the employment is not held then and regardless of the status of the individual at that date. There is a difference between received and remitted. An employee may receive the income proceeds into, say, a foreign bank account, but not remit the money to the UK.

See *British Tax Reporter* ¶406-200.

Overseas Aspects

11040   Double tax treaties

Many such treaties provide that a resident of a foreign country who can claim the protection of the treaty will not be liable to UK tax on emoluments for duties performed in the UK if:

(1)   the individual is present in the UK for periods not exceeding in total 183 days in any tax year;

(2)   the emoluments are paid by an employer who is not resident in the UK; and

(3)   the cost of the emoluments is not borne by a permanent establishment or fixed base that the employer has in the UK.

Treaties often exclude public entertainers and sports people from the protection of such a provision, and their earnings are often paid under deduction of tax.

See *British Tax Reporter* ¶171-100.

UK DOMICILED EMPLOYEES ABROAD

11100   Introduction

Domicile will not affect the taxation treatment of UK domiciled individuals working abroad. The taxation of such individuals will be based on their residence status. However, if they are not resident and not ordinarily resident they will only be liable to tax on duties performed in the UK.

UK domiciliaries

Income tax

A UK-domiciled individual coming to the UK will normally be treated as resident and ordinarily resident here from the date of his arrival, in which case he is liable to UK income tax on his worldwide income. The table shows the liability to tax on employment income according to:

(1)   the individual's residence status; and

(2)   the place where the duties of the job are performed.

Duties performed	In UK	Abroad
R & OR	Liable	Liable
R but not OR	Liable	Liable if remitted to UK
Not R	Liable	Not liable

R = resident
OR = ordinarily resident

The next table shows the position with respect to investment income:

Source of income	UK	Foreign	FOTRA
R & OR	Liable	Liable	Liable
R but not OR	Liable	Liable if remitted to UK	Liable
Not R but OR	Liable	Not liable	Liable
Not R and not OR	Liable	Not liable	Not liable

FOTRA = Free of tax to residents abroad

The investment income table contains some oversimplifications. The liability of non-residents is restricted to tax deducted at source.

Source: HMRC6: *Residents and non-residents. Liability to tax in the United Kingdom* (http://www.hmrc.gov.uk/cnr/hmrc6.pdf)

See *British Tax Reporter* ¶111-350.

11110   Foreign pensions

These are taxed on the arising basis with a ten per cent deduction. Pensions paid as a result of Nazi persecution are not taxable.

See *British Tax Reporter* ¶370-100.

NON-DOMICILED INVESTORS IN THE UK

11150   Income tax

United Kingdom source income is liable to UK income tax even in the hands of a non-resident individual. There are two main exceptions:

(1)   interest that is paid gross is treated as exempt unless a resident agent is involved in collecting it – the non-resident individual can apply to have the interest paid gross from the bank or building society, but the split year concessions do not apply;

(2)   interest on certain UK gilts is exempt if they are owned by a person not ordinarily resident in the UK.

11160   Capital gains tax

An individual who is neither resident nor ordinarily resident is not liable to CGT on gains from UK-situated assets. An individual who is either resident or ordinarily resident or both, but is non-domiciled, is liable to CGT on gains from overseas assets only to the extent that the gains are remitted to the UK (but see 11200 below for rules applying from 6 April 2008). Transfers between spouses or civil partners are still made at no gain or loss even when the transferor is resident but the transferee is not. However, the husband and wife, or civil partners, must be living together and this, together with the rules on temporary non-residence, might make this exemption more difficult.

Non-residents can be liable to income tax on capital gains from transactions in development land under anti-avoidance legislation.

11170   Inheritance tax

A non-domiciled person is liable to inheritance tax on gifts, in lifetime or on death, of property situated in the UK but not property situated abroad. A person with an overseas domicile becomes domiciled in the UK for inheritance tax purposes only with effect from the beginning of the seventeenth year of residence in any consecutive 20 tax years. Domicile for inheritance tax continues for three years after domicile has been lost for other circumstances.

The spouse/civil partner exemption is limited to £55,000 where the donor spouse (or civil partner) is UK domiciled and the donee is not. The donor spouse/civil partner could use the nil rate band to transfer more property to the other spouse/civil partner. A larger gift could escape tax as a potentially exempt transfer.

11180   Location of source of income or asset

It is clear from the foregoing that this is a matter of vital importance. There is a set of statutory rules for CGT. The rules for income tax and inheritance tax are based on case law but are not markedly different. For example, shares are located where they are registered or principally registered (if in more than one place) or where the certificates are kept if they are bearer shares. A debt is located where the debtor resides, an intangible right where it can be enforced or, as with patents or copyrights, where it is registered. A debt under seal is located where the document is kept (though HMRC challenge this for income tax).

By holding assets *through* a foreign company or trust rather than directly, an individual may be able to have a foreign source of income or asset separate from the underlying source or asset of the company or trust which may well be located in the UK. Anti-avoidance legislation exists. The capital gains of overseas companies that would be close companies if they were resident in the UK can be attributed to UK-resident shareholders. Shareholders must be domiciled in the UK and either resident or ordinarily resident. Details of overseas trusts are at 11600ff.

See *British Tax Reporter* ¶370-500.

11200 Annual £30,000 charge

Major changes apply to the tax position of certain individuals using the remittance basis from 6 April 2008. Broadly, adult non-domiciled, or not ordinarily resident, individuals who have been in the UK more than seven of the past 10 tax years, may continue to access the remittance basis of taxation on payment of an annual charge of £30,000 charged on the foreign income and gains they leave outside the UK, unless their unremitted foreign income and gains are less than £2,000.

Prior to 6 April 2008, UK residents who were either not domiciled or not ordinarily resident in the UK could access the remittance basis of taxation without any UK tax being charged on the foreign income and gains they left outside the UK. So the remittance basis meant that income and gains arising overseas were only taxed in the UK when they were brought into the UK.

On and after 6 April 2008, non-UK domiciled and/or not ordinarily resident adults who claim the remittance basis of taxation, who have been resident in the UK more than seven of the past ten tax years, will have to pay a £30,000 annual tax charge in respect of the foreign income and gains they leave outside the UK. This £30,000 charge is in addition to any tax due on UK income and gains or foreign income and gains remitted to the UK.

The £30,000 annual tax charge is payable through the self-assessment system. If the adult pays the £30,000 tax charge from an offshore source directly to HMRC by cheque or electronic transfer, the £30,000 will not itself be taxed as a remittance. If the £30,000 is repaid it will be taxed as a remittance at that point.

Individuals who have access to the remittance basis of taxation can choose each year whether they wish to claim the remittance basis of taxation or pay tax on their worldwide income and gains. Adults will not have to pay the £30,000 minimum tax charge for a particular year if they do not claim the remittance basis for that year.

The £30,000 charge will be income tax or capital gains tax and should be treated as such for the purposes of Double Taxation Agreements. The tax will also be available to cover Gift Aid donations.

Law: FA 2008, s. 25 and Sch. 7

UK DOMICILED INVESTORS ABROAD

11250 Income tax

If resident, a UK domiciled individual investing abroad will be liable to tax under ITTOIA 2005 (former Sch. D, Case IV or V (e.g. foreign interest, dividends, and rents)). From 6 April 1993, foreign dividends are taxed on a similar basis to UK source dividends. This contrasts with the position of a non-domiciled resident who receives dividends from abroad where those dividends are taxed on the remittance basis. Such dividends are taxed at the individual's marginal rate of tax.

The rules of property income apply to overseas properties as they do for overseas properties. This means that loan interest and other expenses are deducted in calculating profits.

One issue that can be encountered by UK residents is ITA 2007, Pt 13, Ch 2. This deals with the transfer of assets abroad. It applies where, as a result of a transfer of assets abroad, income becomes payable to a person resident or domiciled outside the UK and an individual ordinarily resident in the UK either has power to enjoy the income or receives a capital sum. The section applies wherever the transfer takes places and whether or not in conjunction with associated operations. Only the transferor, or joint transferors, or a person who has procured another to make a transfer, can be taxed and on all the income arising but a non-transferor can also be taxed on the value of any benefit he receives under ITA 2007.Pt 13, Ch 2.

There is an exception if the individual can show that avoidance of tax was not one of his purposes or that the transfer and any associated operations were bona fide commercial transactions not designed to avoid tax.

Law: ITA 2007, Pt 13, Ch 2

11260 Capital gains tax

A UK-resident or ordinarily resident individual will remain liable to tax on gains from disposals of overseas assets but there is some scope for the use of foreign trusts.

Temporary non-residence

Rules were introduced from 17 March 1998 to catch those who go abroad on a temporary basis and realise gains whilst abroad. The rules require the period of non-residence to last for at least five tax years. The details of the rules are that they apply where:

* an individual is UK-resident in the year of assessment of return to the UK;
* that individual was not UK-resident for one or more years before the return;
* four out of the seven years preceding the year of departure are years of residence;
* there are fewer than five years between the year of return and the year of departure.

Where the rules apply, the individual is taxed to capital gains on any gains accruing overseas as if they were gains arising during the year of return. However, any capital losses occurring overseas which are not usually allowed against UK gains, will be treated as accruing in the year of return and will be treated as any other capital loss. Gains realised in the tax year of departure will be chargeable in that year.

Extra-statutory Concession D2 allowed the split year concession. Under that concession the year of arrival or departure was split so that, even though the residence status applied for the full year, the Revenue would treat residence as starting or ending on the date of departure from the UK. The concession was revised with effect from 17 March 1998 to take account of the changed rules. In the year of arrival, an individual is not charged to CGT in respect of gains made in the year but before the date of arrival. This concession applies if the individual has not been resident or ordinarily resident in the UK at any time during the five tax years immediately preceding the year of arrival. An individual who becomes not resident or ordinarily resident is not charged to CGT on gains made after the date of departure. Again, this concession only applies if the individual was not resident and not ordinarily resident in the UK for the whole of at least four out of the seven tax years immediately preceding the year of departure.

Gains on assets acquired whilst non-resident will not be caught by the re-entry charge.

Source: ESC D2

11270   Inheritance tax

United Kingdom domiciled individuals are liable to inheritance tax on gifts they make of property wherever situated.

See *British Tax Reporter* ¶370-000.

REMITTANCES

11350   Income remitted to the UK

Remittances of income to the UK are taxable and include remittances payable in the UK or consisting of property imported but bought from foreign income. Travellers' cheques and payments on credit cards can be similarly caught.

Legislation contained in *Finance Act* 2008 removed various loopholes and anomalies which allowed remittance basis users to remit income and gains to the UK without paying tax on them. The changes are outlined in the following sections.

It is important to be able to demonstrate clearly the source of a remittance and it may be necessary to have separate bank accounts for arising basis income, remittance basis income, capital gains and capital.

Ceased sources

Prior to 6 April 2008, foreign savings and investment income were not taxed when remitted to the UK if the source of the income no longer existed in that year. From 6 April 2008 the rules were amended so that where the remittance basis has been claimed for a year, income of that year will be liable to tax if it is remitted to the UK, even where the source of the income has ceased in a previous year.

Cash only

Prior to 6 April 2008, relevant foreign income could only be taxed if it was brought into the UK as cash. If a remittance basis taxpayer turned relevant foreign income into an asset outside the UK and then imported that asset, no UK tax could be charged on the income unless and until the asset was sold or turned into cash in the UK. The legislation has been amended from 6 April 2008 so that money, property and services derived from relevant foreign income brought into the UK will be treated as a remittance and will be taxed as such.

There are exemptions for personal effects (that is, clothes, shoes, jewellery and watches), assets costing less than £1,000, assets brought into the UK for repair and restoration and assets in the UK for less than a total nine-month period purchased out of relevant foreign income. There is also a new exemption from a remittance basis tax charge for works of art brought into the UK for public display (see 11717).

Any asset purchased out of untaxed relevant foreign income which an individual owned on 11 March 2008 will be exempt from a charge under the remittance basis, for so long as that individual owns it, even if that asset is currently outside the UK and later imported. Any asset in the UK on 5 April 2008 will also be exempt from a charge under the remittance basis, for so long as the current owner owns it, even if that asset is later exported and then reimported. The existing charge that arises if such an asset is sold in the UK will remain. *Finance Act* 2009 extended these rules, with retrospective effect from 6 April 2008, to include property purchased out of foreign employment income and foreign chargeable gains, as well as relevant foreign income.

Claims mechanism

Prior to 6 April 2008, foreign savings and investment income arising in a year in which the remittance basis was claimed were not taxed if remitted in a subsequent year in which no claim to the remittance basis was made. The rules were amended from 6 April 2008 so that foreign savings and investment income arising in a year in which the remittance basis is claimed will be taxed if it is remitted to the UK, irrespective of the year in which it is remitted and whether or not a claim to the remittance basis is made in the year in which the remittance is made.

Mixed funds

Formerly there were no statutory rules on the treatment of remittances from funds which include some combination of untaxed relevant foreign income, employment income, capital gains, taxed income or gains and capital. *Finance Act* 2008 contains clear statutory rules for determining how much of a transfer from a mixed fund is treated as the individual's income or chargeable gains, and the manner in which these amounts are chargeable to tax.

Alienation

Prior to 6 April 2008, the law allowed overseas income and gains to be alienated by a non-domiciled or not ordinarily resident individual to a third party, such as an offshore vehicle or a close relative. That alienated income or gains could then be brought into the UK in such a way that the individual whose income or gain it originally was had the use or enjoyment of it in the UK without attracting a charge to tax. From 6 April 2008, legislation will have effect where an individual arranges for money or property to be brought into the UK, or services and benefits to be provided in the UK, that were funded out of untaxed foreign income or gains. Where that individual, or their immediate family, benefits in any way then that individual will be taxed on that money, property, services or benefits under the remittance basis rules of taxation.

The definition of an individual's 'immediate family' is limited to spouses, civil partners, individuals living together as spouses or civil partners and their children or grandchildren under 18. It also covers close companies, or foreign companies that would be close if in the UK, of which any of them are participators and trusts of which any of them are settlors or beneficiaries.

Offshore mortgages

Previously individuals paying tax on the remittance basis who borrowed money from a non-UK institution could repay the interest on that loan out of untaxed foreign income without giving rise to a tax charge on the remittance basis, even if the loan was advanced into the UK. Legislation in *Finance Act* 2008 includes grandfathering provisions such that untaxed relevant foreign income used to fund interest repayments on existing mortgages secured on a residential property in the UK, will not be treated as a remittance on or after 6 April 2008. This grandfathering has effect for repayments for the remaining period of the loan, or until 5 April 2028, whichever is shorter. In addition if the terms of the loan are varied or any further advances made after 12 March 2008 then the repayments will be treated as remittances from that point.

Non-resident companies

Formerly, anti-avoidance legislation designed to prevent UK residents from realising chargeable gains free of tax through a holding in a non-UK resident company did not have effect for non-domiciled individual participators. From 6 April 2008, these anti-avoidance rules have been amended to ensure that UK participators of foreign companies will be taxed on the chargeable gains accruing to the company irrespective of the participator's domicile.

Transfer of assets abroad

Anti-avoidance legislation designed to prevent individuals from avoiding income tax by transferring assets abroad apply to non-domiciled individuals. The remittance basis will apply to remittance basis users.

Accrued income scheme

Prior to 6 April 2008, income tax charges under the accrued income scheme applied to domiciled individuals but not to the non-domiciled. This has changed from 6 April 2008 so that the income tax charge now has effect for non-domiciled individuals as well as domiciled individuals.

Capital gains tax losses

Formerly, non-domiciled individuals got no capital gains tax relief for losses arising offshore as the remittance basis of taxation was compulsory for them with respect to capital gains tax. From 6 April 2008, individuals will be able to elect in and out of the remittance basis on a year-by-year basis so a non-domiciled individual could pay capital gains tax on unremitted foreign gains in a year they are taxed on the arising basis. The capital gains tax legislation has been amended so that non-domiciled individuals taxed on the arising basis who have not claimed the remittance basis from 2008–09 will get relief for foreign losses. Individuals who claim the remittance basis from 2008–09 will be able to elect into a regime that enables them to get relief for their foreign losses in the UK in years they are taxed on the arising basis. That election will be irrevocable and as it will require non-domiciles to disclose details of unremitted capital gains the election will be optional.

Law: FA 2010, s. 33;FA 2009, s. 51 and Sch. 27; FA 2008, s. 25 and Sch. 7

See *British Tax Reporter* ¶370-500.

WITHHOLDING TAXES

11400 PAYE

Any employer must withhold PAYE tax, even if both the employer and the employee are non-resident, provided the employer has a trading presence in the UK and the remuneration is liable to UK income tax. Class I National Insurance contributions must also be withheld.

See *British Tax Reporter* ¶494-050.

11410 Rent and lease premiums

Income tax must be withheld at the basic rate if the payment is made directly to a person whose usual abode is outside the UK. Tax is deducted by the letting agent, if there is one, or the tenant if there is no agent. A landlord may apply to receive rent gross.

Website: *The Non-resident Landlords Scheme* – www.hmrc.gov.uk/cnr/nr_landlords.htm

See *British Tax Reporter* ¶303-200.

11420   Interest

Annual interest paid by a company, or by any other person to another person whose usual place of abode is outside the UK, must be paid net of income tax (unless the recipient is another company within the charge to corporation tax on the interest). Short interest is excluded and so is interest paid by or to a bank carrying on a UK banking business.

Failure to withhold may cause a loss of a deduction for the interest as a trading expense.

See *British Tax Reporter* ¶226-600.

11430   Royalties, alimony, etc.

Tax must be deducted at the basic rate from patent royalties, alimony and other annual payments and also from copyright royalties if the owner's usual place of abode is outside the UK (unless the recipient is another company within the charge to corporation tax on the payment, or is a person entitled to relief from UK tax on royalties under a double tax treaty). The liability to deduct tax does not apply if the royalty is received by the originator of the copyright, i.e. the author. See 1683 for details of disposals of patent rights.

See *British Tax Reporter* ¶171-300.

11450   Price of goods and services

There is no general requirement for withholding tax. Withholding tax at the basic rate will apply to payments to non-resident entertainers and sportsmen, whether made directly or indirectly, for UK services.

11460   Sale of UK land

A withholding tax can apply where a capital gain of a non-resident is taxable as income but there must be a specific direction made to the payer in advance of the payment.

11470   Double tax treaties

These may eliminate or reduce withholding taxes.

See *British Tax Reporter* ¶170-050.

Overseas Aspects

DOUBLE TAX RELIEF AND TREATIES

11550 Treaties and relief

The UK has entered into numerous double tax treaties with other countries to mitigate the effect of double taxation of income and capital gains but far fewer in relation to gifts and inheritances.

Treaties are made with one country in each case but members of the OECD have subscribed to a model form and many treaties follow that form. Where a treaty applies it explains when UK domestic tax law applies and where the overseas tax law applies. The treaty does not override UK tax law in that the treaty cannot impose a liability. It can say which authority has the taxing rights if they exist and there would, otherwise, be double taxation. Double taxation arises because different countries employ different criteria to found their tax jurisdiction. For example, a US citizen who is taxable in the UK as a resident or because of a UK source of income will remain liable to US tax on world-wide income and gains by virtue of US citizenship.

A UK-resident may claim double tax relief even where no treaty is in force. This relief is called unilateral relief. Relief will be given by a credit equal to the lower of the UK tax or foreign tax on the overseas income or capital gains. If there is no UK tax on the income such as where profits are covered by current year losses, the foreign tax can be deducted in calculating the income or gains for UK tax.

A treaty will normally go further than allowing credit by assigning exclusive taxing jurisdiction to one country or other by limiting withholding taxes (e.g. on dividends, interest and royalties). Treaties can apply to dual residents but usually require an individual to be treated as a resident of only one country, determined by criteria in order of priority (e.g. permanent home, centre of vital interests, and nationality). They usually permit a country to tax business profits only if derived from a local permanent establishment. The permanent establishment is usually a fixed place of business defined in some detail. However, a permanent establishment might be a temporary site office or mobile home or caravan. The terms of the specific treaty must be checked. It is possible for a person to be taxed in one country on one type of income or profit but in another country for another type of income.

Credit is also available for overseas tax similar to inheritance tax charged on the gift of an asset, in lifetime or on death. Few treaties have been negotiated and many do not adequately cover lifetime gifts because they were negotiated when the former estate duty was in force. In addition to deductions and credit they also lay down useful criteria for determining and so resolving conflicts over the domicile of an individual and the location of assets.

There is also an agreement known as the arbitration convention, whereby different tax authorities will agree on corresponding adjustments if one country applies its transfer-pricing rules to increase tax in that country.

Source: Digest of Double Taxation Treaties (available online at www.hmrc.gov.uk/cnr/dtdigest.pdf)

Website: www.hmrc.gov.uk/cnr/dtcompany.pdf
www.hmrc.gov.uk/cnr/double-taxation-treaty.htm

See *British Tax Reporter* ¶170-550.

FOREIGN TRUSTS AND ESTATES

11600   Income tax

Non-resident trustees of trusts established by a non-domiciled settlor will be liable to income tax only if they invest in UK-source income. If they do, their income may be taxable at the basic rate or the rate applicable to trusts, which is 50 per cent from 6 April 2010.

Common rules apply from 6 April 2007 to determine the residence of trustees. Trustees are together treated as if they were a single person and the deemed person is treated as resident and ordinarily resident in the UK when all of the trustees are resident; or at least one trustee is resident and at least one is not and the settlor is ordinarily resident or domiciled in the UK when the settlement was created.

United Kingdom resident beneficiaries will be taxable on income from overseas trusts (but on the remittance basis for a non-domiciled beneficiary).

If the trust is established by a UK domiciled settlor the same results follow. If the settlor was ordinarily resident the anti-avoidance legislation in ITA 2007, Pt 13, Ch 2 may apply to UK-resident beneficiaries who receive benefits (and they only escape where they are non-domiciled beneficiaries if the benefit is provided outside the UK).

The income from an estate in the course of the administration of a deceased non-domiciled individual is taxed on a resident beneficiary under special rules. Foreign source income escapes tax if the beneficiary is non-domiciled and the income is not remitted.

A non-resident beneficiary can be taxed on estate income arising in the UK.

The rules concerning settlements by parents on their unmarried minor children and where a settlor retains an interest, etc. do not apply to income that would be taxable only on the remittance basis. A settlement by a UK domiciled individual under which the settlor can benefit but where the trust receives no income will often be caught by ITA 2007, Pt 13, Ch 2 if the trustees own an underlying company that pays no dividends.

United Kingdom resident trustees should allow foreign income to be paid direct to non-resident beneficiaries, wherever possible. This may avoid liability or the need for repayment claims where a tax treaty exempts from liability.

Overseas Aspects

Law: ITA 2007, Pt 13, Ch 2

See *British Tax Reporter* ¶350-800.

11610   Capital gains tax

Non-resident trustees are not liable to UK CGT. Their capital gains can be taxed on beneficiaries receiving capital payments if the beneficiaries are UK domiciled and either UK-resident or ordinarily resident provided the settlor was also domiciled and resident or ordinarily resident when the settlement was made or is so resident at the date of the payment. There is a risk that a payment received in an earlier year can be caught if gains arise in a later year. Gains are not taxed unless and until a payment is made.

The *Finance Act* 1991 tightened up the rules on non-resident trusts by:

(1)   imposing a deemed charge when UK-resident trustees retire in favour of non-residents;

(2)   taxing the settlor on trust gains where the settlor retained an interest;

(3)   charging additional tax where capital payments distributing trust gains are made more than one year later.

Extensive changes to the capital gains tax regime for non-resident trusts apply from 6 April 2008. Non-domiciled beneficiaries of non-resident trusts who claim the remittance basis will be taxed on the remittance basis on all UK and offshore assets. Trustees may to make an irrevocable election to rebase assets held as at 6 April 2008 for the purpose of excluding any part of a chargeable gain relating to the period before 6 April 2008 from being taxed on non-domiciled beneficiaries. Settlors and beneficiaries of non-resident trusts will not be required to disclose information to HMRC about trust assets in relation to which a remittance arose, or details of the trustees, provided they have made a correct return of their tax liabilities. Beneficiaries of non-resident trusts may be required to provide additional information to HMRC where the trustees choose to make an election to rebase trust assets or where HMRC enquire into a beneficiary's tax return.

The revised remittance regime included transitional provisions which prevent certain income which arises before 6 April 2008 from being taxed as a remittance if it is brought to the UK on or after that date. *Finance Act* 2009 extended these provisions to ensure that they operate as intended in their application to individuals who are taxed under the settlements legislation in ITTOIA 2005, Part 5, Ch. 5.

Law: FA 2009, s. 51 and Sch. 27

Source: HMRC Budget 2008 supplementary document: *Residence and Domicile: Taxation of distributions to beneficiaries of non-resident trusts*

11620   Inheritance tax

A trust is outside the scope of inheritance tax if the settlor was domiciled outside the UK when the settlement was made and the settled property is located abroad. There is no charge just because property in such a settlement becomes located abroad. All other settlements are within the scope of inheritance tax.

See *British Tax Reporter* ¶351-100.

MISCELLANEOUS MATTERS

11700   Personal allowances and reliefs

All UK residents are entitled to a personal tax allowance and reliefs (see 1850) for income tax and the annual exemption allowance (see 6150) for capital gains. The majority also pay tax on their worldwide income and gains even if that income and gains remains offshore. UK residents who are either not domiciled, or not ordinarily resident, in the UK can pay tax on the remittance basis which means that income and gains arising overseas are taxed in the UK only when, and if, they are brought into the UK.

On and after 6 April 2008, individuals who claim use of the remittance basis will not be entitled to any of the personal income tax allowances. This includes the basic personal allowance and age-related allowances, blind person's allowance, tax reductions for married couples and civil partners and relief for life insurance payments. Remittance basis users will also lose access to the annual exemption allowance for capital gains. There is, however, a de minimis limit, so that remittance basis users who have unremitted foreign income and gains of less than £2,000 a year will be able to retain access to any of the personal income tax allowances to which they are entitled and the annual exemption allowance for capital gains.

To ensure compliance with certain aspects of the *Human Rights Act* 1998, legislation was introduced in *Finance Act* 2009, effective from 6 April 2010, to withdraw the entitlement for non-resident individuals who previously qualified for UK personal tax allowances and reliefs solely by virtue of being a Commonwealth citizen. Whilst the vast majority of individuals affected will still benefit through other means such as Double taxation Treaties, citizens of Bahamas, Cameroon, Cook Islands, Dominica, Maldives, Mozambique, Nauru, Niue, St Lucia, St Vincent & the Grenadines, Samoa, Tanzania, Tonga, and Vanuatu may be affected.

Payments made under UK obligations are deductible from UK source income of non-residents according to the applicable rules (e.g. interest, alimony, charitable covenants).

Law: FA 2009, s. 5; FA 2008, s. 25 and Sch. 7

See *British Tax Reporter* ¶158-000.

11705 Foreign dividend income

Prior to 6 April 2008, remittance basis users who were higher rate taxpayers were liable at 32.5 per cent on foreign dividend income remitted to the UK. ITTOIA 2005 mistakenly changed the rate at which foreign dividend income was charged to tax on these remittance basis users from 40 per cent to 32.5 per cent. This anomaly has been corrected from 6 April 2008 so that remittance basis users liable at the higher rate will be taxed at 40 per cent on foreign dividend income remitted to the UK.

Law: FA 2008, s. 25 and Sch. 7

Source: HMRC *Brief* 76/09

See *British Tax Reporter* ¶132-550.

11710 Special privileges

Diplomats, consular officials and representatives of international agencies may enjoy special exemptions and treaties may accord these also to students, professors, government employees, etc.

11715 Gurkhas

The earnings of members of the Brigade of Gurkhas from their duties performed overseas, which were previously exempt, are subject to UK income tax with effect from 16 June 2006. A similar change affects NICs. Previously the earnings of Brigade members recruited in Nepal from their employment with the Brigade were disregarded for NICs purposes. This 'disregard' ceased to apply from 5 July 2006.

Law: ITEPA 2003, s. 28(5); *Social Security (Categorisation of Earners) (Amendment) Regulations* 2006 (SI 2006/1530)

Website: www.opsi.gov.uk/si/em2006/uksiem_20061530_en.pdf

11717 Art for public display

From 6 April 2008, works of art are exempt from being taxed under the remittance basis if they are brought into the UK for public display. This exemption applies to art purchased overseas from unremitted untaxed employment income, capital gains or relevant foreign income.

Case Table

(References are to paragraph numbers)

C

	Paragraph
Higgs v Olivier [1952] Ch 311; (1952) 33 TC 136	630
Hill v Davison [1997] BTC 191	406
Hoare [2010] TC 00394	2648
Hochstrasser v Mayes [1960] AC 376; (1959) 38 TC 673 & 702; [1959] 3 All ER 817	273; 8816
Hoechst Finance Ltd v Gumbrell [1983] BTC 66	4557
Holdings Ltd v IR Commrs (1997) Sp C 117	4557; 4558
Holmes v Mitchell [1991] BTC 28	5490
Honig v Sarsfield (1986) 59 TC 337; [1986] BTC 205	2678
Honour v Norris [1992] BTC 153	6224
Hood (John) & Co Ltd v Magee (1918) 7 TC 327	3014
House (t/a P & J Autos) v C & E Commrs [1996] BVC 116	8612
HSBC Life (UK) Ltd v Stubbs (2001) Sp C 295	3036
Hunt v Murphy [1992] BTC 28	323
Hunter v Dewhurst (1932) 16 TC 605; [1932] All ER 753	438
Hutchinson 3G UK Ltd v C & E Commrs (Case C-369/04)	7746
Huxley, ex parte (1916) 7 TC 49	224

I

	Paragraph
Imperial Chemical Industries plc v Colmer (Case C-264/96) [1998] BTC 304; [1999] BTC 440	3809; 3812
Imperial Tobacco Co Ltd v Kelly (1943) 25 TC 292; [1943] 2 All ER 119	650
IR Commrs v Aken [1990] BTC 352	573
IR Commrs v Anglo Brewing Co Ltd (1925) 12 TC 803	2240
IR Commrs v Biggar (1982) 53 TC 254; [1982] BTC 332	940
IR Commrs v Blott [1921] 2 AC 171	3065
IR Commrs v Botnar [1999] BTC 267	1700
IR Commrs v Brackett [1986] BTC 415	1700
IR Commrs v Brander & Cruickshank [1971] 1 WLR 212; (1971) 46 TC 574; [1971] 1 All ER 36	438
IR Commrs v Carron Co (1968) 45 TC 18	2152; 2244
IR Commrs v Castlemaine (Lady) (1943) 25 TC 408	1038
IR Commrs v Cock Russell & Co Ltd (1949) 29 TC 387; [1949] 2 All ER 889	652
IR Commrs v Crawley [1987] BTC 112	1368

	Paragraph
IR Commrs v Dimsey & Allen [1999] BTC 335	2659
IR Commrs v Eversden [2003] BTC 8,028	6786
IR Commrs v Eurocopy plc [1991] BTC 459	328
IR Commrs v Falkirk Ice Rink Ltd (1975) 51 TC 42	640
IR Commrs v Fraser (1942) 24 TC 498; 1942 SC 493	562
IR Commrs v Glasgow Musical Festival Association (1926) 11 TC 154; 1926 SC 920	901
IR Commrs v Gordon [1991] BTC 130	675; 6302
IR Commrs v Gray [1994] BTC 8,034	6573
IR Commrs v Hawley [1928] 1 KB 578; (1928) 13 TC 327	1038
IR Commrs v Helen Slater Charitable Trust Ltd [1982] Ch 49; (1981) 55 TC 230; [1981] 3 All ER 98	5800
IR Commrs v Herd [1993] BTC 245	410; 2784
IR Commrs v Hinchy [1960] AC 748; (1960) 38 TC 625; [1960] 1 All ER 505	180
IR Commrs v Levy (1985) 56 TC 68; [1982] BTC 235	1071
IR Commrs v Liverpool School for Performing Arts [1999] BTC 5,189	8144
IR Commrs v Livingstone (1926) 11 TC 538; 1927 SC 251	568
IR Commrs v Lloyd's Private Banking Ltd [1998] BTC 8,020	6903
IR Commrs v Lysaght [1928] AC 234; (1928) 13 TC 511	180; 216
IR Commrs v Maxse [1919] 1 KB 647; (1919) 12 TC 41	586
IR Commrs v Miller [1930] AC 222	1003
IR Commrs v Mills [1975] AC 38; (1974) 49 TC 367; [1974] 1 All ER 722	1071
IR Commrs v Mulligan [1990] BTC 135	2659
IR Commrs v National Book League [1957] Ch 488; (1957) 37 TC 455; [1957] 2 All ER 644	901
IR Commrs v Nelson (1939) 12 TC 716; 1939 SC 689	574
IR Commrs v Newmarket Income Tax Commrs, ex parte Huxley (1916) 7 TC 49	224
IR Commrs v Nuttall [1990] 1 WLR 631; [1990] BTC 107	2645
IR Commrs v Oldham Training and Enterprise Council [1996] BTC 539	900

Case Table

Paragraph

IR Commrs v Parker (1966) 43 TC 396 1416
IR Commrs v Plummer [1980] AC 896; (1979) 54 TC 1; [1979] 3 All ER 775 1071
IR Commrs v Quigley [1995] BTC 356 402
IR Commrs v Redford [1988] BTC 5,252 2659
IR Commrs v Reed International plc [1995] BTC 373 328
IR Commrs v Reinhold (1953) 34 TC 389; 1953 SC 49 571
IR Commrs v Richards (Exors of) [1971] 1 WLR 571; (1971) 46 TC 626; [1971] 1 All ER 785 .... 5223; 5695
IR Commrs v Scottish and Newcastle Breweries Ltd [1982] 1 WLR 322; (1982) 55 TC 252; [1982] BTC 187 2360
IR Commrs v Spencer-Nairn [1991] BTC 8,003 7153
IR Commrs v Tennant (1942) 24 TC 215 1085
IR Commrs v Tyre Investment Trust Ltd (1924) 12 TC 646 4553
IR Commrs v Ufitec [1977] 3 All ER 924 10160
IR Commrs v Universities Superannuation Scheme Ltd [1997] BTC 3 1422
IR Commrs v Wachtel [1971] Ch 573; (1971) 46 TC 543; [1971] 1 All ER 271 1085
IR Commrs v Werner [1998] BTC 202 2659
IR Commrs v Wilkinson [1992] BTC 297 .... 2678; 2807
IR Commrs v Willoughby [1997] BTC 393 .... 1485; 1700
Island Consultants Ltd v R & C Commrs (2007) Sp C 618 265

J

Jaggers (t/a Shide Trees) v Ellis [1997] BTC 571 556
J & R O'Kane & Co v IR Commrs (1922) 22 TC 303 574
Jarrold v Boustead [1964] 1 WLR 1357; (1964) 41 TC 701; [1964] 3 All ER 76 .... 275; 277
Jay's the Jewellers Ltd v IR Commrs (1947) 29 TC 274; [1947] 2 All ER 762 642
Jeffrey v Rolls-Royce Ltd [1962] 1 WLR 425 630
Jeffs v Ringtons Ltd [1985] BTC 585 2152
Jenkins v Brown [1989] BTC 281 5555

Paragraph

Jenkins v IR Commrs (1944) 26 TC 265; [1944] 2 All ER 491 1085
Jenkinson v Freedland (1961) 39 TC 636 568
Jenners, Princes Street Edinburgh Ltd v IR Commrs (1998) Sp C 166 2150
Joffe v Thain (1956) 36 TC 199 1600
Johnson v Jewitt (1961) 40 TC 231 204
Johnson v Johnson [1946] P 205 1370
Johnson v Prudential Assurance Co Ltd [1998] BTC 112 4606
Johnston v Heath [1970] 1 WLR 1567; (1970) 46 TC 463; [1970] 3 All ER 915 564
Johnston Publishing (North) Ltd v R & C Commrs [2008] BTC 443 3687
Jonathan David Ltd v R & C Commrs [2009] TC 00233 2787
Jones v Garnett [2007] BTC 476 265
Jones v Wright (1927) 13 TC 221 993
JP Commodities v R & C Commrs [2008] BTC 5,563 7978

K

Kellogg Brown & Root Holdings Ltd v R & C Commrs (2008) Sp C 693 51301
Kelsall Parsons & Co v IR Commrs (1938) 21 TC 608; 1938 SC 238; 1938 SLT 239 .... 630; 652
Kempton (Executrix of Kempton) v Special Commrs [1992] BTC 553 2621
Kidson v MacDonald [1974] Ch 339; (1973) 49 TC 503; [1974] 1 All ER 849 5555
Kirby v Thorn EMI plc [1988] 1 WLR 445; [1987] BTC 462; [1988] 2 All ER 947 5080
Kirkby v Hughes [1993] BTC 52 558
Kirkham v Williams [1991] BTC 196 566
Klincke v R & C Commrs [2009] TC 00122 5865
Kneen v Martin [1935] 1 KB 499; (1935) 19 TC 33 1603
Koenigsberger v Mellor [1995] BTC 292 558
Kretztechnik AG v Finanzamt Linz (Case C-465/03) [2006] BVC 66 8174
Kwok Chi Leung Karl (Exor of Lamson Kwok) v Commr of Estate Duty [1988] 1 WLR 1035; [1988] BTC 8,073 6550

L

Laerstate BV v R & C Commrs [2009] TC 00162 3014
Laidler v Perry [1966] AC 16; (1965) 42 TC 351; [1965] 2 All ER 121 288

Lai

1,639

Legislation Finding List

(References are to paragraph numbers)

Inheritance Tax Act 1984 – continued

Taxation of Chargeable Gains
Act 1992 – continued

Index to Concessions and Statements

(References are to paragraph numbers)

Inland Revenue Statements of
   Practice – continued

Index

(References are to paragraph numbers)

Cla